# ABNORMAL PSYCHOLOGY and LIFE

## A DIMENSIONAL APPROACH

## Second Edition

# ABNORMAL PSYCHOLOGY and LIFE

## A DIMENSIONAL APPROACH

**Christopher A. Kearney**
*University of Nevada, Las Vegas*

**Timothy J. Trull**
*University of Missouri, Columbia*

CENGAGE
Learning·

Australia • Brazil • Mexico • Singapore • United Kingdom • United States

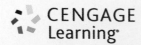

*Abnormal Psychology and Life: A Dimensional Approach,*
**Second Edition, Christopher A. Kearney and Timothy J. Trull**

Product Director: Jon David Hague

Product Manager: Tim Matray

Content Developer: Tangelique Williams-Grayer

Content Coordinator: Jessica Alderman

Product Assistant: Nicole Richards

Media Developer: Mary Noel

Marketing Director: Jennifer Levanduski

Market Development Manager: Melissa Larmon

Content Project Manager: Matt Ballantyne

Art Director: Vernon Boes

Manufacturing Planner: Karen Hunt

Rights Acquisition Specialist: Dean Dauphinais

Production Service: Graphic World Inc.

Text Designer: Parallelogram Graphics

Cover Designer: Terri Wright

Cover Image: © Austin MacRae

Compositor: Graphic World Inc

For product information and technology assistance, contact us at
**Cengage Learning Customer & Sales Support, 1-800-354-9706**
For permission to use material from this text or product,
submit all requests online at **www.cengage.com/permissions.**
Further permissions questions can be emailed to
**permissionrequest@cengage.com.**

Library of Congress Control Number: 2013951250

ISBN-13: 978-1-285-05234-2
ISBN-10: 1-285-05234-X

Cengage Learning
200 First Stamford Place, 4th Floor
Stamford, CT 06902
USA

Cengage Learning is a leading provider of customized learning solutions with office locations around the globe, including Singapore, the United Kingdom, Australia, Mexico, Brazil and Japan. Locate your local office at **international. cengage.com/region.**

Cengage Learning products are represented in Canada by Nelson Education, Ltd.

For your course and learning solutions, visit **www.cengage.com.**
Purchase any of our products at your local college store or at our preferred online store **www.cengagebrain.com.**
**Instructors:** Please visit **login.cengage.com** and log in to access instructor-specific resources.

Printed in China
3  4  5  6  7  18  17  16  15

To my wife, Kimberlie, and my children, Derek and Claire,
for their great patience and support.

—CHRISTOPHER A. KEARNEY

To my wife, Meg, for her love and support.
To Molly, Janey, and Neko for their smiles and laughter.

—TIMOTHY J. TRULL

# About the Authors

**Christopher A. Kearney, Ph.D.,** is Distinguished Professor of Psychology, Director of Clinical Training, and Director of the UNLV Child School Refusal and Anxiety Disorders Clinic at the University of Nevada, Las Vegas. He is a Fellow of the American Psychological Association, a licensed clinical psychologist, and the author of numerous journal articles, book chapters, and books related to school refusal behavior, social anxiety, shyness, and selective mutism in youth. He has also published a work on general child psychopathology, *Casebook in Child Behavior Disorders* (Wadsworth), and is or has been on the editorial boards of *Journal of Consulting and Clinical Psychology, Behavior Therapy, Journal of Clinical Child and Adolescent Psychology, Journal of Abnormal Child Psychology, Journal of Psychopathology and Behavioral Assessment, Journal of Anxiety Disorders,* and *Journal of Gambling Studies.* Dr. Kearney has received several awards for his research, teaching, and mentoring, including the Harry Reid Silver State Research Award among others. In addition to his clinical and research endeavors, Dr. Kearney works closely with school districts and mental health agencies to improve strategies for helping children attend school with less distress.

**Timothy J. Trull, Ph.D.,** is Professor of Psychological Sciences at the University of Missouri, Columbia. Dr. Trull received his Ph.D. from the University of Kentucky and completed his internship at New York Hospital–Cornell Medical Center. His research interests are in the areas of diagnosis and classification of mental disorders, borderline personality disorder, substance use disorders, clinical assessment, professional issues in clinical psychology, and ambulatory assessment methods. Dr. Trull has received several awards and honors for his teaching and mentoring, including Psi Chi Professor of the Year, the Robert S. Daniels Junior Faculty Teaching Award, and most recently the MU Graduate Faculty Mentor Award. He enjoys teaching Abnormal Psychology and Introduction to Clinical Psychology; his textbook *Clinical Psychology* (Wadsworth) is used in classes across the United States and internationally. Dr. Trull is a licensed psychologist, and he continues to train future clinical psychologists in the assessment, prevention, and treatment of psychological disorders.

# Brief Contents

Preface      xxviii

CHAPTER **1** Abnormal Psychology and Life      1

CHAPTER **2** Perspectives on Abnormal Psychology      20

CHAPTER **3** Risk and Prevention of Mental Disorders      50

CHAPTER **4** Diagnosis, Assessment, and Study of Mental Disorders      72

CHAPTER **5** Anxiety, Obsessive-Compulsive, and Trauma-Related Disorders      100

CHAPTER **6** Somatic Symptom and Dissociative Disorders      144

CHAPTER **7** Depressive and Bipolar Disorders and Suicide      176

CHAPTER **8** Eating Disorders      220

CHAPTER **9** Substance-Related Disorders      248

CHAPTER **10** Personality Disorders      288

CHAPTER **11** Sexual Dysfunctions, Paraphilic Disorders, and Gender Dysphoria      320

CHAPTER **12** Schizophrenia and Other Psychotic Disorders      358

CHAPTER **13** Developmental and Disruptive Behavior Disorders      392

CHAPTER **14** Neurocognitive Disorders      432

CHAPTER **15** Consumer Guide to Abnormal Psychology      462

Appendix: Stress-Related Problems      486
Glossary      G-1
References      R-1
Name Index      I-1
Subject Index      I-26

# Contents

Preface xxviii

## CHAPTER 1
# Abnormal Psychology and Life   1

**CASE:** *Travis*   2

**Introduction to Abnormal Psychology**   2

**What Is a Mental Disorder?**   3

**CASE:** *Treva Throneberry*   3

Deviance from the Norm   3

Difficulties Adapting to Life Demands   4

Experience of Personal Distress   5

Defining Abnormality   6

Dimensions Underlying Mental Disorders Are Relevant to Everyone   6

Interim Summary   9

Review Questions   10

**History of Abnormal Psychology**   10

Early Perspectives   10

Early Greek and Roman Thought   10

Middle Ages   11

Renaissance   11

Reform Movement   11

Modern Era   12

Interim Summary   12

Review Questions   12

**Abnormal Psychology and Life: Themes**   12

Dimensional Perspective   13

Prevention Perspective   13

Consumer Perspective   14

Diversity   14

Stigma   14

Interim Summary   17

Review Questions   17

Final Comments   17

Key Terms   18

Media Resources   18

**SPECIAL FEATURES**

**BOX 1.1** | Focus on Diversity: Emotion and Culture   5

**CONTINUUM FIGURE 1.2** Continuum of Emotions, Cognitions, and Behaviors   8

**BOX 1.2** | Focus on Law and Ethics: Heal Thyself: What the Self-Help Gurus Don't Tell You   13

**PERSONAL NARRATIVE 1.1** Alison Malmon   16

CHAPTER

# 2 Perspectives on Abnormal Psychology 20

CASE: *Mariella* 22

**Introduction 22**

**The Biological Model 23**
Nervous Systems and Neurons 24
Brain 25
Biological Assessment and Treatment 25
Evaluating the Biological Model 25
Interim Summary 26
Review Questions 28

**The Psychodynamic Model 28**
Brief Overview of the Psychodynamic Model 29
Psychodynamic Assessment and Treatment 31
Evaluating the Psychodynamic Model 32
Interim Summary 32
Review Questions 32

**The Humanistic Model 33**
Abraham Maslow 34
Carl Rogers 34
Rollo May 35
Humanistic Assessment and Treatment 35
Evaluating the Humanistic Model 35
Interim Summary 36
Review Questions 36

**The Cognitive-Behavioral Model 36**
Behavioral Perspective 36
Cognitive Perspective 37

A Cognitive-Behavioral Model 38
Cognitive-Behavioral Assessment and Treatment 39
Evaluating the Cognitive-Behavioral Model 40
Interim Summary 41
Review Questions 41

**The Sociocultural Model 41**
Culture 42
Gender 43
Neighborhoods and Communities 44
Family 44
Sociocultural Assessment and Treatment 44
Evaluating the Sociocultural Model 47
Interim Summary 47
Review Questions 47
Final Comments 47
Key Terms 48
Media Resources 48

**SPECIAL FEATURES**

BOX 2.1 | Focus on Violence: A More Complex Approach 28

BOX 2.2 | Focus on Law and Ethics: Dangerousness and Commitment 33

BOX 2.3 | Focus on Gender: A More Complex Approach 41

PERSONAL NARRATIVE 2.1 An Integrative Psychologist: Dr. John C. Norcross 46

CHAPTER

# 3 Risk and Prevention of Mental Disorders 50

CASE: *DeShawn* 52

## The Diathesis-Stress Model 52

Diathesis, Stress, and Mental Health 53

Diathesis-Stress: The Big Picture 53

Diathesis-Stress: The Little Picture 53

Implications of the Diathesis-Stress Model 54

Interim Summary 54

Review Questions 54

## Epidemiology: How Common Are Mental Disorders? 54

Prevalence of Mental Disorders 55

Treatment Seeking 57

Treatment Cost 58

Interim Summary 58

Review Questions 59

## Risk, Protective Factors, and Resilience 59

CASE: *Jana* 59

Risk Factors 59

Protective Factors 61

Interim Summary 63

Review Questions 64

## Prevention 64

Prevention on a Continuum 66

Three Types of Prevention 66

Prevention Programs for Mental Disorders 67

Interim Summary 69

Review Questions 70

Final Comments 70

Key Terms 71

Media Resources 71

## SPECIAL FEATURES

BOX 3.1 | John Snow: A Pioneer in Epidemiology and Prevention 55

BOX 3.2 | Focus on Gender: Suicide and College Students 61

BOX 3.3 | Focus on Violence: Prevention of Femicide 64

BOX 3.4 | Focus on Law and Ethics: Constructs Related to Insanity 69

PERSONAL NARRATIVE 3.1 **Kim Dude and the Wellness Resource Center** 70

CHAPTER

# 4 Diagnosis, Assessment, and Study of Mental Disorders 72

CASE: *Professor Smith* 74

## Defining Abnormal Behavior and Mental Disorder 74

Dimensions and Categories 74

*DSM* 75

Advantages of Diagnosis 75

Interim Summary 76

Review Questions 76

## Classifying and Assessing Abnormal Behavior and Mental Disorder 76

Assessing Abnormal Behavior and Mental Disorder 77

Reliability, Validity, and Standardization 78

Interview 80

Intelligence Tests 81

Personality Assessment 82

Behavioral Assessment 86

Biological Assessment 87

Psychophysiological Assessment 88

Neuropsychological Assessment 90

Interim Summary 91

Review Questions 91

## Culture and Clinical Assessment 91

Culture and the Development of Mental Disorders 91

Culture and Clinical Assessment 92

Interim Summary 92

Review Questions 93

## Studying Abnormal Behavior and Mental Disorder 93

Experiment 93

Correlational Studies 95

Quasi-Experimental Methods 95

Other Alternative Experimental Designs 96

Developmental Designs 97

Case Study 97

Consuming the Media's Research 98

Interim Summary 98

Review Questions 98

Final Comments 98

Key Terms 98

Media Resources 99

## SPECIAL FEATURES

**BOX 4.1** | Focus on Diversity: Culture and Diagnosis 77

**PERSONAL NARRATIVE 4.1 Anonymous** 78

**BOX 4.2** | Focus on Law and Ethics: Who Should Be Studied in Mental Health Research? 94

CHAPTER

# 5 Anxiety, Obsessive-Compulsive, and Trauma-Related Disorders 100

**CASE:** *Angelina* 102

**Worry, Anxiety, Fear, and Anxiety, Obsessive-Compulsive, and Trauma-Related Disorders: What Are They? 103**

**Anxiety, Obsessive-Compulsive, and Trauma-Related Disorders: Features and Epidemiology 104**

Panic Attack 105

Panic Disorder 106

Social Phobia 107

Specific Phobia 108

Generalized Anxiety Disorder 109

**CASE:** *Jonathan* 110

Obsessive-Compulsive Disorder 110

Obsessive-Compulsive-Related Disorders 111

Posttraumatic Stress Disorder and Acute Stress Disorder 111

**CASE:** *Marcus* 112

Separation Anxiety Disorder and School Refusal Behavior 115

Epidemiology of Anxiety, Obsessive-Compulsive, and Trauma-Related Disorders 117

**Stigma Associated with Anxiety, Obsessive-Compulsive, and Trauma-Related Disorders 120**

Interim Summary 121

Review Questions 122

**Anxiety, Obsessive-Compulsive, and Trauma-Related Disorders: Causes and Prevention 122**

Biological Risk Factors for Anxiety, Obsessive-Compulsive, and Trauma-Related Disorders 122

Environmental Risk Factors for Anxiety, Obsessive-Compulsive, and Trauma-Related Disorders 126

Causes of Anxiety, Obsessive-Compulsive, and Trauma-Related Disorders 129

Prevention of Anxiety, Obsessive-Compulsive, and Trauma-Related Disorders 130

Interim Summary 131

Review Questions 132

**Anxiety, Obsessive-Compulsive, and Trauma-Related Disorders: Assessment and Treatment 132**

Assessment of Anxiety, Obsessive-Compulsive, and Trauma-Related Disorders 132

Biological Treatment of Anxiety, Obsessive-Compulsive, and Trauma-Related Disorders 134

Psychological Treatments of Anxiety, Obsessive-Compulsive, and Trauma-Related Disorders 135

What if I Have Anxiety or an Anxiety Related Disorder? 141

Long-Term Outcome for People with Anxiety, Obsessive-Compulsive, and Trauma-Related Disorders 141

Interim Summary 142

Review Questions 143

Final Comments 143

Thought Questions    143

Key Terms    143

Media Resources    143

SPECIAL FEATURES

CONTINUUM FIGURE 5.1  Worry, Anxiety, and Fear
Along a Continuum    104

CONTINUUM FIGURE 5.2  Continuum of Emotions,
Cognitions, and Behaviors Regarding Anxiety-Related
Disorders    104

BOX 5.1 | Focus on Gender: Are There True Gender
Differences in Anxiety-Related Disorders?    119

BOX 5.2 | Focus on Diversity: Anxiety-Related Disorders
and Sociocultural Factors    120

THE CONTINUUM VIDEO PROJECT

*Darwin:* PTSD    130

PERSONAL NARRATIVE 5.1  Anonymous    132

BOX 5.3 | Focus on Law and Ethics: The Ethics of
Encouragement in Exposure-Based
Practices    142

# CHAPTER

# 6  Somatic Symptom and Dissociative Disorders    144

Somatic Symptom and Dissociative
  Disorders: A Historical
  Introduction    146

CASE: *Gisela*  146

Somatization and Somatic Symptom
  Disorders: What Are They?    146

Somatic Symptom Disorders: Features
  and Epidemiology    148

Somatic Symptom Disorder    148

Illness Anxiety Disorder    149

Conversion Disorder    150

Factitious Disorder and Malingering    150

Epidemiology of Somatic Symptom Disorders    151

Stigma Associated with Somatic Symptom
  Disorders    152

Interim Summary    152

Review Questions    153

Somatic Symptom Disorders: Causes
  and Prevention    153

Biological Risk Factors for Somatic Symptom
Disorders    153

Environmental Risk Factors for Somatic Symptom
Disorders    153

Causes of Somatic Symptom Disorders    155

Prevention of Somatic Symptom Disorders    156

Interim Summary    156

Review Questions    156

Somatic Symptom Disorders: Assessment
  and Treatment    157

Assessment of Somatic Symptom Disorders    157

Biological Treatment of Somatic Symptom
Disorders    157

Psychological Treatments of Somatic Symptom
Disorders    158

What If I or Someone I Know Has a Somatic Symptom
Disorder?    159

Long-Term Outcome for People with Somatic Symptom Disorders   159

Interim Summary   159

Review Questions   159

## Dissociative Disorders   160

CASE: *Erica*   160

## Normal Dissociation and Dissociative Disorders: What Are They?   161

## Dissociative Disorders: Features and Epidemiology   161

Dissociative Amnesia   161

Dissociative Identity Disorder   162

Depersonalization/Derealization Disorder   165

Epidemiology of Dissociative Disorders   166

## Stigma Associated with Dissociative Disorder   166

Interim Summary   168

Review Questions   168

## Dissociative Disorders: Causes and Prevention   168

Biological Risk Factors for Dissociative Disorders   168

Environmental Risk Factors for Dissociative Disorders   169

Causes of Dissociative Disorders   171

Prevention of Dissociative Disorders   171

Interim Summary   171

Review Questions   171

## Dissociative Disorders: Assessment and Treatment   171

Assessment of Dissociative Disorders   172

Biological Treatment of Dissociative Disorders   172

Psychological Treatments of Dissociative Disorders   173

What If I or Someone I Know Has a Dissociative Disorder?   173

Long-Term Outcome for People with Dissociative Disorders   174

Interim Summary   174

Review Questions   174

Final Comments   174

Thought Questions   174

Key Terms   175

Media Resources   175

## SPECIAL FEATURES

**CONTINUUM FIGURE 6.1 Continuum of Somatization and Somatic Symptom Disorders   148**

BOX 6.1   Focus on Violence: Terrorism and Medically Unexplained Symptoms   156

**CONTINUUM FIGURE 6.4 Continuum of Dissociation and Dissociative Disorders   162**

**PERSONAL NARRATIVE 6.1 Hannah Emily Upp   164**

BOX 6.2   Focus on Law and Ethics: Recovered Memories and Suggestibility   167

BOX 6.3   Focus on Diversity: Dissociation and Culture   167

BOX 6.4   Focus on Violence: Dissociative Experiences and Violence Toward Others   170

## THE CONTINUUM VIDEO PROJECT

*Lani and Jan:* **Dissociative Identity Disorder   174**

CHAPTER

# 7 Depressive and Bipolar Disorders and Suicide  176

CASE: *Katey*  178

## Normal Mood Changes and Depression and Mania: What Are They?  179

## Depressive and Bipolar Disorders and Suicide: Features and Epidemiology  179

Major Depressive Episode  179

Major Depressive Disorder  181

Persistent Depressive Disorder (Dysthymia)  182

Other Depressive Disorders  183

Manic and Hypomanic Episodes  183

Bipolar I Disorder  185

Bipolar II Disorder  189

Cyclothymic Disorder  189

Suicide  189

Epidemiology of Depressive and Bipolar Disorders  191

Epidemiology of Suicide  194

## Stigma Associated with Depressive and Bipolar Disorders  195

Interim Summary  195

Review Questions  196

## Depressive and Bipolar Disorders and Suicide: Causes and Prevention  196

Biological Risk Factors for Depressive and Bipolar Disorders and Suicide  196

Environmental Risk Factors for Depressive and Bipolar Disorders and Suicide  201

Causes of Depressive and Bipolar Disorders and Suicide  204

Prevention of Depressive and Bipolar Disorders and Suicide  205

Interim Summary  206

Review Questions  207

## Depressive and Bipolar Disorders and Suicide: Assessment and Treatment  207

Interviews and Clinician Ratings  207

Self-Report Questionnaires  208

Self-Monitoring and Observations from Others  209

Laboratory Assessment  210

Assessment of Suicide  210

Biological Treatment of Depressive and Bipolar Disorders and Suicide  210

Psychological Treatments for Depressive and Bipolar Disorders and Suicide  214

What If I Am Sad or Have a Depressive or Bipolar Disorder?  217

Long-Term Outcome for People with Depressive and Bipolar Disorders and Suicide  217

Interim Summary  218

Review Questions  218

Final Comments  219

Thought Questions  219

Key Terms  219

Media Resources  219

### SPECIAL FEATURES

CONTINUUM FIGURE 7.1 Continuum of Sadness and Depression  180

**CONTINUUM FIGURE 7.2** Continuum of Happiness, Euphoria, and Mania   180

**PERSONAL NARRATIVE 7.1** Karen Gormandy   184

**BOX 7.1** | Focus on Gender: Forms of Depression Among Women   186

THE **CONTINUUM** VIDEO PROJECT

*Emilie:* Bipolar Disorder   206

**BOX 7.2** | Focus on Law and Ethics: Ethical Dilemmas in Electroconvulsive Therapy   214

**BOX 7.3** | Focus on Diversity: Depression in the Elderly   215

# CHAPTER 8
# Eating Disorders   220

**CASE:** *Sooki*   222

**Weight Concerns, Body Dissatisfaction, and Eating Disorders: What Are They?**   222

**Eating Disorders: Features and Epidemiology**   223

Anorexia Nervosa   223

Bulimia Nervosa   224

**CASE:** *Lisa*   224

Binge Eating Disorder   225

Epidemiology of Eating Disorders   226

**Stigma Associated with Eating Disorders**   231

Interim Summary   231

Review Questions   231

**Eating Disorders: Causes and Prevention**   232

Biological Risk Factors for Eating Disorders   232

Environmental Risk Factors for Eating Disorders   234

Causes of Eating Disorders   236

Prevention of Eating Disorders   237

Interim Summary   237

Review Questions   238

**Eating Disorders: Assessment and Treatment**   238

Assessment of Eating Disorders   238

Treatment of Eating Disorders   241

Biological Treatments of Eating Disorders   241

Psychological Treatments of Eating Disorders   241

What If I Have Weight Concerns or an Eating Disorder?   245

Long-Term Outcome for People with Eating Disorders   245

Interim Summary   246

Review Questions   246

Final Comments   246

Thought Questions   247

Key Terms   247

Media Resources   247

**SPECIAL FEATURES**

**CONTINUUM FIGURE 8.1** Continuum of Body Dissatisfaction, Weight Concerns, and Eating Behavior   224

**PERSONAL NARRATIVE 8.1** Kitty Westin (Anna's mother) 226

**BOX 8.1** | Focus on Gender: Why Is There a Gender Difference in Eating Disorders? 230

**THE CONTINUUM VIDEO PROJECT**

*Sara:* Bulimia Nervosa 233

**PERSONAL NARRATIVE 8.2** Rachel Webb 239

**BOX 8.2** | Focus on Law and Ethics: How Ethical Are Pro-Ana (Pro-Anorexia) Websites? 243

CHAPTER

# 9 Substance-Related Disorders 248

**CASE:** *Elon* 250

**Normal Substance Use and Substance-Related Disorders: What Are They?** 250

**Substance-Related Disorders: Features and Epidemiology** 251

Substance Use Disorder 251

Substance Intoxication 252

Substance Withdrawal 252

Types of Substances 253

Epidemiology of Substance-Related Disorders 263

**Stigma Associated with Substance-Related Disorders** 265

Interim Summary 265

Review Questions 266

**Substance-Related Disorders: Causes and Prevention** 266

Biological Risk Factors for Substance-Related Disorders 266

Environmental Risk Factors for Substance-Related Disorders 269

Causes of Substance-Related Disorders 274

Prevention of Substance-Related Disorders 275

Interim Summary 276

Review Questions 276

**Substance-Related Disorders: Assessment and Treatment** 276

Interviews 276

Psychological Testing 277

Observations from Others 277

Laboratory Testing 277

Biological Treatment of Substance-Related Disorders 280

Psychological Treatment of Substance-Related Disorders 282

What If I or Someone I Know Has a Substance-Related Problem or Disorder? 284

Long-Term Outcome for People with Substance-Related Disorders 284

Interim Summary 286

Review Questions 286

Final Comments 286

Thought Questions 286

Key Terms 286

Media Resources 286

## SPECIAL FEATURES

**CONTINUUM FIGURE 9.1** Continuum of Substance Use and Substance-Related Disorders   252

**BOX 9.1** | The Sam Spady Story   258

**BOX 9.2** | The "Meth" Epidemic   261

**BOX 9.3** | Focus on Gender: Date Rape Drugs   263

## THE CONTINUUM VIDEO PROJECT

*Mark:*  **Substance Use Disorder**   271

**BOX 9.4** | Focus on Violence: Alcohol and Violence   272

**PERSONAL NARRATIVE 9.1** One Family's Struggle with Substance-Related Disorders   278

**BOX 9.5** | Focus on Law and Ethics: Drug Testing   281

# CHAPTER 10 Personality Disorders   288

**CASE:** *Michelle*   290

## Personality Traits, Unusual Personality, and Personality Disorder: What Are They?   291

## Organization of Personality Disorders   292

## Odd or Eccentric Personality Disorders: Features and Epidemiology   293

Paranoid Personality Disorder   293

Schizoid Personality Disorder   293

Schizotypal Personality Disorder   293

**CASE:** *Jackson*   294

Epidemiology of Odd or Eccentric Personality Disorders   295

Interim Summary   296

Review Questions   296

## Dramatic Personality Disorders: Features and Epidemiology   296

**CASE:** *Duane*   296

Antisocial Personality Disorder   296

Borderline Personality Disorder   297

Histrionic Personality Disorder   297

Narcissistic Personality Disorder   298

Epidemiology of Dramatic Personality Disorders   299

Interim Summary   300

Review Questions   300

## Anxious/Fearful Personality Disorders: Features and Epidemiology   300

Avoidant Personality Disorder   301

Dependent Personality Disorder   301

**CASE:** *Betty*   301

Obsessive-Compulsive Personality Disorder   301

Epidemiology of Anxious/Fearful Personality Disorders   302

## Stigma Associated with Personality Disorders   303

Interim Summary   304

Review Questions   304

## Personality Disorders: Causes and Prevention   304

Biological Risk Factors for Odd or Eccentric Personality Disorders   304

Environmental Risk Factors for Odd or Eccentric Personality Disorders    304

Causes of Odd or Eccentric Personality Disorders    305

Biological Risk Factors for Dramatic Personality Disorders    305

Environmental Risk Factors for Dramatic Personality Disorders    306

Causes of Dramatic Personality Disorders    306

Biological Risk Factors for Anxious/Fearful Personality Disorders    306

Environmental Risk Factors for Anxious/Fearful Personality Disorders    307

Causes of Anxious/Fearful Personality Disorders    308

Prevention of Personality Disorders    308

Interim Summary    309

Review Questions    309

## Personality Disorders: Assessment and Treatment    309

Assessment of Personality Disorders    309

Biological Treatments of Personality Disorders    312

Psychological Treatments of Personality Disorders    313

What If I or Someone I Know Has a Personality Disorder?    315

Long-Term Outcomes for People with Personality Disorders    315

Interim Summary    318

Review Questions    318

Final Comments    318

Thought Questions    318

Key Terms    318

Media Resources    318

## SPECIAL FEATURES

**CONTINUUM FIGURE 10.1** Continuum of Normal Personality and Personality Disorder Traits Related to Impulsivity    290

**BOX 10.1**    Focus on Violence: Personality Disorders and Violence    300

**BOX 10.2**    Focus on Gender: Mirror Images of Personality Disorders?    303

**BOX 10.2**    Focus on Law and Ethics: Personality and Insanity    312

## THE CONTINUUM VIDEO PROJECT

*Tina:* **Borderline Personality Disorder    315**

**PERSONAL NARRATIVE 10.1** Anonymous    316

CHAPTER

# 11 Sexual Dysfunctions, Paraphilic Disorders, and Gender Dysphoria    320

## Normal Sexual Behavior and Sexual Dysfunctions: What Are They?    322

CASE: *Douglas and Stacy*    322

## Sexual Dysfunctions: Features and Epidemiology    323

Male Hypoactive Sexual Desire Disorder    323

Female Sexual Interest/Arousal Disorder    323

Erectile Disorder    323

Female Orgasmic Disorder    324

Delayed Ejaculation    324

Premature (Early) Ejaculation    326

Genito-Pelvic Pain/Penetration Disorder    327

Epidemiology of Sexual Dysfunctions    327

## Stigma Associated with Sexual Dysfunctions    327

Interim Summary    328

Review Questions    329

## Sexual Dysfunctions: Causes and Prevention    329

Biological Risk Factors for Sexual Dysfunctions    330

Psychological Risk Factors for Sexual Dysfunctions    330

Causes of Sexual Dysfunctions    331

Prevention of Sexual Dysfunctions    331

Interim Summary    332

Review Questions    333

## Sexual Dysfunctions: Assessment and Treatment    333

Assessment of Sexual Dysfunctions    333

Biological Treatment of Sexual Dysfunctions    334

Psychological Treatments of Sexual Dysfunctions    334

What If I or Someone I Know Has a Sexual Dysfunction?    335

Long-Term Outcomes for People with Sexual Dysfunctions    336

Interim Summary    336

Review Questions    337

## Normal Sexual Desires, Paraphilias, and Paraphilic Disorders: What Are They?    337

## Paraphilic Disorders: Features and Epidemiology    337

Exhibitionistic Disorder    337

CASE: *Tom*    338

Fetishistic Disorder    338

Frotteuristic Disorder    340

Pedophilic Disorder    340

Sexual Masochism and Sexual Sadism    341

Transvestic Disorder    342

Voyeuristic Disorder    342

Atypical Paraphilic Disorders    342

Epidemiology of Paraphilic Disorders    342

Interim Summary     344

Review Questions     344

## Paraphilic Disorders: Causes and Prevention     345

Biological Risk Factors for Paraphilic Disorders     345

Environmental Risk Factors for Paraphilic Disorders     345

Causes of Paraphilic Disorders     347

Prevention of Paraphilic Disorders     347

Interim Summary     348

Review Questions     348

## Paraphilic Disorders: Assessment and Treatment     348

Assessment of Paraphilic Disorders     348

Biological Treatment of Paraphilic Disorders     349

Psychological Treatment of Paraphilic Disorders     349

What If I or Someone I Know Has a Paraphilic Disorder?     350

Long-Term Outcomes for People with Paraphilic Disorders     350

Interim Summary     351

Review Questions     351

## Normal Gender Development and Gender Dysphoria: What Are They?     351

CASE: *Austin*     351

## Gender Dysphoria: Features and Epidemiology     351

## Gender Dysphoria: Causes and Prevention     353

## Gender Dysphoria: Assessment and Treatment     354

Assessment of Gender Dysphoria     354

Biological Treatment of Gender Dysphoria     354

Psychological Treatment of Gender Dysphoria     354

What If I or Someone I Know Has Questions About Gender or Gender Dysphoria?     354

Long-Term Outcomes for People with Gender Dysphoria     355

Interim Summary     355

Review Questions     355

Final Comments     355

Thought Questions     355

Key Terms     356

Media Resources     357

## SPECIAL FEATURES

**CONTINUUM FIGURE 11.1 Continuum of Sexual Behavior and Sexual Dysfunctions     322**

BOX 11.1 | Focus on Gender: Gender Biases in Sexual Dysfunctions and Disorders     330

**CONTINUUM FIGURE 11.4 Continuum of Sexual Behavior and Paraphilic Disorders     336**

BOX 11.2 | Focus on Violence: Rape     345

BOX 11.3 | Focus on Law and Ethics: Sex Offender Notification and Incarceration     350

## THE CONTINUUM VIDEO PROJECT

*Dean:* **Gender Dysphoria     355**

**PERSONAL NARRATIVE 11.1 Sam     356**

CASE: *James*  360

**Unusual Emotions, Thoughts, and
Behaviors and Psychotic Disorders:
What Are They?     361**

**Psychotic Disorders: Features
and Epidemiology     361**

Schizophrenia     361

Phases of Schizophrenia     365

Schizophreniform Disorder     367

Schizoaffective Disorder     368

Delusional Disorder     370

CASE: *Jody*  370

Brief Psychotic Disorder     371

Epidemiology of Psychotic Disorders     371

**Stigma Associated with
Schizophrenia     373**

Interim Summary     375

Review Questions     375

**Psychotic Disorders: Causes
and Prevention     375**

Biological Risk Factors for Psychotic
Disorders     375

Environmental Risk Factors for Psychotic
Disorders     379

Causes of Psychotic Disorders     380

Prevention of Psychotic Disorders     382

Interim Summary     382

Review Questions     383

**Psychotic Disorders: Assessment
and Treatment     383**

Interviews     383

Behavioral Observations     383

Cognitive Assessment     384

Physiological Assessment     384

Biological Treatments of Psychotic Disorders     385

Psychological Treatments of Psychotic Disorders     386

What If I or Someone I Know Has a Psychotic
Disorder?     389

Long-Term Outcome for People with Psychotic
Disorders     389

Interim Summary     389

Review Questions     390

Final Comments     390

Thought Questions     390

Key Terms     390

Media Resources     390

**SPECIAL FEATURES**

**CONTINUUM FIGURE 12.1** Continuum of Unusual
Emotions, Cognitions, and Behaviors and Psychotic
Disorder  362

**PERSONAL NARRATIVE 12.1** John Cadigan  368

**BOX 12.1** | Focus on Diversity: Ethnicity and Income Level
in Schizophrenia  373

**BOX 12.2** | Focus on Violence: Are People with
Schizophrenia More Violent?  374

**THE CONTINUUM VIDEO PROJECT**

*Andre:* **Schizophrenia   382**

**BOX 12.3** | Focus on Law and Ethics: Making the Choice of
Antipsychotic Medication  385

CHAPTER

# 13 Developmental and Disruptive Behavior Disorders 392

**Developmental and Disruptive Behavior Disorders   394**

CASE: *Robert   394*

**Normal Development and Developmental Disorders: What Are They?   395**

**Developmental Disorders: Features and Epidemiology   395**

Intellectual Disability   395

Autism Spectrum Disorder   397

Learning Disorder   399

CASE: *Alison   399*

Epidemiology of Developmental Disorders   401

**Stigma Associated with Developmental Disorders   402**

Interim Summary   402

Review Questions   402

**Developmental Disorders: Causes and Prevention   402**

Biological Risk Factors for Developmental Disorders   402

Environmental Risk Factors for Developmental Disorders   406

Causes of Developmental Disorders   406

Prevention of Developmental Disorders   407

Interim Summary   408

Review Questions   408

**Developmental Disorders: Assessment and Treatment   408**

Cognitive Tests   408

Achievement Tests   409

Interviews   410

Rating Scales   410

Behavioral Observation   410

Biological Treatment for Developmental Disorders   410

Psychological Treatments for Developmental Disorders   411

What If I Think Someone Has a Developmental Disorder?   413

Long-Term Outcome for People with Developmental Disorders   413

Interim Summary   413

Review Questions   414

**Disruptive Behavior Disorders   414**

**Normal Rambunctious Behavior and Disruptive Behavior Disorders: What Are They?   414**

CASE: *Will   415*

**Disruptive Behavior Disorders: Features and Epidemiology   415**

Attention-Deficit/Hyperactivity Disorder   415

Oppositional Defiant Disorder and Conduct Disorder   416

Epidemiology of Disruptive Behavior Disorders   417

**Stigma Associated with Disruptive Behavior Disorders   418**

Interim Summary   419

Review Questions   419

**Disruptive Behavior Disorders: Causes and Prevention   419**

Biological Risk Factors for Disruptive Behavior Disorders   419

Environmental Risk Factors for Disruptive Behavior Disorders   421

Causes of Disruptive Behavior Disorders   423

Prevention of Disruptive Behavior Disorders   423

Interim Summary   424

Review Questions   424

**Disruptive Behavior Disorders: Assessment and Treatment   424**

Interviews   424

Rating Scales   425

Behavioral Observation   425

Biological Treatments for Disruptive Behavior Disorders   425

Psychological Treatments for Disruptive Behavior Disorders   426

What If I Think a Child Has a Disruptive Behavior Disorder?   427

Long-Term Outcome for Children with Disruptive Behavior Disorders   427

Interim Summary   429

Review Questions   429

Final Comments   430

Thought Questions   430

Key Terms   430

Media Resources   430

**SPECIAL FEATURES**

**CONTINUUM FIGURE 13.1** Continuum of Normal Development and Developmental Disorder   394

**BOX 13.1** Focus on Law and Ethics: Key Ethical Issues and Developmental Disorders   403

**BOX 13.2** Focus on Diversity: Testing for People with Developmental Disorders   409

**THE CONTINUUM VIDEO PROJECT**

*Whitney:* **Autism Spectrum Disorder   411**

**CONTINUUM FIGURE 13.4** Continuum of Disruptive Behavior and Disruptive Behavior Disorder   416

**PERSONAL NARRATIVE 13.1** Toni Wood   428

**BOX 13.3** Focus on Violence: Juvenile Arrests and "Diversion"   428

CHAPTER

# 14 Neurocognitive Disorders   432

**CASE:** *William and Laura*   434

**Normal Changes During Aging and Neurocognitive Disorders: What Are They?   435**

**Neurocognitive Disorders: Features and Epidemiology   436**

Delirium   436

Dementia and Major and Mild Neurocognitive Disorder   438

Alzheimer's Disease   439

Lewy Bodies   441

Vascular Disease   441

Parkinson's Disease   442

Pick's Disease   443

Other Problems 443

Epidemiology of Neurocognitive Disorders 444

## Stigma Associated with Neurocognitive Disorders 446

Interim Summary 446

Review Questions 447

## Neurocognitive Disorders: Causes and Prevention 447

Biological Risk Factors for Neurocognitive Disorders 447

Environmental Risk Factors for Neurocognitive Disorders 450

Causes of Neurocognitive Disorders 452

Prevention of Neurocognitive Disorders 453

Interim Summary 454

Review Questions 454

## Neurocognitive Disorders: Assessment and Treatment 454

Assessment of Neurocognitive Disorders 454

Biological Treatments of Neurocognitive Disorders 456

Psychological Treatments of Neurocognitive Disorders 457

What If Someone I Know Has a Neurocognitive Disorder? 459

Long-Term Outcome for People with Neurocognitive Disorders 459

Interim Summary 460

Review Questions 461

Final Comments 461

Thought Questions 461

Key Terms 461

Media Resources 461

### SPECIAL FEATURES

**CONTINUUM FIGURE 14.1 Continuum of Thinking and Memory Problems and Neurocognitive Disorder 436**

**BOX 14.1** Focus on Violence: Maltreatment of the Elderly 446

### THE CONTINUUM VIDEO PROJECT

*Myriam:* **Alzheimer's Disease 448**

**BOX 14.2** Focus on Gender: Grief in the Spouse Caregiver 458

**BOX 14.3** Focus on Law and Ethics: Ethical Issues and Dementia 460

CHAPTER

# 15 Consumer Guide to Abnormal Psychology 462

## Introduction to the Consumer Guide 464

## Becoming a Mental Health Professional 464

Types of Therapists and Qualifications 464

Preparing to Be a Mental Health Professional 465

## Becoming a Client 468

## Treatment at the Individual Level 469

Active Ingredients of Treatment 469

Process Variables in Treatment 471

Does Treatment Work? 472

Prescriptive Treatment 473

Interim Summary     473

Review Questions     473

## Treatment at the Community Level     473

Self-Help Groups     473

Aftercare Services for People with Severe Mental Disorders     474

Residential Facilities for People with Developmental Disorders     475

Criminal Justice System     476

Public Policy and Mental Health     476

Interim Summary     476

Review Questions     477

## Limitations and Caveats About Treatment     477

Client-Therapist Differences     477

Cultural Differences     478

Managed Care     478

Differences Between Clinicians and Researchers     478

Quick Fixes     479

Misuse of Research     479

Weak Research and How to Judge a Research Article     479

Negative Therapist Characteristics     479

Lack of Access to Treatment     480

## Ethics     481

General Principles     481

Assessment     481

Treatment     481

Public Statements     483

Research     483

Resolving Ethical Issues     483

Interim Summary     484

Review Questions     484

Final Comments     484

Thought Questions     484

Key Terms     485

Media Resources     485

## SPECIAL FEATURES

**BOX 15.1** | Focus on Gender: Graduate School and Mentors     469

**PERSONAL NARRATIVE 15.1 Julia Martinez, Graduate Student in Clinical Psychology     470**

**PERSONAL NARRATIVE 15.2 Tiffany S. Borst, M.A., L.P.C.     474**

**BOX 15.2** | Focus on Law and Ethics: Rights of Those Hospitalized for Mental Disorder     477

**BOX 15.3** | Focus on Diversity: Lack of Diversity in Research     478

**PERSONAL NARRATIVE 15.3 Christopher A. Kearney, Ph.D.     480**

**BOX 15.4** | Focus on Law and Ethics: Sexual Intimacy and the Therapeutic Relationship     483

**Appendix: Stress-Related Problems     486**

**Glossary     G-1**

**References     R-1**

**Name Index     I-1**

**Subject Index     I-26**

# Preface

When we, the authors, decided to write this textbook, we wanted to create something different for our students. We wanted to create a book that appealed to students by helping them understand that symptoms of psychological problems occur in many people in different ways. We wanted to avoid characterizing mental disorders from a "yes–no" or "us–them" perspective and focus instead on how such problems affect many people to varying degrees in their everyday lives. In essence, we wanted to illustrate how abnormal psychology was really about the struggles that all of us face in our lives to some extent. We represent this approach in our title: *Abnormal Psychology and Life*.

Abnormal psychology is one of the most popular courses on college campuses. Students are eager to learn about unusual behavior and how such behavior can be explained. Many students who take an abnormal psychology course crave a scientific perspective that can help prepare them well for graduate school and beyond. Other students take an abnormal psychology course because they are curious about themselves or people they know and thus seek application and relevance of the course information to their daily lives. Our book is designed to appeal to both types of students. The material in the book reflects state-of-the-art thinking and research regarding mental disorders but also emphasizes several key themes that increase personal relevance. These themes include a dimensional and integrative perspective, a consumer-oriented perspective, and emphases on prevention and cultural diversity. Personal relevance is also achieved by providing information to reduce the stigma of mental disorder; by illustrating comprehensive models of mental disorder that include biological, psychological, and other risk factors; and by employing various pedagogical aids, visually appealing material, and technological utilities.

## A Dimensional and Integrative Perspective

A focus on how abnormal psychology is a key part of life comes about in this book in different ways. One main way is our focus on a *dimensional perspective toward mental disorder*. We believe that thoughts, feelings, and behaviors associated with mental disorders are present, to some degree, in all of us. Everyone experiences some level of anxiety, sadness, odd physical symptoms, worry about sexual behavior, and memory problems from time to time, for example. Throughout our chapters we vividly illustrate how different mental disorders can be seen along a continuum of normal, mild, moderate, severe, and very severe emotions, thoughts, and behaviors.

We also provide examples along this continuum that parallel common scenarios people face, such as interactions with others and job interviews.

Our dimensional perspective is discussed within the context of an integrative perspective that includes an extensive discussion of risk and protective factors for various mental disorders. Such factors include biological (e.g., genetic, neurochemical, brain changes), personality, psychological (e.g., cognitive, learning, trauma), interpersonal, family, cultural, evolutionary, and other domains. We emphasize a diathesis-stress model and provide sections that integrate risk factors to present comprehensive models of various mental disorders. We also provide an appendix of medical conditions with contributing psychological factors that includes a biopsychosocial perspective to explain the interplay of physical symptoms with stress and other key contributing variables.

## A Consumer-Oriented Perspective

Our book is also designed to recognize the fact that today's student is very *consumer-oriented*. Students expect textbooks to be relevant to their own lives and to deliver information about diagnostic criteria, epidemiological data, brain changes, and assessment instruments in visually appealing and technologically sophisticated ways. This textbook adopts a consumer approach in several ways. The chapters in this book contain suggestions for those who are concerned that they or someone they know may have symptoms of a specific mental disorder. These suggestions also come with key questions one could ask to determine whether a problem may be evident. In addition, much of our material is geared toward a consumer approach. In our discussion of neurocognitive disorders such as Alzheimer's disease, for example, we outline questions one could ask when considering placing a parent in a nursing home.

The consumer orientation of this book is also prominent in the last chapter when we discuss topics such as becoming a mental health professional, becoming a client in therapy, treatments available at the community level such as self-help groups, and how to judge a research article, among other topics. Throughout our chapters, we also focus special attention on issues of gender, ethnicity, law and ethics, and violence in separate boxes. We offer visually appealing examples of a dimensional model for each major mental disorder, brain figures, and engaging tables and charts to more easily convey important information. The book is also linked to many technological resources and contains 15 chapters, which fits nicely into a typical 15-week semester.

We also include several pedagogical aids to assist students during their learning process. The chapters are organized in a similar fashion throughout, beginning with initial sections on normal and unusual behavior and followed by discussions of features and epidemiology, stigma, causes and prevention, assessment, treatment, and prognosis. The chapters contain interim summaries and review questions at periodic intervals to help students check their understanding of what they just learned. Bold key terms are placed throughout the chapters and corresponding definitions are placed in the margin. *What Do You Think?* questions appear after the chapter-opening case study, which help students focus on important aspects of the case. Boxes that direct readers to related videos from the Continuum Video Project are featured in the disorder chapters (Chapters 5-14). More information on the Continuum Video Project is on page xxxi. Final comments are also provided at the end of each chapter to link material to previous and future chapters. Broad-based thought questions are also at the end of each chapter to challenge students to apply what they have learned to their daily lives. The writing style of the book is designed to be easy to follow and to succinctly convey key information.

## Prevention

Another important theme of this book is *prevention*. Most college students function well in their environment, but everyone has some level of risk for psychological dysfunction or distress. We thus emphasize research-based ways to prevent the onset of psychological problems throughout this textbook. We offer specific sections on prevention and provide a detailed discussion of risk factors for mental disorder and how these risk factors could be minimized. We also provide a discussion of protective factors and strategies that could be nurtured during one's life to prevent psychological problems. Examples include anxiety and stress management, emotional regulation, appropriate coping, healthy diet, and adaptive parenting.

Much of our discussion in this area focuses on primary and secondary prevention, which has great appeal for students. Many prevention programs target those who have not developed a mental disorder or who may be at risk due to individual or environmental factors. A focus on prevention helps students understand what they could do to avert problematic symptoms or to seek help before such symptoms become more severe. Prevention material in the book also focuses on tertiary prevention and relapse prevention, so students can understand what steps people can take to continue healthy functioning even after the occurrence of a potentially devastating mental disorder. The prevention material in this book thus has broad appeal, relevance, and utility for students.

## Cultural Diversity

Mental health professionals have made a more concerted effort to achieve greater cultural diversity in their research, to apply findings in laboratory settings to greater numbers of people,

and to shine a spotlight on those who are traditionally underserved. We emphasize these greater efforts in this textbook. In addition to the special boxes on diversity, we provide detailed information about cultural syndromes; how symptoms and epidemiology may differ across cultural groups; how certain cultural factors may serve as risk and protective factors for various disorders; how diagnostic, assessment, and treatment strategies may need to be modified for different cultural groups; and how cultural groups may seek treatment or cope differently with symptoms of mental disorder.

Our discussion of cultural diversity applies to various ethnic and racial groups, but diversity across individuals is represented in many other ways as well. We focus heavily on gender differences, sexual orientation, sociocultural factors, migrant populations, and changes in symptoms as people age from childhood to adolescence to adulthood to late adulthood. Our emphasis on cultural and other types of diversity is consistent with our life-based approach for the book: Symptoms of mental disorder can occur in many people in many different ways in many life stages.

## Stigma

A focus on a dimensional approach to mental disorder helps us advance another key theme of this book, which is to *reduce stigma*. Stigma refers to socially discrediting people because of certain behaviors or attributes that may lead to them being seen as undesirable in some way. People with schizophrenia, for example, are often stigmatized as people who cannot function or who may even be dangerous. Adopting a dimensional perspective to mental disorder helps reduce inaccurate stereotypes and the stigma associated with many of these problems. You will also see throughout this book that we emphasize people first and a mental disorder second to reduce stigma. You will not see us use words or phrases such as *schizophrenics* or *bulimics* or *the learning disabled*. Instead, you will see phrases such as *people with schizophrenia, those with bulimia,* or *children with learning disorder*. We also provide special sections on stigma throughout the chapters as well as boxes that contain information to dispel common myths about people with mental disorders that likely lead to negative stereotyping.

## Clinical Cases and Narratives

Our dimensional perspective and our drive to reduce stigma is enhanced as well by extensive use of clinical cases and personal narratives throughout the book. Clinical cases are presented in chapters that describe a particular mental disorder and are often geared toward cases to which most college students can relate. These cases then reappear throughout that chapter as we discuss features of that disorder as well as assessment and treatment strategies. We also include personal narratives from people who have an actual mental disorder and who can discuss its symptoms and other features from direct experience. All of these cases reinforce the idea that symptoms of mental disorder are present to some degree in many people, perhaps including those easily recognized by a student as someone in his or her life.

# New to the Second Edition

The second edition contains many new and exciting changes. Readers will see that the most obvious change is an adaptation to the new edition of the *Diagnostic and Statistical Manual of Mental Disorders* (DSM), the DSM-5. The chapters remain aligned as they were previously to enhance teaching in a typical semester and to reflect empirical work that has been done for each set of disorders. DSM-5 criteria are presented to help illuminate symptoms of mental disorders better for students and to convey the dimensional aspects introduced more in the new manual. Examples include continua based on severity, number of symptoms or behavioral episodes, and body mass index, among many others. We also emphasize other aspects of the DSM-5 that are dimensional in nature, such as the alternative model of personality disorders (Chapter 10). We also make clear how the DSM-5 has changed with respect to various disorders and how that affects the terminology in the chapters. We hope this helps provide a seamless transition for students and instructors alike.

The second edition also contains more boxes devoted to gender, diversity, violence, and law and ethics. For example, new material has been added regarding concepts related to insanity and to mentoring in graduate school. The second edition also contains new, separate sections regarding stigma for each chapter that covers a set of mental disorders (i.e., Chapters 5–14). These new sections illustrate our commitment to this important topic and present fascinating research with respect to others' views of someone with a mental disorder and treatment and other strategies that have been developed to reduce stigma toward those with mental disorder.

An important process as well has been a thorough review of the material to ensure that students continue to be presented with state-of-the-art research and most current thinking regarding mental disorders, including epidemiology. Several sections of the book have thus been redone or reworked to reflect new data, and hundreds of new citations have been added, most of which are very current. Other sections are new, such as an expansion of research designs in Chapter 4 and a discussion of sleep disorders in the appendix. One thing that has not changed, however, is our deep devotion and commitment to this work and to our students and their instructors.

A brief summary of key changes and additions for each chapter in the second edition is provided here. This is not an exhaustive list but provides some general guidance for those familiar with the first edition.

## Chapter 1: Abnormal Psychology and Life

- New case, Travis, at beginning of chapter to match other chapters and give students a specific example to help illustrate concepts in the chapter.
- Diversity material added, including multicultural psychology.
- Information regarding college students and stigma.

## Chapter 2: Perspectives on Abnormal Psychology

- Update of heritability information.
- New boxes on violence, law and ethics, and gender, including material on dangerousness and commitment.
- Changes in culture section to match DSM-5, such as cultural syndromes.

## Chapter 3: Risk and Prevention of Mental Disorders

- New law and ethics box on constructs related to insanity.
- Updated information on treatment cost and other figures regarding college student suicide.

## Chapter 4: Diagnosis, Assessment, and Study of Mental Disorders

- New section on classifying abnormal behavior and mental disorder to reflect DSM-5 changes and to emphasize dimensional assessments, especially with respect to Professor Smith's case.
- Substantial revision of culture and development of mental disorders section to reflect new changes.
- Substantial revision of culture and clinical assessment section to reflect DSM-5 cultural formulation (and related interview).
- New material in research design sections, including double- and triple-blind designs and natural, analogue, and single-subject experiments.

## Chapter 5: Anxiety, Obsessive-Compulsive, and Trauma-Related Disorders

- DSM-5 clarification regarding these disorders as well as description of new obsessive-compulsive-related disorders such as hoarding and trichotillomania.
- New stigma material regarding anxiety, obsessive-compulsive, and trauma-related disorders.
- Updated heritability and other etiology information.
- Updated assessment and treatment information, such as biological challenges.

## Chapter 6: Somatic Symptom and Dissociative Disorders

- DSM-5 clarification regarding new somatic symptom disorders.
- New stigma material regarding somatic symptom and dissociative disorders.
- Revamped genetics and long-term outcome sections for somatic symptom disorders.

## Chapter 7: Depressive and Bipolar Disorders and Suicide

- *DSM-5* clarification regarding new disorders such as disruptive mood dysregulation disorder.
- New stigma material regarding depressive and bipolar disorders.
- Reorganization of manic and hypomanic episode descriptions.

## Chapter 8: Eating Disorders

- *DSM-5* clarification regarding eating disorders.
- Revamped epidemiology, genetics, brain changes, and prognosis sections.

## Chapter 9: Substance-Related Disorders

- *DSM-5* clarification regarding substance-related disorders and revamping of early section on features.
- New stigma material regarding substance-related disorders.
- New material on college student expectancies regarding alcohol use and treatment of college students with substance use problems.
- New material regarding impulsivity and substance use.
- Revamped section on prevention to reflect changes in the field.

## Chapter 10: Personality Disorders

- *DSM-5* clarification regarding personality disorders as well as description of *DSM-5* alternative dimensional model of personality disorders.
- Updated heritability estimates for the personality disorder clusters and brain change.
- New stigma material regarding personality disorders.
- Revamped prognosis section for personality disorders.
- New law and ethics box on personality and insanity, including the concepts of guilty but mentally ill and diminished capacity.

## Chapter 11: Sexual Dysfunctions, Paraphilic Disorders, and Gender Dysphoria

- *DSM-5* clarification regarding sexual dysfunctions, paraphilic disorders, and gender dysphoria.
- New stigma material regarding sexual dysfunctions.
- Updated prognosis and other information.

## Chapter 12: Schizophrenia and Other Psychotic Disorders

- *DSM-5* clarification regarding psychotic disorders as well as revamping of dimensions of schizophrenia.
- New stigma material regarding psychotic disorders.

## Chapter 13: Developmental and Disruptive Behavior Disorders

- *DSM-5* clarification regarding psychotic disorders as well as revamping of dimensions of schizophrenia.
- New stigma material regarding psychotic disorders.

## Chapter 14: Neurocognitive Disorders

- *DSM-5* clarification regarding neurocognitive disorders as well as dimensions of neurocognitive functioning.
- New stigma material regarding neurocognitive disorders.

## Chapter 15: Consumer Guide to Abnormal Psychology

- Editing throughout to enhance clarity as well as reference updating.
- New gender box on graduate school and mentoring.

## Appendix: Stress-Related Problems

- New prevalence information.
- New section on sleep disorders.
- Key updates regarding Type A and D personalities.

## SUPPLEMENTS

### Continuum Video Project

The Continuum Video Project provides holistic, three-dimensional portraits of individuals dealing with psychopathologies. Videos show clients living their daily lives, interacting with family and friends, and displaying—rather than just describing—their symptoms. Before each video segment, students are asked to make observations about the individual's symptoms, emotions, and behaviors and then rate them on the spectrum from normal to severe. The Continuum Video Project allows students to "see" the disorder and the person as a human; and helps viewers understand abnormal behavior can be viewed along a continuum.

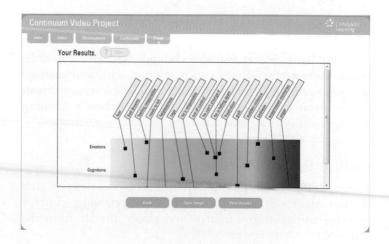

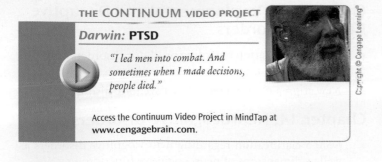

## MindTap

MindTap for Kearney and Trull's *Abnormal Psychology and Life: A Dimensional Approach* is a highly personalized fully online learning platform of authoritative content, assignments, and services offering you a tailored presentation of course curriculum created by your instructor. MindTap guides you through the course curriculum via an innovative learning path where you will complete reading assignments, annotate your readings, complete homework, and engage with quizzes and assessments. MindTap includes the Continuum Video Project.

Go to **cengagebrain.com** to access MindTap.

## Online Test Bank

Available online for instructors, the Test bank is an extensive collection of multiple-choice questions for objective tests, all closely tied to the text chapters. We're confident that you will find this to be a dependable and usable test bank.

## Online Instructor's Resource Manual

Also available online for instructors, the Instructor's Resource Manual is available as a convenient aid for your educational endeavors. It provides a thorough overview of each chapter and includes a wealth of suggestions organized around the content of each chapter in the text.

## Cengage Learning Testing Powered by Cognero

The Test Bank is also available through Cognero, a flexible, online system that allows you to author, edit, and manage test bank content as well as create multiple test versions in an instant. You can deliver tests from your school's learning management system, your classroom, or wherever you want.

## Online Power Points

These vibrant, Microsoft PowerPoint lecture slides for each chapter assist you with your lecture, by providing concept coverage using images, figures, and tables directly from the textbook!

All of these instructor supplements are available online for download.

Go to **login.cengage.com** to create an account and log in.

## Acknowledgments

Producing this book required the joint efforts of Wadsworth and Graphic World Publishing Services. We thank our editor, Tim Matray, and our product developer, Tangelique Williams-Grayer. We thank Cassie Carey at Graphic World for management of the book's production and Dharanivel Baskar for photo research. We are grateful for Nicole Richards, editorial assistant; Matt Ballantyne, content project manager; Vernon Boes, art director; Mary Noel, media editor; and Jessica Alderman, assistant editor. We also appreciate the work of Jennifer Levanduski, marketing director; and Angeline Low, marketing coordinator.

We would like to recognize and thank Ileana Arias, Marianne Taflinger, Jaime Perkins, and Kate Barnes for their help with this text's initial development.

We also want to thank those who agreed to contribute their personal stories for this book. Their narratives were essential to this book and helped bring the material to life.

The feedback and comments from the reviewers of the chapters of this book were extremely helpful. We would like to thank the second edition reviewers:

Polly McMahon, Spokane Falls Community College
Kira Banks, St. Louis University
Adam Wenzel, Saint Anselm College
Stephanie Stein, Central Washington University
Randolph Arnau, University of Southern Mississippi
Wendy Dunn, Coe College
Regan Murray, Briar Cliff University
Ashlea Smith, Paradise Valley Community College
Scott Stehouwer, Calvin College
Beth Wiediger, Lincoln Land Community College

We also thank the following First Edition reviewers, as well as those who wished to remain anonymous:

Craig Abrahamson, James Madison University; Dave Alfano, Community College of Rhode Island; Stephen Balsis, Texas A&M University; Ollie Barrier, Park University at Parkville; Lee Ann Bartolini, Dominican University of California; Evelyn Behar, University of Illinois-Chicago; Kathryn Bell, Northern Illinois University-Dekalb; Laurie Berkshire, Erie Community College; James Bexendale, Cayuga Community College; Amy Badura Brack, Creighton University; Nicole Bragg, Mount Hood Community College; Jo Anne Brewster, James Madison University; Seth Brown, University of Northern Iowa; Emily Bullock, University of Southern Mississippi; David Carpenter, Texas State University; Sherri Chandler, Muskegon Community College; Bryan Chochran, University of Montana; Brian Cowley, Park University–Parkville; Trina Cyterski, University of Georgia; Dale Doty, Monroe Community College; Anthony Drago, East Stroudsburgh University; Wendy Dunn, Coe College;

Christopher Echkhardt, Purdue University at West Lafayette; Georg Eifert, Chapman University; Carlos A. Escoto, Eastern Connecticut State University; Joe Etherton, Texas State University; Gabriel Feldmar, Nassau Community College; Meredyth Fellows, West Chester University; David Fresco, Kent State University; Gina Golden-Tangalakis, California State University, Long Beach; Barry Greenwald, University of Illinois-Chicago; Ron Hallman, Emmanuel Bible College; Julie Hanauer, Suffolk Community College at Ammerman; Kevin Handley, Germanna Community College; April Hess, Southwest Virginia Community College; Cecil Hutto, University of Louisiana-Monroe; Robert Rex Johnson, Delaware Community College; Samuel Joseph, Luzerne County Community College; Guadalupe King, Milwaukee Area Technical College-Downtown; Laura Knight, Indiana University of Pennsylvania; Victor Koop, Goshen College; Martha Lally, College of Lake County; Steve Lee, University of California, Los Angeles; David Lester, The Richard Stockton College of New Jersey; Don Lucas, Northwest Vista College; Susan Meeks, University of Louisville; Rafael Mendez, Bronx Community College; Paul Moore, Quinnipiac University; Francis P. O'Neill, Montgomery County Community College–West Campus; Leanne Parker, Lewis-Clark State College; Deborah S. Podwika, Kankakee Community College; Skip Pollack, Mesa Community College; Jay Pope, Fresno Pacific University; Frank J. Provenzano, Greenville Technical College; Kelly Quinn, East Texas Baptist University; Barry Ries, Minnesota State University at Mankato; Eric Rogers, College of Lake County; John Roop, North Georgia College & State University; Patricia Sawyer, Middlesex Community College; Kerry Schwanz, Coastal Carolina University; Norman A. Scott, Iowa State University; William Scott, Liberty University; Laura Seligman, University of Toledo; Nancy Simpson, Trident Technical College; Randyl Smith, Metropolitan State College of Denver; Betsy Stern, Milwaukee Area Technical College-Downtown; Joanne Hoven Stohs, California State University, Fullerton; Diane Tarricone, Eastern Connecticut State University; Ronald Theobald, SUNY–Jefferson Community College; Ayme Turnbull, Hofstra University; Michelle Vanbuskirk, Monroe Community College; Fabian Vega, Baltimore City Community College at Liberty Campus; J. Celeste Walley-Jean, Clayton State University; Stephen Weiss, Adams State College; Gene White, Salisbury University; Fred Whitford, Montana State University at Bozeman; Amy Williamson, Moraine Valley Community College.

In addition, we thank those who helped us create the supplements for this text, including Fred Whitford, author of the Instructor's Manual, and Kelly Henry, the Test Bank and PowerPoint preparer. Finally, we thank all of the instructors who use this textbook, as well as the students who take their courses. As always, we welcome your comments and suggestions regarding the book.

# Abnormal Psychology and Life

**1**

**CASE:** *Travis*

**What Do You Think?**

**Introduction to Abnormal Psychology**

**What Is a Mental Disorder?**

**CASE:** *Treva Throneberry*

   Interim Summary
   Review Questions

**History of Abnormal Psychology**
   Interim Summary
   Review Questions

**Abnormal Psychology and Life: Themes**
   Interim Summary
   Review Questions

FINAL COMMENTS

KEY TERMS

MEDIA RESOURCES

## SPECIAL FEATURES

**BOX 1.1** | Focus on Diversity: Emotion and Culture   5

**CONTINUUM FIGURE 1.2** Continuum of Emotions, Cognitions, and Behaviors   8–9

**BOX 1.2** | Focus on Law and Ethics: Heal Thyself: What the Self-Help Gurus Don't Tell You   13

**PERSONAL NARRATIVE 1.1** Alison Malmon   16–17

## CASE: Travis

**Travis** is a 21-year-old college junior who has been struggling recently. He and his longtime girlfriend broke up 2 months ago, and he took this very hard. Travis and his girlfriend had been together for 17 months, and she was his first serious romantic relationship. However, the couple eventually became emotionally distant from one another and mutually decided to split following several arguments. Travis initially seemed fine after the breakup but then became a bit sullen and withdrawn about a week later. He began to miss a few classes and spent more time in his dorm room and on his computer.

Since the breakup several weeks ago, Travis seems to be getting worse each day. He rarely eats, has trouble sleeping, and stays in bed much of the day. He "zones out" by playing video games, watching television, or staring out the window for hours per day. Travis has lost about 10 pounds in recent weeks and looks tired and pale. He has also been drinking alcohol more in recent days. In addition, his classroom attendance has declined significantly, and he is in danger of failing his courses this semester.

Travis says little about the breakup or his feelings. His friends have tried everything they can think of to help him feel better, with no success. Travis generally declines their offers to go out, attend parties, or meet other women. He is not mean-spirited in his refusals to go out but rather just shakes his head. Travis's friends have become worried that Travis might

Peter Banos/Alamy

hurt himself, but they cannot be with him all the time. They have decided that Travis should speak with someone at the psychological services center on campus and plan on escorting him there today.

### What Do You Think?

1. Which of Travis's emotional or behavioral problems concern you the most? Why?

2. What do you think Travis should do?

3. What would you do if you had a friend who was experiencing difficulties like Travis?

4. What emotional or behavioral problems have you encountered in yourself or in others over the past year?

5. Are you surprised when people you know experience emotional or behavioral problems? Why or why not?

## Introduction to Abnormal Psychology

You and your classmates chose to take this course for many reasons. The course might be required, or perhaps you thought learning about abnormal, deviant, or unusual behavior was intriguing. Or you might be interested in becoming a mental health professional and thought this course could help prepare you for such a career. Whatever the reason, you have likely known or will eventually know someone with a **mental disorder**. A mental disorder is a group of emotional (feelings), cognitive (thinking), or behavioral symptoms that cause distress or significant problems. About one of four American adults has a mental disorder over the course of a year (Kessler, Chiu, Demler, & Walters, 2005). A survey of students taking classes like this one indicated that almost 97 percent knew at least one person with a mental disorder (Connor-Greene, 2001). Almost 63 percent said they or an immediate family member—such as a parent, sibling, or child—had the disorder. The most commonly reported disorder was depression, a problem that Travis seemed to be experiencing.

**Abnormal psychology** is the scientific study of problematic feelings, thoughts, and behaviors associated with mental disorders. This area of science is designed to evaluate, understand, predict, and prevent mental disorders and help those who are in distress. Abnormal psychology has implications for all of us. Everyone has feelings, thoughts, and behaviors, and occasionally these become a problem for us or for someone we know. Travis's situation at the beginning of the chapter represents some daily experiences people have with mental disorders. Some of us may also be asked to help a friend or sibling struggling with symptoms of a mental disorder. In addition, all of us are interested in knowing how to improve our mental health and how to prevent mental disorders so we can help family members and friends.

In this book, we provide information to help you recognize mental problems and understand how they develop. We also explore methods used by professionals to prevent and treat mental distress and disorder. Knowing this material will not make you an expert, but it could make you a valuable resource. Indeed, we will present information you can use to make informed decisions and direct yourself and others to appropriate sources of support and help. Based on information in Chapters 5 and 7, for example, you will become knowledgeable about how anxiety and depression affect health and behavior in yourself and others as well as ways of dealing with these common problems.

# What Is a Mental Disorder?

As we mentioned, a mental disorder is a group of emotional (feelings), cognitive (thinking), or behavioral symptoms that cause distress or significant problems. Abnormal psychology is the scientific study of problematic feelings, thoughts, and behaviors associated with mental disorders. At first glance, defining problematic or abnormal behavior seems fairly straightforward—isn't abnormal behavior simply behavior that is not normal? In a way, yes, but then we first must know what *normal* behavior is. We often refer to normal behavior as that which characterizes most people. One normal behavior for most people is to leave home in the morning to go to school or work and to interact with others. If a person was so afraid of leaving home that he stayed inside for many weeks or months, this might be considered abnormal—the behavior differs from what most people do.

But what do we mean by *most* people? How many people must engage in a certain behavior for the behavior to be considered normal? And, which group of people should we use to decide what is normal—women, men, people of a certain ethnicity, everyone? You can see that defining normal and abnormal behavior is more complicated than it might appear. Consider the following case:

## CASE: Treva Throneberry

**Treva Throneberry** was born in Texas. Her sisters describe their family as a peaceful and loving one, but Treva paints a different picture. At age 15 years, Treva accused her father of sexual molestation. She later recanted her accusation but was removed from her parents' home and placed in foster care. At age 17 years, Treva ran away from her foster home and was found wandering alone by a roadside before spending time in a mental hospital. A year later, Treva moved into an apartment but soon vanished from town. In 2000, she was charged by Vancouver police with fraud and forgery. Her fingerprints matched those of Treva Throneberry, who was born in 1970, but Treva said she was an 18-year-old named Brianna Stewart. She had been attending Evergreen High School in Vancouver for the past two years, where she was known by everyone as Brianna Stewart. This was the basis for the fraud and forgery charges.

Since her disappearance from Texas, Treva was known by many other names in places across the country. In each town, she initially presented herself as a runaway 15- or 16-year-old in need of shelter who then left suddenly before her new identity turned age 18 years. She would then move to another town and start again as a 15- or 16-year old. Her foster care mother said Treva could not envision living beyond age 18 years.

Treva was examined by a psychiatrist and found competent to stand trial. At her trial, Treva represented herself. She would not plea-bargain because she insisted she was Brianna Stewart and not Treva Throneberry. She argued in court that she was not insane and did not have a mental disorder that caused her to distort reality or her identity. Despite her claims, however, Treva was convicted of fraud and sentenced to a 3-year jail term. She continues to insist she is Brianna Stewart (White, 2002).

You may think Treva's behavior is abnormal, but why? To address this question, we may consider one of three criteria commonly used to determine whether an emotion, thought, or behavior is abnormal: (1) *deviance from the norm,* (2) *difficulties adapting to life's demands* or difficulties functioning effectively (including dangerous behavior), and (3) *experience of personal distress.*

## Deviance from the Norm

Treva's actions are certainly not typical of most teenagers or young adults. Because Treva's behavior is so different from others—*so different from the norm*—her behavior would be considered abnormal. Defining abnormal behavior based on its difference or deviance from the norm is common and has some mass appeal—most people would agree Treva's behaviors are abnormal. Do you? Mental health professionals also rely on deviance from the norm to define abnormal behavior, but they often do so *statistically* by measuring how frequently a behavior occurs among people. Less frequent or less probable behaviors are considered to be abnormal or statistically deviant. Suddenly disappearing from home and assuming a new identity, as Treva did, is a very infrequent behavior that is statistically far from normal behavior.

An objective, statistical method of defining abnormality involves determining the probability of a behavior for a population. Note the bell curve in **Figure 1.1**. This curve shows how likely a behavior is based on its frequency in large groups of people. In this case, a 0 to 100 rating scale indicates level of physical activity among 10-year-olds during a 30-minute recess period. In this graph, 0 = no physical activity and 100 = continuous physical activity. The left axis of the scale shows how many children received a certain activity score: you can see that almost all children received scores in the 20 to 80 range. Based on this distribution of scores, we might statistically define and label the physical activity of children scoring 0 to 19 or 81 to 100 as "abnormal." Note that extremely low *and* extremely high scores are considered abnormal. Some physical activity is the norm, but too little or too much is not. A mental health professional might thus focus on underactive and overactive children in her scientific studies.

Statistical deviance from the norm is attractive to researchers because it offers clear guidelines for identifying emotions, thoughts, or behaviors as normal or abnormal.

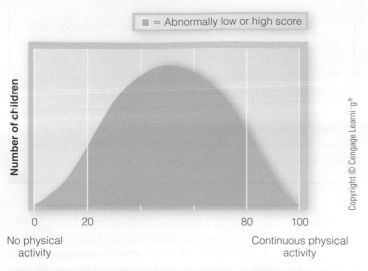

FIGURE 1.1 A STATISTICAL METHOD OF DEFINING ABNORMALITY Extremely low *and* extremely high levels of activity are considered abnormal from a statistical perspective.

However, this approach has some disadvantages. One major disadvantage is that people who differ significantly from an average score are technically "abnormal" or "disordered." But does this make sense for all behaviors or characteristics? Think about intelligence. Using a deviance-from-the-norm criterion, people who score extremely high on an intelligence test would be considered abnormal! But high intelligence is certainly not a disorder. In fact, high intelligence is valued in our society and often associated with success instead of failure. A deviance approach to defining abnormality is thus easy to apply but may fall short for determining what is abnormal.

Another disadvantage of the deviance-from-the-norm criterion is that cultures differ in how they define what is normal. One culture might consider an extended rest period during the workday to be normal, and another culture might not. Likewise, symptoms of mental disorders differ from culture to culture. We often consider self-critical comments and expressions of sadness as indicators of depression, but such behaviors are not always viewed the same way in East Asia (see **Box 1.1**). This is important for mental health professionals to consider when treating someone. Mental health professionals must recognize their own cultural biases and refrain from applying these views inappropriately to someone from another culture. Mental health professionals must also understand that deviance within a culture can change over time—what was deviant 50 years ago may be acceptable today.

Using a statistical definition of deviance, Albert Einstein would be considered "abnormal" because of his high intelligence.

A final problem with the deviance-from-the-norm criterion is that deciding the statistical point at which a behavior is abnormal can be arbitrary and subject to criticism. The method does not tell us what the correct cutoff should be. Refer again to Figure 1.1. If a child has an activity score of 81, she might be considered abnormal. Realistically, however, is a score of 80 (normal) much different from a score of 81 (abnormal)? Where should the cutoff be, and how do we know if that cutoff point is meaningful?

## Difficulties Adapting to Life Demands

Because several problems exist with the deviance-from-the-norm criterion, other judgments are sometimes made to define abnormal behavior. One key judgment often made by mental health professionals is whether a behavior interferes with a person's ability to function effectively. One could argue that Treva's behaviors greatly interfered with her ability to function effectively. She continued to behave in ways that prevented her from adopting an adult role and that eventually landed her in jail. In the case of Travis presented at the beginning of the chapter, you can see his depression kept him from interacting with others and could even lead to self-harm. Indeed, *dangerous behavior* toward oneself or others clearly interferes with an ability to function effectively.

Everyone occasionally has feelings of sadness and discouragement, especially after a tough event such as a breakup. Most people, however, are eventually able to focus better on school, work, or home regardless of these feelings. For other people like Travis, however, feelings of sadness or discouragement become maladaptive. A **maladaptive behavior** is one that interferes with a person's life, including ability to care for oneself, have good relationships with others, and function well at school or at work. Feelings of sadness and discouragement, which at first can be normal, can lead to maladaptive behaviors such as trouble getting out of bed, concentrating, or thinking.

Think about Sasha, who has been very worried since her mother was diagnosed with breast cancer last year. Her mother is currently doing well, and the cancer seems to be in remission, but Sasha cannot stop worrying that her mother's cancer will return. These worries cause Sasha to be so anxious and upset that she cannot concentrate on her schoolwork, and she finds herself irritable and unable to spend much time with her friends. Sasha's worries and behavior, which were understandable at first, have become maladaptive. According to the difficulties-adapting-to-life-demands criterion, Sasha's behaviors might be considered abnormal. Her continual thoughts about her mother's health, coupled with irritability and trouble concentrating,

## BOX 1.1 Focus on Diversity

### Emotion and Culture

Emotional experience and expression are clearly influenced by culture (Mesquita & Walker, 2003). Pride is promoted in the United States, an individualist culture, through praise, encouragement, and awards for personal accomplishments. As a result, Americans may be more self-focused and individual-achievement oriented. In contrast, non-Western collectivist cultures, as in East Asia, prioritize modesty, social obligations, and interpersonal harmony. People are expected to fit in with others and avoid behaviors that bring individual attention or that create group conflict. An American student asked to present a top-notch paper to her class may quickly accept this invitation and invite friends to her presentation. A Japanese student, however, may be less receptive to such a prospect. The American student came from a culture that promotes individual achievement and recognition, whereas the Japanese student came from a culture that promotes group belongingness and not individual recognition.

Consider another example. Expression of self-criticism is more typical of East Asian culture and does not necessarily indicate a mental disorder. In addition, expressions of depression are more likely labeled abnormal by Americans, but anger

Public expressions of anger are less common, and more likely to be seen as deviant, in certain cultures.

is more likely labeled abnormal by East Asians. Expressions of anxiety—especially over fitting in with a group—may be more common or normal in East Asians, but expressions of anger—especially when asserting one's individual rights—may be more common or normal in Americans. If deviance from the norm is used to define abnormal behavior, then cultural identity must be considered. An American psychologist should not, for example, apply her norms regarding emotional expression to someone from East Asia.

---

prevent her from functioning well as a family member, student, and friend. In fact, Sasha may benefit from some professional intervention at this point. In this case, the focus is not on deviance or norms but on the extent to which a behavior or characteristic interferes with daily functioning.

One advantage of this approach is that problems in daily living—as in school, work, or relationships—often prompt people to seek treatment. Unfortunately, the difference between good functioning and maladaptive behavior is not always easy to measure. In addition, the difference between good functioning and maladaptive behavior differs from person to person. Another problem with this criterion is that different people may view a certain behavior differently. Sasha's family members might see her behaviors as caring and thoughtful, but one of her professors might see her behavior as laziness. Mental health professionals often struggle with how to determine whether a person's behavior is maladaptive or truly interferes with a person's daily functioning.

Another problem with the difficulties-adapting-to-life-demands criterion is that people may engage in very odd behaviors but experience little interference in daily functioning. Consider Henry, a telemarketer living alone in Seattle. He never leaves home because of fear of contamination by airborne ra-

dioactivity and bacterial spores released by the Central Intelligence Agency. Henry does not consider himself dysfunctional because he works at home, gets things delivered to him, and communicates to friends or family via telephone and e-mail. Most would agree Henry limits his options by not leaving home and that his thinking is quite peculiar and unrealistic. But is Henry experiencing interference in daily functioning if he is happy the way things are for him? Hasn't he adapted well to his environment? Does he truly need treatment?

### Experience of Personal Distress

Maladaptive behavior is not always a source of concern for people like Henry, so they may not seek treatment. Therefore, another criterion used by mental health professionals to define abnormal behavior is experience of personal distress. Consider Margarette, who has irrational fears of entering tunnels or bridges while traveling by car or bus. She is extremely distressed by this and recognizes that these fears are baseless. Unfortunately, Margarette must travel through tunnels or bridges given her residence in Manhattan. She is desperate for treatment of these irrational fears because they cause her so much distress. In Margarette's case, extreme levels of distress created by a behavior such as fear may be important for defining her behavior as abnormal. In other cases, a behavior could cause great distress for others, which may prompt them to initiate treatment for a person. A child with highly disruptive behavior in school may not be particularly distressed about his actions but may be referred to treatment by his parents.

A personal-distress definition of abnormality has strengths and weaknesses. Personal distress is a hallmark feature of many mental disorders and often prompts people to seek treatment. In addition, most people can accurately assess whether they experience significant emotional and behavioral problems and can share this information when asked. However, some people (like Henry, mentioned earlier) do not report much personal distress even when exhibiting unusual behavior. And, even if a person *is* distressed, no clear guidelines exist for establishing a cutoff point that indicates an abnormal behavior. How much personal distress is too much personal distress?

## Defining Abnormality

As you can see, these three approaches to defining abnormality have several strengths and weaknesses. A successful approach to defining abnormality has thus been to combine the perspectives to merge their strengths and avoid their weaknesses (see **Table 1.1**). At least one of three characteristics must be present for abnormality to be defined as such. We refer to emotions, thoughts, or behaviors as abnormal when they

- violate social norms or are statistically deviant (like Treva's unusual behavior, insisting she was another person)
- interfere with functioning (like Sasha's worries that kept her from performing well at school)
- cause great personal distress (like Margarette's fears of tunnels and bridges)

Agreeing on a definition of *mental disorder* is important to **psychopathologists,** who study mental problems to see how disorders develop and continue and how they can be prevented or treated. A lack of consensus on a definition of abnormal behavior can have adverse consequences. Consider partner abuse, a significant problem in the United States. Much research has been conducted by psychologists and other mental health professionals to identify causes of partner abuse so effective treatments can be designed. Some researchers, however, define partner abuse as physical violence, whereas others work from a broader definition that includes physical, emotional, or sexual violence against an intimate partner. A standard or consistent definition of partner abuse is important because individuals who are physically violent against a partner may differ from those who are emotionally or sexually violent. Likewise, individuals using one form of violence may differ from those using multiple forms of violence against intimate partners. If so, treatments that are effective for one type of abuser may not be effective for other types of abusers. Varying definitions of a problem can thus impede our understanding of abnormal psychology.

Michael Blann/Digital Vision/Jupiter Images

This man has not left his home in two years, but he functions fairly normally and is not distressed. Is his behavior abnormal?

## Dimensions Underlying Mental Disorders Are Relevant to Everyone

Our discussion to this point might suggest a person's behavior is either abnormal or not, but this is not really so. Along with many experts in abnormal psychology, we view the abnormality of emotions, thoughts, or behaviors as a matter of degree, not of kind. In other words, *emotions, thoughts, and behaviors associated with mental disorders are present, to some degree, in all of us.* This statement may seem strange or even shocking to you at first, but let's explore it a little more. Abnormal behaviors are not simply present or absent but exist along a *continuum* in everyone to some degree. Think about sex drive, motor coordination, anxiety, or sadness. Each characteristic is present to some degree in everyone at different times. We all have some sex drive and coordination, and we all become anxious or sad at times. These characteristics may also change over time—it's likely you are more coordinated now than you were at age 5! Different people also show different levels of these characteristics—you may know people who tend to be more anxious or sad than others.

Deciding whether a behavior is different or deviant from the norm is a matter of degree. Earlier we discussed children's

## Table 1.1

| Definitions of Abnormal Psychology | | |
|---|---|---|
| Definition | Advantages | Limitations |
| Deviance from the norm | ▶ We use our own judgment or gut feeling. <br> ▶ Once statistical or objective cutoff scores are established, they are easy to apply. | ▶ Different cultures have different ideas about what normal behavior is. <br> ▶ "Statistically deviant" behaviors may be valued (e.g., high intelligence). <br> ▶ Arbitrary cutoffs (e.g., is a score of 80 much different from a score of 81?). |
| Difficulties adapting to life's demands | ▶ Typically easy to observe if someone is having difficulty. <br> ▶ Often prompts people to seek psychological treatment. | ▶ Unclear who determines impairment or whether a consensus about impairment is required. <br> ▶ Thresholds for impairment not always clear. |
| Experience of personal distress | ▶ Hallmark of many forms of mental disorder. <br> ▶ Individuals may be able to accurately report this. | ▶ Some psychological problems are not associated with distress. <br> ▶ Thresholds or cutoffs for distress are not always clear. |

activity level—children may be underactive, overactive, and even hyperactive. Deciding whether a behavior is maladaptive also is a matter of degree. Some students concerned about their parents' health cope better than others. Even personal distress is displayed in different degrees. Some people are much more distressed about driving through tunnels than others. All these differences make us unique in some way, which is a good thing. The important thing to remember is that anxiety, sadness, anger, and other emotions and behaviors can be best described along a dimension or continuum from extremely low to extremely high levels. Sometimes we do make pronouncements about people who are "anxious" or "depressed," but this is just a convention of language. These features—like all emotions, thoughts, and behaviors—exist on a continuum. **Figure 1.2** is an example of the full range of emotions, thoughts, and behaviors that might follow from problems in college. Think about where Travis might be on this continuum.

The idea that emotions, thoughts, and behaviors exist in varying degrees on a continuum in people has important implications. When a mental health professional evaluates an individual for symptoms of mental disorder, these three dimensions—emotion, thought, and behavior—figure prominently. Various forms of mental disorder comprise emotions such as anxious or depressed mood, thoughts such as excessive worry, and behaviors such as avoidance of others or hyperactivity.

To explore this continuum idea more deeply, consider **Figure 1.3**. Ricardo started a job as a financial analyst 6 months ago and has been feeling anxious, worried, and overwhelmed for the past 3 weeks. His overall mood, or *emotional state,* has been highly anxious—he has great difficulty eating, sleeping,

and interacting with friends. His *cognitive style* can be characterized by intense worry—almost all his thoughts involve what he is doing wrong at his new job and fear that his coworkers and friends will discover the difficult time he is having at work. Because of his anxiety and worry, Ricardo has started to avoid coworkers and friends. This avoidance *behavior* is causing problems for Ricardo, however, because he must meet with clients almost every day.

Consider Yoko as well. Yoko is a young adult with many symptoms related to anxiety. After college, she was hired as a manual writer for a large software company. Yoko has dealt with bouts of anxious mood for most of her life—she almost always feels "on edge" and sometimes has physical symptoms that suggest her body is "on high alert," such as rapid heartbeat, muscle tension, and sweating. These anxiety symptoms worry Yoko, and she often wonders if something is physically wrong with her. Because of her job, however, Yoko can work at home and spends most days without much human contact. This suits Yoko fine because she has never felt completely comfortable around other people and prefers to be alone. Her job requires her to meet with her boss only at the beginning and end of each project. Yoko can tolerate this relatively infrequent contact without much difficulty. So her preference and choice to be alone most of the time does not cause major problems for her.

The combination of psychological symptoms exhibited by Ricardo characterizes social anxiety disorder, which we discuss in Chapter 5. As you can see, though, the emotions, thoughts, and behaviors associated with this disorder exist on a continuum. As this example illustrates, mental disorders include characteristics found among most, if not all, people. Only when levels of these characteristics cross a threshold—when they are

**CONTINUUM FIGURE 1.2    Continuum of Emotions, Cognitions, and Behaviors**

| | Normal | Mild |
|---|---|---|
| **Emotions** | Good alertness and positive emotional state. | Feeling sad or down temporarily, but not for long |
| **Cognitions** | "I'm not getting the grades I want this semester, but I'll keep trying to do my best." | "I'm struggling at school this semester. I wish I could study better, or I'll fail." |
| **Behaviors** | Going to classes and studying for the next round of tests. Talking to professors. | Going to classes with some trouble studying. Less contact with others. |

If people cannot overcome fears they experience when performing an everyday activity such as taking the subway, the fear may be abnormal.

statistically deviant, associated with maladaptiveness, or cause great distress—are they considered abnormal. At one time or another, you have certainly felt anxious, had worrisome thoughts, or had the desire to be alone—similar emotions and thoughts, and their accompanying behaviors, are present to some degree in all of us. In Ricardo's case, however, the degree to which these features are present over the past 3 weeks hinders his daily life.

Figure 1.3 visually depicts this perspective and focuses on several important features of abnormal psychology. Each dimension of abnormality is shown along a continuum, be it

*emotional* (e.g., anxious mood), *cognitive* (e.g., worry intensity), or *behavioral* (e.g., avoidance of others) features. Other factors associated with abnormality can be understood from a dimensional perspective as well. The degree to which one is distressed or experiences interference in daily functioning, for example, can be represented on a continuum. As Figure 1.3 shows, Ricardo and Yoko show similar levels of anxious mood, worry intensity, and avoidance behavior. On a scale of 0 (none) to 100 (extremely high), their anxious mood can be rated 85 (very high), their worry intensity can be rated 50 (moderate), and their avoidance can be rated 70 (high). In Yoko's case, however, these symptoms are associated with *lower levels of distress* (rating = 45) and *impairment* (rating = 50). As we noted, Ricardo's level of dysfunction is severe enough to warrant a diagnosis of *social anxiety disorder,* a mental disorder that is characterized by avoidance of social situations, intense anxiety, and clinically significant impairment in functioning. Yoko, however, does not warrant this or any other anxiety diagnosis because her symptoms are not associated with significant impairment in daily functioning. Indeed, she copes with her symptoms so they do not cause her great personal distress.

You might be wondering if the literature and research on anxiety disorders is relevant to Ricardo, Yoko, and even people with much lower levels of anxious symptoms. The answer is yes, absolutely! Features of mental disorder, personal distress, and impairment are all dimensional or continuous in nature. In fact, research suggests that the same causal factors are responsible for these anxiety-related symptoms whether the symptoms are mild, moderate, or severe. Because everyone will experience some of the symptoms discussed in this textbook or know someone who has or will experience these symptoms, abnormal psychology is relevant to all of us. Abnormal psychology is a part of life.

As you read this textbook and understand more that abnormal psychology is a part of life, you will identify with some of the symptoms and disorders we discuss. This does *not* mean, however, that you or someone you know has a mental disorder. Some people, for example, are extremely neat and tidy and do

| Moderate | Mental Disorder — less severe | Mental Disorder — more severe |
|---|---|---|
| Feeling sad, but a strong positive experience such as a good grade could lift mood. | Intense sadness most of the day with some trouble concentrating and some loss of appetite. | Extreme sadness all the time with great trouble concentrating and complete loss of appetite. |
| "These bad grades really hurt. This may set me back for a while. I'm really worried." | "I'm so worried about these grades that my stomach hurts. I don't know what to do." | "These bad grades just show what a failure I am at everything. There's no hope; I'm not doing anything today." |
| Skipping a few classes and feeling somewhat unmotivated to study. Avoiding contact with professors and classmates. | Skipping most classes and unable to maintain eye contact with others. Strong lack of motivation. | Unable to get out of bed, eat, or leave the house. Lack of energy and frequent crying. |

Commercial Eye/Getty Images

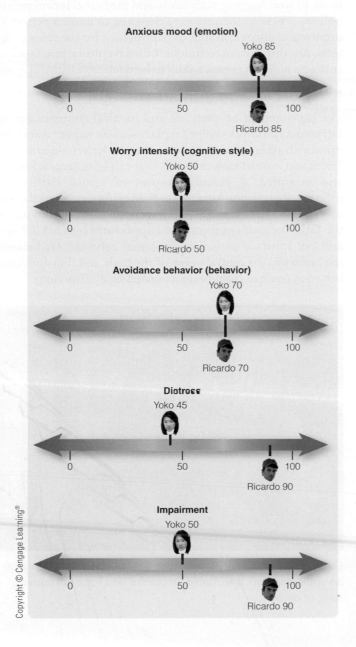

not like things to be disorderly. In fact, they may feel uncomfortable when things are not lined up and organized. If this applies to you or someone you know, you may be tempted to believe you or the person has obsessive-compulsive disorder (Chapter 5). You might share an interest in neatness with someone who has obsessive-compulsive disorder, but you are probably able to tolerate this need for neatness and order and can function even if you were prevented from keeping everything organized. People with very high levels of a characteristic, like a need for neatness, are indeed at risk for developing a condition such as obsessive-compulsive disorder, especially under conditions of high stress. We hope to make you more aware of who is vulnerable for a mental disorder and what can be done to maximize mental health. In doing so, we also emphasize *prevention* of mental disorder, or how people can lower the probability of developing mental disorders.

## INTERIM SUMMARY

▶ A mental disorder is a group of emotional (feelings), cognitive (thinking), or behavioral symptoms that cause distress or significant problems.

▶ About one of four American adults has a mental disorder each year.

▶ Abnormal psychology is the scientific study of troublesome emotions, thoughts, and behaviors associated with mental disorders.

▶ Emotions, thoughts, and behaviors are considered abnormal when they deviate greatly from the norm, interfere with daily functioning, or cause substantial personal distress.

**FIGURE 1.3  RICARDO AND YOKO** Ricardo and Yoko have similar levels of anxious mood, worry intensity, and avoidance behavior. However, they differ on amount of distress experienced and levels of impairment created by their symptoms. *(Photos courtesy of © 2010 Design Pics/Jupiterimages Corporation [Yoko]; ©Istockphoto.com/Carole Gomez [Ricardo].)*

Fancy/Jupiter Images

One of four adults in the United States experiences a mental disorder every year. In addition, features of mental disorders are present, to some degree, in all of us.

► Psychopathologists study mental problems to see how disorders develop and continue and how they can be prevented or alleviated.

► Abnormal behaviors and characteristics are not necessarily only present or absent but actually occur to some degree in all of us.

## REVIEW QUESTIONS

1. Think about Treva. Using each of the three features that characterize abnormal behavior, evaluate whether Treva's behavior would be considered abnormal.

2. What are advantages and disadvantages of each characteristic of abnormal behavior?

3. How might one merge these three characteristics into one definition?

4. What is meant by a dimension of abnormality, and what are implications of this perspective?

# History of Abnormal Psychology

Knowing a little about the history of abnormal psychology will help you better understand some of the ideas and forces that have shaped how we view and treat mental disorders. The model a society uses to understand mental disorder will influence how that disorder is treated. Historically, not much emphasis was placed on research and the scientific method to understand mental health or well-being. In addition, ideas about mental health and disorders were often shaped by social, political, and economic forces. During times of political conservatism and economic hardship, for example, people tend to emphasize individual and physical causes of abnormal behavior as well as biological treatments such as psychosurgery and medication.

During times of political liberalism and economic strength, people tend to emphasize environmental causes of abnormal behavior as well as psychological treatments and sociocultural approaches (Grob, 1994). In the next few sections, we examine the development of abnormal psychology over time, which helps us understand modern-day attitudes and conceptualizations of abnormal behavior as well as treatments.

## Early Perspectives

Early writings of the Egyptians, Chinese, Greeks, and Hebrews identify patterns of, and concerns about, treating abnormal behavior. Early theoreticians frequently attributed abnormal behavior to supernatural causes such as possession by demons or evil spirits. The behavior was viewed spiritually, so the primary form of treatment was **exorcism**, or an attempt to cast out a spirit possessing an individual. Various exorcism techniques were used, including magic, noisemaking, incantations, prayer, flogging, starvation, and medicinal techniques or potions. These techniques were designed to make a person an unpleasant, uncomfortable, or painful host for the spirit or demon. Another ancient technique, called **trephination**, involved cutting a hole in a person's skull to help release a harmful spirit.

## Early Greek and Roman Thought

The development of medicine and medical concepts among Egyptians and Greeks helped replace ancient supernatural theories with natural ones. Natural theories reject supernatural forces and instead look to things that can be observed, known, and measured as potential causes of events. Particularly influential in moving forward the field of abnormal psychology was Hippocrates (460–377 B.C.), a Greek physician known as the father of modern medicine. Hippocrates rejected demons and evil spirits as causes of abnormal behavior. He believed the brain was the central organ of the body and that abnormal behavior resulted from brain disorders or dysfunctions.

National Gallery, London/Art Resource, NY

Early treatments for mental disorder attempted to make a person an unpleasant, uncomfortable, or painful host for a possessive spirit or demon.

Hippocrates recommended treatments for abnormal behavior that would restore brain functioning, including special diets, rest, abstinence from alcohol, regular exercise, and celibacy. Hippocrates' work had great impact on later Greek and Roman physicians. Throughout Greece and Rome, physicians emphasized a scientific approach to learning about causes of abnormal behavior. Because of limited knowledge about human anatomy and biology—experimentation on humans and dissection of human cadavers was illegal—questionable practices such as bleeding and purging were employed. However, treatment of abnormal behavior focused primarily on creating therapeutic environments that included healthy diets, regular exercise, massage, and education. These treatments remain good ideas even today.

Hippocrates rejected demons and evil spirits as causes of abnormal behavior and hypothesized that abnormal behavior resulted from disorders or dysfunction of the brain.

## Middle Ages

The scientific aspects and advances of Greek medicine continued in the Middle East. However, the fall of the Roman Empire brought a return to supernatural theories in Europe. Demon possession again became a prominent explanation of abnormal behavior, and treatment focused on prayer, holy objects or relics, pilgrimages to holy places, confinement, and exorcism. A dramatic emergence of **mass madness** in Europe also appeared during the last half of the Middle Ages. Groups of individuals would be afflicted at the same time with the same disorder or abnormal behaviors.

An example of mass madness was a dancing mania in Italy known as *tarantism*. In tarantism, individuals became victims of a tarantula's "spirit" after being bitten. The possession led to raving, jumping, dancing, and convulsions. *Lycanthropy* also developed in some groups; this is a belief that a person has been transformed into a demonic animal such as a werewolf. Another form of mass madness, *St. Vitus's dance,* or rapid, uncoordinated jerking movements, spread to Germany and other parts of Europe. What caused these and other instances of mass hysteria remains unclear. One possibility is that people in highly emotional states tend to be suggestible. High levels of fear and panic may have led some to believe they had been "taken over" by an outside force or spirit and that these odd behaviors were contagious.

Philippe Pinel advocated more humane treatment of persons with mental problems.

Another possibility is that people inadvertently ate substances such as fungi on food that led to odd beliefs and visions.

## Renaissance

A rebirth of natural and scientific approaches to health and human behavior occurred at the end of the Middle Ages and beginning of the Renaissance. Once again, physicians focused on bodily functioning and medical treatments. In addition, Paracelsus (1490–1541), a Swiss physician, introduced the notion of psychic or mental causes for abnormal behavior and proposed a treatment initially referred to as bodily magnetism and later called hypnosis. Another new approach to treating mental disorders during the Renaissance involved special institutions known as **asylums**. Asylums were places set aside for people with mental disorder. Unfortunately, asylums were originally created simply to remove people with mental disorder from the general population because they were not able to care for themselves. As such, early asylums did not provide much treatment, and living conditions for residents were usually poor.

## Reform Movement

The conditions of asylums or mental hospitals in Europe and America were generally deplorable and in need of great change. A key leader of change was Philippe Pinel (1745–1826), who was in charge of a Paris mental hospital called La Bicêtre. Shocked by the living conditions of the patients, Pinel introduced a revolutionary, experimental, and more humane treatment. He unchained patients, placed them in sunny rooms, allowed them to exercise, and required staff to treat them with kindness. These changes produced dramatic results in that patients' mental states generally improved and order and peace was restored to the hospital. Pinel later assumed charge of a similar facility, La Salpêtrière, and replicated changes and effects seen at La Bicêtre.

Pinel's reforms in France soon spread to other places. William Tuke (1732–1822) created the York Retreat in England and Benjamin Rush (1745–1813) encouraged humane treatment of people with mental disorder in the United States. Dorothea Dix (1802–1887) is credited with making the most significant changes in treating those with mental disorder and in changing public attitudes about these conditions in America. She raised awareness, funds, and political support and established more than 30 hospitals. The humane type of care emphasized during the reform movement period, sometimes referred to as **moral treatment**, paved the way for the modern approach to mental disorders.

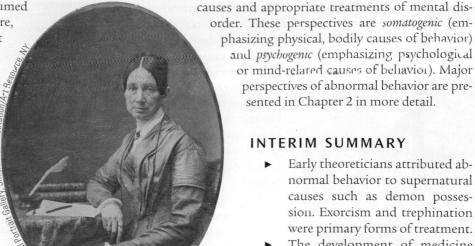

Activist Dorothea Dix is credited with helping to reform treatment of persons with mental disorder in the United States.

## Modern Era

The modern approach to abnormal psychology includes accepting those with mental disorder as people who need professional attention; scientific, biomedical, and psychological methods are used to understand and treat mental disorder. Of special note in this regard was the **mental hygiene** movement that emerged from Clifford Beers's 1908 book, *A Mind That Found Itself.* In the book, Beers described his own experiences with mental disorder and his subsequent treatment in an institution. His description of maltreatment while hospitalized sparked a mental health reform movement in the United States and later across the world. Following his recovery, Beers founded the Connecticut Society for Mental Hygiene in 1908 and the National Committee for Mental Hygiene in 1909. These groups were designed to improve quality of care for those with mental disorder, help prevent mental disorder, and disseminate information to the public about mental disorder. These goals are just as relevant and important today as they were a century ago.

Clifford Beers's autobiography recounted his experiences as a patient in a mental institution and helped launch the mental hygiene movement in the United States.

Several theoretical perspectives were developed during the late 19th century and throughout the 20th century to guide work on understanding and treating mental disorder. These perspectives include biological, psychodynamic, cognitive, behavioral, sociocultural, and other theories of abnormal behavior. Each perspective has important applications for determining causes and appropriate treatments of mental disorder. These perspectives are *somatogenic* (emphasizing physical, bodily causes of behavior) and *psychogenic* (emphasizing psychological or mind-related causes of behavior). Major perspectives of abnormal behavior are presented in Chapter 2 in more detail.

## INTERIM SUMMARY

▶ Early theoreticians attributed abnormal behavior to supernatural causes such as demon possession. Exorcism and trephination were primary forms of treatment.

▶ The development of medicine among Egyptians and Greeks helped replace ancient supernatural theories with natural ones. Treating abnormal behavior focused on creating therapeutic environments via healthy diets, exercise, massage, and education.

▶ The fall of the Roman Empire led again to supernatural theories of abnormal behavior such as demon possession. Treatment thus focused on prayer, holy objects or relics, pilgrimages to holy places, confinement, and exorcism.

▶ During the end of the Middle Ages and beginning of the Renaissance, natural and scientific approaches to health and human behavior reemerged. Asylums were built for those with mental disorder, but generally provided poor care and treatment.

▶ The Reform Movement introduced significant changes to treating mental disorder and led to a modern approach, which includes accepting those with mental disorder as individuals needing treatment and applying biomedical and psychological methods.

## REVIEW QUESTIONS

1. Give two examples of how society and culture influence ideas about causes and treatment of mental disorder.
2. What events were responsible for rejecting supernatural explanations of mental disorder?
3. Consider Treva. What different treatments for her problems would have been used during the Middle Ages, Renaissance, and Modern Era?

## Abnormal Psychology and Life: Themes

When we developed plans for this textbook, we wanted to take a specific approach to abnormal psychology. In particular, we wanted to focus on how abnormal psychology applies to your daily life. You will notice in the following chapters that we try to maximize the personal relevance of the textbook material. We also adopted several other themes for this book that are highlighted here, including a focus on dimensions of abnormal psychology as well as prevention. We hope you keep these themes in mind as you read, think about, and apply material we present in later chapters.

## Dimensional Perspective

You may recall we discussed dimensions, or a continuum, of emotions, thoughts, and behaviors that characterize mental disorder. This theme is worth highlighting again because it is a core principle that guides our text. An important implication of a dimensional perspective is that research on emotions, thoughts, and behavior is relevant to all of us. Everyone, you may recall, feels anxious or sad at times—this is normal. When these normal emotions or thoughts become frequent or severe, however, a mental disorder may be present. Many people are sometimes nervous about driving, especially in a new place. If a person is so anxious when driving that he cannot go to school, however, then the anxiety might be considered abnormal. A dimensional perspective thus involves the notion that people differ only in their *degree* of symptoms.

## Prevention Perspective

The average college student functions pretty well, but many students may be at some risk for mental dysfunction or distress. Therefore, we emphasize *prevention* of mental disorder throughout this textbook. Prevention stems from the concept of *mental hygiene*, or the science of promoting mental health and thwarting mental disorder through education, early treatment, and public health measures. You may recall this approach was developed and promoted by Clifford Beers about a century ago. Prevention and mental hygiene have greatly influenced modern approaches to understanding and treating mental disorders.

We hope this emphasis on prevention will help you recognize symptoms of mental disorder, become aware of early warning signs or risks for these problems, and take steps to prevent psychological distress in yourself or others. Risk and protective factors associated with specific mental disorders will be identified in later chapters. We also present strategies for responding to, or coping with, these risk factors.

A prevention approach is consistent with a **public health model** that focuses on promoting good health and good health practices to avert disease. This model applies well to abnormal psychology. Different aspects of our lifestyles contribute greatly to poor physical and mental health and even death. Examples include poor diet and insufficient exercise, social isolation, and

---

### BOX 1.2 Focus on Law and Ethics

Iqoncept/Shutterstock.com

## Heal Thyself: What the Self-Help Gurus Don't Tell You

We all try to help ourselves. In Western societies such as the United States, the notion of personal responsibility is common, even in the area of mental health. Imagine watching television, listening to the radio, or browsing in a bookstore without being exposed to advice from "Dr. So-and-So" (usually a first name!) about how to deal with family or relationship problems, stress, or some kind of drug, food, sex, or Internet addiction. But does advice from these so-called experts work? Some argue the self-help movement sometimes fails to deliver results and can be actually harmful to our mental health (Harwood & L'Abate, 2010; Salerno, 2005).

The self-help industry promotes *victimization* and *empowerment*. Victimization is the idea that your current state results from factors beyond your control. A common example is thinking about a problem as a "disease" that has been thrust upon you. The logical extension of this viewpoint is that you have no personal responsibility for your problem. According to Salerno, victimization dominated from the 1960s through the 1980s

and is now manifested in a culture of blame—misfortunes are not your fault and society "owes you one." Self-help books and programs that capitalize on victimization are successful because they make individuals feel less guilty about their problems. Conversely, the *empowerment* approach to self-help emphasizes that everything is under your control. In other words, you can do it—with willpower! This viewpoint has dominated American culture over the past decade and emphasizes building self-esteem. Just listen to an interview with an athlete ("If I just put my mind to it, I know we will win") and witness the rising popularity of "life coaches."

The potential harm caused by adopting these perspectives is that victimization may lead you to accept no personal responsibility, whereas empowerment may lead you to be overly confident in your abilities. Either perspective is likely to lead to problems and negative feelings. If you do not get better after adopting the self-help gurus' prescriptions (which may have dubious value), victimization suggests you are still a slave to your problem or disease. On the other hand, empowerment suggests your "failure" reflects a lack of desire or effort. You lose either way, and that must mean it is time for the next book, show, or program to figure out why. Or not—you choose.

unhealthy interpersonal relationships. In addition, mental disorders discussed in this textbook have been linked to declines in physical health. Public health practitioners and researchers are thus motivated to address psychological health and functioning to improve overall quality of life.

In Chapter 3, we further discuss the important topic of prevention and how this concept applies to mental health. At this point, we briefly discuss how prevention interfaces with the study of abnormal psychology. Historically, emphasis has been placed on treating mental disorder once it developed, and certainly this is an important focus. However, the field of abnormal psychology has advanced enough to allow the identification of *risk factors* that help produce many mental disorders. This textbook presents what is currently known in this regard. Information about risk factors can also inform us about what makes someone vulnerable to psychological problems, what can be done to prevent symptoms of mental disorder, and what methods can be used to ameliorate these symptoms if they do develop.

## TYPES OF PREVENTION

Three types of prevention are commonly considered within abnormal psychology. **Primary prevention** involves targeting large groups of people, sometimes the entire public, who have not yet developed a mental disorder. Antidrug commercials to reduce excessive substance use are one example. Other primary prevention examples include programs to reduce job discrimination, enhance school curricula, improve housing, teach parenting skills, and provide educational assistance to children from single-parent homes.

**Secondary prevention** involves addressing emerging problems while they are still manageable and before they become resistant to intervention. A good example of secondary prevention is early detection and treatment of college students with potentially damaging drinking problems. In this case, people at risk for a particular problem are addressed to prevent a full-blown disorder.

Finally, **tertiary prevention** involves reducing the severity, duration, and negative effects of a mental disorder after it has occurred. Tertiary prevention differs from primary and secondary prevention in that its aim is to lessen the effects of an *already* diagnosed disorder. Examples include various medical and psychological treatments for mental disorders. Throughout this textbook, we emphasize primary and secondary prevention in addition to treatments for already existing mental disorders.

## Consumer Perspective

Another major theme of this book is a *consumer perspective*. Our goal is to help you become a more informed *consumer* of scientific information on mental health that is often presented in the popular press. For example, recent reports suggest that certain antidepressant medications, in some highly publicized cases, *increased* suicidal thoughts and behaviors in children and adolescents. We hope material presented in Chapter 7 will inform you about features of depression, how these features vary across age groups, and how these features can be treated using research-supported biological and psychological methods. We hope to help you see through the media hype and understand the true nature of various disorders and their treatment.

Another goal as authors is to show how you can apply research-based information to your own life. Throughout this textbook, for example, you will find strategies for improving self-esteem, communication skills, emotional regulation, intimate relationships, and coping strategies. Doing so is also consistent with the prevention theme we discussed earlier. We also present information on career paths. Some of you may have enrolled in this course because you are interested in certain mental health professions. Once you have learned about different mental disorders, Chapter 15 will help you navigate the field of mental health professions. Consistent with our consumer theme, we also present material in Chapter 15 about seeking a therapist should you ever decide to do so.

## Diversity

Diversity involves differences across males and females, people of assorted racial or ethnic backgrounds, and those with various sexual identities or orientations, among other groups (Hall, 2006). Great progress has been made in recent years with respect to understanding how mental disorders vary across these groups. For example, we know that depression tends to be more common among women than men (Chapter 7) and that certain immigrant populations of ethnic minority status are at increased risk for psychotic disorder (Chapter 12). **Multicultural psychology** refers to examining the effect of culture on the way people think, feel, and act (Hall, 2009). Multicultural psychology is important, among other reasons, for understanding what causes mental disorders and how to better and more specifically assess and treat mental disorders.

Diversity and multicultural psychology are important parts of this textbook. For each major mental disorder, we discuss group differences that have been reported by researchers. In addition, we have special "focus on diversity" and "focus on gender" boxes throughout the textbook that further highlight cultural and gender differences. We also have detailed sections on culture and the sociocultural model of mental disorder (Chapter 2), gender and race and culture as risk factors for mental disorder (Chapter 3), and culture and clinical assessment (Chapter 4). Our goal is to help you understand how cultural, gender, and other group variations impact the presentation, assessment, and treatment of mental disorders.

## Stigma

Another important aspect of this textbook, and one related to a dimensional perspective of abnormal behavior, is stigma. **Stigma** is a characterization by others of disgrace or reproach based on an individual characteristic. People with certain medical disorders are sometimes shunned or rejected by others even though their illness is no fault of their own. Such stigma can also apply to mental disorders. Children with a learning disorder are sometimes treated differently by teachers, and adults with social anxiety disorder are sometimes ridiculed by coworkers. Indeed, stigma is often associated with discrimination and social avoidance. Stigma is also a major reason why people do not seek treatment for mental distress (Corrigan, 2004). This is so alarming that government reports proposed a national campaign to reduce the stigma associated with seeking treatment for psychological problems (President's New Freedom Commission on Mental Health, 2003; U.S. Department of Health and Human Services, 1999). In specific sections throughout the textbook, we discuss what may lead to stigma, the effects of stigma, and ways to combat stigma associated with particular mental disorders.

Stigma and mental disorder are aligned for various reasons. Stigma likely arises from a stereotype that people with a mental disorder are unpredictable, dangerous, violent, incompetent, or responsible for their own fate (Corrigan, 2004). As you read this textbook, however, you will see that these stereotypes are inaccurate and often based on infrequent and isolated events. The vast majority of people with a mental disorder are not much different from you or your classmates, as a dimensional approach to mental disorder suggests. People with mental disorder generally are not violent, unpredictable, incompetent, or to blame for their plight.

Stigma also occurs when government or other institutional policies negatively affect opportunities for people who may be seen as threatening, dangerous, or less deserving of support. One example of this *structural stigma* can be seen in state laws that limit health insurance coverage for mental health problems. Stereotypes and public misperceptions about mental disorder also come from the media via newspaper stories and editorials, television reports and shows, and movies (Penn et al., 2005). The media's focus on negative aspects and consequences of mental disorder, whether accurate or not, promotes prejudice and discrimination.

Consider this example. A study of 70 major American newspapers examined stories containing the terms "mental," "psych," and "schizo" over a 6-week period (Corrigan et al., 2005). A total of 3,353 stories was identified, all of which were examined for stigmatizing themes. Many (39%) stories conveyed a theme of dangerousness, mainly violent crime. In addition, stories about violence and crime committed by someone with a mental disorder were usually given prominent placement in the newspapers. The fact that about two of five stories concerning mental disorder had dangerousness or violence as a theme is striking. These news stories may strengthen the public's perception that mental disorder and dangerousness are linked, thereby increasing stigma toward those with psychological problems.

## EFFECTS OF STIGMA

Stigma affects people in different ways (**Figure 1.4**). One type of stigma is **public stigma**, which refers to the general disgrace the public confers on people with mental disorder that can result in prejudice, stereotyping, and discrimination. People with mental disorder, for example, may experience difficulty securing employment, housing, and health care coverage. Public stigma can also hinder treatment of mental disorders by restricting opportunities for care and by limiting insurance benefits. Think about neighborhood complaints that arise when an agency wants to build a group home for people with intellectual disability (Chapter 13). In a sense, public stigma is a type of social injustice (Corrigan, 2004).

Another way stigma can affect people is **self-stigma**, which refers to disgrace people assign themselves because of public stigma (Corrigan, 2004). Some people adopt the public notion that a mental disorder is something to be ashamed of; this can affect self-esteem or cause an individual to deny a problem exists. Self-stigma can lead as well to damaging behaviors such as reluctance to seek treatment. You can imagine that self-stigma is especially pertinent to children. Imagine a child who is told he has a learning

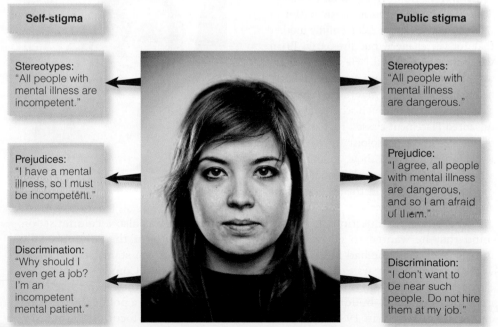

**Self-stigma**

Stereotypes:
"All people with mental illness are incompetent."

Prejudices:
"I have a mental illness, so I must be incompetent."

Discrimination:
"Why should I even get a job? I'm an incompetent mental patient."

**Public stigma**

Stereotypes:
"All people with mental illness are dangerous."

Prejudice:
"I agree, all people with mental illness are dangerous, and so I am afraid of them."

Discrimination:
"I don't want to be near such people. Do not hire them at my job."

Photo: Istockphoto.com/Joan Vicent Cantó Roig

**FIGURE 1.4** PUBLIC STIGMA AND SELF-STIGMA Public stigma may lead some people to avoid the label of mental disorder by not seeking services that might be helpful. Self-stigma may lead people with mental disorder to feel incompetent and unworthy of help. *(From Corrigan, P. How stigma interferes with mental health care. American Psychologist, 59, 614–625, Figure 1. Copyright © 2004 by the American Psychological Association. Reprinted by permission.)*

disorder—how might this knowledge affect his motivation to work in the classroom? Others have found as well that substantial personal stigma often prevents college students from seeking help for mental health issues (Eisenberg, Downs, Golberstein, & Zivin, 2009).

## FIGHTING STIGMA

Stigma can be fought in two key ways: *education* and *promoting personal contact*. Educational efforts to combat stigma range from distributing flyers and brochures that present factual information about mental disorder to semester-long courses regarding the truth about mental disorder (Penn et al., 2005). Educational efforts to combat stigma do have short-term effects on participants' attitudes, and some evidence indicates that education facilitates helping behaviors such as donating funds to organizations (Corrigan & Penn, 1999).

Promoting personal contact involves increased contact with someone with a mental disorder to dispel myths and stereotypes. Methods of promoting personal contact include encouraging volunteer activities in mental health settings and providing classroom experiences in which individuals whose lives are touched by mental disorder present their stories. These encounters have significant and long-lasting effects

on attitudes about mental disorder (Couture & Penn, 2003). The effects appear strongest when the audience consists of students (versus professionals) and when contact is not a required part of the curriculum (Kolodziej & Johnson, 1996).

This textbook strives to fight stigma in several ways. First, by providing factual information about mental disorders we hope to dispel many myths about them. Second, we emphasize that symptoms of mental disorders are present to some degree in all of us. Indeed, material in this textbook is likely to be personally relevant to your life or the lives of people you know because mental disorders are so prevalent. Third, we emphasize people first and mental disorders second. Throughout this book, we refer to people with schizophrenia (not "schizophrenics"), children with a learning disorder (not "the learning disabled"), and individuals with mental disorder (not "the mentally ill"). After all, if someone you know has cancer, you would not call her a "cancer"! People should not be viewed by the disorder they have but by their own singular characteristics.

Finally, a unique feature of this textbook is use of *narratives* (like Alison Malmon's narrative presented in this chapter). These features are first-person accounts of people who experience and deal with symptoms of mental disorder in

## Personal Narrative 1.1

### *Alison Malmon*

I was 18 years old when my world crumbled. Shortly after spring break in my freshman year of college, I got a call from my mother that forever changed our lives. "Ali, Brian shot himself," she said. "He's dead." Brian was my only sibling. Born 4 years and 4 days before me, he was an extraordinary child. He rose to the top of our high school, taking all Advanced Placement classes. He was captain of the debate team, soloist in the annual Rock and Roll Revival show, announcer for school football games, and a columnist for our local paper. He had friends, was smart and funny, and was my role model.

There was no question in Brian's mind that he wanted to go to college in New York City—he had fallen in love with the city a few years earlier and was determined to one day own one of its infamous tall black buildings. So as I entered high school in 1995, Brian was on his way to Columbia University. Four years later, he had stormed Columbia just as he did in high school: He had joined an a cappella group and become

Matthew Worden

**Alison Malmon**

president. He was also a columnist for, and sports editor of, the Columbia daily newspaper and the star of the school's Varsity Music and Comedy show. In addition, he was on the Dean's List every semester, pursuing a political science degree with a strong focus on journalism, with plans to go on to law school.

So when Brian came home for a weekend in November of his senior year to "de-stress," I wasn't too surprised. But

that weekend quickly turned into a week, a week into a month, and a month into the rest of the semester. Before I knew it, Brian was home for basically my entire senior year of high school. He began seeing a psychiatrist, and only then did we discover Brian was suffering from schizoaffective disorder and had been since February of his freshman year at Columbia. He had been hearing voices typical of schizophrenia and experiencing depressive episodes for almost 3 years. He had been walking the streets at night, and packing up his dorm room in boxes, because voices told him to. He had been sleeping days at a time and hated to leave his dorm room because he was so depressed. But he never told anyone. In retrospect, his friends at school remember that he "sometimes went into a funk," but no one ever confronted him about it.

By the time he sought help and came home, Brian had already lost hope. He suffered through what was supposed to be the best time of his life in pain, fear, and complete isolation; no matter how much therapy and medications he tried once

themselves or family members. Common themes throughout these narratives are that stigma directed toward those with mental disorder is inappropriate and that we all have a vested interest in advocating for those with mental disorder. We trust these accounts will be informative, will make these conditions more personally relevant, and will inspire all of us to advocate for the rights and needs of those with mental disorder.

## INTERIM SUMMARY

▶ Emotions, thoughts, and behaviors associated with abnormal psychology and mental disorder are present, to some degree, in all of us.

▶ Mental hygiene refers to the science of promoting mental health and preventing mental disorder through education, early treatment, and public health measures.

▶ Primary prevention targets groups of people who have not developed a disorder to decrease overall rates of a given problem.

▶ Secondary prevention addresses problems while they are still manageable and before they become resistant to intervention.

▶ Tertiary prevention reduces duration and negative effects of a mental disorder after it occurs in an individual.

▶ Stigma associated with mental disorder can result in discrimination, social avoidance, and failure to seek treatment.

▶ Stigma can be fought via education and by promoting personal contact with those with a mental disorder.

## REVIEW QUESTIONS

1. How might Treva Throneberry's behavior be considered dimensional in nature?

2. What are implications of a dimensional viewpoint?

3. What are different types of prevention, and how might each be used to address a problem like depression?

4. How is abnormal psychology relevant to your life? What instances of stigma have you seen?

## Final Comments

The goal of this chapter has been to introduce the field of abnormal psychology and important relevant concepts. Major definitions of abnormal psychology have advantages and disadvantages, and no gold standard exists to define what is abnormal. However, each of these definitions taps an

---

he came home, the pain was too much to bear. On March 24, 2000—during my freshman year at the University of Pennsylvania—Brian took his own life. He was just 22.

I can't even try to describe what it was, and continues to be, like since Brian's death. I lost my big brother, my other half; I am now an only child. My family has been torn apart and our entire fabric has had to be rewoven as well as we know how. A loss to suicide is truly something only other suicide survivors can understand. I live every day with the "what ifs?," the guilt, and the devastation. The unbearable pain has lessened and I am able to get through each day a little easier, but my life will never be the same. Brian was such a promising young man with so much of his life ahead of him. I simply feel sad for anyone whose life he did not have the chance to touch.

When Brian first died, one of the most salient emotions I felt was fear. I became scared thinking that, had I been in his situation and began suffering from a mental disorder in college,

I probably would have done exactly what Brian had. I would have felt responsible, kept my symptoms to myself, and suffered in silence. Nobody was talking about mental health issues on my campus; no one was educating students about signs and symptoms of various disorders, where they could get help, and that they could get better. The stigma surrounding the issues was causing too many people to suffer in shame and isolation. And I knew that if I would have kept quiet like Brian did, too many of my peers were also suffering in silence.

So I formed a campus group called Active Minds (www.activeminds.org) to educate my peers about these issues and get people talking. With more young adults talking, sharing what they and their family and friends had gone through, we would break down walls of silence and more of my peers might feel comfortable getting help they deserved. We were the ones suffering. We were the ones watching our friends suffer. It was time for young adults to be engaged in and educated about mental health issues

and to tell each other: "This can happen to you. I know, because it happened to me. But you can get help for what you're going through, and you can feel better."

This idea of education and discussion to reduce stigma was extremely well supported at my school and within the mental health community. Just 18 months after starting that group at Penn, I formed my own nonprofit organization with the goal to introduce this concept to young adults nationwide. I now work full time as the executive director of the organization Active Minds, Inc., developing and supporting chapters of Active Minds at high schools and colleges around the country, and helping to give a voice to young adults in this field. Every time a young person shares her story, or concentrates his energy to combat stigma he has encountered, our voice is strengthened.

I would give anything to have my brother Brian back with me today. But since I can't, I will do everything in my power to ensure no other young adult has to suffer in silence like he did, and no other sister has to lose her big brother to suicide.

important facet of abnormal behavior that "rings true" to some extent. In addition, emotions, thoughts, behaviors, distress, and impairment from abnormal behavior are dimensional and thus present to some degree in all of us. As authors, we advocate the public health model as a viable and effective way to conceptualize, prevent, and treat mental disorders. Throughout this book, we emphasize themes of dimensionality of abnormal behavior, prevention of mental disorders, a consumer perspective, diversity, and stigma. We hope you find the material engaging and useful not just today but throughout your lifetime.

## Key Terms

| | |
|---|---|
| mental disorder   2 | mental hygiene   12 |
| abnormal psychology   2 | public health model   13 |
| maladaptive behavior   4 | primary prevention   14 |
| psychopathologists   6 | secondary prevention   14 |
| mass madness   11 | tertiary prevention   14 |
| asylums   11 | stigma   14 |

## Media Resources

### MindTap

MindTap for Kearney and Trull's *Abnormal Psychology and Life: A Dimensional Approach* is a highly personalized fully online learning platform of authoritative content, assignments, and services offering you a tailored presentation of course curriculum created by your instructor. MindTap guides you through the course curriculum via an innovative learning path where you will complete reading assignments, annotate your readings, complete homework, and engage with quizzes and assessments. MindTap includes the Continuum Video Project.

Go to **cengagebrain.com** to access MindTap.

# Perspectives on Abnormal Psychology

**2**

**CASE:** *Mariella*

**What Do You Think?**

Introduction

**The Biological Model**
Interim Summary
Review Questions

**The Psychodynamic Model**
Interim Summary
Review Questions

**The Humanistic Model**
Interim Summary
Review Questions

**The Cognitive-Behavioral Model**
Interim Summary
Review Questions

**The Sociocultural Model**
Interim Summary
Review Questions

FINAL COMMENTS
KEY TERMS
MEDIA RESOURCES

**SPECIAL FEATURES**

**BOX 2.1** | Focus on Violence: A More Complex Approach   28

**BOX 2.2** | Focus on Law and Ethics: Dangerousness and Commitment   33

**BOX 2.3** | Focus on Gender: A More Complex Approach   41

**PERSONAL NARRATIVE 2.1  An Integrative Psychologist: Dr. John C. Norcross   46**

## CASE: Mariella

**Mariella**, a 19-year-old college freshman, has been repeatedly asking herself, "What's going on?" and "What should I do?" Something was not right. Mariella was outgoing, bright, and cheery in high school but was now fatigued, blue, and pessimistic in college. She was starting her second semester and thought the tough college adjustment period her friends and family talked about should be over by now. Were her feelings of fatigue and discontent just a temporary "funk," or was something seriously wrong?

Mariella's fatigue and discontent began early in her first semester and worsened toward finals week. She enrolled in five classes and was soon overwhelmed by extensive reading assignments, large classes, and fast-approaching deadlines. She struggled to finish her work, often seemed isolated from others, and felt unimportant in the huge academic setting. Mariella believed no one cared whether she was in class, and she longed for days in high school when she interacted with a close-knit group of teachers and friends. Her college professors seemed to treat her like a number and not a student, and her classmates always seemed to be rushing about with little time to talk.

Mariella was an "A" student in high school but was now struggling to get Cs in her college classes. She had great trouble concentrating on what she read, which led to low test scores. Mariella did talk to her friends and family members back home about her troubles, but no one truly understood what she was going through. Instead, they thought Mariella was experiencing simple, normal homesickness that would soon end.

Mariella began spending more time alone as her first semester approached mid-November. She often slept, watched television, listened to her iPod, and surfed the Internet. She no longer found much enjoyment doing things that used to appeal to her, such as going to the movies and playing the guitar. Mariella declined invitations from others to go out, and her roommate noticed that Mariella seemed sad and lonely. Unfortunately, no one took the time to ask Mariella if something serious might be wrong.

Mariella also lost significant weight her first semester. When she went home for Thanksgiving, her family members were surprised at how she looked. Mariella had noticed no major change except for occasional hunger, but in fact she had lost 10 pounds from her 120-pound frame. Unfortunately, she received flattering comments on how she looked, so the larger problem of her sad mood went undetected. Her concentration and eating problems continued when she returned to school to finish her first semester, and Mariella struggled to finish her final examinations and receive passing grades.

Mariella was happy to return home for the winter break and hoped her feelings of fatigue and discontent were simply related to school. Unfortunately, she remained sad, did not regain lost weight from the previous semester, and continued to sleep much of the day. She dreaded returning to school but felt pressure from others to do so. Mariella became quite despondent when she returned to school in mid-January. She knew something would have to change to endure this second semester, but she felt confused and unsure. Once again she was asking, "What's going on?" and "What should I do?"

### What Do You Think?

1. Why do you think Mariella feels the way she does?

2. What should Mariella do? What would you do if in her situation?

3. Which aspects of Mariella's story concern you most?

4. Do you know people who have had similar experiences? What did they do?

5. What should Mariella's friends and family do to help?

*Nika Fadul/Flickr/Getty Images*

## Introduction

If Mariella had lived centuries ago, demonic possession might have been a common explanation for her problems. Scientists and mental health professionals today, however, focus on a person's biology, environment, and other factors to help people like Mariella. Scientists and mental health professionals develop perspectives or **models**—ways of looking at things—to piece together why someone like Mariella has problems.

Perspectives or models are systematic ways of viewing and explaining what we see in the world. When you try to explain high gasoline prices, you might think about the economic model of *supply and demand* to conclude everyone wants fuel but supplies are limited. Or if a friend of yours is sick, you might think about the disease model of *germ theory* to ask whether she was around a sick person or if she ate spoiled food. Mental health professionals use models to help explain unusual behavior or mental disorders in people like Mariella. Five main models to explain mental disorders are described in this chapter:

- The *biological model* focuses on genetics, neurotransmitters, brain changes, and other physical factors.

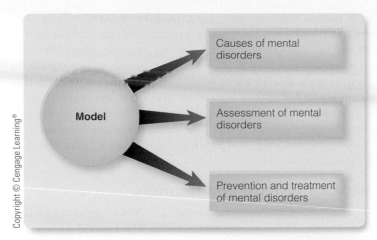

Copyright © Cengage Learning®

**FIGURE 2.1 THE USE OF MODELS** Models or perspectives affect the way we think about causes of mental disorder, our methods of assessment, and our methods of prevention and treatment.

- The *psychodynamic model* focuses on internal personality characteristics.
- The *humanistic model* focuses on personal growth, choice, and responsibility.
- The *cognitive-behavioral model* focuses on specific thoughts and learning experiences.
- The *sociocultural model* focuses on external environmental events and includes the family systems perspective.

These models dominate the mental health profession today and influence the way we think about, assess, and treat mental disorders (see **Figure 2.1**). Each model has strengths and weaknesses, but each provides mental health professionals with ways of understanding what is happening to someone like Mariella. In this chapter, we show how each model could be used to explain Mariella's problems and help her. Many mental health professionals also integrate these models to study and explain mental disorders.

## The Biological Model

The **biological model** rests on the assumption that mental states, emotions, and behaviors arise from brain function and other physical processes. This model has been in use for centuries and is stronger than ever today. Read a newspaper or magazine, watch television, or surf the Internet—countless articles, documentaries, and advertisements are available about medications and other substances to treat mental conditions. Some drug or herb always seems available to cure depression, anxiety, or sexual dysfunction. Despite the

Emil Kraepelin is considered by many to be the father of psychiatric classification and a key contributor to the biological model.

Interfoto/Alamy

incessant advertising, however, the biological model of mental disorder, including the use of medications, is supported by scientific research that links genetics, neurochemistry, and brain changes to various psychological problems.

The biological model of mental disorder was pioneered by Emil Kraepelin (1856-1926), who noticed various **syndromes** or clusters of symptoms in people. Mariella had a cluster of symptoms that included concentration problems, oversleeping, sadness, and weight loss. Her symptoms are commonly described within the syndrome of *depression* (Chapter 7). Kraepelin believed, as do many psychiatrists and other mental health professionals today, that syndromes and symptoms have biological causes. Kraepelin proposed two major types of mental disorders, each with different biological causes: *dementia praecox* (similar to schizophrenia, discussed in Chapter 12) and *manic-depressive psychosis* (similar to bipolar disorder, discussed in Chapter 7).

Kraepelin also believed syndromes to be separate from one another, like mumps and measles, and that each syndrome has unique causes, symptoms, and outcomes. In Mariella's case, her symptom of sadness seemed partly caused by her separation from home and led to outcomes such as poor grades. Kraepelin and many psychiatrists also believe each syndrome has its own biological cause. A psychiatrist may feel Mariella's sadness was caused by depression that ran in her family (genetics), by a chemical (neurotransmitter) imbalance, or by some brain change. We discuss these biological causes next.

### Genetics

Do you think Mariella's sadness may have been present as well in some of her family members? Many mental disorders such as depression do seem to run in families. Genetic material may be involved when symptoms of a mental disorder are passed from parents to children. Genetic material refers to genetic "codes" contained in the nucleus of every human cell (Watson, 2003). *Genes* are the smallest units of inheritance that carry information about how a person will appear and behave. Genes carry information about hair and eye color, weight and height, and even vulnerability to diseases such as lung cancer or mental disorders such as depression. Human genes are located on 46 *chromosomes* or threadlike structures arranged in 23 pairs. A person's chromosomes come half from the biological mother and half from the biological father.

The genetic composition of a person is known as a **genotype** and is fixed at birth. Genotypes produce characteristics such as eye color that do not change over time. An observable characteristic of a person is known as a **phenotype**, which *can* change over time.

Observable characteristics can include intelligence, as well as symptoms of a mental disorder such as difficulty concentrating. Phenotypes can change because they result from genetic *and* environmental influences. Your intelligence is partly determined by genetics from your parents but also by the type of education you received as a child. Scientists are interested in knowing which genetic and environmental influences impact the development of emotions, cognitions, and behavior (DiLalla, 2004). This research specialty is known as **behavior genetics**.

Behavior geneticists are interested in the degree to which a mental disorder is determined by genetics. *Heritability* refers to the amount of variation in a phenotype attributed to genetic factors, often expressed as a number ranging from 0 to 1. Some mental disorders such as anxiety-related disorders have modest heritability, but many major mental disorders have more substantial genetic influences in their development (see **Figure 2.2**). Disorders with particularly high heritability include bipolar disorder and schizophrenia (Kendler, 2005).

Behavior geneticists also focus on what *specific* genes are inherited and how these genes help produce a mental disorder. Researchers in the field of **molecular genetics** analyze *deoxyribonucleic acid* (DNA)—the molecular basis of genes—to identify associations between specific genes and mental disorders. Molecular genetics is quite challenging for several reasons. First, most mental disorders are influenced by multiple genes, not just one. When you hear a media report that researchers found a gene for Alzheimer's disease, keep in mind they likely found only one of many genes. Second, the same symptoms of a mental disorder may be caused by different genes in different people. Third, each human cell contains about 30,000 to 40,000 genes, so finding specific ones related to a certain disorder is like finding a needle in a haystack. Despite these challenges, advances in molecular genetics will likely lead to findings that help scientists determine how and if disorders are genetically distinct from one another. Knowledge of specific genes can also help researchers determine how genes influence physical changes in the body, which we discuss next.

## Nervous Systems and Neurons

Physical structures in our body are affected by genetics, and this can contribute to mental disorder. The **central nervous system** includes the brain and spinal cord and is responsible for processing information from our sensory organs such as eyes and ears and prompting our body into action. The **peripheral nervous system** helps control muscles and voluntary movement, regulates the cardiovascular and endocrine (hormone) systems, assists with digestion, and adjusts body temperature. The nervous systems are composed of billions of **neurons**, or nerve cells, that have four major components: cell body, dendrites, axon, and terminal buttons (see **Figure 2.3**).

A small gap called the **synapse** exists between neurons. Neurons communicate with each other using **neurotransmitters**, or chemical messengers that allow information to cross the synapse. Not all neurotransmitters released into the synapse are used, so an unused neurotransmitter is reabsorbed and recycled in a process called **reuptake**. Medications influence neurotransmitter systems to treat mental disorders. Medications may *block synapses* to decrease neurotransmitter levels or *block reuptake* to increase neurotransmitter levels. People with depression often take drugs such as Prozac or Paxil to increase availability of certain neurotransmitters for improved energy and mood. Six major neurotransmitters are discussed throughout this textbook: serotonin, norepinephrine, dopamine, gamma-aminobutyric

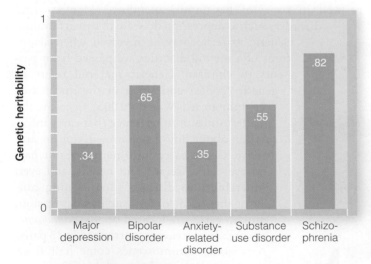

**FIGURE 2.2** HERITABILITY OF MAJOR MENTAL DISORDERS
*Adapted from Merikangas, K.R., & Risch, N. (2005). Will the genomics revolution revolutionize psychiatry? In N.C. Andreasen (Ed.), Research advances in genetics and genomics: Implications for psychiatry (pp. 37–61). Washington, DC: American Psychiatric Publishing; Kendler, K.S., Chen, X., Dick, D., Maes, H., Gillespie, N., Neale, M.C., & Riley, B. (2012). Recent advances in the genetic epidemiology and molecular genetics of substance use disorders. Nature Neuroscience, 15, 181-189.*

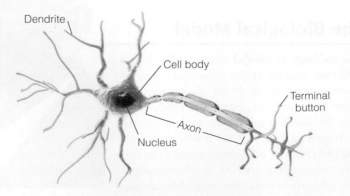

**FIGURE 2.3** BASIC PARTS OF A NEURON *Adapted from Josephine F. Wilson, Biological foundations of human behavior, Fig. 2.6, p. 30. Reprinted by permission of the author.*

acid (GABA), acetylcholine, and glutamate. **Table 2.1** lists functions associated with each.

## Brain

The brain is our most complex and important organ and comprises *140 billion* neurons (Freides, 2002). The brain consists of two cerebral hemispheres that are mirror images of each other. The *right hemisphere* controls movement for the left side of the body, influences spatial relations and patterns, and impacts emotion and intuition. The *left hemisphere* controls movement for the right side of the body, influences analytical thinking, and impacts grammar and vocabulary. The two hemispheres do communicate with each other, however. Complex behaviors such as playing a piano or using language are influenced by both hemispheres.

The **cerebral cortex** covers much of each hemisphere and is largely responsible for consciousness, memory, attention, and other higher-order areas of human functioning. The brain itself is divided into four main lobes (see left side of **Figure 2.4**). The **frontal lobe** is in the front portion of the brain and has many important functions such as movement, planning and organization, inhibiting behavior or responses, and decision making. The frontal lobe is thus a central focus of many mental health researchers. The **parietal lobe** is behind the frontal lobe and is associated with touch. The **temporal lobe** is at the base of the brain and is associated with hearing and memory. The **occipital lobe** is behind the parietal and temporal lobes and is associated with vision.

### Table 2.1

| Major Neurotransmitter Systems Associated with Mental Disorders ||
| --- | --- |
| **Neurotransmitter system** | **Functions** |
| Serotonin | Processing of information; regulation of mood, behavior, and thought processes |
| Norepinephrine | Regulation of arousal, mood, behavior, and sleep |
| Dopamine | Influences novelty-seeking, sociability, pleasure, motivation, coordination, and motor movement |
| Gamma-aminobutyric acid (GABA) | Regulation of mood, especially anxiety, arousal, and behavior |
| Acetylcholine | Important in motor behavior, arousal, reward, attention, learning, and memory |
| Glutamate | Influences learning and memory |

The brain may also be organized along the *forebrain, midbrain,* and *hindbrain*. The forebrain contains the **limbic system** (see right side of Figure 2.4), which regulates emotions and impulses and controls thirst, sex, and aggression. The limbic system is important for several mental disorders and is composed of the hippocampus, cingulate gyrus, septum, and amygdala. Farther down the forebrain, the **basal ganglia** help control posture and motor activity. The **thalamus** and **hypothalamus** are at the crossroads of the forebrain and midbrain and relay information between the forebrain and lower brain areas. The midbrain also contains the *reticular activating system,* which is involved in arousal and stress or tension. The hindbrain includes the *medulla, pons,* and *cerebellum*. These structures are involved in breathing, heartbeat, digestion, and motor coordination.

## Biological Assessment and Treatment

How can knowledge about genetics, neurotransmitters, and brain changes be used to evaluate and treat people with mental disorders? A biologically oriented mental health professional such as a psychiatrist would first give a diagnostic interview (Chapter 4) to better understand a person's problems. Biologically oriented health professionals also use assessment methods to obtain images of brain structure and functioning. *Magnetic resonance imaging* (MRI) provides high-quality brain images to reveal tumors, blood clots, and other structural abnormalities. **Figure 2.5** compares MRI images of a youth with autism to a youth without autism. Other methods for brain imaging are described in Chapter 4.

Biologically oriented mental health professionals decide on treatment once a comprehensive evaluation is complete. Psychiatric medications are commonly used to treat mental disorders by affecting neurotransmitter systems. Medications that decrease *dopamine* generally have antipsychotic effects to ease symptoms of schizophrenia. Medications that increase *norepinephrine* or *serotonin* often have antidepressant effects. Medications that increase *GABA* often have antianxiety effects.

## Evaluating the Biological Model

The biological model is respected because genetics, neurotransmitters, and brain areas clearly influence problems such as anxiety (Chapter 5), depression and bipolar disorder (Chapter 7), schizophrenia (Chapter 12), intellectual disability and autism (Chapter 13), and Alzheimer's disease (Chapter 14). Findings from this model have led to better knowledge about which genes are inherited, how neurotransmitter effects and medications can help treat mental disorder, and how brain changes over time lead to abnormal behavior. The biological perspective comprises much of the material in this textbook.

The biological perspective also has some limitations. First, biological factors do not provide a full account of *any* form of mental disorder. Some disorders have substantial genetic contributions, such as schizophrenia or bipolar disorder, but environmental or nonbiological factors are clearly influential as well. An exclusive focus on biological factors would also deny crucial information about cultural, family, stress, and other factors

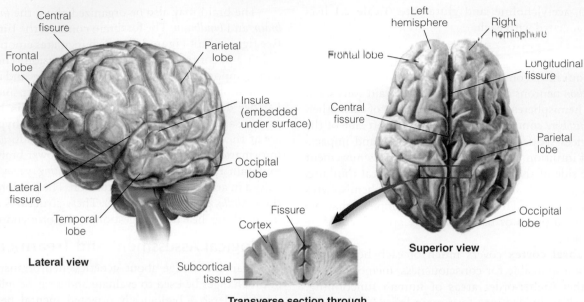

**FIGURE 2.4** MAJOR FEATURES OF THE HUMAN BRAIN

| Structure | Location and Description |
|---|---|
| **Central fissure** | Deep valley in the cerebral cortex that divides the frontal lobe from the rest of the brain |
| **Cerebellum** | Located within the hindbrain; coordinates muscle movement and balance |
| **Cerebral cortex** | Outer-most layer of the brain. Covers almost all of each hemisphere of the brain; referred to as the grey matter of the brain (named after its characteristic coloring). |
| **Frontal lobe** | Located in the front of the brain (in front of the central fissure). The frontal lobe is the seat of a number of very important functions, including controlling movement, planning, organizing, inhibiting behavior or responses, and decision-making. |
| **Hemisphere (left)** | Controls the right half of the body, is typically responsible for analytic thinking, and is responsible for speech |
| **Hemisphere (right)** | Controls the left side of the body, is involved in the determination of spatial relations and patterns, and is involved in emotion and intuition |
| **Lateral fissure** | Deep valley in the cerebral cortex that is above the temporal lobe |
| **Longitudinal fissure** | Deep valley in the cerebral cortex that divides the left and right hemispheres of the brain |
| **Occipital lobe** | Located behind the parietal and temporal lobes of the brain; associated with vision |
| **Parietal lobe** | Located behind the frontal lobe of the brain and above the lateral fissure; associated with the sensation of touch. |
| **Prefrontal cortex** | Controls attention and impulse control; used in problem solving and critical thinking |
| **Subcortical tissue** | Brain tissue immediately below the cerebral cortex |
| **Temporal lobe** | Located below the lateral fissure of the brain; associated with auditory discrimination. |

that influence all of us. Second, we do not know yet exactly how biological factors *cause* mental disorder. We can only say biological changes appear to be significant risk factors for mental disorder. Biological risk factors also clearly interact with environmental risk factors, as we discuss throughout this textbook.

## INTERIM SUMMARY

▶ The biological model assumes that mental states, emotions, and behaviors arise largely from physical processes.

▶ A genetic approach to mental disorder focuses on heritability and molecular genetics.

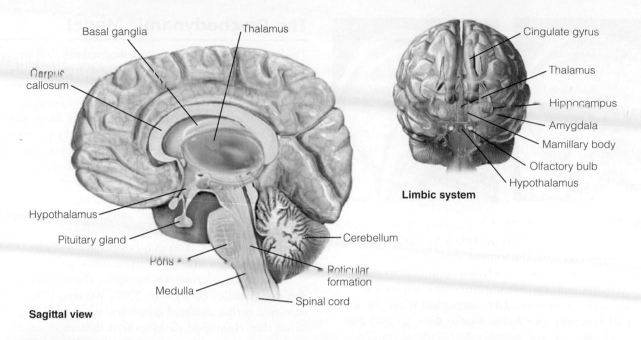

**Sagittal view**

| Structure | Location and Description |
|---|---|
| **Amygdala** | Structure in the limbic system that is involved in emotion and in aggression |
| **Basal ganglia** | Brain structures that control posture, motor activity, and anxiety level |
| **Corpus callosum** | A band of nerve fibers that connects the two hemispheres of the brain, allowing for communication between the right and left sides of the brain. |
| **Hindbrain** | Most posterior part of the brain; includes the medulla, pons, and cerebellum; these structures are involved in important "automatic" activities of the body like breathing, heartbeat, and digestion. In addition, the cerebellum controls motor coordination. |
| **Hypothalamus** | Regulates basic biological needs like hunger, thirst, and body temperature |
| **Hippocampus** | Part of the limbic system involved in memory and learning |
| **Limbic system** | Regulates emotions and impulses, and is also responsible for basic drives like thirst, sex, and aggression. The limbic system consists of several structures that are implicated in psychological disorders: the hippocampus, cingulate gyrus, septum, and amygdala. |
| **Medulla** | Located in the hindbrain; involved in regulating breathing and blood circulation |
| **Pituitary gland** | Regulates other endocrine glands and controls growth; sometimes called the "master gland." |
| **Pons** | Located in the hindbrain; involved in sleep and arousal |
| **Reticular formation** | Internal structures within the midbrain that are involved in arousal and stress or tension |
| **Spinal cord** | Transmits information between the brain and the rest of the body; controls simple reflexes |
| **Thalamus** | Relay signals to and from the cerebral cortex to other brain structures |

**FIGURE 2.4—cont'd**

▶ Neurons are the basic unit of the nervous systems and communicate using chemical messengers or neurotransmitters.

▶ The brain is composed of billions of neurons, as well as several lobes and other structures important for basic functioning.

▶ The biological model is important for understanding many components of major mental disorders, but it cannot explain all aspects of the disorders.

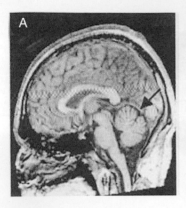
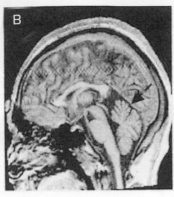

**FIGURE 2.5** MRI SCANS FROM THE CEREBELLAR AREAS OF A 16-YEAR-OLD BOY WITH AUTISM (A) AND A 16-YEAR-OLD BOY WITHOUT AUTISM (B) Note the somewhat smaller cerebellar area in the youth with autism, which may contribute to abnormal motor movements and cognitive impairments often seen in people with autism. *From Palmen, J.M.C., van Engeland, H., Hof, P.R., & Schmitz, C. 2004. Neuropathological findings in autism.* Brain, 127, 2572–2583.

## REVIEW QUESTIONS

1. How might the biological model explain Mariella's problems?
2. Explain the concepts of behavior genetics, heritability, and molecular genetics.
3. Identify some major neurotransmitter systems implicated in mental disorders.
4. What are major structures of the brain, and which ones might be most important for Mariella's condition?
5. What might a biologically oriented mental health professional recommend as treatment for Mariella?

## The Psychodynamic Model

The biological model focuses on internal physical structures related to mental disorder. The **psychodynamic model** also focuses on internal structures but mental ones rather than physical. The psychodynamic model comes from *Freudian theory* that assumes mental states and behaviors arise from motives and conflicts within a person. The term *intrapsychic* refers to psychological dynamics that occur within a person's mind, so this term is often used to describe the psychodynamic model. The psychodynamic model represents one of the most sweeping contributions to the mental health field; its influence permeates our culture. Psychodynamically oriented words or phrases such as *ego, unconscious,* and *Freudian slip* have become part of our common vernacular. You may have even come across aspects of Freudian thought in art, literature, films, and textbooks.

Several basic principles comprise the psychodynamic perspective (Bradley & Westen, 2005; Westen, 1998). One basic principle is that *childhood experiences shape adult personality*. The belief that childhood development influences adult behavior is almost universally accepted. You can likely identify certain childhood experiences that shaped who you are today. You are a product of your biology, youthful experiences, and events happening now. Ignoring any of these factors means we lose much information about your personality and history with others. Imagine if we focused only on Mariella's problems for the past few months—we would lose other information such as her high school experiences that may influence her current symptoms.

A second key principle of the psychodynamic perspective is that *causes and purposes of human behavior are not always obvious but partly unconscious*. Unconscious means the part of

## BOX 2.1  Focus on Violence

### A More Complex Approach

Violence and aggression are complex behaviors that cannot necessarily be explained by single models such as a biological one. Instead, a more complex and developmental approach is often needed. One example is aggression in adolescents with delinquent behavior or conduct disorder (Chapter 13). Dodge and Pettit (2003) proposed that some youth have certain biological qualities that may predispose them to conduct problems such as aggression, although not all youth with these qualities necessarily become aggressive. Those who are more likely to become aggressive tend to experience harsh parental discipline, emotional neglect, lack of teaching from parents, and conflicts with aggressive peers. These experiences then interact with academic and social

problems, which can lead to association with deviant peers in middle or high school. If parents' supervision declines during this time, then the child may not develop adequate social skills to control anger and aggression. In this scenario, many contributing factors are involved, including biological, psychological, and social factors.

A more in-depth approach may be necessary to explain forms of violence in adulthood as well. Intimate partner violence is a significant problem among college students but one that cannot be fully explained just by learning or sociocultural factors. Moore and colleagues (2011) examined college students in dating relationships who used a handheld computer to record daily instances of interpersonal violence. Students were much more likely to engage in physical and psychological interpersonal violence on days they were drinking alcohol. Odds of violence were greater with lower relationship satisfaction and higher levels of past violence.

the mind where mental activity occurs but of which a person is unaware. Scientists in disciplines such as cognitive and social psychology and neuroscience have found that certain cognitive and behavioral processes do not appear to be under cognitive control (e.g., Lau & Passingham, 2007). The implication is that realms of emotion, cognition, and behavior exist of which we are not consciously aware. These hidden realms of emotion, thought, and behavior may also affect motives that drive us to act in certain ways. This is known as **unconscious motivation**. Healthy behavior is considered behavior for which a person understands the motivation (do you know why you are doing what you are doing?). Unhealthy behavior results when we do not fully understand the unconscious causes of our behavior. The goal of psychodynamic therapy is thus to make the unconscious more conscious.

A third key principle of the psychodynamic perspective is that *people use defense mechanisms to control anxiety or stress.* **Defense mechanisms** are strategies to cope with anxiety or stressors such as conflict with others. Psychodynamic theorists believe most humans can adapt to challenges and stressors by using healthy defense mechanisms. Some people with a mental disorder over-rely on less effective defense mechanisms, or defense mechanisms do not work well for them and they become quite stressed.

A fourth key principle of the psychodynamic model is that *everything we do has meaning and purpose and is goal-directed.* This is known as **psychic determinism**. Mundane and bizarre behavior, dreams, and slips of the tongue all have significant meaning in the psychodynamic model. Behaviors may in fact have different meanings. Think about Mariella's weight loss: Was her behavior motivated by a simple desire to lose weight, or was it a signal to others that she needed help?

## Brief Overview of the Psychodynamic Model

We now provide an overview of the major concepts of the psychodynamic model. This includes a description of the structure of the mind, as well as an explanation of psychosexual stages and defense mechanisms.

### STRUCTURE OF THE MIND

A major component of the psychodynamic model of personality and mental disorders is *structure of the mind.* According to Freud and other psychodynamic theorists, the mind (and hence personality) is composed of three basic structures in our unconscious: *id, ego,* and *superego* (see **Figure 2.6**). The **id** is the portion of the personality that is present at birth. The purpose of the id is to seek immediate gratification and discharge tension as soon as possible. This process is the **pleasure principle**. The id propels us to meet demands of hunger, thirst, aggression, or sexual or physical pleasure as soon as possible. The id is thus hedonistic and without values, ethics, or logic. Think about a baby who cries when she wants something and does not want to wait for it. Babies, and maybe even some adults you know, have "id-oriented" personalities.

The id uses a **primary process** form of thinking if gratification is not immediate—this involves manufacturing a fantasy

Bettmann/Corbis

The roots of the psychodynamic model can be traced back to the life and times of the Viennese physician Sigmund Freud (1856–1939).

or mental image of whatever lessens the tension. You might want to date someone but are convinced he or she will reject your invitation, so you simply fantasize about being with that person. Or you might think about food when you are hungry. Dreaming is also a form of primary process. Primary processes cannot provide real gratification such as a date or food, however, so we must develop a second personality structure to help us address real-life demands—the ego.

The **ego** is an organized, rational system that uses higher-order thinking processes to obtain gratification. The ego is

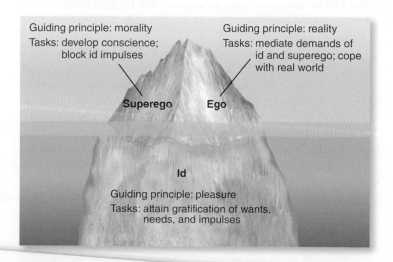

Guiding principle: morality
Tasks: develop conscience; block id impulses

Guiding principle: reality
Tasks: mediate demands of id and superego; cope with real world

**Superego**    **Ego**

**Id**

Guiding principle: pleasure
Tasks: attain gratification of wants, needs, and impulses

**FIGURE 2.6** **FREUD'S STRUCTURE OF THE MIND** *Adapted from Rathus,* Psychology: Concepts and Connections, *9th ed., Fig. 11.1, p. 402. Copyright © 2005 Wadsworth, a part of Cengage Learning. Reproduced by permission. www.cengage.com/permissions.*

the executive of the personality and operates along the **reality principle**, or need to delay gratification of impulses to meet environmental demands. If you badly want an iPad, then your id might urge you to steal it. This would land you in trouble, however, so the ego tries to mediate demands of the id and demands of the environment. The ego uses **secondary process** to do this. Secondary process involves learning, perception, memory, planning, judgment, and other higher-order thinking processes to plan a workable strategy. The ego might plan to schedule some overtime shifts at work so you can earn extra money to buy the iPad. The id thus receives what it wants eventually but in a socially acceptable way. A strong ego is often considered by psychodynamic theorists to be the hallmark of mental health.

The third component of the personality is the **superego**. The superego develops in early childhood and represents societal ideals and values conveyed by parents through rewards and punishments. The superego is essentially one's sense of right and wrong. Punished behavior becomes part of one's *conscience*, and rewarded behavior becomes a part of one's *ego ideal*. The conscience punishes individuals by making them feel guilty or worthless for doing something wrong, whereas the ego ideal rewards individuals by making them feel proud and worthy for doing something right. The role of the superego is to block unacceptable id impulses, pressure the ego to pursue morality rather than expediency, and generate strivings toward perfection. Your superego might punish you by using guilt, shame, and worry if you decide to shoplift an iPad.

## FREUD'S PSYCHOSEXUAL STAGES

Not all psychodynamic theorists adhere strictly to Freudian principles, but they do agree childhood is extremely important in shaping a person's character and personality. Freud himself proposed that each person progresses through **psychosexual stages of development**. These stages occur early in life and are marked by *erogenous zones,* or areas of the body through which hedonistic id impulses are expressed. **Table 2.2** provides a description of each stage.

Severe difficulties experienced by a child at a psychosexual stage may be expressed later in life as symptoms of mental disorders. These difficulties are marked by excessive frustration or overindulgence at a psychosexual stage and can result in **fixation**, or delayed psychosexual development. The particular stage at which such frustration or overindulgence is encountered will determine the nature of later symptoms. A child neglected or deprived during the oral stage of development may compensate in adulthood by engaging in excess oral behaviors such as smoking, talking, or drinking too much alcohol. A child overindulged by parents during toilet training in the anal stage may compensate in adulthood by being overly neat or compulsive. A psychodynamic theorist might say Mariella's basic needs of nurturance and safety were unsatisfied during her oral stage of development, and so she remained fixated at this stage. Her depression may thus be a signal to others that she craves social attention and comfort.

**Table 2.2**

### Freud's Psychosexual Stages of Development

| Stage | Age | Focus |
|---|---|---|
| Oral stage | 0–6 months | Mouth is the chief means of reaching satisfaction. |
| Anal stage | 6 months–3 years | Attention becomes centered on defecation and urination. |
| Phallic stage | 3–6 years | Sexual organs become the prime source of gratification. |
| Latency stage | 6–12 years | Lack of overt sexual activity or interest. |
| Genital stage | 12 years to adulthood | Mature expression of sexuality. |

Copyright © Cengage Learning®

## DEFENSE MECHANISMS

The ego experiences *anxiety* when the id urges it to seek impulsive gratification or when the superego imposes shame and guilt. Anxiety is a painful emotion that warns the ego to quell the threat and protect the organism. The ego uses secondary processes of memory, judgment, and learning to solve problems and stave off external threats. But these measures are less useful when internal threats arise from the id or superego. What then? The ego has at its disposal various tactics called defense mechanisms, which are unconscious mental processes used to fend off conflict or anxiety.

We all use defense mechanisms, such as when we claim we did not really want to date someone who just turned down our invitation. Use of defense mechanisms becomes a problem, however, when we use them excessively or when we use a select few defense mechanisms exclusively. If we constantly deny reality and continue to ask out people who are likely to reject us, then we may get depressed. Moderation and variety are important for mental health, including use of defense mechanisms.

**Table 2.3** lists many defense mechanisms proposed by psychodynamic theorists. Let's discuss some of the primary ones. **Repression** is a basic ego defense that occurs when a person banishes from consciousness threatening feelings, thoughts, or impulses, like a strong sexual desire for a stranger. **Regression** involves returning to a stage that previously gave a person much gratification—think of a middle-aged man under stress who begins to act as if he were a teenager. **Reaction formation** occurs when an unconscious impulse is consciously expressed by its behavioral opposite. "I love you" is thus expressed as "I hate you," a phenomenon common among teens who like someone but who are afraid of rejection. **Projection** occurs when unconscious feelings are attributed to another person. A spouse who feels guilty about cheating on her husband may accuse her husband of infidelity.

## Table 2.3

### Examples of Defense Mechanisms

| Defense mechanism | Description |
|---|---|
| Denial | Refusing to accept or acknowledge reality |
| Displacement | Expressing one's unacceptable feelings onto a different object or person than the one that is truly the target of the feelings |
| Fantasy | Imagining some unattainable desire |
| Identification | Modeling another person's behavior or preferences to be more like them |
| Intellectualization | Providing an in-depth intellectual analysis of a traumatic or other situation to distance oneself from its emotional content |
| Overcompensation | Emphasizing strength in one area to balance a perceived weakness in other area |
| Projection | Attributing one's own unacceptable motives or impulses to another person |
| Rationalization | Developing a specific reason for an action, such as justifying why one did not purchase a particular car |
| Reaction formation | Expressing an unconscious impulse by engaging in its behavioral opposite |
| Regression | Returning to an earlier psychosexual stage that provided substantial gratification |
| Repression | Keeping highly threatening sexual or aggressive material from consciousness |
| Sublimation | Transforming emotions or sexual or aggressive material into more acceptable forms such as dancing or athletic or creative activity |
| Undoing | Reversing an unacceptable behavior or thought using extreme means |

## Psychodynamic Assessment and Treatment

Psychodynamic theorists believe symptoms of mental disorders are caused by unresolved conflicts. A psychodynamically oriented therapist treating Mariella's depression might explore a history of loss, such as loss of important relationships. Mariella's relationships with friends and family at home were indeed affected by attending college. Psychodynamic theorists also believe we unconsciously harbor anger and resentment toward those we love. Mariella may have been unconsciously jealous of, and angry at, her friends and family members who did not move far away and who did not fully appreciate her problems in college. Perhaps she internalized feelings of resentment by directing the feelings toward herself—anger turned inward. This may have led to symptoms of depression such as low self-esteem and sadness. Mariella's depression may have been caused by this unconscious conflict of emotions.

How does a psychodynamic theorist know what unconscious material exists for a client? A psychodynamic mental health professional often assesses unconscious motivations and conflicts using *projective techniques*. Projective techniques are based on the **projective hypothesis**, or an assumption that people project unconscious needs and conflicts onto ambiguous stimuli such as inkblots. People *impose their own structure* on unstructured stimuli and thus reveal something of themselves. Unconscious material is thus uncovered. In Chapter 4, we discuss two major projective tests used to access unconscious material—the *Rorschach* and the *Thematic Apperception Test* (TAT). However, we present next an overview of projective assessment within the context of Mariella's case.

A psychodynamic theorist might expect a depressed client like Mariella to respond to projective tests in ways that indicate underlying anger and hostility. Such findings would support the psychodynamic explanation of depression as "anger turned inward" in response to loss. Mariella might be given an inkblot from the Rorschach and asked "What might this be?" or asked to develop a story about characters depicted in the TAT. Mariella could reveal unconscious material about herself because she must impose some structure, organization, and interpretation onto ambiguous materials. She may respond to an inkblot by saying it represents "two bears fighting with each other" or develop a story from a TAT card about a woman who is mad at a friend. A psychodynamic theorist might conclude from these responses that Mariella is "projecting" her anger and hostility onto the neutral stimulus of an inkblot or TAT card. This "projected" anger and hostility is considered to be unconscious material.

Psychodynamic theorists also use other techniques to access unconscious material. **Free association** means asking a client to say whatever comes to mind during the session, without exercising censorship or restraint. This is not easy (try it) because the client must stop censoring or screening thoughts that may seem ridiculous, aggressive, embarrassing, or sexual. A psychodynamic therapist is looking for slips of the tongue, or Freudian slips, that reveal quick glimpses of unconscious material. Mariella could be speaking during free association and "accidentally" say she has always resented her mother for pushing her to do things outside the home.

A related technique is **dream analysis**. Dreams are thought to reveal unconscious material because ego defenses are lowered during sleep. The **manifest content** of a dream is what actually happens during the dream. The manifest content of a dream may be, for example, that the dreamer is confronted with two large, delicious-looking ice cream cones. The **latent content** of a dream, however, is its symbolic or unconscious meaning. Dreaming about ice cream cones may symbolically represent a longing to return to the mother's breast.

How might psychodynamic theorists use information from projective tests, free association, and dreams to treat Mariella? A key goal of psychodynamic treatment is to help clients gain *insight* into their current problems. **Insight** means understanding the unconscious determinants of irrational emotions, thoughts, or behaviors that create problems or distress. The need for defense mechanisms and psychological symptoms should disappear once these unconscious reasons are fully confronted and understood. A psychodynamic theorist believes Mariella can improve by understanding the true, underlying reasons for her depression, including feelings of anger turned inward.

Psychodynamic theorists interpret past experiences and information from projective assessments to help accomplish insight. **Interpretation** is a cornerstone of psychodynamic therapy and the method by which unconscious meanings of emotions, thoughts, and behavior are revealed. A mental health professional will "translate" for a client what may be causing current symptoms involving emotions, thoughts, or behaviors. Significant insight or behavioral change rarely comes from a single interpretation but rather a slow process in which meaning behind certain emotions, thoughts, and behaviors is repeatedly identified in one context after another. A psychodynamic therapist might point out Mariella's various child, adolescent, and adult experiences, as well as projective assessment responses to illustrate a history of becoming angry with others but bottling up such anger and becoming depressed. Certain dreams and Freudian slips would be instructive as well.

A client's behavior with a therapist can also illuminate the unconscious and reveal conflicts with others. **Transference** is a key phenomenon in psychodynamic therapy that occurs when a client reacts to a therapist as if the latter is an important figure from childhood. Positive and negative feelings can be transferred. Conflicts and problems that originated in childhood are thus reinstated in the therapy room. Mariella might one day yell at her therapist to reflect anger toward her mother.

Client–therapist interactions provide important clues about the nature of a client's problems but are also an opportunity for the therapist to carefully and supportively interpret transference in an immediate and vital situation. A client will then hopefully recognize the irrational nature and origins of transference feelings and cope with these in more rational ways. The client can begin to control such reactions in real-world settings and to use them as a basis for further interpretation and analysis.

## Evaluating the Psychodynamic Model

As mentioned, the most influential principle of the psychodynamic perspective may be that childhood experiences greatly affect adult functioning. The influence of this principle can be seen in popular media as well as in psychology and psychiatry. Think about how we value the health, welfare, and education of children. We also emphasize the negative consequences of child maltreatment, poor parenting, and inadequate education. Children are not little adults who can roll with the punches or easily avoid the stress of a dysfunctional family or dangerous home or neighborhood. Psychodynamic theory has certainly helped us focus on providing better environments for our children. The psychodynamic theory of defense mechanisms also makes intuitive sense. Many of us use defenses to ward off anxiety and cope with psychological threats in our environment.

A strict view of the psychodynamic perspective does reveal some limitations, however. Perhaps the biggest weakness is that little empirical support exists for many of the major propositions and techniques of the perspective. Psychodynamic theory was mostly formed from anecdotal evidence, and many concepts such as the id are abstract and difficult to measure. If we cannot measure an important variable reliably and with confidence, then its usefulness is questionable. Psychodynamic theorists were accused for many years of being "antiscientific" because they accepted Freud's propositions as simple truth. This stance, predictably, divides people into believers and nonbelievers. Believers thought empirical research was unnecessary, and nonbelievers saw no point to empirically testing the theory. Psychodynamic theory has thus lost much of its broad, mainstream appeal, but a short-term therapy approach based on the theory remains popular among some mental health professionals (Lewis, Dennerstein, & Gibbs, 2008).

## INTERIM SUMMARY

▶ The psychodynamic model rests on the assumption that mental states and behaviors arise from unconscious motives and intrapsychic conflicts.

▶ Two major assumptions of this perspective are psychic determinism and unconscious motivation.

▶ According to psychodynamic theorists, the id, ego, and superego comprise the mind.

▶ Psychosexual stages are developmental stages that influence personality and abnormal behavior.

▶ We use defense mechanisms to cope with life demands and intrapsychic conflict.

▶ Problems occur when we use defense mechanisms exclusively or excessively.

▶ Strengths of the psychodynamic perspective include defense mechanisms and an emphasis on how childhood experiences influence adult personality.

▶ A major weakness of the psychodynamic perspective is the relative lack of research support for its major assumptions.

## REVIEW QUESTIONS

1. How might the psychodynamic model explain Mariella's problems?

2. How might a psychodynamically oriented therapist assess and treat Mariella?

## BOX 2.2  Focus on Law and Ethics

### Dangerousness and Commitment

Determining whether someone is dangerous to oneself or others is extremely difficult. Behaviors such as suspiciousness, excitability, uncooperativeness, and tension are not good predictors of dangerousness. Making the task more difficult is that a large majority of people with mental disorders are *not* dangerous (Fulero & Wrightsman, 2009). A psychologist's ability to predict dangerous behavior may be better in the short-term than the long-term, although errors still occur. Some variables may help predict dangerousness, including psychopathy, history of school maladjustment and excessive substance use, violent criminal history, early age of onset of violent behaviors, injury to victims, and psychotic symptoms (Camilleri & Quinsey, 2011; Norko & Baranoski, 2005).

The issue of predicting dangerousness relates to committing someone to a mental hospital against his will. The conflict between individual rights to be free versus societal rights to be protected from dangerous people has been an issue for centuries. Detaining and separating people perceived as dangerous to the general population has become an accepted practice. **Civil commitment** refers to involuntary hospitalization of people at serious risk of harming themselves or others or people who cannot care for themselves (Levenson, 2003). Commitment in this regard can occur on an *emergency* basis for a few days or more *formally* for extended periods by court order.

**Criminal commitment** refers to involuntary hospitalization of people charged with a crime. A person may be hospitalized to determine her competency to stand trial or after acquittal by reason of insanity. **Competency to stand trial** refers to whether a person can participate meaningfully in his own defense and can understand and appreciate the legal process. Such competency is often questioned for people who commit crimes while experiencing intellectual disability, psychotic disorders, dementia, or substance use problems (Pirelli, Gottdiener, & Zapf, 2011).

**Insanity** is a legal term that refers to mental incapacity at the time of a crime, perhaps because a person did not understand right from wrong or because the person was unable to control personal actions at the time of the crime. A person judged to be insane is not held criminally responsible for an act but may be committed as a dangerous person, sometimes for extensive periods of time. The insanity defense has always been controversial, but very few defendants (about 1 percent) actually use this defense. This may change as researchers discover high rates of intellectual disability among people awaiting trial (Crocker, Cote, Toupin, & St-Onge, 2007).

3. Describe the following features of the psychodynamic perspective and how they can help us understand Mariella's symptoms: psychic determinism, unconscious motivation, structure of the mind, psychosexual stages, defense mechanisms.
4. Review the list of defense mechanisms in Table 2.3. Which have you used, and which do you use the most?
5. What are strengths and limitations of the psychodynamic perspective?

## The Humanistic Model

Biological and psychodynamic perspectives focus primarily on internal factors such as genetics and unconscious conflicts. Some theorists have reacted to these models with disdain because the models do not emphasize personal growth, free will, or responsibility. Biological and psychodynamic theorists concentrate heavily on how factors such as genetics and unconscious conflicts automatically shape human behavior. Other theorists, however, focus more on how people can make choices that influence their environment and how they can take responsibility for their actions.

One group of theorists that emphasize human growth, choice, and responsibility adopt a **humanistic model** of psychology. The humanistic model was developed in the 1950s and retains some relevance today. A main assumption of the humanistic model is that people are naturally good and strive for personal growth and fulfillment. Humanistic theorists believe we seek to be creative and meaningful in our lives and that, when thwarted in this goal, become alienated from others and possibly develop a mental disorder. A second key assumption of the model is that humans have choices and are responsible for their own fates. A person with a mental disorder may thus enhance his recovery by taking greater responsibility for his actions.

Humanistic theorists adopt a **phenomenological approach**, which is an assumption that one's behavior is determined by perceptions of herself and others. Humanistic theorists believe in a subjective human experience that includes individual awareness of how we behave in the context of our environment and other people. To fully understand another person, therefore, you must see the world as he sees it and not as you see it. We all have different views of the world that affect our behavior. Humanistic theory was shaped greatly by the works of Abraham Maslow, Carl Rogers, and Rollo May.

We explore these theorists next to expand on our discussion of the humanistic model.

## Abraham Maslow

*Abraham Maslow* (1908–1970) believed humans have basic and higher-order needs they strive to satisfy during their lifetime (see **Figure 2.7**). The most basic needs are physiological and include air, food, water, sex, sleep, and other factors that promote *homeostasis,* or maintenance of the body's internal environment. We feel anxious or irritable when these needs are not met but feel a sense of well-being when the needs are met and when we have achieved homeostasis. These needs must be largely fulfilled before a person can meet other needs. *Safety needs* include shelter, basic health, employment, and family and financial security. *Love and belongingness needs* include intimacy with others and close friendships—a strong social support network. *Esteem needs* include confidence in oneself, self-esteem, achievement at work or another important area, and respect from others. These needs are thought to apply to everyone and have even been adapted to the care of dying patients (Zalenski & Raspa, 2006).

The highest level of need is **self-actualization**, defined as striving to be the best one can be. Maslow believed humans naturally strive to learn as much as they can about their environment, seek beauty and absorb nature, create, feel close to others, and accomplish as much as possible. Self-actualized people are also thought to be moral beings who understand reality and can view things objectively. Pursuit of self-actualization normally occurs after other basic needs have been met, although some people may value other needs such as respect from others more highly than self-actualization.

Maslow believed healthy people are motivated toward self-actualization and become mature in accepting others, solving problems, seeking autonomy, and developing deep-seated feelings of compassion and empathy for others. Unhealthy people, however, experience personal or other obstacles to self-actualization and may develop mental problems as a result. Compare Rachel, who takes whatever classes she wants and excitedly pursues her degree, with Colby, who is pressured by his parents toward a career in which he has no interest. Colby is more likely to experience frustration in his goal toward personal self-actualization and become depressed. Recall as well that Mariella felt considerable pressure from family members to return to college for her second semester. Her feelings of sadness may have been related to diversion from more desired life goals.

## Carl Rogers

*Carl Rogers* (1902–1987) expanded on Maslow's work to become one of the leading proponents of the humanistic model of psychology. Rogers also believed humans strive for self-actualization and that frustration toward this goal could lead to mental problems such as depression. Rogers believed people raised in the right environment could work toward self-actualization and a strong *self-concept* in which one feels differentiated from others in a positive way. Think of someone who is rightfully proud to be the first in her family to graduate from college.

What is the right environment for self-actualization? Rogers presented the concepts of conditional and unconditional positive regard. **Conditional positive regard** refers to an environment in which others set the conditions or standards for one's life. Think about someone like Colby whose major life decisions are made by parents, teachers, or other influential people. People like Colby may feel a sense of loss of control over events and thus feel helpless to change anything. Their drive toward self-actualization and psychological health is thus thwarted. People who feel a sense of loss of control over life events do indeed seem to be at risk for anxiety disorders (Chapter 5).

**Unconditional positive regard** refers to an environment in which a person is fully accepted as she is and allowed to pursue her own desires and goals. Someone like Rachel who is given freedom to choose her own way in life is more predisposed toward self-actualization and psychological health than Colby. Mariella might also have felt less sad if her family members recognized her signs of depression and offered different ideas about what she could do in her life.

Rogers developed **client-centered therapy** that relies heavily on unconditional positive regard and *empathy*. A client-centered therapist establishes a therapeutic environment in which a client is completely accepted and unjudged. Unconditional positive regard in therapy refers to respecting a client's feelings, thoughts, and actions and providing a sympathetic understanding of the client's statements. Many client-centered therapists allow clients to speak freely without assigning blame, criticism, or even feedback about what to do. The therapist instead concentrates on trying to see the world as the client sees it and often reflects a client's statements so the client can

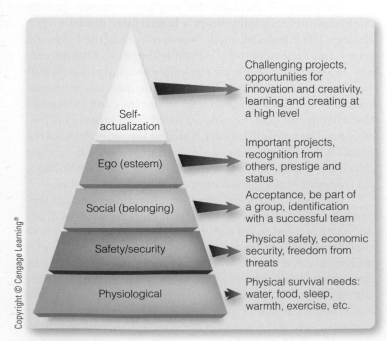

**FIGURE 2.7** MASLOW'S HIERARCHY OF NEEDS

develop his own solution to a problem. Consider the following exchange between a client-centered therapist and Colby:

**Colby:** I've been feeling so down lately, I get so tired of my life.

**Therapist:** It sounds as though things are upsetting you.

**Colby:** Yeah, my parents are always on my case to be a lawyer because my dad and grandfather were lawyers.

**Therapist:** That sounds like a lot of pressure.

**Colby:** It is a lot of pressure. Sometimes I just want to tell them to leave me alone so I can do whatever I want.

**Therapist:** I can understand that. Tell me more about that.

**Colby:** I think I need to have a heart-to-heart talk with my dad. I just can't take this anymore.

The client-centered therapist in this exchange did not tell Colby what to do but instead displayed empathy and allowed Colby to speak freely without worrying about being judged. The therapist also reflected Colby's feelings and statements so he could arrive at his own solution (Rautalinko, Lisper, & Ekehammar, 2007). Client-centered therapists believe many mental problems result from *other-centeredness,* or oversensitivity to demands, criticisms, and judgments of others. Colby's therapist treated him as a responsible adult who needed to become more *person-centered* and find his way back to a path of self-actualization. Client-centered therapists believe clients are their own best experts of their problems and that healthy functioning requires more autonomous decision making.

## Rollo May

*Rollo May* (1909–1994) adopted a similar approach to humanistic psychology. May's *existential psychology* is heavily based on the concept of *authenticity,* or how closely one adheres to one's personality. Someone who is authentic is true to his nature and honest in his interactions with others. Someone who is not authentic may develop a façade and act like someone else in social situations. Perhaps you know someone who tries to be extroverted when really he is introverted or someone who conforms to the "in" crowd so she will be liked. People who are not authentic are thought to be at risk for alienation from others. We discuss several personality disorders in Chapter 10 that involve odd behaviors that often result in social isolation.

Existential theorists believe people are alone in the world and may therefore develop a sense of *meaninglessness.* People who feel meaningless in their world and who are not authentic may be at risk for anxiety and other problems. Existential therapists help their clients discover reasons for their anxiety, manage their anxiety in healthier ways, seek social support from others, develop strong moral values, and act more honestly with others (Spillers, 2007). For example, someone who is introverted could acknowledge that he is less willing to talk in social situations and develop friendships through good listening and other nonverbal support.

## Humanistic Assessment and Treatment

Humanistic theorists believe in a *qualitative* model of assessment. Qualitative assessment focuses on unique characteristics of an individual and often includes general questions about one's perceptions of the world. Humanistic theorists do not group people together to identify common characteristics and often shun formal psychological testing (Chapter 4; Friedman & MacDonald, 2006). A client-centered therapist interviewing Colby would focus on how Colby perceives his world and might thus ask certain questions such as "How might you speak to your father about your concerns?" Specific questions for Colby would not likely be used for Mariella, however, because Mariella's way of viewing the world is completely different than Colby's.

Treatment from a humanistic perspective is *nondirective,* meaning the therapist does not adopt a paternalistic or commanding tone for therapy. A psychiatrist might tell you what medication to take, and a psychodynamic therapist might tell you what your dream means, but a nondirective therapist does not impose her worldview or opinions onto her client. The therapist instead engages in reflective listening so a client can develop solutions, relieve tension, and resume a path toward self-actualization. Nondirective treatments are sometimes considered to be *pretherapy,* or actions taken first in treatment to develop a good relationship with a client (Prouty, 2003). Nondirective treatments thus fit well with most other kinds of therapy.

## Evaluating the Humanistic Model

The humanistic model has several strengths, particularly its focus on human choice and growth. The humanistic model is optimistic and tied to contemporary *positive psychology,* which refers to the study of what factors allow people to thrive in their environments. The humanistic model also emphasizes responsibility. Biological theorists focus on disease models of mental disorder, so treatment usually involves medication or some external agent of behavior change. Psychodynamic theorists focus on personality models of mental disorder, so treatment usually involves better insight with the help of a therapist. Humanistic theorists, however, emphasize that clients themselves must take responsibility for their recovery. Such an approach would seem useful for people with disorders such as anxiety, depression, and substance use. People who actively participate in treatment often have better outcomes than those who participate less (Jackson, 2008).

Rogers's client-centered approach has also contributed greatly to the way therapists approach their clients in session. Many therapists, especially in the first few sessions of therapy, develop a warm, supportive environment for their clients to enhance self-disclosure. We discuss in Chapter 15 different *process variables* that contribute to treatment success. Process variables are factors common to all treatments that seem to help clients. One particularly helpful process variable is a therapeutic environment based on *respect, empathy,* and *full acceptance* of client expressions. A client must feel free to communicate private thoughts without fear of rejection or ridicule (Jordan, 2000; Shamasundar, 2001). Humanistic therapies may thus be helpful for people who need to express grief or discuss difficult personal issues (Goodman, Morgan,

Juriga, & Brown, 2004). Nondirective treatment may also be useful for clients highly mistrustful of, or hostile toward, a therapist.

The humanistic perspective is partly represented in ethical guidelines that psychologists adhere to when treating clients. Psychologists are expected to refrain from biases from possible prejudices toward people of a different culture, sexual orientation, age, gender, or political affiliation, among other factors (American Psychological Association, 2002). Psychologists are expected to respect a client's dignity and rights, including the right to self-determination. If a psychologist feels he cannot be unbiased with a client and this interferes with his ability to conduct therapy, then a referral to another therapist should be made.

The humanistic approach has several limitations as well. The theory is an unscientific one that largely lacks empirical support. Concepts such as self-actualization are difficult to define and test. Many factors other than human perceptions of the world also influence behavior and mental disorder. Client-centered therapy has been criticized as well for its inability to address people with a severe mental disorder such as schizophrenia or those who are suicidal or in pain (Machado, Azevedo, Capanema, Neto, & Cerceau, 2007). The therapy is also more effective for people who are verbal, social, intelligent, and willing to talk. Several groups of people, such as children and people with intellectual disability, are thus not good candidates for this kind of therapy. Some have argued as well that few therapists can realistically be completely nonbiased with a client (Ellis, 2000).

## INTERIM SUMMARY

► The humanistic model focuses on how humans can make choices that influence their environment and how they can take responsibility for their actions.

► The phenomenological approach is based on the assumption that one's behavior is determined by perceptions of herself and others.

► Abraham Maslow outlined a series of human needs; the highest level is self-actualization, or pursuit of one's full potential.

► Carl Rogers developed client-centered therapy, which focuses on unconditional positive regard, or complete acceptance of a client, and empathy.

► Rollo May's existential approach emphasized authenticity, or how closely one adheres to one's personality, as well as anxiety about alienation from others.

► The humanistic perspective relies on qualitative assessment of an individual's perceptions of himself and the world as well as nondirective therapy.

► Strengths of the humanistic perspective include its emphasis on personal responsibility for recovery and process variables important for treatment.

► Weaknesses of the humanistic perspective include relative lack of research support and poor utility for certain groups of people.

## REVIEW QUESTIONS

1. How might the humanistic model explain Mariella's problems?
2. How might a client-centered therapist assess and treat Mariella?
3. Describe the following features of the humanistic perspective and how they can help us understand Mariella's symptoms: phenomenological approach, self-actualization, conditional positive regard, authenticity.
4. What are strengths and limitations of the humanistic perspective?

# The Cognitive-Behavioral Model

The psychodynamic and humanistic perspectives we have covered so far focus specifically on internal variables, lack empirical support, or seem not to apply well to many people with a mental disorder. Another perspective of mental disorders focuses on external as well as internal factors, has good empirical support, and is relevant to many people with a mental disorder. The *behavioral perspective* focuses on external acts and the *cognitive perspective* focuses on internal thoughts. Some textbooks discuss these perspectives separately, but many contemporary researchers and therapists understand the limitations of working within just one model. Many mental health professionals now combine these perspectives into a singular *cognitive-behavioral model*. We discuss these perspectives next and then note how combining the two provides a good explanation for mental disorders and treatment.

## Behavioral Perspective

The **behavioral perspective** developed in reaction to psychodynamic theory that dominated psychology in the early 20th century. Many psychologists were concerned that variables such as id and unconscious were difficult to measure and not important to mental health outcomes. The behavioral perspective instead focuses on environmental stimuli and behavioral responses—variables that can be directly observed and measured. The behavioral perspective is based on the assumption that all behavior—normal or abnormal—is learned. The behavioral model dominated psychology in the mid-20th century because learning principles received much empirical support and applied to many topics of psychological research. Treatment approaches from a behavioral perspective were also found to be quite effective for many problems such as anxiety disorders and intellectual disability. The behavioral perspective is based heavily on a learning approach, so a discussion of key learning principles is important.

### LEARNING PRINCIPLES

Two key learning principles are critical to the behavioral perspective: classical conditioning and operant conditioning. *Classical conditioning* essentially refers to learning by association and was studied initially by *Ivan Pavlov* (1849–1936), a Russian physiologist. Pavlov was interested in the digestive system but made some interesting observations during his experiments with dogs. Pavlov gave meat powder repeatedly to dogs to produce salivation, and he found the dogs often salivated *beforehand*, such as when hearing approaching footsteps. Pavlov was intrigued and explored the nature of this reaction. He rang a bell immediately before a dog received meat powder. This was repeated several times and resulted in dogs salivating after the bell but *before* the meat powder. The dogs learned to salivate to a stimulus, in this case a ringing bell that should not by itself cause salivation. The dogs had learned by association: the bell meant food.

This important experiment led ultimately to **classical conditioning** theory ("conditioning" means learning). Learning occurs when a *conditioned stimulus* (CS) (bell) is paired with an *unconditioned stimulus* (UCS) (meat powder) so future presentations of the CS (bell) result in a conditioned response (CR) (salivation). Classical conditioning theory also suggests that problems such as trauma-based disorders might develop because classical conditioning once took place. Posttraumatic stress disorder involves avoiding situations or people that remind someone of a traumatic experience. Rape victims with this disorder often avoid certain parts of a city associated with the assault, or may feel anxious when they see someone who reminds them of their attacker. These behavioral and emotional reactions might be understood via classical conditioning: a location or physical feature (CS) was paired with an assault (UCS), and now the CS produces the classically conditioned response (CR) of intense fear and avoidance (see **Figure 2.8**).

**Operant conditioning** is based on the principle that behavior followed by positive or pleasurable consequences will likely be repeated but behavior followed by negative consequences such as punishment will not likely be repeated (Shull, 2005; Skinner, 1953). Reinforcement is thus an important aspect of operant conditioning. **Positive reinforcement** involves giving a pleasant event or consequence after a behavior. A child praised or rewarded for cleaning his room is likely to repeat the behavior in the future. Positive reinforcement can also maintain maladaptive behavior, as when someone with depression receives sympathy from others or when parents allow a child to miss school and play video games.

**Negative reinforcement** involves removing an aversive event following a behavior, which also increases the future likelihood of the behavior. Why do you wear deodorant? You likely do not do so for all the wonderful compliments you get during the day but rather to avoid negative comments about body odor! Negative reinforcement can also explain why some fears are maintained over time. Someone afraid of spiders may avoid closets because spiders like to live in dark places. Such avoidance is reinforced because spiders are not encountered and so the aversive event of fear is removed. Such avoidance is also likely to continue in the future (see **Figure 2.9**).

Behavior can also be "shaped" through reinforcement. Students might shape a professor's teaching style by rewarding more interesting lectures. Students might provide strong

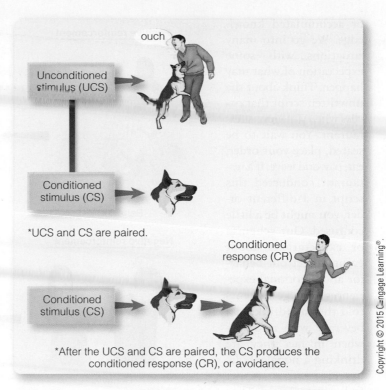

**FIGURE 2.8** PRINCIPLES OF CLASSICAL CONDITIONING

reinforcement by maintaining eye contact, asking questions, or saying, "That is really interesting!" when a professor provides multiple examples or case illustrations. You can see where this is headed. When students reinforce successive approximations of this lively lecture style, they have the power to make the class more engaging, fresh, and interesting. If you try this on your professors, please do not let them know the source of the idea, and please do not keep them completely under your control!

## Cognitive Perspective

The **cognitive perspective** arose from the behavioral perspective because people often behave in ways that have little to do with reinforcement. How did Tony develop an intense fear of heights when he never had a traumatic experience involving heights? An understanding of thoughts, perceptions, and emotions may better account for Tony's fear and avoidance. Not everything can be explained by simple principles of classical and operant conditioning. The cognitive perspective instead suggests that emotions and behavior are influenced by how we perceive and think about our present and past experiences. Learning principles help comprise the behavioral perspective, but other principles comprise the cognitive perspective. These are discussed next.

### COGNITIVE PRINCIPLES

Each of us actively processes and interprets our experiences. Such processing and interpretation is influenced by **cognitive schemas**, or beliefs or expectations that represent a network of accumulated knowledge. We go into many situations with some expectation of what may happen. Think about the unwritten script that occurs when you enter a restaurant. You wait to be seated, place your order, eat, pay, and leave. If a restaurant conducted this script in a different order, you might be a little confused. Our schemas or expectations about events affect our behavior and emotional experiences. College students told they are drinking a beverage with alcohol—when in fact they are drinking a nonalcoholic beverage—often report feeling intoxicated. They talk loudly or become silly as though they are intoxicated. Their *expectancies* of what they are like when intoxicated influence their behavior, even when not drinking alcohol!

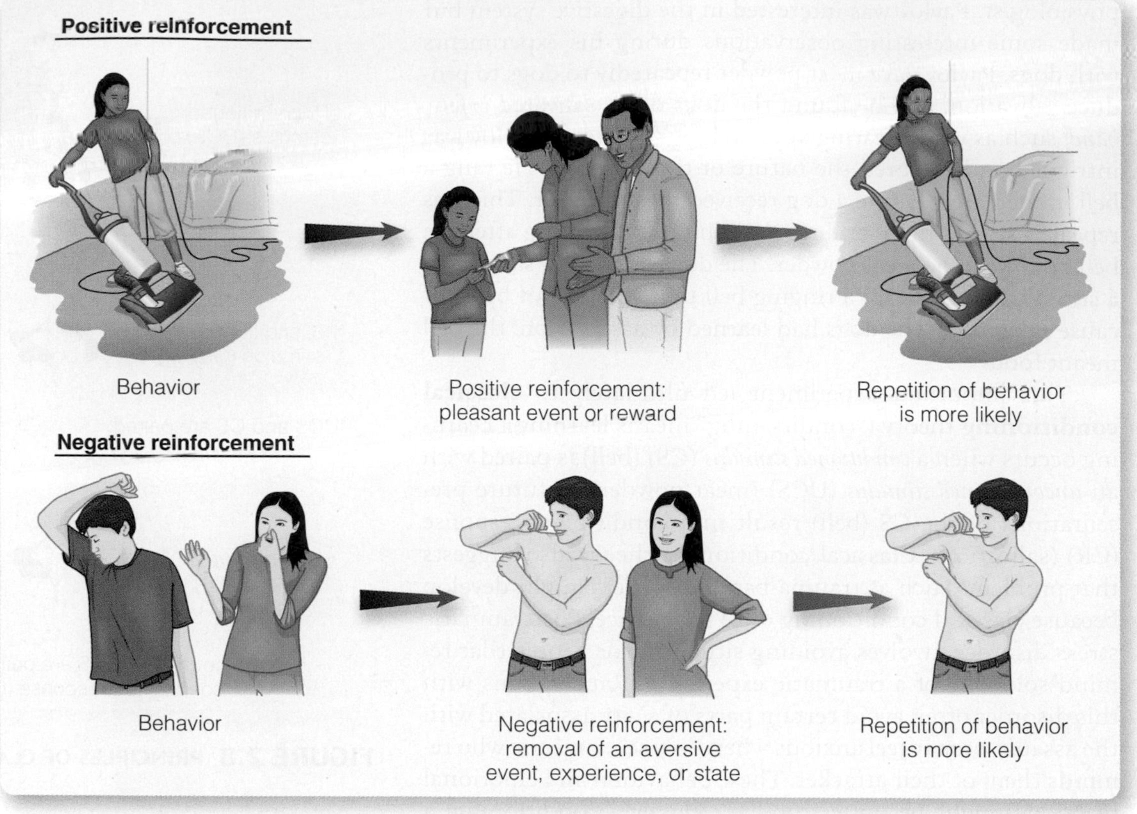

**Positive reinforcement**

Behavior → Positive reinforcement: pleasant event or reward → Repetition of behavior is more likely

**Negative reinforcement**

Behavior → Negative reinforcement: removal of an aversive event, experience, or state → Repetition of behavior is more likely

**FIGURE 2.9** PRINCIPLES OF OPERANT CONDITIONING

**Cognitive distortions** are another important principle of the cognitive perspective and refer to irrational, inaccurate thoughts people have about environmental events. Aaron Beck's cognitive theory (Beck, 2005; Beck, Rush, Shaw, & Emery, 1979) holds that mental disorder may result if one has negative views of oneself ("I'm not good at anything"), other people in the world ("No one cares about anyone except himself"), and the future ("Things will never get easier for me").

Cognitive distortions often come in the form of *arbitrary inference,* which means reaching a conclusion based on little evidence. A professor may see that 2 out of 50 students fell asleep during one lecture and assume she is a bad teacher. The professor ignored the greater evidence that most people did pay attention and instead focused on the two who did not. As professors, we also see students who agonize over one or two mistakes at the expense of seeing the greater value of their examination or project.

Another common cognitive distortion is *personalization,* or erroneously blaming oneself for events. If a coworker refused to speak to you one day, you might personalize the event by wondering what offense you committed. You are ignoring other, more reasonable explanations for what happened—perhaps your coworker just had a fight with her spouse or was worried about a sick child. Cognitive distortions are common to many mental disorders such as anxiety, depressive, eating, and sexual disorders. Indeed, we discuss them throughout this textbook.

## A Cognitive-Behavioral Model

The cognitive perspective highlights the idea that information processing and learning are *active,* not passive, processes. Contemporary psychologists have generally combined behavioral and cognitive approaches into a *cognitive-behavioral model.* This model rests on the assumption that learning principles *and* cognitions interact to influence a person's behavior. This assumption is evident when considering **modeling**, which refers to learning by observing and imitating others. People often learn by watching others, such as when they watch others operate a piece of machinery or use drugs. We process this information, judge how good someone is modeling the behavior, and decide to practice the behavior ourselves. Modeling, also known as *vicarious conditioning,* implies that cognitive mechanisms such as thoughts, beliefs, or perceptions influence learning. A combined cognitive-behavioral perspective helps explain why certain behaviors are learned through observation and not simple reinforcement.

Learning principles and cognitions also interact to help explain specific disorders. Many people are afraid of airplanes even though airplanes are not very dangerous or threatening. Classical and operant conditioning may help explain why fear in these situations is maintained, but why do people *start* avoiding harmless objects or situations in the first place? People who avoid a harmless stimulus internalized something that *now motivates or drives subsequent avoidance behavior.* A type of learning called **avoidance conditioning** is thus often proposed. Avoidance conditioning combines classical and operant conditioning and accommodates an internal state like fear as a *motivating or driving factor* that influences behavior. This internal state is the cognitive aspect of phobia development.

Consider Shawn's flying phobia (see Figure 2.10). A neutral stimulus such as flying on an airplane is paired with an unpleasant unconditioned stimulus such as nausea—classical conditioning. The conditioned stimulus (flying on an airplane) then produces the aversive state (nausea). Shawn then avoids flying because *fear* of experiencing nausea drives him to do so. The internalized aversive state that drives Shawn's avoidance could not be explained by simple classical or operant conditioning. The cognitive component instead provides a more complete account of why Shawn's phobia developed and continued over time.

Contemporary models of mental disorders often include a combination of learning principles and cognitive influences such as expectancies and motivations. Substantial research also supports the idea that cognitive schemas and distortions influence forms of mental disorder. The combination of behavioral/learning and cognitive principles has also led to many important assessment and treatment strategies, some of which are discussed next.

## Cognitive-Behavioral Assessment and Treatment

Behavior therapy represented a novel way of treating mental disorders when introduced in the 1950s and initially included treatments based on principles of classical and operant conditioning. The scope of behavior therapy has since expanded to include other forms of treatment such as cognitive therapy (Goldfried & Davison, 1994; Rathod, Kingdon, Weiden, & Turkington, 2008). Many mental health professionals today endorse a cognitive-behavioral orientation that recognizes the importance of classical and operant conditioning as well as cognitive theories of mental disorders.

A key assessment approach within the cognitive-behavioral perspective is **functional analysis**. Functional analysis refers to evaluating antecedents and consequences of behavior, or what preceded and followed certain behaviors. This is often done by observing a person. A mental health professional might note that Mariella's depressive symptoms were preceded by school-based stressors and loneliness and followed by rewards such as greater attention from family members and friends.

Cognitive variables must also be considered during assessment. Mariella may have certain cognitive distortions, such as believing her troubles in school were related to lack of ability, that others did not care about her, and that things would not improve in the future. Her symptoms may have been at least partly caused by these kinds of cognitive schemas or beliefs that are linked to depression. A therapist would assess for these cognitive processes as well during a functional analysis.

How might a cognitive-behavioral therapist treat Mariella's symptoms? **Cognitive-behavioral therapy** refers to a large collection of treatment techniques to change patterns of thinking and behaving that contribute to a person's problems. These techniques have much empirical support and are among the most effective forms of therapy. Cognitive-behavioral therapy has been shown to be equal or superior to alternative psychological or psychopharmacological treatments for adults and youth (Bandelow, Seidler-Brandler, Becker, Wedekind, & Ruther, 2007; DeRubeis & Crits-Christoph, 1998; Kazdin & Weisz, 1998).

Aaron Beck has been a pioneer in developing cognitive-behavioral treatments for various clinical problems. His model uses cognitive *and* behavioral techniques to modify problematic thinking patterns. Under this model, the following techniques might be used to treat Mariella's depression:

1. Scheduling activities to counteract her inactivity and her focus on depressive feelings. Mariella might be given "homework assignments" to go to the movies with friends or play the guitar before others.
2. Mariella might be asked to imagine successive steps leading to completion of an important task, such as attending an exercise class, so potential barriers or impediments can be identified, anticipated, and addressed. This is called *cognitive rehearsal*.
3. Mariella might engage in assertiveness training and role-playing to improve her social and conversational skills.
4. Mariella might be asked to identify thoughts such as "I can't do anything right" that occur before or during feelings of depression.
5. The reality or accuracy of Mariella's thoughts might be examined by gently challenging their validity ("So you don't think there is *anything* you can do right?").
6. Mariella might be taught to avoid personalizing events for which she is not to blame. She may be shown that her classmates' busy behaviors reflect their own hectic lives and not attempts to rebuff Mariella.
7. Mariella could be helped to find alternative solutions to her problems instead of giving up.

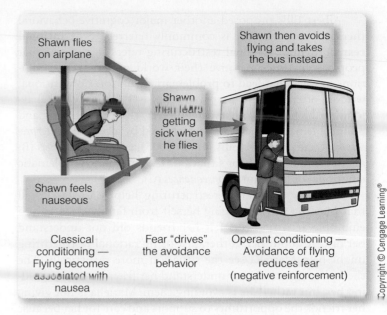

Classical conditioning — Flying becomes associated with nausea

Fear "drives" the avoidance behavior

Operant conditioning — Avoidance of flying reduces fear (negative reinforcement)

**FIGURE 2.10  AVOIDANT CONDITIONING** Shawn is conditioned to avoid flying.

Albert Ellis proposed another major cognitive-behavioral therapy approach that is commonly referred to as **rational restructuring**. Rational restructuring refers to the idea that people sometimes perceive their world and make assumptions in ways that lead to problematic behavior. Conventional wisdom often suggests that events cause emotional and behavioral problems. Ellis believed, however, that problematic and nonproblematic behavior is determined by a person's *interpretation* of those events. Ellis (1962, 2005) argued that *beliefs* (B) about *activating* events or situations (A) determine problematic emotional or behavioral *consequences* (C).

How might rational restructuring help Mariella? Recall that Mariella was distancing herself from family, friends, and enjoyable activities. She felt her friends did not understand her or care about her. A therapist using rational restructuring might help Mariella see the situation more realistically. The therapist might help her understand her friends are not avoiding her, but rather she is avoiding them. Mariella is not giving her friends the opportunity to support and care for her because Mariella is isolating herself. A therapist using rational restructuring will be quite direct with Mariella, using discussions and making arguments that Mariella is viewing her situation irrationally. Irrational beliefs such as "My friends don't care about me" are unfounded and lead to depression. The therapist may also try to teach Mariella to "modify her internal sentences." Mariella might be taught when feeling depressed to pause and ask herself what her immediate thoughts are. The therapist would then ask Mariella to objectively evaluate these thoughts and make corrections. The therapist might thus have her imagine particular problem situations and ask her to think more realistically in these situations.

Other cognitive-behavioral techniques are used to treat mental disorders as well. **Systematic desensitization** is an approach used to treat anxiety-related concerns. A client is first taught to relax, typically via progressive muscle relaxation techniques. The therapist and client then construct a hierarchy of situations or objects related to the feared stimulus. Items at the bottom of the hierarchy arouse anxiety at low levels; for a person afraid of dogs, for example, this might mean watching a dog in a film. More anxiety-provoking items are further along the hierarchy. Contact with an actual feared situation, such as petting a dog, is at the top of the hierarchy. Clients reach a state of relaxation and progressively encounter each object or situation on the hierarchy. If a client becomes too anxious, the procedure is halted so the client can once again become relaxed. Progression along the hierarchy is then restarted. A person is thus desensitized to the previously feared stimulus or situation. From a classical conditioning perspective, the client has learned to respond to a previously feared stimulus with relaxation instead of anxiety.

A key element of systematic desensitization is **exposure treatment**, which involves directly confronting a feared stimulus. This can be done gradually or, in the case of *flooding*, the client does not relax in advance but is instead exposed immediately to a feared stimulus. Exposure treatment can be done by having clients imagine the presence of a feared stimulus or by facing the feared stimulus or situation in real life. Clients are understandably fearful in these situations but, if they continue to stay in the presence of the stimulus, fear diminishes. A non-fearful response becomes associated with a previously feared stimulus or situation through repeated exposure sessions.

Systematic desensitization and exposure treatment are based on classical conditioning, but other behavior therapy techniques are based on operant conditioning, which emphasizes reinforcement. A relatively simple application is when a mental health professional stops reinforcing a problematic behavior and reinforces more adaptive and acceptable behavior. Or, a therapist might help parents manage consequences for their children to increase positive behavior such as completing homework and decrease negative behavior such as aggression.

Operant conditioning principles are also apparent in token economies to modify behaviors of institutionalized populations such as people with intellectual disability or schizophrenia. A **token economy** is a reinforcement system for certain behaviors in which tokens or points are given for positive behaviors and exchanged later for tangible rewards. Someone with schizophrenia on an inpatient ward may earn points for positive behaviors such as attending group therapy sessions and showering. These points could later be exchanged for privileges such as day passes from the hospital. Token economies are also used to improve social and academic skills and other behaviors in children.

## Evaluating the Cognitive-Behavioral Model

The cognitive-behavioral perspective has contributed greatly to our understanding and treatment of mental disorders. The behavioral approach and its emphasis on learning principles revolutionized the study and treatment of mental disorders following psychodynamic theory. The model has been broadened to include thought processes, expectancies, and other internal states. A combined cognitive-behavioral model is among the most influential for conceptualizing the development and maintenance of problematic behavior. The perspective also offers a broad array of treatment choices for many mental disorders. These cognitive-behavioral treatments often have been shown to be effective and efficient, often requiring fewer than 20 sessions.

Limitations of the cognitive-behavioral model should be noted, however. Most problematic might be the model's concept of how mental disorders first develop. Many cognitive-behavior theorists reduce complex behaviors such as depression to simple learning history or cognitive schemas, but this does not seem plausible. Many biological, personality, and social factors also contribute to depression and other disorders. The "chicken and egg" problem is also relevant to cognitive-behaviorism: Did problematic thoughts, beliefs, or expectancies *cause* Mariella's depression, or did these cognitive patterns *result* from her depression?

The cognitive-behavioral perspective appears less able to provide clear and comprehensive historical accounts of how problematic behavior developed in the first place. The cognitive-behavioral perspective seems best suited to explain and address *current* functioning and highlight targets of change that can be used in treatment. The perspective is particularly good for identifying specific symptoms that need change, such as Mariella's isolated behavior and cognitive distortions.

## INTERIM SUMMARY

▶ The behavioral perspective on mental disorders is based on the assumption that behavior is learned.

▶ Two major learning principles underlie the behavioral approach: classical conditioning and operant conditioning.

▶ The cognitive perspective suggests that problematic symptoms and behavior develop from the way we perceive and think about our present and past experiences.

▶ Key principles of the cognitive perspective include schemas and cognitive distortions.

▶ Behavioral and cognitive perspectives have been combined to form the cognitive-behavioral model.

▶ Major cognitive-behavioral treatment approaches include cognitive-behavioral therapy, rational restructuring, systematic desensitization, exposure, and token economy.

▶ Strengths of a cognitive-behavioral model include its broad array of effective treatments.

▶ A major limitation of the cognitive-behavioral model is its poor account of how mental problems originally develop.

## REVIEW QUESTIONS

1. How might the cognitive-behavioral model explain Mariella's problems?

2. What treatments might a cognitive-behavioral therapist use to treat Mariella's problems?

3. Describe the following learning principles and how they might help us understand Mariella's symptoms: classical conditioning, operant conditioning, modeling.

4. What are strengths and limitations of a cognitive-behavioral perspective on mental disorders?

## The Sociocultural Model

The models of mental disorder we have discussed so far in this chapter—biological, psychodynamic, humanistic, and cognitive-behavioral—focus primarily on individuals and their personal characteristics. We do not live in a vacuum, however—many outside factors affect how we feel, think, and behave. Biological, psychodynamic, humanistic, and cognitive-behavioral perspectives do acknowledge some environmental role in psychological problems. The **sociocultural perspective** differs from these models in its greater emphasis on environmental factors; its core assumption is that outside influences play a *major* role in creating a person's psychological problems. The sociocultural perspective focuses on influences that social institutions and other people have on a person's mental health.

Many sociocultural factors potentially impact the development, symptom expression, assessment, and treatment of mental disorders. We highlight here several prominent examples of sociocultural influences on mental health. This is not an exhaustive list, but these examples best highlight this perspective and current areas of investigation. We begin with more global influences, such as culture and gender and neighborhoods, and finish with a topic closer to home—family.

---

### BOX 2.3  Focus on Gender

©Deneg/Shutterstock.com

#### A More Complex Approach

Different models are useful for understanding symptoms, causes, and treatment of mental disorder. The use of a single model to describe a mental disorder can be a problem, however, when gender differences arise. For example, a well-established finding is that female and male children experience similar rates of depression but female adults experience depression at twice the rate of male adults. To explain this finding using just a psychodynamic or cognitive-behavioral model would be difficult. Instead, researchers are moving toward integrative models to help explain gender differences. Hyde and colleagues (2008), for example, proposed an integrative model that focused on negative life events as well as biological, cognitive, and emotional factors. A girl may experience sexual maltreatment as a child, develop a negative cognitive style, experience increased biological arousal, and display emotional difficulties into adulthood that include depression. These factors may pertain more to girls than boys, which may help explain gender differences in adult depression.

Another problem that differs by gender is excessive alcohol use, which is much more common in males than females by late adolescence. Single models such as the humanistic or sociocultural perspective cannot fully account for this difference. Instead, an integrative model may be best. Schulte and colleagues (2009) argued that, early in life, certain biological and psychological factors that predispose alcohol use appear to be similar for boys and girls. During adolescence, however, some important changes take place. Boys start to show more physiological response to alcohol, experience brain maturation later than girls, and report higher estimates of perceived alcohol use by peers than girls. These factors predispose boys to disruptive drinking more than girls.

Culture can influence such problems as anthrophobia (left) and dissociative identity disorder (right).

## Culture

**Culture** refers to the unique behavior and lifestyle shared by a group of people (Smedley & Smedley, 2005; Tseng, 2003). Culture is composed of viewpoints, beliefs, values, and preferences that are evident in rituals, food, customs, laws, art, music, and religion. Culture is not innate but external, learned, and transmitted to others. Culture is not the same as **ethnicity**, which refers to clusters of people who share cultural traits and who use those traits to distinguish themselves from others. Culture is also different from **race**, which refers to a category typically based on physical characteristics.

One difference between ethnicity and race is that ethnic groups identify themselves as such. The concept of race, however, evolved from early attempts to categorize people based on physical characteristics such as skin color, hair texture, and facial features (Smedley & Smedley, 2005). However, analyses of genetic material (DNA) actually reveal more differences *within* racial groups than *between* racial groups (American Anthropological Association, 1999). This reinforces the idea that race is *not* biologically based but rather socially defined. Culture includes but is not limited to concepts of ethnicity and race, and culture is learned from others and passed on to succeeding generations.

Culture can contribute to mental disorder in several ways (Tseng, 2003). First, culture might serve as a distant but *direct cause* of mental disorders. Culturally shared beliefs and ideas can lead to particular forms of stress that, in turn, lead to specific forms of problems called **cultural syndromes** (American Psychiatric Association, 2013). *Dhat syndrome*, for example, is an anxiety-related belief observed in Indian men that one is "losing" semen through nocturnal emissions, masturbation, or urination. The cultural belief driving the fear is that excessive semen loss results in illness (Ranjith & Mohan, 2006).

Culture can help cause mental disorder but can also *influence the way individuals cope with stressful situations.* Two examples

are amok and family suicide. *Amok* is a condition in South Asian and Pacific Islander cultures in which a person attacks and tries to kill others. Cultures in which this condition is observed are often characterized by passivity and nonconfrontation, so amok is seen as a failure to cope with extreme stress (Tseng, 2003). The English phrase "running amok" is derived from this condition (although its meaning is not literal!). *Family suicide* is sometimes observed in Japanese culture when parents and children commit suicide together. This act may be preceded by financial debt or a disgraceful event that causes extreme stress. Family suicide is seen as a coping response, albeit a maladaptive one, because cultural values discourage living disgracefully after a shameful event (Tseng, 2003).

Culture can also influence mental disorders by *shaping the content of symptoms.* Examples include anthrophobia and brain fag. *Anthrophobia,* a phobia of interpersonal relations, is observed in Japanese culture and involves fears of one's body odor, flushing or blushing, and eye contact. These symptoms reflect the culture's hypersensitivity to being looked at or looking at others as well as concern about how one's own behavior is viewed by others (Tseng, 2003). *Brain fag* involves symptoms of intellectual and visual impairment and other body complaints in Nigerian and Ugandan cultures. This condition develops during periods of intensive reading and study, such as before an academic examination, and appears influenced by a culture that promotes family-oriented education. This places intense pressure on a student to be academically successful for the family's sake (Morakinyo & Peltzer, 2002).

Disorders found primarily in Western societies also contain unique symptoms and features. *Multiple personality disorder,* now termed *dissociative identity disorder* (American Psychiatric Association, 2013), is one example. Someone with this disorder may not report being "possessed" by animals or spirits (as is the case in other cultures) but reports being possessed by other selves or personalities that control his behavior. Culture thus influences the possession source: in non-Western cultures possession may be by animals or spirits, but in Western cultures possession may be by other personalities (Tseng, 2003).

*Anorexia nervosa* (Chapter 8) involves excessive concern about being overweight and severe weight loss that threatens one's health. This condition is often observed in American and European cultures but is relatively absent in Samoa and the Pacific Islands where food is scarce or where being overweight is considered attractive. A sociocultural theory stipulates that anorexia nervosa is more prevalent in food-abundant societies that stress an "ideal body" as thin (Lindberg & Hjern, 2003). Culture thus affects the development of psychological problems in various ways (see **Table 2.4**).

## Gender

Mental disorders affect men and women, but some problems seem more common in one gender than the other. Men are more likely to have antisocial personality and substance use disorder, but women are more likely to have anxiety-related and depressive disorders (Kessler et al., 1994). Gender differences may be explained by differences in biology, gender identity, socialization, and social situations in which women and men find themselves (Stewart & McDermott, 2004). Biological differences in sex hormones may help explain why more men than women have sexual disorders (Chapter 11).

*Gender identity* refers to one's awareness of being male or female or perceived degree of masculinity or femininity. Gender identity is influenced by parenting style and interactions with others and can be related to mental disorder. People who are androgynous in their personality, as opposed to strictly masculine or feminine, tend to have fewer symptoms of eating disorders (Hepp, Spindler, & Milos, 2005).

Men are also less likely to find themselves in certain situations compared with women, especially as victims of domestic violence and sexual assault. This may help explain why men have fewer anxiety-related disorders than women (Chapter 5). Our *expectations of men and of women*, or socialization differences, also play a role in developing symptoms of mental disorders. We generally expect men to be less emotionally expressive. Men who are anxious and depressed may thus be more likely to use alcohol and other drugs to self-medicate their symptoms, whereas women may be more likely to talk to friends or see a therapist.

Gender differences are most evident for depression, where women have much higher rates than men, and social support seems to be a key factor. Women generally have more social support than men with respect to number of close relationships and level of intimacy of these relationships (Taylor et al., 2000). If social support suffers, however, women may be more susceptible to depression because they rely more on social support for their well-being (Kendler, Myers, & Prescott, 2005) Recall that Mariella's separation from family members and friends near home was related to her sadness.

Women may be more likely than men to respond to stress by "tending-and-befriending" (Taylor et al., 2000, 2002).

Millennium Images/Superstock

Anorexia nervosa is a condition that occurs most often in European and American cultures.

Women often respond to stress by nurturing and protecting offspring (tend) and by affiliating with others to reduce risk of harm (befriend). Doing so may have an evolutionary component. When a threat existed, quieting offspring and blending into the environment was adaptive because one was not seen as a threat. Affiliating with a social group following a threat also increased the chance one would be protected. This tending and befriending pattern has also been linked to neurobiological systems that characterize attachment to others and caregiving,

**Table 2.4**

| How Does Culture Contribute to Mental Disorders? | |
|---|---|
| **Method** | **Examples** |
| Direct cause: culturally shared belief leads to stress, and then to symptoms of mental disorder | Dhat syndrome |
| Influences the way individuals cope with stress | Amok<br>Family suicide |
| Shapes the content of the symptoms or the symptoms themselves | Anthrophobia<br>Brain fag<br>Dissociative identity disorder<br>Anorexia nervosa |

and these are specific to women. This theory and related findings illustrate that understanding gender differences can help us explain mental disorders and develop treatments. Mariella could volunteer to help others to help reduce her social isolation and depression.

## Neighborhoods and Communities

Another influence on our mental well-being is our surrounding neighborhoods and communities. Several neighborhood characteristics are associated with poorer mental health (Goodman, Fleitlich-Bilyk, Patel, & Goodman, 2007; Wandersman & Nation, 1998). First, neighborhoods with high rates of poverty, turnover among residents, and families headed by females and single parents often have high rates of juvenile delinquency and childhood maltreatment. Second, people in neighborhoods characterized by physical (abandoned buildings, vandalism) and social (public drunkenness, gangs, noisy neighbors) decline often have substantial anxiety, depression, and physical complaints. Third, neighborhoods characterized by noise, crowding, and pollution are often associated with high rates of depression, aggression, and childhood behavior problems.

Why do certain neighborhood characteristics relate to poor mental health? A common theme appears to be stress (Cutrona, Wallace, & Wesner, 2006). Certain neighborhoods generate many stressful life events. People from these neighborhoods also have few resources to handle these stressors, so their ability to cope is taxed. Individual differences exist, however, with respect to how able and how well one can cope with such stressors. Some people are "resilient" to such stressors, and psychologists have focused more on features and mechanisms of this resilience. Knowledge about resilience can help psychologists prevent negative mental health outcomes even for people who live under adverse conditions. We discuss resilience in more detail in Chapter 3 within the context of risk and prevention.

## Family

Many theorists believe that positive family relationships decrease risk for psychological problems but that family conflict can increase risk. A **family systems perspective** assumes that each family has its own rules and organizational structure, or hierarchy of authority and decision making (Goldenberg & Goldenberg, 2004). When family members keep this organization and obey the rules, a sense of homeostasis or stability is created. Dysfunctional families, however, experience problems and distress because the structure and rules are not optimal (Nichols & Schwartz, 2004). Some problematic family relationships and environmental variables are discussed next.

### PROBLEMATIC FAMILY RELATIONSHIPS

*Inflexible* families are overly rigid and do not adapt well to changes within or outside the family. This can lead to substantial conflict, especially as a child reaches adolescence and wants more independence. *Enmeshed* families are characterized by family members who are overly involved in the private lives of other family members—everything is everyone's business. This can lead to overdependence of family members on one another

and feelings of being controlled by others. A family systems theory of anorexia nervosa suggests some individuals try to regain control over their lives by refusing to eat in reaction to parents' excessive involvement and control.

*Disengaged* families are characterized by family members who operate independently of one another with little parental supervision. This family structure might predispose children to develop conduct problems or get into legal trouble. Families can also be characterized by *triangular relationships,* or situations where parents avoid talking to each other or addressing marital conflicts by keeping their children involved in all conversations and activities.

### PROBLEMATIC FAMILY ENVIRONMENT

*Family environment* refers to features or dimensions of family functioning. One feature of family environment is *family affect,* or the degree to which a family is cohesive, organized, and free of conflict. Another feature is *family activity,* or the degree to which families engage in cultural, recreational, and religious activities together. *Family control* is the degree to which a family is rigid or flexible when adapting to new situations or challenges (Black & Lobo, 2008; Jacob & Windle, 1999).

Family environment does seem to influence the mental health of individual family members. Jester and colleagues (2005) followed 335 children at risk for substance use disorders and impulsivity. Parents rated family cohesiveness, organization, and conflict when children were aged 3 to 5 years. Children were assessed for problems of inattention, hyperactivity, and aggression at each 3-year period to adolescence. Children in families with lower levels of cohesion and organization and higher levels of conflict were more aggressive but not inattentive or hyperactive across time. Family environment was a specific risk factor for later aggression but not necessarily other behavior problems.

**Expressed emotion** is the degree to which family interactions are marked by emotional overinvolvement, hostility, and criticism. A parent in a family with high expressed emotion might say to his son: "You never get out of the house. You are never going to amount to anything if you keep it up." Communications like this, although perhaps intended to motivate the son, likely lead to stress and negative feelings of self-worth. People with schizophrenia living in families with high expressed emotion, especially criticism, are at greater risk for relapse compared with people living in families with low expressed emotion (Marom, Munitz, Jones, Weizman, & Hermesh, 2005). Interventions have thus been developed to help family members understand how their actions can negatively affect someone who has, or who is at risk for, a mental disorder.

## Sociocultural Assessment and Treatment

Socioculturalists believe psychological problems largely develop because of the impact of social institutions and other people. What sociocultural factors may have affected Mariella, who was Latina? Mariella's culture is typically *collectivist,* meaning less emphasis on the self and more emphasis on interdependence with others such as friends and family members.

Social support is thus likely quite important for Mariella, and her isolation at school may have influenced her sadness and pessimism. The importance of Mariella's academic achievement from a cultural and family perspective is also important to consider. Mariella may have experienced intense pressure to do well at college, which in turn led to added stress. Her family's dismissive reaction to her depressive symptoms when she was home for Thanksgiving may have led to further pessimism and self-criticism as well.

Mariella's identity as a Latina may have influenced her college experience. Latinas, compared with their male counterparts, may be more passive and less competitive. Mariella may have been experiencing some ambivalence about pursuing advanced academic training given her gender as well. Overall, many potential cultural, gender role, and familial issues may have influenced the development and maintenance of Mariella's depressive symptoms.

Clinicians should thus conduct a thorough assessment of an individual's culture. A cultural assessment does not simply include race but also a person's self-defined ethnicity, sources of social support, affiliations and interactions with social institutions, and larger worldview factors such as religious preference. A person's gender role within a cultural context as well as important neighborhood and community factors should also be assessed. A thorough evaluation of family structure, dynamics, and environment is necessary for understanding a person's mental health as well.

Sociocultural assessment methods are less advanced than those of other models of mental disorder. Measures are available for social stressors, social support, and family environment, but few measures are available for features of culture, gender role, and neighborhood or community variables. A mental health professional, therefore, may be limited to using an unstructured interview when conducting these assessments. (Unstructured interviews are problematic assessment tools; we discuss this in Chapter 4.)

Treatment from a sociocultural perspective focuses on addressing a person's difficulties at global and individual levels. Globally, sociocultural interventions focus on decreasing or preventing stress created for people through sexism, racism, or age or religious discrimination. Consider discrimination based on race or ethnicity, which places additional burden and stress on people and may lead to economic hardship and limited resources for education, health care, and employment. People who experience discrimination because of lack of economic resources are also likely to live in stressful neighborhoods or communities  neighborhoods with high rates of unemployment, poverty, crime, and substance use problems. Unremitting stress from these circumstances can have a significant negative impact on a person's mental health (Hammen, 2005; Schneiderman, Ironson, & Siegel, 2005). Racial and ethnic disparities also exist with respect to access to physical and mental health care (Smedley & Smedley, 2005).

A comprehensive program is clearly needed to address the influence of racial and ethnic discrimination on mental health and access to services. This would include programs to make community members aware of the discrimination, public policy and laws to prevent such discrimination, and efforts to decrease disparities in employment, housing, and economic well-being.

Treatment from a sociocultural perspective also focuses on addressing a person's difficulties at individual levels. *Family therapy* or *couples therapy*—in which multiple family members meet with a therapist at the same time— are used by various kinds of mental health professionals (Goldenberg & Goldenberg, 2004; Nichols & Schwartz, 2004). These therapies allow for better assessment of a family's problems and provide the opportunity to intervene with all members. Many family and couples therapists directly coach individuals on what to say to other family members and provide feedback about their interactions.

Family and couples therapists also identify and fix problems in communication. Therapists emphasize that nothing is wrong with the family or dyad itself but instead focus on particular relationship issues or communication patterns. One family member might be exhibiting more emotional distress or behavioral

Nancy Sheehan/PhotoEdit

Family therapy is a commonly used treatment in the sociocultural model of mental disorder.

## Personal Narrative 2.1

### An Integrative Psychologist: Dr. John C. Norcross

In the early days of psychotherapy, an ideological cold war reigned as clinicians were separated into rival schools—biological, psychodynamic, cognitive-behavioral, humanistic, sociocultural, and so on. Clinicians traditionally operated from within their own theoretical frameworks, often to the point of being blind to alternative conceptualizations and potentially superior treatments.

As the field of psychotherapy has matured, integration has emerged as a clinical reality and the most popular approach. Clinicians now acknowledge the inadequacies of any one theoretical school and the potential value of many perspectives. Rival therapy systems are increasingly viewed not as adversaries but as partners; not as contradictory but as complementary.

My practice and research is devoted to *integration:* a dissatisfaction with single-school approaches and a concomitant desire to look across school boundaries to see how patients can benefit from other ways of conducting treatment. The goal is to enhance the effectiveness and applicability of psychotherapy by tailoring it to the singular needs of each client. Clients frequently require an eclectic mix or hybrid of different perspectives.

Applying identical treatments to all patients is now recognized as inappropriate and probably unethical. Imagine if a physician delivered the same treatment—say, neurosurgery or an antibiotic—to every single patient and disorder. Different folks require different strokes. That's the mandate for integration.

How do we select treatment methods and relationship stances that fit? On the basis of research evidence, clinical experience, and patient preferences. A client who denies the existence of an obvious problem (the precontemplation stage), for example, will profit from a different relationship and treatment than a client who is committed to changing her behavior right now (the action stage). Or a client who seeks more insight into the early childhood antecedents of a problem, for another example, will probably secure better results in psychodynamic therapy than one who seeks psychoactive medication (biological therapy) or specific skills in restructuring thoughts (cognitive therapy). And a client who responds negatively to external guidance and direct advice (high reactance) will surely require a different treatment than one who enjoys them (low reactance). Decades of research can now direct us in making better marriages between some treatments and certain disorders and client characteristics.

Courtesy of Dr. John C. Norcross

Dr. John C. Norcross

The integrative psychotherapist leads by following the client. An empathic therapist works toward an optimal relationship that enhances collaboration and results in treatment success. That optimal relationship is determined by both patient preferences and the therapist's knowledge of the client's personality and preferences. If a client frequently resists, for example, then the therapist considers whether she is pushing something that the client finds incompatible (preferences), or the client is not ready to make changes (stage of change), or is uncomfortable with a directive style (reactance).

*Integration* refers typically to the synthesis of diverse systems of psychotherapy, but we need not stop there. We can combine therapy formats—individual, couples, family, and group. We frequently integrate medication and psychotherapy, also known as combined treatment. Integration gets us beyond either/or to both/and.

In practice, integrative psychologists are committed to the synthesis of practically all effective, ethical change methods. These include integrating self-help and psychotherapy, integrating Western and Eastern perspectives, integrating social advocacy with psychotherapy, integrating spirituality into psychotherapy, and so on. When asked about my doctrine, I reply with the words of the Buddha: "anything that can help to alleviate human suffering."

As a university professor teaching abnormal psychology and clinical psychology, I find that my students naturally favor integration. Theoretical purity, they remind me, is for textbooks, not people. And as a clinical psychologist in part-time independent practice, I find my clients overwhelmingly require an integrative or eclectic approach. Rigid therapy, they teach me, is bad therapy.

Integrative therapy brings evidence-based flexibility and empathic responsiveness to each clinical encounter. Integrative therapy offers the research evidence and clinician flexibility to meet the unique needs of individual patients and their unique contexts. For these reasons, integration will assuredly be a therapeutic mainstay of the 21st century. Come join us!

problems than others, but this is thought to reflect problems within a family or couple. All family members must thus engage in treatment and change the way they interact with other family members.

## Evaluating the Sociocultural Model

The sociocultural perspective has much strength for understanding mental disorders. First, the perspective highlights the importance of social influences on emotions, cognitions, and behaviors. Humans are indeed social beings and so our mental health is clearly influenced by people and institutions around us. Second, the sociocultural perspective provides a good understanding of different sources of stress that have an impact on a person and how that person copes with stress. Sources of stress may occur at global and individual levels. Finally, the sociocultural perspective emphasizes the critical role that family members have in influencing mental health.

Limitations of the sociocultural model should be noted, however. First, evidence linking social, cultural, or environmental factors to mental health is largely correlational. Whether these factors *cause* symptoms of mental disorders is unclear. Second, we do not yet know why people exposed to adverse influences have various outcomes: Some will develop various psychological problems, and some will not. Why does one child living in a poor neighborhood and raised by a dysfunctional family become delinquent but another becomes depressed? Why does one child with abusive parents commit suicide but his sibling succeeds in college with few psychological effects? The sociocultural perspective has great strength, but its account of how psychological problems develop remains incomplete.

## INTERIM SUMMARY

▶ A sociocultural perspective focuses on how other people, social institutions, and social forces influence a person's mental health.

▶ Culture is the unique behavior and lifestyle shared by a group of people.

▶ Gender differences, including our expectations of men and of women, may help instigate certain mental disorders.

▶ Demographic, physical, and stressful aspects of neighborhoods and communities are associated with changes in mental health.

▶ Family structure and functioning, as well as maltreatment and expressed emotion, can impact the psychological well-being of individuals.

▶ A strength of the sociocultural perspective is its focus on social and environmental factors and family on mental health.

▶ A limitation of the sociocultural perspective is the lack of evidence that adverse environments cause mental disorders.

## REVIEW QUESTIONS

1. How can the sociocultural model explain Mariella's problems?
2. Describe what is meant by "culture." How might culture influence the development of Mariella's problems?
3. Discuss how gender roles may influence Mariella's mental health.
4. What aspects of neighborhoods and communities are associated with stress and mental health?
5. How might family structure, functioning, and environment be associated with Mariella's problems?
6. What socioculturally based treatment might a mental health professional use to help Mariella?
7. What are strengths and limitations of the sociocultural perspective?

# Final Comments

You might wonder which major perspective of abnormal behavior is the best one, but no clear answer can be given. Each perspective has its own strengths and limitations and none provides a complete and comprehensive account of all psychological problems. Many mental health professionals thus adopt the notion of a *biopsychosocial model* to mental disorder. A biopsychosocial model stipulates that mental disorder can be attributed to many biological (e.g., genetic, brain changes), psychological (thought, emotional changes), and social (family, societal) variables. These variables work in tandem to produce healthy or unhealthy behavior.

In Chapter 3, we present a general theoretical model, the *diathesis-stress model,* that resembles the biopsychosocial model and addresses the issue of how mental health problems develop. This model incorporates notions of *diathesis,* or predisposition or vulnerability to mental disorder, and *stress,* which can be environmental, interpersonal, or psychological. This model, because of its flexible, wide-ranging definition of diathesis and stress, can accommodate the five perspectives covered in this chapter as well as combinations of these perspectives. The diathesis-stress model is perhaps the best way to think about mental health issues. Chapter 3 begins with a detailed description of this model and its implications for studying, treating, and preventing psychological problems.

## Key Terms

models  22
biological model  23
syndromes  23
genotype  24
phenotype  24
behavior genetics  24
molecular genetics  24
central nervous system  24
peripheral nervous
  system  24
neurons  24
synapse  24
neurotransmitters  24
reuptake  24
cerebral cortex  25
frontal lobe  25
parietal lobe  25
temporal lobe  25
occipital lobe  25
limbic system  25
basal ganglia  25
thalamus  25
hypothalamus  25
psychodynamic model  28
unconscious motivation  29
defense mechanisms  29
psychic determinism  29
id  29
pleasure principle  29
primary process  29
ego  29
reality principle  30
secondary process  30
superego  30
psychosexual stages of
  development  30
fixation  30
repression  30
regression  30
reaction formation  30
projection  30
projective hypothesis  31
free association  31
dream analysis  31

manifest content  31
latent content  32
insight  32
interpretation  32
transference  32
civil commitment  33
criminal commitment  33
competency to stand trial  33
insanity  33
humanistic model  33
phenomenological
  approach  33
self-actualization  34
conditional positive
  regard  34
unconditional positive
  regard  34
client-centered therapy  34
behavioral perspective  36
classical conditioning  37
operant conditioning  37
positive reinforcement  37
negative reinforcement  37
cognitive perspective  37
cognitive schemas  37
cognitive distortions  38
modeling  38
avoidance conditioning  38
functional analysis  39
cognitive-behavioral
  therapy  39
rational restructuring  40
systematic desensitization  40
exposure treatment  40
token economy  40
sociocultural perspective  41
culture  42
ethnicity  42
race  42
cultural syndromes  42
family systems
  perspective  44
expressed emotion  44

## Media Resources

### MindTap

MindTap for Kearney and Trull's *Abnormal Psychology and Life: A Dimensional Approach* is a highly personalized fully online learning platform of authoritative content, assignments, and services offering you a tailored presentation of course curriculum created by your instructor. MindTap guides you through the course curriculum via an innovative learning path where you will complete reading assignments, annotate your readings, complete homework, and engage with quizzes and assessments. MindTap includes the Continuum Video Project.
Go to **cengagebrain.com** to access MindTap.

# Risk and Prevention of Mental Disorders

**CASE: *DeShawn***

**What Do You Think?**

**The Diathesis-Stress Model**
Interim Summary
Review Questions

**Epidemiology: How Common
Are Mental Disorders?**
Interim Summary
Review Questions

**Risk, Protective Factors, and Resilience**

**CASE: *Jana***
Interim Summary
Review Questions

**Prevention**
Interim Summary
Review Questions

FINAL COMMENTS

KEY TERMS

MEDIA RESOURCES

**SPECIAL FEATURES**

**BOX 3.1** | John Snow: A Pioneer in Epidemiology and
Prevention 55

**BOX 3.2** | Focus on Gender: Suicide and College
Students 61

**BOX 3.3** | Focus on Violence: Prevention of Femicide 64

**BOX 3.4** | Focus on Law and Ethics: Constructs Related
to Insanity 69

**PERSONAL NARRATIVE 3.1** Kim Dude *and the*
**Wellness Resource Center** 70–71

## CASE: DeShawn

**DeShawn** is a 21-year-old business major who has been attending a large public university for 3 years. DeShawn was initially anxious about attending college because no one else in his family had done so. He thought the transition to college was going to be tough and unlike anything he had experienced previously. His actual transition to college was a "mixed blessing." On one hand, DeShawn was invigorated by his classes and by meeting so many new people. He liked interacting with his professors and looked forward to graduating with an eye toward an M.B.A.

On the other hand, DeShawn had never been to so many parties. His experience was far beyond his expectations about the party scene at college. His experience began during his first semester when DeShawn was invited to a party at the dorm room of a new acquaintance. The beverage that night was "trash-can punch" that tasted good and had plenty of alcohol. DeShawn thus felt poorly the next day when he woke up around noon, but he could not turn down an invitation for another party later that

evening. DeShawn kept telling himself he would eventually slow down, but that was 3 years ago. DeShawn did not drink every night but seemed to attend a party at least 4 nights a week—every sporting and campus event and weekend was an opportunity for someone to throw a big party.

DeShawn met hundreds of people at these parties in 3 years, but there was a clear downside. DeShawn's drinking increased over the years to the point where he could get tipsy only after 6 to 10 drinks. Of course, DeShawn did not usually stop at 6 to 10 drinks and so felt miserable the next day. Over time he tried to schedule his classes in the late afternoon or early evening to accommodate his "social" activities, but even these classes he often skipped because they conflicted with "Happy Hour." DeShawn's studying suffered tremendously, and he almost failed school his first semester, first year, and two semesters since then. He accumulated only three semesters worth of credits during his 3 years at school.

DeShawn's parents were unhappy about their son's progress. He did his best to hide his grades, but the registrar regularly informed parents about poor academic performance. DeShawn's parents could not understand why their son was doing so poorly in college because he had been a straight-A student in high school. They did not know about the parties, however, and DeShawn was certainly not going to tell them about his social life. DeShawn thus rarely went home on weekends—too many parties to miss,

and who wants to get "grilled" by their parents?—but promised his parents via telephone and e-mail that he would concentrate better and improve his grades.

DeShawn felt he had things under control until he looked in his rearview mirror one night to see flashing lights. He had been drinking heavily and was weaving across lanes. He was a bit confused and even wondered if he had accidentally hurt someone. He was processed at the police station, and DeShawn knew he faced his greatest challenge. What was he going to tell his parents about this "driving under the influence" charge? They were going to go ballistic. He had trouble believing what was happening but resigned himself to the possibility that his college days might be over.

### What Do You Think?

1. Do you think DeShawn has a problem with alcohol? Why or why not?

2. Why do you think DeShawn is drinking so much?

3. What should DeShawn do? Should he tell his parents? To whom should he turn for help?

4. Do you know people who have had similar experiences? What did they do?

5. Do you think DeShawn's situation could have been prevented? If so, how?

## The Diathesis-Stress Model

Why do some college students like DeShawn develop problems with alcohol use but others do not? College is stressful for most students, but not everyone develops a drinking problem. Did DeShawn have a certain genetic structure, an oral fixation, or a maladaptive cognitive schema that led to his drinking problems? Or was some combination of these factors within a stressful college environment responsible?

We discussed different models of mental disorder in Chapter 2 that have various strengths and limitations. We also introduced the *diathesis-stress model* as a way of integrating these models to explain mental disorders. The diathesis-stress model not only integrates perspectives but is consistent with a continuum of mental health and mental disorder. We thus begin this chapter by examining the diathesis-stress model in detail and discussing its implications for studying, treating, and preventing mental disorders.

## Diathesis, Stress, and Mental Health

A **diathesis** is a biological or psychological predisposition to disorder. Diatheses are often genetic or biological, but some diatheses are psychological. Some people expect alcohol use to make them more sociable and fun to be around. These people are more likely than others to drink alcohol. This expectancy is thus a psychological predisposition to use alcohol excessively. DeShawn expected that drinking would make him more sociable, so he is more likely to drink and use alcohol excessively.

Another psychological predisposition is *impulsivity,* or acting too quickly without thinking of the consequences. Impulsive people may predispose themselves to dangerous situations such as drinking too much and then driving. Cognitive schemas can also be considered psychological diatheses or predispositions. Recall Mariella from Chapter 2. Her negative views or schemas about herself, the world, and the future can be viewed as a diathesis or predisposition for her depression.

Biological or psychological diatheses *do not guarantee* one will develop disorders like alcoholism or depression. A diathesis is a *vulnerability*—you can be vulnerable to a certain disorder, but this does not mean you will necessarily develop it. Many people have a genetic predisposition for lung cancer but never develop the disease. Why? Because they never smoke tobacco! DeShawn's expectancies about alcohol or Mariella's cognitive style predispose them toward certain disorders but do not guarantee these disorders will occur. Something must *trigger* these predispositions, such as smoking cigarettes or experiencing the stress of college life. Traumatic experiences such as assault are another stressor linked to many of the mental disorders we discuss in this textbook.

A *combination* of predisposition *and* stress produces psychological problems according to the diathesis-stress model. Stress can be environmental, interpersonal, or psychological, but it must *interact* with a predisposition for a disorder to occur. Predispositions and stressors also occur on a continuum from weak to strong (or low to high). This is consistent with current research and this textbook's dimensional approach to mental health. We need to examine the diathesis-stress model in general (the big picture) and more specifically (the little picture) to understand it better.

## Diathesis-Stress: The Big Picture

Let's examine the big picture of the diathesis-stress model using DeShawn as an example. **Figure 3.1** illustrates predisposition, stress, and a potential psychological problem involving alcohol use on a continuum. This model shows the interaction of a predisposition (impulsivity) with stress along a continuum as they contribute to levels of alcohol use. Predisposition to be impulsive is on a continuum because people are impulsive to *varying degrees.* Some people may even have no impulsivity traits (labeled *Predisposition to impulsivity absent* in Figure 3.1). One of DeShawn's friends, Kira, is quite conscientious about her life and always considers decisions carefully. Kira is not impulsive and would not likely develop alcoholism even when faced with substantial stress.

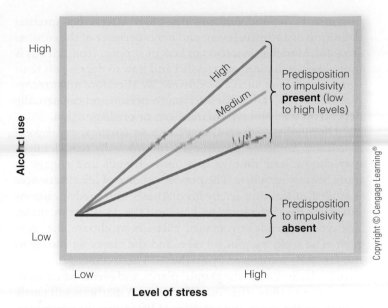

**FIGURE 3.1** A DIATHESIS-STRESS MODEL OF ALCOHOL USE

Most people have *some* degree of diathesis or predisposition or vulnerability, whether low or high. Most of us are impulsive to *some* extent, and this is illustrated in Figure 3.1 as multiple lines bracketed by *Predisposition to impulsivity present.* Each line represents a different impulsivity level. Higher levels of a predisposition—impulsivity in this case—even with smaller amounts of stress result in more alcohol use. Lower levels of impulsivity, even with high stress, result in less alcohol use. *However, the combination of strong predisposition and high stress results in the most alcohol use.*

This model helps us understand why two people exposed to the same level of stress do or do not develop a certain mental disorder. DeShawn and Kira's college stress is likely similar, but their predispositions for high alcohol use are quite different. Many soldiers in Afghanistan will develop posttraumatic stress disorder (Chapter 5), but many will not. Why? Because soldiers (and people in general) differ considerably with respect to their vulnerability to posttraumatic stress disorder.

Diatheses such as impulsivity are clearly important but interact with stressors that can also be viewed along a continuum (Figure 3.1). Two people with the same level of impulsivity may show different outcomes based on level of stress. Mariella may have been troubled because significant college stress triggered her predisposition for depression. Her friend Gisela, however, who had the same type of predisposition but who stayed home after high school, showed no symptoms of depression.

## Diathesis-Stress: The Little Picture

Let's also examine the little picture of the diathesis-stress model by showing how diatheses and stressors can interact in subtle ways. One example is that a diathesis or predisposition can *influence a person's perception of stress.* Stress is subjective, and so one event can be perceived and experienced as much more stressful by one person than another who has a different level of diathesis or vulnerability. Mariella's cognitive predisposition for depression—viewing the world as disappointing, unsympathetic, and unforgiving—likely affects her internal definition of a stressful event and her experience of the event as stressful. Mariella's rejection or lack of support from friends is more likely to be seen as stressful and lead to depression than someone without such a worldview. We therefore must recognize that stress varies from person to person and can actually depend on level and type of diathesis or predisposition.

Our predispositions also *influence our life course and choice of experiences.* Someone predisposed toward a shy temperament may choose over time to have fewer friends and engage in more solitary activities. The person's choice of life experiences is guided, at least in part, by his diathesis. Our predispositions can affect the preferences we have and the decisions we make. The type of friends or romantic partners we choose, the experiences we seek, the jobs we take, and the places we choose to live are likely influenced by diatheses. These choices and experiences also influence the people, places, and events we encounter in life and thus affect our life course. A diathesis will partly determine the range and varieties of life events we experience, and some of these may be seen as stressful. A shy person who surrounds himself with only a few close friends may be more likely than others to feel deliberately alienated at work.

DeShawn's impulsivity may have predisposed him to quickly attending parties and drinking as well as a preference for encountering new people and exciting environments. These preferences helped expose him to certain environments and experiences where excessive alcohol use is more likely to occur. Some of these experiences may also have created stress from poor grades and nagging parents, which may have led to more drinking to cope with the stress. The diathesis of high impulsivity affects a person's life choices and life course. The opposite is also true—less impulsive people will not seek these experiences and will not be exposed to some of these stressors.

## Implications of the Diathesis-Stress Model

The diathesis-stress model has many implications for studying, treating, and preventing psychological problems. A key implication is that we must study certain diatheses or vulnerabilities to mental disorder to fully understand why and how these disorders develop. We must understand the **etiology,** or cause, of mental disorders. A diathesis-stress model does so by including aspects of all theoretical models discussed in Chapter 2. All possible diatheses are considered, such as genetics, neurochemical and brain changes, unconscious processes, learning experiences, thought patterns, and cultural and family factors. Knowing these diatheses is also important for treating mental disorders when they occur and for preventing mental disorders before they begin.

Diatheses or vulnerabilities are *risk factors* for mental disorders. Risk factors are discussed later in this chapter and all chapters describing mental disorders. Researchers study risk factors by comparing people with many symptoms of a disorder to people with few or no symptoms of a disorder. Differences between these groups may represent risk factors or vulnerabilities for the disorder. People like DeShawn with excessive alcohol use can be compared to people like Kira with less

alcohol use. We may find key differences such as genetic structure, impulsivity, and stress, and some of these differences could be useful for treatment and prevention. College freshmen found to be impulsive and stressed could undergo an awareness program to decrease excessive alcohol use. The search for risk factors intersects with the study of patterns of mental disorder in the general population, a topic we turn to next.

### INTERIM SUMMARY

▶ A diathesis is a biological or psychological predisposition or vulnerability to disorder.

▶ A combination or interaction of diathesis and stress produces mental disorder.

▶ A diathesis can influence perception and experience of stress as well as life course and choice of experiences.

▶ A diathesis-stress model integrates theoretical perspectives of mental disorder and provides information about etiology (cause), treatment, and prevention.

### REVIEW QUESTIONS

1. What is a diathesis, and how does a diathesis affect the way we view and experience stressful events?
2. Why might two people exposed to the same traumatic event act differently afterward?
3. How is a diathesis-stress model consistent with a dimensional or continuum approach to mental disorder?
4. How might a diathesis-stress model help us understand mental disorders?

## Epidemiology: How Common Are Mental Disorders?

**Epidemiology** is the study of patterns of disease or disorder in the general population. Epidemiology can involve any physical or mental condition related to poor health or mortality among children and adults. **Epidemiologists** are scientists who investigate the extent of a public health problem such as a mental disorder by making observations, surveying people, and using other methods. **Box 3.1** presents a famous example of epidemiology: John Snow's discovery of the cause of a cholera outbreak and subsequent prevention of new disease cases. Prevention is an important application of information gathered from epidemiological research.

Epidemiologists often focus on incidence and prevalence of mental disorder. **Incidence** refers to *new* cases of a mental disorder within a specific time period such as a month or year. A *1-year incidence* of a mental disorder is the percentage of people who, for the first time, developed that disorder in the previous 12 months. **Prevalence** refers to *all* cases of a mental disorder, including new and existing cases, within a specific time period such as a month or year. A *1-year prevalence* of depression includes all cases of existing depression during the previous 12 months, regardless of when the disorder began.

Epidemiologists also provide **lifetime prevalence** estimates of mental disorders. Lifetime prevalence refers to the

## BOX 3.1

### John Snow: A Pioneer in Epidemiology and Prevention

John Snow (1813–1858) is often referred to as the "Father of Epidemiology." His investigation of a catastrophe is considered classic among epidemiologists, and his simple intervention is a fine example of prevention. An outbreak of cholera occurred in 1854 London primarily among people living near Cambridge and Broad Streets; 500 deaths were reported in this area over a 10-day period. Snow thought people were contracting cholera from a contaminated water source, so he obtained information on cholera deaths from the General Register Office. He used this information and surveyed the scene of the deaths to determine that nearly all deaths occurred a short distance from the Broad Street pump (a water source for this area). He went to each address of the deceased and calculated the distance to the nearest water pump, which was usually the Broad Street pump. He also determined that some of the deceased recently drank from this pump. These data supported his theory of the spread of cholera through water, and he concluded that the water source for the Broad Street pump was contaminated. Snow presented his findings to local authorities, the handle to the pump was removed, and the local cholera outbreak ended. This is a great example of

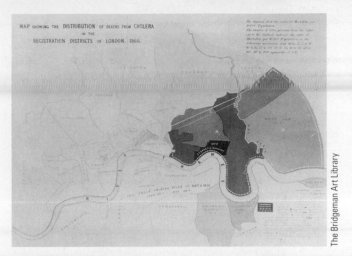

The Bridgeman Art Library

Map showing the distribution of deaths from cholera in the Registration Districts of London, 1866 (litho) (b/w photo), English School (19th century).

epidemiological findings leading to a preventive intervention—one that saved untold lives.

Although the map featured here is faded, it shows the distribution of cholera deaths in a London area. The darker sections indicate the way the deaths were concentrated in one region, leading John Snow to question whether the source of the outbreak originated there.

proportion of those who have had a certain mental disorder *at any time in their life* up to the point they were assessed. Lifetime prevalence indicates risk for certain disorders over the entire life span, whereas smaller prevalence times such as a year provide a snapshot of whether people have recently been diagnosed with a specific disorder. Both prevalence types help us understand the likelihood of mental disorder and are discussed in more detail next and throughout this textbook.

## Prevalence of Mental Disorders

Epidemiologists help determine the prevalence of mental disorders. A major epidemiological survey of Americans, the *National Comorbidity Survey-Replication* (NCS-R), is a representative, community-based survey of about 10,000 people aged 18 years and older. The survey included structured interviews to assess people for major mental disorders and serves as the basis for the next several sections.

### OVERALL PREVALENCE AND SEVERITY

NCS-R data revealed that 46.4 percent of Americans experience a mental disorder at some point in their life (Kessler, Berglund, Demler, Jin, & Walters, 2005). This percentage may seem high, but keep two key points in mind. First, not

everyone who meets criteria for a mental disorder is in treatment. Most people who experience psychological symptoms do not seek a mental health professional during the first year of their diagnosis (Wang, Lane et al., 2005). Friends, peers, or family members may not even know about a person's symptoms. Many symptoms of mental disorders are not obvious, such as sadness, so other people may not recognize a person has a serious problem. Such may have been the case for Mariella.

Second, mental disorders differ with respect to severity and many people show only mild symptoms. This point reinforces a major theme of this textbook—symptoms of mental disorders are present to some extent in all of us and can be represented along a continuum. People with certain symptoms or diagnoses are not qualitatively different from those without. Mariella's symptoms of depression are something we all feel from time to time. Her symptoms may be more severe than ours at the moment, but the symptoms are something with which we can identify.

NCS-R data included serious, moderate, and mild levels of severity (Kessler, Chiu et al., 2005). Each level was defined by certain features associated with a disorder. For example, *serious severity* was defined by features such as suicide attempt

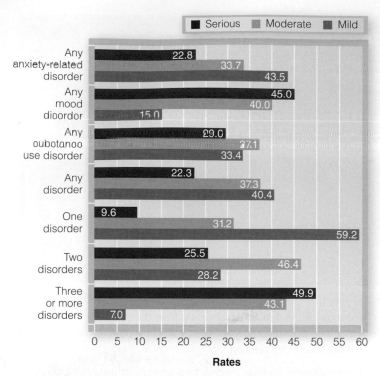

**FIGURE 3.2 SEVERITY OF 12-MONTH MAJOR MENTAL DISORDERS** *Rates* indicate the proportion of people in the United States with the mental disorder at each level of severity (serious, moderate, mild). *Adapted from Kessler, Chiu, et al. (2005).*

with lethal intent, occupational disability, psychotic symptoms, or intense violence. **Figure 3.2** illustrates percentage of severity levels for some major mental disorders. Mental disorder was generally classified as serious (22.3 percent), moderate (37.3 percent), or mild (40.4 percent) in severity. Serious severity was most evident with respect to mood (i.e., depressive and bipolar) disorders (45.0 percent).

## SPECIFIC PREVALENCE RATES

Prevalence information for specific disorders is crucial so we know where to assign treatment and prevention resources. **Figure 3.3** outlines lifetime and 12-month prevalence rates for some major mental disorders. Lifetime prevalence rates for anxiety-related disorders (28.8 percent), including specific phobia (12.5 percent) and social phobia (12.1 percent), are substantial. Mood disorders (20.8 percent) are also relatively common. Lifetime prevalence for substance use disorders in general was 14.6 percent and for alcohol use disorder in particular was 13.2 percent.

The NCS-R also provided *12-month prevalence rates,* which are lower than lifetime prevalence rates because of the shorter time frame. Researchers found that more than one-fourth of Americans (26.2 percent) had one or more mental disorders over the previous year (Kessler, Chiu et al., 2005). Anxiety-related (18.1 percent), mood (9.5 percent), and substance use (3.8 percent) disorders were quite common (Figure 3.3).

## COMORBIDITY

**Comorbidity** refers to the presence of two or more disorders in a person and is a significant concern for mental health professionals. This is so because recovery among people with two or more mental disorders is less likely than among people with one mental disorder. According to the NCS-R, 27.7 percent of Americans will have more than one mental disorder in their lifetime, and 11.8 percent will have had more than one mental disorder in the past year (Kessler, Berglund et al., 2005; Kessler, Chiu et al., 2005). A significant percentage of Americans thus experience more than one mental disorder. Comorbidity is also clearly related to severity of mental disorder. Data from Figure 3.2 indicate that a much higher percentage of those with three or more disorders (49.9 percent) were classified as serious severity than those with only one disorder (9.6 percent).

## AGE OF ONSET

A unique aspect of the NCS-R was that questions were asked about the *onset* of mental disorder (Kessler, Berglund et al., 2005). People who received a diagnosis for a mental disorder at some point in their lives were asked if they could remember when their symptoms started and how their symptoms progressed. Several interesting findings emerged (see **Figure 3.4**). First, the median age of onset for a mental disorder is 14 years. Second, *anxiety-related* disorders have an earlier onset (age 11 years) than *substance use* (age 20 years) or *mood* (age 30 years) disorders. Not everyone diagnosed with these disorders has these exact ages of onset, of

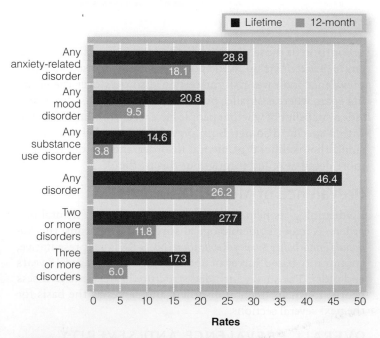

**FIGURE 3.3 LIFETIME AND 12-MONTH PREVALENCE OF MAJOR MENTAL DISORDERS** *Lifetime* and *12-month rates* represent the proportion of U.S. residents with the mental disorder. *Adapted from Kessler, Berglund, et al. (2005); Kessler, Chiu, et al. (2005).*

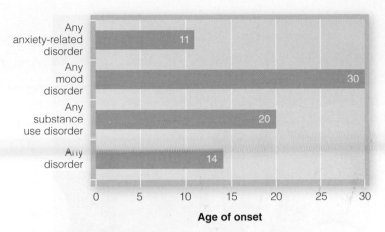

**FIGURE 3.4** MEDIAN AGE OF ONSET OF MAJOR MENTAL DISORDERS *Adapted from Kessler, Berglund, et al. (2005); Kessler, Chiu, et al. (2005).*

course, but these estimates do indicate that many mental disorders first appear in adolescence or young adulthood.

## COHORT EFFECTS AND CHILDREN

**Cohort effects** are significant differences in disorder expression depending on demographic features such as age or gender. Younger Americans may be more likely to develop substance use disorders compared with older Americans. Why? One possible reason is that alcohol was not as available to adolescents 30 years ago as it is today. Our views on underage college drinking have also changed over the years, and the behavior may be more tolerated now than in the past. Attention-deficit deficit/hyperactivity disorder is also diagnosed more now than in the past. Another example is addiction to online gambling such as poker. Which group might have this problem more—older Americans with less expertise about computers or college students raised in a technological era?

**Figure 3.5** presents NCS-R data on mental disorders by age. People aged 18 to 59 years have higher lifetime rates of some major (anxiety-related, mood, substance use) mental disorders than people aged 60 years or older. Why these age differences exist is unclear. Higher lifetime prevalence rates for younger people may be due to greater willingness to admit psychological problems, or adults may underreport or forget symptoms as they get older and further from their disorder onset.

What about youth? Epidemiologists estimate that about 21 to 25 percent of American children and adolescents have a mental disorder. Children and adolescents are most likely to be diagnosed with anxiety-related, disruptive, mood, and substance use problems (Costello, Egger, & Angold, 2005; U.S. Department of Health and Human Services, 1999). Many American children are also reported by their parents to have emotional or behavioral difficulties that interfere with family, academic, and social functioning (Federal Interagency Forum on Child and Family Statistics, 2005).

Mental disorders will generally affect about half of us in our lifetime, and many of these disorders begin in adolescence or early adulthood. Many of us will experience more than one mental disorder, and younger people tend to report higher rates of mental disorder than older people. Mental disorders can be of varying severity, and even people without a formal diagnosis may experience symptoms to some degree. Mental disorders and their symptoms are dimensional, and that is why the study of abnormal psychology is a key part of life in general. The high prevalence of mental disorder also means people often seek treatment, which is discussed next.

## Treatment Seeking

The NCS-R researchers asked people with anxiety-related, mood, or substance use disorders about their use of mental health services in the previous year (Wang, Lane et al., 2005). Many (41.1 percent) used services, including 21.7 percent who used mental health services, 22.8 percent who used general medical services, and 13.2 percent who used non–health care services such as alternative medicine (some used two or more types of service). People who sought treatment were generally younger than age 60 years, female, from a non-Hispanic white racial background, previously married, more affluent, and living in urban areas. People who sought treatment also tended to have more severe mental disorders or two or more mental disorders.

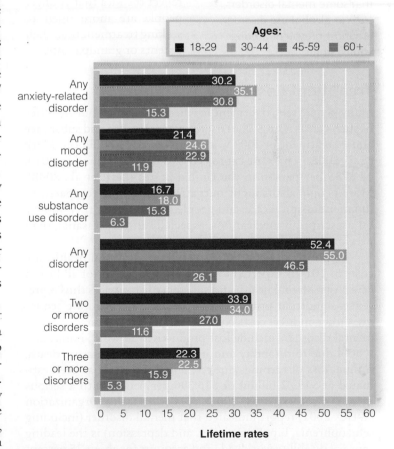

**FIGURE 3.5** LIFETIME PREVALENCE OF MENTAL DISORDERS BY AGE *Lifetime rates represent the proportion of U.S. residents with a mental disorder. Adapted from Kessler, Berglund, et al. (2005).*

Epidemiological studies show that some mental disorders, such as alcohol use disorder, are most prevalent among young adults.

Many people with a mental disorder do eventually seek treatment. Unfortunately, a lengthy delay often occurs between onset of a disorder and first treatment contact. Wang and colleagues (2005) estimated that less than half of those with a mental disorder sought treatment within the first year of onset. The typical delay between diagnosis and treatment for many disorders was *10 years or more*. Less delay was evident for mood disorders but greater delay was evident for anxiety-related disorders. Younger people are more likely to seek treatment, and a later age of onset is linked to more timely treatment contact. This may reflect the idea that younger people are more open to seeking treatment than their parents or grandparents.

## Treatment Cost

Many people seek treatment for mental disorder, but the price of such care is rising. The cost for mental health and substance abuse treatment in 2001 was estimated at $104 billion (Mark et al., 2005). This cost is projected to be $239 billion in 2014, or $735 per person in the United States (Levit et al., 2008). More people also sought outpatient treatment compared to inpatient hospital care, and people spent more of their money on prescription medications, especially antidepressants, than previously (Mark et al., 2005).

To put this in context, $239 billion in mental health care costs in 2014 is expected to represent 6.9 percent of all health care costs. Mental health and substance use services thus represent a significant proportion of the overall health care economy. Other, indirect costs compound this issue. Indirect costs of mental disorders include lost productivity at work, home, and school due to disability and impairment or premature death. Annual loss of earnings due to mental disorder has been estimated at $193.2 billion or $16,306 per person with a serious mental disorder (Insel, 2008). A World Health Organization (WHO, 2001) report indicated that mental disorder (including schizophrenia, bipolar disorder, and depression) is the leading cause of disability worldwide and accounts for about 25 percent of all disability across major industrialized countries. This figure approaches 36 percent if one considers disability associated with substance use disorders. This rate of disability far exceeds

Most people eventually seek treatment for their psychological problems but only after a delay of many years.

that with cardiovascular disease, respiratory disease, and cancer (see **Figure 3.6**).

## INTERIM SUMMARY

▶ Epidemiology is the study of patterns of disease or disorder in the general population.

▶ Incidence refers to number of new cases of a mental disorder within a specific time period, and prevalence refers to all cases present during a specific time period.

▶ Lifetime prevalence refers to proportion of those who have had a certain mental disorder at any time in their life up to the point they were assessed.

▶ About half of American adults have a diagnosable mental disorder, although many are not in treatment or have mild symptoms.

▶ Anxiety-related, mood, and substance use disorders are especially common.

▶ Comorbidity refers to the presence of two or more disorders in a person and is related to greater severity of mental disorder.

▶ Most mental disorders first appear in adolescence or early adulthood.

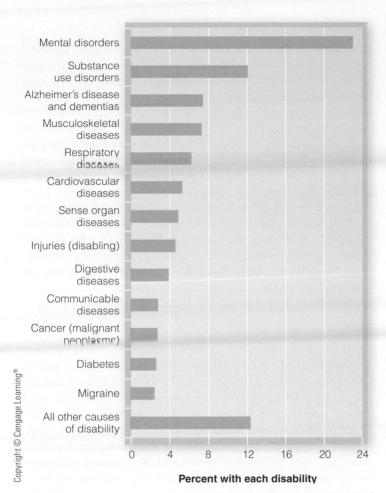

**FIGURE 3.6 MENTAL DISORDERS ARE THE LEADING CAUSE OF DISABILITY** *Adapted from President's New Freedom Commission on Mental Health (2003).* Achieving the promise: Transforming mental health care in America. *Rockville, MD: U.S. Department of Health and Human Services, Substance Abuse and Mental Health Services Administration, Center for Mental Health Services, National Institutes of Health, National Institute of Mental Health.*

► Cohort effects refer to significant differences in expression of mental disorder depending on demographic features such as age and gender.

► Mental disorders are more common among youth and younger adults than older adults, although underreporting in older adults may be a factor.

► Many people eventually seek treatment for a mental disorder, but many others delay treatment for several years.

► The cost of mental health care is prohibitive because mental disorder is a leading cause of disability worldwide.

## REVIEW QUESTIONS

1. What is epidemiology, and how do epidemiologists help us understand mental disorders?
2. What is the difference between incidence and prevalence?
3. What do we know about the prevalence of mental disorders among Americans?
4. What factors are associated with treatment seeking?
5. Describe the financial and disability costs of mental disorders.

# Risk, Protective Factors, and Resilience

## CASE: Jana

**Jana** is a 22-year-old college student with a long history of psychological problems. Jana often feels depressed and anxious, has trouble controlling her moods, and can lash out at others for no reason. This has affected her relationships because many people are afraid they might "set her off." Jana has frequently cut herself with razor blades when under stress or when she is angry at herself. Jana has wanted to die many times and has made several suicide attempts over the past 10 years. She tends to make bad decisions and does so impulsively, which has landed her in legal trouble for shoplifting and writing bad checks. Jana has also struggled with excessive alcohol and other drug use for years. Her friends say Jana often "zones out" for 30 minutes or so when she gets upset, as though she is not really there. Jana has seen many mental health professionals over the years. When they ask what may have caused her problems, Jana points to her childhood, when an uncle maltreated her sexually.

How do mental health professionals understand problems like Jana's? A diathesis-stress model helps us understand factors involved in the development of mental disorder. Some factors are *diatheses* or *vulnerabilities*: features or attributes within a person. Other factors comprise the "stress" part of the model and are typically seen as "environmental": outside a person and perhaps more transient in nature. Diatheses and stressors may be *risk* factors for a mental disorder, but, as we have seen, not everyone with a predisposition for a mental disorder necessarily develops one. Something must therefore *protect* some people from developing a mental disorder. We next discuss further the concepts of *risk* and *protective factors*.

## Risk Factors

A **risk factor** is an individual or environmental characteristic that precedes a mental disorder and is correlated with that disorder. Risk factors can be biological, psychological, or social. Jana's severe childhood sexual maltreatment is a risk factor for problems she experienced in adulthood. Risk factors are associated with an increased probability a disorder will develop, but they do not imply cause. Jana has a mental disorder called *borderline personality disorder* (Chapter 10). A childhood history of severe sexual maltreatment is more common in people with borderline personality disorder than those without the disorder. Recall that risk factors are often identified by comparing prevalence of the risk factor in those with and without a certain disorder. Factors more common in people with a mental disorder may be the ones that place them "at risk" for developing the disorder.

Some risk factors are "fixed," such as gender or family history of a disorder. Other risk factors are dynamic and can change over time, such as social support. Risk factors can also vary across age, gender, or culture. Risk factors for excessive alcohol use in a 21-year-old African American college student like DeShawn are not the same as those for a 45-year-old European American businessman. Many risk factors also exist for a particular mental disorder and may interact with each other in complex ways to influence the development of the disorder.

Risk factors must *precede* the development of a condition, so the mental disorder itself cannot cause its risk factors. We would not consider DeShawn's college struggles to be a risk factor for his excessive alcohol use. Excessive alcohol use instead led to skipping classes and poor grades. For someone else, however, poor grades could trigger stress that then leads to excessive alcohol use. For this person, poor grades are a risk factor.

Identifying risk factors can lead to better treatment and prevention. Childhood sexual maltreatment is a risk factor for borderline personality disorder, as with Jana, so those seeking to prevent borderline personality disorder might focus on preventing such maltreatment. This might be accomplished by educating parents and children about appropriate and inappropriate intimacy and by informing parents and children about resources available to them if problems occur (such as a state Department of Family and Protective Services). We discuss how identifying risk factors can lead to prevention efforts later in this chapter. We next discuss several key risk factors identified in epidemiological studies (Kessler, Berglund et al., 2005; Kessler et al., 1994; Robins, Locke, & Regier, 1991; WHO, 2001).

Women are at greater risk for developing anxiety-related and depressive disorders. Men are at greater risk for developing antisocial personality disorder and substance use disorders.

## GENDER

Risk of mental disorder is different for men and women. Lifetime prevalence for any mental disorder was 36 percent for men and 30 percent for women in the classic *Epidemiological Catchment Area* (ECA) study conducted on Americans (Robins et al., 1991). Not all studies support this finding, however (WHO, 2001). A more consistent finding is that males are more likely than females to have substance use, antisocial personality, sexual, and developmental disorders (Chapters 9, 10, 11, and 13, respectively).

Women are at greater risk for developing anxiety-related disorders and depression (Chapters 5 and 7, respectively). They are also more likely to have neurocognitive disorders such as Alzheimer's disease because they live longer than men (Chapter 14). Women are also more likely than men to have more than one mental disorder at any point in time (Kessler et al., 1994; WHO, 2001). **Box 3.2** discusses how a very serious problem in college students—suicide—affects female college students in their mid to late 20s more than their male peers.

## AGE

Age is also a significant risk factor for mental disorders (Kessler, Amminger et al., 2007). Highest lifetime and 1-year prevalence rates of mental disorders in the ECA study were among people aged 18 to 29 and 30 to 44 years. Lowest rates were among people aged 65 years or older (Robins et al., 1991). These trends were also found in the NCS-R (Figure 3.5). More than 75 percent of people with a mental disorder develop their first symptoms before age 24 years, and 90 percent do so before age 38 years. Unfortunately, early onset of a disorder is related to poorer chance for recovery.

## RACE AND ETHNICITY

The extent to which race and ethnicity are risk factors for mental disorder has been difficult to establish. The ECA study found African Americans to have higher lifetime and 1-year prevalence rates of mental disorder than non-Hispanic European Americans or Latinos and that Latinos did not differ from European Americans (Robins et al., 1991). Kessler et al. (1994) found no such differences, however, and the NCS-R found non-Hispanic European Americans to have higher lifetime prevalence rates for anxiety-related, mood, and substance use disorders than African Americans and Latinos (Kessler, Berglund et al., 2005).

Bodily concerns and phobias may be more common among African Americans than European Americans, but major depression is less likely (U.S. Department of Health and Human Services, 2001). Latino youth experience more anxiety-related and delinquency problems, depression, and substance use than European American youth. Interestingly, adult Mexican *immigrants* had *lower* rates of mental disorder than Mexican Americans born in the United States. Migrant and immigrant populations around the world are often at increased risk for severe mental disorder, however. Finally, adult Puerto Ricans living on the island tended to have lower rates of depression than Puerto Ricans living on the mainland United States.

Prevalence rates of mental disorder among Asian American/Pacific Islanders are similar to European Americans but, when

## BOX 3.2  Focus on Gender

### Suicide and College Students

One of the leading causes of death among young adults is suicide, especially those in college (Brownson, Drum, Smith, & Denmark, 2011). The *Big Ten Suicide Study* (Silverman, Meyer, Sloane, Raffel, & Pratt, 1997) examined rates of completed suicide on Big Ten university campuses. Rate of suicide among these college students (about 7.5 per 100,000) was about half that of peers who were not attending college, and the rate of suicide for undergraduate women was roughly half that of undergraduate men. These gender differences disappeared, however, when rates for older students were examined—suicide rates for women age 25 years or older resembled that of same-age men. Furthermore, the rate for college women in this age group was *higher* than

similar-age peers who were not in college. College women in their mid to late 20s thus seemed to be at greater risk for suicide than other age and gender groups.

One explanation may be the stress of college (Suicide Prevention Resource Center, 2004). Such stress may come from leaving family and peers, facing new academic demands, or even date rape. These stressors may create new psychological difficulties or exacerbate existing ones. Older students and women in particular may experience more stress during college (Silverman, 2004). They are more likely to commute and be alienated from campus life, have left the workforce, have greater financial burden, and have greater worries about the future job market. Older students may also have more dependents and thus additional time and financial burdens. These findings illustrate the utility of epidemiological data for discovering what may cause psychological problems and for developing treatment and prevention efforts.

symptom scales are used, Asian American/Pacific Islanders show more depressive symptoms than European Americans. Large-scale studies of mental disorder among American Indians/Alaska Natives are lacking, but smaller studies indicate rates of depression around 10 to 30 percent. American Indian/Alaska Native children also exhibit high rates of excessive substance use, especially alcohol use among American Indian children. Some specific ethnic differences may be evident, but we cannot yet conclude that race and ethnicity are general risk factors for mental disorder. We discuss specific racial and ethnic differences in greater detail for each disorder throughout this text.

### EDUCATION, SOCIOECONOMIC STATUS, AND MARITAL STATUS

Individuals who do not complete high school are more likely to have a mental disorder than those who complete or go beyond high school (Robins et al., 1991). This seems especially true for substance use disorders (Kessler, Berglund et al., 2005). Unemployed people and people with unskilled jobs are also more likely to develop mental disorder than employed people and people with skilled jobs. Poverty is a well-established risk factor for mental disorder (Robins et al., 1991; WHO, 2001).

Marital status is a significant and consistent risk factor for mental disorder as well. The prevalence of mental disorder is highest among divorced and separated men and women and lowest among married men and women (Baumeister & Harter, 2007; Robins et al., 1991). Marital disruption is most strongly associated with a higher risk for anxiety-related, mood, and substance use disorders, as well as suicide (Kessler, Berglund et al., 2005). A summary of risk factors for mental disorder is found in **Table 3.1**.

### OTHER RISK FACTORS

Other risk factors seem to represent more general vulnerabilities to mental disorder (U.S. Department of Health and Human Services, 2001). *Individual risk factors* include genetic predisposition, low birth weight and premature birth, neuropsychological deficits, language disabilities, chronic physical illness, below-average intelligence, and history of child maltreatment. *Family risk factors* include severe marital discord, overcrowding or large family size, paternal criminality, maternal mental disorder, and admission to foster care. *Community* or *social risk factors* include violence, poverty, community disorganization, inadequate schools, and racism, sexism, and discrimination. We also covered many other risk factors in Chapter 2 when discussing biological, psychodynamic, humanistic, cognitive-behavioral, and sociocultural models of mental disorder. Understanding these many risk factors is important for developing effective treatments and preventing mental disorders before they start. This is also true for protective factors, which are discussed next.

## Protective Factors

We must identify risk factors to determine who is vulnerable to mental disorder, but we must also identify **protective factors** associated with *lower risk* of mental disorder. Protective factors are the flip side of risk factors. Poor social support is a risk factor for depression, therefore strong social support can be thought of as a protective factor. Those with strong social support from friends and family are *less likely* to develop depression than those with poor social support. Perhaps you have been thanked by a friend for being caring and supportive during a difficult period in her life. Your support, and the support of others, may have protected her from becoming severely depressed.

Paul Burns/Digital Vision/Jupiter Image

One epidemiological study found European Americans to have higher lifetime prevalence rates for anxiety-related, mood, and substance use disorders than African Americans and Latinos. Some specific ethnic differences like these are evident, but we cannot yet conclude that race and ethnicity are general risk factors for mental disorder.

Research on protective factors has not been as extensive as that for risk factors, but **Table 3.2** provides some examples. Like risk factors, protective factors can be biological, psychological, or social and can operate at individual, family, or community levels. Happily married people have the lowest lifetime and 1-year prevalence rates of mental disorder. Social support or contact with friends and others, and level of satisfaction with these social contacts, are important protective factors as well (Reblin & Uchino, 2008). Personality and psychological factors such as self-efficacy, problem-solving skills, hopefulness, and a focus on positive events also protect people against mental disorder (Snyder et al., 2000; Southwick, Vythilingam, & Charney, 2005).

## RESILIENCE

Recall from Chapter 2 that some people function well even in terrible circumstances such as poverty and maltreatment. Some people adapt well in these circumstances because of **resilience,** or ability to withstand and rise above extreme adversity (Luthar, Cicchetti, & Becker, 2000). Resilient people can adapt and prosper despite odds against them. Psychologists have become increasingly interested in studying factors associated with resilience, especially among children at risk for negative outcomes due to unfavorable environments such as war, domestic violence, or poverty (see **Figure 3.7**).

## Table 3.1

### Summary of Risk Factors for Mental Disorders

| Risk factor | Findings |
|---|---|
| Age | The highest rates of mental disorders are in the 18–29 and 30–44 age groups. |
| Education | Individuals who do not complete high school are significantly more likely to be diagnosed with a mental disorder, especially substance use disorders, than those who complete or go beyond high school. |
| Employment | Individuals who are unemployed are more likely to develop psychological problems than those who are employed. |
| Gender | Men are more likely than women to be diagnosed with antisocial personality disorder and substance use disorders. Women are at greater risk for developing anxiety-related and depressive disorders. Women are more likely than men to be diagnosed with more than one mental disorder at any point in time. |
| Marital status | Marital disruption (divorce or separation) is associated with mental disorders in general and with anxiety-related, mood, and substance use disorders in particular. |
| Race and ethnicity | Research has demonstrated mixed results in general, with some specific differences. Body concerns and phobias appear more common among African Americans than among whites, but major depression is less likely. Latino youth experience more anxiety-related and delinquency problems, depression, and excessive substance use than white youth. Prevalence rates of diagnosable disorders among Asian American/Pacific Islanders are similar to those of the white population. Large-scale studies of mental disorders among American Indians/Alaska Natives are lacking, but smaller studies have found rates of depression ranging from 10 to 30 percent. American Indian/Alaska Native children exhibit higher rates of substance use, almost all accounted for by alcohol use among American Indian children. |

## Table 3.2

### Protective Factors Against Mental Disorders and Problems

| | |
|---|---|
| Individual | Positive temperament |
| | Above-average intelligence |
| | Social competence |
| | Spirituality or religion |
| Family | Smaller family structure |
| | Supportive relationships with parents |
| | Good sibling relationships |
| | Adequate monitoring and rule-setting by parents |
| Community or social | Commitment to schools |
| | Availability of health and social services |
| | Social cohesion |

Source: U.S. Department of Health and Human Services, 2001, p. 14.

Resilience was originally studied among children of parents with schizophrenia (Chapter 12). A child with a biological parent with schizophrenia is at genetic and environmental risk for schizophrenia, but most children with these risk factors do not develop the disorder and actually adapt quite well (Garmezy 1991; Masten, 2011). These children are exposed to several risk factors for schizophrenia, but they can still thrive.

The study of resilience has since expanded to include traumatic events or adverse environmental or social situations. Many people developed symptoms of posttraumatic stress disorder following the 9/11 terrorist attacks. They became anxious, depressed, lost sleep, and had great difficulty concentrating. These symptoms were very distressing and caused many people to wonder if their mental health would ever improve. But not everyone exposed to these tragic events developed posttraumatic stress disorder. What characterized people who adapted well despite exposure to such tragic events? What were their *resiliency factors*?

Key resiliency factors among children include good social and academic competence and effectiveness in work and play situations. Key resiliency factors among minority populations include supportive families and communities as well as spirituality and religion (U.S. Department of Health and Human Services, 2001). A landmark study of children of Vietnamese refugees confirms this. This study followed refugees exposed to many traumatic and stressful events in Vietnam and the United States as part of resettling in a new country. Many more of these children than might be expected had good academic success in high school. Factors that characterized these resilient youth were strong family ties, community support, and "selective Americanization"—adopting the best values from American as well as Vietnamese culture (Zhou & Bankston, 1998).

Spirituality and religion are also linked to greater life satisfaction and well-being (U.S. Department of Health and Human Services, 2001). African Americans report higher levels of religiosity than other racial or ethnic groups, and religiosity seems to protect against higher rates of psychological problems. But how does religiosity or spirituality provide an advantage? Perhaps people with strong religiosity or spirituality adhere to healthier lifestyles (such as not smoking or drinking alcohol), provide and receive higher levels of social support (such as a church community), or promote positive, optimistic beliefs related to faith (Levin, 1996; Powell, Shahabi, & Thoresen, 2003).

Resiliency factors are associated with good outcome, but whether they *cause* good outcome remains unclear. Still, strong attachments or bonds with family members and the community, as well as good problem-solving and coping skills, seem to buffer people against adverse circumstances. Studies of resilience and competence also help mental health professionals in several practical ways. These studies guide the development of interventions to prevent or eliminate risk factors, build resources, enhance relationships, and improve self-efficacy and self-regulation (Masten & Coatsworth, 1998; Vanderbilt-Adriance & Shaw, 2008).

## INTERIM SUMMARY

▶ A risk factor is an individual or environmental characteristic that precedes a mental disorder and is correlated with that disorder.

▶ Men are at greater risk for substance use, antisocial personality, sexual, and developmental disorders; women are at greater risk for anxiety-related and depressive disorders.

▶ Mental disorder appears more prevalent among younger than older adults.

▶ The extent to which race and ethnicity are risk factors for mental disorder has been difficult to establish, but some specific differences have been reported.

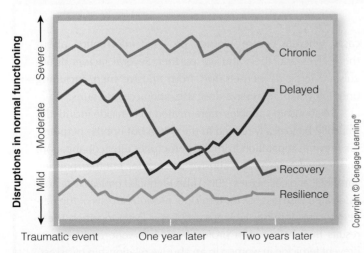

**FIGURE 3.7** TYPICAL PATTERNS OF DISRUPTION IN NORMAL FUNCTIONING ACROSS TIME FOLLOWING A TRAUMATIC EVENT
*Adapted from G.A. Bonanno,* American Psychologist, 59, *Fig. 1, p. 21. Copyright © 2004 by the American Psychological Association. Used with permission.*

Colorblind/Photodisc/Jupiter Images

Spirituality and religion may serve as a protective factor against psychological problems.

▶ Lower educational and socioeconomic levels, as well as divorce or separation from a partner, are general risk factors for mental disorder.

▶ Other risk factors include individual, family, and community or social factors.

▶ Protective factors are associated with lower rates of mental disorder.

▶ Resilience refers to the ability to withstand and rise above extreme adversity and may protect people from developing mental disorder.

▶ Resiliency and protective factors vary across age, gender, race, and ethnicity.

### REVIEW QUESTIONS

**1.** What is the difference between risk factors and protective factors?

**2.** What are major risk factors for mental disorders?

**3.** What features do protective factors and resiliency factors have in common?

**4.** Why is it important to identify risk, protective, and resiliency factors?

## Prevention

Our discussion of risk factors and protective factors such as resilience leads naturally to a focus on one of the main themes of this textbook—prevention. **Prevention** refers to thwarting the development of later problems and may be more efficient and effective than individual treatment after a mental disorder occurs (Evans et al., 2005). Those engaging in prevention often use risk and protective factors to identify people who need more help before major problems develop. Prevention is therefore a guiding principle of many public health programs.

Many prevention programs aim to reduce risk and increase protective factors regarding mental disorder. Child maltreatment, such as that Jana experienced, is a key risk factor for several mental disorders. Many prevention programs therefore try to reduce the prevalence of childhood maltreatment. Prevention programs may also aim to *enhance protective factors*.

---

### BOX 3.3 Focus on Violence

## Prevention of Femicide

Femicide, the murder of women, is a leading cause of premature death among females. American women are killed by intimate partners more frequently than any other type of perpetrator, and physical maltreatment of the woman by the man often precedes the homicide. Identifying risk factors for femicide in abusive relationships may thus help us understand what leads from physical maltreatment to homicide. This is a foundation for prevention efforts.

Campbell and colleagues (2003) studied factors associated with 220 cases of femicide and 343 control cases of intimate partner abuse. Knowledgeable friends and relatives were interviewed about the victim and perpetrator in femicide

cases, whereas control women provided information about themselves and their abusive partner. Several factors distinguished femicide perpetrators from abusive men, including unemployment, excessive drug use, and access to guns.

Relationship variables more related to femicide included a stepchild biologically related to the victim but not the perpetrator, previous separation from the perpetrator after cohabitation, and leaving a physically abusive partner for another partner. Campbell and colleagues (2003) also identified *protective* factors associated with less risk for femicide: previous arrests of the perpetrator for domestic violence and never living together. These results may help health professionals intervene and perhaps prevent femicide in women in an abusive relationship by assessing a perpetrator's access to guns, encouraging women to contact police and use domestic violence resources, and advising women to avoid the perpetrator when leaving the relationship.

Protective factors for children include good social and academic competence and growing up in a positive home environment. Prevention programs could thus be designed to help kids make friends and do well in school and educate parents about proper child-rearing methods. Prevention programs often focus on children and families who are "at risk" for certain disorders based on these kinds of characteristics.

**Table 3.3** presents various techniques to prevent child maltreatment in children in high-risk families (Krugman, Lane, & Walsh, 2007; Peterson & Brown, 1994). This particular

**Table 3.3**

| A Sample Treatment Plan: Preventing Child Maltreatment in Children in High Risk Families | |
|---|---|
| Basic problem-solving training | Learn to recognize and define typical life problems |
| Positive parenting: enjoying the child | ▶ Gain education on the child's development and how to enjoy the child's unfolding abilities<br>▶ See the world through the child's eyes<br>▶ Learn activities for parent and child together: child-led play and mutual reinforcement |
| Parenting skills | Learn general skills such as how to<br>▶ *Define behaviors and goals*<br>▶ *Recognize developmentally appropriate goals*<br>▶ *Identify antecedents and consequences*<br>▶ *Identify rewards*<br>▶ *Identify a reasonable level of control* |
| | Learn request skills such as how to<br>▶ *Make requests to ensure compliance (alpha commands)*<br>▶ *Make reasonable requests* |
| | Learn how to reduce the frequency of undesirable behaviors:<br>▶ *Ignore*<br>▶ *Reward the absence of negative behaviors*<br>▶ *Implement time-out*<br>▶ *Get past the "testing the limits" phase* |
| | Learn how to increase desirable behaviors:<br>▶ *Use praise*<br>▶ *Use explicit rewards: appropriate rewards, token economy* |
| Extending parenting | Learn about child safety, especially the following:<br>▶ *Discipline and abuse—how discipline can slip into abuse, outcomes of abuse*<br>▶ *Responsibility for selecting nonabusive care agents*<br>▶ *Other kinds of injury, "child proofing"*<br>▶ *Supervision*<br>▶ *Child as precious to parent: work to protect* |
| Anger management | Learn how to see oneself through the child's eyes:<br>▶ *Recall one's own parents and parental anger*<br>▶ *Characterize how being the focus of anger feels* |
| | Learn to control your own emotions:<br>▶ *See your anger as a feeling, a color, or a state* |
| | Learn behavioral treatments:<br>▶ *Power to alter your state*<br>▶ *Relaxation*<br>▶ *Becoming aware of anger triggers*<br>▶ *Safety valves*<br>▶ *Self-esteem* |
| | Learn to see successful parenting as anger reducing |

Adapted from "Integrating Child Injury and Abuse-Neglect Research: Common Histories, Etiologies, and Solutions," by L. Peterson and D. Brown, 1994, *Psychological Bulletin, 116*, 293-315. Copyright © 1994 by the American Psychological Association. Reprinted with permission.

program emphasizes different aspects of parenting and caring for a child that may serve to "protect" against maltreatment. The program provides basic education and training in positive parenting, problem-solving skills, and anger management. The hope is that a successful program such as this one will lead to less maltreatment.

## Prevention on a Continuum

The basis of *prevention* is to build mental health and limit the scope of problems, including mental health problems, before they occur or worsen. Individuals do benefit from prevention and treatment programs along a continuum of intervention for mental disorders (Evans et al., 2005; Weisz, Sandler, Durlak, & Anton, 2005). This continuum is represented in the following way: *prevention* occurs before a disorder develops, *treatment* occurs after a disorder develops (or as a disorder is developing), and *maintenance* occurs long after a disorder has developed for people whose symptoms require ongoing attention (see **Figure 3.8**; Institute of Medicine, 2009).

## Three Types of Prevention

Mental health professionals have adopted three major approaches to prevention. These approaches were introduced in Chapter 1 and are discussed in more detail next.

### PRIMARY AND UNIVERSAL PREVENTION

The purest form of prevention is **primary prevention,** where an intervention is given to people with no signs of a disorder (Feldman & Jacova, 2007). Primary prevention practices are administered to prevent *new cases* of a disorder. This type of prevention is a radical departure from traditional ways of addressing mental disorder in which interventions are given *after* significant problems develop. **Universal prevention** is

similar to primary prevention in that large groups of people not affected by a particular problem are targeted to reduce new cases of a disorder (Figure 3.8). Advertisements to educate the public about the dangers of excessive alcohol and other drug use are an example. Universal prevention interventions target everyone, however, so they can be costly.

Other examples of primary or universal prevention are also available. Newborn children are regularly screened for phenylketonuria (PKU), a disorder that can result in intellectual disability (Chapter 13). Children with PKU can be placed on a special diet that prevents intellectual disability from occurring. Other examples of primary prevention include mandatory car seats for preschoolers to prevent accident fatalities and parenting classes to prevent child maltreatment (Table 3.3). Primary prevention also includes programs to reduce job discrimination, enhance school curricula, improve housing, and help children in single-parent homes. About 59 to 82 percent of participants in primary prevention programs have significantly better outcomes than nonparticipants (Durlak & Wells, 1997).

### SECONDARY AND SELECTIVE PREVENTION

**Secondary prevention** refers to addressing problems while they are manageable and before they are more resistant to treatment (Yung et al., 2007). Secondary prevention is designed to "nip a problem in the bud" before it progresses to a full-blown disorder. Secondary prevention programs promote the early identification of mental health problems as well as treatment at an early stage so mental disorders do not develop (Durlak, 1997).

A secondary prevention approach suggests that many people will be screened for early signs of mental health problems. These people are not necessarily seeking help and may not even appear to be at risk. Such screening may be conducted by community-service personnel such as psychologists, physicians, teachers, clergy, police, court officials, social workers, or others. May 1 of each year is set aside as National Anxiety Disorders Screening Day, which helps provide quick assessment for those who may be struggling with initial panic or other anxiety symptoms. Early identification of problems is followed, of course, by appropriate referrals for treatment.

**Selective prevention** is similar to secondary prevention in that people at risk for a particular problem are targeted (Figure 3.8). Selective prevention practices target individuals or subgroups of the population who are more likely than the general population to develop a particular mental disorder. Targeted individuals are identified on the basis of biological, psychological, or social risk factors associated with the onset of a disorder. A program to find and help youth genetically predisposed to schizophrenia would be an example of selective prevention.

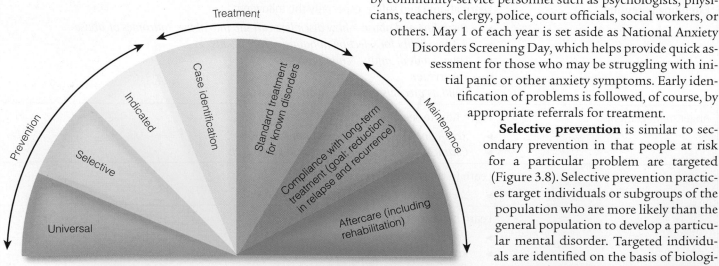

**FIGURE 3.8 PREVENTION EXISTS ON A CONTINUUM OF INTERVENTION FOR MENTAL HEALTH PROBLEMS** *Adapted from Institute of Medicine,* Summary: Reducing risks for mental disorders: Frontiers for preventive intervention research, *Fig. 2.1, p. 8. Washington, DC: National Academy Press. Copyright © 1994, National Academy of Sciences. Reprinted with permission from the National Academies Press.*

A famous prevention program in this regard is the *Rochester Primary Health Project*, which was designed to screen and treat children in early grades for signs of school maladjustment (Cowen et al., 1996). Participants in secondary prevention programs improve about 70 percent more so than control participants (Durlak & Wells, 1998). Children, especially younger ones, tend to benefit more from secondary prevention programs that use cognitive-behavioral and social problem-solving strategies (Elliott, Orr, Watson, & Jackson, 2005).

## TERTIARY AND INDICATED PREVENTION

**Tertiary prevention** refers to reducing the duration and additional negative effects of a mental disorder *after onset*. Tertiary prevention differs from primary and secondary prevention in that new cases of mental disorder are not reduced. Instead, the goal is to stabilize symptoms, provide rehabilitation, prevent relapse, improve a person's quality of life, and lessen effects of an *existing* mental disorder (Lee, McGlashan, & Woods, 2005). Tertiary prevention programs often focus on (1) educating peers and family members to reduce stigmatization, (2) providing job training to increase competence, and (3) teaching independent living skills to help someone be more self-reliant. A person recovering from an episode of schizophrenia might need help in these areas to avoid rehospitalization.

A key goal of tertiary prevention is to prevent additional problems from occurring. Tertiary prevention programs are not much different from traditional treatment of individuals with mental disorders. The focus remains, however, on preventing *other* problems; thus, tertiary prevention does share something in common with primary and secondary prevention. The goal of each prevention form is to reduce problems associated with mental disorder on a community- or population-wide basis.

**Indicated prevention** targets individuals (not groups) who are at very high risk for developing extensive problems in the future (Figure 3.8). These "high-risk" individuals are identified as having many risk factors and few protective factors for a certain mental disorder. Unlike tertiary prevention, indicated prevention focuses on people who have not yet developed a full-blown mental disorder.

## Prevention Programs for Mental Disorders

Prevention programs have been quite successful or promising in areas such as school adjustment, learning and health problems, injuries from accidents, pregnancy, and child maltreatment (Brindis, 2006; Durlak, 1997; Kendrick, Barlow, Hampshire, Polnay, & Stewart-Brown, 2007; Klevens & Whitaker, 2007). Areas of limited success include prevention of complex problems such as excessive substance use and delinquency in adolescents (McMahon, Holly, Harrington, Roberts, & Green, 2008; Thomas & Perera, 2006). A key advantage of prevention is that enormous resources can be saved that otherwise would go toward future treatment, hospitalization, and/or incarceration of people with mental disorder (Evans et al., 2005). Specific examples of prevention programs to address problems commonly experienced by young adults are presented next.

## PRIMARY/UNIVERSAL PREVENTION OF ALCOHOL USE DISORDERS ON COLLEGE CAMPUSES

DeShawn's problems at college come as little surprise given that excessive alcohol use is widespread on college campuses today. DeShawn often engaged in what is known as *binge drinking*, which means consuming five or more drinks on one occasion for men and four or more drinks on one occasion for women. Binge drinking is associated with poorer academic performance, risk for violence or physical injury, risky sexual behavior, and health problems, among other things. Approximately 44 percent of college students describe themselves as binge drinkers (Wechsler, Lee, Kuo, & Lee, 2000). Because binge drinking among college students is a major problem, efforts to prevent it are a top priority.

Many college campuses have prevention programs to curb excessive or binge drinking. These programs can be thought of as *primary* or *universal* prevention programs because all students, not just those at risk for alcohol use disorder, are exposed to these efforts. These programs include general education during freshman orientation, special events during the academic year such as "Alcohol Awareness Week," and peer education programs in which students themselves support their peers' healthy attitudes and lifestyle choices regarding alcohol use (Vicary & Karshin, 2002).

The *Wellness Resource Center (WRC)* at the University of Missouri sponsors a prevention program targeting excessive alcohol use. Major components of the program include promoting responsible decision making and providing accurate information about how much alcohol is consumed by college students (called *social norming*). Peers provide much of the information about drinking and its related problems to fellow students. The WRC's responsible decision-making program is administered by trained peer educators who visit residence halls, fraternity and sorority houses, classrooms, and junior high and high schools to speak about alcohol and other drug issues and making healthy lifestyle choices about eating, exercising, and smoking. Another intervention to promote responsible decision making is the virtual reality CD-ROM *Alcohol 101+*, which is available to Missouri students. *Alcohol 101+* depicts scenarios a student might face in social situations involving alcohol and reinforces good decision making. The CD-ROM has modules especially relevant to first-year college students, fraternity/sorority members, and athletes.

*Social norming* is an important component of many substance use prevention programs. This approach is based on the assumption that students often overestimate how much other students drink and that students drink in amounts they perceive others to drink. Programs like the WRC correct this misperception by educating students about the actual amount of alcohol their peers drink. Survey data reveal that Missouri students believed 60 percent of their peers drink three times a week or more, but actual data from students themselves reveal that only 33 percent do so. The WRC corrects students' norms for drinking by placing weekly ads in the student newspaper, distributing posters and flyers across campus, giving away bookmarks, and placing mouse pads with this information in student computer labs.

The CD-ROM *Alcohol 101+* or its accompanying website have a virtual campus that students can explore to learn more about the effects of alcohol.

The WRC also sponsors prevention organizations such as PARTY (Promoting Awareness and Responsibility Through You), a peer education organization that promotes responsible decision making; GAMMA (Greeks Advocating the Mature Management of Alcohol), an organization of fraternity/sorority students who promote responsible alcohol use; and CHEERS, a statewide program of student volunteers who work with local bars and restaurants to provide designated drivers with free soft drinks. You can see this prevention program is quite comprehensive and extensive.

## PRIMARY/UNIVERSAL PREVENTION OF SUICIDAL BEHAVIOR IN HIGH SCHOOL STUDENTS

Earlier in the chapter we saw that Jana, a 22-year-old college student, had been suicidal many times over the past few years. Suicidal behavior among teenagers and college students is not as rare as you might think. Suicide is one of the leading causes of death among 15- to 24-year-olds. Among American college students aged 20 to 24 years, suicide is the third leading cause of death (Suicide Prevention Resource Center, 2004). In addition, 6% of undergraduates and 4% of graduate students have seriously considered suicide in the past 12 months (Brownson et al., 2011). The need for early and effective suicide prevention programs is thus clear. These programs may help people like Jana who struggle with thoughts of suicide and self-harm.

*Signs of Suicide (SOS)* is a school-based prevention program with two main components (Aseltine & DeMartino, 2004). An educational component involves the review of a video and a discussion guide. These materials highlight the link between suicide and depression, show that suicidal behavior is not a normal reaction to emotional distress, and provide guidelines for recognizing signs and symptoms of depression in oneself and others. Students are also taught what to do (ACT) if signs of depression are present in a peer: *acknowledge* (A) the signs and take them seriously, let the person know you *care* (C), and *tell* (T) a responsible adult about the situation. The video has interviews of people who have been touched by suicide and provides ways of reacting if a peer has signs of depression or suicide. The second component involves a self-screening: Individuals evaluate themselves for signs of depression and suicidal thoughts and are prompted to seek help if necessary.

The SOS program appears to be successful at helping to prevent suicidal behavior. A study of 2,100 high school students found that SOS participants showed a 40 percent decrease in suicide attempts for 3 months after the intervention compared with nonparticipants (Aseltine & DeMartino, 2004). SOS participants also had greater knowledge of depression and more adaptive attitudes about depression and suicide than nonparticipants. This program has also been adapted for graduating seniors who are college-bound, emphasizing how to access resources on campus and in the community. A program like SOS might have helped Jana learn about her signs of depression and distress, realize suicidal behavior is not a good way to cope with depression or stress, and develop a plan for getting social support when she felt overwhelmed. These skills may have reduced Jana's suicidal behaviors.

The Signs of Suicide (SOS) prevention program helps prevent suicide attempts and increase knowledge about depression.

## SECONDARY/SELECTIVE PREVENTION OF PANIC DISORDER

Researchers have also evaluated secondary prevention programs for college students. Gardenswartz and Craske (2001) conducted such a program to prevent panic disorder in "at risk" college students. Panic disorder is characterized by sudden anxiety attacks (Chapter 5). People fear these attacks indicate a heart attack or other physical problem. This anticipatory fear can lead to additional attacks and avoidance of public situations that may lead to embarrassment if a panic attack occurs. Recall that secondary or selective prevention targets people who do not currently have a certain mental disorder but who may be at risk for developing additional symptoms of the disorder.

Gardenswartz and Craske (2001) targeted psychology undergraduates with moderate to severe "anxiety sensitivity," or a tendency to view anxiety symptoms or physiological arousal as harmful or threatening. Anxiety sensitivity is a risk factor for panic disorder, and students in this study had at least one panic attack in the past year but no diagnosis of panic disorder. Students targeted by the researchers thus appeared to be at risk for developing full-blown panic disorder. Approximately half of the "at-risk" participants were randomly assigned to a 5-hour preventative workshop. This workshop provided education about the nature of panic disorder and avoidance, cognitive skills training to correct misinterpretations of bodily sensations, and instructions about how to confront one's fears.

The workshop was effective for preventing full-blown panic disorder. A 6-month follow-up assessment revealed that only one workshop participant (2 percent) but nine nonparticipants (14 percent) developed panic disorder. Workshop participants also reported a greater decrease in panic and avoidance symptoms over the follow-up period than nonparticipants. This intervention shows promise for preventing panic disorder among at-risk individuals and may be particularly attractive because the workshop approach is relatively inexpensive and efficient (Gardenswartz & Craske, 2001). Prevention programs can thus successfully "buffer" young people from developing psychological problems. We present many examples of primary, secondary, and tertiary prevention of mental disorders throughout this textbook.

## INTERIM SUMMARY

- ► Prevention refers to thwarting the development of later problems and guides many mental health programs.
- ► Prevention can be viewed along a continuum with treatment and maintenance.
- ► Primary prevention refers to providing intervention to people with no signs of a particular disorder.
- ► Universal prevention targets large groups of people without a particular problem to reduce new cases of a disorder.
- ► Secondary prevention refers to addressing manageable problems before they become more resistant to treatment.
- ► Selective prevention targets people at risk for a particular problem.
- ► Tertiary prevention refers to reducing the duration and negative effects of a mental disorder after its onset.

---

### BOX 3.4  Focus on Law and Ethics

### Constructs Related to Insanity

Recall from Chapter 2 that *insanity* is a legal term that refers to mental incapacity at the time of a crime. The concept of insanity has been shaped by some key historical standards. One standard is the **M'Naghten rule**, which refers to the idea that a criminal defendant is not guilty by reason of insanity if, at the time of the crime, he did not know the nature or quality of his actions or did not know the difference between right and wrong. The M'Naghten rule means that defendants must have the cognitive ability to know right from wrong. If a defendant did not know the difference, such as someone experiencing a psychotic episode (Chapter 12) or someone with severe intellectual disability (Chapter 13), then this could be the basis for an insanity defense.

Another important historical standard is the **irresistible impulse** or *control* rule. In this situation, one could argue for an insanity defense if a person had a mental disorder that did not allow him to control his actions during a crime. A person may have known the difference between right and wrong but still could not exercise behavioral control. In addition, the **Durham rule** refers to the idea that a person may not be responsible for a criminal act if the act was due to a "mental disease or defect." Both of these standards, however, have been criticized as being too broad (Kolla & Brodie, 2012).

The *American Law Institute* (ALI) attempted to address this concern in 1955 by blending the M'Naghten and irresistible impulse concepts. The ALI recommended that a person could use an insanity defense if a mental disorder prevented him from knowing right from wrong or prevented him from being able to control his actions. The *American Psychiatric Association* (APA) in 1983 recommended paring the ALI definition to include only the first part (i.e., to the M'Naghten rule). Many states and the federal government use the APA distinction today though some states have eliminated the insanity defense altogether.

## Personal Narrative 3.1

### Kim Dude and the Wellness Resource Center

I began my student affairs career in residential life where my role was to encourage students to be successful by helping them make healthy, safe, and responsible decisions in all aspects of their lives. In 1990, I wrote a grant to the U.S. Department of Education to create an alcohol and drug abuse office and became the Director of ADAPT (Alcohol and Drug Abuse Prevention Team). In 1995, the mission of ADAPT expanded, and it became the Wellness Resource Center (WRC).

The students and staff of the Wellness Resource Center realize that one single approach or one single event is not sufficient in helping college students make responsible decisions concerning alcohol or other aspects of their health. Four theoretical models guide the WRC's prevention efforts: (1) responsible decision making, (2) social norming, (3) harm reduction, and (4) environmental management. It takes a comprehensive yearlong effort to have an impact on student behavior.

The responsible decision-making approach is used through peer educator presentations and major campus-wide events such as Alcohol Responsibility

Courtesy of Kim Dude

Kim Dude

Month, Safe Spring Break, Safe Holiday Break, and Wellness Month. The WRC challenges students to make informed, responsible decisions regarding all aspects of their health, and presents between 150 and 200 outreach programs per year.

The WRC implements a social norms approach. Social norms theory suggests that students' misperceptions and overestimations of their peers' alcohol and drug use increase problem behaviors and decrease healthy behaviors because students are acting in accordance with what they think is "normal." Our research on University of Missouri students indicates

a significant difference between student perceptions and the reality of peer alcohol and other drug use. By correcting misperceptions of the norm, the WRC has decreased problem behavior and seen an increase in healthy behavior. The WRC's social norming efforts are comprehensive and incorporate not only an extensive marketing campaign but also educational outreach programs and training.

A harm reduction approach accepts that students sometimes make risky choices and that it is important to create safety nets to keep them from hurting themselves or someone else. The WRC created and supports Project CHEERS, a designated-driver program in which more than 50 bars in Columbia give free soda to designated drivers. Additionally, the WRC provides an educational intervention called BASICS (Brief Alcohol Screening Intervention for College Students) for students caught in violation of the alcohol and drug policies of the university and/or for students who are concerned about their use. The program is composed of a two-hour interactive workshop and a one-hour individual follow-up session led by two Ph.D.-level counseling psychology graduate students.

---

▶ Indicated prevention targets individuals at very high risk for developing extensive problems in the future.

▶ Many prevention programs target children, adolescents, and young adults.

### REVIEW QUESTIONS

1.  What is prevention? What prevention programs are on your college campus?
2.  How might prevention be viewed along a continuum? What are advantages in doing so?
3.  Describe a primary, secondary, and tertiary prevention program for alcohol use disorder in college students. Who would these programs target?
4.  What are important features of prevention for mental disorders in college students?

### Final Comments

The diathesis-stress model is a useful way of thinking about various influences on mental disorders. Diatheses (predispositions) and stressors can be thought of as risk factors for mental disorders. Most mental disorders begin in adolescence or early adulthood when the burden of mental disorder is high. This highlights the need for early prevention efforts to address risk factors and thwart disorder development. Prevention programs are more efficient and cost-effective in the long run than traditional treatment because enormous costs related to disability and tertiary care can be lessened. We discuss effective treatments but also contemporary and personal approaches for preventing various psychological problems throughout this textbook. Examples include suggestions for reducing anxiety and sadness (Chapters 5 and 7), enhancing prenatal care to prevent

The WRC also takes an environmental management approach by actively working to influence the campus and community environment through the campus and community coalition called the Access to Alcohol Action Team. The Columbia Tobacco Prevention Initiative works with all three high schools in Columbia as well as Columbia College and Stephens College on the tobacco control issues. The WRC has also created two statewide coalitions called Missouri Partners In Prevention and Partners In Environmental Change, composed of the 13 state colleges and universities in Missouri. Both PIP and PIEC provide technical assistance, training, and programmatic support for the campus, and are funded by the Missouri Division of Alcohol and Drug Abuse.

My professional journey has been filled with many challenges. Our society glamorizes the misuse and abuse of alcohol through the media, movies, television, music, magazines, and even campus traditions. We have faced a long list of obstacles including the lack of power to make significant change, strong campus

organizations that revolve around alcohol, territory issues with other professionals, and the opinions that student alcohol abuse is simply a rite of passage. Additionally, because the WRC is more than 80 percent grant funded, securing and maintaining funding has been one of the biggest obstacles we have faced.

Another great challenge is trying to change the environment. The WRC cannot do this alone. As the saying states, "It takes a village to raise a child." Everyone in the community needs to be part of the solution: parents, law enforcement, community leaders, educators, business owners, etc. I am a product of the '60s, and I was taught that if you are not part of the solution, you are part of the problem. We all need to be part of the solution and help change laws, policies, and practices so that we have an environment that supports and encourages good decision making.

I am proud to say that the WRC has been successful over the years despite its obstacles and has been recognized as one of the top prevention programs in the country.

So much of our survival and our success is the result of a positive attitude and the desire to never give up. I want to share a story that I love. A woman was walking down a street in a large city past a construction site. She came across three construction workers and asked them each a simple question. "Excuse me sir, what are you doing?" The first man said he was laying bricks, the second man said he was building a wall, and the third man stated proudly that he was building a great cathedral. All three men were doing the same task and yet each viewed it differently. Ultimately, we are all playing a part in building a great cathedral. Some days we may feel like we are just laying bricks, but we are part of a much bigger picture. We are taking part in the great task of building a community that encourages and supports good decision making by all. My philosophy in life is embodied in this quote from Leon Joseph Cardinal Suenens: "Happy are those who dream dreams and are ready to pay the price to make them come true."

*Kim Dude was recognized by the U.S. Department of Education's Network: Addressing Collegiate Alcohol and Other Drug Issues as the recipient of the Outstanding Contribution to the Field award in 2003. Kim has also been honored by the Phoenix Programs in Columbia, Missouri, with the Buck Buchanan Lifetime Service Award for her prevention efforts.*

intellectual disability (Chapter 13), and improving memory to limit cognitive decline (Chapter 14). We turn our attention in Chapter 4 to methods used by mental health professionals to assess, diagnose, classify, and study mental disorders. This discussion will further provide the foundation for understanding the mental disorders we discuss in Chapters 5 through 14.

## Key Terms

diathesis  53
etiology  54
epidemiology  54
epidemiologists  54
incidence  54
prevalence  54
lifetime prevalence  54
comorbidity  56
cohort effects  57
risk factor  59

protective factors  61
resilience  62
prevention  64
primary prevention  66
universal prevention  66
secondary prevention  66
selective prevention  66
tertiary prevention  67
indicated prevention  67

## Media Resources

### MindTap

MindTap for Kearney and Trull's *Abnormal Psychology and Life: A Dimensional Approach* is a highly personalized fully online learning platform of authoritative content, assignments, and services offering you a tailored presentation of course curriculum created by your instructor. MindTap guides you through the course curriculum via an innovative learning path where you will complete reading assignments, annotate your readings, complete homework, and engage with quizzes and assessments. MindTap includes the Continuum Video Project.

Go to **cengagebrain.com** to access MindTap.

# 4

# Diagnosis, Assessment, and Study of Mental Disorders

## CASE: *Professor Smith*

**What Do You Think?**

Defining Abnormal Behavior and Mental Disorder
Interim Summary
Review Questions

Classifying and Assessing Abnormal Behavior and Mental Disorder
Interim Summary
Review Questions

Culture and Clinical Assessment
Interim Summary
Review Questions

Studying Abnormal Behavior and Mental Disorder
Interim Summary
Review Questions

FINAL COMMENTS

KEY TERMS

MEDIA RESOURCES

## SPECIAL FEATURES

BOX 4.1 | Focus on Diversity: Culture and Diagnosis   77

PERSONAL NARRATIVE 4.1 Anonymous   78

BOX 4.2 | Focus on Law and Ethics: Who Should Be Studied in Mental Health Research?   94

## CASE: Professor Smith

Forty-five-year-old **Professor Smith** could not understand what had been happening to him over the past 6 months. He had been experiencing strange sensations throughout his body, including chest pains and headaches. He felt short of breath, light-headed, shaky, and hot throughout his chest and arms during these episodes. These symptoms came on abruptly, sometimes even during sleep, but ended within 15 minutes. Professor

Studio 101/Alamy

Smith had a number of recent setbacks, including denial for promotion to full professor, so this was the last thing he needed.

What could be wrong? Professor Smith had several medical tests to rule out heart problems, a brain tumor, and other maladies. His physician reassured him nothing was medically wrong, but the symptoms persisted. Professor Smith found it harder to concentrate on his work and his career seemed to be on hold. Despite looming deadlines, he struggled to read books and journals and could not concentrate long enough to write a paragraph. His teaching was suffering as well, and he cancelled several classes because of his physical symptoms.

Professor Smith felt he needed to know what was happening but had no clear answer. Even worse, these symptoms and problems at work were creating a strain on his family and friendships. Those who cared about him wanted to help but had trouble doing so because Professor Smith became more isolated, frustrated, and depressed. This

depression seemed to worsen recently as he had trouble sleeping, felt fatigued much of the day, and lost 20 pounds. Finally, he agreed to see a clinical psychologist after constant pleas from his wife and at the suggestion of his physician. He was skeptical, but what harm could it do at this point?

### What Do You Think?

1. Is Professor Smith's behavior abnormal? Do you think he has a mental disorder?

2. Do you know anyone with problems like Professor Smith's?

3. What other information about his condition would be useful to know?

4. What do you think would be the best way to find out more about his problems? Do you think interviews, psychological evaluations, or other medical tests would help?

5. What kind of treatment might give Professor Smith some relief?

## Defining Abnormal Behavior and Mental Disorder

Professor Smith's case illustrates how certain symptoms can limit someone's ability to live comfortably, maintain a career, and even talk to others. These symptoms are indeed quite distressing to him and seem out of the ordinary. Professor Smith has consulted a psychologist to find out what is wrong and what can be done to help. What do mental health professionals do when they address people with mental disorder? Mental health professionals define, classify, assess, and study mental disorders; we discuss these endeavors in this chapter, starting with definition.

### Dimensions and Categories

Mental health professionals often focus on **dimensions** and **categories** to define abnormal behavior and mental disorder. A *dimensional approach* refers to defining abnormal behavior along a continuum or spectrum. Recall three definitions of abnormal behavior from Chapter 1: (1) behavior that deviates from the norm, (2) behavior associated with

difficulty adapting to life's demands, and (3) behavior accompanied by personal distress. Each definition lies on a continuum. Some behaviors deviate a little from the norm and involve slight adaptation problems or distress, and some behaviors deviate substantially from the norm and involve significant adaptation problems and distress. Recall from Chapter 2 how Mariella's symptoms of depression reflected to some extent a normal reaction to being separated from family and friends but also that some of her depressive symptoms seemed problematic. Recall from Chapter 3 our discussion of mild, moderate, and severe intensity of symptoms. These examples show abnormal behavior on a continuum or from a dimensional perspective.

One way to think about abnormal behavior from a dimensional perspective is to consider its many forms. Abnormal behavior actually consists of *emotional states*, *cognitive styles* or ways of thinking, and *physical behavior*. We can view each form along a continuum or dimensional perspective. Professor Smith experiences *emotional* sadness, *cognitive* worry, and *behavioral* avoidance. His symptoms are severe, but all of us become sad and worrisome and avoid things from time to time. We show emotions, thoughts, and behaviors along a spectrum of intensity or oddity.

A different way of defining abnormal behavior or mental disorder is a *categorical approach*. A category is a large class of frequently observed syndromes (mental disorders) composed of abnormal behaviors or features that occur in a person. Many chapters in this book represent broad categories of mental disorder, such as anxiety, depressive, psychotic, personality, developmental, and neurocognitive disorders.

Depression is a widely recognized syndrome or mental disorder that often includes sad mood, sleep and appetite disturbance, and suicidal thoughts. A certain number of symptoms must be present from a categorical perspective before a person's behavior can be considered abnormal—for depression, five of nine main symptoms must be present. Someone with only three or four symptoms of depression would not be considered to have a mental disorder. A **diagnosis** from a categorical perspective is defined by rules that outline how many and what features of a mental disorder must be present.

The categorical approach can be thought of as a "yes–no" approach: One either has or does not have a mental disorder. The approach is derived from a medical model that makes sense when you consider a disease such as measles. We can guarantee you either have measles right now or you do not (pick one!). A "yes–no" approach works well for physical disorders but perhaps less well for mental disorders. Imagine if someone visited a psychologist and complained of sad mood, trouble sleeping, suicidal thoughts, and no other symptoms. This person has *no mental disorder* from a strict categorical perspective because not enough symptoms of depression are evident. But doesn't the person have a problem that should be treated?

We have indicated throughout this textbook that we can best view abnormal behavior along a continuum. Still, many mental health professionals adopt a common categorical approach to classifying mental disorder, and we describe this approach next. Our approach throughout this textbook will be to organize mental disorders by general categories but explain the dimensional aspects of each category in detail.

## DSM

A categorical approach to mental disorder commonly used in the United States and much of the world is the *Diagnostic and Statistical Manual of Mental Disorders (DSM*; American Psychiatric Association [APA], 2013). General features of mental disorder according to the *DSM* include the following:

- A group of emotional, cognitive, or behavioral symptoms, called a **syndrome**, that occur within a person.

- These symptoms are usually associated with emotional distress or disability (impairment) in life activities.

- The syndrome is not simply an expected or culturally approved response to a specific event, such as grief and sadness following death of a loved one.

- The symptoms are considered to reflect dysfunction in psychological, biological, or developmental processes.

A syndrome (or mental disorder or diagnosis) includes a group of abnormal behaviors or number of symptoms *associated with* distress, significant work or interpersonal problems, or likelihood of future problems. Recall Ricardo and Yoko from Chapter 1 who had symptoms of anxiety. Ricardo qualified for a *DSM* diagnosis of social phobia because his symptoms interfered with daily functioning. Yoko's anxiety symptoms, however, were not accompanied by significant impairment in daily functioning, and so she did not qualify for a diagnosis.

This description of syndrome or mental disorder incorporates definitions of abnormal behavior from Chapter 1 and this chapter. The description focuses on behavior that deviates from the norm, behavior associated with difficulty adapting to life's demands, and behavior accompanied by distress. The *DSM* definition of mental disorder is restrictive because it focuses on *clusters* of abnormal behaviors associated with distress or disability. Several abnormal behaviors must be present at the same time *and* cause significant problems for someone to qualify for a diagnosis of a mental disorder.

## Advantages of Diagnosis

Several advantages do exist regarding diagnoses, however. A primary advantage of diagnosis is *communication*—a wealth of information can be conveyed in a single term. A colleague once referred a person with a diagnosis of schizophrenia to one of your authors, Tim. A symptom pattern immediately came to Tim's mind even though he knew nothing about the person: delusions, hallucinations, severe social/occupational dysfunction, and continuous symptoms for at least 6 months. You can think of a diagnosis as "verbal shorthand" for describing features of a mental disorder. We do not have to ask so many questions about a person's symptoms when we know his or her diagnosis.

A second advantage of diagnosis is that standard rules are provided for defining mental disorders and for seeking the cause of these disorders. We must group people based on symptoms they share to study the cause of a mental disorder. Important comparisons between groups can then be made about developmental characteristics, personality features, performance on experimental tasks, or other variables that could shed light on risk factors and cause. We mentioned in Chapter 3 that childhood sexual maltreatment is a risk factor for borderline personality disorder. A reliable and systematic way of defining borderline personality disorder was necessary first, however, to even reach this conclusion. Use of diagnoses assists this process.

A third advantage of diagnosis is that, because everyone uses the same system, clinicians can find useful assessment strategies, such as questionnaires for depression, and researchers can examine prevalence rates of a certain mental disorder at local, state, and national levels. Managed care agencies also rely on diagnostic codes to reimburse people for mental health services. Diagnoses are most important because *they may suggest which treatment is most effective*. A diagnosis of schizophrenia, for example, suggests that antipsychotic medication is likely to be more effective than psychodynamic therapy. More than one treatment is often effective for mental disorders, however.

Diagnoses thus serve many useful functions, and researchers and practitioners commonly use them to understand mental disorder. Laypeople also use diagnoses to understand what is wrong. If you were diagnosed with a strange-sounding disease, you would likely "Google" it to get more information. Diagnoses also ease the sense of uniqueness or loneliness people feel when something is wrong. Professor Smith learned his condition was called "panic disorder" and that the problem can be successfully treated. How do you think he felt once he learned this?

## INTERIM SUMMARY

► Mental health professionals often focus on dimensions and categories to define abnormal behavior and mental disorder.

► A dimensional approach refers to defining abnormal behavior along a continuum.

► A category is a large class of frequently observed syndromes or mental disorders.

► A diagnosis is defined by rules that outline how many and what features of a mental disorder must be present.

► Mental disorder from the *DSM* categorical approach involves a group of abnormal behaviors associated with distress or disability.

► Advantages of diagnosis include enhanced communication, improved definition and understanding of mental disorder, coordinated research, and ideas about which treatment is likely to be most effective for a given disorder.

## REVIEW QUESTIONS

1. What is it about Professor Smith's behavior and symptoms that led his therapist to diagnose him with a mental disorder?
2. Which general features of the *DSM* definition of mental disorder are highlighted in Professor Smith's case?
3. Why do you think the *DSM* definition of mental disorder requires the presence of significant distress or disability?
4. How might diagnosis allow mental health professionals to communicate about Professor Smith's problems, study what caused his problems, and determine what treatment might be effective for him?

## Classifying and Assessing Abnormal Behavior and Mental Disorder

Recall that mental health professionals define, classify, assess, and study mental disorders. We have discussed definition. **Classification** is next and refers to arranging mental disorders into broad categories or classes based on similar features. The *DSM* is a primary method of classification that was recently revised (*DSM-5*; APA, 2013) to update criteria and research-based information about mental disorders listed in the manual. As a result, some material in the chapters will have occasional references to the previous *DSM* version, the *DSM-IV* (APA, 2000).

Some of the diagnostic categories discussed in this textbook may be familiar to you because of their prevalence and media coverage. You may have heard a lot about anxiety, depression, attention-deficit/hyperactivity disorder, Alzheimer's disease, alcohol use disorder, and anorexia nervosa. Other diagnoses may be less familiar to you, such as somatic symptom disorder and paraphilic disorders. Researchers have studied these disorders in one form or another for decades and the disorders are often the focus of clinical attention because of their prevalence and severity.

The *DSM-5* relies on categories to organize mental disorder but also encourages clinicians to use dimensional assessments in addition to diagnoses. Recall that "dimensional" means viewing behavior or symptoms along a continuum. One type of dimensional assessment might include ratings of a person's symptoms as mild, moderate, or severe in intensity. Another dimensional assessment could involve a person's degree of insight into, or recognition of, his mental condition. Dimensional assessments allow clinicians to consider fluctuations in symptoms, to track a client's progress in therapy, and to evaluate all of a client's symptoms, not simply those that are part of an assigned diagnosis. Other types of dimensional assessments are discussed throughout the textbook.

How might such a categorical and dimensional approach work for Professor Smith? Professor Smith's therapist assigned two diagnoses based on his symptoms. The primary diagnosis (initial focus of treatment) was panic disorder. Professor Smith's "episodes" suggest he has periodic panic attacks with chest pain, shaking, breathlessness, hot flashes, and light-headedness (Chapter 5). These attacks are recurrent and unexpected, and Professor Smith has been concerned about additional attacks and their implications ("Am I having a heart attack?"). Professor Smith also received a diagnosis of major depressive disorder (Chapter 7). He has had sad mood, insomnia, difficulty concentrating, fatigue, weight loss, and poor appetite for more than 2 weeks. These symptoms characterize depression.

Professor Smith's therapist also used dimensional assessments. One type of dimensional assessment involved symptom intensity ratings along a continuum (i.e., mild, moderate, severe). For example, some of Professor Smith's anxiety and depressive symptoms were mild to moderate in nature. These included his headaches and sad mood. In contrast, some of his anxiety and depressive symptoms were severe in nature. These included his shortness of breath, light-headedness, trouble sleeping, and fatigue.

Another dimensional assessment involved the impact of Professor Smith's symptoms on different areas of his life. Professor Smith's symptoms such as his inability to concentrate or finish projects had the greatest negative impact on his career. His symptoms also had some impact on his marriage, but his wife was supportive of him during this difficult time. These dimensional assessments allowed the therapist to concentrate treatment first on those symptoms that caused Professor Smith the most amount of distress and that seemed most urgent. You can see that a dimensional approach adds substantial information to a simple diagnosis. We continue to emphasize this dimensional approach as we discuss mental disorders throughout this textbook.

## BOX 4.1  Focus on Diversity

### Culture and Diagnosis

Culture impacts our thoughts, personal perspectives and worldviews, emotional expression, and behavior. Culture must be considered when a person is evaluated for psychological problems, and mental health professionals must be aware of their own biases when they evaluate people of other cultures. What may be considered unusual in one culture may not be in another culture. Consider Gusti A., a 34-year-old Indonesian man:

As a student he was often sick and pondered on life and why one suffered sickness and death. He was puzzled as to the meaning of life and death. He spent a lot of his time alone in his room trying to solve these problems. Then he found he could not sleep and his condition got worse to the point that he rarely went to classes or tried to study or even bothered to look after himself properly. His friends became concerned about his condition and wondered if he was going mad. Then one of his friends found him talking to himself and thought he had finally gone crazy. His friend took him home because he was afraid something would happen to him if he were left alone. His condition continued for over six months, and then he began to have strange experiences. One day he was walking with a friend who suddenly collapsed unconscious in front of him. Feeling a strong desire to help his friend, Gusti A. placed his hand on the unconscious man's head and tried to transfer energy to him. He then instructed his friend to wake up, and he did. Gusti A. was not sure if his friend had recovered as a result of his action or not, but he tried to test his ability to heal others. He also had various premonitions that proved accurate, such as seeing in his mind an accident at the university before it happened, and feeling worried about his grandmother and shortly afterwards discovering she was seriously ill. He was finally convinced he did possess special powers and believed his grandfather, father, and cousin had similar abilities. He began to learn from books about spiritual healing and began to use his inner power to heal people (Stephen & Suryani, 2000, p. 19).

Gusti A.'s beliefs and behaviors may seem quite unusual or even evident of a serious mental disorder like schizophrenia. But people like Gusti A. are viewed as traditional healers (the *balian*) in Bali, Indonesia. Many anthropologists and cross-cultural psychiatrists and psychologists argue that states of consciousness, beliefs, and behaviors of these traditional healers are distinct from behaviors that characterize mental disorders such as schizophrenia or dissociative disorder. Stephen and Suryani (2000) noted that this case might be mistakenly diagnosed as mental disorder by those not culturally informed. Gusti A. successfully completed his university studies, his own personal distress ended once he realized he had special abilities to heal others, and he is a respected and well-functioning member of the community. Stephen and Suryani suggested that becoming a *balian* is like a religious conversion rather than a sign of serious psychosis or dissociation associated with a *DSM*-defined mental disorder.

The *DSM-5* includes a Cultural Formulation Interview to help mental health professionals gain information about how a person's culture may affect his symptoms and treatment (APA, 2013). Questions surround how a person understands and explains his condition, what social stressors and supports he may have, whether his cultural background or identity affects his symptoms, what cultural factors may influence his ability to cope and to seek help, and concerns about his therapist or the mental health setting. Mental health professionals are also encouraged to be aware of how a person's culture can influence risk factors and the course of a disorder (Kleinman, 2012).

## Assessing Abnormal Behavior and Mental Disorder

Defining and classifying mental disorder are important tasks that involve detailed clinical assessment. **Clinical assessment** involves evaluating a person's strengths and weaknesses and understanding the problem at hand to develop a treatment (Trull & Prinstein, 2013). This may include providing a diagnosis for the person. We describe in this next section assessment procedures implemented in clinics, hospitals, and offices of mental health professionals.

The clinical assessment process begins with a *referral*. Someone—perhaps a parent, teacher, spouse, friend, judge, or a person himself—asks a question: "Why is Samantha struggling at her job?" "Why are my child's moods so unstable?" "Why do I feel anxious all the time?" "Why does Professor Smith keep canceling his classes?" People may then be referred to a therapist who might provide a *DSM-5* diagnosis but who will also examine emotional, cognitive, personality, and biological issues that must be addressed. Mental health professionals try to understand precisely what a client seeks or needs and use a wide array of procedures and measures to do so.

### Anonymous

I glanced at the clock on the opposite wall, taking a break from staring at a worn patch in the carpet near my feet. It was nearly 5 P.M.; the last time I looked up was about 1 P.M. My only motivation was to determine where we were in the rhythm of the day, to see how much longer I had to bear before I could retreat to my room. There, my eyes heavy from sleeping pills and emotional exhaustion, I could succumb to the only thing that brought relief from my depression: sleep. It had not taken me long to discover that the most time-consuming activity on psychiatric units was doing nothing other than waiting for something to happen. Waiting to see your psychiatrist. Your social worker. Your nurse. Waiting for a therapy group. For art therapy. Pet therapy (if you're lucky). Waiting for a shower. To brush your teeth. Waiting for morning meds. Afternoon meds. Evening meds. Night meds. Breakfast. Lunch. Dinner. How did I get here?

My depression during my sophomore year in college was not my first episode. I had gone through periods of depression twice during high school, received antidepressant treatment and counseling, and recovered. I took having a depressive disorder seriously and was diligent about seeking and getting help. I did not share my condition with other people, but I did not feel stigmatized. In an age of depressed Zoloft balls bouncing on the TV screen, depression seemed common in society. A little like having mild asthma or high blood pressure. I never thought of myself as someone who was truly "sick"—I saved that term for people with schizophrenia or bipolar disorder, people I assumed spent most of their lives in secluded state institutions, receiving antipsychotics and getting "shock therapy." If someone suggested I would know someday what it's like to be in a hospital, to take a plethora of drugs, and to be considered severely and chronically disordered, I would have found the notion bizarre and comical, if not impossible. That was not me.

Near the end of my sophomore year, I noticed some familiar feelings that, in the past, heralded depression. Over the course of a few weeks, I lost my appetite. Things I normally found engaging—reading, being with friends, participating in groups on campus—had no allure. I lacked the concentration to read more than a page or two or even follow a conversation. As my mood sunk, family and friends became concerned. I became increasingly depressed and despondent over a matter of weeks, and even though I recognized the symptoms and was educated about treatments, I did not want to admit that I was experiencing a relapse of the disorder I thought had ended with my adolescence.

Ultimately, a close friend realized what was happening. Fearing for my safety, he made an urgent appointment with a local psychiatrist; I did not have the energy to protest. The psychiatrist spoke with me about my history, my current symptoms and thoughts of suicide, and determined that I needed to be hospitalized. My recollections of this decision, my admission, and the first few days in the hospital are foggy. My primary emotional response was shock and bewilderment, tempered only by the deadening apathy that engulfed my mood. I couldn't quite get my head around how things had gotten "this far." I was on a locked unit with severely disordered men and women, many acutely psychotic. I was watched constantly by an aide, denied access to my shoelaces, and allowed to make calls only from a phone in the "day room." But despite the indignities and trauma of this experience, I can say now it saved my life. I was discharged after a few weeks, not completely over my depression but on the way to feeling well again. I had started treatment and begun to feel optimistic about my future. Within a month of getting back to school, I truly

## Reliability, Validity, and Standardization

An important expectation of mental health professionals is that they use assessment measures that are strong psychometrically. This means the measures should be reliable, valid, and standardized. We discuss each of these concepts separately.

### RELIABILITY

**Reliability** refers to consistency of scores or responses. Three main ways of evaluating reliability include *test–retest, interrater,* and *internal consistency reliability* (see **Table 4.1**). Each type of reliability is used to examine consistency of assessment data. **Test–retest reliability** is the extent to which a person provides similar answers to the same test items across time. If Karl provides different scores on the same anxiety questionnaire on two consecutive Mondays, then the data may not be very useful. If we interview someone and find that her diagnosis changes

**Table 4.1**

**Types of Reliability for Psychological Tests and Structured Interviews**

| Type of reliability | Definition |
|---|---|
| Test–retest reliability | Consistency of test scores or diagnoses across some period of time |
| Interrater reliability | Agreement between two or more raters or judges about level of a trait or presence/absence of a feature or diagnosis |
| Internal consistency reliability | Relationship among test items that measure the same variable |

felt all this sadness and strife was behind me, and I never imagined that things could become even more challenging and complicated.

Right before my junior year I experienced symptoms that, unlike those during my depressions, I did not find troubling. I was always someone who needed a good 9 hours of sleep to feel well rested, but I started getting by on dramatically less. Some nights I would not touch the bed (if I was even home), other nights I would fall asleep for 2 or 3 hours and then jolt awake, energized and ready to go. My waking hours became filled with frenzied activity—I never felt smarter, more able, or more confident. My thinking was swift and sharp and seemed to reach near superhuman perfection. These feelings continued, but the ecstasy soon devolved into agitation. Every annoyance seemed like a concerted, even conspiratorial, effort to thwart my plans. When my psychiatrist saw me in his office, he knew immediately what was wrong. I was experiencing a manic episode. An ambulance was called and I was brought to the hospital. I was enraged and scared at the same time, but eventually acquiesced to treatment. New medications—antipsychotics and mood stabilizers this time—were used to control my mood.

Most of my symptoms abated within a few weeks, but the medications left me sedated and feeling somewhat dull. New medications for a new diagnosis: bipolar I disorder.

I came away from this traumatic experience dismayed and disheartened, my self-image shattered. I had already come to terms with being a "psychiatric patient" and acknowledged that my first hospitalization was necessary (although at the time I had no doubt it would be my last). But during my first manic episode, I was "publicly" sick in a way I hadn't been before. I was embarrassed and humiliated. Being told I had a disorder only "other people" got—"other people" being unfortunates who lived their lives in drug-induced stupors in institutions or group homes—compounded my feelings of defeat.

As I recovered, I reevaluated some of these feelings and saw things more realistically. I also met other young adults, through a support group, who struggled with the same disorder. It was enlightening and heartening to hear many of their stories, and they provided invaluable advice and support. My ideas as to what it meant to have a mental disorder shifted largely as a result of these conversations, allowing me to approach my own situation with more hope and strength.

I began to see medications and therapy as my toolbox for maintaining a stable life in which I could achieve my goals. This involved tinkering to find the best combination of medicines and trade-offs in terms of putting up with some side effects if my overall health was good.

Coming to terms with having bipolar disorder and learning how to effectively take care of myself has been a process of peaks and valleys. After 3 years of feeling well, I relapsed and experienced episodes of mania and depression. Both required hospitalization and medication changes. Experiencing relapse after a few years of feeling great was a wake-up call. I secretly felt I was somehow "past" that sort of thing. Since then I've tried to be optimistic while still recognizing I have a chronic disorder, and the chance of having more episodes in the future is very high. Thankfully, when I am stable, I have no lingering symptoms. My goal is no longer to avoid getting sick again but to keep myself stable and healthy for as long a stretch as possible. Despite my disorder, I've graduated college and entered graduate school. I've had lasting and meaningful relationships. I live on my own and have traveled widely. My disorder hasn't defined my life, and despite the inevitable challenges ahead, I don't believe it ever will.

*Used with permission.*

from week to week, this would demonstrate poor test–retest reliability for the interview. Recall that Professor Smith received a primary diagnosis of panic disorder. If he came back the next week for a follow-up interview and no longer met criteria for panic disorder, how useful would this interview be? Panic disorder does not come and go this rapidly.

Test–retest reliability is important, but the consistency of scores or diagnoses will naturally diminish as time between test and retest grows longer. This may reflect actual change. Professor Smith may not meet criteria for panic disorder 2 years from now, but this may reflect the fact that he received treatment and no longer shows symptoms of the disorder.

**Interrater reliability** is the extent to which two raters or observers agree about their ratings or judgments of a person's behavior. Interrater reliability is often used to examine the usefulness of a diagnostic interview. Two mental health

professionals may give Professor Smith the same diagnostic interview on the same day and arrive at the same diagnosis. This would reflect good interrater reliability.

**Internal consistency reliability** refers to whether items on a test appear to be measuring the same thing. You would expect items on a test of anxiety to generally relate to one another. If they do not, then the items may not be measuring the same thing or may be measuring something else. Some child self-report measures of anxiety have been criticized for measuring depression more than anxiety. For us to consider them useful, test items should have high internal consistency reliability.

## VALIDITY

**Validity** is the extent to which an assessment technique measures what it is supposed to measure. Key types of validity include *content, predictive, concurrent,* and *construct validity*

## Table 4.2

| **Common Types of Validity** | |
|---|---|
| Type of validity | Definition |
| Content validity | How well test or interview items adequately measure various aspects of a variable, construct, or diagnosis |
| Predictive validity | How well test scores or diagnoses predict and correlate with behavior or test scores that are observed or obtained at some future point |
| Concurrent validity | How well test scores or diagnoses correlate with a related but independent set of test scores or behaviors |
| Construct validity | How well test scores or diagnoses correlate with other measures or behaviors in a logical and theoretically consistent way |

(see **Table 4.2**). **Content validity** is the degree to which test or interview items actually cover aspects of the variable or diagnosis under study. If a test of depression contained items only about sad mood, the test would not have high content validity because depression also involves problematic thinking patterns and withdrawn behavior.

**Predictive validity** refers to whether test or interview results accurately predict some *future* behavior or event. A test of school success has good predictive validity if current scores relate to children's school achievement 2 years from now. **Concurrent validity** refers to whether current test or interview results relate to an important *present* feature or characteristic. A child's diagnosis of conduct disorder should reflect his current level of misbehavior.

**Construct validity** refers to whether test or interview results relate to other measures or behaviors in a logical, theoretically expected fashion. Recall DeShawn's impulsivity and alcohol problems from Chapter 3. A valid test of impulsivity might be expected to correlate with a diagnosis of alcohol use disorder, school or work problems, and lower levels of the neurotransmitter serotonin. If this test does so, then we can be more confident in its construct validity. If people with problems similar to DeShawn's scored high on this test of impulsivity, this would also support the test's construct validity.

## STANDARDIZATION

**Standardization** refers to administering or conducting assessment measures in the same way for everyone. When you took the SAT or ACT, you may have noticed all the rules and guidelines for administering, scoring, and interpreting the test. Proctors gave the test in a standardized or similar way for all high school students in the country.

Assessment measures can be standardized in several ways. First, the same test items and testing procedures, such as time limits or item order, can be used for everyone. Second, the way the test is scored can be the same for everyone. Everyone's SAT verbal scores are based on the same scoring system. Third, our interpretation of test scores can be standardized by collecting normative data from large groups of people across age, gender, and race. Test scores can thus be compared among members of these groups. Scores obtained by a 25-year-old Latina student, for example, can be compared with typical scores obtained by Latina students in this age range. We can then interpret these scores by seeing whether they are higher or lower than average scores obtained by members of the appropriate normative group.

Reliability, validity, and standardization are important for developing and refining clinical assessment techniques. We next explore different methods of clinical assessment. We begin with a discussion of *interviews,* which mental health professionals use to gather information about a person's concerns, symptoms, and history.

## Interview

The interview is the most common assessment technique and is used to solicit a wide range of information about mental disorders. Interviewers often ask questions about the frequency and nature of symptoms of different mental disorders. Interview questions also focus on events or experiences that preceded symptom onset, such as child maltreatment or death of a parent. Interviews have a range of applications and can be easily adapted to match a person's situation.

Interviews differ in two key ways. First, interviews differ with respect to *purpose.* The purpose of one interview may be to evaluate the history and concerns of a person seeking psychological help for the first time, but another interview might focus solely on *DSM-5* diagnoses. Second, interviews may be *unstructured* or *structured.* **Unstructured interviews** allow an interviewer to ask any question that comes to mind in any order. This type of interview is often unreliable because two clinicians evaluating the same person may arrive at different ideas of what is happening. **Structured interviews** require an interviewer to ask standardized questions in a specified sequence. Interviewers ask people the same questions, so two clinicians who evaluate the same person are more likely to arrive at the same diagnosis or conclusion.

Several structured diagnostic interviews are available. The *Structured Clinical Interview* (SCID-I; First, Spitzer, Gibbon, & Williams, 2002) is a popular structured diagnostic interview for major mental disorders. The SCID-I gives clear instructions to the interviewer about what questions to ask and in what order to ask them. Structured interviews like the SCID-I standardize questions to be asked and help interviewers obtain relevant information. Structured interviews are available for various mental disorders as well as many psychological and other variables such as personality and family history of mental disorder.

The clinical interview is the most commonly used assessment technique.

Diagnoses and ratings from structured diagnostic interviews are generally reliable across raters and have high content validity because they are based on specific criteria. Many structured interviews appear to have high construct validity as well. Structured interview diagnoses or ratings usually relate to scores and ratings from other psychological, behavioral, or biological tests in expected ways.

A disadvantage of structured diagnostic interviews is the time necessary to administer and score them. These interviews are comprehensive and can take several hours to conduct. In many clinical settings, clients are seen for only an hour at a time and often for only a few sessions, so these interviews may be less attractive as assessment devices. Structured diagnostic interviews are thus particularly common to research settings.

## Intelligence Tests

**Intelligence tests** are probably the most common form of clinical assessment after the interview. Intelligence tests assess cognitive functioning and provide estimates of a person's intellectual ability. Mental health professionals are interested in assessing cognitive processes such as memory, language, comprehension, reasoning, and speed with which we process and interpret information. Many people associate intelligence tests with assessment of learning disorder and brain dysfunction,

but information provided by these tests can also be used to understand symptoms of mental disorders such as schizophrenia or depression.

Most intelligence tests include multiple *subscales* or *subtests* to measure specific aspects of cognitive functioning such as memory, arithmetic, mastery of general information, or visual-perceptual organization. Some subtests require a person to answer direct questions, but other subtests require people to complete tasks or solve problems. Scores on these subtests are typically combined and compared to normative data from people of similar age and gender. This form of standardization allows an individual's scores to be interpreted as low, average, or high.

The *Wechsler Adult Intelligence Scale—Fourth Edition* (WAIS-IV) (Wechsler, 2008) is one of the most popular intelligence tests. Items regarding a particular domain such as arithmetic are placed in one section (subtest) and arranged in order of increasing difficulty. Item scores from each subtest are converted to *scaled scores*, which represent standardized scores within an age group. Scaled scores are added to derive *intelligence quotients* (IQs), which are general measures of intellectual functioning. Several WAIS-IV subtests are described in **Table 4.3** and a simulated WAIS-IV item is illustrated in **Figure 4.1**.

Intelligence quotients often include *full-scale, performance,* and *verbal* IQs. The full-scale IQ may be most familiar to you; it gives an estimate of overall intellectual ability. Verbal IQ specifically represents use and comprehension of language, and performance IQ specifically represents spatial reasoning. Individual IQs are calculated in relation to normative data. The score of a 20-year-old male, for example, is compared with the scores of other 20-year-old males. To make scores easier to interpret, the mean for each age group is 100; this makes the IQ scale consistent across age groups.

Intelligence test scores can give mental health professionals a sense of a person's strengths and weaknesses. This information is important for diagnosing, assessing, and treating psychological problems. Some disorders, such as Alzheimer's

### Table 4.3

| Simulated Examples of Wechsler Adult Intelligence Scale Subtests | |
|---|---|
| Vocabulary | The examinee must define words. For example, "What does the word *impede* mean?" |
| Similarities | The examinee must explain how two objects are alike. For example, "How are a *wheel* and *ski* alike?" |
| Digit span | Two lists of digits are read aloud by the examiner. For the first list, the examinee must repeat the digits in the order they were read. For example, "2-8-3-9-6." For the second list, the digits must be repeated backward. |

Source: Wechsler (2008).

**FIGURE 4.1 SIMULATED ITEM FROM THE WAIS-IV PICTURE COMPLETION SUBTEST:** Can you find what's missing in this picture? *Simulated items similar to those found in the* Wechsler Adult Intelligence Scale, *Fourth Edition (WAIS-IV). Copyright © 2008 NCS Pearson, Inc. Reproduced with permission. All rights reserved. "Wechsler Adult Intelligence Scale" and "WAIS" are trademarks, in the United States and/or other countries, of Pearson Education, Inc. or its affiliates.*

disease, are defined primarily by cognitive deficits that may be assessed by intelligence tests. Other disorders have cognitive and behavioral features that intelligence tests can at least tap. Intelligence tests are therefore administered to many clients in clinical and research settings.

Intelligence test scores must be interpreted with caution. IQ scores do not indicate how smart a person is but rather how well she is likely to do in future academic work. Most intelligence tests focus on verbal and spatial ability, but do not measure other forms of competence such as social skill, creativity, and mechanical ability. Intelligence tests have also been criticized for bias because people across cultures think differently. A test that is completely "culture-free" has not been developed, but researchers have identified nonverbal intelligence subtests (e.g., digit span) that may be "culture-fair" because scores do not differ much between ethnic groups (Sattler, 2008; Shuttleworth-Edwards, Donnelly, Reid, & Radloff, 2004).

## Personality Assessment

A clinical assessment measure that may be more familiar to you is personality assessment. **Personality assessment** refers to instruments that measure different traits or aspects of our character. Most of us could name or describe at least one

personality or psychological test based on what we have read in books or seen on television shows or films. Many of us have seen a movie or television show that portrayed the "inkblot test" as a measure of personality. Thousands of other personality assessment measures are available, however. These can be divided into objective and projective tests.

### OBJECTIVE PERSONALITY MEASURES

**Objective personality measures** involve administering a standard set of questions or statements to which a person responds using set options. Objective tests often use a *true/false* or *yes/no* response format, but others provide a *dimensional scale* such as 0 = *strongly disagree*, 1 = *disagree*, 2 = *neutral*, 3 = *agree*, and 4 = *strongly agree*. Self-report, paper-and-pencil questionnaires are popular objective tests of general or limited aspects of personality, and many types are discussed throughout this textbook. Examples include the *Social Phobia and Anxiety Inventory* (Chapter 5) and *Beck Depression Inventory* (Chapter 7). These questionnaires are economical, impartial, simple to administer and score, and more reliable and standardized than other assessment methods.

We briefly illustrate here the *Minnesota Multiphasic Personality Inventory—2* (MMPI-2), which clinicians have used for more than 60 years and which is still considered the most important general personality questionnaire (Butcher, 2011; Tellegen et al., 2003). Thousands of studies using the MMPI/MMPI-2 have been published (Graham, 2005), and scores from the scale have been used to measure everything from psychosis to marriage suitability.

The developers of the original MMPI believed the content of a test item mattered less than whether people with the same mental disorder endorsed the same items. Do people with depression endorse the item "I like mechanics magazines" more so than people without depression? If so, then the item might appear on a scale of depression. An item that does not appear on the surface to be related to depression may thus become an item on the depression scale.

The MMPI-2 includes 567 items to which a person answers "True," "False," or "Cannot Say." The MMPI-2 can be administered to people aged 13 years or older, to those who can read at an eighth-grade level, and to individuals or groups. An adolescent version (MMPI-A) is also available (Ben-Porath, Graham, Archer, Tellegen, & Kaemmer, 2006; Williams & Butcher, 2011). The MMPI-2 is usually computer-scored.

A potential problem with questionnaires such as the MMPI-2 is susceptibility to distortion. Some people might wish to place themselves in a favorable light, and others may "fake bad" to receive aid, sympathy, or a military discharge. Other people tend to agree with almost any item regardless of content. If a mental health professional is unaware of these response styles in a given client, the test can be misinterpreted. The following **MMPI-2 validity scales** are used to detect people who are trying to look a certain way or who are defensive or careless when taking the test:

1. *? (cannot say) scale*: This is the number of items left unanswered.
2. *F (infrequency) scale*: These items are seldom answered a certain way ("true" or "false") by people. A high F score may

suggest unusual approaches to taking the test or the presence of odd emotional states, thinking patterns, and behavior.

3. *L (lie) scale*: Endorsing these items places someone in a very positive light. People are unlikely, however, to endorse too many items such as, "I like everyone I meet."

4. *K (defensiveness) scale*: These items suggest defensiveness in admitting certain problems. Items such as "Criticism from others never bothers me." purportedly detect "faking good" but are more subtle than L or F items.

Validity scales help us understand someone's motives and test-taking attitudes. Attempts to present oneself in an overly favorable light will likely be detected by the *Lie* or *Defensiveness* scale and a tendency to exaggerate one's problems or symptoms usually results in an elevated *F (Infrequency)* scale (Graham, 2005). A mental health professional might disregard the test as well under these circumstances.

Scores on 10 **MMPI-2 clinical scales** are also calculated. These scales were originally developed to identify people likely to have certain diagnoses. The MMPI-2 retained the original names of the scales despite newer diagnostic labels introduced since the scale was developed. Each clinical scale with a short description and an abbreviated item is in **Table 4.4**.

Scores from the MMPI-2 can suggest diagnoses, but they also indicate various problematic behaviors and personality styles. How does a mental health professional interpret MMPI-2 profiles? Think about Professor Smith, who agreed to consult with a clinical psychologist after struggling with panic attacks and depression for many months. The clinical psychologist asked Professor Smith to complete the MMPI-2 before their first session, and this information was used with a clinical interview. The following excerpt is from a report based on Professor Smith's MMPI-2 profile (see **Figure 4.2**):

Professor Smith approached testing in a frank manner, and his responses suggest a valid MMPI-2 profile. His scores indicate concern about his present mental state and a willingness to receive help to overcome his problems. The MMPI-2 clinical profile highlights several problems and symptoms Professor Smith experienced during initial treatment. His responses suggest he is anxious, nervous, tense, and high-strung. He worries excessively and expects more problems to occur in the future. Professor Smith also has concerns about his health and body. He may complain of feeling fatigued, exhausted, and

## Table 4.4

### MMPI-2 Clinical Scales and Abbreviated Items

| | |
|---|---|
| 1. Hypochondriasis (Hs) | High scores indicate excessive concern with bodily functions ("Upset stomach"). |
| 2. Depression (D) | High scores indicate pessimism, hopelessness, and slowing of action and thought ("Work atmosphere tense"). |
| 3. Hysteria (Hy) | High scores indicate tendency to use physical and mental problems to avoid conflicts or responsibility ("Feel band around head"). |
| 4. Psychopathic deviate (Pd) | High scores indicate a disregard for social custom, shallow emotions, and inability to profit from experience ("Haven't led a good life"). |
| 5. Masculinity-femininity (Mf) | Items on this scale differentiate traditional gender roles ("Likes mechanic magazines"). High scores indicate a tendency to endorse a nontraditional gender role. |
| 6. Paranoia (Pa) | High scores indicate unusual suspiciousness and possible delusions of grandeur or persecution ("Insulting, vulgar things are said about me"). |
| 7. Psychasthenia (Pt) | High scores indicate obsessions, compulsiveness, fears, guilt, and indecisiveness ("Have strange thoughts"). |
| 8. Schizophrenia (Sc) | High scores indicate bizarre or unusual thoughts or behavior, withdrawal, hallucinations, and delusions ("Unusual experiences"). |
| 9. Hypomania (Ma) | High scores indicate emotional overexcitement, flight of ideas, and overactivity ("Sometimes thoughts race"). |
| 10. Social introversion (Si) | High scores indicate shyness, disinterest in others, and insecurity ("Easily defeated in argument"). |

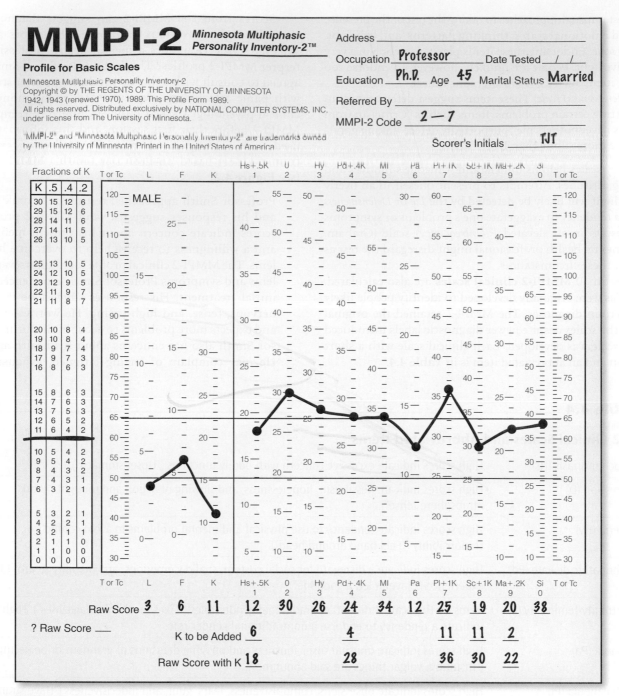

**FIGURE 4.2** PROFESSOR SMITH'S PRETREATMENT MMPI-2 CLINICAL PROFILE *Reproduced by permission of the University of Minnesota Press. All rights reserved. "MMPI®" and "Minnesota Multiphasic Personality Inventory®" are trademarks owned by the University of Minnesota.*

pained. Professor Smith appears depressed, pessimistic, and discouraged about his current situation and may feel lonely and insecure. He has great difficulty concentrating on his work and is likely to be indecisive. Professor Smith may blame himself for his current problems and feel guilty or disappointing to others. His responses also indicate little zest for life and preoccupation with inability to accomplish personal goals.

You can see that MMPI-2 interpretation does not rely on a single score but rather a profile of a client based on all scores. Profiles like Professor Smith's can then be interpreted using certain guidelines. These guidelines, or "cookbooks" as they are sometimes called, outline frequently obtained profiles and descriptions of typical symptoms, complaints, and characteristics of those who produce these profiles. These guidelines help mental health professionals standardize the interpretation of the MMPI-2.

## PROJECTIVE PERSONALITY MEASURES

Not all personality tests emphasize standardized administration, scoring, and interpretation as the MMPI-2 does. Some tests require mental health professionals to use their skill and judgment to interpret an individual's responses. **Projective tests** are based on the assumption that people faced with an ambiguous stimulus such as an inkblot will "project" their own needs, personality, and conflicts. One person looking at a particular inkblot might see a monster's face but another person might see two children playing near a stream. Projective techniques differ drastically from objective questionnaires like the MMPI-2 because (1) responses are not linked to certain scales and (2) responses are interpreted as individual characteristics, such as one's unconscious processes. Projective tests include *sentence completion tasks,* in which people complete a series of unfinished sentences, and *drawing tests,* in which people are asked to draw a figure such as a house or their family. We briefly discuss two other popular projective tests next: the Rorschach and the Thematic Apperception Test.

**Rorschach.** Hermann Rorschach was a Swiss psychiatrist who experimented with inkblots as a way to diagnose psychological problems. The *Rorschach* test consists of 10 inkblot cards that are symmetrical from right to left. Five cards are black and white (with shades of gray) and five are colored. A simulated Rorschach card is shown in **Figure 4.3**.

The Rorschach can be administered in different ways, but many clinicians give a client the first card and say, "Tell me what you see—what it looks like to you." All cards are shown to a client in order, and the clinician writes down every word the client says. The clinician then moves to an *inquiry* phase: She reminds the client of each previous response and asks what prompted each response. The client also indicates the exact location of various responses for each card and may elaborate or clarify responses. Many clinicians focus on these major aspects of responses:

- *Location* refers to area of the card to which the client responded—examples include the whole blot, a large detail, a small detail, or white space.
- *Content* refers to nature of the object seen, such as an animal, person, rock, or fog.
- *Determinants* refer to aspects of the card that prompted a client's response, such as the inkblot's form, color, texture, apparent movement, and shading.

Scoring the Rorschach involves computing the ratio of certain responses—such as responses to colored parts of the inkblots—to total number of responses. Clinicians may also compute the ratio of one set of responses to another, such as number of responses describing human movement to number of color responses. Many mental health professionals do not formally score the Rorschach but rely instead on their clinical impressions of a client's responses.

The utility of the Rorschach is hotly debated. Research-oriented psychologists often question the reliability and

**FIGURE 4.3** INKBLOT SIMILAR TO RORSCHACH INKBLOTS
*From Timothy Trull,* Clinical Psychology *(7th ed.), Fig. 8.2. Copyright © 2005 Wadsworth, a part of Cengage Learning. Reproduced with permission. www.cengage.com/permissions*

validity of Rorschach scores. Some Rorschach proponents argue that interrater and test–retest reliability are excellent but others remain unconvinced (Lilienfeld, Ammirati, & David, 2012; Viglione & Hilsenroth, 2001). Evidence exists to support the predictive validity of some Rorschach scores with respect to thought disturbance, psychotherapy prognosis, and dependency (Lilienfeld, Wood, & Garb, 2000).

**Thematic Apperception Test.** Another popular projective test to assess motivations and interpersonal style is the *Thematic Apperception Test* (TAT). The TAT is a series of pictures like the one in **Figure 4.4**. Most TAT cards depict people in various situations, but some cards contain only objects. Clinicians typically select 6 to 12 cards to give to a client. Clients are asked to say what is happening in the picture now and in the future. Instructions vary from clinician to clinician, but many say something such as, "I want you to make up a story about each of these pictures. Tell me who the people are, what they are doing, what they are thinking or feeling, what led up to the scene, and how it will turn out." The client's stories are then transcribed word-for-word by the clinician.

A mental health professional can learn about a client's personality from these stories. One person might say the picture in Figure 4.4 shows a mother worried about her daughter who is leaving home, but another might say a woman is constantly

**FIGURE 4.4** THEMATIC APPERCEPTION TEST (TAT) CARD

Spencer Grant / PhotoEdit

fighting with her mother and now refuses to talk to her. These different stories help us understand how a client relates to others. The TAT is not generally used to derive specific diagnoses but rather to make judgments about personality themes such as hostility, defensiveness, jealousy, and rebelliousness. The reliability and validity of this test, however, has not received much attention or support (Lilienfeld et al., 2000).

## Behavioral Assessment

The purpose of **behavioral assessment** is to measure overt behaviors or responses shown by a person (Hersen, 2006). Instead of relying only on Professor Smith's report of how fearful and anxious he is when lecturing in class, a behavioral assessor might also observe Professor Smith in this situation. Behavioral assessment provides a snapshot of an actual problem behavior. Traditional assessments such as intelligence or personality tests rely on responses as indirect indicators of underlying traits or characteristics. Behavioral assessment relies on as little interpretation or inference as possible—the behavior observed is the main interest.

Behavioral assessment often involves a functional analysis of behavior. This involves understanding **antecedents**, or

what precedes a behavior, and **consequences**, or what follows a behavior. A functional analysis for Professor Smith might reveal that certain student questions (antecedents) led to stress and panic attacks and that letting class out early (consequences) helped ease these anxious feelings, which is reinforcing. Consequences are often reinforcers of problematic behavior.

Careful and precise description of antecedents, behavior, and consequences is crucial to functional analysis. Important antecedents that you could easily measure and observe include student questions, time spent lecturing, and class attendance. You would also have to specify behaviors of interest, such as frequency and length of Professor Smith's chest pains. Important consequences that you could easily measure and observe include the number of minutes Professor Smith let class out early and the number of times he excused himself from class. You would also have to obtain similar level of detail for other situations in which Professor Smith had a panic attack because antecedents and consequences of behavior often differ from situation to situation.

Behavioral therapists often broaden functional analysis to include organismic variables. **Organismic variables** include a person's physiological or cognitive characteristics that may help the therapist understand a problem and determine treatment. A major organismic variable for Professor Smith is worry about future panic attacks and fear that certain physical sensations indicate an impending attack. Organismic variables such as worries and cognitions are also sometimes assessed via self-report questionnaires.

### NATURALISTIC OBSERVATION

Behavioral assessors often use observation to conduct a functional analysis. One form is **naturalistic observation**, in which a client is directly observed in his or her natural environment. A naturalistic observation might involve observing Professor Smith in his office, classroom, and home for a week. You can see, though, that naturalistic observation can be impractical, difficult, time-intensive, and expensive. Observers also cannot know for sure the problem behavior will even occur, so they sometimes must be present for long periods to capture a certain behavior.

### CONTROLLED OBSERVATION

**Controlled observation** is a more practical and less expensive form of observation, and involves analogue tests; these tests involve tasks that approximate situations people face in real life and that may elicit a certain problem behavior (Miltenberger, 2012). A person anxious about public speaking could be asked to give a short presentation before others in a psychologist's office. Or a troubled married couple might be asked to solve a hypothetical problem. A person's responses are observed and analyzed in each case. This information helps us understand precise mistakes the person makes when speaking before others or the couple makes when solving a problem. These observations can then lead to a treatment plan that might include relaxation and interpersonal skills training for the anxious public speaker and problem-solving and communication skills training for the troubled couple.

## SELF-MONITORING

Controlled observations are more practical than naturalistic observations but can be difficult to arrange. Many behavior assessors thus rely on **self-monitoring**, where a person observes and records his own emotions, thoughts, and behaviors. Professor Smith could be asked to complete a daily diary to record the frequency, intensity, and duration of his panic attacks, related thoughts and emotions, and antecedents and consequences of his panic attacks. Self-monitoring can be informal or more structured like a *dysfunctional thought record* (see **Figure 4.5**). Dysfunctional thought records help identify and monitor situations, thoughts, responses, and outcomes associated with problems

such as depression. A therapist and client can thus better understand what precedes and follows these problems. Technological advances also mean clients can record their emotions, thoughts, and behaviors during their everyday lives. Handheld computers, beepers, and laptop computers have been used to collect self-monitoring data (Hurlburt & Ahkter, 2008).

## Biological Assessment

Recall from Chapter 2 that mental disorders often involve abnormalities in brain structure or function. Many medical tests are available for examining general central nervous system dysfunction, such as from a stroke, but technological advances have led to amazing assessment techniques that can measure very specific central nervous system changes. Brain imaging techniques now provide detailed and precise evaluations of

Directions: When you notice your mood getting worse, ask yourself, "What's going through my mind right now?" and as soon as possible jot down the thought or mental image in the Automatic Thought(s) column

| Date/time | Situation | Automatic thought(s) | Emotion(s) | Adaptive response | Outcome |
|---|---|---|---|---|---|
| | 1. What actual event or stream of thoughts, or daydreams or recollection led to the unpleasant emotion? <br><br> 2. What (if any) distressing physical sensations did you have? | 1. What thought(s) and/or image(s) went through your mind? <br><br> 2. How much did you believe each one at the time? | 1. What emotion(s) (sad/anxious/ angry/etc.) did you feel at the time? <br><br> 2. How intense (0–100%) was the emotion? | 1. (optional) What cognitive distortion did you make? <br><br> 2. Use questions at bottom to compose an adaptive response to the automatic thought(s). <br><br> 3. How much do you believe each response? | 1. How much do you now believe each automatic thought? <br><br> 2. What emotion(s) do you feel now? How intense (0–100%) is the emotion? <br><br> 3. What will you do (or did you do)? |
| Friday 2/23 10 A.M. | Talking on the phone with Donna. | She must not like me anymore. 90% | Sad 80% | Maybe she's upset about something else. 60% | A little bit/Less sad (50%)/I will ask Donna if she is upset with me. |
| Tuesday 2/27 12 P.M. | Studying for my exam. | I'll never learn this. 100% | Sad 95% | Maybe I can't learn all of this, but I can learn some of this. 50% | Somewhat/More motivated (60%)/I will study as hard as I can and ask someone to help me. |
| Thursday 2/29 5 P.M. | Thinking about my economics class tomorrow. | I might get called on and I won't give a good answer. 80% | Anxious 80% | Doing my best is all I can do. 70% | To some extent/A little better (70%)/I'll just give the best answer I can. |
| | Noticing my heart beating fast and my trouble concentrating | What's wrong with me? | Anxious 80% | I'm just nervous; I'm not having a heart attack. 90% | Less so/More calm (80%)/Relax and steady my breathing. |

Questions to help compose an adaptive response: (1) What is the evidence that the automatic thought is true? Not true? (2) Is there an alternative explanation? (3) What's the worst that could happen? Could I live through it? What's the best that could happen? What's the most realistic outcome? (4) What's the effect of my believing the automatic thought? What could be the effect of my changing my thinking? (5) What should I do about it? (6) If _____ [friend's name] was in the situation and had this thought, what would I tell him/her?

**FIGURE 4.5** **AN EXAMPLE OF A DYSFUNCTIONAL THOUGHT RECORD:** The dysfunctional thought record is a type of self monitoring diary or log used to identify what may prompt and what may follow negative emotions. *Adapted from J S Beck, Cognitive Therapy: Basics and Beyond, New York: Guilford, 1995. Copyright © 1995 by Guilford Publications, Inc. Reprinted by permission.*

brain structure and function. We next provide an overview of neuroimaging and other biological tests used to assess psychopathology, although these tests are typically used in research settings or in cases involving clear brain dysfunction from problems such as stroke.

## NEUROIMAGING

Brain images can be derived in several ways. **Computerized axial tomography (CT scan)** assesses *structural abnormalities* of the brain. A CT scan can detect brain tumors and other structural abnormalities such as enlarged ventricles or hollow spaces in the brain sometimes seen in people with schizophrenia or other mental disorders. The CT scan is essentially an X-ray of a cross-section of the brain. X-ray dye (iodine) is injected into the person, and the CT scan assesses brain tissue density by detecting the amount of radioactivity from a moving beam of X-rays that penetrates the tissue. A computer then interprets this information to provide a two-dimensional picture of that cross-section of the brain.

Creatas Images/Jupiter Images

Cell phones and laptop and tablet computers can be used to monitor emotions, thoughts, and behaviors as they occur.

**Magnetic resonance imaging (MRI)** produces higher-quality brain images without radiation. MRI is costly but is better than CT scans in detecting brain tumors, blood clots, and other structural abnormalities. A person lies in a large cylindrical magnet, and radio waves are beamed through the magnetic field. Sensors read the signals, and a computer integrates the information to produce a high-resolution brain image. **Functional MRI (fMRI)** goes a step further in that pictures are taken rapidly to assess metabolic changes in the brain. fMRI thus assesses how the brain is *working*. This can have important implications for understanding risk factors of mental disorder. If fMRI results reveal a person's frontal lobes to be poorly activated during a decision-making task, then frontal lobe dysfunction may be associated with a learning or thought disorder.

**Positron emission tomography (PET scan)** is an invasive procedure to evaluate brain structure *and* function. Radioactive molecules are injected into the bloodstream and emit a particle called a positron. Positrons collide with electrons, and light particles emit from the skull and are detected by the PET scanner. A computer uses this information to construct a picture of how the brain is functioning. PET scans can identify seizure activity and even brain sites activated by psychoactive drugs (see **Figure 4.6**).

## NEUROCHEMICAL ASSESSMENT

**Neurochemical assessment** is a biological assessment of dysfunctions in specific *neurotransmitter* systems. Recall from Chapter 2 that neurotransmitters are brain chemicals that can activate or inhibit neurons and are often part of several main systems such as: *serotonin, norepinephrine, gamma-aminobutyric acid* (GABA), and *dopamine.* Many symptoms of mental disorder are influenced by dysfunction of one or more of these neurotransmitter systems in certain regions of the brain.

No technology allows us to *directly* assess how much neurotransmitter is in a specific brain region, but we can *indirectly* assess this by focusing on neurotransmitter **metabolites**. Metabolites are by-products of neurotransmitters that can be detected in urine, blood, and cerebral spinal fluid. Low levels of a metabolite suggest a low level of the associated neurotransmitter and vice versa. We will see later in this textbook how scientists have used this methodology to evaluate neurochemical theories of depression (low levels of serotonin) and schizophrenia (high levels of dopamine).

## Psychophysiological Assessment

**Psychophysiological assessment** involves evaluating bodily changes possibly associated with certain mental conditions. We experience certain bodily changes when we are highly anxious, such as increased heart rate or sweating (yes, measures exist for sweating!). These kinds of bodily changes could be examined in someone like Professor Smith who is seeking treatment for an anxiety disorder.

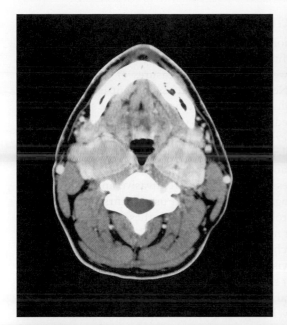

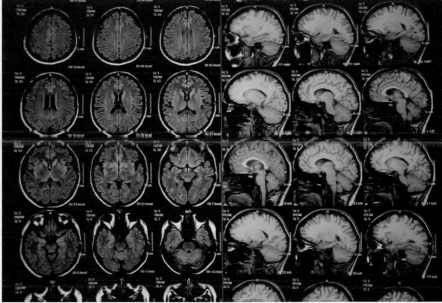

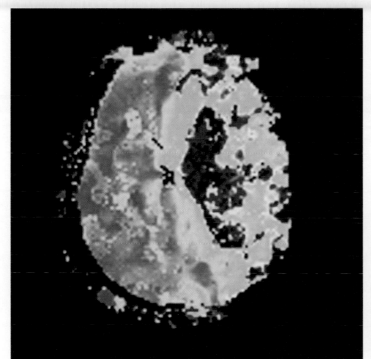

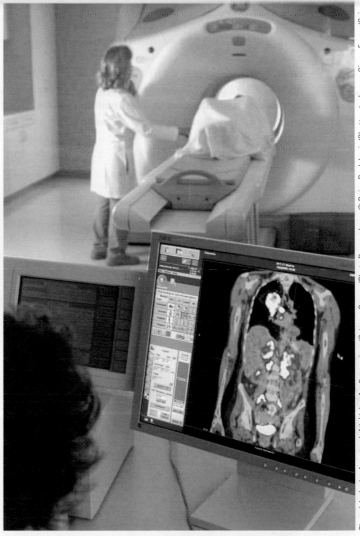

**FIGURE 4.6** EXAMPLES OF BRAIN IMAGING TECHNIQUES:
Several brain imaging techniques are used in biological
assessment. Here are some examples: (top left) A CT scan;
(top right) an MRI scan; (bottom left) an fMRI scan; and
(bottom right) a PET scan.

A common type of psychophysiological assessment is an **electrocardiogram**, which measures heart rate. Electrodes are placed on a person's chest, and the electrical impulse produced by the heartbeat and detected by each electrode is fed to an instrument that measures and integrates this information. Heart rate has been used to assess various emotional states. Those with generalized anxiety disorder (Chapter 5) tend to have a relatively higher heart rate (King, Tsai, & Chentsova-Dutton, 2002). We might also expect Professor Smith's heart rate to be elevated, even when he is not experiencing a panic attack, because his fear of future attacks makes him anxious most of the time.

**Galvanic skin conductance** is another index of emotional state. Some emotional states increase sweat gland activity and thus electrical conductance of the skin (electricity moves faster through skin when a person sweats). This is especially true for people with anxiety. Some people, however, may display *lower* levels of skin conductance. This is true for some people with antisocial personality disorder who manipulate and harm others without guilt (Chapter 10; King et al., 2002). People with antisocial personality disorder often have lower anxiety and fear about negative consequences to their behavior. They may be thus more likely than the rest of us to commit illegal or harmful acts.

The **electroencephalogram (EEG)** is a measure of brain activity. Electrodes are placed at various locations on the scalp so electrical activity in various brain areas can be assessed. Abnormal activity may indicate a lesion or tumor in that area or even seizure activity or epilepsy. Observation of possible abnormal brain wave activity might be followed by additional testing such as MRI.

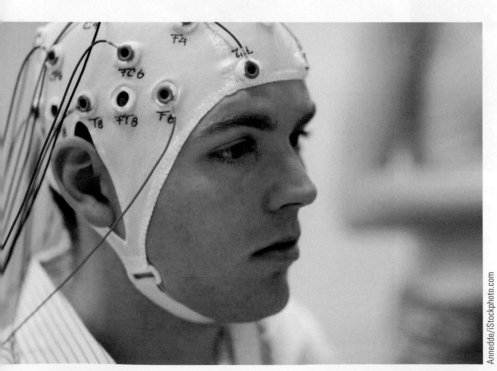

One form of psychophysiological assessment is the electroencephalogram (EEG).

## Neuropsychological Assessment

Methods of biological assessment are *direct* measures of brain and physical function. Methods of **neuropsychological assessment**, however, are *indirect* measures of brain and physical function. Neuropsychological assessment is a noninvasive method of evaluating brain functioning via one's performance on standardized tests and tasks that indicate brain-behavior relationships (Lezak, Howieson, Bigler, & Tranel). Many mental disorders involve some cognitive impairment, so neuropsychological tests can help identify or rule out physical problems. Biological assessment methods are invasive and expensive, so neuropsychological tests are often used as first-line screening measures. If problems are noted from these tests, then biological assessment may follow.

Neuropsychological tests typically assess abstract reasoning, memory, visual-perceptual processing, language functioning, and motor skills. Two general approaches are used for neuropsychological testing. One approach is to employ commonly used neuropsychological batteries such as the *Halstead-Reitan Battery*. These batteries involve various subtests that tap many cognitive and behavioral functions. The following descriptions of two Halstead-Reitan subtests provide good examples:

- *Tactual performance test*: The examinee is blindfolded and asked to place 10 variously shaped blocks into proper slots on a board using touch only. This is done once for each hand (dominant and nondominant) and once with both hands. The blindfold is then removed, and the examinee draws the board and located blocks from memory. This subtest assesses damage to the brain's right parietal lobe and tactile and spatial memory.

- *Seashore rhythm test*: The examinee hears 30 pairs of rhythmic acoustic patterns and states whether the patterns are the same or different. This subtest assesses damage to the brain's anterior temporal lobes and nonverbal auditory perception.

A second approach to neuropsychological testing is to administer one or more standardized tests to evaluate a specific area of brain functioning. This is known as *focal testing*. Suppose a neuropsychologist is primarily concerned with a person's memory functioning. The neuropsychologist might administer the *Benton Visual Retention Test*, which measures memory for designs (**Figure 4.7**). Ten cards are presented for 10 seconds each. After each presentation, the examinee draws the design from memory, and the examiner looks at number and type of errors in the drawings. A related test is the *Bender Visual-Motor Gestalt Test* (Bender-Gestalt II), which contains 14 stimulus cards and may be used for anyone aged 3 years or older (Brannigan & Decker, 2006).

Annedde/iStockphoto.com

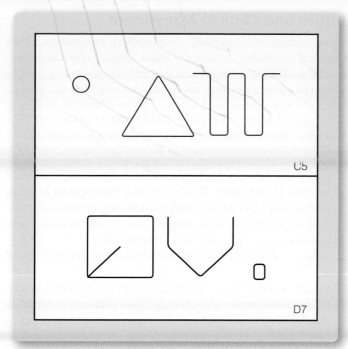

**FIGURE 4.7 EXAMPLES FROM THE BENTON VISUAL RETENTION TEST:** Two cards from the Benton Visual Retention Test that assesses memory for designs. *Adapted from M.D. Lezak, D.B. Howieson, E.D., Bigler, D. Tranel. (2012). Neuropsychological Assessment (5th ed.), New York: Oxford University Press.*

These tests assess immediate memory, spatial perception, and perceptual-motor coordination.

## INTERIM SUMMARY

- Classification refers to arranging mental disorders into broad categories or classes based on similar features.
- The *DSM-5* is a main system of classification that includes diagnoses but also allows for dimensional assessments.
- Clinical assessment involves evaluating a person's strengths and weaknesses as well as understanding a problem to develop treatment.
- Reliability refers to consistency of scores or responses and includes test–retest, interrater, and internal consistency reliability.
- Validity is the extent to which an assessment technique measures what it is supposed to measure and includes content, predictive, concurrent, and construct validity.
- Standardization refers to administering and conducting clinical assessment measures in the same way for everyone.
- Structured and unstructured interviews are the most common type of assessment.
- Intelligence tests are commonly used to assess cognitive aspects of mental disorders but must be viewed with caution, especially when comparing scores across cultures.
- Objective personality measures involve administering a standard set of questions or statements to which a person responds using set options.

- Objective personality measures such as the MMPI-2 are economical, relatively simple to administer and score, and reliable.
- Projective tests such as the Rorschach and TAT rely on the assumption that people project their needs, conflicts, and personality when responding to ambiguous stimuli.
- Behavioral assessment measures overt behaviors or responses and is often conducted via functional analysis of antecedents and consequences of behavior.
- Observational methods used in behavioral assessment include naturalistic and controlled observation and self-monitoring.
- Biological assessment includes neuroimaging techniques as well as procedures for assessing neurochemistry and body physiology.
- Neuropsychological assessment indirectly evaluates brain function via performance on standardized tests and tasks that indicate brain–behavior relationships.

## REVIEW QUESTIONS

1. Why is it important to use reliable, valid, and standardized measures to assess people?
2. What can intelligence tests tell us about clients like Professor Smith?
3. Compare and contrast information you might obtain about Professor Smith from objective and projective personality tests.
4. How does behavioral assessment differ from other forms of assessment?
5. What information from a biological assessment of Professor Smith might complement that obtained from interviews, personality tests, and behavioral assessment?

# Culture and Clinical Assessment

Recall from Chapter 2 the sociocultural perspective of mental disorder, which focuses on influences that social institutions and other people have on one's mental health. We next address the important topic of cultural considerations when assessing mental disorder, beginning with how culture might influence the development of psychological problems.

## Culture and the Development of Mental Disorders

As we discussed in Chapter 2, culture refers to unique behaviors and lifestyles that distinguish groups of people. Culture represents a unique worldview and is reflected in customs, laws, art, and music. Culture can also influence the development of mental disorders in several ways (Tseng, 2001, 2003).

1. *Culture may cause stress and psychological problems.* Culturally shared beliefs or ideas may lead to extreme stress and symptoms of mental disorders. A form of mental disorder may be unique to a culture because of specific ideas or beliefs that are part of that culture. *Ataque de nervios* is a syndrome

common to Latinos (APA, 2013). A person with this syndrome may sense losing control, shout uncontrollably, experience attacks of crying and trembling, and faint or feel suicidal. These symptoms typically result from a stressful family event. Latino culture emphasizes family well-being and stability, so a family crisis can be extremely stressful and produce *ataque de nervios.*

2. *Culture may influence a person's reaction to stress.* Certain cultures may disapprove of certain reactions to stressful events, such as becoming depressed. Some people may thus be expected to react to stress in only limited ways. A Japanese businessman's financial failure might lead to suicide because the disgrace and shame of publicly acknowledging bankruptcy would be too painful.

3. *Culture may influence which symptoms of a disorder are expressed and the content of the symptoms.* Symptoms of depression differ among people of various cultures. Societies or cultures that do not emphasize the concept of "guilt," as in Indonesia, are less likely to have depressed clients who feel guilty. The content of phobias or delusions can also depend on culture. People from poorly developed countries may be less likely to fear airplanes or believe their mind is controlled by satellites.

4. *Culture may reinforce certain forms of mental disorder.* The prevalence of certain mental disorders varies as a function of culture. General lifestyle patterns and attitudes, as well as acceptance of a disorder by the culture, likely influence prevalence. Anorexia nervosa is more prevalent in societies such as ours that emphasize and reward thinness (Chapter 8).

## Culture and Clinical Assessment

Culture clearly influences the development and presentation of mental disorders, so culture must impact clinical assessment as well. This is important not only for assessing people from other countries but also for assessing diverse groups within the United States. This does present unique challenges to many clinicians, however. Tseng (2001) identified four main areas that should be considered during assessment.

1. *Clinicians must overcome a language barrier if one exists.* An interpreter with a background in mental health should be used if necessary. This is not the best option because people may feel uncomfortable disclosing certain information to more than one person. The translator could also misinterpret or mistranslate information.

2. *Clinicians must obtain information about the cultural background of a client.* This might involve reading clinical books on diversity or consulting with cultural experts. A mental health professional must also distinguish behavior collectively shared by a culture and a client's responses or behaviors. A helpful question to a client or family members thus might be, "How do your friends and other members of your community typically react in similar situations?"

3. *Clinicians must be culturally sensitive.* Mental health professionals must be aware that culture influences emotions, thoughts, and behavior. Psychological problems should also be understood and interpreted from a cultural perspective. Many people from East Asian cultures are more reserved, soft-spoken, and passive than people from the West. A mental health professional must be careful not to misinterpret this style as evidence of an interpersonal problem or depression.

4. *Clinicians must be knowledgeable about cultural variations in psychological problems.* Mental health professionals must find assessment and other materials that consider cultural variations in mental disorder. The *DSM-5* presents general categories of information relevant to cultural considerations. First, for many mental disorders, a description of culture-related diagnostic issues is included: how cultural background may influence the cause or presentation of symptoms, preferred terms for distress, and/or prevalence of the disorder. Second, cultural syndromes are discussed; these are covered throughout this textbook. Third, an outline is presented for cultural formulation of presenting problems (see **Table 4.5**).

### INTERIM SUMMARY

► Culture may cause stress and psychological problems.

► Culture may influence a person's reaction to stress.

Culture can influence the development of psychological problems, and mental health professionals and medical doctors must consider cultural influences when conducting a clinical assessment or physical examination.

Sean Justice /Stone/Getty Images

## Table 4.5

### DSM-5 Cultural Formulation

*DSM-5* (APA, 2013) suggests that a mental health professional supplement traditional diagnostic formulations with a cultural formulation of presenting symptoms of clients whose cultural background differs from the treating mental health professional. Information is obtained to address the following topics:

**Cultural identity of the client:** Note the client's ethnic or cultural reference groups as well as language abilities and preferences.

**Cultural ideas of distress:** Note how the identified cultural group might explain the present symptoms and how these symptoms compare with those experienced by those in the cultural reference group.

**Cultural factors related to the social environment:** Note how the cultural reference group might interpret the social stresses, as well as availability of social supports and other resources that may aid treatment.

**Cultural influences on the relationship between the client and the mental health professional:** Indicate differences in cultural and social status between the client and mental health professional that might influence diagnosis and treatment.

**Overall cultural assessment:** Summarize how cultural factors and considerations are likely to influence the assessment and treatment of the client.

From APA, 2013.

- ▶ Culture may influence which symptoms of a disorder are expressed and the content of the symptoms.
- ▶ Culture may reinforce certain forms of mental disorder.
- ▶ Mental health professionals must overcome a language barrier if one exists, obtain information about a client's culture, be culturally sensitive, and be aware of cultural variations in psychological problems.

## REVIEW QUESTIONS

1. How might culture influence the development of psychological problems?
2. What considerations regarding culture are important for clinical assessment?
3. Consider the assessment methods and instruments discussed earlier in this chapter. How might cultural considerations affect the use of these?

## Studying Abnormal Behavior and Mental Disorder

We have so far discussed classification, assessment, and cultural considerations regarding mental disorder. Mental health professionals also rely on the scientific method to study, describe,

explain, predict, and treat disorders. The **scientific method** has three basic steps: generating a hypothesis, developing a research design, and analyzing and interpreting data to test the hypothesis. We present first the most powerful scientific method: the *experiment*.

## Experiment

An **experiment** is a research design that allows us to draw cause-and-effect conclusions about particular variables or events. Researchers generally follow a specific path to draw such conclusions, beginning with a hypothesis.

### HYPOTHESIS

A **hypothesis** is a statement about the cause of an event or about the relationship between two events. We might hypothesize that treatment A is more effective than treatment B for depression. Hypotheses are educated guesses based on previous studies but must be *testable* and *refutable*. This means hypotheses must contain constructs that can be measured or observed so others can try to replicate the study. Recall from Chapter 2 that one criticism of the psychodynamic perspective was that its constructs could not be measured or observed. Constructs such as id and unconscious cannot be directly or accurately measured, and so a cause–effect relationship between these constructs and behavior cannot be established.

If we develop a testable and refutable hypothesis regarding treatment for depression, then we must specify how we define depression and exactly what comprises treatments A and B. We might define depression as scores on a questionnaire or number of hours a person sleeps during the day. We might define treatment A as a specific drug such as Prozac given at 60 milligrams (mg)/day and define treatment B as Prozac given at 20 mg/day. Our hypothesis is now *testable:* We can measure or observe depression and provide specific doses of a medication. Our hypothesis is also *refutable:* Other people can clearly understand what we did, and they can try to replicate these results. We may also find no differences between our two groups, which refutes or contradicts our hypothesis.

### RESEARCH DESIGN

The next step in the scientific experimental method is to develop a *research design* that allows us to test the hypothesis, or in this case tell us if treatment A is indeed more effective than treatment B. Research designs comprise dependent and independent variables. **Dependent variables** are those that measure a certain outcome the researcher is trying to explain or predict. Dependent variables in our experiment might include scores on a depression questionnaire or number of hours a person sleeps during the day. An **independent variable** is a manipulated variable that researchers hypothesize to be the cause of the outcome. The independent variable in our experiment is *treatment:* Some people will receive treatment A, and some people will receive treatment B.

Once we develop a testable and refutable hypothesis with dependent and independent variables, we must then test the hypothesis. We can do so by choosing people with depression from the general population and randomly assigning them to an experimental group and a control group. **Randomization** means assigning people to groups so each person has the same chance of being assigned to any group. The goal of randomization is to make sure our groups represent the general population with respect to age, gender, cultural background, income level, or other variables that could influence the dependent variable. If we examined only Hispanic males in our study, then our results would probably not be too useful to everyone.

The **experimental group** is one that receives the active independent variable, in this case medication at two levels. We actually need two experimental groups for our study: one receiving medication at 60 mg/day and one receiving medication at 20 mg/day. The **control group** is one that does not receive the active independent variable. We may thus include people who are on a wait list for medication and monitor them over time to see if changes occur. They will receive no medication for a certain period of time, so we will see if changes in the experimental group are significantly different than changes in the control group. If our hypothesis is correct, then manipulation of the independent variable in the experimental group will lead to less depression, but this change will not occur in the control group.

We will assign 50 people (participants) with depression to treatment A (experimental group 1; 60 mg/day), 50 people with depression to treatment B (experimental group 2; 20 mg/day), and 50 people with depression to the control group (0 mg/day) for our experiment. Some control groups in an experiment such as this one receive a **placebo** or a substance or treatment that has no actual therapeutic effect. In this example, control group participants could receive a pill with no active treatment ingredient. Experimenters use placebos to control for *bias* or the possibility that a person receiving a medication will show

improved symptoms simply because he expects to improve. Some experiments also use **double-blind designs**, meaning that neither the experimenter nor the participants know who received a placebo or an active treatment. In this case, perhaps only an independent pharmacist knows who received a placebo or active treatment. **Triple-blind designs** are experiments in which participants, experimenters, independent raters of outcome, and even data managers are unaware of who received a placebo or active treatment (Miller & Stewart, 2011). Blinded designs are meant to control for as much bias from different people as possible.

In our experiment, we will then monitor our participants over several weeks by examining their scores on a depression measure and tracking the number of hours they sleep during the day. We may find after 3 months that people in experimental group 1 experienced a substantial drop in depression, people in experimental group 2 experienced a slight drop in depression, and people in the control group experienced no change in depression. This is done by analyzing and interpreting data, the third step in the scientific method. We could then conclude our hypothesis was correct: treatment A (60 mg/day) was indeed more effective than treatment B (20 mg/day). We could also conclude treatment is better than no treatment under these conditions.

Results such as these are a powerful testament to the causal role of treatment for reducing symptoms of depression. The groups were similar at the beginning of the experiment with respect to depression. The only difference between the groups was level of medication given. Differences in depression at the conclusion of the experiment can thus be attributed confidently to the manipulation differences between the groups—those receiving higher amounts of antidepressant medication experienced greater improvement.

---

## BOX 4.2 Focus on Law and Ethics

### Who Should Be Studied in Mental Health Research?

Much concern has been expressed over the relative lack of women and diverse participants in mental health research. Some feel that many studies use samples composed predominantly of male European Americans. This is a problem because results about causes and treatment of mental disorders in male European Americans may not generalize to others. Important biological differences exist between men and women (like hormones) that may affect the development and expression of psychological problems. Diverse ethnic groups are also subject to different types and degrees of environmental stressors, and these differences may influence mental health as well.

Conclusions about psychological problems and their treatment in male European Americans may not be valid for women or people of color.

These concerns have heightened clinical psychologists' awareness of these issues, and more formal requirements for studies supported by the U.S. government are now in place. The National Institutes of Health (NIH) has a policy about including women and members of minority groups in studies of human participants. These groups must be represented in NIH-supported projects unless some clear and compelling rationale exists for not doing so. Researchers must also provide a detailed and specific plan for the outreach and recruitment of women and minority subjects in their study. Researchers can thus address whether general conclusions for men or European Americans also hold for women and diverse groups.

Results such as these can be contaminated by variables other than the independent variable, however. If differences existed between the experimental and control groups, then we would have trouble concluding our treatment was effective. Imagine if the experimental group was mostly male African Americans and the control group was mostly female European Americans. How confident could we be in our results? Factors such as this affect the **external validity** of a study, or the extent to which results can be generalized to the whole population.

If the experimental group experienced something other than the manipulation, or treatment, then our conclusions would also be affected. Imagine if some members of the experimental group were attending therapy sessions in addition to their medication but members of the control group were not. How confident could we then be that medication was the major cause of improved symptoms? Factors such as this can decrease the **internal validity** of an experiment, or the extent to which a researcher can be confident that changes in the dependent variable (depression symptoms) truly resulted from manipulation of the independent variable (medication).

The experiment remains the best strategy for testing hypotheses about mental disorder. Unfortunately, researchers are not able to use this strategy as much as they would like. Experiments are costly in time and resources and require many people to study. Experiments are sometimes criticized for being unethical as well. Making people wait in the control group for medication that could help their depression sooner might raise some questions. If we wanted to study the effects of alcohol use on women and their unborn children, we would not want to deliberately introduce alcohol consumption to their diets. Because experiments can be costly and difficult to conduct, researchers often use correlational studies.

## Correlational Studies

A correlation is an association or relationship between two variables. **Correlational studies** allow researchers to make statements about the association or relationship between variables based on the extent to which they change together in a predictable way. A dependent variable and an independent variable may be related to each other such that high scores on one are associated with high scores on the other and vice versa. You would expect number of hours spent studying for an abnormal psychology test to be associated with higher grades. Height and weight in people are also closely associated. These examples indicate **positive correlations** where two variables are highly related to one another—as one goes up, the other does as well.

Dependent and independent variables may also be related to each other such that low scores on one are associated with high scores on the other and vice versa. You might expect greater dosage of medication to be related to lower scores on a depression measure. This would indicate a **negative correlation** in which two variables are also highly related to one another—as one goes up, the other goes down.

Correlations or associations between two variables are represented by a *correlation coefficient,* which is a number from +1.00 to −1.00. The sign of the coefficient, + or −, refers to type of association between variables. A positive sign indicates a positive correlation, and a negative sign indicates a negative correlation. The *absolute value* of the correlation coefficient, how high the number is regardless of its sign, refers to the *strength* of the association between the two variables.

The closer a correlation is to +1.00 or −1.00, the stronger the association. A correlation coefficient of exactly +1.00 or −1.00 means two variables are perfectly related: As one variable changes, the other variable always changes as well. Knowing someone's score on the independent variable thus allows us to predict a person's score on the dependent variable with 100 percent accuracy. A correlation coefficient of 0.00 means no relationship exists between the two variables: Knowing someone's score on the independent variable allows no prediction about a score on the dependent variable.

Correlations of +1.00 or −1.00 are rare. Correlation coefficients of +0.50 to +0.99 or −0.50 to −0.99 reflect strong association between two variables. Correlation coefficients of +0.30 to +0.49 or −0.30 to −0.49 reflect moderate association between two variables. Correlation coefficients of +0.01 to +0.29 or −0.01 to −0.29 reflect weak association between two variables. Examples of correlation coefficients are in **Figure 4.8**.

A correlation between two variables does not mean one variable *causes* another. *Correlation does not imply causation.* A problem with correlational methods is that we cannot rule out other explanations for the relationship between two variables because correlation does not control for the influence of third variables. This is the *third variable problem.* One of your authors lives in Las Vegas and has seen a strong correlation between number of churches built and number of violent crimes. The more churches built in Las Vegas, the more crime such as murder, rape, and robbery! Can we conclude church-building *caused* more violent crime? Of course not. A *third variable* explains this effect: massive population growth. More people are moving to Las Vegas, so more churches and greater prevalence of crime are to be expected.

Another problem with correlation methods is *directionality.* We know a correlation exists between marital fighting and adolescent delinquency. This effect might at first seem easy to explain—parents who fight a lot increase family stress, model violence as a way to solve problems, and fail to supervise their children. But the *opposite direction* is also possible—some children get into trouble in their teenage years and cause their parents to fight about how best to handle this situation. We may have a strong correlation, but we cannot know for sure which variable is the cause and which is the effect. We would have to conduct an experiment to know for sure.

## Quasi-Experimental Methods

An alternative approach to experiments and correlations is **quasi-experimental methods** or mixed designs. Mixed designs do not randomly assign people to experimental and control groups like a true experiment does. An experimenter instead examines groups that already exist. People already diagnosed with depression might be compared to people without depression. We could compare these groups along different variables such as family history of depression and

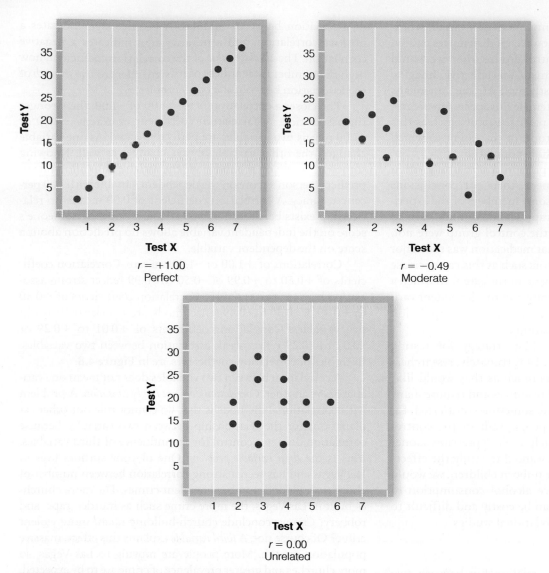

may try to ensure their groups are similar with respect to gender, age, race, income level, and symptoms of a specific disorder such as depression. Unfortunately, researchers cannot identify every variable necessary to match groups and protect internal validity. Experimental and control groups may still differ along important dimensions even after matching.

## Other Alternative Experimental Designs

Other designs also serve as alternatives to a large-scale true experiment. A **natural experiment** is an observational study in which nature itself helps assign groups. Recall John Snow from Chapter 3 who found that some residents getting sick from tainted drinking water were accessing a particular pump, whereas other residents not getting sick were accessing a different pump. The "natural" independent variable in this case was the source of drinking water. Natural experiments also commonly occur following disasters such as tsunamis or hurricanes. Grattan and colleagues (2011) studied different communities affected by the Gulf of Mexico Deepwater Horizon Oil Spill in 2010. One community was indirectly affected, whereas another community was directly exposed to coastal oil. The researchers found that people with spill-related income loss had significantly greater anxiety and depression than those with more stable incomes. Such a study could not be "created" without the tragedy that took place.

**FIGURE 4.8 SCATTERPLOTS SHOWING DIFFERENT STRENGTHS AND SIGNS OF CORRELATIONS.** (Top left) Perfect positive correlation; (top right) moderate negative correlation; (bottom) no correlation. *From Timothy Trull, Clinical Psychology (7th ed.), Fig. 4.2, p. 94. Copyright © 2005 Wadsworth, a part of Cengage Learning. Reproduced with permission. www.cengage.com/permissions*

stressful life events. We could even examine subgroups within the depressed group to see what medications they are taking and whether any effects can be seen. We could also calculate correlations between level of depression and many other variables such as age, income level, and family size.

Quasi-experiments involve no randomization, so researchers who use quasi-experiments must minimize confounds in their investigation. **Confounds** are factors that may account for group differences on a dependent variable. If we examine people with and without depression regarding stressful life events, then we should beware of these other factors. People with depression may have more stressful life events than people without depression, but people with depression may simply be more likely to *remember* stressful life events than people without depression. Confounds such as this impact the internal validity of results.

Researchers often try to *match* people in their groups on many variables to guard against these kinds of problems. They

Another alternative experimental design is an **analogue experiment** that involves simulating a real-life situation under controlled conditions. Often this simulation is done because re-creating certain events or conditions is not ethical. Ehring and colleagues (2009) were interested in examining trauma-related thoughts and memories, but obviously subjecting their research participants to an actual trauma was out of the question. Instead, the researchers conducted an analogue experiment in which participants watched a distressing video and then were monitored afterward. The study provided valuable information about different kinds of coping strategies that might be relevant to posttraumatic stress disorder (Chapter 5).

Researchers also use **single-subject experimental designs** that involve one person or a small group of persons who are examined under certain conditions. Single-subject designs still have experimental and control conditions to observe and measure behavior but do so in innovative ways. One type of single-subject experimental design is an *ABAB* or *reversal* design. In this case, "A" may represent a control condition, and "B" may represent a treatment condition. If a research participant consistently benefits from the "B" condition but not the "A" condition, then we have some evidence that a treatment is working. Such a design is sometimes used for unusual behaviors where obtaining large groups would be difficult. Anglesea and colleagues (2008) used a reversal design to show that a vibrating pager was helpful for reducing rapid eating in three teenage boys with autism.

## Developmental Designs

Researchers also use developmental designs to examine new participants or already-existing groups to see how a certain problem or mental disorder unfolds over time. Developmental designs consist of longitudinal, cross-sectional, and sequential studies. **Longitudinal studies** involve examining the same group of people over a long period of time. Researchers sometimes follow youths whose parents had schizophrenia during childhood and adolescence to see what risk factors eventually lead to the mental disorder.

Longitudinal studies are important for examining behavior change and development, but you can see that a major drawback is the time needed to complete the study. Some longitudinal studies last 20 years or more. Longitudinal studies also run the risk of *attrition,* which means some participants will drop out of the study over time or can no longer be contacted by the researcher. If 100 children begin a study but only 15 are left at the end of adolescence, how useful would the results be?

An alternative approach to longitudinal studies is a **cross-sectional study,** which involves examining different groups of people at one point in time. If a researcher were interested in examining children of parents of schizophrenia, then she might find children at different ages—say, 2, 7, 12, and 17 years—and study them right now. Cross-sectional studies are highly useful

but suffer from *cohort effects*. This means children at different ages are being raised in different eras, which may affect their functioning. Think about the fast-paced changes in technology that occur in our society today. A 2-year-old child will likely have access to different kinds of experiences than a 17-year-old did. These differences will be reflected in their behavior to some extent.

Some researchers thus blend aspects of longitudinal and cross-sectional studies into a **sequential design**. A sequential design begins as a cross-sectional study, but the groups are examined over a short time frame. From the example above, 2-, 7-, 12-, and 17-year-old children whose parents had schizophrenia may be examined now and over a 5-year period. Cross-sectional and longitudinal changes can thus be examined.

## Case Study

The research designs discussed so far are useful but not always practical. A researcher using the **case study method** makes careful observations of one person over time. The researcher may describe in great detail types of symptoms, assessment, and treatment relevant to that case. Substantial data are made available about one person, but no experimental manipulation occurs and no internal validity is present. We also cannot generalize results from one person to the overall population, so no external validity is present.

Case studies are useful for several reasons, especially for describing rare phenomena. People with multiple personalities, for example, are too few to allow for a large experiment. Or a person may have an unusual presentation of symptoms and family background. One of the authors published a case study about a young girl with selective mutism who refused to speak at school and whose parents largely spoke Spanish at home (Vecchio & Kearney, 2007). Case studies are also useful for testing new treatments on a few people to judge their effect and safety. Data from these "pilot studies" can then be used to justify further studies with more people.

You can see researchers use many methods to study mental disorders and that each method has its advantages and limitations (**Table 4.6**). Information derived from each of these

## Table 4.6

### Strengths of Major Research Methods Used for Studying Mental Disorders

|  | True experiment | Correlational methods | Quasi-experiment/ mixed designs | Case study methods |
|---|---|---|---|---|
| Detailed information |  |  |  | + |
| Internally valid results | + |  | + |  |
| Externally valid results | + | + | + |  |
| Can determine causality | + |  | + |  |

*Detailed information:* extensive information about a particular person
*Internal validity:* extent to which a researcher can be confident that changes in the dependent variable truly resulted from manipulation of the independent variable
*External validity:* extent to which results can be generalized to the whole population
*Causality:* the relation between a cause and an effect

methods is presented throughout this textbook. We thus encourage you to keep in mind each method's strengths and weaknesses.

## Consuming the Media's Research

You can see that many types of research can be conducted, and some types (e.g., experiments) allow for stronger conclusions than others (e.g., case studies). This is important to remember when reading a media report about a research finding regarding a mental disorder. Media outlets often focus on sensational aspects of a research study, especially differences found between men and women. When you read these reports, pay close attention to the study that is cited and whether the study is an experiment or something less rigorous. Take the extra step of reading the original research paper to get a sense of what the researchers truly found and what drawbacks exist for the study. Don't just fall for the headline—be a wise consumer of media reports on psychological research.

## INTERIM SUMMARY

▶ The scientific method involves generating a hypothesis, designing a research plan, and analyzing data to test the hypothesis.

▶ An experiment allows a researcher to draw cause-and-effect conclusions about variables.

▶ A hypothesis is a statement about the cause of an event or about the relationship between two events.

▶ Dependent variables are those measuring a certain outcome, and independent variables are those manipulated by a researcher to test a hypothesis.

▶ Experimental and control groups are key to an experiment, which must include randomization of participants.

▶ Internal validity and external validity are important components of an experiment that allow researchers to be confident about their results and generalize their results to the overall population.

▶ Experimenters use certain procedures to control for bias such as placebos and blinded designs.

▶ Correlational studies allow researchers to examine associations between variables and often include evaluating positive and negative correlations.

▶ Correlation does not imply causation because of third variable and directionality problems.

▶ Quasi-experiments involve examining groups that already exist along an independent variable.

▶ Other alternative experimental designs include natural experiments, analogue experiments, and single-subject research designs.

▶ Researchers often examine the development of mental disorders via longitudinal, cross-sectional, and sequential designs.

▶ Researchers use the case study method to make careful observations of one person.

## REVIEW QUESTIONS

1. Describe three major steps used in the scientific method.
2. Discuss various steps and components of an experiment.
3. Describe the correlational approach to research and its problems.
4. Describe the main characteristics of natural experiments, analogue experiments, and single-subject research designs.
5. Describe developmental designs and their advantages and disadvantages.
6. What is a case study, and why would a researcher conduct one?

## Final Comments

You can see that mental health professionals take seriously the precise definition, classification, assessment, and study of psychological problems. This is done to better understand, treat, and prevent mental disorders. If we have a well-defined mental disorder that can be more easily assessed, we can actively work to identify risk factors for the disorder that allow for early detection and prevention of symptoms. We have now reached the point in the book where we begin to describe major mental disorders at length. Each of the following chapters cover important information about features, epidemiology (including diversity), stigma, risk factors, prevention, assessment, and treatment of these disorders. Keep in mind that the behaviors we describe can be seen along a continuum or spectrum. We all have many aspects of these problems to some extent at some point in our lives. We begin by discussing some of the most common forms of mental disorder, the anxiety, obsessive-compulsive, and trauma-related disorders.

## Key Terms

dimensions 74
categories 74
diagnosis 75
syndrome 75
classification 76
clinical assessment 77
reliability 78
test–retest reliability 78
interrater reliability 79
internal consistency reliability 79
validity 79
content validity 80
predictive validity 80
concurrent validity 80
construct validity 80
standardization 80
unstructured interviews 80
structured interviews 80
intelligence tests 81
personality assessment 82

objective personality measures 82
MMPI-2 validity scales 82
MMPI-2 clinical scales 83
projective tests 85
behavioral assessment 86
antecedents 86
consequences 86
organismic variables 86
naturalistic observation 86
controlled observation 86
self-monitoring 87
computerized axial tomography (CT scan) 88
magnetic resonance imaging (MRI) 88
functional MRI (fMRI) 88
positron emission tomography (PET scan) 88

neurochemical
  assessment  88
metabolites  88
psychophysiological
  assessment  88
electrocardiogram  88
galvanic skin
  conductance  90
electroencephalogram  90
neuropsychological
  assessment  90
scientific method  93
experiment  93
hypothesis  93
dependent variables  93
independent variable  93
randomization  94
experimental group  94
control group  94

placebo  94
double-blind design  94
triple-blind design  94
external validity  95
internal validity  95
correlational studies  95
positive correlations  95
negative correlation  95
quasi-experimental
  methods  95
confounds  96
natural experiment  96
analogue experiment  96
single-subject experimental
  design  97
longitudinal studies  97
cross-sectional study  97
sequential design  97
case study method  97

## Media Resources

### MindTap

MindTap for Kearney and Trull's *Abnormal Psychology and Life: A Dimensional Approach* is a highly personalized fully online learning platform of authoritative content, assignments, and services offering you a tailored presentation of course curriculum created by your instructor. MindTap guides you through the course curriculum via an innovative learning path where you will complete reading assignments, annotate your readings, complete homework, and engage with quizzes and assessments. MindTap includes the Continuum Video Project.

Go to **cengagebrain.com** to access MindTap.

# Anxiety, Obsessive-Compulsive, and Trauma-Related Disorders

CASE: *Angelina*

**What Do You Think?**

Worry, Anxiety, Fear, and Anxiety, Obsessive-Compulsive, and Trauma-Related Disorders: What Are They?

Anxiety, Obsessive-Compulsive, and Trauma-Related Disorders: Features and Epidemiology

CASE: *Jonathan*

CASE: *Marcus*

Interim Summary
Review Questions

Stigma Associated with Anxiety, Obsessive-Compulsive, and Trauma-Related Disorders

Anxiety, Obsessive-Compulsive, and Trauma-Related Disorders: Causes and Prevention
Interim Summary
Review Questions

Anxiety, Obsessive-Compulsive, and Trauma-Related Disorders: Assessment and Treatment
Interim Summary
Review Questions

FINAL COMMENTS
THOUGHT QUESTIONS
KEY TERMS
MEDIA RESOURCES

## SPECIAL FEATURES

**CONTINUUM FIGURE 5.1** Worry, Anxiety, and Fear Along a Continuum   104

**CONTINUUM FIGURE 5.2** Continuum of Emotions, Cognitions, and Behaviors Regarding Anxiety-Related Disorders   104

BOX 5.1 | Focus on Gender: Are There True Gender Differences in Anxiety-Related Disorders?   119

BOX 5.2 | Focus on Diversity: Anxiety-Related Disorders and Sociocultural Factors   120

## THE CONTINUUM VIDEO PROJECT

*Darwin:* PTSD   130

**PERSONAL NARRATIVE 5.1 Anonymous   132**

BOX 5.3 | Focus on Law and Ethics: The Ethics of Encouragement in Exposure-Based Practices   142

## CASE: Angelina

**Angelina** was 25 years old when she was referred to a specialized outpatient clinic for people with anxiety-related disorders. Angelina came to the clinic following a scary episode in which she nearly got into a car accident. Angelina said she was driving across a high bridge when she suddenly felt her heart start to race, her breath become short, and her vision become blurry. These feelings were so intense she thought she might wreck the car and hurt herself or others. She was able to pull the car off to the shoulder of the bridge as she struggled with her symptoms. The symptoms seemed to ease a bit after a few minutes. Angelina then waited another 20 minutes, still shaken from the experience, before driving straight home to where she felt safe.

The therapist who spoke to Angelina asked if such an episode had happened before. Angelina said the experience had occurred several times, usually when she was driving or surrounded by many people. Angelina generally felt she could handle her symptoms during these episodes. This last episode, though, and two more that followed, were much more intense than what she had felt before. She recently saw an emergency room doctor and a cardiologist to determine any potential medical causes for her symptoms, but none were found. Angelina was then referred for outpatient psychological treatment.

The therapist asked more about Angelina's history with these symptoms. Angelina said she had always been "the nervous and worried type" and that her anxiety worsened as she attended college. She had particular trouble driving to school and walking into class where other people were sitting and possibly looking at her. Angelina usually sat in the back of the class in case she had to exit quickly to calm herself. The therapist asked Angelina if she worried something

©gyn9037/Shutterstock

bad might happen. Angelina said she was most concerned about the professor looking at her or being asked a question for which she did not have an answer. She was also concerned other people would notice her physical symptoms of anxiety.

Angelina's nervousness escalated a year earlier when she began to experience specific episodes of intense anxiety. Angelina said her first "anxiety attack" happened as she walked into class to take a midterm examination. Her heart began racing, and she was short of breath. When the professor handed her the test, she was shaking and having much trouble concentrating. Angelina said she felt she "wasn't even there" and that "everything was moving in slow motion." Worse, she felt she could not concentrate well enough to take the test. She did complete the test, however, and received a "B-minus" (she was normally an "A/B" student). Other "anxiety attacks" after that point tended to occur when she was going to school or about to enter a classroom. These attacks happened about once a week but not typically on weekends or when she was not in school.

Over the past few months, Angelina's "attacks" became more frequent and affected other, similar situations. Angelina would sometimes have trouble driving to a local mall and shopping among hundreds of people. She was also reluctant to date because she might "seize up" and look foolish. Her greater concern,

however, was that she might have to drop out of college even though she was near graduation. This belief arose from the fact that on her way to her first day of class, Angelina had driven across the bridge that led to her worst anxiety attack. The two other attacks that followed also caused her to miss so many classes, she felt she had to drop all of them. Angelina was thus sad and tearful, feeling she would not be able to return to college and finish her degree.

Angelina now spent her days at home, and her mother had driven her to the therapist's office. She had trouble going to the supermarket or restaurants and preferred to avoid them altogether. Even speaking to the therapist now led Angelina to report an anxiety rating of 8 on a 0 to 10 scale. The therapist asked her what she would like to see different in her life, and Angelina said she wanted to be like her old self, someone who went to school, saw her friends, dated, and enjoyed life. The therapist asked her if she could commit to a full-scale assessment and treatment program, and Angelina agreed to do so.

## What Do You Think?

1. Which of Angelina's symptoms seem typical of someone in college, and which seem very different?

2. What external events and internal factors might be responsible for Angelina's feelings?

3. What are you curious about regarding Angelina?

4. Does Angelina remind you in any way of yourself or someone you know? How so?

5. How might Angelina's anxiety affect her life in the future?

Anxiety involves a sense of apprehension that something bad might happen.

## Worry, Anxiety, Fear, and Anxiety, Obsessive-Compulsive, and Trauma-Related Disorders: What Are They?

Have you ever been *concerned* that something bad will happen? Have you ever been *nervous* about an upcoming event? Have you ever been *afraid* of something, like Angelina was? Some people worry a lot about what could happen in the future. Other people become nervous or anxious at the thought of going on a date, speaking in public, or taking a test. For others, the sight of a snake or an airplane causes intense and immediate fear. For people like Angelina, worry, anxiety, and fear can spiral into an uncontrollable state that makes them want to avoid many things such as school. But what are worry, anxiety, and fear, and what are the differences among them?

**Worry** is a largely cognitive or "thinking" concept that refers to concerns about possible future threat. People who worry tend to think about the future and about what painful things might happen. A person might worry about failing to pay bills on time or a future terrorist attack. Worry is not necessarily a bad thing because it helps people prepare for future events and solve problems (Jonasen & Perilloux, 2012). If you have a test next week and have not prepared for it, you may feel a sense

of dread and develop a study schedule to prevent failure. Worry is thus normal and even adaptive. Worry is often a gradual process that starts slowly for a distant event (oh, yeah, that test is coming) but becomes more intense as the event draws closer (uh-oh, better get studying). If the event draws closer and seems even more threatening, as when a test draws nearer and one is still not prepared, then *anxiety* may occur.

**Anxiety** is an emotional state that occurs as a threatening event draws close. Worry is more cognitive in nature, but anxiety has three key parts: *physical feelings, thoughts, and behaviors*. Physical feelings may include heart racing, sweating, dry mouth, shaking, dizziness, and other unpleasant symptoms. Thoughts may include beliefs that one will be harmed or will lose control of a situation. Behaviors may include avoiding certain situations or constantly asking others if everything will be OK (Ouimet, Gawronski, & Dozois, 2009; Rector, Kamkar, Cassin, Ayearst, & Laposa, 2011). If you have a test tomorrow, and have not studied, then you may feel muscle tension (physical feeling), believe you will not do well (thought), and skip the test (behavior). Anxiety, like worry, is a normal human emotion that tells us something is wrong or needs to change.

The three parts of anxiety often occur in a sequence. Think about a blind date. You might feel physically nervous as you are about to meet the other person for the first time—perhaps you will sweat, tremble a bit, or feel your heart race. You may then start to think the other person will notice your symptoms and that you will look foolish and be judged negatively. You may also be apprehensive about awkward pauses in the conversation or what the other person will say or look like. You may even decide to shorten the date or cancel it because of these feelings and beliefs. Many people with anxiety have a combination of troublesome physical feelings, thoughts, and behaviors. Think about Angelina—what were her major physical feelings, thoughts, and behaviors?

**Fear** is an intense emotional state that occurs as a threat is imminent or actually occurring. Fear is a *specific* reaction that is clear and immediate: fright, increased arousal, and an overwhelming urge to get away (Baumeister, Vohs, DeWall, & Zhang, 2007; Craske et al., 2009). A fear reaction is usually toward something well defined. If you take a quiz you have not studied for, you may experience severe physical arousal and dread and leave the situation quickly. Many people are afraid of snakes. If someone places a cobra nearby, you may immediately become frightful and physically aroused, and run away as quickly as possible. Fear is an ancient human feeling that tells us we are

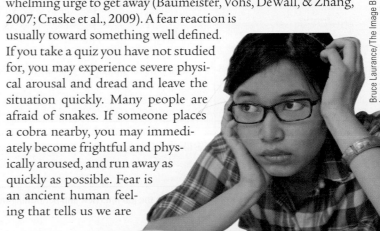

People often worry about daily events such as school or job-related tasks or finances.

| Worry | Anxiety | Fear |
|---|---|---|
| Potential threat | Approaching threat | Imminent threat |
| Little arousal (physical feelings) | Moderate arousal | Severe arousal |
| Heavily cognitive | Moderately cognitive | Scarcely cognitive |
| Little avoidance | Moderate avoidance | Severe avoidance |
| General and slow reaction (caution) | More focused and quicker reaction (apprehensiveness) | Very focused and fast reaction (fight or flight) |

**CONTINUUM FIGURE 5.1**  Worry, Anxiety, and Fear Along a Continuum

in danger and that we may have to fight whatever is before us or flee the situation as quickly as possible (fight or flight). Fear is thus normal and protects us from potential harm, like when we jump away from a snake. Fear that is very intense and severe is *panic*.

Differences among worry, anxiety, and fear can be illustrated along a continuum or dimension (see **Figure 5.1**). Worry occurs in reaction to *potential* threat, anxiety occurs in reaction to *approaching* threat, and fear occurs in reaction to *imminent* threat. Worry is a largely cognitive concept that involves fewer physical feelings and less avoidance than anxiety or fear. A person may experience more physical feelings (arousal) and greater desire to avoid or escape, however, as a threatening event such as a test comes closer in time and distance. Worry also tends to be a general and slow reaction that is cautionary, whereas moderate anxiety or apprehensiveness is more specific and often spurs a person into action (start studying!). Fear involves an immediate and focused reaction so a person can confront or flee a certain situation.

Worry, anxiety, and fear can also be viewed along a dimension of *severity*. Worry, anxiety, and fear are normal human emotions, so all of us experience them to some extent. We worry about the safety of our children, become anxious when about to perform or interview before others, and are frightened when airplanes experience severe turbulence. These experiences are a common part of life, and many people learn to cope with them successfully. Many people go on blind dates even when nervous, and they eventually relax and have a good time. Worry, anxiety, or fear may become more intense, however, to the point where a person finds it difficult to concentrate, finish a task, or relax (see **Figure 5.2**).

Worry, anxiety, and fear may even become *severe* and create enormous trouble for a person—this could be an *anxiety, obsessive-compulsive, or trauma-related disorder* (we sometimes refer to these collectively as **anxiety-related disorders** in this chapter). People like Angelina with these kind of disorders have persistent episodes of severe worry, anxiety, or fear that keep them from doing things they would normally like to do, such as shop, drive, attend school, or get a new job (Figure 5.2). An anxiety-related disorder can be *less severe*, as when a person worries so much about getting into a car accident that driving is difficult. Or an anxiety-related disorder can be *more severe*, as when a person is so fearful of germs that she never leaves the house. People with anxiety-related disorders generally experience worry, anxiety, or fear that is severe, that lasts for long periods of time, and that interferes with daily living. We next cover the major anxiety-related disorders that cause many people like Angelina so much distress.

## Anxiety, Obsessive-Compulsive, and Trauma-Related Disorders: Features and Epidemiology

The following sections summarize the major features and characteristics of the most commonly diagnosed anxiety-related disorders. Many of the disorders in this chapter have anxiety

|  | **Normal** | **Mild** |
|---|---|---|
| **Emotions** | Slight physical arousal but good alertness. | Mild physical arousal, perhaps feeling a bit tingly, but with good alertness. |
| **Cognitions** | "I'm going on a job interview today. I hope they like me. I'm going to show them what I've got!" | "I'm going on a job interview today. I wonder if they will think badly of me. I hope my voice doesn't shake." |
| **Behaviors** | Going to the job interview and performing well. | Going to the job interview but fidgeting a bit. |

**CONTINUUM FIGURE 5.2**  Continuum of Emotions, Cognitions, and Behaviors Regarding Anxiety-Related Disorders

as a key component and were historically studied as one diagnostic group. In the fifth edition of the *Diagnostic and Statistical Manual of Mental Disorders* (*DSM-5*), the disorders were separated into smaller diagnostic groups labeled anxiety, obsessive-compulsive, and trauma- and stressor-related disorders (we

Fear is an intense emotional state that occurs when some threat is imminent.

shorten this latter label in this chapter). We first discuss the concept of a panic attack, which serves as a key part of several anxiety-related disorders.

## Panic Attack

Have you ever felt scared for no reason? Perhaps you were just sitting or standing and suddenly felt intense fear out of the blue. If so, you may have experienced a panic attack similar to the ones Angelina reported. A **panic attack** involves a period of time, usually several minutes, in which a person experiences intense feelings of fear, apprehension that something terrible will happen, and physical symptoms. A panic attack is not a diagnosis but an event that commonly occurs in people with anxiety disorders. Features of a panic attack are listed in **Table 5.1** (APA, 2013).

Common physical symptoms include accelerated heart rate, shortness of breath, chest pain or discomfort, dizziness, and feelings of choking. People having a panic attack also often worry about dying, going "crazy," or losing control and doing something terrible. Angelina's panic attack in her car led her to think she might crash. Panic attacks may also involve feelings that surrounding events are not real (*derealization*) or that a person is watching himself go through the situation (*depersonalization*). Recall Angelina's feeling of detachment when taking her test.

Panic attacks that occur out of the blue, or without warning or predictability, are *unexpected panic attacks*. This can make panic attacks pretty scary. Some people even have panic attacks during sleep (Sarisoy, Boke, Arik, & Sahin, 2008). Over time, a person with panic attacks may be able to predict when these attacks are more likely to occur. Angelina said her panic attacks tended to occur when she was driving or among crowds. An *expected panic attack* has a specific trigger; for example, a person may experience severe panic symptoms when speaking in public. Panic attacks thus involve many troubling physical symptoms and thoughts, two components of anxiety described earlier.

| Moderate | Anxiety-Related Disorder—less severe | Anxiety-Related Disorder—more severe |
|---|---|---|
| Moderate physical arousal, including shaking and trembling, with a little more difficulty concentrating. | Intense physical arousal, including shaking, dizziness, and restlessness, with trouble concentrating. | Extreme physical arousal with dizziness, heart palpitations, shaking, and sweating with great trouble concentrating. |
| "Wow, I feel so nervous about the interview today. I bet I don't get the job. I wonder if I should just forget about it?" | "Oh, no that interview is today. I feel sick. I just don't think I can do this. They will think I'm an idiot!" | "No way can I do this. I'm a total loser. I can't get that job. Why even bother? I don't want to look foolish!" |
| Drafting two emails to cancel the interview but not sending them. Going to the interview but appearing physically nervous. | Postponing the interview twice before finally going. Appearing quite agitated during the interview and unable to maintain eye contact. | Canceling the interview and staying home all day. |

## Table 5.1

### DSM-5 Panic Attack

**Note:** Symptoms are presented for the purpose of identifying a panic attack; however, panic attack is not a mental disorder and cannot be coded. Panic attacks can occur in the context of any anxiety disorder as well as other mental disorders (e.g., depressive disorders, posttraumatic stress disorder, substance use disorders) and some medical conditions (e.g., cardiac, respiratory, vestibular, gastrointestinal). When the presence of a panic attack is identified, it should be noted as a specifier (e.g., "posttraumatic stress disorder with panic attacks"). For panic disorder, the presence of panic attack is contained within the criteria for the disorder and panic attack is not used as a specifier.

An abrupt surge of intense fear or intense discomfort that reaches a peak within minutes, and during which time four (or more) of the following symptoms occur:

**Note:** The abrupt surge can occur from a calm state or an anxious state.

1. Palpitations, pounding heart, or accelerated heart rate.
2. Sweating.
3. Trembling or shaking.
4. Sensations of shortness of breath or smothering.
5. Feelings of choking.
6. Chest pain or discomfort.
7. Nausea or abdominal distress.
8. Feeling dizzy, unsteady, light-headed, or faint.
9. Chills or heat sensations.
10. Paresthesias (numbness or tingling sensations).
11. Derealization (feelings of unreality) or depersonalization (being detached from oneself).
12. Fear of losing control or "going crazy."
13. Fear of dying.

**Note:** Culture specific symptoms should not count as one of the four required symptoms.

American Psychiatric Association. (2013). *Diagnostic and statistical manual of mental disorders* (5th ed.). Arlington, VA: American Psychiatric Association.

## Table 5.2

### DSM-5 Panic Disorder

A. Recurrent unexpected panic attacks. A panic attack is an abrupt surge of intense fear or intense discomfort that reaches a peak within minutes, and during which time four (or more) of the following symptoms occur:
   **Note:** The abrupt surge can occur from a calm state or an anxious state.
   1. Palpitations, pounding heart, or accelerated heart rate.
   2. Sweating.
   3. Trembling or shaking.
   4. Sensations of shortness of breath or smothering.
   5. Feelings or choking.
   6. Chest pain or discomfort.
   7. Nausea or abdominal distress.
   8. Feeling dizzy, unsteady, light headed, or faint.
   9. Chills or heat sensations.
   10. Paresthesias (numbness or tingling sensations).
   11. Derealization (feelings of unreality) or depersonalization (being detached from oneself).
   12. Fear of losing control or "going crazy."
   13. Fear of dying.

   **Note:** Culture specific symptoms should not count as one of the four required symptoms.

B. At least one of the attacks has been followed by 1 month (or more) of one or both of the following:
   1. Persistent concern or worry about additional panic attacks or their consequences.
   2. A significant maladaptive change in behavior related to the attacks.

C. The disturbance is not attributable to the physiological effects of a substance or another medical condition.

D. The disturbance is not better explained by another mental disorder.

American Psychiatric Association. (2013). *Diagnostic and statistical manual of mental disorders* (5th ed.). Arlington, VA: American Psychiatric Association.

## Panic Disorder

People who regularly experience *unexpected* panic attacks have **panic disorder**, a diagnosis involving the *DSM-5* criteria in **Table 5.2** (APA, 2013). At least one of these attacks must be followed by a month or more of concern about having another attack, worry about what the panic attack might mean, or a change in behavior. Angelina did indeed worry about having more attacks and wondered if she might have to drop out of school because of her attacks. Her driving behavior also changed drastically. Panic attacks and panic disorder must not be a result of substance use or a medical condition. Panic disorder is different from other anxiety disorders (see following sections) in which panic attacks are more closely linked to specific (or expected) situations such as public speaking.

Panic disorder is a frightening condition for several reasons. First, a person often has little idea when a panic attack might happen. Panic attacks can occur frequently during the day or be spaced out across several days. Imagine going places and always wondering if a panic attack might strike. Second, panic attacks are not harmful, but many people with panic disorder become terrified of their own internal sensations of dizziness, heart palpitations, or other panic attack symptoms. Some people with panic disorder may believe their symptoms indicate something serious such as a terminal heart condition or illness. People with panic disorder thus fear the onset of more panic attacks.

People with panic disorder, like Angelina or Professor Smith from Chapter 4, might avoid situations in which they may have panic symptoms. Some people with panic disorder may thus be diagnosed with agoraphobia. **Agoraphobia** refers to anxiety about being in places where panic symptoms may occur, especially places where escape might be difficult. Agoraphobia also refers to *avoiding* those places or enduring them with great anxiety or dread (see **Table 5.3**) (APA, 2013). In one large study, 40.6 percent of people with panic disorder developed agoraphobia within 24 weeks of panic disorder onset. Agoraphobia appears more common among people with severe or chronic panic disorder (Kikuchi et al., 2005; Perugi, Frare, & Toni, 2007; Wittchen, Gloster, Beesdo-Baum, Fava, & Craske, 2010).

Recall that behavioral avoidance is a main component of anxiety. Angelina did not want to go to a restaurant because she might have a panic attack and look foolish. Many people with panic disorder stay close to exits or avoid potentially embarrassing situations. Some also develop agoraphobia so severe they cannot leave home. This can obviously lead to severe marital, occupational, academic, and other problems. Angelina was certainly on that path.

## Social Phobia

Do you feel nervous when doing something in front of others? Do you cringe when asked to speak in public or meet someone for the first time? Many people feel nervous in these situations, which is normal. We are concerned about what other people think of us and what the consequences might be if they respond negatively to us. Most of us, however, can control or disregard our anxiety in these situations and function well. For other people, social anxiety is a crippling phenomenon that makes casual conversations or other interactions extremely difficult.

**Social phobia**, also called *social anxiety disorder,* is marked by intense and ongoing fear of potentially embarrassing social or performance situations. A diagnosis of social phobia involves the *DSM-5* criteria in **Table 5.4** (APA, 2013). Social situations include interactions with others, such as dating, having conversations, or attending parties. Performance situations include some evaluation from others, such as taking a test, giving an oral presentation, or playing a musical instrument at a recital. People with social phobia are extremely fearful they will act in a way that causes great personal embarrassment or humiliation in these situations.

People with social phobia may have *expected panic attacks* in social and performance settings and avoid these settings. Or they endure the settings with great anxiety or dread. Angelina had trouble dating, answering questions in class, and shopping and eating in front of others. These are all situations where she could be negatively evaluated. Social avoidance can obviously interfere with one's ability to live a normal life. People with social phobia find it difficult to attend school, take high-profile jobs, and make and keep friends.

---

**Table 5.3**

### DSM-5  Agoraphobia

A. Marked fear or anxiety about two (or more) of the following five situations:
  1. Using public transportation.
  2. Being in open spaces.
  3. Being in enclosed places.
  4. Standing in line or being in a crowd.
  5. Being outside of the home alone.

B. The individual fears or avoids these situations because of thoughts that escape might be difficult or help might not be available in the event of developing panic-like symptoms or other incapacitating or embarrassing symptoms.

C. The agoraphobic situations almost always provoke fear or anxiety.

D. The agoraphobic situations are actively avoided, require the presence of a companion, or are endured with intense fear or anxiety.

E. The fear or anxiety is out of proportion to the actual danger posed by the agoraphobic situations and to the sociocultural context.

F. The fear, anxiety, or avoidance is persistent, typically lasting for 6 months or more.

G. The fear, anxiety, or avoidance causes clinically significant distress or impairment in social, occupational, or other important areas of functioning.

H. If another medical condition is present, the fear, anxiety, or avoidance is clearly excessive.

I. The fear, anxiety, or avoidance is not better explained by the symptoms of another mental disorder—for example, the symptoms are not confined to specific phobia, situational type; do not involve only social situations (as in social anxiety disorder); and are not related exclusively to obsessions (as in obsessive-compulsive disorder), perceived defects or flaws in physical appearance (as in body dysmorphic disorder), reminders of traumatic events (as in posttraumatic stress disorder), or fear or separation (as in separation anxiety disorder).

**Note:** Agoraphobia is diagnosed irrespective of the presence of panic disorder. If an individual's presentation meets criteria for panic disorder and agoraphobia, both diagnoses should be assigned.

American Psychiatric Association. (2013). *Diagnostic and statistical manual of mental disorders* (5th ed.). Arlington, VA: American Psychiatric Association.

**Table 5.4**

### DSM-5 Social Anxiety Disorder (Social Phobia)

A. Marked fear or anxiety about one or more social situations in which the individual is exposed to possible scrutiny by others.

   **Note:** In children, the anxiety must occur in peer settings and not just during interactions with adults.

B. The individual fears that he or she will act in a way or show anxiety symptoms that will be negatively evaluated (i.e., will be humiliating or embarrassing; will lead to rejection or offend others).

C. The social situations almost always provoke fear or anxiety.

   **Note:** In children, the fear or anxiety may be expressed by crying, tantrums, freezing, clinging, shrinking, or failing to speak in social situations.

D. The social situations are avoided or endured with intense fear or anxiety.

E. The fear or anxiety is out of proportion to the actual threat posed by the social situation and to the sociocultural context.

F. The fear, anxiety, or avoidance is persistent, typically lasting for 6 months or more.

G. The fear, anxiety, or avoidance causes clinically significant distress or impairment in social, occupational, or other important areas of functioning.

H. The fear, anxiety, or avoidance is not attributable to the physiological effects of a substance or another medical condition.

I. The fear, anxiety, or avoidance is not better explained by the symptoms of another mental disorder, such as panic disorder, body dysmorphic disorder, or autism spectrum disorder.

J. If another medical condition is present, the fear, anxiety, or avoidance is clearly unrelated or is excessive.

American Psychiatric Association. (2013). *Diagnostic and statistical manual of mental disorders* (5th ed.). Arlington, VA: American Psychiatric Association.

**Table 5.5**

### DSM-5 Specific Phobia

A. Marked fear or anxiety about a specific object or situation.

   **Note:** In children, the fear or anxiety may be expressed by crying, tantrums, freezing, or clinging.

B. The phobic object or situation almost always provokes immediate fear or anxiety.

C. The phobic object or situation is actively avoided or endured with intense fear or anxiety.

D. The fear or anxiety is out of proportion to the actual danger posed by the specific object or situation and to the sociocultural context.

E. The fear, anxiety, or avoidance is persistent, typically lasting for 6 months or more.

F. The fear, anxiety, or avoidance causes clinically significant distress or impairment in social, occupational, or other important areas of functioning.

G. The disturbance is not better explained by the symptoms of another mental disorder.

American Psychiatric Association. (2013). *Diagnostic and statistical manual of mental disorders* (5th ed.). Arlington, VA: American Psychiatric Association.

## Specific Phobia

We mentioned that most people are leery of snakes, so this kind of fear is normal. For other people, though, fear is so strong and pervasive that it interferes with daily functioning. Think about a fear of snakes so strong a person cannot walk in his yard or go to the park. Such is the case for some people with **specific phobia**.

A specific phobia is an excessive, unreasonable fear of a particular object or situation. A diagnosis of specific phobia involves the *DSM-5* criteria in **Table 5.5** (APA, 2013). People with specific phobia may have *expected panic attacks* when they encounter a dog, airplane, clown, or whatever they fear. Specific phobias are arranged into five types:

- *Animal phobias* involve fears of—you guessed it, animals—especially dogs, rodents, insects, and snakes or other reptiles.
- *Natural environment phobias* involve fears of surrounding phenomena such as heights, water, and weather events such as thunderstorms.
- *Blood-injection-injury phobias* involve fears of needles, medical procedures, and harm to self.
- *Situational phobias* involve fears of specific areas such as enclosed spaces in airplanes and elevators.
- *Other phobias* involve any other intense fear of a specific object. Examples include more common ones such as *iophobia* (fear of poison) but also unusual ones such as *levophobia* (fear of things to one's left), *arachibutyrophobia* (fear of peanut butter sticking to the roof of the mouth), and *hippopotomonstrosesquippedaliophobia* (you guessed it—fear of long words).

Many people with social phobia believe they will do something "dumb" or "crazy" to make them appear foolish before others. They may fear stuttering, fainting, freezing, or shaking around other people. They know their fear is excessive and unreasonable, but they still have trouble doing what they must, such as chatting during a job interview (Heimberg, Brozovich, & Rapee, 2010). People with social phobia may even have trouble with simple things like using a debit card in a store, using a public restroom, or getting together with friends at a mall. If someone with social phobia fears only speaking or performing in public, then the disorder is specified as *performance only*.

## Generalized Anxiety Disorder

Do you ever get concerned about many things, large and small? If you do, welcome to the human race, especially if you are a student. Many people worry about what could happen, especially in this day and age with threats everywhere. We seem to read every day about terrible events such as terrorist attacks and devastating hurricanes and earthquakes. Knowing about these things and wondering if they might happen to us naturally makes us uptight and worried. Such worry is normal.

We mentioned that worry is an adaptive phenomenon that helps us prepare for and solve problems. Worry is also something most of us can control and put aside when we have to concentrate. Many people can put aside their worries about the upcoming weekend as they prepare a Wednesday dinner. Worry is thus usually normal and controllable. For other people, though, worry is so strong and persistent it interferes with their ability to work, make decisions, and relax.

Pierre Perrin/Zoko/Sygma/Corbis

Many people are afraid of spiders, but a phobia of spiders, known as arachnophobia, involves a more intense and irrational fear.

**Generalized anxiety disorder** involves extreme levels of worry about various events or activities. A diagnosis of generalized anxiety disorder involves the *DSM-5* criteria in **Table 5.6** (APA, 2013). People with generalized anxiety disorder have trouble controlling their worry and thus often have trouble concentrating, sleeping, or resting. Those with generalized anxiety disorder often worry excessively about minor things such as paying bills or picking up their children on time. Such worry is *not in proportion* to actual risk or problems. Many people worry about paying bills when their homes are near foreclosure, but people with generalized anxiety disorder might worry about paying bills when no financial problems exist. Other common worries of those with generalized anxiety disorder include health issues, chores, being on time, work-related tasks, and competence in different activities.

You may have noticed from Table 5.6 that people with generalized anxiety disorder do not usually experience panic attacks but rather have muscle tension or trouble sleeping and concentrating. Generalized anxiety disorder and worry are largely *cognitive* concepts, so physical and behavioral symptoms are less prominent than what is seen in panic disorder and social and specific phobias (Craske & Waters, 2005; Wells, 2002). People with generalized anxiety disorder do not focus on internal symptoms of panic but more on potential external threats. They also believe these threats to be very dangerous or full of dire consequences. One might worry excessively that not paying a bill 15 days *early* will result in a damaged credit rating and inability to buy a new car.

The key aspect of generalized anxiety disorder, worry, is reported by many people to be a lifelong problem. Generalized anxiety disorder is often the first of several anxiety and other mental disorders a person may have (Craske & Hazlett-Stevens,

---

### Table 5.6

#### DSM-5 Generalized Anxiety Disorder

A. Excessive anxiety and worry (apprehensive expectation), occurring more days than not for at least 6 months, about a number of events or activities.

B. The individual finds it difficult to control the worry.

C. The anxiety and worry are associated with three (or more) of the following six symptoms (with at least some symptoms having been present for more days than not for the past 6 months):
   **Note:** Only one item is required in children.
   1. Restlessness or feeling keyed up or on edge.
   2. Being easily fatigued.
   3. Difficulty concentrating or mind going blank.
   4. Irritability.
   5. Muscle tension.
   6. Sleep disturbance.

D. The anxiety, worry, or physical symptoms cause clinically significant distress or impairment in social, occupational, or other important areas of functioning.

E. The disturbance is not attributable to the physiological effects of a substance or another medical condition (e.g., hyperthyroidism).

F. The disturbance is not better explained by another mental disorder (e.g., anxiety or worry about having panic attacks in panic disorder).

American Psychiatric Association. (2013). *Diagnostic and statistical manual of mental disorders* (5th ed.). Arlington, VA: American Psychiatric Association.

2002). Recall Angelina said she was always the "nervous and worried type." Generalized anxiety disorder that develops early in life is not associated with a specific life event, or trigger, but later-onset generalized anxiety disorder often *is* related to a particular stressor such as bankruptcy. Generalized anxiety disorder is perhaps the least reliably diagnosed of the major anxiety disorders. Uncontrollable worry, muscle tension, and scanning the environment for threats, however, are key symptoms that separate generalized anxiety disorder from other anxiety disorders (Hudson, Devenoy, & Taylor, 2005).

## CASE: Jonathan

Jonathan was a 33-year-old man in therapy for behaviors that recently cost him his job and that were threatening his marriage. Jonathan said he had overwhelming urges to check things to see if they were in place and to order things if they were not. Jonathan said he would go to work and spend the first 3 hours organizing his desk, office, e-mail messages, and computer files. He would also check other offices to see if things were grossly out of place, such as plants, wastebaskets, and pencils. He did this so often his coworkers complained that Jonathan spent more time with them than in his own office. Jonathan did get some work done, but he usually could not concentrate for more than 3 hours per day. He was fired for his lack of productivity.

Jonathan said he often had troubling thoughts about things being out of order. He told his therapist he worried that disorganization would lead him to forget important pieces of information such as what bills needed to be paid and what reports were due. He spent so much time organizing items at work and home, however, that he could accomplish little else. His wife recently threatened to leave if Jonathan did not seek professional help. Jonathan also said he felt depressed and wished he "could think like a normal person."

## Obsessive-Compulsive Disorder

Many of us have little rituals or habits, or **compulsions**, we do every day to keep order or check on things, but not to the extent Jonathan does. Keeping things in place has its advantages in a competitive workplace or if you want to find something at home. Checking the windows and doors at night before going to bed can also protect against disaster. For other people, rituals or compulsions are associated with painful thoughts, or **obsessions**, and become overly time-consuming, distressing, and destructive. Obsessions can also come in the form of constant ideas, impulses, or even images.

**Obsessive-compulsive disorder** involves (1) obsessions, or troublesome thoughts, impulses, or images, and/or (2) compulsions, or ritualistic acts done repeatedly to reduce anxiety from the obsessions. A diagnosis of obsessive-compulsive disorder involves the *DSM-5* criteria in **Table 5.7** (APA, 2013).

Obsessions occur spontaneously, frequently, and intrusively, meaning they are unwanted by the person but uncontrollable. Obsessions may also be quite strange—one might have images or thoughts of massive bacteria on doorknobs or coins. This is a *contamination* obsession. Other common obsessions include the following:

- *Doubt*, such as concern about leaving the front door open
- *Need for order*, such as need to have shoes organized by size and type or food organized by expiration date
- *Impulses toward aggression*, such as intolerable thoughts about harming an infant
- *Sexual imagery*, such as recurrent mental pictures of pornography

### Table 5.7

#### DSM-5 Obsessive-Compulsive Disorder

A. Presence of obsessions, compulsions, or both:

Obsessions are defined by (1) and (2):
1. Recurrent and persistent thoughts, urges, or images that are experienced, at some time during the disturbance, as intrusive and unwanted, and that in most individuals cause marked anxiety or distress.
2. The individual attempts to ignore or suppress such thoughts, urges, or images, or to neutralize them with some other thought or action (i.e., by performing a compulsion).

Compulsions are defined by (1) and (2):
1. Repetitive behaviors (e.g., hand washing) or mental acts (e.g., repeating words silently) that the individual feels driven to perform in response to an obsession or according to rules that must be applied rigidly.
2. The behaviors or mental acts are aimed at preventing or reducing anxiety or distress, or preventing some dreaded event or situation; however, these behaviors or mental acts are not connected in a realistic way with what they are designed to neutralize or prevent, or are clearly excessive.
   **Note:** Young children may not be able to articulate the aims of these behaviors or mental acts.

B. The obsessions or compulsions are time-consuming or cause clinically significant distress or impairment in social, occupational, or other important areas of functioning.

C. The obsessive-compulsive symptoms are not attributable to the physiological effects of a substance or another medical condition.

D. The disturbance is not better explained by the symptoms of another mental disorder (e.g., excessive worries, as in generalized anxiety disorder).

American Psychiatric Association. (2013). *Diagnostic and statistical manual of mental disorders* (5th ed.). Arlington, VA: American Psychiatric Association.

Many people with obsessive-compulsive disorder will perform certain rituals more often than usual, such as this woman, who trims her hedges with a pair of scissors several hours every day.

Compulsions are motor behaviors or mental acts performed in response to an obsession. Someone who obsesses about the front door being open will keep checking the door to make sure it is closed and locked. This may continue so many times in a row that the person misses school or work that day. Compulsions other than checking include hand washing, ordering, counting, silently repeating words or phrases, and seeking reassurance from others. Hand washing usually occurs in response to a contamination obsession—a person may obsess about massive bacteria on her hand and then wash vigorously and often to compensate. Obsessions and compulsions occur nearly every day and interfere with a person's ability to concentrate or work.

Compulsions may take place at least *1 hour per day,* but often last much longer. Counting your change when you get home from school might be normal, but counting the change so many times you take hours doing so might indicate obsessive-compulsive disorder. Many people with little rituals are not disturbed by their behavior, but people with obsessive-compulsive disorder find their obsessions and compulsions to be extremely distressing.

## Obsessive-Compulsive-Related Disorders

*DSM-5* includes disorders that are related to obsessive-compulsive disorder. *Hoarding disorder* refers to people who have persistent difficulty parting with possessions, who feel they need to save items, and who experience cluttered living areas. Other related disorders include people who continually pull out their own hair (*trichotillomania*) or pick their skin (*excoriation disorder*).

Another disorder in this section, **body dysmorphic disorder,** was once grouped with somatic symptom disorders (Chapter 6) but is now thought to be more closely related to obsessive-compulsive behavior. A diagnosis of body dysmorphic

disorder involves the *DSM-5* criteria in **Table 5.8** (APA, 2013). People with body dysmorphic disorder are preoccupied with an imaginary or slight "defect" in their appearance. Many people with this disorder worry excessively about minor alterations in facial features, hair, wrinkles, skin spots, and size of body parts like noses or ears. Many of us are concerned with our appearance, but people with body dysmorphic disorder are so preoccupied they may spend hours per day checking and grooming themselves or they may visit cosmetic surgeons and undergo several surgeries to correct imagined or minor flaws (Crerand, Menard, & Phillips, 2010). People with body dysmorphic disorder may be unable to date or work because of deep embarrassment about some perceived body flaw.

Body dysmorphic disorder has some similarities to *koro,* a syndrome among people in West Africa and Southeast Asia who fear that external genitalia and body parts such as nipples or breasts will shrink into one's body and cause death (Dzokoto & Adams, 2005; Phillips, 2004). The disorder may also be similar to *shubo-kyofu,* a phobia among some Japanese who fear a deformed face or body (Iwata et al., 2011).

## Posttraumatic Stress Disorder and Acute Stress Disorder

The disorders discussed so far are often linked to *regularly* occurring events like public speaking. Other disorders—posttraumatic stress and acute stress disorder—follow a *specific traumatic event. DSM-5* lists these as *trauma- and stressor-related disorders.*

---

### Table 5.8

#### DSM-5 Body Dysmorphic Disorder

A. Preoccupation with one or more perceived defects or flaws in physical appearance that are not observable or appear slight to others.

B. At some point during the course of the disorder, the individual has performed repetitive behaviors (e.g., mirror checking, excessive grooming, skin picking, reassurance seeking) or mental acts (e.g., comparing his or her appearance with that of others) in response to the appearance concerns.

C. The preoccupation causes clinically significant distress or impairment in social, occupational, or other important areas of functioning.

D. The appearance preoccupation is not better explained by concerns with body fat or weight in an individual whose symptoms meet diagnostic criteria for an eating disorder.

American Psychiatric Association. (2013). *Diagnostic and statistical manual of mental disorders* (5th ed.). Arlington, VA: American Psychiatric Association.

## CASE: Marcus

Marcus was a 27-year-old man in therapy for symptoms following a traumatic event. Marcus was about to enter a shopping mall at night two months ago when two men threatened him with a gun and demanded his wallet. Marcus was initially shocked the event was occurring and thus hesitated, which prompted one of the men to strike him in the face. Marcus then gave his wallet to the men, who fled. A shaken Marcus called police to report the incident and was taken to the hospital for treatment. The two assailants had not yet been caught at the time of Marcus's therapy.

Marcus said he had been having trouble sleeping at home and concentrating at work. The latter was especially problematic because he was an accountant. He also felt he was living his life in a "slow motion fog" and that people seemed very distant from him. He increasingly spent time at home and avoided major shopping areas and large parking lots, especially at night. Marcus also feared the gunmen would find and rob him again because they had his driver's license. Most distressing, however, were Marcus's recurring images of the event; he said, "I just can't get the whole scene out of my mind." He thus tried to block thoughts about the trauma as much as possible, with little success.

Have you ever been in a situation where you felt terrified, helpless, or extremely vulnerable? Some people experience traumatic events in their life, events so disturbing they produce changes in behavior and personality. Think about people victimized by the 9/11 terrorist attacks, Hurricane Katrina, the tsunami in Japan, recent earthquakes, or soldiers who faced constant danger in Iraq or Afghanistan. Some people can eventually deal with these stressors as they fade in memory over time. Other people like Marcus, however, find recovery from trauma to be a long and painful process.

**Posttraumatic stress disorder** is marked by frequent reexperiencing of a traumatic event through images, memories, nightmares, flashbacks, or other ways. A diagnosis of posttraumatic stress disorder (PTSD) involves the *DSM-5* criteria in **Table 5.9** (APA, 2013). Marcus's images of his trauma constantly entered his mind. He also became upset at reminders of the trauma, such as walking through a large parking lot at night, and avoided many discussions of the event. People with posttraumatic stress disorder may also feel detached from others, have fewer positive emotional responses than before the event, and expect additional harm or negative consequences. A person may believe others will not want to socialize with her because of the trauma. The person may also experience substantial physical arousal and have problems sleeping, concentrating, or completing everyday tasks.

Symptoms of posttraumatic stress disorder must last at least 1 month for a diagnosis to be made. Some symptoms of posttraumatic stress disorder are delayed more than 6 months from time of trauma, and this refers to *delayed expression*. Most symptoms of posttraumatic stress disorder, however, develop within 3 to 6 months of the trauma (Holeva, Tarrier, & Wells, 2001). *DSM-5* also lists separate criteria for PTSD in children younger than age 7 years (Table 5.9). Young children with PTSD may display reexperiencing symptoms through play, for example.

What about people with problems immediately after the trauma? **Acute stress disorder** refers to distressing memories and dreams, negative mood, dissociation (feelings of detachment from reality or disconnectedness from others), avoidance, and arousal that last between 3 days and 1 month after the trauma. A diagnosis of acute stress disorder involves the *DSM-5* criteria in **Table 5.10** (APA, 2013). People with acute stress disorder may eventually be diagnosed with posttraumatic stress disorder if symptoms continue longer than 1 month. Acute stress disorder is a good predictor of posttraumatic stress disorder (Bryant, Creamer, O'Donnell, Silove, & McFarlane, 2008).

What traumas might lead to acute stress disorder or posttraumatic stress disorder? Key traumas include assault, rape,

Spectators and racers react in the aftermath of the Boston Marathon bombing. Trauma from events such as terrorism can cause posttraumatic stress disorder in some people.

Kelvin Ma/Bloomberg/Getty Images

**Table 5.9**

## DSM-5  Posttraumatic Stress Disorder

**Note:** The following criteria apply to adults, adolescents, and children older than 6 years. For children 6 years and younger, see corresponding criteria below.

A. Exposure to actual or threatened death, serious injury, or sexual violence in one (or more) of the following ways:
1. Directly experiencing the traumatic event(s).
2. Witnessing, in person, the event(s) as it occurred to others.
3. Learning that the traumatic event(s) occurred to a close family member or close friend. In cases of actual or threatened death of a family member or friend, the event(s) must have been violent or accidental.
4. Experiencing repeated or extreme exposure to aversive details of the traumatic event(s) (e.g., first responders collecting human remains; police officers repeatedly exposed to details of child abuse).
   **Note:** Criterion A4 does not apply to exposure through electronic media, television, movies, or pictures, unless this exposure is work related.

B. Presence of one (or more) of the following intrusion symptoms associated with the traumatic event(s), beginning after the traumatic event(s) occurred:
1. Recurrent, involuntary, and intrusive distressing memories of the traumatic event(s).
   **Note:** In children older than 6 years, repetitive play may occur in which themes or aspects of the traumatic event(s) are expressed.
2. Recurrent distressing dreams in which the content and/or affect of the dream are related to the traumatic event(s).
   **Note:** In children, there may be frightening dreams without recognizable content.
3. Dissociative reactions (e.g., flashbacks) in which the individual feels or acts as if the traumatic event(s) were recurring. (Such reactions may occur on a continuum, with the most extreme expression being a complete loss of awareness of present surroundings.)
   **Note:** In children, trauma-specific reenactment may occur in play.
4. Intense or prolonged psychological distress at exposure to internal or external cues that symbolize or resemble an aspect of the traumatic event(s).
5. Marked physiological reactions to internal or external cues that symbolize or resemble an aspect of the traumatic event(s).

C. Persistent avoidance of stimuli associated with the traumatic event(s), beginning after the traumatic event(s) occurred, as evidenced by one or both of the following:
1. Avoidance of or efforts to avoid distressing memories, thoughts, or feelings about or closely associated with the traumatic event(s).
2. Avoidance of or efforts to avoid external reminders (people, places, conversations, activities, objects, situations) that arouse distressing memories, thoughts, or feelings about or closely associated with the traumatic event(s).

D. Negative alterations in cognitions and mood associated with the traumatic event(s), beginning or worsening after the traumatic event(s) occurred, as evidenced by two (or more) of the following:
1. Inability to remember an important aspect of the traumatic event(s) (typically due to dissociative amnesia and not to other factors such as head injury, alcohol, or drugs).
2. Persistent and exaggerated negative beliefs or expectations about oneself, others, or the world (e.g., "I am bad," "No one can be trusted," "The world is completely dangerous," "My whole nervous system is permanently ruined").
3. Persistent, distorted cognitions about the cause or consequences of the traumatic event(s) that lead the individual to blame himself/herself or others.
4. Persistent negative emotional state (e.g., fear, horror, anger, guilt, or shame).
5. Markedly diminished interest or participation in significant activities.
6. Feelings of detachment or estrangement from others.
7. Persistent inability to experience positive emotions (e.g., inability to experience happiness, satisfaction, or loving feelings).

E. Marked alterations in arousal and reactivity associated with the traumatic event(s), beginning or worsening after the traumatic event(s) occurred, as evidenced by two (or more) of the following:
1. Irritable behavior and angry outbursts (with little or no provocation) typically expressed as verbal or physical aggression toward people or objects.
2. Reckless or self-destructive behavior.

*continued*

— **Table 5.9** —

**DSM-5 Posttraumatic Stress Disorder—cont'd**

3. Hypervigilance.
4. Exaggerated startle response.
5. Problems with concentration.
6. Sleep disturbance (e.g., difficulty falling or staying asleep or restless sleep).

F. Duration of the disturbance (Criteria B, C, D, and E) is more than 1 month.

G. The disturbance causes clinically significant distress or impairment in social, occupational, or other important areas of functioning.

H. The disturbance is not attributable to the physiological effects of a substance (e.g., medication, alcohol) or another medical condition.

*Specify* whether:

**With dissociative symptoms:** The individual's symptoms meet the criteria for posttraumatic stress disorder, and in addition, in response to the stressor, the individual experiences persistent or recurrent symptoms of either of the following:

1. **Depersonalization:** Persistent or recurrent experiences of feeling detached from, and as if one were an outside observer of, one's mental processes or body (e.g., feeling as though one were in a dream; feeling a sense of unreality of self or body or of time moving slowly).
2. **Derealization:** Persistent or recurrent experiences of unreality of surroundings (e.g., the world around the individual is experienced as unreal, dreamlike, distant, or distorted).
**Note:** To use this subtype, the dissociative symptoms must not be attributable to the physiological effects of a substance (e.g., blackouts, behavior during alcohol intoxication) or another medical condition (e.g., complex partial seizures).

*Specifiy* if:

**With delayed expression:** If the full diagnostic criteria are not met until at least 6 months after the event (although the onset and expression of some symptoms may be immediate).

**Posttraumatic Stress Disorder for Children 6 Years and Younger**

A. In children 6 years and younger, exposure to actual or threatened death, serious injury, or sexual violence in one (or more) of the following ways:
1. Directly experiencing the traumatic events(s).
2. Witnessing, in person, the event(s) as it occurred to others, especially primary caregivers.
**Note:** Witnessing does not include events that are witnesses only in electronic media, television, movies, or pictures.
3. Learning that the traumatic event(s) occurred to a parent or caregiving figure.

B. Presence of one (or more) of the following intrusion symptoms associated with the traumatic event(s), beginning after the traumatic event(s) occurred:
1. Recurrent, involuntary, and intrusive distressing memories of the traumatic event(s).
**Note:** Spontaneous and intrusive memories may not necessarily appear distressing and may be expressed as play reenactment.
2. Recurrent distressing dreams in which the content and/or affect of the dream are related to the traumatic event(s).
**Note:** It may not be possible to ascertain that the frightening content is related to the traumatic event.
3. Dissociative reactions (e.g., flashbacks) in which the child feels or acts as if the traumatic event(s) were recurring. (Such reactions may occur on a continuum, with the most extreme expression being a complete loss of awareness of present surroundings.) Such trauma-specific reenactment may occur in play.
4. Intense or prolonged psychological distress at exposure to internal or external cues that symbolize or resemble an aspect of the traumatic event(s).
5. Marked physiological reactions to reminders of the traumatic event(s).

C. One (or more) of the following symptoms, representing either persistent avoidance of stimuli associated with the traumatic event(s), or negative alterations in cognitions and mood associated with the traumatic event(s), must be present, beginning after the event(s) or worsening after the event(s):
**Persistent Avoidance of Stimuli**
1. Avoidance of or efforts to avoid activities, places, or physical reminders that arouse recollections of the traumatic event(s).
2. Avoidance of or efforts to avoid people, conversations, or interpersonal situations that arouse recollections of the traumatic event(s).

---

**Table 5.9**

### DSM-5 Posttraumatic Stress Disorder—cont'd

**Negative Alterations in Cognitions**
3. Substantially increased frequency of negative emotional states (e.g., fear, guilt, sadness, shame, confusion).
4. Markedly diminished interest or participation in significant activities, including constriction of play.
5. Socially withdrawn behavior.
6. Persistent reduction in expression of positive emotions.

D. Alterations in arousal and reactivity associated with the traumatic event(s), beginning or worsening after the traumatic event(s) occurred, as evidenced by two (or more) of the following:
1. Irritable behavior and angry outbursts (with little or no provocation) typically expressed as verbal or physical aggression toward people or objects (including extreme temper tantrums).
2. Hypervigilance.
3. Exaggerated startle response.
4. Problems with concentration.
5. Sleep disturbance (e.g., difficulty falling or staying asleep or restless sleep).

E. The duration of the disturbance is more than 1 month.

F. The disturbance causes clinically significant distress or impairment in relationships with parents, siblings, peers, or other caregivers or with school behavior.

G. The disturbance is not attributable to the physiological effects of a substance (e.g., medication or alcohol) or another medical condition.

*Specifiy* whether:
   **With dissociative symptoms:** The individual's symptoms meet the criteria for posttraumatic stress disorder, and the individual experiences persistent or recurrent symptoms of either of the following:
   1. **Depersonalization:** Persistent or recurrent experiences of feeling detached from, and as if one were an outside observer of, one's mental processes or body (e.g., feeling as though one were in dream; feeling a sense of unreality of self or body or of time moving slowly).
   2. **Derealization:** Persistent or recurrent experiences of unreality of surroundings (e.g., the world around the individual is experienced as unreal, dreamlike, distant, or distorted).
   **Note:** To use this subtype, the dissociative symptoms must not be attributable to the physiological effects or a substance (e.g., blackouts) or another medical condition (e.g., complex partial seizures).

*Specify* if:
   **With delayed expression:** If the full diagnostic criteria are not met until at least 6 months after the event (although the onset and expression of some symptoms may be immediate).

American Psychiatric Association. (2013). *Diagnostic and statistical manual of mental disorders* (5th ed.). Arlington, VA: American Psychiatric Association.

---

war, severe physical or sexual maltreatment, natural disasters such as tornados or floods, robbery, home invasion, or witnessing horrifying events (Ruggiero, Morris, & Scotti, 2001). More common events such as a car accident, learning of a trauma to a close friend or relative, or experiences of first responders (e.g., police, fire personnel) can also result in either disorder. Not everyone who experiences a traumatic event necessarily develops acute stress disorder or posttraumatic stress disorder, however.

## Separation Anxiety Disorder and School Refusal Behavior

Some anxiety-related disorders are more common in youth. Many young children experience anxiety that is normal for their age. One of the author's children, when she was 2 years old, commonly got upset when Dad dropped her off at preschool in the morning—that's normal. Some toddlers also need their parents close to them when it is time for sleep at night. Some children, however, fear separation so much they refuse to attend school or sleep over at a friend's house. This behavior can be quite disruptive for some families, especially if parents are late for work, conflict occurs, or no one can sleep.

**Separation anxiety disorder** is marked by substantial distress when separation from a major attachment figure occurs or is expected to occur. This distress must last at least 4 weeks in children, so initial distress about going to school is excluded. The separation anxiety must also be developmentally inappropriate. This means a child is at an age, perhaps in elementary school, where separation should not be a problem

## Table 5.10

### DSM-5 Acute Stress Disorder

A. Exposure to actual or threatened death, serious injury, or sexual violation in one (or more) or the following ways:
   1. Directly experiencing the traumatic event(s).
   2. Witnessing, in person, the event(s) as it occurred to others.
   3. Learning that the event(s) occurred to a close family member or close friend. Note: In case of actual or threatened death of a family member or friend, the event(s) must have been violent or accidental.
   4. Experiencing repeated or extreme exposure to aversive details of the traumatic event(s) (e.g., first responders collecting human remains, police officers repeatedly exposed to details of child abuse).
   **Note:** This does not apply to exposure through electronic media, television, movies, or pictures, unless this exposure is work related.

B. Presence of nine (or more) of the following symptoms from any of the five categories of intrusion, negative mood, dissociation, avoidance, and arousal, beginning or worsening after the traumatic event(s) occurred:

**Intrusion Symptoms**
   1. Recurrent, involuntary, and intrusive distressing memories of the traumatic event(s). Note: In children, repetitive play may occur in which themes or aspects of the traumatic event(s) are expressed.
   2. Recurrent distressing dreams in which the content and/or affect of the dream are related to the event(s). Note: In children, there may be frightening dreams without recognizable content.
   3. Dissociative reactions (e.g., flashbacks) in which the individual feels or acts as if the traumatic event(s) were recurring. (Such reactions may occur on a continuum, with the most extreme expression being a complete loss of awareness of present surroundings.) Note: In children, trauma-specific reenactment may occur in play.
   4. Intense or prolonged psychological distress or marked physiological reactions in response to internal or external cues that symbolize or resemble an aspect of the traumatic event(s).

**Negative Mood**
   5. Persistent inability to experience positive emotions.

**Dissociative Symptoms**
   6. An altered sense of the reality of one's surroundings or oneself.
   7. Inability to remember an important aspect of the traumatic event(s) (typically due to dissociative amnesia and not to other factors such as head injury, alcohol, or drugs).

**Avoidance Symptoms**
   8. Efforts to avoid distressing memories, thoughts, or feelings about or closely associated with the traumatic event(s).
   9. Efforts to avoid external reminders (people, places, conversations, activities, objects, situations) that arouse distressing memories, thoughts, or feelings about or closely associated with the traumatic event(s).

**Arousal Symptoms**
   10. Sleep disturbance.
   11. Irritable behavior and angry outbursts (with little or no provocation), typically expressed as verbal or physical aggression toward people or objects.
   12. Hypervigilance.
   13. Problems with concentration.
   14. Exaggerated startle response.

C. Duration of the disturbance (symptoms in Criterion B) is 3 days to 1 month after trauma exposure.

**Note:** Symptoms typically begin immediately after the trauma, but persistence for at least 3 days and up to a month is needed to meet disorder criteria.

D. The disturbance causes clinically significant distress or impairment in social, occupational, or other important areas of functioning.

E. The disturbance is not attributable to the physiological effects of a substance or another medical condition and is not better explained by brief psychotic disorder.

American Psychiatric Association. (2013). *Diagnostic and statistical manual of mental disorders* (5th ed.). Arlington, VA: American Psychiatric Association.

but is. A diagnosis of separation anxiety disorder involves the *DSM-5* criteria in **Table 5.11** (APA, 2013). A child with separation anxiety disorder will often have trouble going to school or sleeping alone, throw a tantrum when a parent wants to go someplace without him, and have physical complaints such as a stomachache when away from a parent.

One symptom of separation anxiety disorder is "persistent reluctance to go to school," but **school refusal behavior** can also be due to other reasons. Kearney (2001) outlined four major reasons why children refuse school:

- To avoid something related to school that causes great distress, such as a teacher, bus, bully, or going from class to class

- To escape uncomfortable social and/or performance situations such as conversations, performances, or tests

- To spend time with, or get attention from, parents

- To get tangible rewards outside of school, such as time with friends, television, or sleeping late

Many children thus have trouble going to school for reasons other than separation anxiety (Kearney & Albano, 2004). Many teenagers occasionally "skip" classes to have fun, but they eventually graduate. Ongoing or chronic absences, however, can lead to long-term problems such as delinquency, school dropout, and occupational and marital problems in adulthood (Kearney, 2008). Youths who refuse school for a combination of the reasons listed above may also be at particular risk for school failure or dropout.

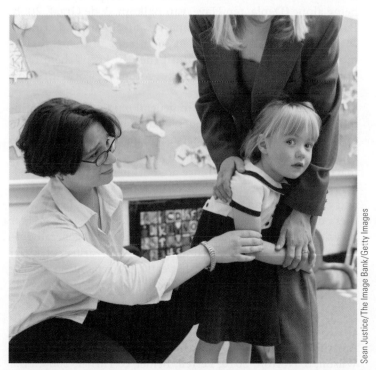

Many children have separation anxiety when they are younger, but some continue to have the problem even during school-age years.

Sean Justice/The Image Bank/Getty Images

## Epidemiology of Anxiety, Obsessive-Compulsive, and Trauma-Related Disorders

Anxiety-related disorders are commonly found in the general population, affecting 28.8 percent of Americans at some point in their lives and 18.1 percent in the past 12 months (Kessler, Chiu, Demler, & Walters, 2005; Kessler, Berglund et al., 2005). Lifetime and 12-month prevalence rates for the major anxiety-related disorders are outlined in **Figure 5.3**. Social phobia and specific phobia are especially common, affecting about 1 in 8 people.

---
**Table 5.11**

### DSM-5   Separation Anxiety Disorder

A. Developmentally inappropriate and excessive fear or anxiety concerning separation from those to whom the individual is attached, as evidenced by at least three of the following:

  1. Recurrent excessive distress when anticipating or experiencing separation from home or from major attachment figures.
  2. Persistent and excessive worry about losing major attachment figures or about possible harm to them, such as illness, injury, disasters, or death.
  3. Persistent and excessive worry about experiencing an untoward event (e.g., getting lost) that causes separation from a major attachment figure.
  4. Persistent reluctance or refusal to go out, away from home, to school, to work, or elsewhere because of fear of separation.
  5. Persistent and excessive fear of or reluctance about being alone or without major attachment figures at home or in other settings.
  6. Persistent reluctance or refusal to sleep away from home or to go to sleep without being near a major attachment figure.
  7. Repeated nightmares involving the theme of separation.
  8. Repeated complaints of physical symptoms when separation from major attachment figures occurs or is anticipated.

B. The fear, anxiety, or avoidance is persistent, lasting at least 4 weeks in children and adolescents and typically 6 months or more in adults.

C. The disturbance causes clinically significant distress or impairment in social, academic, occupational, or other important areas of functioning.

D. The disturbance is not better explained by another mental disorder.

American Psychiatric Association. (2013). *Diagnostic and statistical manual of mental disorders* (5th ed.). Arlington, VA: American Psychiatric Association.

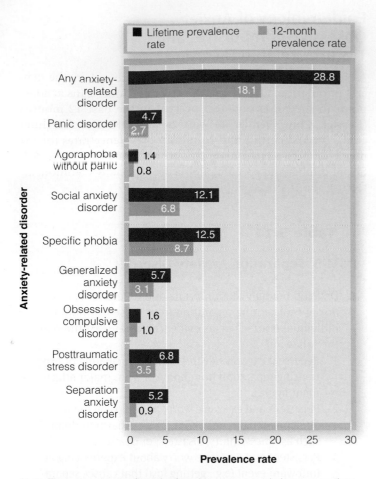

*Note:* These numbers reflect the fact that some people have more than one anxiety-related disorder.

**FIGURE 5.3** LIFETIME AND 12-MONTH PREVALENCE RATES FOR THE ANXIETY-RELATED DISORDERS Adapted from Kessler, Chiu, Demler, & Walters (2005) and Kessler et al. (2005).

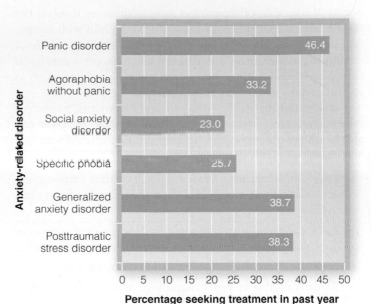

**FIGURE 5.4** PERCENTAGE OF PEOPLE WITH AN ANXIETY-RELATED DISORDER SEEKING TREATMENT IN THE PAST YEAR Adapted from Kessler et al. (1999).

Anxiety is even more problematic when you consider other facts. First, many people experience *symptoms* of anxiety-related disorders that do not necessarily rise to the level of a formal diagnosis. About 20 to 50 percent of college students report recent panic-like attacks that are less severe or less frequent compared with those experienced by people with panic disorder (Deacon & Valentiner, 2000; Norton, Dorward, & Cox, 1986). Many people also have persistent and debilitating worry that may not rise to the level of generalized anxiety disorder (Ruscio et al., 2005).

Second, many people delay seeking treatment for an anxiety-related disorder. Only a minority of people with such a disorder sought some form of treatment in the past year (see **Figure 5.4**; Kessler et al., 1999; Ruscio et al., 2008). Most people with panic disorder experience full-blown symptoms in their early to mid-20s, as Angelina did, but they may delay psychological treatment because they visit medical doctors first to rule out physical conditions (Lynch & Galbraith, 2003). Many people with social or

performance anxiety are also generally shy and may not believe their condition to be serious (Henderson & Zimbardo, 2010).

Strong fears of specific items are common in the general population, especially fears of snakes and other animals, heights, flying in airplanes, enclosed spaces, illness or injury, blood, water, death, bad weather, medical procedures, and being alone (Depla, ten Have, van Balkom, & de Graaf, 2008; Pull, 2008). Recall that Angelina was afraid around crowds. Many people say they have had such fears all their life, but most do not seek treatment until the fear keeps them from doing something important like going to work (Stinson et al., 2007).

Anxiety-related disorders in general tend to be more common among females than males, although the female-to-male ratio for some of these disorders is greater than for others (see **Figure 5.5**; Kessler, Berglund et al., 2005). Several reasons that may account for this difference are outlined in **Box 5.1**. Anxiety-related disorders tend to be fairly equal among young boys and girls. During adolescence and early adulthood, however, as these disorders become more common, females show greater prevalence than males. Anxiety-related disorders generally begin at age 19 to 31 years, although somewhat earlier for social phobia (median age of onset, 13 years) and separation anxiety disorder (median age of onset, 7 years; Kessler, Berglund et al., 2005, Kessler, Angermeyer et al., 2007).

Few racial differences have been found with respect to anxiety-related disorders among European Americans, African Americans, and Hispanics within the United States (Barrera, Wilson, & Norton, 2010; Ferrell, Beidel, & Turner, 2004; Pina & Silverman, 2004). One study, however, indicated a slightly

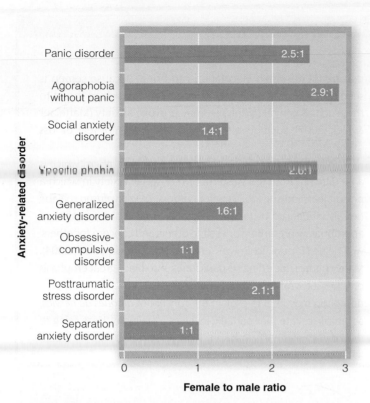

**FIGURE 5.5** **FEMALE TO MALE RATIOS FOR ANXIETY-RELATED DISORDER PREVALENCE RATES** Adapted from APA (2013), Kessler et al. (1994), Kessler et al. (1995), and Offord et al. (1996).

greater risk for anxiety-related disorders among European Americans than African Americans or Hispanics (Kessler, Berglund et al., 2005).

Major anxiety-related disorders are more prevalent in certain countries such as the United States, Colombia, New Zealand, and France. Disorder rates are particularly low for people in Japan, Israel, China, Nigeria, and Spain (Kessler et al., 2007), although some researchers have found fewer cultural differences in prevalence and other characteristics of major anxiety-related disorders (Warah & Brodbeck, 2000; Weissman et al., 1994). People of one culture may fear certain stimuli more so than people of another culture because of environmental experiences. A person living in a dense forest, for example, may be more afraid of animals than a person living in a large urban setting (see also the later section on cultural factors). The nature of how anxiety-related disorders are expressed can also differ from culture to culture. The following are examples of anxiety-related disorders across the globe (see also **Box 5.2**):

- *Koro:* intense fear of one's penis or nipples retracting into the body or shrinking in size (South and East Asia)
- *Taijin kyofusho:* intense fear of offending other people, perhaps through one's own body odor, inept conversation, or physical abnormality (Japan)
- *Dhat:* anxiety about loss of semen (India, Sri Lanka, China)
- *Pa-leng:* intense fear of cold that may lead to wearing layers of clothes even in hot weather (Asia)

---

## BOX 5.1 Focus on Gender

### Are There True Gender Differences in Anxiety-Related Disorders?

Females have more anxiety-related disorders than males (Figure 5.5). This is often reported, but is it actually true, and why? Are women just more nervous than men? Or are women more likely to report anxiety and more willing to seek therapy than men, who may prefer to keep their anxiety private or self-medicate their anxiety using alcohol or other drugs? These are common explanations for the gender difference in anxiety-related disorders.

A closer look at this gender difference reveals more intricate explanations. Women experience more physical and sexual trauma than men, and as many as 69 percent of women suffer physical maltreatment from their partners in their lifetime (Ruiz-Perez, Plazaola-Castano, & Vivas-Cases, 2007). Women are more likely to be raped or sexually assaulted and are thus

predisposed to develop acute or posttraumatic stress or other anxiety-related disorders. Women also worry more than men (Masho & Ahmed, 2007; Robichaud, Dugas, & Conway, 2003).

Therapist bias may also be a contributing factor. Therapists may be more likely to assign an anxiety-related diagnosis to a female based on misguided expectations or assumptions about that gender. Some researchers argue the gender difference in anxiety-related disorders is real because men are more likely on a daily basis to be exposed to events, objects, and situations that produce anxiety (Craske, 1999; McClean & Anderson, 2009). Some men spend more time working outside, speaking to others, or driving during the day. Perhaps men have greater opportunities for exposure to—and thus treatment for—anxiety-provoking phenomena and so truly have fewer anxiety-related disorders than women. Controversy about a true gender difference in anxiety-related disorder is not likely to end anytime soon because many plausible explanations are supported by research.

## BOX 5.2 Focus on Diversity

### Anxiety-Related Disorders and Sociocultural Factors

The anxiety-related disorders described in this chapter are those listed in the *DSM*, a manual written largely by American psychiatrists. Anxiety-related disorders are experienced differently across cultures, however, and sociocultural factors certainly influence why some people experience different kinds of anxiety symptoms. Some examples are described here. One thing that does not change across cultures, though, is the amount of distress these problems bring to people's lives.

Recall that *koro* represents an intense fear of one's penis or nipples shrinking into one's body. One sociocultural factor that may influence this phenomenon is strong religious or Taoist beliefs about the need for sexual restraint and the harm that frequent semen ejaculation can bring. Because semen is seen as a source of energy or strength, any perceived threat to this, such as genital shrinkage, may provoke anxiety (Mattelaer & Jilek, 2007). Such beliefs may also affect *dhat,* or fear of loss of semen.

*Taijin kyofusho* represents a fear of offending others, which is a bit different from the Western form of social anxiety in which a person fears looking foolish before others. *Taijin kyofusho* may be heavily influenced by Japanese emphases on the importance of appropriately presenting oneself to others and concern for others' well-being (Tarumi, Ichimiya, Yamada, Umesue, & Kuroki, 2004). Many cultures, including Hispanic ones, also place great emphasis on physical symptoms to express distress or anxiety. Such a phenomenon may help to explain the concept of *ataques de nervios,* a panic-like state that partially involves a feeling of heat rising to the head (Diefenbach, Robison, Tolin, & Blank, 2004).

- *Ataques de nervios:* a panic-like condition of uncontrollable episodes of shouting, crying, and trembling as well as feelings of heat rising to the head and aggression (Puerto Rico)
- *Latah:* an exaggerated startle response mixed with shouting obscenities (Malaysia)

Anxiety-related disorders are highly comorbid, or associated with, other mental disorders (see **Table 5.12**). People with one anxiety-related disorder often have another anxiety-related disorder. Recall that generalized anxiety disorder often leads to other anxiety-related disorders and is commonly associated with social phobia (Mennin, McLaughlin, & Flanagan, 2009). Anxiety-related disorders and depression are also commonly seen in the same individual because the disorders share many features such as irritability, restlessness, and withdrawal. Combined anxiety and depression is sometimes referred to as *negative affectivity* (Hirshfeld-Becker, Micco, Simoes, & Henin, 2008). People with anxiety-related disorders are also at particular risk for suicide (Hawgood & De Leo, 2008).

Anxiety-related disorders and substance use disorder are commonly comorbid as well because many people who are anxious self-medicate or ease their symptoms by using alcohol or other drugs (Castle, 2008; Cosci, Schruers, Abrams, & Griez, 2007). Anxiety-related disorders and substance use may also share common causal factors, however, and a direct relationship between the two problems is likely influenced by factors such as gender or accessibility to alcohol (Morris, Stewart, & Ham, 2005).

Anxiety-related disorders are also associated with eating disorders and avoidant and dependent personality disorders (Chapters 8 and 10; Cox, Pagura, Stein, & Sareen, 2009; Swinbourne

& Touyz, 2007). As mentioned, obsessive-compulsive disorder is sometimes associated with hoarding and with *trichotillomania,* or a compulsion to pull out one's hair, eyelashes, eyebrows, and other body hair (Chamberlain et al., 2007). Separation anxiety disorder can be associated with other conditions such as panic, social anxiety, and obsessive-compulsive disorders (Brucki et al., 2007).

## Stigma Associated with Anxiety, Obsessive-Compulsive, and Trauma-Related Disorders

Recall from Chapter 1 that an important aspect of this textbook is addressing *stigma,* which refers to characterizing others with disgrace or reproach based on an individual characteristic. People with anxiety-related disorders may feel stigma or negative judgment when nervously speaking before others or when having trouble boarding an airplane. Researchers have also found that people sometimes have negative attitudes toward those with generalized anxiety disorder. One survey revealed that a substantial percentage of people felt that those with generalized anxiety disorder were unstable (16.7 percent), that generalized anxiety disorder was not a real mental disorder (13.0 percent), that people with an anxiety-related disorder were not suitable employees (7.8 percent) or were self-centered (6.4 percent), and that anxiety-related disorder was a sign of personal weakness (6.0 percent). Others endorsed the belief that people with an anxiety-related disorder were lazy, shameful, dangerous, or to blame for their problems (Griffiths, Batterham, Barney, & Parsons, 2011). Teenagers of parents with obsessive-compulsive

**Table 5.12**

| Comorbidity of Current Major Anxiety-Related Disorders with Each Other and with Depression | | | | | | |
|---|---|---|---|---|---|---|
| **Current Comorbid Disorder** | **Current Anxiety-Related Disorder** | | | | | |
| | PD/A | SAD | SP | GAD | OCD | PTSD |
| Panic disorder with or without agoraphobia | — | 3 | 5 | 18 | 9 | 23 |
| Social anxiety disorder | 15 | | 9 | 36 | 26 | 15 |
| Specific phobia | 15 | 8 | — | 12 | 12 | 15 |
| Generalized anxiety disorder | 16 | 13 | 5 | — | 12 | 23 |
| Obsessive-compulsive disorder | 7 | 8 | 3 | 4 | — | 23 |
| Posttraumatic stress disorder | 4 | 3 | 0 | 1 | 0 | — |
| Major depressive disorder | 23 | 14 | 3 | 26 | 22 | 69 |

Numbers represent percentages of comorbid diagnoses for that group (e.g., 15% of people with PD/A [top row] have social anxiety disorder [column] and 4% have posttraumatic stress disorder [column]).
PD/A: panic disorder with or without agoraphobia, SAD: social anxiety disorder, SP: specific phobia, GAD: generalized anxiety disorder, OCD: obsessive-compulsive disorder, PTSD: posttraumatic stress disorder.
Source: Brown et al. (2001).

disorder also worry about what others might think of their parent's condition and feel stigmatized as a result (Griffiths, Norris, Stallard, & Matthews, 2011).

People with an anxiety-related disorder who feel stigmatized may be less likely to admit a problem or to seek treatment. This may be especially evident in military personnel who have returned from Iraq and Afghanistan and who often have PTSD and related disorders. Unfortunately, only 54.3 percent of military personnel referred for a mental health evaluation actually follow through on a mental health visit, suggesting possible reluctance due to stigma (Hoge, Auchterlonie, & Milliken, 2006). Greden and colleagues (2010) tried to address this issue by training "soldier peers" who encourage military personnel to enter treatment and then monitor adherence to treatment. A key aspect of this program is to convey the idea that seeking treatment is a sign of strength and to remove military cultural barriers such as stigma that prevent seeking treatment.

## INTERIM SUMMARY

▶ Anxiety is composed of three parts: physical feelings, thoughts, and behaviors.
▶ Anxiety-related disorders often involve excessive worry, anxiety, or fear.
▶ Panic attacks involve (1) intense physical feelings such as heart racing, sweating, and dizziness and (2) thoughts that one will lose control, go crazy, or die. Panic attacks may be expected or unexpected.
▶ Panic disorder refers to regular unexpected panic attacks and worry about the consequences of these attacks.

▶ People with panic disorder may also have agoraphobia, or avoidance of situations in which a panic attack might occur.
▶ Social phobia refers to intense and ongoing fear of potentially embarrassing situations in the form of expected panic attacks.
▶ Specific phobia refers to excessive, unreasonable fear of an object or situation.
▶ Generalized anxiety disorder refers to extreme levels of persistent, uncontrollable worry.
▶ Obsessive-compulsive disorder refers to the presence of obsessions, or troublesome and recurring thoughts, and compulsions, or physical or mental acts performed in response to an obsession to lessen distress.
▶ Posttraumatic stress disorder refers to constant reexperiencing of a traumatic event through images, memories, nightmares, flashbacks, or other ways.
▶ Acute stress disorder refers to short-term anxiety and dissociative symptoms following a trauma.
▶ Separation anxiety disorder refers to children with excessive worry about being away from home or from close family members. The disorder may be associated with school refusal behavior.
▶ Anxiety-related disorders are common to the general population and especially females. Many anxiety-related disorders develop at age 19 to 31 years. Anxiety-related disorders are often associated with other anxiety-related disorders, depression, and substance use.
▶ People with anxiety-related disorders may feel stigma from others and thus may be less likely to seek treatment.

## REVIEW QUESTIONS

1. How do Angelina's symptoms differ from normal worry, anxiety, or fear?
2. Identify different kinds of panic attacks and the main features of panic disorder.
3. Describe anxiety-related disorders that involve severe social anxiety, fear of a specific object, worry, bizarre ideas and behaviors, and symptoms following a trauma.
4. Which anxiety-related disorder applies mostly to children, and what troublesome behavior is sometimes associated with it?
5. Describe the epidemiology of anxiety-related disorders, including issues of gender and culture.

# Anxiety, Obsessive-Compulsive, and Trauma-Related Disorders: Causes and Prevention

We have now covered the major features and epidemiology of anxiety-related disorders, so we turn our attention next to factors that cause the disorders. We also discuss how knowing about these factors might help us prevent anxiety-related disorders.

## Biological Risk Factors for Anxiety, Obsessive-Compulsive, and Trauma-Related Disorders

Why do people have such intense physical feelings, strange thoughts, and urges to avoid situations? Recall from Chapter 3 that mental disorders are often viewed from a diathesis-stress model, which attributes causes to a combination of biological and environmental variables. Many people are born with a genetic or biological predisposition toward certain personality characteristics and mental conditions. These biological predispositions are sometimes strong and sometimes weak, but they are almost always influenced or triggered to some degree by life events. So when talking about risk factors that may lead to anxiety-related disorders, we must consider biological predispositions *and* environmental events. Biological predispositions in people with anxiety-related disorders may include genetics, brain features, neurochemical features, behavioral inhibition, and evolutionary influences.

### GENETICS

Genetic researchers often rely on *family studies*, in which a certain disorder is examined in people and their close relatives. If many more close, or *first-degree*, relatives have the disorder compared with the general population, the disorder is said to "run in the family" and perhaps have a genetic basis. First-degree relatives include parents, siblings, and children. Researchers also conduct *twin studies*, in which identical twins and nonidentical, or fraternal, twins are compared. Identical (monozygotic) twins share much more genetic material with each other than fraternal/nonidentical (dizygotic) twins. Researchers examine

the *concordance rate,* or percentage of cases in which each twin has the disorder. A concordance rate of 70 percent means 70 percent of a group of twins had the same disorder. If a much higher concordance rate is found among identical than fraternal twins, such as 70 percent versus 30 percent, then the disorder is thought to have some genetic basis.

Family and twin studies indicate that anxiety-related disorders do have some moderate genetic basis. First-degree relatives of people with *panic disorder* are 3 to 21 times more likely than control participants to have panic disorder (Low, Cui, & Merikangas, 2008; Smoller & Tsuang, 1998). This association applies more to females than males and is even somewhat true for more distant relatives. Twin studies also indicate higher concordance rates of panic disorder among identical (24–73 percent) than fraternal (0–17 percent) twins (Shih, Belmonte, & Zandi, 2004). The heritability (Chapter 2) of panic disorder has been reported to be 0.55 (Kendler et al., 2011).

Studies also reveal *social phobia* to be more common in close family relatives compared to controls (Merikangas, Lieb, Wittchen, & Avenevoli, 2003; Tillfors, Furmark, Ekselius, & Fredrikson, 2001). Somewhat more concordance for the disorder may also be seen in identical (24.4 percent) than fraternal (15.3 percent) female twins (Kendler, Neale, Kessler, Heath, & Eaves, 1992). The heritability of social phobia has been reported to be 0.57 (Kendler et al., 2011).

*Specific phobia* also seems to run in families: 33 percent of first-degree relatives of people with phobia report having a phobia themselves, compared with 11 percent of control participants. This is especially true for females (Fyer et al., 1990; Hettema, Neale, & Kendler, 2001). The heritability of specific phobia has been reported to be 0.55 (Kendler et al., 2011). Family members often share the same type of phobia as well. A family member with an animal or blood-injection-injury phobia may be more likely than controls to have relatives with that phobia type (Van Houtem et al., 2013). These data do not necessarily mean a specific gene is responsible for phobias, just that the mental condition seems common among family members. Other factors, including environmental ones such as learning, may also be influential.

*Generalized anxiety disorder* also seems to run in families and occurs in 19.5 percent of first-degree relatives of people with the disorder compared with only 3.5 percent for controls (Coelho, Cooper, & Murray, 2007; Noyes et al., 1987). Substantially greater concordance for generalized anxiety disorder among identical than fraternal twins is also seen, although this effect might be better explained by comorbid depression or panic disorder (Craske, 1999; Hettema, 2008). That is, people with generalized anxiety disorder *and* depression or panic disorder may have a stronger genetic predisposition toward generalized anxiety disorder than people with generalized anxiety disorder *without* depression or panic disorder. The heritability of generalized anxiety disorder has been reported to be 0.51 (Kendler et al., 2011).

Family data indicate *obsessive-compulsive disorder* to be more common among first-degree relatives of people with the disorder (10.3 percent) compared with control participants

(1.9 percent). Children with obsessive-compulsive disorder are also more likely than control participants to have parents with the disorder (Black, Noyes, Goldstein, & Blum, 1992; Calvo, Lazaro, Castro, Morer, & Toro, 2007). Twin data also indicate moderately higher concordance for obsessive-compulsive disorder among identical than fraternal twins (Grados & Wilcox, 2007). The heritability of obsessive-compulsive symptoms has been reported to be 0.49 (Mathews et al., 2007). Stein and colleagues (2002) found genetic influences for symptoms of *posttraumatic stress disorder* to be modest but higher for people like Marcus exposed to assault compared with people exposed to nonassault trauma such as car accidents or natural disasters. The heritability of posttraumatic stress disorder has been reported to be 0.46 (Sartor et al., 2012).

What can thus be said about these different genetic studies? Anxiety-related disorders do tend to run in families, and some people appear to be more genetically predisposed toward certain anxiety-related disorders. The contribution of genetics to the cause of anxiety-related disorders is less than other major mental disorders such as schizophrenia, however (Chapter 12). No single gene or set of genes leads *directly* to an anxiety-related disorder. Genetics may instead help produce brain or neurochemical features or temperaments that help lead to an anxiety-related disorder or otherwise interact with environmental events to predispose the person to development of an anxiety-related disorder. We next discuss some potential brain features that are associated with anxiety-related disorders.

## BRAIN FEATURES

Recall from Chapter 2 that several areas of the brain are important for certain kinds of normal and abnormal behavior. Particularly important brain areas for increased physical arousal and anxiety-related disorders include the amygdala and the septal-hippocampal system (Blackford & Pine, 2012; Small, Schobel, Buxton, Witter, & Barnes, 2011) (see **Figure 5.6**). The *amygdala* is a brain area long associated with fearful responses. The amygdala can be activated by a scary face or an imminent threat such as a nearby snake, and helps produce physical symptoms such as fast heart rate and sweating and emotional states of anxious apprehension and fear (see **Figure 5.7**,

Robinson, Charney, Overstreet, Vytal, & Grillon, 2012). This helps a person cope with threat.

Key changes in the amygdala might be related to over-arousal and excessive startle responses in people with different anxiety-related disorders (Kent & Rauch, 2009). Such changes may thus be closely associated with specific or social phobia. People with obsessive-compulsive disorder or posttraumatic stress disorder also show significant activity in the amygdala when exposed to reminders of their trauma or other anxiety-provoking stimuli (Mahan & Ressler, 2012; Milad & Rauch, 2012). Changes in the amygdala may be influenced by certain genes but more research in this area is needed.

Connections from the amygdala to other key areas of the brain seem even more pertinent to anxiety-related disorders. One such area is the *septal-hippocampal system,* which may help a person respond to threats and remember and learn about highly anxiety-provoking situations (Grupe & Nitschke, 2013).

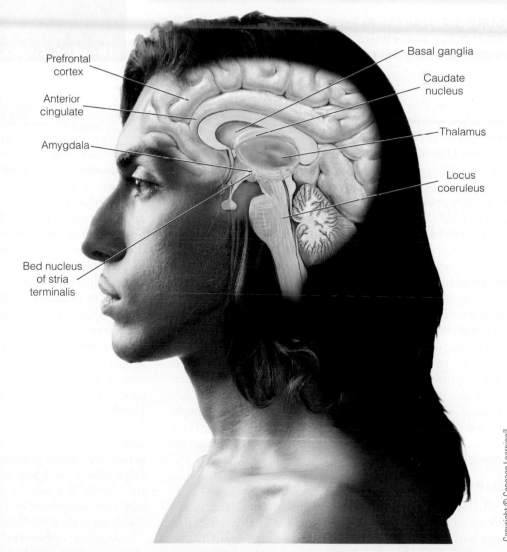

**FIGURE 5.6** KEY BRAIN AREAS IMPLICATED IN THE ANXIETY-RELATED DISORDERS
© 2010 Plush Studios/Bill Reitzel/Jupiterimages Corporation

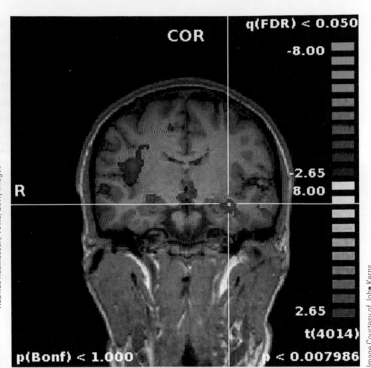

**FIGURE 5.7** FEAR CAN BE EXPRESSED AS A FACIAL IMAGE (LEFT) AND AS A BRAIN IMAGE (RIGHT). IN THIS fMRI (RIGHT) OF A PERSON EXPERIENCING FEAR, THE AMYGDALA IS ACTIVE.

Unfortunately, this area may remain activated even when no threat exists, so a person with an anxiety-related disorder could be worried or anxious or fearful of something not threatening or, as with Marcus, could continue to vividly remember aspects of trauma. This area may be particularly affected by antianxiety drugs (Yeung, Treit, & Dickson, 2012). The amygdala and the septal-hippocampal system connect as well to the *prefrontal cortex* and *bed nucleus of the stria terminalis,* brain structures also heavily involved in behavioral and emotional aspects of anxiety (Yassa, Hazlett, Stark, & Hoehn-Saric, 2012).

Other brain features seem very specific to certain disorders. People with obsessive-compulsive disorder can have altered functioning of the *orbitofrontal cortex, basal ganglia, caudate nucleus, anterior cingulate,* and *thalamus* (Sadock & Sadock, 2007). People with this disorder may experience increased or decreased volume (size) or activity in these areas. Such changes may result in intrusive thoughts, repetitive motor behaviors, depression, and disruptions in information processing (Milad & Rauch, 2012). Panic attacks and disorder have been specifically linked to changes in the *locus coeruleus,* which is a main norepinephrine center in the brain (see next section; Wemmie, 2011). These brain areas interact with various neurotransmitters, which are discussed next.

## NEUROCHEMICAL FEATURES

Recall from Chapter 2 that neurotransmitters affect a person's mood and behavior, so it may come as little surprise that people with anxiety-related disorders have significant neurochemical changes. Neurotransmitters most closely linked to anxiety-related disorders include serotonin, norepinephrine,

and gamma-aminobutyric acid (GABA; Garakani, Murrough, Charney, & Bremner, 2009). Changes in these neurotransmitter and related systems, as with the brain features just discussed, may be partly the result of genetic influences.

*Serotonin* is closely related to mood and motor behavior. Changes in serotonin have been found in people with many anxiety-related disorders, especially panic, obsessive-compulsive, and generalized anxiety disorders (see **Figure 5.8**). Serotonin receptors may be particularly sensitive in people with these disorders, creating hyperactivity in different parts of the brain. Medications effective for people with anxiety-related disorders often help normalize serotonin activity in the brain to produce calm (Mathew, Hoffman, & Charney, 2009). Serotonin is also related to depression (Chapter 7), so changes in this neurotransmitter may help explain the high comorbidity between anxiety and depression.

*Norepinephrine* is related to excessive physical symptoms of anxiety, partly because the locus coeruleus is heavily concentrated with norepinephrine receptors. This is especially pertinent to people with panic, phobic, and posttraumatic stress disorders. Some people with anxiety-related disorders may have poor regulation of norepinephrine, which can lead to sporadic bursts of activity and related physical symptoms, as in panic attacks. *GABA* helps inhibit nerve cells related to anxiety. This neurotransmitter may be deficient in people with anxiety-related disorders and thus contribute to excessive worry and panic symptoms (Goddard et al., 2010; Kalueff & Nutt, 2007).

Another important neurochemical change in people with anxiety-related disorders involves the *hypothalamic-pituitary-adrenal* (HPA) system and a substance called *cortisol*

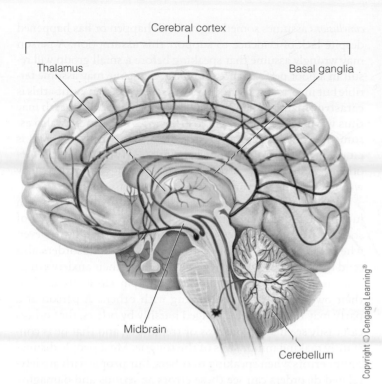

Cerebral cortex

Thalamus

Basal ganglia

Midbrain

Cerebellum

Copyright © Cengage Learning®

**FIGURE 5.8  SEROTONIN PATHWAYS OF THE BRAIN**

(Reagan, Grillo, & Piroli, 2008). The HPA system is responsible for helping a person respond to stressful situations by releasing substances allowing the body to confront or flee a threatening stimulus (fight or flight). One such substance is cortisol, levels of which elevate when a person is faced with threat but that diminish over time as the threat fades. You may see your professor administering a pop quiz and become quite physically aroused as your cortisol level increases. Your cortisol level drops, however, as you calm down and focus.

In some people with excess arousal and anxiety-related disorders, cortisol levels remain high *even when threat subsides*. They may thus be agitated, watchful of threat, or physically anxious for little reason (Vreeburg et al., 2010). This is not always the case, however; some people with posttraumatic stress disorder have *suppressed* levels of cortisol (McFarlane, Barton, Yehuda, & Wittert, 2011). Therefore, more work must be done to see exactly what role cortisol plays with respect to the cause of these disorders.

## BEHAVIORAL INHIBITION

Have you ever known someone who did not like new things or preferred to be near only familiar people and situations? Genetic contributions or brain features could predispose someone for certain personality patterns, or temperaments, that have an impact on anxiety-related disorders. One such pattern is **behavioral inhibition**, or withdrawal from unfamiliar or new stimuli (Kagan, 2012). Perhaps 10 to 15 percent

of people are born with behavioral inhibition, which comes in the form of irritability, shyness, fearfulness, overcautiousness, and physical feelings of anxiety. Toddlers and children with behavioral inhibition are subdued and react fearfully to new people or situations, often preferring to be close to their parents. Such behavior is normal for many young children, who eventually outgrow early shyness or fearfulness of new things, but behavioral inhibition in some youths is relatively stable across the life span (Clauss & Blackford, 2012).

People with behavioral inhibition seem to be at risk for developing anxiety-related disorders, which makes sense because many people with these disorders avoid new situations, stay close to home (like Angelina), or become nervous or worry about unfamiliar circumstances. Long-term studies reveal children with behavioral inhibition to be more likely than control participants to develop anxiety-related disorders (Hirshfeld-Becker, Micco, Simoes et al., 2008). Social phobia is especially more likely to be diagnosed among youths with (17 percent) than without (5 percent) behavioral inhibition (Biederman et al., 2001). Children with behavioral inhibition are also more likely to have parents with an anxiety-related disorder than are children without behavioral inhibition. Socially and generally anxious adults also report more aspects of behavioral inhibition in childhood than controls (Gladstone, Parker, Mitchell, Wilhelm, & Malhi, 2005).

Many children with behavioral inhibition later develop an anxiety-related disorder, but most children with such inhibition do not. Not all people with anxiety-related disorders show behavioral inhibition either. Factors such as a supportive family and social network likely protect some people from developing an anxiety-related disorder (Kearney, 2005). Other personality characteristics may also interact with behavioral inhibition to contribute to anxiety-related disorders, such

©BrantLeeMedia/Shutterstock.com

Some children are naturally hesitant or even fearful in new situations, such as getting one's first haircut.

as neuroticism or general distress, desire to avoid harm, and anxiety sensitivity (see anxiety sensitivity section below; Doty, Japee, Ingvar, & Underleider, 2013).

## EVOLUTIONARY INFLUENCES

Evolutionary influences may also contribute to anxiety-related disorders. *Preparedness* is the idea that humans are biologically prepared to fear certain stimuli more than others. People of all cultures seem particularly afraid of snakes and spiders but rarely of trees and flowers. We may have realized as we evolved that snakes and spiders represent true threats to be avoided but that trees and flowers are rarely threatening. People today are thus more likely, or prepared, to develop a phobia of snakes or spiders than a phobia of trees or flowers (Mineka & Oehlberg, 2008).

Evolutionary theories have also been proposed for other anxiety-related disorders. Social anxiety may help preserve social order by inducing people to conform to social standards, form clear hierarchies, and avoid conflict (Gilbert, 2001). Compulsive behaviors such as checking, hoarding, or washing may have been historically adaptive when hunting and gathering food (Polimeni, Reiss, & Sareen, 2005). Fainting after a skin injury such as a needle injection may be an adaptive response to inescapable threat (Bracha, 2004).

## Environmental Risk Factors for Anxiety, Obsessive-Compulsive, and Trauma-Related Disorders

We have covered some of the biological or early-life risk factors for anxiety-related disorders, so we turn our attention next to environmental risk factors that may develop over a person's lifetime. These include cognitive risk factors, anxiety sensitivity, family factors, learning experiences, and cultural factors.

## COGNITIVE RISK FACTORS

An environmental risk factor closely related to anxiety-related disorders is negative thought patterns, or **cognitive distortions**. People with anxiety-related disorders often have *ongoing* thoughts about potential or actual threat from external events (Cisler & Koster, 2010). We mentioned that people with generalized anxiety disorder often scan their environment looking for threats or things to worry about. They generally see events in a *negative light* or look first at how they might be harmed (Rinck, Becker, Kellermann, & Roth, 2003). Angelina's concern that her professor might look at her was based on an assumption she would be called on, not know the answer to a question, and look foolish. She did not consider other possibilities like the fact she was a good student who probably did know the answer.

Common cognitive distortions in people with anxiety-related disorders include jumping to conclusions, catastrophizing, and emotional reasoning (Beck & Dozois, 2011; Ghahramanlou-Holloway, Wenzel, Lou, & Beck, 2007). Someone who *jumps to*

*conclusions* assumes something bad will happen or has happened despite lack of evidence to support this assumption. A person may wrongly assume that speaking before a small group will result in a poor performance. Similarly, someone may assume terrible but incorrect consequences will result from an event—this is **catastrophizing**. A person who makes mistakes in a speech may thus wrongly assume he will lose his job. A person may also assume her physical feelings reflect how things truly are—this is **emotional reasoning**. People who are nervous speaking before others, and who have strong physical feelings of anxiety, may wrongly assume everyone can tell how nervous they are.

People with anxiety-related disorders also make errors in judgment about their skill. Many underestimate their level of social skill, believing they are less competent than others even when it is not true. People with anxiety-related disorders also tend to view social events negatively, believe their anxiety symptoms to be highly visible to others, and pay close attention to their own errors when interacting with others. A person at a party may feel he is being judged harshly by others, that others can easily see his nervousness or trembling, and that he is constantly making minor slips of the tongue. Most people dismiss minor errors when speaking to others, but people with anxiety-related disorders can see these errors as serious and damaging (Clark & McManus, 2002; Hirsch, Clark, Mathews, & Williams, 2003; Muris, Rapee, Meesters, Schouten, & Geers, 2003).

Many people with anxiety-related disorders think negatively and then avoid anxious situations. They subsequently feel better after avoiding these situations because their physical arousal goes away. This rewards their negative way of thinking and avoidance. People with generalized anxiety disorder may believe worrying helps prevent bad things from happening. Anxiety-related disorders are thus maintained over time. Angelina assumed terrible things would happen if she had a panic attack, avoided situations where a panic attack might occur, and felt relieved when those terrible things did not happen. Patterns like this keep many people from seeking treatment, and they kept Angelina from shopping, dating, and attending school.

People with obsessive-compulsive disorder have catastrophic beliefs about their own thoughts. Jonathan and others with obsessive-compulsive disorder are greatly troubled by their intrusive and spontaneous thoughts, feeling guilty or blaming themselves for having them. This may be tied to **thought-action fusion**, in which one believes thinking about something, such as hurting a baby, means he is a terrible person or that the terrible thing is more likely to happen (Berle & Starcevic, 2005). Many people with obsessive-compulsive disorder also view their thoughts as dangerous, and this increases physical arousal and triggers even more obsessions. People with the disorder also try to suppress their thoughts, but this only leads to more obsessions (Purdon, 2004). Try *not* to think about "blue dogs" for the next minute. What happens?

Cognitive theories of anxiety-related disorders also focus on **emotional processing**, or a person's ability to think about a past anxiety-provoking event without significant anxiety (Brewin & Holmes, 2003; Rachman, 2004). Think about a person once trapped in an elevator and intensely fearful. Good emotional processing means the person can later talk about the story, listen to others' accounts of being trapped in an elevator, or even ride elevators without anxiety. People with anxiety-related disorders, however, often have trouble processing difficult events. Poor emotional processing helps explain why many forms of anxiety are maintained for long periods of time even when no threat is present. This is especially relevant to people like Marcus with posttraumatic stress disorder. Marcus continued to experience reminders of the event in the form of nightmares and intrusive thoughts. He had not yet reached the point where he had fully processed or absorbed what had happened and was therefore still unable to function well on a daily basis.

## ANXIETY SENSITIVITY

Related to cognitive distortions is the erroneous belief that internal physical sensations are dangerous. Many of us are naturally concerned about our health, but some people become extremely worried about even minor physical changes. **Anxiety sensitivity** is a fear of the potential dangerousness of internal sensations (Hayward & Wilson, 2007; Olatunji & Wolitsky-Taylor, 2009). A person may experience a minor change in heart rate and excessively worry he is having a heart attack. Recall that Angelina went to an emergency room doctor and a cardiologist because she felt her symptoms were dangerous. Symptoms of panic are not actually dangerous, but many people wrongly think the symptoms mean a serious medical condition, insanity, loss of control, or imminent death.

Children and adults with anxiety symptoms and anxiety-related disorders, especially those with panic attacks and panic disorder, often show high levels of anxiety sensitivity (Schmidt et al., 2010; Starcevic & Berle, 2006). This makes sense when you consider that people with panic attacks often fear another panic attack and thus more negative physical symptoms and consequences. Anxiety sensitivity may be a characteristic learned over time, or it might be a type of temperament that is present early in life and related to certain biological predispositions.

## FAMILY FACTORS

Family-based contributions to anxiety-related disorders are also important. Parents of anxious children may be overcontrolling, affectionless, overprotective, rejecting, and demanding. Rejecting parents could trigger a child's worry about being left alone or anxiety about handling threats from others without help. Overprotective or controlling parents may restrict a child's access to friends or other social situations or prematurely rescue a child from an anxious situation, thus rewarding anxiety. Parents of anxious children may also encourage avoidance in their children and discourage prosocial behaviors ("OK, you don't have to go to that birthday party"). Such parents also tend to avoid or withdraw from various situations themselves (Rapee, 2012; Woodruff-Borden, Morrow, Bourland, & Cambron, 2002).

Parents of anxious children also overemphasize opinions of, and negative evaluations from, others. Families of anxious children tend to be isolated or unstable and avoid many social situations. Parents may also serve as a model for their child's anxiety (Fisak & Grills-Taquechel, 2007; Rapee, Schniering, & Hudson, 2009). A parent with panic disorder may avoid anxious situations, appear physically nervous, attend closely to internal sensations, or withdraw from chores after having an attack. Some children may view these behaviors as ways of coping with anxious situations and do the same. Another important family variable involves insecure or anxious/resistant attachment patterns, which are more common in children with anxiety-related disorders than controls (Brown & Whiteside, 2008; Manassis, 2001).

Anxiety-related disorders also seem prevalent among people maltreated by their parents. Two thirds of youths sexually or physically maltreated met criteria for posttraumatic stress disorder in one study. Maltreated youths with posttraumatic stress disorder also met criteria for several other anxiety-related disorders (see **Figure 5.9**) (Linning & Kearney, 2004). Female adults maltreated as children also have higher rates of posttraumatic stress disorder than controls, and this seems related to negative effects on the hypothalamic-pituitary-adrenal system discussed earlier (Shea, Walsh, MacMillan, & Steiner, 2004).

How might these parent/family experiences interact to produce an anxiety-related disorder? Some suggest that parental

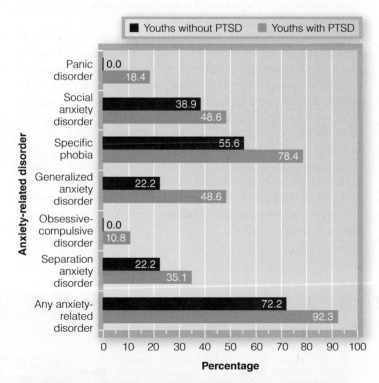

**FIGURE 5.9 COMORBID ANXIETY-RELATED DIAGNOSES IN MALTREATED YOUTHS** Adapted from Linning and Kearney (2004).

practices, modeling, and insecure attachment lead to reduced opportunities for a child to practice anxiety management skills in different social and evaluative situations (Dadds & Roth, 2001). A child's demands for close physical proximity to a parent may be frequently rewarded, and a child and parent may have an overdependent relationship that prevents effective separation. Many children refuse school because of anxiety about social and evaluative situations and about being away from parents or home. Some parents also feel anxious about this separation and encourage a child to stay home. Factors such as maltreatment can cause physical brain changes that lead to anxiety-related disorder as well.

## LEARNING EXPERIENCES

Excessive fear can also be a learned response. Modeling parent behavior is one learned pathway, but children can also become fearful through *direct learning* or *information transfer* (Dadds, Davey, & Field, 2001). Direct learning may involve *classical conditioning* and *operant conditioning*. Classical conditioning is derived from Ivan Pavlov's famous experiment in which he saw dogs instinctively salivate at the sight and smell of food (see **Figure 5.10**). Food is an *unconditioned stimulus,* and salivation is an *unconditioned response* because no learning occurs—the salivation is automatic. Pavlov then associated the food/unconditioned stimulus with a ringing bell and conditioned his dogs to eventually salivate to the bell. The food/unconditioned stimulus became associated with the bell, a *conditioned* (or learned) *stimulus*. Repeated pairings or associations of the food and bell then produced a situation where the conditioned stimulus (bell) produced a *conditioned response,* in this case salivation.

Such a process can also occur for the development of fears. Think about someone who walks through a park and is bitten by a vicious dog. The bite is an unconditioned stimulus because it immediately causes pain and fear or an unconditioned response—no learning is necessary. If negative experiences with a dog happened repeatedly, then any exposure to a dog (now a conditioned stimulus) would result in fear of that dog (now a conditioned response). This fear may then become *generalized,* as when a person becomes afraid of many dogs, even those that have not bitten her. Such a model is often used to explain phobias, but many intense panic attacks also occur following stressful life events (Venturello, Barzega, Maina, & Bogetto, 2002).

Direct learning of fears may also involve operant conditioning, or subsequent rewards for fearful behavior. Parents often reinforce certain apprehensions in their children, such as wariness around strangers. Too much reinforcement in this area could lead to a situation in which a child rarely interacts with other peers or adults and then does not develop good social or communication skills. Social anxiety may thus result when the child later tries to interact with others but does so in an awkward way that leads to social rejection and further social anxiety (Kearney, 2005).

Fears are also reinforced by avoidance. If you are nervous about an upcoming dental appointment, then you might cancel it. The feeling of relief you then experience is quite rewarding and may motivate you to cancel more appointments in the future. Some fears develop from classical *and* operant conditioning. A person bitten by a dog may associate dogs with pain and fear and then avoid dogs for the rest of her life. The fear thus remains even though no additional trauma is taking place (Mineka & Zinbarg, 2006).

Another factor in fear development is information transfer. A child may hear stories from other children or adults about the dangerousness of certain stimuli such as spiders and thus develop a fear of them. Many people also seem predisposed to fear certain things such as spiders, snakes, strangers, separation from loved ones, heights, and water. We may have developed an innate sense of fear about certain things that could harm us as we evolved. This is sometimes called a *nonassociative theory of fear* because no trauma is needed for someone to show the fear (Coelho & Purkis, 2009).

Learning experiences may also lead a person to develop a sense of *lack of control* over, or sense of *unpredictability* about, life events (Armfield, 2007; Chorpita & Barlow, 1998). Difficulties at school and subsequent avoidance of evaluative situations there could lead a person to excessively worry about her competence and place in the surrounding world. Children maltreated by their parents have difficulty knowing who they can trust and may develop a sense of lack of control about their environment. Marcus experienced a severe threat to his safety and later felt a sense of unpredictability regarding future threats.

## CULTURAL FACTORS

We mentioned that many anxiety-related disorders are present worldwide and often come in different forms across cultures. Still, ethnic groups may be more susceptible to certain kinds of

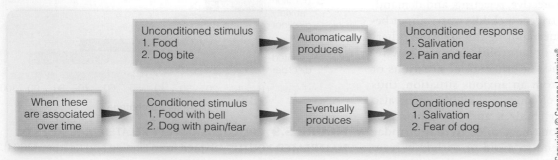

**FIGURE 5.10** CLASSICAL CONDITIONING MODEL OF FEAR

anxiety-related disorders because of where they live and because of difficult conditions they experience. One group of researchers examined rates of posttraumatic stress disorder among African Americans in an inner-city mental health clinic (Schwartz, Bradley, Sexton, Sherry, & Ressler, 2005). Many of the 184 adults (43 percent) met criteria for posttraumatic stress disorder, and many had been exposed to traumatizing events. Other researchers have also demonstrated that African Americans are commonly exposed to high levels of stress (Giscombe & Lobel, 2005). Some have also found that Hispanic police officers are at increased risk for PTSD, especially those with greater dissociation, self-blame, perceived racism, and less social support (Pole, Best, Metzler, & Marmar, 2005).

Posttraumatic stress and other anxiety-related disorders in people around the world have also been linked to mass trauma through natural disasters and terrorism, war zones, and genocide. People exposed to Hurricane Katrina were prone to symptoms of posttraumatic stress disorder (Kessler et al., 2008). People exposed to earthquakes, volcanic eruptions, typhoons, and other natural disasters also commonly develop symptoms of posttraumatic stress and depression (Goenjian et al., 2005, Kokai, Fujii, Shinfuku, & Edwards, 2004).

People exposed to terrorism, war zones, and genocide are also vulnerable to anxiety-related disorders. Examples include U.S. soldiers in Afghanistan, bombing survivors in Northern Ireland, Palestinian and Israeli youths, and Vietnamese, Sudanese, and Cambodian refugees (Bolea, Grant, Burgess, & Plasa, 2003; Gidron, 2002; Hinton, Pham et al., 2004; Hinton, Pich, Chhean, Pollack, & Barlow, 2004; Lapierre, Schwegler, & Labauve, 2007; Lavi & Solomon, 2005; Solomon & Lavi, 2005). Symptoms of posttraumatic stress were evident among flight attendants, Pentagon employees, and children and pregnant women close to the World Trade Center during the September 11, 2001, terrorist attacks (Corey et al., 2005; Engel, Berkowitz, Wolff, & Yehuda, 2005; Grieger, Waldrep, Lovasz, & Ursano, 2005; Saigh, Lee, Ward, & Wilson, 2005).

Many people with anxiety-related disorders in various cultures also show different kinds of anxiety symptoms, often in the form of physical symptoms. Cambodian refugees have common panic-like symptoms that include feelings of paralysis during and after sleep and images of a being approaching them in the night (Hinton, Pich, Chhean, & Pollack, 2005; Hinton, Pich, Chhean, Pollack, & McNally, 2005). Certain ethnic groups may thus be at particular risk for anxiety-related disorder because of the circumstances in which they live. These studies also indicate that clinicians must be sensitive to these issues when conducting assessment and treatment.

## Causes of Anxiety, Obsessive-Compulsive, and Trauma-Related Disorders

Now that you understand the many risk factors for anxiety-related disorders, let us explore how these factors might interact to produce an anxiety-related disorder. Researchers emphasize integrative, diathesis-stress models or pathways to help explain the cause of different anxiety-related disorders (Barlow, 2002; Zvolensky, Kotov, Antipova, & Schmidt, 2005). These theorists

believe certain people are born with *biological vulnerabilities* to experience high anxiety. Some people have genetic predispositions or various brain or neurochemical features that cause them to feel highly physically aroused and upset when negative life events occur. Others may have certain temperaments, such as behavioral inhibition, that predispose them to anxiety-related disorders as well.

People also develop a *psychological vulnerability* toward anxiety-related disorders. Some people continue to have anxiety-provoking thoughts, family experiences that reinforce anxious behavior, and anxiety-related learning experiences. Some people may also feel they lack control over many situations in their lives. Still others could experience anxiety-provoking trauma in the form of maltreatment, surrounding threats, or exposure to terrorism or natural disasters.

Kearney (2005) outlined one possible developmental pathway to social phobia in youth that might serve as a good illustration (see **Figure 5.11**). Some youth are clearly born with predispositions toward overarousal and behavioral inhibition,

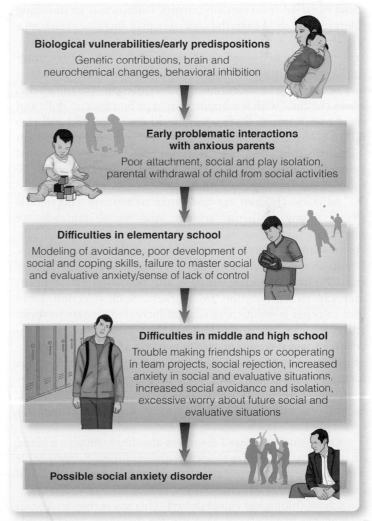

**Biological vulnerabilities/early predispositions**
Genetic contributions, brain and neurochemical changes, behavioral inhibition

**Early problematic interactions with anxious parents**
Poor attachment, social and play isolation, parental withdrawal of child from social activities

**Difficulties in elementary school**
Modeling of avoidance, poor development of social and coping skills, failure to master social and evaluative anxiety/sense of lack of control

**Difficulties in middle and high school**
Trouble making friendships or cooperating in team projects, social rejection, increased anxiety in social and evaluative situations, increased social avoidance and isolation, excessive worry about future social and evaluative situations

**Possible social anxiety disorder**

**FIGURE 5.11** SAMPLE DEVELOPMENTAL PATHWAY OF SOCIAL ANXIETY DISORDER

THE **CONTINUUM** VIDEO PROJECT

*Darwin:* **PTSD**

*"I led men into combat. And sometimes when I made decisions, people died."*

Access the Continuum Video Project in MindTap at **www.cengagebrain.com**.

demonstrating fear and excitability, particularly in new situations. These predispositions may be the result of genetics and key brain and neurochemical features. These infants may be raised by parents who are themselves predisposed toward anxious and avoidant behavior. The early infant–parent relationship could thus be marked by poor attachment and problematic social interactions. As these infants grow into toddlerhood, they may isolate themselves from others by playing alone or be subject to social isolation from nervous parents. Parents may be unwilling to expose the child to birthday parties, play dates, or preschool.

If a toddler remains socially isolated and if his social interactions with parents are problematic, this could set the stage for later difficulties. The child may imitate the parents' behaviors of avoiding or withdrawing from different situations; this leaves the child with few opportunities to build social skills and receive appropriate feedback from others. The child will also fail to control social anxiety or develop good coping skills in different situations. Children not in preschool or surrounded by peers, or those neglected or otherwise maltreated, might be more at risk for such outcomes.

As these children age and enter elementary and middle school, many academic, athletic, and social demands are placed on them. Youths are expected to cooperate with others on school projects, play on teams, and develop friendships. Unfortunately, children already predisposed to social anxiety and who have had early isolation and poor skill development may experience rejection from others. Such rejection could lead to other consequences such as increased anxiety in social and evaluative situations, thoughts that interactions with others and anxiety symptoms are dangerous, increased avoidance of others, arrested social skill development, and worry about future social and evaluative situations. As these youths enter high school, their patterns of social anxiety and avoidance may become ingrained, and they may meet diagnostic criteria for social phobia.

Other anxiety-related disorders also likely involve a blend of biological and psychological vulnerabilities. Some people with panic disorder are naturally high in physical arousal and easily get upset or worried about stressful life events like starting school (biological vulnerability). This stress may lead to an unexpected panic attack, as it did for Angelina. Most people who have a panic attack dismiss the event as merely unpleasant but some, like Angelina, feel the panic attack is uncontrollable

and will cause terrible things like a car accident (psychological vulnerability). They then fear another panic attack and avoid situations in which attacks may occur. A person might also monitor her internal sensations such as heart rate to see if a panic attack is about to happen. Of course, doing so will increase physical arousal, likely trigger another panic attack, and increase worry that even more will occur. The person is thus always *worrying* about having a panic attack or actually *having* a panic attack. Such was the case for Angelina.

Other anxiety-related disorders involve more specific causal factors. People with specific phobias may have had a direct traumatic experience, such as a dog bite, that caused intense fear. People with posttraumatic stress disorder must, by definition, have experienced a traumatic event for the disorder to occur. The presence of trauma and later recollections of the trauma likely converge with one's belief that these events are uncontrollable. The person may continue to experience high levels of physical arousal (just like during the trauma) and scan the environment looking for threats or reminders of the trauma. Unwanted thoughts about the trauma can also continue.

People with generalized anxiety disorder, a largely cognitive condition, may believe negative life events will happen frequently, suddenly, and uncontrollably. A person may even look for threats when they are not there. Worry about minor life events may be reinforced because it lowers physical arousal and keeps someone from thinking about more serious emotional or fearful issues. A person with obsessive-compulsive disorder may also believe his thoughts are dangerous. All anxiety-related disorders, however, involve an intricate combination of different biological and psychological vulnerabilities.

## Prevention of Anxiety, Obsessive-Compulsive, and Trauma-Related Disorders

Given what we know about risk factors and cause of anxiety-related disorders, what could be done to prevent them? Many fears and anxiety-related disorders begin in adolescence or early adulthood, so thinking of prevention during childhood and adolescence makes sense. Researchers have identified several goals that might be important for prevention. These goals center on building a child's ability to control situations that might lead to anxiety.

Some suggest children should be taught the difference between dangerous and nondangerous situations and learn which situations should definitely be avoided, such as being in the middle of the street (Donovan & Spence, 2000). Children could also be taught strategies to address potentially threatening situations such as bullies, busy roads, and swimming pools. Rules about safety, talking to a teacher, and being with friends could be covered. Children could also be taught social and coping skills necessary when unfortunate events do occur. Youths may be taught how to cope with being turned down for a date, failing a test, or being cut from a team. The general idea is to teach children to successfully handle stressful situations and not resort to avoidance or feelings of loss of control. Other aspects of prevention that might be important include changing negative thoughts, having parents model good ways of handling stress, improving parent attitudes toward their children, reducing parent anxiety, reducing actual harmful situations, and identifying and providing therapy for children with anxious parents (Bienvenu & Ginsburg, 2007).

An anxiety prevention program for children—the FRIENDS workbook—concentrates on educating children about anxiety, teaching them to relax, challenging and changing negative self-statements, coping with troublesome situations, rewarding themselves for approach behavior and not avoidant behavior, and practicing these steps in real-life situations (Barrett & Pahl, 2006). FRIENDS stands for:

- **F**eeling worried
- **R**elax and feel good
- **I**nner thoughts
- **E**xplore plans
- **N**ice work so reward yourself
- **D**on't forget to practice
- **S**tay cool

A child is encouraged to recognize when she is feeling anxious, work to control physical feelings of anxiety, and think more realistically (see later treatment sections). She would also be expected to practice situations, such as social and performance situations, to reduce anxiety in those situations. The FRIENDS program does reduce the prevalence of anxiety symptoms in children (Barrett, Farrell, Ollendick, & Dadds, 2006).

Anxiety prevention strategies also apply to adults. Recall from Chapter 3 a study about a 5-hour workshop of education, relaxation training, and exposure (see later treatment section) that effectively prevented panic disorder in adults (Gardenswartz & Craske, 2001). Similar efforts to change problematic feelings, thoughts, and behaviors related to anxiety have been conducted for anxious college students, physical and sexual assault victims, those with public-speaking anxiety, and people with agoraphobia or stressful lifestyles (Regehr, Alaggia, Dennis, Pitts, & Saini, 2013; Roe-Sepowitz, Bedard, & Thyer, 2005; Rothbaum et al., 2008). These programs help individuals relax, change problematic thoughts, develop social skills, and reduce avoidance and other behavior symptoms by confronting whatever provokes anxiety.

Other adult prevention programs are more government-based and focus on the general population. These programs have come in the form of media-based education and screening for anxiety-related disorders. Media-based education involves teaching the public about symptoms of anxiety and that these symptoms can be successfully treated before they get worse. Examples include telephone information lines, websites, public service announcements, printed material, and cooperation with local mental health agencies. May 1 of each year is set aside as National Anxiety Disorders Screening Day, which helps provide quick assessment for those struggling with panic or other anxiety symptoms (Roe-Sepowitz, et al., 2005). Those identified with problematic anxiety can then be referred for professional treatment.

## INTERIM SUMMARY

- ▶ Family and twin studies indicate a moderate genetic basis for many anxiety-related disorders.
- ▶ Several brain areas have been implicated in anxiety-related disorders, especially the amygdala and septal-hippocampal regions, which are associated with physical arousal, emotion, and memories surrounding fearful and anxiety-provoking stimuli. Other brain areas are specific to certain anxiety-related disorders, such as the anterior cingulate in obsessive-compulsive disorder and the locus coeruleus in panic disorder.
- ▶ Neurotransmitters most implicated in anxiety-related disorders include serotonin, norepinephrine, and gamma-aminobutyric acid (GABA).
- ▶ People with behavioral inhibition—a temperamental pattern of irritability, shyness, fearfulness, overcautiousness, and physical feelings of anxiety—seem predisposed to disorders such as social phobia.
- ▶ Anxiety may be influenced by evolutionary processes in that some avoidance behaviors seem adaptive in certain contexts.
- ▶ Cognitive risk factors include distorted thinking about the dangerousness of various stimuli, assumptions that something bad will happen, assumptions of terrible consequences, and assumptions that others can easily notice one's anxiety.
- ▶ Anxiety sensitivity refers to fear of the potential dangerousness of one's own internal sensations such as dizziness and increased heart rate.
- ▶ Family factors may contribute to anxiety-related disorders, especially overcontrolling, affectionless, overprotective, rejecting, and demanding parents. Parents may also model

Photo and Co/Riser/Getty Images

Children have to be taught the difference between dangerous and nondangerous situations. This mother shows her children how to safely cross a street.

anxiety-based responses or induce anxiety by maltreating their children.

▶ People can learn aspects of fear and anxiety through direct experience, information transfer, or reinforcement for fear of strangers or other stimuli.

▶ Cultural factors influence the development of anxiety-related disorders, particularly in people more commonly exposed to traumas.

▶ Biological and environmental risk factors can make a person vulnerable to anxiety-related disorder.

▶ Preventing an anxiety-related disorder involves building ability to control situations that might lead to anxiety, education about dangerous and nondangerous situations, changing negative thoughts, coping better with stress, and practicing skills in real-life situations.

## REVIEW QUESTIONS

1. Describe data that support a genetic contribution to anxiety-related disorders.

2. What key brain and neurochemical features may be related to anxiety-related disorders? What temperamental characteristic occurs early in life and may predict anxiety-related disorders? How so?

3. What are some cognitive distortions associated with anxiety-related disorders, and what is anxiety sensitivity?

4. How might family factors, learning experiences, and cultural backgrounds help cause anxiety-related disorders?

5. Describe an overall causal model for anxiety-related disorders.

6. What factors might be important for a program to prevent anxiety-related disorders?

# Anxiety, Obsessive-Compulsive, and Trauma-Related Disorders: Assessment and Treatment

We have covered risk factors for anxiety-related disorders and will next cover assessment and treatment methods most relevant to people with these disorders. We discuss assessment and treatment methods in general because most of these strategies apply to each anxiety-related disorder. However, we also provide tables that contain treatment information specific to each major anxiety-related disorder. The assessment and treatment methods we discuss next are extremely important for people who are plagued by crippling fears and obsessions (see **Personal Narrative 5.1**), as well as other problems we discuss in this textbook.

## Assessment of Anxiety, Obsessive-Compulsive, and Trauma-Related Disorders

We mentioned in Chapter 4 that mental health professionals use various methods to examine people. The primary methods to evaluate or assess people with anxiety-related disorders include interviews, self-report questionnaires, self-monitoring and observations from others, and psychophysiological assessment.

---

## Personal Narrative 5.1

### *Anonymous*

From as far back as I can remember, my life had been plagued by mental disorder. As a child and through adolescence, obsessions and compulsions wreaked havoc on my brain and my life. I used to have irrational fears of catching fatal illnesses or getting abducted by aliens.

The obsessions could be best described as chaos occurring in my head. Any thought I had was accompanied with that current obsession. There was no complete joy in any activity, because at no point was my day free from anxiety. I became a prisoner of my own brain. Furthermore, I would complete certain rituals, such as adding numbers in my head, or placing items in my pockets in the exact same order every day; if I didn't

do this, I feared something bad would happen.

As time went on, these obsessions and compulsions occurred periodically in my life, lasting for a few weeks or a few months at a time. During my last few years of high school and freshmen year of college, the obsessions subsided and were at worst mild and short-lived. However, they reared their ugly head my sophomore year in college, and it was at this point that I knew I had a mental disorder; I realized a normal brain wouldn't function this way. I knew these fears and thoughts were completely irrational, but I couldn't help them.

I began to seek help during the summer; by that time the obsessions had ceased, but a horrible feeling came

over me as I drove to school for that fall semester. That feeling I felt, which progressively got worse throughout the semester, was depression. It's a feeling that sucks the life out of you.

I finally saw a psychiatrist in the fall, and he prescribed me psychotropic medication. The depression began to ease for a while, but when the winter came, depression reclaimed my entire body. I spent months trapped in the dark cloud of depression. I couldn't sleep, couldn't eat and after a while, questioned how I could live like this much longer. I saw my doctor more frequently during this time period, and after a while, we were able to work out the proper medications that were able to completely alleviate my symptoms.

From that moment on, every day has been a gift to be alive. Now to

## INTERVIEWS

What would you be curious to know about Angelina, Jonathan, and Marcus? Mental health professionals who treat people with anxiety-related disorders are often curious about thoughts and physical feelings, daily activities and avoidance, targets of anxiety and fear, and long-term goals. This information is important for knowing how to treat someone with an anxiety-related disorder because specific client characteristics can be identified and addressed. Angelina's therapist was able to uncover some interesting information about what exactly happens during her panic attack while driving:

**Therapist:** What kinds of thoughts do you have when driving?
**Angelina:** I think I'm going to crash the car because it keeps swerving in the lane.
**Therapist:** What do you usually think and do next?
**Angelina:** I focus a lot on my symptoms, like my heart racing or dizziness, and try to look around fast to see where I can pull the car over . . . I think I'm going to smash into someone because I'm not being too careful.
**Therapist:** Are you able to get the car over to the shoulder?
**Angelina:** Yes, I've never had an accident, but you never know, the next time could be the time I really hurt someone!

Many therapists prefer unstructured interviews, but structured interviews usually rely on diagnostic criteria and contain a list of questions a therapist asks each client with a possible mental disorder. A common interview for people with anxiety-related disorders is the *Anxiety Disorders Interview Schedule* (ADIS; Brown, DiNardo, & Barlow, 2004). The ADIS is primarily useful for evaluating anxiety disorders, but other disorders can be assessed as well. A child version of the ADIS is also available (Lyneham, Abbott, & Rapee, 2007; Silverman & Albano, 1996).

## SELF-REPORT QUESTIONNAIRES

Anxiety-related disorders consist of many internal symptoms such as increased heart rate or negative thoughts, so clients are often asked to rate symptoms on questionnaires. The *Anxiety Sensitivity Index—3* evaluates fear of the dangerousness of one's internal sensations, a key aspect of panic disorder. Selected items from this scale are in **Table 5.13** (Osman et al., 2010; Taylor et al., 2007). Other commonly used questionnaires for people with anxiety-related disorders are in **Table 5.14**.

## SELF-MONITORING AND OBSERVATIONS FROM OTHERS

People with anxiety-related disorders are often asked to monitor and keep a record of their symptoms on a daily basis (Silverman & Ollendick, 2005). This serves several purposes. First, monitoring symptoms every day cuts down on having to remember what happened the previous week, such as what happened during a certain episode of worry, and helps provide material for discussion in a therapy session. Second, monitoring increases a person's self-awareness of the frequency, intensity, and change in anxiety symptoms over time, such as panic attacks. Third, monitoring helps keep a person focused on a task such as exposure to anxiety instead of distracting or avoiding. Others who know the client well may also keep records of her more obvious anxiety symptoms, such as avoidance. This applies especially to children and adolescents.

say that every day from then on has been the best day of my life would be a lie. However, I was almost dead; I now have a new lease on life and I appreciate all things in life to a greater degree.

Besides my new lease on life, this experience also had another powerful effect on me. From then on I decided to be an advocate for mental health. I had formed a chapter of the National Alliance on Mental Illness (NAMI) at my school. In overcoming this past experience, I felt as if I had been to the gates of hell and back, and now it was time to use my experience to make sure no one goes to those gates, at least not alone.

In my eyes I've always viewed it as an obligation to speak about my disorder and help others. God blessed me with numerous gifts to help me become a successful student and person. I knew that if I told others I dealt with depression and anxiety, they would be completely shocked. I was also pretty certain that the people who knew me wouldn't view me any differently. Therefore, I felt that I wouldn't face much stigma. It still wasn't the easiest step to take, but I decided at that point to carry this cross of mental disorder everywhere I go. I want to assure people they can be successful and break down the stigma every chance I get, and most importantly making sure no one feels as I did on those desolate earlier days.

The stigma of mental disorder causes problems in many aspects of society. People don't want to receive treatment due to the perceived notion of being embarrassed, or fear of the unknown. This hurts the economy, the health care system, education, and, most importantly, people's individual lives. To eliminate this stigma, those in the mental health field must work tirelessly against this prejudice. Those with a mental disorder should not be ashamed of their disorder; some of the smartest and most creative people in the world had a mental disorder. As more people step out of the seclusion caused by stigma, the stigma itself will disappear. People will realize how commonplace mental disorder is in this society, how real of a medical condition it is, and how to treat it effectively.

Used with permission.

**Table 5.13**

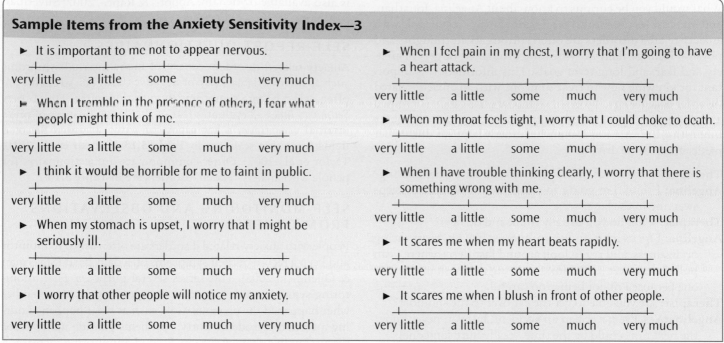

### Sample Items from the Anxiety Sensitivity Index—3

▶ It is important to me not to appear nervous.

very little    a little    some    much    very much

▶ When I tremble in the presence of others, I fear what people might think of me.

very little    a little    some    much    very much

▶ I think it would be horrible for me to faint in public.

very little    a little    some    much    very much

▶ When my stomach is upset, I worry that I might be seriously ill.

very little    a little    some    much    very much

▶ I worry that other people will notice my anxiety.

very little    a little    some    much    very much

▶ When I feel pain in my chest, I worry that I'm going to have a heart attack.

very little    a little    some    much    very much

▶ When my throat feels tight, I worry that I could choke to death.

very little    a little    some    much    very much

▶ When I have trouble thinking clearly, I worry that there is something wrong with me.

very little    a little    some    much    very much

▶ It scares me when my heart beats rapidly.

very little    a little    some    much    very much

▶ It scares me when I blush in front of other people.

very little    a little    some    much    very much

Anxious clients are usually asked to record episodes of panic attacks and/or specific physical symptoms, thoughts, and behaviors (Labrecque, Dugas, Marchand, & Letarte, 2006). Angelina's therapist asked her to track her panic attacks, list her thoughts during and after each attack, and rate her symptoms of accelerated heart rate and trouble breathing. **Behavioral avoidance tests** may also be done to see how close someone with an anxiety-related disorder can get to a feared situation or object (Ollendick, Lewis, Cowart, & Davis, 2012). Marcus's therapist accompanied him as he drove near the spot he was attacked, but Marcus did not get very far before stopping.

## PSYCHOPHYSIOLOGICAL ASSESSMENT

Psychophysiological assessment is sometimes done to measure severity of physical symptoms in people with anxiety-related disorders. Common measures include heart rate, blood pressure, and respiration, but more sophisticated measures may be used in research settings. These include skin conductance and resistance, electromyogram (for muscle tension), and measures of vasomotor activity. In *skin conductance*, electrodes are placed on a person's fingertip and wrist and a small, nonpainful electrical current is introduced to one electrode. A computer measures the time the current takes to travel from one electrode to another. An anxious person may have more active sweat glands and thus conduct the electricity faster than a nonanxious person (Dindo & Fowles, 2008). Some researchers also use *biological challenge procedures* during assessment. These procedures may involve inducing panic-like symptoms (e.g., increased heart rate) using a certain agent such as carbon dioxide to safely assess how a person typically responds to anxious symptoms (Kutz, Marshall, Bernstein, & Zvolensky, 2010). Psychophysiological assessment may reveal rich information about a client, but it is costly and time-intensive. This kind of assessment is most often seen in research or medical settings.

## Biological Treatment of Anxiety, Obsessive-Compulsive, and Trauma-Related Disorders

How do you think the various people discussed in this chapter might be treated for their anxiety-related disorders? Recall that anxiety consists of three components: physical feelings, thoughts, and behaviors. Treating anxiety-related disorders may thus involve biological interventions, or medications, to quell physical feelings and enhance approach behaviors.

Antianxiety medication has become a leading method of treating people with anxiety-related disorders. Some of the most common antianxiety medications are listed in **Table 5.15**. One particular class of antianxiety drug is the *benzodiazepines*, or drugs that produce a sedating effect. Recall that one risk factor for anxiety-related disorder seems to be excess neurochemical activity in different areas of the brain. Benzodiazepines help modify this excess activity to make a person feel more calm. These drugs may also enhance the GABA system of the brain to produce a more inhibiting effect on anxiety. Benzodiazepines are often used to treat people with panic disorder (Mitte, 2005; Watanabe, Churchill, & Furukawa, 2007).

Another major class of drugs for anxiety-related disorders is the *antidepressants* (see also Chapter 7), specifically, drugs that moderate serotonin levels in the brain. Recall that serotonin levels are not always well regulated in people with anxiety-related disorders, so antidepressants sometimes help provide this regulation. Antidepressant drugs are often used to treat people with social and generalized anxiety and obsessive-compulsive and posttraumatic stress disorders (Cooper, Carty, & Creamer, 2005; Fineberg & Gale, 2004; Ipser, Kariuki, & Stein, 2008; Schmitt et al., 2005).

Drug treatment is effective for 60 to 80 percent of adults with anxiety-related disorders but less so for people with

---

**Table 5.14**

| Common Questionnaires for Assessing Anxiety-Related Disorders | |
| --- | --- |
| Questionnaire | What does it assess? |
| Beck Anxiety Inventory | General symptoms of anxiety |
| Children's Manifest Anxiety Scale | Worry, oversensitivity, concentration problems, and physical feelings of anxiety |
| Fear Questionnaire | Avoidance due to agoraphobia, blood injury phobia, or social phobia |
| Fear Survey Schedule for Children–Revised | Fears of failure and criticism, the unknown, injury and small animals, danger and death, and medical procedures |
| Impact of Event Scale | Hyperarousal, reexperiencing, and avoidance/numbing symptoms of posttraumatic stress disorder |
| Maudsley Obsessional-Compulsive Inventory | Checking, washing, doubting, and slowness/repetition |
| Mobility Inventory | Agoraphobia-related avoidance behavior |
| Multidimensional Anxiety Scale for Children-2 | Harm avoidance and physical, separation, and social anxiety |
| Panic and Agoraphobia Scale | Severity, frequency, and duration of panic attacks and avoidance |
| Penn State Worry Questionnaire | Intensity and excessiveness of worry |
| School Refusal Assessment Scale–Revised | Why a child refuses to attend school |
| Social Anxiety Scale for Children—Revised | Fear of negative evaluation, social avoidance and distress, and generalized social distress |
| Social Interaction Anxiety Scale | Anxiety about interpersonal interactions |
| Social Phobia and Anxiety Inventory | Physical, cognitive, and behavioral components to social anxiety |
| State-Trait Anxiety Inventory | Anxiety symptoms at this moment and anxiety symptoms felt much of the time |
| Symptom Checklist 90-R Crime-Related PTSD Scale | Symptoms of posttraumatic stress disorder |

severe, long-term anxiety comorbid with other mental disorders. Relapse rates can also be high when a person stops taking the drug (Denys & de Geus, 2005; Simon et al., 2002). Medication side effects can be unpleasant as well. Possible side effects of benzodiazepines include motor and memory problems, fatigue, depression, and irritability and hostility. Possible side effects of antidepressants include nausea, drowsiness, dizziness, and sexual dysfunction (Westenberg & Sandner, 2006). Antidepressants have not been found to be addictive, but their sudden discontinuation can lead to unpleasant physical symptoms. People who use benzodiazepines, however, can become dependent on the drugs (Chouinard, 2004).

## Psychological Treatments of Anxiety, Obsessive-Compulsive, and Trauma-Related Disorders

Psychological interventions have also been designed to address each of the three anxiety components—physical feelings, thoughts, and behaviors.

## PSYCHOEDUCATION AND SOMATIC CONTROL EXERCISES

Many anxiety-related disorders involve uncomfortable levels of physical arousal. Such arousal can come in the form of increased heart rate, dizziness, short breath, hot flashes, and other symptoms. People with generalized anxiety disorder can also have severe muscle tension. Physical feelings of anxiety can trigger unpleasant thoughts and then avoidance, so an important first step of treatment is to educate a person about the three components of anxiety and how these components relate to her. This process is **psychoeducation**. Examples are listed in **Table 5.16**.

Angelina's therapist knew her client often had unpleasant and intense physical symptoms during her panic attacks. These symptoms then led to worries about harm from a panic attack and avoidance of places where an attack could occur. Teaching people with anxiety-related disorders about their symptoms and about how their physical feelings, thoughts, and behaviors influence each other is important to develop a good treatment plan, to ease concerns about the disorder, to emphasize

**Table 5.15**

### Common Medications for People with Anxiety-Related Disorders

**Benzodiazepines**

► Alprazolam (Xanax)
► Lorazepam (Ativan)
► Clonazepam (Klonopin)
► Diazepam (Valium)
► Chlordiazepoxide (Librium)
► Temazepam (Restoril)
► Oxazepam (Serax)

**Antidepressants**

► Fluoxetine (Prozac)
► Paroxetine (Paxil)
► Sertraline (Zoloft)
► Fluvoxamine (Luvox)
► Citalopram (Celexa)
► Escitalopram oxalate (Lexapro)

that many people have these symptoms, and to convey that the symptoms can be successfully treated. Clients are sometimes taught **somatic control exercises** to address physical feelings of anxiety. Somatic control exercises help clients manage physical arousal so it is less strong and threatening. Common somatic control exercises include relaxation training and breathing retraining (see Table 5.16 for examples for each anxiety-related disorder).

In **relaxation training**, a person is taught to tense and release different muscle groups to diffuse tension (Jorm et al., 2004). The therapist may ask a person to sit in a comfortable chair, close his eyes, make a fist, and hold tightly for 10 seconds. The person then releases the fist quickly and repeats the process (try it). This is done for other muscle groups as well, such as those in the shoulders, face, stomach, and legs. The therapist encourages the client to attend to the difference between a tense muscle and a relaxed one. Many people with anxiety-related disorders have trouble even knowing they are tense. The procedure is often audiotaped and the person practices at home.

Another procedure to reduce physical feelings of anxiety is **breathing retraining** (Leahy, Holland, & McGinn, 2012). This procedure involves having a person change her breathing

**Table 5.16**

### Psychoeducation and Somatic Control Exercise Examples for People with Anxiety-Related Disorders

| Disorder | Psychoeducation example | Somatic control exercise example |
|---|---|---|
| Panic disorder | Education about typical panic attack symptoms and a person's sequence of physical feelings to thoughts to behaviors | Correct breathing and muscle relaxation during a panic attack |
| Social phobia | Education about common worries and avoidance associated with social and evaluative anxiety | Muscle relaxation during a public speaking assignment |
| Specific phobia | Education about the irrational and excessive nature of fear and how avoidance interferes with quality of life | Correct breathing and muscle relaxation during exposure to a feared stimulus such as a dog |
| Generalized anxiety disorder | Education about excessive, uncontrollable worry and difficulty sleeping and other physical consequences | Muscle relaxation before bedtime to ease transition to sleep |
| Obsessive-compulsive disorder | Education about the nature and content of key thoughts (obsessions) and how they can lead to specific behaviors (compulsions) | Muscle relaxation following getting one's hand dirty |
| Posttraumatic stress disorder | Education about how one's trauma has led to symptoms of reexperiencing, physical arousal, and avoidance of certain places | Correct breathing during a trip near where the trauma occurred |
| Separation anxiety disorder | Education to parents and children about worries regarding harm befalling a parent or the child | Muscle relaxation upon having to enter school without parents |

From Craske et al., 2000.

during anxious times to include long, deep breaths in through the nose and out through the mouth. The person is encouraged to feel the breaths in the diaphragm (diaphragmatic breathing) by holding her fingers below her stomach. Breaths should be slow, deep, and regular (try it a few times). One advantage of this strategy is that a person can use it in public situations without drawing much attention.

## COGNITIVE THERAPY

Recall that another aspect of anxiety-related disorder is negative thoughts. Angelina was concerned a panic attack might cause extensive harm to her or others. Therapists often use **cognitive therapy** to change these negative thought patterns. Cognitive therapy involves examining negative statements a person may be making and encouraging the person to challenge the thought (Beck & Dozois, 2011). Cognitive therapy helps people change their way of reasoning about the environment, think more realistically, and see the positive side of things as well as the negative. Examples of cognitive therapy for different anxiety-related disorders are listed in **Table 5.17**.

Recall that many people with anxiety-related disorders engage in cognitive distortions such as catastrophizing, or incorrectly assuming terrible things will happen from a certain event. Angelina catastrophized by assuming she would lose control, go crazy, or harm herself or others during a panic attack. A first step in cognitive therapy is to educate the person about her cognitive distortions and have her keep track of them during the week (Leahy et al., 2012). Angelina was asked to keep a daily log of panic attacks as well as thoughts that accompanied the attacks. She was also shown how many of her thoughts led to her avoidant behaviors.

Clients are encouraged to dispute negative thoughts by *examining the evidence* for and against a certain thought (O'Donohue & Fisher, 2012). A person is encouraged to look realistically at what is happening instead of assuming the negative in a situation. Angelina was convinced panic would lead to a car accident. She was asked if she had ever had a car accident before from a panic attack, and she said no. She was also asked what she did when she did panic while driving, and she said she usually went to the side of the road. The therapist helped her examine evidence about the situation:

**Therapist:** You said earlier you think you will crash the car when having a panic attack. What evidence do you have this will happen?

## Table 5.17

### Cognitive Therapy Examples for People with Anxiety-Related Disorders

| Disorder | Cognitive therapy example |
|---|---|
| Panic disorder | Examine evidence whether heart palpitations truly indicate a heart attack. Discuss worst-case scenario of having a panic attack in a department store and how the person could control panic symptoms without avoidance. |
| Social phobia | Test a client's hypothesis that if she calls a coworker for information that the coworker will become irritated and hang up on her. Have the client guess the probability of this happening and then make the call to see if her prediction is accurate. |
| Specific phobia | Examine the worst-case scenario for what could happen if the client were exposed to something he feared, such as a snake. Explore the realistic probabilities of unlikely scenarios such as being attacked by the snake. |
| Generalized anxiety disorder | Examine a client's belief that worry itself has successfully stopped disaster from happening. Instead, help the client understand that worrying about some disaster does not make the disaster less likely to happen. |
| Obsessive-compulsive disorder | Consider a client's concern that taking risks will lead to disaster. A client may be persuaded to deliberately make mistakes and realize that disaster will not result. Or a therapist may convey that compulsions such as checking and handwashing do not necessarily guarantee safety or total cleanliness. |
| Posttraumatic stress disorder | Investigate a client's belief that all thoughts about the trauma must be suppressed. Teach the client that thoughts about the trauma are not harmful and that a full processing of these thoughts is necessary for recovery. |
| Separation anxiety disorder | An older child or adolescent may be encouraged to consider alternative explanations for a parent being late to pick her up from school. Examples include traffic congestion and unexpected errands and not necessarily a car accident, which is a low-probability occurrence. |

**Angelina:** I'm swerving a bit and feel I have to pull over because of my symptoms.

**Therapist:** But earlier you said you've never been in a car accident, right? So what is the evidence against the idea you might crash?

**Angelina:** Well, I am a very careful driver, and especially when I feel these symptoms coming on. I drive slower and usually stay in the right lane so I can get over to the shoulder. Plus, I've never gotten a ticket for my driving.

**Therapist:** That sounds like a lot of evidence against crashing.

**Angelina:** Yes, I guess that's true, maybe I can handle the symptoms while driving better than I thought.

The therapist pointed out to Angelina, using several driving examples, that not only was there *no evidence* she would get into a car accident while having a panic attack, but that even if she did have a panic attack while driving, she had the ability to protect herself by pulling over. Angelina was encouraged during future panic attacks to examine evidence that something harmful was going to happen. Little evidence was available to suggest this in almost all cases.

Clients may also engage in *hypothesis testing* to see what the actual chances are that something bad will happen (Beck & Dozois, 2011). Angelina was asked to rate the probability she would "go crazy" and be institutionalized for a panic attack in the upcoming week. Angelina regularly replied that the odds of this happening were 60 to 80 percent, although the therapist would give estimates closer to 1 percent. Angelina came to see over time that the therapist's hypotheses were more accurate than hers, and her estimates of disaster decreased.

Clients are also encouraged to *decatastrophize* by thinking about the worst that could happen in a situation and thinking about whether this is really so bad (Craske & Barlow, 2007). Angelina was terrified of shopping at the mall for fear of a panic attack. The therapist calmly asked her, "What is the worst thing that could happen if you had a panic attack at the mall?" Angelina said she would feel her physical symptoms. Again the therapist asked, "So? What's the worst thing about that?" Angelina was surprised at the therapist's calm and said she would feel embarrassed. The therapist challenged this again by saying, "OK. Have you ever felt embarrassed before?" Angelina had, of course, and saw that being embarrassed was an uncomfortable but controllable and temporary state of mind. She came to see over time that, even if she had a panic attack, the consequences were not severe and she could handle them.

A key goal of cognitive therapy is to increase a person's ability to challenge negative thoughts and develop a sense of control over anxious situations. Cognitive therapy can be used to help people control fears of symptoms, negative consequences, threat, obsessions, and reexperiencing images or thoughts (Table 5.17). Many studies have shown cognitive therapy to be a useful component for treating people with anxiety-related disorders (Beck, 2005; Butler, Chapman, Forman, & Beck, 2006). Cognitive therapy may be supplemented with a related technique known as *stress inoculation training*, where a client is taught problem-solving skills to reduce stress in general and cope with difficult life events (Meichenbaum, 2007). A client may also practice self-statements during a task to stay focused and not escape the task.

## EXPOSURE-BASED PRACTICES

Face your fears. Have you heard that phrase before? This is one of the most important aspects of treatment for people with anxiety-related disorders. **Exposure-based practices** are typically used to draw a person closer to whatever he is anxious or fearful about (Shearer, 2007). A person's fear tends to increase as he approaches a feared object or situation. As the person continues to stay in the situation, however, he becomes more used to it, and fear tends to fade. The problem many people with anxiety-related disorders have is they avoid a situation or escape it as fear becomes severe. A person engaged in exposure-based practices is asked to stay in the situation, such as a mall, to experience high levels of fear and learn (1) the fear will eventually decrease over time and/or (2) the person can control the fear. Examples of exposure-based practices for different anxiety-related disorders are listed in **Table 5.18**.

Exposure can be gradual or fast-paced. Gradual exposure may occur during **systematic desensitization**, in which a person slowly approaches a feared situation while practicing relaxation training and/or cognitive therapy (Sisemore, 2012). An anxiety hierarchy is formed (see an example in **Figure 5.12**) that lists items ranging from easy to hard. The person is then exposed to the easiest (bottom) item until his anxiety level is low. He is then exposed to each subsequent step on the hierarchy until he reaches the final goal.

Angelina's therapist accompanied her on various driving trips, excursions to the mall and restaurants, and classes at school (items in Figure 5.12). Angelina was also given homework assignments to practice these and other exposures on her own, including calling friends, going on dates, and driving across a high bridge. She was encouraged during these times to change her thoughts and note her control over her anxiety symptoms:

**Therapist:** OK, we're in the car driving on the freeway, what are you feeling and thinking?

**Angelina:** I feel a little shaky, and my heart is pounding. My lungs feel tight. I'm afraid of having a panic attack and crashing and killing my therapist.

**Therapist:** What are the odds of that?

**Angelina:** Pretty low. It's not likely to happen. I've never crashed the car before even when having a panic attack.

**Therapist:** And what about your physical feelings?

**Angelina:** I can control my breathing and stay steady. I know I can do this!

**Therapist:** Great! I know you can too. Let's keep driving.

Real-life exposures are *in vivo* exposures, but other exposures can be *imaginal*. The latter may involve describing difficult or grotesque stories to a person to have her think about negative events. We obviously do not want to re-create a trauma for someone with posttraumatic stress disorder. Many with

**Table 5.18**

### Exposure-Based Therapy Examples for People with Anxiety-Related Disorders

| Disorder | Exposure-based therapy example |
|---|---|
| Panic disorder | Ride in a car with a client who fears panic attacks while driving. This may consist of sitting in a car, then driving in a parking lot, then driving on an empty road, then driving on a busier road, and then driving on a freeway |
| Social phobia | Gradually increase the number of minutes a person is expected to stay at a social function. Have the client practice social- and performance-based tasks such as introducing oneself, maintaining a conversation, or speaking in public. |
| Specific phobia | Gradually approach a feared stimulus such as a dog. This may begin with watching films of dogs, then visiting a pet store, then visiting an animal shelter, then visiting a park, and then slowly approaching a friendly dog. |
| Generalized anxiety disorder | Ask a client to expose herself to worry instead of suppressing it but to consider alternative explanations for events. Also, practice refraining from checking, cleaning, or other "worry behaviors." |
| Obsessive-compulsive disorder | Ask a client to plunge his hands into a pile of dirt and not wash. Or ask him to park near a Dumpster but breathe normally, throw shoes haphazardly into a closet and refrain from ordering them, or drive to work after checking the oven just once. |
| Posttraumatic stress disorder | Gradually approach a setting where a trauma took place or visit a key gravesite. Engage in discussions about the traumatic event instead of suppressing reminders about the event. |
| Separation anxiety disorder | Require a child to attend school without her parents initially for 1 hour per day. On subsequent days, add an extra 15 to 30 minutes until full-time school attendance is achieved. |

posttraumatic stress disorder continue to try to avoid thinking about the event, which of course triggers more memories and flashbacks. A person doing imaginal exposure thinks first about minor aspects of the trauma and later thinks about more detailed descriptions of the entire event. Anxiety tends to fade as a person thinks more about the event and talks about it.

Exposure for posttraumatic stress disorder can be supplemented as well with a technique known as *eye movement desensitization and reprocessing* (EMDR). EMDR involves inducing back-and-forth eye movements in people as they recall and process traumatic memories. This process is similar to rapid eye movement during sleep and may help reduce the strength of traumatic memories in the hippocampus, as well as anxiety triggered by the amygdala (Harper, Rasolkhani-Kalhorn, & Drozd, 2009). EMDR remains somewhat controversial, however, and requires additional research.

Another type of exposure that simulates in vivo experiences is *virtual reality therapy,* which involves asking a client to wear a headset and watch computer-generated images. These images can be related to stimuli people fear, such as being on an airplane, sitting in an enclosed space, or standing in a high place. A virtual environment can also be set up for people with public speaking anxiety. Virtual reality therapy is effective for people with phobias and is particularly useful for people with unusual or difficult-to-treat phobias (Meyerbroker & Emmelkamp, 2010).

Exposure can also be fast-paced and intensive, as in **flooding** (Moulds & Nixon, 2006). Flooding involves exposing a person to fear with little preparation. A person afraid of dogs could be placed in a room with a dog (in a safe situation, of course) until intense fear subsides and he can approach the dog. Exposure can also be made to internal sensations as well as external items. This refers to **interoceptive exposure** and is most useful for those with panic attacks (Wald & Taylor, 2007). A person undergoing interoceptive exposure is exposed to her most terrifying physical feeling and asked to endure it or engage in relaxation training. A person afraid of increased heart rate might be asked to run up and down a flight of stairs for 1 minute and then calm down and realize the symptom is not dangerous nor does it have to be avoided.

Exposure-based therapies are useful for all anxiety-related disorders (Stewart & Chambless, 2009). This is true even for obsessive-compulsive disorder, for which exposure and **response (or ritual) prevention** are often used (Bjorgvinsson, Hart, & Heffelfinger, 2007). A person may be exposed to her obsession and not allowed to engage in the compulsion. A person with a contamination obsession might be asked to plunge his hands into dirt and then refrain from washing. His anxiety will initially be high, but over time he will learn that anxiety decreases without having to wash and that the thought is not harmful. Response prevention for someone with body dysmorphic disorder might involve limiting the number of times she can check some perceived flaw or groom herself.

A similar procedure is used for people with generalized anxiety disorder. A person is asked during **worry exposure** to concentrate on her anxious thought and then think of as many alternatives to the event as possible (Hoyer et al., 2009). A father worried about his teenager getting into a car accident because she is late coming home would think about this scenario and then give more believable alternatives—perhaps the teenager was caught in traffic or dropped off a friend. People with generalized anxiety disorder are also encouraged to stop their "worry behaviors" such as constantly checking on loved ones or cleaning their house (Roemer & Orsillo, 2002). Managing time and prioritizing tasks (those to be done today, tomorrow, the next day) is also important.

Exposure-based practices are often integrated with other behavioral procedures such as *modeling* and *biofeedback*. A client during modeling watches someone else engage in an approach behavior and then practices it himself. Someone afraid of dogs could gradually approach a dog as her therapist pets the dog to model lack of fear. Clients during biofeedback are attached to a device that gives them visual feedback about heart rate, respiration rate, or brain wave activity. Clients are taught to relax and control their arousal by seeing how relaxation lowers heart and respiration rates. This process is sometimes tied to exposures. A client may be asked to perform a stressful task such as counting backward by sevens and then relax and note how heart and respiration rates decline (Hammond, 2005; Meuret, Wilhelm, & Roth, 2004).

Exposure therapy for people with phobias often means actual physical contact with the feared stimulus.

## MINDFULNESS

Traditional cognitive-behavioral therapies work well for many people with anxiety-related disorders, but not all, particularly those with severe or complicated symptoms. Clinical researchers have thus designed a relatively new set of therapies to help people understand and accept their anxiety symptoms but still live a normal life. The therapist helps a client develop **mindfulness**, or greater daily awareness and acceptance of his symptoms and how the symptoms can be experienced without severe avoidance or other impairment (Hofmann & Asmundson, 2008; Toneatto & Nguyen, 2007).

A therapist might ask Jonathan, who had severe obsessions and compulsions, how he could accept his thoughts and

| Item | Anxiety rating (0-10) | Avoidance rating (0-10) |
|------|-----------------------|-------------------------|
| Driving across a high bridge | 9 | 9 |
| Going on a date | 9 | 9 |
| Attending class | 9 | 8 |
| Shopping in a large department store | 9 | 7 |
| Eating in a restaurant | 8 | 7 |
| Driving along a flat road | 7 | 6 |
| Walking along campus | 5 | 5 |
| Going to a supermarket | 4 | 3 |
| Riding in the car with someone driving | 3 | 2 |
| Attending a therapy session | 2 | 2 |

**FIGURE 5.12** SAMPLE ANXIETY HIERARCHY FOR ANGELINA

Virtual reality therapy for people with phobias is an innovative treatment that works well for difficult cases.

behavioral urges but still get work done at his job. Someone with social phobia at a party could be asked to accept the fact she is anxious but still consider what she needs to say and do to interact with others. Therapists using mindfulness help people recognize they are anxious but focus on how the anxiety can be "set aside" or how to allow thoughts to "pass through their body" so they can still function socially and occupationally. Mindfulness approaches are promising but remain in development (Hofmann, Sawyer, Witt, & Oh, 2010).

## What If I Have Anxiety or an Anxiety-Related Disorder?

People are often screened for anxiety-related disorders, and the answers to some basic questions may indicate whether further assessment or even treatment is warranted. Some of these questions are listed in **Table 5.19**. If you find yourself answering "yes" to most of these questions, then you may wish to consult a clinical psychologist, psychiatrist, or other mental health professional (see also Chapter 15). Cognitive-behavioral therapy and/or medication for your anxiety may be best.

If you feel you have unpleasant anxiety but not necessarily an anxiety-related disorder, then teaching yourself to relax, changing your thoughts, and facing your fears may be best. Talk about your feelings with your family and friends or attend an anxiety screening. Further information about screening and treatment for anxiety disorders can be found at the websites of the Anxiety Disorders Association of America (www.adaa.org) and the Association for Behavioral and Cognitive Therapies (www.abct.org). Anxiety and anxiety-related disorders can be quite painful; if they are for you, do not wait to seek more information.

## Long-Term Outcome for People with Anxiety, Obsessive-Compulsive, and Trauma-Related Disorders

What is the long-term picture, or *prognosis*, for people with anxiety-related disorders? Factors that predict better treatment outcome include treatment compliance and completion, longer treatment (especially exposure), better social skills and social support, less depression and other comorbid disorders, less severe trauma and anxiety symptoms, fewer negative thinking patterns, and fewer stressful life events (Francis, Moitra, Dyck, & Keller, 2012; Hofmann et al., 2007; Simpson et al., 2011; Steketee et al., 2011; Thrasher, Power, Morant, Marks, & Dalgleish, 2010).

Angelina's long-term prognosis was probably good because she sought treatment soon after her most severe panic attacks, was motivated and did complete treatment successfully, had supportive friends and family, and did not have other major disorders such as depression or substance use. Jonathan's prognosis might be poorer because his symptoms seem more ingrained and severe. Marcus's prognosis may depend on how well he can face and address the trauma he experienced.

Contestants on the TV show *Fear Factor* engaged in a feat of "flooding" when they faced their fears. In this example, a contestant must overcome a fear of heights.

## BOX 5.3 Focus on Law and Ethics

### The Ethics of Encouragement in Exposure-Based Practices

Imagine you are the therapist treating Angelina for her panic attacks and agoraphobia. Imagine also that one of your treatment sessions involves accompanying Angelina to a local mall she has not visited for several months. She greatly fears having a panic attack, but your job is to expose her to the setting so she can realize her intense anxiety will subside and she can control her panic symptoms. People with panic disorder and agoraphobia are often able to successfully complete their anxiety hierarchy. In other cases, though, fear is so intense it takes a lot of encouragement, even prodding, by the therapist.

How much prodding is too far? Don't people have a right to live their lives the way they want to, even if it means avoiding

some places? On the other hand, don't therapists have an obligation to their client to end their distress, even if it means short-term fear? The ethical guidelines of the American Psychological Association stipulate that psychologists are expected to "make reasonable efforts to answer patients' questions and to avoid apparent misunderstandings about therapy." The client should thus know ahead of time what will occur in therapy, including difficult real-life exposures, and agree to it. This also involves **informed consent,** which means people entering therapy should be fully informed about all potential risks and benefits of therapy.

Angelina expressed a lot of hesitation about the exposure process, but the therapist made sure she was fully educated about what to expect—such as a possible panic attack—as well as what benefits successful therapy might bring, such as ability to return to school. In this way, no surprises awaited Angelina, and she was more accepting of the therapy process.

### Table 5.19

**Screening Questions for Anxiety-Related Disorder**

Do you find that many of the anxiety symptoms described in this chapter apply to you?

Are there many things you would like to do but can't because you feel too anxious?

Are you greatly troubled by your anxiety symptoms?

Do other people notice your anxiety or encourage you to seek help?

Does your anxiety last much of the time, even when nothing stressful is happening?

Has your work or social life or sleep suffered a lot because of anxiety or worry?

Do you get extremely upset over even little things most of the time?

Have you experienced a traumatic event that you just can't seem to put behind you?

Do you feel sad, irritable, tense, and pessimistic much of the time?

If you could improve your life, would it include feeling less anxious?

Researchers have also looked at the long-term functioning of children with anxiety and anxiety-related disorders. Many fears and worries in childhood are temporary, such as a 4-year-old's fear of monsters in the closet. Some traits related to anxiety, however, are more stable over time. These include behavioral inhibition and shyness (Chronis-Tuscano et al., 2009). Disorders that stem from these characteristics, like social phobia, may be fairly chronic over time. We also mentioned that childhood problems such as separation anxiety disorder and school refusal behavior can lead to long-term problems if left untreated. Obsessive-compulsive disorder is fairly stable for children and adolescents in severe cases as well (Micali et al., 2010). The best approach for addressing anxiety-related disorders at any age is early and complete treatment.

### INTERIM SUMMARY

- Interviews, self-report questionnaires, and observations are used to collect information about people with anxiety-related disorders because of the internal nature of the symptoms.
- Psychophysiological assessment of anxiety-related disorders can consist of determining heart rate, muscle tension, sweat gland activity, and other symptoms to measure their severity.
- Effective treatment for anxiety-related disorders addresses unpleasant physical feelings, negative thoughts, and avoidant behaviors. Biological treatment for anxiety-related disorders includes medications such as benzodiazepines and antidepressants.
- Psychological treatments for people with anxiety-related disorders often begin with psychoeducation and somatic control exercises like relaxation training or breathing retraining.

▶ Cognitive therapy can involve techniques such as examining the evidence, hypothesis testing, and decatastrophizing.

▶ Exposure-based practices are important to help a person reduce anxious avoidance.

▶ Exposure may be done quickly or more gradually through systematic desensitization.

▶ Long-term outcome for people with anxiety-related disorders is best when they receive early and longer treatment, have a good social life, and have less severe symptoms.

## REVIEW QUESTIONS

1. Outline the major assessment techniques for anxiety-related disorders, including interviews, self-report questionnaires, observations, and psychophysiological measurement.
2. What different methods may be used to control physical symptoms of anxiety?
3. What techniques might be used to help an anxious person change negative thoughts?
4. What strategies could a mental health professional use to help someone with anxiety eliminate avoidance?
5. What is the prognosis or long-term outcome for people with anxiety-related disorders?

## Final Comments

People with anxiety and anxiety-related disorders suffer substantial distress from scary physical feelings, negative thoughts, and avoidance of things they normally like to do. This is important to remember the next time someone you know does something like speak in front of others or fly nervously in an airplane. Fear and anxiety are normal, but there can be situations in which the emotions get out of control. If they do, talking to someone about it or contacting a qualified mental health professional is a good idea.

## Thought Questions

1. Think about television shows or films you have seen that have anxious characters in them. Do you think these characters display realistic or unrealistic symptoms of anxiety? How so?
2. What situations make you most anxious? How do you feel physically, what do you think in those situations, and what do you do? Would you change anything after having read this chapter?
3. What would you now say to a friend who might be very anxious?

4. What separates "normal" anxiety from "abnormal" anxiety? Do you think anxiety has more to do with personal, family, or other factors? Why?
5. What do you think could be done socially to reduce anxiety in people?

## Key Terms

worry 103
anxiety 103
fear 103
anxiety-related disorder 104
panic attack 105
panic disorder 106
agoraphobia 107
social phobia 107
specific phobia 108
generalized anxiety
    disorder 109
compulsions 110
obsessions 110
obsessive-compulsive
    disorder 110
body dysmorphic
    disorder 111
posttraumatic stress
    disorder 112
acute stress disorder 112
separation anxiety
    disorder 115
school refusal behavior 117
behavioral inhibition 125
cognitive distortions 126

catastrophizing 126
emotional reasoning 126
thought-action fusion 127
emotional processing 127
anxiety sensitivity 127
behavioral avoidance
    tests 134
psychoeducation 135
somatic control
    exercises 136
relaxation training 136
breathing retraining 136
cognitive therapy 137
exposure-based
    practices 138
systematic
    desensitization 138
flooding 139
interoceptive exposure 139
response (or ritual)
    prevention 139
worry exposure 140
mindfulness 140
informed consent 142

## Media Resources

### MindTap

MindTap for Kearney and Trull's *Abnormal Psychology and Life: A Dimensional Approach* is a highly personalized fully online learning platform of authoritative content, assignments, and services offering you a tailored presentation of course curriculum created by your instructor. MindTap guides you through the course curriculum via an innovative learning path where you will complete reading assignments, annotate your readings, complete homework, and engage with quizzes and assessments. MindTap includes the Continuum Video Project.

Go to **cengagebrain.com** to access MindTap.

# Somatic Symptom and Dissociative Disorders

**6**

Somatic Symptom and Dissociative Disorders: A
   Historical Introduction

Somatization and Somatic Symptom Disorders: What
   Are They?

CASE: *Gisela*

**What Do You Think?**

Somatic Symptom Disorders: Features and
   Epidemiology

Stigma Associated with Somatic Symptom Disorders
   Interim Summary
   Review Questions

Somatic Symptom Disorders: Causes and Prevention
   Interim Summary
   Review Questions

Somatic Symptom Disorders: Assessment and
   Treatment
   Interim Summary
   Review Questions

Dissociative Disorders

CASE: *Erica*

**What Do You Think?**

Normal Dissociation and Dissociative Disorders:
   What Are They?

Dissociative Disorders: Features and Epidemiology

Stigma Associated with Dissociative Disorders
   Interim Summary
   Review Questions

Dissociative Disorders: Causes and Prevention
   Interim Summary
   Review Questions

Dissociative Disorders: Assessment and Treatment
   Interim Summary
   Review Questions

FINAL COMMENTS
THOUGHT QUESTIONS
KEY TERMS
MEDIA RESOURCES

## SPECIAL FEATURES

**CONTINUUM FIGURE 6.1** Continuum of
Somatization and Somatic Symptom Disorders   148

**BOX 6.1** | Focus on Violence: Terrorism and Medically
       | Unexplained Symptoms   156

**CONTINUUM FIGURE 6.4** Continuum of Dissociation
and Dissociative Disorders   162

**PERSONAL NARRATIVE 6.1** Hannah Emily Upp   164

**BOX 6.2** | Focus on Law and Ethics: Recovered Memories
       | and Suggestibility   167

**BOX 6.3** | Focus on Diversity: Dissociation and
       | Culture   167

**BOX 6.4** | Focus on Violence: Dissociative Experiences
       | and Violence Toward Others   170

**THE CONTINUUM VIDEO PROJECT**

*Lani and Jan:* **Dissociative Identity Disorder**   174

# Somatic Symptom and Dissociative Disorders: A Historical Introduction

This chapter is actually like two mini-chapters: one on somatic symptom disorders and one on dissociative disorders. Somatic symptom and dissociative disorders were once seen as related but are now considered distinct disorders. Somatic symptom disorders generally involve physical symptoms with great distress and impairment. Dissociative disorders often involve a disturbance of consciousness, memory, or identity (American Psychiatric Association [APA], 2013).

In the past, people believed that both somatic symptom disorders and dissociative disorders were the result of psychological factors such as trauma (Brown, Schrag, & Trimble, 2005). Psychodynamic theorists believed strange or "hysterical" behaviors resulted from unconscious conflicts related to personal trauma. An adult severely neglected as a child may relate to others with difficulty, seek attention through constant physical complaints, or channel distress into bizarre and medically unexplained sensory-motor symptoms. These symptoms may include glove anesthesia (numbness in the hand only), paralysis, and sudden blindness or deafness (Aybek, Kanaan, & David, 2008). Or a person may develop amnesia about traumatic events in childhood that allows him to detach or dissociate from those events.

As perspectives other than the psychodynamic perspective gained traction within clinical psychology, disorders related to physical symptoms and disorders related to consciousness, memory, or identity were differentiated. Researchers now study somatic symptom and dissociative disorders as largely distinct entities, so we describe the disorders separately here. We begin our discussion with somatic symptom disorders.

## Somatization and Somatic Symptom Disorders: What Are They?

We get more aches and pains as we age (trust us). Many additional aches and pains result from normal wear in joints, muscles, and tendons. We also take longer to heal as we age and often cannot do what we could when we were 20 years old (trust us again). We thus spend more time in doctors' offices as we age. All of this is normal. Many of us also visit health professionals for regular checkups and preventive care.

Many people also engage in **somatization**, or a tendency to communicate distress through physical symptoms and to pursue medical help for these symptoms (Hurwitz, 2004). The prefix "soma" means body; therefore, anything "somatic" refers to the physical body. Many of us become concerned with strange symptoms that compel us to visit a physician. We may be told nothing is wrong or that the problem is minor and not to be dwelled on. We then experience relief and usually let the matter rest. Other times physicians prescribe a general remedy for a vague problem like moderate back pain, which typically addresses the problem to our satisfaction. All of these are normal occurrences.

---

## CASE: Gisela

**Gisela** was referred to psychological treatment by her physician. Gisela was 29 years old and had a 5-year history of physical complaints that medical tests could not explain. She often complained of general abdominal and back pain but no specific physical trauma. Gisela visited the physician several times a year, typically with some variation of the same complaint, and asked for waivers and doctors' notes to help her miss work. The physician conducted a wide array of tests multiple times over several years but concluded that Gisela's constant complaints were due to stress, child rearing, marital issues, or another psychological variable.

Following two cancellations, Gisela met with a clinical psychologist who often accepted referrals from physicians. Gisela was emotional during her initial interview and said she had difficulty caring for her two small children and her husband while working full time. She said she often felt pain in her "lower gut," as well as different places in her back. Gisela could not specify an area of pain, instead saying, "It just hurts all over." The therapist asked Gisela about when or how often pain occurred, but she gave vague answers such as "all the time," "when I am at work or working at home," and "I don't know exactly." Gisela added she sometimes felt numbness in her feet, a symptom her doctors could not explain. She also had occasional nausea and vomiting.

The psychologist asked how long Gisela had been in pain, and she replied, "It feels like I've had it all my life." She also could not connect her symptoms to any physical trauma.

She had not been, for example, in a car accident or the victim of a crime. The psychologist then suggested that Gisela's back pain might be due to the psychological and physical stress of caring for two small children. Gisela dismissed this notion, however, saying the pain could not be explained by simply lifting children because the pain was often sharp, severe, and debilitating. She thus felt unable to complete chores, go to work, or drive when her pain flared.

The psychologist also explored other concerns Gisela had, such as her fear that "something is really wrong with me." Gisela worried she had a serious condition such as Epstein-Barr virus, lupus, or Lyme

AAGAMIA/Iconica/Getty Images

Many people naturally worry about various health concerns as they age, but excessive worry can become a problem.

Other people like Gisela make frequent doctor visits for physical symptoms with no clear biological cause. Physicians are struck by the number of visits these patients request or number of surgeries they want. These patients are not relieved by constant reassurances from their physicians that no real problem exists. Hostility is thus common between physicians and these patients, and many of the patients visit multiple doctors and hospitals for relief or to understand what is wrong with them. Many resist suggestions their physical symptoms have some psychological basis. Gisela dismissed the psychologist's suggestion that stress or family issues caused her symptoms.

People with extreme somatization may have a **somatic symptom disorder** (see **Figure 6.1**). A person with a somatic symptom disorder experiences physical symptoms that may or may not have a discoverable physical cause. These symptoms may resemble minor complaints such as general achiness or pain in different areas of the body. Complaints that are more moderate may include loss of sexual desire, nausea and vomiting, and bloating. The person is highly distressed by the symptoms.

Other disorders are related to somatic symptom disorder, although the term *somatic symptom disorders* is used in this chapter to collectively refer to all of these disorders (APA, 2013). For example, some people are excessively preoccupied with the consequences of various physical symptoms. These people may be less concerned with general symptoms, but they fear they have some serious disease. In addition, other people have symptoms that are quite severe and include sudden blindness, deafness, or paralysis. These

disease. She also became defiant when the psychologist mentioned her doctor tested for these disorders multiple times with negative results. Gisela said she did not trust her doctor to care adequately for her. She also revealed she had seen other doctors in the past but complained they seemed overwhelmed by their numbers of patients and did not have time to consider all possibilities for her symptoms.

The psychologist received permission from Gisela to speak to her husband, physician, and boss. Each said Gisela was a sweet, decent person who truly loved her children and husband. Each commented, however, about Gisela's great need for attention, continual symptom complaints, and desire for reassurance. Her husband and boss described Gisela as a manipulative person who would

bend the truth to get something she wanted. Her husband said Gisela sometimes embellished difficulties to avoid obligations or gain attention and volunteered that she was no longer interested in sex.

Gisela also revealed that she often evaluated herself for physical problems. She often noted her pulse rate and blood pressure, kept a diary of times when her pain flared, and concentrated on minor changes in her physical condition. These factors seemed related to a somatic symptom disorder. Gisela's psychologist suggested a treatment approach that would include physical and psychological components, although Gisela remained more interested in alleviating her physical symptoms than any psychological problem.

## What Do You Think?

1. Which of Gisela's symptoms seem typical or normal for someone with family and job demands, and which seem very different?

2. What external events and internal factors might be responsible for Gisela's dramatic presentation of physical symptoms?

3. What are you curious about regarding Gisela?

4. Does Gisela remind you in any way of yourself or someone you know? How so?

5. How might Gisela's physical complaints affect her life in the future?

| | Normal | Mild |
|---|---|---|
| Emotions | Optimism regarding health. | Mild physical arousal and feeling of uncertainty about certain physical symptoms. |
| Cognitions | No concerns about health. | Some worry about health, perhaps after reading a certain magazine article. |
| Behaviors | Attending regular, preventive checkups with a physician. | Checking physical body a bit more or scheduling one unnecessary physician visit. |

ADAM GAULT/Science Photo Library/Jupiter Images

**CONTINUUM FIGURE 6.1** Continuum of Somatization and Somatic Symptom Disorders

physical symptoms may be linked to anxiety and depression. Finally, other people deliberately induce symptoms in themselves.

A psychological component likely contributes to somatic symptom disorders. Such components often involve stress, conflict, isolation, or trauma. You may have heard the term *psychosomatic* to describe people with physical symptoms that seem "all in their head." A person may be constantly complaining about real physical symptoms or diseases, but the complaints seem a little exaggerated or far-fetched. Psychosomatic and somatic symptom disorders are not exactly the same, but our body and mind are closely connected, so disturbances in one area can lead to problems in the other. We next describe the most commonly diagnosed somatic symptom disorders.

## Somatic Symptom Disorders: Features and Epidemiology

Major somatic symptom disorders in *DSM-5* include somatic symptom disorder, illness anxiety disorder, conversion disorder, and factitious disorder.

### Somatic Symptom Disorder

Do you ever have strange, unexplained feelings in your body? Many people do, such as a sudden pain in the head or a twinge in the abdomen. Most of us pay little attention to these changes because they are not severe and do not last long. Other people like Gisela pay much attention to these physical symptoms and complain about them for many years. A diagnosis of somatic symptom disorder may thus apply.

Somatic symptom disorder involves at least one physical symptom that causes a person great distress as well as impairment in daily functioning. A key part of the disorder, however, is that the person has recurrent thoughts that the symptom is serious or has great anxiety about the symptom or one's health. The person may also devote substantial time and energy to the symptom, such as visiting doctors. Gisela's symptoms caused her to experience distress, miss work, and fail to complete obligations

at home. Keep in mind the symptoms the person feels are real—they are not "faked"—and the symptoms may or may not have a medical explanation. Somatic symptom disorder in the fifth edition of the *Diagnostic and Statistical Manual of Mental Disorders* (*DSM-5*) is related to somatization disorder and pain disorder in *DSM-IV*, and many of those with the older diagnoses are expected to meet criteria for somatic symptom disorder (APA, 2013). Much of the research literature thus concerns somatization and pain disorders and is presented in this chapter.

A diagnosis of somatic symptom disorder involves the *DSM-5* criteria in **Table 6.1** (APA, 2013). Some people with somatic

---

**Table 6.1**

### DSM-5 Somatic Symptom Disorder

A. One or more somatic symptoms that are distressing or result in significant disruption of daily life.

B. Excessive thoughts, feelings, or behaviors related to the somatic symptoms or associated health concerns as manifested by at least one of the following:
1. Disproportionate and persistent thoughts about the seriousness of one's symptoms.
2. Persistently high level of anxiety about health or symptoms.
3. Excessive time and energy devoted to these symptoms or health concerns.

C. Although any one somatic symptom may not be continuously present, the state of being symptomatic is persistent (typically more than 6 months).

Specify if symptoms primarily involve pain, if symptoms have a persistent course, and if severity is mild (one criterion B symptom), moderate (two criterion B symptoms), or severe (2-3 criterion B symptoms with multiple somatic complaints or one very severe somatic symptom).

American Psychiatric Association. (2013). *Diagnostic and statistical manual of mental disorders* (5th ed.). Arlington, VA: American Psychiatric Association.

| Moderate | Somatic Symptom Disorder — less severe | Somatic Symptom Disorder — more severe |
|---|---|---|
| …oderate physical arousal and greater uncertainty …out one's health. | Intense physical arousal misinterpreted as a sign or symptom of some terrible physical disorder. | Extreme physical arousal with great trouble concentrating on anything other than physical state. |
| …ong worry about aches, pains, possible disease, or …pearance. Fleeting thoughts about death or dying. | Intense worry about physical state or appearance. Intense fear that one has a serious disease. Common thoughts about death and dying. | Extreme worry about physical state. Extreme fear of having a serious potential disease. Frequent thoughts about death and dying |
| …heduling more doctor visits but generally feeling …ieved after each one. | Regular doctor-shopping and requests for extensive and repetitive medical tests with little or no relief. Checking body constantly for symptoms. | Avoidance of many social and work activities. Scheduling regular surgeries, attending specialized clinics, or searching for exotic diseases. |

symptom disorder experience significant pain. Gisela reported pain in several areas of her body. People with somatic symptom disorder may complain of pain in areas of the body difficult to assess for pain. Common examples include the back, neck, face, chest, pelvic area, abdomen, sciatic nerve, urinary system, and muscles. Some people initially experience pain from a physically traumatic event but continue to report pain even when fully healed. A burn victim may continue to report pain even when grafts and dressings are finished and when no medical explanation for pain exists. Other people undergo limb amputation and still report pain in that limb, a condition known as *phantom pain* that may have psychological and physical causes (Vase et al., 2011).

Other common complaints include fatigue, shortness of breath, dizziness, and heart palpitations (Iezzi, Duckworth, & Adams, 2004). People with somatic symptom disorder may also have certain personality traits or patterns—they may be attention seeking, seductive, manipulative, dependent, and/or hostile toward family, friends, and clinicians. They may show aspects of personality disorders marked by dramatic or unstable behavior (Chapter 10) (Mai, 2004).

Somatization problems may be "functional" or "presenting." *Functional somatization* refers to what we just described—medically unexplained symptoms not part of another mental disorder. *Presenting somatization* refers to somatic symptoms usually presented as part of another mental disorder, especially anxiety or depression (Boutros & Peters, 2012). Someone with depression may feel fatigued or have low sexual drive, but these physical symptoms are because of the depression. Overlap may occur between functional and presenting somatization. Mental conditions such as depression and stress are strong predictors of whether someone with chronic illness will seek doctor visits and pursue hospitalization (De Boer, Wijker, & De Haes, 1997; Keeley et al., 2008).

## Illness Anxiety Disorder

Other people are less concerned with *symptoms* than of some overall *disease*. People with **illness anxiety disorder** are preoccupied with having some serious disease that may explain general bodily changes. Someone with illness anxiety disorder may worry about

having hepatitis or AIDS based on minor changes in pulse rate, perspiration, or energy level. Recall that Gisela worried about illnesses such as Lyme disease. Illness anxiety disorder in *DSM-5* is related to hypochondriasis in *DSM-IV*, and many of those with the older diagnosis are expected to meet criteria for illness anxiety disorder (APA, 2013). Much of the research literature thus concerns hypochondriasis and is presented in this chapter.

A diagnosis of illness anxiety disorder involves the *DSM-5* criteria in **Table 6.2** (APA, 2013). People with illness anxiety disorder may worry about having a particular disease even after medical tests prove otherwise. A person may receive a negative HIV test but still worry about having AIDS. Such a preoccupation must

Back pain is one of the most common complaints reported by people with somatic symptom disorder.

**Table 6.2**

### DSM-5 Illness Anxiety Disorder

A. Preoccupation with having or acquiring a serious illness.

B. Somatic symptoms are not present or, if present, are only mild in intensity. If another medical condition is present or there is a high risk for developing a medical condition, the preoccupation is clearly excessive or disproportionate.

C. There is a high level of anxiety about health, and the individual is easily alarmed about personal health status.

D. The individual performs excessive health-related behaviors or exhibits maladaptive avoidance.

E. Illness preoccupation has been present for at least 6 months, but the specific illness that is feared may change over that period of time.

F. The illness-related preoccupation is not better explained by another mental disorder.

Specify whether medical care is frequently used (care-seeking type) or medical care is rarely used (care-avoidant type).

American Psychiatric Association. (2013). *Diagnostic and statistical manual of mental disorders* (5th ed.). Arlington, VA: American Psychiatric Association.

**Table 6.3**

### DSM-5 Conversion Disorder (Functional Neurological Symptom Disorder)

A. One or more symptoms of altered voluntary motor or sensory function.

B. Clinical findings provide evidence of incompatibility between the symptom and recognized neurological or medical conditions.

C. The symptom or deficit is not better explained by another medical or mental disorder.

D. The symptom or deficit causes clinically significant distress or impairment in social, occupational, or other important areas of functioning or warrants medical evaluation.

Specify symptom type, if symptoms are acute (less than 6 months) or persistent (6 months or more), and if symptoms occur with or without a psychological stressor.

American Psychiatric Association. (2013). *Diagnostic and statistical manual of mental disorders* (5th ed.). Arlington, VA: American Psychiatric Association.

last at least 6 months and cause substantial distress or impairment in daily functioning. A diagnosis of illness anxiety disorder can also involve frequent medical care such as testing, or avoidance of doctors and hospitals.

People with illness anxiety disorder may have other unique characteristics. Thoughts about having an illness are constant and may resemble those of obsessive-compulsive disorder (Chapter 5). People with illness anxiety disorder may also have significant fears of contamination and of taking prescribed medication. They are intensely aware of bodily functions, and many complain about their symptoms in detail (unlike those with somatic symptom disorder). This may be because they want to help their physician find a "diagnosis" and a "cure" even though an actual disease may not exist. Many people with illness anxiety disorder fascinate themselves with medical information and have *autosuggestibility*, meaning that reading or hearing about an illness can lead to fear of having that disease (Fink et al., 2004). This may be particularly problematic in the age of the Internet with its many websites that offer self-diagnostic tools.

## Conversion Disorder

People with **conversion disorder** experience motor or sensory problems that *suggest* a neurological or medical disorder, even though one has not been found. Examples include sudden blindness or deafness, paralysis of one or more areas of the body, loss of feeling or ability to experience pain in a body area, feeling of a large lump in the throat (*globus hystericus*), and **pseudoseizures**, or seizure-like activity such as twitching or loss of consciousness without electrical disruptions in the brain.

A diagnosis of conversion disorder involves the *DSM-5* criteria in **Table 6.3** (APA, 2013). Symptoms related to the disorder

are real—again, they are not "faked"—but have no medical explanation. The symptoms are also not part of a behavior or experience that is part of one's culture. Many religious and healing rituals in different cultures involve peculiar changes such as loss of consciousness, but this is not conversion disorder.

Psychological, not physical, stressors generally trigger symptoms of conversion disorder. Examples include trauma, conflict, and stress. A soldier may suddenly become paralyzed in a highly stressful wartime experience. A psychodynamic theorist might say the terror of trauma is too difficult to bear, and so distress is "converted" into a sensorimotor disability that is easier to tolerate (Hurwitz, 2004). You might guess that these symptoms cause substantial distress and significantly interfere with daily functioning. However, many people with conversion disorder also experience *la belle indifférence*, meaning they are relatively unconcerned about their symptoms. This seems odd because most of us, if we suddenly developed a severely disabling condition, would be distraught. A lack of concern, however, may indicate other psychological factors are at play, perhaps including dramatic or attention-seeking behavior (Fadem, 2013).

## Factitious Disorder and Malingering

**Factitious disorder** refers to deliberately falsifying or producing physical or psychological symptoms (see **Table 6.4**) (APA, 2013). A person with factitious disorder may fabricate physical complaints such as stomachaches or psychological complaints such as sadness to assume the sick role. People with factitious disorder may purposely make themselves sick by taking medications or inducing fevers. Factitious disorder is thus different from somatic symptom and illness anxiety disorders in which a person does not deliberately cause his symptoms.

## Table 6.4

### DSM-5  Factitious Disorder

**Factitious Disorder Imposed on Self**

A. Falsification of physical or psychological signs or symptoms, or induction of injury or disease, associated with identified deception.

B. The individual presents himself or herself to others as ill, impaired, or injured.

C. The deceptive behavior is evident even in the absence of obvious external rewards.

D. The behavior is not better explained by another mental disorder, such as delusional disorder or another psychotic disorder.

**Factitious Disorder Imposed on Another (Previously Factitious Disorder by Proxy)**

A. Falsification of physical or psychological signs or symptoms, or induction of injury or disease, in another, associated with identified deception.

B. The individual presents another individual (victim) to others as ill, impaired, or injured.

C. The deceptive behavior is evident even in the  absence of obvious external rewards.

D. The behavior is not better explained by another mental disorder, such as delusional disorder or another psychotic disorder.

> **Note:** The perpetrator, not the victim, receives this diagnosis.
>
> Specify if there is a single episode or recurrent episodes of falsification of illness and/or induction of injury.

American Psychiatric Association. (2013). *Diagnostic and statistical manual of mental disorders* (5th ed.). Arlington, VA: American Psychiatric Association.

**Munchausen syndrome** is a factitious disorder in which a person causes symptoms and claims he has a physical or mental disorder. This could involve mimicking seizures or injecting fecal bacteria into oneself. The disorder may be somewhat more common among women visiting obstetricians and gynecologists, including women who deliberately induce vaginal bleeding. Some people with Munchausen syndrome may experience stressful life events or depression or have aspects of borderline or antisocial personality disorder (Babe, Peterson, Loosen, & Geracioti, 1992; Rabinerson, Kaplan, Orvieto, & Dekel, 2002). The prevalence of factitious disorder among hospital patients is 0.3 to 0.8 percent; Munchausen syndrome is rare (Gregory & Jindal, 2006; Lad, Jobe, Polley, & Byrne, 2004). No specific treatment currently exists for factitious disorder (Eastwood & Bisson, 2008).

*Munchausen syndrome by proxy* (or *factitious disorder imposed on another*) refers to adults who deliberately induce illness or pain into a child and then present the child for medical care

(Table 6.4) (Stirling, 2007). The parent is usually the perpetrator and often denies knowing the origin of the child's problem (Shaw, Dayal, Hartman, & DeMaso, 2008). The child generally improves once separated from the parent. Most child victims of Munchausen syndrome by proxy are younger than age 4 years, and most perpetrators are mothers. A main motive for these terrible acts is attention and sympathy the parent receives from others (Frye & Feldman, 2012).

External incentives are absent in factitious disorder, but **malingering** refers to deliberate production of physical or psychological symptoms *with some external motivation*. Malingering is not a formal *DSM-5* diagnosis like factitious disorder but rather an additional condition that may be a focus of clinical attention. A person may complain of back pain or claim he hears voices to avoid work or military service, obtain financial compensation or drugs, or dodge criminal prosecution (APA, 2013). Malingering may be present in 20 to 60 percent of cases of mild head injury, particularly in cases involving litigation (Aronoff et al., 2007). Malingering is present in 20 to 50 percent of cases in people with chronic pain who have some financial incentive to appear disabled (Greve, Ord, Bianchini, & Curtis, 2009).

Physicians are often encouraged to note when reported symptoms do not match findings from medical tests (McDermott & Feldman, 2007). Mental health professionals may use neuropsychological testing or tests such as the Minnesota Multiphasic Personality Inventory—2 (MMPI-2) (Chapter 4) to identify someone with malingering. People who malinger sometimes deliberately do worse on certain tests that even grossly impaired people can do (Williams, 2011). Mental health professionals generally avoid promises of external commitments such as financial benefits and gently confront a malingering client to keep him focused on immediate and verifiable problems (Murdach, 2006).

## Epidemiology of Somatic Symptom Disorders

*DSM-5* diagnostic labels are used in the following sections for continuity purposes, but keep in mind that the research base is largely from parallel *DSM-IV* diagnoses of somatization and pain disorders (akin to somatic symptom disorder) and hypochondriasis (akin to illness anxiety disorder). Many people with somatic symptom disorders remain in the medical system and not the mental health system, and many have vague symptoms, so data regarding epidemiology remain sparse. Complicating matters is that several known medical conditions include vague, undefined symptoms that make it difficult to tell whether a person has a true physical disorder. Examples of these conditions include fibromyalgia (widespread pain in muscles and soft tissue), chronic fatigue syndrome, lupus (an autoimmune disorder causing organ damage), and irritable bowel syndrome (see Appendix) (Fadem, 2013; Mai, 2004).

Many people display moderate somatization and not a formal somatic symptom disorder. People in the United Kingdom presenting to general practitioners often have multiple unexplained physical symptoms (35 percent) and unexplained medical symptoms (19 percent) as their *primary* clinical problem.

Others (9 percent) had high levels of health anxiety (Peveler, Kilkenny, & Kinmouth, 1997). Rates may be similar in the United States (olde Hartman et al., 2009). Children and adolescents also commonly report physical symptoms such as abdominal and chest pain, headache, nausea, and fatigue. Among teenagers, 11 percent of girls and 4 percent of boys report distressing somatic complaints (Silber & Pao, 2003). Moderate somatization thus seems to be a common phenomenon.

Epidemiological research reveals the median prevalence rate of somatic symptom disorder (somatization disorder) in the general population to be 0.4 percent (see **Table 6.5**). This rises to 5.2 percent among medical inpatients. The prevalence of *DSM-IV* pain disorder, now part of somatic symptom disorder, is 0.6%. Somatic symptom disorder appears related to female gender, lower education levels, and physical disability (Creed & Barsky, 2004; Creed et al., 2012; Fink, Hansen, & Oxhoj, 2004).

The mean prevalence rate of illness anxiety disorder (hypochondriasis) in the general population is reportedly about 4.8 percent. This figure seems consistent in medical inpatients as well. Unlike somatic symptom disorder, no clear link appears between illness anxiety disorder and gender or educational level (Creed & Barsky, 2004; Fink et al., 2004). Illness anxiety disorder is associated with increased disability and health costs, as well as degree of worry about illness. People may become more concerned about illness when they already have a true disability and may thus seek even more extensive medical support.

Conversion disorder has been less studied epidemiologically and is probably more rare. Conversion disorder may be present in only 0.3 percent of the general population, but this rate likely differs across cultures (Deveci et al., 2007; Faravelli et al., 1997). About 30 percent of neurological inpatients, however, have no medical explanation for their somatic complaints (Allet & Allet, 2006; Ewald, Rogne, Ewald, & Fink, 1994). Some evidence indicates that somatic symptom disorders are more common among non–European Americans. The most common medically unexplained symptoms across cultures are *gastrointestinal problems* and *strange skin sensations* such as feelings of burning, crawling, and numbness. Unexplained medical symptoms are particularly prevalent among Latinos (especially Puerto Ricans), South Americans, Asians, Nigerians, and those from Caribbean countries and India (Escobar & Gureje, 2007; Gureje, Simon, Ustun, & Goldberg, 1997). Many people of non-Western nations express distress (depression and anxiety) in more somatic than cognitive forms. Certain cultures may socially reinforce somatic expressions of distress (Lam, Marra, & Salzinger, 2005).

Somatic symptom disorders are closely related to depression and anxiety, and somatic complaints often *precede* depression and anxiety-related disorder (Aragones, Labad, Pinol, Lucena, & Alonso, 2005; Gleason & Yates, 2004; Phillips, Siniscalchi, & McElroy, 2004). Somatic symptom and illness anxiety disorders have features similar to panic, generalized anxiety, and obsessive-compulsive disorders. Somatic symptom and illness anxiety disorders may also present together in up to 60 percent of cases (Creed & Barsky, 2004). Overlap between somatic symptom and personality disorders, especially personality disorders involving dramatic or erratic behavior, has also been noted (Bornstein & Gold, 2008; Garcia-Campayo, Alda, Sobradiel, Olivan, & Pascual, 2007).

## Stigma Associated with Somatic Symptom Disorders

People of different cultures may report various types of psychological symptoms depending on local norms and whether stigma is present. For example, those from Asian cultures such as China or India tend to use somatic complaints to express depression because doing so is less stigmatizing than admitting emotional sadness (Lauber & Rossler, 2007; Raguram, Weiss, Channabasavanna, & Devins, 1996). In addition, fear of stigma appears to delay treatment among some people with somatic symptom disorders (Freidl, Spitzl, & Aigner, 2008). Indeed, family members, friends, and even physicians may view a person with a somatic symptom disorder as more of a nuisance than someone who needs psychological help (Hale & Reck, 2010).

Stigma can affect illness behaviors as well. People with unexplained medical symptoms, such as those with chronic fatigue syndrome, often face blame or dismissal from others who attribute their symptoms to emotional problems. This may affect their decision to seek treatment (Kirmayer & Looper, 2006). People with somatization concerned about stigma will also continue to emphasize somatic and not psychological explanations for their symptoms (Rao, Young, & Raguram, 2007). Such stigma concerns even affect people with severe medical conditions such as epilepsy (Freidl et al., 2007).

### INTERIM SUMMARY

▶ Somatic symptom and dissociative disorders were once thought to be linked, but they are now seen as largely separate entities.

▶ Somatization is a tendency to communicate distress through physical symptoms and to pursue medical help for these symptoms.

▶ Somatic symptom disorder refers to medically explained or unexplained pain or other physical symptoms that cause distress and impairment.

**Table 6.5**

| Prevalence Rates of Major Somatic Symptom Disorders | |
|---|---|
| Somatic symptom disorder | 0.4% |
| Illness anxiety disorder | 4.8% |
| Conversion disorder | 0.3% |

▶ Illness anxiety disorder refers to excessive concern that one has a serious disease.

▶ Conversion disorder refers to medically unexplained pseudoneurological symptoms.

▶ Factitious disorder refers to deliberately inducing symptoms in oneself or others, whereas malingering refers to doing so for some external motivation.

▶ Somatization is common among medical patients, but formal somatic symptom disorders are less prevalent. Somatic symptom disorder and illness anxiety disorder are more common than conversion disorder.

▶ Medically unexplained symptoms are more common among people in non-Western countries; such symptoms are closely related to depression and anxiety and personality disorders.

▶ Fear of stigma could delay treatment among some people with somatic symptom disorders.

## REVIEW QUESTIONS

**1.** What is the difference between somatization and a somatic symptom disorder?

**2.** Define and contrast different somatic symptom disorders.

**3.** How does functional somatization differ from presenting somatization?

**4.** How common are different somatic symptom disorders?

**5.** How might stigma affect somatic symptom disorders?

# Somatic Symptom Disorders: Causes and Prevention

Data regarding the cause of somatic symptom disorders have emerged slowly. Key factors related to the development of these disorders may include genetics, brain changes, illness behavior, and cognitive, cultural, evolutionary, and other factors.

## Biological Risk Factors for Somatic Symptom Disorders

### GENETICS

Somatic symptom disorder may have a moderate genetic basis, with a heritability estimate of 0.44 (Kendler et al., 2011). Illness anxiety disorder may also have a moderate genetic basis, with a reported heritability estimate of 0.49 based on a personality inventory (Gizer, Seaton-Smith, Ehlers, Vieten, & Wilhelmsen, 2010). Somatic symptom disorders often cluster among family members, particularly female relatives and between parents and children (Schulte & Petermann, 2011). Several aspects of somatic symptom disorders have a genetic basis as well, especially anxiety, anxiety sensitivity (Chapter 5), depression (Chapter 7), and alexithymia (difficulty understanding one's emotions; Rief, Hennings, Riemer, & Euteneuer, 2010; Silber, 2011).

### BRAIN FEATURES

Another biological risk factor for somatic symptom disorders may be brain changes, especially in areas relevant to emotion, perception, and physical feeling. Key aspects of the brain thus include the amygdala and limbic system, hypothalamus, and cingulate, prefrontal, and somatosensory cortices (see **Figure 6.2**; Garcia-Campayo, Fayed, Serrano-Blanco, & Roca, 2009; Kanaan, Craig, Wessely, & David, 2007). These areas may be overactive in some people with somatic symptom disorders (Henningsen, 2003). Some people may thus perceive or "feel" bodily changes and experiences that are not actually occurring. Recall from Chapter 5 that the amygdala is associated with fearful emotional responses and physical symptoms such as increased heart rate and sweating. An overactive amygdala may thus explain why people with somatic symptom disorders experience many physical changes and concern about the changes.

Others propose that changes in these brain areas interfere with inhibitory behavior and promote hypervigilance about symptoms, as well as increased central nervous system activity and stressful responses (Thayer & Brosschot, 2005). Some disruption is occurring in communications between the brain and body (Kirmayer, Groleau, Looper, & Dao, 2004). Some people with somatic symptom disorders may thus feel they must constantly check physical status indicators such as heart rate, blood pressure, and respiration.

Recall from our earlier discussion that some people report feeling pain in a recently amputated limb. People with phantom limb pain appear to have changes in the brain's motor and somatosensory cortices. The brain initially seems to have trouble adjusting to the missing limb because motor and somatosensory cortices must undergo a neuronal reorganization to account for the missing limb (Karl, Muhlnickel, Kurth, & Flor, 2004). Other researchers have also noted a relationship between somatization and increased epilepsy, multiple sclerosis, cortisol, and blood pressure (Mai, 2004).

Other biological evidence also suggests that people with somatic symptom disorders have brain changes that lead to distractibility, difficulty growing accustomed to continuous stimuli such as physical sensations, and limited cognitive functioning (Iezzi et al., 2004). These brain changes may include dysfunction in the frontal lobe and right hemisphere. Changes in the right hemisphere may help explain why many somatic complaints tend to be on the left side of the body.

Neuroimaging evidence also reveals possible changes in blood flow to key brain areas. Researchers have found changes in different areas of the cortex among people with conversion disorder (Bryant & Das, 2012; Vuilleumier, 2005). Decreased blood flow may occur in areas of the prefrontal cortex and other aspects of the brain related to loss of sensory and motor function as seen in conversion disorder (Black, Seritan, Taber, & Hurley, 2004; see **Figure 6.3**).

## Environmental Risk Factors for Somatic Symptom Disorders

Environmental risk factors are also likely for people with somatic symptom disorders, especially those preoccupied with disease. These factors include illness behavior and reinforcement, as well as cognitive, cultural, evolutionary, and other factors.

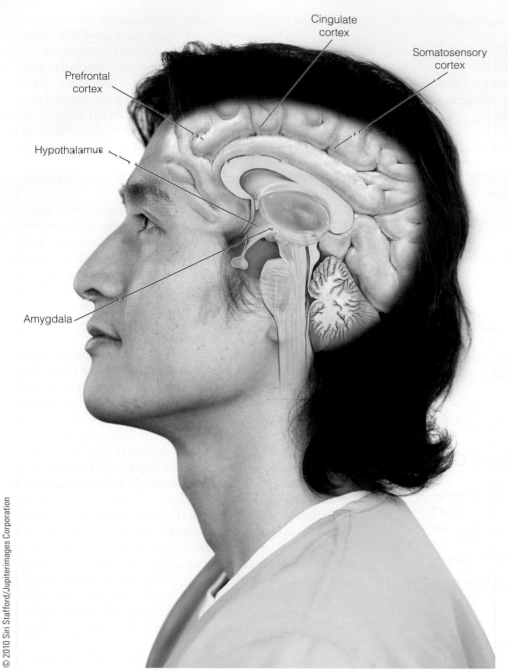

Prefrontal cortex

Cingulate cortex

Somatosensory cortex

Hypothalamus

Amygdala

**FIGURE 6.2** BRAIN AREAS IMPLICATED IN SOMATIC SYMPTOM DISORDERS

Copyright © Cengage Learning®.

## ILLNESS BEHAVIOR AND REINFORCEMENT

*Illness behavior* is a key concept of somatic symptom disorders and refers to behaviors one does when sick (Rief, Martin, Klaiberg, & Brahler, 2005). Examples include resting in bed, seeing a physician, and taking medication. Partners, family members, and friends may reinforce these behaviors by giving sympathy, attention, and comfort. This may help explain the phenomenon of *la belle indifference* in people with conversion disorder. We also generally accept sickness as a socially appropriate means of withdrawing from obligations, so negative

reinforcement can be powerful as well. For people with somatic symptom disorders, like Gisela, social reinforcement for constant complaints or doctor visits may help explain why these disorders persist for long periods. Such demands for attention may intersect as well with someone's dramatic personality structure or disorder.

Another form of comfort relevant to this population is *reassurance*. Many of us feel reassured by medical tests and doctor reports that give us a "clean bill of health," but people with somatic symptom disorders may not. Reassurance is also an effective anxiety-reducer in the short term but not the long term. People like Gisela may thus pursue ongoing, repetitive, and lengthy medical tests and visits. Some believe children model parents' use of reassurance seeking as they age (Burton, 2003; Mai, 2004). Children may copy parents' frequent complaints about physical symptoms or calls to friends for sympathy.

*Secondary gain* sometimes refers to receiving social reinforcement for somatic complaints. Psychodynamic theorists view *primary gain* as unconscious use of physical symptoms to reduce psychological distress. People who pay close attention to minor physical symptoms thus reduce attention toward some internal or external stressor (Hurwitz, 2004). Some people may find it easier to concentrate on minor bodily changes than major life stressors such as marital conflict, financial troubles, or academic failure.

## COGNITIVE FACTORS

Related to illness behaviors are *illness beliefs* or *attributions,* or perceived causes of physical symptoms. People may believe a virus, a psychological condition such as depression, or an external problem such as working too much causes their illness or physical sensation (Henningsen, Jakobsen, Schiltenwolf, & Weiss, 2005). People with somatic symptom disorders tend to adopt biological or illness explanations for their symptoms compared with people with other disorders, who adopt psychological explanations. A person coming home from a long and difficult day at work may adopt a physical explanation for his fatigue (I am sick), whereas many of us would adopt a psychological explanation (I am stressed out).

Those with somatic symptom disorders also see themselves as particularly vulnerable to illness and thus engage in more

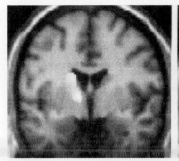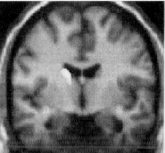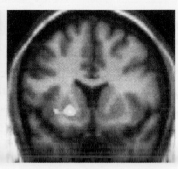

**FIGURE 6.3** BRAIN IMAGING OF BLOOD FLOW IN PEOPLE WITH CONVERSION DISORDER
From Black, D.N., Seritan, A.L., Taber, K.H., & Hurley, R.A. (2004). Conversion hysteria: Lessons from functional imaging. *Journal of Neuropsychiatry and Clinical Neuroscience, 16,* 245-251.

illness behaviors (Hilbert, Martin, Zech, Rauh, & Rief, 2010; Rief, Nanke, Emmerich, Bender, & Zech, 2004). The presence of anxiety and depression, problems also related to cognitive distortions, seem closely linked to increased health anxiety and internal illness beliefs as well (Lieb, Meinischmidt, & Araya, 2007; Muse, McManus, Hackmann, Williams, & Williams, 2010).

Another cognitive factor in somatic symptom disorders is *somatosensory awareness,* or a tendency to notice and amplify physical sensations (Burton, 2003). This is a condition also seen in those with panic disorder and refers to people who attend closely to minor bodily changes. The changes thus become amplified and seem more severe than they are. Indeed, overlap exists between illness anxiety disorder and panic disorder (Deacon & Abramowitz, 2008). Try it. Concentrate intensely on your heart rate for a few minutes and see if you notice any changes or a feeling your heart is "pounding" more so than before. Such intense awareness of internal sensations relates to persistent heart palpitations over time (Barsky, 2001).

## CULTURAL FACTORS

We mentioned that people of non-Western nations tend to express feelings of depression and anxiety as physical symptoms more than people of Western nations do. Psychological conditions are highly stigmatizing in non-Western countries, so a greater emphasis on physical symptoms may be more acceptable. Many cultures have "cultural idioms of distress" to make various experiences seem more normal (Hinton & Lewis-Fernandez, 2010). Consider the Vietnamese notion of *phong tap,* which refers to general aches and pains and distress attributable to fatigue and cold. Attributing one's mental distress to external factors beyond one's control is acceptable practice. This may fit into the notion we mentioned earlier that social reinforcement in a culture is important for how people express their distress.

## EVOLUTIONARY AND OTHER FACTORS

Evolutionary theories of somatic symptom disorders are sparse, but some researchers have theorized that symptoms of conversion disorder developed as an adaptive way of coping with inescapable threats to life (Bracha, Yoshioka, Masukawa, & Stockman, 2005). People faced with warfare or massacre may show debilitating

symptoms such as blindness as a signal to others that one is not a danger; this may help ward off harm. Displaying somatic complaints relates to social closeness and adaptive coping among people faced with loss of a close relative (Segal & Blozis, 2002). This may help increase support or care from others.

Other general factors may also apply to somatic symptom disorders. Examples include poor medical attention and care, unnecessary or incompetent medical treatment, stressful life events, and general emotional arousal (Mai, 2004). Poor medical attention and care may include insufficient feedback by a general physician to someone worried about a particular disease. Stressful life events relate closely to severity of conversion disorder symptoms (Nicholson, Stone, & Kanaan, 2011). These general factors seemed evident for Gisela. Her life was clearly stressful because she had two small children and a full-time job, and she became overexcited quickly. Her point that her doctors seemed overwhelmed by their numbers of patients may also have been valid. Some also point to large-scale events such as terrorism as potentially related to medically unexplained symptoms (see **Box 6.1**).

## Causes of Somatic Symptom Disorders

Different factors likely cause somatic symptom disorders, but much controversy remains about exactly how these problems originate. Some believe the best way to view somatic symptom disorders is as changes in perception, control, and attention (Brown, 2004). Some people misinterpret or *misperceive* sensory experiences as real and dangerous symptoms of some serious medical problem. One might think of general gastrointestinal discomfort as stomach cancer. Someone with somatic symptom disorder may also view internal sensory experiences as *uncontrollable,* meaning the symptoms are beyond her ability to influence or treat. This makes the experiences more frightening.

The way people with somatic symptom disorders misperceive internal sensations is similar to the way some people with anxiety-related disorders, especially panic disorder, do (Chapter 5). Recall that somatic symptom and anxiety-related disorders are closely linked (Hanel et al., 2009). One possibility for this link is that physical symptoms of anxiety, such as heart palpitations or dizziness, become part of a powerful memory later used to explain minor physical discomfort (Brown, 2004). An anxious person might have chest pain and worry (wrongly) she is having a heart attack. This person may later have slightly blurred vision and worry (wrongly) she has a brain tumor.

Many people with somatic symptom disorders also *overattend* to even minor changes in their body (Stuart, Noyes, Starcevic, & Barsky, 2008). If you constantly and intensively concentrate on your heart or respiration rate, you may notice some changes over time. These are normal, of course. For some

## BOX 6.1 Focus on Violence

### Terrorism and Medically Unexplained Symptoms

Do terrorist attacks and suicide bombings create physical changes in people exposed to these events? Somatization and somatic symptom disorders are certainly related to various psychological factors and personal trauma, but some have claimed that even large-scale traumas such as terrorism may have a causal role. Following the 9/11 terrorist attacks, some predicted an increase in referrals to physicians for stress-related medically unexplained symptoms (Hassett & Sigal, 2002). The authors noted that many studies linked exposure to terrorism with somatic complaints such as headaches, backaches, sleep problems, breathing and gastrointestinal difficulties, and even

neurological changes. This connection was found in people in Israel who face frequent terrorist acts, as well as survivors of the Oklahoma City bombing. Stress related to fear of attack at an unknown moment can create intense physiological changes in some people.

Recent data bear this out. Holman and colleagues (2000) examined 2,592 adults who completed a health survey before 9/11 and an assessment of acute stress responses after the attacks. The researchers examined cardiovascular ailments in these people over a 3-year period. People with worry and acute stress responses to the terrorist attacks had a 53 percent greater chance of experiencing hypertension and heart problems. Many people across the country were thus traumatized by the terrorist attacks and had medical symptoms as a result.

people with somatic symptom disorders, however, overattention amplifies the intensity of their symptoms and contributes to worries about their meaning. They may come to believe they have some serious disease. Not surprisingly, such overattention exists in people with anxiety-related and depressive disorders (Chapters 5 and 7). All of these processes—sensory misperception, feelings of uncontrollability, and overattention—can then lead to illness behaviors, social reinforcement for playing the "sick role," avoidance of daily activities, and a somatic symptom disorder (Brown, 2004; Rief & Broadbent, 2007).

## Prevention of Somatic Symptom Disorders

Data are scarce regarding the prevention of somatic symptom disorders, but information about the disorders in children and adolescents may be instructive. Youths with somatization are often female, and their parents are often of lower socioeconomic status and educational level. Stressful life events, traumatic experiences such as maltreatment, history of physical disease, unnecessary medical interventions, and the presence of other mental disorders such as anxiety and depression also relate to somatization in youths (Bisht, Sankhyan, Kaushal, Sharma, & Grover, 2008; Schulte & Petermann, 2011). Others have stated as well that some youths receive substantial attention from parents for somatic complaints, and this serves as a reinforcer (Silber & Pao, 2003).

Given this information, strategies to prevent the development of somatic symptom disorders may include several components. Examples include educating children and parents about dangerous and nondangerous physical symptoms, attending to serious but not common bodily changes, helping youths cope with traumatic events and related mental disorders, ensuring adequate and competent health care, and practicing anxiety management (Chapter 5). Given that somatic

symptom disorders may endure over time, addressing risk factors for the problems as early as possible is important.

### INTERIM SUMMARY

▶ Biological risk factors for somatic symptom disorders may include genetic predispositions, as well as key brain changes in the amygdala, hypothalamus, limbic system, and cingulate, prefrontal, and somatosensory cortices.

▶ Environmental risk factors for somatic symptom disorders include illness behaviors, which involve medically related behaviors potentially reinforced by significant others.

▶ Cognitive factors are likely powerful influences in somatic symptom disorders because many people with these disorders use somatic explanations for even minor bodily changes.

▶ Cultural and other factors may influence somatic symptom disorders as well. Poor medical attention and care, problematic medical treatment, stressful life events, and emotional arousal may be risk factors.

▶ A causal model of somatic symptom disorders focuses on misperception of symptoms, feelings of uncontrollability about symptoms, and overattention to minor bodily changes.

▶ Risk factors in children and adolescents may inform strategies for preventing somatic symptom disorders. Examples include stressful life events, traumatic experiences, unnecessary medical interventions, and comorbid anxiety and depression.

### REVIEW QUESTIONS

1. Describe how certain brain changes may be associated with somatic symptom disorders.
2. What forms of social reinforcement relate to somatic symptom disorders?
3. What cognitive factors relate to somatic symptom disorders?

4. Describe an overall causal theory to explain Gisela's somatic symptom disorder.
5. Outline a prevention strategy for a youth at risk for medically unexplained symptoms.

# Somatic Symptom Disorders: Assessment and Treatment

We turn next to strategies for assessing and treating somatic symptom disorders. Keep in mind the psychological assessment of someone with a possible somatic symptom disorder should be done in conjunction with a comprehensive medical evaluation.

## Assessment of Somatic Symptom Disorders

Assessing someone like Gisela with a somatic symptom disorder usually involves interviews, questionnaires, and personality assessment. We discuss each method next.

### INTERVIEWS

Interviews to gather information about people with somatic symptom disorders include structured, research-based ones such as the *Structured Clinical Interview, Composite International Diagnostic Interview, Somatoform Disorders Schedule,* and *International Diagnostic Checklists* (First, Spitzer, Gibbon, & Williams, 2002; Hiller & Janca, 2003; Hiller, Zaudig, & Mambour, 1996). These interviews cover diagnostic criteria for various somatic symptom disorders.

Questions given to someone like Gisela with a possible somatic symptom disorder should involve a detailed history of physical and psychological problems. Somatic symptom disorders can be complex and long-standing, and we know these disorders often begin in childhood and adolescence, so questions about one's history should extend far into the past. Pertinent topics include early and recent life experiences and stressors, medication and substance use history, others' reactions to somatic complaints, cognitive distortions, interference in daily functioning, and motivation for seeking and pursuing psychological treatment for what the client may believe is mostly a medical problem.

Gisela hesitated about using psychological treatment to address what she thought were simply medical problems. Interviewing a person with a somatic symptom disorder thus requires a therapist to develop good rapport with her client. Guidelines for communicating with a person with a somatic symptom disorder are in **Table 6.6**.

### QUESTIONNAIRES

Screening instruments also exist for possible somatic symptom disorders. Common ones include the *Screening for Somatoform Disorders (SOMS)* and *SOMS-7,* which cover diagnostic criteria and measure a person's medically unexplained physical symptoms (Rief & Hiller, 2003). Cognitive distortions and illness behaviors are often a part of somatic symptom disorders, so some questionnaires assess these constructs. Examples include the *Cognitions about Body and Health Questionnaire* and *Scale for the*

### Table 6.6

**Guidelines for a Therapist Communicating with a Person with Possible Somatic Symptom Disorder**

| |
|---|
| Acknowledge that the symptoms are real and distressing to the client. |
| Accept the need to address somatic complaints. |
| Avoid attempts to convince the client of a psychological cause for symptoms. |
| Continue to gently refer to the role of tension and stress. |
| Discuss various topics, not just symptoms. |
| Schedule regular visits not predicated on complaints. |
| Develop goals in conjunction with the client. |
| Discuss how symptoms limit a client's functioning instead of what might be physically wrong. |
| Maintain empathy with a client but set limits on behavior. |

From Maynard (2003).

*Assessment of Illness Behavior* (Rief, Hiller, & Margraf, 1998; Rief, Ihle, & Pilger, 2003).

Other questionnaires specific to hypochondriasis include the *Whiteley Index, Illness Behaviour Questionnaire, Illness Attitude Scales,* and *Somatosensory Amplification Scale* (SAS). These scales measure diagnostic symptoms, perceptions of illness, and awareness of internal sensations (Fava, Sonino, & Wise, 2012). Sample SAS items are in **Table 6.7**.

### PERSONALITY ASSESSMENT

Recall that somatic symptom disorders and unrealistic health concerns sometimes relate to certain personality traits or disorders. Assessment for this population may thus include personality inventories. The *Minnesota Multiphasic Personality Inventory—2* (MMPI-2) includes clinical subscales for hypochondriasis, somatic complaints, and health concerns (Aragona, Tarsitani, De Nitto, & Inghilleri, 2008; Butcher, Graham, Williams, & Ben-Porath, 1990). The hypochondriasis and health concerns subscales help discriminate people with chronic pain from control participants. Chronic pain relates as well to elevated anxiety and depression scores (Slesinger, Archer, & Duane, 2002). Others have found the MMPI useful for screening women with somatic symptom disorder (Wetzel et al., 1999).

## Biological Treatment of Somatic Symptom Disorders

People with somatic symptom disorders often experience comorbid anxiety and depression, so a key treatment approach has been medication to address these conditions. The most

## Table 6.7

**Sample Items from the Somatosensory Amplification Scale**

| |
|---|
| I am often aware of various things happening within my body. |
| When I bruise myself, it stays noticeable for a long time. |
| I can sometimes feel the blood flowing in my body. |
| I can sometimes hear my pulse or my heartbeat throbbing in my ear. |
| I am quick to sense the hunger contractions in my stomach. |
| Even something minor, like an insect bite or a splinter, really bothers me. |
| I have a low tolerance for pain. |

*Note:* Items are scored on a 1-to-5 scale reflecting how much each item characterizes a person (5 equals more so).
Barsky, A.J., Wyshak, G., & Klerman, G.L. (1990). The Somatosensory Amplification Scale and its relationship to hypochondriasis. *Journal of Psychiatric Research, 24,* 323-334. Reprinted by permission of Elsevier.

common medications for this population have been selective serotonergic reuptake inhibitors (Chapters 5 and 7) such as escitalopram (Lexapro), fluoxetine (Prozac), fluvoxamine (Luvox), and paroxetine (Paxil). Use of these drugs for somatic symptom and illness anxiety disorders helps improve anxiety and depression, as well as fears of disease, symptom preoccupation, and overall functioning. Specific pain is not generally affected (Fallon et al., 2003; Muller et al., 2008; Sumathipala, 2007). Antidepressant medication may help reduce the number of pain *episodes,* however (Fallon, 2004). Much work remains regarding these medications because most drug studies in this area have not included control groups (Ipser, Sander, & Stein, 2009).

## Psychological Treatments of Somatic Symptom Disorders

Somatic symptom disorders are associated with problematic illness behaviors and significant cognitive factors, so the use of psychological treatments for these disorders has begun to garner more research attention. You might not be surprised that psychological treatments for somatic symptom disorders resemble the treatments for anxiety-related disorders (Chapter 5). Keep in mind, however, that many people with somatic symptom disorder resist the idea of treatment from a mental health professional. Clients like Gisela might have to first recognize that their symptoms may have some psychological basis, but this is often not easy for them to do.

### COGNITIVE THERAPY

Cognitive therapy for anxiety-related disorders involves examining inaccurate statements a person may be making and encouraging the person to challenge the thought and think more realistically. This therapy works the same way for treatment of people with somatic symptom disorders. People with somatic symptom disorders should first understand the connection between their problematic thoughts and their physical symptoms. Someone who constantly worries about having a disease and who checks her body constantly for changes may amplify those changes and misperceive them as dangerous. Cognitive therapy helps a person examine evidence to dispute this thought process. A person may come to realize that minor physical sensations and changes are not dangerous because all humans have them and because the symptoms are often temporary and controllable.

A client with a somatic symptom disorder may also benefit from logically examining her thoughts about the consequences of physical symptoms. Someone like Gisela may constantly worry her physical symptoms will devastate her life. A therapist might help Gisela understand she can effectively cope with or control physical symptoms and additional stressors in her life. Biofeedback, in which a person learns to consciously control bodily functions such as heart rate, can be useful in this regard (Nanke & Rief, 2003).

The various somatic symptom disorders involve problematic thought processes that can be treated with cognitive therapy. People with illness anxiety disorder fear their symptoms indicate a serious disease. A cognitive therapist may help a client with illness anxiety disorder discuss evidence for and against a disease belief, assess realistic probabilities for a certain physical symptom, and understand that a 100 percent certainty of knowing one is not ill is never possible. A person with abdominal distress should list all possible reasons and probabilities for such distress, including cancer but also gas, indigestion, and other common but harmless conditions (Allen & Woolfolk, 2010). When conducting cognitive therapy for anyone with a somatic symptom disorder, clinicians generally avoid blaming a client for her symptoms and focus on reducing concurrent anxiety and depression (Greenberg & Wilhelm, 2011).

### BEHAVIOR THERAPY

Behavior therapy for somatic symptom disorder helps a person reduce excess behaviors such as checking symptoms and visiting doctors. Behavior therapy aims to reduce the excess attention-seeking and reassurance-seeking behaviors that many people with somatic symptom disorders engage in; these behaviors cause others to reinforce their symptoms. **Contingency management** involves educating family members and friends about a person's somatic symptom disorder and encouraging them to reinforce "well" behaviors such as going to work, finishing chores, and staying active. This seems especially important for treating *conversion disorder,* in which an emphasis is placed on removing medical and social attention for abnormal sensory-motor conditions, administering physical therapy to restore normal movement, and helping clients cope with stress and trauma (Krem, 2004; Thomas & Jankovic, 2004).

The primary behavioral treatment components for somatic symptom disorders are relaxation training, exposure, response prevention, and social skills and assertiveness training (Iezzi et al., 2004). You may notice these treatments are similar to those mentioned in Chapter 5 for anxiety-related disorders, especially obsessive-compulsive disorder. Somatic symptom disorders often have an anxious component, so treatments aimed at anxiety may work well for this population. Relaxation training and exposure are often conducted together to help ease muscle tension, which aggravates physical symptoms, and reduce anxiety when a person confronts anxiety-provoking stimuli. Such stimuli usually include avoided situations such as social interactions, dating, and work. Gisela's therapist worked with her to establish a regular pattern of work attendance. Response prevention involves limiting the number of times a person can monitor physical symptoms or engage in some other excess behavior. Many therapists use behavioral procedures with cognitive therapy to treat people with somatic symptom disorders.

Cognitive plus behavioral therapy for people with somatic symptom disorders is quite helpful in some cases (Bleichhardt, Timmer, & Rief, 2004; Magarinos, Zafar, Nissenson, & Blanco, 2002). Exposure, response prevention, and cognitive therapy in one study helped 75 percent of people with illness anxiety disorder show meaningful improvement (Visser & Bouman, 2001). Success rates for people with somatic symptom disorders are generally less positive, however, than for people with anxiety disorders or depression. This is because people with somatic symptom disorders often show multiple symptoms over long periods (Rief & Sharpe, 2004). The most useful approach for this population will likely include medication *and* comprehensive psychological treatment within medical and mental health settings.

## What If I or Someone I Know Has a Somatic Symptom Disorder?

If you suspect you or someone you know might have features of a somatic symptom disorder, then seeking a full medical and psychological examination is important. You may also want to think about related problems of stress, anxiety, or depression that aggravate physical symptoms or worries about having some disease (Chapters 5 and 7). Somatic symptom disorders can be distressing and often greatly interfere with one's ability to accomplish even simple tasks. Encouraging someone who may have features of a somatic symptom disorder to continue to stay active and "work through" his symptoms is a good idea as well.

## Long-Term Outcome for People with Somatic Symptom Disorders

Longitudinal studies indicate that many people (50 to 75 percent) with medically unexplained symptoms or somatic symptom disorder show improvement over time but that about 10 to 30 percent deteriorate. People with illness anxiety disorder often have a more chronic course, with 50 to 70 percent maintaining their symptoms over time. Predictors of more chronic course of somatic symptom disorder include greater severity of symptoms such as degree of pain or illness behavior as well as poor physical functioning. Other possible predictors have support in some studies but not others and include female gender, comorbid mood problems, and unrealistic fears of illness (olde Hartmann et al., 2009).

How do people with somatic symptom disorders fare after treatment? People do respond to treatment for these problems, although researchers have found certain characteristics related to better long-term outcome. These characteristics include less anxiety and fewer pretreatment symptoms, comorbid conditions, cognitive distortions about bodily functioning, and hospital stays (Hiller, Leibbrand, Rief, & Fichter, 2002; Nakao, Shinozaki, Ahern, & Barsky, 2011; Phillips, Pagano, Menard, Fay, & Stout, 2005). As we mention throughout this textbook, the more severe one's symptoms, the more difficult successful treatment will be.

## INTERIM SUMMARY

- ▶ Therapists use interviews and questionnaires to assess people with somatic symptom disorders. These measures concentrate on diagnostic criteria, history of symptoms, illness behaviors and beliefs, personality patterns, and other relevant topics.

- ▶ Biological treatments for people with somatic symptom disorders include antidepressant medication to ease comorbid depression, fears of disease, and symptom preoccupation.

- ▶ Psychological treatments for people with somatic symptom disorders involve cognitive-behavioral strategies to reduce illness behaviors and avoidance, improve physical functioning, address trauma, and limit checking and other excessive behaviors.

- ▶ The long-term outcome of people with somatic symptom disorders is variable but may be somewhat worse for people with illness anxiety disorder. Severity of symptoms and degree of comorbid conditions are good predictors of outcome.

## REVIEW QUESTIONS

1. Describe various methods of assessing people with somatic symptom disorders.
2. What medications might be best for people with somatic symptom disorders?
3. What issues might arise when trying to get family members involved in treating someone with a somatic symptom disorder?
4. Describe psychological treatments for people with somatic symptom disorders.
5. Outline the long-term outcome for people with somatic symptom disorders.

# Dissociative Disorders

## CASE: Erica

**Erica** was attending outpatient therapy for depression and "strange experiences." The 25-year-old was attending therapy sessions for about 3 months after a breakup with her boyfriend. Her romantic relationship lasted only a few months but was conflictive and occasionally violent. Erica said her interactions with her boyfriend were "intense" because they engaged in frequent sexual contact but also constant fighting about time spent together, progression of the relationship, and failure to communicate verbally. Erica said her boyfriend hit her on more than one occasion, although hospitalization or the police were never involved. Erica and her boyfriend mutually agreed to part after a serious decline in the quality of their relationship.

Erica said she was depressed and tearful about the breakup and especially about being alone. She said she was having trouble eating and sleeping and missed several days of work to stay in bed. Erica's therapist was able, however, to help her client gradually gain control of her life and improve her mood. Erica became more active in seeing her family members and friends, resumed work on a regular basis, thought about new dating opportunities, and engaged in cognitive therapy to reduce self-blame about her past relationship.

Therapy progressed in these areas but remained stagnant in other areas. Erica often had trouble remembering things from the past week or even the day before, seemed distracted in therapy sessions, and even missed some sessions. The therapist sometimes asked Erica if anything was wrong, but Erica would only say she was having some recent memory difficulties and felt "strange."

When asked for details, Erica said she would sometimes come home to find her apartment a mess even though she was a very neat person. She also received two speeding tickets in the mail but did not remember a police officer stopping her. Erica also said she sometimes forgot what day of the week it was.

Erica's therapist tried to go into detail about these experiences, but with little success. The therapist also thought it strange that Erica was generally unwilling or unable to talk about past relationships or even her childhood. When asked about these periods in her life, Erica became ashen and said she could not "really remember my birthdays or anything specific" about childhood. Following several unfruitful sessions, Erica's therapist decided a more in-depth discussion of Erica's past would help her fully understand her current depression and relationship problems.

The therapist called Erica one night at home to ask if she could delve into Erica's past in more detail. This might involve conversations with Erica's parents and others who had known her for a long time. Erica answered the telephone and listened to the therapist before excusing herself. The therapist waited about 4 minutes before a young voice came on the telephone. The therapist was confused because Erica lived alone and had no children. The young voice on the line told the therapist, "I can't let you talk to her about those things." The therapist, startled and alarmed, asked the voice to explain. The voice said, "We can't talk about those bad things," paused, and said, "We just can't." The therapist asked the voice to identify itself but the voice only said, "It's me," before hanging up.

The therapist called back, but no one answered.

Erica came to her therapy session the next day as if nothing had happened. The therapist told her about the telephone conversation but Erica was perplexed and did not know how to respond. The therapist then asked Erica about recent days and times that she could not remember, and the previous night was one of those times. The therapist delicately explained to Erica that she may be experiencing episodes of dissociation whenever stressful events occurred and that Erica may have a separate personality structure. Erica was confused but listened intently because the description of dissociation fit her history. Erica did say, somewhat out of the blue, that the young voice her therapist heard was likely 7 years old. She did not know why she thought this to be the case. Erica's therapist believed her client was likely having symptoms of a dissociative disorder and perhaps even had multiple personalities.

## What Do You Think?

1. Which of Erica's symptoms seem normal, and which seem odd for someone with intense, recent life stressors such as hers?

2. What external events and internal factors might be responsible for Erica's odd symptoms?

3. What are you curious about regarding Erica?

4. Does Erica remind you in any way of yourself or someone you know? How so?

5. How might Erica's odd symptoms affect her life in the future?

## Normal Dissociation and Dissociative Disorders: What Are They?

Have you ever been in a stressful situation where you felt "out of it"? Perhaps you were taking a test or talking before a group of people and suddenly felt as if you were watching yourself do the task or floating above yourself? These experiences, though somewhat odd, are normal and represent **dissociation**. Dissociation refers to some separation of emotions, thoughts, memories, or other inner experiences from oneself. In other words, we feel as if we have split from ourselves.

Such separation is often mild and temporary and can include things like daydreaming, being absorbed by a film, "spacing out," or highway hypnosis, in which a person drives for a distance but cannot recall how he arrived at his destination (Cerezuela, Tejero, Choliz, Chisvert, & Monteagudo, 2004). In other cases, separation is moderate, meaning a person may feel temporarily outside of her body or walk through hallways as if in a fog. Or a person may feel he cannot recall all details of a certain event (see **Figure 6.4**).

These episodes of dissociation are normal because they are temporary and do not interfere with daily life. A person may take an important test and feel dissociated for the first few minutes. She may feel as if she is watching herself take the test and have trouble concentrating on the questions. Usually, however, this feeling dissipates quickly, and the ability to concentrate returns. We may feel we are "coming back to the test" and see it more clearly than before. Another person may see a terrible accident and feel as if events are progressing in dreamlike slow motion. Everything might then suddenly snap back to "real time." Minor dissociation may help us temporarily handle stress by keeping it at arm's length. The dissociation usually dissipates as we adjust to the stressful situation, calm ourselves, and do what we need to do.

In some cases, however, separation can be severe and lead to **dissociative disorders**. Dissociative disorders often involve disturbance in consciousness, memory, or identity (APA, 2013).

A person may experience some form of dissociation for lengthy periods of time or in some extremely odd way. Erica may have coped with recent or past stress by forgetting information that reminded her of trauma. She may have even developed a separate personality at age 7 years that "kept" traumatic memories of that time hidden so she would not have to think about them. Such extreme dissociation may be reinforced over time because it works so well—in other words, the person does not have to address a particular trauma. Unfortunately, as with Erica, long-term dissociation can cause significant problems in social relationships and even legal status.

## Dissociative Disorders: Features and Epidemiology

Dissociative disorders include dissociative amnesia, dissociative identity disorder, and depersonalization/derealization disorder. We next discuss features of these challenging disorders.

### Dissociative Amnesia

Do you ever forget things for no reason? Of course you do! We all forget things from time to time, and forgetfulness increases with age (Chapter 14). Normal forgetfulness is nothing much to worry about because the items we forget are minor and can easily be remembered with a cue. For some people like Erica, however, forgotten items are highly *personal*—examples include childhood experiences, family members, and even identifying information like one's name. A diagnosis of **dissociative amnesia** may thus apply (see **Table 6.8**) (APA, 2013).

Dissociative amnesia involves forgetting highly personal information, typically after some traumatic event. A person may have trouble remembering his name after a car accident or assault. To be defined as dissociative amnesia, such forgetfulness is not caused by substance use or neurological or other medical disorder. The memory loss can, however, cause distress and impair one's ability to function on a daily basis. Imagine being unable to remember who you are—this would cause enormous

Brief episodes of dissociation, such as depersonalization, are common and normal.

Jason Bourne, Matt Damon's character in *The Bourne Identity*, has dissociative amnesia and spends much of the film attempting to discover his true identity.

| | Normal | Mild |
|---|---|---|
| **Emotions** | Feeling good connection with others and environment. | Mild physical arousal, especially when forgetting something. |
| **Cognitions** | No concerns about forgetfulness. | Slight worry about lack of concentration on an examination or about increasing forgetfulness as one ages. |
| **Behaviors** | Occasional forgetfulness but little problem remembering with a cue. | Daydreaming during class, minor "spacing out" during a boring abnormal psychology lecture, mild forgetfulness. |

**CONTINUUM FIGURE 6.4** Continuum of Dissociation and Dissociative Disorders

---

### Table 6.8

#### DSM-5 Dissociative Amnesia

A. An inability to recall important autobiographical information, usually of a traumatic or stressful nature, that is inconsistent with ordinary forgetting.

   **Note:** Dissociative amnesia most often consists of localized or selective amnesia for a specific event or events; or generalized amnesia for identity and life history.

B. The symptoms cause clinically significant distress or impairment in social, occupational, or other important areas of functioning.

C. The disturbance is not attributable to the physiological effects of a substance or a neurological or other medical condition.

D. The disturbance is not better explained by dissociative identity disorder, posttraumatic stress disorder, acute stress disorder, somatic symptom disorder, or major or mild neurocognitive disorder.

   Specify if with dissociative fugue, or travel or wandering associated with amnesia for identity or other autobiographical information.

American Psychiatric Association. (2013). *Diagnostic and statistical manual of mental disorders* (5th ed.). Arlington, VA: American Psychiatric Association.

---

stress and would obviously prevent you from working and even taking care of yourself.

Dissociative amnesia can come in several forms. People with dissociative amnesia may have only one severe episode of forgetfulness or several smaller or equally severe episodes. This may depend on the degree of trauma in their life. Recollection of important personal information may return suddenly for some but more gradually in others. Oddly, a person may forget *personal information* but remember historical events or how to drive a car. Such semantic or procedural memory can be lost in some cases, however (van der Hart & Nijenhuis, 2001). Dissociative amnesia seems common among soap opera characters, but loss of widespread personal information is actually quite rare.

Dissociative amnesia can also include **dissociative fugue**. Some people develop amnesia about personal events and suddenly move to another part of the country or world. People with dissociative fugue cannot recall their past, and sometimes their identity, and end up living and working far away from family and friends. The person often assumes a new identity or is greatly confused about personal identity. Dissociative fugue most often occurs after a traumatic event. A man about to be publicly embarrassed in a scandal may suddenly move to another part of the country and assume a new name and job. Fugue states are characterized by dissociation, so in this case the person did not consciously plan to move. Instead, he likely had little recollection of what happened to him in the past. Fugue states can eventually disappear and a person may resume his old life, although memories of the original trauma may still be poor (Santos & Gago, 2010).

## Dissociative Identity Disorder

Other people with dissociative disorder experience *identity* problems that involve formation of different personalities. Those with **dissociative identity disorder** actually have two or more distinct personalities within themselves (this disorder was once called *multiple personality disorder*). These personalities may wrest control of a person's consciousness and for a time become the dominant personality (see **Table 6.9**) (APA, 2013). When this happens, as it did for Erica, a person may feel as if strange events are happening around her. The person may have trouble recalling personal information and have memory gaps about childhood or recent events. To be defined as dissociative identity disorder, the development of multiple personalities must not result from substance use or a medical condition. Identity "splitting" is often due to a traumatic event or set of events such as child maltreatment (Ross & Ness, 2010).

What is remarkable about dissociative identity disorder is that *true* differences supposedly exist among the personalities. Each personality may have its own distinctive voice, behavior, memories, age, gender, handedness, allergies, and eyesight (Birnbaum &

| Moderate | Dissociative Disorder — less severe | Dissociative Disorder — more severe |
|---|---|---|
| Greater difficulty concentrating, feeling more alienated from others and one's environment. | Intense difficulty concentrating and feelings of estrangement from others. | Feelings of complete alienation and separation from others or one's environment. |
| Greater worry about minor dissociation, such as sitting in a car at the supermarket and wondering how one arrived there. | Intense worry about substantial dissociation or "gaps" in memory or little realization that something is wrong. | Potential lack of insight or thought about one's personal identity or changed living situation. |
| Highway hypnosis, more frequent forgetfulness, or acting as if in a fog or a dream. | Infrequent episodes of depersonalization, intense forgetfulness, or missing appointments with others. | Severe and frequent episodes of dissociation, constant amnesia or fugue, presence of multiple personalities. |

© iStockphoto.com/Sharon Dominick

The Olympian/McClatchy-Tribune/MCT/Getty Images

In 2006, Jeffrey Ingram (pictured with his wife) woke up on a sidewalk in downtown Denver with no memory of who he was. Doctors believed he was in a dissociative fugue state.

## Table 6.9

### DSM-5 Dissociative Identity Disorder

A. Disruption of identity characterized by two or more distinct personality states, which may be described in some cultures as an experience of possession. The disruption in identity involves marked discontinuity in sense of self and sense of agency, accompanied by related alterations in affect, behavior, consciousness, memory, perception, cognition, and/or sensory-motor functioning. These signs and symptoms may be observed by others or reported by the individual.

B. Recurrent gaps in the recall of everyday events, important personal information, and/or traumatic events that are inconsistent with ordinary forgetting.

C. The symptoms cause clinically significant distress or impairment in social, occupational, or other important areas of functioning.

D. The disturbance is not a normal part of a broadly accepted cultural or religious practice.

**Note:** In children, the symptoms are not better explained by imaginary playmates or other fantasy play.

E. The symptoms are not attributable to the physiological effects of a substance (e.g., blackouts or chaotic behavior during alcohol intoxication) or another medical condition (e.g., complex partial seizures).

American Psychiatric Association. (2013). *Diagnostic and statistical manual of mental disorders* (5th ed.). Arlington, VA: American Psychiatric Association.

Thomann, 1996)! Keep in mind a person with dissociative identity disorder is *not pretending* to be someone different, such as when an adult acts and talks like a child. Instead, true differences exist in behavior and other characteristics that make someone unique. Some researchers, however, question the existence of multiple personalities and see only differences in representations of different emotional states (Merckelbach, Devilly, & Rassin, 2002). Others maintain that dissociative identity disorder is a valid diagnosis but one that should involve a clearer definition of symptoms (Gleaves, May, & Cardena, 2001).

Many people with dissociative identity disorder have a *host personality* and *subpersonalities,* or alters. A host personality is the one most people see and is likely present most of the time. A host personality is like your general personality that changes from time to time but is not dramatically different. Subpersonalities, however, are additional, distinct personalities within a person

that occasionally supplant the host personality and interact with others. This may help explain memory gaps. A different personality may have temporarily dominated Erica's consciousness, trashed her apartment, and sped recklessly while driving. This would help explain some of Erica's odd experiences and her difficulty remembering recent events. Subpersonalities also have their own set of memories, such as the 7-year-old Erica who

## Personal Narrative 6.1

### Hannah Emily Upp

The young woman was floating face down in the water, about a mile southwest of the southern tip of Manhattan. Wearing only red running shorts and a black sports bra, she was barely visible to the naked eye of the captain of the Staten Island Ferry. Less than four minutes later, a skiff piloted by two of the ferry's deckhands pulled up alongside the woman. One man took hold of her ankles while the other grabbed her shoulders. As she was lifted from the water, she gasped.

"I went from going for a run to being in the ambulance," the woman said several months later in describing her ordeal. "It was like 10 minutes had passed. But it was almost three weeks." On Aug. 28, a Thursday, a 23-year-old schoolteacher from Hamilton Heights named Hannah Emily Upp went for a jog along Riverside Drive. That jog is the last thing that Ms. Upp says she remembers before the deckhands rescued her from the waters of New York Harbor on the morning of Tuesday, Sept. 16 [2008].

Rumors and speculation abounded about what befell Ms. Upp. She disappeared the day before the start of a new school year at Thurgood Marshall Academy, a Harlem school, where she taught Spanish. She left behind her wallet, her cellphone, her ID, and a host of troubling questions. It was as if the city had simply opened wide and swallowed her whole—until she was seen on a security camera at the Midtown Apple store checking her e-mail. Then she vanished again. And then reappeared, not only at the Apple store but also at a Starbucks and several

Nicole Bengiveno/The New York Times/Redux

New York Sports Clubs, where news reports said she went to shower. Was she suffering from bipolar disorder? Running away from an overly demanding job? Did she forage for food? Where did she sleep? Most baffling of all, how did she survive for so long without money or any identification in one of the world's busiest and most complex cities?

After her rescue, while she was recovering from hypothermia and dehydration, she was told that she was suffering from dissociative fugue.

"It's weird," Ms. Upp said. "How do you feel guilty for something you didn't even know you did? It's not your fault, but it's still somehow you. So it's definitely made me reconsider everything. Who was I before? Who was I then—is that part of me? Who am I now?"

The answer to that last question, at least on the surface, is a bright, introspective young woman with an easy laugh and an expansive smile. She looked like any other recent college graduate negotiating the rapidly narrowing space between youth and adulthood. Her questions about her identity are, to some degree,

no different from those of her peers who haven't had to deal with highly publicized memory loss.

"When you're just starting out, you have one job to your name: There's your professional identity and then there's who you are," she said. She may be questioning who she is after her experience, she added, "but everybody is." She laughed and added, "This is just extra."

Before she jogged out of her life that August day, Ms. Upp had a demanding schedule. The previous fall, after graduating from Bryn Mawr, she began teaching Spanish to more than 200 seventh and eighth graders at Thurgood Marshall Academy while studying for a master's degree in education at Pace University. It was a challenging job, but one she loved.

Ms. Upp credits the police with helping her piece together what happened during the missing weeks. Though details like where she ate and slept remain elusive to her, security camera footage and conversations with police detectives have provided some clues to the where if not the why. According to police reports, Ms. Upp spent a lot of time in places like Riverside Drive, "where if you're in running gear, no one's going to look at you twice," she said. When she revisited Riverside Drive after leaving the hospital, Ms. Upp said, "it seemed to make sense to me. Not only is it one of my favorite places, but there's something soothing about the sound of water and just not feeling trapped in the concrete jungle."

Ms. Upp's doctors have helped her make sense of other clues, like her stops at the Apple store, where she was seen both checking her e-mail and speaking with a fellow Pace student. "I was on a computer,

---

may have been hiding memories of severe maltreatment from the host personality.

The relationships between subpersonalities and between subpersonalities and the host personality can be complex. Different relationship possibilities exist for the various personalities of the person with dissociative identity disorder, including the following:

- A *two-way amnesiac* relationship means the personalities are not aware of the existence of one other.

- A *one-way amnesiac* relationship means some personalities are aware of other personalities, but this awareness is not always reciprocated.

- A *mutually aware* relationship means the personalities are aware of all other personalities and may even communicate with one another (Dorahy, 2001; Huntjens et al., 2005).

Erica was clearly unaware of at least one subpersonality, but the subpersonality was aware of Erica, who was the

but there's no evidence in my Gmail account of any e-mails being sent or read," Ms. Upp said. She did log in, something her doctors attributed to a muscle memory: How many times in our lives have we typed in our name and password without even thinking? "So their theory," Ms. Upp said, "is that I thought, hey, this is a computer, this is what I do with a computer." But once she opened her e-mail, she couldn't figure out who Hannah was and why everyone was looking for her. "So I logged out and left." Her conversation with the Pace student had a similarly surreal quality. While Ms. Upp says she does not recall the meeting, a store security camera showed her speaking with the young man, who had asked her if she was the missing student everyone was trying to find. She said she wasn't.

The one tangible clue to the extent of her travels was the large blister on her heel. In addition to the hypothermia, dehydration, and a sunburn, the blister was the only physical record of her three weeks spent on the move, and it suggests why she eventually left the city's streets for its waterways: Her feet hurt.

"They think that just as I was wandering on land, I wandered in the water," Ms. Upp said. "I don't think I had a purpose. But I had that really big blister, so maybe I just didn't want my shoes on anymore.

"From what I can piece together, I left Manhattan late at night," she said. "I've gone back over lunar records to figure out if there was a full moon then, which sounds right. At that point in the tidal records, the current would have been in my favor, so whether I was Olympic swimming or doggy paddling, I

could have made it." Made it, that is, to Robbins Reef, where she pulled herself ashore after swimming for several hours. She believes that she spent the next day sitting on the rocks around the lighthouse, a theory supported by the fresh sunburn she sported when she was rescued. She remained on the island until she returned to the water around 11 the following morning.

"At 11:50 a.m. I noticed something in the water that didn't belong there," Captain Covella said. About 200 feet away from Ms. Upp, who was floating face down, the men were lowered into the water. When they reached her, [they] turned her face up, and . . . lifted her into the skiff. Three minutes later, they were at the Staten Island Ferry terminal.

## The Next Steps

Initially, Ms. Upp said she believed that once she returned to her apartment, she would leave her ordeal in the past. But in some ways, it was just beginning. Never mind the reporter who showed up on her doorstep two hours after she arrived home; the larger question was whether she could resume her daily life without worrying about stumbling into another fugue. And would she forever be known as "that missing teacher"?

Ms. Upp considered leaving New York altogether. But, ultimately, she decided to stay.

"I didn't want my life to change in such a way that the things I enjoy I couldn't enjoy anymore," she said. "It was just, I can't let New York win."

Recovery has been slow. Simple social routines like seeing friends and taking a dance class have helped her

re-establish her personal identity. Figuring out her professional identity has been harder. Ms. Upp is on leave from her teaching job, and though the post is still open to her, she is uncertain about returning. Was it significant, she wonders, that she disappeared the day before school started?

"There's a lot of room for self-doubt and confusion there," she said. "And, well, I don't know. I certainly would never have intended to do that, but it makes you wonder." She wonders, too, about what caused the fugue state. So far, a possible catalyst has yet to emerge.

"That's the hardest thing," Ms. Upp acknowledged. "If I don't feel confident about the trigger, how do you start with prevention?"

She has learned, however, that fugues are usually isolated events.

"If you work through it, you can usually go on to live a normal life," she said. "Obviously, the hardest part is the period right after. It's textbook that you feel shame, you feel embarrassed, you feel guilt—all things I've definitely felt."

She has also experienced something rarely afforded to anyone in this city: the chance to slow down.

"If anything," she said, "I've gotten a time to really appreciate what normal life is like. I've never had a moment in my life where I've just stopped and said, hold on, let's re-evaluate everything."

*Adapted from http://www.nytimes.com/ 2009/03/01/nyregion/thecity/01miss.html? _r=1&emc=eta1&pagewanted=all# (Rebecca Flint Marx and Vytenis Didziulis, "A Life, Interrupted," New York Times, Feb. 27, 2009. Copyright © 2009 New York Times Co. Reprinted by permission.*

host personality. This is common to many people with dissociative identity disorder, especially at the beginning of therapy.

## Depersonalization/Derealization Disorder

Another dissociative disorder is **depersonalization/ derealization disorder**, which involves persistent experiences of detachment from one's body as if in a dream state (see **Table 6.10**) (APA, 2013). People with this disorder maintain a

sense of reality but may feel they are floating above themselves, watching themselves go through the motions of an event, or feel as if they are in a movie or like a robot. Depersonalization often exists with *derealization,* or a sense that surrounding events are not real (Simeon et al., 2008). Think about suddenly waking up to an odd noise—you perhaps feel disoriented or feel the surrounding environment is a bit surreal.

Depersonalization or derealization episodes can be short or long, but a person may have trouble feeling sensations or

Judy Castelli and her art. Judy has been diagnosed with 44 personalities.

emotions. These episodes cause great distress and significantly interfere with daily functioning. The depersonalization or derealization episodes should not occur because of another mental disorder such as panic disorder, or substance use or a medical condition. However, people with panic and other anxiety-related disorders commonly report depersonalization and derealization. Brief episodes of depersonalization are common in the general population and are not a mental disorder (APA, 2013). Symptoms of depersonalization and fugue are also sometimes difficult to tease apart.

---

### Table 6.10

#### DSM-5 Depersonalization/Derealization Disorder

A. The presence of persistent or recurrent experiences of depersonalization, derealization, or both:
   1. Depersonalization: Experiences of unreality, detachment, or being an outside observer with respect to one's thoughts, feelings, sensations, body, or actions.
   2. Derealization: Experiences of unreality or detachment with respect to surroundings.

B. During the depersonalization or derealization experiences, reality testing remains intact.

C. The symptoms cause clinically significant distress or impairment in social, occupational, or other important areas of functioning.

D. The disturbance is not attributable to the physiological effects of a substance (e.g., a drug of abuse, medication) or another medical condition (e.g., seizures).

E. The disturbance is not better explained by another mental disorder.

American Psychiatric Association. (2013). *Diagnostic and statistical manual of mental disorders* (5th ed.). Arlington, VA: American Psychiatric Association.

---

## Epidemiology of Dissociative Disorders

You can understand how researchers have a difficult task when studying people with dissociative disorders. Symptoms of these disorders are often hidden, and many people with dissociative disorders do not seek therapy. Many people who attend therapy for some *other disorder,* however, also experience symptoms of dissociation. Erica's original reason for attending therapy was symptoms of depression. Among people with other psychiatric disorders, about 17 to 25 percent also have a dissociative disorder, especially depersonalization/derealization disorder (Friedl, Draijer, & de Jonge, 2000; Lipsanen et al., 2004; Mueller, Moergeli, Assaloni, Schneider, & Rufer, 2007).

The prevalence of pathological dissociation among Americans is about 2.0 to 3.4 percent (Maaranen et al., 2005; Seedat, Stein, & Forde, 2003). Researchers have reported prevalence rates for depersonalization/derealization (1–2 percent) and dissociative identity (1 percent) disorders (Hunter, Sierra, & David, 2004; Rifkin, Ghisalbert, Dimatou, Jin, & Sethi, 1998). The prevalence of dissociative amnesia, however, is highly debatable. Some researchers claim this is a rare phenomenon, but others believe the disorder is more common than previously thought. The discrepancy derives from controversy as to whether adults can suddenly recall long-forgotten events from childhood (see **Box 6.2**; Loftus, 2003).

Pathological dissociation may be more common in younger people and in men more than women (Seedat et al., 2003). Others, however, report no gender differences for dissociative experiences (Spitzer, Klauer, et al., 2003). Dissociative experiences appear somewhat more commonly in African Americans than European Americans (Aderibigbe, Bloch, & Walker, 2001). Some speculate that African Americans use dissociation as a coping strategy for operating as a minority group or that this group is more susceptible to dissociation (Seedat et al., 2003). Unfortunately, no clear reason has emerged for this difference (see **Box 6.3**).

Aspects of dissociative disorders seem highly comorbid with other mental disorders, especially those involving trauma. This is particularly so for posttraumatic stress disorder and conversion disorder (Sar, Akyuz, Kundakci, Kiziltan, & Dogan, 2004; Wilkeson, Lambert, & Petty, 2000). About 15 percent of people exposed to a traumatic event report high levels of dissociative symptoms (Dominguez, Cohen, & Brom, 2004). Dissociative behavior is also quite common among homeless and runaway youths and adolescents who have experienced trauma (McCarthy & Thompson, 2010; Tyler, Cauce, & Whitbeck, 2004).

## Stigma Associated with Dissociative Disorders

Stigma may be an important issue in dissociative disorders. Freidl and colleagues (2007) surveyed people with dissociative and other disorders and found that nearly 60% believed that most people would not allow someone with a mental disorder to take care of their children and that most young women would be reluctant to date a man who had a mental disorder. Most of the respondents also believed that potential employers would bypass applications of psychiatric patients. In addition, a majority of those surveyed

## BOX 6.2 Focus on Law and Ethics

### Recovered Memories and Suggestibility

Reports have appeared in the media over the years about people accused of child maltreatment or domestic violence by others who suddenly recall these events after many years. People who suddenly recall these memories are indeed adept at suppressing anxious autobiographical thoughts (Geraerts, McNally, Jelicic, Merckelbach, & Raymaekers, 2008). A heated controversy in this area, however, is the topic of *recovered memories.* Recall that Erica's subpersonality seemed to have memories of severe maltreatment from childhood. In other people with dissociative disorders, memories of past maltreatment emerge as amnesia or fugue dissipates during treatment. The validity of these recovered memories remains unclear, however. This takes on greater meaning when a prosecutor decides to indict someone based on recovered memories.

This controversy stems from the fact that children, adolescents, and even adults may be susceptible to leading questions about past events. This is *suggestibility*. In one study, maltreated children were asked misleading questions about a recent physical examination. One question was "There was no window in the room, was there?" when in fact there was a window. Young children were more prone to "fall" for misleading questions than older children and adolescents (Eisen, Qin, Goodman, & Davis, 2002).

Researchers have thus called for strict ethical guidelines for assessing people with memories of maltreatment. These guidelines include warning clients about the possibility of recovering false memories, outlining limits to confidentiality, obtaining special training for eliciting memories, making conclusions only with corroborating evidence, and always acting in the best interests of a client (Cannell, Hudson, & Pope, 2001; Pettifor, Crozier, & Chew, 2001).

## BOX 6.3 Focus on Diversity

### Dissociation and Culture

Dissociation is evident across many cultures, although many other conditions seem related to the Western concept of dissociation. One such condition is *possession disorder,* in which a person believes he is possessed by some other entity (Tseng, 2003). In Japan, animal and other spirits are commonly thought to influence people's behavior. In Thailand, *phii bob* refers to the belief that the spirit of another living person can enter a person's body and cause behavioral changes. One particular Islamic belief is that of *jinn,* or genies, that can cause harm to humans sometimes through possession (Khalifa & Hardie, 2005). These phenomena underscore the importance of considering a person's cultural background when addressing a possible case of dissociative disorder.

Some authors contend that certain cultures may be more predisposed to dissociative experiences such as depersonalization. Sierra and colleagues (2006) believe that depersonalization experiences might be more common to people of Western countries. This is because a person's "sense of self" in these countries tends to be highly individualistic and autonomous,

People in a trance-like state may show behaviors that resemble a dissociative disorder.

and thus more susceptible to separation from one's social context. Non-Western societies tend to emphasize a more collectivist orientation involving greater social integration and interdependence. People who adopt a collectivist sense of self may thus be less predisposed to depersonalization or other dissociative experiences.

believed that people in the general population saw psychiatric patients as less intelligent, trustworthy, and valued with respect to their opinions. Negative beliefs such as these could lead to reluctance to rely on others for support or to seek treatment if psychological symptoms persisted or worsened.

## INTERIM SUMMARY

▶ Normal dissociation refers to separation of emotions, thoughts, memories, or other inner experiences from oneself. Dissociation that occurs in a severe or very odd way may be a dissociative disorder.

▶ Dissociative amnesia refers to loss of memory for highly personal information. This may be related to dissociative fugue, which involves sudden movement away from home or work with loss of memories for personal and other information.

▶ Dissociative identity disorder refers to two or more distinct personality states within a person. These states may include a host personality and subpersonalities that can differ in their awareness of each other.

▶ Depersonalization/derealization disorder refers to persistent experiences where a person feels detached from his body as if in a dream state.

▶ Dissociation is common in people with mental disorders, although the prevalence of formal dissociative disorders in the general population is less common. Dissociative disorders are often associated with trauma and trauma-related mental disorders.

▶ Many people with dissociative symptoms feel stigmatized by others.

## REVIEW QUESTIONS

1. What is the difference between normal and abnormal dissociation?
2. Discuss features of major dissociative disorders.
3. What is a host personality and subpersonalities?
4. What types of relationships might subpersonalities have with one another?
5. How common are dissociative experiences?

## Dissociative Disorders: Causes and Prevention

The cause of dissociative disorders remains unclear, but evidence is emerging that key brain changes and trauma are important risk factors. These factors likely work in tandem in diathesis-stress fashion to help produce dissociative disorders.

## Biological Risk Factors for Dissociative Disorders

Brain and memory changes are key risk factors of dissociative disorders. We discuss these risk factors next.

### BRAIN FEATURES

A key aspect of dissociative disorders is disintegration of consciousness, memory, and identity. Brain areas responsible for integrating incoming information may thus be altered in some way. Key brain areas for integration include the amygdala, locus coeruleus, thalamus, hippocampus, anterior cingulate cortex, and frontal cortex (see **Figure 6.5**; Hopper, Frewen, van der Kolk, & Lanius, 2007; Scaer, 2001). Some believe disintegration or dissociation in times of stress creates an arousal threshold in these brain areas. Reaching this threshold triggers increased alertness but also inhibition of strong emotional responses such as anxiety (Sierra, 2008; Sierra & Berrios, 1998).

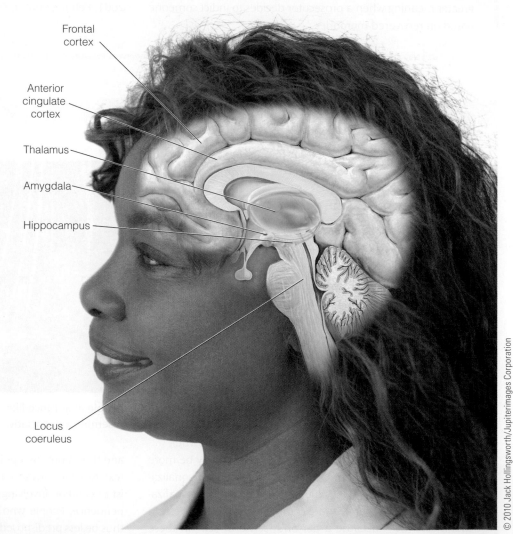

Frontal cortex
Anterior cingulate cortex
Thalamus
Amygdala
Hippocampus
Locus coeruleus

**FIGURE 6.5** MAJOR BRAIN AREAS IMPLICATED IN THE DISSOCIATIVE DISORDERS
Copyright © Cengage Learning®.

We may detach ourselves from a terrible event so we can control our responses and react adaptively. A person in a car accident may feel she is floating above the crash scene but at the same time can rescue others, talk to police, and call family members. Her alertness is increased, but excesses in emotion and physical arousal are temporarily blunted. This person may later appreciate the full weight of what happened and experience nightmares or flashbacks of the trauma. People with acute stress or posttraumatic stress disorder commonly have dissociation (Chapter 5) (Lanius et al., 2010).

Dissociative disorders, especially depersonalization/derealization and perhaps amnesia/fugue, may also be due to problems in connections between various brain areas, especially between sensory systems (eyesight, hearing) and the limbic system. A possible consequence of such disruption is that a person sees an event, especially a strongly negative event, but is able to "detach" herself and experience little emotional response. Such disconnection can also lead to blunted pain experiences and a decrease in irrelevant thoughts. Evidence indicates that people undergoing depersonalization have blunted reactions to arousing stimuli (Sierra & David, 2011). Others have found that neurochemical changes in serotonin, endogenous opioid, and glutamate systems relate to depersonalization as well (Stein & Simeon, 2009).

## MEMORY CHANGES

Work in the area of memory changes and dissociative disorder remains in development, but some suggest that intense negative emotions lead to key memory changes, especially of *compartmentalization* and *difficulty retrieving information* (Holmes et al., 2005). Exposure to a negative event and intense negative emotions may instigate a segregation or "compartmentalization" of one part of the mind from other areas. This appeared to happen with Erica—her therapist later discovered that her client's 7-year-old alter personality held memories of childhood trauma. Compartmentalization may help explain why certain memories or personalities are not "known" by the host personality.

Compartmentalization may not be complete, however. When one personality learns new information, interference in learning in another personality can occur. One personality may also retrieve information learned by another personality (Dorahy, 2001). This provides support for the existence of mutually aware or one-way amnesiac relationships among personalities. Transfer of information across different personalities may depend, however, on emotional and personal content of the information. Evidence from one case indicates that a host personality often reported positive memories, whereas a child subpersonality often reported negative memories. The child personality contained memories of sexual maltreatment that occurred during a woman's childhood. These memories were available to the host personality in fragmented forms, however (Bryant, 1995; van der Hart, Bolt, & van der Kolk, 2005).

Difficulty retrieving information is also common in people with dissociative identity disorder and dissociative amnesia. People with these disorders may have trouble distinguishing true and false memories, especially of childhood. People with these disorders often have deficits in short-term memory and working memory, which is the ability to hold information while completing another task. Problems in these areas of memory, which may result from increased emotional arousal, may relate to irrelevant thoughts and dissociative experiences (Dorahy, 2001; Dorahy, Irwin, & Middleton, 2004; Dorahy, Middleton, & Irwin, 2005).

Think about trying to remember someone's telephone number as you are driving a car (working memory). If you are extremely upset about something at this time, you may temporarily forget the telephone number because you are thinking about other things and "spacing out" a bit. People with dissociative disorders may have such problems on a grander scale. What causes these memory changes to begin with, however, remains unclear. One possibility is that people with dissociative amnesia and identity disorder have reduced blood flow in the right frontotemporal cortex (see **Figure 6.6**; Markowitsch, 2003; Sar, Unal, & Ozturk, 2007). Excessive stress and trauma may create these metabolic changes.

## Environmental Risk Factors for Dissociative Disorders

We next discuss important environmental risk factors for dissociative disorders such as trauma and cultural influences.

### TRAUMA

Traumatic experiences and posttraumatic stress disorder are closely linked to dissociative disorders. Adult dissociation often follows a severe traumatic event such as child maltreatment (Hall, 2003; Whiffen & MacIntosh, 2005). Consider a 4-year-old child experiencing severe physical maltreatment from a parent. The options available to this child are few: He is unlikely to run away, kill the parent, or commit suicide. An alternative coping strategy is to dissociate or detach from the trauma in a psychological way. Such dissociation may be mild in the form of thinking about something else or more severe in the form of developing amnesia or even a different personality. Perhaps this occurred in Erica's case.

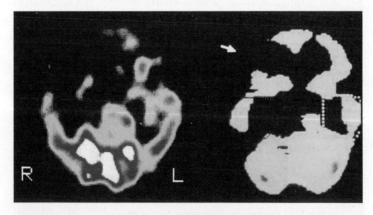

**FIGURE 6.6**  **REDUCED BLOOD FLOW IN THE FRONTAL LOBE OF A PERSON WITH DISSOCIATIVE AMNESIA** From Plate 2 of Markowitsch, H.J. (1999). Functional neuroimaging correlates of functional amnesia. *Memory, 7,* 561-583.

Traumatic problems may follow dissociation in other cases. A good predictor of posttraumatic stress disorder is dissociation *during* a traumatic event (Bryant et al., 2011). Someone who dissociates during a traumatic event may not cognitively process all relevant stimuli in that situation. Such avoidance can help produce symptoms of posttraumatic stress disorder, and exposure to reminders of the trauma is a key part of treatment for posttraumatic stress disorder (Chapter 5). A person who is assaulted may dissociate somewhat and even describe her attacker to police. She may cognitively avoid other stimuli associated with the event, however, such as the parking lot where the assault occurred. If she walks through that parking lot in the future, doing so may trigger posttraumatic stress.

Dissociation may thus be a way of temporarily coping with a terrible event. This is especially likely if the event involved intense fears of death, loss, or lack of control. Such fears are in addition to the terror of the trauma and increase the likelihood one will experience long-term emotional distress or posttraumatic stress disorder (Bryant et al., 2011). Other researchers, however, refute a causal relationship between dissociation

and trauma because some third variable may explain the relationship. A third variable such as intense family conflict could explain trauma *and* dissociation in an adolescent (so trauma or dissociation may not have caused the other). People with dissociative disorders also do not remember earlier traumatic events with great accuracy (Merckelbach & Muris, 2001).

### CULTURAL FACTORS

Cultural factors may also relate to dissociation because cases of dissociative identity disorder seemed to peak before 1920 and after 1970. Some speculate that changes in how the concept of "self" is defined from generation to generation may affect the prevalence of dissociative identity disorder (Kihlstrom, 2005). Some people may rely on "an alternate personality" explanation to avoid personal responsibility for certain acts, even violent ones. We sometimes refer to ourselves and others in terms of Dr. Jekyll and Mr. Hyde (see **Box 6.4**).

Little research is available about dissociative disorders in other countries. Researchers have recognized dissociative amnesia and depersonalization in Uganda and found the disorders

---

## BOX 6.4  Focus on Violence

### Dissociative Experiences and Violence Toward Others

A key component of different dissociative disorders is that a person becomes detached from reality at one time or another. An interesting question, however, is whether people in dissociative states are particularly violent toward other people. Occasionally we see people charged with a violent crime who claim no memory of their act or that "a different part of themselves" was responsible.

One of the "Hillside Stranglers"—responsible for the rape and strangulation of several young women in California in 1977 and 1978—later claimed to have alter personalities. Films such as *Psycho* reinforce the impression as well that dissociative experiences are associated with violence. Some have also speculated that men often commit violent acts when dissociated and end up in prison, whereas women with dissociation are more likely to be less aggressive

In the film *Psycho*, the character Norman Bates appeared to have different personalities; some were meek and some were violent.

"Hillside Strangler" Kenneth Bianchi at one point falsely claimed he had alter personalities responsible for his killings.

© Bettmann/Corbis

and enter therapy. About 25 percent of prison inmates report severe dissociative experiences (Moskowitz, 2004).

Violence and dissociation may be linked in a couple of ways. First, a person may experience dissociative/traumatic flashbacks, believe he is in danger, and lash out at others. Second, dissociation may occur during the commission of a violent crime of passion. A man who strangles another person during an intense argument may have trouble grasping the enormity of his act and experience a sense of depersonalization. These possibilities underscore the importance of closely monitoring a person's dissociative symptoms in treatment (Moskowitz, 2004).

followed traumatic circumstances as they often do in Western cultures. Dissociative fugue and dissociative identity disorder, however, were usually confused with other, local concepts of dementia (Chapter 14) or *possession trance disorder* (Van Duijl, Cardena, & De Jong, 2005). Possession trance disorder (or dissociative trance disorder) refers to a sense that a new identity attributable to a spirit or other entity replaces one's identity and controls a person's behavior and possibly his memory. This underscores the need to consider local contexts and beliefs before assigning a *DSM-5* diagnosis.

## Causes of Dissociative Disorders

Some researchers have proposed *neurodevelopmental approaches* to explain how disparate factors such as brain and memory changes interact with trauma to help cause dissociative disorders. Consider what normally happens in a positive childhood. First, children grow to develop strong and positive attachments to family members and caregivers, emotional regulation, and adaptive brain structure. Children learn to associate well with others, control excess emotions such as rage, and adapt to normal life changes.

Second, young children begin to coordinate different aspects of thinking and emotions into a consolidated *sense of self*. A youngster gains information from different situations and learns that certain rules apply and that he has some control over what will happen. A sense of self develops as children realize who they are and how the world works.

Third, loving parents accelerate this process by setting rules, providing support, and helping a child gain control of emotions and behaviors. We teach our children to listen carefully, come to us when scared, and communicate and develop self-control—"Use your words!" We also encourage them to explore different aspects of life while protecting them from harm. Many parents also develop daily routines for their children so youngsters feel safe in knowing what comes next.

A maltreated child, however, may not develop a strong and unified sense of self. The child is unsure about which rules apply, who to trust, and what happens next. An integrated sense of self and control over different life situations is thus lacking. This could lead to overarousal and development of different personalities or dissociative states. A lack of unified self may relate to changes in the orbitofrontal cortex, an area of the brain largely responsible for memory and consciousness (Webber, 2011). Empirical data to support these ideas remain necessary, however.

## Prevention of Dissociative Disorders

Data are lacking regarding prevention of dissociative disorders, but preventing traumatic events that might lead to dissociative disorders may be instructive. An important traumatic event is child maltreatment. No studies have shown that reducing child maltreatment necessarily prevents dissociative disorders, but this is certainly possible. Efforts to prevent child maltreatment generally focus on the following:

- Teaching children to resist maltreatment by reporting it to others.
- Educating children about unsafe situations.

- Educating parents about normal child development and high-risk situations that often lead to maltreatment, such as family transitions and stress.
- Teaching parents appropriate disciplinary practices.
- Implementing home visitation programs staffed by nurses, physicians, social workers, paraprofessionals, or others, especially following a child's birth.
- Providing support groups for parents.
- Encouraging pediatricians, psychologists, and other health professionals to report suspected incidents of maltreatment.

Prevention programs involving these components have shown variable success. Getting children to report maltreatment is difficult to do. The long-term effectiveness of home visitation programs is also unclear (Paradise, 2001; Rubin, Lane, & Ludwig, 2001). Still, helping parents raise their children in a safe environment can only increase a family's quality of life and perhaps prevent maltreatment and even later dissociative experiences for a given child.

## INTERIM SUMMARY

▶ Biological risk factors for dissociative disorders may include key brain changes in areas most responsible for memory and consciousness integration.

▶ Memory changes in people with dissociative disorders often involve compartmentalization of personal material and failure to retrieve information.

▶ Trauma and dissociation are linked but the causal relationship between the two remains unclear.

▶ Neurodevelopmental models of dissociative disorder concentrate on how young maltreated children fail to develop a unified sense of self.

▶ Prevention of dissociative disorders has not received much research attention, but prevention of child maltreatment may be helpful in this regard.

## REVIEW QUESTIONS

1. What brain changes may be associated with dissociative disorders?
2. What memory changes seem central to dissociative disorders?
3. How are trauma and dissociation linked?
4. Describe a general causal theory of dissociation in early life.
5. Outline a strategy for preventing child maltreatment.

# Dissociative Disorders: Assessment and Treatment

We have covered the major features and causes of dissociative disorders, so we turn next to ways of assessing and treating these devastating problems. A full medical examination must first rule out biological conditions that may explain dissociative symptoms. Biological conditions with similar symptoms could include epilepsy, migraine headache, and brain injury or disease, among others (Lambert, Sierra, Phillips, & David, 2002).

## Assessment of Dissociative Disorders

Assessing someone like Erica with a possible dissociative disorder may be accomplished using interviews and questionnaires. We describe these next.

### INTERVIEWS

Interviewing people with dissociative disorder can be a difficult task for several reasons. First, many people with these disorders, such as those with amnesia or fugue, do not seek therapy for dissociation. Second, recollection of memories from dissociative states is often poor. Third, accessing different personalities in someone with dissociative identity disorder can be quite challenging.

Still, interviews are available to assess for dissociative symptoms and disorders. Prominent ones include the *Clinician-Administered Dissociative States Scale* and *Structured Clinical Interview for Dissociative Disorders—Revised* (SCID-D-R; Bremner et al., 1998; Steinberg, 2000). The SCID-D-R is a semistructured interview for symptoms of amnesia, depersonalization, derealization, identity confusion, and identity alteration. The interview also covers severity of these symptoms and degree to which they interfere with daily functioning. Sample SCID-D-R questions include the following:

- Have you ever felt as if there were large gaps in your memory? (amnesia)
- Have you ever felt that you were watching yourself from a point outside of your body, as if you were seeing yourself from a distance (or watching a movie of yourself)? (depersonalization)
- Have you ever felt as if familiar surroundings or people you knew seemed unfamiliar or unreal? (derealization)
- Have you ever felt as if there was a struggle going on inside of you? (identity confusion)
- Have you ever acted as if you were a completely different person? (identity alteration)

An interview of someone with a possible dissociative disorder should include a detailed history of trauma and symptoms of acute stress or posttraumatic stress disorder. Recall that many people with dissociative disorder have experienced recent or past traumatic events. Erica's therapist embarked on a long assessment process that included interviews of Erica and her 7-year-old personality, who named herself Erica-Bad. The therapist compiled a detailed history about severe maltreatment of Erica-Bad by her father, who was now deceased. The therapist also explored recent stressors such as Erica's breakup with her boyfriend to know why the subpersonality suddenly appeared to the therapist. The conflict and distress of Erica's relationship and breakup seemed to have triggered intense, compartmentalized memories of maltreatment in childhood.

### QUESTIONNAIRES

Questionnaires are also available to assess dissociative symptoms; one commonly used questionnaire is the *Dissociative Experiences Scale* (DES; Carlson et al., 1993; Ruiz, Poythress, Lilienfeld, & Douglas, 2008). The DES covers 3 main categories of dissociative symptoms: dissociative amnesia, absorption and imaginative

involvement, and depersonalization/derealization. Absorption and imaginative involvement refer to engaging in fantasy to such an extent that reality and fantasy are blurred.

An adolescent version of this scale (A-DES) covers dissociative amnesia, absorption and imaginative involvement, passive influence, and depersonalization and derealization (Armstrong, Putnam, Carlson, Libero, & Smith, 1997; Keck Seeley, Perosa, & Perosa, 2004). Passive influence refers to the experience of not having full control over one's body and physical sensations. The DES and A-DES are useful for identifying people with pathological levels of dissociative symptoms. Sample A-DES items are in **Table 6.11**.

Other popular scales contain items or subscales relevant to dissociative symptoms. Examples include MMPI-2 items and the dissociation scale from the *Trauma Symptom Checklist for Children* (Briere, 1996; Butcher et al., 1990; Sadowski & Friedrich, 2000). Researchers generally encourage the use of multiple measures to assess dissociation (Friedrich et al., 2001; Spitzer, Liss, et al., 2003). This is because dissociative symptoms are often complex, hidden, and unpredictable.

## Biological Treatment of Dissociative Disorders

The biological treatment of dissociative disorders largely involves medication to ease comorbid symptoms of anxiety, posttraumatic stress, depression, and related disorders such as personality disorders. The most commonly used drugs are anxiolytics, antidepressants, and antipsychotic and anticonvulsant medications. Much of the research in this area comes from case study material, and some people with dissociative disorders do improve in their symptoms when taking these medications. Other researchers, however, report little effect (Philpsen, Schmahl, & Lieb, 2004; Simeon, Guralnik, Schmeidler, & Knutelska, 2004; Simeon & Knutelska, 2005).

One problem with using these drugs to treat dissociative disorders is that side effects of these medications, especially antipsychotic drugs, can include feelings of dissociation (Lacy & Mathis, 2003). Another issue is that medications used for

---

### Table 6.11

**Sample Items from the Adolescent Dissociative Experiences Scale**

I get so wrapped up in watching TV, reading, or playing video games that I don't have any idea what's going on around me.

People tell me I do or say things that I don't remember doing or saying.

I feel like I'm in a fog or spaced out and things around me seem unreal.

I don't recognize myself in the mirror.

I find myself someplace and don't remember how I got there.

*Note:* Items are scored on a 0-to-10 scale where 0 = *never* and 10 = *always*.

dissociative symptoms were designed for other mental disorders, so little information is available about the biological treatment of dissociative disorders per se (Brand, Classen, McNary, & Zaveri, 2009). Medication may be an adjunct to psychological treatment for dissociation.

## Psychological Treatments of Dissociative Disorders

Psychological treatments for dissociative disorders are often geared toward reducing comorbid problems of anxiety, posttraumatic stress, and depression. Many of the cognitive-behavioral approaches we discussed in Chapter 5 also apply to people with dissociative disorders. The goals of these approaches are also the same: help people cope with trauma, develop skills to think rationally and realistically, and reduce avoidance of social and other activities. Cognitive-behavioral treatment of symptoms of posttraumatic stress disorder is usually essential for addressing the problems of people with dissociative disorders (Brand et al., 2012). Additional approaches to treat the core symptoms of dissociation, especially with respect to dissociative identity disorder, are sometimes necessary as well. We discuss these approaches next.

### PSYCHOTHERAPY

A key goal of psychological treatment for dissociative disorders is to help a person reintegrate memories, personalities, and other aspects of consciousness (Pais, 2009). For dissociative amnesia, the goal is to help a person recall previous aspects of certain trauma or past events in a supportive and safe way and ease her transition back to a normal routine (Jasper, 2003). For depersonalization/derealization disorder, the goal is to help a person reinterpret symptoms as nonthreatening, increase safety behaviors, and decrease avoidance (Hunter, Baker, Phillips, Sierra, & David, 2005).

For dissociative identity disorder, treatment is often long and complex. The average length of treatment was reportedly 2.8 years in one study (Sno & Schalkin, 1999). Several clinical researchers use a psychodynamic stage approach for this population. One method involves the following stages (Brand et al., 2011; Kluft, 1999):

1. Create a safe, empathic environment in therapy to build a strong therapist-client relationship that also includes all subpersonalities.
2. Enhance a person's ability to function on a daily basis, which includes communicating with and gaining cooperation from subpersonalities.
3. Gather detailed information about all subpersonalities, especially their personal histories.
4. Discuss and process traumatic events associated with each subpersonality, sometimes using hypnosis. Processing means repeated and detailed discussions of these events.
5. Encourage cooperation, empathy, and communication among all subpersonalities as these traumatic events are processed.
6. Integrate subpersonalities into one another, perhaps beginning with those sharing similar histories or personality

traits. A single personality is sought, but a collection of fewer subpersonalities may be the final result.
7. Learn coping skills as an alternative to dissociation to address difficult daily events, especially in social relationships.
8. Engage in long-term follow-up to help prevent relapse toward dissociation.

### HYPNOSIS

*Hypnosis* refers to a relaxed and focused state of mind in which a person is highly suggestible. People with dissociative disorders may undergo hypnosis to increase continuity of memory and identity. A person may undergo hypnosis to try to retrieve forgotten memories, access hidden personalities, or integrate different dimensions of consciousness (Bob, 2008). Some use hypnosis as well to derive more information about traumatic experiences that led to dissociative states (Lynn & Cardena, 2007). Hypnosis may be useful but data to support this approach largely involve case reports (Brandt & Van Gorp, 2006). Hypnosis may also lead to distorted memories (Gleaves, Smith, Butler, & Spiegel, 2004).

### OTHER PSYCHOLOGICAL APPROACHES

People with dissociative identity disorder may benefit from supportive family therapy as they enter the reintegration process and address past traumas. These people may also benefit from emotional expression through art, music, dance, and poetry (Kluft, 1999). Techniques are sometimes necessary to address suicidality in subpersonalities as well (Chapter 7; Ringrose, 2012). Dissociative experiences among youths may be associated with ongoing maltreatment, so eliminating maltreatment and providing a safe environment are obviously important (Haugaard, 2004). The psychological treatment of dissociative disorders generally involves helping a person develop a unified sense of self and daily cohesiveness with respect to emotions, thoughts, and behaviors.

Erica's therapist devoted 2 years to detailed discussions of past trauma. Erica's siblings participated in therapy to help confirm previous aspects of maltreatment and provide support. The therapist was able to establish a good working relationship with Erica-Bad, the 7-year-old subpersonality. The child personality gave important information about the past, including physical and sexual maltreatment from Erica's father and uncle. This process was a long and painful journey that required antidepressant medication and interventions to address intermittent suicidal urges. Many people erroneously believe, perhaps based on the films *The Three Faces of Eve* or *Sybil,* that once a person remembers past trauma, all subpersonalities disappear.

## What If I or Someone I Know Has a Dissociative Disorder?

Knowing if you or someone you know has a dissociative disorder can be difficult because the symptoms of these disorders are often murky. Pay attention to ongoing forgetfulness, odd experiences, and detachment from others, among other sudden peculiarities. If you suspect someone you know might be

**THE CONTINUUM VIDEO PROJECT**

### *Lani and Jan:* Dissociative Identity Disorder

*"It's like living with 13 room-mates...and your responsibility is to make sure everyone's needs get met."*

Access the Continuum Video Project in MindTap at **www.cengagebrain.com**.

experiencing symptoms of a dissociative disorder, then referring her for a full medical examination and even an emergency room consultation is important. The possible consequences of being in a state of dissociation can be devastating.

## Long-Term Outcome for People with Dissociative Disorders

The long-term outcome for people with dissociative disorders is variable because integration of consciousness is difficult and because the problems usually extend from childhood. Some people with dissociative amnesia or fugue are able to recover and return to their past lifestyles. Others continue to have problems with information recall and disruption in their lives. They may experience more episodes of severe memory loss as well (Coons, 1999; MacDonald & MacDonald, 2009).

Many people with dissociative identity disorder do respond positively to biological and psychological treatment. Improvements occur with respect to dissociation, anxiety, depression, and suicidality as a person addresses traumas and integrates subpersonalities (Brand et al., 2009; Ellason & Ross, 1996, 1997). A person's initial degree of depression, other psychopathology, and trauma may be good predictors of whether full personality integration can be achieved (Powell & Powell, 1998).

Erica did not achieve full integration of her host personality and subpersonality (Erica-Bad). Over time and with extended treatment, however, appearances by Erica-Bad became fewer and Erica herself experienced less disruption in her daily life. She also felt less depressed, began to forge good relationships with her siblings, and considered new dating opportunities.

### INTERIM SUMMARY

▶ Interviews to assess people with dissociative disorders often cover recent and past stressors and the presence of amnesia, depersonalization, derealization, identity confusion, and identity alteration.

▶ Questionnaires screen for dissociative symptoms such as amnesia, absorption and imaginative involvement, depersonalization, and passive influence.

▶ The biological treatment of dissociative disorders usually includes medication for concurrent symptoms of anxiety, depression, and other problems.

▶ Psychotherapy for dissociation helps a person reintegrate consciousness, process traumatic events, and learn to cope with daily events without using dissociation.

▶ The long-term outcome of people with dissociative disorders is variable and likely depends on severity of past trauma and current degree of psychopathology.

### REVIEW QUESTIONS

1. Describe various methods to assess people with dissociative disorders, and devise an assessment strategy you think might be most helpful.

2. What medications might be best for people with dissociative disorders?

3. What aspects of psychotherapy might be best for people with dissociative disorders?

4. How might expressive and other psychological therapies help people with dissociation?

5. Describe the long-term outcome for people with dissociative disorders.

## Final Comments

Somatic symptom and dissociative disorders are among the strangest but most fascinating disorders we discuss in this textbook. Perhaps you noticed many of the similarities among these sets of disorders and the anxiety-related disorders in Chapter 5; related factors include apprehension, trauma, interpersonal difficulties, cognitive distortions, and avoidance of social and other situations. Treatments for these problems often overlap. In the next chapter, we discuss another set of disorders closely related to those we have discussed so far: the depressive and bipolar disorders.

## Thought Questions

1. If you were a medical doctor, what would you say and do in response to a patient who presents with somatic symptom or illness anxiety disorder?

2. Think about people in the news who have claimed that some dissociative experience has kept them from remembering a crime or other event. Do you believe them? Why or why not?

3. What would you say to a friend who told you that his relative seems to be "spacing out" a lot in his life?

4. What separates "normal aging" from somatization and "normal forgetfulness" from dissociation? At what point does one "cross the line" from regular changes in thinking, memory, and behavior to more serious problems?

5. How might we reduce the prevalence of somatic symptom and dissociative disorders in the general population?

## Key Terms

somatization 146

somatic symptom
    disorder 147

illness anxiety disorder 149

conversion disorder 150

pseudoseizures 150

factitious disorder 150

contingency
    management 158

Munchausen syndrome 151

malingering 151

dissociation 161

dissociative disorders 161

dissociative amnesia 161

dissociative fugue 162

dissociative identity
    disorder 162

depersonalization/
    derealization
    disorder 165

## Media Resources

### MindTap

MindTap for Kearney and Trull's *Abnormal Psychology and Life: A Dimensional Approach* is a highly personalized fully online learning platform of authoritative content, assignments, and services offering you a tailored presentation of course curriculum created by your instructor. MindTap guides you through the course curriculum via an innovative learning path where you will complete reading assignments, annotate your readings, complete homework, and engage with quizzes and assessments. MindTap includes the Continuum Video Project.

Go to **cengagebrain.com** to access MindTap.

# Depressive and Bipolar Disorders and Suicide

## CASE: *Katey*

**What Do You Think?**

**Normal Mood Changes and Depression and Mania:**
**What Are They?**

**Depressive and Bipolar Disorders and Suicide:**
**Features and Epidemiology**

**Stigma Associated with Depressive and Bipolar**
**Disorders**
Interim Summary
Review Questions

**Depressive and Bipolar Disorders and Suicide:**
**Causes and Prevention**
Interim Summary
Review Questions

**Depressive and Bipolar Disorders and Suicide:**
**Assessment and Treatment**
Interim Summary
Review Questions

FINAL COMMENTS
THOUGHT QUESTIONS
KEY TERMS
MEDIA RESOURCES

## SPECIAL FEATURES

**CONTINUUM FIGURE 7.1** Continuum of Sadness and
Depression   180–181

**CONTINUUM FIGURE 7.2** Continuum of Happiness,
Euphoria, and Mania   180–181

**PERSONAL NARRATIVE 7.1** Karen
Gormandy   184–185

**BOX 7.1** | Focus on Gender: Forms of Depression Among
| Women   186

## THE CONTINUUM VIDEO PROJECT

*Emilie:* **Bipolar Disorder   206**

**BOX 7.2** | Focus on Law and Ethics: Ethical Dilemmas in
| Electroconvulsive Therapy   214

**BOX 7.3** | Focus on Diversity: Depression in the
| Elderly   215

## CASE: Katey

**Katey** was a 30-year-old woman referred for outpatient therapy following a stay in an inpatient psychiatric unit. Katey's hospital visit came after police found her atop a tall building threatening to jump. Her behavior at the time was somewhat bizarre: the police said Katey was talking very fast and claiming she could fly. Katey was difficult to converse with, but police officers eventually convinced her to move away from the edge of the building and come with them to the psychiatric hospital.

At the hospital, Katey said she had been feeling strange over the past several weeks. She rarely slept and instead wanted to "meet new and interesting people." She frequented dance clubs and bars and fearlessly walked down alleyways to meet people. These actions led to some potentially dangerous situations and interactions, especially given the provocative way Katey dressed, but fortunately no physical harm had come to her. She also said she needed to talk fast because "so many thoughts fly through my head." Katey had lost her job recently and much of her contact with family members. She was also in danger of losing her apartment because she had spent her savings on lavish clothes.

Katey's therapist asked what happened the night the police found her. Katey said she had been drinking at a dance club and could not remember how she arrived at the top of the building. Her memory of that night was poor, although she did recall bits and pieces of conversations. Katey received medication at the hospital and slept for most of 3 days, saying she felt much more "normal" and "with it" afterward.

Katey said she had always battled moodiness and substance use problems. She said her "mood swings" began in adolescence after her first breakup with a boyfriend and continued during her college and early career years. She often compensated for mood changes by drinking alcohol and working hard. Katey said she could occasionally go 2 or 3 days working with little sleep, and this intense activity seemed to alleviate some sadness. She remained haunted, however, by her often-changing mood.

Katey said she was married briefly several years ago, but the marriage ended because both partners tired of the other's "drama." Since that time, Katey continued her work as a legal assistant and received substantial raises over the years. Her work during recent months, however, was sloppy and tardy, and she was often absent. Katey's boss fired her 3 months ago after several warnings. Katey said her firing triggered much anxiety for her and prompted her current string of strange behaviors.

Katey also said she occasionally thought about hurting herself. These thoughts usually came when she felt unhappy but intensified recently as her unusual behavior became more stressful. Katey reluctantly admitted she once tried halfheartedly to kill herself in college.

Her attempt followed a night of drinking during which she became sad and found some pills (unknown kind) in her roommate's bathroom. She took several pills but woke the next morning in a daze and with a severe headache. Katey said she had not attempted suicide from that point to the night when police found her atop the building.

Katey cried in session and felt her life was in disarray. She had no job, few friends, was barely hanging on to a place to live, and had not spoken with her family in months. Her recent emotional states seemed to propel her toward self-destruction. Katey said she desperately wanted to regain control of her moods and her life in general. Her therapist assured her that Katey's compliance with medication and therapy attendance would go a long way in helping her do so.

## What Do You Think?

1. Which of Katey's symptoms seem typical of a young adult, and which seem very different?

2. What external events and internal factors might be responsible for Katey's feelings?

3. What are you curious about regarding Katey?

4. Does Katey remind you in any way of yourself or someone you know? How so?

5. How might Katey's mood changes affect her life in the future?

# Normal Mood Changes and Depression and Mania: What Are They?

Have you ever been very sad or "down in the dumps" like Katey? Have you ever reacted badly to a stressful life event like a break-up? Have you ever felt you could not control your behavior or ever had thoughts about hurting yourself? For most people, sadness is a natural reaction to unfortunate events that happen in their lives. Many of us become sad when we receive a poor grade, have an argument with a loved one, or discover a friend is sick. Such sadness is usually mild and temporary.

Other times our sadness can be more intense and last for a longer period. We are particularly sad when a family member dies, when lengthy separation from loved ones occurs, or when overwhelmed by life's demands. This sadness generally lingers but eventually fades as we cope with the stressor more effectively. We often rely on our friends and family members to help us through life's "tough patches."

For people like Katey, however, sadness lingers for a long time, occurs for little reason, or is so intense that interacting with others is difficult. The sadness often prevents a person from functioning effectively at school or work. A person may have trouble eating, sleeping, or concentrating; feel responsible for things beyond her control; and feel extremely fatigued. Sadness or a sense of hopelessness can become so intense that harming oneself or committing suicide seems like the only way to stop the pain. These symptoms refer to *depression,* which is at the far end of the sadness continuum (see **Figure 7.1**).

Sadness is an emotion or mood, and its natural opposite is happiness. Many events and people make us happy, and all of us strive to be happy when we can. Most of us find happiness in the little things of life, such as coming home and hugging one's children, talking to close friends, and accomplishing significant goals at work. Sometimes we even get carried away with our happiness, such as laughing a little too loudly at a social event. Such behaviors might even cause us some embarrassment!

Other people sometimes experience an intense state of happiness called *euphoria.* Euphoria is a wonderful feeling many people sense immediately after hearing good news or after a joyous event like childbirth. Euphoria is usually a short-term feeling that fades as a person becomes accustomed to whatever experience they had—the joy of having a newborn quickly gives way to exhaustion! Euphoria is not generally harmful as long as it is temporary.

Euphoria can be lingering or ongoing for some people. People with chronic euphoria often have constant feelings of being "on the go," thoughts "racing" through their head, a sense of pressure to keep talking, and chronic loss of sleep. They are also distracted and make poor personal decisions, as Katey did. One may also have a sense of *grandiosity,* or a belief that he is especially powerful or talented when this is not actually true. These symptoms can be so severe they lead to extreme irritability and self-destructive or even suicidal behavior. These symptoms refer to *mania,* which is at the far end of the happiness and euphoria continuum (see **Figure 7.2**).

# Depressive and Bipolar Disorders and Suicide: Features and Epidemiology

People whose depression or mania becomes so severe it interferes with daily functioning may have a **depressive disorder** or a **bipolar disorder**. Depressive and bipolar disorders are sometimes collectively referred to as mood disorders. Someone with only depression may have a unipolar (one pole) disorder, as in *unipolar depression* or *depressive disorder.* Depression and mania can occur in the same individual, however, as they do in Katey's case. This person may have a bipolar (two pole) disorder. We next cover major depressive and bipolar disorders that cause people like Katey so much distress. We also discuss suicide, which is often associated with depressive and bipolar disorders.

## Major Depressive Episode

A **major depressive episode** involves a period of time, typically at least 2 weeks but usually longer, in which a person experiences sad or empty moods most of the day, nearly every day (see Criteria A-C in **Table 7.1**; American Psychiatric Association [APA], 2013). A major depressive episode does not refer to temporary sadness that may last a day or two or for only part of a day. Instead, the problem refers to a lengthy period in which a person is depressed during different times of the day and almost every day of the week. The sadness is usually intense, to the point that the person has trouble functioning in her daily life. Such was true for Katey.

People experiencing a major depressive episode also lose pleasure doing things they used to enjoy. A person may have always enjoyed being with friends or family, pursuing a hobby, or working at his job. Following a major depressive episode, however, he may withdraw from these activities or no longer get much pleasure from them. Katey became increasingly withdrawn from her family. We have also seen in other chapters

People with depression are often sad and isolated from others.

**CONTINUUM FIGURE 7.1** Continuum Of Sadness and Depression

|  | Normal | Mild |
|---|---|---|
| **Emotions** | Good mood. | Mild discomfort about the day, feeling a bit irritable or down. |
| **Cognitions** | Thoughts about what one has to do that day. Thoughts about how to plan and organize the day. | Thoughts about the difficulty of the day. Concern that something will go wrong. |
| **Behaviors** | Rising from bed, getting ready for the day, and going to school or work. | Taking a little longer than usual to rise from bed. Slightly less concentration at school or work. |

(on anxiety-related and somatic symptom/dissociative disorders) that people with mental disorders often avoid or withdraw from social contact. You will see throughout this textbook that many people with mental disorder often have problems interacting with others.

Major depressive episodes also may involve severe changes in appetite, weight, and sleep (Lam, 2012). People who are depressed often fail to eat or they overeat, perhaps to help compensate for sadness. People who are depressed also have trouble sleeping and may wake up very early each morning, lying in bed until it is time to rise for the day (*early morning wakening*). Conversely, though, many people with depression have a heavy feeling of fatigue and loss of energy that leads to oversleeping. Such *hypersomnia* may also be a way to escape painful life events or extreme feelings of sadness.

A key characteristic of a major depressive episode is a feeling of "slowness," or trouble gathering much physical energy. A person may simply want to lie on the couch all day, passively surf the Internet at work, or sleep a lot. People with very severe cases

of depression, or *melancholia,* may be so slowed down they do not move any muscles for hours. Although depressive episodes can resemble anxiety-related disorders in many respects (Chapter 5), this melancholic feeling of slowness is much more characteristic of depression (Harald & Gordon, 2012). Following is a conversation between a therapist and a client who is severely depressed:

**Therapist:** Can you tell me what you have planned for today?
**Client:** (after long pause) Well ... not sure ... might get up today.
**Therapist:** OK, you might get up—what do you think you could do next?
**Client:** Well ... (very long pause)
**Therapist:** Yes, keep going.
**Client:** I don't know, I can't really think about it ... I just want to sleep.

People experiencing a major depressive episode tend to feel worthless and guilty about many things, including life events beyond their control. They may blame themselves for not preventing a friend's divorce. Trouble concentrating or making

**CONTINUUM FIGURE 7.2** Continuum of Happiness, Euphoria, and Mania

|  | Normal | Mild |
|---|---|---|
| **Emotions** | Feeling good. | Happiness about good events that day, such as an unexpected check in the mail. Feeling a "bounce" in one's step. |
| **Cognitions** | Thoughts about the pleasant aspects of the day. | Thoughts about the good things in life. |
| **Behaviors** | Normal daily activity. | Completing daily tasks with great vigor. Being quite social and talkative. |

| Moderate | Depression — less severe | Depression — more severe |
|---|---|---|
| Feeling upset and sad, perhaps becoming a bit teary-eyed. | Intense sadness and frequent crying. Daily feelings of "heaviness" and emptiness. | Extreme sadness, very frequent crying, and feelings of emptiness and loss. Strong sense of hopelessness. |
| Dwelling on the negative aspects of the day, such as a couple of mistakes on a test or a cold shoulder from a coworker. | Thoughts about one's personal deficiencies, strong pessimism about the future, and thoughts about harming oneself (with little intent to do so). | Thoughts about suicide, funerals, and instructions to others in case of one's death. Strong intent to harm oneself. |
| Coming home to slump into bed without eating dinner. Tossing and turning in bed, unable to sleep. Some difficulty concentrating. | Inability to rise from bed many days, skipping classes at school, and withdrawing from contact with others. | Complete inability to interact with others or even leave the house. Great changes in appetite and weight. Suicide attempt or completion. |

decisions is also common in this population and often leads to problems at work or school, as was true for Katey. The most serious symptom of a major depressive episode is thoughts or ideas about death or suicide, or an actual suicide attempt. Many people facing a major depressive episode, like Katey, have morbid thoughts and fantasies about dying, their own funeral, and cutting or otherwise hurting themselves. These thoughts sometimes precede actual attempts to harm oneself. Tragically, these attempts are sometimes fatal.

A major depressive episode must interfere with daily functioning and not be directly caused by a medical condition or substance. People temporarily *bereaved* following loss of a loved one may not necessarily receive a diagnosis of a major depressive episode because grief is a normal human reaction. Feelings of sadness in children are more difficult to identify, so irritable mood can replace obvious signs of unhappiness. Failure to gain weight may also be symptomatic of a major depressive episode in youths.

## Major Depressive Disorder

**Major depressive disorder**, sometimes called *major depression* or *unipolar depression,* usually involves a longer period during which a person may experience multiple major depressive episodes (see **Figure 7.3** and Table 7.1). A 2-month interval of normal mood must occur for episodes to be considered separate from one another (APA, 2013). Major depressive disorder can be diagnosed, however, in someone who has only a single or first episode of depression. Major depressive disorder may be mild, moderate, or severe and may occur with or without *psychotic features* such as bizarre ideas or hearing voices that are not real (we discuss psychotic features in more detail in Chapter 12). Depressive symptoms may also be *peripartum* or *postpartum,* occurring during pregnancy or after the birth of a child (see **Box 7.1**). In addition, depression in some people occurs more in fall or winter months, or *seasonal depression* (O'Hara, 2009; Rohan, Roecklein, & Haaga, 2009; Tonna, De Panfilis, & Marchesi, 2012). People with seasonal

| Moderate | Mania— less severe | Mania — more severe |
|---|---|---|
| Sense of temporary euphoria about some grand life event such as a wedding or birth of a newborn. Feeling on "cloud nine." | Intense euphoria for a longer period. Feelings of agitation and inflated self-esteem. | Extreme euphoria for very long periods, such as months. Sense of grandiosity about oneself, such as the belief that one is a great playwright. |
| Thoughts racing a bit about all the changes to one's life and how wonderful life is. | Intense, racing thoughts that lead to distractibility and difficulty concentrating. | Racing thoughts almost nonstop that lead to complete inability to concentrate or speak to others coherently. |
| Some difficulty sleeping due to sense of elation. | Less need for sleep, pressure to talk continuously, working for hours on end. | Engaging in pleasurable activities that lead to damage, such as racing a car down a residential street or spending all of one's money. |

## Table 7.1

### DSM-5  Major Depressive Disorder

A. Five (or more) of the following symptoms have been present during the same 2-week period and represent a change from previous functioning; at least one of the symptoms is either (1) depressed mood or (2) loss of interest or pleasure.
   **Note:** Do not include symptoms that are clearly attributable to another medical condition

   1. Depressed mood most of the day, nearly every day, as indicated by either subjective report (e.g., feels sad, empty, hopeless) or observation made by others (e.g., appears tearful). (**Note:** In children and adolescents, can be irritable mood.)
   2. Markedly diminished interest or pleasure in all, or almost all, activities most of the day, nearly every day (as indicated by either subjective account or observation).
   3. Significant weight loss when not dieting or weight gain (e.g., a change of more than 5% of body weight in a month), or decrease or increase in appetite nearly every day. (**Note:** In children, consider failure to make expected weight gain.)
   4. Insomnia or hypersomnia nearly every day.
   5. Psychomotor agitation or retardation nearly every day (observable by others, not merely subjective feelings of restlessness or being slowed down).
   6. Fatigue or loss of energy nearly every day.
   7. Feelings of worthlessness or excessive or inappropriate guilt (which may be delusional) nearly every day (not merely self-reproach or guilt about being sick).
   8. Diminished ability to think or concentrate, or indecisiveness, nearly every day (either by subjective account or as observed by others).
   9. Recurrent thoughts of death (not just fear or dying), recurrent suicidal ideation without a specific plan, or a suicide attempt or a specific plan for committing suicide.

B. The symptoms cause clinically significant distress or impairment in social, occupational, or other important areas of functioning.

C. The episode is not attributable to the physiological effects of a substance or to another medical condition.
   **Note:** Criteria A–C represent a major depressive episode.
   **Note:** Responses to a significant loss may include the feelings of intense sadness, rumination about the loss, insomnia, poor appetite, and weight loss noted in Criterion A, which may resemble a depressive episode. Although such symptoms may be understandable or considered appropriate to the loss, the presence of a major depressive episode in addition to the normal response to a significant loss should also be carefully considered. This decision inevitably requires the exercise of clinical judgment based on the individual's history and the cultural norms for the expression of the distress in the context of loss.

D. The occurrence of the major depressive episode is not better explained by schizoaffective disorder, schizophrenia, schizophreniform disorder, delusional disorder, or other specified and unspecified schizophrenia spectrum and other psychotic disorders.

E. There has never been a manic episode or hypomanic episode.
   **Note:** This exclusion does not apply if all of the manic-like or hypomanic-like episodes are substance-induced or are attributable to the physiological effects of another medical condition.

American Psychiatric Association. (2013). *Diagnostic and statistical manual of mental disorders* (5th ed.). Arlington, VA: American Psychiatric Association.

---

depression often experience reduced energy, poor motivation, and anxiety with depressed mood (Gill & Saligan, 2008).

## Persistent Depressive Disorder (Dysthymia)

Another mood disorder similar to major depression is **persistent depressive disorder**, commonly called *dysthymia,* which is a chronic feeling of depression for at least 2 years (see **Table 7.3**; APA, 2013). People with persistent depressive disorder may not have all the severe symptoms of major depression but instead have "low-grade" symptoms that persist for much of their life. A mixture of symptoms is often seen involving appetite and sleep changes, fatigue, low self-esteem, trouble concentrating or making decisions, and feeling hopeless (Moch, 2011).

Persistent depressive disorder still involves an intense feeling of sadness most of every day, with relief from symptoms never longer than 2 months at a time (see **Figure 7.4**). Some people with dysthymia also have one or more major depressive episodes during the 2-year course of their disorder. The presence of dysthymia *and* a major depressive episode at the same time is *double depression* (Klein, Shankman, & Rose, 2008). Double depression is difficult to spot unless a client has seen a therapist for some time and the therapist notices a sudden or gradual worsening of the client's symptoms.

Persistent depressive disorder must not be caused by a medical condition or substance, and the disorder must significantly interfere with daily functioning. The disorder may be classified as *early* or *late onset* depending on whether symptoms developed before age 21 years or at age 21 years or older. Persistent depressive disorder may be diagnosed in children and adolescents after a *1-year* period of depressed *or* irritable mood.

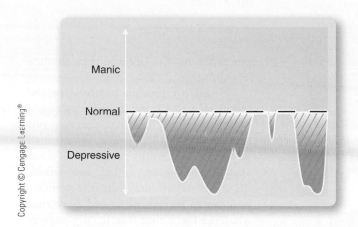

**FIGURE 7.3** **CYCLE OF MAJOR DEPRESSIVE DISORDER** Major depressive disorder may involve one or more major depressive episodes.

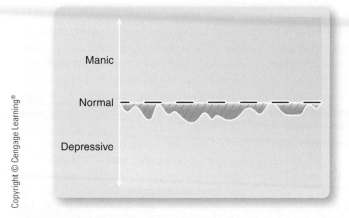

**FIGURE 7.4** **CYCLE OF PERSISTENT DEPRESSIVE DISORDER** Persistent depressive disorder (or dysthymia) involves low-grade symptoms of depression for at least 2 years.

## Other Depressive Disorders

Other formal depressive disorders were added to the *Diagnostic and Statistical Manual of Mental Disorders (DSM-5)*. *Disruptive mood dysregulation disorder* refers to youth aged 6 to 18 years with recurrent temper outbursts that are severe and well out of proportion to a given situation (see **Table 7.4**; APA, 2013). The outbursts occur at least 3 times per week, and the child is often irritable or angry. Symptoms must be present for at least 1 year and be seen in multiple settings. Onset is before age 10 years. The disorder was meant to address the fact that many children with these symptoms may have been diagnosed and treated for bipolar disorder (discussed later in the chapter). More research is needed on this disorder. Another new formal depressive disorder is *premenstrual dysphoric disorder,* which was once a condition for further study (see Box 7.1).

## Manic and Hypomanic Episodes

Have you ever felt euphoric or had seemingly boundless elation? We hope you have! As we mentioned, euphoria for a short time is usually not harmful. Feelings of euphoria that

continue uncontrollably for long periods, however, can lead to destructive behavior. A **manic episode** is a period during which a person feels highly euphoric or irritable (see **Table 7.5**; APA, 2013). The person has key symptoms that may lead to severe problems during this period of euphoria. She may have a sense of *grandiosity,* or a feeling she can do something unlikely or impossible (Hawke & Provencher, 2012). Katey felt she might be able to fly. A person may also pursue pleasurable activities to such an extent that the activities become self-destructive. A person in a manic episode may engage in a shopping or sexual spree, pour money into foolish investments, or joyride in a car at high speeds. Severe problems in functioning at school or work can also result from extreme *distractibility* many people have during a manic episode.

People experiencing a manic episode also tend to speak rapidly, as if their mind is generating so many thoughts they cannot express them quickly enough. Such *flight of ideas* was true for Katey at times. Following is part of a conversation

People with depression often sleep a lot or have trouble sleeping and do not take pleasure in many activities.

## Personal Narrative 7.1

### Karen Gormandy

Karen Gormandy

*Courtesy of Karen Gormandy*

Falling into depression was slow and deceptively delicious. By all accounts, it should have never been. There were no signs or clues when I was very young. In fact, my childhood was a blast.

But by the time I was 12, I was someone else. Not the wild child who was dubbed the "Queen of Play" but a confused adolescent whose actions, thoughts, and desires were motivated by a desire to disengage and become numb. I'm not sure what happened or how it started, but I remember beginning to feel the inward pull when I was 12 years old, when within months of arriving to New York from Trinidad my mother moved out. No one said anything for days. She was just not there. Days later, my father called me into his bedroom and told me she was gone and he didn't know when she'd be back. I was 15 before it was full-blown, almost immobilizing depression.

I would get up, go to school, and simply sit—inattentive and spaced out in class—the teachers' voices, when I did hear them, sounded like distorted noise and incomprehensible static. It wasn't long before I wasn't doing assignments; pretty soon I was cutting classes. I would get all the way to school and stand in front of the building knowing full well I was not going to set foot in there; I would turn tail and head home.

I would take the subway as far as Lexington Avenue and without leaving the station, would catch a train back to Queens, stop off at the candy store, get a Twix bar for lunch and a monthly Harlequin, and share the last leg of my trip home on the bus with a smattering of MTA workers returning home from the graveyard shift.

Before I knew it, when my father flicked the light on for me to get me up for school, I would follow the sound of his footsteps down the carpeted stairs, listen for the front door to close and instead of getting up, I'd turn over and go back to sleep.

I don't think anyone noticed that I spent my entire sophomore year of high school in my room. I left it only when everyone else was in bed to indulge my one pleasure—the late and then the late late show.

When my mother returned to the family, I was 17 and firmly ensconced under sheets and blankets that had not been changed in weeks and surrounded by books that took me far away from anything that resembled my world. All she could think to do was sprinkle holy water in my room and pray that whatever force that was having its way with me would leave. I don't remember how I came to get up and out and back to school. It may have had something to do with a threat from the Board of Education.

My second major depressive episode didn't last quite a year. I had started college on a high note, excited and expectant. But there was a part of me that was knotted up. My husband had taken a job out of state and my teenage son, Justin, was spending more and more time with his friends. I thought my going to school would give me something to replace my lost identity as wife and my dwindling presence as mother. Displacement was not so easy. School could not cover up or replace the shock of being left by my husband and not needed as much by my son.

I lasted a year, and then my resolve started to collapse. I had studied architecture in San Francisco and at the University of Colorado, and I continued

---

between a therapist and a client experiencing flight of ideas with some grandiosity:

**Therapist:** Can you tell me what you have planned for today?

**Client:** Oh yeah! Lots of things, lots of things, lots of things!

**Therapist:** OK, can you . . .

**Client:** (interrupting) Gonna drive, gonna fly, gonna bus, gonna ride!

**Therapist:** (speaking quickly to get a word in) Where do you want to go?

**Client:** Anywhere, anytime, Rome, Greece, wherever I go, I can go!

Those in a manic state may be highly agitated and pursue a certain goal with great enthusiasm. They may "pour themselves" into a project at work and seem to accomplish a lot, although closer examination reveals the project to be riddled

*Getty Images/Comstock (RF)/Jupiter Images*

People in a state of mania often do things that may be self-destructive, such as indulging in a shopping spree that they cannot afford.

on and enrolled as an architecture major at Montana State University. After the second semester, my work was becoming more and more unarchitectural and wilder. I drew curves and lines that had no order and created work outside the perimeters of the assignments.

My son was also falling off the edge of adolescence. He started hanging out with potheads and the high school clique of marginal characters. He was edgy and moody and rebelling against something.

By the time winter came, I was ready to jump out of my own skin. I was agitated, grumpy, and unhappy. I would get up, see Justin off to school, go to class but not do the assignments. After a few weeks, I would go to one class and skip all my other classes, work frantically to catch up on the schoolwork, and when it became too hard to catch up, I stopped going. Justin moved out at 16, and I stopped getting up in the morning.

Days went by and aside from getting out of bed to go to the bathroom, or to watch TV—my attention span lasted an hour or so before I got drowsy and went back to bed—I stayed under a cocoon of covers. When Justin dropped in, I got out of bed and pretended to be a mother. I can't remember where the time went; I hibernated and lost track of days and nights.

I started to cry. I cried a lot. I cried in front of the university bursar when he asked me why I hadn't paid the rent. Too much in shock to think of a polite answer, I just blurted out the truth: that I wasn't sure if I was married, that I wasn't sure what was happening with my son. He recommended a university therapist.

Jim Murphy was a compassionate, sensitive therapist. He had red hair and the old 1970s trick of wearing a full beard so that he wouldn't be mistaken for a student. My moods were easy to read: invisible—when I stuffed my wild hair under a baseball cap and kept my eyes trained to the ground, or defiant—I let my wooly mane loose and uncombed, glared at all the young, hopeful students (who I was furiously jealous of!) in the eye and defied them to stare back. I got brave enough to insist Justin see a doctor. The doctor said he tested positive for marijuana, but otherwise he was fine.

After four sessions, I was on Zoloft and academic probation instead of being suspended. I could reapply for financial aid and get myself back into the university's good graces.

With Jim's help, I rethought my future and changed my major from architecture to film, enrolled in art classes to begin in summer, and spent the spring alone. I went for long walks and drives, and borrowed movies and TV series

and watched them again and again. I laughed again.

My fall was slow and almost sensual. My journey up and out is a daily decision. The inclination not to give up and to shut down is like fighting a powerful force of nature that is as strong and as unyielding as gravity. There are days when I am repelled by the sight of myself in the mirror and the surges of self-loathing are incapacitating.

I am in talk therapy. Therapy is a safe place to be raw and vulnerable, maybe it has something to do with just acknowledging the existence of my demons. For whatever reason, it's what I need. My moods undulate not in an up/down, happy/sad way, but more in a hanging on, keeping it together, being distracted kind of way. At this writing it's pretty horrible. The sadness seems ever present and I have to return to meds.

A place to be honest about my feelings, a few very good and empathetic friends and supportive community—such as NAMI (National Alliance on Mental Illness)—keeps me out of the hole. Sometimes I can even remember and smile at the wild child I used to be.

with mistakes. Katey worked hard, but her sloppiness cost her job. Someone in a manic episode usually requires little sleep to feel fully rested. Manic episodes last at least 1 week but could be much longer, perhaps lasting weeks or months. The manic episode must interfere with daily functioning and not be caused by a medical condition or substance.

Other people experience what is known as a **hypomanic episode**. Have you ever suddenly had a huge burst of energy or inspiration and completely cleaned the house or finished a project at work? Many of us have felt a "rush" like this, although the experience never lasts more than a few hours or a couple of days. A hypomanic episode, however, comprises the same symptoms as a manic episode but may not cause severe impairment in daily functioning. Unlike "bursts of energy" that many of us occasionally have, hypomanic episodes last at least 4 days (see **Table 7.6**; APA, 2013).

## Bipolar I Disorder

**Bipolar I disorder** refers to one or more manic episodes in a person. The disorder is sometimes called *manic-depression* because a person may alternate between episodes of major depression and mania or hypomania. Such was likely true for Katey. Bipolar I disorder may involve just a single manic episode, however. People with bipolar I disorder often have a major depressive episode that lasts weeks or months, followed by an interval of normal mood before another manic or hypomanic episode (see **Table 7.7 and Figure 7.5a**; APA, 2013). Other people with bipolar I disorder have *mixed features,* which refers to mania with symptoms of depression that do not rise to the level of a major depressive episode.

Some people with bipolar I disorder experience *rapid cycling*, which means they frequently switch from depression to mania and back again with little or no period of normal mood.

## BOX 7.1 Focus on Gender

### Forms of Depression Among Women

Women report more depression than men, and this difference may be due to genetic factors as well as stressful marital and other relationships. However, conditions specific to women may also help to explain this difference. Examples include premenstrual dysphoric disorder and postpartum depression.

**Premenstrual dysphoric disorder** is a controversial condition that refers to depressive or other symptoms during most menstrual cycles in the past year (**Table 7.2**; APA, 2013). These symptoms include depressed, anxious, or angry mood; mood swings; fatigue; trouble concentrating; eating and sleeping changes; feeling out of control; and physical symptoms such as bloating or joint pain. The symptoms mainly occur in the week prior to menses and must cause distress or interfere with a woman's daily functioning. About 3 to 9 percent of women may have this condition, which may link to hormonal changes that alter serotonin levels. Treatment thus usually involves antidepressant medication (Shah et al., 2008).

### Table 7.2

#### DSM-5 Premenstrual Dysphoric Disorder

A. In the majority of menstrual cycles, at least five symptoms must be present in the final week before the onset of menses, start to *improve* within a few days after the onset of menses, and become *minimal* or absent in the week postmenses.

B. One (or more) of the following symptoms must be present:
   1. Marked affective lability.
   2. Marked irritability or anger or increased interpersonal conflicts.
   3. Marked depressed mood, feelings of hopelessness, or self-deprecating thoughts.
   4. Marked anxiety, tension, and/or feelings of being keyed up or on edge.

C. One (or more) of the following symptoms must additionally be present, to reach a total of *five* symptoms when combined with symptoms from Criterion B above.
   1. Decreased interest in usual activities.
   2. Subjective difficulty in concentration.
   3. Lethargy, easy fatigability, or marked lack of energy.
   4. Marked changes in appetite; overeating; or specific food cravings.
   5. Hypersomnia or insomnia.
   6. A sense of being overwhelmed or out of control.
   7. Physical symptoms such as breast tenderness or swelling, joint or muscle pain, sensation of "bloating," or weight gain.
   **Note:** The symptoms in Criteria A–C must have been met for most menstrual cycles that occurred in the preceding year.

D. The symptoms are associated with clinically significant distress or interference with work, school, usual social activities, or relationships with others.

E. The disturbance is not merely an exacerbation of the symptoms of another disorder, such as major depressive disorder, panic disorder, persistent depressive disorder (dysthymia), or a personality disorder (although it may co-occur with any of these disorders).

F. Criterion A should be confirmed by prospective daily ratings during at least two symptomatic cycles. (**Note:** The diagnosis may be made provisionally prior to this conformation.)

G. The symptoms are not attributable to the physiological effects of a substance or another medical condition.

American Psychiatric Association. (2013). *Diagnostic and statistical manual of mental disorders* (5th ed.). Arlington, VA: American Psychiatric Association.

## BOX 7.1 Focus on Gender—cont'd

**Peripartum depression** or **postpartum depression** refers to symptoms of depression or a major depressive episode that occurs during pregnancy or in the weeks following childbirth (APA, 2013). Postpartum depression is not simply the "blues" that many women face after childbirth, which may be caused by hormonal changes or social isolation. Instead, postpartum depression is a severe condition that affects about 13 percent of women after they give birth. Postpartum depression is commonly associated with depression and anxiety during pregnancy (peripartum), stressful life events during pregnancy, lower social support, and previous history of depression (Reid & Meadows-Oliver, 2007; Robertson, Grace, Wallington, & Stewart, 2004). Women with these risk factors should thus be monitored closely before and after childbirth in case suicidal ideation is present.

Mark Wilson/Getty Images

Brooke Shields has been an outspoken educator about postpartum depression in women since the birth of her child.

## Table 7.3

### DSM-5 Persistent Depressive Disorder (Dysthymia)

A. Depressed mood for most of the day, for more days than not, as indicated by either subjective account or observations by others, for at least 2 years.
   **Note:** In children and adolescents, mood can be irritable and duration must be at least 1 year.

B. Presence, while depressed, of two (or more) of the following:
   1. Poor appetite or overeating.
   2. Insomnia or hypersomnia.
   3. Low energy or fatigue.
   4. Low self-esteem.
   5. Poor concentration or difficulty making decisions.
   6. Feelings of hopelessness.

C. During the 2 year period (1 year for children or adolescents) of the disturbance, the individual has never been without the symptoms in Criteria A and B for more than 2 months at a time.

D. Criteria for a major depressive disorder may be continuously present for 2 years.

E. There has never been a manic episode or a hypomanic episode, and criteria have never been met for cyclothymic disorder.

F. The disturbance is not better explained by a persistent schizoaffective disorder, schizophrenia, delusional disorder, or other specified or unspecified schizophrenia spectrum and other psychotic disorder.

G. The symptoms are not attributable to the physiological effects of a substance (e.g., a drug of abuse, a medication) or another medical condition (e.g., hypothyroidism).

H. The symptoms cause clinically significant distress or impairment in social, occupational, or other important areas of functioning.

Specify if in partial or full remission, early (before age 21 years) or late (after age 21 years), and mild, moderate, or severe.

American Psychiatric Association. (2013). *Diagnostic and statistical manual of mental disorders* (5th ed.) . Arlington, VA: American Psychiatric Association.

___ **Table 7.4** ___

## DSM-5 Disruptive Mood Dysregulation Disorder

A. Severe recurrent temper outbursts manifested verbally and/or behaviorally that are grossly out of proportion in intensity or duration to the situation or provocation.

B. The temper outbursts are inconsistent with developmental level.

C. The temper outbursts occur, on average, three or more times per week.

D. The mood between temper outbursts is persistently irritable or angry most of the day, nearly every day, and is observable by others.

E. Criteria A–D have been present for 12 or more months. Throughout that time, the individual has not had a period lasting 3 or more consecutive months without all of the symptoms in Criteria A–D.

F. Criteria A and D are present in at least two of three settings and are severe in at least one of these.

G. The diagnosis should not be made for the first time before age 6 years or after age 18 years.

H. By history or observation, the age at onset of Criteria A–E is before 10 years.

I. There has never been a distinct period lasting more than 1 day during which the full symptom criteria, except duration, for a manic or hypomanic episode have been met.
**Note:** Developmentally appropriate mood elevation, such as occurs in the context of a highly positive event or its anticipation, should not be considered as a symptom of mania or hypomania.

J. The behaviors do not occur exclusively during an episode of major depressive disorder and are not better explained by another mental disorder.
**Note:** This diagnosis cannot coexist with oppositional defiant disorder, intermittent explosive disorder, or bipolar disorder, though it can coexist with others, including major depressive disorder, attention-deficit/hyperactivity disorder, conduct disorder, and substance use disorders. Individuals whose symptoms meet criteria for both disruptive mood dysregulation disorder and oppositional defiant disorder should only be given the diagnosis of disruptive mood dysregulation disorder. If an individual has ever experienced a manic or hypomanic episode, the diagnosis of disruptive mood dysregulation disorder should not be assigned.

K. The symptoms are not attributable to the physiological effects of a substance or to another medical or neurological condition.

American Psychiatric Association. (2013). *Diagnostic and statistical manual of mental disorders* (5th ed.). Arlington, VA: American Psychiatric Association.

___ **Table 7.5** ___

## DSM-5  Manic Episode

A. A distinct period of abnormally and persistently elevated, expansive, or irritable mood and abnormally and persistently increased goal-directed activity or energy, lasting at least 1 week and present most of the day, nearly every day (or any duration if hospitalization is necessary).

B. During the period of mood disturbance and increased energy or activity, three (or more) of the following symptoms (four if the mood is only irritable) are present to a significant degree and represent a noticeable change from usual behavior:
   1. Inflated self-esteem or grandiosity.
   2. Decreased need for sleep.
   3. More talkative than usual or pressure to keep talking.
   4. Flight of ideas or subjective experience that thoughts are racing.
   5. Distractibility, as reported or observed.
   6. Increase in goal-directed activity (either socially, at work or school, or sexually) or psychomotor agitation.
   7. Excessive involvement in activities that have a high potential for painful consequences.

C. The mood disturbance is sufficiently severe to cause marked impairment in social or occupational functioning or to necessitate hospitalization to prevent harm to self or others, or there are psychotic features.

D. The episode is not attributable to the physiological effects of a substance or to another medical condition.
   **Note:** A full manic episode that emerges during antidepressant treatment (e.g., medication, electroconvulsive therapy) but persists at a fully syndromal level beyond the physiological effect of that treatment is sufficient evidence for a manic episode and, therefore, a bipolar I diagnosis.

American Psychiatric Association. (2013). *Diagnostic and statistical manual of mental disorders* (5th ed.). Arlington, VA: American Psychiatric Association.

___ **Table 7.6** _____

### DSM-5 Hypomanic Episode

A. A distinct period of abnormally and persistently elevated, expansive, or irritable mood and abnormally and persistently increased activity or energy, lasting at least 4 consecutive days and present most of the day, nearly every day.

B. During the period of mood disturbance and increased energy and activity, three (or more) of the following symptoms (four if the mood is only irritable) have persisted, represent a noticeable change from usual behavior, and have been present to a significant degree:
  1. Inflated self-esteem or grandiosity.
  2. Decreased need for sleep.
  3. More talkative than usual or pressure to keep talking.
  4. Flight of ideas or subjective experience that thoughts are racing.
  5. Distractibility as reported or observed.
  6. Increase in goal-directed activity or psychomotor agitation.
  7. Excessive involvement in activities that have a high potential for painful consequences.

C. The episode is associated with an unequivocal change in functioning that is uncharacteristic of the individual when not symptomatic.

D. The disturbance in mood and the change in functioning are observable by others.

E. The episode is not severe enough to cause marked impairment in social or occupational functioning or to necessitate hospitalization. If there are psychotic features, the episode is, by definition, manic.

F. The episode is not attributable to the physiological effects of a substance.
  **Note:** A full hypomanic episode that emerges during antidepressant treatment (e.g., medication, eletroconvulsive therapy) but persists at a fully syndromal level beyond the physiological effect of that treatment is sufficient evidence for a hypomanic episode diagnosis. However, caution is indicated so that one or two symptoms (particularly increased irritability, edginess, or agitation following antidepressant use) are not taken as sufficient for diagnosis of a hypomanic episode, nor necessarily indicative of a bipolar diathesis.

American Psychiatric Association. (2013). *Diagnostic and statistical manual of mental disorders* (5th ed.). Arlington, VA: American Psychiatric Association.

At least four cycles occur per year in these cases (Hajek et al., 2008). Still others with the disorder, especially females and those with psychotic symptoms, experience *ultra-rapid cycling* or even *continuous (ultradian) cycling* in which sharp changes in mood toward depression or mania occur almost daily for a certain period (Burgy, 2011; Wilk & Hegerl, 2010).

### Bipolar II Disorder

**Bipolar II disorder** comprises episodes of hypomania that alternate with episodes of major depression. Full-blown manic episodes are not seen as they are in bipolar I disorder (see **Table 7.8** and **Figure 7.5b**; APA, 2013). Hypomanic episodes could worsen and become manic episodes, however, so bipolar II may become bipolar I disorder. For a diagnosis of bipolar II disorder to be made, the condition must not be caused by a medical problem or substance. Hypomanic episodes by themselves may not cause significant impairment in functioning, but hypomanic episodes with major depressive episodes (bipolar II disorder) do significantly interfere with daily functioning.

### Cyclothymic Disorder

**Cyclothymic disorder**, sometimes called *cyclothymia*, refers to symptoms of hypomania and depression that fluctuate over at least a 2-year period (see **Table 7.9**; APA, 2013). People with cyclothymic disorder do not have full-blown *episodes* of depression, mania, or hypomania. Instead, general *symptoms* of hypomania and depression cycle back and forth, perhaps with intermediate

___ **Table 7.7** _____

### DSM-5 Bipolar I Disorder

A. Criteria have been met for at least one manic episode (Criteria A–D under "Manic Episode").

B. The occurrence of the manic and major depressive episode (s) is not better explained by schizoaffective disorder, schizophrenia, schizophreniform disorder, delusional disorder, or other specified or unspecified schizophrenia spectrum and other psychotic disorder.

American Psychiatric Association. (2013). *Diagnostic and statistical manual of mental disorders* (5th ed.). Arlington, VA: American Psychiatric Association.

periods of normal mood (see **Figure 7.5c**). A diagnosis of cyclothymic disorder requires that these symptoms not be absent for more than 2 months. Cyclothymic symptoms may last only 1 year in children and adolescents. Cyclothymic disorder must not be caused by a medical condition or substance but must significantly interfere with daily functioning.

### Suicide

**Suicide** refers to killing oneself and is commonly associated with depressive and bipolar disorders. Suicide is not a mental disorder but is the most serious aspect of depressive and bipolar

## Table 7.8

### DSM-5 Bipolar II Disorder

A. Criteria have been met for at least one hypomanic episode (Criteria A–F under "Hypomanic Episode") and at least one major depressive episode (Criteria A–C under "Major Depressive Episode").

B. There has never been a manic episode.

C. The occurrence of the hypomanic episode(s) and major depressive episode(s) is not better explained by schizoaffective disorder, schizophrenia, schizophreniform disorder, delusional disorder, or other specified or unspecified schizophrenia spectrum and other psychotic disorder.

D. The symptoms of depression or the unpredictability caused by frequent alternation between periods of depression and hypomania causes clinically significant distress or impairment in social, occupational, or other important areas of functioning.

American Psychiatric Association. (2013). *Diagnostic and statistical manual of mental disorders* (5th ed.). Arlington, VA: American Psychiatric Association.

## Table 7.9

### DSM-5 Cyclothymic Disorder

A. For at least 2 years (at least 1 year in children and adolescents) there have been numerous periods with hypomanic symptoms that do not meet criteria for a hypomanic episode and numerous periods with depressive symptoms that do not meet criteria for a major depressive episode.

B. During the above 2-year period (1 year in children and adolescents), the hypomanic and depressive periods have been present for at least half the time and the individual has not been without the symptoms for more than 2 months at a time.

C. Criteria for a major depressive, manic, or hypomanic episode have never been met.

D. The symptoms in Criterion A are not better explained by schizoaffective disorder, schizophrenia, schizophreniform disorder, delusional disorder, or other specified or unspecified schizophrenia spectrum and other psychotic disorder.

E. The symptoms are not attributable to the physiological effects of a substance or another medical condition.

F. The symptoms cause clinically significant distress or impairment in social, occupational, or other important areas of functioning.

American Psychiatric Association. (2013). *Diagnostic and statistical manual of mental disorders* (5th ed.). Arlington, VA: American Psychiatric Association.

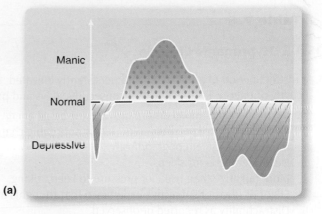

(a)

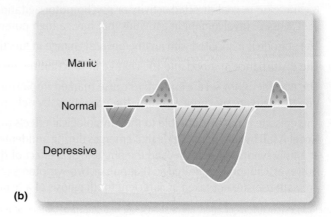

(b)

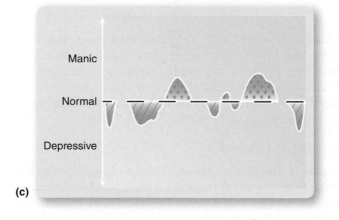

(c)

Copyright © Cengage Learning®

**FIGURE 7.5** COMPARISON OF CYCLES OF BIPOLAR I DISORDER, BIPOLAR II DISORDER, AND CYCLOTHYMIC DISORDER (a) Bipolar I disorder may involve alternating manic and major depressive episodes. (b) Bipolar II disorder may involve alternating hypomanic and major depressive episodes. (c) Cyclothymic disorder may involve alternating symptoms of hypomania and depression.

disorders. Suicide also occurs in people with other mental disorders or no mental disorder. Different aspects of suicide include suicidal ideation, suicidal behavior, suicide attempt, and suicide completion (see **Figure 7.6**) (Chiles & Strosahl, 2005). *Suicidal ideation* refers to thoughts about death, killing oneself, funerals, or other morbid ideas related to one's death. Thinking about suicide does not mean a person will commit suicide, but such thoughts can be a risk factor. *Suicidal behavior,* sometimes called *parasuicidal behavior* or *deliberate self-harm,* refers to self-destructive behavior that may or may not indicate a wish to die. Examples include cutting or burning oneself.

*Suicide attempt* refers to severe self-destructive behavior in which a person is trying to kill herself. Common methods of suicide attempt include firearms, hanging, alcohol/ substance/medication overdose, carbon monoxide poisoning, and jumping from a high place. A suicide attempt may or may not lead to *suicide completion,* which refers to people who do kill themselves. All aspects of suicide are commonly associated with people with depressive, bipolar, and other mental disorders.

Some theorists have proposed different types of suicide. One influential theorist was *Emile Durkheim* (1858–1917), a French sociologist who studied people and their relationship to society. Durkheim believed some people commit suicide for different reasons related to social integration. *Egoistic suicide* refers to a situation in which a person's social integration is weak, and so he believes committing suicide comes at little cost to others. Think of a teenager who believes no one cares for him—social alienation is indeed a risk factor for suicide (Langhinrichsen-Rohling, Friend, & Powell, 2009). *Anomic suicide* refers to a situation in which a person has great difficulty adapting to disrupted social order created by events such as economic crises. A surge of suicide in China relates somewhat to massive economic changes there (Law & Liu, 2008).

*Fatalistic suicide* refers to a situation in which a person feels oppressed by society and that his only means of escape is through death. Some people may feel condemned by fate, such as a woman who cannot have children—childlessness in women is indeed a risk factor for suicide attempt (Muller et al., 2005). *Altruistic suicide* refers to a situation in which a person commits

**FIGURE 7.6 SUICIDALITY SPECTRUM** Suicidality can be viewed along a spectrum from thoughts of suicide to actual death.

suicide to benefit society or others around him. Think of a soldier who sacrifices his life in Afghanistan to save comrades (Braswell & Kushner, 2012).

## Epidemiology of Depressive and Bipolar Disorders

General feelings of sadness are quite common: As many as 20 percent of adults and 50 percent of youths report recent symptoms of depression (Kessler & Wang, 2010). Feelings of sadness can intensify and result in diagnoses of major depressive disorder or dysthymia. The lifetime prevalence of major depressive disorder is 16.6 percent, and 6.7 percent of adults had the disorder in the previous year (see **Figure 7.7**). The lifetime prevalence of dysthymia is 2.5 percent, and 1.5 percent of adults had the disorder in the previous year (Kessler, Berglund, et al., 2005; Kessler, Chiu, Demler, & Walters, 2005). The prevalence of major depression and dysthymia in adolescents is 11.7% (Merikangas et al., 2010).

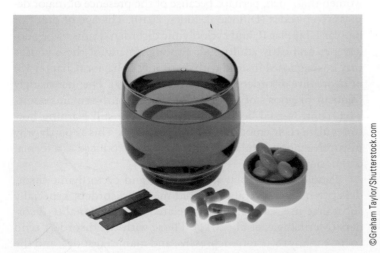

Common means of committing suicide include overdosing, cutting, hanging, jumping from a high place, or shooting.

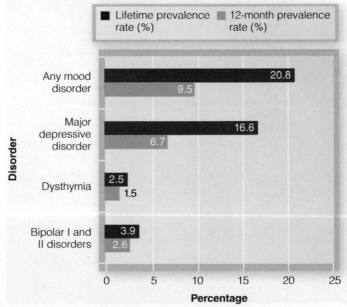

*Note:* These numbers reflect the fact that some people have more than one mood disorder.

**FIGURE 7.7** LIFETIME AND 12-MONTH PREVALENCE RATES FOR THE MAJOR DEPRESSIVE AND BIPOLAR DISORDERS.

Depression in females increases significantly around the beginning of adolescence, and female adolescents and adults are generally depressed at twice the rate of males (Hyde, Mezulis, & Abramson, 2008; Zahn-Waxler, Shirtcliff, & Marceau, 2008). Women may be more willing to admit symptoms of depression than men, but several studies indicate women to be more likely to have a first episode of depression, longer episodes of depression, and more recurrent episodes of depression than men. This gender difference may relate to frequency of stressors and other events in the lives of women (Essau, Lewinsohn, Seeley, & Sasagawa, 2010; Young & Korszun, 2010; see Box 7.1). Women also become depressed during certain seasons such as winter and have anxious depression more so than men (Grigoriadis & Robinson, 2007).

Rates of depression and treatment-seeking for depression differ around the world (see **Figures 7.8** and **7.9**). Rates of depression are relatively high in Lebanon, France, Chile, Brazil, Italy, New Zealand, and several European cities. Among Americans, depression seems equally prevalent among European and African Americans but higher in Puerto Ricans and lower in Asian Americans. These findings reveal significant cross-cultural differences with respect to depression (see later section on cultural influences; Bhugra & Mastrogianni, 2004).

Severe depression and dysthymia usually begin in late adolescence or early adulthood (especially mid-20s), but they could occur at any age. Many people have the disorders for

Nineteen-year-old Army Pfc. Ross McGinnis died saving the lives of four comrades in Iraq in 2006 by voluntarily jumping on a grenade tossed into their military vehicle. He received the Medal of Honor for what may have been an example of altruistic suicide.

several years before seeking treatment, and most adults are diagnosed at age 30 to 59 years (Kessler, Berglund, et al., 2005). Many people with dysthymia do not seek treatment until severe depression develops. Others do not seek treatment because they assume depressive symptoms are simply part of their shy or withdrawn personality. Less than half of people with depressive or bipolar disorders sought treatment for the problem in the previous year (see **Figure 7.10**).

Severe depression and dysthymia are highly comorbid with many other mental disorders, particularly anxiety-related and personality disorders and substance use problems (Blanco et al., 2010; Davis, Uezato, Newell, & Frazier, 2008; Levy, Edell, & McGlashan, 2007). Even on its own, depression is especially harmful—many with the disorder experience work and school difficulties and problems with interpersonal and marital relationships (Kessler et al., 2003; McKnight & Kashdan, 2009). Does this remind you of Katey?

Bipolar disorders are somewhat less common. The lifetime prevalence of bipolar I and bipolar II disorders is 3.9 percent among American adults. In addition, 2.6 percent of American adults had the disorders in the previous year (Kessler, Berglund, et al., 2005; Kessler, Chiu, et al. 2005). Bipolar II disorder is different from bipolar I disorder because manic episodes are not seen, but one study indicated that 17.4 percent of people with bipolar II disorder eventually progressed to bipolar I disorder (Alloy et al., 2012). Bipolar I and II disorders are also present in 2.7 percent of adolescents (Merikangas et al., 2010). Cyclothymic disorder occurs in 0.4 to 2.5 percent of the general population. About one-third to two-thirds of those with cyclothymic disorder eventually develop bipolar I or bipolar II disorder (Van Meter, Youngstrom, & Findling, 2012).

Bipolar I and cyclothymic disorders seem equally present in men and women and among people of different cultures (see **Figure 7.11**; Johnson, 2004; Kawa et al., 2005). Caribbean and African groups are less likely to experience depression but more likely to experience psychotic symptoms before mania compared with white Europeans (Kennedy, Boydell, van Os, & Murray, 2004). Bipolar II disorder may be somewhat more common in women than men, perhaps because of the presence of major depressive episodes (Diflorio & Jones, 2010). The age of onset of bipolar I, bipolar II, and cyclothymic disorders seems to be adolescence and early adulthood, although many of these youths may be diagnosed instead with disruptive behavior (Chapter 13) or depressive disorders (Joshi & Wilens, 2009). The increasingly frequent diagnosis of bipolar disorder in youth remains somewhat controversial because many youth are still learning how to regulate their emotions (Birmaher, 2012). This is partly why disruptive mood regulation disorder was introduced as a formal diagnosis in *DSM-5*.

People with bipolar I, bipolar II, and cyclothymic disorders often have several comorbid mental disorders, especially substance use, eating, anxiety-related, and personality disorders (Merikangas et al., 2011). Those with the disorders tend to have many recurrent depressive and manic episodes, and the disorders can lead to severe consequences with respect to daily functioning (Judd et al., 2008).

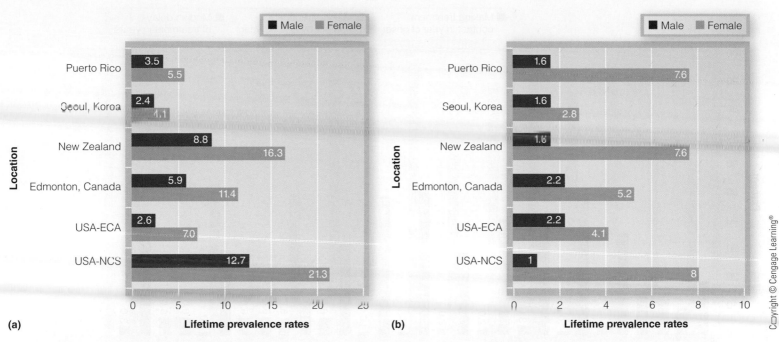

(a) Lifetime prevalence rates

(b) Lifetime prevalence rates

**FIGURE 7.8 RATES OF MAJOR DEPRESSION AND DYSTHYMIA BY GENDER IN COMMUNITY SURVEYS.** Gender differences in rates of major depression (a) and dysthymia (b) vary in different areas of the world. ECA, Epidemiologic Catchment Area; NCS, National Comorbidity Study.

(a) Current depression

| Total | 10.4% |
| Male | 0.0% |
| Female | 12.4% |

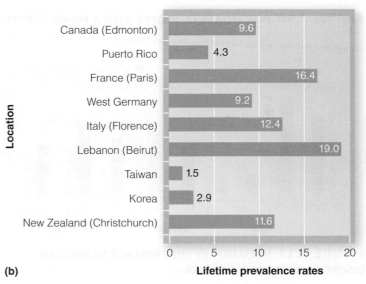

(b) Lifetime prevalence rates

**FIGURE 7.9 TRANSCULTURAL VARIATION IN THE PREVALENCE OF DEPRESSION** (a) Current depression rate in selected countries. (b) Lifetime prevalence rate of depression in selected countries.

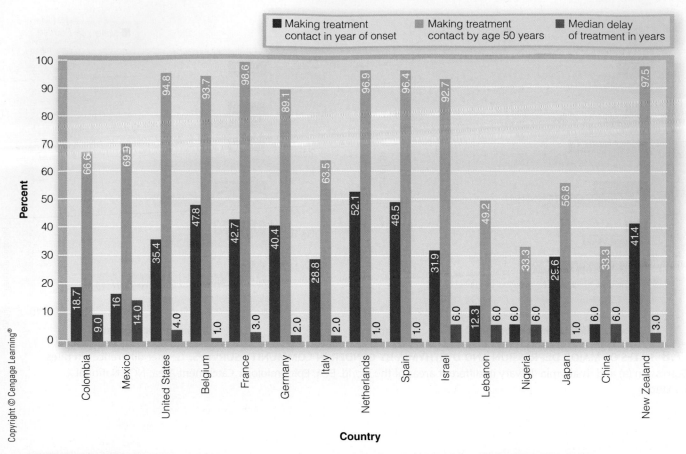

FIGURE 7.10  PERCENTAGE OF PEOPLE WITH A MAJOR DEPRESSIVE OR BIPOLAR DISORDER SEEKING TREATMENT

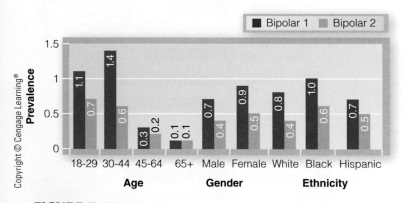

FIGURE 7.11  VARIATION IN THE PRESENCE OF BIPOLAR DISORDER BY SEVERAL FACTORS

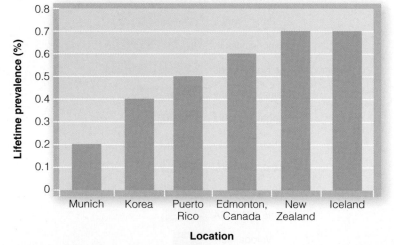

## Epidemiology of Suicide

An estimated 782,000 lives were lost due to suicide worldwide in 2008 (Varnick, 2012). The National Center for Health Statistics reports that 38,364 Americans committed suicide in 2010, representing 1.6 percent of all deaths. Suicide is the tenth leading cause of death overall, third among young adults, and common among the elderly (Crosby, Han, Ortega, Parks, & Gfroerer, 2011). About 1 to 12 percent of the population have

attempted suicide, and 8.3 million Americans think about suicide each year—although only a fraction (0.3 percent) go on to commit suicide (Chiles & Strosahl, 2005; Crosby et al., 2011). Approximately 6% of undergraduate and 4% of graduate students have seriously contemplated suicide within the past year (Brownson, Drum, Smith, & Denmark, 2011).

Most suicides come from firearms, suffocation, and poisoning, although many people deliberately kill themselves in cars and other "accidents" to save family members and friends from additional grief. Men are more likely than women to use particularly lethal methods of suicide such as firearms and hanging. Men thus actually complete suicide at four times the rate of females (Callanan & Davis, 2012).

Suicide rates are highest in Eastern Europe but considerably lower in the United States, Taiwan, Korea, Japan, China, and Canada and lowest among Latin American and Muslim countries (see **Figure 7.12**; Mann et al., 2005). Among Americans, suicide is more common among European Americans, Protestants, professionals, nonheterosexuals, and unmarried people (see **Figure 7.13**). Rates of adolescent suicide have increased substantially over the past several decades, and adolescent and adult Native Americans are at particular risk. African Americans, Hispanics, and Asian/Pacific Islanders tend to have the lowest rates of suicide. People who are unemployed and/or socially isolated also tend to be at higher risk for suicide (Anderson, 2002; Bhugra & Mastrogianni, 2004; Blakely, Collings, & Atkinson, 2003; Duberstein et al., 2004; Gould, Greenberg, Velting, & Shaffer, 2003).

Suicide *attempts* are much more common in women than men, perhaps because women try to commit suicide in ways that take longer and have a higher chance of rescue. Examples include drug overdose and carbon monoxide poisoning. This disparity may be culture-specific, however. More women than men commit suicide in China (Chiles & Strosahl, 2005; Law & Liu, 2008).

Suicide often occurs in people with bipolar disorder (11–15 percent) or depression (15–19 percent; Ebmeier, Donaghey, & Steele, 2006; Miklowitz & Johnson, 2006). About 48 percent of those with depression have suicidal ideation (Richards, 2011). Suicidality is also associated with many other mental disorders, as well as states of anxiety, stress, anger, boredom, frustration, and guilt. Suicidality also relates to inflexibility, impatience, aggression, and impulsivity. Alcohol use and stressful life events are also closely linked with suicidal behavior (Arsenault-Lapierre, Kim, & Turecki, 2004; Cherpitel, Borges, & Wilcox, 2004; Chiles & Strosahl, 2005).

## Stigma Associated with Depressive and Bipolar Disorders

People with depressive and bipolar disorders may experience substantial stigma given the debilitating nature of their symptoms. McNair and colleagues (2002) surveyed hundreds of people with current or past depression. Many said family members and friends were unsupportive because they equated clinical depression with "normal" sadness or with an emotional state that would pass with time. Part of this was because family members and friends saw no outward signs of a problem. Others with depression dared not tell coworkers that they were taking antidepressant medication or even that they had depressive symptoms due to fears of discrimination. Many people with depression reported that health care providers downplayed the significance of their symptoms, and so they often declined to seek more intensive treatment. High levels of stigma have also been found among people with bipolar disorder. Many reportedly believe that the public holds negative attitudes toward people with a mental disorder (Brohan et al., 2011).

Some have tried interventions to reduce stigma associated with depression. Griffiths and colleagues (2004) asked people with depression to review two websites. One website included education about aspects of depression such as symptoms, causes, sources of help, prevention, and the need to seek treatment. The site also contained short biographies of famous people with depression. A second website was devoted to cognitive behavioral methods to help people think more realistically, solve problems more effectively, and cope better with relationship difficulties or events that could trigger depressive symptoms. Perceived stigma was reduced significantly more for the website intervention group compared to controls who did not review online materials. The study supports our assertion in Chapter 1 that education is a powerful antidote to stigma.

### INTERIM SUMMARY

► Depressive and bipolar disorders refer to extreme emotional states of sadness or euphoria.

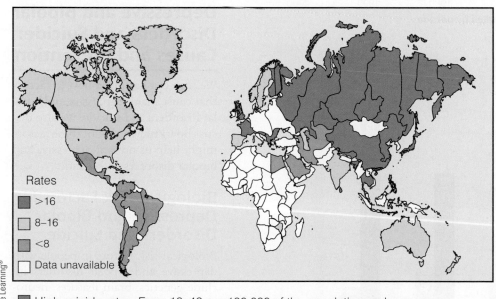

Rates
- ■ >16
- □ 8–16
- ■ <8
- □ Data unavailable

■ High suicide rates. From 16–46 per 100,000 of the population and over.

□ Intermediate suicide rates. From 8–16 per 100,000 of the population.

■ Low suicide rates. Under 8 per 100,000 of the population.

□ Data not available.

**FIGURE 7.12** TRANSCULTURAL VARIATION IN SUICIDE RATES

► A major depressive episode is a lengthy period of sad or empty mood, eating and sleeping problems, concentration difficulties, fatigue, sense of worthlessness, and suicidal thoughts or attempts. Major depressive disorder may involve several major depressive episodes.

► Persistent depressive disorder (dysthymia) is a chronic feeling of depression for at least 2 years.

► Other formal depressive disorders include disruptive mood dysregulation disorder and premenstrual dysphoric disorder.

► A manic episode is a period of uncontrollable euphoria and potentially self-destructive behavior. Hypomanic episodes are similar to manic episodes but with less impaired functioning.

► Bipolar I disorder involves one or more manic episodes. Bipolar II disorder refers to hypomanic episodes with major depressive episodes.

► Cyclothymic disorder refers to symptoms of hypomania and depression that fluctuate over a long time.

► Depressive and bipolar disorders are common in the general population and often occur with anxiety-related, personality, eating, and substance use disorders.

► Suicide is commonly seen in people with depressive and bipolar disorders, especially among men, European Americans, nonmarried people, and the elderly.

► Many people with depressive and bipolar disorders feel stigmatized for their condition by family members and others.

## REVIEW QUESTIONS

1. What are depressive and bipolar disorders, and how do these differ from normal sadness or happiness?

2. What are characteristics of depression?

3. Describe differences between bipolar I, bipolar II, and cyclothymic disorder.

4. Describe different dimensions of suicide.

5. How common are depressive and bipolar disorders and suicide? What populations are most at risk?

# Depressive and Bipolar Disorders and Suicide: Causes and Prevention

We turn our attention next to factors that cause major depressive and bipolar disorders and suicide. We also discuss how knowing about these factors might help us prevent depressive and bipolar disorders and suicide.

## Biological Risk Factors for Depressive and Bipolar Disorders and Suicide

Biological risk factors in people with depressive and bipolar disorders include genetics, brain features, neurochemical and hormonal features, and sleep deficiencies.

## GENETICS

Researchers rely on family and twin studies to evaluate genetic contributions to mental conditions such as

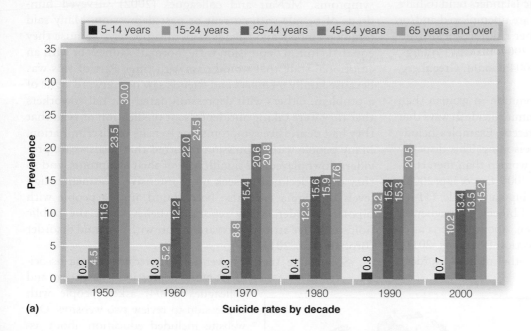

(a) Suicide rates by decade

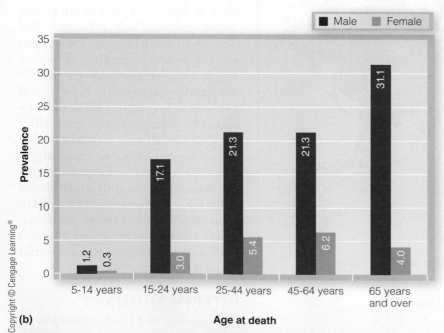

(b) Age at death

**FIGURE 7.13** DEATH RATES FOR SUICIDE ACCORDING TO DECADE, AGE, RACE, AND GENDER FOR THE UNITED STATES, 1950–2002

depressive and bipolar disorders. *Family studies,* in which researchers assess family members of a person with a mental disorder, indicate that depression does run in families. First-degree relatives of people with depression have depression themselves **2.8** times more than the general population (Shyn & Hamilton, 2010). Children of depressed parents are up to 4 times more likely to have a mood disorder than children of nondepressed parents (Beardslee, Gladstone, & O'Connor, 2011). Bipolar disorder also runs in families. Relative risk for bipolar disorder has been found to be 6.4 times greater in children and 7.9 times greater in siblings of persons with bipolar disorder (Lichtenstein et al., 2009).

*Twin studies* also suggest that depressive and bipolar disorders have a genetic basis. Identical twin males and females have been found concordant for depression 31.1 percent and 47.6 percent of the time, respectively, compared with nonidentical twin males and females (25.1 percent and 42.6 percent concordance, respectively) (see **Figure 7.14**; Kendler & Prescott, 1999). Studies of bipolar disorder indicate that identical twins share the disorder about 38.5 to 62 percent of the time, a concordance rate much higher than that of fraternal twins (4.5–9.1 percent; Smoller & Finn, 2003). Identical twins share *any* depressive or bipolar disorder about 81 percent of the time compared with only 23 percent in control participants (Vehmanen, Kaprio, & Lonnqvist, 1995).

Several genes for depression have been implicated, especially those on chromosome 17 that may be involved with serotonin (we discuss serotonin in a later section; Middeldorp et al., 2009). Many researchers believe depression results from an *oligogenic transmission,* in which a small set of genes work interactively to cause this complex mental disorder (Demirkan et al., 2011). Researchers of bipolar disorder have focused on genes on chromosomes 2, 4, 5, 11, 12, 16, 18, 21, and X (Farmer, Elkin, & McGuffin, 2007). About one third of people with bipolar disorder also have red-green color blindness; both conditions link to genes on the X chromosome (Dubovsky &

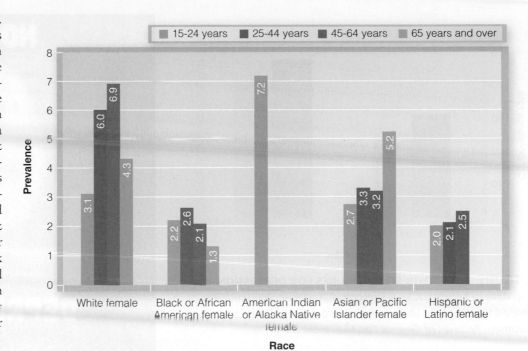

(c)    *Note:* Data for the American Indian or Alaska Native group are incomplete.

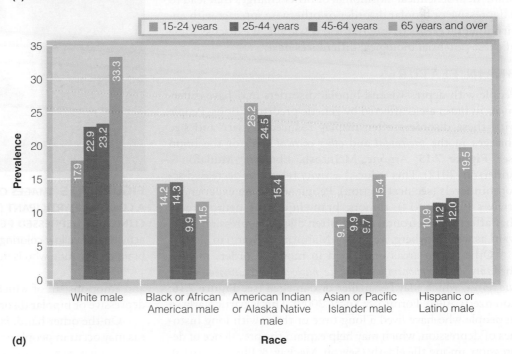

(d)    **Race**

**FIGURE 7.13**  continued

Dubovsky, 2002). However, genes on different chromosomes may work in an oligogenic fashion to help produce bipolar disorder (Greenwood et al., 2012).

Some people seem genetically predisposed toward certain depressive and bipolar disorders, although no one gene or set of genes likely leads *directly* to the disorders. Genetics account for only about 37 to 50 percent of depression symptoms, but heritability for bipolar disorder is about 75 to 80 percent (Farmer et al., 2007; Hamet & Tremblay, 2005; Sullivan, Daly, & O'Donovan, 2012). Genetics may instead help produce

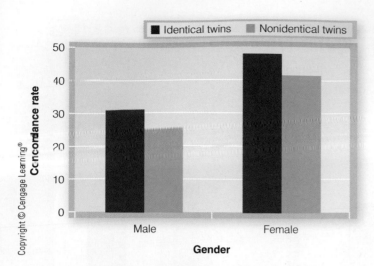

**FIGURE 7.14** **TWIN STUDY FIGURES FOR DEPRESSION** Based on data in Kendler, K.S., & Prescott, C.A. (1999). A population-based twin study of lifetime major depression in men and women. *Archives of General Psychiatry, 56,* 39-44.

brain, neurochemical, hormonal, or other changes that lead to a depressive or bipolar disorder or otherwise interact with environmental events to lead to these disorders. We discuss some of these potential biological differences next.

## BRAIN FEATURES

People with depressive and bipolar disorders may have differences in brain areas affected by genetic predispositions. People with these disorders often display reduced activity and size changes in the *prefrontal* and *other cortical areas* of the brain (see **Figure 7.15**; Arnone, McIntosh, Ebmeier, Munafo, & Anderson, 2012). This reduced activity relates to decreased serotonin levels (see next section). People who have experienced strokes (Chapter 14), tumors, brain injury, or neurosurgery that affect the prefrontal cortex often display depression afterward as well (Mayberg, Keightley, Mahurin, & Brannan, 2004).

Other brain areas implicated in mood disorders include the *amygdala, hippocampus, caudate nucleus,* and *anterior cingulate cortex,* which may be smaller or damaged (see **Figure 7.16**; Lorenzetti, Allen, Fornito, & Yucel, 2009). This is particularly so in people who have lived a long time or those with long histories of depression, which may help explain the prevalence of depression among the elderly (Sexton, Mackay, & Ebmeier, 2013). These brain areas are involved in goal-directed behavior and inhibition of negative mood and troublesome thoughts. Someone with less activation of these areas (depression) may thus fail to pursue important work goals and have recurrent negative thoughts. Memory difficulties among people with depression might also relate to these brain changes (Price & Drevets, 2012).

Subtle damage to certain brain areas may also contribute to mood disorders in general and depression in particular, especially damage to *white matter, basal ganglia,* and the *pons* (Davidson, Pizzagalli, & Nitschke, 2010). These brain areas may be involved in regulation of attention, motor behavior, memory,

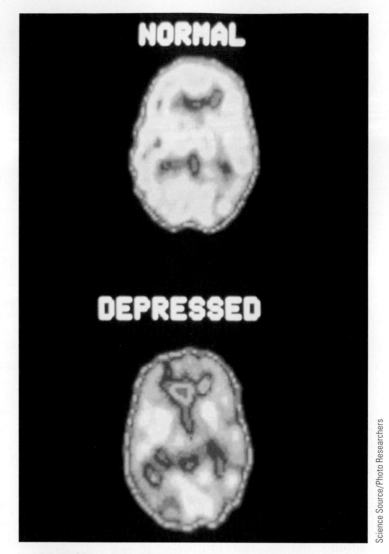

**FIGURE 7.15** **IMAGES COMPARING THE BRAIN OF A CONTROL PARTICIPANT (TOP) WITH THE BRAIN OF A CLINICALLY DEPRESSED PERSON (BOTTOM)** Note the lower activity (less yellow coloring) of the cortex and other areas in the brain of someone who is depressed.

and emotions, all of which can be problematic in people with depressive or bipolar disorders.

On the other hand, *increased* activity of these key brain areas may occur in people with bipolar disorder (see **Figure 7.17**). Heightened activity in the anterior cingulate and increased size of the *putamen* relate to mania (Bernstein et al., 2013; Cui et al., 2011). These areas work with other brain structures to influence motor activity, so hyperactivity in these areas may help explain constant restlessness, movement, and goal-directed activity in people with bipolar disorder. In addition, changes in areas such as the hippocampus that affect depression do not always seem evident in people with bipolar disorder (Geuze, Vermutten, Bremner, 2005). Instead, areas such as the amygdala and hippocampus seem intact.

Some evidence indicates that certain brain areas are reduced in size in some people with bipolar disorder, and these

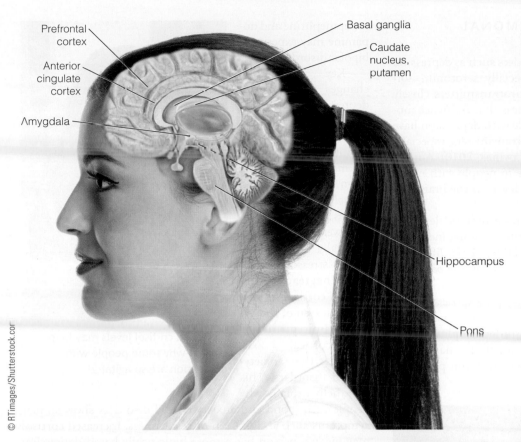

FIGURE 7.16 BRAIN AREAS MOST IMPLICATED IN THE DEPRESSIVE AND BIPOLAR DISORDERS

changes may relate somewhat to changes seen in people with schizophrenia (Chapter 12; Daban et al., 2006). Indeed, the two disorders have some symptoms in common (see **Figure 7.18**). People with symptoms of mania with or without symptoms of schizophrenia may have reduced white and gray matter in the brain (Bora & Pantelis, 2011; Cui et al., 2011). Such abnormalities may interfere with connections among important brain areas, which could lead to disruptive thought patterns seen in people with bipolar disorder and schizophrenia.

Brain changes for depression generally seem to involve cortical-limbic circuits, whereas brain changes for bipolar disorder generally seem to involve limbic-thalamic-cortical circuits, so some overlap is apparent (Radenbach et al., 2010). These changes may come from early effects such as genetics, maternal stress during pregnancy and altered hormonal levels, reduced blood flow to the fetus, poor prenatal care, or pregnant mothers' use of antidepressant medication, among other reasons (Garcia-Bueno, Caso, & Leza, 2008; Goodman, 2008). Not everyone who experiences these early effects necessarily develops a mood disorder, however. Brain changes affecting depressive and bipolar disorders likely intersect with neurochemical and hormonal features, which we discuss next.

FIGURE 7.17 THE BRAIN OF A PERSON WITH BIPOLAR DISORDER SHOWS INCREASED ACTIVITY COMPARED TO THE BRAIN OF A PERSON WITH UNIPOLAR DEPRESSION *From Mayberg, H.S., Keightley, M., Mahurin, R.K., & Brannan, S.K. (2004). Neuropsychiatric aspects of mood and affective disorders. In S.C. Yudofsky & R.E. Hales (Eds.), Essentials of neuropsychiatry and clinical neurosciences (pp. 489-517). Washington, DC: American Psychiatric Publishing.*

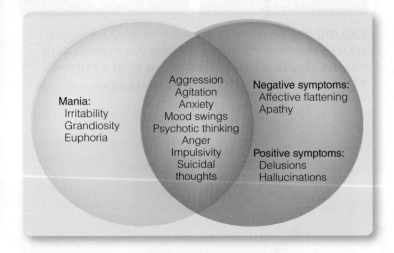

FIGURE 7.18 SYMPTOM OVERLAP BETWEEN SCHIZOPHRENIA AND BIPOLAR DISORDER *From C. Daban et al., (2006). Specificity of cognitive deficits in bipolar disorder versus schizophrenia: A systematic review. Psychotherapy and Psychosomatics, 75, 72-84. Reprinted by permission of S. Karger AG, Basel.*

# NEUROCHEMICAL AND HORMONAL FEATURES

Recall from Chapter 3 that mental disorders such as depression involve certain neurotransmitters, especially serotonin, norepinephrine, and dopamine. These neurotransmitters closely link to limbic and other key brain systems that influence motivation level and emotional state. People with depression have lower than normal levels of these neurotransmitters, especially serotonin (see **Figure 7.19**; Werner & Covinas, 2010). Antidepressant medications are often effective in people with mood disorders because they boost serotonin levels in the brain (see later treatment section).

People with bipolar disorder also have reduced levels of serotonin but *higher* than normal levels of norepinephrine (Newberg, Catapano, Zarate, & Manji, 2008). This difference from depression led some researchers to develop the *permissive hypothesis* (see **Figure 7.20**; Goodwin & Jamison, 2007). According to this theory, low serotonin levels may predispose a person for a mood disorder. Other neurotransmitter levels may determine the specific *direction* of the mood disorder. People with low serotonin plus low norepinephrine and dopamine may experience depression, whereas people with low serotonin plus high

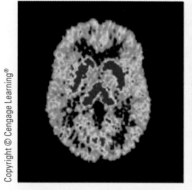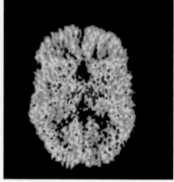

**FIGURE 7.19** POSITRON EMISSION TOMOGRAPHY (PET) SCAN OF LOWER SEROTONIN FUNCTION IN A PERSON WITH MAJOR DEPRESSION (RIGHT) COMPARED WITH A PERSON WITHOUT DEPRESSION (LEFT) *Original source unknown.*

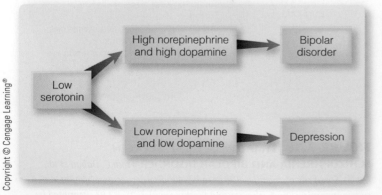

**FIGURE 7.20** PERMISSIVE HYPOTHESIS FOR DEPRESSIVE AND BIPOLAR DISORDERS

norepinephrine and dopamine may experience bipolar disorder.

Key hormonal changes also occur in depressive and bipolar disorders. People with depression and cognitive deficits such as memory problems often have increased *cortisol* levels (Mannie, Barnes, Bristow, Harmer, & Cowen, 2009). This is especially true following a stressor. Recall from Chapter 5 that increased cortisol, as well as disruption of the hypothalamic-pituitary-adrenocortical axis, impacts the anxiety-related disorders. This may help explain why

Increased cortisol levels may help explain why some people with depression are so agitated.

people with mood and anxiety-related disorders show similar symptoms such as agitation or restlessness. Increased cortisol may mean a person has a more biologically based depression best treated with medication (Hinkelmann et al., 2012).

Other hormonal changes also relate to depressive and bipolar disorders. People with underactive thyroid conditions (and correspondingly low levels of thyroid hormones) often experience symptoms of depression (Page & Azar, 2012). A key thyroid hormone, *triiodothyronine*, interacts significantly with serotonin and is sometimes used with antidepressants to relieve depression (Chang, Sato, & Han, 2013). Rapid cycling in bipolar disorder relates to a less active thyroid as well, so treating the latter condition is often important (Chakrabarti, 2011). People with depression also have suppressed levels of growth hormone and the hormones somatostatin and prolactin (Thase, 2010). These deficiencies, along with increased cortisol, may help explain the sleep and mood changes seen in people and especially premenopausal women with depression. We describe these sleep deficiencies next.

## SLEEP DEFICIENCIES

People with depressive and bipolar disorders often have disruptions in their normal sleep–wake cycle. Those with depression often have insomnia or hypersomnia and usually feel tired during the day. On the other hand, people with bipolar disorder in a manic state usually sleep very little. What might explain these effects?

People with depression tend to enter *rapid eye movement* (REM) sleep more quickly and display less slow-wave, or deep, sleep than normal (Riemann, 2007). Depression also seems related to intense but less stable REM sleep. These factors can disrupt sleep and cause fatigue. Sleep problems affect about 45 to 83 percent of people with depression and likely relate to genetic factors and changes in hormones and neurotransmitters such as serotonin (Thase, 2006). A disruption in *circadian rhythms,* or one's internal sleep–wake clock, may also occur in people with early morning wakening or depression in winter months. The latter may occur because sunlight is less available to help regulate a person's internal clock (Germain & Kupfer, 2008).

People with bipolar disorder may also have disrupted REM and slow-wave sleep, and some sleep deprivation may trigger manic episodes and especially rapid cycling (Plante & Winkelman, 2008). Changes in one's social routine during the day—such as loss of a spouse or partner, travel across time zones, or birth of a newborn—may disrupt biological rhythms that surround sleep. This likely occurs more so for people predisposed to sensitive internal biological clocks or those with poor coping skills. Disruption of circadian rhythms may spiral out of control and contribute to a manic state (Westrich & Sprouse, 2010). Such may have been true for Katey, whose late night attendance at clubs may have helped trigger a manic episode.

## Environmental Risk Factors for Depressive and Bipolar Disorders and Suicide

We turn our attention next to environmental risk factors that develop over time to create depressive or bipolar disorders. These include stressful life events and cognitive, interpersonal, and family factors. We also discuss cultural and evolutionary influences.

### STRESSFUL LIFE EVENTS

We all experience negative life events that cause us to struggle, but we often "bounce back" with the help of others. For people predisposed to depression, however, stressful life events seem more frequent, painful, and difficult to cope with. Stressful life events that help predict depression symptoms in college students include relationship breakup, illness, and relocation to college (Reyes-Rodriguez, Rivera-Medina, Camara-Fuentes, Suarez-Torres, & Bernal, 2013). Interethnic difficulties and conflicts as well as achievement stress also contribute to depression symptoms in Asian American, African American, and Latino/a American college students (Wei et al., 2010). Stressful life events often precede depressive symptoms, though their relationship to *ongoing* depression is less clear. Stressful life events may help trigger manic symptoms as well, as Katey's job loss did (Havermans, Nicolson, & Devries, 2007; Stroud, Davila, & Moyer, 2008).

Why do some people develop depression after a stressful life event but others do not? The *severity* and *meaning* of the stressful life event are clearly important (Espejo, Hammen, & Brennan, 2012; Monroe, 2008). People who become depressed tend to experience major, uncontrollable, and undesirable events highly significant to them. Examples include death of a child or partner, job loss, marital infidelity, business failure, and serious illness. Social support and ability to cope with a negative event are also important. A person who recently lost a loved one may be less depressed if she has a supportive partner and maintains regular eating and sleeping patterns. Personality traits may be important as well, including dependency, rumination, conscientiousness, and self-criticism (Klein, Kotov, & Bufferd, 2011). The impact of stressful life events often interacts with a person's cognitive misinterpretations of these events, and we discuss these risk factors next.

### COGNITIVE FACTORS

An environmental risk factor closely related to depressive and bipolar disorders is negative thought patterns, or **cognitive distortions**. You may recall we mentioned cognitive distortions in Chapter 5 because many people with anxiety-related disorders have unrealistic thoughts about potential or actual threat from internal sensations or external events. Examples of unrealistic thoughts include jumping to conclusions, catastrophizing, and emotional reasoning (see **Figure 7.21**)

Aaron Beck and others contend that some people with depression develop overly distorted, pessimistic views of themselves, the world around them, and their future. This is the **negative cognitive triad**. Some people view a certain event in a negative way and have catastrophic thoughts about the event (Beck & Dozois, 2011; Goldberg, Gerstein, Wenze, Welker, & Beck, 2008). These thoughts tend to be **automatic thoughts**, meaning they constantly repeat over the course of a day.

Consider Victor, who recently failed his math test, as an example of the negative cognitive triad. Following his grade, Victor believed he was not too bright (oneself), thought others would see him as a complete failure (world), and thought he would have to drop out of school (future). Victor gave a single negative event much more weight than should be the case. Many people with depression focus their thoughts on themes of loss and personal failure, inadequacy, and worthlessness (Abramson et al., 2002).

David Oliver/Stone/Getty Images

Stressful life events such as caring for two young children while working full time can help trigger depressive or bipolar disorders.

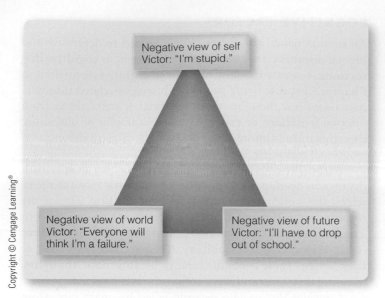

**FIGURE 7.21** **NEGATIVE COGNITIVE TRIAD INVOLVING COGNITIVE DISTORTIONS ABOUT THE SELF, WORLD, AND FUTURE**

A similar cognitive theory of depression, **hopelessness** (or attribution) **theory**, focuses on attitudes or *attributions* people make about an event (Abramson et al., 1999; Hankin, 2008). People with depression experience a negative life event, assume the event will last a long time (*stable*), and believe the event will affect most areas of their life (*global*). Victor assumed a single bad performance on a math test would doom the entire semester and would affect other courses and even his interpersonal relationships.

Hopelessness may also result from *internal* attributions because a person could excessively blame himself for a negative life event and develop low self-esteem. Hopelessness develops because a person believes that, no matter what he does, his efforts will not lead to change. A person may believe increased studying will not lead to passing grades or college graduation. This sense of **learned helplessness** might relate to excessive dependency on others (Abramson et al., 2002).

The concept of learned helplessness comes from experiments with dogs exposed to inescapable shock. Once the dogs "learned" they could not escape, they simply sat in a corner and passively accepted the shock. Learned helplessness continued even in later situations in which the dogs could obviously escape. The dogs may have learned that nothing they did had any effect on their environment (Maier & Watkins, 2005; Seligman & Maier, 1967). Such beliefs may occur in people as well. Cognitive theories of depression generally relate to mild or moderate cases of depression or what is sometimes called nonbiological, environmentally based, or *exogenous* depression.

Cognitive risk factors can also be important for bipolar disorder. Cognitive distortions in this regard often refer to beliefs that one can do something she cannot actually do (recall Katey's belief she might be able to fly) or beliefs that using medication will be harmful. These beliefs may lead people to stop using medication. People entering a manic or hypomanic episode will also adopt a more carefree attitude, underestimate risk,

develop an overly optimistic outlook, emphasize immediate gratification, minimize problems, experience increased speed of thoughts, and have trouble concentrating and paying attention (Newman, Leahy, Beck, Reilly-Harrington, & Gyulai, 2002).

## INTERPERSONAL FACTORS

Depression also seems linked to interpersonal difficulties such as social skill deficits, communication problems, and relationship or marital conflict. People with depression see themselves as socially ineffective with others. Other people who observe a person with depression may also reject the person and rate him as having poor social skills (Tse & Bond, 2004). Social skill problems may involve poor eye contact, sad facial expression, head drooping, little smiling, or lack of motivation to communicate or to be expressive. Social skill deficits do predict levels of depression (Segrin & Rynes, 2009).

People with depression also have communication problems. They speak slowly and softly, have flat affect or little emotion when speaking, and pause a long time before responding to others (Segrin, 2011). People with depression also frequently seek reassurance and choose topics of conversation that surround sadness, negative self-evaluation ("I'm no good"), and personal flaws ("I'm clumsy around others") (Hames, Hagan, & Joiner, 2013).

Marital conflict closely relates to depression, especially among people who married early in life to relieve depression. Depression often leads to marital problems in men but marital problems often lead to depression in women (Gabriel, Beach, & Bondemann, 2010). Depression and marital problems may co-occur because one spouse becomes withdrawn or angry, because sexual relations suffer, or because problems are not solved well. The relationship between marriage and depression is likely complex, however. Men become more depressed by financial pressures, whereas women become more depressed by family problems (Kessler, 2003).

Depression may relate to amount of social reinforcement one receives for certain behaviors (Carvalho & Hopko, 2011). Some people receive attention, reassurance, comfort, and sympathy from others when depressed. Friends and family

The concept of learned helplessness grew out of experiments with dogs that showed passivity after being subjected to inescapable electric shock.

members may call or visit more, offer to help with children and chores, and listen to problems. Conversely, prosocial behavior is ignored or taken for granted—a person may thus revert to depressive behavior to receive more attention. A social behavioral theory of depression may help explain why some depressive behaviors continue over time.

## FAMILY FACTORS

Children of parents with a depressive or bipolar disorder have more of these disorders themselves compared with the general population. Genetics may play a role in this connection, but problems among family members are also likely a factor. One such problem involves attachment. Impaired attachment to parents at an early age, especially anxious or ambivalent or avoidant attachment, can lead to later depression that surrounds overdependency on others, loss, fear of abandonment, poor self-worth, self-criticism, and anger toward parents and oneself (Morley & Moran, 2011). Recall that Katey had little contact with her family members. Later in therapy, she also said her relationship with her parents had never been particularly close.

Depression in mothers can also be a strong risk factor for depression in children. Depressed mothers often display inadequate parenting, tend to disengage from their children, and show many negative and few positive behaviors toward their children. Depressed mothers may withdraw from or ignore child-rearing situations that demand supervision and discipline, and focus on criticism and not affection toward their children. Depressed fathers also tend to be withdrawn, indecisive, cynical, and irritable (Spector, 2006). Children may thus model depressive symptoms in their parents and develop overly negative views of themselves. Such parenting especially affects young children who come from low-income families (Goodman, Fleitlich-Bilyk, Patel, & Goodman, 2007).

Families of children with depression are often marked by less available parents and little support and nurturance for the child. These families may have high levels of **expressed emotion**, or hostility, conflict, and overinvolvement (Silk et al., 2009). This means family members often fight but remain deeply involved in the details of one another's lives. Family stressors such as marital

problems, maltreatment, and poverty also relate to child depression (Beardslee, Gladstone, & O'Connor, 2011). Children may thus develop cognitive and attributional distortions and poor social skill with respect to communication, problem solving, and assertiveness. These problems relate to interpersonal difficulties, social withdrawal, and depression (Katz, Conway, Hammen, Brennan, & Najman, 2011).

Children whose parents have bipolar disorder are also at high risk for developing the disorder themselves. This is especially so if a parent has other mental disorders such as a substance use or personality disorder. Marital conflict and poor parenting and family cohesion closely relate to childhood bipolar disorder (Belardinelli et al., 2008; Du Rocher Schudlich, Youngstrom, Calabrese, & Findling, 2008). Poor parenting includes substantial criticism and other negative behaviors toward a child. Expressed emotion also relates to poor outcome in youth with bipolar disorder (Keenan-Miller & Miklowitz, 2011). How such parent and family problems specifically lead to bipolar disorder remains unclear. One possibility is that unstable parent and family behaviors hinder a child's ability to control her emotions.

## CULTURAL FACTORS

We mentioned that rates of depression vary across areas of the world and even among subgroups of a country like the United States. One possible explanation is that depression and other mental disorders are especially high among immigrant and migrant populations (we discuss a similar finding for schizophrenia in Chapter 12). In the United States, the Hispanic population is one of the fastest growing subgroups. Many Latinos are Mexicans who immigrate to the United States for better working conditions but who have high rates of health problems, stress, and depression (Sullivan & Rehm, 2005). High rates of depression and other mental health problems also occur among migrant workers in Europe (Carta, Bernal, Hardoy, & Haro-Abad, 2005). However, some researchers also believe that more acculturated immigrants,

Marital problems may be a key trigger for depression.

Mothers with depression are at significant risk for having children with depression.

or those who adopt more practices of the mainstream culture such as music and food, tend to be more depressed than those less acculturated. Those who stay close to others who share a common cultural identity may experience some protection from depression (Bhugra & Gupta, 2011).

Bipolar disorders are seen fairly equally across cultures, but researchers have found some interesting cultural differences when examining specific aspects of these disorders. One group of researchers examined people experiencing a first episode of mania in the United Kingdom and found African-Caribbean and African groups to be much less likely than white Europeans to have depression before the onset of their mania (Kennedy et al., 2004). African groups had more psychotic symptoms during their first manic episode. All groups had similar symptoms of bipolar disorder, but types of symptoms associated with the disorder were quite different.

These differences may have been due to environmentally or genetically determined ethnic differences, or the minority populations may have been less likely to seek earlier help for depressive symptoms. Initial failure to properly diagnose bipolar disorder has been found among Hispanic adolescents referred for major depressive disorder (Dilsaver & Akiskal, 2005). These studies indicate that mental health services are not always readily available to diverse individuals, that diverse individuals may hide symptoms or seek help only when symptoms are severe, and that clinicians must be sensitive to differences in culture and ways mental disorders are expressed.

## EVOLUTIONARY INFLUENCES

Evolutionary theories also exist for depressive and bipolar disorders. Some believe depressed states evolved so certain people could withdraw from social interactions. Perhaps certain people feel their value to others is low and their burden on others is high. A person may feel at risk for exclusion from the social group and

thus minimize contact with the group. This might help explain depressive symptoms such as sensitivity to comments of others and low risk-seeking behavior (Allen & Badcock, 2003). Others believe depression evolved so people could ruminate over problems until a proper solution is found, that depressive behaviors signal to others the need for help, or that depression and withdrawal from difficult situations helps lower stress (Nesse & Ellsworth, 2009; Watson & Andrews, 2002).

Evolutionary theories of mania are sparser, although some speculate that hypomanic states help improve physical fitness, facilitate invading or settling a new territory, enhance reproductive opportunities, and display positive personal characteristics attractive to potential mates (Brody, 2001). Others propose that cyclothymic tendencies increase creativity that helps in sexual seduction and increases chances for leadership of a group (Akiskal & Akiskal, 2005).

## Causes of Depressive and Bipolar Disorders and Suicide

Researchers emphasize integrative models to explain how many risk factors can produce depressive and bipolar disorders (Garcia-Toro & Aguirre, 2007; see **Figure 7.22**). Certain people are likely born with a *biological vulnerability* to experience different depressive or bipolar disorders. Some people

Migrant workers and immigrants have been shown to be especially susceptible to depression.

David R. Frazier Photolibrary, Inc. / Alamy

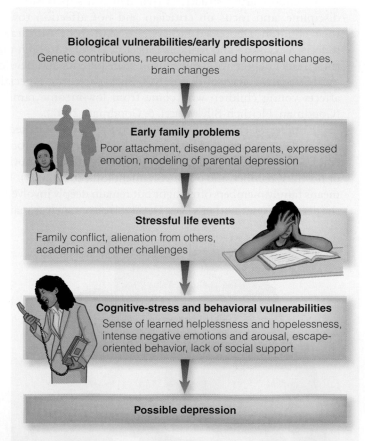

**FIGURE 7.22** SAMPLE DEVELOPMENTAL PATHWAY OF DEPRESSION

clearly have a genetic predisposition toward depression or bipolar disorder. These genetic factors may interact with or predispose someone toward important neurochemical, hormonal, and brain changes that affect ability to control mood and related behavior.

People also develop a *psychological vulnerability* toward depressive and bipolar disorders. Some people experience stressful and life-changing events such as loss of one's mother in early childhood, come to believe they have little control over life events, and experience interpersonal and family problems that contribute to their disorder or deprive them of social support.

Think about depression. Some people are naturally predisposed, perhaps via genetics and/or low serotonin and norepinephrine levels or prefrontal brain changes, to experience depressed mood and lack of motivation or energy (*biological vulnerability*). As these people develop as children, sad mood and slow motor behavior may interact with various parental and family factors we mentioned earlier. These factors include poor attachment, disengaged parenting, family dysfunction, and modeling depressive behaviors. In turn, these factors can lead to a child's problems controlling emotions, solving problems rationally, and interacting with others.

During adolescence and young adulthood, more stressful life events are likely to occur. These events include family changes and conflict, alienation from peers and others, illness, or academic challenges and problems. A cognitive vulnerability may develop in which one believes he has little control over these events and develops a sense of hopelessness about changing negative experiences (*cognitive-stress psychological vulnerability*). Some may try to escape depression by marrying or having a child early in life, but this strategy is not generally effective. If a person also experiences poor social support and is overdependent on others, then depression may be even more likely.

Some people have a strong biological vulnerability to depression that requires few environmental triggers. People with biologically oriented, or *endogenous,* depression often develop sadness for little apparent reason. Other people have a weak biological predisposition toward depression but still become depressed when frequent, overwhelming, and negative life events occur. People with environmentally oriented, or *exogenous,* depression develop sadness primarily because they cope poorly with major life stressors. Exogenous or *reactive* depression often follows some major event.

People with bipolar disorders likely have a strong biological vulnerability toward recurrent manic or hypomanic episodes. Genetic predispositions and neurochemical changes are well documented in this population. Little environmental influence may be needed to trigger the disorders. Some psychological factors relate to onset and duration of bipolar symptoms, including stressful life events, family hostility and conflict, lack of social support, cognitive distortions, and personality disturbances (Treuer & Tohen, 2010). Katey's therapist discovered that Katey's mother also had symptoms of bipolar disorder and that Katey was alienated from her family.

What about suicide? One popular multidimensional model stipulates that suicidality generally has four main components:

1. Intense negative emotions from stressful life events and difficulty handling stress
2. Tendency to solve problems by avoiding and escaping them
3. Short-term reductions in distress when thinking about or attempting suicide
4. Long term increases in negative arousal and distress when thinking about or attempting suicide

These factors can be aggravated by poor social support and depression or bipolar disorder. A person who reaches the point of suicide feels unable to escape torment and feels such pain is intolerable and will last a long time. Severe hopelessness develops such that a person has trouble thinking about problem solutions other than suicide (Chiles & Strosahl, 2005).

## Prevention of Depressive and Bipolar Disorders and Suicide

Depressive and bipolar disorders often begin in adolescence or early adulthood, so it makes sense to think of prevention during childhood and adolescence. Several target areas might be important for prevention. These targets involve coping with stressful life events and addressing individual, cognitive, and family factors. Individual factors include social skill and interpersonal problems, medical illness, and academic difficulties, among others. Cognitive factors include low self-esteem, attributional distortions, and hopelessness, among others. Family factors include marital conflict and disengaged or hostile parents, among others (Munoz, Beardslee, & Leykin, 2012).

Prevention programs for depressive disorders typically address (1) people without any symptoms of the disorders; (2) people at risk for developing the disorders, such as children of parents with depressive disorders; and (3) people who have a depressive disorder and wish to prevent relapse. For people without symptoms of depressive disorder, researchers have evaluated large-scale primary or universal prevention programs (Waddell, Hua, Garland, Peters, & McEwan, 2007). One such program was developed by Ian Shochet and colleagues; its two sections are the *Resourceful Adolescent Program-Adolescents* (RAP-A) and the *Resourceful Adolescent Program-Family* (RAP-F). The RAP-A program involves an 11-session group approach to teach adolescents to:

- Declare existing strengths, such as being a good student or son/daughter
- Manage stress in difficult situations
- Modify negative and irrational thoughts to think more realistically
- Solve problems effectively
- Develop and use social support networks such as friends and other social groups

- Develop strategies to reduce family and interpersonal conflict, such as negotiating solutions and repairing relationships
- Enhance social skill and recognize other people's perspectives

The RAP-F program, which focuses on parents, involves stress management, education about normal teenager development, promotion of self-esteem, and strategies to reduce family conflict. Symptoms of depression and hopelessness declined significantly for RAP-A and RAP-F groups compared with control participants. A nice advantage of this program is that it is based in schools where more adolescents might have access (Shochet et al., 2001).

For people at risk for developing depressive disorders, researchers have evaluated large-scale secondary or selected/indicated prevention programs (Munoz et al., 2012). Gregory Clarke and colleagues evaluated a program that focused on adolescents whose parents had major depression or dysthymia. Teenagers participated in 15 sessions to identify and challenge unrealistic thoughts, especially thoughts related to their depressed parents ("I will be just like my parents"). Parents also attended education sessions. At-risk adolescents who received the prevention program displayed fewer symptoms of depression and suicide over time than controls (Clarke et al., 2001). An advantage of this study is that one key intervention ingredient—cognitive restructuring—was found so effective. Cognitive restructuring, or cognitive therapy, as we discussed in Chapter 5, involves examining negative statements a person may be making and encouraging the person to challenge the thought and think more realistically (see also later treatment section).

For people with a depressive disorder, researchers have evaluated relapse prevention programs (Apil, Hoencamp, Haffmans, & Spinhoven, 2011). People with depression often need help identifying situations such as solitary places that place them at risk for future depression, managing stress, coping with and resolving difficult situations such as marital conflict, and enhancing self-confidence (Richards & Perri, 2010). Relapse prevention for depression also involves helping people remain on antidepressant medication and increasing mindfulness regarding their behaviors (Bieling et al., 2012; Bondolfi et al., 2010).

Little work is available regarding prevention of bipolar disorder, although youth whose parents have the disorder are certainly at risk themselves. Early prevention research in this area has concentrated on youth just beginning to show symptoms of bipolar disorder and who have thus received medication (Geller & DelBello, 2008). For people with bipolar disorder, relapse prevention focuses on maintaining medication and increasing family and social support (Beynon, Soares-Weiser, Woolacott, Duffy, & Geddes, 2008).

Preventing suicide must also be a priority among people with depressive and bipolar disorders. General programs to prevent suicide focus on adolescents and involve school-based suicide awareness programs, screening teenagers at risk for suicide, enhancing problem-solving and coping skills, educating peers and teachers to identify high-risk behaviors, and providing crisis intervention to those at risk. Other suicide prevention strategies include community-based crisis centers and hotlines. These programs do help reduce suicide rates among youth (Gould et al., 2003; Miller, Eckert, & Mazza, 2009).

Suicide prevention programs for adults also focus on awareness and education among the public, such as helping people understand risk factors associated with suicide and reducing stigma of mental disorder. These programs also focus on primary care physicians, clergy, pharmacists, and other "first responders" to help them recognize and treat suicidal tendencies in people who come for help. Screening programs to help identify early suicidal behaviors are an avenue to get people help via medication and psychotherapy. Follow-up care after a suicide attempt is critical as well to prevent a second attempt. These programs have also been moderately successful for lowering suicide rates in specific groups (Mann et al., 2005).

## INTERIM SUMMARY

► Biological risk factors for depressive and bipolar disorders include genetics, brain changes, neurochemical and hormonal differences, and sleep deficiencies.

► Environmental risk factors for depressive and bipolar disorders include stressful and uncontrollable life events, negative thought processes and misattributions, problematic interpersonal relationships, and parent and family factors that help create an unstable living environment for a child. Cultural and evolutionary factors may also be influential.

► Biological and environmental risk factors can make a person vulnerable to a depressive or bipolar disorder. These risk factors inhibit one's ability to control emotions, cope with stress, solve problems, and relate to others effectively.

► Depressive and bipolar disorders may result from a combination of (1) early biological factors and (2) environmental factors related to ability to cope, think rationally, and develop competent social and academic skills.

► Preventing depressive and bipolar disorders involves building one's ability to control situations that might lead to symptoms.

**THE CONTINUUM VIDEO PROJECT**

### *Emilie:* **Bipolar Disorder**

*"When I'm feeling the worst, my brain tells me that I am worthless, that the kids would be better off without me...I'm just a drain."*

Copyright © Cengage Learning.®

Access the Continuum Video Project in MindTap at **www.cengagebrain.com**.

## REVIEW QUESTIONS

1. Describe data that support a genetic contribution to depressive and bipolar disorders.
2. What key brain, neurochemical, and hormonal brain changes relate to depressive and bipolar disorders, and how might sleep deficiencies contribute?
3. Describe two main cognitive theories of depression.
4. How might interpersonal and family factors help cause depressive and bipolar disorders?
5. Describe an overall causal model for depressive and bipolar disorders.
6. What factors might be important in designing a program to prevent depressive and bipolar disorders as well as suicide?

# Depressive and Bipolar Disorders and Suicide: Assessment and Treatment

Primary methods to assess people with depressive and bipolar disorders include interviews, self-report questionnaires, self-monitoring, observations from others, and physiological measurement. A person suspected of having a depressive or bipolar disorder should always have a full medical examination as well. Medical conditions related to depression, for example, include neurological impairments, brain injuries, cardiovascular problems, hormonal changes, immune disorders, and terminal illnesses (see **Table 7.10**). Symptoms of depressive and bipolar disorders may also relate to drug intoxication, withdrawal, or side effects. If a physical condition or substance contributes to a person's depressive or bipolar symptoms, then medical treatment or expanded psychological treatment is necessary to address the condition or drug problem.

## Interviews and Clinician Ratings

Katey's therapist had many questions for her client, especially about her behaviors and thoughts during the day. The therapist was also interested in how Katey felt about her symptoms and what Katey would like to be doing weeks or months from now. Recall from Chapter 5 that therapists typically ask these and other questions in unstructured or structured interviews. Structured interviews usually cover diagnostic criteria and contain questions a therapist asks each client with a possible depressive or bipolar disorder.

Structured interviews for people with depressive and bipolar disorders include the *Schedule for Affective Disorders and Schizophrenia* and *Structured Clinical Interview* (Arbisi, 1995; First, Spitzer, Gibbon, & Williams, 1997). The *Washington University in St. Louis Kiddie Schedule for Affective Disorders and Schizophrenia* is useful for youths (Geller et al., 2001). Other interview-format instruments determine how severe a person's symptoms are or how a person is responding to treatment. Examples include the *Brief Psychiatric Rating Scale* and *Hamilton Rating Scale for Depression* (see **Table 7.11**, Biancosino, Picardi,

**Table 7.10**

### Disorders Associated with Depression

| Neurological disorders | Systemic disorders |
|---|---|
| **Focal lesions:** Stroke, Tumor, Surgical ablation, Epilepsy | **Endocrine disorders:** Hypothyroidism and hyperthyroidism, Adrenal diseases (Cushing's, Addison's), Parathyroid disorders |
| **Regional degenerative diseases:** Parkinson's disease, Huntington's disease, Pick's disease, Fahr's disease, Progressive supranuclear palsy, Carbon monoxide exposure, Wilson's disease | **Inflammatory/infectious diseases:** Systemic lupus erythematosus, Neurosyphilis, AIDS, Tuberculosis, Mononucleosis, Sjögren's syndrome, Chronic fatigue syndrome |
| **Diffuse diseases:** Alzheimer's disease, AIDS dementia, Multiple sclerosis | **Metabolic disorders:** Uremia, Porphyria, Vitamin deficiencies |
| **Miscellaneous disorders:** Migraine, Paraneoplastic syndromes | **Miscellaneous disorders:** Medication side effects, Chronic pain syndromes, Sleep apnea, Cancer, Heart disease |

Marmai, Biondi, & Grassi, 2010; Romera, Perez, Menchon, Polavieja, & Gilaberte, 2011).

Katey's therapist used the Hamilton Rating Scale for Depression to note Katey's depressed mood, difficulties sleeping, thoughts about inability to work, and agitation. The therapist saw that many of Katey's sentences contained sadness or bleakness. Katey was also restless at night and disturbed by constant thoughts about her condition. Fortunately, however, Katey did not wish she were dead, although she did occasionally wonder if life was worth living. Following is an excerpt from Katey's interview:

**Katey:** Yeah, I just find it so hard to get up in the morning sometimes.
**Therapist:** What do you think about in the morning?
**Katey:** How hard the day will be, who I'll have to meet, what I have to do—it just seems so overwhelming at times.
**Therapist:** Do you think about ways you can cope with events during the day?
**Katey:** I don't really see the point. What difference does it make? The day is going to be a big flop no matter what I do.

## Table 7.11

### Hamilton Rating Scale for Depression

**Instructions:** For each item, select the number that corresponds to the statement that best characterizes the patient.

1. Depressed mood (sadness, hopeless, helpless, worthless)
   - 0    Absent
   - 1    These feeling states indicated only on questioning
   - 2    These feeling states spontaneously reported verbally
   - 3    Communicates feeling states non-verbally—i.e., through facial expression, posture, voice, and tendency to weep
   - 4    Patient reports VIRTUALLY ONLY these feeling states in his spontaneous verbal and nonverbal communication

2. Feelings of guilt
   - 0    Absent
   - 1    Self reproach, feels he has let people down
   - 2    Ideas of guilt or rumination over past errors or sinful deeds
   - 3    Present illness is a punishment. Delusions of guilt
   - 4    Hears accusatory or denunciatory voices and/or experiences threatening visual hallucinations

3. Suicide
   - 0    Absent
   - 1    Feels life is not worth living
   - 2    Wishes he were dead or any thoughts of possible death to self

   - 3    Suicidal ideas or gestures
   - 4    Attempts at suicide (any serious attempt rates 4)

4. Insomnia early
   - 0    No difficulty falling asleep
   - 1    Complains of occasional difficulty falling asleep i.e., more than 1/2 hour
   - 2    Complains of nightly difficulty falling asleep

5. Insomnia middle
   - 0    No difficulty
   - 1    Patient complains of being restless and disturbed during the night
   - 2    Waking during the night—any getting out of bed rates 2 (except for purposes of voiding)

6. Insomnia late
   - 0    No difficulty
   - 1    Waking in early hours of the morning but goes back to sleep
   - 2    Unable to fall asleep again if he gets out of bed

From Hamilton M. (1967). Development of a rating scale for primary depressive illness, *British Journal of Social & Clinical Psychology*, 6(4):278-296. Reproduced with permission from The British Psychological Society. Reprinted with permission from John Waterhouse and the British Psychological Society.

Therapists commonly use unstructured interviews to assess people with depressive and bipolar disorders. Important topics to cover during such an interview include:

- Past and present mood symptoms
- Risk factors such as interpersonal and cognitive factors
- Medical and treatment history
- Ongoing problems and comorbid diagnoses
- Motivation for change
- Social support
- Suicidal thoughts and behaviors (see Assessment of Suicide section)

Katey's therapist asked many questions about her family and symptom history. Katey's symptoms had been ongoing for some time, and her mother had some intense mood changes. Other questions related to Katey's current ability to function and what daily social supports she could access. Many questions were also devoted to Katey's thought patterns and her willingness to take prescribed medication.

Therapists must also understand that people with depressive and bipolar disorders often speak at a different pace, bias their information in negative (depression) or positive (manic) ways, and may be uncomfortable sharing personal information. Building rapport is thus very important. Therapists can also examine nonverbal behaviors in an interview to help determine symptoms and severity of a depressive or bipolar disorder. Important nonverbal behaviors for depression, for example, include reduced facial expression and poor eye contact, slow movement, muted affect, low energy level, and minimal smiling or laughter (Annen, Roser, & Brune, 2012).

## Self-Report Questionnaires

Depressive and bipolar disorders involve severe changes in emotions and thoughts, so clients are often asked to rate their symptoms on questionnaires. Self-report questionnaires for people with depression focus on recent depressive symptoms, problematic thoughts, and hopelessness. A common self-report measure is the *Beck Depression Inventory—II*, which addresses negative attitudes toward oneself, level of impairment due to depression, and physical symptoms (Beck, Steer, & Brown, 1996; Vanheule, Desmet, Groenvynck, Rosseel, & Fontaine, 2008). A child version of this scale is also available; selected items are listed in **Table 7.12** (Garcia, Aluja, &

## Table 7.12

### Sample Items from the Children's Depression Inventory

*Choose one:*
► am sad once in a while.
► am sad many times.
► am sad all the time.

*Choose one:*
► do not think about killing myself.
► think about killing myself, but I would not do it.
► want to kill myself.

*Choose one:*
► nobody really loves me.
► am not sure if anybody loves me.
► am sure that somebody loves me.

## Table 7.13

### Automatic Thoughts Questionnaire-Revised

Instructions: Listed below are a variety of thoughts that pop into people's heads. Please read each thought and indicate how frequently, if at all, the thought occurred to you over the last week. Please read each item carefully and circle the appropriate answers in the following fashion: 0 = "not at all," 1 = "sometimes," 2 = "moderately often," 3 = "often," and 4 = "all the time."

| Responses | Thoughts |
|---|---|
| 0 1 2 3 4 | 1. I feel like I'm up against the world. |
| 0 1 2 3 4 | 2. I'm no good. |
| 0 1 2 3 4 | 3. I'm proud of myself. |
| 0 1 2 3 4 | 4. Why can't I ever succeed? |

Remember, each sentence that you read is a thought that you may have had often, less frequently, or not at all. Tell us how often over the last week you have had each of the thoughts.

| Responses | Thoughts |
|---|---|
| 0 1 2 3 4 | 5. No one understands me. |
| 0 1 2 3 4 | 6. I've let people down. |
| 0 1 2 3 4 | 7. I feel fine. |
| 0 1 2 3 4 | 8. I don't think I can go on. |
| 0 1 2 3 4 | 9. I wish I were a better person |
| 0 1 2 3 4 | 10. No matter what happens, I know I'll make it. |
| 0 1 2 3 4 | 11. I'm so weak. |
| 0 1 2 3 4 | 12. My life's not going the way I want it to. |
| 0 1 2 3 4 | 13. I can accomplish anything. |
| 0 1 2 3 4 | 14. I'm so disappointed in myself. |
| 0 1 2 3 4 | 15. Nothing feels good anymore. |
| 0 1 2 3 4 | 16. I feel good. |
| 0 1 2 3 4 | 17. I can't stand this anymore. |

Del Barrio, 2008; Kovacs, 1996). The *Beck Hopelessness Scale* assesses level of pessimism about the future and strongly relates to suicidal behavior (Beck & Steer, 1988; Hanna et al., 2011). The *Automatic Thoughts Questionnaire—Revised* assesses negative thoughts common to people with depression (see **Table 7.13**; Safren et al., 2000).

The interview remains a dominant psychological approach for assessing people with bipolar-related disorders (Miller, Johnson, & Eisner, 2009). However, some measures assess self-reported symptoms of mania and hypomania. Examples include the *General Behavior Inventory* and *Hypomanic Personality Scale* (Schalet, Durbin, & Revelle, 2011; Youngstrom, Findling, Danielson, & Calabrese, 2001). Reports from significant others in a person's environment may also be useful, and we discuss these methods next.

## Self-Monitoring and Observations from Others

People with depressive and bipolar disorders can monitor and log their own symptoms on a daily basis. We discussed in Chapter 5 that daily self-monitoring reduces the need to recall events and increases focus and self-awareness on one's symptoms. For people with depressive and bipolar disorders, important information to record each day may include ratings of sadness or euphoria, activities with others, attendance at work or school, negative or suicidal thoughts, eating and sleeping patterns, and unpleasant physical symptoms, among other topics. Others who know a client well can also record her more obvious mood symptoms, such as grandiosity like Katey's one-time belief she could fly. This applies especially to people with bipolar disorder—Katey's therapist made sure family members and friends helped monitor Katey's mood and behavior between treatment sessions.

## Laboratory Assessment

People with depressive disorders can have marked changes in hormones or neurotransmitters, so laboratory assessment techniques may apply. The *dexamethasone suppression test* (DST) involves injecting a person with dexamethasone, which is a corticosteroid. Dexamethasone is similar to cortisol and decreases the pituitary gland's release of adrenocorticotropic hormone, which in turn decreases release of cortisol from the adrenal gland. Recall that people with depression have differences in the hypothalamic-pituitary-adrenal axis. Cortisol levels from dexamethasone decline over time for most people but remain high—or not suppressed—in people with major depression (see **Figure 7.23**).

Some researchers have found DST results to relate closely to depression, but the results can also characterize people with other mental and medical or hormonal disorders such as Cushing's syndrome (Aytug, Laws, & Vance, 2012; Sher, 2006). Other laboratory assessments for this population include tests for neurotransmitter and hormonal or thyroid levels as well as sleep studies. Laboratory assessments are costly and require a lot of time, however, and so are more common in research than clinical settings.

## Assessment of Suicide

Recall that suicidality is common in people with depression and mania, as it was for Katey. A critical area of assessing depressive and bipolar disorders, therefore, is suicidal thoughts and behaviors. Therapists usually address suicidality by asking clients if they have thoughts of harming themselves. Most people accurately answer this question. Therapists also study a person's history and current risk factors to determine the likelihood he may commit suicide. We mentioned earlier that high-risk factors for suicide include being male, elderly, single, European American, unemployed, or socially isolated.

People at risk for suicidal behavior also tend to have a mental disorder, have experienced a recent and stressful life event, feel socially alienated and a burden to others, and are sad, agitated, or angry (Anestis, Bagge, Tull, & Joiner, 2011; Stolberg, Clark, & Bongar, 2002). People who feel a strong sense of **hopelessness**, or a feeling they have no options or control over situations in their lives, are at high risk for suicide (Hawton, Comabella, Haw, & Saunders, 2013). This was true for Katey, although she did not currently have thoughts of harming herself. Still, her therapist continued to assess for possible suicidality during treatment.

Hirschfeld created a system for assessing suicide (see **Figure 7.24**; Hirschfeld, 2001; Hirschfeld & Russell, 1997). Following a consideration of major risk factors, therapists are encouraged to ask about recent symptoms of depression or anxiety and substance use. Risk can then be determined even further by asking specific questions about the detail of one's plan to commit suicide. Someone who has a carefully designed plan will tend to be at high risk for doing so. Questions should also surround access to weapons, willingness to die, psychotic symptoms such as hearing voices, previous suicide attempts, family history of suicide, and ability to resist the act of suicide (Simon & Hales, 2012). If a person is at high and imminent risk for committing suicide, a therapist must take drastic action to prevent the act. We discuss these clinical actions further in the later treatment section.

Researchers also use *retrospective analysis* to examine people who have attempted or completed suicide. Retrospective analysis, sometimes called a *psychological autopsy,* may involve interviewing family members and friends, examining suicide notes, and evaluating medical records (Conner et al., 2011). One retrospective study of youth revealed that interpersonal conflicts often led to suicide attempt or completion. These conflicts most often involved a fight with parents, end of a relationship, or a disagreement with a significant other. Financial problems, maltreatment, and mental disorder were also commonly present (Hagedorn & Omar, 2002).

## Biological Treatment of Depressive and Bipolar Disorders and Suicide

Biological treatments for people with depressive and bipolar disorders include medication, electroconvulsive therapy, repetitive transcranial magnetic stimulation, and light therapy.

### MEDICATION

Antidepressant medications are often helpful for people with depression. Recall from Chapter 2 that antidepressants increase serotonin and norepinephrine in the brain, often by blocking reuptake of these neurotransmitters. Many antidepressants are thus called **selective serotonin reuptake inhibitors**, or SSRIs (see **Table 7.14**). SSRIs are popular because they affect serotonin-based areas of the brain specifically and not other neurotransmitter systems. Side effects thus tend to be limited, although they do exist.

Common side effects of SSRIs include nausea, headache, agitation, sweating, gastrointestinal problems, sexual dysfunction, and insomnia (Howland, 2007). SSRIs have been associated with increased risk of self-harm and suicide attempt, especially for children and adolescents (Gunnell, Saperia, & Ashby, 2005; Hetrick,

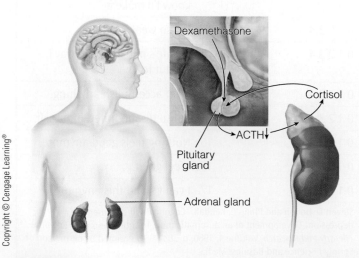

**FIGURE 7.23  PRIMARY BODILY FUNCTIONS INVOLVED IN THE DEXAMETHASONE SUPPRESSION TEST (DST)**

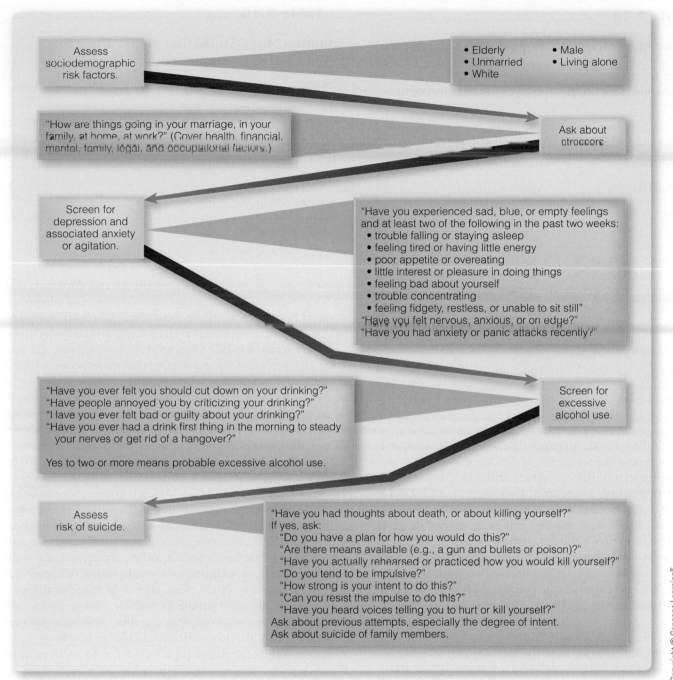

**FIGURE 7.24** SCHEMATIC FOR ASSESSMENT OF SUICIDALITY

Merry, McKenzie, Sindahl, & Proctor, 2007). SSRIs may relate to suicide attempt because a person with depression has more energy after taking the drugs but uses this energy for self-harm.

SSRIs have largely replaced **tricyclic antidepressants** (see Table 7.14) that produced the same neurotransmitter effect but had more side effects. Tricyclics affect serotonin as well as norepinephrine and other neurotransmitter systems. Side effects of tricyclics include a wide range of cardiovascular, muscular, allergic, gastrointestinal, endocrinological, and other symptoms. Tricyclics and SSRIs are both effective, but many

physicians and patients prefer SSRIs because of their fewer side effects (Arroll et al., 2005). Tricyclics may be used if a person does not respond well to an SSRI.

Other antidepressants are available if SSRIs or tricyclics are not effective (see Table 7.14). **Monoamine oxidase inhibitors** (MAOIs) enhance *tyramine* to increase norepinephrine and serotonin. Unfortunately, this also means a person on MAOIs must abstain from various foods such as aged cheese and substances such as cold medications, or a toxic reaction could occur. Severe side effects are common to these drugs

## Table 7.14

### Common Medications for People with Depression

| Selective serotonin reuptake inhibitors (SSRIs): | Tricyclic antidepressants: |
|---|---|
| Citalopram (Celexa) | Anafranil (Clomipramine) |
| Escitalopram oxalate (Lexapro) | Elavil (Amitriptyline) |
| Fluoxetine (Prozac) | Norpramin (Desipramine) |
| Fluvoxamine (Luvox) | Sinequan (Doxepin) |
| Paroxetine (Paxil) | |
| Sertraline (Zoloft) | |
| **Monoamine oxidase inhibitors (MAOIs):** | **Others:** |
| Marplan (Isocarboxazid) | Effexor (Venlafaxine) |
| Nardil (Phenelzine) | Wellbutrin (Bupropion) |
| Parnate (Tranylcypromine) | Remeron (Mirtazapine) |
| | Duloxetine (Cymbalta) |

## Table 7.15

### Common Mood-Stabilizing Medications for People with Bipolar Disorder

| |
|---|
| Carbamazepine (Tegretol) |
| Divalproex (Depakote) |
| Lamotrigine (Lamictal) |
| Lithium (Eskalith) |
| Olanzapine (Zyprexa) |
| Thorazine (Chlorpromazine) |

as well, including agitation, manic-like symptoms, weakness, dizziness, and nausea.

In addition to SSRIs, tricyclics, and MAOIs, other antidepressants include *Wellbutrin* (bupropion) and *Effexor* (venlafaxine) to increase norepinephrine (see Table 7.14; Hewett et al., 2010). Side effects of these drugs can be quite severe: side effects of Wellbutrin include dizziness, tachycardia (fast heart rate), nausea, weight loss, excessive sweating, severe headache, blurred vision, insomnia, and agitation. Many people with depression also take *St. John's wort,* an herbal extract found in any drugstore. However, its effectiveness for depression seems no different from placebo (Hypericum Depression Trial Study Group, 2002).

Antidepressants work well for people with depression, but they may take 6 weeks or more to achieve an adequate effect (Rayner et al., 2011). Overdose of antidepressants is also a common method of suicide. Adding other crisis management procedures is thus indicated when a person is suicidal (see later section). Antidepressants may be less effective when a person's depression has psychotic features, is seasonal in nature, or is extremely severe. Antidepressants by themselves are effective in about 60 to 70 percent of cases compared with 30 percent for placebo control participants (Gitlin, 2010). Medication is more effective for people with fewer comorbid disorders, less severe depression, and better social support (Bagby, Ryder, & Cristi, 2002; Fournier et al., 2010).

Medication for people with bipolar disorder involves **mood-stabilizing drugs** (see **Table 7.15**; Berk, Dodd, & Berk, 2005). *Lithium* is most effective for preventing future manic episodes and

suicide because it decreases norepinephrine and dopamine and increases serotonin. The drug also affects thyroid and adrenocorticotropic hormones, which we mentioned earlier with respect to the dexamethasone suppression test (Chenu & Bourin, 2006).

Lithium can be highly toxic, so periodic blood tests are necessary. Lithium's toxicity and the fact that many people with bipolar disorder want to keep their euphoria or have poor insight can make compliance to the medication problematic (Busby & Sajatovic, 2010). Side effects of lithium can include vomiting, weakness, cardiovascular and urinary problems, thyroid abnormalities, dizziness, confusion, muscle tremor, and drowsiness.

If lithium is not effective alone, then *divalproex* may also be prescribed. Divalproex is an anticonvulsant drug that increases gamma-aminobutyric acid (GABA) levels and creates a sedating effect (Johannessen Landmark, 2008). The drug may be especially useful for people with rapid cycling and mixed features (Kemp et al., 2009). In severe cases of bipolar disorder, lithium and divalproex are used with another anticonvulsant such as *carbamazepine* or antipsychotic medications (Chapter 12; Li, Frye, & Shelton, 2012). Side effects of mood-stabilizing drugs include digestive problems, muscle tremor and weakness, dizziness, nausea, vomiting, diarrhea, and thrombocytopenia (low blood platelets, which could lead to bleeding).

Mood-stabilizing drugs are effective for 46 to 58 percent of people with acute mania compared to 30 percent for placebo (Baldessarini, 2013). The combination of lithium and carbamazepine seems more effective than either drug alone, and *lamotrigine* (another anticonvulsant) seems better for preventing depression after a manic episode than treating mania per se (Cookson & Elliott, 2006; Goodnick, 2006). People who respond best to these drugs have less severe bipolar disorder and continue to take their medication (Baldessarini, Perry, & Pike, 2008; Maj, 1999). Katey took lithium and divalproex and did appear calmer during treatment.

### ELECTROCONVULSIVE THERAPY

An unusual but often effective treatment for people with very severe or melancholic depression is **electroconvulsive therapy**, or ECT. Sometimes known as "shock therapy,"

ECT involves placing one or two electrodes on a person's head and deliberately inducing a seizure into the brain via shock for 0.5 to 2.0 seconds. The person first receives sedative medication to prevent convulsions. People with severe depressive symptoms such as difficulty moving who have not responded to medication may receive ECT in an inpatient psychiatric setting. The process usually requires 6 to 12 sessions over 2 to 4 weeks, and common side effects include temporary memory loss and confusion (APA, 2001; Porter, Douglas, & Knight, 2008).

ECT is generally effective for people with very severe depression, even more so than medication, especially if two electrodes and higher dosage is used. Relapse rates can be high, however (UK ECT Review Group, 2003). People with mania can also benefit from ECT, particularly those who do not respond to medication (APA, 2001; Mohan, Tharyan, Alexander, & Raveendran, 2009). How ECT works is not completely clear, but repeated electroconvulsive shock in primates produces new neurons in the hippocampus (Perera et al., 2007). ECT remains a common but still controversial treatment (see **Box 7.2**).

## REPETITIVE TRANSCRANIAL MAGNETIC STIMULATION

An alternative to ECT is **repetitive transcranial magnetic stimulation** (rTMS), which involves placing an electromagnetic coil on a person's scalp and introducing a pulsating,

high-intensity current. The current produces a magnetic field lasting 100 to 200 microseconds, and the procedure is less invasive than ECT (Couturier, 2005). rTMS may increase the brain's metabolism of glucose and blood flow to the prefrontal cortex, but the procedure remains somewhat controversial and perhaps less effective than other treatment methods (George et al., 2009). People with major depression respond better to rTMS (24.7 percent) compared to placebo (6.8 percent) (Berlim, Van den Eynde, & Daskalakis, 2012). rTMS may also be effective for people with mania (Praharaj, Ram, & Arora, 2009).

## LIGHT THERAPY

An innovative treatment for people with seasonal depression, especially those primarily depressed in winter months, is *light therapy*. Light therapy generally consists of having a person sit before a bright light of 2,000 to 10,000 lux (a unit of illumination) for 30 to 120 minutes per day during the winter. Traditional light therapy involved large light "boxes," but modern devices include smaller towers a person can see while reading or working on a computer. The therapy is usually administered in the morning or evening and may work by enhancing photon absorption or by adjusting circadian rhythms or melatonin levels. More than half of people with seasonal

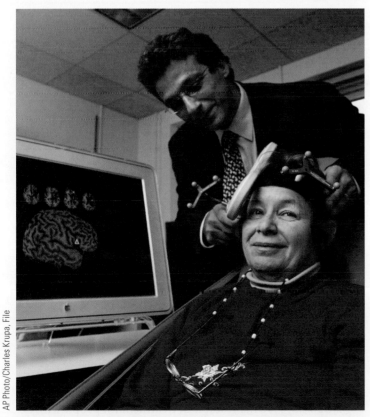

Repetitive transcranial magnetic stimulation (rTMS) is a treatment for people with depression.

Light therapy may be especially useful for people with seasonal depression.

---

## BOX 7.2 Focus on Law and Ethics

### Ethical Dilemmas in Electroconvulsive Therapy

Electroconvulsive therapy (ECT) is an effective treatment for people with severe depression. Still, ECT remains controversial because many people view the procedure with alarm and because researchers are still unsure how ECT works. Ottosson and Fink (2004) outlined several ethical principles for therapists who consider ECT. These principles include *beneficence* (does the procedure help the person?), *nonmaleficence* (does the procedure harm the person in any way?), *respect for autonomy* (is the person fully informed of the benefits and risks of the procedure?), and *justice* (does the procedure preserve the person's dignity?).

These principles can create ethical dilemmas. Ottosson and Fink outlined these dilemmas in vignettes. One vignette involves an elderly woman with cardiovascular problems and severe depression. Even if ECT is the preferred choice of treatment in this situation, should it be used at the risk of worsening her cardiovascular symptoms? In another vignette, a person with severe depression is hospitalized after a suicide attempt and too distraught to speak with doctors. Even if ECT might work, would doing so be advisable because the person cannot give proper consent or understand the treatment?

Other vignettes create additional questions. What if a person gives consent for ECT but family members adamantly oppose the treatment? What if ECT allows a person to become legally competent to stand trial for a terrible crime? What if a person refuses ECT but continues to be suicidal? Answering these questions is difficult and requires a thorough review of the ethical principles outlined by Ottosson and Fink. What would you do in these situations?

---

depression respond positively to light therapy, and the procedure may also be useful for some people with nonseasonal depression (Even, Schroder, Friedman, & Rouillon, 2008; Rastad, Ulfberg, & Lindberg, 2008).

## Psychological Treatments for Depressive and Bipolar Disorders and Suicide

Psychological treatments are quite effective for mild and moderate mood problems and include behavioral activation, cognitive therapy, mindfulness, interpersonal therapy, and family and marital therapy. Most of these apply best to depression but some can apply to bipolar disorder as well. We next discuss psychological treatments for depressive and bipolar disorders and suicide.

### BEHAVIORAL ACTIVATION AND RELATED THERAPIES

People with depression often isolate themselves from others and lose interest in previously pleasurable activities. Others may then provide sympathy and attention and socially reinforce depressed behavior. Therapists rely on *behavioral activation* to address this process. Essential components of behavioral activation include psychoeducation about depression, increasing daily activities and exercise, and rewarding progress. Specific activities a therapist may focus on include the following:

- Educational and creative activities such as learning a musical instrument or engaging in photography
- Domestic activities such as housecleaning or cooking
- Health and appearance activities such as going to the dentist and shopping for new clothes

- Leisure activities such as walking in the park and increased exercise
- Religious activities such as going to church

The overall goal of behavioral activation is to get a person more involved with daily social activities that will help produce positive feelings of self-esteem (Lejuez, Hopko, Acierno, Daughters, & Pagoto, 2011; Sturmey, 2009). Behavioral activation may be combined with other behavioral approaches as well:

- *Contingency management* may involve teaching significant others not to reinforce depressive behavior and instead reinforce active, prosocial behavior.
- *Self-control therapy* may involve having a person reinforce herself for active, nondepressed behaviors.
- *Social skills training* may help a person, especially an adolescent with depression, improve methods of social interaction, including making eye contact, smiling more, and discussing topics other than depression.
- *Coping* or *problem-solving skills training* may be used to help people find effective solutions for problems instead of avoiding them.

Therapists often combine behavioral techniques with other psychological approaches such as reminiscence therapy (see **Box 7.3**) and cognitive therapy, which we describe next.

### COGNITIVE THERAPY

*Cognitive therapy* is a main staple of treatment for people with depressive and bipolar disorders. We discussed in Chapters 5 and 6 that cognitive therapy involves examining a person's negative

## BOX 7.3 Focus on Diversity

### Depression in the Elderly

Many people think of depression as a condition that largely affects adolescents and young adults, but researchers have focused on another population that has more than its share of depression: the elderly. Estimates are that as many as 10 to 25 percent of people aged over 65 years have symptoms of depression and 1 to 5 percent have major depressive disorder. Rate of suicide in this group has also greatly increased over the past several decades, especially among people ages 80 to 84 years (Blazer, 2002).

Depression among the elderly is sometimes difficult to detect for several reasons. First, many older people with depression focus on complaints of physical symptoms of their depression rather than mood. Second, symptoms of depression such as withdrawal or motivation loss may be thought of by others as a desire to relax during retirement or simply signs of "old age." Third, symptoms of sadness may be dismissed as simple bereavement over friends who begin to pass away. Fourth, symptoms of depression often mimic those seen in dementia (see Chapter 14), especially slowed speech and movement and difficulties in memory and concentration. What might initially appear to be Alzheimer's disease may actually be depression.

Treating depression in the elderly often involves cognitive and family therapy as well as medication. One treatment designed specifically for older people with depression is **reminiscence therapy.** Reminiscence therapy involves a systematic review and discussion of each phase of a person's life, from birth to present, with a particular focus on trying to resolve conflicts and regrets. The therapy seems generally effective for older people with depression, but more research is needed to see what types of people might benefit most (Chiang et al., 2010).

*Jochem Wijnands/Picture Contact BV/Alamy*

---

statements and encouraging her to challenge her thoughts. Cognitive therapy helps people change their ways of reasoning about the environment and see the positive and realistic side of things as well as the negative. A person also learns about the relationship between thoughts, emotion, and behavior. One may believe he will fail a test, become sullen and withdrawn from others, and fail to study or prepare for the test. Becoming aware of these kinds of sequences and using cognitive techniques will help him refrain from such catastrophic thinking and problematic behaviors.

Cognitive therapy for depression entails examining evidence for and against a certain thought, hypothesis testing to see the actual chances something bad will happen, and decatastrophizing worst-case scenarios. The main goals of cognitive therapy for depression are to increase a person's ability to challenge negative thoughts and develop a sense of control over life events that seem unpredictable and overwhelming. Cognitive therapy helps a person who believes he will fail an upcoming test to learn how to realistically appraise whether failure will *actually* happen and how to properly study so failure is less likely to happen.

Cognitive therapy for depression is certainly better than no treatment and appears to be as effective as medication. Cognitive therapy may produce better longer-term results than medication because clients have learned specific skills to combat depressive thoughts. Cognitive therapy with medication is a standard treatment for depression in many clinical settings, but the therapy may be less effective for people with severe depression or those actively suicidal (Fournier et al., 2009; Gibbons et al., 2010).

Cognitive therapy can also be effective for bipolar disorder (Ball et al., 2006; Lam, Hayward, Watkins, Wright, & Sham, 2005). One main goal of this approach, as with depression, is to challenge and change unrealistic beliefs. Many people with bipolar disorder mistakenly believe that euphoria will improve their quality of life when in fact it often leads to self-destructive behavior. Cognitive therapy for bipolar disorder also concentrates on improving problem-solving skills, organization, memory, social support, and safety behaviors; avoiding high-risk behaviors such as substance use; and recognizing early warning signs of mania. This may also involve daily thought records, consultations with friends and family members, and strategies to delay impulsive behaviors (Newman et al., 2002). Cognitive therapy for bipolar disorder also aims to enhance medication compliance.

## MINDFULNESS

Recall from Chapter 5 that mindfulness is a relatively new therapy to help people understand and accept their symptoms but still live a normal life. We discussed how mindfulness for anxiety-related disorder involves greater awareness and acceptance of symptoms and how symptoms can be experienced without severe avoidance or other impairment. Therapists also apply mindfulness to people with depression and focus on helping people experience the present rather than dwell on past failures or negative expectations about the future. A therapist encourages a client to be aware of her body and movement in the here and now and to use meditation to enhance this awareness (Kingston, Dooley, Bates, Lawlor, & Malone, 2007).

Some of the most problematic aspects of depression are troublesome emotions, thoughts, and physical behaviors. A therapist engaging in mindfulness thus encourages a client to view sad mood, thoughts, and physical feelings as events that pass through the mind and not as indicators of reality (Ma & Teasdale, 2004). Clients are encouraged to disengage from habitual thoughts and focus on "being" in the moment. Therapists often combine mindfulness with cognitive therapy for individuals or groups. Mindfulness is effective for treating depression and may be especially helpful for preventing relapse (Piet & Hougaard, 2011).

## INTERPERSONAL THERAPY

Another psychological approach to treating depressive and bipolar disorders is *interpersonal therapy,* or IPT. The basis of IPT is that a person's attachment or relationships with others are key to mental health. IPT focuses on repairing problematic relationships or coping with loss of close relationships (Weissman, 2007; Weissman & Verdeli, 2012). IPT concentrates on four main categories of relationship difficulty:

1. *Grief* due to the loss of a loved one
2. *Role disputes* with others such as a spouse, partner, parent, coworker, or friend
3. *Role transitions* or major changes in a person's life, such as ending a relationship, starting a new job, coping with an illness, or retiring from one's career
4. *Interpersonal deficits* such as lack of social skill and trouble maintaining relationships with others

Interpersonal therapy is an *eclectic* approach, or one that uses techniques from different theoretical orientations such as psychodynamic, cognitive, behavioral, and family systems approaches. Therapists who use IPT for depression concentrate on exploring a person's unrealistic expectations of others, solving interpersonal problems effectively, finding new friends, and improving methods of good communication. IPT is especially useful if a person's depression stems from problematic relationships with others, but it is useful as well as part of an overall treatment plan with cognitive therapy and medication (Cuijpers et al., 2011; Weissman & Markowitz, 2002). IPT may also be useful for people with bipolar disorder, especially when therapists link the approach to scheduling regular patterns of sleep (Miklowitz & Scott, 2009).

## FAMILY AND MARITAL THERAPY

Family and marital therapy for depressive and bipolar disorders may be conducted within the context of IPT or separately. Family therapy is especially helpful for families marked by high expressed emotion, or excessive hostility, criticism, and overinvolvement. Family therapy is particularly useful for adolescents with depression. Family therapists focus on improving communication and problem-solving skills among family members. Contingency management, in which a person with depression is encouraged to be active and associate with others, is a common ingredient of family therapy as well. Parents who show withdrawn behavior may also receive treatment for their depression or counseling regarding their child-rearing practices. Therapy focusing on family members or parents regarding depression is generally effective for parents and children (Diamond et al., 2010; Lemmens, Eisler, Buysse, Heene, & Demyttenaere, 2009).

Katey's treatment did include family members who provided social and financial support and who helped her remain on medication. Katey's mother also had symptoms of bipolar disorder, so family members learned about the condition and what symptoms to monitor. Katey eventually moved in with her parents to help stabilize her condition, so therapy also involved reducing role conflicts and improving communication among family members. Family therapy for bipolar disorder is often important to prevent relapse, as was true for Katey (Zaretsky, Rizvi, & Parikh, 2007).

Marital therapy is also commonly used to treat depression, especially in women. A marital therapist will try to improve communication and problem-solving skills and increase mutually pleasurable and prosocial behavior such as scheduling activities that a husband *and* wife like to do. Cognitive-behavioral components for treating depression are used as well. Marital therapy can be an effective treatment for depression, especially when marital issues are a main reason for depression and when medication is also used (Pampallona, Bollini, Tibaldi, Kupelnick, & Munizza, 2004). A person with depression is also more likely to remain in therapy if his or her partner attends therapy than if the person only takes medication (Leff et al., 2000; Mead, 2002). Intervention that includes partners may be useful as well for helping people

Marital therapy is an effective treatment for depression, especially in women.

with bipolar disorder remain on their medication (D'Souza, Piskulic, & Sundram, 2010).

Psychological treatments for depression are quite effective by themselves but are commonly supplemented by medication. Psychological treatments for bipolar disorder, however, are *almost always* supplemented with medication, as was true for Katey. In severe cases of depressive or bipolar disorder, biological treatments are often used first and may be much more effective than psychological treatments.

## TREATMENT OF SUICIDALITY

What should a therapist do if someone is suicidal? Therapists usually determine if risk of suicide is imminent, meaning the person is likely to commit suicide if left alone. In cases of suicidality, ethical issues of therapist–client confidentiality are not as important as client safety, so a therapist must do what is necessary to protect a client's life. If suicide seems imminent, as was true for Katey, then a therapist typically arranges hospitalization in an inpatient psychiatric unit. If a person calls a therapist and threatens suicide, the therapist may call an ambulance or the police to have the person transferred to a hospital. Often this also involves informing people close to the person, such as a spouse or partner, and working closely with hospital staff to help the person cope with their current crisis. Medication, group therapy, and constant supervision are strategies to address people in hospital settings who are suicidal (Tishler & Reiss, 2009).

If a person is not at imminent risk for suicide but might be so in coming hours or days, therapists may draft a *no-suicide contract*. This is an agreement, often signed by a therapist and client, in which the client agrees to contact and speak with the therapist before any self-destructive act. Contracts are not a perfect intervention, but clients may adhere to the contracts and refrain from impulsive behavior. Others argue that a client's *commitment to a treatment statement* is more effective than a no-suicide contract. A commitment to treatment statement represents an agreement between a therapist and client that the client will commit to the treatment process and to living, openly communicate about suicidal thoughts and urges, and access emergency care when needed (Rudd, Mandrusiak, & Joiner, 2006).

A therapist will also contact the person frequently during the week and encourage significant others, with the client's permission, to closely supervise the client and remove potentially lethal items such as firearms and medications from the home. Issues related to thoughts of suicide, such as a recent stressful life event or substance use, are addressed as well (Chiles & Strosahl, 2005; Hirschfeld & Russell, 1997).

## What If I Am Sad or Have a Depressive or Bipolar Disorder?

The answers to some basic questions (**Table 7.16**) may help you decide if you wish further assessment or even treatment for a possible depressive or bipolar disorder. If you find the answer to most of these questions is yes, then you may wish to consult a clinical psychologist, psychiatrist, or other mental health

**Table 7.16**

| Screening Questions for Depressive and Bipolar Disorder |
| --- |
| Do you find any of the mood symptoms described in this chapter apply to you much more so than most people your age? |
| Are there many things you would like to do but cannot because you feel too sad? |
| Are you greatly troubled by your mood symptoms? |
| Do other people notice your sadness or euphoria or encourage you to seek help? |
| Does your sadness or euphoria last much of the time, even when nothing stressful is happening? |
| Has your work or social life or sleep suffered a lot because of sadness or euphoria? |
| Do you get extremely upset over even little things most of the time? |
| Have you experienced a stressful life event that you just cannot seem to put behind you? |
| Do you feel sad, irritable, tense, and pessimistic much of the time? |
| If you could make your life better, would it include feeling less sad? |

professional (Chapter 15). Additional professional information is available from the Association for Behavioral and Cognitive Therapies (www.abct.org) and the National Alliance for Research on Schizophrenia and Depression (www.narsad.org).

If you think you have a depressive or bipolar disorder, consult with a mental health professional that specializes in this problem. Do not diagnose yourself. If you think you have sadness or euphoria but not necessarily a depressive or bipolar disorder, then becoming more socially active, changing your thoughts, and resolving interpersonal conflicts may be best. Talk about your feelings with family and friends, or attend a depression screening in your community. If you think you have severe symptoms, however, then be sure to seek consultation from a qualified therapist.

## Long-Term Outcome for People with Depressive and Bipolar Disorders and Suicide

What is the long-term picture, or prognosis, for people with depressive and bipolar disorders like Katey? Factors that predict good treatment outcome for depression include better treatment compliance and completion, longer and more complex treatment, early recovery from depression, and fewer past episodes of major depression and residual symptoms. Other factors related to good outcome include fewer stressful life events and comorbid diagnoses, good family and marital relationships, effective communication skills, high self-esteem, and older age of onset (Fournier et al., 2009;

Pampallona et al., 2004; Sherrington, Hawton, Fagg, Andrew, & Smith, 2001).

For people who have experienced a major depressive episode, risk of a second episode in their lifetime is about 50 percent. For people who have experienced two major depressive episodes, risk of a third episode is about 70 percent. For people who have experienced three or four major depressive episodes, risk of more episodes is about 80 to 90 percent. About 27 percent of people with major depression have three or more major depressive episodes in their lifetime, with the average being four. Men with depression are also more likely to die from cardiovascular and other problems than people without depression (Dubovsky & Dubovsky, 2002; Richards, 2011). Recurring depression is related to younger age of onset, medication discontinuation, persistent symptoms of dysthymia and other mental disorders, and chronic medical illness (Eaton et al., 2008; Merikangas et al., 2003).

For those in treatment for bipolar disorder, similar prognostic factors are evident. People with bipolar disorder who respond well to treatment tend to have more classic forms of the disorder, with less rapid cycling or mixed features. Good treatment outcome is related to medication compliance and effectiveness (especially *early* in the disorder), better cognitive functioning, fewer comorbid diagnoses, less expressed emotion in families, ongoing contact with mental health professionals, good occupational status, and female gender (Green, 2006; Keck, 2006).

People with bipolar disorder tend to go in three different directions over time (Goldberg, Garno, & Harrow, 2005). About 15 to 20 percent of people with bipolar disorder eventually have *good* overall functioning, meaning they generally remain on their medication and have few symptoms of mania or depression. About 10 to 15 percent of people with bipolar disorder eventually have *poor* overall functioning, meaning they continue to experience severe manic or depressive episodes that require hospitalization. Poor outcome is linked to fast recurrences of these episodes, rapid cycling, substance use, and family history of the disorder. About 50 to 60 percent of people with bipolar disorder eventually have *moderate* overall functioning, meaning their symptoms and ability to function on a daily basis wax and wane over time (Goldberg & Harrow, 1999; Treuer & Tohen, 2009).

What about people released from a hospital following suicidal behavior? About 6 percent of people hospitalized following suicidal behavior commit suicide within 1 week of hospital discharge. People who commit suicide soon after discharge tend to be female, single, and have a depressive or psychotic disorder. This group also chooses suicidal methods that are readily available, such as drowning, jumping, or hanging (Pirkola, Sohlman, & Wahlbeck, 2005). Short-term functioning for people with suicidality is good, although long-term outcome is variable.

Katey's long-term prognosis remains unclear. On the plus side, she was currently in treatment and sticking with it, and seemed to have good family support. On the minus side, her mental condition lasted for years without adequate treatment,

she used alcohol and had suicidal behaviors, and she lost her life savings and job. Good outcome will likely have to include ongoing and intense medication and psychological treatment as well as strong support from significant others.

## INTERIM SUMMARY

▶ Assessing people with depressive and bipolar disorders often includes structured and unstructured interviews and self-report questionnaires.

▶ Observations and information from therapists, spouses, partners, children, parents, and others are important for assessing depressive and bipolar disorders.

▶ Laboratory assessments for depression include the dexamethasone test.

▶ Assessing risk of suicide is critical in depressive and bipolar disorders and often focuses on detail of suicide plan, access to weapons, and support from others.

▶ Biological treatment of depressive and bipolar disorders includes selective serotonin reuptake inhibitors (SSRIs), tricyclics, monoamine oxidase inhibitors (MAOIs), and mood-stabilizing drugs.

▶ Electroconvulsive therapy (ECT) involves deliberately inducing a brain seizure to improve very severe depression. Repetitive transcranial magnetic stimulation (rTMS) involves placing an electromagnetic coil on a person's scalp and introducing a current to relieve depressive symptoms.

▶ Light therapy is often used for people with seasonal depression.

▶ Psychological treatment of depressive and bipolar disorders includes behavioral approaches to increase activity and reinforcement from others for prosocial behavior. Cognitive therapy is also a main staple for depressive and bipolar disorders and may be linked to mindfulness.

▶ Interpersonal and marital and family therapists concentrate on improving a person's relationships with others to alleviate symptoms of depressive and bipolar disorders.

▶ Addressing suicidal behavior, sometimes via hospitalization, is a critical aspect of treating people with depressive and bipolar disorders.

▶ Long-term outcome for people with depressive and bipolar disorders is best when they receive early treatment, remain on medication, have fewer comorbid diagnoses, and experience good support from others.

## REVIEW QUESTIONS

1. Outline major assessment techniques for depressive and bipolar disorders, including interviews, self-report questionnaires, observations, and laboratory assessment.
2. What medications help control symptoms of depressive and bipolar disorders? How do they work?
3. Describe electroconvulsive, repetitive transcranial magnetic, and light therapies.
4. What psychological treatment strategies could a mental health professional use to help someone improve interpersonal functioning and mood? How so?

5. What is the prognosis or long-term outcome for people with depressive and bipolar disorders?

# Final Comments

People with depressive and bipolar disorders suffer tremendous distress from swings of emotion, hopelessness, troubling thoughts, and self-destructive behavior. This is important to remember if you or someone you know feels sad or withdrawn from others. Occasional feelings of sadness and euphoria are normal, but they can sometimes linger and get out of control. If they do, then talking to someone about it or contacting a qualified mental health professional is a good idea. You can see how symptoms of depression and anxiety cause so much distress for people, and these symptoms occur together in people with eating disorders, which we discuss in the next chapter.

# Thought Questions

1. Think about television shows or films you have seen that have characters with mood problems. Do you think these characters display realistic or unrealistic symptoms of mood changes? How so?
2. Think about situations that make you most sad, such as illness of a loved one or breakup of a relationship. Think about situations that make you most euphoric, such as a great test grade or a new baby relative. How do you feel physically, what do you think in those situations, and what do you do? Having read the chapter, would you change anything?
3. What would you say to a friend who might be very sad or euphoric and who might be considering suicide?
4. What separates "normal" from "abnormal" mood? Do you think depressive and bipolar disorders have more to do with personal, family, or other factors? Why?
5. What do you think family members and friends could do to reduce severe mood changes in people they know?

# Key Terms

depressive disorder 179
bipolar disorder 179
major depressive episode 179
major depressive disorder 181
persistent depressive disorder (dysthymia) 182
manic episode 183
hypomanic episode 185
premenstrual dysphoric disorder 186
peripartum depression 187
postpartum depression 187
bipolar I disorder 185
bipolar II disorder 189
cyclothymic disorder 189
suicide 189
cognitive distortions 201

negative cognitive triad 201
automatic thoughts 201
hopelessness theory 201
learned helplessness 202
expressed emotion 203
hopelessness 210
selective serotonin reuptake inhibitors (SSRIs) 210
tricyclic antidepressants 211
monoamine oxidase inhibitor (MAOI) 211
mood-stabilizing drugs 212
electroconvulsive therapy (ECT) 212
repetitive transcranial magnetic stimulation (rTMS) 213
reminiscence therapy 215

# Media Resources

## MindTap

MindTap for Kearney and Trull's *Abnormal Psychology and Life: A Dimensional Approach* is a highly personalized fully online learning platform of authoritative content, assignments, and services offering you a tailored presentation of course curriculum created by your instructor. MindTap guides you through the course curriculum via an innovative learning path where you will complete reading assignments, annotate your readings, complete homework, and engage with quizzes and assessments. MindTap includes the Continuum Video Project.

Go to **cengagebrain.com** to access MindTap.

# Eating Disorders

# 8

**CASE:** *Sooki*

**What Do You Think?**

**Weight Concerns, Body Dissatisfaction, and Eating Disorders: What Are They?**

**Eating Disorders: Features and Epidemiology**

**CASE:** *Lisa*

**Stigma Associated with Eating Disorders**
Interim Summary

**Eating Disorders: Causes and Prevention**
Interim Summary
Review Questions

**Eating Disorders: Assessment and Treatment**
Interim Summary
Review Questions

FINAL COMMENTS
THOUGHT QUESTIONS
KEY TERMS
MEDIA RESOURCES

## SPECIAL FEATURES

**CONTINUUM FIGURE 8.1** Continuum of Body Dissatisfaction, Weight Concerns, and Eating Behavior   224–225

**PERSONAL NARRATIVE 8.1** Kitty Westin (Anna's mother)   226–227

**BOX 8.1** | Focus on Gender: Why Is There a Gender Difference in Eating Disorders?   230

## THE CONTINUUM VIDEO PROJECT

*Sara:* **Bulimia Nervosa**   233

**PERSONAL NARRATIVE 8.2** Rachel Webb   239

**BOX 8.2** | Focus on Law and Ethics: How Ethical Are Pro-Ana (Pro-Anorexia) Websites?   243

## CASE: Sooki

**Sooki** is a 19-year-old Asian American college student who is 5 feet 4 inches tall and weighs 90.4 pounds. Friends have not noticed that Sooki has lost so much weight over the last year (25 pounds!) because she wears baggy clothes. About a year ago, Sooki became extremely afraid of becoming fat. She was convinced that weight gain would be the worst thing possible and that her college life would be ruined. Sooki began skipping meals and, when she did eat once or twice a day, consumed only a "salad" or other small items. Her salad consists of four lettuce leaves, part of a carrot, an apple slice, and no dressing. Sooki is preoccupied with food and calories. Every bite of food she eats is carefully considered, and she carries charts that list calories per serving of many foods. She drinks only water and diet soda.

Sooki is obsessed with how much she weighs and how she looks. She owns two scales: one is near her bed and one is in her bathroom. She weighs herself 10 or more times a day. Sooki has told others her butt is too big and her stomach is "poochy." Sooki is markedly underweight but frequently checks her body in the mirror to make sure she is not becoming fat. Her self-esteem depends heavily on her body weight. When Sooki weighs more than 90.0 pounds, she feels bad about herself; when she weighs less than 90.0 pounds, she is perkier. Sooki views weight loss as an impressive achievement in self-discipline. Family members have noticed her weight change and have told Sooki she is underweight. Still, Sooki does not see her eating and low weight as a problem. She hopes to lose more weight by eliminating "fattening" foods from her diet such as apple slices and diet soda. Sooki has kept to herself recently and leaves her room only to attend class.

### What Do You Think?

1. Which of Sooki's symptoms seem typical for a college student, and which seem very different?

2. What external events and internal factors might be responsible for Sooki's problems?

3. What are you curious about regarding Sooki?

4. Does Sooki remind you in any way of yourself or someone you know? How so?

5. How might Sooki's eating problems affect her life in the future?

*©Cameramannz/Shutterstock.com*

## Weight Concerns, Body Dissatisfaction, and Eating Disorders: What Are They?

Have you ever looked at yourself in the mirror and worried you were overweight? Have you ever been concerned about how much you eat? These questions are common for many people, especially in an age when the dangers of obesity seem always to be on the news. Concern about weight is normal and can be adaptive. Achieving and maintaining normal weight is important for reducing risk of heart disease, diabetes, stroke, and other potentially fatal conditions. Regular exercise and good eating habits also improve our mood and reduce stress. Most of us weigh ourselves every so often to check where we are, and this is normal.

Other people take concern about weight to a higher level. People with **weight concerns** feel overweight much of the time, even when they are not, and view their weight negatively. Perhaps you know someone with a thin physique who thinks a lot about weight and exercises vigorously. People with weight concerns focus on how much they weigh during different times of the day and often have a *drive for thinness*. People with weight concerns focus intently on certain areas of their body they would like to tone or decrease in size. Weight concerns are not a problem if a person is not distressed, remains in a normal weight range, and avoids physical damage from overexercising.

Some people with weight concerns adopt a negative self-evaluation of what their body looks like. **Body dissatisfaction** refers to dissatisfaction or distress with one's appearance, an overinvestment in the way one appears, and avoidance of certain situations or things because they elicit body concerns (Grabe & Hyde, 2006; Wojtowicz & von Ranson, 2012). People with body dissatisfaction are more than just concerned about their weight. They are constantly unhappy about their weight and think about what could be different with their appearance. They spend substantial money on exercise equipment and gym memberships but avoid social and other situations in which people might judge their weight negatively. Sooki eventually avoided most situations other than class.

Weight concerns and body dissatisfaction are dimensional constructs, meaning we all have these characteristics to some degree. Some people have *intense* weight concerns and body dissatisfaction that escalate toward an **eating disorder.** People with eating disorders have great worry and distress about their weight and body. Sooki was quite *fearful* of gaining weight. Weight concerns and body dissatisfaction are two of the three key components of an eating disorder. The third major component is **eating problems**, which

their social activities, and experience significant emotional, behavioral, and even medical consequences. People with these characteristics, like Sooki, have an eating disorder.

Eating disorders can be less severe, as when people are highly bothered by their weight and appearance but still eat occasionally (Figure 8.1). Eating disorders can also be more severe, however, when a person stops eating and essentially starves herself to death. Severe eating disorders also involve intense distress and sadness. We cover next the major eating disorders that affect many people like Sooki.

## Eating Disorders: Features and Epidemiology

This section summarizes the major features and other characteristics of the most common eating disorders: anorexia nervosa, bulimia nervosa, and binge eating disorder.

### Anorexia Nervosa

People with **anorexia nervosa** refuse to maintain a minimum, normal body weight, have an intense fear of gaining weight, and show disturbance in the way they view their body shape and weight (see **Table 8.1**; American Psychiatric Association [APA], 2013). Sooki likely met diagnostic criteria for anorexia nervosa because of her low body weight, intense fear of being fat, and disturbed body image. Severity of anorexia nervosa is based partly on body mass index (Table 8.1).

You might think people with anorexia nervosa have no appetite, but they do. In fact, people with anorexia nervosa

A drive for thinness can lead to eating problems or an eating disorder.

involve restricted eating or excessive dieting and lack of control of eating.

**Restricted eating**, or **dieting**, refers to deliberate attempts to limit food intake or change types of foods that are eaten. People with eating disorders focus intently on foods that result in weight gain or loss. Such focus is driven by weight concerns or body dissatisfaction. Sooki rarely ate and maintained very low calorie meals because she believed she was too fat.

**Lack of control over eating** involves inability to keep oneself from eating large amounts of food. People who lack control over eating consume excessive quantities of food. This feature thus has cognitive (believing one has lost control) and behavioral (eating too much) components. People who lack control over eating can gain substantial weight and be considered overweight for someone of their height, age, and gender. Some people may develop *obesity* as a result, but obesity is not considered an eating disorder.

Weight concerns, body dissatisfaction, and eating problems occur along a continuum (see **Figure 8.1**). Most of us have occasional weight concerns or body dissatisfaction that we address or can cope with. Intense weight concerns or body dissatisfaction cause some people, however, to go to extremes to control their weight. These extremes include severely restricted eating, excessive exercise or taking medicine or laxatives that lead to weight loss. These people are highly distressed, limit

**Table 8.1**

**DSM-5 Anorexia Nervosa**

A. Restriction of energy intake relative to requirements, leading to a significantly low body weight in the context of age, sex, developmental trajectory, and physical health. *Significantly low weight* is defined as a weight that is less than minimally normal or, for children and adolescents, less than that minimally expected.

B. Intense fear of gaining weight or of becoming fat, or persistent behavior that interferes with weight gain, even though at a significantly low weight.

C. Disturbance in the way in which one's body weight or shape is experienced, undue influence of body weight or shape on self-evaluation, or persistent lack of recognition of the seriousness of the current low body weight.

Specify if restricting or binge-eating/purging type, partial or full remission, and current severity as mild (BMI ≥ 17 kg/m²), moderate (BMI 16-16.99 kg/m²), severe (BMI 15-15.99 kg/m²), or extreme (BMI < 15 kg/m²).

American Psychiatric Association. (2013). *Diagnostic and statistical manual of mental disorders* (5th ed.). Arlington, VA: American Psychiatric Association.

**CONTINUUM FIGURE 8.1**    Continuum of Body Dissatisfaction, Weight Concerns, and Eating Behavior

| | Normal | Mild |
|---|---|---|
| **Emotions** | Positive feelings about oneself. | Some anxiety about one's body shape and weight. |
| **Cognitions** | "I feel pretty good about my body and about my weight." | "I wish I were more fit and weighed a little less. Maybe I could cut back a bit on my eating." |
| **Behaviors** | Eating without concerns. | Tries to eat less at meals and may skip a meal every now and then. |

Image Source/Jupiter Images

often think about food, as Sooki did, and even prepare elaborate meals for others. Unfortunately, people with anorexia nervosa have an intense dissatisfaction with their bodies and thus fear gaining weight. They are driven to thinness and often look for ways to reduce weight.

People with anorexia nervosa lose weight mainly by eating less and exercising excessively. If they do eat, they avoid foods with the most calories. Many people with anorexia nervosa initially lose weight by eliminating soft drinks or fattening foods such as desserts from their diets. Over time, however, they eliminate more and more foods and increasingly skip meals. These **restricting behaviors** form the basis for one subtype of anorexia nervosa (Table 8.1). Sooki is a member of this restricting subtype.

Others with anorexia nervosa lose weight by binge eating (see later section) and purging. **Purging** refers to ridding oneself of food or bodily fluids (and thus weight) by self-induced vomiting, misusing laxatives or diuretics, or performing enemas. Binge eating and purging form the basis for a second subtype of anorexia nervosa (Table 8.1).

A particularly fascinating feature of anorexia nervosa is a person's belief she is fat despite overwhelming evidence to the contrary. Sooki lost 25 pounds, nearly 20 percent of her body weight, but still saw her buttocks as large and her stomach as "poochy." People with anorexia nervosa have extreme misperceptions about how they look, feeling fat even when clearly emaciated. A good analogy would be the accentuation and distortion of body size and shape that happens to a reflection in a fun house mirror.

People with anorexia nervosa may not appreciate the serious physical and medical consequences of their very low weight. Individuals with anorexia nervosa become emaciated, dehydrated, and hypotensive (low blood pressure). Anemia, kidney dysfunction, cardiovascular problems, dental problems, electrolyte imbalance, and osteoporosis may result as well. Some people with anorexia nervosa eventually die by self-starvation or suicide (see **Personal Narrative 8.1**).

## Bulimia Nervosa

### CASE: Lisa

**Lisa** is a 25-year-old woman in therapy for an eating disorder. She has been overconcerned about her body for many years and said she never felt good about school, friends, or herself if she thought she was overweight. Lisa was never skinny but was not overweight either—it just seemed to her that she was overweight. Lisa was constantly trying to limit her eating and weight by dieting. Unfortunately, her appetite would build over time and erupt into an eating feast. Lisa stocked her house with foods like whole cakes, quarts of ice cream, and packages of Oreos and ate these foods voraciously during her binges. Lisa felt panicked and out of control of her eating when this happened.

Lisa's episodes of overeating became more frequent in the last year, occurring about 5 times a week. This made Lisa even more fearful of gaining weight. She was also embarrassed by the way she dealt with her overeating, which involved vomiting after each binge. She hid her vomiting from others, but her teeth were soon eroding as a result. Lisa's binging and purging continued until one day when she noticed a substantial amount of blood in her vomit. She realized she needed help.

Have you ever eaten so much your stomach hurt? How about feeling guilty after a huge meal? Most of us have overindulged at a buffet or felt self-conscious about eating too many sweets, and this is normal. We are usually concerned about how much we eat and what the consequences might be if we eat too much. Most of us can control our eating and

| Moderate | Eating Disorder — less severe | Eating Disorder — more severe |
|---|---|---|
| Moderately anxious and feels down about body shape and weight. | Intense anxiety and sadness over apparent inability to lose enough weight. | Severe anxiety and depression over one's body shape and weight. |
| "Wow, I feel fat. I need to start cutting back on eating If I don't cut back, I'm going to get even fatter." | "I feel fat all the time, and I wish my body were thinner. I've got to get rid of all these awful calories in my body!" | "I'm extremely fat, and I hate my body! I have to stop eating now! No one understands." |
| Regularly skips meals and eats low calorie foods only. Starts exercising more to lose weight. | Eats one meal a day, usually a salad with no dressing. May purge after meals or take laxatives. | Eats only rarely and when forced to do so: exercises excessively and purges frequently to lose more weight. |

Andrew Fox / Alamy

Obesity, while not physically healthy, is not considered an eating disorder.

understand that overeating occasionally happens. For others like Lisa, however, episodes of overeating are frequent and cause many problems.

**Bulimia nervosa** is marked by binge eating, inappropriate methods to prevent weight gain, and self-evaluation greatly influenced by body shape and weight (see **Table 8.2**; APA, 2013). **Binge eating** means eating an amount of food in a limited time—such as 2 hours or less—that is much larger than most people would eat in that circumstance. Binge eating typically occurs in private and may be triggered by depression, stress, or low self-esteem. Binge eating is also accompanied by lack

of control over eating. Many people who binge are ashamed of their eating problem and hide their symptoms.

People with bulimia nervosa use inappropriate behaviors, or **compensatory behaviors**, to prevent weight gain (see **Table 8.3**). Lisa induced vomiting after a binge, and this method is used by 80 to 90 percent of those who seek treatment for bulimia nervosa. Vomiting is negatively reinforcing (Chapter 2) because it reduces stomach discomfort as well as fear of weight gain. *Purging* compensatory behaviors include vomiting, misuse of laxatives or diuretics, or enemas. *Nonpurging* compensatory behaviors include fasting for several days or exercising excessively (Table 8.3). Compensatory behaviors can lead to serious physical and medical complications. Excessive vomiting can lead to dental problems, swelling of salivary glands, or esophageal problems. Overusing laxatives and diuretics can lead to chronic diarrhea or bowel problems.

People with bulimia nervosa, like those with anorexia nervosa, emphasize body shape and weight to evaluate themselves. The major difference between the disorders is that people with anorexia nervosa are characterized by excessively low weight, whereas people with bulimia nervosa may be normal weight or overweight. Severity of bulimia nervosa is based partly on number of episodes of compensatory behavior per week (Table 8.2).

## Binge Eating Disorder

Some people have recurrent episodes of binge eating but *without* compensatory behaviors like purging, excessive exercise, or fasting. People with **binge eating disorder** experience lack of control over eating during a certain period that leads to discomfort (see **Table 8.4**; APA, 2013). To be diagnosed as such, binge eating must occur, on average, once a week for at least 3 months. Other features of binge eating episodes include eating more rapidly than normal, eating despite feeling uncomfortably full, eating large amounts even when not hungry, eating alone because of embarrassment over quantity of food consumed, and

### Kitty Westin (Anna's mother)

Anna Selina Westin was born on November 27, 1978. I remember her birthday like it was yesterday. She was a beautiful, healthy baby with bright blue eyes, curly blond hair, and a "rose bud" mouth. She grew and developed into a young woman full of life and love, and she had hopes, dreams, and a future full of promise until she became ill with a deadly disorder that affects millions: anorexia. When Anna was 16 years old, she was first diagnosed with anorexia, and on February 17, 2000, Anna committed suicide after struggling with anorexia for 5 years. Anna was only 21 years old when she died.

I write about my experience with Anna hoping that people reading our story will better understand the seriousness of the disorder and how it affects the family. But before I go on, I would like to say that my husband and I are very proud of Anna and the effort she put into fighting her disorder. We feel no shame that she had the disorder or that she committed suicide. We both understand that anorexia is a disorder, not a choice. By telling our story honestly and openly we hope to dispel the stigma and shame often associated with an eating disorder and suicide. Since we made the decision to talk honestly about Anna's life and death, we have opened ourselves up to questions—frequently asked questions are *What were Anna's symptoms?* and *When did you first notice them?*

Photo courtesy of Kitty Westin, The Anna Westin Foundation

Anna Westin

In retrospect, Anna most likely showed signs of developing an eating disorder long before we recognized them. When Anna was a young girl, she was perfectionistic and high achieving and needed to get everything "just right." She was dissatisfied with herself when she had difficulties and was intolerant of her own perceived imperfections. She showed signs of anxiety and had periods of depression from a young age.

Anna was petite, and I remember that she began talking about her size and shape when she was about 15 years old. I recall the day she came home from school very upset because an acquaintance had made a remark about the size of her thighs. This may have been the start of her obsession with being thin. Soon after that incident, she announced she had decided to become a vegetarian. At the time I was not concerned about this (although I was confused). I questioned her commitment to this "lifestyle," and she assured me that she would eat a healthy and balanced diet. I did not know at the time that this behavior was the beginning of restricting and that within a few months Anna would restrict almost all foods. It seemed that almost overnight Anna went from being a personable, caring, and spirited adolescent to being hostile, angry, withdrawn, and uncommunicative. Her weight dropped noticeably, and she avoided all situations with the family that involved food, including family meals.

Anna continually denied that she had any problems eating or issues with her size, but it became apparent that she was ill and getting sicker by the day. We brought her to our family physician for a checkup. The doctor referred her for an evaluation for an eating disorder. Anna was diagnosed with anorexia nervosa. Like most families suddenly faced with the trauma of caring for a seriously ill member, we were not prepared and woefully ignorant when we learned our daughter's diagnosis. Unlike so many other problems like diabetes, cancer, and heart disease, there was little information and support available to help us understand anorexia. We did not know where to turn for education, support, and guidance. We were often confused, always afraid, and sometimes angry.

Anna was first diagnosed and treated for anorexia when she was 16 years

---

feeling disgusted, depressed, or guilty after overeating. Individuals with binge eating disorder are greatly distressed about their behavior. They typically have varying degrees of obesity and may have enrolled in weight control programs.

Binge eating disorder is similar to bulimia nervosa except people with bulimia nervosa regularly engage in compensatory behaviors to prevent weight gain (Thomas, Vartanian, & Brownell, 2009). People with binge eating disorder also binge over a much longer period of time and their binging may be less frantic than those with bulimia nervosa. Severity of binge eating disorder is based partly on number of binge eating episodes per week (Table 8.4).

## Epidemiology of Eating Disorders

Eating disorders are not as common as the anxiety and depressive disorders we discussed in previous chapters, but they do occur frequently enough to be of great concern to mental health professionals. Lifetime prevalence rates for major eating disorders are in **Table 8.5.** Symptoms of eating disorders are also common among adolescents and young adults with other mental disorders. The medical complications of eating disorders can also be quite severe, so researchers have paid great attention to these problems.

Peak age of onset for anorexia nervosa is 15 to 19 years, and the disorder is more common in industrialized societies

old. She was treated successfully in an outpatient program and seemed to recover fully. At that time I did not understand that the relapse rate for eating disorders is high and that we should remain vigilant for a number of years. I wish that someone had told me that the average time between diagnosis and recovery is 7 years; that may have alerted me to the dangers of relapse and we may have done some things differently.

Anna seemed to do well after completing her first treatment for anorexia and she graduated from high school and went on to college. During the ensuing years, she had bouts of depression and anxiety, especially when under stress, but overall she reported feeling healthy and happy. Her anorexia returned, however, and this time she was gravely ill by the time we were able to get her the care she needed. We have tried to determine what triggered her relapse, and nothing has stood out, so we conclude that her biochemistry must have been the primary factor. We were able to get Anna admitted to a specialized eating disorders treatment program, and because she had responded so well the first time, we were not overly concerned and had no reason to doubt that she would fully recover. Anna was a "typical" eating-disordered patient: resistant, angry, and in denial. However, once she was in the program getting the support she needed and restoring her health, she realized the seriousness of her disorder and the importance of the treatment and she became much more cooperative and receptive. Anna was getting the best care available and the program she was in used a multidisciplinary approach that included medical doctors, psychologists, psychiatrists, social workers, registered nurses, dietitians, tutors, physical and occupational therapists, and care managers. In addition to Anna's individual and group therapy, we were involved in family therapy and education groups. We finally felt like we were learning what we needed to know to help Anna. However, the effects anorexia was having on the family were enormous. My husband and I argued over many things including how best to deal with Anna, and our anger and frustration was often directed toward each other. Our younger daughters struggled to understand the disorder and found it difficult to accept that their sister was ill and could possibly die. We all walked on eggshells fearing that if we did or said the wrong thing, we would upset Anna and exacerbate the situation. It was hard to know when we should back off and when to get involved. We were advised not to watch Anna eat, but you tell me how we could do this when we were afraid that our child would die unless she ate? After all, food was the "medicine," and aren't parents supposed to make sure their child takes the medicine required to treat a disorder?

In spite of these things, treatment seemed to be going well. We were able to maintain confidence that Anna was on the road to recovery. Then suddenly we ran into a roadblock we did not expect and it changed everything. The roadblock was our insurance company. They refused to pay for most of the care Anna's medical team recommended, stating it was not medically necessary. Our family was forced to guarantee payment to keep her in the hospital. When Anna heard this, she felt guilty and like she was a burden on our family. We assured her that she needed to concentrate and put her energy into healing and we would worry about the money, but I don't think she was able to hear this. Anna committed suicide a few months later. I don't "blame" the insurance company for her death; I know that anorexia killed her. However, insurance did contribute to her death because they added to her feelings of worthlessness and hopelessness.

There are no adequate words to describe the grief and loss our family felt and continues to feel since Anna died. However, we have been able to transform some of these powerful emotions into something positive by starting a foundation in Anna's name and joining the fight against eating disorders.

Used with permission.

(Bulik et al., 2005). Mortality is significantly associated with anorexia nervosa in many countries, and eating disorder has the highest death rate of any major mental disorder (Arcelus, Mitchell, Wales, & Nielsen, 2011; Signorini et al., 2007). Mean age at time of death is reportedly 49 to 61 years (Reas et al., 2005).

Prevalence rates for eating disorders may seem low but consider other related facts. Many people have *symptoms* of eating disorder that do not rise to the level of a formal diagnosis. About 6 percent of undergraduate women have concern about anorexia or bulimia, and 25 to 40 percent report moderate problems regarding weight control, worry about body image, and lack of control over eating (Schwitzer et al., 2008). Many people also do not seek treatment for their eating disorder. Only 23.2 percent of those with an eating disorder seek mental health care (Hart, Granillo, Jorm, & Paxton, 2011). People may shun treatment for eating disorders because they feel embarrassed or stigmatized. Many people with eating disorders are secretive about their symptoms and feel they do not have a problem. Sooki viewed restricted food intake and weight loss as a virtue and not a problem to be acknowledged and treated.

Eating disorders are much more common among females than males. Several reasons may account for this gender

## Table 8.2

### DSM-5  Bulimia Nervosa

A. Recurrent episodes of binge eating. An episode of binge eating is characterized by both of the following:
   1. Eating, in a discrete period of time, an amount of food that is definitely larger than what most individuals would eat in a similar period of time under similar circumstances.
   2. A sense of lack of control over eating during the episode.

B. Recurrent inappropriate compensatory behaviors in order to prevent weight gain, such as self-induced vomiting; misuse of laxatives, diuretics, or other medications; fasting; or excessive exercise.

C. The binge eating and inappropriate compensatory behaviors both occur, on average, at least once a week for 3 months.

D. Self-evaluation is unduly influenced by body shape and weight.

E. The disturbance does not occur exclusively during episodes of anorexia nervosa.

Specify if partial or full remission and severity as mild (1-3 episodes of inappropriate compensatory behaviors per week), moderate (4-7 episodes of inappropriate compensatory behaviors per week), severe (8-13 episodes of inappropriate compensatory behaviors per week), or extreme (14+ episodes of inappropriate compensatory behaviors per week).

American Psychiatric Association. (2013). *Diagnostic and statistical manual of mental disorders* (5th ed.). Arlington, VA: American Psychiatric Association.

## Table 8.3

### Compensatory Behaviors

Compensatory behaviors to prevent weight gain after binge eating include the following:

▶  Misuse of laxatives

▶  Misuse of enemas

▶  Excessive exercise

▶  Misuse of diuretics

▶  Fasting

▶  Self-induced vomiting

## Table 8.4

### DSM-5  Binge-Eating Disorder

A. Recurrent episodes of binge eating. An episode of binge eating is characterized by both of the following:
   1. Eating, in a discrete period of time, an amount of food that is definitely larger than what most people would eat in a similar period of time under similar circumstances.
   2. A sense of lack of control over eating during the episode.

B. The binge-eating episodes are associated with three (or more) of the following:
   1. Eating much more rapidly than normal.
   2. Eating until feeling uncomfortable full.
   3. Eating large amounts of food when not feeling physically hungry.
   4. Eating alone because of feeling embarrassed by how much one is eating.
   5. Feeling disgusted with oneself, depressed, or very guilty afterward

C. Marked distress regarding binge eating is present.

D. The binge eating occurs, on average, at least once a week for 3 months.

E. The binge eating is not associated with the recurrent use of inappropriate compensatory behavior as in bulimia nervosa and does not occur exclusively during the course of bulimia or anorexia nervosa.

Specify if partial or full remission and severity as mild (1-3 binge-eating episodes per week), moderate (4-7 binge-eating episodes per week), severe (8-13 binge-eating episodes per week), or extreme (14+ binge-eating episodes per week).

American Psychiatric Association. (2013). *Diagnostic and statistical manual of mental disorders* (5th ed.). Arlington, VA: American Psychiatric Association.

## Table 8.5

### Lifetime Prevalence Rates (%) for Major Eating Disorders

| Eating disorder | Women | Men |
|---|---|---|
| Anorexia nervosa | 0.9 | 0.3 |
| Bulimia nervosa | 1.5 | 0.5 |
| Binge eating disorder | 3.5 | 2.0 |

Source: Hudson, J.I., Hiripi, E., Pope, H.G., & Kessler, R.C. (2007). The prevalence and correlates of eating disorders in the National Comorbidity Survey Replication. *Biological Psychiatry, 61*, 348-358.

difference (see **Box 8.1**). A large sociocultural role might contribute to eating disorder symptoms in girls and women. Many theorists focus on "objectification" of women, media models of thinness for women, stress from maltreatment and sexual harassment, poor recognition of achievements, and excessive attention to beauty and body shape. Self-objectification, self-surveillance, and disordered eating are more common among former and current ballet dancers than control participants (Ringham et al., 2006; Tiggeman & Slater, 2001). Symptoms of eating disorder have also been linked to actresses, models, and elite female athletes in sports requiring thinness (Guisinger, 2003; Smolak, Murnen, & Ruble, 2000).

Males with eating disorders are not as well studied as females, but some interesting findings have emerged. Eating disorders appear to be on the rise among male athletes, especially in sports in which leanness may lead to a competitive advantage. Examples include wrestling, rowing, boxing, and possibly ski jumping (Bratland-Sanda & Sundgot-Borgen, 2012; Glazer, 2008). One study of 135 males with eating disorders indicated that many had major depressive disorder (54 percent), substance use disorder (37 percent), or a personality disorder (26 percent). Some had a family history of mood disorder (29 percent) or alcoholism (37 percent). Many (46 percent) also had bulimia nervosa; 22 percent had anorexia nervosa; and 32 percent had an eating disorder not otherwise specified (Carlat, Camargo, & Herzog, 1997).

Any racial or ethnic gap in eating disorders among Americans appears to be small. Rates of core eating disorder symptoms such as fear of being fat, body weight and shape concerns, and binge eating are similar for European American, Asian American, Latina, and African American girls and women aged 11 to 26 years (Franko, Becker, Thomas, & Herzog, 2007; Shaw, Ramirez, Trost, Randall, & Stice, 2004). Rates of risk factors for eating disorders—such as pressure to be thin, body dissatisfaction, and dieting—were also similar among these groups. The strength of the relationship between risk factors and eating disorder symptoms did not differ among these groups either. Racial and ethnic differences for eating disorder in the United States appear minimal at this time.

Eating disorders have been described as *cultural syndromes*, or problems that appear only in certain cultures and Western, industrialized nations. A deeper look, however, reveals a more nuanced finding. Anorexia nervosa is reported in most countries around the world and cannot be solely attributed to the influence of Western ideals favoring thinness. Rates of anorexia nervosa differ little in Western and non-Western countries. Cases of bulimia nervosa in non-Western countries, however, are linked to Western ideals, and prevalence rates of bulimia are lower in non-Western than

Western countries. Bulimia nervosa may be a cultural syndrome (Keel, Brown, Holland, & Bodell, 2012).

Eating disorders are highly comorbid with other mental disorders, including other eating disorders. Up to 50 percent of those with anorexia nervosa develop bulimia nervosa symptoms, and some with bulimia nervosa develop anorexia nervosa symptoms (Bulik, Sullivan, Fear, Pickering, 1997; Tozzi et al., 2005). Eating disorders are also comorbid with depression, body dysmorphic disorder, self-injurious behavior, and suicide (Bulik et al., 2008; Godart, Perdereau, Jeammet, & Flament, 2005; Svirko & Hawton, 2007). People with anorexia nervosa like Sooki are often socially isolated, sad, and less interested in sexual activity. They often report problems getting close to others and experience shame and guilt. People with binge eating disorder report their overeating often occurs during a depressed state and precedes guilt and shame. Obesity occurs in about 65 percent of those with binge eating disorder (Yager, 2008). People with eating disorders often exhibit symptoms of anxiety-related disorders as well. Anorexia nervosa is often present with symptoms of obsessive-compulsive disorder, including obsessions about food and body shape and compulsive behavior such as hoarding food. Anxiety disorder symptoms prominent in bulimia nervosa include those related to social phobia such as fear of social situations and being evaluated by others (Jordan et al., 2008; Kaye, Bulik, Thornton, Barbarich, & Masters, 2004).

Personality and substance use disorders are also common in people with bulimia nervosa and binge eating disorder. These disorders likely overlap because they share the symptom of impulse-control problems. People with bulimia

The changing male body ideal. (Left) Actor Burt Lancaster circa 1946. (Right) Rapper and actor LL Cool J circa 2004.

## BOX 8.1 Focus on Gender

### Why Is There a Gender Difference in Eating Disorders?

Females have more eating disorders than males—but why? A prominent explanation for gender differences in eating disorders concerns gender roles (Blashill, 2011). Our society values a female gender role resembling the "superwoman"—a woman with a great career, happy marriage and family, active social life, and good looks. The superwoman role emphasizes thinness, perfectionistic striving, and some autonomy from the family because of career. Striving for thinness, perfectionism, and loneliness or isolation are also correlates of eating disorders, so this role model may influence some females to develop symptoms of eating disorders.

The superwoman ideal intersects as well with how "ideal" women are portrayed in the media—thin—and this can affect how girls and women evaluate themselves. Women's bodies are also more likely to be "objectified" by being looked at, evaluated, and sexualized. This reinforces the culture of thinness, leads to more maltreatment and sexual harassment, and may keep women from achieving as much as men in their careers (Dour & Theran, 2011; Fredrickson & Roberts, 1997).

Biological factors almost certainly contribute to eating disorders, but whether these factors contribute to the difference in eating disorder prevalence rates between the genders remains unclear. Certain biological vulnerabilities may be expressed differently in women and men. Dieting to reduce weight may lower serotonin functioning more in women than men (Kaye, 2008; Soloff, Price, Mason, Becker, & Meltzer, 2010). Reduced serotonin is associated with overeating and carbohydrate craving. Another possible reason involves natural physical development. As boys and girls enter puberty, boys become more muscular and closer to the "ideal" for men, but girls obtain increased body fat and curves and move away from the "ideal" for women.

Are we teaching young girls that thin is the way to be? Barbie embodies the tall, thin, glamorous look.

---

nervosa have relatively higher rates of borderline personality disorder, a condition characterized by high levels of impulsivity (Chapter 10). Those with bulimia nervosa also experience higher rates of excessive alcohol and stimulant use. Use of stimulants may begin as a way of controlling weight and appetite but then becomes an addiction (Baker, Mitchell, Neale, & Kendler, 2010).

Some symptoms of eating disorders may be due to semistarvation and malnutrition (APA, 2013). Prisoners of war and those who experienced starvation or dieted often develop preoccupation with food, hoard food, and engage in binge eating once food is available. These individuals may also exhibit depression, obsessions, apathy, and irritability, but

The changing female body ideal. (Left) Actress Jane Russell circa the mid-1950s. (Right) Actress Cameron Diaz circa 2003.

more research is needed in this area (Bachar, Canetti, & Berry, 2005).

# Stigma Associated with Eating Disorders

Perhaps you know someone with an eating disorder. Many men (20 percent) and women (24 percent) in the United Kingdom said they knew someone with an eating disorder (Crisp, 2005). Respondents were asked whether they agreed to certain statements regarding people with various mental disorders (**Table 8.6**). Many respondents felt people with eating disorders are to blame for their problems and that they could pull themselves together if they chose to. People often view eating disorders as "self-inflicted" and related to willpower. Recall from Chapter 1 that attitudes such as these result in viewing others as weak in character and "different" from the rest of us.

These results were largely replicated in an American survey. Residents from two metropolitan areas rated their agreement with statements regarding a person with anorexia nervosa, schizophrenia, or asthma (Stewart, Keel, & Schiavo, 2006). Residents rated people with anorexia nervosa as better able to pull themselves together if they wanted to, more to blame for their condition, and more likely to be acting to get attention compared with those with schizophrenia or asthma. Respondents also rated the following factors as more relevant to anorexia nervosa than other diagnostic groups: lack of social support, lack of self-discipline, and poor parenting. Stigma associated with anorexia nervosa may thus be driven by perceptions that those with the disorder are largely responsible for their own problems.

## Table 8.6

### Agreement with Stigmatizing Statements

Respondents were asked whether they agreed to certain statements regarding people with certain mental disorders.

| Statement | Eating disorders 1998 | Eating disorders 2003 | Alcoholism 1998 | Alcoholism 2003 | Depression 1998 | Depression 2003 |
|---|---|---|---|---|---|---|
| Danger to others | 7 | 7 | 65 | 64 | 23 | 19 |
| Unpredictable | 29 | 27 | 71 | 70 | 56 | 53 |
| Hard to talk to | 38 | 33 | 59 | 55 | 62 | 56 |
| Feel different from us | 49 | 33 | 35 | 25 | 43 | 30 |
| They are to blame | 34 | 33 | 60 | 54 | 13 | 11 |
| Could pull themselves together | 38 | 35 | 52 | 50 | 19 | 17 |
| Treatment would not help | 9 | 10 | 11 | 12 | 16 | 15 |
| Will never fully recover | 11 | 15 | 24 | 29 | 23 | 25 |

Adapted from Crisp (2005). All numbers are percentages.

Copyright © Cengage Learning®

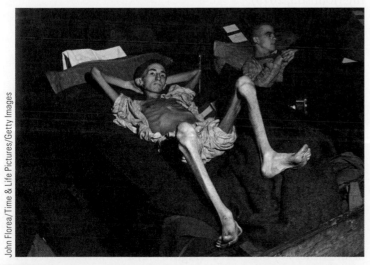

Starvation can cause many of the symptoms associated with eating disorders. Private Joe Demler suffered from starvation as a prisoner of war in 1945.

John Florea/Time & Life Pictures/Getty Images

## INTERIM SUMMARY

▶ Major features of eating disorders include weight concerns, body dissatisfaction, and eating problems. Eating problems include restricted eating or dieting and lack of control over eating.

▶ Eating disorders include anorexia nervosa, bulimia nervosa, and binge eating disorder.

▶ Women are about 10 times more likely to have anorexia nervosa or bulimia nervosa than men, and many people with an eating disorder do not seek treatment.

▶ Similar rates of eating disorder symptoms are found among many major racial and ethnic groups in the United States.

▶ Anorexia nervosa has been observed in countries around the world and does not appear to be a cultural syndrome; bulimia nervosa is primarily found in Western cultures and may be a cultural syndrome.

▶ People often view those with eating disorders as responsible for their behavior, which may stigmatize this population.

## REVIEW QUESTIONS

1. How do Sooki's symptoms differ from normal concern about body shape or weight?

2. Identify main features of, and major differences between, anorexia nervosa, bulimia nervosa, and binge eating disorder.

3. Describe the epidemiology of eating disorders, including issues of gender and culture.

4. How might people with eating disorder be stigmatized by others?

# Eating Disorders: Causes and Prevention

We turn our attention next to factors that cause eating disorders and discuss how knowing about these factors might help us prevent these conditions.

## Biological Risk Factors for Eating Disorders

Recall from previous chapters that mental disorders are often viewed from a *diathesis-stress model*, or a combination of biological and environmental variables. Many people are born with a genetic or biological predisposition toward certain neurological features or personality characteristics. Environmental conditions or life events often influence or trigger these biological predispositions. Biological predispositions in people with eating disorders include genetics, brain features, neurochemical features, and personality traits such as perfectionism and impulsivity.

### GENETICS

Eating disorders do run in families, and some people seem genetically predisposed toward certain eating disorders (Bulik et al., 2010; Mitchell et al., 2010; see **Table 8.7**). Modest heritability (0.42) has also been reported for eating disorder in general (Kendler et al., 2011). Genes on chromosomes 1, 4, and 10 may contribute to these predispositions (Klump, Bulik, Kaye, Treasure, & Tyson, 2009). Genetic influences may be stronger for certain subtypes of eating disorder, especially the restricting subtype of anorexia nervosa (Scherag, Hebebrand, & Hinney, 2010).

No one gene or set of genes leads *directly* to an eating disorder, however. Studies to find genetic markers for eating disorders in general have produced inconsistent results, but drive for thinness

### Table 8.7

**Genetic Basis of Eating Disorders**

| Eating disorder | Percent of variance due to genetic basis |
|---|---|
| Anorexia nervosa | 28%–74% |
| Bulimia nervosa | 54%–83% |
| Binge eating disorder | 41%–57% |

Source: Thornton, L.M., Mazzeo, S.E., & Bulik, C.M. (2010). The heritability of eating disorders: Methods and current findings. In R.A.H. Adan & W.H. Kaye (Eds.), *Behavioral neurobiology of eating disorders* (pp. 141-156). Berlin: Springer-Verlag.

may link to genes on chromosomes 1, 2, and 13 (Trace, Baker, Penas-Lledo, & Bulik, 2013). This may be especially true for females compared with males (Baker et al., 2009). Genetics likely set the stage for brain or neurochemical features or temperaments that help lead to eating disorders or interact with environmental events to trigger eating disorders. We next discuss some brain features found in those with eating disorders.

### BRAIN FEATURES

Recall from Chapter 2 that the *hypothalamus* is the brain structure that regulates hunger and eating and is involved in appetite (see **Figure 8.2**). Eating disorder researchers thus focus on this structure. Damage to the lateral hypothalamus leads to weight and appetite changes in animals (Stratford & Wirtshafter, 2012). Others have focused on the connection of the lateral hypothalamus to the *amygdala*. This connection seems related to learned cues that surround eating. These cues override feelings of fullness and thus promote more eating (Johnson, 2013).

The nucleus accumbens has also been implicated in eating disorders because this brain structure is linked to the lateral hypothalamus as well as sensory pleasure from food (Berridge, 2009). Other brain regions such as the prefrontal, orbitofrontal, and somatosensory cortexes are associated with the rewarding aspects of food and may play a part in eating disorders (Volkow, Wang, & Baler, 2011). In addition, the thalamus is potentially involved in excess food intake (Avena & Bocarsly, 2011).

Animal models of brain structures and eating disorder may not completely relate to humans, however. Recall that people with anorexia nervosa *do have an appetite*—they just choose not to eat. An animal model also does not explain body image disturbance or fear of becoming fat in anorexia nervosa or bulimia nervosa. The hypothalamus and amygdala and other key brain areas (Figure 8.2) are likely involved in eating disorders, but structural or functional problems with these brain structures cannot completely account for symptoms of these disorders.

Bubbles Photolibrary / Alamy

Is it biological makeup or bad habits that lead to obesity?

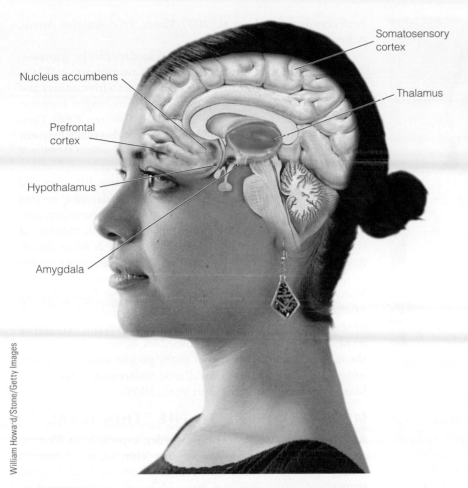

Somatosensory cortex

Thalamus

Nucleus accumbens

Prefrontal cortex

Hypothalamus

Amygdala

William Howard/Stone/Getty Images

**FIGURE 8.2** BRAIN AREAS IMPLICATED IN EATING DISORDERS

## NEUROCHEMICAL FEATURES

The neurotransmitter most closely linked to eating disorders is *serotonin* (Lee & Lin, 2010). Serotonin influences mood regulation, obsessive thinking, impulsivity, and eating behavior. Serotonin is also responsible for **satiety**, or feeling full from eating. People with anorexia nervosa who engage in food restriction may disrupt their serotonin functioning. People with bulimia nervosa and binge eating disorder may have low levels of serotonin, which can cause malfunction in the body's satiety feedback mechanism, leading to binges.

Anorexia nervosa and bulimia nervosa are characterized by reduced serotonin activity, and people with anorexia nervosa and bulimia nervosa also show limited responsivity to serotonin-stimulating medications (Flament, Bissada, & Spettigue, 2012). Serotonin dysfunction is also associated with features common to anorexia nervosa or bulimia nervosa, including self-destructive behavior, impulsivity, compulsivity, obsessive thinking, and depression. We discussed in Chapter 7 how serotonin closely relates to depression, and some research indicates a shared genetic risk between anorexia nervosa and major depression (Slane, Burt, & Klump, 2011).

*Dopamine* may also play a role in eating disorders. Dopamine is linked to pleasurable aspects of food as well as motivation to obtain food (Broft, Berner, Martinez, & Walsh, 2011). Dysfunction in the dopamine system might lead those with anorexia nervosa to have less motivation to obtain food, whereas the opposite would be true for those with bulimia nervosa and binge eating disorder. One might thus expect differences in dopamine functioning between those with anorexia nervosa and those with other forms of eating disorders characterized by binging.

**Endogenous opioids** are bodily chemicals that reduce pain, enhance positive mood, and suppress appetite. These chemicals are released during starvation and after intense exercise, so they may have an impact on eating disorders. Endogenous opioid release is rewarding, so this may reinforce self-starvation and excessive exercise in anorexia nervosa. Low levels of endogenous opioids promote *craving of food* and thus may characterize bulimia. Craving food may lead to binges and then stress relief or euphoria, so binging is reinforced (Hill, 2007). We turn next to more observable factors that may be influenced by neurochemical substances and that contribute to the development and maintenance of eating disorders.

## PERSONALITY TRAITS

Perfectionism is often cited as a risk factor for eating disorders, especially among people with an obsessive drive for thinness. People with anorexia nervosa have fixed or rigid thoughts of ideal body type, compensatory and almost ritualistic behavior to lose weight, and strict adherence to certain patterns of eating (or not eating). People with bulimia nervosa also have an ideal body type in mind and perfectionism often drives dieting that perpetuates the binge–purge cycle. Perfectionism appears to be associated with, but not necessarily a cause of, eating disorder (Sassaroli et al., 2008).

Impulsivity is another personality feature cited as a risk factor for bulimia nervosa. Binge eating is often characterized by a desperate, urgent quality. Those who binge describe these

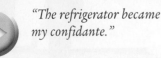

THE **CONTINUUM** VIDEO PROJECT

*Sara:* **Bulimia Nervosa**

*"The refrigerator became my confidante."*

Copyright © Cengage Learning.®

Access the Continuum Video Project in MindTap at **www.cengagebrain.com**.

Perfectionism appears to be associated with, but not necessarily a cause of, eating disorder.

*Jamie Grill/Iconica/Getty Images*

perfectionism (Jacobs et al., 2009; Yanez, Peix, Atserias, Arnau, & Brug, 2007).

Families of people with eating disorders can be intrusive, controlling, hostile, disorganized, and unsupportive (Claes, Vandereycken, & Vertommen, 2004). Conflict with mothers and fathers and less maternal intimacy relate to weight concerns during adolescence (May, Kim, McHale, & Crouter, 2006). Family members of people with eating disorders also make frequent and negative comments about body shape and weight (Hanna & Bond, 2006; Wade, Gillespie, & Martin, 2007).

Other family factors contribute to eating disorders *and* to many other major mental disorders we describe in this textbook. *Expressed emotion*, a concept involving hostility, conflict, and overinvolvement (Chapter 7), relates to families of those with eating disorder (Di Paola, Faravelli, & Ricca, 2010). Recall also from Chapter 7 that insecure attachment relates to depression and seems to relate to eating disorders as well. Many people with eating disorders also report family history of childhood trauma such as neglect or emotional, physical, or sexual maltreatment. Child maltreatment is not necessarily a risk factor specific to eating disorders, however. You will see throughout this textbook that many people with mental disorders report high rates of childhood maltreatment (Dunkley, Masheb, & Grilo, 2010; Gilbert et al., 2009).

## MEDIA EXPOSURE TO THE "THIN IDEAL"

Another risk factor for eating disorder, especially in Western society, is media promotion of the "thin ideal." American beauty queens, models, and Playboy bunnies have become increasingly thin over the past 50 years (see **Figure 8.3**). Young people, especially young girls, are influenced by the media's depiction of attractiveness and ideal body type—Selena

episodes as driven and uncontrollable. We also mentioned that substance use and personality disorders are comorbid with eating disorders and especially bulimia nervosa. These substance use and personality disorders are characterized by high levels of impulsivity. Impulsivity does not likely lead directly to an eating disorder but does seem to predispose some people toward symptoms of bulimia (Waxman, 2009).

## Environmental Risk Factors for Eating Disorders

We turn our attention next to environmental risk factors that develop over a person's lifetime. These include family factors, media exposure to the "thin ideal," and cognitive and cultural factors.

### FAMILY FACTORS

A leading factor in eating disorder is substantial reinforcement given by family members to a person who has lost significant weight and who is thus thought to possess great self-discipline and self-control (Treasure, Schmidt, & Macdonald, 2010). Some family members also express a preference for their children to be thin. Mothers of girls with eating disorders often diet, have an eating disorder, and display

*Hemis/Alamy*

Real or perceived pressure from others to look a certain way could spur excessive dieting and even eating disorder.

Gomez and Taylor Swift are not overweight. Body types for many celebrities and athletes seem to set a standard, but many of these "models" are severely underweight and thin. Women on television and in magazines are generally much thinner than most American women.

This media ideal clashes with the fact that size and weight of the average woman have increased over the years. Many of us are not biologically inclined to be "waiflike" either. The media provides few examples of non thin women comfortable with their weight and appearance. An adolescent girl thus sees a big difference between what is portrayed in the media and what she sees in the mirror. Some of these girls (and boys) try to achieve the media ideal but find they can only do so via severely restricted eating, excessive exercise, or purging. Media depictions do influence body dissatisfaction and eating disorder symptoms in children as young as age 5 years (Hill, 2006; Levine & Murnen, 2009).

## COGNITIVE FACTORS

Major cognitive risk factors for eating disorder include *body dissatisfaction* and *body image disturbance*. We have seen that family and media influences can affect body dissatisfaction. For some people, a discrepancy occurs between actual body size and weight and a perceived "ideal" body size and weight equated with attractiveness. Body dissatisfaction is a risk factor as well as a maintenance factor for eating disorders (Stice, Ng, & Shaw,

2010). Body image disturbance refers to faulty self-evaluation of one's body weight and shape despite contradictory evidence (Sherry et al., 2009). Recall that Sooki thought she was fat even though others told her she was underweight. Distorted self-evaluation often leads to restricting diet and food consumption, as was true for Sooki.

## CULTURAL FACTORS

We mentioned that eating disorders are present worldwide and that bulimia nervosa may be seen more in Western cultures. Anorexia nervosa may also be less common in certain countries where food is scarce or where being "plump" or slightly overweight is valued. A mental disorder involving distorted body image and self-starvation is less likely in these countries. Research into cultural factors of eating disorder is thus most prevalent in the United States.

As we noted earlier, few racial or ethnic differences in America have been found for eating disorder (Shaw et al., 2004). European American women do not differ from Latinas or Asian American women with respect to body dissatisfaction. European American women do, however, report higher levels of body dissatisfaction than African American women. This may reflect greater acceptance of body weight

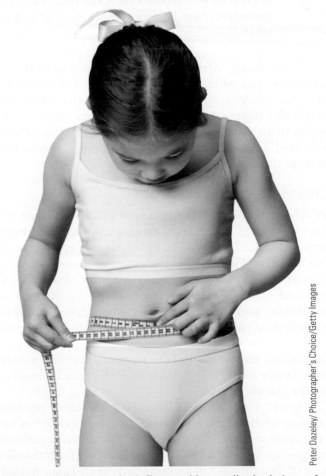

How much do popular TV shows like *Project Runway* influence body image?

Gregorio T. Binuya/Everett Collection

Even young children can be influenced by media depictions of the thin ideal.

Peter Dazeley/ Photographer's Choice/Getty Images

FIGURE 8.3 PERCENTAGE OF EXPECTED WEIGHT REFERS TO THE RATIO OF ACTUAL WEIGHT TO WHAT IS TYPICAL FOR WOMEN OF A PARTICULAR HEIGHT AND AGE Playboy centerfolds and Miss America contestants have become thinner and farther below the norm over time. (Photos: left, Landov; right, Ethan Miller/Getty Images)

and shape among African American women as well as the possibility that African American women are raised to be more independent, strong, and self-reliant than other women of color (Grabe & Hyde, 2006). This may make African American girls and women less susceptible to the thin ideal promoted by the media and more willing to accept themselves as they are.

## Causes of Eating Disorders

We discussed in earlier chapters how a diathesis-stress model could be used to integrate various risk factors to explain mental disorder, and the same model can apply to eating disorders (see **Figure 8.4**). Biological diatheses, or vulnerabilities, include genetics or brain or neurochemical features that lead some people to have trouble regulating mood or behavior and to react strongly when upset or stressed. Psychological vulnerabilities include low self-esteem, perfectionism, impulsivity, body dissatisfaction, and a distorted body image. Environmental stressors such as child maltreatment, family conflict, and social or media-based pressures to be thin also play a role.

Figure 8.4 shows how biological vulnerabilities, psychological vulnerabilities, and stressors or sociocultural factors interact to cause severely restricted eating. Two different paths then emerge—one leads to anorexia nervosa and one leads to bulimia nervosa. Two subtypes of anorexia nervosa are characterized by restricted eating and by binging and purging. Both subtypes,

In some non-Western cultures, being heavy is more desirable than being thin.

however, involve *excessive weight loss*. Binging and purging are also evident in bulimia nervosa but normal or above normal weight is maintained. Eating disorders thus involve interplay between diatheses and stressors.

# Prevention of Eating Disorders

Many risk factors for eating disorder occur at an early age, so prevention of these problems usually begins in childhood or adolescence. Preventing eating disorder is important for two key reasons. First, eating disorders are associated with significant impairment, inpatient hospitalization, suicide attempts, and mortality. Second, less than one third of people with eating disorders receive treatment, and treatment is not effective for all those with eating disorders.

Eating disorder prevention programs emphasize education about eating disorders and consequences, resisting sociocultural pressures for thinness, healthy weight control behaviors, and interactive exercises to address risk factors such as body dissatisfaction. *National Eating Disorders Awareness Week* involves a media campaign to educate people about eating disorder and quick screening assessments in selected clinics for those struggling with eating problems. People with problematic eating patterns or concerns can then be referred for professional treatment.

About 51 percent of eating disorder prevention programs reduce risk factors and 29 percent reduce current or future eating disorder (Stice, Shaw, & Marti, 2007). These prevention efforts thus show modest effects. Prevention of eating problems among college students is more successful if people learn not

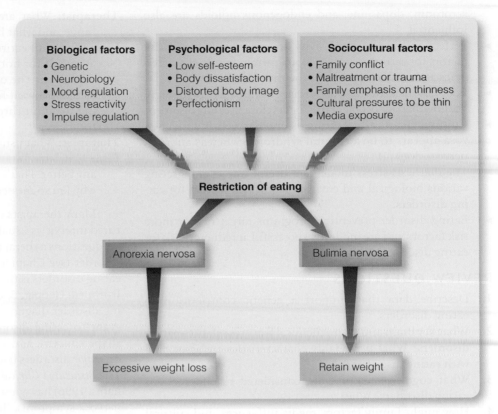

**FIGURE 8.4**  CAUSAL MODEL OF EATING DISORDERS

to internalize the "thin ideal" and if media literacy programs are available to counter overly thin images of women and overly muscular images of men (Yager & O'Dea, 2008).

"Student Bodies" is an 8-week program administered via the Internet (Jacobi, Volker, Trockel, & Taylor, 2012; Winzelberg et al., 2000). The program combines a structured cognitive-behavioral curriculum with a discussion group. People are screened for risk factors and then invited to participate. Primary goals are to reduce excessive weight concerns and body dissatisfaction. Participants log onto a website with updated content each week. The program involves reading the content, completing assignments, and participating in a moderated online discussion group. Participants also self-monitor and write entries in a Personal Journal of Body Image. College women report that this program does reduce weight concerns (Taylor et al., 2006). The program also reduced onset of eating disorders among people with an elevated body mass index (see Assessment of Eating Disorders section) and among some who use compensatory behaviors to prevent weight gain. Prevention programs like this one hold promise for reducing the incidence of eating disorder symptoms.

## INTERIM SUMMARY

▶ Eating disorders have some genetic basis, but environmental risk factors are also important in the development of these disorders.

▶ Brain structures likely involved in eating problems are the hypothalamus and amygdala. Neurochemicals such as

African American women may be less susceptible to the thin ideal than other women in the United States.

serotonin, dopamine, and endogenous opioids are also influential.

▶ Perfectionism and impulsivity are personality-based risk factors for eating disorders, as are certain family characteristics and media exposure to the thin ideal.

▶ Body dissatisfaction and body image disturbance are cognitive features that put people at risk for developing eating disorders.

▶ Cultural factors affect eating disorder as well; bulimia nervosa appears to be a cultural syndrome, whereas anorexia nervosa does not.

▶ The diathesis-stress model is a useful way of integrating various biological and environmental risk factors for eating disorders.

▶ Eating disorder prevention programs target one or more risk factors and are modestly successful at reducing risk for eating disorders.

## REVIEW QUESTIONS

1. Describe data that support a genetic contribution to eating disorders.
2. What key brain and neurochemical features relate to eating disorders? What personality characteristics are associated with eating disorders?
3. What cognitive features are considered risk factors for eating disorders? Why?
4. How might family factors, media influences, and cultural backgrounds help cause eating disorders?
5. What topics are typically addressed in programs to prevent eating disorders?

# Eating Disorders: Assessment and Treatment

We next discuss different methods of assessing and treating eating disorders. These methods are important for people like Sooki, Lisa, and Rachel (see **Personal Narrative 8.2**) who struggled with symptoms of eating disorders.

## Assessment of Eating Disorders

Mental health professionals use various methods to examine people with eating disorders. The primary methods they use include interviews, self-report questionnaires, self-monitoring, and physical assessment.

## INTERVIEWS

Mental health professionals who assess people with eating disorders often inquire about current height and weight, thoughts and physical feelings about eating, thoughts and feelings about body shape and image, behaviors to prevent weight gain, and long-term goals. This information is important for knowing how to treat someone with an eating disorder because specific client characteristics can be identified and addressed. Lisa's therapist discovered some interesting information about what happens when her eating is out of control:

**Therapist:** What happens when you binge?
**Lisa:** I eat lots of sweets, like cake, ice cream, cookies, and candy bars.

**Therapist:** What are you usually thinking about during a binge, and what happens next?
**Lisa:** While I'm eating, I just don't feel I can stop. I get mad at myself for not being able to stop my eating, and I feel depressed. The only thing I can do right after the binge to make myself feel better is to throw up. It's embarrassing to admit throwing up so much, but it does make me feel better.
**Therapist:** What usually happens after you throw up?
**Lisa:** Well, later, I start feeling guilty and thinking I'll never get any better. That's when the depression kicks in . . . I wonder why I'm so messed up.

Many therapists prefer unstructured interviews, but structured interviews usually rely on diagnostic criteria and contain set questions a therapist asks each client with a possible mental disorder (see Chapter 4). A common structured interview for eating disorders is the *Eating Disorders Examination* (EDE 16.0D; Fairburn, Cooper, & O'Connor, 2008). The EDE provides eating disorder diagnoses as well as scores on four subscales relevant to eating disorder problems: restraint, eating concern, shape concern, and weight concern. Most interviews focused on *major* disorders have sections for eating disorder symptoms. The *Structured Clinical Interview* (First, Spitzer, Gibbon, & Williams, 1996) has questions about anorexia nervosa and bulimia nervosa symptoms. Binge eating disorder can also be assessed with this interview.

## SELF-REPORT QUESTIONNAIRES

Self-report questionnaires are often used to screen for eating problems. The *Eating Disorder Diagnostic Scale* (Krabbenborg et al., 2012; Stice, Telch, & Rivzi, 2000) provides diagnostic information for eating disorders. Scores can be calculated for key components of eating disorders like body dissatisfaction and binge eating. Selected items from this scale are in **Table 8.8**. A list of other questionnaires that mental health professionals use when assessing people with eating disorders is in **Table 8.9**.

Some prevention programs for eating disorders are administered over the Internet.

## Personal Narrative 8.2

### *Rachel Webb*

*Ana and Mia are nicknames for anorexia nervosa and bulimia nervosa.*

Dear Mia,

We've come a long way together, but I'm afraid I'm going to have to ask you to leave. You have become that last drunken guest at the party that is my life. I'm not sure who invited you, but every time I've almost pushed you out the door you come crashing back in.

You arrived early, long before I was conscious of your presence. You waited in the corner, through years of taunting and abuse until my deeply buried self-hatred could no longer be ignored. That's when you decided we needed each other.

I needed a way to deal with my world; a way to silently punish myself for my many shortcomings in a way no one else would see. You needed someone you could seduce and brainwash. You needed someone who would believe the things you whispered in her ear.

"You're defective."
"You're ugly."
"You're stupid."
"You're worthless."

Funny how the things you were telling me were the same things I heard every day at school. It must have been most convenient for you that I already believed those things about myself.

You convinced me that despite the rosy suburban childhood my parents tried to give me, I was miserable. Despite my loving family and supportive adult friends, I was unlovable. Despite my wall full of swimming medals and writing awards, I was talentless. Despite my ability to build a career, I was a failure.

Photo courtesy of Rachel Webb

Rachel Webb

Through all of that, you stayed. You were waiting for me to crash diet before I tried on bridal gowns for the wedding I would call off. You were waiting for my boyfriend to dump me. Waiting for me to have a bad day, or just to be tired and bored. The day my parents told me I was fat fully announced your arrival.

But our time is over. For all of our time together, I have realized that I am stronger than you.

The beginning of the end came 2 years ago, on that morning when I was semiconscious on my bathroom floor, covered in my own vomit. That's when you went too far. The shadows in the corner parted, and I saw you for what you really are.

I decided then and there that you had to leave. But no matter how hard I try (cleaning up the dirty glasses, vacuuming the floor, saying how early I have to get up in the morning), you refuse to leave and your presence is still puzzling.

All I know is you helped me start a war with my body. You prevented me from enjoying myself and my family and my friends. From being able to eat meals like a normal person. From experiencing the normal cycle of being hungry, eating, and stopping when I felt full.

I'm not sure what I could have done to prevent our relationship. It really all goes back to fifth grade, doesn't it? When I couldn't get through a day at school without being ostracized or punched. You followed me through my teenage years, and we flirted and played until you lucked out. When I was in college, I dated a jerk, and all of the things I learned about myself in fifth grade were confirmed.

Once we were well acquainted, you disintegrated my muscle tone until I couldn't carry a bag of groceries, change the tank on my office water cooler, or walk more than a block or two without needing to sit down. You've given me an irregular heartbeat and low blood pressure that causes me to faint if I stand still for too long. I'm certain you've given me cavities, but I'm too afraid to go to the dentist. Time will only tell as to whether you've given me osteoporosis.

Somehow, after all this time, I have grown stronger than you. I have regained my muscle and am prepared to throw you out with an imprint of a combat-booted foot planted squarely in your backside. At this point, you need a willing host, and I am no longer willing.

So please, take your tingling fingertips and bruised knuckles. Take your sunken eyes and your cracked lips. Take your perpetually sore throat and your raging headaches. Take the self-doubt and self-loathing that you brought with you.

And whatever you do, don't come back. Because I am stronger than you are, and I know how much you hate that.

## SELF-MONITORING

People with eating disorders can monitor and record their daily symptoms and behaviors. Daily recording is likely more accurate than a retrospective report of the past week. A person can also focus on what happened immediately before or after a symptom or behavior. The act of self-monitoring itself can lead to fewer symptoms and behaviors—we generally do an excess behavior less if we record each time it happens. We become more aware of our behaviors and gain better control over them.

Self-monitoring can be accomplished using a paper diary to indicate frequency of behaviors such as binge eating,

## Table 8.8

### Sample Items from the Eating Disorder Diagnostic Scale

**Body dissatisfaction/fear of gaining weight**

Over the past 3 months . . .

▶ Have you felt fat?

▶ Have you had a definite fear that you might gain weight or become fat?

▶ Has your weight influenced how you think about (judge) yourself as a person?

▶ Has your shape influenced how you think about (judge) yourself as a person?

Note: Each of these items is rated as 0 ("not at all"), 1, 2 ("slightly"), 3, 4 ("moderately"), or 5 or 6 ("extremely").

**Binge Eating**

During these episodes of overeating and loss of control did you . . .

▶ Eat much more rapidly than normal?

▶ Eat until you felt uncomfortably full?

▶ Eat large amounts of food when you didn't feel physically hungry?

▶ Eat alone because you were embarrassed by how much you were eating?

▶ Feel disgusted with yourself, depressed, or very guilty after overeating?

▶ Feel very upset about your uncontrollable overeating or resulting weight gain?

Note: These questions are answered *yes* or *no*.
Source: Stice, E., Telch, C. F., & Rizvi, S. L. (2000). Development and validation of the Eating Disorder Diagnostic Scale: A brief self-report measure of anorexia, bulimia, and binge-eating disorder. *Psychological Assessment, 12*, 123-131. Reprinted by permission of the authors.

## Table 8.9

### Common Questionnaires for Assessing Eating Disorders

General Diagnosis of Eating Disorders

*Eating Disorders Inventory-2* (EDI-2)
*Kids Eating Disorders Survey* (KEDS)

Body Dissatisfaction/Body Image Disturbance

*Body Shape Questionnaire* (BSQ)
*Body Image Avoidance Questionnaire*

Dietary Restraint

*Dutch Eating Behavior Questionnaire* (DEBQ)
*Three-Factor Eating Questionnaire* (TFEQ-R)

Binge Eating

*The Binge Eating Scale*

Source: Pike, K.M. (2005). Assessment of anorexia nervosa.

purging, or excessive exercise; emotions and thoughts that preceded these behaviors; and consequences after the behavior such as stress relief, comfort, or guilt. Paper diaries can also be used to track and record meals eaten and calories consumed. This information can be extremely helpful for understanding one's eating problem and for planning treatment.

A high-tech version of self-monitoring involves using **electronic diaries** such as Palm Pilots or certain smartphone applications to record behavior. Sooki might be asked to carry an electronic diary to document meals, thoughts about her body, and fear of becoming fat. She could also indicate her mood state before and after restricting her eating as well

as events before and after skipping meals. Women with anorexia nervosa who use electronic diaries show many changes in mood throughout the day. They also endorse many eating disorder symptoms and rituals such as skipping meals, checking joints and bones for fat, and consuming fluids to curb appetite. Electronic diaries can thus provide rich data for mental health professionals who plan treatment (Haedt-Matt & Keel, 2011).

## PHYSICAL ASSESSMENT

People with eating disorders should always have a thorough medical examination. Many eating disorder symptoms are physical, such as low weight, and eating disorders can result in serious medical symptoms and life-threatening outcomes. A physical examination can focus on height and weight to determine body mass index (BMI; **Table 8.10**), heart rate and rhythm, and muscle tone and strength. Physical assessment can also help physicians and mental health professionals decide the first step of treatment. Someone with anorexia nervosa found to be severely malnourished may require inpatient hospitalization to insert and maintain a nasogastric tube for feeding. Common laboratory tests to assess people with eating disorders include the following:

● Metabolic panel to assess for electrolyte imbalance due to poor nutrition

● Blood count to check for anemia

● Enzyme tests to rule out severe malnutrition

● Serum amylase tests to suggest purging behavior

● Bone scans to rule out calcium deficiency or bone mass loss

Electronic diaries can be used to monitor one's mood, thoughts, and eating behavior.

## Treatment of Eating Disorders

Recall that eating disorders have symptoms involving emotional, physical, cognitive, and behavioral features. The general aims of biological and psychological treatment for eating disorder are thus to (APA, 2006):

- Return the person to a healthy weight
- Treat physical complications
- Increase motivation to restore healthy eating patterns
- Educate the person about healthy eating patterns
- Help the person recognize and change core problematic feelings, thoughts, and behaviors about the eating disorder
- Enlist family support for change
- Prevent relapse

## Biological Treatments of Eating Disorders

Biological treatments for eating disorders involve controlled weight gain and medication.

### CONTROLLED WEIGHT GAIN

Many people with anorexia nervosa lose so much weight that their condition becomes life-threatening. About 50 percent of people with anorexia nervosa who seek treatment are admitted to inpatient care involving *controlled weight gain* and

nutrition guidance (Guarda, 2008). Controlled weight gain can include a nighttime nasogastric tube to increase basic nourishment, improve vital functioning, and provide a minimal amount of energy. Those with anorexia may also be given regular snacks and small meals under staff supervision as well as praise for their eating (Rigaud, Brondel, Poupard, Talonneau, & Brun, 2007).

Controlled weight gain is often conducted in conjunction with a nutritionist who educates a person about healthy food choices. A mental health professional should expect only small gains in weight per week, usually about 2 to 4 pounds per week (Guarda, 2008). People with anorexia who start to gain weight may become increasingly anxious, depressed, or irritable as they do so, so these mood states must also be managed. Controlled weight gain is thus often used in conjunction with medication.

### MEDICATION

We mentioned that serotonin changes contribute to eating disorders and that depression, which is associated with low serotonin, is highly comorbid with eating disorders. Medication for eating disorders has thus primarily involved *selective serotonin reuptake inhibitors* (SSRIs) like Prozac and others (Chapter 7). These medications are not overly helpful with people with anorexia nervosa because the drugs do not necessarily increase weight (Mitchell, Roerig, & Steffen, 2013). SSRIs are helpful, however, for treating comorbid depression, anxiety, obsessional thinking, and purging (if present). Antipsychotic medications (Chapter 12) may also be used for cases involving severe obsessional thinking or delusional body image disturbances (Mehler-Wex, Romanos, Kirchheiner, & Schulze, 2008). Research regarding antipsychotics for eating disorders has produced mixed results, however (Lebow, Sim, Erwin, & Murad, 2013).

SSRIs and psychological treatment (discussed in the next section) do significantly reduce binge eating and purging and help ease impulse control problems reported by many people with bulimia nervosa and binge eating disorder (Vocks et al., 2010). Appetite suppressants are sometimes used to help with weight loss in these groups as well. The drugs reduce eating but mental health professionals must ensure that clients on these drugs monitor heart rate and blood pressure (McElroy, Guerdjikova, Mori, & O'Melia, 2012).

## Psychological Treatments of Eating Disorders

Psychological treatments for eating disorders involve family therapy and cognitive-behavioral therapy.

### FAMILY THERAPY

Family therapy is useful for many people with eating disorders but is particularly helpful for adolescents with anorexia nervosa. A popular form of family therapy for those with anorexia nervosa is a family systems or Maudsley model approach. This approach initially focuses on obtaining cooperation from all family members, examining family patterns of eating and attitudes toward a client's symptoms, and improving eating and weight gain (Keel & Haedt, 2008). Family therapy can begin

## Table 8.10

### Body Mass Index (BMI) Chart

| BMI (kg/m²) Height (in.) | 19 | 20 | 21 | 22 | 23 | 24 | 25 | 26 | 27 | 28 | 29 | 30 | 35 | 40 |
|---|---|---|---|---|---|---|---|---|---|---|---|---|---|---|
| | | | | | | | Weight (lb.) | | | | | | | |
| 58 | 91 | 96 | 100 | 105 | 110 | 115 | 119 | 124 | 129 | 134 | 138 | 143 | 167 | 191 |
| 59 | 94 | 99 | 104 | 109 | 114 | 119 | 124 | 128 | 133 | 138 | 143 | 148 | 173 | 198 |
| 60 | 97 | 102 | 107 | 112 | 118 | 123 | 128 | 133 | 138 | 143 | 148 | 153 | 179 | 204 |
| 61 | 100 | 106 | 111 | 116 | 122 | 127 | 132 | 137 | 143 | 148 | 153 | 158 | 185 | 211 |
| 62 | 104 | 109 | 115 | 120 | 126 | 131 | 136 | 142 | 147 | 153 | 158 | 164 | 191 | 218 |
| 63 | 107 | 113 | 118 | 124 | 130 | 135 | 141 | 146 | 152 | 158 | 163 | 169 | 197 | 225 |
| 64 | 110 | 116 | 122 | 128 | 134 | 140 | 145 | 151 | 157 | 163 | 169 | 174 | 204 | 232 |
| 65 | 114 | 120 | 126 | 132 | 138 | 144 | 150 | 156 | 162 | 168 | 174 | 180 | 210 | 240 |
| 66 | 118 | 124 | 130 | 136 | 142 | 148 | 155 | 161 | 167 | 173 | 179 | 186 | 216 | 247 |
| 67 | 121 | 127 | 134 | 140 | 146 | 153 | 159 | 166 | 172 | 178 | 185 | 191 | 223 | 255 |
| 68 | 125 | 131 | 138 | 144 | 151 | 158 | 164 | 171 | 177 | 184 | 190 | 197 | 230 | 262 |
| 69 | 128 | 135 | 142 | 149 | 155 | 162 | 169 | 176 | 182 | 189 | 196 | 203 | 236 | 270 |
| 70 | 132 | 139 | 146 | 153 | 160 | 167 | 174 | 181 | 188 | 195 | 202 | 207 | 243 | 278 |
| 71 | 136 | 143 | 150 | 157 | 165 | 172 | 179 | 186 | 193 | 200 | 208 | 215 | 250 | 286 |
| 72 | 140 | 147 | 154 | 162 | 169 | 177 | 184 | 191 | 199 | 206 | 213 | 221 | 258 | 294 |
| 73 | 144 | 151 | 159 | 166 | 174 | 182 | 189 | 197 | 204 | 212 | 219 | 227 | 265 | 302 |
| 74 | 148 | 155 | 163 | 171 | 179 | 186 | 194 | 202 | 210 | 218 | 225 | 233 | 272 | 311 |
| 75 | 152 | 160 | 168 | 176 | 184 | 192 | 200 | 208 | 216 | 224 | 232 | 240 | 279 | 319 |
| 76 | 156 | 164 | 172 | 180 | 189 | 197 | 205 | 213 | 221 | 230 | 238 | 246 | 287 | 328 |

### Body weight in pounds according to height and body mass index.

| BMI | Weight class |
|---|---|
| 18.5 or less | Underweight |
| 18.5–24.9 | Normal |
| 25.0–29.9 | Overweight |
| 30.0–34.9 | Obese |
| 35.0–39.9 | More Obese |
| 40 or greater | Extremely Obese |

as early as the controlled weight gain program in an inpatient setting. Family members can praise an adolescent for gaining weight and refraining from pressures to stay thin.

Family therapy after a person has left the hospital may focus on reducing conflict among family members and ensuring everyone can maintain appropriate patterns of food preparation and consumption. Family therapists also address expressed emotion to ease overinvolvement, criticism, and hostility among family members (Rutherford & Couturier, 2007). Parents are initially encouraged to take control of what their adolescent eats, but over time this responsibility shifts to the teen (Wilson, 2005). Family therapy generally lasts 6 months to 3 years and tends to work better in the short term than the long term (Fisher, Hetrick, & Rushford, 2010). Family therapy may be more effective if combined with medication or the cognitive-behavioral approaches we discuss next.

## COGNITIVE-BEHAVIORAL THERAPY

Recall that we previously separated cognitive and behavioral approaches to therapy for anxiety-related, somatic symptom, and depressive and bipolar disorders. Therapists who treat eating disorders, however, often combine cognitive and behavioral therapies into a singular approach we describe here. Cognitive-behavioral therapy (CBT) is a dominant approach for treating many different eating disorders and especially bulimia nervosa and binge eating disorder (Agras & Apple, 2007). CBT often focuses on binging and purging cycles as well as cognitive aspects of body dissatisfaction, overconcern with weight and shape,

and perfectionism. The therapy is often conducted in conjunction with a nutrition and medication program and possibly family therapy.

CBT for bulimia nervosa rests on cognitive and behavioral factors that influence development and maintenance of symptoms (see **Figure 8.5**; Murphy, Straebler, Cooper, & Fairburn, 2010). People with bulimia nervosa have a rigid idea of an ideal body shape and weight, which leads them to overly restrict food intake to increase self-esteem. This rigid stance makes a person psychologically and physiologically vulnerable to periodically lose control over their eating (binge). These episodes are negatively reinforced because they reduce distress and negative feelings from restrictive dieting. People then feel compelled to purge (vomit) to prevent weight gain after a binge. Purging is also negatively reinforced because anxiety following the binge is reduced. Unfortunately, those with bulimia often feel guilty and depressed following a binge–purge cycle, which leads again to low self-esteem. This cycle thus brings them back to the initial situation—excessive dieting to improve self-esteem.

We can see this cycle develop with Lisa. Lisa was preoccupied with her weight and often limited her eating and weight by dieting. Dieting made her feel good about herself in the short term, but pressures of daily life and continued worry about her weight led to high stress. Lisa reduced her stress by eating, which in her case led to loss of control and overeating. Lisa felt better after a binge but then panicked and felt deep shame about her excess behavior. She then vomited to reduce her distress. Unfortunately,

---

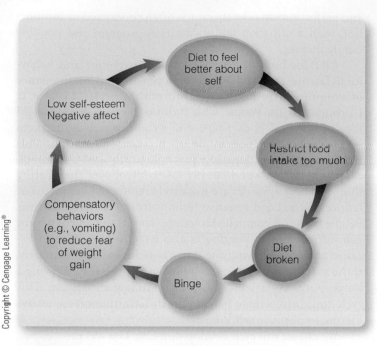

**FIGURE 8.5** A MODEL OF BULIMIA NERVOSA: THE BINGE–PURGE CYCLE

her usual stressors and worries about weight awaited her the next day and the cycle began again.

Cognitive-behavioral therapists try to interrupt this cycle by (1) questioning social standards for physical attractiveness, (2) challenging beliefs that encourage severe food restriction, and (3) developing normal eating patterns and habits. Several strategies are thus used, including the following:

- Self-monitoring eating, thoughts, urges, and behaviors
- Education about the model for bulimia nervosa and need for change
- Weekly weighing
- Education about body weight regulation, adverse effects of dieting, and consequences of purging
- Problem solving
- Changing rigid dieting
- Cognitive restructuring to address concerns about eating, body weight, and body shape
- Exposure methods to increase acceptance of body weight and shape
- Relapse prevention training

Cognitive-behavioral treatment for bulimia nervosa lasts about 18 weeks (Mitchell et al., 2011). In *Stage 1*, the therapist explains the cognitive-behavioral model of bulimia nervosa, begins weekly weighing, and teaches the client to self-monitor eating, drinking, the contexts in which these occur, and associated

thoughts and feelings. A typical monitoring sheet is shown in **Figure 8.6.** A therapist will review these monitoring sheets and other homework assignments in subsequent sessions. The therapist also provides education about the nature of bulimia nervosa and gives feedback about eating as well as how to limit purging or vomiting. Lisa was taught to delay the time between a binge and her purging to see that her distress level would drop by itself without having to vomit.

*Stage 2* of cognitive-behavioral treatment addresses all forms of dieting, concerns about weight and shape, perfectionism, low self-esteem, and problem solving skills. Lisa was taught to prepare healthy foods, limit types of food she brought into the house, discuss what she valued about herself other than weight, and how to avoid times and places that put her at risk for binging. She also enlisted the help of friends who helped monitor her eating behavior. The aim of *Stage 3* is to prevent relapse.

Individualized maintenance plans, like that outlined in **Figure 8.7,** can be developed so a client can anticipate and plan for future eating problems and setbacks. Nutritionists can also help with structured meal plans and exercise regimens to address weight control issues during these stages. Evidence supports the effectiveness of cognitive-behavioral treatment for binge eating

| Day _____ | | | Date _____ |
|---|---|---|---|

| Time | Food and liquid consumed | Place | Context |
|---|---|---|---|
| 7:35 | 1  grapefruit<br>1  cup black coffee } | Kitchen | Feel really fat. |
| 11:10 | 1  apple | Work | |
| 3:15 | 2  Twix<br>1  bread roll | High St.<br>" | |
| | a  fruit cake | Market | Everyone looked at me in the market. I'm out of control. I hate myself. I can't stop crying. |
| 3:30 | 2  chocolate eggs<br>2  bread rolls<br>1/2  pint of milk | "<br>Kitchen<br>" | |
| 5:10 | 1  bowl of cereal<br>1  bowl of cereal<br>1  pita bread with<br>   cottage cheese | "<br>"<br>" | |
| 6:00 | 1  glass water | " | |
| | a  baked potato<br>1  can diet soda | Outside<br>" | Weighed myself<br>   lost 8 lbs – too heavy |
| 9:00 | 1  cup soup<br>1  ice cube<br>1  cup coffee } | Kitchen<br>"<br>" | Feel fat and ugly. |
| 9:20 | | | |
| 10:00 | | | Why do I do this? I want to be thin. I can't help it |
| 11:20 | 1  coffee (black) | Sitting room | |
| | 1  coffee (black)<br>6  shortbread biscuits<br>4  pieces of chocolate<br>2  pieces of toast<br>2  glasses of water | Kitchen<br>"<br>"<br>"<br>" | Weighed myself<br>   lost 7 lbs – fat<br><br>Took 24 Nylax. |

**FIGURE 8.6** A MONITORING SHEET USED IN COGNITIVE-BEHAVIORAL TREATMENT FOR BULIMIA NERVOSA

but less so for weight control (Grilo, Masheb, Wilson, Gueorguieva, & White, 2011).

## What If I Have Weight Concerns or an Eating Disorder?

People are often screened for eating disorders, and the answers to some basic questions may indicate whether further assessment or even treatment is warranted. Some of these questions are listed in **Table 8.11**. If you find yourself answering "yes" to most of these questions, then you may wish to consult a clinical psychologist, psychiatrist, or other mental health professional (Chapter 15). Cognitive-behavioral therapy and/or medication may be best.

If you feel you have eating concerns but not necessarily an eating disorder, then teaching yourself to gain better control over your eating patterns and change your thoughts about your body may be best. Talk about your concerns with family members and friends or attend an eating disorders screening. Further information about

Eating problems may recur at times of stress. You should regard your eating problem as an Achilles' heel: It is the way you are prone to react at times of difficulty. You discovered during treatment that certain techniques helped you regain control over eating. The techniques that you found most helpful are listed below. These should be reinstituted under two sets of circumstances:

> 1. If your eating problem is getting worse
> 2. If you sense you are at risk of relapse

At such times there will often be some underlying problem. You must therefore examine what is happening in your life and look for any events or difficulties that might be of relevance. If any problems seem relevant, you should consider all possible solutions in order to construct a plan of action. In addition, you should use one or more of the following strategies to address your eating:

1. Set some time aside so that you can reflect on the current situation. You need to devise a plan of action. Reckon on formally reevaluating your progress every day or so. Some strategies may have worked; some may not.

2. Restart monitoring everything you eat, when you eat it.

3. Confine your eating to three planned meals each day, plus two planned snacks.

4. Plan your days ahead. Avoid both long periods of unstructured time and overbooking. If you are feeling at risk of losing control, plan your meals in detail so that you know exactly what and when you will be eating. In general, you should try to keep one step ahead of the problem.

5. Identify the times at which you are most likely to overeat (from recent experience and the evidence provided by your monitoring sheets) and plan alternative activities that are not compatible with eating, such as meeting friends, exercising, or taking a bath or shower.

6. If you are thinking too much about your weight, make sure that you are weighing yourself no more than once a week. If necessary, stop weighing altogether. If you want to reduce weight, do so by cutting down the quantities that you eat at each meal rather than by skipping meals or avoiding certain foods. Remember, you should accept a weight range, and gradual changes in weight are best.

7. If you are thinking too much about your shape, this may be because you are anxious or depressed. You tend to feel fat when things are not going well. You should try problem solving in order to see whether you can identify any current problems and do something positive to solve, or at least minimize, them.

8. If possible, confide in someone. Talk through your problem. A trouble shared is a trouble halved. Remember, you would not mind any friend of yours sharing his or her problems with you.

9. Set yourself limited realistic goals. Work from hour to hour. One failure does not justify a succession of failures. Note down any progress, however modest, on your monitoring sheets.

**FIGURE 8.7** **A MAINTENANCE PLAN FOLLOWING COGNITIVE-BEHAVIORAL TREATMENT FOR BULIMIA NERVOSA** *From Fairburn, C. G., Marcus, M. D., & Wilson, G. T. (1993). Cognitive behaviour therapy for binge eating and bulimia nervosa: A comprehensive treatment manual. In C. G. Fairburn & G. T. Wilson (Eds.), Binge eating: Nature, assessment, and treatment (pp. 361-404). New York: Guilford. Copyright © 1993 by Guilford Publications, Inc. Reprinted by permission.*

screening and treatment for eating disorders can be found at the websites of the National Eating Disorders Association (www.nationaleatingdisorders.org) or the National Association of Anorexia Nervosa and Associated Eating Disorders (www.anad.org).

## Long-Term Outcome for People with Eating Disorders

What is the long-term picture, or *prognosis*, for people with eating disorders? The picture is not particularly bright for those with anorexia nervosa. Anorexia nervosa has the highest mortality rate of any mental disorder, including depression—about

10 percent of those with anorexia nervosa eventually die via starvation or suicide (Arcelus et al., 2011). Another 40 percent remain chronically impaired, with symptoms waxing and waning over time. The better news is that many people with anorexia nervosa show improved though not totally absent symptoms over time (Wade, Bergin, Tiggemann, Bulik, & Fairburn, 2006). Sooki eventually sought treatment but dropped out after only a few sessions. Her prognosis over time is thus likely to be variable or poor.

Treatment outcomes for people with anorexia nervosa vary and can range from good (27.5 percent) or intermediate (25.3 percent) to poor (39.6 percent) or deceased (7.7 percent;

## Table 8.11

### Screening Questions for Eating Disorders

▶ Are you constantly thinking about your weight and food?

▶ Are you dieting strictly and/or have you lost a lot of weight?

▶ Are you more than 10% below your healthy weight?

▶ Are people concerned about your weight?

▶ Is your energy level down?

▶ Do you constantly feel cold?

▶ Are you overeating and feeling out of control?

▶ Are you vomiting, using laxatives or water pills, herbal agents, or trying to fast as a way to control your weight?

▶ Are you overexercising or do others consider your exercise excessive?

▶ Does your weight drastically fluctuate?

▶ Do any of the above interfere with your enjoyment of life, relationships, or everyday functioning?

Note: *These questions are not intended to diagnose an eating disorder.* They are simply designed to indicate that a person may be thinking too much about food, weight, etc., or engaging in potentially eating-disordered behaviors. *Yes* answers to more than five of these questions could indicate a problem that should be evaluated by a professional. For a list of mental health professionals and support groups in your area, visit the National Association of Anorexia Nervosa and Associated Eating Disorders at www.anad.org.

Source: National Association of Anorexia Nervosa and Associated Eating Disorders (www.anad.org).

Fichter, Quadflieg, & Hedlund, 2006). People who seek treatment for anorexia nervosa generally do better if they have less purging behavior and shorter duration of the disorder. Those treated for anorexia nervosa generally do worse if they continue to have a compulsion to exercise, have poor social relationships and a hostile attitude toward their family, and have other mental disorders such as depression (Berkman, Lohr, & Bulik, 2007). Many people with anorexia eventually develop bulimia nervosa or binge eating disorder and must seek treatment for these conditions as well (Fichter & Quadflieg, 2007).

The picture is more optimistic for bulimia nervosa. People with bulimia nervosa can have an intermittent course involving recurring symptoms and symptom-free periods. Symptoms of bulimia nervosa often diminish over time. Other people with bulimia nervosa have a more chronic course, however, in which symptoms persist (Fichter, Quadflieg, & Hedlund, 2008). The course for binge eating disorder is also variable, with remission rates of 25% to 80% (Keel & Brown, 2010). Binge eating disorder is associated with health problems such as obesity, hypertension, diabetes, coronary heart disease, sleep apnea, stroke, and certain cancers (Bulik & Reichborn-Kjennerud, 2003).

People who seek treatment for bulimia nervosa show full recovery (45%), considerable improvement (27%), or chronic course that includes crossing over to another eating disorder or mortality (28%; Steinhausen & Weber, 2009). Some show various improvements in dysfunctional dieting, weight loss, and body image. Cognitive-behavioral treatment is more effective than medication or other psychological treatments for bulimia nervosa, though medication is often used in conjunction with psychological treatment (Mitchell et al., 2011; Wilson, 2005). People who seek treatment for bulimia nervosa generally do better if they respond early to treatment and have better impulse control and less depression. Such was the case for Lisa. People who seek treatment for bulimia nervosa generally do worse if they have poor social adjustment or a lifetime history of anorexia (Berkman, Lohr, & Bulik, 2007).

### INTERIM SUMMARY

▶ Major approaches to assess eating disorders include interviews, self-report questionnaires, self-monitoring, and physical assessment.

▶ Treatments for eating disorders share some general aims: returning to a healthy weight; increasing motivation to restore healthy eating patterns; providing education about healthy eating; aiding recognition of problematic feelings, thoughts, and behaviors; enlisting support from others; and preventing relapse.

▶ Controlled weight gain and medication are prominent biological approaches to treating eating disorders.

▶ Family and cognitive behavioral therapies are the most effective psychological treatments for eating disorders.

▶ Of the eating disorders, the prognosis, course, and treatment outcome for bulimia nervosa is most favorable, followed by binge eating disorder and anorexia nervosa.

### REVIEW QUESTIONS

1. Describe major assessment techniques for eating disorders, including interviews, self-report questionnaires, self-monitoring, and physical assessment.

2. What different methods may be used to treat anorexia nervosa?

3. What different methods may be used to treat bulimia nervosa?

4. What strategies could a mental health professional use to help someone with binge eating disorder?

5. What is the long-term outcome for people with eating disorders?

## Final Comments

Eating disorders are not as prevalent as other disorders we discuss in this textbook, but they are serious conditions with many adverse physical outcomes. These disorders are especially relevant to college-age, young adults. Eating problems lie on a continuum, so many people likely share eating concerns and symptoms with those who meet criteria for an eating disorder. Help is available, so if you or someone you know has concerns about body weight and shape or eating behaviors, talking to someone about it or contacting a qualified mental health professional is a good idea.

## Thought Questions

1. Think about models or television or film stars that seem markedly underweight or overweight. Do you think they have symptoms of an eating disorder? Which disorders, and why?

2. Have you ever been concerned about your body shape or weight? How about your own eating behavior? What factors may have influenced this? What information in this chapter seems most relevant to you?

3. What would you now say to a friend who might have concerns about her body weight or shape or about her eating behaviors?

4. What separates "normal" eating or weight concerns from "abnormal" eating or weight concerns?

5. Do you think eating disorders have more to do with biological, family, cultural, or other factors? Why?

## Key Terms

weight concerns 222
body dissatisfaction 222
eating disorder 222
eating problems 222
restricted eating 223
dieting 223
lack of control over
   eating 223
anorexia nervosa 223
restricting behaviors 223

purging 223
bulimia nervosa 225
binge eating 225
compensatory
   behaviors 225
binge eating disorder 225
satiety 233
endogenous opioids 233
electronic diaries 240

## Media Resources

### MindTap

MindTap for Kearney and Trull's *Abnormal Psychology and Life: A Dimensional Approach* is a highly personalized fully online learning platform of authoritative content, assignments, and services offering you a tailored presentation of course curriculum created by your instructor. MindTap guides you through the course curriculum via an innovative learning path where you will complete reading assignments, annotate your readings, complete homework, and engage with quizzes and assessments. MindTap includes the Continuum Video Project.

Go to **cengagebrain.com** to access MindTap.

# 9

# Substance-Related Disorders

---

## CASE: *Elon*

**What Do You Think?**

Normal Substance Use and Substance-Related Disorders: What Are They?

Substance-Related Disorders: Features and Epidemiology

Stigma Associated with Substance-Related Disorders
Interim Summary
Review Questions

Substance-Related Disorders: Causes and Prevention
Interim Summary
Review Questions

Substance-Related Disorders: Assessment and Treatment
Interim Summary
Review Questions

FINAL COMMENTS
THOUGHT QUESTIONS
KEY TERMS
MEDIA RESOURCES

## SPECIAL FEATURES

CONTINUUM FIGURE 9.1 Continuum of Substance Use and Substance-Related Disorders 252–253

BOX 9.1 | The Sam Spady Story 258
BOX 9.2 | The "Meth" Epidemic 261
BOX 9.3 | Focus on Gender: Date Rape Drugs 263
BOX 9.4 | Focus on Violence: Alcohol and Violence 272

### THE CONTINUUM VIDEO PROJECT

*Mark:* Substance Use Disorder 271

PERSONAL NARRATIVE 9.1 One Family's Struggle with Substance-Related Disorders 278–279

BOX 9.5 | Focus on Law and Ethics: Drug Testing 281

## CASE: Elon

**Elon** was a student at a large public college who enjoyed the party scene even more than his friend DeShawn (Chapter 3). DeShawn entered college with an eye toward academics, but Elon entered college with an eye toward socializing and having as much fun as possible. Elon was an 18-year-old African American male who achieved good grades in high school and received an academic scholarship for the first 2 years of college. Elon's good performance in high school courses was due more to his intellectual talent than hard work. He was therefore able to enter college, but he found himself overwhelmed by professors' demands for extensive writing projects, reading assignments, and oral presentations.

Elon was somewhat impulsive but also extroverted and gregarious. He blended into parties, made friends, and found sexual partners with ease. Elon drank alcohol excessively at these parties, as he had sometimes done in high school, and smoked marijuana on occasion. Using these drugs eased his concern about the demands of school and

Image Source/Jupiter Images

satisfied his personal need for attention and companionship. Unfortunately, Elon failed all but one course his first semester.

Elon received academic probation and vowed to improve his reading and studying during his second semester. This strategy worked for the first 2 weeks, but Elon became bored with the course material and again started to attend campus parties. He also became bored with his usual social and party scene, however, and began to experiment with creative sexual practices and different drugs. Elon began using cocaine to boost effects of his alcohol use and used marijuana to calm himself after using too much cocaine.

Elon was soon almost out of money from buying alcohol and other drugs. He stopped attending classes and spent much of his day watching television, sleeping, and playing videogames. At night, Elon found a party or sought people who could give him illicit drugs. He remained sexually active but his ability to perform was impaired. He thus sought more powerful drugs and drug combinations to satisfy his need for a "high."

Elon secured a loan from his parents and began spending more time in areas of the city with significant drug activity. He tried different drugs and drug combinations, and he settled on a personal favorite called PNP—"party and play"—that involved crystal methamphetamine and sildenafil (a drug such as Viagra

or Cialis that helps men achieve penile erections). This combination allowed Elon to experience greatly enhanced mood, feelings of invulnerability, and sexual performance. The drug combination was quickly addictive and Elon eventually spent nearly all his time seeking or using the drug cocktail.

Elon continued his drug use despite an arrest for lewd conduct and a visit to the emergency room for a seizure (a side effect of methamphetamine with sildenafil). Elon's parents finally found their son sleeping half-naked in a downtown alleyway. Elon had no recollection of the past few days, and his parents took him to a drug rehabilitation facility. Elon was about to undergo the painful process of drug withdrawal and the even more painful process of admitting to his parents what happened to him.

### What Do You Think?

1. Which of Elon's symptoms seem typical for a college student, and which seem very different?

2. What external events and internal factors might be responsible for Elon's drug use?

3. What are you curious about regarding Elon?

4. Does Elon remind you in any way of yourself or someone you know? How so?

5. How might Elon's drug use affect his life in the future?

## Normal Substance Use and Substance-Related Disorders: What Are They?

How many people do you know who regularly use some kind of drug? The number might surprise you. Many of us have a glass of wine, smoke a cigarette, drink soda, or take prescribed pain or sleep medication during the day or night. Each substance

contains a key drug—alcohol, nicotine, caffeine, or a morphine derivative in these cases—that affects behavior. Many people drink alcohol to unwind after a hard day, smoke cigarettes to relax, drink caffeinated beverages to boost energy, and take medication for pain. Many of us engage in **substance use** that somehow affects our behavior. Such use is normal and may not lead to significant problems if we use the drug carefully.

Other people engage in substance use a bit more frequently. You may know someone who drinks a couple of alcoholic beverages or smokes a half-pack of cigarettes every day. This is substance use on a grander scale but is not necessarily a problem if he can stop using the drug or if he is not physically addicted to the drug. Someone going through a rough time of life may drink alcohol more frequently than before but not necessarily drive and wreck a car when drinking. Or, a person may smoke cigarettes occasionally but have no daily cravings for nicotine. No impairment occurs in daily functioning, and no substantial physical harm takes place.

Some people continue to engage in substance use and do so to a greater degree, however. You may know people who get drunk more than once a week or who seem hooked on painkillers. Daily functioning *does* seem impaired, or some physical harm *is* taking place in these cases. A person may attempt to drive while drunk, fight with others over use of painkillers, or have trouble getting up in the morning to go to work. A person may thus be engaging in substance use to a moderate or intense degree (see **Figure 9.1**).

For people like Elon, substance use becomes so severe that many areas of life are greatly impaired. Elon's extensive and varied drug use caused his academic failure, financial ruin, and legal troubles. He was also endangering his life because of physical addiction to drugs. Elon was spending nearly all his time looking for and using legal and illegal drugs. He must have known his lifestyle was self-destructive, but he reached a point where he could not control his own drug-seeking behavior. Elon was experiencing substance use to a *severe degree*, or a **substance-related disorder**. We discuss features of this tragic and rampant problem in this chapter.

## Substance-Related Disorders: Features and Epidemiology

Substance-related disorders include substance use disorder as well as substance intoxication and withdrawal. Substance use disorder combines previous diagnostic categories of substance abuse and substance dependence. We discuss these problems next.

### Substance Use Disorder

**Substance use disorder** involves *repeated* use of substances to the point that recurring problems are evident. Diagnostic criteria for alcohol use disorder, for example, are listed in **Table 9.1** (American Psychiatric Association [APA], 2013). Severity of substance use disorder is based partly on the number of diagnostic criteria shown by a person (Table 9.1). Substance use disorders generally involve impaired control, social impairment, risky use, and tolerance and/or withdrawal.

*Impaired control* means the person has difficulty cutting down on his substance use, ingests more and more of the drug over time, spends a great amount of time looking for the drug or recovering from its use, and has intense craving for the drug. DeShawn and Elon tried to reduce their substance use but were unsuccessful in doing so. Elon eventually spent so much time searching for drugs (drug-seeking behavior) that he gave up many of his academic and social activities. Drug-seeking

### Table 9.1

#### DSM-5  Alcohol Use Disorder

A. A problematic pattern of alcohol use leading to clinically significant impairment or distress, as manifested by at least two of the following, occurring within a 12-month period:
   1. Alcohol is often taken in larger amounts or over a longer period than was intended.
   2. There is a persistent desire or unsuccessful efforts to cut down or control alcohol use.
   3. A great deal of time is spent in activities necessary to obtain alcohol, use alcohol, or recover from its effects.
   4. Craving, or a strong desire or urge to use alcohol.
   5. Recurrent alcohol use resulting in a failure to fulfill major role obligations at work, school, or home.
   6. Continued alcohol use despite having persistent or recurrent social or interpersonal problems caused or exacerbated by the effects of alcohol.
   7. Important social, occupational, or recreational activities are given up or reduced because of alcohol use.
   8. Recurrent alcohol use in situations in which it is physically hazardous.
   9. Alcohol use is continued despite knowledge of having a persistent or recurrent physical or psychological problem that is likely to have been caused or exacerbated by alcohol.
   10. Tolerance, as defined by either of the following:
       a. A need for markedly increased amounts of alcohol to achieve intoxication or desired effect.
       b. A markedly diminished effect with continued use of the same amount of alcohol.
   11. Withdrawal, as manifested by either of the following:
       a. The characteristic withdrawal syndrome for alcohol.
       b. Alcohol (or a closely related substance, such as a benzodiazepine) is taken to relieve or avoid withdrawal symptoms.

Specify if in early or sustained remission and if in a controlled environment as well as mild (2-3 symptoms), moderate (4-5 symptoms), or severe (6+ symptoms).

American Psychiatric Association. (2013). *Diagnostic and statistical manual of mental disorders* (5th ed.). Arlington, VA: American Psychiatric Association.

behavior sometimes relates to *psychological dependence* on a drug, meaning a person believes she needs the drug to function effectively (Narita et al., 2005). A person may use cocaine at work because she feels she needs it to present well before others or accomplish a substantial amount of work in a short period.

*Social impairment* means the person is experiencing key problems in his life because of substance use. Such problems could include missing many work or school days, neglecting or otherwise maltreating children, driving or operating heavy machinery

**CONTINUUM FIGURE 9.1** Continuum of Substance Use and Substance-Related Disorders

| | Normal | Mild |
|---|---|---|
| Emotions | Stable mood. | Mild discomfort about the day; feeling a bit irritable or down. |
| Cognitions | No concern about substance use | Thoughts about the difficulty of the day. Worry that something will go wrong at work |
| Behaviors | Occasional but appropriate alcohol use or use of medication. | Drinking a bit more than usual; relying on medication to sleep. |

while impaired, legal troubles, fighting, or arguing with partners or friends about intoxication. Elon clearly had a substance use disorder because he was missing classes, withdrawing from old friends and family members, and driving while impaired.

*Risky use* means that the person continues taking the drug despite the fact that it places him in hazardous situations. The person's use of the drug continues even though he may know that doing so is harmful or that it creates physical or psychological problems. Elon knew his lifestyle was destructive, but he could not stop using drugs.

Finally, people with substance use disorder often show *tolerance and/or withdrawal*. **Tolerance** refers to the need to ingest greater and greater quantities of a drug to achieve the same effect. Someone who regularly drinks three beers a day will find over time that the same physiological "high" from this amount no longer exists. The person must thus drink more beer or switch to another, more powerful drug to achieve the same effect. Withdrawal refers to maladaptive behavioral changes when a person stops using a drug (see Substance Withdrawal section).

## Substance Intoxication

Have you known someone who got drunk but, when you spoke to him the next day, seemed fine despite a hangover? He perhaps experienced **substance intoxication**, a usually reversible condition brought on by excessive use of a drug such as alcohol. Diagnostic criteria for alcohol intoxication, for example, are listed in **Table 9.2** (APA, 2013). A person who becomes intoxicated experiences maladaptive changes in behavior—he may become aggressive, make inappropriate sexual advances, and show impaired judgment and rapid shifts in mood. Impaired judgment may lead to a poor decision to drive, and rapid shifts in mood may lead to depression.

An intoxicated person may also have difficulty staying awake, thinking clearly, or even walking. Some people may be intoxicated for short periods, but others go on *binges* and remain intoxicated for lengthy periods. Elon later vaguely recalled to a drug counselor that he once used meth

### Table 9.2

#### DSM-5 Alcohol Intoxication

A. Recent ingestion of alcohol.

B. Clinically significant problematic behavioral or psychological changes that developed during, or shortly after, alcohol ingestion.

C. One (or more) of the following signs or symptoms developing during, or shortly after, alcohol use:
  1. Slurred speech.
  2. Incoordination.
  3. Unsteady gait.
  4. Nystagmus.
  5. Impairment in attention or memory.
  6. Stupor or coma.

D. The signs or symptoms are not attributable to another medical condition and are not better explained by another mental disorder, including intoxication with another substance.

American Psychiatric Association. (2013). *Diagnostic and statistical manual of mental disorders* (5th ed.). Arlington, VA: American Psychiatric Association.

(methamphetamine) for 6 straight days. Keep in mind that intoxication is not generally considered abnormal *without* maladaptive behavioral changes. A person who comes home after a long week at work, drinks several margaritas, and falls asleep, does not have a mental disorder.

## Substance Withdrawal

**Substance withdrawal** refers to maladaptive behavioral changes when a person stops using a drug. Diagnostic criteria for alcohol withdrawal, for example, are listed in **Table 9.3** (APA, 2013). When a person stops taking a drug, severe physical and

| Moderate | Substance-Related Disorder — less severe | Substance-Related Disorder — more severe |
|---|---|---|
| Considerable stress and sadness (note that opposite emotions occur when drug is used). | Intense stress, sadness, and feelings of emptiness; agitation about not having access to a specific drug or drugs. | Extreme stress, sadness, and feelings of emptiness. Extreme agitation when drug is not available. |
| Dwelling on negative aspects of the day; worry about threats to one's job or marriage. Thoughts about ways to hide excessive substance use. | Frequent thoughts about using substances and worry about harm to personal health. | Thoughts focused almost exclusively on drug use and self-destruction of one's lifestyle. |
| Drinking alcohol regularly at night; occasionally missing work; heavy use of medication. | Regular intoxication such that many days are missed from work; arguments with spouse about substance use; arrests for impairment. | Very frequent intoxication; loss of job or marriage; physical addiction to a drug; seeking to secure or use drugs most of the time. |

## Table 9.3

### DSM-5  Alcohol Withdrawal

A. Cessation of (or reduction in) alcohol use that has been heavy and prolonged.

B. Two (or more) of the following, developing within several hours to a few days after the cessation of (or reduction in) alcohol use described in Criterion A:
   1. Autonomic hyperactivity (e.g., sweating or pulse rate greater than 100 bpm).
   2. Increased hand tremor.
   3. Insomnia.
   4. Nausea or vomiting.
   5. Transient visual, tactile, or auditory hallucinations or illusions.
   6. Psychomotor agitation.
   7. Anxiety.
   8. Generalized tonic-clonic seizures.

C. The signs or symptoms in Criterion B cause clinically significant distress or impairment in social, occupational, or other important areas of functioning.

D. The signs or symptoms are not attributable to another medical condition and are not better explained by another mental disorder, including intoxication or withdrawal from another substance.

Specify if with perceptual disturbances.

American Psychiatric Association. (2013). *Diagnostic and statistical manual of mental disorders* (5th ed.). Arlington, VA: American Psychiatric Association.

behavioral changes can occur. These changes are usually the opposite of the intoxicating effect of a drug and may include nausea, vomiting, tremors, fever, seizures, hearing voices or seeing things not actually there (hallucinations), and death. Behavioral changes such as anxiety, depression, and other mood states may also occur. A well-known feature of alcohol withdrawal is *delirium tremens* (DTs), which involves severe confusion and autonomic overactivity in the form of sweating, heart palpitations, and trembling (Thiercelin, Lechevallier, Rusch, & Plat, 2012).

The *DSM-5* lists many kinds of substances or drugs that a person could experience problems with (APA, 2013). Not all of these drugs necessarily involve a substance use disorder (e.g., caffeine), intoxication (e.g., tobacco), or withdrawal (e.g., hallucinogens), however. A list of substances and relevant diagnostic categories is in **Table 9.4**. We next discuss the specific characteristics of these substances.

## Types of Substances

A brief description of major substances that are used excessively as well as their street names and effects is listed in **Table 9.5**. Drugs fall into several main categories based on effects they have on behavior. Several categories were discussed in previous chapters, such as anxiolytics in Chapter 5 and antidepressants in Chapter 7. We also briefly mentioned neuroleptic, or antipsychotic, drugs in previous chapters (these are discussed in more detail in Chapter 12). Other main categories of drugs we discuss in this chapter include depressants, stimulants, opiates, hallucinogens, marijuana, and others.

### DEPRESSANTS

**Depressant**, or sedative, drugs are those that inhibit aspects of the central nervous system. Common depressants include alcohol, anesthetics for surgery, antiseizure medications for epilepsy, barbiturate drugs people use to calm themselves (largely replaced now by antianxiety drugs, discussed in Chapter 5), and hypnotic drugs people use to go to sleep. Popular examples of the latter include zolpidem (Ambien) and eszopiclone (Lunesta).

*Alcohol* is the most well-known and widely used depressant drug. You might be wondering why alcohol is classified as a depressant when, after a couple of drinks, a person feels elated or relieved. This is because alcohol initially affects a

## Table 9.4

### DSM-5 Diagnoses Associated with Substance Class

| | Psychotic disorders | Bipolar disorders | Depressive disorders | Anxiety disorders | Obsessive-compulsive and related disorders |
|---|---|---|---|---|---|
| Alcohol | I/W | I/W | I/W | I/W | |
| Caffeine | | | | I | |
| Cannabis | I | | | I | |
| Hallucinogens | | | | | |
|   Phencyclidine | I | I | I | I | |
|   Other hallucinogens | I* | I | I | I | |
| Inhalants | I | | I | I | |
| Opioids | | | I/W | W | |
| Sedatives, hypnotics, or anxiolytics | I/W | I/W | I/W | W | |
| Stimulants** | I | I/W | I/W | I/W | I/W |
| Tobacco | | | | | |
| Other (or unknown) | I/W | I/W | I/W | I/W | I/W |

Note. X= The category is recognized in DSM-5
I = The specifier "with onset during intoxication" may be noted for the category.
W = The specifier "with onset during withdrawal" may be noted for the category.
I/W = Either "with onset during intoxication" or "with onset during withdrawal" may be noted for the category.
P = The disorder is persisting.
*Also hallucinogen persisting perception disorders (flashbacks).
**Includes amphetamine-type substance, cocaine, and other or unspecified stimulants.
Reprinted with permission from the *Diagnostic and Statistical Manual of Mental Disorders*, Fifth Edition, (Copyright ©2013). American Psychiatric Association. All Rights Reserved.

## Table 9.5

### Common Substances and Their Street Names

| Drug | Street names |
|---|---|
| Acid (LSD) | Acid, blotter, and many others |
| Club drugs | XTC, X (MDMA); Special K, Vitamin K (ketamine); liquid ecstasy, soap (GHB); roofies (Rohypnol) |
| Cocaine | Coke, snow, flake, blow, and many others |
| Ecstasy/MDMA (methylene-dioxymethamphetamine) | XTC, X, Adam, hug, beans, love drug |
| Heroin | Smack, H, ska, junk, and many others |
| Inhalants | Whippets, poppers, snappers |
| Marijuana | Pot, ganga, weed, grass, and many others |
| Methamphetamine | Speed, meth, chalk, ice, crystal, glass |
| PCP/phencyclidine | Angel dust, ozone, wack, rocket fuel, and many others |
| Prescription medication | Commonly used opioids include oxycodone (OxyContin), propoxyphene (Darvon), hydrocodone (Vicodin), hydromorphone (Dilaudid), meperidine (Demerol), and diphenoxylate (Lomotil); common central nervous system depressants include barbiturates such as pentobarbital sodium (Nembutal), and benzodiazepines such as diazepam (Valium) and alprazolam (Xanax); stimulants include dextroamphetamine (Dexedrine) and methylphenidate (Ritalin) |

Source: National Institute on Drug Abuse and National Institute on Alcohol Abuse and Alcoholism.

| Sleep disorders | Sexual dysfunctions | Delirium | Neurocognitive disorders | Substance use disorders | Substance intoxication | Substance withdrawal |
|---|---|---|---|---|---|---|
| I/W | I/W | I/W | I/W/P | X | X | X |
| I/W |  |  |  |  | X | X |
| I/W |  | I |  | X | X | X |
|  |  | I |  | X | X |  |
|  |  | I |  | X | X |  |
|  |  | I | I/P | X | X |  |
| I/W | I/W | I/W |  | X | X | X |
| I/W | I/W | I/W | I/W/P | X | X | X |
| I/W | I | I |  | X | X | X |
| W |  |  |  | X |  | X |
| I/W | I/W | I/W | I/W/P | X | X | X |

neurotransmitter system most responsible for inhibition, the gamma-aminobutyric acid (GABA) system. Recall from Chapter 5 that impairment in the GABA system may relate to excess activity that manifests in the form of panic attacks. Alcohol is thus inhibiting a key inhibitory brain system. This process is **disinhibition**. A person may thus do things he might not do normally, such as talk a little more, dance, or make a sexual advance. He may feel a "high" or sense of well-being but is actually experiencing reduced central nervous system activity.

Alcohol effects closely relate to **blood alcohol level**, or concentration of alcohol in the blood. Various blood alcohol levels related to alcohol intake for males and females of different sizes are listed in **Table 9.6**. Common effects of alcohol use at different levels are listed in **Table 9.7**. People usually start feeling intoxicated at a blood alcohol level of 0.08, which is the legal cutoff for "driving under the influence" (DUI). **Lethal dose**, or LD, is the dose of a substance (alcohol in this case) that kills a certain percentage of test animals. LD1 is the dose at which 1 percent of test animals die at a certain blood alcohol level (McKim & Hancock, 2013). An LD50 kills about half and, in humans, occurs at a blood alcohol level of 0.40. This blood alcohol level is therefore extremely dangerous.

As a person drinks more alcohol past the disinhibition stage, she becomes more intoxicated as *excitatory* areas of the

Ianni Dimitrov / Alamy

Binge drinking can lead to many untoward consequences.

## Table 9.6

### Relationships among Gender, Weight, Alcohol Consumption, and Blood Alcohol Level

| Absolute alcohol (ounces) | Beverage intake* | Blood alcohol levels (mg/100 ml) | | | | | |
|---|---|---|---|---|---|---|---|
| | | Female (100 lb) | Male (100 lb) | Female (150 lb) | Male (150 lb) | Female (200 lb) | Male (200 lb) |
| 1/2 | 1 oz spirits† 1 glass wine 1 can beer | 0.045 | 0.037 | 0.03 | 0.025 | 0.022 | 0.019 |
| 1 | 2 oz spirits 2 glasses wine 2 cans beer | 0.090 | 0.075 | 0.06 | 0.050 | 0.045 | 0.037 |
| 2 | 4 oz spirits 4 glasses wine 4 cans beer | 0.180 | 0.150 | 0.12 | 0.100 | 0.090 | 0.070 |
| 3 | 6 oz spirits 6 glasses wine 6 cans beer | 0.270 | 0.220 | 0.18 | 0.150 | 0.130 | 0.110 |
| 4 | 8 oz spirits 8 glasses wine 8 cans beer | 0.360 | 0.300 | 0.24 | 0.200 | 0.180 | 0.150 |
| 5 | 10 oz spirits 10 glasses wine 10 cans beer | 0.450 | 0.370 | 0.30 | 0.250 | 0.220 | 0.180 |

* In 1 hour.
† 100-proof spirits.
From Ray, O. (1978). *Drugs, society, and human behavior* (2nd ed.). St. Louis, MO: C.V. Mosby, p. 147. Reprinted by permission.

brain become depressed or inhibited. These excitatory areas of the brain include the reticular activating system, the limbic system, and the cortex. You may notice that someone who continues to drink alcohol experiences changes in behavior and personality, perhaps becoming more surly or aggressive. Reflexes and other motor behaviors also become impaired, judgment and reasoning become clouded, and attention and concentration become difficult to maintain. You can see this is a recipe for disaster should the person decide to drive.

Other common effects of alcohol at this stage include increased sexual desire but poor performance, an erroneous belief that problem-solving ability is adequate as one is becoming sober, and memory impairment. You may have difficulties remembering the name of a new person you met the night before while drinking. People who continue drinking may also mix their alcohol with other drugs, which can lower the dose necessary for death. This is because mixing different drugs (polysubstance use) causes a *synergistic* or multiplicative, not additive, effect. Drinking 3 shots of whiskey and snorting 3 lines of cocaine, for example, does

not add to 6 units of effect but rather multiplies to 9. Interaction effects of alcohol with other common drugs are shown in **Table 9.8**.

As alcohol use intensifies and a person becomes extremely drunk, strong changes in personality and behavior occur. Many people become depressed, stupefied, or unconscious. Walking and talking become difficult, and a person may have trouble breathing. As the alcohol depresses areas of the brain necessary for involuntary actions, such as the medulla that controls breathing, a person is at risk for asphyxiation and death.

*Binge drinking* involves ingesting large amounts of alcohol in a short period and relates to many college student deaths and problems (Courtney & Polich, 2009). A college student at Colorado State University died after binge drinking over an 11-hour period (see **Box 9.1**). According to the National Institute of Alcoholism and Alcohol Abuse, binge drinking corresponds to 5 or more drinks for males and 4 or more drinks for females in a 2-hour period. A College Alcohol Study conducted by the Harvard School of Public Health

**Table 9.7**

### Blood Alcohol Levels (BALs) and Expected Behavior

| Percent BAL | Behavior |
|---|---|
| 0.01 | Few overt effects, slight feeling of relaxation |
| 0.03 | Relaxed with slight exhilaration, decrease in visual tracking, minimal impairment in mental functions |
| 0.05 | Feeling relaxed and warm, some release of inhibition, some impaired judgment, lowered alertness, slight decrease in fine motor skills, mild reduction in visual capability in tracking and glare recovery |
| 0.06 | Mild relaxation, slight impairment in fine motor skills, increase in reaction time, slurred speech, poor muscle control, exaggerated emotions |
| 0.08 | Legal evidence of intoxication and DUI; vision impaired, increased loss of motor functions, may stagger |
| 0.09 | Judgment now clouded, lessening of inhibitions and self-restraint, reduced visual and hearing acuity, increased difficulty in performing motor skills |
| 0.10 | Slowed reaction times, slurred speech, drowsiness, nausea, deficits in coordination, impaired motor functioning, and difficulty in focusing, judging moving targets, and glare recovery |
| 0.15 | Major impairment in physical and mental functions, difficulty in standing, walking and talking; disturbed perception, blurred vision, large increases in reaction times, falling asleep, vomiting |
| 0.20 | Marked depression of sensory and motor functions, mentally confused, gross body movements can be made only with assistance, unable to maintain an upright position, incoherent speech, needs assistance to walk, has difficulty staying awake, vomiting |
| 0.25 | Severe motor disturbance, sensory perceptions greatly impaired, staggering, as well as behaviors seen at 0.20 |
| 0.30 | Stuporous but conscious, severe mental confusion, difficulty in reacting to stimuli, general suppression of sensibility, little comprehension of what is going on, respiratory depression, brain functions severely depressed, repeatedly falling down, passes out, may be in coma |
| 0.40 | Almost complete anesthesia, reflexes are depressed, breathing and heartbeat may stop, unconscious and may be dead |
| 0.50 | Completely unconscious, deep coma if not dead |
| 0.60 | Death most likely; depression of brain centers that control heart rate and breathing |

From R.J. Craig, *Counseling the alcohol and drug dependent client: A practical approach* (p. 93) New York: Pearson, 2004. Reprinted by permission of Pearson Education, Inc.

surveyed 14,941 students at 140 American colleges and universities. Some of the study's most important findings include the following (Wechsler & Wilson, 2008):

- Within the past 30 days, 22 percent of students drank on 10 or more occasions, 45 percent binged when drinking, 29 percent were drunk 3 or more times, and 47 percent drank to get drunk.
- Only 19 percent of students abstained from alcohol.
- More students drank alcohol than used cocaine, marijuana, or cigarettes combined.
- The strongest predictor of binge drinking was fraternity or sorority residence or membership.
- Other risk factors for binge drinking are male gender, athletic status, European American background, and age less than 24 years.
- Frequent binge drinkers are 17 times more likely to miss a class, 10 times more likely to vandalize property, and 8 times more likely to be injured because of their drinking.
- 10 percent of female students who are frequent binge drinkers were reportedly raped or subjected to nonconsensual sex compared with 3 percent of female non–binge drinkers.

People addicted to alcohol (alcoholism) are clearly at risk for other health problems. Withdrawal symptoms can be particularly severe and include delirium tremens, mentioned earlier. Extensive alcohol use is also associated with increased risk for suicide, homicide, unprotected sexual activity, sexual assault, and traffic and other accidents (Schermer, 2006; Thompson, 2006). People who chronically and excessively use alcohol also commonly experience **cirrhosis of the liver** in which scar tissue replaces liver tissue, leading to loss of

## Table 9.8

### Alcohol–Drug Interactions

| Drug | Prescribed purpose | Interaction |
| --- | --- | --- |
| Anesthetics (e.g., Diprivan, Ethrane, Fluothane) | Administered before surgery to render a patient unconscious and insensitive to pain | ▶ Increased amount of drug required to induce loss of consciousness<br>▶ Increased risk of liver damage |
| Antibiotics | Used to treat infectious diseases | ▶ Reduced drug effectiveness<br>▶ Nausea/vomiting<br>▶ Headache<br>▶ Convulsions |
| Antidepressants (e.g., Elavil) | Used to treat depression and other forms of mental disorder | ▶ Increased sedative effects<br>▶ May decrease effectiveness of antidepressant<br>▶ Potential for dangerous rise in blood pressure |
| Antihistamines (e.g., Benadryl) | Used to treat allergic symptoms and insomnia | ▶ Intensified sedation<br>▶ Excessive dizziness |
| Antiulcer medications (e.g., Tagamet, Zantac) | Used to treat ulcers and other gastrointestinal problems | ▶ Prolonged effect of alcohol<br>▶ Increased risk of side effects |
| Narcotic pain relievers (morphine, codeine, Darvon, Demerol) | Used to alleviate moderate to severe pain | ▶ Intensified sedation<br>▶ Increased possibility of a fatal overdose |
| Nonnarcotic pain relievers (aspirin, ibuprofen, acetaminophen) | Used to alleviate mild to moderate pain | ▶ Increased risk of stomach bleeding<br>▶ Increased risk of the inhibition of blood clotting<br>▶ Increased effects of consumed alcohol<br>Note: acetaminophen (Tylenol) taken during or after drinking may significantly increase one's risk of liver damage. |
| Sedatives and hypnotics (Valium, Dalmane, Ativan, sleeping pills) | Used to alleviate anxiety and insomnia | ▶ Severe drowsiness<br>▶ Depressed cardiac and respiratory functions<br>▶ Increased risk of coma or fatality |

Adapted from the National Institute on Alcohol Abuse and Alcoholism. (1995, January). Alcohol Alert (Publication No. 27 PH 355). Bethesda, MD: NIAAA.

---

### BOX 9.1

#### The Sam Spady Story

On September 5, 2004, an undergraduate student at Colorado State University died after binge drinking both beer and shots over an 11-hour period. The student, Samantha Spady, was a homecoming queen, cheerleading captain, and honor student in high school. She was a business major with big ambitions, but instead of fulfilling them, she became one of 1,400 college students aged 18 to 24 years who die from alcohol-related incidents each year (*USA Today*, 2006). Her story is now the subject of a DVD documentary (*Death by Alcohol: The Sam Spady Story*) available via a website established to honor Samantha and educate others about the dangers of binge drinking. The website (http://www.samspadyfoundation.org) also lists key signs that someone might be suffering from alcohol poisoning after binge drinking and needs *immediate help*:

- Unconscious or semiconscious
- Breathing less than 10 times per minute or irregular (check every 2 minutes)
- Cold, clammy, pale, or bluish skin
- Can't be awakened by pinching, prodding, or shouting
- Vomiting without waking up

Courtesy of Sam Spady Foundation

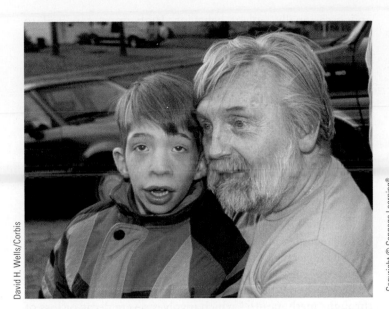

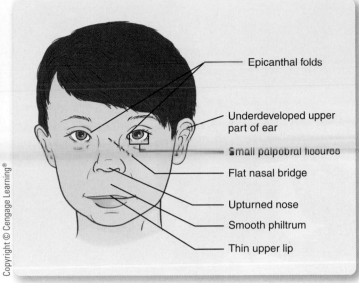

Epicanthal folds

Underdeveloped upper part of ear

Small palpebral fissures

Flat nasal bridge

Upturned nose

Smooth philtrum

Thin upper lip

Copyright © Cengage Learning®

David H. Wells/Corbis

**FIGURE 9.2** CHARACTERISTIC FACIAL FEATURES OF YOUTHS WITH FETAL ALCOHOL SYNDROME

function and possibly death (Rehm et al., 2010). **Korsakoff's syndrome**, a problem also discussed in Chapter 14, involves confusion, memory loss, and coordination difficulties because of thiamine deficiency from extended alcohol use (Kril & Harper, 2012).

The harmful effects of alcoholism have a wide reach and include children of people with alcoholism. These children are at increased risk of neglect or other maltreatment and at risk for developing substance-related problems later in life (Kelley et al., 2010; Yau et al., 2012). Some (1 percent) newborns exposed to maternal alcohol use during pregnancy have **fetal alcohol syndrome**. Fetal alcohol syndrome is a condition that produces facial abnormalities (see **Figure 9.2**), slowed physical growth, cognitive impairment, and learning problems throughout elementary school (Riley, Infante, & Warren, 2011). Alcohol use by pregnant mothers, particularly binge drinking, can produce more general *fetal alcohol effects* as well. These effects on the child include reduced verbal intelligence and increased delinquent behavior and learning problems (Mattson, Crocker, & Nguyen, 2011).

## STIMULANTS

**Stimulant** drugs activate or stimulate the central nervous system. Common stimulants include bronchodilators to ease breathing and treat asthma, methylphenidate to treat attention-deficit/hyperactivity disorder (Chapter 13), and drugs that we focus on here: caffeine, nicotine, cocaine, and amphetamines.

*Caffeine* is a legal drug, of course, commonly found in soda, coffee, tea, and chocolate. Many people use caffeine to boost energy, as evidenced by a Starbucks on nearly every corner and a plethora of high-caffeine drinks such as Red Bull and Monster. Caffeine helps release epinephrine

and norepinephrine, so mood, alertness, and cardiovascular activity become elevated. Moderate caffeine use is not dangerous, but someone who ingests large amounts for an extended period is susceptible to withdrawal symptoms such as headaches, irritability, sleepiness, anxiety, vomiting, and muscle tension and pain (Juliano, Huntley, Harrell, & Westerman, 2012).

People generally ingest *nicotine* via cigarettes and other tobacco products. Most cigarettes contain about 0.5 to 2.0 mg of nicotine and about 10 percent of this is absorbed during smoking. Nicotine is an extremely deadly poison—if you ingested 30 to 60 mg of pure nicotine, you would die within minutes (Solarino, Rosenbaum, RieBelmann, Buschmann, & Tsokos, 2010). Nicotine's effect on the brain is similar to caffeine, and many people who smoke find increased cardiovascular activity and motor tremors but also relaxation. The relaxation may come from increased serotonin following nicotine ingestion. Nicotine is an extremely addictive substance and can produce withdrawal symptoms of restlessness, irritability, and concentration and sleep problems. About one quarter of college students (25.1 percent) smoke cigarettes regularly (Moran, Wechsler, & Rigotti, 2004). Of this group of smokers:

- Most (64 percent) were female, 90 percent were aged 18 to 24 years, 81 percent were European American, and 62 percent lived off campus.

- Most (65 percent) smoked occasionally and not every day, but 12 percent smoked 1 to 9 cigarettes, 15 percent smoked 10 to 19 cigarettes, and 8 percent smoked more than 19 cigarettes per day.

- Some (18 percent) smoked a cigarette within 30 minutes of waking in the morning.

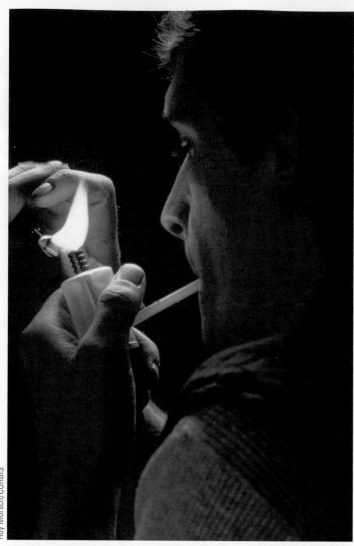

Cocaine is often smoked in the form of crack.

and occasionally violent behavior. High doses can lead to heart attacks and respiratory failure and death. Cocaine can be physically addictive, and a strong psychological dependence develops toward the drug. Withdrawal from cocaine can cause severe depression, overeating, and sleep problems. According to the Office of National Drug Control Policy, 9.5 percent of college students have tried cocaine and 6.6 percent have done so in the past year.

Amphetamines are also powerful stimulants that primarily increase dopamine and norepinephrine. About 90 percent of all excessive amphetamine use today involves methamphetamine, or crank (see **Box 9.2**). Methamphetamine can be snorted or smoked and results in a sudden "high" that can last hours. A person may feel empowered to do many things, as Elon did, or feel invulnerable to harm. Sexual desire may be enhanced as well. A person may become psychologically or physically addicted to methamphetamine after just a few doses. People addicted to methamphetamine are sometimes identifiable through "meth mouth," which involves severe decay or loss of teeth from exposure to the drug's toxic chemical composition (Ravenel et al., 2012).

People who use methamphetamine often use force to obtain another dose; violence and theft are common among users, as are anxiety, confusion, insomnia, and paranoia. In Las Vegas, home to one of your textbook authors, desperate methamphetamine users sometimes wait in the desert for discarded meth labs so they can scrounge for drug remnants. Children of meth users are often neglected as well. Withdrawal from meth can be severe; common symptoms include depression, anxiety, fatigue, paranoia, and intense cravings for the drug. According to the Office of National Drug Control Policy, 5.2 percent of college students have tried methamphetamine and 2.9 percent have done so in the past year.

- More than half (54 percent) tried to quit at least once in the past year.
- Most (58 percent) had no plan to quit in the next year.
- Among those who smoked in the past 30 days, 55 percent engaged in binge drinking in the past 2 weeks and 57 percent socialized with friends more than 2 hours per day.

*Cocaine* is a powerful stimulant usually ingested by sniffing or snorting crystals or smoking in the form of crack. People may mix cocaine with other drugs such as alcohol or heroin, the latter known as a "speed ball." Cocaine stimulates dopamine, norepinephrine, and serotonin systems to produce euphoria, high energy similar to mania, and bizarre, paranoid,

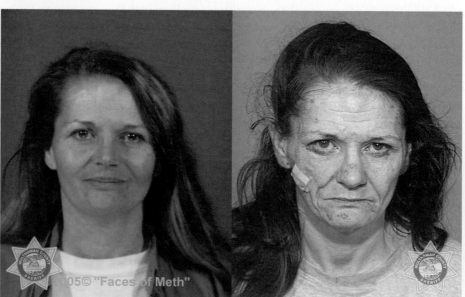

These are booking photographs of a woman arrested for methamphetamine use. The photo on the right was taken only 2.5 years after the photo on the left.

## BOX 9.2

### The "Meth" Epidemic

Many drugs have been cause for concern in America's "drug war," but perhaps none is as insidious and dangerous as methamphetamine. According to the Substance Abuse and Mental Health Services Administration, a review of 15 states revealed 102,378 admissions in 2004 for methamphetamine use compared with 73,454 admissions for cocaine and heroin use *combined* (see accompanying table; Gannett News Service, 2006). Unfortunately, treatment facilities specifically for methamphetamine use are not as prevalent as for other drugs. Many people desperate for methamphetamine, like Elon, thus resort to illegal activities and end up in prison.

Why has methamphetamine use become such an epidemic? The pleasurable effects of meth are extremely intense and include strong euphoria, enhanced sexual drive and stamina, and lowered sexual inhibition. The drug helps stimulate pleasure centers in the brain to release large amounts of dopamine. The drug is also becoming easier to obtain throughout the country. The physical downsides of using meth are extremely numerous, however, and include brain and liver damage, malnutrition, skin infections, immune system problems, convulsions, stroke, and death. Many people like Elon who use meth experience such a powerful high, however, that they completely ignore these physical effects.

| State | Meth | Cocaine and Heroin | State | Meth | Cocaine and Heroin |
|---|---|---|---|---|---|
| Arizona | 3,301 | 1,091 | Nevada | 3,257 | 1,932 |
| Arkansas | 4,072 | 2,926 | North Dakota | 373 | 43 |
| California | 60,235 | 54,956 | Oklahoma | 3,876 | 2,281 |
| Hawaii | 2,381 | 433 | Oregon | 8,561 | 3,948 |
| Idaho | 2,299 | 142 | South Dakota | 668 | 146 |
| Iowa | 5,563 | 2,125 | Utah | 3,665 | 1,816 |
| Montana | 1,185 | 192 | Wyoming | 878 | 88 |
| Nebraska | 2,064 | 735 | | | |

Source: Substance Abuse and Mental Health Services Administration

## OPIATES

**Opiates** (sometimes called narcotics or *opioids*) are drugs commonly used to relieve pain or cough, such as morphine or codeine. Morphine and codeine can be used excessively, but a related opiate, heroin, is overused more. Heroin is a derivative of morphine that is typically injected. The drug produces a sudden "rush" of euphoria followed by alternating periods of drowsiness and wakefulness. Long-term effects include increased risk for cancer and infertility. Opiates work by stimulating different types of opiate receptors in the brain across the hippocampus, amygdala, thalamus, and locus coeruleus. Heroin is extremely addictive and can result in severe withdrawal symptoms of agitation, chills, drowsiness, cramps, vomiting, sweating, and diarrhea. According to the Office of National Drug Control Policy, 0.9 percent of college students have tried heroin and 0.4 percent have done so in the past year.

Modern-day painkillers are also related to morphine and can be highly addictive. Drugs such as OxyContin, Darvon, Vicodin, Percocet, and Percodan are narcotic-based medications that can cause addiction in only a few doses. Prescription drug use is becoming one of the fastest-growing forms of substance-related disorder. According to the Office of National Drug Control Policy, 2.5 percent of college students used OxyContin in the past year.

## HALLUCINOGENS

**Hallucinogens** are drugs that cause symptoms of psychosis such as hallucinations (seeing or hearing things not actually there), disorganized thinking, odd perceptions, and delirium (a cognitive state of confusion and memory problems). Hallucinogen use often involves peyote or LSD (lysergic acid diethylamide), the latter of which seems to spur dopamine in the brain (a phenomenon also linked to psychoses such as schizophrenia). Another drug, *ecstasy* (MDMA or methylenedioxymethamphetamine), acts as both stimulant and hallucinogen. According to the Office of National Drug Control Policy, 10.2 percent of college students have tried MDMA.

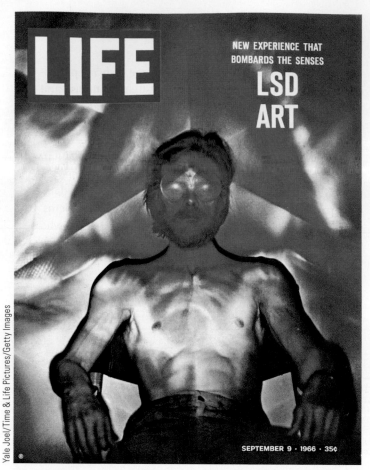

Many people who take LSD reportedly experience psychedelic hallucinations marked by bright colors and shapes. Some artists have tried to represent their experiences with the drug in art, as highlighted in this edition of Life magazine.

Hallucinogens produce powerful changes in perception; a person may "hear" colors or experience sounds in the form of light. Many psychological effects of hallucinogens are unique and unpredictable, however. Tolerance to LSD develops and dissipates quickly, so most people who use the drug do so sporadically. Withdrawal symptoms are not usually seen, though a person with a history of LSD use may experience sudden "flashbacks" that resemble the drug-induced state. According to the Office of National Drug Control Policy, 12 percent of college students have tried hallucinogens and 5.9 percent have done so in the past year.

## MARIJUANA

**Marijuana** comes from *Cannabis sativa,* or the hemp plant, that contains an active ingredient known as THC (delta-9-tetrahydrocannabinol). Marijuana is typically smoked but can be baked into edible pastries as well. Marijuana stimulates cannabinoid receptors throughout the brain and especially the cortex, hippocampus, basal ganglia, and hypothalamus. The drug creates feelings of joy, well-being, humor, and a dreamlike state. Time often feels distorted; attention, vigilance, and short-term memory diminish; creativity is enhanced; and motor behavior

is impaired. Long-term use can also produce infertility (Bari, Battista, Pirazzi, & Maccarrone, 2011).

Marijuana may not be physically addictive for everyone because tolerance is not always present, but heavy users are more at risk. Minor withdrawal symptoms such as sleep problems, anxiety, and irritability may occur. Marijuana is a medical treatment for glaucoma and may quell nausea, vomiting, convulsions, and pain. According to the Office of National Drug Control Policy, 49.1 percent of college students have tried marijuana and 33.3 percent have done so in the past year. Marijuana use can be a gateway to other illicit drug use, although life stress is also a contributing factor (Van Gundy & Rebellon, 2010).

### OTHER DRUGS

Other drugs also relate to excessive substance use:

● *Designer drugs* or *club drugs* represent manmade modifications of psychoactive drugs such as amphetamines and heroin.

Angel Raich is seen with cannabis buds at her home in Oakland, California. She began smoking after her doctor suggested it might ease pain she suffers from an inoperable brain tumor.

*Phencyclidine* (PCP) induces strong perceptual distortions and often highly violent and dangerous behavior. Club drugs may also include *date rape drugs* (see **Box 9.3**).

- *Inhalants* are volatile liquids stored in containers that give off strong fumes; users inhale the fumes to produce feelings of euphoria and lightheadedness. Examples include airplane glue, spray paint, cleaning agents, paint thinner, and gasoline. According to the Office of National Drug Control Policy, 8.5 percent of college students have tried inhalants and 2.7 percent have done so in the past year.

- *Steroids* are synthetic substances to enhance muscle growth and secondary sexual characteristics but are sometimes used excessively by adolescents and athletes to gain a competitive edge. According to the Office of National Drug Control Policy, 1.9 percent of people aged 19 to 28 years have used steroids and 0.5 percent have done so in the past year.

## Epidemiology of Substance-Related Disorders

You can see that substance use is common among college students. Among the general population, use of legal drugs such as alcohol and tobacco is also common. According to the Department of Health and Human Services, 50.3 percent of Americans aged 12 years or older currently use alcohol, and 22.8 percent engaged in binge drinking in the past 30 days. Recent alcohol use is more common among men (59.8 percent) than women (45 percent), and among European Americans (56.2 percent) than Hispanics (43.2 percent), African Americans (38.9 percent), American Indians/Alaska Natives (38.1 percent), and Asian Americans (34.1 percent). In addition, 13.5 percent of Americans had recently driven a motor vehicle under the influence of

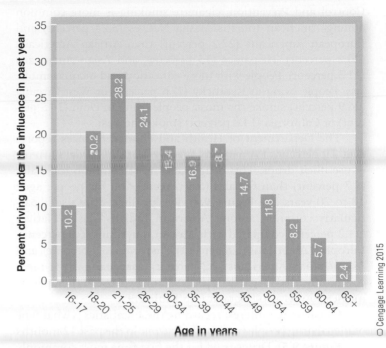

**FIGURE 9.3** DRIVING UNDER THE INFLUENCE OF ALCOHOL IN THE PAST YEAR AMONG PEOPLE AGED 16 YEARS AND OLDER

alcohol (see **Figure 9.3**). Some (11.2 percent) pregnant women also drink alcohol and 4.5 percent engaged in binge drinking in the past month.

Tobacco use is also common. Of Americans aged 12 years and older, 29.2 percent use some tobacco product (85.2 percent of this is cigarette use). This rate rises for adults aged 18 to 25 years (39.5 percent) and males (27.7 percent) compared with females (22.3 percent). According to the U.S. Centers for Disease

## BOX 9.3  Focus on Gender

### Date Rape Drugs

According to the National Women's Health Information Center, date rape drugs are used to induce dizziness, disorientation, and loss of inhibition and consciousness so a woman can be sexually assaulted. Other crimes, such as robbery, may be committed as well while a woman is in a drugged state. Date rape drugs generally include *ketamine* ("special K"), *rohypnol* ("roofies"), and *GHB* (gamma hydroxybutyrate or "liquid ecstasy"). These drugs are generally tasteless, odorless, and colorless and can be slipped into a person's drink. Alcohol also intensifies the effects of these drugs and can lead

to serious physical problems such as slowed heart rate and blood pressure.

What can you do to protect yourself? According to the Center, open all containers yourself, do not share or accept drinks from others, do not drink from open containers such as punch bowls, always be with a nondrinking and trusted friend, and always keep your drink with you, even if using the restroom. If you have to leave a drink behind, then assume the worst and do not drink it again. If you feel you have been drugged and raped—possibly evidenced by memory lapses or genital or other body bruising or other signs—then contact the police or go to an emergency room as soon as possible. Provide a urine sample for a physician as soon as possible (the drugs may still be in your system) and do not urinate, bathe, or change clothes before getting help.

Control and Prevention, cigarette smoking is more common among American Indians/Alaska Natives (33.4 percent) and European Americans (22.2 percent) than African Americans (20.2 percent), Hispanics (15 percent), and Asian Americans (11.3 percent). People with more education and income smoke less. People living in Kentucky (27.6 percent) or West Virginia (26.9 percent) smoke the most; people living in Utah (10.5 percent) or California (14.8 percent) smoke the least.

The Department of Health and Human Services reports that 7.9 percent of Americans aged 12 years and older currently use illicit drugs. This drug use is more common for males (8.7 percent) than females (5.5 percent) and for people aged 18 to 20 years (see **Figure 9.4**). Recent illicit drug use is particularly common among American Indians/Alaska Natives (11.2 percent) compared with African Americans (6.9 percent), European Americans (6.8 percent), Hispanics (5.9 percent), and Asian/Indian Americans (2.2 percent). Marijuana is the most commonly used illegal drug, but nonmedical use of therapeutic medications is also frequent (see **Table 9.9**).

Of particular interest regarding these statistics is what type of illegal drug people used *for the first time* in the past 12 months (see **Figure 9.5**). Drugs tried for the first time most commonly include prescription medications and marijuana. The average age at which people use certain drugs for the first time is outlined in **Figure 9.6**. Inhalants and marijuana tend to be illegal drugs of choice for teenagers and prescription medications tend to be drugs of choice with increased age. All drug use, however, is most common during ages 12 to 30 years.

The lifetime prevalence of any substance-related disorder is 14.6 percent and, for the past 12 months, 3.8 percent. Alcohol use disorder has the highest 12-month and lifetime prevalence rates of the major substance-related disorders (Kessler, Berglund, et al., 2005). According to the Department of Health and Human Services, substance use disorder is much more common among males (12.7 percent) than females (6.2 percent) and among people aged 18 to 25 years (21.2 percent). Substance use disorder is

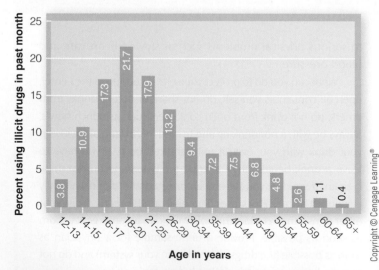

**FIGURE 9.4** PAST MONTH ILLICIT DRUG USE AMONG PEOPLE AGED 12 YEARS AND OLDER

**Table 9.9**

**Types of Illicit Drug Use in Lifetime, Past Year, and Past Month among Persons Aged 12 or Older: Percentages, 2008**

| Drug | Lifetime | Past year | Past month |
|---|---|---|---|
| Illicit drugs | 47.0 | 14.2 | 8.0 |
| Marijuana and hashish | 41.0 | 10.3 | 6.1 |
| Cocaine | 14.7 | 2.1 | 0.7 |
| Crack | 3.4 | 0.4 | 0.1 |
| Heroin | 1.5 | 0.2 | 0.1 |
| Hallucinogens | 14.4 | 1.5 | 0.4 |
| LSD | 9.4 | 0.3 | 0.1 |
| PCP | 2.7 | 0.0 | 0.0 |
| Ecstasy | 5.2 | 0.9 | 0.2 |
| Inhalants | 8.9 | 0.8 | 0.3 |
| Nonmedical use of psychotherapeutics | 20.8 | 6.1 | 2.5 |
| Pain relievers | 14.0 | 4.8 | 1.9 |
| OxyContin | 1.9 | 0.6 | 0.2 |
| Tranquilizers | 8.6 | 2.0 | 0.7 |
| Stimulants | 8.5 | 1.1 | 0.4 |
| Methamphetamine | 5.0 | 0.3 | 0.1 |
| Sedatives | 3.6 | 0.2 | 0.1 |
| Illicit drugs other than marijuana | 30.3 | 8.0 | 3.4 |

higher among American Indians/Alaska Natives (20.2 percent) compared with multiracial individuals (12.2 percent), Hispanics (9.8 percent), European Americans (9.6 percent), African Americans (8.3 percent), and Asian Americans (4.7 percent). People with substance use disorder are also much more likely to be unemployed than employed full-time.

Some (22.7 percent) people with a substance-related disorder sought treatment in the past year, especially for alcohol (Kessler et al., 1999). Most treatment occurred at specialized rehabilitation facilities. Marijuana, cocaine, and pain relievers were the most commonly used nonalcohol drugs. Some (8.8 percent) people need treatment for substance use disorder but do not seek treatment. Common reasons for not seeking treatment include lack of insurance, desire to keep using drugs, poor access to treatment, stigma, and lack of knowledge about where to go for treatment.

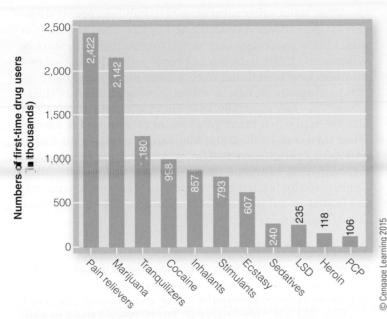

**FIGURE 9.5** PAST YEAR FIRST-TIME USE OF DRUGS

# Stigma Associated with Substance-Related Disorders

People with substance-related disorders often face social discrimination with respect to employment, housing, and interpersonal rejection. One survey of people with substance-related disorder revealed that many felt stigmatized (Luoma et al., 2007). Many in the sample believed that once others knew of the person's substance problem, they treated them unfairly (60%) or were afraid of them (46%). Many in the sample also believed that some family members gave up on them (45%), some friends rejected them (38%), and employers paid them a lower wage (14%). Participants in the survey reported that hearing others say unfavorable or offensive things about people in treatment for substance use was a common stigmatizing experience. Others have found as well that stigma toward individuals with substance-related disorders negatively affected attempts to access treatment services (Myers, Fakier, & Louw, 2009).

Luoma and colleagues (2008) reported one of the few attempts to address stigma among people with substance-related disorders. The researchers examined 88 participants in a 28-day residential treatment program for a substance-related disorder. The intervention involved a 6-hour group format whereby participants were encouraged to accept difficult feelings, emphasize human connection and mutual acceptance, focus more on the process of thinking (i.e., thinking about how thinking happens in the mind) rather than the content of negative thoughts, and explore goals and values in life. The intervention helped reduce internalized shame and stigma. Livingston and colleagues (2011) reviewed several studies in this area and reported that communicating positive stories of people with substance-related disorders may be useful for reducing stigma among the general public.

## INTERIM SUMMARY

► Substance-related disorders include substance use disorder, intoxication, and withdrawal.

► Substance use disorder refers to repeated use of substances that lead to recurring problems.

► Substance intoxication is a usually reversible condition brought on by excessive use of alcohol or another drug.

► Tolerance refers to the need to ingest greater amounts of a drug to achieve the same effect.

► Withdrawal refers to maladaptive behavioral and physiological changes when a person stops taking a drug.

► Substances may be categorized by the effect they have on people. Depressants inhibit the central nervous system, whereas stimulants activate the central nervous system.

► Opiates are drugs commonly used to relieve pain, and hallucinogens are drugs that cause psychosis-like symptoms.

► Marijuana works by stimulating cannabinoid brain receptors and is the most commonly used illicit drug.

► Substance use is extremely common, and substance-related disorders are among the most common mental disorders.

► People with substance-related disorders are often stigmatized via social discrimination with respect to employment, housing, and interpersonal rejection.

Substance-related disorders are comorbid with many other mental disorders, especially anxiety-related, depressive, and personality disorders. Substance-related disorders also relate closely to severe psychological stress, especially among 18- to 25-year-olds. Many more people with a major depressive episode experience substance use disorder compared to people without a major depressive episode. People overusing one drug also commonly overuse another drug (polysubstance use). Approximately two thirds (67.6 percent) of people with a substance-related disorder use alcohol only, but 15.1 percent of people with a substance-related disorder use alcohol *and* an illicit drug.

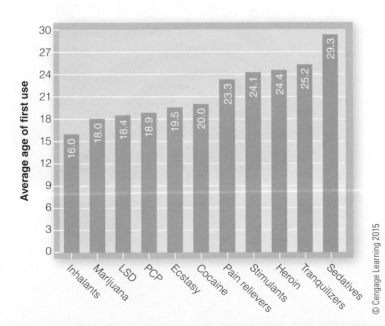

**FIGURE 9.6** AVERAGE AGE OF FIRST USE OF DRUGS

## REVIEW QUESTIONS

1. What is the difference between substance use and substance use disorder?
2. What is substance intoxication and withdrawal?
3. Identify major classes of drugs and their psychological effects.
4. Describe what to do if you ingest a date rape drug.
5. How common are substance-related disorders, and what populations are most at risk?

# Substance-Related Disorders: Causes and Prevention

We turn our attention now to factors that cause substance-related disorders. We also discuss how knowing about these factors might help us prevent substance-related disorders.

## Biological Risk Factors for Substance-Related Disorders

Biological risk factors in people with substance-related disorders include genetics, brain features, and neurochemical characteristics.

### GENETICS

Genetics influence substance-related disorders, especially alcoholism. Heritability estimates for alcoholism are 0.52 to 0.57 (Kendler et al., 2011; Sullivan et al., 2012). Early family studies revealed that people whose family members overused alcohol were 3 to 4 times more likely to overuse alcohol themselves compared with people without such a family history (Walters, 2002). A problem with family studies, however, is that environmental influences could explain the effect. Children could be modeling parental misuse of alcohol instead of receiving a genetic predisposition for the problem. Genetic influences may be stronger for males than females and for severe compared with less severe cases of alcoholism. Alcoholism is likely predisposed by many genes working together (Nieratschker, Batra, & Fallgatter, 2013).

Genetic models for alcoholism are modest, but variables *related to* alcoholism may have a stronger genetic effect. Genetics may affect a person's *metabolism* of alcohol—some people process alcohol faster than others and may be less susceptible to alcoholism (Birley et al., 2009). Genetics may also affect a person's sensitivity to alcohol. Genetics influence *low level of response to alcohol*, and this can predict alcoholism in offspring of people with alcoholism (Schuckit, 2009). People with low response to alcohol must drink more to achieve the same psychological effects and are therefore more at risk than the general population for developing alcoholism. One study indicated that 55.3 percent of heavy drinking college males reported low response to alcohol (Daugherty & Van Tubergen, 2002). Genetics may also affect the brain's neurochemistry to induce *craving* for alcohol or increase disinhibition and sensitivity to alcohol (see neurochemical section later in the chapter; Lenz, Frieling, Kornhuber, Bleich, & Hillemacher, 2011).

What about other substances? Heritability appears strongest for dependence on cocaine and opiates such as heroin or prescription painkillers such as OxyContin (Schwab, Scott, & Wildenauer, 2009). Relatives of people with substance-related disorders have been found to be 8 times more likely than control participants to have a substance-related disorder themselves. This was especially true for opiates and cocaine but also for marijuana. Many genes are likely responsible for this effect (Mayer & Hollt, 2006; Merikangas et al., 1998). Genes may influence receptors, such as opiate receptors, that increase responsiveness to certain drugs (Kendler, Chen, et al., 2012). Genes may also influence development of key brain structures implicated in substance-related disorders. We discuss these brain features next.

### BRAIN FEATURES

Many brain features link to substance-related disorders. Brain changes in substance-related disorders coincide with several inducements toward compulsive drug use: priming, drug cues, cravings, and stress (Pickens et al., 2011). *Priming* refers to a situation in which a single drug dose such as a drink of alcohol or snorted line of cocaine leads to an uncontrollable binge. *Drug cues* refer to stimuli associated with drug use, such as friends, favorite hangouts, and other things that stimulate further drug use. *Cravings* refer to an obsessive drive for drug use, much as Elon had a consuming desire to seek and use drugs to the exclusion of almost all other activities. *Stress* is a common trigger of relapse in people with substance-related disorders. Recall that drug use is commonly associated with anxiety and depression.

Brain features related to each of these areas are primarily part of the **mesolimbic system**, a major dopamine pathway

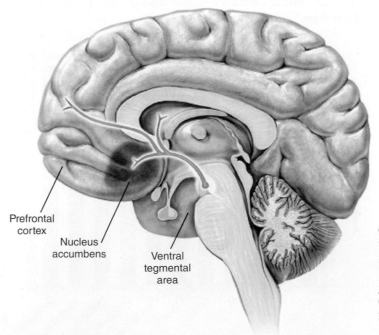

Prefrontal cortex

Nucleus accumbens

Ventral tegmental area

**FIGURE 9.7** MESOLIMBIC PATHWAY IN THE BRAIN

and one strongly implicated in sensations of pleasure, reward, and desire (see neurochemical section later in the chapter). Rats will constantly press a lever to stimulate brain areas related to this pathway (Robinson, Zitzman, & Williams, 2011). The mesolimbic system generally begins in the brain's *ventral tegmental area* and ends in the *nucleus accumbens* (see **Figure 9.7**). Drugs such as crack cocaine greatly stimulate this system and often lead to priming effects and intense cravings (Wu, McCallum, Glick, & Huang, 2011). Continued drug use that stimulates the mesolimbic system can then become associated with certain cues such as a particular bar or group of friends that help perpetuate someone's addiction (Naqvi & Bechara, 2010).

The mesolimbic pathway links as well to other brain areas central to addiction (see **Figure 9.8**; adapted from Adinoff, 2004):

- *Amygdala*, which is involved in assigning a high "reward value" to stimuli such as drugs, stress-induced pursuit of drug use, and conditioning place preferences for drug use such as a particular area of town.

- *Anterior cingulate*, which is involved in self-control and problem solving and may be particularly relevant to emotional salience or excessive preoccupation with particular drugs (Ma et al., 2010).

- *Bed nucleus of the stria terminalis*, which you may recall from Chapter 5 is involved in stress reactions and may be involved in drug-seeking behavior to cope with stress (Nobis, Kash, Silberman, & Windeer, 2011). The amygdala and bed nucleus of the stria terminalis are key aspects of the hypothalamic-pituitary-adrenal axis so heavily implicated in anxiety-related disorders. This may help explain the high association of substance-related and anxiety-related disorders.

- *Hippocampus*, which is involved in acquiring new information and forming new memories and may be instrumental for storing powerful memories of emotionally arousing stimuli such as drug use (Belujon & Grace, 2011).

- *Insular cortex or insula*, which is involved in pain processing, and stimulation of which has been linked to drug craving (Kenny, 2011).

- *Prefrontal cortex*, which is involved in upper-level cognitive processes such as control and regulation and that may be altered by drug use, thus leading to continued drug craving and use. The prefrontal

cortex may also become extremely responsive to stimuli that predict drug availability (Goldstein & Volkow, 2011).

- *Orbitofrontal cortex*, which is involved in decision making in unpredictable or uncertain situations and in which drug-induced changes could result in impulsive behavior, the latter clearly related to drug use, as described later in the section on personality (Lucantonio, Stalnaker, Shaham, Niv, & Schoenbaum, 2012).

Neuroimaging studies support these findings. **Figure 9.9** illustrates a brain scan of a person with a history of excessive cocaine use and one with no such history. Blood flow to the prefrontal cortex, illustrated by brighter colors, diminishes in the person who uses a substance excessively (Goldstein & Volkow, 2011). Euphoria often accompanies less activity in this area, so people may not engage in high-level thinking and reasoning while intoxicated. The prefrontal cortex does, however, become highly stimulated when surrounding stimuli predict drug availability, and this is likely due to a strong connection between the prefrontal cortex and the mesolimbic system and nucleus accumbens. The result is someone who cares little for stimuli other than drugs and whose

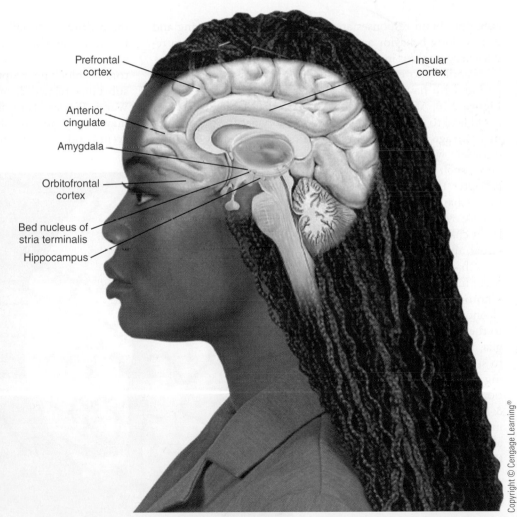

**FIGURE 9.8** MAJOR BRAIN AREAS IMPLICATED IN SUBSTANCE-RELATED DISORDERS

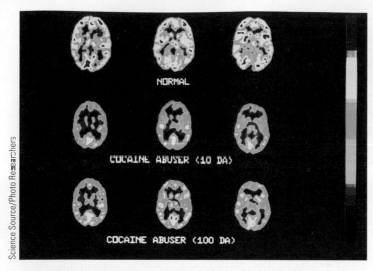

**FIGURE 9.9** BRAIN IMAGE OF PERSON WHO USES COCAINE EXCESSIVELY COMPARED WITH A NORMAL CONTROL PARTICIPANT Normal metabolic activity, indicated by bright red and yellow, is blunted in the person using drugs. Image is from *Science Source/Photo Researchers*.

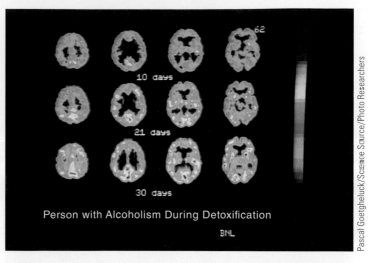

**FIGURE 9.10** BRAIN IMAGE OF PERSON WITH ALCOHOLISM GOING THROUGH DETOXIFICATION Alcohol is a depressant. Brain activity increases (yellow) with increasing time without alcohol. Image is from *Science Source/Photo Researchers*.

excitatory brain responses are not well controlled. Craving and drug-seeking behavior are thus enhanced, but capability to reduce drug intake is impaired (Volkow et al., 2010).

People who excessively use alcohol or nicotine for long periods also have reduced brain size and altered activity (see **Figure 9.10**; Almeida et al., 2008; Buhler & Mann, 2011). This could lead to greater cognitive and memory decline than is normal with age. Reduced brain size occurs in other heavily cognitive disorders we discuss in this textbook, such as psychotic disorders (Chapter 12) and Alzheimer's disease (Chapter 14). Excessive alcohol use over time can also produce brain changes that lead to motor, visual, and speech problems.

Changes in brain function also occur in children with fetal alcohol syndrome whose mothers ingested alcohol during pregnancy. Damage to the corpus callosum, basal ganglia, and cerebellum can contribute to substantial cognitive and learning problems seen in this population (Muralidharan, Sarmah, Zhou, & Marrs, 2013). General reduction in brain size in newborns with fetal alcohol syndrome is evident as well (**Figure 9.11**).

## NEUROCHEMICAL FEATURES

The mesolimbic dopamine pathway appears to be the main neural base for the reinforcing effects of

many drugs, especially alcohol, stimulants, opiates, and marijuana. These drugs increase dopamine release in the nucleus accumbens by stimulating *D2* (specialized dopamine) receptors or blocking reuptake of dopamine. Some people with substance-related disorders have fewer D2 receptors (Volkow, Wang, Fowler, Tomasi, & Telang, 2011). This means they may not be able to obtain much reward from everyday life events and so resort to excesses such as drug use to obtain

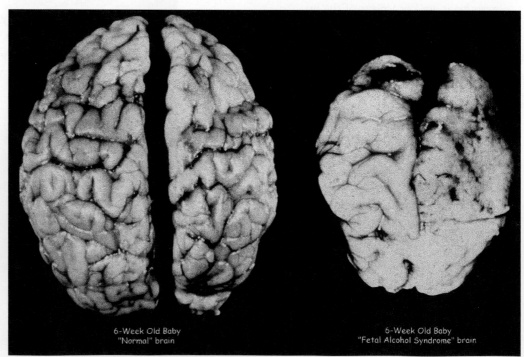

**FIGURE 9.11** BRAIN DAMAGE TO A NEWBORN WITH FETAL ALCOHOL SYNDROME COMPARED TO A NORMAL CONTROL

People often engage in substance use to relieve stress.

sufficient rewards. This is known as **reward deficiency syndrome** (Blum, Gardner, Oscar-Berman, & Gold, 2012).

Opiates like heroin and morphine act directly on opioid receptors in the nucleus accumbens as well as other areas of the brain and spinal cord. Excess dopamine release in the nucleus accumbens relates also to drug relapse and overwhelming drug-seeking behavior (LaLumiere, Smith, & Kalivas, 2012). Stress may activate the prefrontal cortex that, you may recall, has a strong connection to key components of the mesolimbic dopamine pathway: the ventral tegmental area and nucleus accumbens.

Other neurotransmitters influence substance-related disorders as well, but even these neural pathways affect dopamine release in the mesolimbic system. Glutamate, GABA, acetylcholine, serotonin, and norepinephrine have excitatory or inhibitory connections to the mesolimbic dopamine system (Brabant, Alleva, Quertemont, & Tirelli, 2010). GABA appears to have an inhibitory effect on dopamine release in the mesolimbic system. Drugs that suppress this inhibitory effect, therefore, such as alcohol or morphine, may thus help stimulate dopamine release (Matsui & Williams, 2011). Keep in mind that much of these data come from animal studies, so extrapolating results to humans may be problematic.

Dopamine release acts as a powerful reward (euphoria), thus providing an incentive to increase and maintain drug use. Dopamine release also promotes reward-related learning so a person is often seeking rewards such as drugs (Wise, 2009). Such conditioning or learning might explain Elon's extremely driven behavior toward seeking and using methamphetamine. Over time, the reward system becomes specifically attuned to availability of specific drugs. This helps explain why people abstinent from a drug for many years can easily and quickly relapse toward excessive drug use.

## Environmental Risk Factors for Substance-Related Disorders

We turn our attention next to environmental risk factors for substance-related disorders. These include stress, cognitive factors, learning, personality factors, and family factors. We also discuss cultural and evolutionary influences.

### STRESS

Stress is an important trigger for many of the mental disorders we discuss in this textbook; for substance-related disorders this is especially true. Stress can clearly trigger substance use, such as when people have a glass of wine to relax, smoke a cigarette to unwind, or snort a line of cocaine to enhance mood. Recall that people with anxiety and depression often engage in substance use to cope with stressors such as interacting with others and feeling miserable. Ongoing use of substances to cope with stressors can lead to a pattern of overuse. Excessive substance use is closely associated with early physical and sexual maltreatment, poor parental and social support, and chronic distress (Rogosch, Dackis, & Cicchetti, 2011).

Stress is important as well regarding relapse toward substance-related disorders, as when a person has been abstinent for some time but regresses back to old drinking or drug-using habits (falling "off the wagon"). **Stress-induced relapse** involves an activation of certain brain substances related to stress, such as corticotropin-releasing hormone and cortisol, that help us cope but also increase dopamine activity in the mesolimbic pathway. Stress also increases norepinephrine, which helps stimulate key components of the mesolimbic pathway: the bed nucleus of the stria terminalis, nucleus accumbens, and amygdala (Belujon & Grace, 2011). Environmental stress thus triggers dual responses in the brain: coping and desire for reward. Maybe that is why we crave chocolate so much when stressed!

Stress may enhance drug relapse in other key ways as well. Increased glutamate from stress may produce a state of sadness from dopamine depletion to trigger cravings for increased dopamine by using drugs (Kalivas, LaLumiere, Knackstedt, & Shen, 2009). Chronic stress may also weaken a person's ability to cope effectively with difficult situations by creating damage to the prefrontal cortex (Goldstein & Volkow, 2011). A person's ability to sustain attention, recall appropriate coping skills learned in therapy, and inhibit maladaptive responses such as drinking and driving may be impaired.

## COGNITIVE FACTORS

Recall our discussions in earlier chapters of *cognitive distortions* or biases as risk factors for anxiety-related and depressive disorders. These refer to erroneous beliefs one has about oneself and the surrounding world that can lead to maladjustment. Cognitive distortions are also a part of substance-related disorders. One common misperception among people with substance-related disorders is increased *positive expectancies* about effects of various substances and minimization of negative effects. A person may discount or dispute the addictive qualities of a drug and claim she "can stop anytime I want."

Some people believe that using certain substances will lead to grand experiences or life changes, such as enhanced personal or social functioning. A person may falsely believe drug use will increase his social skill with women or facilitate his accomplishments at work. Positive expectancies about alcohol are also evident. College students often have several positive expectancies regarding alcohol use, including enhanced sociability, courage, sexuality, and calmness. These expectancies, however, relate closely to hazardous alcohol use before a social gathering or event (Zamboanga, Schwartz, Ham, Borsari, & Van Tyne, 2010).

Recall from Chapter 3 that another misperception among many people with substance-related disorders, especially college students, is that other people use alcohol and other drug amounts similar or in excess to their own (Cunningham, Neighbors, Wild, & Humphreys, 2012). Such a misperception seemed evident for DeShawn and Elon, who felt their initial drinking was in line with the typical college experience. Such misperception, however, reinforces a person's belief that his drinking or other drug use is not a problem.

People with alcoholism also selectively attend to cues that indicate alcohol is nearby, such as seeing a favorite drinking buddy (Bordnick et al., 2008). People with alcoholism or other drug use problems attend longer to words and pictures that depict substance-related constructs (Field, Munafo, & Franken, 2009). Such selective attention relates to the brain and neurochemical features we discussed earlier and seems particularly relevant to strong emotional cravings for certain drugs. This may lead to a hard-to-break cycle in which selective attention, emotional craving, and dopamine release reinforce each other.

Cognitions affect substance use, but consider also that severe substance use may itself create cognitive changes by altering the prefrontal cortex. Alcohol and other drugs can create massive changes in the brain that affect attention, perception, judgment, memory, problem solving, decision making, and other higher cognitive processes. People with alcoholism often have *blackouts*, in which they remember nothing during a period of heavy drinking, or *grayouts*, in which they can remember events during a heavy period of drinking only when someone reminds them of what happened or if they drink heavily again (McKim & Hancock, 2013).

## LEARNING

Recall from Chapter 5 that many people learn to develop severe anxiety through classical and operant conditioning as well as modeling behavior of others. These learning processes also apply to substance-related disorders. Classical conditioning essentially refers to learning by association, and many people with substance-related disorders associate certain environmental cues with drug use. If a person always seems to use methamphetamine with friends at a local park, he is more likely in the future to use the drug when surrounded by these cues. Treatment for substance use disorder can thus be difficult—a person may become "clean" in a drug rehabilitation center but then relapse quickly when he returns to old stomping grounds where cues for substance use are strong.

A stunning example of classical conditioning was the large-scale remission of heroin addiction by Vietnam veterans. Approximately 20 percent of Vietnam-based soldiers in the 1960s and 1970s were thought addicted to heroin, spurring a firestorm of concern about what would happen when they returned to the United States. Remarkably, however, the addiction rate in these soldiers dropped to 1 percent after they came home. One explanation is that cues surrounding heroin use—such as intense stress, completely different geography, and certain peer groups—disappeared once the soldiers returned home. This story is not a completely happy one, however because many veterans experienced premature death from other causes (Price, Risk, Murray, Virgo, & Spitznagel, 2001).

Drug use can also be rewarding, of course, and therefore maintained by operant conditioning. Recall that reward centers of the brain are highly stimulated by drug use and people can become particularly vulnerable to drug-conditioned stimuli. Positive reinforcers of drug use include fitting in with peers, a sense of euphoria and invulnerability, and feelings of sexual prowess, as was true for Elon. Drug use can also serve as a powerful *negative reinforcer* in that stress, pressure, depression, and withdrawal symptoms recede. Negative reinforcers serve as strong indicators of craving and relapse (Koob, 2011).

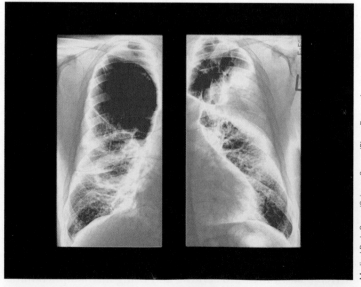

A long-term consequence often minimized by smokers is emphysema. Color enhanced frontal x-ray of the chest showing emphysema. The lungs are colorized blue. A large cavity (right) is infected and filled with fluid.

Furthermore, the negative effects or punishers of drug use are often distant. People who smoke cigarettes enjoy the immediate sense of relief and relaxation but worry little about far-off consequences such as lung cancer and *emphysema* (a lung disease marked by damage to air sacs and difficulty breathing). Nicotine in particular may become associated with other nondrug rewards as well (Donny, Caggiula, Weaver, Levin, & Sved, 2011). How many people do you know smoke cigarettes in certain pleasurable situations such as eating a big meal, drinking alcohol, or after sex?

Modeling or imitating the behavior of others can also be a significant learning-based factor for substance-related disorders. People do not generally pick up a crack pipe or inject heroin themselves but usually model the behavior from others. Modeling may be especially pertinent to adolescents. Adolescents who use substances excessively tend to cluster with deviant, substance-using peer groups, especially if low parent monitoring occurs (Kiesner, Poulin, & Dishion, 2010). Drug use among peers also facilitates social interaction and a sense of belonging.

## PERSONALITY FACTORS

Have you heard the phrase "addictive personality"? The media often adopt this phrase, which refers generally to people who compulsively seek certain things—food, sex, shopping, gambling, drugs—to enhance mood. Researchers who study substance-related disorders do focus on personality traits, though the term "addictive personality" has yet to be supported. One personality trait closely related to substance-related disorder, one we discussed in Chapter 3, is *impulsivity*. Impulsivity generally refers to risk taking, lack of planning, chaotic lifestyle, desire for immediate gratification, and explosiveness (Ivanov, Schultz, London, & Newcorn, 2008). Impulsive sensation seeking is particularly associated with heavy alcohol use in adolescents (Stautz & Cooper, 2013).

Researchers have also linked substance use disorder and impulsive aggression in general with domestic violence, violent crime, and suicide in particular. Knowing which comes first, however, substance use or violence, has not been clearly established (see **Box 9.4**). *Psychopathy* also relates closely to substance-related disorders (Dembo et al., 2007). Psychopathy refers to antisocial behavior, lack of remorse for aggressive behavior, and need for immediate gratification. People with sub-

Impulsivity is a key personality trait associated with substance-related disorders.

stance use disorder are generally less likely to inhibit their behavior and delay gratification (Bornovalova, Lejuez, Daughters, Rosenthal, & Lynch, 2005).

Why might psychopathy or impulsive aggression link to substance-related disorders? People with psychopathy or substance use disorder may react quickly or impulsively to stressors by aggressively facing a perceived threat and/or by using drugs to cope with a threat. Certain brain changes may also be similar in both groups (Anderson & Kiehl, 2012). Another possibility is that people with antisocial and impulsive tendencies have lower thresholds for deviant behaviors such as excessive risk-taking and substance use (Swogger, Walsh, Lejuez, & Kosson, 2010).

Others have found excessive substance use related to disinhibited, disagreeable, depressed, and anxious personality features (Kotov, Gamez, Schmidt, & Watson, 2010; Staiger, Kambouropoulos, & Dawe, 2007). Recall from Chapters 5 and 7 that people with anxiety-related and depressive and bipolar disorders commonly use substances such as alcohol to reduce stress in general and social phobia in particular (Robinson, Sareen, Cox, & Bolton, 2011). Stress is also a key reason for relapse among people with substance-related disorders (Ungless, Argilli, & Bonci, 2010).

**THE CONTINUUM VIDEO PROJECT**

### Mark: **Substance Use Disorder**

▶ *"That's what drugs are, they are your savior but also they are also there to kill, maim, and destroy you. It's awesome, but true."*

Copyright © Cengage Learning.®

Access the Continuum Video Project in MindTap at **www.cengagebrain.com**.

## BOX 9.4  Focus on Violence

### Alcohol and Violence

Alcohol and violence do seem to go hand in hand. According to the U.S. Centers for Disease Control and Prevention, approximately 40 percent of violent and nonviolent crimes were committed under the influence of alcohol, and 40 percent of people convicted of rape and sexual assault claimed they were under the influence of alcohol at the time of the crime. Furthermore, 72 percent of college campus rapes occur when victims are too intoxicated to consent or refuse sex. Nearly 50 percent of child maltreatment cases are associated with parental drug use, and two thirds of victims of domestic violence say alcohol was involved in the violent incident. About 23 percent of suicide deaths are attributable to alcohol as well. Among assailants at an emergency room,

alcohol was involved in 52.3 percent of cases (James, Madeley, & Dove, 2006).

Little information is available as to the direction of these effects. Drinking alcohol may precede domestic assault but may also follow marital problems. Other factors are also present, such as other mental disorder, access to weapons, and stress (Farooque, Stout, & Frost, 2005). Still, some research studies as well as media reports of extreme cases of domestic violence do point to alcohol misuse as a substantial mitigating factor (Parker, 2004). On Independence Day in 2006, for example, a man in California killed himself and his four children after arguing with his wife—empty beer bottles were strewn in the backyard. On the same day in Portland, Maine, a man killed his wife after his 17-year-old son refused his demands to buy more beer. Despite conflicting research evidence about the causal direction of alcohol and domestic violence, these incidents clearly indicate the need for extensive education and prevention.

## FAMILY FACTORS

Family factors play an important role in the onset and maintenance of substance-related disorders. Children of parents with substance-related disorders are much more likely than the general population to use substances themselves. College students with parents with alcoholism are more likely to be current drug users and to begin drinking earlier than peers (Braitman

et al., 2009). Having a parent who smokes is also associated with greater risk of smoking among adolescents (Selya, Dierker, Rose, Hedeker, & Mermelstein, 2012). Children raised in homes where parents smoke are also at increased risk for health problems associated with secondhand smoke, such as chronic ear infections, asthma, bronchitis, pneumonia, fire-related injuries, and *sudden infant death syndrome* (crib death; Oberg, Jaakkola, Woodward, Peruga, & Pruss-Ustun, 2011).

Risk of substance use disorder increases with spikes in family conflict and detachment as well as permissive parent attitudes about drug use (Brook, Brook, Rubenstone, Zhang, & Gerochi, 2006). According to the Department of Health and Human Services, 5.1 percent of youths who said their parents would *strongly disapprove* of their using marijuana actually used the drug in the past month. In contrast, 30 percent of youths who said their parents would only *somewhat disapprove* or *neither approve nor disapprove* of their using marijuana actually used the drug in the past month. One third of college students said their parents would approve of their drinking. This group was much more likely to report having a drinking problem (Boyle & Boekeloo, 2006).

Another family factor linked closely to adolescent drug use is parent psychopathology, especially substance use disorder and antisocial behaviors. Parents who are not well involved in their child's life, who

BananaStock/Jupiter Images

Codependency is a family factor associated with substance-related disorders.

supervise their children poorly, and who do not have affectionate interactions with their children also place their children at much higher risk for substance use disorder (Ryan, Jorm, & Lubman, 2010). History of parental divorce or separation and low expectations of a child also predict excessive substance use in adolescents (Jaffe & Solhkhah, 2004).

The popular media are especially enamored of one particular family factor involved in substance-related disorders; you have probably read about or heard the term **codependency**. Codependency generally refers to dysfunctional behaviors that spouses, partners, children, and others engage in to cope with the stress of having a family member with a substance-related disorder. Codependency often involves intense care of a person with a substance-related disorder to the detriment of one's own health. Spouses and children of a father with alcoholism may constantly help him to bed or call his workplace to explain his absence. Family members thus inadvertently reward—or *enable*—the behavior of the person with alcoholism. People in codependent relationships may also feel responsible for a person's substance problem and tightly control their relationships with others to avoid rejection. Codependent relationships are thus generally considered unhealthy.

Do children whose parents use drugs excessively grow to have significant problems in adulthood? Much of the literature has focused on children of parents with alcoholism, and the answer to this question seems to be yes, to some extent. Adult children of parents with alcoholism are at significant risk for excessive substance use, antisocial behavior such as aggression, anxiety-related disorders and distress, depression, low self-esteem, and difficult family relationships. Adult children of parents with alcoholism tend to have more marital conflict and stress during parenting and lower social support and family cohesion. This group also tends to marry at a younger age and divorce more than the general population. However, these results do not apply to all adult children of parents with alcoholism. Many adult children of parents with alcoholism, particularly those now in college, report few difficulties (Conners et al., 2004; Harter, 2000). The latter findings raise questions about the validity and utility of the concept of codependency.

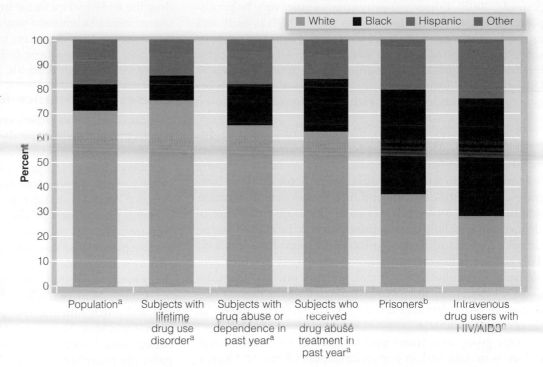

[a] Data from 2002 National Survey on Drug Use and Health (5); Population by Race/Ethnicity in 2002, Percent of Persons 12+ Reporting Any Illicit Drug Use in Lifetime by Race/Ethnicity in 2002, Percent of Persons 12+ Meeting Criteria for Drug Abuse or Dependence in Past Year by Race/Ethnicity in 2002, and Percent of Persons 12+ Reporting They Received Drug Abuse Treatment in the Past Year by Race/Ethnicity in 2002.
[b] Data from Bureau of Justice Statistics Bulletin (10).
[c] Data from Centers for Disease Control and Prevention (11).

**FIGURE 9.12** **DISTRIBUTION OF SELECTED VARIABLES RELATED TO DRUG USE BY ETHNICITY**
*From W.M. Compton et al. Developments in the epidemiology of drug use and drug use disorders.* American Journal of Psychiatry, 162, 1494-1502. Copyright © 2005. *Reprinted by permission of the American Psychiatric Association.*

## CULTURAL FACTORS

Aside from American Indians/Alaska Natives, rates of substance use disorder are fairly equal among European Americans, African Americans, Hispanics, and Asian Americans. The reasons why some American Indians/Alaska Natives have such high rates of substance-related disorder is not completely clear. Substance use disorder in this population is associated with high rates of trauma (Dickerson & Johnson, 2012). Others suggest "craving-for-alcohol" genes on chromosomes 12, 15, and 18 that may be specific to some members of this population (Ehlers, Gizer, Gilder, & Wilhelmsen, 2011).

Rates of lifetime drug use for European Americans, African Americans, and Hispanics resemble rates in the general population (see **Figure 9.12**). However, African Americans and Hispanics are disproportionately more likely than European Americans to experience *severe consequences* from drug use. In particular, African Americans and Hispanics are overrepresented with respect to imprisonment and HIV/AIDS among those who inject drugs (Compton, Thomas, Conway, & Colliver, 2005). African Americans and Hispanics, who are more likely to inject drugs than European Americans, may also be at greater risk for hepatitis B and C infections and overdose

(Estrada, 2005). Ethnic minority communities may be predisposed to substance use disorder because of high poverty and unemployment, easier access to alcohol and other drugs, poor schools, and limited access to mental health services (Cooper, Friedman, Tempalski, Friedman, & Keem, 2005; McNeece & DiNitto, 2005). Ethnic minority drug users also tend to begin injecting substances at an earlier age, often during adolescence (Fuller et al., 2005).

Rates of alcohol consumption and alcoholism also differ around the world. Attitudes toward drinking and whether members of a culture commonly engage in heavy drinking have much to do with these differences. Some cultures integrate alcohol into daily life and meals, as occurs in Mediterranean nations. Other cultures exemplify more abstinence to alcohol and less daily consumption, such as the United States, Canada, and Scandinavian countries. Increased or decreased daily consumption may influence the frequency at which people develop alcoholism, but this remains unclear. Consider that Canadian men and Swedish women have the highest percentage of binge drinkers in the world (Bloomfield, Stockwell, Gmel, & Rehn, 2003).

One group of cultures with historically low rates of alcoholism is in Asia and, in particular, Japan, China, and Korea. Asians are more predisposed to *facial flushing* and other unpleasant physical reactions when drinking alcohol, which tends to suppress desire for alcohol (Sobue, Takeshita, Maruyama, & Morimoto, 2002). Facial flushing and sensitivity to alcohol relate to elevated levels of *acetaldehyde,* a metabolite of alcohol. Among Asians, genetic predispositions may cause acetaldehyde to generate quickly and remain in the body for longer periods. This process produces and prolongs unpleasant physical reactions and may thus provide greater protection from alcoholism (Chai et al., 2005; Eriksson, 2001). Others, however, have not found this to be so, and rates of alcoholism have increased in certain parts of Asia such as Taiwan (Lu et al., 2005; Nishiyori et al., 2005).

## EVOLUTIONARY INFLUENCES

Some have proposed evolutionary theories for substance-related disorders. One evolutionary theory is that the mesolimbic dopamine system is not strictly a reward-based system but one intricately involved in survival motivation. People who view chemical substances as threats to their reproductive ability are generally apt to avoid these substances, whereas people who view chemical substances as boosting their reproductive ability accept these substances (Newlin, Regalia, Seidman, & Bobashev, 2012). Many people such as Elon engage in alcohol and other substance use because they believe it will enhance their social desirability and attractiveness to others.

Another evolutionary view of addiction is that individuals within societies generally pursue positions of dominance and submission to maintain social order. Some advantages to submission exist, such as avoiding aggressive behavior, but such a position also causes stress because one can be excluded from group resources at any time. Coping with such stress may involve

drug use and may be a factor in high drug use in disadvantaged communities. Submission may also lead to a socially dependent relationship with a dominant individual, which may cause maltreatment and subsequent feelings of depression assuaged by substance use (Lende & Smith, 2002).

## Causes of Substance-Related Disorders

Substance-related disorders are quite complicated in terms of risk factors that help cause the problems. To arrange risk factors into a general model of addiction, many theorists and researchers adopt a biopsychosocial approach that incorporates aspects of the *diathesis-stress model* we discussed for other disorders (Garland, Boettiger, & Howard, 2011). Biological factors may predispose a person toward substance use, and environmental factors may trigger this predisposition to produce a substance-related disorder. Some researchers argue as well that we will eventually need different theories of cause because many kinds of substance-related disorders may exist.

Comprehensive models of addiction often divide biological and environmental risk factors into distal or proximal ones (Park, Sher, Todorov, & Heath, 2011). **Distal factors** are background factors that indirectly affect a person and can generally contribute to a mental disorder. Biological distal factors with respect to substance-related disorders include genetic predisposition and perhaps temperaments such as an impulsive personality. Environmental distal factors include association with deviant peers, problematic family relationships, parental drug use, culture, and early learning and drug experiences.

**Proximal factors** are more immediate factors that directly affect a person and more specifically contribute to a mental disorder. Biological proximal factors include activation of the mesolimbic dopamine pathway upon drug use. Environmental proximal factors include stress, depression, peer pressure, positive expectancies about substance use, and availability of substances. Proximal factors may also include consequences of drug use, both positive (e.g., enhanced mood and relief from stress) and negative (e.g., ill physical effects and occupational and legal troubles).

Some of these factors interact to propel a person toward substance use disorder (see **Figure 9.13**). Recall that craving for substances often involves selective attention to cues that remind a person of drug use. This selective attention also appears to have a biological basis in that dopamine is released from brain features of the mesolimbic pathway. This highly rewarding event further reinforces a person's drug-seeking behavior (Volkow et al., 2011). Ongoing stress in a person's life may also lead to long-term excessive alcohol use that creates key changes in the prefrontal cortex. These brain changes can then help produce even more stress as a person's memory and concentration suffer and can lead to even greater focus on obtaining rewarding substances. Key neuronal and other brain changes can also make a person particularly sensitive to craving and desire for future drug use (Pickens et al., 2011).

Various factors seemed to swell into a "perfect storm" that set the stage for Elon's excessive alcohol and other drug use. His

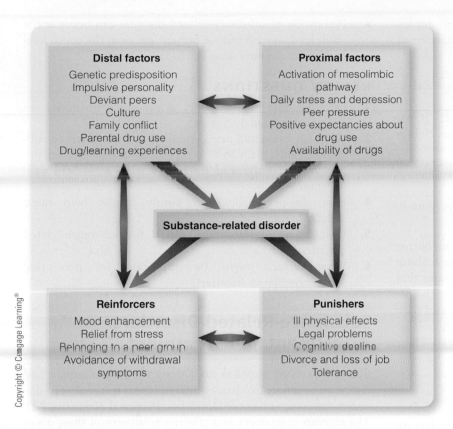

**FIGURE 9.13** Sample causal model of substance-related disorder

distal biological risk factors included an impulsive personality and high levels of arousal assuaged by alcohol use. A family history of alcoholism may have been present as well. Proximal risk factors included entry into college and substantial stress following intense academic demands. Elon also greatly enjoyed the pleasurable aspects of sex and drug use and was clearly exciting key areas of the brain such as the mesolimbic pathway. Elon later expanded and increased his drug use and focused solely on drug-seeking behavior. Many people with substance-related disorders experience a phenomenon they describe as *rock-bottom*, meaning their brain function and behavior are almost singularly geared toward seeking and using drugs. Such devastating effects underscore the need for prevention, and we describe these efforts next.

## Prevention of Substance-Related Disorders

Given the terrible personal and health-based consequences of extended drug use, prevention efforts for substance-related disorders have received much attention. Prevention efforts include those for adults and those for children and adolescents. Recall from Chapter 3 our discussion of a prevention program sponsored by the University of Missouri's Wellness Resource Center. Program components included promoting responsible decision making and providing accurate information about alcohol consumption by college students. Once misperceptions are corrected about the extent and acceptability of student drinking, binge and heavy drinking typically decline. Programs tailored

to college students also include changing positive expectancies about alcohol use and increased use of designated drivers (Cronce & Larimer, 2011).

Prevention programs also aim to reduce alcohol and other drug intake in pregnant mothers to prevent fetal alcohol effects in newborns. These programs focus on screening for alcohol and other drug use, educating mothers about ill effects of such use, managing stress and reducing depression, increasing social support, and visiting the mother's home (Floyd, Weber, Denny, & O'Connor, 2009; Tough, Clarke, & Clarren, 2005). Similar techniques help reduce excessive substance use among the elderly, health care professionals, hospital patients, victims and perpetrators of violence, and people with comorbid mental disorders (Howard, Delva, Jenson, Edmond, & Vaughn, 2005).

Universal efforts to prevent substance use disorder often target the public. Examples include raising the minimum drinking age, lowering the legal limit for defining driving while impaired, airing antidrug commercials, banning advertisements for tobacco in some media, engaging in drug testing in the workplace, and implementing heavy taxation on alcohol and tobacco products. The general effectiveness of these policies for reducing drug use has been relatively modest, however (Howard et al., 2005).

A controversial approach to preventing extended health problems in those addicted to drugs is to reduce needle sharing by supplying new, clean needles or syringes. *Needle exchange* or *harm reduction programs* provide unused needles and syringes to intravenous drug users, cleansing materials such as bleach or skin ointment, education about communicable diseases such as AIDS, and access to mental health services (Delgado, 2004). Some criticize needle exchange programs for potentially maintaining excessive drug use habits, but the programs do effectively reduce bloodborne diseases and risk factors associated with HIV (Marlatt & Witkiewitz, 2010).

*Relapse prevention* is also a key way of reducing further drug use in someone with a substance-related disorder. Relapse prevention involves reducing exposure to alcohol and other drugs, improving motivation to continue abstinence, self-monitoring daily mood and tempting situations, recognizing and coping appropriately with drug cravings, reducing anxiety and depression, modifying irrational thoughts about drug use, and developing a crisis plan if alcohol or other drugs are used again (McGovern, Wrisley, & Drake, 2005). Medication to reduce the pleasurable nature of a specific drug and regular attendance at self-help group meetings may also be useful for relapse prevention (see later treatment section; Drake, Wallach, & McGovern, 2005; Spanagel & Kiefer, 2008). Relapse prevention strategies are more effective for people addicted to nicotine, alcohol, and marijuana (Dutra et al., 2008; Hajek, Stead, West, Jarvis, & Lancaster, 2009).

Other prevention programs target children and adolescents so drug use does not begin in the developmental period. These programs typically focus on:

- Reducing availability of illegal drugs
- Increasing legal consequences for drug use
- School-related media programs such as DARE (Drug Abuse Resistance Education) to educate youth and change drug-related attitudes
- Programs to increase work and leisure opportunities to deflect youths from drug-seeking opportunities
- Peer-based programs to enhance methods of saying no to offers to use drugs

Prevention programs that are comprehensive in nature tend to be more effective than simply educating youth about substance use (Lemstra et al., 2010). Prevention programs that emphasize skills building, such as drug refusal and social life skills, are particularly useful for reducing marijuana and hard drug use and for improving decision-making ability, self-esteem, and peer pressure resistance (Faggiano et al., 2008). These programs may be more effective for boys than girls, however (Vigla-Taglianti et al., 2009).

## INTERIM SUMMARY

- Biological risk factors for substance-related disorders include genetic contributions, especially for metabolism, low response to alcohol, and craving.
- Brain features implicated in substance-related disorders are those closely linked to the mesolimbic pathway and primarily include the amygdala, anterior cingulate, bed nucleus of the stria terminalis, and prefrontal cortex.
- Neurochemical features implicated in substance-related disorders primarily involve dopamine release from the mesolimbic pathway.
- Stress is a major environmental trigger for excessive substance use and often leads to relapse.
- Cognitive factors—especially positive expectancies about substance use and misperceptions about life changes brought about by substance use—help increase substance use.
- Classical and operant conditioning and modeling are important learning processes implicated in substance-related disorders.
- Impulsive personality and related traits can predispose some people toward substance use disorder.
- Family factors such as conflict and poor cohesion are good predictors of later substance use disorder and perhaps codependent relationships.
- Some cultural differences with respect to drug use are present, but the reasons for these differences remain unclear.
- Evolutionary theories of substance use include enhancement of reproductive fitness and easing anxiety and depression from submissive relationships.
- The cause of substance-related disorders is likely multivaried and involves several proximal and distal factors and reinforcers.

- Prevention of substance-related disorder can occur at the adult level, as with relapse prevention, or at the youth level to prevent excessive drug use before it begins.

## REVIEW QUESTIONS

1. Describe data that support a genetic contribution to substance-related disorders.
2. What key brain and neurochemical changes relate to substance-related disorders?
3. Describe cognitive and learning factors associated with substance use.
4. How do personality and family factors help cause substance-related disorders?
5. Describe an overall causal model for substance-related disorders.
6. What factors might be important for preventing substance-related disorders?

# Substance-Related Disorders: Assessment and Treatment

Substance-related disorders are among the most rampant and dangerous mental disorders we discuss in this textbook. The disorders can ravage an entire family (see **Personal Narrative 9.1**). The accurate assessment and effective treatment of these disorders is therefore critical. We next describe key methods, such as interviews, psychological testing, observations from others, and laboratory testing, for assessing substance-related disorders.

## Interviews

Interviews are a frequent means of assessing many mental disorders. Common types of interviews for substance-related disorders include screening interviews and motivational interviews. **Screening interviews** are specifically designed to assess recent and lifetime problems with respect to substance use. Two commonly used screening interviews are the Addiction Severity Index—6 and the Comprehensive Drinker Profile.

The *Addiction Severity Index—6* contains structured questions about medical status, employment, social support, alcohol and other drug use, and legal, family, and psychiatric status. Composite scores from the measure are excellent predictors of substance use disorder (Cacciola, Alterman, Habing, & McLellan, 2011). The *Comprehensive Drinker Profile* is more specific to people with alcohol-use problems. This measure helps clinicians obtain information about past and present drinking patterns, life and medical problems related to alcohol use, and reasons for drinking. The scale has revealed gender differences with respect to alcohol use. Men more so than women drink at an earlier age, drive while drinking, drink beer, and drink away from home. Women report more negative emotional effects after drinking (Darke, 2010; Miller & Cervantes, 1997).

**Motivational interviewing** is an assessment and treatment strategy that involves obtaining information about a person's substance-related problem *and* providing feedback to help increase his readiness for change. An interviewer provides empathy, illustrates discrepancies between what a person is currently doing and what his long-term goals are, and helps a person believe change is possible. Clinicians who use motivational interviewing ask open-ended questions, listen and reflect information carefully, provide treatment choices, outline problems associated with current drug use, support a person's statements about wanting to change, and set specific treatment goals (Miller & Rollnick, 2009). A motivational interviewer actively gives advice and reinforces a person's willingness to change current behavior. Motivational interviewing is effective at reducing alcohol consumption, including college students in a 6-month period (Walters, Vader, Harris, Field, & Jouriles, 2009).

Elon underwent a motivational interview regarding his drug use during his initial days at a drug rehabilitation facility. Following is a brief vignette from the interview:

**Elon:** I just don't know if I can change. The stuff I was taking was . . . I just think about using it all the time.

**Therapist:** You could change if you wanted to, but if you continue the path you're on you will kill yourself.

**Elon:** I understand that, and sometimes I do want to go back to the way things were.

**Therapist:** That's an excellent choice, and there are different ways we can offer you to get back to that point.

**Elon:** It just seems as though I've been using for so long now . . .

**Therapist:** Let's talk about some times in your life when you didn't use drugs but still did pretty well in school and with your friends.

## Psychological Testing

Therapists also use psychological tests to screen and assess for drug use. A well-known test is the *Minnesota Multiphasic Personality Inventory* (MMPI-2) we discussed in Chapter 4. The MMPI-2 has three subscales that assess for drug use. Items on the *Addictions Acknowledgement Scale* detect substance use among people willing to admit such use. Items on the *Addiction Potential Scale* are those typically endorsed by people who use substances more so than those who do not. Items on the *MacAndrew Alcoholism Scale* are general MMPI-2 items that discriminate people who use substances from people who do not (Clements & Heintz, 2002).

Another scale we discuss at more length in Chapter 10 is the *Millon Clinical Multiaxial Inventory—III*. This scale assesses personality disorders but has two subscales for alcohol dependence and drug dependence. Items on these subscales center on diagnostic criteria and concern drug use as well as behaviors associated with drug use. These subscales successfully predict risk for increased or decreased drug use (Hesse, Guldager, & Holm-Linneberg, 2012; Retzlaff, Stoner, & Kleinsasser, 2002).

Other commonly used screening measures include the Michigan Alcoholism Screening Test and the CAGE. These scales are particularly useful for assessing recent and severe use of alcohol (Darke, 2010). The *Michigan Alcohol Screening Test* is a 24-item measure of drinking habits, interpersonal and legal problems related to drinking, and treatment for alcoholism. The *CAGE* is a 4-item measure that includes variations of the following questions. Answering yes to two or more of these questions relates to high risk for substance use disorder (Skogen, Overland, Knudsen, & Mykletun, 2011):

- Have you ever felt you needed to **C**ut down on your drinking?
- Have people **A**nnoyed you by criticizing your drinking?
- Have you ever felt bad or **G**uilty about your drinking?
- Have you ever felt you need a drink first thing in the morning (**E**ye-opener) to steady your nerves or get rid of a hangover?

## Observations from Others

Excessive drug use is often a hidden problem, and many people do not accurately report their alcohol or other drug use. Therapists may thus conduct observations and solicit reports from others. Family members, partners, coworkers, and friends can help monitor a person's behavior and report days missed from work, time away from home, family arguments over drug use, and binges, among other things. This must be done with great care and with knowledge and consent of the person with a substance-related disorder. Observations like these are often part of family therapy for people with substance-related disorders (see treatment section).

## Laboratory Testing

Laboratory tests involve analyzing urine, blood, breath, hair, saliva, or sweat to detect recent drug use. Potential employers and drug treatment facilities often use these measures to determine abstinence from drugs. *Urine screens* are perhaps the most common laboratory measure of recent substance use, though periods of detection differ by drug (see **Table 9.10**). Some drugs such as phencyclidine can be detected as much as 8 days after use, but other drugs such as alcohol cannot be detected past 10 hours.

Urine screens detect presence or absence of certain drugs and are a good initial screening method. A downside of urine screens is the prevalence of wrong results, so the tests may precede other laboratory measures. Urine screens consist of the following processes:

- *Chromatography* separates chemicals into their individual components.

- *Spectrometry* identifies exact molecular structure of certain chemicals and usually follows chromatography.
- *Spectral methods* detect certain luminescence various drugs emit under fluorescent light.
- *Immunoassays* assess for antibodies generated from a substance.

*Blood tests* also assess for recent drug use, especially alcohol. Blood alcohol tests are

Handheld Breathalyzers are available for self-testing one's alcohol level.

## Personal Narrative 9.1

### One Family's Struggle with Substance-Related Disorders

#### The Father

I dreamed that my daughter, Carrick, was perched on the edge of a dock on a lake. I stood behind her. As she slipped into the water, it dawned on me that she was taking a swimming test and I was the only one observing her. Her back arched and her arms plunged in a graceful butterfly stroke, but her head did not emerge. Her skin suddenly blanched, and I sensed she was in trouble. I jumped into the gray chop, landing beyond where her efforts had carried her. As I faced her, she sank feet first, her long hair swirling in the water. She was just inches away but it seemed an infinite distance. I felt responsible, as if my thinking that she might drown made it happen. I wanted to change the direction the dream was taking, but couldn't do it. I knew she would plunge faster than I could dive after her, and that I would not be able to bring her to the surface even if I managed to catch her.

I woke up. My chest felt raw and empty, as if my ribcage had been ripped open. At first I thought the dream was about my feeling that I have something to lose again. But as I've thought about it, I realize that my subconscious was confirming what I've learned the hard way. I cannot "save" my daughter. If she wants, I can only try to help her learn to swim. When it comes to addiction, that's all anybody can do.

For several years, I've lived with the specter of my daughter killing herself. It haunted me whenever the phone rang at a time when it didn't normally, or if a holiday passed without our having heard from her, or when I saw or heard Deirdre, my wife, weeping. However her death happened—a heroin overdose, hypothermia, murder, suicide, AIDS—I knew I would have to find the words to express what had happened, and why.

Carrick started smoking marijuana when she was 12 years old, and worked her way to a heroin addiction by 17. She sees her drug dependencies, as do I, as the inevitable outcome of genes and other influences. We have had a trying journey. When Carrick was using drugs, she often overwhelmed Deirdre, our son Duncan, and me—individually and collectively. We all have different ways of coping. My way has been to try to find some connections to the experiences of others. And so, as part of this journey, I have been writing *The Elephant on Main Street: An Interactive Memoir of Addictions*, which became a website (www.elephantonmain.com).

Thanksgiving 2004 was the first that Carrick spent at home since 1999 when she was 15. In 2000, she was in a wilderness therapy program in the high desert of Utah. In 2001, she was living on the streets of Philadelphia with a lost soul who called himself Chaos Destruction. In 2002, she was hanging with Pete, who had just been released from state prison for drug dealing. In 2003, she and Pete were either incarcerated on Riker's Island or about to be—she was so strung out on heroin and cocaine that one day blended into the next.

After Thanksgiving dinner 2004, our 15-year-old son Duncan surprised us with a box of chocolates and a greeting card. He wrote: "Mom, Dad, Carrick, Pete. I love you guys all. We stick through the hardest times as a family." That's what this small piece of the narrative is all about: sticking together through the hardest times—and telling the story.

#### The Mother

I have alcoholism, which has been in remission since 1987 when I had my last drink. My husband, to whom I have been married almost 30 years, is in recovery and has been sober since 1985. My father was a high-functioning alcoholic, and my 21-year-old daughter is in recovery, having suffered an addiction to heroin, since the age of 17. In 1997, 10 years sober, I developed severe treatment-resistant major depression. I took refuge in sleep, finding even routine activities too overwhelming to accomplish. There seemed no reason to continue living. Suicidal ideation filled my waking hours. Eventually I was hospitalized. Following electro-convulsive therapy, a uniquely designed regimen of antidepressant medications, and talk therapy, I began down another road to recovery.

Courtesy of Thom Forbes
Thom Forbes, Father

Courtesy of Thom Forbes
Deirdre Forbes, Mother

Today I feel better than I ever have about waking up in the morning and facing life's challenges and joys. I've concluded that I want to devote the remainder of my working life to battling the effect of chemical dependency, which often coexists with mental disorder, on individuals, families, and communities. I want people to know the damage addiction and mental disorder can do, but I also want them to see and understand that recovery works. I want people to see I am unusual only because I am part of a minority who speak out about their recovery, not because I am in recovery. Stigma and discrimination keep many in recovery from doing so.

## The Child and Brother

Being the ghost child wasn't that bad in the beginning of the drama between Carrick and my parents. I had freedom really; I got to do whatever I wanted. Like a ghost, I was there but no one really saw me. But I didn't realize that why I was so free was because all of the attention was on my sister. I didn't care at all because everything was going fine for me. I didn't care . . . not yet.

There were times where my sister's problems wouldn't bother me at all, but then there would be other times where I would be in the middle of an argument and be overwhelmed with the drama and tension between my parents and my sister. All I wanted to do was just to walk away from it, let them deal with the problem because hey, it doesn't concern me, it's not my problem, it's Carrick's problem. Or so I thought. But it became my problem, too, in at least four ways:

1.  Money. As the problem got worse, Carrick started asking me for money. Most of the time I would give it to her because I wanted to be a good little brother and I wanted to help her out. Then my parents told me she was just using the money to buy drugs. That's when I just felt like punching a wall. I felt like I should have known why she wanted the money so badly. When I stopped giving her money, she started stealing from me. Then she would deny stealing from me, and that's when Carrick's problem started becoming my problem.

2.  Sleep. There were some nights when my sister and my parents would just argue throughout the whole night, nonstop yelling, and I couldn't sleep at all. They would argue on school nights, and I just wanted to get the hell out of there.

3.  Communication. I could barely talk with my parents because they were always mindful of my sister. If I asked them to do something for me, they would just say things like "Well, after when Carrick comes home," or "I have to take Carrick somewhere." It was always "Carrick, Carrick, Carrick."

4.  Random fights on small things. Sometimes fights would start about the most random things, like television shows. After the problem was resolved, I usually realized it wasn't clean Carrick who was arguing with me over television, it was the mean Carrick, who was high, fighting with me.

I didn't really understand how serious my sister's problem was until I grew older. During her downfall, I thought she was just in a little trouble that wouldn't have a giant effect on her future, and that the problem would eventually go away. As we grew up, and Carrick started controlling her problem and pushing herself to go to school, the attention started shifting toward me. They were afraid that I might head down the wrong road and might end up messing up my life. When I'd go out with my friends, they asked questions like "who, what, when, why, where?" I have to admit; I guess those antidrug commercials really do work for parents.

Overall, Carrick's problem didn't just concern her. It concerned the whole family. Anyone's actions in the family will certainly affect another person's life. A family is like a chain. If you break the chain, you break the family. We all depend on each other. We all need each other.

I also learned a lot from this problem. I'm able to help out people in my school who might have similar problems, or who might be heading down the wrong road. I think I got a lot smarter when it comes to drugs and drinking.

After seeing what drugs have done to my sister, mentally and physically, it gives me a perfect reason to say "No." I'm thankful that I don't have to learn what trouble drugs can cause by doing them. I can just look at what they did to my sister. After all I've been through, I feel like a better man who is able to make the right decisions.

I guess if it weren't for Carrick, I probably wouldn't have any reason not to try drugs or drink. But I'm thankful for my sister, because I have learned so much from her. And I realized that anyone who has a problem in a family always affects someone else in the family.

Courtesy of Thom Forbes

**Duncan Forbes, Brother**

## Table 9.10

### Periods of Detection for Illicit Drugs by Urinalysis

| Drug | Period of detection |
| --- | --- |
| Alcohol | 6–10 hours |
| Amphetamine | 1–2 days |
| Barbiturates | 2–10 days |
| Benzodiazepines | 1–6 weeks |
| Cocaine | 1–4 days |
| Codeine | 1–2 days |
| Hashish | 1 day–5 weeks |
| Heroin | 1–2 days |
| LSD | 8 hours |
| Marijuana | 1 day–5 weeks |
| MDMA (ecstasy) | 1–2 days |
| Mescaline | 2–3 days |
| Methadone | 1 day–1 week |
| Methamphetamine | 1–2 days |
| Morphine | 1–2 days |
| Nicotine | 1–2 days |
| Phencyclidine (PCP) | 2–8 days |
| Tetrahydrocannabinol (THC) | 1 day–5 weeks |

From R.J. Craig, *Counseling the alcohol and drug dependent client: A practical approach* (p. 91), New York: Pearson, 2004. Reprinted by permission of Pearson Education, Inc.

used when a person is suspected of driving under the influence of alcohol, when a person's memory or thinking ability seems impaired, for adolescents, and for people in a drug rehabilitation facility. Earlier we provided a table of different blood alcohol levels and typical behavior associated with those levels (Table 9.7).

A quicker method of assessing recent alcohol use and blood alcohol level is via one's breath, as when a police officer uses a *toximeter* or *Breathalyzer test* that a person breathes into. Several handheld Breathalyzer devices are now available so a person can test herself before driving. Blood alcohol levels will tend to rise more quickly if you are female, have drunk hard liquor, have drunk substantial amounts of alcohol (such as more than one drink per hour), weigh less, are older, have not eaten recently, are using other drugs or medications, or mix alcohol with carbonated beverages, which speeds absorption. For some people, drinking an abundance of water during and after alcohol use slows alcohol absorption and helps them avoid a severe

hangover. Drinking lots of water *and* lots of alcohol, however, will still leave you grossly impaired.

*Hair analysis* is becoming a preferred method of drug testing because someone can detect illicit drug use months after a person ingested a drug. About 60 to 80 strands of hair close to the scalp are analyzed to detect drug use in the past 3 months (Ledgerwood, Goldberger, Risk, Lewis, & Price, 2008). Hair analysis is popular because substances to hide drug use cannot easily contaminate results. Downsides to hair testing are that the amount of drug a person took, and when the person took the drug, cannot be clearly established. Racial bias may also be a factor (see **Box 9.5**). *Saliva* and *sweat* tests for drug use have also been developed. Studies of drivers whose saliva was tested reveal that the most common drugs found are ecstasy and methamphetamine (Vindenes, 2012; Wylie, Torrance, Seymour, Buttress, & Oliver, 2005).

## Biological Treatment of Substance-Related Disorders

You might think it odd that other substances or medications could treat substance-related disorders. Many now believe a combination of medication and psychological treatment may be best to address stubborn substance-related problems. Medications for these disorders include agonists, antagonists, partial agonists, and aversives.

### AGONISTS

**Agonists** are drugs that have a similar chemical composition as the excessively used drug. Agonist drug treatment thus takes advantage of **cross-tolerance**, or tolerance for a drug one has never taken. A good example of agonist drug treatment is *methadone* for people addicted to heroin or related opiates such as morphine or oxycodone. Methadone shares a chemical composition with opiate drugs and so binds to opiate receptors in the brain as opiates do (Matsui & Williams, 2010). Methadone treatment is given as a person reduces opiate use so cravings for, and withdrawal symptoms from, the opiate are less severe. Once a person is fully cleansed of the addictive drug, methadone doses are gradually reduced as well. Another drug, a methadone derivative known as *levo-alpha-acetyl-methadol* (LAAM), lasts longer in the body and may need to be taken only three times a week compared with daily doses for methadone. LAAM is thus more effective than methadone for helping people end opiate addiction (Anglin, Conner, Annon, & Longshore, 2008).

Agonist agents are also used for nicotine addiction. *Nicotine replacement therapy* refers to ingesting safe amounts of nicotine without smoking tobacco. The alternative ingestion comes in the form of a nicotine patch (Nicoderm), gum (Nicorette), inhaler, or nasal spray (Hughes, Peters, & Naud, 2011). No one form is greatly more effective than another, although the patch is the easiest to use and the inhaler the most difficult (Polosa & Benowitz, 2011). These devices also help reduce cravings and withdrawal symptoms, and their strength can be gradually reduced until a person is no longer addicted.

## BOX 9.5 Focus on Law and Ethics

### Drug Testing

Sophisticated methods of drug testing such as hair and saliva analyses are now available, so important ethical questions arise. A key ethical dilemma is one's right to privacy versus a public's right to know of potentially dangerous situations. A flashpoint in this dilemma has been drug testing of current employees for substance use. Some argue employees have a right to safeguard personal information, especially about legal drug use such as alcohol or tobacco. Drug testing may also be humiliating for a person who must urinate before a supervisor, or the testing may be discriminatory if people are chosen because of some visible characteristic such as disability or race. A person conducting hair analysis might also show bias if the type of hair sample identifies a person as a likely ethnic minority (Greenfield & Hennessy, 2008).

Others argue that employers have a right to know if an employee is impaired on the job and might harm others. You would not want airplane pilots or truckers to be drunk when flying or driving. Some have taken a middle ground on this issue, claiming that drug testing is ethical under strict conditions such as establishing policies acceptable to workers *and* employers, engaging in selective but not universal drug testing, providing prior notice of testing, notifying employees of test results, and carefully maintaining confidentiality of drug testing results (DesJardins & Duska, 2003).

Ethical questions regarding drug testing apply to other populations as well. Some claim mandatory drug testing of high school athletes is coercive, lacks informed consent and confidentiality, and unfairly targets a specific group of people (Louria, 2004). Many parents also disagree with professional association statements that drug test results for teenagers be completely confidential—does a parent have a right to know about her son's drug use? (Schwartz, Silber, Heyman, Sheridan & Estabrook, 2003). Finally, some express concern that drug testing on pregnant women could lead to prosecution for harm to the fetus (Stone-Manista, 2009).

## ANTAGONISTS

**Antagonists** are drugs that block pleasurable effects of an addictive drug, with the expectation, and hope, that this will reduce cravings for the addictive drug. A good example is *naltrexone* (Revia), which blocks opiate receptors in the brain, and specifically the nucleus accumbens, to decrease craving for alcohol and reduce its pleasurable effects. The drug is effective for reducing alcohol consumption and craving (Lobmaier, Kunoe, Gossop, & Waal, 2010). A combination of naltrexone with *acamprosate*, a drug that may also have some antagonist properties, is effective as well for preventing relapse in people with alcoholism (Spanagel, & Kiefer, 2008). A related antagonist, *naloxone* (Narcan), is used in emergency rooms to treat opiate overdose (Kim, Irwin, & Khoshnood, 2009).

## PARTIAL AGONISTS

**Partial agonists** are drugs that may act as an agonist or antagonist depending on how much of a neurotransmitter is produced. Dopamine has a close association with substance-related disorders, so a partial agonist will increase dopamine levels when this neurotransmitter is not highly produced in the brain and decrease dopamine levels when this neurotransmitter *is* highly produced in the brain (Crunelle, Miller, Booij, & van den Brink, 2010).

A common partial agonist for substance-related disorders is *buprenorphine* (Subutex), which acts as an agonist at certain opiate receptors but an antagonist at other opiate receptors. The drug helps control craving for opiates by binding to key opiate receptors but has fewer side effects such as sedation than pure agonists such as methadone. Buprenorphine also appears to be nearly if not equally effective as methadone, so the drug may be given if methadone does not work well, or as a transition between methadone and abstinence (McCance-Katz, Sullivan, & Nallani, 2009).

## AVERSIVES

**Aversive drugs** are those that make ingestion of an addictive drug quite uncomfortable. A good example is *disulfiram* (Antabuse). When someone takes this drug, there are no ill effects until he drinks alcohol. Following alcohol intake, the person experiences nausea, vomiting, diarrhea, and blood pressure changes that essentially punish him for alcohol use or create a learned taste aversion. Think about what happens when you eat something at a restaurant and then get sick—you do not want to go back to that restaurant for quite a while!

Disulfiram is an aldehyde dehydrogenase inhibitor, meaning that high levels of acetaldehyde build up quickly. Recall from our discussion of cultural factors that high levels of acetaldehyde may cause several unpleasant symptoms and deter certain people from using alcohol. A person with alcoholism does not take disulfiram every day, but he may take the drug during "high-risk" times such as going on vacation or during a holiday season (Schuckit, 2009). Disulfiram is also effective for treating cocaine use (Devoto, Flore, Saba, Cadeddu, & Gessa, 2012). A related drug, *calcium carbimide* (Temposil), has similar but milder effects than disulfiram.

Another aversive drug is *silver acetate*, a substance placed in gum, lozenges, or mouthwash (Carson et al., 2013). Silver acetate has no major side effects when used alone. When mixed with nicotine, however, as when a person smokes a cigarette after using the mouthwash, mucous membranes are irritated and a foul taste occurs in the person's mouth. Punishment of the response (smoking) or creating a learned taste aversion is thus key. Disulfiram and silver acetate only work if a person is sufficiently motivated to use the substances to deter alcohol and tobacco use.

## OTHER MEDICATIONS

Other medications are used to treat substance-related disorders as well, especially antianxiety and antidepressant drugs (discussed in Chapters 5 and 7). The drugs combat comorbid anxiety and depressive symptoms that may trigger excessive alcohol and other drug use, and the medications may even help reduce some alcohol and cocaine consumption by themselves. Research continues as well on medications to speed drug metabolism to cleanse the body quickly, and vaccines for substance-related disorders (Stowe et al., 2011). The best treatment for substance-related disorders is likely a combination of medication with psychological approaches, which we discuss next.

# Psychological Treatment of Substance-Related Disorders

Psychological treatment of substance-related disorders generally involves inpatient and residential treatment, brief interventions, cognitive-behavioral therapy, family and marital therapy, group therapy, and self-help groups.

## INPATIENT AND RESIDENTIAL TREATMENT

Elon eventually entered a drug rehabilitation facility after substantial drug use and dangerous behavior. People who are intoxicated or dependent on a particular substance often must first undergo *inpatient* or *residential treatment* in which the major focus is detoxification and rehabilitation. **Detoxification** involves withdrawing from a drug under medical supervision, which may include medications mentioned previously. A person may be gradually withdrawn from heroin use by using methadone and sedatives to quell intense withdrawal symptoms. Detoxification also involves providing good nutrition, rest, exercise, and a stress-free environment to cleanse the body of all addicted drugs. Elon was asked to engage in low-temperature saunas, replace vitamins and minerals missing from his diet in the past few months, drink plenty of water, and adhere to a normal routine with set times for sleeping and waking.

**Rehabilitation** from drug use is the next phase of inpatient or residential treatment. Many rehabilitation treatment programs rely on the *Minnesota model*, which emphasizes complete abstinence, education about substance-related disorder and its consequences, effects of addiction on family members, and cognitive-behavioral techniques to prevent relapse (discussed in a later section). Individuals with substance-related disorders often share their experiences with professionals and other residents and confront problems currently facing them.

Elon eventually realized the full consequences of his actions, such as expulsion from college, and how much pain he caused his parents.

Most rehabilitation programs last about 4 weeks but could be longer in some cases. More than half of people who enter rehabilitation programs for alcohol remain abstinent a year after discharge, but only about one fourth remain abstinent 4 years after discharge. Rehabilitation programs are more likely to work if a person volunteered for treatment rather than having been referred by a court or employer. Spousal and family involvement is also important, as is immediate linkage to outpatient interventions discussed next (Dziegielewski, 2005; Weiss, Potter, & Iannucci, 2008).

## BRIEF INTERVENTIONS

*Brief interventions* for substance-related disorders include short-term strategies to change behavior as much as possible in a limited time. Brief interventions include the motivational interviewing technique we discussed earlier, which includes providing feedback about one's excessive substance use and negotiating and setting a goal for change. A therapist may try to get a client to commit to drinking only on weekends or allow a family member or trusted coworker to monitor his alcohol use at home or work. Brief interventions often last up to five treatment sessions (Kaner et al., 2009).

Brief interventions also focus on identifying high-risk situations for excessive substance use, especially when a person is stressed, lonely, bored, or depressed. Exploring the pros and cons of substance use, providing information about substance use and its negative consequences, and bolstering social support are important as well. The goal of brief interventions is not necessarily to achieve complete abstinence but to stabilize or reduce a person's substance use enough so she can pursue the more thorough types of therapy we discuss next. Brief interventions are effective at reducing excessive substance use for up to 6 to 12 months, but more so for men and if combined with medication (Bertholet, Daeppen, Wietlisbach, Fleming, & Burnand, 2005; Madras et al., 2009; McCaul & Petry, 2003).

## COGNITIVE-BEHAVIORAL THERAPY

We have discussed various aspects of cognitive-behavioral therapy for anxiety-related, somatic symptom, depressive, bipolar, and eating disorders. *Cognitive therapy* essentially refers to challenging and changing irrational thoughts about a given situation. Recall that one cognitive mistake commonly made by people who engage in heavy drinking, especially college students, is that others drink as much or more than they do. Correcting this misperception is thus important. Cognitive therapy may also involve modifying cognitive distortions we discussed in Chapters 5 and 7, especially those related to catastrophization. A person with substance use disorder may mistakenly believe if she does not take a certain drug such as cocaine, her performance on a work task will be terrible and she will be fired. Cognitive therapy is thus important for addressing psychological dependence and is usually incorporated into behavior therapy techniques.

*Behavior therapy* refers to changing learning patterns and other maladaptive behaviors associated with a given disorder. **Skills training** is a key behavioral treatment for substance-related disorders. Skills training involves helping a person understand antecedents and consequences of drug use (recall functional analysis from Chapter 4) and recognizing what situations represent a high risk for return to drug use. The stress of school was a strong trigger or antecedent of Elon's drug use, and elation and sexual prowess were potent consequences. He also came to see that certain situations were quite risky for him, especially association with drinking buddies and college parties.

Following this step, a person is encouraged to avoid high-risk situations or somehow cope with them effectively (*stimulus control*). In a high-risk situation, a person may be taught how to appropriately decline offers for alcohol or other drugs, understand one's limit and adhere strictly to it, leave a situation (party) after a certain time, bring a friend to help monitor alcohol or other drug use, or think about negative consequences to drug use. People can also learn to plan for emergencies, such as who to contact when tempted by drug use, and control physical arousal and strong emotions tied to cravings for drugs. People with substance-related disorders must also understand that even small events, such as taking a wrong turn when driving and seeing a liquor store, can produce strong cravings that require an adaptive response like calling a friend (Carroll, 2008).

Skills training may also involve **self-monitoring** in which a person constantly records the amount of drug taken or various situations and emotions that lead to urges for drug use. The idea here is to make a person as aware as possible of antecedents to drug use as well as actual drug use—the more we are aware of our excess behaviors, the less we tend to engage in them. Therapists may combine skills training with **cue exposure therapy** in which a person is exposed to cues such as the sight and smell of alcohol and then uses skills such as relaxation or discussion to successfully decline drug use (Vollstadt-Klein et al., 2011). Therapists use skills training to prevent relapse to excessive drug use and may combine the training with other approaches such as mindfulness (Bowen et al., 2009).

A key aspect of behavior therapy for substance-related disorders is **contingency management**, or rewarding positive behaviors via praise and other reinforcers from family members, friends, and close associates. Elon's parents verified and rewarded their son's abstinence following regular drug screens. Contingency management may also involve incentives in which therapists provide vouchers for various goods and services following drug-free urine or other screening. Contingency management is particularly effective for reducing opiate, nicotine, alcohol, cocaine, and marijuana intake. A downside to contingency management, however, is that effects may diminish if outside rewards do not continue (Hartzler, Lash, & Roll, 2012).

A **community reinforcement approach** to substance-related disorders is similar to contingency management. A person with substance use disorder is not only rewarded by others for abstinence but also encouraged to change conditions in his environment—such as those at work, home, and recreationally—to make them more rewarding than substance use. Therapists

often combine this approach with vouchers, medication, and ongoing drug testing. The approach seems particularly effective for excessive cocaine use (Meyers, Roozen, & Smith, 2011).

## FAMILY AND MARITAL THERAPY

Substance-related disorders involve great harm to family members, and better treatment outcomes for people with these disorders usually relate to good marital and family environments. Family and marital therapies are thus important components of treatment. These treatments involve the spouse or partner or other family members of a person with a substance-related disorder to help motivate a person to seek treatment, increase positive communications within the family, solve problems effectively, and monitor a person's substance use. The general goal of these techniques is to foster a living environment that helps prevent relapse to excessive alcohol or other drug use and that reduces the "enabling" behaviors we discussed earlier (O'Farrell & Clements, 2012).

Films and reality television shows sometimes portray family members having an "intervention" with someone with a substance use or other problem. Such intervention usually involves suddenly confronting or shocking a person with a family meeting to increase insight and encourage the person to seek help for a substance use problem. Unfortunately, this strategy has shown to be more harmful than helpful because the identified person may feel threatened or singled out as a "scapegoat" for family or marital problems. Many families also fail to follow through with intervention plans (O'Farrell & Clements, 2012).

Clinicians often use family therapy to treat adolescents with substance use problems, and **multidimensional family therapy** is a popular form. Multidimensional family therapy consists of a 12-week program that focuses on developing a strong adolescent–parent bond, enhancing good negotiation and family problem-solving skills, improving supervision of the adolescent, and correcting learning and school-based problems. The therapy has been shown to be as or more effective than cognitive-behavioral therapy for improving family cohesion and peer relations and for reducing future arrests and excessive substance use. Establishing a strong adolescent-parent alliance appears to be crucial for family members to remain in treatment and complete the program successfully (Liddle, 2010; Robbins et al., 2006).

## GROUP THERAPY

*Group therapy* has always been a popular form of treatment for people with substance-related disorders. The group meets together with a therapist with the goal of helping to reduce alcohol and other drug use. Group therapy approaches can differ widely based on the orientation of the therapist, but common practices include providing education about the consequences of excessive drug use, encouraging commitment to change, enhancing social support, recognizing cues that lead to excessive substance use, restructuring destructive lifestyles and relationships, and identifying alternative ways of coping with stress. The effectiveness of group therapy is not fully clear but may be better if treatment targets reduced substance use and comorbid psychological problems such as depression and personality disorder (Brook, 2008; Khantzian, Golden-Schulman, & McAuliffe, 2004).

## SELF-HELP GROUPS

**Self-help groups** are similar to group therapy in that several people with a substance-related disorder meet to support one another and encourage abstinence. Most self-help groups are led not by a professional therapist but by people with a particular substance use problem. Perhaps the most well-known self-help group is *Alcoholics Anonymous*, which relies on a 12-step and 12-tradition program that leads one (hopefully) to abstinence under the guidance of a sponsor or senior member (see **Table 9.11**). The general philosophy of Alcoholics Anonymous is that alcoholism is a disease controlled only by complete abstinence. Self-help groups are a highly cost-effective means of assisting people with substance-related disorders.

Approximately two thirds (67.4 percent) of people with alcoholism seek help through Alcoholics Anonymous (Timko, Moos, Finney, & Lesar, 2000). People are more likely to join Alcoholics Anonymous if their drinking is particularly severe and if they have few friends or family members for support (Tonigan & Connors, 2008). Related 12-step groups include *Narcotics Anonymous* or *Cocaine Anonymous* for mind-altering substances as well as groups for family members of people with alcoholism or other substance-related disorder, including *Al-Anon/Alateen* and *Nar-Anon*. Many groups, such as *Double Trouble in Recovery*, address people with substance-related disorders *and* another mental disorder such as depression.

Do 12-step groups work for people with substance-related disorders? This is hard to know because these groups differ with respect to their structure and who attends, but Alcoholics Anonymous and related groups are moderately effective. Self-help groups often work because they provide good social and abstinence support but rely heavily on individual motivation to attend meetings regularly. A key downside of self-help groups is dropout. About 40 percent of people drop out of these groups after 1 year, although this rate may not differ much from people in traditional therapy. People who remain in self-help groups longer tend to be African American and more motivated to change, connected to religious activities, socially involved, and accepting of the disease model of addiction (Bogenschutz, Geppert, & George, 2006; Kelly, Kahler, & Humphreys, 2010).

## What If I or Someone I Know Has a Substance-Related Problem or Disorder?

If you or someone you know wants to cut down on drinking or smoking, then working with family members to monitor substance use, consulting self-help guides, and discovering other ways of coping with stress and other triggers may be sufficient. Substance-related problems can be devastating, however, and can easily lead to severe consequences such as a car accident, arrest, or loss of a job. If you or someone you know has a serious substance-related problem, such as with cocaine, methamphetamine, or alcohol, then seeking medical and psychological help as soon as possible is very important. We recommend consulting a qualified professional who specializes in substance use treatment.

## Long-Term Outcome for People with Substance-Related Disorders

Treating people with substance-related disorders can be complicated and involves many pharmacological and psychological components. Relapse is also common in this population. Regarding adolescents, treatment effectiveness is about 38 percent at 6 months after treatment and 32 percent at 12 months after treatment. Adolescents who do better in treatment are those who actually complete a treatment program, who had less severe substance use, and who have peers and parents that provide positive social support and do not condone substance use (Willams, Chang, et al., 2000; Winters, Botzet, & Fahnhorst, 2011).

Some (31 percent) adults with substance-related disorders achieve abstinence at posttreatment compared with 13 percent of people in control groups (Dutra et al., 2008). Success in treatment is related to quality of treatment, less severe substance use, commitment to abstinence, and treatment tailored to individual characteristics of a client, such as women with eating disorders (Clifford, Maisto, Stout, McKay, & Tonigan, 2006; Greenfield et al., 2007). Maintaining therapeutic contact over time is also crucial for continued success, especially in more severe cases (McKay et al., 2010).

Treatment for college students with drinking problems is relatively successful. Many programs use motivational interviewing, alcohol education, normative comparisons, and moderation strategies. Most studies reveal significant improvements in alcohol-related knowledge, attitudes toward drinking, normative beliefs about drinking, and intentions to reduce alcohol intake (Scott-Sheldon, Demartini, Carey, & Carey, 2009). Personalized feedback about one's drinking seems especially effective for people who drink for social reasons and for heavy drinkers (Vader, Walters, Prabhu, Houck, & Field, 2010).

What is the long-term outcome of people with substance-related disorders? Much of this literature has focused on people with alcoholism. One comprehensive study of 636 males with alcoholism revealed several phases of the disorder. A person with alcoholism in his 20s may escalate heavy drinking to the point that, by his 30s, significant interference occurs in areas such as marriage and work. A person with alcoholism in his 40s had very serious physical complications from excessive drinking, such as hepatitis, severe withdrawal symptoms, and hallucinations (Hu et al., 2005; Schuckit, Smith, Anthenelli, & Irwin, 1993). Long-term dependence on alcohol relates closely to intense craving for alcohol, family history of alcoholism, greater alcohol intake, history of other drug use, and presence of legal and other problems related to drinking (De Bruijn, Van Den Brink, De Graaf, & Vollebergh, 2005; Schuckit & Smith, 2011).

**Table 9.11**

## The Twelve Steps and Traditions of Alcoholics Anonymous

| The twelve steps of Alcoholics Anonymous | The twelve traditions of Alcoholics Anonymous |
|---|---|
| 1. We admitted we were powerless over alcohol—that our lives had become unmanageable. | 1. Our common welfare should come first; personal recovery depends upon A.A. unity. |
| 2. Came to believe that a Power greater than ourselves could restore us to sanity. | 2. For our group purpose, there is but one ultimate authority—a loving God as He may express Himself in our group conscience. Our leaders are but trusted servants; they do not govern. |
| 3. Made a decision to turn our will and our lives over to the care of God *as we understood Him.* | 3. The only requirement for A.A. membership is a desire to stop drinking. |
| 4. Made a searching and fearless moral inventory of ourselves. | 4. Each group should be autonomous except in matters affecting other groups or A.A. as a whole. |
| 5. Admitted to God, to ourselves and to another human being the exact nature of our wrongs. | 5. Each group has but one primary purpose—to carry its message to the alcoholic who still suffers. |
| 6. Were entirely ready to have God remove all these defects of character. | 6. An A.A. group ought never endorse, finance, or lend the A.A. name to any related facility or outside enterprise, lest problems of money, property, and prestige divert us from our primary purpose. |
| 7. Humbly asked Him to remove our shortcomings. | 7. Every A.A. group ought to be fully self-supporting, declining outside contributions. |
| 8. Made a list of all persons we had harmed, and became willing to make amends to them all. | 8. Alcoholics Anonymous should remain forever non-professional, but our service centers may employ special workers. |
| 9. Made direct amends to such people whenever possible, except when to do so would injure them or others. | 9. A.A., as such, ought never be organized; but we may create service boards or committees directly responsible to those they serve. |
| 10. Continued to take personal inventory and when we were wrong promptly admitted it. | 10. Alcoholics Anonymous has no opinion on outside issues; hence the A.A. name ought never be drawn into public controversy. |
| 11. Sought through prayer and meditation to improve our conscious contact with God, *as we understood Him,* praying only for knowledge of His will for us and the power to carry that out. | 11. Our public relations policy is based on attraction rather than promotion; we need always maintain personal anonymity at the level of press, radio, and films. |
| 12. Having had a spiritual awakening as the result of these steps, we tried to carry this message to alcoholics, and to practice these principles in all our affairs. | 12. Anonymity is the spiritual foundation of all our traditions, ever reminding us to place principles before personalities. |

Source: The Twelve Steps are reprinted with permission of Alcoholics Anonymous World Services, Inc. ("AAWS"). Permission to reprint the Twelve Steps does not mean that AAWS has reviewed or approved the contents of this publication, or that AAWS necessarily agrees with the views expressed herein. A.A. is a program of recovery from alcoholism only—use of the Twelve Steps in connection with programs and activities which are patterned after A.A., but which address other problems, or in any other non-A.A. context, does not imply otherwise.

The degree of stability for use of other drugs ranges widely. Almost all (96 percent) people who smoke cigarettes reportedly continue over a 5-year period. Contrast this with follow-up rates for alcohol (82 percent), cocaine (74 percent), marijuana (66 percent), stimulants other than cocaine (60 percent), opiates (55 percent), and sedatives (33 percent). This study included people who were in public and private chemical dependency treatment settings. Stability over time for all drugs was greater for men than women (Culverhouse et al., 2005). Substance-related problems are thus quite resistant to treatment and stable over time.

## INTERIM SUMMARY

► Assessing people with substance-related disorders often includes screening and motivational interviews as well as psychological testing and observations from others.

► Laboratory testing for substance-related disorders includes urine, blood, hair, saliva, and sweat screens for toxins.

► Biological treatment for substance-related disorders includes medications such as agonists, antagonists, partial agonists, and aversives.

► Inpatient and residential treatment for substance-related disorders focuses on short-term detoxification and rehabilitation.

► Brief interventions for substance-related disorders involve stabilizing or reducing substance use enough so more thorough forms of treatment can be applied.

► Cognitive-behavioral therapy for substance-related disorders involves modifying irrational cognitions about drug use and identifying and changing high-risk situations that could lead to relapse.

► Family, marital, and group therapies provide social support and reinforcement for abstinent behavior.

► Self-help groups involve meetings of people with similar substance use problems who share support and experiences to maintain abstinence.

► About half of people who seek treatment for a substance-related disorder successfully control the problem, but many people experience severe problems much of their life.

## REVIEW QUESTIONS

1. Outline major assessment techniques for substance-related disorders, including interviews, psychological testing, and laboratory assessment.
2. What medications help control symptoms of substance-related disorders? How do they work?
3. Describe inpatient therapy for substance-related disorder.
4. What psychological treatment strategies could a mental health professional use to help someone achieve abstinence? How so?
5. What is the long-term outcome for people with substance-related disorders?

# Final Comments

Substance use is common and accepted in our society, as demonstrated by widespread use of caffeine, alcohol, and tobacco. Some people thus "cross the line" into using more dangerous drugs or using legal drugs to a severe extent. Many of us might think of the typical person with alcoholism as the "old, homeless guy," but the reality is that substance use disorder could easily be affecting the person next to you. This is why we always consider the person first and the disorder second—saying, for example, people with alcoholism instead of alcoholics!

# Thought Questions

1. Think about television shows or films you have seen that have characters with substance use problems. Do you think these characters display realistic or unrealistic symptoms of substance use problems? How so?
2. Think about situations where you engage in substance use. What factors propel you to do so? Why do you think people you know use legal (or illegal) drugs? Having read the chapter, would you change anything about your substance use?
3. What would you now say to a friend who might be using substances too much?
4. What separates "normal" from "abnormal" substance use? Do you think excessive substance use has more to do with biological, personal, family, or other factors? Why?
5. What do you think family members and friends could do to reduce excessive substance use in people they know?

## Key Terms

| | |
|---|---|
| substance use 250 | codependency 273 |
| substance-related disorder 251 | distal factors 274 |
| substance use disorder 251 | proximal factors 274 |
| tolerance 252 | screening interviews 276 |
| withdrawal 252 | motivational interviewing 276 |
| substance intoxication 252 | agonists 280 |
| substance withdrawal 252 | cross-tolerance 280 |
| depressant 253 | antagonists 281 |
| disinhibition 255 | partial agonists 281 |
| blood alcohol level 255 | aversive drugs 281 |
| lethal dose 255 | detoxification 282 |
| cirrhosis of the liver 257 | rehabilitation 282 |
| Korsakoff's syndrome 259 | skills training 283 |
| fetal alcohol syndrome 259 | self-monitoring 283 |
| stimulant 259 | cue exposure therapy 283 |
| opiates 261 | contingency management 283 |
| hallucinogens 261 | community reinforcement approach 283 |
| marijuana 262 | multidimensional family therapy 283 |
| mesolimbic system 266 | self-help groups 284 |
| reward deficiency syndrome 269 | |
| stress-induced relapse 269 | |

## Media Resources

### MindTap

MindTap for Kearney and Trull's *Abnormal Psychology and Life: A Dimensional Approach* is a highly personalized fully online learning platform of authoritative content, assignments, and services offering you a tailored presentation of course curriculum created by your instructor. MindTap guides you through the course curriculum via an innovative learning path where you will complete reading assignments, annotate your readings, complete homework, and engage with quizzes and assessments. MindTap includes the Continuum Video Project.

Go to **cengagebrain.com** to access MindTap.

# Personality Disorders

# 10

**CASE:** *Michelle*

**What Do You Think?**

**Personality Traits, Unusual Personality, and Personality Disorder: What Are They?**

**Organization of Personality Disorders**

**Odd or Eccentric Personality Disorders: Features and Epidemiology**

**CASE:** *Jackson*

Interim Summary
Review Questions

**Dramatic Personality Disorders: Features and Epidemiology**

**CASE:** *Duane*

Interim Summary
Review Questions

**Anxious/Fearful Personality Disorders: Features and Epidemiology**

**CASE:** *Betty*

**Stigma Associated with Personality Disorders**
Interim Summary
Review Questions

**Personality Disorders: Causes and Prevention**
Interim Summary
Review Questions

**Personality Disorders: Assessment and Treatment**
Interim Summary
Review Questions

FINAL COMMENTS
THOUGHT QUESTIONS
KEY TERMS
MEDIA RESOURCES

## SPECIAL FEATURES

**CONTINUUM FIGURE 10.1 Continuum of Normal Personality and Personality Disorder Traits Related to Impulsivity   290–291**

**BOX 10.1** | Focus on Violence: Personality Disorders and Violence   300

**BOX 10.2** | Focus on Gender: Mirror Images of Personality Disorders?   303

**BOX 10.3** | Focus on Law and Ethics: Personality and Insanity   312

THE CONTINUUM VIDEO PROJECT

*Tina:* **Borderline Personality Disorder   315**

**PERSONAL NARRATIVE 10.1 Anonymous   316–317**

## CASE: Michelle

**Michelle** was 23 years old when she was admitted to a psychiatric inpatient unit following her seventh suicide attempt in 2 years. She told her ex-boyfriend that she swallowed a bottle of aspirin, and he rushed her to the emergency room. Michelle had a 5-year history of depressive symptoms that never seemed to ease. She was sad and had poor appetite, low self-esteem, difficulty concentrating, and hopelessness. Michelle's symptoms of depression were never severe enough to warrant hospitalization or treatment, however.

Michelle also had great difficulty controlling her emotions. She became

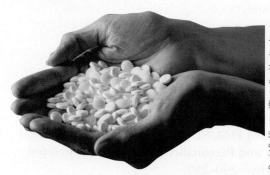

David Buffington/Photodisc/Jupiter Images

intensely sad, irritable, or anxious almost at a moment's notice. These intense negative feelings were often triggered by setbacks or arguments but rarely lasted more than 4 to 5 hours. Michelle also had a long history of impulsive behaviors, such as excessive drug use, indiscriminant sexual activity, and binge eating.

Michelle's anger was also unpredictable and intense. She once used a hammer to smash a wall after receiving a bad grade on a test. Michelle's relationships with her friends, boyfriends, and parents were intense and unstable as well. People often complained that Michelle became angry with them and criticized them for no apparent reason. She also frequently expressed her fear that others (including her parents) might leave or abandon her. Michelle once aggressively clutched a friend's leg to convince her to stay for dinner. Separation was obviously difficult for Michelle.

She tried to leave home and attend college 4 times but always returned home within a few weeks. She told her ex-boyfriend before her hospital admission, "I want to end it all" and "No one loves me."

## What Do You Think?

1. Which of Michelle's behaviors seem typical of a stressed-out 23-year-old, and which seem very different?

2. What external events and internal factors might be responsible for Michelle's troubles?

3. What are you curious about regarding Michelle?

4. Does Michelle remind you in any way of yourself or someone you know? How so?

5. How might Michelle's unusual behaviors affect her life in the future?

**CONTINUUM FIGURE 10.1** Continuum of Normal Personality and Personality Disorder Traits Related to Impulsivity

|  | Normal | Mild |
|---|---|---|
| **Emotions** | Stable mood and low levels of impulsive urge. | Occasional mood swings and impulsive urges. |
| **Cognitions** | Occasional thoughts of spontaneity in a socially adaptive way. | Occasional thoughts of spontaneous activity such as stealing. |
| **Behaviors** | Acts different in different situations depending on the social context. | Acts inappropriately at times in work or social situations. |

# Personality Traits, Unusual Personality, and Personality Disorder: What Are They?

All of us have personality traits that make up who we are. A **personality trait** can be thought of as a readiness to act in a certain way. Think about someone with great integrity. You know this person can be trusted because she is predisposed to be honest and reliable in what she does. You may also know someone who is shy, which means he is more willing to shun social contacts and pursue solitary activities. Common personality traits that everyone has to some degree include the following:

- *Openness:* active imagination and sensitivity; opposite is practicality and routine-oriented
- *Conscientiousness:* self-disciplined and achievement-oriented; opposite is less goal-oriented and more laid-back
- *Extraversion:* socially gregarious behavior; opposite is introversion
- *Agreeableness:* compassionate and cooperative; opposite is suspiciousness and antagonism
- *Neuroticism:* tendency to express negative emotional states; opposite is emotional stability

Some people show extreme levels of personality traits. Perhaps you know people who have trouble controlling their emotions, who always fight with family members, or who are impulsive or suspicious of others. Many people with intense personality traits still function fairly well because others tolerate their idiosyncrasies or because their behavior does not significantly interfere with their job or marriage. Intense personality traits can even be adaptive, as when someone who is overly pushy does well in a sales career.

For people like Michelle, however, personality traits are so extreme, they cause many problems. These people often have unusual, intense, and severe personality traits that appear in many situations. Michelle showed intense impulsivity, anger, and separation anxiety that prevented her from having stable relationships or going to college. People with extreme levels of personality traits that cause great impairment in functioning, especially social and occupational functioning, have a **personality disorder**. Personality disorders lie at the end of a dimensional spectrum (see **Figure 10.1**; Skodol, 2012; Trull, Jahng, Tomko, Wood, & Sher, 2010).

People with a personality disorder have unusual ways of thinking about themselves and others (cognitive feature), experiencing and expressing emotions (affective feature), interacting with others (interpersonal feature), and controlling impulses (impulse control; see **Table 10.1**). Think about someone who is overly suspicious. Suspiciousness is a personality trait with cognitive ("Other people want to hurt me"), affective (angry or hostile outbursts), and interpersonal (keeping others at "arm's length") features. A suspicious person may also show impulse control problems by sending angry, "flaming" e-mails to others at work if he feels threatened.

Personality disorders involve stable, long-standing, and inflexible traits. People with a personality disorder like Michelle often say their traits can be traced back to childhood or adolescence. Inflexible traits are a key aspect of personality disorder. The traits are difficult for a person to change and appear across many situations. Think about someone's impulsive behavior at a party—being spontaneous and taking some risks might seem normal in this situation. Being impulsive and goofing around at a job site or during a funeral, however, would be maladaptive and inappropriate. People with a personality disorder have great difficulty changing their behavior from one situation to another and from one interpersonal context to another. Such inflexibility causes significant distress or impairment in social, occupational, or other areas of functioning.

Personality disorders involve traits that deviate significantly from the expectations of a culture. This is important

| Moderate | Personality Disorder — less severe | Personality Disorder — more severe |
|---|---|---|
| Frequent mood swings and some impulsive urges but little impairment at work or with relationships. | Intense mood swings and impulsive urges with significant impairment at work or with relationships. | Extreme mood swings and impulsive or aggressive urges that lead to self-harm, arrest, or violence. |
| Frequent odd thoughts or thoughts of dangerous activity such as harming self or others. | Intense thoughts of suicide, paranoia, abandonment, attention from others, vengeance, or work. | Extreme and constant thoughts of suicide, paranoia, abandonment, attention from others, vengeance, or work. |
| Problematic personality trait such as impulsivity or emotional reactivity shown in many situations. | Problematic personality traits and dangerous behavior shown in almost all situations. | Problematic personality traits and dangerous behavior shown in almost all situations with intense distress and impairment. |

Mark Scott/Taxi/Getty Images

## Table 10.1

### DSM-5  General Personality Disorder

A. An enduring pattern of inner experience and behavior that deviates markedly from the expectations of the individual's culture. This pattern is manifested in two (or more) of the following areas:
   1. Cognition (i.e., ways of perceiving and interpreting self, other people, and events).
   2. Affectivity (i.e., the range, intensity, lability, and appropriateness of emotional response).
   3. Interpersonal functioning.
   4. Impulse control.

B. The enduring pattern is inflexible and pervasive across a broad range of personal and social situations.

C. The enduring pattern leads to clinically significant distress or impairment in social, occupational, or other important areas of functioning.

D. The pattern is stable and of long duration, and its onset can be traced back at least to adolescence or early adulthood.

E. The enduring pattern is not better explained as a manifestation or consequence of another mental disorder.

F. The enduring pattern is not attributable to the physiological effects of a substance or another medical condition.

American Psychiatric Association. (2013). *Diagnostic and statistical manual of mental disorders* (5th ed.). Arlington, VA: American Psychiatric Association.

## Table 10.2

### DSM-5  Personality Disorders

| Odd/eccentric | Dramatic/erratic/ emotional | Anxious/fearful |
|---|---|---|
| Paranoid | Antisocial | Avoidant |
| Schizoid | Borderline | Dependent |
| Schizotypal | Histrionic | Obsessive-compulsive |
| | Narcissistic | |

American Psychiatric Association. (2013). *Diagnostic and statistical manual of mental disorders* (5th ed.). Arlington, VA: American Psychiatric Association.

to remember because what may appear to be strange or deviant from the perspective of one culture may be quite normal and adaptive in another (Wakefield, 2012). Being "reserved" or "shy" in one culture can be seen as "courteous" and "dignified" in another culture. Clinicians who assess people for possible personality disorder must consider someone's cultural background. We discuss next how personality disorders are organized according to different clusters of traits.

## Organization of Personality Disorders

The fifth edition of the *Diagnostic and Statistical Manual of Mental Disorders* (*DSM-5*) organizes personality disorders into three main clusters based on similarity of traits (see **Table 10.2**). The first cluster is the *odd/eccentric* group, which includes paranoid, schizoid, and schizotypal personality disorders. People with odd/eccentric personality disorders display features that seem bizarre to others. The second cluster is the *dramatic/erratic/emotional* group that includes antisocial, borderline, histrionic, and narcissistic personality disorders. People with dramatic/erratic/emotional personality disorders display features that seem exaggerated to others. The third cluster is the *anxious/fearful* group, which includes avoidant, dependent, and obsessive-compulsive personality disorders. People with

anxious/fearful personality disorders display features that seem apprehensive to others. We discuss each of these clusters separately in this chapter.

The *DSM-5* also contains an alternative model of personality disorder that is based on dimensions of functioning and requires further study. This dimensional model emphasizes impairments in personality functioning and traits rather than specific categories of disorder. For example, a person could have one or two personality traits that are inflexible and maladaptive. The person could show these traits across many situations and experience great impairment. Think about someone who is often impulsively aggressive toward others at work and in personal relationships.

This dimensional model involves four key elements of personality functioning that could be impaired:

- Identity (e.g., have boundaries with others and regulate one's emotions)
- Self-direction (e.g., pursue life goals or self-reflect)
- Empathy (e.g., understand others' perspectives and the effects of one's own behavior on others)
- Intimacy (e.g., be close with others and desire to be with others)

This dimensional model also involves personality traits that can be pathological:

- Negative affectivity (e.g., presence of many negative emotions)
- Detachment (e.g., avoidance of others and restricted emotions)
- Antagonism (e.g., callousness toward others or self-importance)
- Disinhibition (e.g., impulsive behavior and immediate gratification)
- Psychoticism (e.g., odd behaviors and thoughts)

A dimensional model of personality disorders thus involves impairment in personality functioning *and* one or more pathological personality traits. As such, specific categories of personality disorder are emphasized less, and a continuum of personality constructs is emphasized more. The categorical approach to personality disorders remains popular among researchers and therapists, however, and thus provides the structure for the rest of the chapter.

# Odd or Eccentric Personality Disorders: Features and Epidemiology

Odd or eccentric personality disorders include paranoid, schizoid, and schizotypal personality disorders.

## Paranoid Personality Disorder

Many of us have moments when we do not trust certain people or are cautious around others because we fear harm. Moments of suspiciousness can be realistic and adaptive at times, as when a stranger suddenly approaches you. Other people, however, are constantly mistrustful and suspicious of others, even those they know well. **Paranoid personality disorder** involves a general distrust and suspiciousness of others (see **Table 10.3**; American Psychiatric Association [APA], 2013). People with this disorder often read harmful intentions from neutral interactions or events and assume the worst. They blame others for their misfortunes and have trouble working collaboratively or closely with others. Someone with paranoid personality disorder may be rigid, controlling, critical, blaming, and jealous. This person may engage in lengthy and acrimonious legal disputes that are difficult to resolve. People with paranoid personality disorder are sometimes not good coworkers or spouses because they are highly argumentative, hostile, and sarcastic.

## Schizoid Personality Disorder

Many people like to be alone and seem a little awkward around others. Shyness is a personality trait generally accepted in our society as normal and tolerable. In addition, many people who are shy still desire social relationships. Other people, however, show extreme social detachment and isolation and may have **schizoid personality disorder** (see **Table 10.4**; APA, 2013). People with this disorder have little interest in establishing or maintaining relationships with others and show little emotional expression. They have few, if any, friends, rarely marry or have sex, and often do not express joy, sadness, warmth, or intimacy. People with schizoid personality disorder generally do not show the suspiciousness or paranoid ideation of those with paranoid personality disorder but often prefer to work in isolation and may find jobs that involve minimal social contact. If they do marry or become parents, they show little warmth and emotional support and appear neglectful, detached, and disinterested.

## Schizotypal Personality Disorder

Perhaps you know someone who is quirky and unusual in how he acts or dresses. The behavior of some people we meet may seem quite odd or even bizarre. This is not necessarily a problem, however, because different forms of behavior and dress are common to our society. Other people like Jackson (next page), however, have extremely unusual behaviors, perceptions, and

---

**Table 10.3**

### DSM-5 Paranoid Personality Disorder

A. A pervasive distrust and suspiciousness of others such that their motives are interpreted as malevolent, beginning by early adulthood and present in a variety of contexts, as indicated by four (or more) of the following:

  1. Suspects, without sufficient basis, that others are exploiting, harming, or deceiving him or her.

  2. Is preoccupied with unjustified doubts about the loyalty or trustworthiness of friends or associates.

  3. Is reluctant to confide in others because of unwarranted fear that the information will be used maliciously against him or her.

  4. Reads hidden demeaning or threatening meanings into benign remarks or events.

  5. Persistently bears grudges.

  6. Perceives attacks on his or her character or reputation that are not apparent to others and is quick to react angrily or to counterattack.

  7. Has recurrent suspicions, without justification, regarding fidelity of spouse or sexual partner.

B. Does not occur exclusively during the course of schizophrenia, a bipolar disorder or depressive disorder with psychotic features, or another psychotic disorder and is not attributable to the physiological effects of another medical condition.

American Psychiatric Association. (2013). *Diagnostic and statistical manual of mental disorders* (5th ed.). Arlington, VA: American Psychiatric Association.

---

thoughts that cause them significant problems. **Schizotypal personality disorder** involves interpersonal deficits, cognitive and perceptual aberrations, and behavioral eccentricities (see **Table 10.5**; APA, 2013). People with schizotypal personality disorder have extreme social anxiety and perhaps paranoia. They are odd, eccentric, or peculiar in their behavior or appearance;

People with paranoid personality disorder are prone to be suspicious and have difficulty working with others.

## CASE: Jackson

**Jackson** is a 27-year-old man who just started college after taking time off to "explore himself." Jackson entered school to study sociology, philosophy, anthropology, and psychology so he could "explain the human race." Jackson comes to class with blue spiky hair and dressed in dirty T-shirts and long pants. He often talks to classmates when his instructor is speaking and has alienated most of his peers. Jackson has few friends, poor hygiene, and odd mannerisms. He sometimes stands in class to take notes in the middle of the room, asks questions that have little to do with the class topic, and speaks in a monotone voice. Jackson's instructor was concerned when his student claimed events on the local news were about him. Jackson said stories involving fire, abduction, and a car accident mirrored what happened to him that day. He also expressed sadness because his classmates would not work on a group project with him.

### Table 10.4

#### DSM-5 Schizoid Personality Disorder

A. A pervasive pattern of detachment from social relationships and a restricted range of expression of emotions in interpersonal settings, beginning by early adulthood and present in a variety of contexts, as indicated by four (or more) of the following:
1. Neither desires nor enjoys close relationships, including being part of a family.
2. Almost always chooses solitary activities.
3. Has little, if any, interest in having sexual experiences with another person.
4. Takes pleasure in few, if any, activities.
5. Lacks close friends or confidants other than first-degree relatives.
6. Appears indifferent to the praise or criticism of others.
7. Shows emotional coldness, detachment, or flattened affectivity.

B. Does not occur exclusively during the course of schizophrenia, a bipolar disorder or depressive disorder with psychotic features, another psychotic disorder, or autism spectrum disorder and is not attributable to the physiological effects of another medical condition.

American Psychiatric Association. (2013). *Diagnostic and statistical manual of mental disorders* (5th ed.). Arlington, VA: American Psychiatric Association.

display inappropriate or constricted affect; and have few (if any) friends or confidants outside their immediate family. Schizotypal personality disorder differs from paranoid and schizoid personality disorders in that people with schizotypal personality disorder are usually more odd or eccentric in their behavior and more often have perceptual and cognitive disturbances.

Many people with schizotypal personality disorder have unusual ideas, beliefs, and communication. They misinterpret or overpersonalize events, have unusual ideas that influence their behavior (they may think it possible to communicate via telepathy, for example), and have difficulty being understood by others. They may show *ideas of reference* where they believe everyday events somehow involve them when actually they do not (Hummelen, Pedersen, & Karterud, 2012). People with schizotypal personality disorder may drift toward "fringe" groups that support their unusual thinking and odd beliefs. These activities can provide structure for some people with schizotypal personality disorder but also contribute to greater deterioration if psychotic-like or dissociative experiences are encouraged.

People with schizotypal personality disorder are most likely to seek treatment for anxiety-related or depressive disorders. They may show brief or transient psychotic episodes in response to stress. These episodes are relatively short, however, lasting a few minutes to

Writer/Dreamstime.com

Schizoid personality disorder involves a strong desire to be alone.

## Table 10.5

### DSM-5 Schizotypal Personality Disorder

A. A pervasive pattern of social and interpersonal deficits marked by acute discomfort with, and reduced capacity for, close relationships as well as by cognitive or perceptual distortions and eccentricities of behavior, beginning by early adulthood and present in a variety of contexts, as indicated by five (or more) of the following:
  1. Ideas of reference (excluding delusions of reference).
  2. Odd beliefs or magical thinking that influences behavior and is inconsistent with subcultural norms.
  3. Unusual perceptual experiences, including bodily illusions.
  4. Odd thinking and speech.
  5. Suspiciousness or paranoid ideation.
  6. Inappropriate or constricted affect.
  7. Behavior or appearance that is odd, eccentric, or peculiar.
  8. Lack of close friends or confidants other than first-degree relatives.
  9. Excessive social anxiety that does not diminish with familiarity and tends to be associated with paranoid fears rather than negative judgments about self.

B. Does not occur exclusively during the course of schizophrenia, a bipolar disorder or depressive disorder with psychotic features, another psychotic disorder, or autism spectrum disorder.

American Psychiatric Association. (2013). *Diagnostic and statistical manual of mental disorders* (5th ed.). Arlington, VA: American Psychiatric Association.

Reuters TV/Reuters

People with schizotypal personality disorder may seek out others who share their odd beliefs. Although it is not known whether they had schizotypal personality disorder, members of the Heaven's Gate cult showed characteristic behavior of those with this disorder. Thirty-nine Heaven's Gate members committed mass suicide because they believed that after their deaths, a UFO that was hiding behind the Hale-Bopp comet would pick them up. Their leader, Marshall Applewhite (pictured), claimed to be an alien from outer space.

a few hours, and do not typically indicate a psychotic disorder (Chapter 12). Only a small portion of people with schizotypal personality disorder develop schizophrenia, but many develop depression. Some of those with schizotypal personality disorder remain marginally employed, withdrawn, and transient throughout much of their lives.

## Epidemiology of Odd or Eccentric Personality Disorders

Personality disorders occur in about 9 to 15.7 percent of the general population, although estimates are much higher among psychiatric outpatients (Lenzenweger, Lane, Loranger, & Kessler, 2007; Trull, Jahng, Tomko, Wood, & Sher, 2010; Zimmerman, Rothschild, & Chelminski, 2005). Personality disorders are associated with significant social and occupational dysfunction, comorbid psychopathology, lower quality of life, and suicidality (Cramer, Torgersen, & Kringlen, 2006; Trull et al., 2010; Zimmerman et al., 2005). Maladaptive personality traits are also present in many people with a major mental disorder (Widiger, 2011).

Researchers estimate that odd or eccentric personality disorders occur in 2.1 percent of the general population. Specific prevalence rates have been reported for paranoid (1.9 percent),

schizoid (0.6 percent), and schizotypal (0.6 percent) personality disorders (Trull et al., 2010). Many people with odd or eccentric personality disorders either do not seek treatment or seek treatment for other problems. These personality disorders are highly comorbid with anxiety-related, depressive, bipolar, substance use, and psychotic disorders, as well as disruptive behavior disorders such as attention-deficit/hyperactivity disorder. Findings are mixed with respect to gender differences related to odd or eccentric personality disorders (Lenzenweger et al., 2007; Links & Eynan, 2013; Lynam & Widiger, 2007; Trull et al., 2010).

Racial and ethnic differences are not prominent in personality disorders. Race and ethnicity should be closely considered, however, when assessing a client for an odd or eccentric personality disorder. Someone who is angry, frustrated, and guarded does not necessarily have paranoid personality disorder. Consider a recent immigrant to the United States who is unfamiliar with English and American customs. This person would be understandably cautious and suspicious of others. Some people may also appear introverted, isolated, or aloof when these behaviors are a natural part of their culture. A diagnosis of schizoid personality disorder would not apply. Clinicians must also be sure not to confuse symptoms of schizotypal personality disorder with religious experiences, folk beliefs, or linguistic peculiarities shown by certain cultural groups. For example, the *ghost dance* is performed by many Native Americans who believe the ritual allows them to visit relatives or friends who have left their bodies. Such a belief should not be mistaken for evidence of a personality disorder.

## INTERIM SUMMARY

▶ Personality disorders involve dysfunctional and inflexible personality traits that deviate significantly from cultural expectations and are shown across many situations.

▶ Personality disorders include traits that are odd or eccentric; dramatic, erratic, or emotional; and anxious or fearful.

▶ Odd or eccentric personality disorders include paranoid, schizoid, and schizotypal personality disorders.

▶ Paranoid personality disorder involves general distrust and suspiciousness of others.

▶ Schizoid personality disorder involves social isolation and restricted emotional experience and expression.

▶ Schizotypal personality disorder involves social anxiety, paranoid fears, and eccentric behavior, perceptions, and thoughts.

▶ Personality disorders are prevalent throughout the general population, but odd or eccentric personality disorders are more common in clinical samples.

▶ Odd or eccentric personality disorders are comorbid with other mental disorders such as anxiety-related and depressive disorders but are not highly linked to gender, race, or ethnicity.

## REVIEW QUESTIONS

1. What are the main features of a personality disorder?
2. What are the main clusters of personality disorder?
3. What are the main odd or eccentric personality disorders and their features?
4. How common are odd or eccentric personality disorders?
5. What mental disorders are most associated with odd or eccentric personality disorders?

# Dramatic Personality Disorders: Features and Epidemiology

Recall that a second cluster of personality disorder involves dramatic, erratic, or overly emotional behavior that seems exaggerated to others. This group includes antisocial, borderline, histrionic, and narcissistic personality disorders. Consider the case of Duane for antisocial personality disorder (adapted from Lykken, 1995).

## CASE: Duane

**Duane** was a man in his 20s whose father had left when he was a child. Duane frequently encountered trouble as a youth that led to extended stints in reform school or prison. He earned respect from others, however, because of his fearlessness, self-confidence, and intelligence. He eventually became a pilot and businessman and was adept at construction. Duane was charming, especially to women, and helped break up several marriages among his friends and relatives.

Duane was also aggressive toward others and impulsive. He once broke into a friend's safe and traded gunshots with a police officer.

Duane used his charm to become a successful businessman in construction but had little capacity for love or empathy and little interest in the truth. He exaggerated his prowess in hunting and shooting but lacked insight that others could notice his lies. Duane enjoyed being admired and respected by others, but those who knew him well understood he was a manipulator and that his good fellowship was false. Duane used his charm to swindle people out of money and often found dangerous situations such as flying through fog to be thrilling.

Lykken, D.T. (1995). *The antisocial personalities*. Hillsdale, NJ: Erlbaum.

## Antisocial Personality Disorder

Duane exhibits many features of **antisocial personality disorder**. Antisocial personality disorder involves a pattern of behavior that reflects an extreme disregard for and violation of the rights of others (see **Table 10.6**; APA, 2013). Antisocial personality disorder involves deceitfulness, impulsivity, irritability/ aggressiveness, criminal acts, and irresponsibility. Not all people with antisocial personality disorder have criminal records, however. People with the disorder often commit reckless acts that neglect the safety of others, and they lack remorse for harm they inflict. Those with antisocial personality disorder are unlikely to maintain steady employment. Some people with the disorder can obtain professional and criminal success as long as their violations and deceptions are undiscovered. Their success may unravel at some point, however, because of their impulsivity, negligence, and lack of foresight. People with antisocial personality disorder may at first appear charming, fun, and engaging, but many of their social relationships eventually fail because of poor empathy, infidelity, and lack of responsibility as well as episodes of maltreatment, exploitation, and angry hostility.

Antisocial personality disorder is evident in childhood in the form of conduct disorder (Chapter 13). Conduct disorder involves aggression toward people and animals, property destruction, deceitfulness or theft, and serious violations of laws and rules. Evidence of conduct disorder before age 15 years is required for a diagnosis of antisocial personality disorder. Not all children with conduct disorder will eventually meet criteria for antisocial personality disorder, although some do (Howard, Huband, & Duggan, 2012).

**Psychopathy** is a diagnostic construct related to antisocial personality disorder. Psychopathy involves little remorse or guilt, poor behavioral control, arrogance, superficial charm, exploitativeness, and lack of empathy (Kiehl & Sinnott-Armstrong, 2013). Many people with psychopathy are intensely goal-directed toward money, sex, and status. About one third of people with antisocial personality disorder like Duane

**Table 10.6**

### DSM-5  Antisocial Personality Disorder

A.  A pervasive pattern of disregard for and violation of the rights of others, occurring since age 15 years, as indicated by three (or more) of the following:

1.  Failure to conform to social norms with respect to lawful behaviors, as indicated by repeatedly performing acts that are grounds for arrest.
2.  Deceitfulness, as indicated by repeated lying, use of aliases, or conning others for personal profit or pleasure.
3.  Impulsivity or failure to plan ahead.
4.  Irritability and aggressiveness, as indicated by repeated physical fights or assaults.
5.  Reckless disregard for safety or self or others.
6.  Consistent irresponsibility, as indicated by repeated failure to sustain consistent work behavior or honor financial obligations.
7.  Lack of remorse, as indicated by being indifferent to or rationalizing having hurt, mistreated, or stolen from another.

B.  The individual is at least age 18 years.

C.  There is evidence of conduct disorder with onset before age 15 years.

D.  The occurrence of antisocial behavior is not exclusively during the course of schizophrenia or bipolar disorder.

American Psychiatric Association. (2013). *Diagnostic and statistical manual of mental disorders* (5th ed.). Arlington, VA: American Psychiatric Association.

Miramax/Everett Collection

The film character Anton Chigurh in *No Country for Old Men* exhibited many features of psychopathy.

display psychopathy (Coid & Ullrich, 2010). Antisocial personality disorder and psychopathy overlap with respect to antisocial behaviors and impulsivity (Verona, Sprague, & Sadeh, 2012; see **Box 10.1**).

## Borderline Personality Disorder

Some people are dramatic in their behavior but still maintain good social and occupational relationships. Other people like Michelle (the first case study), however, have features of borderline personality disorder (see **Table 10.7**; APA, 2013). **Borderline personality disorder** involves a pattern of impulsivity and unstable affect, interpersonal relationships, and self-image. The term "borderline" reflects a traditional view that the disorder was on the "borderline" of neurosis and psychosis. People with borderline personality disorder frequently experience strong, intense negative emotions and are prone to suicidal threats, gestures, or attempts. They are unsure of their self-image as well as their views of other people. They harbor intense abandonment fears and feelings of emptiness, as Michelle did. Stressful situations may lead to transient paranoid ideation or dissociation. Associated features include self-defeating behavior such as making a bad decision that destroys a good relationship, depressive or substance use disorder, and premature death from suicide. Approximately 10 percent of those with borderline personality disorder commit suicide and 60 to 70 percent attempt suicide (Carpenter, Tomko, Trull, & Boomsma, 2013; see **Box 10.1**).

## Histrionic Personality Disorder

Have you ever known someone who always had to be the center of attention? Some people have quite an entertaining presence and are the life of the party. Other people, however,

Peter Dazeley/Photographer's Choice/Getty Images

Self-harm is a common feature of borderline personality disorder.

---

**Table 10.7**

### DSM-5  Borderline Personality Disorder

A pervasive pattern of instability of interpersonal relationships, self-image, and affects, and marked impulsivity, beginning by early adulthood and present in a variety of contexts, as indicated by five (or more) of the following:

1. Frantic efforts to avoid real or imagined abandonment.
2. A pattern of unstable and intense interpersonal relationships characterized by alternating between extremes of idealization and devaluation.
3. Identity disturbance: markedly and persistently unstable self-image or sense of self.
4. Impulsivity in at least two areas that are potentially self-damaging.
5. Recurrent suicidal behavior, gestures, or threats, or self-mutilating behavior.
6. Affective instability due to a marked reactivity of mood.
7. Chronic feelings of emptiness.
8. Inappropriate, intense anger or difficulty controlling anger.
9. Transient, stress-related paranoid ideation or severe dissociative symptoms.

American Psychiatric Association. (2013). *Diagnostic and statistical manual of mental disorders* (5th ed.). Arlington, VA: American Psychiatric Association.

---

take attention-seeking behaviors to an extreme. People with **histrionic personality disorder** display pervasive and excessive emotionality and attention seeking (see **Table 10.8**; APA, 2013). Hallmarks of histrionic personality disorder include actions that place oneself in the center of attention, provocative or inappropriately intimate behavior, fleeting and superficial emotional expression, and suggestibility. Histrionic personality disorder is different than borderline personality disorder

David South / Alamy

Those with histrionic personality disorder like to be the center of attention.

in that the latter typically involves self-destructive behavior, feelings of deep emptiness and identity disturbance, and angry disruptions in close relationships.

People with histrionic personality disorder experience difficult romantic relationships and friendships. They have trouble balancing strong needs for attention and intimacy with the reality of a situation. They have trouble delaying gratification and tend to act impulsively. People with this disorder have an intense need to be loved, desired, and involved with others on an intimate basis and will use various means toward this end. They may use their physical appearance to draw attention to themselves and be melodramatically emotional or inappropriately seductive. They may perceive a relationship as being more intimate than it is because of their need for romantic fantasy.

## Narcissistic Personality Disorder

Have you ever known someone who talked endlessly about his accomplishments? Some people who promote themselves have a healthy level of self-confidence that might be annoying but not

---

### Table 10.8

#### DSM-5 Histrionic Personality Disorder

A pervasive pattern of excessive emotionality and attention seeking, beginning by early adulthood and present in a variety of contexts, as indicated by five (or more) of the following:

1. Is uncomfortable in situations in which he or she is not the center of attention.
2. Interaction with others is often characterized by inappropriate sexually seductive or provocative behavior.
3. Displays rapidly shifting and shallow expression of emotions.
4. Consistently uses physical appearance to draw attention to self.
5. Has a style of speech that is excessively impressionistic and lacking of detail.
6. Shows self-dramatization, theatricality, and exaggerated expression of emotion.
7. Is suggestible.
8. Considers relationships to be more intimate than they actually are.

American Psychiatric Association. (2013). *Diagnostic and statistical manual of mental disorders* (5th ed.). Arlington, VA: American Psychiatric Association.

---

### Table 10.9

#### DSM-5 Narcissistic Personality Disorder

A pervasive pattern of grandiosity (in fantasy or behavior), need for admiration, and lack of empathy, beginning by early adulthood and present in a variety of contexts, as indicated by five (or more) of the following:

1. Has a grandiose sense of self-importance.
2. Is preoccupied with fantasies of unlimited success, power, brilliance, beauty, or ideal love.
3. Believes that he or she is "special" and unique and can only be understood by, or should associate with, other special or high-status people (or institutions).
4. Requires excessive admiration.
5. Has a sense of entitlement.
6. Is interpersonally exploitative.
7. Lacks empathy: is unwilling to recognize or identify with the feelings and needs of others.
8. Is often envious of others or believes that others are envious of him or her.
9. Shows arrogant, haughty behaviors or attitudes.

American Psychiatric Association. (2013). *Diagnostic and statistical manual of mental disorders* (5th ed.). Arlington, VA: American Psychiatric Association.

---

pathological. Other people, however, have such a strong need to impress others that they experience many social problems. People with **narcissistic personality disorder** display grandiosity, need for admiration, and lack of empathy for others (see **Table 10.9**; APA, 2013). People with this disorder have an exaggerated sense of self-importance and believe they are so unique they can only be understood by similarly "special" people. These views lead to distasteful interpersonal behaviors such as arrogance, exploitation, and a sense of entitlement (Pincus & Lukowitsky, 2010). Narcissistic personality disorder differs from borderline and histrionic personality disorders in that those with narcissistic personality disorder have marked grandiosity but less self-destructiveness, impulsivity, or concerns about abandonment.

People with narcissistic personality disorder seem to have high self-confidence and self-esteem but are actually quite vulnerable to real or perceived threats to their status. People with the disorder may express rage or become vengeful if challenged. They tend to have "serial friendships," meaning relationships end when others no longer express admiration or envy. People with the disorder cannot tolerate criticism or defeat, and this may keep them from high levels of achievement.

## Epidemiology of Dramatic Personality Disorders

Researchers estimate that dramatic personality disorders occur in 5.5 percent of the general population. Specific prevalence rates have been reported for antisocial (3.8 percent) and borderline (2.7 percent) personality disorders (Trull et al., 2010).

Many researchers believe histrionic and narcissistic personality disorders are more rare, however. Specific prevalence rates have been reported for histrionic (0.3 percent) and narcissistic (1.0 percent) personality disorders (Trull et al., 2010).

People with antisocial personality disorder are commonly found in substance use treatment and forensic settings. Approximately 42 percent of people imprisoned worldwide have a personality disorder, including 21 percent with antisocial personality disorder (Fazel & Danesh, 2002). Antisocial personality disorder is more common among men (Trull et al., 2010) and among those from lower socioeconomic classes and urban settings. People with antisocial personality disorder may migrate to urban settings and become socially or economically impoverished, or impoverishment may contribute to the development of antisocial traits. The diagnosis does not apply to someone whose antisocial behavior represents a protective survival strategy, especially in extreme poverty.

Borderline personality disorder is the most frequently diagnosed personality disorder in inpatient and outpatient settings. More women than men reportedly meet criteria for borderline personality disorder, but this is based primarily on clinical studies. Rates of borderline personality disorder in men and women appear to be similar in the general population (Lenzenweger et al., 2007; Lynam & Widiger, 2007; Trull et al., 2010). Borderline personality may be misdiagnosed among adolescents who sometimes become angry and fight with family members. Many youth eventually "grow out" of these behaviors and become responsible adults. People with

## BOX 10.1 Focus on Violence

### Personality Disorders and Violence

The personality disorders most often associated with violence are the dramatic personality disorders, especially borderline personality disorder and antisocial personality disorder (Howard, 2011). These personality disorders involve high levels of impulsivity and risk taking. Violence committed by those with borderline personality disorder is typically directed toward themselves in the form of self-harm, self-mutilation, or suicidal behavior. Violence committed by those with antisocial personality

disorder, however, is typically directed toward others. Antisocial behavior may be marked by psychopathy as well.

Studies of the relationship between psychopathy and violence have produced some interesting findings regarding the nature of violent acts associated with this condition. People with psychopathy, compared with nonpsychopathic criminals, are more likely to commit violence that is predatory (e.g., stalking), callous or cold-hearted, less emotionally driven, and more premeditated (Hare & Neumann, 2008). People with psychopathy—sometimes called psychopaths or sociopaths—appear less likely to commit crimes of passion and are more likely to be detached and ruthless in their violent acts.

---

true borderline personality disorder, however, show chronic and pervasive maladaptive traits into adulthood.

Histrionic personality disorder is more prevalent among women (Trull et al., 2010), but cultural, gender, and age norms must be considered to determine whether a certain behavior indicates this disorder. The diagnostic criteria for this disorder closely resemble traits that define stereotypic femininity, so clinicians may misdiagnose histrionic personality disorder in women (Samuel & Widiger, 2009). Cultural groups also differ with respect to emotional expression. Histrionic personality should be considered only if a person's emotional expression is excessive within her cultural group and causes distress or impairment. Histrionic personality disorder is likely to be diagnosed in some cultural groups more than others. The disorder may be less frequent in Asian cultures and more frequent in Hispanic and Latin American cultures because of cultural differences in the overt expression of sexual interest and seductiveness (Huang et al., 2006).

Narcissistic personality disorder appears to be more prevalent among men (Lynam & Widiger, 2007; Trull et al., 2010). The disorder is a controversial one for several reasons. First, idealism is characteristic of many adolescents and young adults and should not be mistaken for the traits and behaviors of narcissistic personality disorder. The disorder should be diagnosed only when such beliefs are extremely unrealistic and cause significant distress or impairment. Second, not all mental health professionals worldwide recognize narcissistic personality disorder. Pathological narcissism may be a manifestation of a modern, Western society that is self-centered and materialistic and less centered on familial or interpersonal bonds (Campbell & Miller, 2011).

Dramatic personality disorders are highly comorbid with psychological problems and other mental disorders. People with antisocial personality disorder are at significant risk for unemployment, poverty, injury, violent death, excessive alcohol and other drug use, incarceration, recidivism (parole violation), and substantial relationship instability (Fountoulakis, Lecht, & Kaprinis, 2008; Hare & Neumann, 2008). Borderline

personality disorder is closely associated with substance use, depression, and suicidality (Wedig et al., 2012).

### INTERIM SUMMARY

▶ Dramatic, erratic, or emotional personality disorders include antisocial, borderline, histrionic, and narcissistic personality disorders.

▶ Antisocial personality disorder involves an extreme disregard for and violation of the rights of others.

▶ Psychopathy involves problematic interpersonal styles such as arrogance, lack of empathy, and manipulativeness.

▶ Borderline personality disorder involves impulsivity, unstable affect and interpersonal relationships, and suicidality.

▶ Histrionic personality disorder involves an excessive need for attention, superficial and fleeting emotions, and impulsivity.

▶ Narcissistic personality disorder involves grandiosity, need for admiration, and lack of empathy for others.

▶ The most common dramatic personality disorders are antisocial and borderline personality disorders, but all disorders of this group involve substantial distress and/or impairment.

### REVIEW QUESTIONS

1. What are the main features of antisocial personality disorder and psychopathy?

2. What are key features of borderline, histrionic, and narcissistic personality disorders?

3. Describe the epidemiology of the dramatic personality disorders, including issues of gender and culture.

## Anxious/Fearful Personality Disorders: Features and Epidemiology

Recall that a third cluster of personality disorder involves anxious or fearful behavior that seems apprehensive to others. This group includes avoidant, dependent, and obsessive-compulsive personality disorders.

## Avoidant Personality Disorder

Have you ever known someone who was shy and seemed uncomfortable at parties or other social events? We mentioned earlier that shyness is common in our society and usually tolerated well. Many people who are shy have a good self-image. Other people, however, have intense fears of inadequacy and negative evaluation. These people want relationships with others but have extreme difficulty initiating contact. **Avoidant personality disorder** involves a pervasive pattern of anxiety, feelings of inadequacy, and social hypersensitivity (see **Table 10.10**; APA, 2013).

People with avoidant personality disorder often avoid jobs or situations that require significant interpersonal contact; they are seen as "shy" or "loners." People with the disorder avoid others because they see themselves as inept, unappealing, or inferior. They are also afraid of being embarrassed or rejected by others. People with avoidant personality disorder become involved with others only in situations in which they feel certain of acceptance. Those with the disorder want close relationships, so this aspect makes them different from people with schizoid personality disorder. Other features of avoidant personality disorder include hypervigilance in social situations and low self-esteem.

People with avoidant personality disorder often do well at their jobs as long as they can avoid public presentations or leadership. Social functioning and social skills development are usually greatly impaired, however. If a person with

### Table 10.10

#### DSM-5 Avoidant Personality Disorder

A pervasive pattern of social inhibition, feelings of inadequacy, and hypersensitivity to negative evaluation, beginning by early adulthood and present in a variety of contexts, as indicated by four (or more) of the following:

1. Avoids occupational activities that involve significant interpersonal contact because of fears of criticism, disapproval, or rejection.
2. Is unwilling to get involved with people unless certain of being liked.
3. Shows restraint within intimate relationships because of the fear of being shamed or ridiculed.
4. Is preoccupied with being criticized or rejected in social situations.
5. Is inhibited in new interpersonal situations because of feelings of inadequacy.
6. Views self as socially inept, personally unappealing, or inferior to others.
7. Is unusually reluctant to take personal risks or to engage in any new activities because they may prove embarrassing.

American Psychiatric Association. (2013). *Diagnostic and statistical manual of mental disorders* (5th ed.). Arlington, VA: American Psychiatric Association.

avoidant personality disorder does develop a close relationship, he will likely cling to the person dependently. Many people with avoidant personality disorder also have anxiety-related disorders such as social phobia as well as depression.

## Dependent Personality Disorder

### CASE: Betty

**Betty** is a 47-year-old woman who has been married 27 years. She has five children aged 8, 12, 16, 20, and 24 years. Her husband insisted on having children every 4 years in their marriage, and Betty complied. Betty has been a homemaker during her marriage, taking care of her children and husband by assuming all household chores. Her few friends describe Betty as meek, quiet, and subservient. She is not the kind of person who "rocks the boat," and she usually complies with others' requests in PTA, Scout, and church meetings. Betty rises at 5 a.m. and will not go to sleep before 11 p.m. unless all her tasks are completed. She was recently hospitalized for depression and exhaustion but left against medical advice to prepare dinner for her family at home.

Have you ever known someone who was a "follower" and always seemed to conform to what others wanted to do? Many of us occasionally bend to our friend's wishes to go someplace or do something we are not thrilled about doing. At other times, however, we speak up and assert what we want. For people like Betty, however, conformity is a way of life. **Dependent personality disorder** involves a pervasive, excessive need to be cared for, leading to submissiveness, clinging behavior, and fears of separation (see **Table 10.11**; APA, 2013).

People with dependent personality disorder "give their lives over" to others—they ask for advice and guidance about even the smallest of decisions, seem helpless, and readily abdicate responsibility for most areas of their lives. Their fear that others may reject or leave them is so intense, they will not express disagreements with others. They may even volunteer to do unpleasant, demeaning tasks to gain nurturance and approval. People with dependent personality disorder are prone to low self-esteem, self-doubt, self-criticism, and depression and anxiety-related disorders. Their neediness and desperation often prevents them from carefully selecting a person who will protect them and be supportive. The result may be bad choices—they may choose their partners indiscriminately and become quickly attached to unreliable, uncaring, and abusive people.

## Obsessive-Compulsive Personality Disorder

Have you ever known someone who was very organized and attended to all details of a task with great passion? Perhaps you have known someone with a type A personality marked by competitiveness, time-consciousness, impatience,

## Table 10.11

### DSM-5 Dependent Personality Disorder

A pervasive and excessive need to be taken care of that leads to submissive and clinging behavior and fears of separation, beginning by early adulthood and present in a variety of contexts, as indicated by five (or more) of the following:

1. Has difficulty making everyday decisions without an excessive amount of advice and reassurance from others.
2. Needs others to assume responsibility for most major areas of his or her life.
3. Has difficulty expressing disagreement with others because of fear of loss of support or approval.
4. Has difficulty initiating projects or doing things on his or her own (because of a lack of self-confidence in judgment or abilities rather than a lack of motivation or energy).
5. Goes to excessive lengths to obtain nurturance and support from others, to the point of volunteering to do things that are unpleasant.
6. Feels uncomfortable or helpless when alone because of exaggerated fears of being unable to care for himself or herself.
7. Urgently seeks another relationship as a source of care and support when a close relationship ends.
8. Is unrealistically preoccupied with fears of being left to take care of himself or herself.

American Psychiatric Association. (2013). *Diagnostic and statistical manual of mental disorders* (5th ed.). Arlington, VA: American Psychiatric Association.

## Table 10.12

### DSM-5 Obsessive-Compulsive Personality Disorder

A pervasive pattern of preoccupation with orderliness, perfectionism, and mental and interpersonal control, at the expense of flexibility, openness, and efficiency, beginning by early adulthood and present in a variety of contexts, as indicated by four (or more) of the following:

1. Is preoccupied with details, rules, lists, order, organization, or schedules to the extent that the major point of the activity is lost.
2. Shows perfectionism that interferes with task completion.
3. Is excessively devoted to work and productivity to the exclusion of leisure activities and friendships (not accounted for by obvious economic necessity).
4. Is overconscientious, scrupulous, and inflexible about matters of morality, ethics, or values (not accounted for by cultural or religious identification).
5. Is unable to discard worn-out or worthless objects even when they have no sentimental value.
6. Is reluctant to delegate tasks or to work with others unless they submit to exactly his or her way of doing things.
7. Adopts a miserly spending style toward both self and others; money is viewed as something to be hoarded for future catastrophes.
8. Shows rigidity and stubbornness.

American Psychiatric Association. (2013). *Diagnostic and statistical manual of mental disorders* (5th ed.). Arlington, VA: American Psychiatric Association.

and "workaholism." Attention to detail and organization are considered positive traits in our society, although some aspects of type A personality have been linked to heart disease in men. Other people, however, spend inordinate amounts of time on detail and organization. **Obsessive-compulsive personality disorder** involves a preoccupation with orderliness, perfectionism, and control (see **Table 10.12**; APA, 2013). Despite the similarity in name, this personality disorder is different from obsessive-compulsive disorder (Chapter 5) in that those with the personality disorder do not generally have obsessions or compulsions.

People with obsessive-compulsive personality disorder are rigid, stubborn, and perfectionistic to the point that tasks never get completed. Their preoccupation with rules, details, and morality cause them trouble at work and outside of work. They are seen as inflexible and miserly and may be described by others as "control freaks." Other features of this personality disorder include hoarding, indecisiveness, reluctance to delegate tasks, low affection, rumination, and anger outbursts.

Many people with obsessive-compulsive personality disorder are successful at their career. They can be excellent workers to the point of excess, sacrificing their social and leisure activities, marriage, and family for their job. People with this disorder tend to have strained relationships with their spouse and children because of their tendency to be detached and uninvolved but also authoritarian and domineering. A spouse or partner may complain of little affection, tenderness, and warmth. Relationships with colleagues at work may be equally strained by excessive perfectionism, domination, indecision, worrying, and anger. Jobs that require flexibility, openness, creativity, or diplomacy may be particularly difficult for someone with obsessive-compulsive personality disorder.

People with obsessive-compulsive personality disorder may be prone to various anxiety and physical disorders because of their worrying, indecision, and stress. People with the disorder who are angry and hostile may be prone to cardiovascular disorders. Depression may not develop until a person recognizes the sacrifices that have been made by their devotion to work and productivity, which may not occur until middle age. Most people with this personality disorder experience early employment or career difficulties and even failures that may result in depression.

## Epidemiology of Anxious/Fearful Personality Disorders

Researchers estimate that anxious/fearful personality disorders occur in 2.3 percent of the general population. Specific prevalence rates have been reported for avoidant (1.2 percent), dependent (0.3 percent), and obsessive-compulsive (1.9 percent) personality disorders (Trull et al., 2010).

Avoidant personality disorder occurs more frequently in women (Trull et al., 2010). Religious and cultural influences may be responsible for submissive and self-effacing behaviors in some individuals (Hsu et al., 2012). People from an extremely fundamentalist religious background may appear to "avoid" socializing with others, especially at events in which alcoholic beverages are served. One must understand the "avoidant" behavior in the context of someone's strong religious beliefs and prohibitions.

Dependent personality disorder is more common in women (Trull et al., 2010). The prevalence and diagnosis of dependent personality disorder may also vary across cultures, however, because many societies value dependency-related behaviors (Chen, Nettles, & Chen, 2009). Western societies place more emphasis and value on expressions of autonomy and self-reliance, so people in these cultures may be more prone to a diagnosis of dependent personality disorder (Caldwell-Harris & Aycicegi, 2006). Interpersonal connectedness and interdependency are highly valued in Japanese and Indian cultures, so dependency may be seen as pathological less often.

Obsessive-compulsive personality disorder also occurs more frequently in women (Trull et al., 2010). Mental health professionals must be careful not to misdiagnose this disorder because many people are conscientious, devoted to their work, organized, and perfectionistic. Only when these features produce significant distress or impairment can they be considered indicators of obsessive-compulsive personality disorder. Anxious/fearful personality disorders are often comorbid with anxiety-related, depressive, and somatic symptom disorders.

B Busco/ Photographer's Choice/Getty Images

Obsessive-compulsive personality disorder is characterized by perfectionism, excessive dedication to work, and inflexibility.

## Stigma Associated with Personality Disorders

Many people with personality disorders have strong emotions and impulsive behavior. This kind of behavior can increase the chances of being stigmatized. Aviram and colleagues (2006) discussed possible ways in which people with borderline personality disorder may experience stigma. A key problem is that mental health professionals sometimes hold negative

---

### BOX 10.2  Focus on Gender

### Mirror Images of Personality Disorders?

A long-standing debate is whether personality disorders essentially derive from the same causes but go in different directions for men and women. Some disorders do seem more particular to men, especially paranoid, schizoid, schizotypal, antisocial, narcissistic, avoidant, and obsessive-compulsive personality disorders. Other disorders seem more particular to women, especially borderline, histrionic, and dependent personality disorders.

Are certain personality disorders "mirror images" of one another following some childhood trauma? One comparison of people with antisocial and borderline personality disorders revealed that both groups suffered more child maltreatment than control participants. Those who eventually developed borderline personality disorder had cognitive schemas related

to detachment from others, emotional expression, need gratification, helplessness and powerlessness, and feeling worthy of punishment. Those who eventually developed antisocial personality disorder had cognitive schemas related to attacking, bullying, and humiliating others (Lobbestael, Arntz, & Sieswerda, 2005).

Others have found certain precursors to personality disorders in children, some of which may be more pertinent to boys or girls (Geiger & Crick, 2010; Shiner, 2005). Precursors to personality disorder that may be more present in boys include restricted emotion, distant relationships, exaggerated sense of self, and lack of concern for others' needs. Precursors to personality disorder that may be more present in girls are the opposite of those for boys: expressive emotion, overly close relationships, negative sense of self, and overconcern for others' needs. These patterns may have important ramifications for preventing and treating personality disorders.

perceptions of people with borderline personality disorder, especially the belief that these people are annoying, manipulative, demanding, and attention seeking. Other researchers have found that mental health professionals believe that clients with personality disorders are more difficult to manage than clients without personality disorders (Newton-Howes, Weaver, & Tyrer, 2008). Such negative perceptions may lead some mental health professionals to withdraw or keep their emotional distance from those with powerful affective states such as anger or troublesome behaviors such as self-injury or multiple suicide attempts.

Aviram, Brodsky, and Stanley (2006) outlined a scenario in which negative perceptions of a client with borderline personality disorder can actually worsen symptoms. The cycle may begin when a mental health professional expects that a certain client will be difficult and manipulative. The therapist may then withdraw emotionally to avoid being manipulated and assume that the client's behavior is something the client can control but chooses not to. Unfortunately, the unresponsiveness of the therapist can actually trigger a client's tendency to be self-critical and this may lead to self-destructive behavior. This behavior may induce the therapist to withdraw even more, and the client may eventually leave treatment prematurely. Therapists were thus encouraged to overcome preexisting negative perceptions by having extensive discussions with a client before treatment.

## INTERIM SUMMARY

▶ Anxious/fearful personality disorders include avoidant, dependent, and obsessive-compulsive personality disorders.

▶ Avoidant personality disorder involves a pervasive pattern of anxiety, feelings of inadequacy, and social hypersensitivity.

▶ Dependent personality disorder involves a pervasive, excessive need to be cared for, leading to submissiveness, clinging behavior, and fears of separation.

▶ Obsessive-compulsive personality disorder involves a preoccupation with orderliness, perfectionism, and control.

▶ The most common anxious/fearful personality disorders are avoidant and obsessive-compulsive personality disorders, but all disorders of this group involve substantial distress and/or impairment.

▶ Strong emotions and impulsive behavior often associated with personality disorders can be a source of stigma for this population.

## REVIEW QUESTIONS

1. What are the main features of avoidant personality disorder?
2. What are key features of dependent and obsessive-compulsive personality disorders?
3. Describe the epidemiology of the anxious/fearful personality disorders, including issues of gender and culture.

## Personality Disorders: Causes and Prevention

We turn our attention next to risk factors and how our knowledge of these factors might help us prevent personality disorders. Researchers of personality disorders often focus on genetic, neurobiological, family environment, cognitive, and personality factors. The following discussion is organized by cluster of personality disorder; for each cluster, we explore biological risk factors, environmental risk factors, and causes.

### Biological Risk Factors for Odd or Eccentric Personality Disorders

Recall that odd or eccentric personality disorders include paranoid, schizoid, and schizotypal types. Genetics likely play a limited role in the development of odd or eccentric personality disorders, with heritability estimates of just 0.29 to 0.38 (Kendler et al., 2011). Schizotypal personality disorder may share a common genetic risk factor with schizophrenia (Hazlett, Goldstein, & Kolaitis, 2012). This is consistent with the theory that schizotypal personality disorder lies on the "schizophrenia spectrum," a continuum of schizophrenia-like syndromes and symptoms. Schizotypal personality disorder may represent a less severe and less dysfunctional form of schizophrenia (McClure et al., 2010).

Genetics may set the stage for cognitive and perceptual problems important in odd or eccentric personality disorders, especially schizotypal personality disorder. This is known as a *psychobiological theory of personality disorders* (Millon, 2012). Many people with these disorders, such as Michelle from the beginning of the chapter, have trouble attending to and selecting relevant stimuli in the environment. This results in misunderstandings, suspiciousness of others, extreme social detachment, and trouble separating what is real and what is imagined. These problems appear to be somewhat biologically based.

Twin studies of personality traits also suggest a genetic influence on the development of odd or eccentric personality disorders. The personality traits of restricted emotional expression, suspiciousness, and cognitive distortion appear to be influenced by genetic factors. These three traits are central to odd or eccentric personality disorders (Livesley & Jang, 2008). Genetics may also influence changes in the neurotransmitter dopamine that can predispose a person to odd or eccentric behaviors (Reichborn-Kjennerud, 2010).

### Environmental Risk Factors for Odd or Eccentric Personality Disorders

Family factors are also thought to influence the development of odd or eccentric personality disorders. Parental maltreatment, neglect, and emotional withdrawal relate closely to these personality disorders as well as other mental disorders we describe in this textbook (Geiger & Crick, 2010). Odd or eccentric personality disorders are clearly influenced as well by cognitive distortions. Paranoid personality disorder may develop when paranoid beliefs are reinforced by a cognitive set that leads a person to focus on signs of malicious intent in others. Examples of cognitive beliefs that underlie odd or eccentric personality disorders are in **Table 10.13** (Beck et al., 2004).

## Causes of Odd or Eccentric Personality Disorders

Odd or eccentric personality disorders are likely caused by some genetic predisposition as well as stressors that emerge in a person's life (see **Figure 10.2**). A genetic predisposition such as a family history of schizophrenia may influence later changes that help produce an odd or eccentric personality disorder. A genetic diathesis may influence family environment—parents who are emotionally withdrawn themselves may become physically or emotionally abusive to a child. A genetic diathesis may also set the stage for dysfunction in the dopamine neurotransmitter system that leads to cognitive and perceptual deficits associated with odd or eccentric personality disorders.

Neurobiology and family environment also influence each other. Some parents may become withdrawn from a child with odd cognitions or behaviors brought about by dopamine dysfunction. Neurobiological vulnerabilities also influence the development of cognitive beliefs such as mistrust and personality traits such as suspiciousness or restricted emotion that characterize odd or eccentric personality disorders. Cognitive beliefs and personality traits influence each other as well, as when a person who believes coworkers mean him harm becomes generally paranoid and suspicious.

## Biological Risk Factors for Dramatic Personality Disorders

Recall that dramatic personality disorders include antisocial, borderline, histrionic, and narcissistic types. Dramatic personality disorders have moderate genetic predispositions, with heritability estimates of 0.32 to 0.50 (Kendler et al., 2011). Impulsivity/aggression is most associated with borderline and antisocial personality disorder. People high on the impulsive/aggressive dimension, such as Duane with antisocial personality

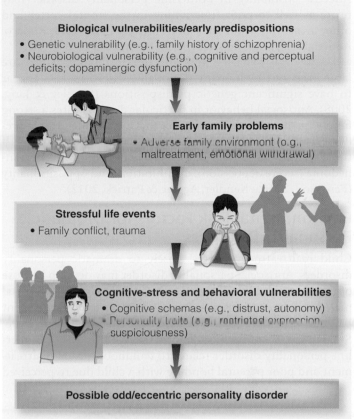

**FIGURE 10.2** CAUSAL MODEL OF CLUSTER A PERSONALITY DISORDERS

disorder, have a low threshold for action and often act without deliberating. They do not anticipate well the potential negative consequences of their actions and do not profit from past experience or knowledge of negative consequences. Impulsive aggression is associated with reduced serotonin (Coccaro, Sripada, Yanowitch, & Phan, 2011).

Psychopathy in adults and conduct disorder in boys are also associated with reduced brain size in areas perhaps related to moral development. These areas include the amygdala, frontal and temporal cortexes, superior temporal gyrus, and hippocampus (Blair, 2010; Koenigs, Baskin-Sommers, Zeier, & Newman, 2011). Impulsivity in borderline personality disorder may relate as well to dysfunction of the orbitofrontal cortex (Wolf et al., 2012).

Another dimension important to dramatic personality disorders is affective instability. People high on this trait are prone to rapid, intense mood shifts when frustrated, criticized, or separated from others. The noradrenergic neurotransmitter system is most closely associated with these mood shifts. People given substances that release catecholamine, which operates on the noradrenergic system, show intense emotional reactivity. People with significant mood shifts may be hypersensitive to fluctuations in the noradrenergic neurotransmitter system.

---

### Table 10.13

**Examples of Cognitions Associated with Odd or Eccentric Personality Disorders**

1. My privacy is more important to me than is closeness to people (schizoid, schizotypal).
2. I shouldn't confide in others (schizoid, schizotypal).
3. I cannot trust other people (paranoid).
4. Other people have hidden motives (paranoid).
5. It isn't safe to confide in other people (paranoid).

Reprinted from Beck et al. (1990), pp. 359-363.

Affective instability in borderline personality disorder may relate as well to poor functioning in the frontal cortex and other areas important for emotion (see **Figure 10.3**; Ruocco, Amirthavasagam, Choi-Kain, & McMain, 2013).

Antisocial behavior and affective instability, which are large parts of the dramatic personality disorders, also appear to have significant genetic predispositions (Livesley & Jang, 2008). Antisocial behavior in particular demonstrates a strong family history (Blazei, Iacongo, & McGue, 2008). Genetic predispositions exist for many other behaviors associated with these conditions as well. These behaviors include anxiety, anhedonia (severe depression), disinhibition, and oppositionality (Ferguson, 2010a; Kendler, Aggen, & Patrick, 2012).

## Environmental Risk Factors for Dramatic Personality Disorders

Child maltreatment relates closely to dramatic personality disorders. Antisocial personality disorder may develop because of traumatic childhood experiences such as physical or sexual maltreatment, aggressive parents, divorce, and inconsistent parental discipline (Blazei et al., 2006; Huizinga et al., 2006; Shi, Bureau, Easterbrooks, Zhao, & Lyons-Ruth, 2012). Borderline personality disorder relates to childhood sexual maltreatment and poor parental bonding with a child due to perceived

abandonment or actual separation (Gratz, Tull, Baruch, Bornovalova, & Lejuez, 2008).

Various parent–child relationships likely influence histrionic personality disorder, including one in which parental love and attention depends on a child's attractiveness and sexual provocativeness (Bornstein & Malka, 2009). One result might be that a daughter's self-worth depends primarily on how her father relates to her, and this pattern may repeat itself in adulthood with other men. Psychosocial theories of narcissistic personality disorder primarily focus on underlying feelings of inadequacy that drive one to seek recognition from others (Pincus & Lukowitsky, 2010).

Several cognitive beliefs also underlie symptoms of dramatic personality disorders (see **Table 10.14**; Beck et al., 2004). Some believe that deception, lying, cheating, and seductiveness are acceptable ways of securing one's needs. These beliefs can lead to aggressive or provocative interpersonal styles and problems that characterize antisocial and other dramatic personality disorders.

## Causes of Dramatic Personality Disorders

Dramatic personality disorders are likely caused by genetic predispositions and family-based stressors (see **Figure 10.4**). A family history of depressive, bipolar, substance use, or antisocial personality disorder likely serves as a genetic diathesis. This genetic diathesis directly influences family environmental (child maltreatment or poor parental bonding) and neurobiological (impulsive aggression, affective instability) factors related to dramatic personality disorders. Family environmental factors influence, and are influenced by, cognitive beliefs such as "I need what I want *now*" and personality traits such as emotional dysregulation that comprise dramatic personality disorders. Neurobiological factors such as noradrenergic dysfunction also influence these cognitive beliefs and personality traits.

## Biological Risk Factors for Anxious/ Fearful Personality Disorders

Recall that anxious/fearful personality disorders include avoidant, dependent, and obsessive-compulsive types. Genetics play a modest role in the development of anxious/fearful personality disorders, with heritability estimates of 0.34 to 0.47 (Kendler et al., 2011). Other dimensions of anxious/fearful personality disorders that may have some genetic basis include behavioral inhibition, tendency to anticipate harm or future negative events, excessive sensitivity to negative events, heightened arousal, and a tendency to read threat or potential harm into benign events (Van Gestel & Van Broeckhoven, 2003).

People with anxious/fearful personality disorders may inherit neurobiological vulnerabilities as well, especially those involving the noradrenergic

Prefrontal cortex

Basal ganglia

Thalamus

Hippocampus

Amygdala

Image Source/Getty Images

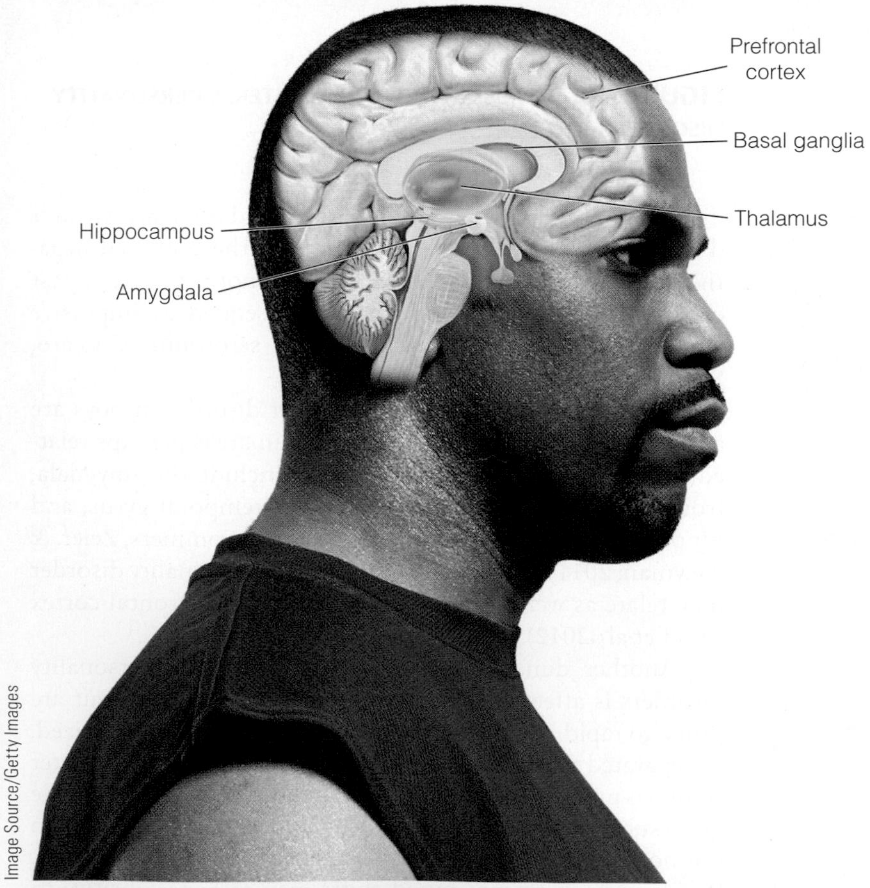

**FIGURE 10.3** **BRAIN FEATURES MOST IMPLICATED IN BORDERLINE PERSONALITY DISORDER.** Copyright © Cengage Learning®

## Table 10.14

### Examples of Cognitions Associated with Dramatic Personality Disorders

1. I should be the center of attention (histrionic).
2. I cannot tolerate boredom (histrionic).
3. Other people should satisfy my needs (narcissistic).
4. Lying and cheating are okay as long as you don't get caught (antisocial).
5. If I want something, I should do whatever is necessary to get it (antisocial).

Reprinted from Beck et al. (1990), pp. 359-363.

and gamma-aminobutyric acid (GABA) neurotransmitter systems. These vulnerabilities lead to heightened fearfulness and sensitivity to potential threat. Inherited personality traits may also contribute to the development of these disorders. Inhibition (avoidant personality disorder), compulsivity (obsessive-compulsive personality disorder), anxiousness, insecure

**FIGURE 10.4** CAUSAL MODEL OF CLUSTER B PERSONALITY DISORDERS

attachment, social avoidance, and submissiveness are traits central to anxious/fearful personality disorders. Twin studies suggest a strong genetic component for these traits (Livesley & Jang, 2008).

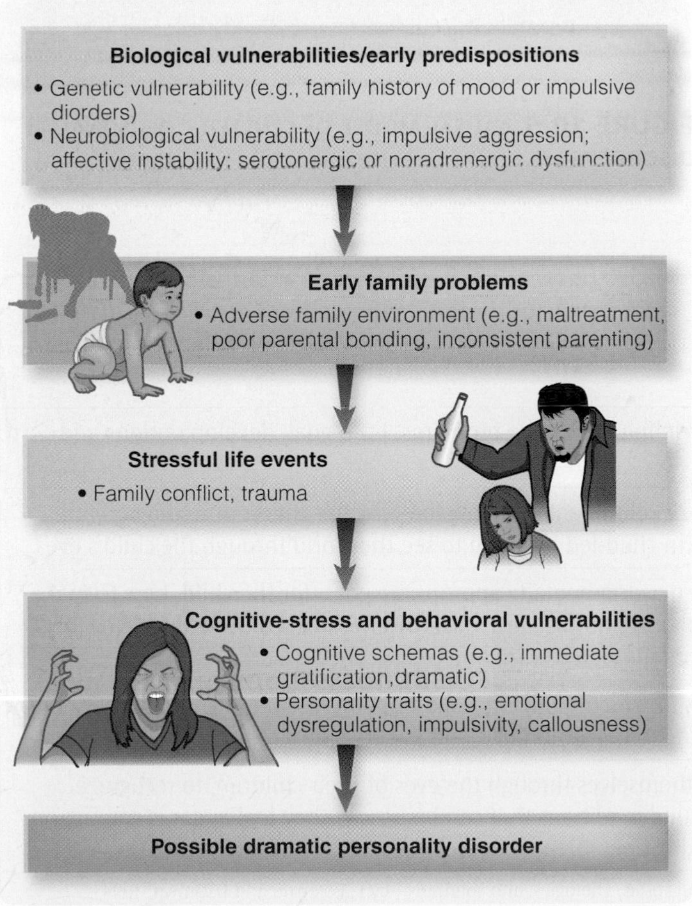

## Environmental Risk Factors for Anxious/Fearful Personality Disorders

Avoidant personality disorder may result when an anxious, introverted, and unconfident person experiences repeated episodes of embarrassment, rejection, or humiliation in childhood. Adolescence may be a particularly difficult time for these individuals because of the importance of attractiveness, popularity, and dating. The interaction of these temperamental traits and negative experiences may lead to cognitive schemas such as excessive self-consciousness or feelings of inadequacy or inferiority that comprise avoidant personality disorder (Beck et al., 2004).

Dependent personality disorder may result from an interaction between an anxious/fearful temperament and insecure attachment to parents (Meyer, Pilkonis, Proietti, Heape, & Egan, 2001). Those with the disorder, such as Betty, rely on others for reassurance, help, and a sense of security because they see themselves as weak and ineffectual. They are also preoccupied with threats of abandonment, and they feel helpless. These cognitive schemas set the stage for those with dependent personality disorder to become depressed when faced with interpersonal loss or conflict (see **Table 10.15**; Beck et al., 2004).

Less is known about family or environmental influences regarding obsessive-compulsive personality disorder. Children who ultimately develop obsessive-compulsive personality disorder may have been well behaved and conscientious but perhaps overly serious and rigid (Mervielde, De Clercq, De Fruyt, & Van Leeuwen, 2005). Cognitive schemas associated with obsessive-compulsive personality disorder include hyper-responsibility for oneself and others, perfectionism, excessive attention to detail, and catastrophic thinking when faced with perceived failure or setback (Beck et al., 1990, 2004).

## Table 10.15

### Examples of Cognitions Associated with Anxious/Fearful Personality Disorders

1. I am needy and weak (dependent).
2. I am helpless when I'm left on my own (dependent).
3. I am socially inept and socially undesirable in work or social situations (avoidant).
4. It is important to do a perfect job on everything (obsessive-compulsive).
5. Any flaw or defect of performance may lead to catastrophe (obsessive-compulsive).

Reprinted from Beck et al. (1990), pp. 359-363.

## Causes of Anxious/Fearful Personality Disorders

Anxious/fearful personality disorders are likely caused by genetic predispositions and family environment problems (see **Figure 10.5**). A family history of anxiety-related disorder serves as the genetic diathesis for anxious/fearful personality disorders and influences the development of family environment, neurobiological, cognitive, and personality risk factors. Insecure attachment to parents or rejection from parents relate to underlying neurobiological vulnerabilities of anxiety or inhibition. Family environment and neurobiological factors influence the development of cognitive beliefs such as those related to low self-esteem or catastrophizing events. These factors also influence personality traits such as anxiousness or inhibition that underlie anxious/fearful personality disorders.

## Prevention of Personality Disorders

Prevention efforts for personality disorders are rare. Researchers have focused, however, on three major risk factors of personality disorders that may be the focus of future prevention efforts in this area. One of these risk factors is child maltreatment (Kim, Cicchetti, Rogosch, & Manly, 2009). Efforts to prevent child maltreatment may help influence the development of personality disorders. Successful prevention of child maltreatment often involves frequent home visits, reducing maternal stress, increasing social support, and parent training (MacMillan et al., 2009). Skills commonly taught to parents to reduce maltreatment are summarized in **Table 10.16**.

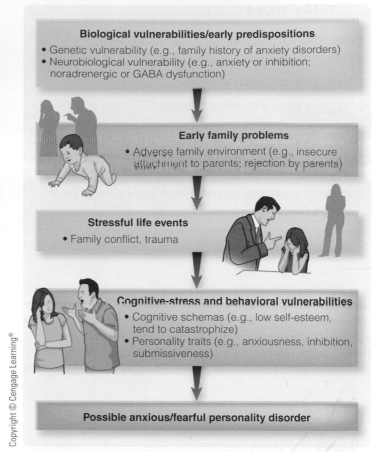

Copyright © Cengage Learning®

**FIGURE 10.5** CAUSAL MODEL OF CLUSTER C PERSONALITY DISORDERS

---

**Table 10.16**

### Prevention of Child Maltreatment

| Skills taught | |
|---|---|
| *Basic problem solving* | Parents are taught to recognize and define typical life problems, list a goal, develop options and plans, and evaluate the outcome. |
| *Positive parenting: enjoying the child* | Parents are taught about normative development and how to enjoy the child's unfolding abilities. In addition, parents learn to engage in child-led play and to see the world through the child's eyes. |
| *Parenting skills* | Parents are taught how to recognize developmentally appropriate goals for the child, how to make requests in a way that ensures compliance, how to decrease unwanted behaviors from the child, and how to increase desired behaviors through reward and praise. |
| *Extending parenting* | Parents are taught about child safety. Instruction includes material on discipline and maltreatment, selecting safe caregivers, childproofing to prevent injury, and supervising children. |
| *Anger management* | This module teaches parents to see themselves through the eyes of their children, to recognize and control anger, to relax, and to build in options that can be used if they feel anger is coming on (for example, distracting oneself, taking deep breaths, removing oneself from the situation). |

Source: Adapted from "Integrating Child Injury and Abuse-Neglect Research: Common Histories, Etiologies, and Solutions," by L. Peterson and D. Brown, 1994, *Psychological Bulletin, 116*, 293-315. Copyright © 1994 by the American Psychological Association. Reprinted with permission.

Another main risk factor for personality disorders is poor interpersonal skills. Many people with personality disorders experience great difficulty in interpersonal contexts such as family relationships, friendships, and work situations (Muralidharan, Sheets, Madsen, Craighead, & Craighead, 2011). Many are socially withdrawn, aggressive, impulsive, insecure, dependent, and highly attention seeking. Efforts to enhance a person's social skills may help prevent troublesome interpersonal styles that characterize personality disorder.

Interpersonal skills training is especially relevant to deficits seen in avoidant personality disorder such as extreme shyness and difficulty initiating relationships. Four main social skills are taught: listening and attending, empathy, appropriate self-disclosure, and respectful assertiveness (Ahmed et al., 2012). Training in each of these skills involves educating a client about the skills, modeling appropriate social interactions, and asking the client to practice the skills.

A third major risk factor for personality disorder is *emotional dysregulation*. Problems in emotional responsiveness such as restricted affect or affective instability characterize many personality disorders. Prevention efforts help people identify, cope with, change, and control negative emotional states. Treatment procedures for borderline personality disorder (discussed in a later section) might be modified for prevention efforts (Chanen & McCutcheon, 2013). People can learn to describe emotional states (love, joy, anger, sadness, fear, shame), identify events or interpretations that prompt these emotions, understand how an emotion is experienced or expressed, and attend to the aftereffects of an emotion. A training plan for emotional regulation of anger is outlined in **Table 10.17**.

## INTERIM SUMMARY

- Genetic influences may be particularly strong for schizotypal personality disorder because of its place on the schizophrenia spectrum.
- A psychobiological theory of personality disorder suggests that genetics set the stage for cognitive and perceptual problems that underlie odd or eccentric and other personality disorders.
- Parental maltreatment and withdrawal as well as cognitive distortions comprise major environmental risk factors for odd or eccentric personality disorders.
- Dramatic personality disorders have significant genetic predispositions, especially with respect to impulsive/aggressive behavior and affective instability.
- Dramatic personality disorders also relate closely to childhood traumas such as severe maltreatment as well as cognitive distortions.
- Anxious/fearful personality disorders may be caused by genetic factors that underlie anxiety and inhibition as well as difficulties in interpersonal contexts such as relationships with parents, friendships, and coworkers.
- Prevention of personality disorders might focus on reducing major risk factors such as child maltreatment, poor interpersonal skills, and emotional dysregulation.

## REVIEW QUESTIONS

1. What aspects of personality disorders have a genetic predisposition?
2. What brain and neurochemical features relate to personality disorders?
3. What personality characteristics relate to personality disorders?
4. What cognitive features relate to personality disorders?
5. What topics might be addressed in programs to prevent personality disorders?

# Personality Disorders: Assessment and Treatment

We divided our discussion of features and risk factors for personality disorders into the three main clusters. Assessment and treatment in this area, however, often cuts across many personality disorders; therefore, we present this section as a general overview.

## Assessment of Personality Disorders

Clinicians often use self-report questionnaires, unstructured clinical interviews, semistructured clinical interviews, and

Programs designed to prevent child maltreatment may decrease the likelihood of personality disorder symptoms in these children when they grow up.

**Table 10.17**

| **Emotion Regulation Training** | | | |
|---|---|---|---|
| ANGER WORDS—examples | | | |
| anger | disgust | grumpiness | rage |
| aggravation | dislike | hate | resentment |
| agitation | envy | hostility | revulsion |
| annoyance | exasperation | irritation | scorn |
| bitterness | ferocity | jealousy | spite |
| contempt | frustration | loathing | torment |
| cruelty | fury | mean-spiritedness | vengefulness |
| destructiveness | grouchiness | outrage | wrath |

1. **Prompting events for feeling anger—examples**
   - Losing power or respect
   - Being insulted
   - Not having things turn out the way you expected
   - Experiencing physical or emotional pain
   - Being threatened with physical or emotional pain by someone

2. **Interpretations that prompt feelings of anger— examples**
   - Expecting pain
   - Feeling that you have been treated unfairly
   - Believing that things should be different
   - Rigidly thinking "I'm right"
   - Judging that the situation is illegitimate, wrong, or unfair

3. **Experiencing the emotion of anger—examples**
   - Feeling out of control or extremely emotional
   - Feeling tightness in your body
   - Feeling your face flush or get hot
   - Teeth clamping together, mouth tightening
   - Crying; being unable to stop tears
   - Wanting to hit, bang the wall, throw something, blow up

4. **Expressing and acting on anger—examples**
   - Gritting or showing your teeth in an unfriendly manner
   - A red or flushed face
   - Verbally or physically attacking the cause of your anger; criticizing
   - Using obscenities or yelling, screaming, or shouting
   - Clenching your hands or fists
   - Making aggressive or threatening gestures
   - Pounding on something, throwing things, breaking things
   - Brooding or withdrawing from contact with others

5. **Aftereffects of anger—examples**
   - Narrowing of attention
   - Attending only to the situation making you angry and not being able to think of anything else
   - Remembering and ruminating about other situations that have made you angry in the past
   - Depersonalization, dissociative experience, numbness

Source: Adapted from *Skills Training Manual for Treating Borderline Personality Disorder* by Marsha Linehan. © 1993 The Guilford Press.

informant reports to assess personality disorders. We discuss each of these methods and their advantages and disadvantages (see **Table 10.18**).

## SELF-REPORT QUESTIONNAIRES

Self-report questionnaires include items that assess symptoms of personality disorder (Samuel et al., 2011). Personality disorder questionnaires are easy to administer and economical with respect to time and effort. Self-report instruments are generally used as screening instruments and not as diagnostic measures because they do not assess level of impairment or distress. Self-report instruments also do not typically assess whether symptoms were evident since young adulthood (Hopwood, Morey, Edelen, Shea, & Grilo, 2008).

A popular self-report of various personality constructs is the *Millon Clinical Multiaxial Inventory—III* (Millon, Davis, Millon, &

Grossman, 2006). The measure consists of 24 scales related to all personality disorders and other problems such as depression and excessive substance use. Child and adolescent versions are also available. Recall as well from Chapter 4 that the *Minnesota Multiphasic Personality Inventory—2* is a well-used self-report measure that can suggest diagnoses but also indicates various problematic behaviors and personality styles. Sample items from another popular personality disorder measure, the *Personality Diagnostic Questionnaire—4*, are shown in **Table 10.19** (Bouvard, Vuachet, & Marchand, 2011; Hyler, 1998).

## INTERVIEWS

Many clinicians use unstructured clinical interviews to assess personality disorders, although researchers prefer the structured interview (Samuel et al., 2011). Unstructured interviews allow a mental health professional to ask any question about

___ **Table 10.18** _____

### Advantages and Disadvantages of Four Major Methods of Personality Disorder Assessment

| | Questionnaire | Unstructured clinical interview | Structured clinical interview | Informant ratings |
|---|---|---|---|---|
| Advantages | Quick, not time-consuming | Easily integrated into standard clinical practice | Tied to diagnostic criteria | Not subject to self-portrayal "bias." |
| | Useful as a screening measure | Natural "flow" | Most empirically supported | Can provide historical perspective |
| Disadvantages | Overdiagnoses | Not directly tied to diagnostic criteria | Potentially long and tedious | Often fails to agree with self-report |
| | Potentially subject to self-portrayal bias | Subject to clinician bias or error | May seem awkward to introduce into typical clinical session | Dependent on extent of informant's knowledge of the target |

personality disorder symptoms. Unstructured interviews are often less reliable and more susceptible to interviewer bias than structured interviews, however (Trull & Prinstein, 2013). Mental health professionals who use unstructured clinical interviews or case review also routinely fail to assess specific

Structured interviews are the gold standard for personality disorder assessment.

___ **Table 10.19** _____

### Examples of Personality Diagnostic Questionnaire—4 (PDQ-4) Items

| Disorder | Example |
|---|---|
| Avoidant | Over the past several years . . . I avoid working with others who may criticize me. |
| Dependent | Over the past several years . . . I can't make decisions without the advice, or reassurance, of others. |
| Borderline | Over the past several years . . . I either love someone or hate them, with nothing in between. |
| Antisocial | Over the past several years . . . I do a lot of things without considering the consequences. |
| Paranoid | Over the past several years . . . I keep alert to figure out the real meaning of what people are saying. |
| Schizotypal | Over the past several years . . . I get special messages from things happening around me. |

Reprinted with permission from Steven E. Hyler, M.D.

personality disorder diagnostic criteria or they express cultural bias (Mikton & Grounds, 2007).

Structured interviews take more time but are systematic, comprehensive, replicable, and objective. Structured interviews for personality disorder provide a mental health professional with useful suggestions for inquiries about various symptoms (Samuel et al., 2011). Sample interview items from the *Structured Interview for DSM-IV Personality* (SIDP-IV) are listed in **Table 10.20** (Pfohl, Blum, & Zimmerman, 1997).

## Table 10.20

| **SIDP-IV Questions Used to Assess a Dependent Personality Disorder Criterion** |
| --- |
| **Dependent Personality Disorder Criterion:** |
| Has difficulty making everyday decisions without an excessive amount of advice and reassurance from others. |
| **Interview Questions:** |
| ▶ "Some people enjoy making decisions and other people prefer to have someone they trust tell them what to do. Which do you prefer?" |
| ▶ "Do you often turn to others for advice about everyday decisions like what to have for lunch or what clothes to buy?" |

Reprinted with permission from the Structured Interview for *DSM-IV* Personality. Copyright © 1997 American Psychiatric Association.

## INFORMANT REPORTS

A disadvantage of self-report questionnaires and interviews is their emphasis on a person's self-report. This is a problem because many people with personality disorders have distorted self-image and self-presentation that can color their answers on these measures. An alternative method of assessing personality disorder is the **informant report** (Cooper, Balsis, & Oltmanns, 2012). Informants such as family members or close friends can provide an important historical perspective on a person's traits, especially if the informants themselves have no mental disorder.

Informant reports do have some downsides, however. These reports often conflict with self-reports and so a clinician may be unsure which perspective is most truthful (Cooper et al., 2012). Relatives and close friends will not know everything about a person that would be necessary to provide a valid description, they may be biased, and they may have false assumptions or expectations about a person. Informant report of personality disorder features remains a promising assessment method, however (Markon, Quilty, Bagby, & Krueger, 2013).

## Biological Treatments of Personality Disorders

People with personality disorders appear to benefit to some degree from various medications. Medication use has been targeted primarily toward those with borderline personality disorder. Medications for this population include antidepressant, antianxiety, and antipsychotic drugs. The beneficial effects of these drugs are usually limited to one area of functioning such as impulsivity or affective instability. Not all studies indicate positive results, however, and many people drop out of medication treatment. No firm conclusions can be drawn regarding a specific medication for a specific personality disorder (Ingenhoven, Lafay, Rinne, Passchier, & Duivenvoorden, 2010).

Medication may be more effective for specific groups of symptoms and not an overall personality disorder. Three main

---

## BOX 10.3 Focus on Law and Ethics

### Personality and Insanity

Some people with personality disorders may be prone toward criminal acts. Could they claim a personality disorder as the basis for an insanity defense? People with antisocial personality disorder generally cannot use this condition as an insanity defense. For example, serial killers cannot claim that being a "psychopath" or "sociopath" is grounds for an insanity plea. Others have argued, however, that a certain personality disorder could nullify responsibility for a criminal act. Recall from Chapter 3 that a common standard for insanity is that a person was unable to distinguish right from wrong at the time of the crime. Kinscherff (2010) argued that the impairments and comorbid disorders found in some personality disorders can be so severe that they mitigate, or lessen, criminal responsibility. An example is someone with borderline personality disorder and a history of severe maltreatment who harmed someone but did so during symptoms of posttraumatic stress disorder and paranoid psychosis.

Gray areas such as this have thus led some states to modify the verdict a jury may give when a defendant asserts an insanity defense. One alternative verdict is **guilty but mentally ill**, which assumes that the defendant is guilty of a crime and that he should receive punishment for the crime. However, the court has discretion to order psychiatric treatment before or after incarceration (Melamed, 2010). Another alternative is **diminished capacity**. This means a person did not have a mental disorder that absolves him or her for responsibility for a crime but did have a diminished mental capacity. Excessive alcohol use or trauma, for example, may have led a defendant to the point that she did not possess the mental state or intent relevant to the crime. Diminished capacity may mean that a person is convicted of a lesser offense (e.g., manslaughter instead of murder) or given a lighter sentence (Edersheim, Brendel, & Price, 2012).

symptom groups that may respond to medication include *cognitive-perceptual, affect,* and *impulsive aggression* (Jones et al., 2011; Olabi & Hall, 2010). Cognitive-perceptual symptoms of odd or eccentric personality disorders may be treated with antipsychotic drugs such as perphenazine, trifluoperazine, or haloperidol (Chapter 12). Affective (emotional) symptoms of dramatic personality disorders may be treated with selective serotonin reuptake inhibitors such as fluoxetine (Chapter 7). Impulsive aggressive problems of people with dramatic personality disorders may be treated with selective serotonin reuptake inhibitors, mood stabilizers such as lithium (Chapter 7), or antipsychotic drugs.

## Psychological Treatments of Personality Disorders

Personality disorders are among the most difficult mental disorders to treat because their symptoms are severe, chronic, long-standing, and associated with intense dysfunction, distress, and impairment. Clinicians in this area usually focus on maladaptive personality traits (Matusiewicz, Hopwood, Banducci, & Lejuez, 2010; Paris, 2009).

Not everyone with a personality disorder seeks treatment, but some do. Some people with personality disorder, particularly those with borderline personality disorder, seek many forms of treatment such as individual, group, and family/couple therapy; day treatment; hospitalization; halfway houses; and medication. People with borderline personality disorder also pursue lengthy treatment (Gunderson & Links, 2008). Many treatment studies in personality disorder thus focus on borderline personality disorder; common therapies used include short-term psychodynamic, cognitive-behavioral, and dialectical behavior therapies.

### SHORT-TERM PSYCHODYNAMIC THERAPY

Short-term psychodynamic therapy involves frequent meetings with a therapist to develop a close alliance and help clients transfer negative emotions. This therapy focuses on conflicts or themes that impede a person's life, such as abandonment, emptiness, jealousy, or aggression. A psychodynamic therapist will explore historical events in a person's life that may have led to problematic personality traits. Issues of child maltreatment or other trauma may also be discussed to help a client develop insight into her symptoms. Interpersonal conflict resolution, appropriate emotional experience, and less self-destructive behavior are key aspects

of short-term psychodynamic therapy as well (Town, Abbass, & Hardy, 2011).

### COGNITIVE-BEHAVIORAL THERAPY

Cognitive-behavioral therapy for personality disorders often focuses on easing symptoms of anxiety and depression (Chapters 5 and 7). Clinicians may use cognitive therapy to modify irrational thoughts, social skills training to improve interpersonal relationships, relaxation training to ease high levels of physical arousal, and behavioral activation to increase social contacts. Marital and family therapy may be used as well to improve communication and problem-solving skills (Gunderson & Links, 2008).

### DIALECTICAL BEHAVIOR THERAPY

One form of cognitive-behavioral treatment, **dialectical behavior therapy**, is quite useful for people with borderline personality disorder (Bedics, Atkins, Comtois, & Linehan, 2012). Dialectical behavior therapy addresses symptoms commonly associated with this disorder, including suicidal gestures/attempts, self-injury, and self-mutilation. Clients learn various skills to change behavioral, emotional, and thinking patterns that cause problems and extreme distress. Treatment strategies address each of the following areas:

- *Interpersonal effectiveness skills training:* Clients learn to manage interpersonal conflict, appropriately meet their desires or needs, and say no to unwanted demands from others.

- *Emotional regulation skills training:* Clients learn to identify different emotional states, understand how emotions affect them and others, engage in behavior likely to increase positive emotions, and counteract negative emotional states.

Family members can provide useful information about someone's personality traits and problems.

An important component of dialectical behavior therapy involves training in various emotional and interpersonal skills.

● *Distress tolerance skills training:* Clients learn to tolerate or "get through" stressful situations using distraction exercises (to ultimately gain a better perspective), self-soothing strategies such as listening to beautiful music, and techniques to improve their experience of the current moment such as imagery or relaxation.

● *Mindfulness skills training:* Clients learn to self-observe their attention and thoughts without being judgmental.

Clinicians often conduct dialectical behavior therapy in a group format, and clients often remain in treatment for several months to a year. Dialectical behavior therapy is effective for reducing suicidal behaviors, excessive substance use, number of days of psychiatric hospitalization, and treatment dropout. The therapy may also improve depression and hopelessness in some clients (Gutteling, Montagne, Nijs, & van den Bosch, 2012). Michelle, our case from the beginning of the chapter, would be a good candidate for dialectical behavior therapy because of her suicidality and her feelings of sadness and hopelessness.

A good way to illustrate dialectical behavior therapy is to present portions of a transcript of an actual therapy session. The client in this scenario was a 30-year-old woman with borderline personality disorder who was hospitalized 10 times in the previous 2 years for suicidal ideation and self-harm in the form of drinking Clorox bleach, cutting and burning herself, and one suicide attempt. A dialectical behavior *therapist* (T) explains the program and goals to the *client* (C) in the following segment (Linehan & Kehrer, 1993, pp. 428–429):

*T:* Now, the most important thing to understand is that we are not a suicide-prevention program, that's not our job. But we are a life enhancement program. The way we look at it, living a miserable life is no achievement. If we decide to work together, I'm going to help you try to improve your life so that it's so good that you don't want to die or hurt yourself. You should also know that I look at suicidal behavior, including drinking Clorox, as problem-solving behavior. I think of alcoholism the same way. The only

difference is that cutting, burning, unfortunately, it works. If it didn't work, nobody would do it more than once. But it only works in the short term, not the long term. So quitting cutting, trying to hurt yourself, is going to be exactly like quitting alcohol. Do you think this is going to be hard?

*C:* Stopping drinking wasn't all that hard.

*T:* Well, in my experience, giving up self-harm behavior is usually very hard. It will require both of us working, but you will have to work harder. And like I told you when we talked briefly, if you commit to this, it is for 1 year. Individual therapy with me once a week, and group skills training once a week. So the question is, are you willing to commit for 1 year?

*C:* I said I'm sick of this stuff. That's why I'm here.

*T:* So you've agreed to not drop out of therapy for a year, right?

*C:* Right.

*T:* And you do realize that if you don't drop out for a year, that really does, if you think about it, rule out suicide for a year?

*C:* Logically, yeah.

*T:* So, we need to be absolutely clear about this, because this therapy won't work if you knock yourself off. The most fundamental mood-related goal we have to work on is that, no matter what your mood is, you won't kill yourself, or try to.

*C:* Alright.

*T:* So that's what I see as our number one priority, not our only one, but our number one, that we will work on that. And getting you to agree, meaningfully of course, and actually following through on staying alive and not harming yourself and not attempting suicide no matter what your mood is. Now the question is, whether you agree to that.

*C:* Yes, I agree to that.

The therapist reinforces the client for using distress tolerance skills when her request for pain medication was refused by her physician in this next segment (Linehan & Kehrer, 1993, p. 433):

*T:* That's good thinking. That's when you're thinking about the advantages and disadvantages of doing it. OK, so at that point the advantages of making it worse were outweighed by the disadvantages. OK. So you keep up the good fight here. Now what else did you try?

*C:* I tried talking about it with other patients.

*T:* And what did they have to say?

*C:* They said I should get pain medication.

*T:* Right. But did they say you should cut yourself or hurt yourself if you didn't get it?

*C:* No. And I tried to get my mind off my pain by playing music and using mindfulness. I tried to read and do crossword puzzles.

*T:* Um hmm. Did you ever try radical acceptance?

*C:* What's that?

*T:* It's where you sort of let go and accept the fact that you're not going to get the pain medication. And you just give yourself up to that situation. You just accept that it ain't going to happen, that you're going to have to cope in some other way.

*C:* Which I did yesterday. I needed a little Ativan to get me there but I got there.

*T:* Yesterday?

*C:* Yeah. I took a nap. When I woke up I basically said, "Hey, they're not going to change, so you've just got to deal with this the best that you can."

*T:* And did that acceptance help some?

*C:* I'm still quite angry about what I believe is discrimination against borderline personalities. I'm still very angry about that.

*T:* OK. That's fine. Did it help though, to accept?

*C:* Um hmm.

*T:* That's good. That's great. That's a great skill, a great thing to practice. When push comes to shove, when you're really at the limit, when it's the worst it can be, radical acceptance is the skill to practice.

## What If I or Someone I Know Has a Personality Disorder?

People are sometimes screened for personality disorders, and the answers to some basic questions may indicate whether further assessment or even treatment is warranted. Some of these questions are in **Table 10.21**. If you find yourself answering "yes" to most of these questions, then you may wish to consult a clinical psychologist, psychiatrist, or other mental health professional (Chapter 15). Cognitive-behavioral therapy or medication may be best.

If you feel concerned about how you relate to others, but do not necessarily have a personality disorder, then teaching yourself to gain better control over moods and impulses and communicating and relating better to others may be helpful. Discuss your concerns with family members and friends as well. Further information about screening and treatment for personality disorders is available from several websites (e.g., http://www.tara4bpd.org/dyn/index.php; http://www.borderlinepersonalitydisorder.com/).

## Long-Term Outcomes for People with Personality Disorders

Personality disorders are generally best treated by cognitive-behavioral and some psychodynamic treatments that reduce symptoms and improve social functioning (Ahmed et al., 2012;

---

**Table 10.21**

### Screening Questions for Personality Disorders

▶ Do you often have difficulty maintaining boundaries with others or managing your emotions?

▶ Do you very often have trouble directing yourself toward your life goals or engaging in self-reflection?

▶ Do you have problems understanding the emotions of other people and the effects of your behavior on others?

▶ Are you unable to be close with others?

▶ Do you find yourself to be often impulsive, aggressive, detached, callous, or odd toward others?

---

Paris, 2009). However, those in therapy experience no more overall personality change than those not in therapy (Ferguson, 2010b). Therapy for antisocial personality disorder in particular has not been highly effective (Davidson et al., 2009). In addition, many people (37%) with personality disorders do not complete treatment (McMurran, Huband, & Overton, 2010). Factors that do predict treatment completion include commitment to change, good therapeutic relationship, and low impulsivity (Barnicot, Katsakou, Marougka, & Priebe, 2011).

Treatment effectiveness for personality disorders may improve if specific treatments are tailored to specific skills and behaviors. Behavioral treatments to lower social fear and improve interpersonal skills are most effective for avoidant personality disorder. Dialectical behavior therapy seems particularly effective for borderline personality disorder (Ahmed et al., 2012; Kliem, Kroger, & Kosfelder, 2010). Other personality disorders may be amenable to specific treatments as well. Examples include empathy training for adolescent boys with psychopathy, social problem-skills training for antisocial adults, and assertiveness skills training for people with dependent personality disorder. Greater research is needed in these areas, however (Hadjipavlou & Ogrodniczuk, 2010).

Symptoms of personality disorder often affect outcome for people with other mental disorders. People with anxiety, depressive, and substance use disorders *and* symptoms of personality disorder generally have poorer long-term outcome than people without symptoms of personality disorder (Pennay et al., 2011; Skodol et al., 2011; Telch, Kamphuis, & Schmidt, 2011). Underlying beliefs related to personality disorders—such as those listed in Tables 10.13, 10.14, and 10.15—may predict negative outcome for cognitive therapy for depression (Carter et al., 2011).

The research on long-term outcome of personality disorders is primarily confined to antisocial and borderline personality disorders. Antisocial behavior develops as conduct disorder in a child and about 50% of youth with conduct disorder later develop antisocial personality disorder (De Brito & Hodgins,

---

**THE CONTINUUM VIDEO PROJECT**

### *Tina:* **Borderline Personality Disorder**

*"I kinda get high off of making people as uncomfortable as they make me. It's almost my way of really connecting with myself."*

Copyright © Cengage Learning.®

Access the Continuum Video Project in MindTap at **www.cengagebrain.com**.

## Personal Narrative 10.1

### Anonymous

I suffer from borderline personality disorder, and because it is often difficult for individuals who don't have a mental disorder to understand what all the intricacies are of living with such a condition, I'm hoping that the following account will shed some light on the matter. More than anything else, the most important point I wish to convey is that individuals with a mental disorder are very much like anyone else—they wish to be treated with respect and understanding and given the opportunity to share their knowledge and talents to make the world a better place.

Living with a mental disorder has probably been the most difficult, and at the same time rewarding, aspect of my life. Even though I've made great strides to learn to manage my disorder over the past several years, I would have to say that I am still at a point where much of my self-definition is determined by my mental disorder. My hopes are that someday I will move beyond this narrowed definition of who I am and be able to more adequately self-identify with aspects that do not include my disorder and that more positively identify the other competencies that I possess.

If I recall correctly, my disorder dates all the way back to the first memories I have. For some reason, I've always sort of felt biologically "off." I can remember experiencing "weird" feelings, but I still to this day cannot identify exactly what they were. I only know that as I was given the proper medication, these feelings decreased substantially. I was 17 when I saw my first psychiatrist.

My parents would now say that, all through my childhood and especially during my adolescence, something was very wrong, but they couldn't put their finger on it. I experienced a fair amount of negative affect, which often seemed to them a bad "attitude." I was never able to clarify for my parents what was wrong, and because I tended to be a rather compliant child in most ways and didn't verbalize my difficulties, they had no idea the extent of my pain.

From the very first moments of my life, it was obvious that I was a very "sensitive" child. Temperamentally, I was hurt by the smallest of things, needed help dealing with very strong emotions (especially negative), needed help in calming myself, was clingy, and felt overly stimulated by certain environments. I sensed subtleties that others did not pick up on. I hated school because teachers I had often were experienced as too harsh, and even the smallest of correction felt painful to me. My perceptions of others (like a teacher getting mad) were magnified because of my enhanced sensitivity, and the pain of even these normal childhood occurrences was too much for me.

I would not say I had any "traumatic" events happen in my life—at least not anything that many others haven't experienced. My parents divorced when I was 5, and my mother remarried when I was 11. I was not abused or neglected, although I only saw my father on weekends, and he usually was too busy with work to pay much attention to me. I had a difficult time living with my mother and stepfather, never really feeling able to adjust. I think the hardest things for me were the fact

that my emotional makeup and that of my family's were very different, and I did not get very important emotional needs met that were imperative to my overall functioning. I was a very expressive child, and my parents were very much the opposite in many ways—they were more reserved, didn't feel the need to talk about feelings as much, and thought that I should be able to "control" my emotions the same way they did. Unfortunately, because of my disorder, this was not possible, and so my pain went underground and unrecognized, and my life got progressively worse.

When I finally did see my first therapist and psychiatrist, I was given some degree of help, but ultimately was never diagnosed properly and therefore never received the appropriate treatment. My parents continued to seek help for me, took me to a plethora of therapists, and still found that no one seemed able to really do anything to help me get better. It was not until many years later (at the age of 25), after years of hospitalizations, one suicide attempt, one unsuccessful treatment of electroconvulsive therapy (ECT), and a failed marriage, that I was finally given the correct diagnosis. And it was my good fortune that, at that time, the treatment I needed was being provided by the county mental health system that I had entered.

After my divorce, I qualified for SSI and entered the county mental health system of care. I had only ever utilized private insurance, so having to go to the county mental health clinic was quite a change—they only served the most severely disturbed and economically challenged of the population.

---

2009). People with antisocial personality disorder experience high rates of mortality, criminality, excessive substance use, unemployment, relationship difficulties, and imprisonment (Gibbon et al., 2010). Many with antisocial personality disorder show fewer symptoms in their 40s; they tend to be less impulsive and commit fewer acts that could lead to arrest or incarceration. Some with antisocial personality disorder continue a chronic pattern even past age 40 years, however, and continue to commit criminal acts or die prematurely (Davies, Clarke, Hollin, & Duggan, 2007; Paris, 2003).

People with borderline personality disorder tend to be most dysfunctional before age 30 years and gradually less symptomatic after age 30 years. The disorder appears to peak in young adulthood but diminish in severity by middle age.

I had grown up in a very educated, middle-class environment, and for me to get on SSI and receive services from the county was a hard adjustment. The ironic thing is that it wasn't until I reached this level of economic need that I finally was offered the proper treatment. None of the private insurances offered this treatment, and knew very little about the diagnosis I had and how to treat it. Unfortunately, to this day, my mental disorder still remains highly stigmatized in the therapeutic community, and many clinicians will not treat individuals like me because they feel our problems to be wearing and intractable.

As I entered the county system, I was given the diagnosis of borderline personality disorder (BPD). Past therapists I had seen had toyed with the idea that I might have this disorder, but few wanted to label me with such a seemingly harsh diagnosis. (Some therapists think that to label someone a borderline is thought to be akin to giving someone the death sentence!) Unfortunately, it was to my detriment. When I started obtaining services from the mental health system, I was told they were just starting a new program for individuals with this disorder and asked me if I would be interested. At that point I was willing to try anything, so I said yes. The treatment was called dialectical behavior therapy (DBT), and is still to this day one of the few empirically supported treatments that work for this population of individuals. I was the first of three individuals to enter this program, and I continued the treatment intensively for the next 4 years.

Because behaviors exhibited by those with BPD can seem outrageous and confusing to many who witness them, analogies may prove helpful to fully understand what these individuals experience. The analogy that resonates closest with my own experience of the disorder relates to the life of a third-degree burn victim. Because burn victims obviously have virtually no skin, any movement or touch may prove excruciatingly painful—great care and sensitivity is needed in all contact. An individual with BPD is very much like a third-degree burn victim, only with no "emotional" skin. Unfortunately, because no one can "see" the condition, the extreme sensitivity and heightened reactivity of people with BPD seem irrational to those around them. Because the smallest of things affect these individuals, our current stressful and fast-paced society is often not conducive to their particular needs.

Another helpful analogy can be described by thinking about the lens of a telescope. Because individuals with BPD constantly struggle with their perceptions of reality due to such frequent and intense emotional states, their ability to retain clarity of thought is much like constantly looking through a telescope lens that is out of focus. You may be aware that the lens is out of focus, but try as you might, those darn emotions keep wanting to run the show! So, even though the reality is that "most people I meet like me," my actual perception is often very different. Most of the time I see myself as extremely flawed, utterly incompetent, and deserving of punishment regardless of the fact that others discount these notions of my reality on a daily basis. It's almost like I just have to accept that during periods of intense emotion (which is much of the time), life may appear hopeless, but the negative feelings will eventually pass.

Currently, I am in the process of finishing my master's degree in marriage and family therapy. I have told no one in my program about my disorder. Unfortunately, because there remains so much stigma regarding BPD, it would not be in my best interests to divulge my condition at this time. Ironically, the fact that I am entering a profession that purports to treat individuals like myself with compassion, and yet continues to berate and ridicule us doesn't seem to make much of a difference at this time. Because of the present gap in transfer of information that so often resides between the research community and the everyday experiences of the practicing clinician, I currently remain unable to come forward. However, even though prejudice runs strong right now, I don't believe this will always be so. As individuals like myself enter the field and use our own successes to help others in similar situations, I do think there will be a reduction in prejudice and a recognition that therapists and patients alike, really aren't all that different after all.

And with that, I'd like to leave a quote that significantly reflects my personal beliefs about what truly constitutes a "life worth living":

---

I have learned that success is to be measured not so much by the position that one has reached in life, as by the obstacles which he has overcome while trying to succeed.—*Booker T. Washington*

---

Many cases of borderline personality disorder remit by age 40 years (75%) and by age 50 years (92%; Paris, 2009). Others report that the remission rate over a 10-year period is 85% (Gunderson et al., 2011). Unfortunately, the suicide rate is up to 10% over time in people with borderline personality disorder, especially among those who are older and who did not experience success in treatment (Paris, 2009). Interpersonal features that are slow to remit include emotional responses to being alone and dependency (Choi-Kain et al., 2010). Positive outcome seems related to lack of childhood sexual maltreatment, no family history of excessive substance use, good work history, no comorbid anxious/fearful personality disorder, low neuroticism, and high agreeableness (Zanarini, Frankenburg, Reich, & Fitzmaurice, 2010; Zanarini, Frankenburg, Hennen, Reich, & Silk, 2006).

Long-term outcome for odd or eccentric and anxious/fearful personality disorders appears to be somewhat stable or generally improved over time (Gunderson et al., 2011; Sanislow et al., 2009). Symptoms that are most stable over time include paranoid ideation and unusual experiences, affective instability, anger, feelings of inadequacy, feeling socially inept, and rigidity. Symptoms that are least stable over time include odd behavior and constricted affect, self-injury, avoidance of certain jobs and social situations, and miserly and strict moral behavior (McGlashan et al., 2005).

## INTERIM SUMMARY

▶ Clinicians who assess symptoms of personality disorder typically use self-report questionnaires, interviews, and informant reports.

▶ Biological treatments for personality disorders involve medications to ease anxiety and depression, stabilize mood, and reduce comorbid psychotic symptoms.

▶ Psychological treatments for personality disorders include short-term psychodynamic therapy, cognitive-behavioral interventions, and dialectical behavior therapy.

▶ Psychological treatment for personality disorders is moderately effective but less so than for other major mental disorders. Effectiveness may improve if specific treatments are tailored to specific personality disorders.

▶ Personality disorders may remit over time but many people experience a chronic course marked by premature death or suicide.

## REVIEW QUESTIONS

1. Describe the major assessment techniques for personality disorders.

2. What medications are primarily used to treat personality disorders?

3. What general psychological approaches may be used to treat personality disorders?

4. What treatment approaches may be useful for specific personality disorders?

5. What is the long-term outcome for people with personality disorders?

# Final Comments

Personality disorders are prevalent in clinical settings and the general population. The disorders produce great distress, social and occupational problems, and serious negative outcomes such as suicide or incarceration. Most symptoms and features of personality disorders develop by young adulthood, so they are especially relevant to young adults. The traits and features that comprise these disorders lie on a continuum, so most of us to some degree, or at least on occasion, experience problems like those with a personality disorder. Personality disorders, unlike many mental disorders we discuss in this textbook, can be chronic. This makes it even more important for those with personality disorders to seek help from a mental health professional.

# Thought Questions

1. Think about television or film characters that portray someone with many interpersonal problems or conflicts. Is this character a good example of a personality disorder? Which disorder, and why?

2. Have you ever been concerned about the way you interact with others? Are you too shy, outgoing, or abrasive? What factors may have influenced the way you are with other people? What information in this chapter seems most relevant to you?

3. What would you now say to friends who might have concerns about their interpersonal style, emotions, or problems with impulse control?

4. What separates "normal" personality quirks from "abnormal" personality traits?

5. Do you think personality disorders have more to do with biological, family, cultural, or other factors? Why?

# Key Terms

personality trait 291
personality disorder 291
paranoid personality disorder 293
schizoid personality disorder 293
schizotypal personality disorder 293
antisocial personality disorder 296
psychopathy 296
borderline personality disorder 297

histrionic personality disorder 298
narcissistic personality disorder 299
avoidant personality disorder 301
dependent personality disorder 301
obsessive-compulsive personality disorder 302
informant report 312
dialectical behavior therapy 313

# Media Resources

## MindTap

MindTap for Kearney and Trull's *Abnormal Psychology and Life: A Dimensional Approach* is a highly personalized fully online learning platform of authoritative content, assignments, and services offering you a tailored presentation of course curriculum created by your instructor. MindTap guides you through the course curriculum via an innovative learning path where you will complete reading assignments, annotate your readings, complete homework, and engage with quizzes and assessments. MindTap includes the Continuum Video Project.

Go to **cengagebrain.com** to access MindTap.

## Table 11.8

### Prevalence of Sexual Problems by Demographic Characteristics (Women)

| | Lacked interest in sex | Unable to achieve orgasm | Experienced pain during sex | Sex not pleasurable | Anxious about performance | Trouble lubricating |
|---|---|---|---|---|---|---|
| **Age, years** | | | | | | |
| 18–29 | 32% | 26% | 21% | 27% | 16% | 19% |
| 30–39 | 32% | 28% | 15% | 24% | 11% | 18% |
| 40–49 | 30% | 22% | 13% | 17% | 11% | 21% |
| 50–59 | 27% | 23% | 8% | 17% | 6% | 27% |
| **Marital status** | | | | | | |
| Currently married | 29% | 22% | 14% | 21% | 9% | 22% |
| Never married | 35% | 30% | 17% | 25% | 18% | 17% |
| Divorced, separated, or widowed | 34% | 32% | 16% | 25% | 15% | 19% |
| **Education** | | | | | | |
| Less than high school | 42% | 34% | 18% | 28% | 18% | 15% |
| High school graduate | 33% | 29% | 17% | 23% | 12% | 20% |
| Some college | 30% | 24% | 16% | 23% | 12% | 21% |
| College graduate | 24% | 18% | 10% | 18% | 10% | 22% |
| **Race or ethnicity** | | | | | | |
| White | 29% | 24% | 16% | 21% | 11% | 22% |
| Black | 44% | 32% | 13% | 32% | 16% | 15% |
| Hispanic | 30% | 22% | 14% | 20% | 12% | 12% |
| Other | 42% | 34% | 19% | 23% | 23% | 17% |

Data are from National Health and Social Life Survey.

denial of the problem and failure to seek treatment (Shabsigh et al., 2010). Men are often embarrassed to discuss the issue, so some researchers have proposed that medical professionals should initiate conversations about erectile dysfunction with their male patients, particularly those with risk factors such as medication use for diabetes or heart disease (Green & Kodish, 2009). In addition, researchers have found that 90% of men with premature ejaculation had not discussed with a physician alternatives to prolong the sexual experience (Brock et al., 2009). To help reduce the stigma associated with premature ejaculation, Seagraves (2010) advocated for a change to the term "rapid ejaculation."

Stigma with respect to sexual dysfunction can apply to women as well. Recurrent painful intercourse is not uncommon among women. However, many women are initially confused about the source of pain, try to pursue strategies for relief that do not work, and are reluctant to seek professional help. In addition, health care providers rarely raise this topic with their patients (Donaldson & Meana, 2011). Binik (2010) argued that sexual pain is a problem that has many concurrent issues and should not be considered a sexual dysfunction. Another source of stigma comes from secondary problems that can result because of sexual pain. These problems include infertility, marital problems, and divorce (Palha & Lourenco, 2011). Peterson and colleagues (2012) proposed that infertility specialists should consider these painful conditions when counseling couples.

### INTERIM SUMMARY

▶ Sexual dysfunctions involve disturbance of the sexual response cycle and may be lifelong or acquired.

- Male hypoactive sexual desire disorder and female sexual interest/arousal disorder involve lack of fantasies or desire to have sexual relations.
- Erectile disorder refers to difficulty obtaining or maintaining a full erection during sex.
- Female orgasmic disorder and delayed ejaculation refer to delay or absence of orgasm during sex.
- Premature (early) ejaculation refers to orgasm that occurs before a man wishes it.
- Genito-pelvic pain/penetration disorder involves problems of pain during intercourse.
- Sexual dysfunctions are common, increase with age, associate with one another and with anxiety and depression, and may link to medical, substance, and cultural factors.
- Sexual dysfunctions can be highly stigmatizing and can affect people's decisions to seek treatment.

## REVIEW QUESTIONS

1. What sexual dysfunctions affect sexual desire and arousal?
2. What sexual dysfunctions affect sexual orgasm?
3. What sexual dysfunction involves pain during intercourse?
4. Discuss the epidemiology of sexual dysfunctions.
5. Discuss stigma surrounding some sexual dysfunctions.

## Sexual Dysfunctions: Causes and Prevention

Risk factors for sexual dysfunctions have not been explored at length but likely include biological and environmental variables. We next discuss these risk factors and prevention of sexual dysfunctions.

**Table 11.9**

### Prevalence of Sexual Problems by Demographic Characteristics (Men)

| | Lacked interest in sex | Unable to achieve orgasm | Climax too early | Sex not pleasurable | Anxious about performance | Trouble maintaining or achieving erection |
|---|---|---|---|---|---|---|
| **Age, years** | | | | | | |
| 18–29 | 14% | 7% | 30% | 10% | 19% | 7% |
| 30–39 | 13% | 7% | 32% | 8% | 17% | 9% |
| 40–49 | 15% | 9% | 28% | 9% | 19% | 11% |
| 50–59 | 17% | 9% | 31% | 6% | 14% | 18% |
| **Marital status** | | | | | | |
| Currently married | 11% | 7% | 30% | 6% | 14% | 9% |
| Never married | 19% | 8% | 29% | 11% | 21% | 10% |
| Divorced, separated, or widowed | 18% | 9% | 32% | 13% | 26% | 14% |
| **Education** | | | | | | |
| Less than high school | 19% | 11% | 38% | 14% | 23% | 13% |
| High school graduate | 12% | 7% | 35% | 6% | 18% | 9% |
| Some college | 16% | 8% | 26% | 9% | 19% | 10% |
| College graduate | 14% | 7% | 27% | 6% | 13% | 10% |
| **Race or ethnicity** | | | | | | |
| White | 14% | 7% | 29% | 7% | 18% | 10% |
| Black | 19% | 9% | 34% | 16% | 24% | 13% |
| Hispanic | 13% | 9% | 27% | 8% | 5% | 5% |
| Other | 24% | 19% | 40% | 9% | 21% | 12% |

Data are from National Health and Social Life Survey.

## BOX 11.1 Focus on Gender

### Gender Biases in Sexual Dysfunctions and Disorders

Sexual dysfunctions and disorders are among the most controversial diagnoses. Part of the reason for this is that possible bias exists against women and men with respect to some of the disorders. Genito-pelvic pain/penetration disorder is an example. Many women are "blamed" by their partners for being "frigid" or for avoiding sexual contact. Some researchers suggest, however, that a condition like genito-pelvic pain/penetration disorder (previously dyspareunia and vaginismus) may be linked to important psychological factors such as symptoms of depression and anxiety, marital problems, and past sexual trauma (Donaldson & Meana, 2011). For some women, the problem they experience is not just sexual and isolated to them, but rather pain-related and linked to stress in their partner relationships. Successful therapy for some of these women requires active involvement of their sexual partner.

Conversely, women rarely if ever are diagnosed with transvestic disorder (cross-dressing for sexual excitement; see later section in paraphilic disorders), perhaps because women are generally allowed to wear masculine or feminine clothing in public. Men, however, are generally penalized if they publicly wear feminine apparel, often receiving stares or negative comments from others. With respect to exhibitionistic disorder (sexual arousal by exhibiting genitals to strangers, see later section in paraphilic disorders), men tend to be penalized more if they reveal more skin than women, for whom such behavior is often considered attractive. Some men clearly commit offenses due to their paraphilic disorder, but others may be viewed as abnormal simply because they choose to express themselves in legal, androgynous ways.

## Biological Risk Factors for Sexual Dysfunctions

We mentioned that biological factors such as medical conditions and substances impact sexual performance. Sexual dysfunctions must not be caused exclusively by a medical condition or a substance; however, researchers often investigate sexual problems that are related to medical conditions or substance use. Medical conditions that impair sexual performance in men include prostate cancer and subsequent treatment as well as cardiovascular problems. Medical conditions that impair sexual performance in women include cervical and other gynecological cancers as well as menopause (Hordern, 2008). Some medical conditions that may affect sexual functioning could also be present in either gender, such as diabetes, general pain, renal disease, multiple sclerosis, and spinal cord injuries or paralysis (Clayton & Ramamurthy, 2008). These medical conditions can lead to sexual pain or difficulties with arousal or orgasm.

Various substances also interfere with normal sexual functioning. Examples include legal substances such as alcohol, nicotine, and some prescription medications and illegal substances such as opioids and marijuana. Alcohol use impairs male and female sexual performance (Johnson, Phelps, & Cottler, 2004). Drugs for psychiatric conditions like depression and schizophrenia can also impair sexual response (Abler et al., 2011).

## Psychological Risk Factors for Sexual Dysfunctions

Psychological factors also impair the sexual response cycle. One key factor is anxiety or worry during sexual performance about satisfactorily pleasing oneself and one's partner. Men may worry about obtaining an erection, ejaculating prematurely, or having enough energy to complete the act. Such was true for Douglas. Women may worry about pain during intercourse and lack of orgasm. Worry about performance may lead to failure that creates more anxiety and avoidance of sex (Gralla et al., 2008).

Men and women may also distract themselves during sex to monitor their own performance. The **spectator role** involves greater concern with evaluating performance than enjoying relaxed sexual activity (Borras-Valls & Gonzalez-Correales, 2004). Sexual experience becomes less enjoyable and less likely to produce a satisfactory sexual response when a person is distracted from erotic thoughts by criticizing his sexual behavior. Men often try to delay ejaculation by thinking of negative or positive sexual experiences or by thinking about irrelevant items such as baseball statistics, but this is usually unhelpful (Hartmann, Schedlowski, & Kruger, 2005).

Failures during sexual performance can also result from poor interactions between partners during sex. Many couples do not speak during sex when a conversation about what a person enjoys and does not enjoy would greatly enhance the experience. A man may wish for more oral gratification and a woman may wish for more manual clitoral stimulation. These interests should be shared with one another, even during intercourse. Marital or relationship problems can also interfere with adequate sexual activity (McCabe et al., 2010). Problems may include fighting, stress, sexual boredom, difficulty with intimacy or fertility, or impulsive behavior.

Historical psychological variables can be important as well for determining sexual dysfunctions. Early sexual experiences for someone may have been traumatic, as when a child or adolescent is sexually maltreated, when a first sexual experience goes badly, or when fear of pregnancy is intense (Desrochers, Bergeron, Landry, & Jodoin, 2008). Future sexual experiences may thus be painful physically and psychologically. Another early factor is family treatment of sex as a "dirty" or repulsive act that was not to be discussed or practiced. Strict religious practices that may lead to punishment of masturbation or other sexual activity may also be a factor (Shabsigh & Anastasiadis, 2003). These family practices could lead to ignorance about the normal sexual process and problems when sex is attempted, such as attempting intercourse too quickly.

General knowledge about sex over time is important as well, as many aging men require greater stimulation for an erection and many women experience less vaginal lubrication (Laumann et al., 2008). Acknowledging these normal changes and making adjustments in one's sexual activity to compensate for them is therefore important. People with mental disorders such as depression or anxiety commonly experience sexual dysfunctions as well. These disorders can help cause sexual dysfunctions and help maintain them over time (Laurent & Simons, 2009).

## CULTURAL FACTORS

Sexual dysfunctions are common across various cultures. Erectile dysfunction in men is common in places as diverse as Brazil, Italy, Uganda, Kenya, Turkey, Malaysia, Japan, Korea, and the United States (Gray & Campbell, 2005; Kamatenesi-Mugisha & Oryem-Origa, 2005; Ku, Park, Kim, & Paick, 2005; Moreira, Lbo, Diament, Nicolosi, & Glasser, 2003; Nicolosi, Moreira, Shirai, Tambi, & Glasser, 2003; Uguz, Soylu, Unal, Diler, & Evlice, 2004). Attitudes about erectile dysfunction are also quite similar across various cultures—most men believe erectile dysfunction is a source of sadness, that they are not "too old for sex," that knowledge about erectile dysfunction is important, and that they would try virtually any remedy for the condition (Perelman, Shabsigh, Seftel, Althof, & Lockhart, 2005).

Among American men, erectile dysfunction seems to affect Hispanics disproportionately. This may be because Hispanic men have poorer care for conditions that can produce erectile dysfunction, such as diabetes or hypertension, or because erectile ability is perceived to be highly important (Smith et al., 2009). Fortunately, drug treatment for erectile dysfunction has been shown to be equally effective across African American, Hispanic, and European American men (Morgentaler, Barada, et al., 2006).

Premature ejaculation is also common to many men and may be particularly so among men with Asian and Islamic backgrounds. The reasons for this are unclear but may be due to strict attitudes or anxiety about sex, genetic or familial reasons, or stress about living in a foreign culture (Moreira, Kim, Glasser, & Gingell, 2006; Richardson & Goldmeier, 2005; Richardson, Wood, & Goldmeier, 2006).

Women of different cultures also experience sexual dysfunction, although the perceived cause of dysfunction can vary. Moroccan couples with sexual problems such as pain or erectile dysfunction commonly use sorcery from some other person as an explanation (Kadri et al., 2002). Women medicated for depression or high blood pressure across cultures may

experience sexual dysfunction as well (Okeahialam & Obeka, 2006; Williams et al., 2006). Sexual dysfunction and depression often co-occur in women, and some speculate that this comorbid condition is especially prevalent in Asian American, Hispanic, and African American women. Possible reasons for this include historical lack of emphasis on sexual needs of Asian American women, greater risk for depression among Hispanic women who experience alteration of sexual capability, and negative impact on sexual attitudes among African American females who may be more likely to have experienced a violent sexual encounter (Dobkin, Leiblum, Rosen, Menza, & Marin, 2006).

African American women are more likely than European American women to report concern about vaginal lubrication, sex appeal, sexually transmitted disease, thinking much about sex, and having an affair. Asian American women show less concern than European American women about lack of interest in sex, orgasm difficulty, sex appeal, unsatisfied sexual needs, and sexual concerns from a partner. Asian American women may be more concerned, however, about sexually transmitted disease and penetration difficulties (see **Table 11.10**; Nusbaum, Braxton, & Strayhorn, 2005).

## Causes of Sexual Dysfunctions

Integrated causal models for sexual dysfunctions have been proposed, and a commonly cited one is in **Figure 11.2** (Janssen, 2011; Nobre, 2010; Wiegel, Scepkowski, & Barlow, 2006). People with dysfunctional sexual performance respond to sexual demands in several negative ways. A person may expect bad things to happen, such as anxiety, lack of erection, or pain. The person may then focus on failure to perform rather than enjoyment of the experience, feel helpless or threatened in sexual situations, and avoid many sexual interactions (McCall & Meston, 2007). Avoiding sexual experiences may not allow a person to experience or practice positive sexual interactions. A cycle is thus created that leads to anxiety, lack of control, expectation of failure, and more avoidance.

Causal factors for sexual dysfunction have also been organized along a "balancing scale" that tilts toward successful or dysfunctional sexual performance (see **Figure 11.3**) (Barlow, 2007; Wincze, 2009). This model includes various biological and psychological risk factors, the presence of which can "tilt" the scale toward one end or another. A person who is depressed, who has negative interactions with a partner, who does not enjoy sexual activity, and who has certain medical conditions may have a certain sexual dysfunction. Douglas and Stacy's sexual experience became dominated by a new, uncomfortable environment that involved exhaustion from child care.

## Prevention of Sexual Dysfunctions

Prevention of sexual dysfunctions has focused primarily on *relapse prevention* with couples. Much of this involves booster sessions or other methods to help couples continue to practice psychological treatment techniques for sexual dysfunction and/or manage comorbid physical or psychological problems (Wincze, 2009). Successful prevention of later problems during sex will continue

## Table 11.10

### Prevalence of Sexual Concerns among White, African American, and Asian American Women

| Sexual concerns | White | African American | Asian American |
|---|---|---|---|
| Lack of interest in sex | 89 | 84 | 72 |
| Difficulty having orgasm | 87 | 79 | 72 |
| Vaginal lubrication | 76 | 63 | 74 |
| Lack of sex appeal | 72 | 62 | 47 |
| Sexual pain | 72 | 77 | 69 |
| Unsatisfied sexual needs | 69 | 73 | 54 |
| Need sex information | 65 | 70 | 55 |
| Desires different than partner's | 62 | 53 | 51 |
| Contraception, family planning, fertility | 62 | 73 | 48 |
| Inability to have orgasm | 61 | 60 | 61 |
| HIV/AIDS | 52 | 76 | 54 |
| Safe sex/sexually transmitted diseases | 52 | 68 | 51 |
| Partner sexual difficulties | 49 | 41 | 41 |
| Difficulty inserting penis | 48 | 44 | 56 |
| Thinking too much about sex | 39 | 44 | 37 |
| Adult sexual coercion | 36 | 46 | 21 |
| Adult emotional/physical maltreatment | 36 | 32 | 22 |
| Childhood emotional/ physical maltreatment | 34 | 36 | 19 |
| Want to have/have had an affair | 34 | 52 | 21 |
| Hard to control sexual urges | 30 | 32 | 25 |
| Sexual orientation | 25 | 28 | 29 |
| Sexual interest in women | 20 | 23 | 20 |
| Childhood sexual coercion | 17 | 20 | 12 |
| Wish to be opposite sex | 16 | 14 | 15 |
| Sexually abusive towards others | 15 | 4 | 8 |

Numbers are percentages. From Nusbaum, M. R., Braxton, L., & Strayhorn, G. (2005). The sexual concerns of African Americans, Asian Americans, and white women seeking routine gynecological care. *Journal of the American Board of Family Medicine, 18*(3), 173, Table 2. Reprinted by permission of the American Board of Family Medicine.

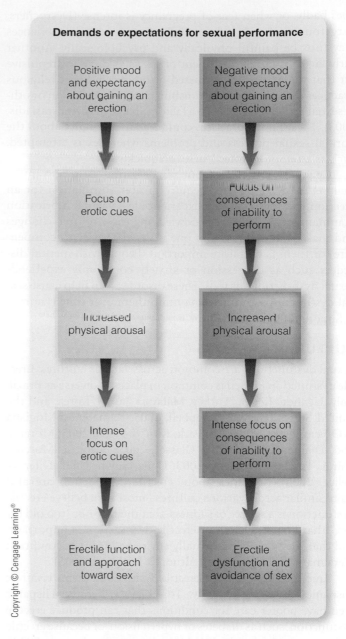

Copyright © Cengage Learning®

**FIGURE 11.2** MODEL OF ERECTILE DYSFUNCTION

to require effort from both sexual partners as well as good communication. Constant pressure from one partner is not productive and should be avoided (McCarthy & McDonald, 2009).

## INTERIM SUMMARY

► Biological risk factors for sexual dysfunctions commonly include illnesses and legal and illegal substances.

► Psychological risk factors for sexual dysfunctions include worry during performance, marital problems, traumatic early sexual experiences, strict family practices regarding sex, and poor sexual knowledge.

► An integrated causal approach to sexual dysfunctions likely involves a combination of biological events and expectations that negative events will occur during sex.

▶ Preventing sexual dysfunctions primarily involves relapse prevention after a couple completes treatment.

## REVIEW QUESTIONS

1. What biological risk factors may influence sexual dysfunctions?
2. What psychological risk factors may influence sexual dysfunctions?
3. What is the spectator role?
4. How might a "balancing scale" help us understand sexual dysfunctions?
5. How might one help a couple prevent future episodes of sexual dysfunction?

# Sexual Dysfunctions: Assessment and Treatment

## Assessment of Sexual Dysfunctions

Sexual dysfunctions involve many psychological and medical ingredients, so a comprehensive assessment is important. A full health assessment should also precede a psychological one to rule out or medically address any physical problem.

### INTERVIEWS

Interviews for people with sexual dysfunctions must be done carefully given the highly sensitive nature of the material being covered. Important areas to cover during an interview include sexual history, knowledge, beliefs, desires, and practices. Other relevant information would necessarily involve relationship issues such as marital conflict, medical history and current medications, stress, lifestyle changes, comorbid psychological problems such as depression, and goals for treatment (Wincze,

2009). The interview should also help build rapport with clients who may find such discussions difficult.

### QUESTIONNAIRES

Self-report questionnaires with respect to sexual dysfunctions generally surround issues of sexual satisfaction, arousal, anxiety, preferences, attitudes, and knowledge (Malatesta & Adams, 2004). These measures are useful but should only be used in conjunction with other assessment measures because self-report may be biased. Common self-report questionnaires for sexual dysfunctions include the following.

- *Derogatis Sexual Functioning Inventory* (Meston & Derogatis, 2002)
- *Female Sexual Desire Questionnaire* (Goldhammer & McCabe, 2011)
- *Female Sexual Function Index* (Wiegel, Meston, & Rosen, 2005)
- *International Index of Erectile Function* (Rosen, Cappelleri, & Gendrano, 2002)
- *Male Sexual Health Questionnaire* (Rosen et al., 2007)
- *Sexual Interest and Desire Inventory* (Sills et al., 2005)

Sample items from the Female Sexual Function Index are listed in **Table 11.11**.

### SELF-MONITORING

Couples may also record information about their daily sexual history. This could involve descriptions of sexual activity, degree of desire or arousal, type of affectionate behaviors, orgasm frequency and quality, satisfaction with the sexual experience, and emotional states and thoughts about the sexual experience (Malatesta & Adams, 2004). Monitoring information from both partners is important and can be compared to see if large discrepancies exist. Self-monitoring is obviously used instead of direct observation by others given the sensitive nature of the behavior. A therapist's observations of other relevant variables such as marital communication can be important, however (Litzinger & Gordon, 2005).

### PHYSIOLOGICAL ASSESSMENT

Physiological assessment of sexual dysfunctions overlaps to some degree with procedures we mention later for paraphilic disorders, such as the *penile plethysmograph*. Physiological assessment of sexual dysfunctions remains underdeveloped, but a common strategy for assessing erectile disorder is *nocturnal penile testing*. Erections during sleep are monitored physiologically because no sexual anxiety or demands for performance are present. If a man continues to have erectile difficulties during sleep, he may be diagnosed with erectile disorder. If erections occur without difficulty during

| | Successful sexual functioning | Dysfunctional sexual functioning |
|---|---|---|
| **Psychological factors** | ▶ Good emotional health<br>▶ Attraction toward partner<br>▶ Positive attitude toward partner<br>▶ Positive sex attitude<br>▶ Focus on pleasure<br>▶ Newness<br>▶ Good self-esteem<br>▶ Comfortable environment for sex<br>▶ Flexible attitude toward sex | ▶ Depression or PTSD<br>▶ Lack of partner attraction<br>▶ Negative attitude toward partner<br>▶ Negative attitude toward sex<br>▶ Focus on performance<br>▶ Routine, habit<br>▶ Poor self-esteem<br>▶ Uncomfortable environment for sex<br>▶ Rigid, narrow attitude toward sex |
| **Physical factors** | ▶ No smoking<br>▶ No excess alcohol<br>▶ No medications that affect sex<br>▶ Good physical health<br>▶ Regular, appropriate exercise<br>▶ Good nutrition | ▶ Smoking<br>▶ Too much alcohol<br>▶ Antihypertensive medication/drugs<br>▶ Poor physical health<br>▶ Heart and blood-flow problems<br>▶ Diabetes |

**FIGURE 11.3** POSITIVE AND NEGATIVE FACTORS THAT AFFECT SEXUAL FUNCTIONING

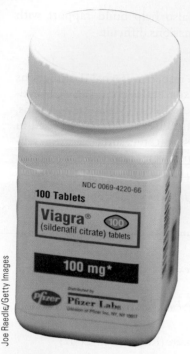

Viagra and related drugs have helped many men with erectile dysfunction.

sleep, then psychological factors such as performance anxiety may need to be addressed. Nocturnal penile testing can be done at a sleep laboratory or using a portable device at home (Elhanbly, Elkholy, Elbayomy, Elsaid, & Abdelgaber, 2009)

## Biological Treatment of Sexual Dysfunctions

Medical treatment for sexual dysfunctions has concentrated most on drugs for erectile disorder. The most well known of these drugs is *sildenafil*, which helps to increase blood flow to the penis and thus to form an erection. Sildenafil—sold under the brand names Viagra, Levitra, and Cialis—comes in pill form, but other drugs may be injected directly into the penis to cause the same effect. The most common is *prostaglandin E*1, which relaxes muscles in the penis to assist an erection.

Other methods to improve erectile quality include *implants* surgically inserted into the penis. These implants may be inflatable, semirigid, or continually rigid to maintain erections, but problems include awkwardness and possible damage to the penis (Liechty & Quallich, 2008). Other surgical procedures may be done as well to correct penile blood flow problems. An alternative to surgery is a *vacuum system* in which a tube is placed around the penis, and a pump helps draw blood into the penis (Hoang, Romero, & Hairston, 2011). The erection is then maintained by placing an elastic band at the base of the penis. Such a device may also be used to enhance clitoral blood flow in women (Bargiota, Dimitropoulos, Tzortzis, & Koukoulis, 2011). Medications remain the primary biological intervention for erectile difficulty, but these surgical and manual methods are also effective.

Other drugs, especially antidepressants, have been used for sexual dysfunctions such as premature ejaculation (Zaazaa et al., 2012). Vaginal lubricants and hormone replacement therapy may be useful for women with painful intercourse (Hickey, Elliot, & Davison, 2012). Medical problems that result in painful sexual intercourse should be resolved as well. People with low sexual desire may receive *testosterone, estrogen,* or *androgen* hormonal treatment (Gass et al., 2011; Maggi, 2012).

## Psychological Treatments of Sexual Dysfunctions

Medical approaches to addressing sexual dysfunctions are often accompanied by psychological approaches, or *sex therapy*. Sex therapy involves different techniques to enhance performance

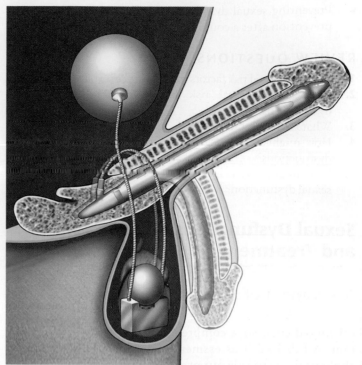

Penile implants help the male organ become rigid for penetration during sex.

during sex. A common technique for premature ejaculation is the **stop–start procedure** (Rowland & Cooper, 2011). The penis is stimulated by the man or a partner until an erection occurs and ejaculation seems close. The top of the penis is then pinched to suppress stimulation, prevent ejaculation, and allow the erection to be maintained longer. As the man becomes more accustomed to controlling his excitement, intercourse begins slowly so ejaculation can be further delayed. In this way, more lengthy intercourse can occur.

For men and women with low sexual desire, sex therapy may consist of initially banning sexual contact and rebuilding a couple's sexual repertoire. This is called **sensate focus** (Crowe, 2012). A couple may be asked to refrain from sex and caress and massage each other only in nonsexual areas—avoiding breasts and genital areas. Both partners can thus become more relaxed and focused on pleasure, and the pressure to perform in intercourse eases. As therapy progresses, partners guide each other's hands to different areas of the body that give the most pleasure for that person. Verbal communication about likes and dislikes during this process is important as well.

Intercourse is gradually reintroduced to the intimacy process as a couple becomes more experienced in relaxing and giving pleasure to a partner during sex. *Fantasy training* and exposure to erotic material to increase the range of sexual fantasies a partner may have during sex may also be done with sensate focus (ter Kuile, Both, & van Lankveld, 2010). Douglas and Stacy were relieved by the initial ban on intercourse, and fantasy training helped start them toward a path of better sensuality.

Joe Raedle/Getty Images

Nucleus Medical Art, Inc./Getty Images

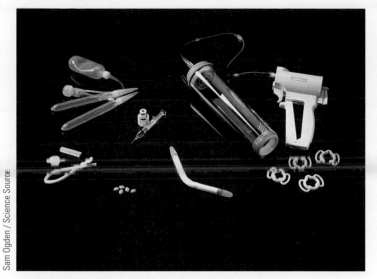

Various treatments for erectile disorder are pictured here, including a penile vacuum (right). It stimulates blood flow into the penis, and the rings are used to keep the blood in.

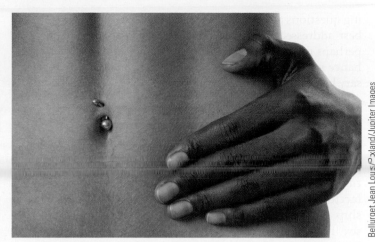

Sensate focus is a sex therapy technique to enhance sexual pleasure for a couple and reduce sexual dysfunction.

**Masturbation training** may also be useful for people with orgasmic problems. A partner practices effective masturbation and stimulation so orgasm is enhanced and brought about more quickly (van Lankveld, 2009). Specific areas of stimulation that help produce orgasm, such as clitoral stimulation, are explored and can then be extended to intercourse with a partner to hopefully bring about orgasm at that time.

Pain during intercourse may be addressed in various ways as well. Psychological treatment generally focuses on initially prohibiting intercourse, gradually inserting dilators to increase vaginal size, practicing relaxation training, and using *Kegel exercises* to strengthen the vaginal area (Cacchioni & Wolkowitz, 2011). Kegel exercises may involve inserting a finger into the vagina and then systematically squeezing and releasing the vaginal muscles. Vaginal lubricants during this process may be helpful as well.

Psychological approaches for sexual problems may also target related issues such as marital conflict, exhaustion, trauma, depression, anxiety, and excessive substance use. Sex may be scheduled at relaxing and convenient times and places, such as early in the morning or at a hotel away from the demands of children. This was especially helpful for Douglas and Stacy. Increasing sexual knowledge between partners, enhancing safe-sex practices, and reducing sexual myths and avoidance are important as well (Wincze, 2009). Couples may appreciate that either partner can initiate sex, that condom use is acceptable, and that orgasm is not always the final product of intercourse.

## What If I or Someone I Know Has a Sexual Dysfunction?

If you feel you or someone you know may have a sexual dysfunction, then consulting with a physician and clinical psychologist who specializes in these problems may be best. Some screen

### Table 11.11

#### Female Sexual Function Index

| Question | Response options |
|---|---|
| Over the past 4 weeks, how often did you feel sexual desire or interest? | 5 = Almost always or always<br>4 = Most times (more than half the time)<br>3 = Sometimes (about half the time)<br>2 = A few times (less than half the time)<br>1 = Almost never or never |
| Over the past 4 weeks, how confident were you about becoming sexually aroused during sexual activity or intercourse? | 0 = No sexual activity<br>5 = Very high confidence<br>4 = High confidence<br>3 = Moderate confidence<br>2 = Low confidence<br>1 = Very low or no confidence |
| Over the past 4 weeks, when you had sexual stimulation or intercourse, how difficult was it for you to reach orgasm (climax)? | 0 = No sexual activity<br>1 = Extremely difficult or impossible<br>2 = Very difficult<br>3 = Difficult<br>4 = Slightly difficult<br>5 = Not difficult |
| Over the past 4 weeks, how often did you experience discomfort or pain during vaginal penetration? | 0 = Did not attempt intercourse<br>1 = Almost always or always<br>2 = Most times (more than half the time)<br>3 = Sometimes (about half the time)<br>4 = A few times (less than half the time)<br>5 = Almost never or never |

ing questions are listed in **Table 11.12**. Sexual dysfunctions are best addressed by a comprehensive medical examination and perhaps medication as well as psychological procedures to enhance sexual performance. Marital therapy may also be necessary before pursuing a sexual solution.

## Long-Term Outcomes for People with Sexual Dysfunctions

We mentioned that some sexual conditions such as erectile problems worsen over time. Other problems such as premature ejaculation may get better over time, and sexual satisfaction often improves as couples mature in their relationship. Other problems, such as pain or lack of interest during sex, may not change much over time (Frank, Mistretta, & Will, 2008).

Many people do, however, respond positively to medical and psychological treatment approaches for sexual dysfunctions. About 52 percent of women who receive testosterone treatment for low sexual desire improve; some effectiveness has also been found for men (Isidori et al., 2005; Kingsberg et al., 2007). Men with erectile disorder using sildenafil (50–100 mg) achieve a strong erection in 35 to 80 percent of cases compared with 0 to 22 percent for placebo. Success rates are similar for men across racial and ethnic groups (Padma-Nathan, 2006). Effects of sildenafil may be enhanced by sex therapy (Aubin, Heiman, Berger, Murallo, & Yung-Wen, 2009).

Psychotherapy for premature ejaculation seems effective for about 64 percent of men, but relapse rates are high (Althof, 2005). More than 80 percent of women can achieve orgasm through masturbation training, but only 20 to 60 percent achieve orgasm with a partner during intercourse (Both & Laan, 2003). Many people drop out of treatment for sexual dysfunctions, however. Much more treatment outcome research is needed with respect to sexual dysfunctions.

Positive outcome in sex therapy may relate to good relationship quality, high partner motivation for improvement, lack of serious comorbid disorders such as depression, physical

### Table 11.12

**Screening Questions for Sexual Dysfunction**

| |
|---|
| Do you or someone you know have difficulty in sexual relations with others? |
| Do you or someone you know have little or no desire for sexual intercourse? |
| Do you or someone you know avoid sex (or conversations about sex) because of performance worries? |
| Do you or someone you know have trouble achieving an orgasm during intercourse? |
| Do you or someone you know experience pain during intercourse? |

Copyright © Cengage Learning®

attraction between partners, and treatment compliance (Balon & Segraves, 2009). Couples like Douglas and Stacy who work on problems together, and do so in a warm, supportive way, seem better destined for success during sex.

### INTERIM SUMMARY

▶ Interviews for sexual dysfunctions cover sexual history, knowledge, beliefs, desires, and practices as well as relevant relationship issues.

▶ Self-report questionnaires are useful for assessing sexual dysfunctions and focus on sexual satisfaction, arousal, anxiety, preferences, attitudes, and knowledge.

▶ Self-monitoring is sometimes used as an assessment technique for sexual dysfunction.

▶ Physiological assessment of sexual dysfunctions includes nocturnal penile testing and other methods.

▶ Medical treatments for sexual dysfunctions include drugs such as Viagra, implants, vaginal lubricants, and hormone therapy.

**CONTINUUM FIGURE 11.4** Continuum of Sexual Behavior and Paraphilic Disorders

| | Normal | Mild |
|---|---|---|
| **Emotions** | Regular arousal and desire to have typical sexual behavior. | Mild physical arousal when thinking about unusual sexual behavior. |
| **Cognitions** | Thoughts about typical sexual behavior. | Thoughts about unusual sexual behavior. |
| **Behaviors** | Engaging in typical sexual behavior. | Surfing Internet sites that cater to unusual sexual behavior. |

▶ Psychological interventions for sexual dysfunctions concentrate on sex therapy to address premature ejaculation, orgasmic problems, pain, and marital relationships.

▶ People with sexual dysfunctions generally respond well to treatment, especially if the couple is attracted to one another, communicates well, and complies with treatment.

### REVIEW QUESTIONS

1. What topics might be covered when using interviews and self-report measures to assess sexual dysfunctions?
2. How can self-monitoring and physiological assessment help a clinician know more about sexual dysfunctions?
3. What medications are available to treat sexual dysfunctions?
4. Describe the start-stop procedure, sensate focus, and masturbation training.
5. What is the long-term outcome for people with sexual dysfunctions?

## Normal Sexual Desires, Paraphilias, and Paraphilic Disorders: What Are They?

Many people engage in regular sexual activity with no problem but have unusual fantasies and desires during sex. These fantasies are usually harmless and do not indicate a clinical problem. Other people have odd sexual fantasies and find a consenting partner to help fulfill the fantasies. If sexual behavior is odd but consensual and legal and causes no harm or distress, then the behavior is considered normal. Many couples mutually agree to engage in sexual "games" that may involve domination, peculiar attire, tickling, videotaping, and other irregular activities (see **Figure 11.4**). Some of these activities can become quite frequent and fervent. **Paraphilias** are preferential, intense, and/or persistent sexual interests that may be odd but are not a mental disorder.

Other people experience unusual sexual fantasies and behaviors that consume much of their time and energy. Someone might spend hours at work on Internet sex sites, spend all day at an adult bookstore, have urges to do something unusual or illegal, and constantly wonder what it would be like to have sex with different partners. These fantasies and behaviors are not necessarily abnormal but do verge on becoming a problem if work, interpersonal relationships, or financial or legal standing are threatened.

For other people, sexual fantasies can become quite distressing, central to their life, or linked to illegal or harmful behaviors that interfere with work, concentration, or regular sexual relationships. **Paraphilic disorders** include problems arising from sexual behavior or fantasies involving highly unusual activities (APA, 2013). A person's Internet role-playing may not necessarily rise to the level of a mental disorder. If he spent so much time satisfying his urges he was arrested for an illegal activity or was distressed by obsessive fantasies, however, then he may have a paraphilic disorder.

## Paraphilic Disorders: Features and Epidemiology

We next summarize major features of the most commonly diagnosed paraphilic disorders. Each paraphilia has a particular focus of sexual fantasies, urges, or behaviors, or paraphilia (**Table 11.13**).

### Exhibitionistic Disorder

The particular focus of **exhibitionistic disorder**, or *exhibitionism* or *flashing* or *indecent exposure,* is exposing one's genitals to strangers who do not expect the exposure (see **Table 11.14**; APA, 2013). Tom exposed himself to unsuspecting teenagers in the hope of getting a strong reaction. Paraphilic disorders such as exhibitionism generally involve acting on one's fantasies or having significant distress or interpersonal problems because of the fantasies. Tom acted on his fantasies *and* was quite distressed by them.

A person with exhibitionism will often expose himself to others and then quickly flee the scene. Usually no actual sexual

| Moderate | Paraphilic Disorder — less severe | Paraphilic Disorder — more severe |
|---|---|---|
| Strong physical arousal when fantasizing about unusual sexual behavior. | Intense physical arousal when fantasizing about or engaging in unusual sexual behavior. | Extreme physical arousal when fantasizing about or engaging in unusual sexual behavior. |
| Sexual fantasies that lead to urges toward highly unusual sexual behaviors. | Sexual fantasies about unusual sexual behavior that become central to a person's life and create distress. | Obsession-like sexual fantasies about unusual sexual behavior that cause great distress. |
| Spending substantial time on the Internet or in adult bookstores, especially regarding unusual sexual behavior. | Inability to concentrate or have regular sexual relationships. Engaging in some unusual sexual behavior. | Engaging in or being arrested for highly unusual sexual behavior such as inappropriate contact with a child. |

# CASE: Tom

**Tom** was 36 years old when he was court-referred for therapy following an arrest for indecent exposure. The incident had occurred 2 months earlier when Tom parked his car on a street near a local high school. Three female teenagers walked by Tom's car and saw him masturbating in the front seat. One teenager grabbed her cell phone and took a picture of Tom's license plate as he quickly drove away. The police were called and, based on the picture of the license plate, arrived at Tom's home to make the arrest. A plea arrangement allowed Tom to stay out of jail but with considerable community service, registration as a sex offender, and court-mandated therapy.

Tom's therapist asked him to provide a history of behavior that led up to the arrest. Tom initially said he always had "kinky" sexual ideas, even from

adolescence, but had never before acted on them. He often daydreamed and fantasized about being a powerful male figure that was highly attractive to women, particularly adolescents and young women. His fantasies ventured into many different scenarios. One fantasy involved watching young women, including teenagers, undress before him or wear schoolgirl outfits that made them look young. Another fantasy involved sadomasochistic interactions with young women in which he controlled

their behavior and attire. Still another key fantasy involved his exposure to young women, who would then (in his fantasy) become very attracted to him and wish to spend time with him.

Tom said he had dominating women in his life, including his mother and teachers, and that his personality was actually shy and meek. He thought his fantasies compensated for a deep sense of inadequacy he often felt around women, although he appeared to be socially skilled and not easily intimidated. Tom said his sex life with his wife was normal, that he had been married 8 years, that he had one child, and that neither his wife nor anyone else was aware of his secret fantasies. He reportedly had no desire to actually practice his fantasies until about 4 years ago.

When asked what changed 4 years ago, Tom said he became more involved

## Table 11.13

### Major Paraphilic Disorders

| Paraphilic disorder | Focus of arousal |
| --- | --- |
| Exhibitionistic | Exposing genitals to strangers |
| Fetishistic | Nonliving object or nongenital body part |
| Frotteuristic | Physical contact with a non-consenting person |
| Pedophilic | Children |
| Sexual Masochism and Sexual Sadism | Humiliation from or to others |
| Transvestic | Dressing as the opposite gender |
| Voyeuristic | Secretly watching others undress or engage in sex |

## Table 11.14

### DSM-5 Exhibitionistic Disorder

A. Over a period of at least 6 months, recurrent and intense sexual arousal from the exposure of one's genitals to an unsuspecting person, as manifested by fantasies, urges, or behaviors.

B. The individual has acted on these sexual urges with a nonconsenting person, or the sexual urges or fantasies cause clinically significant distress or impairment in social, occupational, or other important areas of functioning.

Specify if sexually aroused by exposing genitals to prepubertal children, mature individuals, or both. Specify if in a controlled environment or in full remission.

American Psychiatric Association. (2013). *Diagnostic and statistical manual of mental disorders* (5th ed.). Arlington, VA: American Psychiatric Association.

caught, however, as Tom was, an arrest is often made. Exhibitionism may also occur with *telephone scatalogia*, or sexual arousal via obscene telephone calls to others (Langstrom, 2010).

## Fetishistic Disorder

The particular focus of **fetishistic disorder**, or *fetishism*, is nonliving objects or a nongenital body area to begin or enhance sexual arousal (see **Table 11.15**; APA, 2013). People

contact with others takes place. The person often leaves the scene to masturbate to fantasies that the stranger was sexually aroused by, or somehow enjoyed, the exposure. A person with exhibitionism may misinterpret the stranger's shock or surprise as sexual arousal (Murphy & Page, 2008). If the person is

in Internet chat rooms. He discovered various rooms that catered to his fantasies by allowing him to role-play and learn of others' fantasies that soon became his own. He found himself daydreaming more and more about exhibiting himself to young women, who would then be overwhelmed by his sexual prowess and become very attentive to him. He role-played many versions of this scenario in Internet chat rooms, found websites largely devoted to his fantasies, subscribed to services that provided pictures related to his fantasies, and even found other people in his area who had similar fantasies and who guided him about the best places to act out his fantasies.

Tom eventually confessed about numerous occasions where he had surreptitiously exposed himself before young women. The exposure was so covert the

women did not even know what Tom had done. Tom would then go to a hidden place and masturbate to a fantasy that the young woman had seen his genitals and that she longed to be with him.

Tom engaged in a much more risky exposure on the day of his arrest. He was actively seeking a reaction from one of the teenagers, after which he planned to drive home and masturbate to a fantasy that she was sexually aroused by his presence. Tom was now mortified about what happened and worried about the effect of his arrest on his marriage and career. Tom said he was deeply ashamed of what he had done and wished he could be free of his constant sexual fantasies. He sobbed and said he would do anything to make sure something like this incident would never happen again.

## What Do You Think?

1. How are Tom's fantasies and behaviors different from a typical adult? Would any of his behaviors seem normal in a certain context or for someone of a certain age?

2. What external events and internal factors might be responsible for Tom's fantasies and behaviors?

3. What are you curious about regarding Tom?

4. Does Tom remind you in any way of yourself or someone you know? How so?

5. How might Tom's fantasies and behaviors affect his life in the future?

---

with fetishism often need certain types of clothing or other objects nearby when masturbating or engaging in intercourse. The objects allow the person to become excited during sexual activity, such as obtaining an erection, and to achieve orgasm. Many people with fetishism prefer female underclothes, stockings, high heels or boots, lingerie, or clothing fabrics such as rubber, leather, nylon, or silk. The fetish object is usually held or seen or smelled during masturbation to achieve excitement, or a partner may be asked to wear the fetish object (Kafka, 2010a). Fetishism is not a

mental disorder unless a person is greatly upset by the urges or behaviors or until the behavior interferes with sexual or other areas of functioning. A nondistressed husband whose wife happily wears high heels to bed would not be diagnosed with fetishism. If the husband shoplifted certain shoes for

© Studio 10ne/Shutterstock.com

People with fetishism are sometimes drawn to women's shoes.

### Table 11.15

#### DSM-5 Fetishistic Disorder

A. Over a period of at least 6 months, recurrent and intense sexual arousal from either the use of nonliving objects or a highly specific focus on nongenital body part(s), as manifested by fantasies, urges, or behaviors.

B. The fantasies, sexual urges, or behaviors cause clinically significant distress or impairment in social, occupational, or other important areas of functioning.

C. The fetish objects are not limited to articles of clothing used in cross-dressing (as in transvestic disorder) or devices specifically designed for the purpose of tactile genital stimulation (e.g., vibrator).

Specify if in a controlled environment or in full remission.
Specify if body part, nonliving object, or other.

American Psychiatric Association. (2013). *Diagnostic and statistical manual of mental disorders* (5th ed.). Arlington, VA: American Psychiatric Association.

---

**Table 11.16**

### DSM-5 Frotteuristic Disorder

A. Over a period of at least 6 months, recurrent and intense sexual arousal from touching or rubbing against a non-consenting person, as manifested by fantasies, urges, or behaviors.

B. The individual has acted on these sexual urges with a nonconsenting person, or the sexual urges or fantasies cause clinically significant distress or impairment in social, occupational, or other important areas of functioning.

Specify if in a controlled environment or in full remission.

American Psychiatric Association. (2013). *Diagnostic and statistical manual of mental disorders* (5th ed.). Arlington, VA: American Psychiatric Association.

---

masturbation or for his wife to wear to bed, however, a diagnosis of fetishism might be warranted.

## Frotteuristic Disorder

The particular focus of **frotteuristic disorder**, or *frotteurism*, is physical contact with someone who has not given consent (see **Table 11.16**; APA, 2013). Physical contact often involves rubbing against someone in a very crowded place such as a bar, subway train, or sidewalk. A person with frotteurism may engage in light contact such as "accidentally" rubbing his genitals against another person, or may engage in more extensive contact such as groping a woman's breasts and buttocks. The person often flees the scene quickly and may masturbate to a fantasy of having a long-term relationship with the victim (Langstrom, 2010). The person will likely not see the victim again unless he is caught at the time of the incident.

## Pedophilic Disorder

The particular focus of **pedophilic disorder**, sometimes called *pedophilia*, is sexual attraction to a child (see **Table 11.17**; APA, 2013). Pedophilic disorder is not necessarily the same thing as *child molestation*. Someone who molests children may not be attracted to children but may have sexual contact with them because he lacks partners his age, wishes to hurt the child's parents, is intoxicated, or has cognitive or intellectual deficits (LeVay & Baldwin, 2012). Characteristics of those with pedophilic disorder do overlap to some degree with characteristics of those who molest children, however; both associate child sex with feelings of power, for example (Suchy, Whittaker, Strassberg, & Eastvold, 2009). The term *sex offender* is a legal one that refers to someone convicted of child sexual maltreatment, whether he has pedophilic disorder or not (Blanchard, 2010a).

Pedophilic acts involve behaviors such as observation, exposure, subtle physical contact, fondling, oral sex, and penetration (Quayle, 2011). The exact age at which someone is considered to be pedophilic is controversial but is currently defined as someone at least 16 years old and at least 5 years older than the victim. Pedophilic disorder may not apply to someone in late adolescence who has sex with someone aged 12 to 13 years but could apply if the sexual partner is younger. This remains controversial, however, because many youths have been identified as sexual offenders (Ostrager, 2010). Imagine a 20-year-old who has "consensual" sex with his 15-year-old girlfriend. Some might consider this pedophilic disorder, but others might not. Age-of-consent laws vary from state to state.

Many people with pedophilic disorder or those who molest children have a preferred target, such as girls aged 6 to 13 years who have not yet entered puberty. Many people with pedophilic

People with frotteurism prefer crowded places such as subways to seek victims.

© Alexander Becher/dpa/Corbis

AP Photo/W. A. Harewood

Genarlow Wilson was convicted of aggravated child molestation at the age of 17 years for having consensual oral sex with his 15-year-old girlfriend. He served 2 years in prison before the Georgia Supreme Court overturned his 10-year sentence, saying his crime "does not rise to the level of adults who prey on children."

## Table 11.17

### DSM-5 Pedophilic Disorder

A. Over a period of at least 6 months, recurrent, intense sexually arousing fantasies, sexual urges, or behaviors involving sexual activity with a prepubescent child or children (generally age 13 years or younger).

B. The individual has acted on these sexual urges, or the sexual urges or fantasies cause marked distress or interpersonal difficulty.

C. The individual is at least age 16 years and at least 5 years older than the child or children in Criterion A.

Specify if exclusive to children or nonexclusive, sexually attracted to males or females or both, and limited to incest. Specify if in a controlled environment or in full remission.

American Psychiatric Association. (2013). *Diagnostic and statistical manual of mental disorders* (5th ed.). Arlington, VA: American Psychiatric Association.

disorder target boys *and* girls, however, especially if victims under age 6 years are available (Levenson, Becker, & Morin, 2008). Those with pedophilic disorder may rationalize their behavior by believing sexual acts somehow benefit a child educationally or sensually (Gannon & Polaschek, 2006). John Mark Karr, the man who once claimed he killed JonBenét Ramsey, also claimed he was in love with the child.

Many people with pedophilic disorder are not distressed by their behavior and concentrate on young family members, especially daughters and nieces. Those with pedophilic disorder often "groom" a child by offering extensive attention and gifts, then demanding sexual favors in return. Others may even go as far as abducting children. Children are often threatened with loss of security if they disclose maltreatment to others (Quayle, 2011).

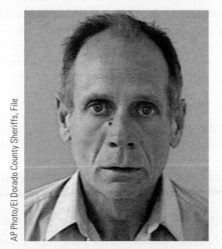

Phillip Garrido was arrested in 2009 and charged with kidnapping fifth-grader Jaycee Lee Dugard in 1990. He admits to fathering her two children during the 18 years he allegedly held her captive in his backyard.

People with pedophilic disorder may be subtyped as well along certain characteristics (from Cohen & Galynker, 2002, and McAnulty, Dillon, & Adams, 2004):

- *Preferred victim* (male, female, or both)
- *Relationship to victim* (family member/incestuous or nonfamily member/nonincestuous)
- *Sexual arousal* (to children only or to people of various ages)
- *Sexual orientation* (homosexual, heterosexual, or bisexual)
- *Aggressiveness* (presence or absence of cruelty during an act of pedophilic disorder)

## Sexual Masochism and Sexual Sadism

The particular focus of **sexual masochism** and **sexual sadism**, is a desire to be humiliated or made to suffer or to humiliate or to make suffer, respectively (see **Table 11.18**; APA, 2013). Sexual masochism involves desire to suffer during sexual activity, often in the form of bondage, pain, treatment as an infant (infantilism), extensive humiliation such as verbal abuse, or oxygen deprivation (*hypoxyphilia* or *asphyxiophilia*). Masochistic desires can be fulfilled during masturbation in the form of self-punishment or by involving others. The physical maltreatment sought by people with masochism can be severe and quite painful. Sexual sadism involves desire to inflict suffering on someone during sexual activity, often in the same forms of maltreatment described for masochism. Sadism is often about *controlling* an individual during sexual activity, and sadistic behavior is sometimes conducted toward someone with masochism (Powls & Davies, 2012).

Sadism and masochism can exist in one person (*sadomasochism*) who enjoys switching roles. Sadomasochistic acts can range in severity from mild slapping or tickling to moderate humiliation to severe pain or restraints to extreme rape, mutilation, or murder. Sadomasochistic acts can also involve children. Wolfgang Priklopil from Austria kidnapped 10-year-old

Wolfgang Priklopil allegedly kidnapped Natascha Kampusch when she was 10 years old and engaged in pedophilic and sadomasochistic acts with her during her 8 year imprisonment.

Natascha Kampusch and held her captive for 8 years in a make-shift dungeon as she referred to him as "master."

## Transvestic Disorder

The particular focus of **transvestic disorder**, or *transvestism*, is dressing as the opposite gender (see **Table 11.19**; APA, 2013). This disorder is often seen in males who dress as women and imagine themselves as females (*autogynephilia*). Transvestism differs from simple fetishism in that women's clothes are not necessary for sexual arousal, but rather help a person engage in the fantasy of being a woman. Cross-dressing in transvestism can be secret, such as wearing panties underneath male clothing, or obvious, such as a drag queen wearing a dress and makeup. Cross-dressing initially occurs for sexual excitement but may be done over time to reduce negative feelings such as anxiety or depression or to feel attractive (Blanchard, 2010b). Some men with transvestism become more uncomfortable with their own gender and may seek to become a woman physically (see later gender dysphoria section)

People with transvestism cross-dress for sexual excitement, sometimes in public.

David Westing/Getty Images

---

### Table 11.18

#### DSM-5 Sexual Masochism and Sexual Sadism

**Sexual Masochism Disorder**

A. Over a period of at least 6 months, recurrent and intense sexual arousal from the act of being humiliated, beaten, bound, or otherwise made to suffer, as manifested by fantasies, urges, or behaviors.

B. The fantasies, sexual urges, or behaviors cause clinically significant distress or impairment in social, occupational, or other important areas of functioning.

**Sexual Sadism Disorder**

A. Over a period of at least 6 months, recurrent and intense sexual arousal from the physical or psychological suffering of another person, as manifested by fantasies, urges, or behaviors.

B. The individual has acted on these sexual urges with a nonconsenting person, or the sexual urges or fantasies cause clinically significant distress or impairment in social, occupational, or other important areas of functioning.

Specify if in a controlled environment or in full remission.
Specify with asphyxiophilia.

American Psychiatric Association. (2013). *Diagnostic and statistical manual of mental disorders* (5th ed.). Arlington, VA: American Psychiatric Association.

---

## Voyeuristic Disorder

The particular focus of **voyeuristic disorder**, or *voyeurism*, is secretly watching others undress or engage in sexual activity without being seen (see **Table 11.20**; APA, 2013). People with voyeurism usually do not want sexual contact with the person(s) being watched. They become sexually aroused by the fact the watched persons placed themselves in such a vulnerable position and by the fact they themselves could be caught. The *risk* of the situation is thus most exciting for the person (Langstrom, 2010). A person with voyeurism often masturbates when watching others or does so later to the fantasy of having sex with the watched person(s).

## Atypical Paraphilic Disorders

Paraphilic disorders may also be diagnosed as *other specified paraphilic disorder* (APA, 2013). Atypical paraphilic disorders also involve some unusual focus of arousal during sexual activity as well as distress or impairment, but are quite rare (Kafka, 2010b). Some examples are listed in **Table 11.21.**

## Epidemiology of Paraphilic Disorders

Charting the exact prevalence of paraphilic disorders is difficult because the behaviors are usually secret and rarely brought to a therapist's attention. Harsh societal stigma against unusual sexual practices often forces people with paraphilic disorders to online activities (Rosenmann & Safir, 2006). Survey

Some researchers claim paraphilic disorders are deviations from common courtship practices.

Voyeurism may have been romanticized in the past but it involves substantial violation of privacy.

---

**Table 11.19**

### DSM-5 Transvestic Disorder

A. Over a period of at least 6 months, recurrent and intense sexual arousal from cross-dressing, as manifested by fantasies, urges, or behaviors.

B. The fantasies, sexual urges, or behaviors cause clinically significant distress or impairment in social, occupational, or other important areas of functioning.

Specify if in a controlled environment or in full remission. Specify if with fetishism or autogynephilia.

American Psychiatric Association. (2013). *Diagnostic and statistical manual of mental disorders* (5th ed.). Arlington, VA: American Psychiatric Association.

---

**Table 11.20**

### DSM-5 Voyeuristic Disorder

A. Over a period of at least 6 months, recurrent and intense sexual arousal from observing an unsuspecting person who is naked, in the process of disrobing, or engaging in sexual activity, as manifested by fantasies, urges, or behaviors.

B. The individual has acted on these sexual urges with a nonconsenting person, or the sexual urges or fantasies cause clinically significant distress or impairment in social, occupational, or other important areas of functioning.

C. The individual experiencing the arousal and/or acting on the urges is at least 18 years of age.

Specify if in a controlled environment or in full remission.

American Psychiatric Association. (2013). *Diagnostic and statistical manual of mental disorders* (5th ed.). Arlington, VA: American Psychiatric Association.

---

data about fantasies are often not helpful because people may answer questions in a socially desirable way and because simple fantasies are not enough to diagnose someone with a paraphilic disorder. The presence of a paraphilic disorder is thus usually determined when a person is arrested or seeks medical or psychological help. Fetishism is often identified only after an arrest for shoplifting items such as lingerie (Vinkers, De Beurs, Barendregt, Rinne, & Hoek, 2011).

Paraphilic disorders are much more common in men than women. Among men clinically evaluated for deviancy, unusual sexual behavior varies, but child molestation is the most prevalent interest (see **Table 11.22**). College men reportedly engaged in voyeurism (42 percent), frotteurism (35 percent), obscene telephone calls (8 percent), coercive sex (5 percent), and exhibitionism (2 percent). Furthermore, 3 percent reported sexual contact with girls under age 12 years, and 5 percent desired sex with such girls (Laws & O'Donohue, 2008; Templeman & Stinnett, 1991). Case reports from around the globe suggest

## Table 11.21

### Some Atypical Paraphilic Disorders

| Paraphilic disorder | Focus of arousal |
|---|---|
| Acrotomophilia/apotemnophilia | Amputees or being an amputee |
| Autagonistophilia | Being observed, filmed, or on stage |
| Autonepiophilia | Pretending to be a baby in diapers |
| Biastophilia | Surprise assault of another person |
| Gynemimetophilia | Sex-reassigned partners |
| Kleptophilia | Stealing from others |
| Klismaphilia | Enemas |
| Narratophilia | Erotic, "dirty" talk between a couple |
| Necrophilia | Contact with corpses |
| Olfactophilia | Odors from certain body areas |
| Partialism | Specific body part such as hair |
| Symphorophilia | Staging an accident and then watching |
| Troilism | Involvement of a third person in sex |
| Urophilia and coprophilia | Urine and feces |
| Zoophilia | Animals |

## Table 11.22

### Males Evaluated for Deviant Sexual Interest

| Deviant sexual interest | Prevalence |
|---|---|
| Child molestation | 35% |
| Voyeurism | 19% |
| Exhibitionism | 13% |
| Fetishism | 12% |
| Frotteurism | 10% |
| Transvestism | 6% |
| Sexual masochism and sexual sadism | 2% |

Source: Abel, G.G., & Osborn, C.A. (2000). The paraphilias. In M.G. Gelder, J.J. Lopez-Ibor, & N. Andreasen (Eds.), *New Oxford textbook of psychiatry* (pp. 897-913). New York: Oxford.

Another key characteristic of paraphilic disorders is that several may be present in a given individual (Kafka, 2010b). Tom had exhibitionism but also fantasies about watching teenagers and young women undress before him without their knowledge. Pedophilic disorder is also comorbid with other mental disorders such as anxiety-related, depressive, substance use, and personality disorders (Bogaerts, Daalder, Vanheule, Desmet, & Leeuw, 2008). Paraphilic disorders are sometimes associated with violent behavior. Acts of child molestation and pedophilic disorder can obviously involve serious damage or death to a child. Rape is sometimes considered sadistic as well, particularly if inflicting pain is sexually arousing for the rapist (Thornton, 2010; see **Box 11.2**).

### INTERIM SUMMARY

▶ People with paraphilic disorders experience sexual urges, fantasies, and behaviors that involve unusual stimuli and cause significant distress or impairment.

▶ Paraphilic disorders include exhibitionism, fetishism, frotteurism, pedophilic disorder, sexual masochism and sexual sadism, transvestism, and voyeurism.

▶ Paraphilic disorders are more common in men and typically begin in adolescence or young adulthood.

▶ Paraphilic disorders can be linked to other mental disorders and violence.

### REVIEW QUESTIONS

**1.** What are major features of a paraphilia?

**2.** What are major targets of sexual arousal in people with different paraphilic disorders?

**3.** What are subtypes of pedophilic disorder?

**4.** How might pedophilic disorder differ from child molestation?

**5.** What are common demographic and clinical features of paraphilic disorders?

that paraphilic disorders are not culture-specific. Paraphilic activity, especially among males, may be universally common (Ahlers et al., 2011).

Paraphilic disorders generally develop during adolescence and the early 20s, and most people with the problems, like Tom, are married (Langstrom, 2010). Pedophilic disorder likely begins in adolescence or young adulthood as many males with the disorder are incarcerated during those periods (Laws & O'Donohue, 2008). Most people with pedophilic disorder are heterosexual or bisexual; the percentage of people with pedophilic disorder who are homosexual is 9 to 40 percent (Hall & Hall, 2007). Many people with transvestism have wives who accept their husband's private behavior. Some people with transvestism, however, eventually engage in public cross-dressing and some do seek sex reassignment surgery (Blanchard, 2010b).

## BOX 11.2 Focus on Violence

### Rape

Acts of sadism can involve severe violence. One such behavior is rape, and rapists tend to fall into certain categories. Rape is not a mental disorder, but some rapists are motivated by anger toward women or anger in general and may have aspects of narcissism or antisocial personality disorder. About 5 to 10 percent of rapists enjoy the suffering they cause to their victims, and this may be categorized as *sadistic rape*. Many rapists are aroused by stimuli that suggest sexual force and control (Harris, Lalumiere, Seto, Rice, & Chaplin, 2012).

Rape can occur within marital or dating relationships. *Acquaintance* or *date rape* affects many female college students and often involves male acceptance of violence, heavy alcohol or other drug use, isolated situations, and miscommunication. Drugs such as *flunitrazepam* (Rohypnol or "roofies") may also be secretly passed on to women to induce a near state of unconsciousness and vulnerability to rape (Chapter 9; Basheer, 2011). Some males who engage in this kind of coercive sexual activity may eventually victimize people they do not know.

Only a fraction of all rapes are reported to police. Sometimes a woman is unsure a crime took place, as in the case of marital or date rape. Other women may take some responsibility for the attack (even though it was clearly not her fault) or be afraid of the consequences of reporting the attack. Whether a rape is reported or not, however, the psychological aftereffects are devastating and can include depression, posttraumatic stress, and anxiety disorders, sleep difficulties, and various sexual and interpersonal problems.

## Paraphilic Disorders: Causes and Prevention

The exact cause of paraphilic disorders is not known, but some biological predispositions and environmental risk factors may exist. We next discuss these causal factors.

### Biological Risk Factors for Paraphilic Disorders

Early and scattered data indicated some general genetic component to sexual deviancy and paraphilic disorders. Recent work, however, does not consistently support a strong genetic component. Genetics may instead influence factors *related* to sexual deviancy such as psychosocial deficits and violence (Hunter, Figueredo, Malamuth, & Becker, 2003). Genetics potentially affect the *reward deficiency syndrome* sometimes implicated in people with pedophilic disorder. Reward deficiency syndrome is a spectrum of impulsive, compulsive, or addictive behaviors such as intense sexual urges (Blum et al., 2012). Men with an extra Y chromosome have also been found to display more sexual deviancy than the general population (Briken, Habermann, Berner, & Hill, 2006).

Neuropsychological problems such as dementia may also lead to less inhibited and more compulsive and abnormal sexual behaviors (Chapter 14; Poetter & Stewart, 2012). This may be due to damage in temporal-limbic brain areas that influence sex drive and in frontal lobe brain areas that influence sexual inhibition (see **Figure 11.5**; Suchy et al., 2009). Hormonal changes may also exist in some people with paraphilic disorders, but consistent evidence remains elusive (Jordan, Fromberger, Stolpmann, & Muller, 2011).

Some personality characteristics seem common to people with paraphilic disorders. Examples include problems controlling sadness and anger as well as poor empathy, social, intimacy, and problem-solving skills (especially around women). Other traits include impulsivity, psychopathy, dependency, sense of inferiority and inadequacy, anger, neuroticism, paranoia, narcissism, and defensiveness (Cohen, Gans, et al., 2002; Cohen, McGeoch, et al., 2002; Curnoe & Langevin, 2002; Gacono, Meloy, & Bridges, 2000; Huprich, Gacono, Schneider, & Bridges, 2004; Kirsch & Becker, 2007; Lee, Jackson, Pattison, & Ward, 2002; Reid, Carpenter, Spackman, & Willes, 2008). Antisocial characteristics and antisocial personality disorder (Chapter 10) also characterize some people with sexual interest in children (Webb, Craissati, & Keen, 2007). One specific personality profile does not fit most people with pedophilic disorder or other paraphilic disorders, however.

### Environmental Risk Factors for Paraphilic Disorders
#### FAMILY CONTRIBUTIONS

Difficult family circumstances also contribute to paraphilic disorder development. People with paraphilic disorders often describe their early home lives as emotionally abusive (Jespersen, Lalumiere, & Seto, 2009). Such early problems could lead to poorly developed social, sexual, and intimacy skills because appropriate parental feedback was not given. People with paraphilic disorders also tend to come from large families and tend to be lower in birth order (Langevin, Langevin, & Curnoe, 2007; Ward & Beech, 2008).

Family factors also contribute to pedophilic disorder, and poor attachment and frequent and aggressive sexual activity within a family may predispose some toward sexual offenses (Whitaker et al., 2008). Contrary to popular belief, however, most people sexually maltreated as children do *not* generally go on to sexually maltreat children as adults (Putnam, 2003). On the other hand, people with pedophilic disorder do report being sexually maltreated as a child more so than control participants (Jespersen et al., 2009).

## LEARNING EXPERIENCES

Many paraphilic disorders begin with a learning experience in which a person associates sexual arousal or orgasm with an unusual object or situation or person. A teenager may have inadvertently and secretly noticed someone undressing and then became sexually aroused. His sexual arousal was classically conditioned with the voyeuristic act, and this association was later reinforced by masturbation and orgasm (Hofmann, 2012). Learning theory is likely a good explanation for some paraphilic disorder development, especially because paraphilic disorders occur more in males (who masturbate more). But learning theory cannot be the sole explanation for paraphilic disorders; if it were, then most people would have paraphilic disorders (LeVay & Baldwin, 2012). Paraphilic behaviors may also be reinforced by family members or others or the behaviors were learned as a way to reduce anxiety or escape from difficult life circumstances. Paraphilic disorders may become

a problem similar to obsessive-compulsive disorder in some cases (Chapter 5; Real, Montejo, Alonso, & Menchón, 2013).

Some contend paraphilic disorders may result when *courtship behaviors* are not properly expressed (Freund & Seto, 1998; Langstrom & Seto, 2006). Courtship among two people generally involves the following stages:

- Finding and evaluating a potential partner
- Communicating with the partner in a nonphysical way, such as smiling or talking
- Physical contact without sexual intercourse, such as kissing or petting
- Sexual intercourse

Voyeurism, exhibitionism, frotteurism, and *preferential rape* (when a man prefers rape more than a consenting partner) may link to disruptions in each of these four stages, respectively. A person with voyeurism may have difficulty finding potential sexual partners and resorts to secretive peeping. Such disruptions could be caused by faulty learning patterns or biological variables, but no definitive conclusions have been made.

## COGNITIVE DISTORTIONS

Many people with paraphilic disorders or those who commit sexual offenses have strong cognitive distortions or irrational beliefs about their peculiar sexual behavior (Snowden, Craig, & Gray, 2011). These beliefs allow a person to justify his behavior. Tom believed the surprised reactions of others to his genital exposure represented sexual arousal on their part or a desire to be with him. People who make obscene telephone calls often misinterpret angry reactions from others as sexual arousal.

Those with pedophilic disorder may also rationalize their behavior by claiming sexual acts somehow benefit a child. Those with pedophilic disorder tend to perceive a child victim as more interested in sexual acts than is actually so, take less responsibility for the acts compared with control participants, and often see children as sexual beings (Mihailides, Devilly, & Ward, 2004). People with fetishism may also misjudge their guilt and self-hatred as sexual arousal, which is temporarily reduced following orgasm (Hyde & DeLamater, 2011).

## CULTURAL AND EVOLUTIONARY FACTORS

Paraphilic disorders are present in different areas of the globe, but some paraphilias may be more prevalent

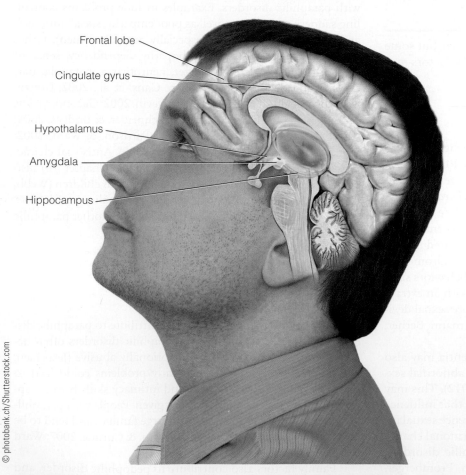

Frontal lobe

Cingulate gyrus

Hypothalamus

Amygdala

Hippocampus

© photobank.ch/Shutterstock.com

**FIGURE 11.5** MAJOR BRAIN AREAS IMPLICATED IN THE PARAPHILIC DISORDERS

in certain cultures that practice greater tolerance for such behavior. Masochism may be more common among Asian populations that emphasize humility and downplaying of success (Kovel, 2000). Cross-dressing has been prominently displayed in Filipino and American films, suggesting some level of cultural acceptance. American films such as *The Bird-cage* and *To Wong Foo, Thanks for Everything! Julie Newmar* display cross-dressing as a core, essential aspect of the plots. Sweeping generalizations regarding culture and paraphilic disorders cannot yet be made, however.

From an evolutionary standpoint, paraphilic disorders may be understood by considering parental investment in offspring. Females are generally more invested in type of offspring they bear, so they may be more discriminating in their sexual interactions and less promiscuous. Men, on the other hand, may be less invested in type of offspring they bear. Men may choose more variable mating strategies and tend toward promiscuity. A minority of men would thus be expected to engage in very deviant sexual behavior. A related evolutionary theory is that humans evolved from strict mating practices seen in animals by becoming more diverse in ways that males try to attract females (Quinsey, 2012; Troisi, 2003).

## Causes of Paraphilic Disorders

Integrated causal models for general paraphilic disorders have not been highly developed, although specific models for pedophilic disorder have been presented. Some researchers focus on neurodevelopmental models of pedophilic disorder in which early risk factors set the stage for other risk factors that then lead to pedophilic disorder. One important early risk factor is abnormal cortical development that leads to sexual hyperarousal and difficulty limiting sexual arousal to adults. Other early risk factors include sexual maltreatment as a child and poor attachment with parents.

These early risk factors could interact with later risk factors such as poor social and sexual skill development, learning experiences leading to deviant sexual arousal toward children, and cognitive distortions and maladaptive personality patterns. The latter may include antisocial tendencies that prevent stoppage of pedophilic acts. These risk factors collectively could help produce pedophilic disorder (Seto & Lalumiere, 2010; Ward & Beech, 2008).

✂ Biological predisposition toward sexual hyperarousal and poor self-regulation may be evident in other paraphilic disorders (Mitchell & Beech, 2011; Stinson, Becker, & Sales, 2008). This predisposition likely interacts with key environmental variables such as unusual sexual learning experiences, cognitive distortions, social skill deficits, paraphilic fantasies reinforced by masturbation, and attempts to suppress paraphilic fantasies, which ironically leads to more fantasies (see **Figure 11.6**). Tom was aroused by various stimuli and had several "successful" exposures without being caught. His acts were reinforced by subsequent masturbation and orgasm, and his attempts to stop his fantasies and behavior were unsuccessful. Much more research is needed regarding the development of specific paraphilic disorders like Tom's.

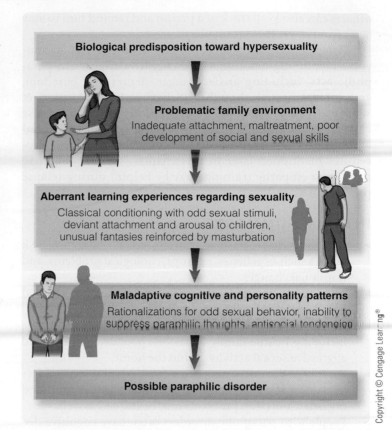

**FIGURE 11.6** SAMPLE DEVELOPMENTAL PATHWAY OF A PARAPHILIC DISORDER

## Prevention of Paraphilic Disorders

Information is scarce regarding prevention of paraphilic disorders despite the importance of this goal. Part of the reason for this is that people with paraphilic disorders often have multiple targets for their sexual desire and because sexual behaviors are usually secretive. Some have proposed guidelines for developing paraphilic disorder prevention programs, however. Prevention programs could focus on developing appropriate social and sexual skills in childhood and adolescence (Hyde & DeLamater, 2011). Youth might thus be better able to engage in prosocial same-gender and cross-gender interactions, understand sexual desire and adaptive sexual activities, and avoid sexism and violence. Interventions to improve family communication and problem-solving skills might be helpful as well.

Prevention of paraphilic disorders often comes in the form of *relapse prevention* after a person has been arrested or seeks help for his problem. Relapse prevention has primarily applied to people with pedophilic disorder or sexual offenders. A key aspect of relapse prevention training is to help a person identify situations that place him at high risk for committing a paraphilic act (Laws & O'Donohue, 2008). Examples of places to avoid might include high schools (pedophilic disorder), college dormitories (voyeurism), empty parking lots (exhibitionism), and crowded bars (frotteurism). Spouses or police officers can also keep track of a person and remind him to stay away from or escape certain places.

Relapse prevention of paraphilic disorders can also involve identifying emotional and cognitive triggers to paraphilic acts, including anxiety, anger, depression, boredom, and intense sexual thoughts (Schaffer, Jeglic, Moster, & Wnuk, 2010). The person is taught skills to manage these emotions and thoughts and to develop appropriate social and intimacy interactions with others. Other treatment procedures mentioned later in this chapter, such as cognitive therapy or empathy training, may be helpful during relapse prevention as well.

## INTERIM SUMMARY

▶ Paraphilic disorders may relate to certain biological risk factors such as genetics, neuropsychological problems, and hormonal changes.

▶ Those with paraphilic disorders may be introverted and have poor social and intimacy skills.

▶ Family variables may contribute to paraphilic disorders, including hostile family behaviors, poor attachment, and aggressive sexual activity within the home.

▶ Paraphilic disorders may come from learning experiences by associating a paraphilic focus with masturbation and orgasm. Courtship problems may be learned as well.

▶ People with paraphilic disorders often have cognitive distortions to justify or rationalize their sexual behavior.

▶ The cause of paraphilic disorders may involve hypersexuality, deviant sexual arousal, learning experiences, social skills deficits, and other important variables.

▶ Preventing paraphilic disorders may involve teaching appropriate social and sexual skills as well as relapse prevention after one has been arrested or seeks treatment.

## REVIEW QUESTIONS

1. What are major biological risk factors for paraphilic disorders?

2. What personality and family characteristics are evident in people with paraphilic disorders?

3. How might learning experiences and cognitive distortions contribute to paraphilic disorders?

4. What is an integrated theory for the cause of pedophilic disorder?

5. What strategies might be used to prevent paraphilic behavior?

# Paraphilic Disorders: Assessment and Treatment

## Assessment of Paraphilic Disorders

Sexual desire and arousal can be subjective, so assessing paraphilic disorders often depends on a person's self-report as well as questionnaires that focus on sexual interests. Physiological measurement has also been used as an assessment tool.

## INTERVIEWS

When interviewing someone with a possible paraphilic disorder, a clinician would likely focus on past and present sexual interests and activities, paraphilic acts, legal problems or sexual offenses, interactions with sexual partners, family and medical history, and comorbid problems like anxiety, depression, and substance use (Laws & O'Donohue, 2008). Other important issues include sense of empathy and responsibility to victims, impulsive and aggressive behavior, and level of insight about the wrongfulness of one's behavior (Craig & Beech, 2009). Interviews must be conducted with care given the delicate nature of the material being covered and the sometimes-hostile nature of an interviewee who is in legal trouble, such as a sex offender. Information from interviews often needs to be supported by legal officials, sexual partners, written documentation, or polygraph testing (Laws & O'Donohue, 2008).

## QUESTIONNAIRES

Questionnaires and screening instruments may be useful for assessing people with paraphilic disorders, but this method may be problematic if someone fears legal consequences or wants to appear socially desirable. Still, some inventories assess sexual history and unusual interests, hypersexuality, and sexually aggressive and pedophilic behavior. Common examples include the following:

- *Attraction to Sexual Aggression Scale* (revised) (Malamuth, 1998)
- *Clarke Sex History Questionnaire for Males* (revised) (Langevin & Paitich, 2002)
- *Multidimensional Assessment of Sex and Aggression* (revised) (Knight & Cerce, 1999)
- *Multiphasic Sex Inventory II* (Nichols & Molinder, 2000)
- *Sex Offender Treatment Intervention and Progress Scale* (McGrath, Lasher, & Cumming, 2012)

Other screening instruments focus on sexual offense histories. The *Screening Scale for Pedophilic Interests* (SSPI) is based on prior pedophilic behavior. The SSPI is useful for identifying people with pedophilic disorder who are likely to harm additional children (Seto & Lalumiere, 2010). Sample items from the SSPI are listed in **Table 11.23**.

## PHYSIOLOGICAL ASSESSMENT

Physiological assessment of paraphilic disorders is often called *phallometric testing*. A person is usually presented with slides or other stimuli such as audiotapes that represent different sexual acts or activities. Subsequent arousal in males is evaluated via *penile plethysmograph* or strain gauge, a rubber ring that measures circumference of the penis. Sexual response in females is measured by examining blood volume in the vaginal area via a *vaginal photoplethysmograph* or perineal (vaginal/anal) muscle function via a *myograph* or *perineometer* (Akerman & Beech, 2012). Sexual interest can also be examined by showing erotic slides or films and measuring how long a person attends to the material (Wilson, Abracen, Looman, Picheca, & Ferguson, 2011).

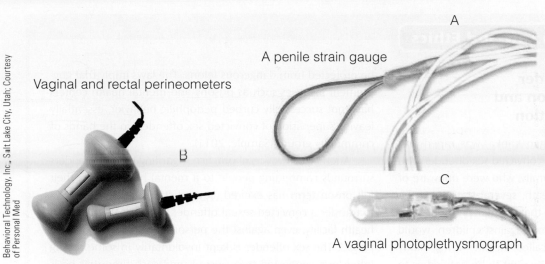

Vaginal and rectal perineometers

A penile strain gauge

A vaginal photoplethysmograph

Physiological assessment devices for sexual response.

Plethysmography can distinguish child sex offenders from nonoffenders and possibly rapists from nonoffenders. Problems with physiological assessment include finding the best stimuli for a particular person and a person's ability to fake responding by suppressing arousal or not paying attention to a sexual stimulus. Test-retest reliability of plethysmography is also limited (Akerman & Beech, 2012).

## Biological Treatment of Paraphilic Disorders

A key treatment of paraphilic disorders is pharmacotherapy to reduce testosterone levels in men and, thus, sexual desire, arousal, and unusual behavior. The main drugs to do so include *medroxyprogesterone acetate* (Depo-Provera), *leuprolide acetate* (Lupron), and *cyproterone acetate* (Cyproterone). These drugs reduce unusual sexual desires or dangerous sexual activity, but severe side effects and noncompliance to taking the medications are common (Gooren, 2011; Jordan et al., 2011).

### Table 11.23

| Items from the Screening Scale for Pedophilic Interests (SSPI) |
| --- |
| Offender has male victim (Yes = 2; No, female victims only = 0) |
| Offender has more than one victim (Yes = 1; No, single victim only = 0) |
| Offender has a victim aged 11 or younger (Yes = 1; No, child victims were 12 or 13 years old = 0) |
| Offender has an unrelated victim (Yes = 1; No, related victims only = 0) |

*Note.* Higher scores indicate greater risk of harming additional children.
Source: Seto, M.C., & Lalumiere, M.L. (2001). A brief screening scale to identify pedophilic interests among child molesters. *Sexual Abuse: A Journal of Research and Treatment*, 13, 15-25.

*Antidepressant medications*, especially selective serotonin reuptake inhibitors (Chapter 7), may reduce sexual urges and diminish performance or relieve depression or compulsive behaviors that trigger paraphilic acts (Garcia & Thibaut, 2011). Side effects and noncompliance can be problematic. Chemical *castration* by injecting certain drugs to eliminate production of testosterone has been advocated by some to treat people with violent sexual behavior, and the procedure does seem to reduce the rate of new offenses (Rice & Harris, 2011). The procedure is obviously a drastic one, however, and may not completely "cure" a person of all unusual sexual desires and behaviors. Programs to monitor sexual predators have thus become more common (see **Box 11.3**).

## Psychological Treatments of Paraphilic Disorders

Behavior therapy has also been explored to reduce paraphilic activities. Relevant forms of behavior therapy include *aversion treatment, covert sensitization*, and *orgasmic reconditioning*. **Aversion treatment** initially involves having a person view slides or stimuli most central to his paraphilic focus, such as a fetish object or pictures of children. The person then obtains an erection and masturbates, but this behavior is then punished via electric shock, foul odors, or something otherwise distasteful (Maggi, 2012). Sexual arousal toward the unusual stimulus may eventually decline but results in outcome studies are mixed. Aversion therapy may also take the form of *shame therapy* whereby a person, usually one with exhibitionism, engages in the paraphilic act before clinic staff members who offer no response or who laugh (Maletsky, 2003).

Related to aversion treatment is **covert sensitization**, which may involve having a person imagine grotesque scenes that remind him of possible negative consequences of his actions and that punish the paraphilic urge. A male with exhibitionism could imagine exposing himself to others from a car as well as subsequent scenes in which his car would not start, where people began to laugh and call the police, and where he felt utterly humiliated. Tom engaged in this technique with some success. A problem with covert sensitization, however, is that the procedure requires someone to imagine vivid scenes and be motivated enough to comply with a therapist's instructions. Positive scenes of escape or successful control of urges, such as a person imagining staying at work to avoid high schools in the afternoon, may thus be introduced as well (Laws & O'Donohue, 2008).

**Orgasmic reconditioning** or *masturbatory reconditioning* also involves initial masturbation to an unusual sexual stimulus or imaginal scenes, but the person switches to more appropriate stimuli or scenes such as intercourse with his partner immediately

## BOX 11.3 Focus on Law and Ethics

### Sex Offender Notification and Incarceration

A 7-year-old New Jersey girl, Megan Kanka, was raped and murdered in 1991 by a previously convicted sex offender who lived across the street from her family, who were unaware of his past history. Following her death, several states and the federal government passed laws that "sexual predators," or those with histories of sexual crimes against children, would have to register with police (so-called Megan's laws). Many of these laws gave communities the right to be notified as to who these people were, even after they served long prison sentences. You may be able to find registered sex offenders in your location listed on a police department website. These laws raise important ethical dilemmas surrounding the conflict between an individual's right to privacy and societal rights to be protected from dangerous felons. The laws imply that government agencies such as prisons and mental health centers have not successfully curbed pedophilic behavior, essentially leaving supervision of convicted sex offenders in the hands of community groups (Sample, 2011).

Another controversial practice regarding sexual offenders surrounds committing people to a mental hospital *after* their full prison term has expired. Several states allow authorities to transfer a convicted sexual offender to an inpatient mental health facility, even against the person's will, for an indefinite period. The sex offender is kept involuntarily in some setting (often one connected to a prison) until such time that he is determined not to be dangerous to the community. Such laws raise an important ethical dilemma—who has more rights, the person who paid a full debt to society for his crimes or community members who wish to be protected against a potentially violent offender? (Birgden & Cucolo, 2011).

---

before orgasm (Laws & O'Donohue, 2008). The pleasurable orgasm is thus associated with appropriate sexual content. Later in therapy, the person can switch to more appropriate scenes much earlier and further away from orgasm. More complete arousal to appropriate stimuli is thus achieved. Orgasmic reconditioning may also link to *masturbatory satiation* in which a person continues to masturbate after orgasm to paraphilic stimuli. The irritating and boring nature of this activity is therefore associated with the paraphilic stimulus, which serves as a mild punishment (Hunter, Ram, & Ryback, 2008).

Therapists may also use *cognitive therapy* to help a person with paraphilic disorder change irrational thoughts. The illogical reasons a person may have to justify illicit sexual behavior can be challenged and modified. A person's belief that a sex act was for a child's benefit can be confronted. Therapy can also involve educating a person to identify and avoid high-risk situations such as playgrounds, teaching social and other skills to control impulses and reduce anxiety and depression, and increasing empathy by having a person identify with the victim and understand the harm he caused (Schaffer et al., 2010). These therapy components may be useful in individual and group settings and in 12-step programs (similar to the ones for substance use disorders discussed in Chapter 9) for people with sexual addictions (Hyde & DeLamater, 2011).

### What If I or Someone I Know Has a Paraphilic Disorder?

If you feel you or someone you know may have a paraphilic disorder, then consulting with a clinical psychologist or other mental health professional who understands these problems may be best. Some screening questions are listed in **Table 11.24**. Paraphilic disorders are best addressed by cognitive-behavioral procedures to enhance appropriate behavior. Medical conditions should be explored as well.

### Long-Term Outcomes for People with Paraphilic Disorders

The long-term prognosis for people with paraphilic disorders is largely unknown, partly because many such people are never identified or they drop out of treatment. Treatments for different paraphilic disorders remain in development, but many people (78.6 to 95.6 percent) seem to respond positively (Maletsky & Steinhauser, 2002). Long-term outcome for many people with paraphilic disorders may simply improve, however, because of reduced sexual arousal with age

### Table 11.24

| Screening Questions for Paraphilic Disorder |
|---|
| Do you know someone whose sexual behavior constantly surrounds unusual urges or possibly illegal activities? |
| Do you know someone who has trouble concentrating or completing daily tasks because of their sexual desires and urges? |
| Do you know someone attracted sexually to children? |
| Do you know someone who has been arrested for unusual sexual activity? |

(Maggi, 2012). Tom's extended therapy and the humiliation of being arrested resulted in successful abstinence from exhibitionistic exposures.

Much of the long-term outcome data for paraphilic disorders has centered on people with pedophilic disorder or those who have committed sexual offenses against children. *Recidivism rates*, or number of people arrested a second time for a pedophilic act, are typically examined. Recidivism rates for pedophilic disorder are 10 to 50 percent. Those who recidivate or show poor treatment response are more likely to have strong sexual arousal to children, be homosexual or bisexual, and show more paraphilic interests and antisocial personality traits. Judging whether someone may harm a child again depends largely on clinical judgment, however (Hall & Hall, 2007; Moulden, Firestone, Kingston, & Bradford, 2009; Seto, 2004).

### INTERIM SUMMARY

▶ Interviews with people with paraphilic disorder often focus on paraphilic thoughts and behaviors as well as personality characteristics and comorbid problems.

▶ Self-report questionnaires may be used to assess sexual history and unusual interests, hypersexuality, and sexually aggressive and pedophilic behavior.

▶ Physiological assessment for paraphilic disorders includes penile plethysmograph, vaginal blood volume, and measuring how long a person views erotic material.

▶ Drug treatment for paraphilic disorders aims to reduce testosterone and sex drive and to improve depression and compulsive behaviors.

▶ Psychological treatments for paraphilic disorders concentrate on aversive techniques to quell behavior, masturbatory procedures to reorient arousal to more appropriate stimuli, and cognitive therapy to change irrational thoughts.

▶ People with paraphilic disorders can respond positively to treatment and tend not to be rearrested, though this may be due to reduced sex drive with age.

### REVIEW QUESTIONS

1. What topics might a clinician cover when interviewing someone with a paraphilic disorder?
2. What self-report questionnaires and physiological procedures might be useful for assessing someone with a paraphilic disorder?
3. What medications are used to treat paraphilic disorders?
4. What psychological interventions are used to treat paraphilic disorders?
5. What long-term outcomes have been suggested for people with paraphilic disorders?

## Normal Gender Development and Gender Dysphoria: What Are They?

Other problems have less to do with sex and more to do with gender. Most children and adolescents develop a strong sense of who they are and to what gender they belong. Think about

### CASE: Austin

**Austin** was a 7-year-old boy referred for treatment by his parents, who were concerned about some of Austin's ongoing behavior. Their son had been insisting for months that he was actually a girl. Austin's parents were not initially concerned by the behavior because many children like to act like someone else, such as a favorite superhero. Over the past few months, however, Austin's insistence he was a girl had not changed and had led to other odd behaviors. Austin persistently entered his mother's closet and drawers to try on her clothes and makeup, often wanted to be "mommy" or other female figures when playing, and generally preferred to be around girls rather than boys at school. He was greatly teased at school for being around girls and for not playing sports. Austin was also somewhat effeminate in his behavior and often tried to act like other girls with respect to walking and toileting. His parents sought treatment following Austin's recent statement that he wished he could "cut off my penis."

an elementary school playground—boys often group themselves together when playing and exclude girls. Likewise, girls congregate with one another and away from boys. This is normal developmental behavior because it prevents premature sexual contact and helps children learn certain gender roles.

Sometimes the gender-learning process goes awry. **Gender dysphoria** involves strong desire to be the opposite gender and strong dislike of one's current sexual anatomy. The problem is more a *gender* issue than a sexual one because many people with gender dysphoria enjoy normal sexual relations. A person with gender dysphoria wants to be the opposite gender and a diagnosis requires that the person experience considerable distress or problems in daily life functioning (see **Table 11.25**; APA, 2013). A boy with gender dysphoria may act like a girl, be ridiculed by his peers, and subsequently refuse to attend school. Gender dysphoria was previously called gender identity disorder, and so the research literature regarding this latter disorder is presented in this chapter.

## Gender Dysphoria: Features and Epidemiology

Austin may have features of gender dysphoria, sometimes called *transsexualism*, which is marked by strong desire to be of the opposite gender and identifying oneself as a person of the opposite gender (APA, 2013). Austin insisted he was a girl and was not simply role-playing. Gender dysphoria is often marked by cross-dressing, but not for sexual excitement as in transvestism. People with gender dysphoria often prefer to be around people of the opposite gender, to act like them, and insist others treat them as someone of the opposite gender.

**Table 11.25**

**DSM-5 Gender Dysphoria**

### Gender Dysphoria in Children

A. A marked incongruence between one's experienced/expressed gender and assigned gender, of at least 6 months' duration, as manifested by at least six of the following (one of which must be Criterion A1):
  1. A strong desire to be of the other gender or an insistence that one is the other gender (or some alternative gender different from one's assigned gender).
  2. In boys (assigned gender), a strong preference for cross-dressing or simulating female attire; or in girls (assigned gender), a strong preference for wearing only typical masculine clothing and a strong resistance to the wearing of typical feminine clothing.
  3. A strong preference for cross-gender roles in make-believe play or fantasy play.
  4. A strong preference for the toys, games, or activities stereotypically used or engaged in by the other gender.
  5. A strong preference for playmates of the other gender.
  6. In boys (assigned gender), a strong rejection of typically masculine toys, games, and activities and a strong avoidance of rough-and-tumble play; or in girls (assigned gender), a strong rejection of typically feminine toys, games, and activities.
  7. A strong dislike of one's sexual anatomy.
  8. A strong desire for the primary and/or secondary sex characteristics that match one's experienced gender.
B. The condition is associated with clinically significant distress or impairment in social, school, or other important areas of functioning.

### Gender Dysphoria in Adolescents and Adults

A. A marked incongruence between one's experienced/expressed gender and assigned gender, of at least 6 months' duration, as manifested by at least two of the following:
  1. A marked incongruence between one's experienced/expressed gender and primary and/or secondary sex characteristics (or in young adolescents, the anticipated secondary sex characteristics).
  2. A strong desire to be rid of one's primary and/or secondary sex characteristics because of a marked incongruence with one's experienced/expressed gender (or in young adolescents, a desire to prevent the development of the anticipated secondary sex characteristics).
  3. A strong desire for the primary and/or secondary sex characteristics of the other gender.
  4. A strong desire to be of the other gender (or some alternative gender different from one's assigned gender).
  5. A strong desire to be treated as the other gender (or some alternative gender different from one's assigned gender).
  6. A strong conviction that one has the typical feelings and reactions of the other gender (or some alternative gender different from one's assigned gender).

Specify with a disorder of sex development and/or posttransition to desired gender.

American Psychiatric Association. (2013). *Diagnostic and statistical manual of mental disorders* (5th ed.). Arlington, VA: American Psychiatric Association.

People with gender dysphoria are also uncomfortable with their own gender, believe they were born as the wrong gender, and may even try to change their gender as adolescents or adults. People with gender dysphoria may be heterosexual or homosexual, and the disorder is usually associated with severe stress, depression, and social isolation (Wallien, Swaab, & Cohen-Kettenis, 2007; Zucker, Bradley, et al., 2012). Gender dysphoria could be but is usually not diagnosed if a person was born with unclear genitalia that forced parents at that time to choose the gender of their child (APA, 2013).

The diagnostic category of gender dysphoria is controversial, however. The diagnosis in children may reinforce stereotypes of masculinity and femininity by tacitly assuming which toys and clothes are appropriate for each gender. Transsexual persons also experience significant discrimination and stigma (Chamberland & Saewyc, 2011). Researchers contend, however, that many youths with gender dysphoria suffer great distress and remain unhappy with their gender into adolescence and adulthood (Zucker, Wood, Singh, & Bradley, 2012).

Gender dysphoria is quite rare, affecting 0.005 to 0.014 percent of men and 0.002 to 0.003 percent of women (APA, 2013). Prevalence rates are often based on referrals for treatment and not the general population, however. American youth aged 4 to 5 years who wish to be the opposite gender may include as many as 1.3 percent of boys and 5.0 percent of girls, although these numbers may not reflect true gender dysphoria and seem to decline with age (Cohen-Kettinis & Pfafflin, 2003; Zucker & Lawrence, 2009). Age of onset is typically before elementary school for girls and before puberty for boys (Okabe et al., 2008).

## Gender Dysphoria: Causes and Prevention

Data are scarce regarding risk factors for gender dysphoria. No strong biological risk factors, including genetics, family history, and physical problems, have been supported. Some point to prenatal sex hormones as somehow related to the disorder. Exposure to opposite-gender hormones such as testosterone sometimes relates to cross-gender behavior (Veale, Clarke, & Lomax, 2010). Possible genetic predisposition has been identified as well (Gomez-Gil et al., 2010). Hormonal and genetic influences can help create many brain changes associated with gender identity (Hines, 2011). Biological risk factors for gender dysphoria are not well established, however.

Psychological risk factors also remain unclear. Children with gender dysphoria often have relationship difficulties with parents (57 percent) and peers (52 percent) and family mental health problems (38 percent). These children also experience considerable harassment or persecution from others (33 percent; Di Ceglie, 2000). Parenting variables might thus be important; examples include parent psychopathology such as depression, tolerance of social isolation and cross-gender behavior in children, or rejection of a child. Boys with gender dysphoria are also less active and rough-and-tumble in their play than boys without the disorder. Girls with gender dysphoria are generally more active than girls without the disorder (Zucker & Bradley, 1999).

Gender dysphoria is a formal diagnostic condition, but changes in gender are commonplace in many parts of the world. A *fa'afafine* is a Polynesian boy voluntarily raised as a girl in a family with too many male children. Many of these boys continue to view themselves, and are viewed by others,

In Polynesia, boys are sometimes raised as girls, even into adulthood, if a family has too many male children. Here, Tafi Toleafa, who was born as a boy and raised as a girl, helps serve food at a family party.

ERIK HILL/Anchorage Daily News/MCT/Landov

as female even into adulthood. A *fakaletti* is a boy from Tonga who dresses and lives as a girl to help with chores and who may choose to continue to live as a woman in adulthood. Males adopt characteristics of females in androgynous and socially acceptable ways in many other cultures as well. Examples include *kathoey* male-to-female dancers in Thailand, *mukhannathun* Islamic males who adopt female appearance and other characteristics, and *evening people* of India who purposely assume colorful, effeminate clothing in a transgender manner. These examples represent culturally normal or accepted practices, which calls into question the universal validity of a diagnosis of gender dysphoria.

The cause of gender dysphoria remains unknown, but early biological predispositions and parental reinforcement of cross-gender behavior in children may be influential (Zucker, Bradley, et al., 2012). Austin's parents tolerated his odd behaviors for some time. Other variables such as attachment to a specific parent (e.g., to mothers in boys), child and parent insecurity, and responses from peers and siblings may be important as well. The lack of knowledge about the cause of gender dysphoria leaves little information about preventing the disorder other than addressing symptoms early in life (see treatment section).

Bill Bachmann/PhotoEdit

Young boys and girls typically play apart, but children with gender dysphoria may identify more with the opposite gender.

# Gender Dysphoria: Assessment and Treatment

## Assessment of Gender Dysphoria

The assessment of youths with gender dysphoria includes interviews, observations of cross-gender behavior, and drawings of oneself and others. Important interview questions include current and future beliefs about one's gender (e.g., are you a boy or girl and what will you be when you grow up?), positive and negative beliefs about the two genders, fantasies about being the opposite gender, and whether one is confused about being a boy or girl. Observations of cross-gender behavior are also important, including cross-dressing, preference for cross-gender toys (and rejection of same-gender toys), and statements about wanting to be the opposite gender. Youths may also be asked to draw pictures of people because children with gender dysphoria often draw someone of the opposite gender first (Zucker, Wood et al., 2012).

Adults with gender dysphoria, especially those considering sex reassignment surgery (see next section), are typically evaluated along personality, projective, intelligence, and other psychological tests to rule out severe problems such as personality disorders (Chapter 10) and ensure a person is truly ready for such a life-changing experience. Information should also be obtained about history of the person's gender dysphoria and peer relationships, medical status, family functioning, and sexual interests (Cohen-Kettenis & Pfafflin, 2003).

## Biological Treatment of Gender Dysphoria

The primary biological treatment for adults with gender dysphoria is **sex reassignment surgery**. For men, external genitalia and facial hair are removed, a vagina is created, and hormones are given to develop breasts and soften more rugged, masculine features. For women, an external phallus is created, internal sexual organs and possibly breasts are removed, and hormones are given to develop more traditionally masculine features. Sex reassignment surgery is done only after an extensive period, perhaps 2 years or more, of psychotherapy and actual living in the role of the opposite gender (Cohen-Kettenis & Pfafflin, 2003).

## Psychological Treatment of Gender Dysphoria

Psychological approaches to treating gender dysphoria focus mainly on behavioral techniques to reduce cross-gender behaviors in children and adolescents and encourage same-gender identification. Parents may be trained to establish token economies or other consequence systems to reward same-gender behavior, such as wearing traditional gender clothing, and to discourage cross-gender behavior. Parents may also tell a child they value him or her as a boy or girl and help the child develop same-gender friendships and social activities (Richmond, Carroll, & Denboske, 2010). Parent groups to provide education and support regarding children with gender dysphoria also reduce stigma (Di Ceglie & Thummel, 2006). Psychological treatment of adolescents and young adults may consist of videotaping behaviors and providing feedback about how cross-gender behaviors can be changed (Moller, Schreier, Li, & Romer, 2009). For example, a male may be given feedback about his effeminate voice.

## What If I or Someone I Know Has Questions About Gender or Gender Dysphoria?

You or someone you know may have questions about the play, dress, and gender-related behavior of a child, or you may have concerns a child may have gender dysphoria. Two important screening questions in this regard are (1) Does the child engage in a great deal of cross-gender behavior? and (2) Is the child dissatisfied with his or her gender? If you feel a child does have strong gender distress, then consulting a clinical psychologist or other mental health professional who understands these issues is important. Keep in mind, however, that cross-gender behavior is common and that gender dysphoria is rare.

Gaffney/Liaison/Getty Images

Renee Richards was a male tennis player who became famous for changing genders and continuing her tennis career.

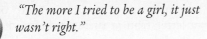

## THE CONTINUUM VIDEO PROJECT

### Dean: Gender Dysphoria

*"The more I tried to be a girl, it just wasn't right."*

Copyright © Cengage Learning.®

Access the Continuum Video Project in MindTap at **www.cengagebrain.com**.

## Long-Term Outcomes for People with Gender Dysphoria

Children with gender dysphoria are thought to respond to behavior therapy better than adolescents with the disorder because their sense of gender orientation as youngsters is more flexible. Adolescents and adults with gender dysphoria may be more successfully treated via sex reassignment surgery. Up to 97 percent of people who undergo sex reassignment are generally satisfied, but 10 to 15 percent of people who have the surgery may experience some regret or have poor outcome (Lawrence, 2003; Sutcliffe et al., 2009). Many people with gender dysphoria experience improvements in psychological symptoms (78%), quality of life (80%), and sexual function (72%) following sex reassignment (Murad et al., 2010).

Youths who continue to show intense cross-gender behavior throughout their childhood may be more likely to develop gender dysphoria or alternative sexual orientations as adolescents or adults (Zucker, 2005). Untreated symptoms of gender dysphoria seem to improve somewhat, but aspects of anxiety, depression, and other psychopathology may remain (Drummond, Bradley, Peterson-Badali, & Zucker, 2008; Wallien & Cohen-Kettenis, 2008). Austin's treatment focused on changing some of his effeminate behaviors, which seemed to be successful. His long-term functioning, including sexual behaviors and any mental disorder, is unclear.

### INTERIM SUMMARY

▶ Gender dysphoria refers to strong desire to be of the opposite gender and identifying oneself as a person of the opposite gender.

▶ Risk factors for gender dysphoria are still being investigated, although some have pointed to early hormonal changes and parenting practices.

▶ The assessment of gender dysphoria may involve asking questions about current and future beliefs about one's gender, positive and negative beliefs about the two genders, fantasies, and confusion about one's gender.

▶ The primary biological intervention for gender dysphoria, particularly in adults, is sex reassignment surgery in which external genitalia and bodily features are modified to fit the characteristics of the opposite gender.

▶ Psychological interventions for gender dysphoria focus on changing cross-gender behaviors.

### REVIEW QUESTIONS

1. What are features of gender dysphoria?
2. What biological risk factors may relate to gender dysphoria?
3. What psychological risk factors may relate to gender dysphoria?
4. What methods are used to assess gender dysphoria?
5. What methods are used to treat gender dysphoria?

## Final Comments

People with sexual dysfunctions, paraphilic disorders, or gender dysphoria suffer enormous daily distress because sexual and gender-related behaviors are so central to human existence. Furthermore, these problems are much more common than previously thought, as evidenced by high demands for sexual therapy and related medications. Sexual problems are sometimes embarrassing to admit, but acknowledging a problem and addressing it appropriately can have an enormous positive impact on quality of life. Openly discussing problems with sexual response and unusual sexual desires with one's partner, and improving communication in general, is critical as well. Open communication and thought about a child's gender and play preferences is also important.

## Thought Questions

1. Are there unusual sexual behaviors you feel should not be classified as a mental disorder, if any? Which unusual sexual behaviors do you feel should definitely be classified as a mental disorder, if any? Why or why not?
2. What is the impact of the Internet on sexual fantasies and behaviors?
3. What guidelines would you recommend for defining pedophilic disorder? Would two young adolescents engaging in sexual activity qualify for the diagnosis?
4. How do you think Viagra and other drugs for sexual activity will affect sexual practices in the United States and elsewhere?
5. What separates "normal" sexual activity from "abnormal" sexual activity? Do you think sexuality has more to do with biological, family, or other factors? Why?
6. What cross-gender behaviors might you tolerate in your child? How far would you allow cross-gender behavior to go in your child before you became worried?

## Personal Narrative 11.1

### Sam

I'm Sam, and there's nothing abnormal about me. There is, however, something incredibly disturbing and sick about a society that wants to hurt and annihilate me simply because I don't fit into its rigid gender binary. I am a transsexual, and I am in the process of being fired from my current job. This is the third job that I have lost due to the discomfort people feel about my gender presentation and my particular embodied journey through life. I have had men in pickup trucks pull up alongside me and shout "Freak!" and follow me home, making threatening gestures. I have had people walking by me shout that I'm going to burn in hell. In this, I am actually one of the lucky ones. Last night I attended the Transgender Day of Remembrance vigil on my campus to light candles and hear the stories of the transgender people who were murdered in the last year. There is, on average, one transgender person per month who is killed somewhere in the United States, and this statistic drastically underrepresents the staggering violence against transgender people, because it only documents those individuals whose murders were reported as transgender murders. This does not account for those bodies that were never recovered, nor does it count those transgender people who end up taking their own lives because they could no longer stand to face the kind of scorn and contempt that is part of living as transgender.

These murders are not just clean and simple killings. The transgender women spoken about at the vigil last night were shot in the chest ten times each. This is typical of such murders—multiple stab wounds, dismemberment. They are crimes of intense hatred and frenzy—signs of a very insecure and disturbed society. And yet it is transgender people who are labeled as mentally disordered.

Transgender people do not possess authority over our own bodies. We are not treated as trustworthy informants about our own experience. For instance, when I decided that I wanted to go on male hormones to effect particular changes in my body—after living as openly transgendered for 13 years, completing a Ph.D. in Gender Studies, and doing extensive research both abroad and within

Sam Bullington

*Courtesy of Sam Bullington*

the United States on transgender issues/communities I was required to obtain a letter from a therapist before I could schedule my appointment with the endocrinologist. This therapist knew far less about transgender issues than I did and I had only been seeing him for a couple of months, but his credentials were required before I could pursue changes to my body. When I met with the endocrinologist, he consulted with his young intern, not with me, about whether he would consent to writing me a prescription for testosterone. His ultimate decision was determined by asking my partner whether *she* thought it was a good idea. I was 40 years old at the time and was treated as though I were 5—though without the lollypop afterward. This is extremely insulting to transgender people—folks who usually have done extensive personal research and often know more about the relevant medical interventions than the doctors themselves (especially those of us, like myself, who live in small towns). This is especially outrageous given the fact that "gender-normative" people can seek body modifications to enhance their gender performance (for instance, breast implants or penile enhancements) without needing permission from a therapist or being diagnosed with a mental disorder.

## Key Terms

sexual dysfunctions 322

male hypoactive sexual desire disorder 323

female sexual interest/arousal disorder 323

erectile disorder 323

female orgasmic disorder 324

delayed ejaculation 324

premature (early) ejaculation 326

genito-pelvic pain/ penetration disorder 327

spectator role 330

stop–start procedure 334

sensate focus 334

masturbation training 335

paraphilias 337

paraphilic disorders 342

exhibitionistic disorder 337

fetishistic disorder 338

frotteuristic disorder 340

pedophilic disorder 340

sexual masochism 341

sexual sadism 341

transvestic disorder 342

voyeuristic disorder 342

aversion treatment 349

covert sensitization 349

orgasmic reconditioning 349

gender dysphoria 351

sex reassignment surgery 354

Society feels compelled to study and try to understand transgender experience because it seems to be so different from the "normal" experience of gender. However, there is nothing remotely normal about gender development in the contemporary United States. Gender socialization is entirely compulsory and usually begins before we are even born. We are given gendered names and pronouns, directed toward certain colors, toys, and hobbies while discouraged away from others, encouraged to express certain aspects of our personalities but warned against expressing others. My students constantly remind me of the often severe penalties of breaking these mandatory rules—being called a "sissy" or "fag," getting beat up, being punished by parents and other authority figures, being a social outcast. It requires an awful lot of policing on the part of society to create something that is supposedly "natural" and inevitable.

Contrary to what we are taught, gender is a spectrum, not a binary—a rainbow of colors, not the limited choices of black and white. Even biologically, research has demonstrated that there is immense variation in our bodies and approximately one in every thousand of us (and this is a very conservative estimate) comes into the world with a body that doesn't neatly fit into the two available choices of "male" and "female." Our gender identities are even more complicated and individualized. Very few of us actually comfortably fit into the masculine men/feminine women poles—many have to commit considerable life energy to meet these expectations and such gender requirements harm all of us, not just transgender people. They inhibit our full range as human beings—from men who have health or family problems because the only emotion they were taught to express was anger, to women who can't access their full power, confidence, and potential because they were socialized to prioritize pleasing others and making their bodies attractive. Transgenderism is part of the beautiful diversity of human life. It is only pathological in a society whose resources are fundamentally allocated on the basis of what genitalia you were born with. If we did not live in a society in which there were so many social advantages to being male over female, it would not matter to which category you were assigned or whether you moved between them—or created your own new categories.

Again, my name is Sam, and there is nothing abnormal about me. I have a Ph.D., I'm an ordained minister, I've been in two 10-year relationships, and I'm currently married (although not legally since in the state of Missouri I'm not actually allowed to be legally married—I cannot marry a woman because I was born female, and I cannot marry a man because I live as a man now). Despite all of these social accomplishments, people constantly look down on me and regard me with suspicion because I am a transsexual. The only thing that is different about my journey is that I sought to look inwardly for my answers about myself, something that I continually recommend to my students. Despite living in a "free country" that prides itself on individualism, we are expected to conform most aspects of ourselves and our life journeys to extremely limited and proscribed paths and we are constantly bombarded with relentless media images telling us how we should look, what we should buy, how much we should weigh, what we should wear, what we should think, continually reinforced by admonitions from our families, religious organizations, educational institutions, and the state. I attempted for several decades to live in this manner and ended up miserable, as many others are currently. My path to happiness and ultimately freedom came from listening to my own heart above the din of all of the other voices trying to define my experience. I highly recommend it to anyone.

## Media Resources

### MindTap

MindTap for Kearney and Trull's *Abnormal Psychology and Life: A Dimensional Approach* is a highly personalized fully online learning platform of authoritative content, assignments, and services offering you a tailored presentation of course curriculum created by your instructor. MindTap guides you through the course curriculum via an innovative learning path where you will complete reading assignments, annotate your readings, complete homework, and engage with quizzes and assessments. MindTap includes the Continuum Video Project.

Go to **cengagebrain.com** to access MindTap.

# Schizophrenia and Other Psychotic Disorders

# 12

CASE: *James*

**What Do You Think?**

Unusual Emotions, Thoughts, and Behaviors and Psychotic Disorders: What Are They?

Psychotic Disorders: Features and Epidemiology

CASE: *Jody*

Stigma Associated with Schizophrenia
    Interim Summary
    Review Questions

Psychotic Disorders: Causes and Prevention
    Interim Summary
    Review Questions

Psychotic Disorders: Assessment and Treatment
    Interim Summary
    Review Questions

FINAL COMMENTS
THOUGHT QUESTIONS
KEY TERMS
MEDIA RESOURCES

## SPECIAL FEATURES

CONTINUUM FIGURE 12.1 Continuum of Unusual Emotions, Cognitions, and Behaviors and Psychotic Disorder   362–363

PERSONAL NARRATIVE 11.1 John Cadigan   368–369

BOX 12.1 | Focus on Diversity: Ethnicity and Income Level in Schizophrenia   373

BOX 12.2 | Focus on Violence: Are People with Schizophrenia More Violent?   374

CONTINUUM VIDEO PROJECT

*Andre:* Schizophrenia   382

BOX 12.3 | Focus on Law and Ethics: Making the Choice of Antipsychotic Medication   385

# CASE: James

**James** was 29 years old when he was referred to an inpatient psychiatric ward at a city hospital. He was brought to the emergency room the night before by police, who initially found him trying to gain illegal access to a downtown FBI building. James fled hysterically down the street, running and screaming loudly, when first confronted by two policemen. He then darted into traffic, nearly causing an accident, before entering a convenience store. The police officers entered the store and found James curled up in a corner and sobbing. They tried to speak to James but said he was unresponsive and frightened. James was eventually led into a patrol car after some coaxing. James told the officers he knew they were going to kill him and asked that they do so quickly. The officers told James they had no intention of hurting him, but James was unconvinced.

James was taken to the hospital for evaluation. This was done because he engaged in self-destructive behavior by running into traffic and because he seemed intoxicated or greatly confused. A physician examined James's physical state in the emergency room. James seemed unhurt and had no signs of external injury. Later, toxicology tests revealed James had been drinking alcohol, but not enough to justify his bizarre behavior. A psychiatrist from the inpatient unit was thus consulted.

The psychiatrist found James terrified of his immediate environment and others around him. James became more receptive to the idea he would not be harmed after considerable discussion and extensive sedative medication. The psychiatrist asked James if he could remember his earlier behavior and piece together what happened that day. James did not recall his entire day but did convey some important bits of information.

James said he was overwhelmed lately with feelings of apprehension and fear that he and someone important were about to be harmed. He could not specify why he felt this way, but he was sure he had special information that the president of the United States was going to be harmed soon and that he, James, would also be harmed because he knew of the plot. These feelings eventually became so strong that James felt he had to leave his apartment and warn someone at the FBI office. James said he thought the police were going to kill him because they were agents responsible for the plot against the president. James was still agitated and worried for his own life despite heavy sedation. Nonetheless, he did provide the psychiatrist with names of people close to him.

James was transferred to the inpatient psychiatric unit and held for observation and medication. The psychiatrist spoke to James again the next morning and conveyed that his wife and parents were to visit him that day. Following their visit, the psychiatrist spoke to each family member to piece together James's personal history. They said James had always been an unusual child and adolescent and that things greatly worsened once he entered college in his early 20s. James would often become sullen, withdrawn, morbid, and focused on what might happen if he or family members

Richard Nowitz/National Geographic/Getty Images

or important people were harmed. These behaviors escalated whenever James was particularly stressed during college, and he barely completed requirements for his degree.

James worked intermittently as an assistant to a financial advisor the past 4 years but was hospitalized twice for severe depression and unusual behaviors. The last hospitalization occurred a year ago when James was reprimanded at work for trying to persuade an important client that her life was in danger. The reprimand triggered bizarre responses in James ranging from agitation to hiding in the basement of his house. James was placed on different medications that eased his agitation, but his wife said he "did not always take his pills." His wife said James was upset over a conversation he overheard at work, one in which a client was bragging about having met the president of the United States. Perhaps James misinterpreted this statement as one of threat toward the president, which triggered his current behavior. James was committed to the inpatient unit for further assessment and treatment.

## What Do You Think?

1. Why do you think James was so agitated and scared?

2. What external events and internal factors might be responsible for James's feelings?

3. What are you curious about regarding James and his family?

4. Does James remind you of a character you have seen in the movies? How so?

5. How might James's behavior affect him in the future?

# Unusual Emotions, Thoughts, and Behaviors and Psychotic Disorders: What Are They?

We have discussed throughout this textbook mental disorders that affect *specific* areas of functioning. Anxiety-related and depressive disorders, for example, affect limited areas of functioning and are sometimes called neurotic disorders or *neuroses*. Someone with social anxiety disorder might have trouble functioning effectively in social situations but can function well in other tasks like caring for oneself or working independently.

Many people also experience odd emotions, thoughts, and behaviors during the course of obsessive-compulsive disorder, illness anxiety disorder, or schizotypal personality disorder. People with these disorders often have odd thoughts, but the thoughts are usually somewhat plausible or believable. A person with obsessive-compulsive disorder may obsess about bacteria growing on his hands, but this is something that could occur. People with illness anxiety disorder worry about having a serious disease, which may be a plausible though untrue explanation for their physical symptoms. Emotional states often associated with these conditions, such as anxiety and depression, are understandable as well. Behaviors associated with these thoughts and emotions, such as excessive hand washing and medical doctor visits, are also unusual but largely an extension of normal things that many people do.

Other mental disorders affect *many* areas of functioning and involve emotions, thoughts, and behaviors so bizarre a person cannot function in most areas of her life. Some of these disorders are **psychotic disorders** or *psychoses* (**Figure 12.1**). People with psychotic disorders may have unusual emotional states or affect. **Flat affect** refers to lack of emotion even in situations that call for great joy or sadness. **Inappropriate affect** refers to a mood that does not match the context of a given situation. A person may laugh hysterically as someone describes a sad story, become enraged for little reason, or break down crying after watching a reality television show. Clearly these kinds of emotional reactions prevent a person from interacting well with others.

People with psychotic disorders also have extremely rigid or bizarre thoughts called **delusions**. James's unyielding belief that others wanted to harm him is an example of a delusion. People with psychotic disorders also have trouble organizing their thoughts to form clear sentences or communicate well with others.

People with psychotic disorders also show highly unusual behaviors. Some hear voices no one else does that tell them to do something. These voices are auditory examples of **hallucinations**, or sensory experiences without a real environmental stimulus. People with psychotic disorders can also display **catatonic** positions by remaining in a near immovable state for hours. Those with psychotic disorders often have trouble going to work or engaging in daily self-care such as washing or getting dressed. This is known as *avolition*.

Psychotic disorders affect a tiny minority of people, but their overall effect on those with the disorders is devastating. People with psychoses, especially those in the active phase of the disorders, cannot work, communicate with others, think rationally, or care for themselves. James's symptoms progressed to the point where he was unable to work, was convinced others wanted to harm him, and was engaged in potentially severe self-destructive behavior.

# Psychotic Disorders: Features and Epidemiology

The most well known of the psychoses, and the one we devote the most attention to in this chapter, is schizophrenia. We also cover other psychotic disorders related to schizophrenia, including schizophreniform, schizoaffective, delusional, and brief psychotic disorders (see **Table 12.1**). Common to each disorder is a debilitating and tragic mental condition that can rob people of their basic personality. Many people with psychotic disorders like James are haunted every day by horrendous and irrational fears, images, thoughts, and beliefs that do not seem like their own.

## Schizophrenia

You may have seen behavior like James's depicted in films such as *A Beautiful Mind*, *The Shining*, or *Spider*. Symptoms of **schizophrenia** are evident in these films and in people like James. Schizophrenia generally consists of two main groups of symptoms: positive and negative. **Positive symptoms** of schizophrenia represent excessive or overt symptoms; **negative symptoms** of schizophrenia represent deficit or covert symptoms (see **Table 12.2**). Positive symptoms of schizophrenia include delusions and hallucinations as well as disorganized speech and

## Table 12.1

| Types of Psychotic Disorders | |
|---|---|
| **Disorder** | **Key features** |
| Schizophrenia | Positive symptoms such as delusions and hallucinations and negative symptoms such as lack of speech or emotion and failure to care for oneself |
| Schizophreniform disorder | Features of schizophrenia for 1 to 6 months but not necessarily with great impairment in daily functioning |
| Schizoaffective disorder | Characteristic features of schizophrenia *and* a depressive or manic episode |
| Delusional disorder | No psychotic symptoms except for one or more delusions |
| Brief psychotic disorder | Several key features of schizophrenia for 1 day to 1 month |

**CONTINUUM FIGURE 12.1**    Continuum of Unusual Emotions, Cognitions, and Behaviors and Psychotic Disorder

| | Normal | Mild |
|---|---|---|
| **Emotions** | Laughing at a joke or crying at a funeral. | Slightly restricted range of emotions, such as not responding to a joke or sad story. |
| **Cognitions** | Ability to organize thoughts and sentences and communicate well. | Slight oddities of thinking, such as belief that a dead relative is in the room. |
| **Behaviors** | Working and interacting with others appropriately. | Slightly peculiar behaviors such as failing to wash or brush one's teeth for a couple of days. |

behavior. Negative symptoms of schizophrenia include lack of speech or emotion and failure to care for oneself (American Psychiatric Association [APA], 2013). We next describe different positive and negative symptoms in more detail.

## DELUSIONS

A key positive symptom of schizophrenia is a delusion. A delusion is an irrational belief involving a misperception of life experiences. Delusions are usually very fixed beliefs, meaning they are highly resistant to others' attempts to persuade the person otherwise, and are often incomprehensible and simply

untrue. James's strong but strange belief that the conversation he overheard at work meant the president of the United States was about to be harmed is a delusion. In the film *A Beautiful Mind*, the lead character John Nash believed he could find secret Soviet codes in magazines and newspapers. Delusions can come in several forms, including persecutory, control, grandiose, referential, and somatic, among others.

*Persecutory delusions* are the type of delusion most commonly seen in people with schizophrenia; these delusions represent irrational beliefs that one is being harmed or harassed in some way (Combs et al., 2009). A person with a persecutory delusion may believe secret government officials are following him and about to do something dire. Persecutory delusions may intersect with *control delusions,* in which a person may believe others are deliberately:

- placing thoughts in her mind without permission (*thought insertion*)
- transmitting his thoughts so everyone can know them (*thought broadcasting*)
- stealing her thoughts and creating memory loss (*thought withdrawal*; Frith, 2005)

*Grandiose delusions* represent irrational beliefs that one is an especially powerful or important person, when actually this is not so (Knowles, McCarthy-Jones, & Rowse, 2011). Delusions of grandiosity are more peculiar than simple beliefs about grandiosity in people with bipolar disorder or narcissistic personality disorder (Chapters 7 and 10). A person with bipolar disorder or narcissistic personality disorder may truly but wrongly believe he is a great writer, but a person with a grandiose delusion may truly but wrongly believe he is a top government official, a company's chief executive officer, or Napoleon! Charles Cullen, a nurse sentenced to 11 consecutive life terms for killing up to 40 patients, may have suffered from a grandiose delusion in claiming at one time he was an "angel of mercy."

## Table 12.2

### Positive and Negative Symptoms of Schizophrenia

| Positive symptoms | Negative symptoms |
|---|---|
| ▶ Delusions (rigid, bizarre, irrational beliefs) | ▶ Alogia (speaking very little to others) |
| ▶ Hallucinations (sensory experiences in the absence of actual stimuli) | ▶ Avolition (inability or unwillingness to engage in goal-directed activities) |
| ▶ Disorganized speech (jumbled speech or speech conveys little information) | ▶ Anhedonia (lack of pleasure or interest in life activities) |
| ▶ Inappropriate affect (showing emotions that do not suit a given situation) | ▶ Flat affect (showing little emotion in different situations) |
| ▶ Catatonia (unusual symptoms marked partly by severe restriction of movement or extreme excitability) | ▶ Lack of insight (poor awareness of one's mental condition) |

| Moderate | Psychotic Disorder — less severe | Psychotic Disorder — more severe |
|---|---|---|
| Greater restrictions in emotions or odd emotional content for a situation, such as getting upset for little reason. | Intense restrictions in mood or intense anger at a coworker for innocuous behaviors such as not responding immediately to an email. | No mood changes whatsoever or extreme inappropriate affect such as laughing for no reason or sobbing loudly during a happy story. |
| Greater oddities of thinking, such as a belief that one's life resembles segments on a television news program, or some difficulty forming clear thoughts. | Delusional or very odd beliefs that seem possible, such as belief that a coworker is deliberately poisoning one's lunch, or greater difficulty forming clear thoughts. | Delusional or extremely odd beliefs that seem impossible, such as a belief that one is being abducted by aliens, or complete inability to form clear thoughts. |
| Greater peculiarity of behavior, such avoiding all television shows because of possible resemblance to one's life or failing to wash for 1-2 weeks. | Intense peculiarity of behavior, such as refusing to go to work for several weeks due to fear of being harmed or great difficulty caring for oneself. | Extremely peculiar behavior such as hearing voices, running wild down a street, not moving at all for hours, or loss of interest in caring for oneself. |

© Wrangler/Shutterstock.com                    Copyright © Cengage Learning®

*Referential delusions* (or delusions of reference) are irrational beliefs that events in everyday life have something special to do with oneself. A person may be watching local television news and believe each story is based on some aspect of her life from that day (Startup, Bucci, & Langdon, 2009). *Somatic delusions* represent irrational beliefs that one's physical body is affected, usually in a negative way and often by an outside source (Spalletta, Prias, Rubino, Caltagirone, & Fagioli, 2013). A person may believe an inability to sleep is caused by excessive microwave radiation outside the house.

## HALLUCINATIONS

Hallucinations are sensory experiences a person believes to be true, when actually they are not. The most common hallucination in schizophrenia is *auditory*, in which a person may hear voices that repeat her thoughts, comment on her appearance or behavior, argue, or command her to do something (Waters et al., 2012). Unlike many media portrayals, however, the voices the person hears are not always threatening or demanding of violent behavior. The voice or voices may be recognizable and comforting to the person, or it may be the person's own voice. The latter may relate to a thought broadcasting delusion, where a person hears his thoughts repeated aloud and assumes others can hear them as well. Imagine how distressing that can be!

Hallucinations can also be *visual* or *tactile*, as when a person sees images or visions not seen by others or feels bizarre sensations on his skin. In the film *A Beautiful Mind*, John Nash was portrayed as seeing a roommate who was not actually there. Sometimes visual and tactile hallucinations are linked in an especially distressing way, as when a person "sees" and "feels" large bugs and snakes crawling up her arms (Lewandowski, De-Paola, Camsari, Cohen, & Ongur, 2009). Hallucinations can obviously be extremely upsetting and interfere with ability to interact with others.

Films such as *Spider* depict the lives of people with delusions or psychotic disorders.

Hallucinations can even be *olfactory*. Following is a brief transcript of a woman seen in an inpatient psychiatric ward by one of your authors:

**Therapist:** Can you describe what changes have been happening to you?

**Patient:** I've been having very strange smells coming to me lately. Just awful.

**Therapist:** What kind of smells? Can you describe them?

**Patient:** Well . . . I know it sounds weird, I know . . . I guess I'm . . . maybe crazy or something, but everything smells to me like . . . garbage.

In the film *A Beautiful Mind*, the character John Nash believed he could find secret Soviet codes in newspapers and magazines.

**Therapist:** Garbage? Really?

**Patient:** Yeah, my food, my clothes . . . even you!

**Therapist:** (retrieving and then presenting a sweet-smelling piece of heated apple pie) Okay, let's test this out a bit. How does this smell to you?

**Patient:** (moving head away quickly) *Ewwww,* awful, like rotten eggs or something. I can't even eat lately . . . *ich* . . . that's so disgusting!

## DISORGANIZED SPEECH

Many people with schizophrenia also show **disorganized speech**. Speech patterns can be so disorganized a person cannot maintain a regular conversation. Verbalizations may be disconnected, jumbled, interrupted, forgotten in midsentence, or mixed in their phrasing (*loose association*). A person might say "store I go to the have to" instead of "I have to go to the store." A person may also simply make up words that do not make sense to anyone (*neologism*), repeat the same words over and over, say words together because they rhyme (*clang association*), or not

speak at all (*alogia*; Goldfarb & Bekker, 2009). A woman with schizophrenia once called one of your authors a "bifalugel," which seemed to have some angry meaning to her but had little meaning to the listener.

Other people with schizophrenia speak quite clearly, stop without warning, and then talk about a completely different topic. This phenomenon, known as *tangentiality*, requires the listener to constantly steer the speaker back to the original topic of conversation. You might guess that interviews with people with schizophrenia can sometimes last hours and may produce only bits of useful information. Consider this interview with someone just committed to an inpatient unit:

**Psychiatrist:** Do you know where you are?

**Patient:** In a room that is in the . . . (voice trails off)

**Psychiatrist:** Yes, go ahead, continue.

**Patient:** (after considerable silence) The room to the park area . . . I see it.

**Psychiatrist:** What are you seeing?

**Patient:** Smell of the chocolate cake.

**Psychiatrist:** Do you see or smell something?

**Patient:** (after more silence) No, I can do it.

**Psychiatrist:** What can you do?

**Patient:** Time to relax.

## DISORGANIZED OR CATATONIC BEHAVIOR

Many people with schizophrenia are disorganized not only in their speech but also in their behavior. A person may be unable to care for herself and not engage in appropriate hygiene, dress, or even eating. The person may be highly agitated as well (like James) or show *inappropriate affect* or emotions in a given situation (Hempel, Hempel, Schonknecht, Stippich, & Schroder, 2003). He may laugh during a sad story. Such behavior is often unpredictable and frightening to others, as was James's behavior when chased by police.

Even more bizarre is **catatonic behavior**, which may include unusual motor symptoms (Ungvari, Mann, & Caroff, 2013). A person with schizophrenia may not react to environmental events such as someone saying hello or may seem completely unaware of his surroundings (*catatonic stupor*). A person's body part, such as an arm, can be moved to a different posture and that posture is maintained for long periods. This is *waxy flexibility* or *catalepsy*. Other people with schizophrenia may:

- show wild or uncontrolled motor activity (*stereotypy* or *agitation*)
- repeat others' words (*echolalia*) or actions (*echopraxia*)
- adopt a rigid posture that is difficult to change (Frith & Johnstone, 2003)

## NEGATIVE SYMPTOMS

Delusions, hallucinations, and disorganized speech and behavior are positive symptoms of schizophrenia. Negative symptoms of schizophrenia refer to pathological *deficits* in

*Everett Collection*

Pictures drawn by artist Louis Wain. Cats were the subject matter of Wain's art even as he experienced intense periods of psychosis.

## OTHER CRITERIA

Other criteria must also be present for a diagnosis of schizophrenia. Symptoms of schizophrenia must interfere significantly with one's ability to function on an everyday basis. James became unable to work or appropriately interact with others. A person's symptoms must not be due to a substance or medical condition (see **Table 12.3**; APA, 2013). Schizophrenia must not be diagnosed with schizoaffective disorder (see later section), depressive or bipolar disorder with psychotic features (Chapter 7), or autism spectrum disorder (Chapter 13) unless prominent delusions and hallucinations are present.

## Phases of Schizophrenia

People with schizophrenia often, but not always, progress through stages of symptoms (**Figure 12.2**). Many begin with a **prodromal phase** that can last days, weeks, months, or even years. This phase is often marked by peculiar behaviors such as minor disturbances

behavior, or showing too little of a certain behavior (Foussias & Remington, 2010). Common negative symptoms in schizophrenia include:

- Flat affect, or showing very little emotion even in situations that seem to demand much emotion, such as a wedding or funeral. A person often speaks in monotone and shows few changes in her facial expression.

- **Alogia**, or speaking very little to other people and appearing withdrawn. Even when a person with schizophrenia does speak, his language is often very basic and brief.

- **Avolition**, or inability or unwillingness to engage in goal-directed activities such as caring for oneself, working, or speaking to others. A person with these negative symptoms may appear depressed.

- **Anhedonia**, or lack of pleasure or interest in life activities.

*Lack of insight* or poor awareness of one's mental condition, a common occurrence in schizophrenia, sometimes links to negative symptoms as well (Antonius et al., 2011). Negative symptoms are not as dramatic or obvious as positive symptoms such as delusions and hallucinations but are nevertheless crucial and damaging aspects of schizophrenia and often more difficult to treat (Lysaker et al., 2011). Positive symptoms of schizophrenia may relate to neurochemical changes amenable to medication, but negative symptoms may relate to structural brain changes not largely affected by medication (we discuss this further in later sections).

People with catatonia may display bizarre motor movements and postures.

## Table 12.3

### DSM-5 Schizophrenia

A. Two (or more) of the following, each present for a significant portion of time during a 1-month period (or less if successfully treated). At least one of these must be (1), (2), or (3):
  1. Delusions.
  2. Hallucinations.
  3. Disorganized speech.
  4. Grossly disorganized or catatonic behavior.
  5. Negative symptoms.

B. For a significant portion of the time since the onset of the disturbance, level of functioning in one or more major areas, such as work, interpersonal relations, or self-care, is markedly below the level achieved prior to the onset (or when the onset is in childhood or adolescence, there is failure to achieve expected level of interpersonal, academic, or occupational functioning).

C. Continuous signs of the disturbance persist for at least 6 months. This 6-month period must include at least 1-month of symptoms (or less if successfully treated) that meet Criterion A (i.e., active-phase symptoms) and may include periods of prodromal or residual symptoms. During these prodromal or residual periods, the signs of the disturbance may be manifested by only negative symptoms or by two or more symptoms listed in Criterion A present in an attenuated form.

D. Schizoaffective disorder and depressive or bipolar disorder with psychotic features have been ruled out because either 1) no major depressive or manic episodes have occurred concurrently with the active-phase symptoms, or 2) if mood episodes have occurred during active-phase symptoms, they have been present for a minority of the total duration of the active and residual periods of the illness.

E. The disturbance is not attributable to the physiological effects of a substance or another medical condition.

F. If there is a history of autism spectrum disorder or a communication disorder of childhood onset, the additional diagnosis of schizophrenia is made only if prominent delusions or hallucinations, in addition to the other required symptoms of schizophrenia, are also present for at least 1 month (or less if successfully treated).

Specify if first episode, multiple episodes, continuous, or unspecified; if with catatonia; and severity.

American Psychiatric Association. (2013). *Diagnostic and statistical manual of mental disorders* (5th ed.). Arlington, VA: American Psychiatric Association.

in speech and thought processes, odd or withdrawn social interactions, perceptual distortions, attention and memory problems, and symptoms of depression and anxiety (Tandon, Shah, Keshavan, & Tandon, 2012). The prodromal phase is often marked by negative symptoms that make it difficult to determine exactly what problem a person has. This phase may resemble severe depression. Positive symptoms in attenuated or lesser form, such as unusual perceptual experiences or beliefs, may be present in the prodromal phase as well.

Following the prodromal phase, a person may enter a **psychotic prephase** marked by the first "full-blown" positive symptom of schizophrenia such as a hallucination (Hafner & Maurer, 2006). A particular stressor may trigger the psychotic prephase, such as James's overheard conversation, and the prephase often lasts less than 2 months. Positive symptoms usually increase at this point and a person is often admitted for treatment. Positive or negative symptoms must last at least 6 months for a diagnosis of schizophrenia, which may constitute the prodromal phase and psychotic prephase.

This 6-month (or longer) period must include a 1-month phase in which the symptoms are especially acute, or an **active phase** (APA, 2013). A person in the active phase usually experiences many

"full-blown" positive and negative symptoms, as James did, and needs hospitalization to protect himself and others. Following treatment, many people with schizophrenia advance to a **residual phase** that usually involves symptoms very similar to the prodromal phase (Jobe & Harrow, 2010). Many people with schizophrenia remain in this residual phase for much of their life.

Many people with schizophrenia show *heterogeneous* behavior, meaning their symptoms are present in different combinations and severity. The *Diagnostic and Statistical Manual of Mental Disorders* (5th edition; *DSM-5*) thus provides a rating scale for *dimensions* of schizophrenia that are fluid and that may apply better to people with mixed symptoms of schizophrenia (APA, 2013). These dimensions represent a continuum of different symptoms a person may have, ranging from not present and equivocal to mild, moderate, and severe.

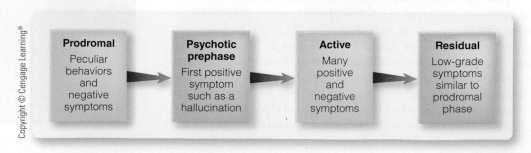

**FIGURE 12.2** PHASES OF SCHIZOPHRENIA

These dimensions include hallucinations, delusions, disorganized speech, abnormal psychomotor behavior (e.g., catatonia), negative symptoms, impaired cognition, depression, and mania (**Figure 12.3**).

Another possible dimension of schizophrenia relates to social disturbance (Potuzak, Ravichandran, Lewandowski, Ongur, & Cohen, 2012). All of these dimensions allow a therapist to describe someone with a psychotic disorder more specifically. James showed a moderate to severe degree of delusions and milder degrees of disorganized speech and negative symptoms. Someone with schizophrenia could have any combination of these problems to any degree in this dimensional approach.

## Schizophreniform Disorder

What about people who experience psychotic symptoms for less than 6 months? People who show features of schizophrenia for 1 to 6 months, and whose daily life functioning may not yet be greatly impaired, may have **schizophreniform disorder** (see **Table 12.4**) (APA, 2013). This disorder is sometimes thought of as a first-episode psychosis (Segarra et al., 2012).

James experienced times in his life, as in college, when he had psychotic features for less than 6 months and was able to function at a basic level. If a person with schizophreniform disorder has psychotic symptoms that last longer than 6 months, then the diagnosis could be changed to schizophrenia. People with schizophreniform disorder may be those *with* or *without*

| Hallucinations | Delusions | Disorganized speech | Abnormal psychomotor behavior |
|---|---|---|---|
| Degree of pressure to respond to voices or being bothered by voices | Degree of pressure to act on beliefs or being bothered by beliefs | Degree of difficulty following person's speech | Degree of bizarre motor behavior or catatonia |

| Negative symptoms | Impaired cognition | Depression | Mania |
|---|---|---|---|
| Degree of decrease in facial expression or gestures or self-initiated behavior | Degree of reduction in cognitive function | Degree of sadness or hopelessness or guilt | Degree of elevated, expansive, or irritable mood or restlessness |

**FIGURE 12.3** DSM-5 DIMENSIONS OF SCHIZOPHRENIA

*good prognostic features* (APA, 2013). Those with good prognostic features, like James, have adequate daily functioning before the onset of psychotic symptoms, confusion during the most active psychotic symptoms, no flat affect, and quick onset of psychotic symptoms after their behavior becomes noticeably different (Addington & Addington, 2005).

## Table 12.4

### DSM-5  Schizophreniform Disorder

A. Two (or more) of the following, each present for a significant portion of time during a 1-month period (or less if successfully treated). At least one of these must be (1), (2), or (3):
   1. Delusions.
   2. Hallucinations.
   3. Disorganized speech (e.g., frequent derailment or incoherence).
   4. Grossly disorganized or catatonic behavior.
   5. Negative symptoms (i.e., diminished emotional expression or avolition).

B. An episode of the disorder lasts at least 1 month but less than 6 months. When the diagnosis must be made without waiting for recovery, it should be qualified as "provisional."

C. Schizoaffective disorder and depressive or bipolar disorder with psychotic features have been ruled out because either 1) no major depressive or manic episodes have occurred concurrently with the active-phase symptoms, or 2) if mood episodes have occurred during active-phase symptoms, they have been present for a minority of the total duration of the active and residual periods of the illness.

D. The disturbance is not attributable to the physiological effects of a substance (e.g., a drug of abuse, a medication) or another medical condition.

   Specify if with or without good prognostic features; if with catatonia; and severity.

American Psychiatric Association. (2013). *Diagnostic and statistical manual of mental disorders* (5th ed). Arlington, VA: American Psychiatric Association.

## John Cadigan

*John Cadigan described living with schizophrenia in a film he made for HBO/Cinemax called People Say I'm Crazy (www.peoplesayimcrazy.org). His woodcuts have been exhibited at museums and galleries nationwide.*

My worst symptom is paranoia. A lot of times my paranoia comes in the form of thinking people hate me, thinking people don't like me just because of the way they look at me or because of what they do with their hands or what they say or what they don't say. At my boarding house, I can tell whether they like me or they don't like me by the way they make my bed. If the sheets are not slick and they are old sheets, with little bumps on them—that means they're sending me a message that they don't like what I'm doing. They're trying to get rid of me, they don't like me. If the sheets are all new and slick—that means I'm doing OK.

My disorder hit when I was in college at Carnegie Mellon. I had my first psychotic break 6 months before graduating, and I've been struggling with a form of schizophrenia ever since. Growing up, sports and art were the most important things in my life. I sometimes fantasized about being a professional soccer player. When I was in fifth grade I was voted most popular, most athletic, and most artistic. My senior year I was voted most quiet, which was pretty much true. I was. I think that was the beginning of my symptoms.

Katie Cadigan

John Cadigan

The first 3 years of my disorder I was sick all the time. I tried every antipsychotic, mood stabilizer and antidepressant on the market. But nothing worked. I couldn't read for a few years. Schizophrenia affects logic and comprehension. I literally could not understand the words. It was even hard to watch television. Basically, what I did all day was pace and drink coffee. And I eventually turned to alcohol and was getting drunk every day.

Finally in the mid-1990s the new generation of medication became available—the first new drugs for schizophrenia in decades. And I began taking one of them. Very very slowly, it started working. And, I got a new doctor, who is wonderful.

When my family realized that my schizophrenia was not going to go away, my mother moved out to California (where I live) from Boston. My disorder brought everyone in my family together.

Since my parents' divorce, my family had been very fractured. But they all united to try and help me.

I'm really close with my oldest sister Katie, who's a filmmaker. I usually go to Katie or my Mom when I'm having a bout of paranoia or depression. In the beginning of my disorder, when we really didn't know what was going on, Katie and her husband let me live with them. I was very sick then, so I wasn't the easiest person to live with. Now I hang out at Mom's house a lot and watch TV. There I can be alone. I can be safe. I'm lucky to have such a supportive family.

A lot of other families don't understand that schizophrenia is a brain disease. One of my best friends, Ann, was disowned by her family. Her children don't talk to her because they think she's crazy and don't want anything to do with her. She doesn't get to see her grandchildren. My mom and I have adopted her into our family. She calls me her adopted son and calls my mom her sister.

Here's what some of my family said when I asked what the hardest part of my disorder was for them:

MY MOM: "The hardest part? To single out one I couldn't do it. There were a hundred hardest parts. Just to watch the amount of suffering.... Once I understood how much having this brain disease was hurting you, how much you struggled with it and how much pain you were in—it felt unbearable to me

## Schizoaffective Disorder

You may have noticed that people with schizophrenia often have symptoms that resemble depression, such as loss of interest in things and decreased movement and talking. A person who meets many of the diagnostic criteria for schizophrenia may *also* meet diagnostic criteria for depression. She may thus qualify for a diagnosis of **schizoaffective disorder** (see **Table 12.5**; APA, 2013).

Schizoaffective disorder includes characteristic features of schizophrenia *and* a depressive or manic episode (Chapter 7). Symptoms of schizophrenia, however, are considered primary—delusions or hallucinations must last at least 2 weeks without prominent symptoms of a mood disorder. A person often develops schizophrenia and later develops depression, which may happen when she experiences negative consequences such as a job loss due to odd behavior. Two subtypes of schizoaffective

and that I couldn't do anything, really, to help you."

MY BROTHER STEVE: "There was a time when we went to see you in the hospital and you couldn't speak. Your eyes had this look of entrapment—that you were trapped inside yourself. And there was just sheer terror in your eyes. That was hard. Really hard."

MY SISTER KATIE: "The very hardest part was when you started getting suicidal. It was about 2 years into your disorder. It was horrible. I didn't want you to die."

People think that schizophrenia means split personality or multiple personality, but they're making a big mistake. The "schizo" prefix doesn't mean personality split—it means a break with reality. I don't know what reality is. I can't trust my own perceptions. The hardest struggle is to know what's real and what's not real. And that's a daily struggle for me.

I have a hard time being around people. Sometimes I feel restless and I feel like I've got to pace. I guess it's my constant fear that people are out to purposely drive me crazy or mess with my mind. Like there's a secret agenda. As if everybody is interconnected and they are slowly and subtly dropping clues. A glance here, and a glance there. It is evil and the evil is after me. It makes it really difficult to communicate to others and to get up the courage to reach out to others and make friends.

These thoughts—they just get in my head and fester in there. Then I tell myself, "It's not true. It's not true. It's not true. It's not true. It's not true. It's not true." And, I try to just say that over and over again. "It's not true. It's not true. It's not true."

My doctor helped me learn how to do reality checks. When I'm having a hard time with terrible thoughts, and I think it might be paranoia, I try to get up my courage to go to a safe person. It might be one of my sisters or my mom, or even my doctor. And I tell them what I'm thinking. And every single time, they tell me, "John, you're wrong. Your perceptions and your thoughts aren't based in reality." It doesn't take away the paranoia, but it helps lessen the intensity.

There are times when I can work and there are times when I can't work. When my thoughts are racing or when I'm incredibly paranoid, those are times when I can't work. It feels awful. It's just a terrible feeling. I don't have much hope. I don't. But I try to keep telling myself that it will pass. It will pass.

I've been volunteering at a food closet with my friend Patrick. He was signed up and it was his first time going and I just decided to go along and help. Clients are allowed two visits a week. They have a little computer there and Patrick checks them in. They move about a ton of food a week. So many people helped me and I get so much support from other people. I think it's good for my own soul to help others. It makes me feel good doing it. I enjoy it. I really enjoy doing it.

At the food closet, everything was fine for a while. Until the paranoia crept in. It all revolved around nametags. My friend Patrick had a nametag and this woman Shelly did and this guy Morris did and so did Gloria. They all had nametags and I didn't. And I thought it was a secret message telling me: "We hate you, John. We don't want you around, John. We think you are an awful person, John." It sounds so stupid when I say it but it really devastates me. This kind of thing happens to me all the time.

I wonder if I am ever going to get better. I know I've gotten better. But I wonder if I'm ever going to get a lot better. Totally better. I'm 30 years old now and have been struggling with this disorder for close to 9 years. Nine years. I remember one thing my friend Ed said to me. He said something like, "when you get to around 50 the symptoms kind of ease up a bit." That's another 20 years for me.

disorder include *depressive type* and *bipolar type,* the latter meaning the co-occurrence of main features of schizophrenia with manic episodes. Recall from Chapter 7 that people with depressive and bipolar disorders can also have psychotic symptoms, but in these cases, the depressive or bipolar disorder is most prominent (Tarbox, Brown, & Haas, 2012).

Schizoaffective disorder is sometimes considered part of a schizophrenia spectrum that includes depression, bipolar disorder, and schizotypal personality disorder (Jager, Haack, Becker, & Frasch, 2011). Clinicians often have a difficult task distinguishing symptoms of severe depressive or bipolar disorder from symptoms of schizophrenia. Imagine someone who is intensely withdrawn, who fails to move for hours at a time, and who has distorted thoughts—this could be someone with severe depression, symptoms of schizophrenia, or both.

## Delusional Disorder

**CASE: Jody**

**Jody** was a 38-year-old office manager who worked for a large law firm. She interacted with lawyers and their private secretaries to conduct financial and other business necessary for the firm to function efficiently. The firm was a competitive environment that involved substantial turnover and jockeying for better positions and offices. Jody was a competent manager, but she consistently wondered if her coworkers deliberately tried to sabotage her to gain her position.

Jody was involved in many discussions with the law partners over the years about these concerns, few of which were substantiated. Problems intensified recently, however, when one of the lawyers was promoted to partner, and his personal secretary was appointed as Jody's assistant. Jody felt threatened by this organizational move and became suspicious of Rachel, her new assistant. These suspicions deepened when Rachel moved her desk near Jody's and when Rachel took initiative to help Jody with daily tasks.

Jody's suspicions became more unusual—she believed Rachel was deliberately poisoning her lunch in an effort to make her sick. Jody thought this was an effort on Rachel's part to eventually secure Jody's position. Jody accused Rachel on several occasions of stealing, inserting substances into, and spitting on her lunch. Rachel vehemently denied all of this, but Jody enlisted the help of others in the office to spy on Rachel and even asked one of the lawyers to represent her in a lawsuit against Rachel. The law partners eventually had to intervene and told Jody she would lose her job if she continued these accusations and that she needed professional help.

People with schizophrenia or schizophreniform or schizoaffective disorder have psychotic symptoms such as delusions, hallucinations, disorganized speech, disorganized or catatonic behavior, and negative symptoms. Other people with a psychotic disorder, such as those with **delusional disorder**, however, have no psychotic symptoms except for one or more delusions (see **Table 12.6**; APA, 2013). A delusion could be nonbizarre or bizarre, the latter meaning it is not plausible. Jody's belief that a coworker poisoned her lunch is plausible, although not true, and thus nonbizarre. People with delusional disorder do not experience significant impairments in daily functioning apart from the impact of the delusion but may be quite distressed.

A person with delusional disorder may have one or more of the following delusions:

- *Erotomanic,* such as the mistaken belief a special person, such as a celebrity, loves the person from a distance

--- Table 12.5 ---

### DSM-5 Schizoaffective Disorder

A. An uninterrupted period of illness during which there is a major mood episode (major depressive or manic) concurrent with criterion A of schizophrenia.
   **Note:** The major depressive episode must include Criterion A1: Depressed mood.

B. Delusions or hallucinations for 2 or more weeks in the absence of a major mood episode (depressive or manic) during the lifetime duration of the illness.

C. Symptoms that meet criteria for a major mood episode are present for the majority of the total duration of the active residual portions of the illness.

D. The disturbance is not attributable to the effects of a substance (e.g., a drug of abuse, a medication) or another medical condition.

   Specify if bipolar or depressive type; if first episode, multiple episodes, continuous, or unspecified; if with catatonia; and severity.

American Psychiatric Association. (2013). *Diagnostic and statistical manual of mental disorders* (5th ed.). Arlington, VA: American Psychiatric Association.

--- Table 12.6 ---

### DSM-5 Delusional Disorder

A. The presence of one (or more) delusions with a duration of 1 month or longer.

B. Criterion A for schizophrenia has never been met.

C. Apart from the impact of the delusion(s) or its ramifications, functioning is not markedly impaired, and behavior is not obviously bizarre or odd.

D. If manic or major depressive episodes have occurred, these have been brief relative to the duration of the delusional periods.

E. The disturbance is not attributable to the physiological effects of a substance or another medical condition and is not better explained by another mental disorder, such as body dysmorphic disorder or obsessive-compulsive disorder.

   Specify if erotomanic, grandiose, jealous, persecutory, somatic, mixed, or unspecified type; if first episode, multiple episodes, continuous, or unspecified; if with bizarre content; and severity.

American Psychiatric Association. (2013). *Diagnostic and statistical manual of mental disorders* (5th ed.). Arlington, VA: American Psychiatric Association.

- *Grandiose,* such as the mistaken belief one is an especially powerful, famous, or knowledgeable person
- *Jealous,* such as the mistaken belief a spouse is having an affair
- *Persecutory,* such as Jody's mistaken belief another person aimed to harm her
- *Somatic,* or a mistaken belief about one's body, such as having some serious medical disease (Wustmann, Pillmann, & Marneron, 2011)

Some people develop a delusion because of their close relationship with another person who also has a delusion. This is sometimes called *folie à deux.* The two people often share similar ideas with respect to the irrational belief. This process could explain why Wanda Barzee, the wife of the man who kidnapped Elizabeth Smart in Utah, consented to and participated in this terrible crime. She appeared to believe, as her husband Brian Mitchell did, that kidnapping Smart was a "revelation from God" and that polygamy (multiple spouses) was acceptable. This process is also sometimes evident in cases of child maltreatment in which both parents believe their maladaptive behavior benefits the child (Wehmeier, Barth, & Remschmidt, 2003). The delusion may weaken in the second person when she is separated from the more dominant, delusional partner.

## Brief Psychotic Disorder

What happens when a person has psychotic symptoms for less than 1 month? A person with such symptoms may qualify for a diagnosis of **brief psychotic disorder**, which involves several key features of schizophrenia occurring for 1 day to 1 month (see **Table 12.7**; APA, 2013). These features include delusions, hallucinations, disorganized speech, and disorganized or catatonic behavior. Symptoms of brief psychotic disorder often occur after an environmental stressor or traumatic event (Tessner, Mittal, & Walker, 2011).

Psychotic symptoms may occur in women after giving birth—**postpartum psychosis** (Spinelli, 2009). Recall from Chapter 7 that some women have postpartum depression; some women experience postpartum depression *and* psychosis. Andrea Yates, a woman from Texas who drowned her five children in a bathtub in her house, appeared to have delusional and depressive symptoms following the birth of her most recent child and the death of her father. Her condition underscores the need for greater knowledge and prevention of postpartum psychosis and depression. Symptoms of brief psychotic disorder often dissipate as a person becomes better able to cope with the stressor, if one exists. The symptoms persist and can lead to disastrous consequences or schizophreniform disorder or schizophrenia in other cases, however.

## Epidemiology of Psychotic Disorders

Schizophrenia occurs in 0.33 to 0.72 percent of the general population (McGrath, Saha, Chant, & Welham, 2008; Saha, Chant, & McGrath, 2008; Tandon, Keshavan, & Nasrallah, 2008). Median age of onset is 22 years (although the disorder could occur at any age), and schizophrenia is somewhat more frequent among males than females (Luoma, Hakko, Ollinen, Jarvelin, & Lindeman, 2008). Males with schizophrenia tend to have symptoms at a younger age than females with

---

### Table 12.7

#### DSM-5  Brief Psychotic Disorder

A. Presence of one (or more) of the following symptoms. At least one of these must be (1), (2), or (3):
   1. Delusions.
   2. Hallucinations.
   3. Disorganized speech (e.g., frequent derailment or incoherence).
   4. Grossly disorganized or catatonic behavior.

B. Duration of an episode of the disturbance is at least 1 day but less than 1 month, with eventual full return to premorbid level of functioning.

C. The disturbance is not better explained by major depressive or bipolar disorder with psychotic features or another psychotic disorder such as schizophrenia or catatonia, and is not attributable to the physiological effects of a substance (e.g., a drug of abuse, a medication) or another medical condition.

American Psychiatric Association. (2013). *Diagnostic and statistical manual of mental disorders* (5th ed.). Arlington, VA: American Psychiatric Association.

Andrea Yates, a Texas woman who drowned her five children (four pictured), may have suffered from a postpartum psychosis.

Wanda Barzee (top right), the reported wife of Brian Mitchell (top left), may have had a delusion with her husband that explained her consent to kidnap Elizabeth Smart.

schizophrenia (Eranti, MacCabe, Bundy, & Murray, 2013). This means men usually have more severe symptoms as well.

One possible reason why men have more severe schizophrenia symptoms than women may be that women have certain biological factors, such as protective hormones or less severe brain changes, which help prevent the development of very severe symptoms. Another possibility is that women function

better than men in work and social settings, which delays onset of schizophrenia symptoms until later in life (Falkenburg & Tracy, 2012). Ethnicity and income level may relate to schizophrenia as well (see **Box 12.1** and later section on cultural influences).

Schizophrenia can be associated with many other mental disorders because of its complex and devastating symptoms. Recall that schizophrenia can be, for some people, the final phase of a psychotic spectrum that initially includes brief psychotic disorder (less than 1 month) and schizophreniform disorder (1–6 months). The odd behaviors associated with schizophrenia, such as unusual perceptual experiences and persecutory thoughts, may also mean schizophrenia is part of a spectrum of disorders that includes schizotypal, schizoid, and paranoid personality disorders (Chapter 10; **Figure 12.4**) (Ritsner, 2011). These disorders generally involve bizarre and suspicious behaviors and thought-related problems that greatly interfere with many aspects of a person's life.

The most common mental disorders otherwise associated with schizophrenia are anxiety-related, depressive, bipolar, and substance use disorders (Buckley, Miller, Lehrer, & Castle, 2009). Depression could develop before schizophrenia and help trigger psychotic symptoms, or the development of psychotic symptoms could lead to a downward spiral involving difficult events such as job loss that causes someone to later become depressed (Rosen, Miller, D'Andrea, McGlashan, & Woods, 2006).

Suicide is also much more common among people with schizophrenia (4.9 percent) than the general population (0.01–0.03 percent). Suicide in people with schizophrenia closely relates to onset of the disorder, depression, excessive substance use, recent loss, agitation, and poor adherence to treatment. People with schizophrenia most at risk for suicide tend to be single, unemployed, and socially isolated males

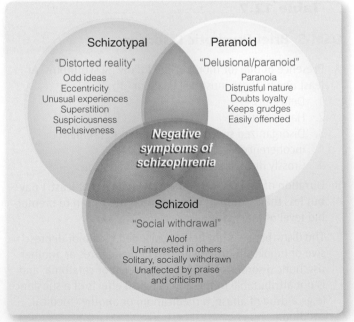

**FIGURE 12.4** SCHIZOPHRENIA SPECTRUM DISORDERS

## BOX 12.1 Focus on Diversity

### Ethnicity and Income Level in Schizophrenia

A controversial issue is whether ethnicity and income level have an impact on schizophrenia. An analysis of different countries generally indicates no large variation in prevalence rates for schizophrenia (Saha, Welham, Chant, & McGrath, 2006). Certain groups of people may be at increased risk for psychotic disorder, however. Schizophrenia is more common in certain immigrant populations of ethnic minority status. People in urban settings may also be at higher risk for schizophrenia than those in rural settings (Vilain et al., 2013).

Possible reasons for these findings include exposure to more pollution and noise, higher rates of excessive substance use, increased risk of infectious diseases and malnutrition, stress from poverty conditions and unemployment, racism,

social isolation, poor availability of treatment services, and the interaction of these conditions with genetic predispositions for psychotic disorder (Mura, Petretto, Bhat, & Carta, 2012). One single factor does not seem responsible, however, for possible ethnic differences in schizophrenia.

Schizophrenia also relates to lower income level. Knowing the direction of this relationship is not easy, however. Some people may develop schizophrenia following the stressors of poverty, but some people may first develop schizophrenia and then drift into lower socioeconomic levels as their disorder progresses and their income declines, such as after job loss. People with more income may also have access to earlier treatment and display less positive symptoms of schizophrenia. People with less income are also more likely to believe their disorder will result in stigma and discrimination from others (Broussard, Goulding, Talley, & Compton, 2012; Muntaner, Eaton, Miech, & O'Campo, 2004).

(Hor & Taylor, 2010). Violence toward others is sometimes but not usually a feature of schizophrenia (see **Box 12.2**).

Schizophreniform disorder is quite similar to schizophrenia, especially the prodromal phase of schizophrenia. Most people with the disorder have thus not yet presented for treatment, and prevalence rates for schizophreniform disorder (0.09 percent) are therefore much lower than for schizophrenia (Goldner, Hsu, Waraich, & Somers, 2002). As many as two-thirds of people with schizophreniform disorder may eventually receive a diagnosis of schizophrenia or schizoaffective disorder (Whitty et al., 2005).

The prevalence of schizoaffective disorder is similar to schizophrenia (0.5–0.8 percent; Malhi, Green, Fagiolini, Peselow, & Kumari, 2008). Those with schizophrenia and bipolar disorder tend to display symptoms at a younger age than those with schizophrenia and depression. Schizoaffective disorder tends to be more prevalent among women than men (Iniesta, Ochoa, & Usall, 2012). This is likely due to frequent presence of depression in schizoaffective disorder.

Unusual beliefs about people or events are common in the general population, but formal delusional disorder is rare (0.01–0.05 percent prevalence rate). Many people with delusional disorder have persecutory (54.5 percent) and/or reference (46.6 percent) delusions (Cardno & McGuffin, 2006; Grover, Biswas, & Avasthi, 2007). The prevalence of formal delusional disorders such as erotomania (15 cases per 100,000 people) is also quite low (Kelly, 2005). Delusional disorder may be slightly more common in women than men, but men with the disorder tend to have more severe symptoms and worse functioning (de Portugal et al., 2010).

Little is known about brief psychotic disorder because the problem is often limited in duration and scope and because many people recover quickly. Brief psychotic disorder is thus considered to be an *acute transient psychosis*. Acute transient psychoses differ from schizophrenia in that they involve more females, a later age of onset, greater anxiety and fluctuation of symptoms, and less social withdrawal (Castagnini & Berrios, 2011). Postpartum psychosis occurs in 1 or 2 of 1,000 births and is often linked to social isolation, confusion, disorganized behavior, sleep deprivation, and severe symptoms of depression and bipolar disorder (Spinelli, 2009). Suicide or harm to a newborn, as was the case with Andrea Yates, can occur in extreme cases as well.

## Stigma Associated with Schizophrenia

Schizophrenia is a severe and debilitating disorder, so stigma associated with the problem is clearly a concern. Brohan and colleagues (2010) surveyed thousands of people with schizophrenia or other psychotic disorders. Many (41.7%) reported moderate to high levels of self-stigma, which referred to loss of previous identities (e.g., as a partner, friend, parent) to adopt a stigmatized view of themselves as someone with a severe mental disorder. In addition, most participants felt the public held negative attitudes toward those using mental health services, and 69.4% reported moderate to high levels of perceived discrimination from others. One bright note, however, was the fact that people with schizophrenia who had more social contacts experienced less self-stigma. The researchers speculated that reduced alienation and greater support from others was important for reducing stigma. Others have found as well that

## BOX 12.2 Focus on Violence

### Are People with Schizophrenia More Violent?

Media portrayals of people with psychotic disorders such as schizophrenia are often skewed toward images of voices commanding a person to commit violent acts. A serial killer in 1970s New York City was murdering women and young lovers with a .44 caliber handgun. The murderer claimed in a letter that "Papa Sam" was commanding him to go out and kill—the murderer was later dubbed the "Son of Sam." David Berkowitz, a man with psychotic delusions about demons telling him to hunt for blood, was eventually arrested for these terrible crimes. Newspaper headlines screamed almost daily about the hunt for Berkowitz and later about his mental state. The widespread and intensive coverage gave people the impression that those with psychoses must necessarily be dangerous. Many voices heard by people with schizophrenia do not command them to kill, but intense media coverage of certain cases such as Berkowitz's does raise the question about whether this population is particularly violent.

People with schizophrenia are arrested for violent acts much more frequently than are members of the general population (see accompanying table) (Brennan, Mednick, & Hodgins, 2000; Hodgins, 2008). Strong risk factors for violence in this population include prior history of violence, excessive substance use, and acute psychotic symptoms such as delusions (Bo, Abu-Akel, Kongerslev, Haahr, & Simonsen, 2011). Furthermore, 3 to 7 percent of men imprisoned in Western countries have a psychotic disorder, which is substantially greater than in the general population (less than 1 percent; Fazel & Danesh, 2002).

Consider other evidence regarding violence and schizophrenia, however. First, the great majority of people in prison do not have psychotic disorders and more have depression than psychotic disorder (Fazel & Seewald, 2012). Second, only about

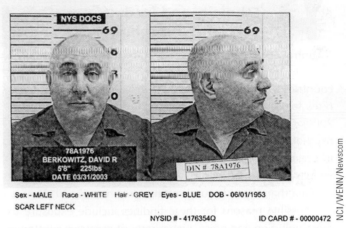

NYS DOCS
78A1976
BERKOWITZ, DAVID R
5'8"  225lbs
DATE 03/31/2003
DIN # 78A1976
Sex - MALE   Race - WHITE   Hair - GREY   Eyes - BLUE   DOB - 06/01/1953
SCAR LEFT NECK
NYSID # - 4176354Q          ID CARD # - 00000472

NCI/WENN/Newscom

The violent crimes of "Son of Sam" David Berkowitz were prominently displayed in newspaper headlines, which may have skewed the public's perception of people with schizophrenia as overly dangerous.

1 in 14 people with first-episode psychosis engage in violence that causes harm to others (Foley et al., 2005). People with first-episode psychosis are much more likely to harm themselves (Tarrier, Khan, Cater, & Picken, 2007). Third, people with severe mental disorder such as schizophrenia were 4 times more likely than the general population to be *victimized* by a violent crime such as rape or robbery in the past year (Teplin, McClelland, Abram, & Weiner, 2005). Some people with schizophrenia are at risk for committing violent crimes, but the vast majority do not do so and are more likely to be victims themselves.

### Arrests for Violent Acts (%)

| Diagnosis | Men | Women |
|---|---|---|
| No diagnosis | 2.7 | 0.1 |
| Schizophrenia | 11.3 | 2.8 |

Source: Brennan, P.A., Mednick, S.A., & Hodgins, S. (2000). Major mental disorders and criminal violence in a Danish birth cohort. *Archives of General Psychiatry*, 57, 494-500.

*stigma resistance*, or one's capacity to counteract stigma, is associated with a social network with a sufficient number of friends (Sibitz, Unger, Woppmann, Zidek, & Amering, 2011). This may especially be the case if supportive friends and family members have knowledge about the psychotic disorder (Smith, Reddy, Foster, Asbury, & Brooks, 2011).

Stigma associated with schizophrenia and other psychotic disorders is important because it affects symptoms and treatment. Staring and colleagues (2009) examined 114 people with schizophrenia spectrum disorders. Participants who had good insight about their condition and who did not perceive much stigmatization tended to have better outcomes with respect to depression, self-esteem, and quality of life compared with those with stigmatizing beliefs. Good insight and less stigma may be associated as well with greater engagement during treatment as well as medication compliance.

## INTERIM SUMMARY

▶ People with psychotic disorders have bizarre emotions, thoughts, and behaviors that greatly interfere with many different areas of daily functioning.

▶ Positive or excessive symptoms of schizophrenia include delusions, hallucinations, and disorganized speech and behavior.

▶ Negative or deficit symptoms of schizophrenia include flat affect, alogia, avolition, and anhedonia.

▶ Schizophrenia may also be rated by severity across dimensions that include positive and negative symptoms as well as impaired cognition, depression, and mania.

▶ Schizophreniform disorder is very similar to schizophrenia but lasts 1 to 6 months and may not involve serious impairment in daily functioning.

▶ Schizoaffective disorder applies to those who have features of schizophrenia and a depressive or manic episode.

▶ Delusional disorder involves one or more delusions that may or may not have bizarre content.

▶ Brief psychotic disorder involves features of schizophrenia that last 1 day to 1 month and can be triggered by a traumatic event.

▶ Schizophrenia is a rare disorder but is more commonly seen in males. The disorder is often viewed along a spectrum of disorders and is associated with depression and suicide and substance use.

▶ Stigma associated with schizophrenia can be severe and affects symptoms and treatment.

## REVIEW QUESTIONS

1. What are key positive and negative symptoms of schizophrenia?
2. Describe the main dimensions of schizophrenia that can be rated.
3. Describe the main features of schizophreniform, schizoaffective, and brief psychotic disorder.
4. What types of delusions are common to people with psychotic disorders?
5. Who most commonly has schizophrenia and what conditions relate to the disorder?

# Psychotic Disorders: Causes and Prevention

Why would someone like James have such bizarre thoughts and behaviors? Recall that many mental disorders are thought to result from a combination of biological and environmental variables. Many people are born with a genetic or biological predisposition toward certain personality characteristics and mental conditions. These biological predispositions are sometimes strong and sometimes weak, but they appear to be quite strong in schizophrenia. We thus concentrate mostly on biological risk factors for schizophrenia but cover environmental factors that may have some impact as well.

## Biological Risk Factors for Psychotic Disorders

Biological predispositions in people with psychotic disorders may involve genetics, brain and neurochemical features, and cognitive deficits.

### GENETICS

Family, twin, and adoption studies indicate that schizophrenia has a strong genetic basis. **Figure 12.5** summarizes studies of the prevalence of schizophrenia in relatives of people with schizophrenia (Fanous & Kendler, 2008; Faraone, Tsuang, & Tsuang, 1999). Recall that schizophrenia is present in less than 1 percent of the general population. Children of people with schizophrenia, however, are about 12 times more likely than the general population to develop schizophrenia. The risk factor is high even among more distant relatives. Grandchildren of people with schizophrenia are about 3 times more likely than the general population to develop schizophrenia. Family data also indicate increased risk for close relatives for schizophreniform, schizoaffective, and aspects of schizotypal and avoidant personality disorders (Fogelson et al., 2010; Goldstein, Buka, Seidman, & Tsuang, 2010).

Twin studies also indicate that schizophrenia has a genetic component. Concordance rates for schizophrenia among identical twins (50–53 percent) are generally much higher than for fraternal twins (4.1–15 percent; Shih, Belmonte, & Zandi, 2004). Adoption studies reveal a similar finding. Children born to mothers with schizophrenia but raised by parents without schizophrenia still show a higher likelihood

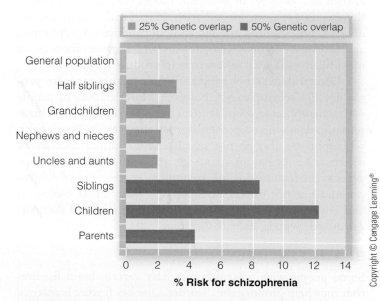

**FIGURE 12.5** **LIFETIME PREVALENCE OF SCHIZOPHRENIA BY DEGREE OF RELATIONSHIP TO A PERSON WITH SCHIZOPHRENIA** *From Faraone, S.V., Tsuang, M.T., & Tsuang, D.W. (1999). Genetics of mental disorders: A guide for students, clinicians, and researchers. New York: Guilford. Copyright © 1999 by Guilford Publications, Inc. Reprinted by permission.*

of developing schizophrenia themselves (11–19 percent) than control groups (0–11 percent). This appears to be especially true if parents have problems communicating with their adoptive children whose biological mothers had schizophrenia (Cantor-Graae & Pedersen, 2007; Cardno, Thomas, & McGuffin, 2002). Heritability for schizophrenia is estimated to be 0.70 to 0.90 (Mulle, 2012).

Several researchers have found linkages to schizophrenia on chromosomes 1-10, 13-15, 17, 20, and 22. This seems especially true for chromosomes 2, 6, 10, and 22 (Chen, Riley, & Kendler, 2009). The data are not consistent, however, because many people with schizophrenia do not show these genetic markers (Crow, 2008). Current research

The Genain quadruplets were identical siblings, all female, who developed schizophrenia. Researchers at the National Institute for Mental Health studied them closely to learn more about genetic contributions to psychosis.

has thus begun to focus on new genetic mutations, especially on chromosome 22, that could lead to schizophrenia (Rodriguez-Murillo, Gogos, & Karayiorgou, 2012).

Many people with schizophrenia may also have multiple genes that work together to help produce the disorder. This is known as a *polygenic* or *multilocus* model (Gejman, Sanders, & Kendler, 2011). Some people with schizophrenia may have individual genes strong enough to help produce schizophrenia, and thus to be recognized by researchers, but even these genes most likely work with others to help produce the disorder.

Genetic data do not paint the whole picture as to why people develop schizophrenia, however. Most relatives of people with schizophrenia, even identical twins of parents with schizophrenia, *do not* develop the disorder themselves. People with schizophrenia also do not usually have children themselves, which raises questions about genetic transmission. Perhaps genetic predispositions are strong for some types of schizophrenia but not others, and perhaps many other biological and environmental variables are responsible as well (Svrakic, Zorumski, Svrakic, Zwir, & Cloninger, 2013).

## BRAIN FEATURES

Some people with schizophrenia have certain brain features that may help produce the disorder. One key feature is *enlarged ventricles,* or spaces or gaps in the brain (**Figure 12.6**). This finding is not specific to schizophrenia, because some people with neurocognitive disorders (Chapter 14) also have enlarged ventricles. This brain feature is a highly replicated biological finding in people with schizophrenia, however (Jaaro-Peled, Ayhan, Pletnikov, & Sawa, 2010).

How might enlarged ventricles lead to schizophrenia? One possibility is that enlarged ventricles mean a general failure in normal brain development or disruption of pathways from one area of the brain to the next. An important disruption may involve neural connections between areas of

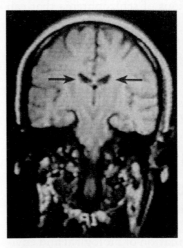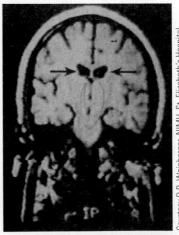

**FIGURE 12.6** COMPARISON OF BRAINS OF PEOPLE WITHOUT (LEFT) AND WITH (RIGHT) SCHIZOPHRENIA. NOTE THE INCREASED VENTRICULAR SIZE IN THE AFFECTED BRAIN.
*From "Regional deficits in brain volume in schizophrenia: A meta-analysis of voxel based morphometry studies," by R. Honea, T.J. Crow, D. Passingham, and C.E. Mackay,* American Journal of Psychiatry, 162, 2005. *Reprinted with permission from the American Journal of Psychiatry, Copyright (2005) American Psychiatric Association.*

the brain that influence cognition and language. Schizophrenia is increasingly seen as a disorder of cortical connectivity (Rapoport, Giedd, & Gogtay, 2012). Another possibility is that added space means critical brain areas are less well developed than they should be. This leads us to the next major finding in this area: differences in lobes of the brain.

Schizophrenia researchers have paid particular attention to poor development of the temporal lobe of the brain, which is partially responsible for auditory processing and language (**Figure 12.7**). People with schizophrenia often have key problems in auditory processing and language, so these problems may be due to differences in temporal lobe areas (Shepherd, Laurens, Matheson, Carr, & Green, 2012). The medial temporal lobe, especially the amygdala and hippocampus, is smaller in people with schizophrenia than in control participants (Karnik-Henry et al., 2012). These areas are partially responsible for verbal and spatial memory processing and emotion, which are problematic as well for people with schizophrenia. Reduced size in the superior and middle temporal gyri, which can affect auditory memory and language processing, has also been linked to people with schizophrenia (Cobia, Smith, Wang, & Csernansky, 2012).

Other researchers have found reductions in total brain size and gray matter, which affect the size of different brain lobes and thus cognition (**Figure 12.8**; Asami et al., 2012). Some have pointed to more specific deficits with respect to the frontal lobe, which is heavily involved in complex information processing and organization of functioning and may contribute to auditory hallucinations (Yamada et al., 2007). Other specific brain differences implicated in schizophrenia, which also often involve smaller size, include the following:

- *Thalamus* and *parietal/occipital lobes,* differences in which may affect the integration of sensory information and visual attention (Shepherd, Laurens, Matheson, Carr, & Green, 2012)

- *Basal ganglia* and *cerebellum,* differences in which may affect motor behavior and output to higher-order brain areas (Glenthoj et al., 2007; Puri et al., 2008)

- *Corpus callosum,* differences in which may affect language and communication between the brain hemispheres (Walterfang et al., 2008)

Enlarged ventricles and reduced brain size in certain areas such as the frontal lobe may help explain negative symptoms of schizophrenia (Galderisi et al., 2000). Differences in other areas such as the temporal lobe may help explain positive symptoms of schizophrenia. Loss of gray matter may start in the parietal lobe, perhaps even during adolescence, and later spread to the frontal and temporal lobes (Thompson et al., 2009). How this loss spreads and the degree to which it does may help determine a person's specific symptoms of schizophrenia.

The other major finding with respect to brain changes and schizophrenia is *lack of asymmetry* in certain areas. Some people with schizophrenia may have differences in the *heteromodal association cortex,* which includes two key brain areas for language processing: *Broca's area* and *planum temporale.* Lack of asymmetry in the planum temporale is a possible risk factor for learning disorder (Chapter 13) and a similar finding has been found for people with schizophrenia (Oertel-Knöchel et al., 2013). Lack of asymmetry in other brain areas has been implicated in schizophrenia as well, including the *anterior cingulate cortex* (Rothlisberger et al., 2012), which is partially responsible for types of decision making.

Studies of brain features represent fascinating advances in the field, but bear in mind that findings are often less than conclusive. How these brain changes might lead to specific symptoms of schizophrenia is not completely known either. These brain changes could be due to genetic predispositions,

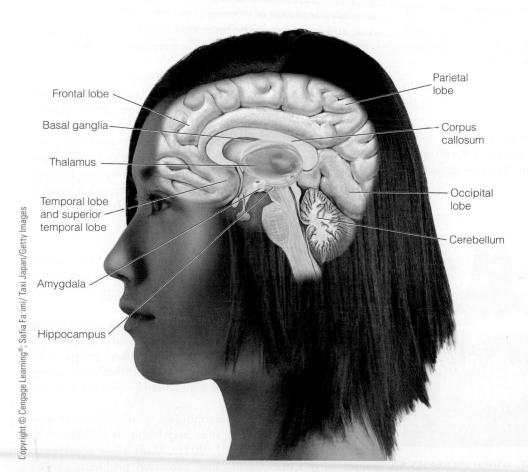

Frontal lobe

Basal ganglia

Thalamus

Temporal lobe and superior temporal lobe

Amygdala

Hippocampus

Parietal lobe

Corpus callosum

Occipital lobe

Cerebellum

**FIGURE 12.7**  BRAIN AREAS MOST IMPLICATED IN SCHIZOPHRENIA

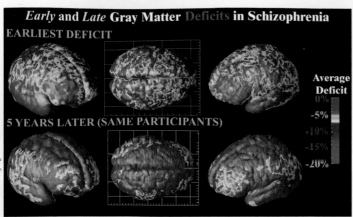

**FIGURE 12.8** **COMPARISON OF BRAINS OF PEOPLE WITH SCHIZOPHRENIA AT AN EARLIER (UPPER ROW) AND LATER (BOTTOM ROW) STAGE** Note progressive loss of gray matter.

simple anatomical differences in the general population, degeneration in the brain over time, environmental factors, or other variables. Not everyone with schizophrenia shows measurable brain differences, which means that other causes, such as the neurochemical features we discuss next, are likely present.

## NEUROCHEMICAL FEATURES

One of the most prominent theories of schizophrenia is that symptoms are caused by an excess of certain neurotransmitters in the brain, especially dopamine (**Figure 12.9**). The *excess dopamine hypothesis* has been popular largely because:

- Many people with positive symptoms of schizophrenia are successfully treated with drugs that lower dopamine levels (discussed later in the treatment section).

- Antipsychotic drugs may actually produce very low levels of dopamine and create side effects similar to Parkinson's disease, which is caused by deficient levels of dopamine (Chapter 14; Esper & Factor, 2008).

- Excess levels of dopamine, from methamphetamine intoxication for example, can lead to motor problems and psychotic symptoms (Callaghan et al., 2012).

- L-dopa, a drug that boosts levels of dopamine in people with Parkinson's disease, can produce psychotic symptoms if taken in excess and can aggravate symptoms of schizophrenia (Jaskiw & Popli, 2004).

- Dopamine receptors, especially D2 receptors, may be denser in the brains of some people with schizophrenia (Seeman, 2011).

The excess dopamine theory was criticized as an *overall* explanation for schizophrenia, however, because it did not explain many *negative* symptoms such as avolition and poor speech (Thaker & Carpenter, 2001). Researchers also reported inconsistent findings as to whether people with schizophrenia actually have more dopamine receptors or turnover (death of some neurons and generation of new ones) as one might expect in this theory (Meyer-Lindenberg et al., 2002).

A revised theory regarding dopamine is that the neurotransmitter itself is less important than is its role in helping to control information processing in the cortex (Murray, Lapin, & Di Forti, 2008). Recall that changes in brain lobes have been implicated in schizophrenia and many of these areas involve large amounts of dopamine receptors. Areas of the brain that link to the cortex, such as the basal ganglia or amygdala, also have large amounts of dopamine receptors. Changes in dopamine and key areas of the brain may interact to help produce symptoms of schizophrenia, but the precise nature of this possibility remains under study.

Other neurotransmitters have been implicated in schizophrenia as well, including noradrenaline, serotonin, gamma-aminobutyric acid, and glutamate (Carlsson, 2006; Craven, Priddle, Crow, & Esiri, 2005). Perhaps these other neurotransmitters, especially serotonin, interact with dopamine and deficits in key brain areas to help produce symptoms of schizophrenia. Less serotonin in the frontal cortex may lead to more activity in this brain area and thus more dopamine activity (Alex, Yavanian, McFarlane, Pluto, & Pehek, 2005).

## COGNITIVE DEFICITS

Brain changes and other biological factors may help explain why many people with schizophrenia have several key cognitive deficits. Key deficits include memory, attention, learning, language, and executive functions such as problem-solving and decision-making abilities (Savla et al., 2012). Memory and attention in particular are problematic for many people with schizophrenia. With respect to memory, many people with schizophrenia have great difficulty recalling information, using cues to aid recall, and retaining information over time (Stone & His, 2011).

Many people with schizophrenia also experience sustained attention problems that may begin in childhood or adolescence (Diwadkar et al., 2011). Many close relatives of people with schizophrenia have attention problems as well (Giakoumaki, Roussos, Pallis, & Bitsios, 2011). Also, many

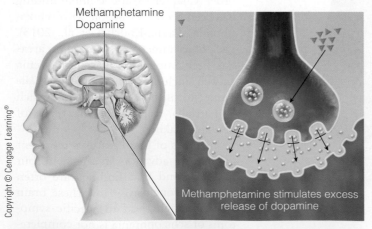

**FIGURE 12.9** **METHAMPHETAMINE USE, WHICH INCREASES DOPAMINE, CAN LEAD TO PSYCHOTIC SYMPTOMS.**

people with schizophrenia have problems processing rapid visual information, tracking objects with their eyes, and concentrating on one subject (Green, Waldron, Simpson, & Coltheart, 2008). Difficulty processing information may lead to sensory overload, and this may help explain positive symptoms such as hallucinations and delusions. Negative symptoms might be the result of withdrawal from this sensory overload (Thoma et al., 2005). Difficulty processing information may also be central to the disorganized speech found in many people with psychotic disorders (Becker, Cicero, Cowan, & Kerns, 2012).

Some researchers believe schizophrenia subtypes could be based on cognitive functioning. Many people with schizophrenia have little cognitive impairment, but others have severe and generalized impairment similar to dementia (Chapter 14; Kayman & Goldstein, 2012). Less cognitive impairment may relate to temporal lobe dysfunction; more severe impairment may relate to frontal lobe dysfunction (Allen, Goldstein, & Weiner, 2001). Severity levels and symptoms of schizophrenia are incredibly diverse and not easily subject to such classification, however (Goldstein, Shemansky, & Allen, 2005). Still, cognitive distinctions may be important for assessment and treatment.

## Environmental Risk Factors for Psychotic Disorders

Early and later environmental factors also influence the development of psychotic disorders. These environmental factors include prenatal complications, adverse life events and excessive substance use, and cultural and evolutionary influences.

### PRENATAL COMPLICATIONS

People with schizophrenia, if they had some developmental delay, tend to have had more prenatal complications than the general population (Clarke et al., 2011). One prenatal complication that seems closely involved in psychotic disorders is *hypoxic ischemia,* or low blood flow and oxygen to the brain. This can lead to enlarged ventricles (see earlier brain features section). Lower birth weight and smaller head circumference are also common to this population (Fineberg, Ellman, Buka, Yolken, & Cannon, 2013).

Prenatal complications can also come in the form of viruses and infections. People with schizophrenia are born disproportionately in late winter or spring months; therefore, the fetus has developed in times involving higher risk for influenza and other diseases (**Figure 12.10**). This risk may be even more so if a child is born in a large urban setting or if his family recently migrated to another country (Stilo, Di Forti, & Murray, 2011). Some have noted also that schizophrenia is most frequent during times of famine (Song, Wang, & Hu, 2009). Exposure to rubella, viral encephalitis, or severe malnutrition could place a fetus at increased risk for schizophrenia and other disorders (Brown, 2011).

### ADVERSE LIFE EVENTS AND EXCESSIVE SUBSTANCE USE

Maternal stress during the prenatal period may lead to important brain changes and later mental disorders, including schizophrenia (Khashan et al., 2008). Later environmental

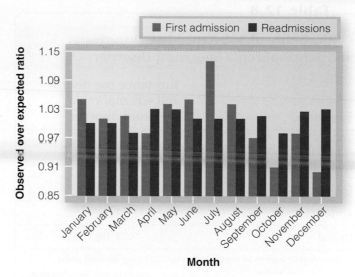

**FIGURE 12.10** **RATES OF FIRST ADMISSIONS AND READMISSIONS OF SCHIZOPHRENIA BY BIRTH MONTH** Note the generally higher rates of first admissions among people born in spring and summer months. *Source. Clarke, M., Moran, P., Keogh, F., Morris, M., Kinsella, A., Larkin, C., Walsh, D., & O'Callaghan, E. (1999). Seasonal influences on admissions for affective disorder and schizophrenia in Ireland: A comparison of first and readmissions.* European Psychiatry, 14, 253.

factors such as adverse life events and excessive substance use could also influence the development of psychotic disorders. Many people with schizophrenia experience stressful life events in weeks and months before the onset of psychotic symptoms, especially if they are emotionally reactive (Docherty, St-Hilaire, Aakre, & Seghers, 2009). Such was the case with James.

People with psychotic disorders are also much more likely to use marijuana excessively than the general population (Casadio, Fernandes, Murray, & Di Forti, 2011). Other drugs could lead to psychotic symptoms as well. Excessive substance use among people with schizophrenia symptoms is common (see **Table 12.8**). Whether stressful life events and excessive substance use trigger psychotic symptoms or whether they develop afterward is not clear. Some people may use alcohol or other drugs to cope with psychotic symptoms, but substance use disorder and schizophrenia also share common risk factors such as increased mesolimbic dopaminergic activity (Addy, Radhakrishnan, Cortes, & D'Souza, 2012).

Traumatic life events and excessive substance use often occur together in people with schizophrenia. Many women with schizophrenia or schizoaffective disorder who also use substances excessively have experienced episodes of child or adult maltreatment, assault, motor vehicle accidents, and post-traumatic stress disorder (46 percent; **Figure 12.11**; Gearon, Kaltman, Brown, & Bellack, 2003). What remains unclear, however, is whether stressful life events trigger psychotic symptoms or whether psychotic symptoms place people in vulnerable positions in which they may be exploited by others.

## Table 12.8

**Comorbidity of Substance Use Disorder and Schizophrenia-Spectrum Disorder**

| Substance | Substance use disorder and schizophrenia spectrum disorder |
|---|---|
| Alcohol | 65.7% |
| Cannabis | 22.7% |
| Cocaine | 23.2% |
| Amphetamine | 1.7% |
| Opioid | 1.1% |

Diagnostic distributions of people with a substance use disorder and a schizophrenia-spectrum disorder. Some people may have had more than one substance use disorder.

From Compton, M.T., Weiss, P.S., West, J.C., & Kaslow, N.J. (2005). The associations between substance use disorders, schizophrenia-spectrum disorders, and Axis IV psychosocial problems. *Social Psychiatry and Psychiatric Epidemiology, 40,* 939–946, Table 1. Reprinted by permission of Springer Science and Business Media.

| Type of trauma | N | % |
|---|---|---|
| **Childhood** | | |
| Sexual maltreatment | 33 | 61 |
| Physical maltreatment | 26 | 48 |
| Witnessed family violence | 35 | 65 |
| **Adulthood** | | |
| Sexual maltreatment | 32 | 59 |
| Physical assault or maltreatment | 44 | 82 |
| Death of a close friend or loved one | 42 | 78 |
| Life-threatening illness | 30 | 56 |
| Robbed with a weapon | 29 | 54 |
| Loved one experienced a life-threatening accident, assault, or illness | 25 | 46 |
| Life threatened with knife or gun | 25 | 46 |
| Motor vehicle accident | 22 | 41 |
| Witnessed a stranger being assaulted | 20 | 37 |
| Revictimization in adulthood of victims of childhood trauma | 36 | 67 |

**FIGURE 12.11** LIFETIME EXPOSURE TO TRAUMATIC EVENTS IN 54 WOMEN WITH SUBSTANCE USE DISORDERS AND SCHIZOPHRENIA

## CULTURAL AND EVOLUTIONARY INFLUENCES

Other factors related to schizophrenia may include culture and evolutionary influences. Schizophrenia does seem more common in people in developing countries and in immigrants and migrant workers than in people in developed countries and native populations. Increased rates of schizophrenia are reported among African Caribbean samples in England compared with native samples (Mitter, Krishnan, Bell, Stewart, & Howard, 2004; Sharpley, Hutchinson, McKenzie, & Murray, 2001). Social isolation and lack of social support among migrant workers may be a key risk factor for schizophrenia.

Sociocultural models of schizophrenia also focus on the issue of *labeling* or assigning someone with a diagnosis of severe mental disorder. The process of labeling someone with a diagnosis like schizophrenia may indeed predispose the person to display symptoms that could be construed as consistent with the disorder. A person just diagnosed with schizophrenia may withdraw from others to avoid discrimination, experience lowered self-esteem and quality of life, become enraged or depressed, and act oddly (Angermeyer & Schulze, 2001).

Labeling can also affect how others view someone. Rosenhan (1973) conducted a famous study in which people without mental disorder went to various hospitals and falsely claimed to hear voices. All of these "pseudo-patients" were hospitalized and kept on an inpatient unit despite the fact that they purposefully displayed normal behavior on the unit. Hospital records indicated that staff members often judged normal behavior such as note-taking as pathological, simply on the basis that the person was admitted to an inpatient unit. The study underscored the fact that stigma can be quite strong and hard to challenge once a diagnosis of severe mental disorder is given.

The issue of social functioning has also been raised with respect to evolutionary hypotheses about schizophrenia. One theory is that humans tolerate greater deviation from normal functioning the more they develop complex social lives farther removed from the basic "hunter-gatherer" status of our distant ancestors. Early groups of humans could not tolerate people incapable of protecting and nourishing the group because of psychotic symptoms, but people with these symptoms today can more easily be assimilated into, and contribute to, society. Another evolutionary hypothesis is that a genetic mutation occurred in some humans as they split from other primates eons ago. This genetic mutation might affect areas of functioning that separate us from other primates—most notably language. Deficits in language, of course, are often central to psychotic disorders (Brune, 2004; Crow, 2004).

## Causes of Psychotic Disorders

How do all of these risk factors interact to produce a psychotic disorder? A popular integrative model for how schizophrenia and other psychotic disorders might develop is the **neurodevelopmental hypothesis** (Owen, O'Donovan, Thapar, & Craddock, 2011). Proponents of this model essentially state that a subtle disease process affects brain areas early in life, perhaps as early as the second trimester of the prenatal period, and progresses gradually to the point where full-blown symptoms are produced (**Figure 12.12**; Piper et al., 2012). Early brain changes could come from disease, famine, and low birth weight, among other variables. Genetic predispositions could also affect fetal and child brain development that may contribute to later symptoms of schizophrenia.

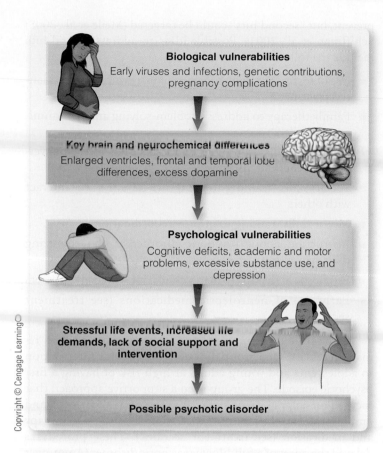

**FIGURE 12.12** SAMPLE DEVELOPMENTAL PATHWAY OF PSYCHOTIC DISORDER

Some theorists believe these early brain changes become especially pertinent when the adolescent brain goes through significant reorganization and increased use. One possibility is that neurons are insufficiently pruned at this time, which means old synaptic connections are not discarded as they are in most people. This can lead to a "packing" of useless neurons in key areas of the brain such as the hippocampus. Such abnormalities can help lead to full-blown symptoms of schizophrenia (Goto & Lee, 2011; Grace, 2010). Another possibility is that a less well-developed brain can no longer handle the increased complexities of life during adolescence and adulthood.

If the neurodevelopmental hypothesis is true, then one might expect signs of early problems and brain changes to emerge as a child develops. Some evidence indicates this to be so. People with schizophrenia often have other physical problems that probably developed about the same time as key brain changes, and some of these problems may be evident in children and adolescents. These physical problems include irregularities of the ears, head, face, tongue, palate, and hands and feet (Compton & Walker, 2009). Some irregularities have been linked to brain ventricle size in schizophrenia (Murphy, 2002). Many people with schizophrenia do not have these irregularities, however, and many people with these irregularities do not have schizophrenia.

Stronger evidence for the neurodevelopmental hypothesis comes from strange motor behaviors often seen in children of parents with schizophrenia or children who eventually develop schizophrenia. Some of these strange motor behaviors have been identified in home movies and videotapes of children whose parents had schizophrenia (Schiffman et al., 2004). These strange motor behaviors may be the result of prenatal complications or genetics that affect brain development, or may have to do with excess levels of dopamine. Many of these children display the following characteristics:

- Irregularities or lags in motor development, such as delayed walking
- Slow head and body growth
- Poor fine and gross motor coordination and perception
- Overactivity
- Odd hand movements and other involuntary movements
- Twitching and grimacing

Keep in mind, however, that these odd motor behaviors sometimes predict other disorders such as depressive and bipolar disorders. Not all people with schizophrenia necessarily had these symptoms in childhood either, and these symptoms do not necessarily mean someone will go on to develop schizophrenia.

Other childhood changes that may provide support for the neurodevelopmental hypothesis include changes in cognitive and social behaviors. Children at risk for developing schizophrenia tend to show a decline in intelligence over time, lower tested intelligence, and more repeated grades and trouble paying attention than controls (Maki et al., 2005). Children who eventually develop schizophrenia tend to have more withdrawn, neurotic, depressive, solitary, aggressive, and disruptive behaviors than control participants (Niemi, Suvisaari, Tuulio-Henriksson, & Lonnqvist, 2003). People with schizophrenia often develop poor social cognition and **theory of mind**, or an understanding of the thoughts and beliefs of others (Koelkebeck et al., 2010). James did not always fully appreciate or understand the perspectives of other people. These cognitive and social changes are quite inconsistent and not always predictive of schizophrenia, however.

As a child develops further, environmental events certainly have an impact on his development and may speed or even prevent the onset of full-blown symptoms of a later psychotic disorder. We mentioned that stressful life events and excessive substance use have been linked to schizophrenia. A child who displays problematic behavior as a youngster may experience stress from loss of family members, academic demands, family conflict, and peer pressures. This may lead to various outcomes such as depression, excessive substance use to cope, or triggered psychotic symptoms. Conversely, environmental support from others and early intervention may help prevent serious symptoms from occurring. We discuss this in the prevention section.

Once full-blown symptoms of schizophrenia begin, levels of functioning tend to remain stable (Bachmann, Bottmer, & Schroder, 2008). This provides even more support for the neurodevelopmental hypothesis, which predicts that early brain changes will outline a fairly consistent course of behavior for a person. Many people with schizophrenia eventually show remission or some improvement in their symptoms over time, meaning early and stable brain changes are more likely a cause for schizophrenia than ongoing brain deterioration (Andreasen et al., 2011).

Whatever the actual cause of schizophrenia and other psychotic disorders, these problems are clearly among the most complex mental disorders. We will likely find over time that many different types of schizophrenia exist and that each has its own developmental pathway. Charting these pathways will require substantial research effort and collaboration among mental health professionals. In the meantime, efforts to prevent these disorders must be a priority.

## Prevention of Psychotic Disorders

Given what we know about risk factors for psychotic disorders, what could be done to prevent them? Early symptoms of psychotic disorders may emerge in adolescence or early adulthood, so it makes sense to think of prevention in the childhood and adolescent years. We know genetics play a large role in schizophrenia, so it might be useful to focus on children whose parents had schizophrenia and look for early signs of stressful life events and motor, cognitive, and social problems. Children identified as at risk could then be taught ways to improve their functioning and perhaps blunt the onset of schizophrenia symptoms.

Some researchers have proposed a *two-hit model of schizophrenia* that may help guide prevention efforts (Rapoport et al., 2012). A child is deemed to be at particular risk for schizophrenia if his close relatives had schizophrenia (the first hit) and if he experienced a severe environmental stressor such as prenatal complications, residence in an institution, or family conflict, among others (the second hit). A special kind of "second hit" involves problems in early child rearing. Children at risk for schizophrenia are much more likely to experience parental inconsistency, hostility, overinvolvement, and early loss of or separation from parents than control participants (Schiffman et al., 2001).

This model may be useful for implementing prevention efforts. At-risk children could be identified by evaluating family history, early environmental stressors, minor physical anomalies, and early problematic behaviors. "First hits" are difficult to

prevent, but "second hits" could be targeted (Meile et al., 2008; Schiffman et al., 2001). Possible ideas to address second hits include the following:

- Use of foster care homes instead of institutions for residential placement
- Family therapy to address problem-solving and communication skills
- Academic skills training to boost sustained attention, verbal skills, and intelligence
- Social skills training to improve abilities to interact with others
- Motor skills training to improve coordination
- Instruction about psychotic disorders and recognizing their symptoms
- Psychosocial therapy to help a child cope with daily stressors
- Early use of neuroleptic medications (see treatment section)

Large-scale prevention studies focused on these ideas remain necessary. One group, however, did provide intervention to adolescents and young adults at high risk of having a first psychotic episode. The group used a supportive approach that focused on helping participants address social, vocational, and family problems in addition to cognitive-behavioral therapy and medication (see treatment sections). These procedures delayed the onset of a full-blown psychotic disorder (Amminger et al., 2011; McGorry et al., 2002).

Another target of prevention in general and relapse prevention in particular is *expressed emotion*. Recall from Chapter 7 that expressed emotion refers to emotional overinvolvement and hostility on the part of family members toward one another as well as inability to cope with a person's mental disorder, in this case schizophrenia. A person with schizophrenia is often blamed for his mental disorder and harshly criticized by families with high expressed emotion (Cechnicki, Bielanska, Hanuszkiewicz, & Daren, 2013).

High levels of expressed emotion produce greater relapse in people with schizophrenia and so expressed emotion may be a good target for relapse prevention (Aguilera, Lopez, Breitborde, Kopelowicz, & Zarate, 2010). Expressed emotion relates to medication compliance and may interact with culture. Some claim family members communicate poorly to someone with a psychotic disorder if the person deviates much from core cultural values and norms (Kymalainen & Weisman de Mamani, 2008). The area of family dynamics and how they relate to further psychotic episodes remains a fascinating area of study.

## INTERIM SUMMARY

- ► Biological risk factors for psychotic disorders include genetics, brain and neurochemical differences, and cognitive deficits.
- ► Environmental risk factors for psychotic disorders include prenatal complications, disease, famine, stressful life events, and excessive substance use.

**CONTINUUM VIDEO PROJECT**

### *Andre:* **Schizophrenia**

*"I believe that other people are pathological liars, and I'm not. So why should I even have to listen to them?"*

Access the Continuum Video Project in MindTap at **www.cengagebrain.com**.

▶ Biological and environmental risk factors can make a person vulnerable to having a psychotic disorder. These risk factors may produce early brain changes that, over time, do not allow a person to fully address life's stressful and complex tasks.

▶ One causal theory for psychosis is a neurodevelopmental model in which an early disease state leads to key brain changes and stable psychotic symptoms.

▶ Preventing psychosis may involve assessing for markers early in life, enhancing skills that deteriorate in one's lifetime, and reducing expressed emotion in families.

## REVIEW QUESTIONS

1. Describe data supporting a genetic contribution to psychotic disorders.
2. What key brain changes and environmental factors relate to psychotic disorders?
3. Explain the neurodevelopmental model of schizophrenia.
4. What factors might be important for a program to prevent psychotic disorders?
5. What is expressed emotion?

# Psychotic Disorders: Assessment and Treatment

Psychotic disorders often involve multiple and severe deficits, so assessment can be quite difficult. Information often comes from spouses, children, family members, and friends to piece together a history of symptoms and behavior patterns. Such was true for James. Clinical observations by mental health professionals who have experience with this population are invaluable as well. We discuss each of these methods in the following sections.

A full medical examination should always precede a psychological assessment of schizophrenia because certain medical conditions could produce psychotic symptoms. Examples include epilepsy, brain trauma such as stroke, central nervous system infections such as AIDS, endocrine and metabolic disorders, vitamin deficiency, and autoimmune disorders. Substances such as amphetamines, marijuana, phencyclidine (PCP), and LSD could produce psychotic symptoms as well. Alcohol and barbiturate withdrawal can also lead to psychotic-like symptoms (Paparelli, Di Forti, Morrison, & Murray, 2011).

## Interviews

Interviews are difficult for many people with psychotic disorders because of delusions, hallucinations, suspicion, and disorganized thoughts and behaviors. Still, unstructured interviews may be conducted to get as much useful information as possible. Information about the following areas should be a priority:

● Current level of functioning and specific problem behaviors and deficits
● Recent life events and personal history
● Medication and treatment history and degree of compliance

● Comorbid medical and psychological conditions
● Financial resources and support from significant others

A semistructured interview often used for people with severe mental disorder is the *Schedule for Affective Disorders and Schizophrenia* (SADS; Arbisi, 1995). This interview concentrates on background and demographic characteristics as well as past and present symptoms of various disorders including psychoses. The interview (and other similar ones) can take a long time to administer, requires much expertise to give, and may not be useful for someone with highly disorganized thoughts.

Brief rating scales used as semistructured interviews are thus sometimes used. These scales focus mainly on negative and positive symptoms of schizophrenia as well as impaired thinking. The scales are usually completed by mental health professionals who obtain information from chart reviews, observations, or discussions with a person with schizophrenia, significant others, and other professionals. An individual may also be asked to complete certain scales if possible.

A common rating scale is the *Brief Psychiatric Rating Scale*, which measures thought disturbance, disorganized behavior, problematic affect, and withdrawn behavior (Mueser, Curran, & McHugo, 1997). Other rating scales include the *Positive and Negative Syndrome Scale* (Kay, Fiszbein, & Opler, 1987; Lancon, Auquier, Nayt, & Reine, 2000) and *Symptom Checklist—90—Revised* (SCL-90-R; Derogatis, 1994). Simulated items from the SCL-90-R psychoticism subscale are in **Table 12.9**.

## Behavioral Observations

Behavioral observations of people with psychotic disorders are useful to evaluate social and self-care skills. Important skills to observe include starting and maintaining a conversation, solving problems, managing stress and one's symptoms, taking medications, engaging in basic hygiene, working well with others, and maintaining appropriate facial expressions and affect, among others (Semkovska, Bedard, Godbout, Limoge, & Stip, 2004). Side effects of medications should also be observed closely. One could also evaluate "neurological soft signs" that may indicate some brain change (Chan, Xu, Heinrichs, Yu, & Wang, 2010). These signs include poor balance and coordination, awkward movements and reflexes, tremors, and speech and sleep problems.

The most common method for evaluating these behaviors is to carefully monitor a person with a psychotic disorder and get information from family and friends. Behavioral observations are most useful if they occur in multiple settings, especially at home, work, and during recreational activities. Role-play or scales that measure social and self-care skills may be helpful with observations in these areas as well (Leifker, Patterson, Heaton, & Harvey, 2011; Park, Ku, et al., 2011). Consider the following role-play between a therapist and a person with residual schizophrenia:

**Therapist:** How are you doing today?
**Patient:** (saying something in a mumbled voice, head down)
**Therapist:** Can you look at me when you say that? And I need to hear you a bit better.

**Table 12.9**

| Simulated Items from the Psychoticism Subscale of the Symptom Checklist 90-R | Not at all (0) | A little bit (1) | Moderately (2) | Quite a bit (3) | Extremely (4) |
|---|---|---|---|---|---|
| **How much were you distressed by:** | | | | | |
| The idea that someone else can control your thoughts | | | | | |
| Hearing voices that other people do not hear | | | | | |
| Other people being aware of your private thoughts | | | | | |
| Having thoughts that are not your own | | | | | |
| The idea that you should be punished for your sins | | | | | |
| The idea that something serious is wrong with your body | | | | | |
| The idea that something is wrong with your mind | | | | | |

Source: Simulated items similar to those found in the Symptom Checklist—90—Revised (SCL-90-R). Copyright © 1975, 2004 Leonard R. Derogatis, Ph.D. Reproduced with permission. Published exclusively by NCS Pearson, Inc. All rights reserved. SCL-90-R is a registered trademark of Leonard R. Derogatis, Ph.D.

**Patient:** (more clearly) I said fine . . . (voice trailing off a bit).

**Therapist:** Great! I could hear you much better that time.

**Patient:** (silence)

**Therapist:** How about responding to what I just said? What could you say in reply?

**Patient:** Um, well . . . ah . . . thanks?

**Therapist:** Yes, great! You're welcome! Let's keep this conversation going.

## Cognitive Assessment

Many people with schizophrenia and other psychotic disorders have difficulties with language and verbal ability, attention and concentration, memory, problem solving, decision making, and sensory-perceptual functioning. Tests to evaluate these areas of cognitive function in this population are thus often crucial.

Tests of language and verbal ability are often derived from certain subtests of intelligence and achievement tests. These include verbal subtests from the *Wechsler Adult Intelligence Test* (4th edition; WAIS-IV) and reading subtests from the *Wide Range Achievement Test* (4th edition; WRAT-4; Wechsler, 2008; Wilkinson & Robertson, 2006). One should look for problems in language fluency, perception, production, and syntax as well as differences in scores on these tests. Reading scores on the WRAT-4 may not deteriorate even after development of a severe mental disorder or brain dysfunction, so these scores may be used as a premorbid (before disorder) level of functioning. These scores can then be compared with WAIS-IV verbal subtest scores, which indicate current functioning, to see what changes have taken place. This assessment strategy may be less helpful, however, for someone with severely disorganized symptoms or intense reading problems. Attention or concentration deficits

may be evaluated using the *Continuous Performance Test II,* which requires a person to react to a long series of stimuli presented at regular intervals (Conners & MHS staff, 2000).

Other neuropsychological tasks such as sorting objects into categories like color are also used to assess frontal cortex problems in schizophrenia, especially problems in decision making, problem solving, and verbal memory. People with psychotic disorders often have motor problems, so specific subtests of neuropsychological measures that evaluate finger tapping and grip strength in dominant and nondominant hands may be useful as well. Other subtests may be used to evaluate sensory perceptual problems in vision, hearing, or touch. An example is the Fingertip Number Writing subtest of the Halstead-Reitan test where a person closes his eyes and identifies what number is written on his fingertip by the examiner. This test can differentiate people with and without brain dysfunction. Tests most often used to assess these neuropsychological tasks include the following:

- *California Verbal Learning Test—II* (Delis, Kramer, Kaplan, & Ober, 2000)
- *Halstead-Reitan Neuropsychological Test Battery* (Reitan & Wolfson, 1993)
- *Stroop Color and Word Test* (Golden & Freshwater, 2002)
- *Wechsler Memory Scale—IV* (Wechsler, 2009)
- *Wisconsin Card Sorting Test* (Heaton & PAR Staff, 2003)

## Physiological Assessment

People with psychotic disorders often have intense symptoms that may have a strong biological basis, so competing medical explanations should be ruled out first. Laboratory

### Making the Choice of Antipsychotic Medication

Making the independent choice to take medication is a crucial step toward recovery for many people with mental disorders. Controversy arises, however, with respect to antipsychotic medication and what to do if a person is legally incapable of making choices about treatment. Imagine someone referred by police to an inpatient psychiatric unit who has acute delusions and hallucinations. If his ability to understand reality is impaired, and he cannot give consent about antipsychotic medication, then what?

Most jurisdictions allow physicians to administer antipsychotic medication without consent of the individual in situations that involve emergencies, obvious incompetence of the individual, and/or dangerousness to self or others (as with

James). Even in these cases, however, every attempt should be made to include the person in the consent process as soon and as much as possible, to consult with family members about treatment options, and to provide only enough treatment to help the person make competent decisions about further treatment.

A more serious issue is *forced medication*. Should the government mandate that someone arrested for a crime and who is acutely psychotic receive antipsychotic medication against his will for the purpose of increasing legal competence and the possibility of imprisonment? This issue has been raised in several court cases and has deep ramifications for other practices. Could government agencies eventually mandate medications for children and adults with certain other mental disorders? How would the line be drawn for other kinds of treatments as well? For now, these questions are answered only on a case-by-case basis by the courts.

tests such as urine and blood analyses may also be done to examine excess levels of neurotransmitters and legal and illegal drugs. Such tests are often done to monitor a person's compliance with prescribed medication as well as potentially dangerous interactions with other drugs. These tests are not foolproof, however, so behavioral observations and rating scales may be used with laboratory testing (Braff, Freedman, Schork, & Gottesman, 2007).

## Biological Treatments of Psychotic Disorders

Someone like James with a severe psychotic disorder clearly needs intense treatment for bizarre and complex symptoms. Schizophrenia and other psychotic disorders have a strong biological component, so treatment often begins with medication (see **Box 12.3**). Medication for psychotic symptoms is sometimes called *antipsychotic* or *neuroleptic medication*. These medications are typically divided into **typical antipsychotics** and **atypical antipsychotics** (see **Table 12.10**; Crossley, Constante, McGuire, & Power, 2010).

Typical antipsychotics such as phenothiazines are traditionally used for this population and focus primarily on reducing excess levels of dopamine in the brain. These drugs were introduced in the 1950s and led to a widespread decline in people hospitalized for severe mental disorders such as schizophrenia (**Figure 12.13**). Typical antipsychotics are helpful but have several problems (Bounthavong & Okamoto, 2007):

- Many people with psychotic disorders do not respond well to these drugs.

- The drugs are useful for treating positive symptoms of psychotic disorders such as delusions and hallucinations but not negative symptoms.

- Side effects may be extremely unpleasant or irreversible in some cases (discussed later).

Atypical antipsychotic drugs are newer (or second-generation) agents developed to treat more people with psychotic disorders,

## Table 12.10

### Common Medications for People with Psychotic Disorders

| Typical antipsychotics | Atypical antipsychotics |
|---|---|
| Chlorpromazine (Thorazine) | Clozapine (Clozaril) |
| Fluphenazine (Prolixin) | Olanzapine (Zyprexa) |
| Haloperidol (Haldol) | Quetiapine (Seroquel) |
| Loxapine (Loxitane) | Risperidone (Risperdal) |
| Molindone (Moban) | Ziprasidone (Geodon) |
| Pimozide (Orap) | |
| Thioridazine (Mellaril) | |
| Thiothixene (Navane) | |
| Trifluoperazine (Stelazine) | |

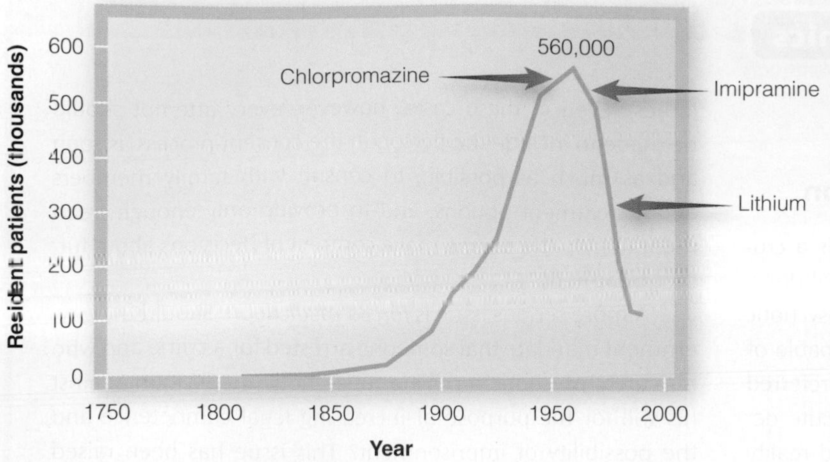


**FIGURE 12.13 THE POPULATION IN STATE AND COUNTY HOSPITALS** The number of people hospitalized for severe mental disorders such as schizophrenia declined greatly after 1960 partly because of the introduction of antipsychotic drugs. *Source: From Stroup, A.L. and Manderscheid, R.W. (1988). "The development of the state mental hospital system in the United States: 1840–1980," Journal of the Washington Academy of Sciences, 78, 59-68. Reprinted by permission.*

address depressive and negative symptoms, and minimize side effects. These newer drugs affect various dopamine receptors as well as other neurotransmitter systems such as serotonin (Meltzer & Massey, 2011).

Typical and atypical antipsychotic drugs do work better than no drug treatment. Typical and atypical antipsychotic drugs are similar in effectiveness with respect to rehospitalization rates, but atypical antipsychotics appear more effective for severe cases of schizophrenia (Stargardt, Weinbrenner, Busse, Juckel, & Gericke, 2008). Other data indicate the long-term effectiveness of atypical antipsychotics is better than typical antipsychotics (Meltzer, 2013).

Antipsychotic medication is useful for people with schizophrenia and is often necessary for someone to complete even basic self-care tasks. Still, key problems remain. First, the drugs are not effective for all people with psychotic disorders. Second, many people experience significant side effects from antipsychotic medication. Common side effects of typical antipsychotics include muscle spasms and rigidity, restlessness, pacing, fixed facial expression, sedation, and seizures. Involuntary movements of the body, or **extrapyramidal effects**, are also common. Another side effect of typical antipsychotics, *tardive dyskinesia,* is a potentially irreversible condition marked by involuntary tics of the face, mouth, tongue, and upper body (Woods et al., 2010). Side effects of atypical antipsychotics tend to be less severe but may include low blood pressure, diabetes, sedation, weight gain, concentration problems, and seizures, among others (Ananth, Parameswaran, & Gunatilake, 2004).

Another problem with medication is that one must take the drug for it to work. Compliance rates for taking medication are not always strong for people with psychotic disorders (Barkhof, Meijer, de Sonneville, Linszen, & de Haan, 2012). People often struggle with multiple medications, memory and thought difficulties, stressful life events, side effects, excessive substance use, and transportation to pharmacies and doctors' offices. The cost of atypical antipsychotic drugs is also much higher than typical antipsychotic drugs (Meltzer, 2013). A person with a psychotic disorder has a high chance of relapse if she delays or stops taking prescribed medication (Higashi et al., 2013). Methods of increasing compliance are part of the psychological treatment approach for psychotic disorders.

## Psychological Treatments of Psychotic Disorders

Medications are a mainstay ingredient of many treatment plans for psychotic disorders, but they are typically supplemented with psychological approaches. Psychological approaches usually aim to improve medication compliance, social and self-care skills, employment duration, support from relevant others, mood, and cognitive abilities. Psychological approaches for this population are designed to enhance a person's quality of life and help prevent relapse.

### MILIEU THERAPY AND TOKEN ECONOMY

Two psychological techniques adopted on inpatient psychiatric units for people with acute psychotic symptoms are milieu therapy and token economy. **Milieu therapy** involves establishing an environment in which prosocial and self-care skills are encouraged. Mental health professionals, physicians, nurses, and other staff continually praise and encourage a person with psychotic symptoms to dress, eat, groom, attend therapy services, interact appropriately with others, and engage in other positive behaviors (Borge, Angel, & Rossberg, 2013).

Milieu therapy is sometimes linked to a **token economy** in which prosocial and self-care skills are tangibly rewarded via points (or other items) later exchanged for privileges such as day trips outside the hospital. A token economy might involve rewards for teeth brushing and eating dinner with others. James was allowed more time outside the hospital as he attended inpatient group therapy sessions. These inpatient strategies help reduce symptoms, improve social behavior, and facilitate earlier discharge (Dickerson, Tenhula, & Green-Paden, 2005).

### COGNITIVE-BEHAVIORAL AND SUPPORTIVE PSYCHOTHERAPIES

You might think psychotherapy for someone with strong psychotic symptoms would not be useful, but think again! Cognitive-behavioral and supportive psychotherapies do help prevent relapse (Jones, Hacker, Cormac, Meaden, & Irving, 2012). Cognitive-behavioral therapy is typically better than routine care for people with schizophrenia and

Tim Page/Corbis

People with schizophrenia on an inpatient unit are often encouraged, via milieu therapy, to be together to build social skills and support and reduce isolation.

aims to achieve the following (Rathod, Kingdon, Weiden, & Turkington, 2010):

- Create a strong therapeutic alliance with a client built on acceptance, support, and collaboration

- Educate a client about his psychosis and reduce stigma associated with symptoms

- Reduce stress associated with psychotic symptoms

- Decrease delusions and hallucinations and change erroneous expectancies and thoughts about them

- Address comorbid conditions such as excessive substance use, anxiety, and depression

- Lower chances of relapse by identifying and eliminating triggers such as stress, family conflict, and forgotten medication

Recall that Jody had delusions about her coworkers harming her and that her employers asked her to seek professional help. Her therapist helped Jody separate more realistic from less realistic thoughts and reduce life stress to help prevent her suspiciousness. Jody learned to examine evidence for and against her thoughts, talk to others about her concerns in a socially appropriate way, and pursue enjoyable activities outside of work.

## MEDICATION COMPLIANCE

People with schizophrenia and other psychotic disorders often need to stay on medication to function on a daily basis, so helping them comply with medication is important. Behavioral strategies to do so include discussions about benefits of taking medication and disadvantages of not taking medication, education about medications and their main and side effects, pairing medication use with an essential part of a daily routine such as eating dinner, putting medication in obvious places so it is remembered, and rewarding appropriate medication use, perhaps using a token economy (Barkhof et al., 2012). Significant others or an electronic device may also monitor a person

closely and even count pills, especially after her hospitalization or during times of high stress (Acosta et al., 2009).

## SOCIAL SKILLS TRAINING

Many people with schizophrenia have great difficulty interacting with others, either because of their developmental history or current symptoms. They are thus at risk for social withdrawal, depression, and other problems. Social skills training has been used to enhance contact with others, decrease distress, and prevent relapse. Social skills training usually consists of repeated modeling and practice and feedback regarding small behaviors first (Bellack, Mueser, Gingerich, & Agresta, 2004). A person with schizophrenia could watch two people have a short conversation and then try the same task with her therapist. The therapist closely watches for key behaviors such as lack of eye contact, inaudible or incoherent speech, interruptions, poor emotional control, and other important problems.

Feedback to educate a client about these deficiencies is crucial, and a person should continue to practice until the skill is well developed. The person should practice her skills in natural settings with different people, be rewarded for her efforts, and later advance to more difficult tasks such as introducing herself and participating in long conversations. Social skills training could be done individually but is quite effective when done with a group of people. Such training is useful in therapy settings, but good generalization of skills to more natural settings requires extensive and ongoing practice (Galderisi et al., 2010).

## COGNITIVE AND VOCATIONAL REHABILITATION

Psychotherapy for people with psychotic disorders also involves rehabilitation of cognitive and vocational deficits. Many people with schizophrenia have great problems in attention, memory, and decision-making and problem-solving skills. The main goal of cognitive rehabilitation is to improve performance in these areas and integrate performance into social interactions. Examples of cognitive rehabilitation techniques include repeated instruction and practice on neuropsychological tests, computer exercises, use of self-instructions to maintain focus and guide performance in social situations, careful listening to others' statements, software training of specific tasks that require attention and memory, and ongoing vigilance and encoding of important information (Dickinson et al., 2010; Velligan, Kern, & Gold, 2006). Reinforcement of these tasks is important as well. These techniques are generally effective for improving cognitive skills, but questions remain about whether they can lead to long-lasting and broad changes (Wykes, Huddy, Cellard, McGurk, & Czobor, 2011).

Vocational rehabilitation aims to reintegrate a person with a psychotic disorder into a productive occupational environment. Vocational rehabilitation concentrates mainly on job training, support, and employment in an area a person is motivated to work. Other areas of vocational rehabilitation include practicing language and cognitive skills in a work setting, detailed work performance feedback, and resolution of job-related difficulties. These efforts successfully increase job performance for this population (Lysaker, Davis, Bryson, & Bell, 2009).

Family therapy is often a key treatment for people with schizophrenia to improve communication and medication compliance and to solve problems effectively.

## FAMILY THERAPY

Recall that expressed emotion, or family hostility and criticism and overinvolvement, is a risk factor for psychotic disorders and relapse. Many people with schizophrenia also return to their spouses or families for care. Family therapy is thus an important component of treatment for this population. Therapy usually concentrates on educating family members about a psychotic disorder, providing support, decreasing highly emotional communications within the family, decreasing stress and depression, helping family members cope with caring for a relative with a psychotic disorder, managing crises, and improving problem-solving skills (Bird et al., 2010).

Family therapy may be conducted for a single family or done within a support group of many people. Family therapy may also be done in early or later stages of a person's psychotic disorder. Family therapy at any stage should be coordinated closely with other psychological and drug treatments. Family therapy does contribute to lower relapse rates for people with schizophrenia (Gleeson et al., 2010).

## COMMUNITY CARE

A person with a psychotic disorder is often treated for acute symptoms in a hospital setting, but simple discharge afterward is not a suitable care strategy. This is especially true if families are initially overwhelmed with the task of caring for the person. Extensive support is thus offered to a person via community or residential treatment (**Figure 12.14**; Meuser & Jeste, 2008). A person may live in a group home or another living arrangement for persons with severe mental disorder. This approach involves case managers to assist and supervise a person, mental health services, help with work and money management and self-care skills, efforts to improve social and verbal skills, and family therapy (Lloyd-Evans, Slade, Jagielska, & Johnson, 2009). The eventual goal for the person is often to return to the care of family members or perhaps live more independently. James was eventually discharged from the hospital once his mental condition was stable. He was placed in a group home with 5 other individuals with severe mental disorder and staff members who served as case managers.

Another model of community care is *assertive community treatment*. A person with schizophrenia may live independently but receive frequent (assertive) contact from psychiatrists and other mental health professionals. Treatment often occurs at a person's home or nearby area such as a park. Emphasis is placed on community integration, family support, employment, and long-term physical and mental health services. Assertive community treatment is effective for maintaining patient contact and for reducing hospitalizations and homelessness (Meuser, Deavers, Penn, & Cassisi, 2013).

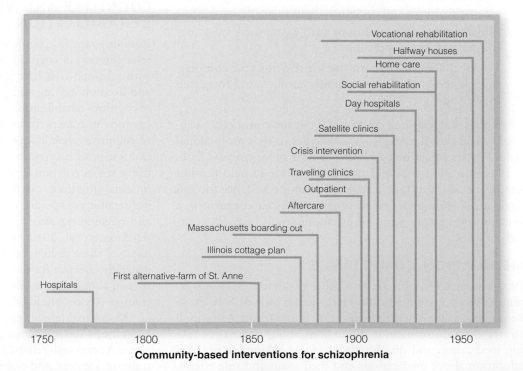

**Community-based interventions for schizophrenia**

**FIGURE 12.14 ALTERNATIVES TO PSYCHIATRIC HOSPITALS** Community-based alternatives to hospital care for people with psychotic disorders have been developed historically to help prevent relapse and rehospitalization. *From A. Kales et al., Recent Advances in Schizophrenia, New York: Springer-Verlag, 1990, Figure 1. Reprinted by permission of Springer Science and Business Media.*

## What If I or Someone I Know Has a Psychotic Disorder?

Knowing if someone is developing a psychotic disorder can be hard, but some telltale signs may suggest that further evaluation or treatment is warranted. Some screening questions are listed in **Table 12.11**. If you find the answer to most of these questions is yes, then you or the person you know may wish to consult a clinical psychologist, psychiatrist, or other mental health professional (Chapter 15). You may wish to contact mental health professionals affiliated with local inpatient psychiatric units and/or community care settings for people with severe mental disorder. Provide detailed information about the person's thought patterns, behaviors, and positive symptoms such as delusions and hallucinations. Signs of depression and excessive substance use should be monitored closely as well. Talk to family and friends about your concerns. Early symptom recognition and intervention is often the best approach to prevent potentially life-threatening behaviors. Additional professional information is available from the National Alliance for Research on Schizophrenia and Depression (www.narsad.org) and the National Institute of Mental Health (www.nimh. nih.gov/health/publications/schizophrenia/complete-index.shtml).

## Table 12.11

| Screening Questions for Psychotic Disorder |
|---|
| Do you find that any of the psychotic symptoms described in this chapter apply to someone you know much more so than most people your age? |
| Does someone you know show very peculiar behaviors that impair his ability to function in daily life (e.g., go to work, do well in school)? |
| Does someone you know have great suspicions or paranoia about others? |
| Is someone you know greatly troubled by symptoms of impaired attention, concentration, or other higher-order thought processes? |
| Does someone you know have greater problems organizing and expressing thoughts? |
| Does someone you know seem very socially withdrawn for the first time? |
| Has someone you know recently experienced a traumatic event that seems to have triggered very bizarre behaviors? |
| Does the person you are concerned about have a family history of severe mental disorders? |

## Long-Term Outcome for People with Psychotic Disorders

What is the long-term picture, or prognosis, for people like James and Jody with psychotic disorders? Many people with psychotic disorders have a fairly stable course of symptoms, but 74 percent display good outcome marked by improved symptoms over time. Most work (78.8 percent), although not always in paid positions (37.5 percent), and most report satisfactory quality of paid work (85.2 percent, Hopper et al., 2001). Factors that predict good outcome include less brain volume reduction and substance use, shorter length of untreated symptoms, preserved cognitive function, good social and work skills, supportive family, good response to antipsychotic drugs, treatment adherence, and female gender (Hoffmann, Kupper, Zbinden, & Hirsbrunner, 2003; Schennach, Musil, Moller, & Riedel, 2012; Silverstein & Bellack, 2008).

Up to 90 percent of people with a first psychotic episode relapse within 5 years, however, often because of medication maintenance problems (Gaebel et al., 2002; Perkins, Gu, Boteva, & Lieberman, 2005). Other people with schizophrenia show a chronic course not largely amenable to any treatment. People with severely chronic schizophrenia show progressive deterioration in frontal and temporal brain lobes, increased ventricle size, and frequent need for hospitalization over time (Hulshoff Pol & Kahn, 2008; Mitelman & Buchsbaum, 2007). Other factors related to poor outcome include early and insidious or slow onset of psychosis, poor insight, poor early adjustment, delusions, flat affect and other negative symptoms, and substantial impairment after the first episode of psychotic symptoms (Emsley, Chiliza, & Schoeman, 2008; Ho, Nopoulos, Flaum, Arndt, & Andreasen, 2004; Malla & Payne, 2005).

James's long-term prognosis was thought to be fair because he did receive treatment soon after each of his episodes of strange behavior, because he had extensive social support, because his cognitive functioning was still relatively good (if bizarre), and because each of his episodes was triggered by a specific event such as an overheard conversation. Jody's long-term prognosis is good because she was intelligent, had good cognitive functioning, and pursued effective therapy. The best approach for addressing psychotic disorders at any age is early and complete treatment.

### INTERIM SUMMARY

▶ Assessing people with psychotic disorders is important because of their complicated symptoms and is often based on family discussions and observations.

▶ Interviews have been created for people with psychotic disorders, although brief rating scales in the form of interviews are often used.

▶ Behavioral observations of people with psychotic disorders often focus on social and self-care skills.

▶ Cognitive assessment of people with psychotic disorders involves intelligence, neurological, and attention-based tests that can be linked to physiological assessment.

▶ Treating psychotic disorders often involves a biological approach first, and many typical and atypical neuroleptic drugs are available. Side effects, compliance, and relapse are common problems, however.

▶ Psychological treatments for people with psychotic disorders aim to improve quality of life and focus on milieu therapy, token economy, cognitive-behavioral and supportive psychotherapies, compliance with medication, social skills training, cognitive and vocational rehabilitation, and family therapy.

▶ Long-term outcome for people with psychotic disorders is best for females and those with less brain volume reduction, less neurological soft signs, less severe positive symptoms, fewer side effects of medication, shorter length of untreated symptoms, above average intelligence, good social skills, and a clear trigger such as a stressful life event.

## REVIEW QUESTIONS

1. Outline major assessment techniques for psychotic disorders, including interviews, brief rating scales, observations, and cognitive and physiological measurements.

2. What biological methods may be used to manage symptoms of psychoses, and what are some problems associated with these methods?

3. What psychological strategies could a mental health professional use to help someone with a psychotic disorder on an inpatient unit?

4. What psychological strategies could a mental health professional use to help someone with a psychotic disorder in an outpatient clinical or residential setting?

5. What is the long-term outcome for people with psychotic disorders?

# Final Comments

People with psychotic disorders suffer substantial distress and impairment from their symptoms. Imagine hearing voices, believing others can hear your personal thoughts, having trouble forming sentences, and being unable to work or go to school. These problems are devastating, so be as compassionate and helpful as possible when addressing someone with a psychotic disorder. Try to consider the person first and his disorder second—a person with schizophrenia, not a schizophrenic. Try also to get help for someone you may come across in your life who begins to have these symptoms.

# Thought Questions

1. Think about television shows or films with characters with psychotic symptoms in them. Do you think these characters display realistic or unrealistic symptoms of psychosis? Do you think the entertainment industry has skewed the public's view of psychotic disorders?

2. What symptoms of psychotic disorders do you think many people experience to a lesser degree at different times of their lives?

3. What would you now say to a friend who might be developing symptoms of a psychosis? Has what you have learned here helped you understand those symptoms and become more compassionate?

4. What separates "normal" thought patterns from "abnormal" thought patterns? How can you tell if someone's thinking processes are affected?

5. What do you think could be done socially to reduce psychotic experiences in people?

## Key Terms

psychotic disorders   361
flat affect   361
inappropriate affect   361
delusions   361
hallucinations   361
catatonic   361
schizophrenia   361
positive symptoms   361
negative symptoms   361
disorganized speech   364
catatonic behavior   364
alogia   365
avolition   365
anhedonia   365
prodromal phase   365
psychotic prephase   366

active phase   366
residual phase   366
schizophreniform
   disorder   367
schizoaffective disorder   368
delusional disorder   370
brief psychotic disorder   371
postpartum psychosis   371
neurodevelopmental
   hypothesis   380
theory of mind   381
typical antipsychotics   385
atypical antipsychotics   385
extrapyramidal effects   386
milieu therapy   386
token economy   386

## Media Resources

### MindTap

MindTap for Kearney and Trull's *Abnormal Psychology and Life: A Dimensional Approach* is a highly personalized fully online learning platform of authoritative content, assignments, and services offering you a tailored presentation of course curriculum created by your instructor. MindTap guides you through the course curriculum via an innovative learning path where you will complete reading assignments, annotate your readings, complete homework, and engage with quizzes and assessments. MindTap includes the Continuum Video Project.

Go to **cengagebrain.com** to access MindTap.

# Developmental and Disruptive Behavior Disorders

**CASE:** *Robert*

**What Do You Think?**

**Normal Development and Developmental Disorders: What Are They?**

**Developmental Disorders: Features and Epidemiology**

**CASE:** *Alison*

**Stigma Associated with Developmental Disorders**
Interim Summary
Review Questions

**Developmental Disorders: Causes and Prevention**
Interim Summary
Review Questions

**Developmental Disorders: Assessment and Treatment**
Interim Summary
Review Questions

**Disruptive Behavior Disorders**

**Normal Rambunctious Behavior and Disruptive Behavior Disorders: What Are They?**

**CASE:** *Will*

**What Do You Think?**

**Disruptive Behavior Disorders: Features and Epidemiology**

**Stigma Associated with Disruptive Behavior Disorders**
Interim Summary
Review Questions

**Disruptive Behavior Disorders: Causes and Prevention**
Interim Summary
Review Questions

**Disruptive Behavior Disorders: Assessment and Treatment**
Interim Summary
Review Questions

**FINAL COMMENTS**
**THOUGHT QUESTIONS**
**KEY TERMS**
**MEDIA RESOURCES**

## SPECIAL FEATURES

**CONTINUUM FIGURE 13.1 Continuum of Normal Development and Developmental Disorder   394-395**

**BOX 13.1** | Focus on Law and Ethics: Key Ethical Issues and Developmental Disorders   403

**BOX 13.2** | Focus on Diversity: Testing for People with Developmental Disorders   409

## THE CONTINUUM VIDEO PROJECT

*Whitney:* **Autism Spectrum Disorder   411**

**CONTINUUM FIGURE 13.4 Continuum of Disruptive Behavior and Disruptive Behavior Disorder   416-417**

**PERSONAL NARRATIVE 13.1 Toni Wood   428-429**

**BOX 13.3** | Focus on Violence: Juvenile Arrests and "Diversion"   428

**CONTINUUM FIGURE 13.1** Continuum of Normal Development and Developmental Disorder

| | Normal | Mild |
|---|---|---|
| Emotions | Good control of emotions and appropriate emotional experiences. | Mild delays in impulse, anger, or other emotional control. |
| Cognitions | Normal intelligence and thinking. | Below average intelligence but little interference in daily functioning. |
| Behaviors | Good self-care skills and academic achievement. | Low academic achievement and perhaps delay in some self-care skills. |

© Morgan Lane Photography/Shutterstock.com

# Developmental and Disruptive Behavior Disorders

We have discussed many disorders in this textbook that apply largely to adults, such as somatic symptom, personality, and psychotic disorders. Other mental disorders, however, apply more to children and adolescents than adults, although the disorders often persist into adulthood. Examples include developmental disorders (or developmental disabilities) and disruptive behavior disorders. We focus on these disorders in this chapter.

**Developmental disorders** involve delay in normal maturity, especially with respect to intellect, cognition, learning, and methods of self-care (**Figure 13.1**). Examples of developmental disorders include intellectual disability, autism, and learning disorder. Disruptive behavior disorders involve *externalizing* or obvious behavior problems that include overactivity, impulsivity, inattention, aggression, noncompliance, and other disturbances. Examples of disruptive behavior disorders include attention-deficit/hyperactivity disorder and oppositional defiant and conduct disorders.

## CASE: Robert

**Robert** was a 17-year-old male recently transferred to a small residential facility (group home) for people with severe developmental disorders. He was transferred to the facility after several years of living with his family at home or with peers in a large developmental center. He was often placed in the developmental center when he was overly aggressive or emotional and when his parents feared he might hurt himself or others. His behavior generally improved over the past year, but Robert's parents said they were no longer able to physically care for their son. They approved his transfer to the group home where trained staff members could supervise and help him.

Robert had several developmental delays in language, social and motor skills, and cognitive ability during childhood. He rarely interacted with others and preferred to play by himself. He had enormous difficulty in school and was placed in special education after being diagnosed with autism. Robert assaulted other people as an adolescent and was on medication to control an explosive temper. His transfer to the smaller group home was designed to simulate family-type living but in an environment where his behavior toward others could be monitored frequently.

Brand New Images/ Photodisc/Jupiter Images

### What Do You Think?

1. How are Robert's behaviors different from a typical child or young adult? Which of his behaviors might seem normal for a child or adolescent?

2. What external events and internal factors might be responsible for Robert's behaviors?

3. What are you curious about regarding Robert?

4. Does Robert remind you in any way of someone you know? How so?

5. How might Robert's behaviors affect his life in the future?

| Moderate | Developmental Disorder — less severe | Developmental Disorder — more severe |
|---|---|---|
| oderate delays in impulse, anger, or other motional control. | Substantial delays in emotional control that may lead to instances of aggression or self-injury. | Extremely poor emotional control that may lead to frequent aggression or self-injury. |
| elow average intelligence and some difficulty with nguage. | Severely impaired intelligence with considerable difficulty forming and expressing thoughts. | Profoundly impaired intelligence with extreme difficulty forming and expressing thoughts. |
| iling subjects at school and greater difficulty ring for oneself. | Inability to function in a normal classroom and in need of considerable assistance in daily living. | Extreme delays in functioning and inability to eat, dress, and wash, requiring complete assistance in daily living. |

Developmental and disruptive behavior disorders may be comorbid, occurring together in a particular child. Youths with autism are sometimes aggressive and impulsive and fail to pay close attention to others. Youths with attention-deficit/hyperactivity disorder commonly have learning problems such as difficulty reading. Researchers generally study these sets of disorders—developmental and disruptive—as separate entities, however, so we describe them separately here. We will occasionally identify in this chapter instances in which developmental and disruptive behavior disorders intersect. Consider, for example, Robert's case, which opened this chapter.

## Normal Development and Developmental Disorders: What Are They?

We develop many skills during childhood necessary for us to become independent and function well in various situations. We learn how to speak clearly, dress and feed ourselves, interact with others, tell time, read, use complex arithmetic, drive a car, and balance a checking account. Many of these skills we now take for granted because we learned them at an early age and practiced them repeatedly during our life. Think about all the basic things you did this morning to get ready for the day. You generally do these things automatically or with little thought.

Some children, however, become "stuck" in a particular area of development. These children may be slower than peers to learn to speak in a grammatically correct way or to read. These children may have **limited developmental disorders** because one area but not many areas of functioning are affected. A learning disorder is one example (see later in this chapter). A child with trouble learning to read is often of normal intelligence, has friends, and performs fine in other school subjects. People with limited developmental disorders can often function independently and care for themselves adequately as adults.

For other children, *many* areas of normal development are delayed. These areas include intellect and cognition, language, social interactions, and even physical growth. Skills may fail to develop or may develop much more slowly compared to peers. These delays are often so severe a youth cannot care for himself. Robert was unable to learn to read and his language development was very slow for many years. His ability to interact with others was also severely impaired and he was sometimes aggressive to himself and others.

Robert had a **pervasive developmental disorder**. His delays were evident in many areas and interfered with his ability to communicate with, or function independently of, others. Robert was thus unable to live on his own. People with pervasive developmental disorders often have unique talents, but almost all have deficient cognitive ability or intelligence. Examples of pervasive developmental disorders include severe forms of intellectual disability as well as autism. We discuss these pervasive and limited developmental disorders in the next section.

## Developmental Disorders: Features and Epidemiology

This section summarizes the major features of the most commonly diagnosed developmental disorders. Various symptoms of intellectual disability, autism, and learning disorder are discussed.

### Intellectual Disability

Have you ever known someone unable to attend regular classroom settings or learn things like tying a shoe or putting on a jacket? Perhaps you have seen television shows or films that depict people who have trouble understanding basic aspects of life. People with these problems are often diagnosed with a pervasive developmental disorder known as **intellectual disability** (previously called mental retardation). Intellectual disability can be the sole diagnosis given to a child, although the disorder is often part of other pervasive developmental disorders such as autism (Matson & Shoemaker, 2009). We thus first cover major features of intellectual disability.

Intellectual disability consists of three main features (see **Table 13.1**; American Psychiatric Association [APA], 2013). The first main feature is poor cognitive (thinking) development, sometimes defined as a score of less than 70 on an intelligence test. Clinical judgment or alternative testing may be used to assess cognitive delay, however. The second main feature of intellectual disability is deficits in **adaptive functioning**, which refers to the ability to complete everyday tasks that allow one to be independent (Tasse et al., 2012). Consider these important areas of adaptive functioning and think how hard your life might be if you were unable to do them:

Many of us take for granted social and work skills that are often a struggle for people with developmental disorders.

- *Language*: stating one's desires, understanding others, and asking for help
- *Social interaction*: conversing, initiating activities, and being assertive
- *Academic*: studying, taking tests, reading, and using numbers
- *Self-care*: eating, washing, dressing, toileting, driving, and telling time
- *Home living*: paying bills, doing yard work, cleaning the house, and caring for a child
- *Community*: shopping, taking a bus, and using mail or money
- *Self-direction*: deciding on a career, marriage, or whether to have children
- *Leisure*: seeing a movie or playing a sport, game, or musical instrument
- *Health*: knowing when to see a doctor, take medications, and apply first aid
- *Safety*: preventing fire and theft and knowing what to do in an emergency
- *Work*: filing an application, cashing a paycheck, and delegating tasks

The third main feature of intellectual disability is that the disorder must begin during the developmental period, usually before age 18 years, which excludes certain people. A person who suffers a head injury at age 30 years and now has trouble thinking and dressing would not be diagnosed with intellectual disability. A 65-year-old with Alzheimer's disease (Chapter 14), who may have cognitive and adaptive functioning problems for the first time, also would not be diagnosed with intellectual disability.

## Table 13.1

### DSM-5 Intellectual Disability

Intellectual disability (intellectual developmental disorder) is a disorder with onset during the developmental period that includes both intellectual and adaptive functioning deficits in conceptual, social, and practical domains. The following three criteria must be met:

A. Deficits in intellectual functions, such as reasoning, problem solving, planning, abstract thinking, judgment, academic learning and learning from experience, confirmed by both clinical assessment and individualized, standardized intelligence testing.

B. Deficits in adaptive functioning that result in failure to meet developmental and socio-cultural standards for personal independence and social responsibility. Without ongoing support, the adaptive deficits limit functioning in one or more activities of daily life, such as communication, social participation, and independent living, across multiple environments, such as home, school, work, and community.

C. Onset of intellectual and adaptive deficits during the developmental period.

Specify mild, moderate, severe, or profound severity.

American Psychiatric Association. (2013). *Diagnostic and statistical manual of mental disorders* (5th ed.). Arlington, VA: American Psychiatric Association.

People with intellectual disability often appreciate and enjoy relationships as much as anyone else.

Intellectual delay, deficits in adaptive functioning, and onset during the developmental period must occur *together* for a diagnosis of intellectual disability. This is important because a low score on an intelligence test does not necessarily mean a person has intellectual disability. A person may score low on an intelligence test but still be able to earn a living by working independently at a lower-paying job and managing a place to live. A diagnosis of intellectual disability would thus not apply. Intellectual disability is a diagnosis that should be given only after a thorough assessment of cognitive *and* adaptive functioning.

Intellectual disability can be subtyped by mild, moderate, severe, and profound severity. These subtypes were previously based on intelligence test scores but such groupings are not always helpful; someone who scores a 52 on an intelligence test could have better adaptive functioning than someone who scores a 60. Grouping people with intellectual disability based on how much help they need in daily living is preferable to IQ scores; the following categories have been defined (APA, 2013; Luckasson & Schalock, 2013):

- *Intermittent or mild*: support when needed, such as moving, shopping for groceries, or seeking a new job

- *Limited or moderate*: consistent support, such as transportation, employment training, or help paying bills

- *Extensive or severe*: regular, daily support, such as preparing food, getting dressed, or bathing

- *Pervasive or profound*: constant, intense support, such as ongoing medical attention or complete care

## Autism Spectrum Disorder

Have you worked with people with developmental disorders? Perhaps you noticed a certain group who always seem by themselves and who show strange behaviors, like Robert. Perhaps you have seen certain films such as *Rain Man* or *Fly Away* that show people with these strange behaviors. These people have another pervasive developmental disorder associated with multiple cognitive and social deficits: **autism spectrum disorder** (sometimes called *autism*, *autistic disorder*, or *infantile autism*). People with autism often have intellectual disability, but autism is a distinctly different disorder in certain key ways.

Autism is marked by three main sets of symptoms (see **Table 13.2**; APA, 2013). The first set involves severe impairment in *social interaction*. People with autism do not generally interact

Autism is a devastating developmental disorder, but some people with the disorder, like Jason McElwain, who scored six 3-pointers in his high school basketball game, offer heartwarming stories of accomplishment.

with others, preferring instead to be by themselves (the prefix "auto" meaning "self"). Robert often squirmed away from others and failed to develop good relationships. This is an important difference between people with autism and people with intellectual disability—the latter do enjoy playful social interactions (Balling, Jones, Noone, & Hastings, 2012).

People with autism generally avoid eye contact, show few facial expressions and bodily gestures, and fail to develop friendships (Kasari & Patterson, 2012). People with autism do not share their experiences with others or reciprocate emotions like joy. A child with autism would not typically show her parents a new finger-painting (as many children would) or react strongly to praise or criticism. Social interaction is a painful process for many people with autism.

The second set of autistic symptoms is severe impairment in *communication* with others. This problem overlaps to some extent with intellectual disability, though language deficits are often more extreme and bizarre in people with autism (Boucher, 2013). Many people with autism like Robert are mute or show a long delay in language. Even if a person with autism does have some speech, the speech is often unusual.

Some people with autism have *echolalia*, or repeating what one has just heard (Grossi, Marcone, Cinquegrana, & Galluci, 2012). One of your authors who worked with children with autism would greet them at the bus before escorting them to class. One 7-year-old girl named Hope would get off the bus each day and be greeted with "Hi, Hope!," to which she replied "Hi, Hope!" This *immediate* echolalia occurred for several months despite daily efforts to correct her response. Echolalia can also be *delayed* as a person suddenly blurts out something recalled from several days earlier. Other strange speech patterns include *pronoun reversal*, such as switching "I" for "you," and *incoherent sentences*, such as jumbling words together in a nonsensical way (Evans & Demuth, 2012).

The third main set of autistic symptoms is *bizarre behavior patterns*. Many children with autism do not engage in pretend play, and they often fail to imitate others, as most young children do. Their play is instead marked by withdrawal and preoccupation with parts of objects, such as spinning a wheel on a toy truck for hours (Wong & Kasari, 2012). People with autism also tend to be routine-oriented,

Many people with autism find social attention and touch to be aversive.

## Table 13.2

### DSM-5 Autism Spectrum Disorder

A. Persistent deficits in social communication and social interaction across multiple contexts, as manifested by the following, currently or by history:
1. Deficits in social-emotional reciprocity.
2. Deficits in nonverbal communicative behaviors used for social interaction.
3. Deficits in developing, maintaining, and understanding relationships.

**Severity is based on social communication impairments and restricted, repetitive patterns of behavior.**

B. Restricted, repetitive patterns of behavior, interests, or activities, as manifested by at least two of the following, currently or by history:
1. Stereotyped or repetitive motor movements, use of objects, or speech.
2. Insistence on sameness, inflexible adherence to routines, or ritualized patterns of verbal or nonverbal behavior.
3. Highly restricted, fixated interests that are abnormal in intensity or focus.
4. Hyper- or hyporeactivity to sensory input or unusual interest in sensory aspects of the environment.

**Severity is based on social communication impairments and restricted, repetitive patterns of behavior.**

C. Symptoms must be present in the early developmental period.

D. Symptoms cause clinically significant impairment in social, occupational, or other important areas of current functioning.

E. These disturbances are not better explained by intellectual disability or global developmental delay.

Specify if with intellectual impairment, language disturbance, catatonia, or medical factor or mental disorder.

American Psychiatric Association. (2013). *Diagnostic and statistical manual of mental disorders* (5th ed.). Arlington, VA: American Psychiatric Association.

and disruptions in their routine can lead to tantrums or aggression. Many people with autism also show socially inappropriate *self-stimulatory behavior*, such as excessive rocking, hand flapping, or walking on their toes (Boyd, McDonough, & Bodfish, 2012).

People with autism are sometimes aggressive toward themselves or others. *Self-injurious behavior* can include biting or hitting oneself or banging one's head against a wall (Duerden, Szatmari, & Roberts, 2012). About 50 to 70 percent of people with autism have intellectual disability, though most people with intellectual disability do not have autism (Matson & Shoemaker, 2009). Autism is also marked in some cases by special *savant* skills, such as superior memory, calendar, mathematical, or artistic abilities (Howlin, Goode, Hutton, & Rutter, 2009). Such skills were apparent in Dustin Hoffman's character in *Rain Man*. Savant skills appear to be linked to well-developed memory systems in the brain that lead to narrow but very deep abilities (Treffert, 2009).

Many children with autism engage in strange, repetitive motor behaviors known as self-stimulation.

The severity of autism spectrum disorder depends on the level of deficits in social communication and restricted, repetitive behaviors (see **Table 13.3**; APA, 2013). A previously diagnosed condition, *Asperger's disorder*, involved impairment in social interaction with some unusual behavior patterns but not major deficits in language, cognitive development, or adaptive functioning. People previously diagnosed with Asperger's disorder would now likely be diagnosed with autism spectrum disorder at Level 1 (Table 13.3; APA, 2013). People with Asperger's disorder or those at Level 1 autism spectrum disorder may be able to function more independently later in life than people with severe intellectual disability or autism (Robinson, Curwen, & Ryan, 2012).

## Learning Disorder

The developmental disorders we discussed so far involve delays or problems in *multiple* areas of functioning. Developmental disorders can also be *limited* in scope, however, affecting just one or two areas of functioning. People with limited developmental disorders usually function much better than people with pervasive developmental disorders but still struggle in key areas. One type of limited developmental disorder is learning disorder.

Dustin Hoffman's character in *Rain Man* illustrates someone with savant skills.

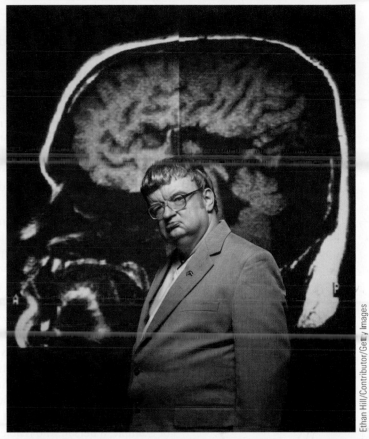

Kim Peek is the basis for the character in *Rain Man*.

## CASE: Alison

**Alison** was an 8-year-old girl experiencing great trouble in school. She consistently failed reading and spelling assignments despite enormous effort. Her teacher said Alison's work was barely legible and often contained basic errors of writing, such as misspelled words and incomplete letters. These errors were beginning to affect her arithmetic work as well because many of the math problems contained stories and symbols. Alison was still working at a first-grade level by the middle of third grade.

Alison regularly struggled when asked to read a story in a group setting. She read very slowly, paused often, and had trouble answering basic questions about the story afterward. Her teacher was particularly confused by Alison's performance because the girl seemed bright, capable, motivated, and alert. Alison performed well in other subjects such as science, music, art, and physical education. She also had no problem with basic self-care skills and showed no behavior problems in class. Alison's teacher did notice, however, that her student was becoming quite frustrated with her homework and was turning in fewer assignments on time.

**Table 13.3**

## DSM-5 Severity Levels for Autism Spectrum Disorder

| Severity level | Social communication | Restricted, repetitive behaviors |
|---|---|---|
| Level 3 "Requiring very substantial support" | Severe deficits in verbal and nonverbal social communication skills cause severe impairments in functioning, very limited initiation of social interactions, and minimal response to social overtures from others. For example, a person with few words of intelligible speech who rarely initiates interaction and, when he or she does, makes unusual approaches to meet needs only and responds to only very direct social approaches. | Inflexibility of behavior, extreme difficulty coping with change, or other restricted/repetitive behaviors markedly interfere with functioning in all spheres. Great distress/difficulty changing focus or action. |
| Level 2 "Requiring substantial support" | Marked deficits in verbal and nonverbal social communication skills; social impairments apparent even with supports in place; limited initiation of social interactions; and reduced or abnormal responses to social overtures from others. For example, a person who speaks simple sentences, whose interaction is limited to narrow special interests, and who has markedly odd nonverbal communication. | Inflexibility of behavior, difficulty coping with change, or other restricted/repetitive behaviors appear frequently enough to be obvious to the casual observer and interfere with functioning in a variety of contexts. Distress and/or difficulty changing focus or action. |
| Level 1 "Requiring support" | Without supports in place, deficits in social communication cause noticeable impairments. Difficulty initiating social interactions, and clear examples of atypical or unsuccessful responses to social overtures of others. May appear to have decreased interest in social interactions. For example, a person who is able to speak in full sentences and engages in communication but whose to-and-fro conversation with others fails, and whose attempts to make friends are odd and typically unsuccessful. | Inflexibility of behavior causes significant interference with functioning in one or more contexts. Difficulty switching between activities. Problems of organization and planning hamper independence. |

Have you or someone you know ever struggled in a particular subject at school such as reading, spelling, or math? For some people like Alison, learning a certain academic skill can be a trying and fruitless experience. Many youth cannot read or spell words correctly, solve basic arithmetic problems, or write a paragraph even though their intelligence is normal. These children may have a learning disorder.

A **learning disorder** (or *specific learning disorder*) is marked by difficulties in reading, spelling, math, or written expression, which could mean a student is failing that particular subject (see **Table 13.4**; APA, 2013). A learning disorder cannot be explained by intellectual disability, however, because the person's intelligence is usually normal (Wong & Butler, 2012). A large *discrepancy* may exist between the person's actual school achievement (below normal) and their potential to learn (normal).

A learning disorder is not due to sensory problems such as visual or hearing impairments, although a child with these problems could still be diagnosed with learning disorder (Handler & Fierson, 2011). Learning disorder is not a result of simple lack of motivation in school or environmental disadvan-

Fuse/Jupiter Images

Dysgraphia refers to a learning problem involving writing.

## Table 13.4

### DSM-5  Specific Learning Disorder

A.  Difficulties learning and using academic skills, as indicated by the presence of at least one of the following symptoms that have persisted for at least 6 months, despite the provision of interventions that target those difficulties:
 1.  Inaccurate or slow and effortful word reading.
 2.  Difficulty understanding the meaning of what is read.
 3.  Difficulties with spelling.
 4.  Difficulties with written expression.
 5.  Difficulties mastering number sense, number facts, or calculation.
 6.  Difficulties with mathematical reasoning.

B.  The affected academic skills are substantially and quantifiably below those expected for the individual's chronological age, and cause significant interference with academic or occupational performance, or with activities of daily living, as confirmed by individually administered standardized achievement measures and comprehensive clinical assessment. For individuals age 17 years and older, a documented history of impairing learning difficulties may be substituted for the standardized assessment.

C.  The learning difficulties begin during school-age years but may not become fully manifest until the demands for those affected academic skills exceed the individual's limited capacities (e.g., as in timed tests, reading or writing lengthy complex reports for a tight deadline, excessively heavy academic loads).

D.  The learning difficulties are not better accounted for by intellectual disabilities, uncorrected visual or auditory acuity, other mental or neurological disorders, psychosocial adversity, lack of proficiency in the language of academic instruction, or inadequate educational assessment.

Specify if impairment in reading, written expression, or mathematics and severity as mild, moderate, or severe.

American Psychiatric Association. (2013). *Diagnostic and statistical manual of mental disorders* (5th ed). Arlington, VA: American Psychiatric Association.

tage such as poor teaching. A true learning disorder is likely related to changes in the person's brain (Stein & Kapoula, 2012).

*Dyslexia* is sometimes used to refer to learning problems in reading and spelling. Some people with dyslexia reverse letters when seeing them, but not all do. Dyslexia is instead a broader term that includes trouble with reading or spelling (Snowling, 2013). *Dyscalculia* is sometimes used to refer to problems learning mathematics and can relate to dyslexia because a person may have trouble reading mathematical symbols or story problems (Butterworth, Varma, & Laurillard, 2011). Other terms related to learning disorder include the following:

- *Dysgraphia:* problems of written expression, such as writing very slowly or off a page

- *Dysnomia:* problems naming or recalling objects, such as saying "fork" when seeing a "spoon"

- *Dysphasia:* problems comprehending or expressing words in proper sequence, such as failing to understand what others say or trouble speaking logically to others

- *Dyspraxia:* problems of fine motor movements, such as trouble buttoning a shirt

- *Dyslalia:* problems of articulation or trouble saying words clearly and understandably

## Epidemiology of Developmental Disorders

Intellectual disability occurs in 1.04 percent of the population (Maulik, Mascarenhas, Mathers, Dua, & Saxena, 2011). The disorder is much more common in boys than girls and is typically diagnosed in preschool and elementary school-age years when a child is compared academically with peers (Burack, Hodapp, Iarocci, & Zigler, 2012). Intellectual disability can be comorbid with autism and is commonly associated with anxiety, depression, dementia, and psychotic disorders (Einfeld, Ellis, & Emerson, 2011). The onset of intellectual disability is usually gradual because early developmental delays are sometimes hard to spot or are confused with other possible problems such as hearing impairment.

Intellectual disability appears more common in less developed nations than wealthier ones and among people of low socioeconomic status (Maulik et al., 2011). Intellectual disability is also more common among African Americans than other racial groups. Some speculate that this may be due to racial segregation, economic disadvantage, culturally inappropriate testing, or higher rates of diabetes and other disease in mothers (Boyle et al., 2011; Leonard & Wen, 2002).

Narrowly defined autism occurs in 17 of 10,000 births worldwide and broadly defined autism spectrum disorder occurs in 62 of 10,000 births worldwide (Elsabbagh et al., 2012). The prevalence of autism is increasing (Matson & Kozlowski, 2011). The disorder is 2 to 5 times more common in boys than girls, but girls with autism often have more severe symptoms, such as lower intelligence (Rivet & Matson, 2011). People with autism are not often diagnosed with comorbid psychiatric disorders, perhaps because of restricted emotions, but symptoms of anxiety and depression are common (Mayes, Calhoun, Murray, & Zahid, 2011). Autism is associated with medical problems such as seizures and hearing and visual problems, however. Autism is less associated with race (Mayes & Calhoun, 2011). The onset of autism tends to be more sudden than intellectual disability as tendencies such as self-stimulatory behavior and social withdrawal are more apparent in toddlerhood.

Learning disorder affects 7.2 percent of students, although problems in specific areas may be more common (Elsabbagh et al., 2012). About 15.1 to 20 percent of American children have basic reading problems (Shaywitz & Shaywitz, 2005). Learning disorder is more common among boys than girls, especially if processing deficits are severe (Liederman, Kantrowitz, & Flannery, 2005). European American children have a greater prevalence of learning disorder with attention-deficit/hyperactivity disorder than Hispanic or African American children (Pastor & Reuben, 2005).

Learning disorder may be comorbid with any other disorder but is linked in many cases (45.1 percent) with attention-deficit/hyperactivity disorder (DuPaul, Gormley, & Laracy, 2013; see later section on disruptive behavior disorders). Problems with social skills, aggression, and substance use are also common to youths with learning disorder. Onset of learning disorder is gradual and often marked by early language delays and medical conditions (McBride-Chang et al., 2011).

## Stigma Associated with Developmental Disorders

Children are especially susceptible to stigma because they are more vulnerable and powerless than adults. This applies especially to children with developmental disorders and their parents. Gray (2002) found that parents of children with autism often encountered avoidance, hostile staring, and rude comments from others. Part of this may be because children with autism appear normal physically but can display severe behavior problems. Self-stigma can occur as well, as some parents blame themselves or their parenting style for their child's autism (Farrugia, 2009). Some teachers may also be less empathetic toward children with autism and some may see such children as dangerous (Ling, Mak, & Cheng, 2010). These studies illustrate the importance of educating the public about pervasive developmental disorders.

### INTERIM SUMMARY

▶ People with pervasive or limited developmental disorders experience delays in key areas of functioning and impaired cognitive ability or intelligence.

▶ Intellectual disability is a pervasive developmental disorder involving early deficits in cognitive ability and adaptive functioning.

▶ Autism is a pervasive developmental disorder involving severe impairments in social interaction and communication as well as bizarre behavior patterns.

▶ Asperger's disorder is now part of autism spectrum disorder and involves impairment in social interaction with some unusual behavior patterns but not major deficits in language, cognitive development, or adaptive functioning.

▶ Learning disorder is a limited developmental disorder involving deficits in a subject like reading, math, spelling, or writing.

▶ Stigma is an important part of developmental disorders and can affect others' view of a child.

### REVIEW QUESTIONS

1. What are major features and subtypes of intellectual disability?
2. What are major symptoms of autism?
3. Outline differences between pervasive and limited developmental disorders.
4. Describe major features of learning disorder and its related terms.
5. Describe the epidemiology of pervasive and limited developmental disorders.

## Developmental Disorders: Causes and Prevention

We turn our attention next to factors that cause developmental disorders. We also discuss how understanding these factors might help prevent developmental disorders.

### Biological Risk Factors for Developmental Disorders

Many mental disorders are caused by a combination of biological and environmental variables. This is also true for developmental disorders, though biological predispositions tend to be very strong. These predispositions include genetic influences, chromosomal aberrations, and prenatal and perinatal problems that lead to brain changes.

### GENETIC INFLUENCES: GENE DAMAGE

*Genes* represent individual units on a *chromosome* that contain important information about a person's traits and characteristics. Thousands of genes are part of each of the typically 46 chromosomes in a human. Genes predispose us to become whoever we are but may also become damaged and lead to developmental disorders. Many cases of severe intellectual disability relate to genetic and other organic defects.

**Fragile X syndrome** is a condition that results when the *FMR1* gene of the X chromosome narrows, breaks, or otherwise becomes mutated. Fragile X syndrome affects 1 in 4,000 to 6,000 males but is less common in females (1 in 7,000--10,000) because they have another X chromosome to help compensate for damage (Hagerman, 2008). Females may, however, suffer from effects of fragile X syndrome or be carriers of the problem—they may have the genetic mutation but not the full-blown syndrome. The genetic mutation leads to certain brain changes (see brain changes section). People with fragile X syndrome show hyperactivity, self-stimulatory and self-injurious behavior, aggression, poor social skills, perseveration (doing the same thing over and over), and bizarre language. Most have intellectual

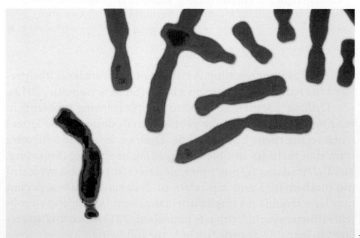

Newscom

People with fragile X syndrome often experience narrowing or breakage in the X chromosome.

disability. Fragile X syndrome may account for up to 30 percent of X-linked forms of intellectual disability (Raymond, 2005).

Another example of how genetics influence intellectual disability is **phenylketonuria (PKU)**. PKU is also caused by a genetic mutation, this time on chromosome 12. PKU is an *autosomal recessive disorder*, meaning the defective gene must be inherited from both parents for problems to occur (Frye & Rossignol, 2012). The defective gene leads to the body's inability to break down *phenylalanine*, an amino acid. Excess phenylalanine in the body can damage the liver and brain (Jorns et al., 2012). Check out a diet soda can—it warns the product contains phenylalanine.

Untreated PKU may create physical problems such as awkward gait and spasms and cognitive problems such as severe language delay, learning disorder, and intellectual disability. Fortunately, however, early screening can detect newborns with PKU, and a special diet limiting phenylalanine intake can prevent many of these problems (Di Ciommo, Forcella, & Cotugno, 2012). People on this special diet must usually refrain from meat, fish, eggs, dairy products, nuts, and corn, among other items. PKU occurs in 1 in 15,000

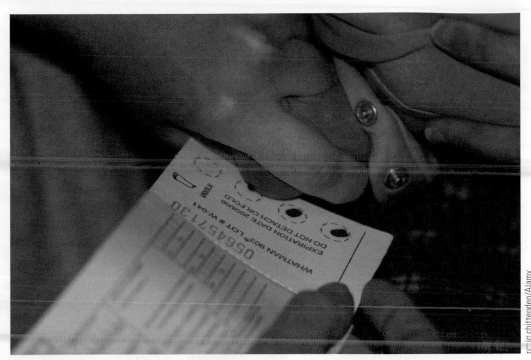

rc in chittenden/Alamy

Newborns are tested for PKU by a heel-prick and given a special diet if they test positive.

American births, although many more people may be carriers. Carriers have the defective gene from only one parent, so no symptoms develop (Blau, van Spronsen, & Levy, 2010).

Genetic influences can lead to intellectual disability in other ways as well. People with **sickle cell disease**, which affects 1 of 600 live births, especially African Americans, experience damaged red blood cells, slow blood move-

---

## BOX 13.1 Focus on Law and Ethics

### Key Ethical Issues and Developmental Disorders

People with developmental disorders are often children or those who have trouble speaking for themselves, so many ethical dilemmas arise with this population. One dilemma that arises almost immediately is the question of what parents should do if they discover, through genetic testing, that their fetus has a severe and potentially fatal developmental disorder. A related question surrounds the decision to have children if a person knows a developmental disorder will likely be genetically transmitted. What would you do in these situations, and why?

Another key issue for this population surrounds quality of life and level of choice that should be made available to someone with a pervasive developmental disorder (Brown &

Brown, 2009). How much choice should Robert have in his living environment, and could too much freedom lead to harm toward others or lack of progress toward his educational goals? All people have the right to available and effective treatment that causes the least amount of restriction on freedom (Chapter 15). For Robert, this meant placement in a group home that simulated family living as opposed to a more impersonal developmental center.

Ethical considerations for people with developmental disorders also concern medication and punishment, which are often used without a person's explicit consent (and usually with the consent of others). Is it fair to medicate, restrain, or severely punish someone for misbehavior when they have not given consent? What if a behavior such as head-banging is life-threatening? An ethical dilemma such as this involves juxtaposing an individual's right to expression with societal right to prevent harm. What might you do in this situation?

ment, and less oxygenation to the body. The problem has been linked to a genetic mutation (HbS) and could lead to severe brain damage and intellectual disability, especially early in life (Swanson, Grosse, & Kulkarni, 2011). People with **Tay-Sachs disease**, which affects 1 in 300,000 births, especially Ashkenazi Jews, experience severe motor and sensory impairments, intellectual disability, and death at age 2 to 4 years. Several genetic mutations have been linked to this disorder as well (Haghighi et al., 2011).

## GENETIC INFLUENCES: CONCORDANCE

A genetic component seems at least partially responsible for causing autism. Concordance rates of autism are 60 to 92 percent in identical twins but 0 to 10 percent in fraternal twins. Autism also runs in families—siblings of a child with autism have a 2 to 8 percent chance of having autism themselves. Abnormalities on chromosomes 7, 15, and 16 have been implicated in autism (Miles, 2011). Parents of children with autism are not more likely than the general population to have autism themselves, however. Because identical twin concordance rates for autism are not 100 percent, influences other than genetic must be contributing as well.

A genetic component also accounts for about 54 to 65 percent of the cause of learning disorder, especially reading problems (dyslexia). One twin study of 264 pairs of identical twins and 214 pairs of fraternal twins revealed concordance rates of 62 to 63 percent and 15 to 29 percent, respectively (Hawke, Wadsworth, & DeFries, 2005). These data supplement other studies that show dyslexia to run in families. About 23 to 65 percent of children with dyslexia may have parents with dyslexia and 40 percent may have siblings with dyslexia. Genetic defects responsible for learning disorder, especially reading problems, may be on chromosomes 2, 3, 6, 15, and 18 (Shaywitz & Shaywitz, 2005).

## CHROMOSOMAL ABERRATIONS

Changes in sections of a chromosome or an entire chromosome also influence about 25 percent of severe developmental problems (Ropers, 2010). Almost all (95 percent) cases of **Down syndrome** are due to an extra chromosome 21. Most people with Down syndrome thus have 47 chromosomes in their cells. This "extra" genetic information leads to several distinct characteristics, especially physical ones such as a large tongue, upward-slanting eyes, short fingers, brittle blond hair, and visual, hearing, and cardiac problems (Dierssen & De La Torre, 2012).

People with Down syndrome often develop symptoms of Alzheimer's disease after age 40 to 50 years (Chapter 14; Ness et al., 2012). Down syndrome affects 1 in 600 live births, but the

chances of having a child with the condition increase greatly with maternal age. A 20-year-old mother has a 1 in 1,441 chance of giving birth to a child with Down syndrome, but a 46-year-old mother has a 1 in 31 chance. This is likely due to problems in chromosome separation at conception (Sherman, Allen, Bean, & Freeman, 2007). Other syndromes and chromosomal aberrations linked to intellectual disability are in **Table 13.5**.

Rhea Anna/ Aurora/Getty Images

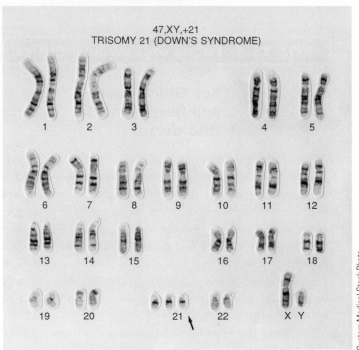

47,XY,+21
TRISOMY 21 (DOWN'S SYNDROME)

Custom Medical Stock Photo

Children with Down syndrome often have an extra chromosome 21 and intellectual disability but can still participate in and enjoy many typical childhood activities.

## Table 13.5

### Other Syndromes and Chromosomal Aberrations That May Lead to Intellectual Disability

| Syndrome | Possible cause | Prevalence |
| --- | --- | --- |
| Prader-Willi syndrome | Deletion on chromosome 15 | 1/10,000–15,000 births |
| Klinefelter syndrome | Males with extra X chromosome(s) | 1/600–900 male births |
| Turner syndrome | Females with one X chromosome | 1/2,000–3,000 female births |
| Noonan syndrome | May be similar to Turner syndrome | 1/1,000–2,500 births |
| Neurofibromatosis | Deletion on chromosomes 17 or 22 | 1/4,000 births |
| Williams syndrome | Deletion on chromosome 7 | 1/20,000 births |
| Smith-Magenis syndrome | Deletion on chromosome 17 | 1/25,000 births |
| Angelman syndrome | Deletion on chromosome 15 | 1/15,000–30,000 births |
| Rett's disorder | Mutation on MECP2 gene on X chromosome | 1/10,000-15,000 births |

Sources: Brandes & Mesrobian (2005); Dykens & Cassidy (1999); Neul, 2012; Powell & Schulte (1999); Rovet, Netley, Keenan, Bailey, & Stewart (1996).

## PRENATAL AND PERINATAL PROBLEMS

Genetic and chromosomal changes are obviously very important, but other biological phenomena can also lead to developmental disorders. **Teratogens** are conditions that negatively impact physical development of a child during prenatal (before birth) or perinatal (during birth) periods. Teratogens that occur early in pregnancy can lead to many structural changes because this is a key time for organ development. Teratogens that occur later in pregnancy, or even during birth, can also affect brain development and may produce a developmental disorder in conjunction with genetic/chromosomal problems (Ellison, Rosenfeld, & Shaffer, 2013).

A key teratogen is maternal use of alcohol and other drugs during pregnancy. A child exposed to alcohol prenatally may develop fetal alcohol syndrome (FAS; see Chapter 9) or broader *fetal alcohol effects* (Riley, Infante, & Warren, 2011). Children with fetal alcohol effects tend to have a small head size, facial and heart defects, and lower intelligence, the latter of which may last for years. These children also show problems in learning, memory, hyperactivity, impulsivity, and communication

and social skills (Mattson, Crocker, & Nguyen, 2011). Maternal use of other drugs such as nicotine, narcotics, and stimulants can also lead to lower birth weight, premature birth, behavioral problems, inattention, and developmental disorders (Burd et al., 2007; Schempf, 2007). Other important teratogens include diseases such as HIV and toxins such as lead and mercury.

Excessive maternal stress can increase adrenaline and thus limit oxygen to a fetus. Malnourished fetuses are especially likely to perish or have malformations, low birth weight, or premature birth. Some children also experience a lack of oxygen, termed *anoxia* or *hypoxia*, during birth from delays in the birth canal or choking by the umbilical cord (Nair & Russell, 2012). All of these experiences could lead to brain damage and thus severe developmental delay. We next discuss specific brain areas affected by genetic, chromosomal, and teratogenic influences.

## BRAIN FEATURES

Researchers have focused on key brain changes with respect to intellectual disability, including gross malformations and subtle markers of brain damage. Gross malformations include induction and migration defects. **Induction defects** are problems in closure of the neural tube (linking the spinal cord to the brain), proper development of the forebrain, and completion of the corpus callosum, the part of the brain linking left and right hemispheres (**Figure 13.2**). **Migration defects** refer to problems in cell growth and distribution in the second to fifth month of pregnancy, which can lead to underdeveloped brain areas (Barkovich, Guerrini, Kuzniecky, Jackson, & Dobyns, 2012).

Subtle markers of brain damage usually involve minor changes in size and shape of certain brain areas. A larger than normal cerebellum has been found in youth with developmental delays, and a smaller cerebellum has been found in adults with fragile X syndrome (Greco et al., 2011; Webb et al., 2009). Developmental disorders have also been linked to *enlarged ventricles*, a phenomenon we discussed for schizophrenia in Chapter 12 (Jary, De Carli, Ramenghi, & Whitelaw, 2012).

Other developmental disorders have even more specific types of brain changes. Autism seems associated with enlargement of the overall brain, especially with respect to the midsagittal area, limbic system, amygdala, and occipital, parietal, and temporal lobes (Courchesne, Campbell, & Solso, 2011). Increased brain size relates to less well-connected neurons. This may help explain unusual emotional and social behaviors seen in people like Robert.

People with autism tend to have a smaller corpus callosum, which may affect motor coordination and emotion regulation (Frazier, Keshavan, Minshew, & Harden, 2012). Those with autism also may have fewer *Purkinje cells*, which relate to behavioral inhibition (Sudarov, 2013). Autism has also been linked to high levels of serotonin, a neurotransmitter involved in motor activity (Harrington, Lee, Crum, Zimmerman, & Hertz-Picciotto, 2013). These latter changes may be related to self-stimulatory behavior and perseveration. People with what was previously labeled Asperger's disorder may have changes in the amygdala-prefrontal cortex pathway that affect facial expressions of emotion (Yu, Cheung, Chua, & McAlonan, 2011).

developmental problems such as learning disorder. Autism is largely unrelated to culture, but some have noted a higher prevalence among immigrant populations (Keen, Reid, & Arnone, 2010). Recall this same kind of finding for people with schizophrenia (Chapter 12).

Developmental disorders can also result from accidents or other traumas that lead to brain damage. About 1,200 to 1,400 children are severely shaken each year, which can lead to death or permanent brain damage (Newton & Vandeven, 2005). Most of those who shake babies are males in their early 20s, many of whom are frustrated by a child's crying or toileting problems (Starling et al., 2004). Other forms of physical child maltreatment could cause brain damage as well. Brain injury can also result from hitting one's head on the sidewalk after a fall from a bike, a near-drowning experience, a car accident, poisoning from lead or cleaners, or being punched in the face. Neurological damage could also come from diseases such as meningitis (Higginson, Martin, & Cook, 2010). Most of these problems are preventable, and education about ways to protect children from brain injury is crucial.

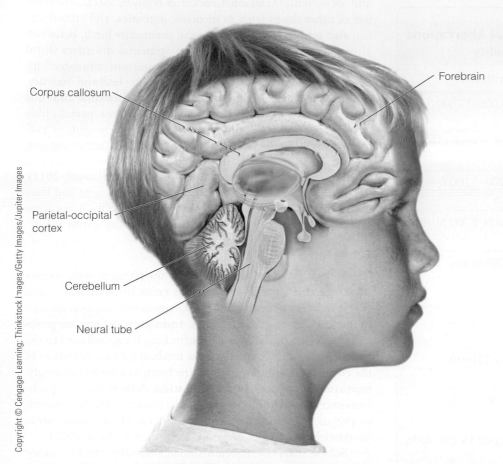

**FIGURE 13.2** MAJOR BRAIN AREAS IMPLICATED IN DEVELOPMENTAL DISORDERS

Corpus callosum, Forebrain, Parietal-occipital cortex, Cerebellum, Neural tube

Children with learning disorder often show brain *symmetry*, in which opposing sides of a brain area are nearly equal in size. Most people have asymmetry, where one side is larger than the other. Brain areas most implicated in learning disorder, especially reading and language problems, are the *planum temporale* and *parietal lobe* (Bloom, Garcia-Barrera, Miller, Miller, & Hynd, 2013; Cabeza, Ciaramelli, & Moscovitch, 2012). These areas may not be as well developed as they are for people without learning disorder. Disruptions of the posterior (rear) areas of the left hemisphere closely link to learning disorder (Shaywitz & Shaywitz, 2012).

## Environmental Risk Factors for Developmental Disorders

Environmental and cultural factors can also be important for shaping developmental disorders. This pertains most to mild forms of intellectual disability, which can result from family variables such as poor language stimulation, neglect of a child's educational needs, or inconsistent parenting. This is sometimes referred to as **cultural-familial intellectual disability** and may account for up to 50 percent of cases of intellectual disability. Children in this group tend to live in poverty and have parents lower in intelligence (Hodapp, Griffin, Burke, & Fisher, 2011). Lack of attention to education can also prolong other

## Causes of Developmental Disorders

How do these risk factors interact to produce a developmental disorder? Strong biological factors clearly predispose certain people to have intellectual disability and/or autism. These biological factors lead to brain changes that cause problems or delays in thinking, reasoning, decision making, judgment, and other higher-order cognitive processes. These problems then lead to severe deficits in self-care, academic, communication, and other crucial skills. Environmental factors could also help cause critical brain changes or maintain a developmental disorder over time.

You may find it difficult to sort out all the biological influences related to developmental disorders. Consider a model called the *final common pathway* (Anagnostou, 2012; **Figure 13.3**). In this model, various biological factors conspire or interact in different ways for children with different disorders. One child may have a certain genetic predisposition in addition to a key neurotransmitter change, such as increased serotonin, that leads to autism. Another child may have a certain chromosomal aberration in addition to anoxia at birth that leads to moderate intellectual disability. Another child may have been exposed to alcohol prenatally and was born prematurely, which may lead to learning disorder. In the final common pathway model, any combination of biological factors could lead to certain key brain

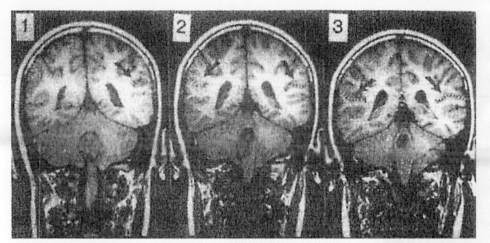

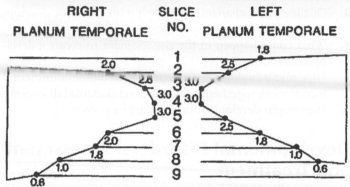

RIGHT                                          LEFT
PLANUM TEMPORALE    SLICE NO.    PLANUM TEMPORALE

Children with reading problems often show symmetry of a key brain area known as the planum temporale. The upper images illustrate the location of the planum temporale and the lower image illustrates graphically the similarity or symmetry of the size of the planum temporale in a child with learning disorder.

changes that then lead to a specific type of developmental disorder.

## Prevention of Developmental Disorders

Developmental disorders begin early in life, so it makes sense to think of prevention before and immediately after birth. Prevention may thus involve genetic testing and counseling, fetal care, screening of newborns, and early medical care for babies. Preventing accidents and other factors that could lead to brain damage is also imperative. Delivering educational services to at-risk children may be helpful as well.

Prenatal genetic testing can occur in different ways, most commonly through *chorionic villus sampling* or *amniocentesis*. These methods involve DNA extraction as a fetus develops. DNA testing can be easily done after birth as well by examining hair, skin, or blood. These methods are done to check number of chromosomes or conduct a more thorough DNA assessment to find missing or defective genes. Genetic testing is often done for adolescent and older mothers, when a family history exists of a

certain problem, or when a child shows signs of a genetically based disorder (Toriello, 2011). If a fetus has a genetic disorder or chromosomal aberration, then genetic counseling would follow to explore all options with the parents.

Prenatal care of the fetus is also crucial for prevention of developmental disorders, and this can involve proper diet, especially folic acid, regular visits to a medical doctor, and avoidance of drugs, high stress, toxins, and diseases. Proper diet includes limits on caffeine and plenty of grains, fruits, vegetables, water, and sources of protein such as nuts and beans. Vitamin supplements are also important. Pregnant women should also consult a physician before taking medications or exercising vigorously (Vidaeff, Franzini, & Low, 2003).

Screening newborns is another important prevention technique, and not just for PKU. Many diseases potentially related to developmental disorders, such as HIV, can be identified after birth. Early medical care for babies and insurance coverage for minimum hospital stays following birth are also important. Adherence to immunization schedules, proper diet, and ongoing checkups is critical as well (O'Hagen & Rappuoli, 2004).

Accident prevention is a large part of pediatric psychology as well. This includes preventing head injury, such as wearing helmets when bike riding, using proper car seats and cribs, and providing safe toys. Prevention must also include denying access to poisons, eliminating items that could choke a child, locking cabinets and toilets and pools, placing gates before

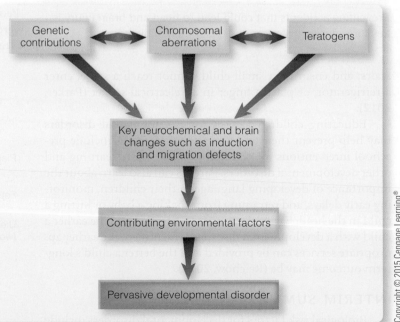

**FIGURE 13.3** SAMPLE FINAL COMMON PATHWAY OF PERVASIVE DEVELOPMENTAL DISORDER

Preventing accidents that could lead to head and brain injury is key for reducing instances of developmental disorder.

stairs, and ensuring a small child cannot reach a stove, enter a refrigerator, or place a finger in an electrical socket (Parker, 2012).

Educating children at risk for developmental disorders may help prevent their onset or severity. Services include preschool interventions for children predisposed to learning and other developmental disorders. Parents can also learn about the importance of developing language in their children, monitoring early delays, and refraining from shaking a baby or hitting a child in the head. Early screening is critical as well. The earlier a child with a developmental disorder is identified, the earlier appropriate services can be provided and the better a child's long-term outcome may be (Reichow, 2012).

## INTERIM SUMMARY

▶ Biological risk factors for developmental disorders include genetic contributions, chromosomal aberrations, prenatal teratogens, perinatal problems, and induction and migration brain defects.

▶ Environmental risk factors for developmental disorders include family variables and traumatic brain injury.

▶ Biological and environmental risk factors can create brain changes that impair cognition and ability to live an independent life.

▶ Preventing developmental disorders often involves genetic testing and counseling, prenatal care, newborn screening, early medical care for babies, accident prevention, and delivering educational services to at-risk children and parents.

## REVIEW QUESTIONS

1. Explain how genetic and chromosomal problems can lead to developmental disorder.
2. Define teratogens and indicate how they can lead to developmental disorder.
3. Outline brain changes associated with different developmental disorders.
4. What could happen in the environment to create a developmental disorder?
5. How might biological predispositions and environmental factors work together to cause a developmental disorder?
6. How might developmental disorder be prevented?

# Developmental Disorders: Assessment and Treatment

Mental health professionals use various methods to examine people with developmental disorders. These methods include cognitive, achievement, and other tests as well as interviews, rating scales, and behavioral observation.

## Cognitive Tests

People with developmental disorders often experience severe cognitive and intellectual deficits, so a basic assessment strategy is to use tests that assess for overall intellectual and

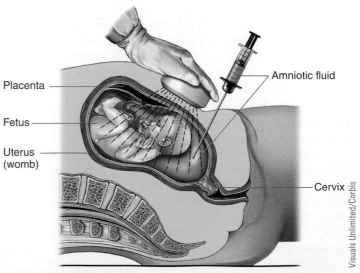

Amniocentesis involves obtaining a sample of amniotic fluid to detect possible genetic defects.

problem-solving functioning. We described commonly used intelligence tests in Chapter 4. Intelligence tests generally assess two types of cognitive ability: *verbal* and *performance*. Verbal tasks that intelligence tests address include knowledge of general information and vocabulary, comprehension of verbal material, and drawing comparisons. Performance tasks include sequencing items, arranging designs, putting pieces together to form a whole, identifying missing parts, and recalling information. Collectively, these tasks are used to assess for attention, concentration, anxiety, short-term and long-term memory, practical knowledge, social judgment, motivation and persistence, visual discrimination, mental processing speed, distractibility, visual association, conceptual thinking, ordering and planning ability, and perceptual and spatial ability.

Many intelligence tests are *norm-referenced*, which means test scores are compared with those from thousands of people who previously took the test. The norms are age-based, so Robert's performance could be compared with people his age. Most intelligence tests are based on a mean of 100 and a standard deviation of 15. Recall that intellectual disability may partly involve a score less than 70 (or 2 standard deviations below the mean) on a standardized intelligence test. Robert's early score on one of these tests was 55.

Intelligence tests are highly useful for gathering information about cognitive ability and potential for future scholastic achievement. They are not a measure of how "smart" one is, however. The tests measure global problem-solving ability, not what specific information a person knows (Sattler, 2008). Intelligence tests must be used carefully (see **Box 13.2**). One should never diagnose a developmental disorder based *only* on an intelligence test score. Test results should be combined with other information (described below) to determine diagnosis and functioning level.

*Neuropsychological testing* may also be used if brain damage is suspected in a person with developmental disorder. These tests are more specific than intelligence tests and assess for sensation, motor speed and strength, perceptual ability, memory, language, attention, abstract and flexible thought processes, and orientation or knowledge of time, people, and places. We described common neuropsychological tests in Chapter 4.

Some children may be too young to be formally tested. An examiner could thus rely on developmental tests such as the *Bayley Scales of Infant and Toddler Development—Third Edition* (Bayley, 2005). The Bayley assesses youngsters aged 1 to 42 months by comparing performance on certain tasks to normal developmental milestones. For example, children commonly recognize themselves at age 12 months (a cognitive ability) and can walk up stairs alone at age 21 to 25 months (a motor ability). The test covers cognitive, language, motor, adaptive, and social-emotional abilities.

Developmental tests are also available for newborns, such as the *Neonatal Intensive Care Unit Network Neurobehavioral Scale*; these tests assess muscle tone, motor activity, and stress (Lester & Tronick, 2004). Developmental test scores relate to intelligence test scores but are not exactly the same. Performance on these tests, however, may help identify developmental delay and predict how well a child may function over time.

## Achievement Tests

Intelligence tests measure general problem-solving ability, but *achievement tests* measure more specific types of knowledge. Achievement tests are often *criterion-referenced*, meaning they measure a child against a level of performance. Children are assessed on reading, spelling, and arithmetic tasks to determine their grade level on the *Wide Range Achievement Test 4* (Wilkinson

---

### BOX 13.2 Focus on Diversity

### Testing for People with Developmental Disorders

Many cognitive, achievement, and other tests are available for assessing people with developmental disorders. These tests are standardized on thousands of people and have shown excellent reliability and validity. Still, questions remain about how applicable these tests are to minorities and people from disadvantaged backgrounds. Concerns have arisen that the tests unfairly predispose certain groups toward diagnoses of developmental disorder and placement in special education settings.

According to American Psychological Association (2002) ethical guidelines, those who use tests must recognize situations in which assessment techniques may not apply to certain people

based on their gender, age, ethnicity, religion, sexual orientation, disability, language, socioeconomic status, and other key distinctions. Examiners must always be aware that certain tests may not be the best method of gathering information about a particular child. Many children have parents who speak only Spanish at home, for example, and these children may be penalized on an intelligence test that assumes good English-speaking ability.

The best approach to evaluating people with developmental disorders is to rely on a *multimethod, multisource assessment approach*. This means, in addition to testing, that one should rely on other assessment methods such as rating scales, interviews, and observation. One should also speak to parents, siblings, peers, teachers, and other sources who know a person well. A more complete picture can thus be gathered about a person's functioning in his environment and whether a diagnosis of developmental disorder is truly necessary.

& Robertson, 2006). A fourth-grader who scores at the 2.5 grade level would thus be considered low achieving. Achievement tests are popular for assessing children with learning disorder, but scores do not always correspond well with school performance.

## Interviews

Interviews are also used to assess people with developmental disorders, although the measures are obviously limited if someone cannot or will not communicate. Some structured diagnostic interviews have been designed specifically for people with developmental disorders using only pictures (Valla, Bergeron, & Smolla, 2000). Interviews specific to autism have also been designed, such as the *Autism Diagnostic Interview—Revised* and *Parent Interview for Autism—Clinical Version* (de Bildt et al., 2004; Stone, Coonrod, Pozdol, & Turner, 2003). Questions when interviewing people with developmental disorders often surround mental status, concerns about one's environment, individual choice and quality of life, communication ability, relationships with others, anxiety and depression, and needed support.

Interviews can also shed light on a person's abilities to function independently and adaptively. A common instrument is the *Vineland Adaptive Behavior Scales, Second Edition* (VABS-II; Sparrow, Cicchetti, & Balla, 2005). The VABS-II covers four primary domains of adaptive functioning: communication, daily living skills, socialization, and motor skills. Like intelligence tests, the measure is based on a mean of 100 and a standard deviation of 15. People who know a person well, such as parents and siblings, can also be interviewed regarding a person with a developmental disorder.

## Rating Scales

Rating scales are also available to assess people with a developmental disorder and can be very useful when testing and interviewing is not possible. Many scales focus on adaptive and problem behaviors and are completed by mental health professionals or caregivers. A common example is the *Adaptive Behavior Scale—Residential and Community: Second Edition* (Nihira, Leland, & Lambert, 1993). Other rating scales are more specific to a certain disorder, like autism, to help diagnose the problem. A common example is the *Childhood Autism Rating Scale, Second Edition* (CARS2; Schopler, Van Bourgondien, Wellman, & Love, 2010), sample items of which are listed in **Table 13.6**. Rating scales have the advantage of providing fast information but should generally be supplemented with behavioral observations.

## Behavioral Observation

Direct behavioral observation of a person with a developmental disorder is very important when examining specific behavior problems. Direct observation is often used to gauge the frequency and severity of self-injurious and self-stimulatory behaviors, aggression, and tantrums. One could also observe adaptive behaviors regarding social interactions and language (Neal, Matson, & Belva, 2013).

For children with learning disorder, direct observation is used to measure inattention, motivation, out-of-seat behavior, and actual schoolwork behaviors such as on-task and test-taking

---

**Table 13.6**

### Sample Items from Childhood Autism Rating Scale, Second Edition (CARS2) Rating Sheet for "Relating to People"

Relating to people

1—No evidence of difficulty or abnormality in relating to people (The child's behavior is appropriate for his or her age. Some shyness, fussiness, or annoyance at being told what to do may be observed, but not to an atypical degree.)

1.5-2—Mildly abnormal relationships (The child may avoid looking the adult in the eye, avoid the adult or become fussy if interaction is forced, be excessively shy, not be as responsive to the adult as is typical, or cling to parents somewhat more than most children of the same age.)

2.5-3—Moderately abnormal relationships (The child shows aloofness [seems unaware of adult at times]. Persistent and forceful attempts are necessary to get the child's attention at times. Minimal contact is initiated by the child.)

3.5-4—Severely abnormal relationships (The child is consistently aloof or unaware of what the adult is doing. He or she almost never responds or initiates contact with the adult. Only the most persistent attempts to get the child's attention have any effect.)

---

behavior and organization and study skills. Reviewing a child's schoolwork and home behavior is also important (Mautone, Marshall, Costigan, Clarke, & Power, 2012). Behavioral observations can be formally structured but more often involve a rater who simply watches a person and records the presence and severity of certain behaviors in short time intervals.

## Biological Treatment for Developmental Disorders

Medications may be used to treat specific aspects of developmental disorders. Seizures are quite common in people with autism, so anticonvulsant medications are often prescribed (Robinson, 2012). Sedative and neuroleptic medications may be used to control agitation or dangerous behaviors such as aggression and self-injury (Williamson & Martin, 2012). *Fenfluramine* leads to decreased serotonin levels and has been used with limited success to treat dangerous motor behaviors in people with autism (Chadman, Guariglia, & Yoo, 2012). Medications may also be used to ease comorbid symptoms of attention-deficit/hyperactivity, anxiety-related, depressive, bipolar, and sleep disorders (Rowles & Findling, 2010). Medication use in this population must be considered carefully because many who take the drugs cannot give consent or accurately report side effects.

**Gene therapy** may also be a key biological treatment in the future for people with developmental disorders (Chapter 14). Examples include replacing fragile X and other genetic mutations with healthy genes to reverse or stem developmental delay. Early work with mice is promising, but gene therapy for humans is still a distant hope (van Bokhoven, 2011).

## Psychological Treatments for Developmental Disorders

Psychological treatments for people with developmental disorders, like Robert, often target individual areas of functioning. We next cover treatments to improve language, social relationships, self-care and academic skills, and problem behaviors. These treatments are based largely on behavioral principles and models of learning (Chapter 2) and have been found to be quite effective for people with developmental disorders.

### LANGUAGE TRAINING

Many developmental disorders involve language problems, and language skills are an excellent predictor of long-term functioning in this population. A child must first pay attention, however, to learn language and other skills. This is especially important for children with autism, many of whom vigorously avoid social and eye contact with others. **Discrete-trial training** may be used to increase eye contact. A teacher issues a command ("Look at me") and rewards the child if he complies. If not, the teacher holds a desirable item such as a cookie near her own eye to entice the child to make eye contact. Such training must eventually eliminate use of the cookie, but the training successfully increases eye contact and attention (Turan, Moroz, & Croteau, 2012).

Language training can begin once good attention is established. Such training often focuses first on building *receptive labeling ability* for various objects. A child may be shown four pictures, one of which is a chair, and told to "Point to the chair." Rewards are given for correct answers; incorrect answers are met with prompts toward the correct response. Pictures usually include items commonly used by the child or that are important for daily functioning such as eating utensils, types of food or drink, the toilet, or clothing. A main goal is to enhance later expressive speech and give a child a way to communicate his wants. This is also important for reducing problem behaviors—a child pointing to a toilet to indicate a need to go

is less likely to be as aggressive in communicating that desire as a child with no language (Kurtz, Boelter, Jarmolowicz, Chin, & Hagopian, 2011).

Language training then involves more *expressive speech* (Ingersoll & Dvortcsak, 2010). Early expressive language programs often focus on *shaping*, or rewarding approximations of talking. A child might first be given a reward every time he makes a vocalization, even babbling, yelling, or crying. As the child vocalizes more, these sounds are shaped into basic speech sounds. A child's lips could be pressed together to make the "m" sound. Easier sounds are trained first, then more difficult ones such as "j" and "q." These sounds may be shaped eventually into words and sentences. Unfortunately, such training can last years and is often incomplete (Vismara & Rogers, 2010).

Language training can also involve *speech imitation* in which a teacher places an object before a child, names it, and asks a child to repeat the name. The child may eventually be asked to name the object without help. The child will hopefully learn to make requests of different items independently and generalize his language to request other items. *Natural incidental training* is used as a person's language develops further. Extensive language is taught in a more natural way (Duffy & Healy, 2011). A teacher may look at a child and wait a few seconds for a request for an item. Appropriate requests are then rewarded with the item or the teacher prompts the request by telling the child he needs to communicate what he wants.

Language training is best if a child has some language before age 5 years, even echolalia, and if the intervention is intensive. If formal language training is not working, then *sign language* may be taught (Vismara & Rogers, 2010). Sign language is an especially desirable option for children with autism who often have excellent motor skills but who resist language training. Robert learned signs for 15 objects. Sign language is useful but has limitations because many other people do not recognize the signs. Technological assistance to help with communication may thus be useful (Shane et al., 2012).

### SOCIALIZATION TRAINING

Another key aspect of treating people with developmental disorders is *socialization training*. A person is taught to perform and use social skills such as making eye contact, conversing appropriately, playing and cooperating with others, and expressing affection (Walton & Ingersoll, 2013). Basic socialization training consists of *imitation and observational learning*. A teacher will model certain social behaviors as a child watches, then prompt imitation on the child's part. Initial social behaviors often include basic play actions such as stacking blocks, group activities such as rolling a ball to others, and manipulating objects such as opening a door. Advanced training involves generalization to other settings and behaviors, use of language, and quicker imitation of others (Koegel, Kuriakose, Singh, & Koegel, 2012). Parent involvement is also important.

Another socialization training method involves *social play groups* where children are rewarded for play with peers instead of solitary play. Children may also be taught to act out different imaginary scenes to build pretend play, use appropriate facial

A key treatment for children with developmental disorders, especially autism, is socialization training.

expressions and verbalizations to express affection, and cooperate with others (Reichow & Volkmar, 2010). Another socialization training method is *peer-mediated interventions* in which children without developmental disorders teach different social skills to children with developmental disorders (Sperry, Neitzel, & Engelhardt-Wells, 2010). Peers or siblings could ask a child with autism to share an object, join a group activity, give a hug, carry on a short conversation, or make eye contact. Teaching children to initiate social contacts on their own and learn social cognitive abilities such as understanding others' emotions is also an important part of socialization training (Laugeson, Frankel, Gantman, Dillon, & Mogil, 2012).

## SELF-CARE SKILLS TRAINING

For people with severe developmental disorders, improving self-care skills is often necessary. These skills lie at the heart of adaptive functioning and one's ability to be independent, so developing these skills is usually a top priority. Self-care skills training programs are most effective for toileting, eating, dressing, and grooming.

Self-care skills training programs typically involve *task analysis, chaining,* and *feedback and reinforcement* (Detrich & Higbee, 2010). A skill is divided into steps in task analysis. If a person wants to put on a jacket, steps might include picking up the jacket, placing one arm in the correct sleeve, placing the other arm in the other sleeve, pulling the jacket over the shoulders, and zippering the jacket. In a *forward* chaining process like this one, a person is taught each step from beginning to end. Frequent feedback and rewards for completing the step correctly are given.

In a *backward* chaining process, a person is taught each step from end to beginning. A teacher could help a person put on a jacket using all steps except final zippering, which the person would do herself. As that step was mastered, the teacher would work backward until each step was accomplished independently. Some adaptive behaviors can only be done in a forward way, of course—you cannot brush your teeth or apply deodorant backward!

## ACADEMIC SKILLS TRAINING

Academic skills training programs are most pertinent for children with learning disorder, though they can certainly apply to people with pervasive developmental disorders. Academic skills can include *readiness* skills such as holding a pencil, using scissors, staying in a seat, and raising a hand to talk. For people with learning disorder, however, academic skills training must also include detailed educational programs that target and improve specific deficits in reading, spelling, writing, and mathematical ability (Shapiro, 2011).

Educational programs for reading generally center on helping children recognize and decode words that delay reading. This often involves a *phonetic* approach to reading that requires children to "break down" the sounds of difficult words. A teacher may present a child with a book passage and ask a child to note words that might be difficult. The child then sounds out a word, writes it several times, and perhaps looks it up in the dictionary. The teacher then reads the passage to the child as she follows along. The child is then asked to read the passage, with special attention to the difficult words. Reading programs for children with learning disorder focus on being aware of basic speech sounds, understanding the relationship between sounds and symbols, blending speech sounds together, and reading and writing certain texts (Shapiro, 2011).

Teachers who address writing problems focus on handling a pencil correctly, tracing and saying letters, writing from memory, and having a child describe what she is writing, such as a circle and tail for "Q." A focus is made as well on organizing writing tasks and producing coherent written products. Computers may also be used to increase writing efficiency (Evmenova, Graff, Jerome, & Behrmann, 2010).

Programs for spelling problems can include the *write–say method*, which involves asking a child to take practice spelling tests and rewriting and saying aloud missed words (Kearney, Alvarez, & Vecchio, 2005). Teachers who address mathematical problems concentrate on a student's ability to read symbols,

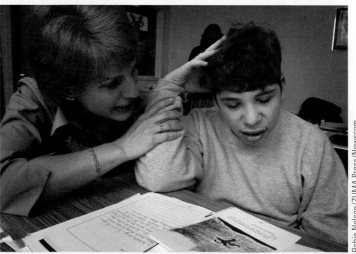

Children with learning disorder often benefit from individualized teaching in special education.

Technology is often used to help children with learning disorder develop better reading, spelling, mathematical, and writing skills.

count efficiently without using fingers, recall basic arithmetic facts and words such as "divide," and follow logical steps to solve a problem (Moeller, Fischer, Cress, & Nuerk, 2012).

## ADDRESSING PROBLEM BEHAVIORS

Recall that people with developmental disorders often show problem behaviors such as self-stimulation, self-injury, aggression, tantrums, and noncompliance. Several behavioral procedures are thus used to reduce these misbehaviors:

- *Time-out,* or isolating a person to extinguish attention-seeking misbehavior.

- *Token economy,* or establishing a set system of points or tokens for appropriate behavior later exchanged for rewards such as special food or playtime. This may also include *response cost,* or losing points for misbehavior.

- *Differential reinforcement of incompatible behavior,* or rewarding behaviors that cannot be done at the same time as the misbehavior. One could write on a piece of paper, a behavior incompatible with slapping someone. *Differential reinforcement of other behavior* involves rewarding the absence of a certain misbehavior following a time interval such as 5 minutes.

- *Restitution and practice positive overcorrection,* or requiring a person to practice appropriate behavior after some disruptive behavior, such as cleaning one's deliberate spill as well as others' messes.

- *Punishment,* or using restraint or other aversive procedures following misbehavior. Punishment is often used with other procedures because it may suppress but not eliminate misbehavior.

## What If I Think Someone Has a Developmental Disorder?

Children are often screened for developmental disorders in school, especially learning disorder. If you feel a child you know is struggling in school or having difficulty with language or social skills, then you may wish to consult a clinical or school

psychologist, special education teacher, or other mental health professional (Chapter 15).

## Long-Term Outcome for People with Developmental Disorders

What is the long-term picture for people like Robert? Those with severe developmental disorders such as profound intellectual disability or autism generally have a poor prognosis. About 78 to 90 percent of this population will continue to have extremely poor outcomes related to social behavior, intellectual functioning, and independence (Billstedt, Gillberg, & Gillberg, 2005). For many of these people, lifelong care in a supervised living setting is necessary.

Other people with developmental disorders show substantial improvement and function fairly independently. People with Down syndrome often live and work independently with some assistance. People with less severe autism may become more expressive and empathetic over time, and others get married and are employed. Some (35 percent) experience greater vulnerability to anxiety-related and depressive disorders, however (Khouzam, El Gabalawi, Pirwani, & Priest, 2004; Tantam, 2000; Volkmar & Klin, 2000).

Severe social awkwardness, thought disturbance, and desire to be left alone are still seen in many people with less severe autism (Robinson, Curwen, & Ryan, 2012). Good prognosis for people with pervasive developmental disorders relates to language before age 5 years, early and intensive intervention, higher intelligence (IQ above 50), responsiveness to sounds and others, less delay in major developmental milestones, less neurological impairment, and fewer genetic/chromosomal problems (Levy & Perry, 2011; Rice, Warren, & Betz, 2005).

Children with learning disorder continue to experience several difficulties into adolescence and adulthood. Children with reading problems often have continued trouble naming words quickly, recognizing basic speech sounds, spelling, and reading symbols. Many eventually have anxiety and antisocial behavior problems and few enroll in college (Gregg, 2013). Many schools are better equipped now to assist students with learning disorder, however, often providing arrangements such as longer test-taking sessions and computer facilities for writing. Positive long-term outcome for this population generally relates to higher intelligence and higher socioeconomic status, early diagnosis and intervention, early language stimulation, fewer comorbid diagnoses, and less severe disorder (Pratt & Patel, 2007).

## INTERIM SUMMARY

- ▶ Cognitive assessment for people with developmental disorders includes intelligence, neuropsychological, and achievement tests.

- ▶ Interviews and rating scales for people with developmental disorders cover current functioning as well as needs, support systems, and behavior problems.

- ▶ Direct observation is often used to assess frequency and severity of problem behaviors but can also be used to examine adaptive and academic behaviors.

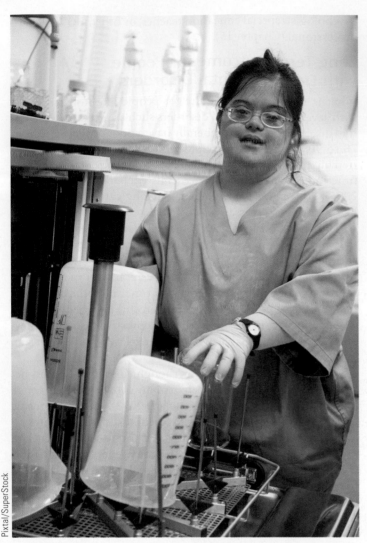

Pixtal/SuperStock

Many people with developmental disorders go on to live productive lives.

▶ Medications for people with developmental disorders are sometimes used for explosive behaviors, seizures, and symptoms of comorbid problems.

▶ Psychological treatment for people with developmental disorders includes attention and language training, socialization training, self-care skills training, and academic tutoring.

▶ Treatments for problem behaviors in people with developmental disorders include time-out, token economy, differential reinforcement of incompatible or other behavior, restitution and practice positive overcorrection, and punishment.

▶ Long-term functioning of many people with developmental disorders is difficult, but good prognostic signs include early language and intervention, higher intelligence, and less severe disorder and neurological impairment.

### REVIEW QUESTIONS

1. Describe methods of cognitive assessment for people with developmental disorders.

2. What are primary aspects of achievement and other tests for people with developmental disorders?

3. Outline main features of attention, language, socialization, and self-care skills training for those with severe developmental disorders.

4. Describe strategies for treating youth with learning disorder.

5. Describe interventions to address problem behaviors in people with developmental disorders.

6. What is the long-term functioning for most people with developmental disorders?

## Disruptive Behavior Disorders

Developmental disorders are not the only kind of mental disorders that occur mostly in children and adolescents. Recall from our discussion at the beginning of the chapter that youth may also have disruptive behavior disorders involving inattention, impulsivity, overactivity, noncompliance, or aggression.

## Normal Rambunctious Behavior and Disruptive Behavior Disorders: What Are They?

Have you ever baby-sat a highly active preschooler? Or perhaps you have small children that constantly test your patience. Watching and raising young children can be an arduous and exhausting task, so much so that many parents look forward to work on Monday morning! Many children are naturally curious about their environment and are egocentric, meaning they have trouble understanding the needs of others. They focus much more on what they want and usually interrupt, throw a tantrum, or even hit someone to get what they want. Young children eventually learn to better control emotions, delay impulses, and act in socially appropriate ways to get what they want. A child may learn that he first needs to pick up some toys or eat dinner using good manners to watch a favorite television program (**Figure 13.4**).

Other children take longer to control their emotions and impulses and might be described as rambunctious. They constantly test limits placed on them by parents and teachers. They may continue, even into the school-age years, to throw tantrums or become upset when something happens they do not like. Or they may continue to be very physically active, always climbing on the furniture or running about. Many of these children are difficult to control but can pay attention and comply with others when they absolutely have to, such as dinnertime or when at church. These children eventually learn appropriate ways to channel their excess energy, such as playing soccer or running as hard as possible during recess.

For other children like Will, severe problems of impulsivity, overactivity, and inattention continue for lengthy periods of time. These problems greatly interfere with their ability to function in daily situations that require behavior control and concentration. Many children are able to adjust their behavior

## CASE: Will

**Will** was an 8-year-old boy referred to a psychologist and psychiatrist for severe disruptive behavior. His behavior problems began in preschool and consisted of running about the classroom, failing to comply with parent and teacher requests, and being aggressive to other children. The problems became so difficult that Will was expelled from two preschools. Will's problems were stable during kindergarten, but his entry into first grade was highly problematic. He ran about his classroom, often disturbing his classmates, and was regularly sent to the principal's office. Will threw a metal object at a child's head on one occasion and was suspended for 3 school days. His teacher described him as a highly

© Antonov Roman/
Shutterstock.com

impulsive child who did not have control over his behavior. Will seemed to do as he pleased, rarely completed class assignments, and was disorganized. He had great trouble comprehending what others were saying to him, perhaps because he was not paying much attention.

Will's entry into second grade was marked by severe escalation of his disruptive behaviors. His teacher said Will was difficult to control, especially because he was physically strong for his age. Repeated attempts by the teacher and principal to engage Will's parents to address their son's behavior were fruitless. Will's parents seemed unfazed by the school's complaints and attributed his behavior to lack of school discipline. They said they were "tired" of their son's misbehavior and learned it was best to just "give him what he wants."

Will's impulsive, hyperactive, and noncompliant behavior became so bad he was failing school at the end of second grade. He also became more brazen

in his aggressiveness toward others, often using obscene language and bullying tactics to get what he wanted. The final straw came when Will was caught with a razor blade at school. He was suspended indefinitely and his parents were told he would be allowed to return to class only after they sought professional help for their son's misbehavior.

### What Do You Think?

**1.** How do Will's behaviors differ from a typical child? Which of his behaviors might seem normal for a child?

**2.** What external events and internal factors might be responsible for Will's behaviors?

**3.** What are you curious about regarding Will?

**4.** Does Will remind you in any way of someone you know? How so?

**5.** How might Will's behaviors affect his life in the future?

---

from recess (wild horseplay) to a classroom (sitting at a desk quietly) within a few minutes. Other children, such as Will, however, cannot do so and continue to be disruptive. They thus have trouble following class rules and concentrating on academic tasks. These children may have **attention-deficit/hyperactivity disorder (ADHD).**

Other children continue to show noncompliance and aggression during and after elementary school. Severe problems of noncompliance comprise **oppositional defiant disorder**, and severe problems of aggression comprise **conduct disorder**. ADHD and oppositional defiant and conduct disorders are **disruptive behavior disorders**. The disorders can occur separately but sometimes occur together in a child like Will. We next discuss major features of disruptive behavior disorders.

## Disruptive Behavior Disorders: Features and Epidemiology

### Attention-Deficit/Hyperactivity Disorder

Children with attention-deficit/hyperactivity disorder (ADHD) have three key behavior problems: *inattention, overactivity,* and *impulsivity* (see **Table 13.7**; APA, 2013). Inattention means a

child has ongoing problems listening to others, attending to details in schoolwork and other tasks such as chores, and organizing work. Such children are constantly distracted by irrelevant stimuli—they may suddenly run to a window to look outside as a teacher is speaking. Children with ADHD, especially those with inattention, are also forgetful, reluctant to complete schoolwork, sloppy, and somewhat absent-minded, meaning they always seem to be losing things and unaware of what is happening around them. Such children may be diagnosed with ADHD that is predominantly *inattentive* (APA, 2013).

Children may also be diagnosed with ADHD that is predominantly *hyperactive-impulsive*. Hyperactive means a particular child always seems to be fidgeting, leaving his seat at school or the dinner table, climbing excessively on furniture or desks, and talking too much. These children are often described as "having no 'off' switch," meaning they are always moving from the time they wake up to the time they go to bed. They also have trouble playing quietly. Impulsive means a particular child often interrupts others, tries to answer questions before a questioner is finished, and has trouble waiting his turn, such as when playing a game.

Children with ADHD may have problems with all three symptoms—inattention, hyperactivity, and impulsivity; this is

**CONTINUUM FIGURE 13.4**  Continuum of Disruptive Behavior and Disruptive Behavior Disorder

| | Normal | Mild |
|---|---|---|
| Emotions | Good control of emotions and appropriate emotional experiences. | Mild problems in impulse, anger, or other emotional control. |
| Cognitions | Rational thoughts about social situations and interactions with parents. | Occasional thoughts of noncompliance or aggression. |
| Behaviors | Good self-control of behavior and compliance toward authority figures. | Occasional rambunctiousness and noncompliance to authority figures. |

© Sally and Richard Greenhill/Alamy

Many children are occasionally disruptive in public, but some show such frequent and intense misbehaviors that they have a disruptive behavior disorder.

ADHD with a *combined presentation*. Will had all these characteristics. A diagnosis of ADHD is made only when a child's behaviors impair his abilities to function in at least two settings, such as home and school. This excludes children who act fine in school but not at home. To be diagnosed as such, symptoms of ADHD must also be present before age 12 years, as was true for Will (APA, 2013). The diagnosis of ADHD is somewhat controversial because many children with true ADHD are often misdiagnosed with oppositional defiant or conduct disorder (see next section). At the same time, however, medications for ADHD may be overprescribed. ADHD may thus be both an underdiagnosed *and* an overdiagnosed disorder (Batstra & Frances, 2012).

## Oppositional Defiant Disorder and Conduct Disorder

Children with oppositional defiant disorder often refuse to comply with others' commands (see **Table 13.8**; APA, 2013). They often seem hostile and angry toward others, argumentative, bullying, spiteful, and overly sensitive. They lose their tempers easily, and these behaviors cause substantial impairment in daily functioning (APA, 2013). Will's mean-spirited attitude toward others meant few children wanted to be near him, much less play with him.

Oppositional defiant disorder may continue over time and eventually evolve into a more severe condition: conduct disorder. Conduct disorder, sometimes equated with *juvenile delinquency*, involves a consistent pattern of violating the rights of others (Henggeler & Sheidow, 2012; see **Table 13.9**; APA, 2013). Symptoms of conduct disorder may be divided into four main categories. First, these youths may be aggressive toward other people or animals, often displaying cruel behavior such as using a weapon or torturing someone (or an animal), assaulting and stealing from someone, or engaging in rape (Lahey & Waldman, 2012). Second, these youths may destroy property, such as setting fires or vandalizing a

| Moderate | Disruptive Behavior Disorder — less severe | Disruptive Behavior Disorder — more severe |
|---|---|---|
| Moderate problems in impulse, anger, or other emotional control. | Substantial problems regulating one's impulses and emotions that create trouble functioning in a classroom. | Extremely poor emotional control or lack of emotion that leads to aggression or explosiveness. |
| Frequent irritation toward others and thoughts of defiance or aggression. | Intense thoughts that others are actively hostile to the person, even in ambiguous situations. | Frequent thoughts of aggression, hostility toward others, and rule-breaking. |
| Significant rambunctiousness and noncompliance at home or school. | Highly disruptive behavior at home and school and/or property destruction and severe noncompliance. | Extreme disruptive behavior and/or aggression to people and animals. |

© 2010 Getty Images/Jupiterimages Corporation

Copyright © Cengage Learning®

school building. Third, many youths with conduct disorder lie to others to get something or to avoid punishment. They may also steal from others in a secretive way, such as shoplifting, and forcibly break into someone's house or car. Finally, many youths with conduct disorder violate laws or rules for their age group, such as missing school or curfew or running away from home. Collectively, these behaviors must cause serious impairment in functioning, such as being expelled from school or being arrested for a crime. Conduct disorder may begin in childhood or adolescence and its symptoms can range from mild to moderate to severe (APA, 2013).

## Epidemiology of Disruptive Behavior Disorders

ADHD occurs in 5 to 12 percent of children, 8.7 percent of adolescents, and 4 percent of adults worldwide. Many general problems are associated with ADHD, including academic and social skill deficits, school failure, low self-esteem, marital conflict, and excessive substance use. Specific mental disorders associated with ADHD include oppositional defiant and conduct disorder, anxiety-related and depressive disorders, and learning disorder. ADHD is much more prevalent among boys than girls. Girls with ADHD tend to have less disruptive behavior problems but greater intellectual impairments than boys with ADHD. ADHD appears to be a worldwide phenomenon not generally linked to cultural factors (Biederman, 2005; Merikangas et al., 2010; Rohde et al., 2005; Spira & Fischel, 2005; Wilens, 2007).

Oppositional defiant disorder affects 2 to 11 percent of 5- to 17-year-olds and is much more common in boys than girls. The disorder is commonly associated with other disruptive behavior and learning problems. Oppositional defiant disorder often evolves into conduct disorder when a child shows severe disruptive behavior at an early age. Only 47 percent of youth with oppositional defiant disorder go on to develop conduct

disorder, however (Burke, Loeber, & Birmaher, 2002; Costello, Egger, & Angold, 2005; Rowe, Costello, Angold, Copeland, & Maughan, 2010).

Conduct disorder affects 2 to 12 percent of 5- to 17-year-olds and is much more common in boys than girls. Girls with conduct disorder usually show more covert and less aggressive behaviors than boys with conduct disorder and are often diagnosed later in adolescence. Conduct disorder is often comorbid with other mental conditions, especially anxiety-related, depressive, learning, and substance use disorders (Beauchaine, Hinshaw, & Pang, 2010; Berkout, Young, & Gross, 2011).

Symptoms of conduct disorder are present in youth worldwide. Most American youths in juvenile detention facilities, many of whom meet criteria for conduct disorder, are African American (54.9 percent). This compares to rates for Hispanics (28.7 percent) and European Americans (16.2 percent). This is

Children with conduct disorder are often aggressive and bullying toward others.

Beau Lark/Fancy (RF)/Jupiter Images

**Table 13.7**

### DSM-5 Attention-deficit/hyperactivity disorder

A.  A persistent pattern of inattention and/or hyperactivity-impulsivity that interferes with functioning or development, as characterized by (1) and/or (2):

1.  **Inattention:** Six (or more) of the following symptoms have persisted for at least 6 months to a degree that is inconsistent with developmental level and that negatively impacts directly on social and academic/occupational activities:
    **Note:** The symptoms are not solely a manifestation of oppositional behavior, defiance, hostility, or failure to understand tasks or instructions. For older adolescents and adults (age 17 and older), at least five symptoms are required.
    a.  Often fails to give close attention to details or makes careless mistakes in schoolwork, at work, or during other activities.
    b.  Often has difficulty sustaining attention in tasks or play activities.
    c.  Often does not seem to listen when spoken to directly.
    d.  Often does not follow through on instructions and fails to finish schoolwork, chores, or duties in the workplace.
    e.  Often has difficulty organizing tasks and activities.
    f.  Often avoids, dislikes, or is reluctant to engage in tasks that require sustained mental effort.
    g.  Often loses things necessary for tasks or activities.
    h.  Is often easily distracted by extraneous stimuli.
    i.  Is often forgetful in daily activities.

2.  **Hyperactivity and impulsivity:** Six (or more) of the following symptoms have persisted for at least 6 months to a degree that is inconsistent with developmental level and that negatively impacts directly on social and academic/occupational activities:
    **Note:** The symptoms are not solely a manifestation of oppositional behavior, defiance, hostility, or failure to understand tasks or instructions. For older adolescents and adults (age 17 and older), at least five symptoms are required.
    a.  Often fidgets with or taps hands or feet or squirms in seat.
    b.  Often leaves seat in situations when remaining seated is expected.
    c.  Often runs about or climbs in situations where it is inappropriate.
    d.  Often unable to play or engage in leisure activities quietly.
    e.  Is often "on the go," acting as if "driven by a motor".
    f.  Often talks excessively.
    g.  Often blurts out an answer before a question has been completed.
    h.  Often has difficulty waiting his or her turn.
    i.  Often interrupts or intrudes on others.

B.  Several inattentive or hyperactive-impulsive symptoms were present prior to age 12 years.

C.  Several inattentive or hyperactive-impulsive symptoms are present in two or more settings.

D.  There is clear evidence that the symptoms interfere with, or reduce the quality of, social, academic, or occupational functioning.

E.  The symptoms do not occur exclusively during the course of schizophrenia or another psychotic disorder and are not better explained by another mental disorder.

Specify if combined, predominantly inattentive, or predominantly hyperactive/impulsive presentation; if in partial remission; severity as mild, moderate, or severe.

American Psychiatric Association. (2013). *Diagnostic and statistical manual of mental disorders* (5th ed). Arlington, VA: American Psychiatric Association.

especially true for youth who lack nurturing parents and live in disadvantaged neighborhoods (Brody et al., 2003; Dogan, Onder, Dogan, & Akyuz, 2004; Heyerdahl, Kvernmo, & Wichstrom, 2004; Shek, 2005; Vermeiren, Jones, Ruchkin, Deboutte, & Schwab-Stone, 2004). ADHD and conduct and oppositional disorders likely affect less than 12 percent of children, but the disorders account for at least 50 percent of referrals to mental health agencies. This is because symptoms of these disorders are usually quite disturbing to parents and teachers.

## Stigma Associated with Disruptive Behavior Disorders

Stigma can affect children with disruptive behavior disorders. Martin and colleagues (2007) found that many survey respondents did not want a child with ADHD to live next door (22.2%) or to have their child befriend a child with ADHD (23.5%). Others said they did not want to spend an

## Table 13.8

### DSM-5 Oppositional Defiant Disorder

A. A pattern of angry/irritable mood, argumentative/defiant behavior, or vindictiveness lasting at least 6 months as evidenced by at least four symptoms from any of the following categories, and exhibited during interaction with at least one individual who is not a sibling.

**Angry/Irritable Mood**
1. Often loses temper.
2. Is often touchy or easily annoyed.
3. Is often angry and resentful.

**Argumentative/Defiant Behavior**
4. Often argues with authority figures or, for children and adolescents, with adults.
5. Often actively defies or refuses to comply with requests from authority figures or with rules.
6. Often deliberately annoys others.
7. Often blames others for his or her mistakes or misbehavior.

**Vindictiveness**
8. Has been spiteful or vindictive at least twice within the past 6 months.

B. The disturbance in behavior is associated with distress in the individual or others in his or her immediate social context, or it impacts negatively on social, educational, occupational, or other important areas of functioning.

C. The behaviors do not occur exclusively during the course of a psychotic, substance use, depressive, or bipolar disorder. Also, the criteria are not met for disruptive mood dysregulation disorder.

Specify if mild (symptoms in one setting), moderate (symptoms in two settings), or severe (symptoms in three or more settings).

American Psychiatric Association. (2013). *Diagnostic and statistical manual of mental disorders* (5th ed.). Arlington, VA: American Psychiatric Association.

evening with a child with ADHD or his or her family (16.9%) or have children with ADHD in their child's classroom (19.3%). Parents and teachers also tend to rate the academic skills of children with ADHD more negatively than children without ADHD (Eisenberg & Schneider, 2007). Stigma can also apply to youths with conduct disorder. Murrie and colleagues (2005) presented case vignettes to juvenile probation officers. Youth in the vignettes with a diagnostic label of conduct disorder were rated by officers as more in need of psychological services and more likely to commit future crimes than youths with no diagnostic label. These studies indicate that educating people about the behaviors of children with disruptive behavior disorders is needed to prevent bias and discrimination.

## INTERIM SUMMARY

▶ Many children may be described as rambunctious, but some have disruptive behavior disorders involving inattention, impulsivity, overactivity, aggression, and noncompliance.

▶ Attention-deficit hyperactivity/disorder refers to intense problems of inattention, impulsivity, and/or overactivity.

▶ Oppositional defiant disorder refers to noncompliance, hostility and anger toward others, argumentativeness, and bullying behavior, among other symptoms.

▶ Conduct disorder refers to intense problems of aggression, property destruction, lying and stealing, and status violations.

▶ Disruptive behavior disorders are common and seen more in boys than girls. The problems seem universal and are often comorbid with one another.

▶ Stigma is an important part of disruptive behavior disorders and can affect others' view of a child.

## REVIEW QUESTIONS

1. How do disruptive behavior disorders differ from normal rambunctious behavior?
2. Define major symptoms and subtypes of attention-deficit/hyperactivity disorder.
3. Outline main symptoms of oppositional defiant disorder.
4. What are main categories of symptoms of conduct disorder?
5. Describe the epidemiology of the disruptive behavior disorders.

# Disruptive Behavior Disorders: Causes and Prevention

Disruptive behavior disorders involve biological and environmental risk factors. ADHD relates especially to biological risk factors and oppositional and conduct disorders clearly relate to many environmental risk factors.

## Biological Risk Factors for Disruptive Behavior Disorders

### GENETIC INFLUENCES

Strong evidence supports a genetic basis for ADHD. First, the disorder runs in families: parents and siblings of children with ADHD are 2 to 8 times more likely than the general population to have ADHD. Second, twin studies worldwide indicate that genetic factors account for about 76 percent of the variance when explaining ADHD onset. Third, findings from adoption studies reveal biological relatives of children with ADHD to have an elevated rate of ADHD compared with the general population (Franke, Neale, & Faraone, 2009).

Studies of the biology of conduct disorder often focus on aggression and emotionality. A key finding is that boys who are highly active and emotional early in life seem to become more aggressive. Such early activity and emotionality may have a moderate genetic basis (Waldman & Gizer, 2006). Others have

**Table 13.9**

### DSM-5 Conduct Disorder

A. A repetitive and persistent pattern of behavior in which the basic rights of others or major age-appropriate societal norms or rules are violated, as manifested by the presence of at least three of the following 15 criteria in the past 12 months from any of the categories below, with at least one criterion present in the past 6 months:

**Aggression to People and Animals**
1. Often bullies, threatens, or intimidates others.
2. Often initiates physical fights.
3. Has used a weapon that can cause serious physical harm to others (e.g., a bat, brick, broken bottle, knife, gun).
4. Has been physically cruel to people.
5. Has been physically cruel to animals.
6. Has stolen while confronting a victim.
7. Has forced someone into sexual activity.

**Destruction of Property**
8. Has deliberately engaged in fire setting with the intention of causing serious damage.
9. Has deliberately destroyed others' property (other than by fire setting).

**Deceitfulness or Theft**
10. Has broken into someone else's house, building, or car.
11. Often lies to obtain goods or favors or to avoid obligations.
12. Has stolen items of nontrivial value without confronting a victim.

**Serious Violations of Rules**
13. Often stays out at night despite parental prohibitions, beginning before age 13 years.
14. Has run away from home overnight at least twice while living in the parental or parental surrogate home, or once without returning for a lengthy period.
15. Is often truant from school, beginning before age 13 years.

B. The disturbance in behavior causes clinically significant impairment in social, academic, or occupational functioning.

C. If the individual is age 18 years or older, criteria are not met for antisocial personality disorder.

Specify if childhood, adolescent, or unspecified onset; if with limited prosocial emotions, lack of remorse or guilt, callous-lack of empathy, unconcerned about performance, shallow or deficient affect; mild, moderate, or severe.

American Psychiatric Association. (2013). *Diagnostic and statistical manual of mental disorders* (5th ed.). Arlington, VA: American Psychiatric Association.

found that impulsive, violent behavior may link to genes that help control amount of neurotransmitters in the brain, most notably norepinephrine, dopamine, and serotonin. Childhood conduct problems may also have a strong genetic component, but much more work is needed in this area before definitive conclusions can be drawn (Cappadocia, Desrocher, Pepler, & Schroeder, 2009).

## NEUROCHEMICAL FEATURES

Neurochemical changes implicated for children with ADHD include deficiencies or imbalances in dopamine and norepinephrine, especially in prefrontal brain areas. Such changes may help explain problems of motor control, behavior inhibition, and cognition. ADHD may be an inability to regulate one's own behavior, so medications to help improve symptoms of ADHD focus on increasing these neurotransmitter levels (del Campo, Chamberlain, Sahakian, & Robbins, 2011).

Serotonin levels have been found to be low among youths with aggression and conduct disorder. Lower levels of cortisol and higher levels of testosterone also appear among youths with disruptive behavior disorders, which is consistent with findings that these youths have lower heart rates and less physiological arousal. Some of these youths may thus lack anxious inhibition to engage in aggressive or other antisocial acts (Matthys, Vanderschuren, Schutter, & Lochman, 2012; Montoya, Terburg, Bos, & van Honk, 2011).

## BRAIN FEATURES

Children with disruptive behavior disorders have characteristic brain changes, some of which may relate to genetic predispositions and that may interact with neurochemical changes. Youths with ADHD have smaller or different volumes of key brain areas, especially the prefrontal cortex, anterior cingulate cortex, basal ganglia, caudate, putamen, pallidum, corpus callosum, and cerebellum. Less blood flow and poor connectivity in key frontostriatal areas is often seen as well. Such changes help explain problems of inattention, overactivity, and impulsivity in this population (Cubillo, Halari, Smith, Taylor, & Rubia, 2012; Konrad & Eickhoff, 2010; Plessen & Peterson, 2009).

Neuroimaging studies of youths with oppositional defiant or conduct disorder are sparse, though some work has focused on aggression and antisocial behavior. The most reliable finding is less volume in the prefrontal cortex, a result that overlaps with ADHD (**Figure 13.5**). Others have implicated changes in the amygdala, basal ganglia, and brain stem. Deficits in these brain areas may help explain trouble controlling excess emotions and aggressive behaviors (Blair, 2010; Fairchild et al., 2011).

## PERSONALITY FACTORS

Personality factors also come into play in youths with disruptive behavior disorders, particularly oppositional defiant or conduct disorder. These personality factors could relate to temperament issues raised earlier and involve *callous-unemotional traits*. Youths with these traits often lack guilt or remorse for their hurtful acts toward others, show little emotion, are unempathetic to others, and manipulate others for their own gratification. A teenager

with this personality pattern might resemble someone with antisocial personality disorder (Chapter 10). He will use others for personal gratification, such as sexually or to obtain goods or services, and do so with little regard for others. This personality pattern seems particularly relevant to youths with severe conduct disorder (Frick, 2012).

## Environmental Risk Factors for Disruptive Behavior Disorders

### TERATOGENS

Recall that teratogens refer to prenatal risk factors such as maternal drug use and exposure to toxins. Youths with disruptive behavior disorders may have been exposed to various prenatal teratogens more than occurs in the general population. Key teratogens related to later disruptive behavior disorders, especially ADHD, include maternal smoking and alcohol use, which closely relate to problems of attention, cognition, and learning. Increased stress during pregnancy, pregnancy and delivery complications, premature birth, and lower birth weight are significant risk factors as well (Konrad & Eickhoff, 2010; Thapar, Cooper, Eyre, & Langley, 2013).

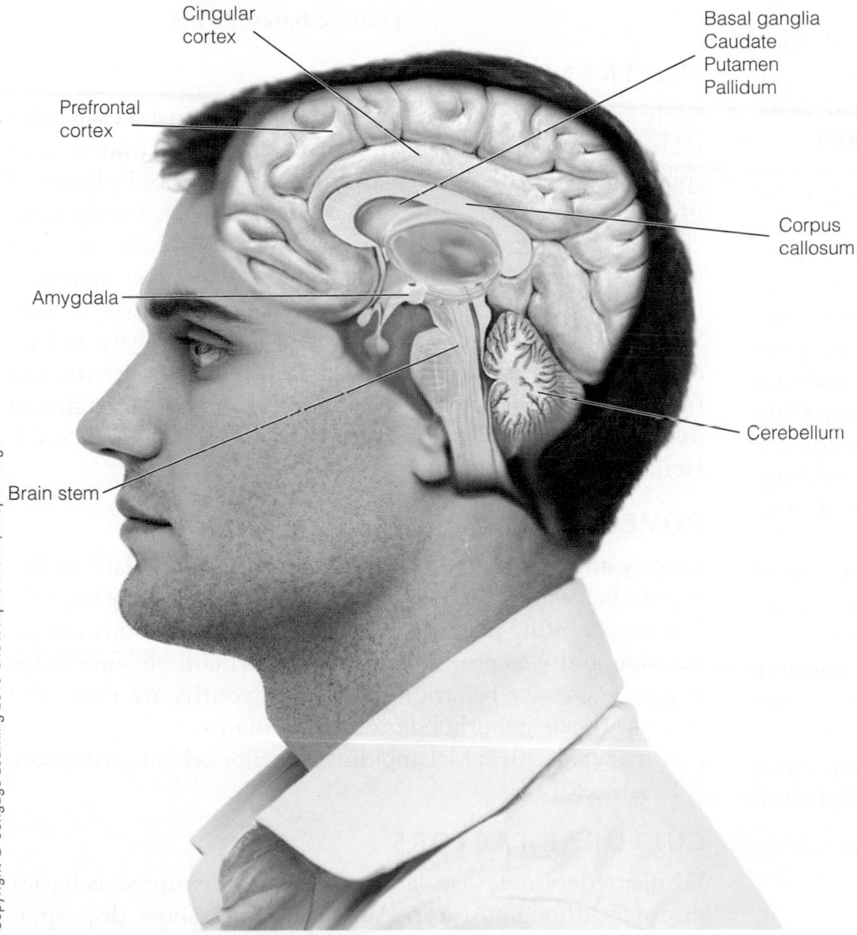

### FAMILY CONFLICT AND PARENTING PRACTICES

Conflict in a marriage and among family members closely relates to disruptive behavior problems in youth. Fright associated with watching parents fight may cause attachment problems and contribute to a child's inability to control his emotions. Youngsters could also model parental aggression as a way to solve problems. Other youths may be rewarded for aggression or overactivity by a parent's unwillingness to address the behavior (Counts, Nigg, Stawicki, Rappley, & von Eye, 2005; Martel, Nikolas, Jernigan, Friderici, & Nigg, 2012).

Poor parenting practices closely relate to disruptive behavior problems. Examples include rewarding child misbehavior by providing positive consequences or removing negative ones. A child could become aggressive and overactive so parents will bribe him to stop the behaviors. Or a child could misbehave in response to parent commands to avoid a chore. Patterns of *coercion* begin early in life, can escalate to extreme forms of misbehavior, and can be accelerated by ineffective parent discipline (Parent et al., 2011; Snyder, Cramer, Afrank, & Patterson, 2005).

Other parenting problems associated with disruptive behavior disorders include poor monitoring of a child's behavior, harsh and uncaring communications, overcontrol, excessive physical punishment, and use of unclear commands. Some parents phrase commands in the form of a question ("Will you please just go to school?"), interrupt or lecture their children when giving a command,

**FIGURE 13.5** MAJOR BRAIN AREAS IMPLICATED IN DISRUPTIVE BEHAVIOR DISORDERS

© Gladskikh Tatiana/Shutterstock

Marital conflict is a key risk factor for children with behavior problems.

no real threat exists. A teenager may be accidentally bumped by someone in a school hallway and immediately assume the person committed the act intentionally and with intent to harm. Such assumptions could help trigger thoughts and behaviors of vengeance or spitefulness.

Youths with conduct disorder also favor aggressive solutions for problems, fail to fully understand the negative consequences of aggression, define problems in hostile ways, and perceive their self-worth as low. A child who hits another child may have done so as a first resort to get something and might have trouble appreciating negative consequences of this act (Dodge, Godwin, & Conduct Problems Prevention Research Group, 2013; Lansford, Malone, Dodge, Petit, & Bates, 2010).

or issue vague commands that leave room for interpretation ("Go clean your room"). This often leads to child noncompliance or defiance (Beauchaine, Webster-Stratton, & Reid, 2005; Seipp & Johnston, 2005; Shaw, Lacourse, & Nagin, 2005).

## DEVIANT PEERS

Youths with disruptive behavior disorders, especially those with conduct disorder, associate more with deviant peers, are rejected by nondeviant peers, and have hostile interpersonal relationships. Many of these youths also have poor social and verbal skills, which contribute to their inability to form positive friendships. Oftentimes such rejection from others leads a child to associate with others who have also been rejected because of aggression. Hostile and aggressive behavior may thus be rewarded by peers (Dishion & Tipsord, 2011).

Association with deviant peers is sometimes linked to bullying behavior. Bullying refers to victimizing someone through aggression and other hostile behavior such as yelling or verbal threats. Bullying appears to be a stable behavior—many children who bully at age 8 years continue to do so at age 16 years. Factors associated with ongoing bullying include disruptive behavior problems, poor social competence, and male gender (Craig & Pepler, 2003; Powell & Ladd, 2010).

## COGNITIVE FACTORS

Older children and adolescents with disruptive behavior disorders, particularly those with conduct disorder, have key information-processing differences. Many of these youth misinterpret actions of others as hostile or threatening when

## MALTREATMENT

Early sexual and physical maltreatment toward a child also relates to disruptive behavior problems. If a child is maltreated during the infancy, toddler, or preschool phases of life, various externalizing behavior problems during later childhood and adolescence are much more likely to occur than if the child was not maltreated. Of course, maltreatment may also occur in response to a child's misbehavior. Why might maltreatment help produce disruptive behaviors? Possibilities include poor attachment to parents, difficulty controlling emotions, and development of cognitive distortions and low self-esteem (King et al., 2011; Oswald, Heil, & Goldbeck, 2010).

## POVERTY

Poverty and low socioeconomic status strongly relate to disruptive behavior disorders in youth. This is partly due to problematic parenting practices and general neighborhood disorganization and violence. Whether neighborhood violence helps trigger aggressive behavior or whether youths are ones who provoke the neighborhood problems remains unclear, however (Latimer et al., 2012; McLaughlin, Costello, Leblanc, Sampson, & Kessler, 2012).

## CULTURAL FACTORS

Ethnicity does not seem largely related to disruptive behavior disorders, though African Americans may show disproportionately more antisocial behavior patterns. This effect may be due to low socioeconomic status, substandard housing, poor educational opportunities, and inadequate access to mental health care. Children with ADHD may be overrepresented among diverse populations as well, but only because these populations are at greater risk for low birth weight newborns and other factors that could lead to ADHD. ADHD and other disruptive behavior disorders do not seem specific to culture, although parenting practices related to these disorders may be (Bauermeister, Canino, Polanczyk, & Rohde, 2010).

## Causes of Disruptive Behavior Disorders

Researchers have focused on *multifactorial* or *biopsychosocial* models of disruptive behavior disorders that combine many risk factors. A multifactorial model of ADHD includes biological and environmental factors that interact to help produce the disorder. Many risk factors have been suggested, with others still to be discovered; therefore, some suggest that multiple pathways to ADHD exist. Some of these pathways could be largely genetic, some largely due to pregnancy and delivery complications, some largely due to stress and other teratogens, and some largely due to a combination of these factors. The latter pathway is the most likely early scenario. These pathways may then lead to key brain and neurochemical changes, especially changes that affect ability to self-regulate behavior. When combined with certain environmental factors such as ineffective parenting, these brain changes help trigger symptoms of inattention, impulsivity, and overactivity (Loeber & Burke, 2011; Pardini & Frick, 2013; **Figure 13.6**).

A multifactorial approach may also apply to oppositional defiant disorder and conduct disorder, although the pathways to these disorders likely rely more heavily on environmental factors. General biological predispositions can set the stage for certain difficult and hostile temperaments as well as tendencies toward aggression and impulsivity. Such predispositions seem strong in children with ADHD but weaker in those with conduct problems. Irritable temperaments and tendencies toward antisocial behavior can, however, set the stage for poor attachment with parents, ineffective parenting, and social and academic problems. A child who inherits a fussy and irritable temperament from parents could be difficult to care for and may be rejected by parents with the same irritable temperament (Moffitt, 2005; Rowe et al., 2010; **Figure 13.7**).

Some of these problems can be resolved early in a child's life if parents provide effective supervision and appropriate consequences for behavior. Some children may resist such efforts or these efforts may break down, however, which can lead to harsh parenting, family conflict, peer rejection, and school failure. Association with deviant peers, exposure to neighborhood violence,

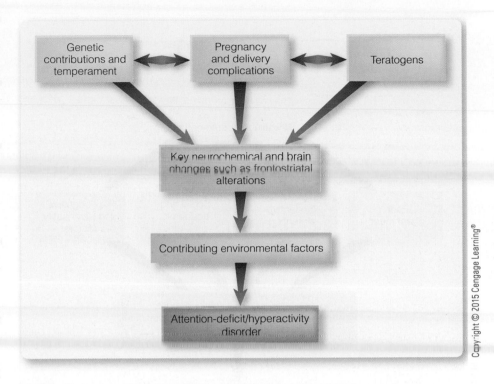

**FIGURE 13.6** SAMPLE MULTIFACTORIAL MODEL OF ATTENTION-DEFICIT/ HYPERACTIVITY DISORDER

and other factors such as excessive substance use or depression can aggravate the situation as well (Boden, Fergusson, & Horwood, 2010; Deault, 2010).

## Prevention of Disruptive Behavior Disorders

Prevention programs for disruptive behavior disorders are largely school-based to help youths improve social and academic competence. One of the most comprehensive prevention programs for these disorders involved classroom-based behavior management. This strategy focused on developing class rules with students, placing students in teams of disruptive and nondisruptive members, and providing group reinforcement so children were encouraged to manage their own and group members' behavior.

If a classroom rule was violated, a teacher would take away a card from several cards at the beginning of class. If at least one card remained following a set period of time, then some reward was given. The frequency of assembling these teams was gradually increased over time to three 1-hour time periods per week. Later phases of prevention involved attention toward prosocial behavior. The procedure helped prevent disruptive behaviors in general, especially for youths with moderate disruptive problems (Spilt, Koot, & van Lier, 2013).

Given the severe nature of many disruptive behavior disorders, however, effective prevention programs will likely have to involve developing appropriate parenting skills, improving social-cognitive skills in children, and providing academic skills training, group interventions, *and* classroom management (Villodas, Pfiffner, & McBurnett, 2012). An

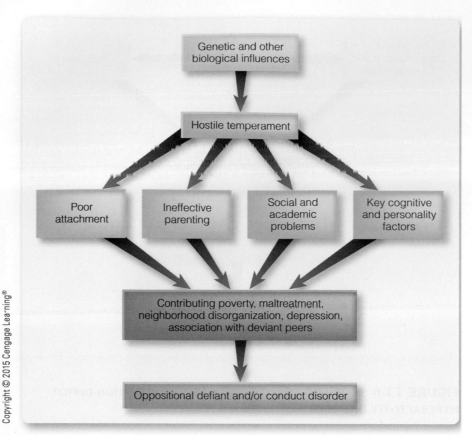

**FIGURE 13.7** SAMPLE MULTIFACTORIAL MODEL OF OPPOSITIONAL DEFIANT DISORDER AND CONDUCT DISORDER

example is the Fast Track model for young children at high risk for conduct problems. This model includes social skill and anger control training, tutoring for academic problems, parent training, and home visits for first-grade youth. In one study, 37 percent of the intervention group was free of conduct problems following third grade compared with 27 percent of a control group. In addition, prevention efforts over 10 years resulted in significantly less use of professional services (Conduct Problems Prevention Research Group, 2002; Jones et al., 2010). These results are encouraging but also indicate great difficulty modifying severe behavior problems. How do you think Will might have responded to such a prevention program?

## INTERIM SUMMARY

► Evidence strongly supports a genetic basis for ADHD but less so for conduct disorder.
► Imbalances of dopamine and norepinephrine have been noted in ADHD and low serotonin has been noted in conduct disorder.
► Youth with disruptive behavior disorders may have smaller brain areas as well as key differences in the prefrontal cortex and other areas.
► Prenatal teratogens implicated in disruptive behavior disorders include maternal drug use.

► Family conflict, poor parenting practices, and association with deviant peers seem especially related to conduct disorder but may also apply to cases of ADHD.
► Youth with disruptive behavior disorders often interpret actions of others as hostile, have other social-cognitive deficits, and have callous-unemotional personality traits.
► Causal theories for disruptive behavior disorders focus on multifactorial models that include biological predispositions and environmental risk factors as well as various pathways that can lead to ADHD or conduct disorder.
► Preventing disruptive behavior disorders may involve a thorough approach targeting skills deficits, parenting, and classroom behavior management.

## REVIEW QUESTIONS

1. What genetic predispositions exist for disruptive behavior disorders?
2. What other biological risk factors exist for disruptive behavior disorders?
3. Describe child-based, parent-based, and community-based factors that may cause disruptive behavior disorders.
4. Outline a multifactorial model for the cause of ADHD and conduct disorder.
5. What methods have been used to prevent disruptive behavior disorders?

# Disruptive Behavior Disorders: Assessment and Treatment

Mental health professionals use various methods to examine children with disruptive behavior disorders. These methods primarily include interviews, rating scales, and behavioral observation.

## Interviews

Interviews of a child and his parents and school officials are essential when assessing a child with a possible disruptive behavior disorder. Questions should surround various aspects of a child's cognitive, emotional, and social development. The presence of risk factors mentioned in this chapter should also be determined. Ongoing risk factors in a child's daily environment should be assessed as well, including parent-child interactions, parenting style and discipline, marital and family interactions, and school-based interactions with peers and teachers. Medical conditions and school performance should also be evaluated (Dirks, De Los Reyes, Briggs-Gowan, Cella, & Wakschlag, 2012).

A thorough history of a child's symptoms must also be obtained, especially the frequency, intensity, and duration of overactivity, impulsivity, inattention, noncompliance, and aggression.

Interviews to assess these problems can be unstructured or structured. A commonly used structured interview for youths with disruptive behavior disorders is the *National Institute of Mental Health Diagnostic Interview Schedule for Children (Version IV;* Shaffer, Fisher, Lucas, Dulcan, & Schwab-Stone, 2000).

## Rating Scales

Parent and teacher rating scales are also available for assessing disruptive behavior in youths. Scales commonly used to assess global levels of disruptive behavior include the *Child Behavior Checklist, Teacher Report Form, Conners Rating Scales (Conners 3),* and *Behavior Assessment System for Children, Second Edition* (Achenbach & Rescorla, 2001; Conners, 2008; Reynolds & Kamphaus, 2004). For youth with ADHD, common rating scales include the *Conners ADHD/DSM-IV Scales, ADHD Rating Scale-IV,* and *ADHD Symptoms Rating Scale* (DuPaul et al., 1998; Holland, Gimpel, & Merrell, 2001). Sample items from the Conners scale are listed in **Table 13.10**. For conduct disorder, a commonly used rating scale is the *Home and School Situations Questionnaire* (Barkley, 2000). Sample items from this questionnaire are listed in **Table 13.11**.

## Behavioral Observation

Observing the behavior of children with disruptive behavior in their natural environments, such as school and home, is an essential part of assessment. Behavioral observations help add information and clarify discrepancies from interview and rating scale data and are useful for examining specific aspects of behavior (Gray et al., 2012). Behavioral observations are also conducted to determine why a child misbehaves over time. Possible reasons include attention from parents, desire to escape situations such as classrooms, or to obtain tangible rewards such as toys. Therapists sometimes link behavioral observations to specific tests for ADHD symptoms. The *Continuous Performance Test* II measures a child's ability to sustain

---

**Table 13.10**

### Sample Items from the Conners ADHD Scales (CADS)—Parent Version

| |
|---|
| Does not follow through on instructions and fails to finish schoolwork, chores, or duties in the workplace (not due to oppositional behavior or failure to understand instructions). |
| Has trouble concentrating in class. |
| Distractibility or attention span a problem. |
| Has difficulty waiting in lines or awaiting turn in games or group situations. |
| Has difficulty playing or engaging in leisure activities quietly. |

*Note.* Items are scored on a 0 to 3 scale where 0 = not at all true, 1 = just a little true, 2 = pretty much true, and 3 = very much true.

---

**Table 13.11**

### Sample Items from the Home and School Situations Questionnaire

**Does your child present any problems with compliance to instructions, commands, or rules for you in any of these situations?**

Playing with other children

Mealtimes

When you are on the telephone

In public places

While in the car

*Note.* Items are scored as yes/no and then on a 1 to 9 scale where 1 = mild and 9 = severe.

attention and limit impulsivity on various tasks (Conners & MHS Staff, 2004).

## Biological Treatments for Disruptive Behavior Disorders

The primary biological treatment for youths with disruptive behavior disorders is *stimulant medication.* This might seem odd when considering ADHD and excessive aggressive behavior—why stimulate those symptoms?! Recall, however, that a major problem in disruptive behavior disorders is trouble regulating one's behavior. Self-regulation deficits may be due to low levels of neurotransmitters such as dopamine and norepinephrine in key brain areas such as the prefrontal cortex (Shiels & Hawk, 2010). Stimulating inhibitory centers of the brain may actually help children regulate their behavior and become less overactive and impulsive.

The main stimulant medication for ADHD is *methylphenidate* (Ritalin or Concerta). About 70 to 77 percent of youths with ADHD benefit from the drug, as do many adults. The drugs help children reduce overactivity and impulsivity, although less strong effects are evident for attention and academic performance (Dodson, 2005; Olfson, 2004; Remschmidt & Global ADHD Working Group, 2005). One problem with stimulant medication is side effects that include headaches, stomachaches, tics, restlessness, weight loss, reduced appetite, and insomnia (Daughton & Kratochvil, 2009). For those with severe side effects, who do not respond to stimulant medication, or who have tic disorders, a nonstimulant medication, *atomoxetine* (Strattera), is also helpful for increasing norepinephrine levels and improving ADHD symptoms (Garnock-Jones & Keating, 2009). Another problem with respect to stimulant medications is illicit use by college students. One study indicated that 20 percent of college students reported illicit use of prescription stimulants, often to improve concentration, stay awake, control appetite, or become high (Judson & Langdon, 2009).

Stimulant medications have also been used for youths with conduct disorder, but the drugs tend to be more effective if a youth has comorbid ADHD symptoms. These medications help reduce classroom disruption, aggression, property destruction, and other conduct problems. Other drugs such as antianxiety, mood stabilizing, and antipsychotic medications are sometimes used as well to help control explosive symptoms such as intense anger outbursts. Psychological treatments for oppositional defiant and conduct disorders are typically recommended as a first resort, however (Nevels, Dehon, Alexander, & Gontkovsky, 2010).

## Psychological Treatments for Disruptive Behavior Disorders

Psychological treatments for disruptive behavior disorders primarily focus on home-, school-, and community-based programs to reduce problematic symptoms and develop academic, social, and self-regulation skills. We describe these treatments next.

### PARENT TRAINING

Ineffective parenting is a key risk factor for disruptive behavior disorders and home-based misbehaviors likely have to be addressed by parents. Parent training programs are thus a key treatment element for this population. Many parent training programs have been proposed, and their effectiveness with youth with disruptive behavior disorders is well documented. Parent training programs typically include the following components:

- Educate parents about a child's behavior problems and how best to address them.

- Teach parents to identify and specifically define problem behaviors, such as "My son will not wash the dishes when told," and establish clear rules for behavior.

- Provide appropriate attention and tangible rewards when a child engages in prosocial behaviors such as completing homework, finishing chores, and eating dinner quietly.

- Ignore minor inappropriate behaviors such as whining.

- Provide appropriate and consistent disciplinary procedures such as time-out or loss of privileges when a child engages in serious misbehaviors.

- Give effective commands that are clear, short, and linked to consequences.

- Use a token economy for prosocial and antisocial behaviors.

- Increase daily monitoring and supervision of a child.

- Teach parents to solve problems effectively and refrain from conflict.

- Increase daily contact with school officials to coordinate treatment and consequences for behavior, such as asking teachers to send home a daily behavior report card (Jones et al., 2013; Webster-Stratton, Reid, & Beauchaine, 2011).

### SCHOOL-BASED BEHAVIOR MANAGEMENT

Children with disruptive behavior disorders pose a challenge to teachers trying to maintain classroom order, so school-based behavior management is also a key treatment for this population. School-based treatment does overlap with parent-based training and the two procedures are often coordinated so a child always faces clear guidelines and consequences regarding his behavior (Farahmand, Grant, Polo, Duffy, & DuBois, 2011). Will's transgressions at school should have been met with school- and home-based consequences such as loss of privileges. School-based strategies for children with ADHD can also include rotating rewards to maintain novelty and interest in them, providing frequent feedback about rules and self-regulation, developing social skills, and encouraging peers to help a child modify his behavior (Reid & Johnson, 2012; Young & Amarasinghe, 2010).

### SOCIAL AND ACADEMIC SKILLS TRAINING

Because children with disruptive behavior disorders have social and academic problems that can lead to further aggression and other misbehaviors, training programs to enhance skills in these key areas are important and effective. These programs focus on helping youth control impulses and anger, develop social and problem-solving skills, cooperate better with others, and enhance academic competence. This may be done by challenging and modifying irrational thoughts, recognizing and addressing early warning signs of anger and impulsivity such as muscle tension, considering alternative explanations for another's behavior, rewarding appropriate participation in prosocial group activities, and receiving extra tutoring and educational support for academic deficits (Daley & Birchwood, 2010; Young & Amarasinghe, 2010).

### RESIDENTIAL TREATMENT

A teenager may have to temporarily leave his family and be placed in residential or community-based treatment if disruptive behavior is severe. Such programs include camps, group homes, or other facilities where adolescents live until they can be reintegrated to their regular home. Residential treatment often consists of group therapy to develop social and self-care skills, anger management, family therapy to reduce conflict and build problem-solving strategies, supervised chores and other work, and systematic consequences for prosocial and

Katherine Frey/The Washington Post/Getty Images

The Freestate Challenge Academy is a residential program for at-risk high school students who have past issues with disruptive behavior.

inappropriate behavior. Residential treatment programs have been shown to produce short-term improvements in disruptive behavior, but their long-term effectiveness is not strong. Many youth who attend these programs eventually commit more crimes or require additional community placement (James, 2011; Wilmshurst, 2002).

## MULTISYSTEMIC TREATMENT

A new way to address severe disruptive behavior in children and adolescents is to provide extensive family services that include many psychological treatments. **Multisystemic treatment** is a family-based approach that includes procedures we described here as well as the following: therapy for parent psychopathology and substance use problems, involvement with appropriate peers, social support, school and vocational achievement, and linkage to agencies that can provide financial, housing, and employment support. This approach is effective in the long-term for reducing aggressive criminal activity, although ongoing access to treatment is likely necessary. This approach is sometimes used as a diversion program for adolescents arrested for a crime (see **Box 13.3**; Henggeler, 2011).

## What If I Think a Child Has a Disruptive Behavior Disorder?

If you suspect your child or someone you know has ADHD or another disruptive behavior disorder, consider the screening questions in **Table 13.12.** If the answer to most of these questions is yes, a good idea would be to consult a clinical child

## Table 13.12

| **Screening Questions for Disruptive Behavior Disorders** |
|---|
| Does a particular child always seem to be in trouble both at home and school? |
| Does a particular child always seem to be "on the go" even at mealtime and bedtime? |
| Does a particular child seem much more inattentive, hyperactive, or impulsive than most kids his age? |
| Can the child in question concentrate well on her homework or chores? |
| Is a particular child often noncompliant with adult requests, much more so than most kids his age? |
| Does a particular child frequently engage in aggression, theft, deceitfulness, and rule-breaking behavior much more so than most kids her age? |
| Has the child in question been arrested? |
| Does a particular child often seem hostile, argumentative, and overly sensitive? |

psychologist and a psychiatrist who specialize in these issues. Consulting both professionals is especially important for ADHD because medication in conjunction with behavior management may be the best treatment approach. Many adults with ADHD symptoms may be helped with these therapies as well. If the answers to these questions are mostly no but you still believe considerable family conflict is resulting from a child's misbehavior, then seeking the help of a family therapist is a good idea.

## Long-Term Outcome for Children with Disruptive Behavior Disorders

Children with disruptive behavior disorders are at serious risk for later aggression and other mental disorders. Severe symptoms of hyperactivity and impulsivity in young children often predict later onset of oppositional defiant disorder. Oppositional defiant disorder is also an excellent predictor of later conduct disorder. The eventual comorbidity of all three disorders is especially likely if strong genetic contributions exist (Dick, Viken, Kaprio, Pulkkinen, & Rose, 2005; Rowe et al., 2010).

Children with ADHD generally experience stable symptoms over time, although these symptoms can change. Preschoolers with ADHD are often difficult to control, overactive, inattentive, and noncompliant. Full-blown symptoms of inattention, overactivity, and impulsivity are seen as these children enter elementary school. Many children with ADHD then experience social and academic problems such as rejection by others, poor social skill development, and school failure. Will was having many of these problems (Jester et al., 2005; Lahey, Pelham, Loney, Lee, & Willcutt, 2005).

Severe levels of overactivity and impulsivity improve somewhat as children with ADHD reach adolescence. Still, 70 to 80 percent continue to experience inattention, restlessness, and difficulty with impulse control. These adolescents are also at serious risk for conduct disorder, excessive substance use, depression, and school dropout. Intense family conflict and inadequate social relationships aggravate these conditions as well (Biederman, Faraone, & Monuteaux, 2002; Kieling & Rohde, 2010). As adults, inattention and impulsivity often remain in the form of poor concentration at work, constant forgetfulness and daydreaming, low frustration tolerance, loss of temper, and difficulty completing a college degree (Barkley, Murphy, & Fischer, 2010).

Three different developmental pathways may mark youths with oppositional defiant or conduct disorder. Two pathways begin in childhood and one in adolescence. The first childhood pathway is largely associated with symptoms of ADHD, especially impulsivity and severe family dysfunction. Such a pathway might apply best to Will. The second childhood pathway is associated with a callous-unemotional personality and difficult temperament. Youth whose conduct problems begin with these pathways likely show enduring antisocial behavior into adolescence and adulthood. Finally, an adolescent-onset pattern is marked by general rebelliousness and association with deviant peers normally associated with adolescence, and usually does not lead to severe adjustment problems in adulthood (Pardini & Frick, 2013; Rowe et al., 2010).

## Personal Narrative 13.1

### Toni Wood

As I sat among piles of unfolded laundry, sorted through junk mail and unpaid bills, and walked through the clutter in the house, my newly received diagnosis of ADHD did not surprise me. What *did* surprise me was not being diagnosed until I was 38 years old. My two boys had already been diagnosed years earlier, the oldest with ADHD inattentive and the youngest with ADHD combined. Both were diagnosed by first seeing a developmental pediatrician and ruling out physical ailments that could mimic symptoms of ADHD. From there they went to a health care practitioner for psychoeducational testing through the local children's hospital. They received comprehensive evaluations, but as an adult I could not utilize the same resources they used.

I started talking to other adults about this once-thought childhood disorder to gauge their reactions and seek referrals. I was mostly met with cynicism and doubt. Adult ADHD was just coming onto the scene as a plausible occurrence. Surprisingly, my search led to a friend

Toni Wood

*Courtesy of Toni Wood*

who had recently been diagnosed. I say surprisingly because at the time, ADHD was not something people talked about openly. In a lot of ways, it still isn't, some 9 years later.

Formally receiving the diagnosis did a number of things for me. It lifted a big weight off my shoulders by providing an answer to so many "why's?" in my

past. But then it opened a bigger chasm by asking another question: "If I'm not who I thought I was, then who am I . . . really?" The diagnosis threw me into confusion as I tried to deal with these questions.

I soon found myself at the door of a therapist's office, certain I would be deemed "crazy." I wasn't. I *was* diagnosed as depressed, though: a common occurrence among adults diagnosed with ADHD. My treatment now included an antidepressant with the stimulant medication for ADHD while in therapy to learn how to integrate this new "person" into my view of myself.

During a period of 4 years or so, I rode the roller-coaster of depression. It took me in and out of valleys, through tunnels, up over mountains where things looked stunning only to plunge back to the valley by way of a long, dark tunnel. I withdrew from life, not trusting what it had to offer. I recall times when my children would walk past and see the glazed look in the general direction of

## BOX 13.3 Focus on Violence

### Juvenile Arrests and "Diversion"

Adolescents with disruptive behavior disorders sometimes display aggression toward others as well as antisocial behavior such as property destruction or stealing. Arrest rates for juveniles remain high. The issue of juvenile violence and other antisocial behavior was widely debated in the 1990s, and many states lowered the age at which juveniles could be arrested and tried as adults for various crimes. Many of these youth were incarcerated with adult prisoners and were at risk for severe exploitation because of their youth and inexperience.

Some states have since reevaluated this practice and instituted "diversion" programs allowing first-time offenders to avoid incarceration (Schwalbe, Gearing, MacKenzie, Brewer, &

Ibrahim, 2012). Examples include wilderness and boot camps, court-based mediation and conflict resolution, and referral to counseling services or group homes. Diversion programs typically focus on detailed assessment of a particular youth, expunging arrest and conviction records, family-based treatment, and linkage to community-based agencies.

A prominent example is the Miami-Dade Juvenile Assessment Center Post-Arrest Diversion Program. This program evaluates and addresses first-time youth offenders by providing treatment services as an alternative to incarceration. Charges against a youth may be dismissed following intense supervision and completion of treatment, often for substance use and family-related problems. This practice helps reduce stigma associated with "delinquency" and allows youths to experience a second chance at entering adulthood without the detriment of an arrest record (Cocozza et al., 2005).

the television, and hear them announce that "Mom's depressed again."

I can't recall that last journey out of the valley, how it was different from the others. I just knew it was. Life began again. The piles had seemed to have taken on a life of their own and the bills were all merged into one heap, as the phone rang off the hook with bill collectors on the other end. Taking the medication and armed with knowledge about myself, I started on the trek out of the abyss, tackling one issue at a time and creating systems that worked with my processing styles. My family looked on with guarded optimism wondering if they could trust what they were seeing.

The biggest change that came about was my desire to help others. Since my youngest son was diagnosed, I advocated for him at his school, getting accommodations, trying to keep his playing field level. I learned what his challenges were, found his strengths, and then went to work getting approval for him to use those strengths to overcome the

challenges. I had learned a lot about myself and what I could do for others. The medication allowed me to focus and follow through on projects. I wanted to put those new skills to work helping others go through their difficult times.

Although I wanted to get to work instantly, I was able to recognize I needed further education. As I looked back, I saw that school had not been easy for me, despite the embossed gold sticker on the diploma. I remembered the long hours reading texts, and then rereading them, taking copious notes in class, feeling like every teacher talked too fast and I wrote too slow, then copying the notes later using different colors to set things apart. Remembering the anxiety around tests brought about its own anxiety; how was I going to survive another go-round? (It had been so long, I thought, since I had been to school.)

And the house—how would I be able to keep up with the bills, feed the kids, do the laundry . . . all the "normal" things others seemed to do so naturally? I didn't

have answers to those questions; I just had the answer to how I was going to use my experience. I had determined it was not going to control me; I was going to control it. Once I made that determination, my life changed.

I learned what I believe to be one of the critical concepts that everyone needs to learn: experiences don't make or mold the person . . . it's what the person does with the experiences that defines who they are. I went back to college, using general education credits from my first degree to apply toward my second bachelor of science degree. With the help of the Disabilities Services office at the university, I graduated 18 months later, feeling much more successful than my first time through college. From there I went on to another challenge, taking an 11-month teleclass to become a coach to fulfill my goal of helping others. There was no Disabilities Services office but I knew enough that I managed just fine, and today I am now a certified coach working out of my home . . . helping others with ADHD.

Persistent ADHD and oppositional defiant/conduct symptoms seem best predicted by severity and complexity. This means that particularly severe symptoms, greater impairment, and substantial comorbidity predict problems throughout adolescence and adulthood. Other high-risk factors include early age of onset and aggression, depression, behavior problems in multiple settings, lower intelligence, excessive substance use, parental psychopathology, and low socioeconomic status (Biederman et al., 2008; Kessler, Adler, Barkley, et al., 2005).

## INTERIM SUMMARY

▶ Methods to assess youths with disruptive behavior disorders include interviews, rating scales, and behavioral observations.

▶ Biological treatment of disruptive behavior disorders includes stimulant medication to address deficits or imbalances in dopamine and norepinephrine.

▶ Parent training for treating disruptive behavior disorders involves defining behavior problems, providing appropriate consequences for child behavior, giving effective commands, and increasing supervision of a child and contact with school officials.

▶ School-based behavior management of disruptive behavior problems is often done in coordination with parent training

and focuses on methods of helping children enhance control over their behavior.

▶ Social and academic skills training is used to help youth control impulses and anger and develop better social and academic skills.

▶ Residential treatment is sometimes used for severe cases of adolescent disruptive behavior disorder and includes placement in community-based settings with an eventual goal of returning a child to his home.

▶ Multisystemic treatment is a strategy for addressing severe disruptive behavior problems by providing treatment at different levels: family, school, and agency.

▶ Children with disruptive behavior disorders often have stable symptoms, especially in cases of early age of onset and aggression, more intense severity and complexity of symptoms, excessive substance use, family dysfunction, and parent psychopathology.

## REVIEW QUESTIONS

1. What are the primary methods of assessing youths with disruptive behavior?

2. What are the main medications for children with ADHD, and what are their side effects?

3.  Outline major goals of parent training and school-based behavior management for youths with disruptive behavior.
4.  Describe social and academic skills training and residential and multisystemic treatments. How might these strategies be combined to address a child with severe disruptive behavior?
5.  What is the long-term outcome for youths with ADHD and/or oppositional defiant and conduct disorder?

## Final Comments

People with developmental disorders suffer many problems functioning on a daily basis. They often rely on others for help and are frustrated with their inability to be fully independent. This is important to remember the next time you see someone struggle to get the right change in line at a store or someone with trouble talking articulately or reading a story quickly. Of course, many of us need help from other people in our daily lives. If you know someone who seems to need a lot of extra help, however, then talking to someone about it or contacting a qualified mental health professional is a good idea.

Think about a child who acts up in a supermarket, movie theater, or airplane. Your first response is likely annoyance, and your second response might be to wonder what is wrong with the parents. Why don't they control their child? Many kids who act up can and should be managed better by parents, but consider the possibility that a parent is trying to address a child with a severe disruptive behavior disorder. Children with ADHD, oppositional defiant disorder, or conduct disorder are enormously difficult to live with, both at home and out in public. When you next see a child being disruptive in public, ask yourself what might be causing the child's misbehavior.

## Thought Questions

1.  When you notice people with developmental disorders portrayed in television shows and films, what strikes you most? How realistic are the portrayals, given what you have learned here?
2.  Who should make decisions for adults with developmental disorders? If you had a relative with mild intellectual disability, how much supervision would you want to provide?
3.  If a friend of yours was pregnant with a child who had a major chromosomal aberration, what would you tell her?
4.  How do you think children with learning disorder should be addressed in schools? Is separation with a special education teacher the best option? Should girls have as many opportunities for arithmetic tutoring as boys have for reading tutoring?

5.  Do you think people with pervasive developmental disorders should have children? Why or why not?
6.  Why do you think disruptive behavior disorders are much more common in boys than girls? How might parents and teachers deal differently with boys and girls?
7.  What are advantages and disadvantages of allowing children with ADHD to be in regular classroom settings?
8.  What is the difference between normal adolescent rebelliousness and conduct disorder?
9.  What are risks of medicating youths with ADHD?

## Key Terms

developmental disorders 394
limited developmental disorders 395
pervasive developmental disorder 395
intellectual disability 395
adaptive functioning 396
autism spectrum disorder 397
learning disorder 400
fragile X syndrome 402
phenylketonuria (PKU) 403
sickle cell disease 403
Tay-Sachs disease 404
Down syndrome 404
teratogens 405
induction defects 405
migration defects 405
cultural-familial intellectual disability 406
gene therapy 411
discrete-trial training 411
attention-deficit/hyperactivity disorder 415
oppositional defiant disorder 415
conduct disorder 415
disruptive behavior disorders 415
multisystemic treatment 427

## Media Resources

### MindTap

MindTap for Kearney and Trull's *Abnormal Psychology and Life: A Dimensional Approach* is a highly personalized fully online learning platform of authoritative content, assignments, and services offering you a tailored presentation of course curriculum created by your instructor. MindTap guides you through the course curriculum via an innovative learning path where you will complete reading assignments, annotate your readings, complete homework, and engage with quizzes and assessments. MindTap includes the Continuum Video Project.

Go to **cengagebrain.com** to access MindTap.

# Neurocognitive Disorders

**14**

## CASE: *William and Laura*

### What Do You Think?

**Normal Changes During Aging and Neurocognitive Disorders: What Are They?**

**Neurocognitive Disorders: Features and Epidemiology**

**Stigma Associated with Neurocognitive Disorders**
Interim Summary
Review Questions

**Neurocognitive Disorders: Causes and Prevention**
Interim Summary
Review Questions

**Neurocognitive Disorders: Assessment and Treatment**
Interim Summary
Review Questions

FINAL COMMENTS
THOUGHT QUESTIONS
KEY TERMS
MEDIA RESOURCES

## SPECIAL FEATURES

### CONTINUUM FIGURE 14.1 Continuum of Thinking and Memory Problems and Neurocognitive Disorder 436

BOX 14.1 | Focus on Violence: Maltreatment of the Elderly 446

### THE CONTINUUM VIDEO PROJECT

**Myriam: Alzheimer's Disease 448**

BOX 14.2 | Focus on Gender: Grief in the Spouse Caregiver 458

BOX 14.3 | Focus on Law and Ethics: Ethical Issues and Dementia 460

# CASE: William and Laura

**William Ponder** and his wife, Laura, were both 83 years old. They had been married 58 years and lived in a rural area much of their lives. The Ponders were arrested after an incident in which their checking account was grossly overdrawn. The bank manager said the couple had written more than $22,000 worth of bad checks during the previous several months. Detectives sought help from the Ponders' two grown sons and discovered that Mr. Ponder simply added zeroes to his checkbook balance whenever he needed to pay bills—he would change a $100 balance to $1,000 as necessary. No actual funds had been placed into the checking account for some time, however.

Detectives found the couple to be agitated, argumentative, and confused. The Ponders insisted no problem existed with their checking account and that they should not be hassled because "we're old and you just want our money." They could not recall their address at times, but other times seemed lucid. Mr. Ponder's memory of events was worse than his wife's memory, and he could no longer drive because of poor motor skills and forgetfulness about where he was. The couple thus depended on Mrs. Ponder's driving and on their two sons, who would check on their parents from time to time.

The presiding judge at a court hearing about the bad checks asked the couple to submit to a neuropsychological examination. The examination was to determine the extent to which Mr. and Mrs. Ponder were impaired and could no longer care for each other or manage their finances. Mrs. Ponder had moderate memory problems and seemed somewhat withdrawn and occasionally confused, and her scores on the test were in the low normal range. Mr. Ponder, however, struggled mightily on many of the items, especially those related to sensory-motor functioning and memory. He struggled to such an extent he began yelling at the examiner and refused to finish the examination.

The neuropsychologist also interviewed the couple's two sons, who said they were stunned at the recent turn of events. They did reveal their parents were not as "sharp" as in years past and that their parents had become more withdrawn from others. Both sons were particularly concerned about their father, who displayed major personality changes over the past 2 years. They described their father as typically mellow and easygoing who was transforming into a belligerent, short-tempered, and tense man. The sons once approached their parents about the possibility of living in an assisted care facility, but their father verbally threatened them for even mentioning the subject.

Mr. Ponder refused a second interview with the neuropsychologist, but Mrs. Ponder agreed. She confirmed her sons' reports and admitted she was sometimes afraid to live with her husband. He was becoming more aggressive and even struck her on two occasions, although he had never done so earlier in their marriage. He spent much of his day consuming alcohol, watching television, and sleeping. She also worried he might wander about and get lost.

Mrs. Ponder conceded she was feeling overwhelmed by having to care for her husband as well as the house. She continued to allow Mr. Ponder to control the couple's finances and worried that "something awful" was going to happen to their retirement account. Mrs. Ponder was reportedly becoming more depressed and confused and was having trouble eating and sleeping. Her mood was somber as she realized her husband was changing, that he was not the same loving man he used to be, and that they could be in severe legal trouble or be forced to sell their home. Mrs. Ponder knew her future must involve enormous change. She worried about where she would live and how much money was left, but mostly she worried about her husband's fading physical and mental health.

The neuropsychologist concluded that Mr. Ponder was likely in middle stages of a neurocognitive disorder, perhaps due to Alzheimer's disease. Mrs. Ponder displayed normal memory changes for someone her age, but she was also depressed and occasionally confused, which may have led to mild thought and memory problems. The neuropsychologist reported to the court his findings and the Ponders were allowed to make proper restitution to various businesses without additional legal trouble. The state department of aging was notified, however, and the Ponders' life as they had known it for decades was about to change dramatically.

Blazej Lyjak/Shutterstock.com

## What Do You Think?

1.  Which of Mr. and Mrs. Ponder's symptoms seem typical of someone in later stages of life and which seem very different?

2.  What external events and internal factors might be responsible for Mr. Ponder's dramatic changes in thoughts and behaviors?

3.  What are you curious about regarding Mr. and Mrs. Ponder?

4.  Do the Ponders remind you in any way of someone you know? How so?

5.  How might the Ponders' memory problems affect their lives in the future?

# Normal Changes During Aging and Neurocognitive Disorders: What Are They?

Most of us experience subtle changes in memory and other thinking processes as we age. As we enter our 30s and 40s, slightly greater problems start to occur with respect to *short-term memory*. Middle-aged adults may start to wonder more why they went upstairs (what was I looking for?), where they misplaced something (what did I do with those keys?), or the name of someone they met last night (who was that guy?). Other people experience changes in *long-term memory*, such as forgetting who won the World Series 5 years ago. Still others experience more problems with *episodic memory*, or ability to recall personal experiences from further in the past, such as the name of their fifth-grade teacher (Shing et al., 2010).

These normal changes may relate to alterations in brain areas most responsible for memory. The *hippocampus* and *frontal lobes* may lose brain cells or be affected by neurochemical changes such as loss of dopamine over time (Backman, Lindenberger, Li, & Nyberg, 2010). These alterations, however, are often slow to develop, only mildly annoying, and do not significantly interfere with daily functioning. Once a person is reminded of something (you went upstairs to look for glue), the sought-after memory is usually retrieved quickly. Still, one can usually tell he is not as "quick" to remember things as in the past. He may experience more of what is known as the *tip-of-the-tongue phenomenon*, or feeling he knows something he cannot immediately remember.

Normal changes occur in the frontal lobe and other brain areas over time, so one might also experience subtle difficulties in other cognitive areas. Such difficulties often involve processing and reasoning speed, decision making, planning for events, paying attention, and exercising good judgment (Salthouse, 2012). A person may find it takes more time than usual to decide which car to buy, has trouble keeping straight all the details of organizing a wedding or concentrating on a long lecture, or cannot navigate a complex driving trip in a strange city. Subtle changes may also occur with respect to computing mathematical problems, sorting objects, and discriminating patterns. A person may begin to have more trouble reading complex music. What makes all of these changes normal, however, is the fact that most everyone experiences them to some extent and that these experiences do not interfere significantly with daily functioning.

General memory, learning, or concentration problems do increase over time: the percentage of people experiencing these problems climbs from 6.3 percent at age 65 to 74 years, to 12.8 percent at age 75 to 84 years, and to 27.7 percent at age 85+ years (U.S. Census Bureau, 2004). These figures are significant but also tell us the large majority of older people *do not* have substantial cognitive problems! People aged 65+ years tend to be married, living in a household, and owners of their own home (U.S. Census Bureau, 2004). These facts dispel the notion that most elderly people must depend on others for their livelihood.

Many older people with dementia begin to withdraw from others.

Yuri Arcurs/INSADCO Photography/Alamy

For some people, however, memory and thinking changes do become much more severe under *certain circumstances* (**Figure 14.1**). Someone's ability to remember information and pay close attention to others is likely impaired when she has been drinking heavily, has just come out of surgery under general anesthesia, or has a high fever. People in these states are often confused and have trouble staying awake. Such impairments in cognition, which are usually temporary and reversible, are often referred to as **delirium**.

For other people, memory and thinking changes become much more severe as they age. Someone's ability to recall information may still be impaired even after a reminder is given, or a person's forgetfulness may become very frequent. A person may start to forget how to do simple things like tying a shoelace or using a microwave oven. She may also have trouble learning new tasks, especially complicated ones, and struggle to have conversations with others. Other problems might include the need to repeat oneself or to constantly ask the same question to get information and remember it. A person in this situation, like Mr. Ponder, might also experience personality changes, loss of social skills, loss of interest

**CONTINUUM FIGURE 14.1**    Continuum of thinking and memory problems and neurocognitive disorder

| | Normal | Mild |
|---|---|---|
| **Emotions** | Stable emotions during thinking and recall. | Mild frustration and concern following memory lapses. |
| **Cognitions** | Good thinking and memory processes. | Occasional lapses of attention or memory or tip-of-the-tongue phenomenon. |
| **Behaviors** | Engaging in good work and social behavior. | Slight delays in work or requests to repeat something someone has said. |

in daily activities, and psychological issues such as worry and sadness about cognitive changes. These cognitive changes are massive, often irreversible, and *do* significantly interfere with daily functioning. People undergoing such dramatic changes in memory and cognition experience **dementia.** In the following sections, we review features of these two major sets of **neurocognitive disorders:** delirium and dementia.

People with delirium often have trouble understanding time and location.

## Neurocognitive Disorders: Features and Epidemiology

### Delirium

Have you ever been in a state of mind where things around you seemed fuzzy or confusing? Perhaps you were just coming out of surgery with general anesthesia, were extremely tired, or stayed a little too long at happy hour. Your ability to think clearly or even to stay awake may have been affected. Delirium exists when someone's normal state of thinking or consciousness is impaired (see **Table 14.1**; American Psychiatric Association [APA], 2013). Impairment due to delirium is typically short-lived, and a person usually recovers fully. Examples include fading of general anesthesia or another drug, becoming rehydrated, recovering from a high fever, or reducing stress or exhaustion.

A person in a state of delirium often has trouble interacting with others and is not clearly aware of surrounding events. She may have great trouble maintaining attention in a conversation or moving attention from one person to another. Focused attention or concentration is difficult in these situations as well (Zimmerman, Rudolph, Salow, & Skarf, 2011). Other higher-order cognitive processes are also impaired, including ability to remember information, speak clearly, or integrate information such as assembling a puzzle. Delirium is sometimes associated with *disorientation,* meaning a person has difficulty remembering personal information, where he is, or even what time it is (Blazer & van Nieuwenhuizen, 2012). A person may have been in a car accident that caused temporary inability to identify oneself, realize she is in a hospital, or recognize day or night. Mrs. Ponder sometimes showed symptoms of delirium when she appeared confused or unsure around others. These symptoms may have been due to sleep deprivation or stress.

Another key aspect of delirium is fluctuation of the problem over hours and days. A person may be lucid and can maintain a conversation at times but seem confused and

| Moderate | Neurocognitive Disorder — less severe | Neurocognitive Disorder — more severe |
|---|---|---|
| Increasing frustration at loss of attention and memory or irritability with others. | Intense anxiety and concern about attention and memory loss. | Dramatically decreased emotional behavior, including apathy about one's condition. |
| Ongoing and regular lapses of attention or memory, especially short-term memory. | Intense decreases in attention, memory, processing speed, planning ability, and judgment. | Extreme loss of attention and memory, such that long-term memories become lost. |
| Greater difficulties organizing and completing work and engaging in conversations. | Ongoing inability to converse well with others; getting lost frequently and wandering. | Dramatically decreased physical behavior; little verbal activity and sleeping much. |

© Monkey Business Images/Shutterstock.com

sleepy at other times (Lundstrom, Stenvall, & Olofsson, 2012). Many people in a state of delirium slip in and out of sleep or conscious awareness. A person's mood may also shift quickly, perhaps from anger to apathy to giddiness within a short time. Motor behavior can change quickly as well, as when someone becomes agitated and then slows down considerably or sleeps

(Meagher et al., 2012). Psychotic-like symptoms of delusions and hallucinations can occur as well, which make states of delirium potentially dangerous. Someone in this state should never drive a car or be left unsupervised.

## Table 14.1

### DSM-5 Delirium

A. A disturbance in attention and awareness (reduced orientation to the environment).

B. The disturbance develops over a short period of time (usually hours to a few days), represents a change from baseline attention and awareness, and tends to fluctuate in severity during the course of a day.

C. An additional disturbance in cognition.

D. The disturbances in Criteria A and C are not better explained by another preexisting, established, or evolving neurocognitive disorder and do not occur in the context of a severely reduced level of arousal, such as coma.

E. There is evidence from the history, physical examination, or laboratory findings that the disturbance is a direct physiological consequence of another medical condition, substance intoxication or withdrawal, or exposure to a toxin, or is due to multiple etiologies.

Specify if due to substance intoxication, substance withdrawal, medication, another medical condition, or multiple etiologies; if acute or persistent; if hyperactive, hypoactive, or mixed level of activity.

American Psychiatric Association. (2013). *Diagnostic and statistical manual of mental disorders* (5th ed.). Arlington, VA: American Psychiatric Association.

Â© J.P. Greenwood/Corbis

Delirium is often induced by alcohol or other drug use.

Delirium is usually caused by general medical conditions or substance intoxication or withdrawal, but many other factors can lead to the problem as well (see **Table 14.2**). Specific medical evidence is usually necessary to assign a diagnosis of delirium, but direct observation can sometimes be enough. If delirium might be due to an electrolyte imbalance, then a medical assessment is likely necessary. If delirium might be due to recent alcohol intake, however, then simply observing the person or interviewing significant others may be sufficient. States of delirium should not be assumed when a person may actually be in a state of dementia, aspects of which we discuss next.

## Dementia and Major and Mild Neurocognitive Disorder

Delirium involves cognitive deficits that are acute, develop quickly, fluctuate, and are typically reversible. Dementia, on the other hand, involves cognitive deficits that (Trzepacz & Meagher, 2012):

- are *chronic*, meaning the deficits last for long periods
- develop *slowly*, meaning gradual onset of the deficits

---

### Table 14.2

| Possible Causes of Delirium |
| --- |
| Substance intoxication |
| Substance withdrawal |
| Metabolic/endocrine disturbance |
| Traumatic brain injury |
| Seizures |
| Neoplastic disease |
| Intracranial infection |
| Systemic infection |
| Cerebrovascular disorder |
| Organ insufficiency |
| Other central nervous system etiologies |
| Other systemic etiologies: |
| Heat stroke |
| Hypothermia |
| Radiation |
| Electrocution |
| Postoperative state |
| Immunosuppression |
| Fractures |

---

- show a *progressive* course, meaning little fluctuation in the deficits
- are usually *irreversible*, meaning the deficits do not improve with time

Cognitive deficits in dementia also involve problems with learning, memory, attention, language, recognition, planning, decision-making, problem-solving, concentration, judgment, and perceptual-motor ability (such as driving). Mr. Ponder had many problems with mathematical ability, memory, and focused attention. Delirium and dementia often occur together and share common etiologies such as general medical conditions, substance use, or some combination of these, and symptoms of each also commonly resemble those of depression and schizophrenia (see **Table 14.3**; Miller & Solai, 2013). Delirium is usually reversible, however, so we concentrate in this chapter on dementia or delirium with dementia.

Dementias may be characterized as a neurocognitive disorder that can differ in severity (see **Table 14.4**) (APA, 2013). A **major neurocognitive disorder** involves significant cognitive decline and interference with daily activities such as paying bills. This was the case for Mr. Ponder. A **mild neurocognitive disorder** involves modest cognitive decline but without interference in daily activities. This was the case for Mrs. Ponder. A mild neurocognitive disorder may eventually progress to a major neurocognitive disorder. The terms dementia and major neurocognitive disorder remain generally synonymous, although dementia sometimes specifically refers to older persons with multiple cognitive problems.

Dementias can also be characterized as presenile or senile. You may have heard the term "senile" sometimes applied to older people. This term is not a clinical one but refers only to some loss of mental ability with age. *Presenile dementia*, however, commonly refers to onset of dementia symptoms before age 65 years, whereas *senile dementia* is a term that commonly refers to onset of dementia symptoms after age 65 years (Vieira et al., 2013). People with presenile (or early onset) dementias typically show more severe symptoms and often die from the disorders much sooner than people with senile dementias. Presenile dementias may have a more aggressive course due to stronger genetic or other biological links than senile dementias (van der Flier, Pijnenburg, Fox, & Scheltens, 2011).

We describe the most common types of neurocognitive disorder in this chapter. You should be aware that many *other* types exist, however. Examples include neurocognitive disorder brought on by HIV disease, Prion disease, Huntington's disease, brain tumor, thyroid problems, malnutrition, blood that collects on the surface of the brain (subdural hematoma), infections, metabolic disorders, and advanced stages of multiple sclerosis (APA, 2013). Creutzfeldt-Jakob disease, a condition that leads to rapid neurological impairment, can also produce neurocognitive disorder and death (Tagliapietra et al., 2013). Various substances or toxins can also lead to neurocognitive disorder if ingested for prolonged periods. Examples include carbon monoxide, inhalants, lead, and mercury (Ghosh, 2010).

## Table 14.3

### Differential Diagnosis of Delirium, Dementia, Depression, and Schizophrenia

|  | Delirium | Dementia | Depression | Schizophrenia |
|---|---|---|---|---|
| Onset | Acute | Insidious[a] | Variable | Variable |
| Course | Fluctuating | Often progressive | Diurnal variation | Variable |
| Reversibility | Usually[b] | Not usually | Usually but can be recurrent | No, but has exacerbations |
| Level of consciousness | Impaired | Unimpaired until late stages | Generally unimpaired | Unimpaired (perplexity in acute stage) |
| Attention and memory | Inattention is primary with poor memory | Poor memory without marked inattention | Mild attention problems, inconsistent pattern, memory intact | Poor attention, memory intact |
| Hallucinations | Usually visual; can be auditory, tactile, gustatory, olfactory | Can be visual or auditory | Usually auditory | Usually auditory |
| Delusions | Fleeting, fragmented, usually persecutory | Paranoid, often fixed | Complex and mood congruent | Frequent, complex, systematized, often paranoid |

[a]Except for large strokes.
[b]Can be chronic (paraneoplastic syndrome, central nervous system adverse events of medications, severe brain damage).
From *Essentials of Neuropsychiatry and Behavioral Neurosciences* (2nd ed.), by Stuart C. Yudofsky, M.D, and Robert E. Hales, M.D., M.B.A., Table 5.3 p. 154. Copyright © 2010 American Psychiatric Publishing, Inc. Reprinted by permission.

## Alzheimer's Disease

One of the most tragic and severe mental problems we discuss in this textbook is **Alzheimer's disease** (see **Table 14.5**; APA, 2013). Some of you may already be familiar with this disorder by reading about famous people who had the disorder, such as Ronald Reagan or Charlton Heston, or by knowing older family members with the disorder. Alzheimer's disease involves slow and irreversible progression of dementia. Alzheimer's disease necessarily involves multiple cognitive deficits, but especially those related to memory. The disorder accounts for about 60 to 70 percent of all cases of dementia (Apostolova & Cummings, 2012).

The following cognitive deficits are likely to occur in someone with Alzheimer's disease:

- *Aphasia*, or impaired ability to use or comprehend spoken language, as when a person has difficulty speaking or cannot understand what is being said to him
- *Apraxia*, or impaired voluntary movement despite adequate sensory and muscle functioning, as when a person can no longer tie her shoes
- *Agnosia*, or impaired ability to recognize people or common objects, as when a person fails to recognize loved ones or basic items such as a spoon

- *Executive functioning deficits*, which include impaired ability to plan or organize daily activities, engage in abstract thinking, or understand the sequence of events, such as maneuvering driving turns to get to and from a grocery store

Herb Winokur, 83, is suffering from dementia and Parkinson's disease. His daughter must decide how to provide the best care for him since his condition makes it virtually impossible for him to complete sentences and maintain his independent lifestyle.

--- **Table 14.4** ---

### DSM-5 Major and Mild Neurocognitive Disorder

**Major Neurocognitive Disorder**

A. Evidence of significant cognitive decline from a previous level of performance in one or more cognitive domains based on:
  1. Concern of the individual, a knowledgeable informant, or the clinician that there has been a significant decline in cognitive function; and
  2. A substantial impairment in cognitive performance, preferably documented by standardized neuropsychological testing or, in its absence, another quantified clinical assessment.

B. The cognitive deficits interfere with independence in everyday activities.

C. The cognitive deficits do not occur exclusively in the context of a delirium.

D. The cognitive deficits are not better explained by another mental disorder.

Specify if due to Alzheimer's disease, frontotemporal lobar degeneration, Lewy body disease, vascular disease, traumatic brain injury, substance/medication use, HIV infection, Prion disease, Parkinson's disease, Huntington's disease, another medical condition, multiple etiologies, or unspecified.

**Mild Neurocognitive Disorder**

A. Evidence of modest cognitive decline from a previous level of performance in one or more cognitive domains based on:
  1. Concern of the individual, a knowledgeable informant, or the clinician that there has been a mild decline in cognitive function; and
  2. A modest impairment in cognitive performance, preferably documented by standardized neuropsychological testing or, in its absence, another quantified clinical assessment.

B. The cognitive deficits do not interfere with capacity for independence in everyday activities.

C. The cognitive deficits do not occur exclusively in the context of a delirium.

D. The cognitive deficits are not better explained by another mental disorder.

American Psychiatric Association. (2013). *Diagnostic and statistical manual of mental disorders* (5th ed.). Arlington, VA: American Psychiatric Association.

--- **Table 14.5** ---

### DSM-5 Major or Mild Neurocognitive Disorder Due to Alzheimer's Disease

A. The criteria are met for major or mild neurocognitive disorder.

B. There is insidious onset and gradual progression of impairment in one or more cognitive domains.

C. Criteria are met for either probable or possible Alzheimer's disease as follows:

*For major neurocognitive disorder:*
**Probable Alzheimer's disease** is diagnosed if either of the following is present; otherwise, **possible Alzheimer's disease** should be diagnosed.
  1. Evidence of a causative Alzheimer's disease genetic mutation from family history or genetic testing.
  2. All three of the following are present:
    a. Clear evidence of decline in memory and learning and at least one other cognitive domain.
    b. Steadily progressive, gradual decline in cognition, without extended plateaus.
    c. No evidence of mixed etiology.

*For mild neurocognitive disorder:*
**Probable Alzheimer's disease** is diagnosed if there is evidence of a causative Alzheimer's disease genetic mutation from either genetic testing or family history.
**Possible Alzheimer's disease** is diagnosed if there is no evidence of a causative Alzheimer's disease genetic mutation from either genetic testing or family history, and all three of the following are present:
  1. Clear evidence of decline in memory and learning.
  2. Steadily progressive, gradual decline in cognition, without extended plateaus.
  3. No evidence of mixed etiology.

D. The disturbance is not better explained by cerebrovascular disease, another neurodegenerative disease, the effects of a substance, or another mental, neurological, or systemic disorder.

American Psychiatric Association. (2013). *Diagnostic and statistical manual of mental disorders* (5th ed.). Arlington, VA: American Psychiatric Association.

These cognitive problems develop slowly and worsen over a period of 5 to 9 years. People with Alzheimer's disease in early stages of the disorder may appear simply forgetful or distracted when speaking to others (Sperling et al., 2011). They may become confused about where they are, take less initiative in daily activities, and have trouble with logical thought. These subtle impairments eventually worsen, however, as people with Alzheimer's disease will often take longer time to complete simple tasks such as making a sandwich or will have greater difficulty with more complicated tasks (Ito et al., 2010). Mr. Ponder could no longer drive himself places or compute complex mathematical problems.

As Alzheimer's disease progresses further, personality changes are seen, and problems start to develop with skills practiced for many years, such as reading and writing (Chertkow, Feldman, Jacova, & Massoud, 2013). Mr. Ponder was becoming more belligerent and tense and clearly had trouble with his checkbook. People with Alzheimer's disease also begin to have enormous problems interacting with others and completing basic motor tasks such as tying shoelaces. Long-term memory and other cognitive areas of functioning eventually become much more impaired, even to the point where a person cannot recognize others or care for himself (Donix et al., 2013). Mr. Ponder needed assistance doing everyday activities such as getting dressed and may get to the point where he will not recognize his wife of nearly 60 years. Basic abilities such as speech, walking, feeding, and toileting are severely impaired in final stages of Alzheimer's disease. Someone with the disorder is often placed under supervised care and usually dies from pneumonia or other diseases (Moschetti, Cummings, Sorvillo, & Kuo, 2012).

## Lewy Bodies

Another neurocognitive disorder that is similar to Alzheimer's disease involves **Lewy bodies** (see **Table 14.6**; APA, 2013). This disorder, sometimes called *Lewy body disease*, includes most of the key features of Alzheimer's disease, but may also include visual hallucinations, muscle tremors, and a more fluctuating course of symptoms (Harciarek & Kertesz, 2008). A person with advanced Lewy body disease may speak normally at one time of day and later experience great difficulty interacting with others. The problem is linked mostly to *Lewy bodies* in the cortex, substantia nigra, and other brain areas (Sreenath & Barber, 2009). Lewy bodies are accumulations of certain proteins in neurons that lead to cell damage. Lewy body disease may account for about 20 percent of cases of dementia, although significant overlap with Alzheimer's disease is often seen (Watson & O'Brien, 2012).

## Vascular Disease

**Vascular disease**, sometimes also referred to as *cerebrovascular disease*, is another common form of neurocognitive disorder but one caused by problems with blood vessels that supply the brain with oxygen and other nutrients. The most common blood vessel problem that leads to vascular-based neurocognitive disorder, sometimes called *vascular dementia*, is a *stroke*. A stroke occurs when a blood vessel is blocked or bursts, which denies oxygen to parts of the brain; various areas of the

**Table 14.6**

### DSM-5 Major or Mild Neurocognitive Disorder with Lewy Bodies

A. The criteria are met for major or mild neurocognitive disorder.

B. The disorder has an insidious onset and gradual progression.

C. The disorder meets a combination of core diagnostic features and suggestive diagnostic features for either probable or possible neurocognitive disorder with Lewy bodies.
   **For probable major or mild neurocognitive disorder with Lewy bodies,** the individual has two core features, or one suggestive feature, with one or more core features.
   **For possible major or mild neurocognitive disorder with Lewy bodies,** the individual has only one core feature, or one or more suggestive features.
   1. Core diagnostic features:
      a. Fluctuating cognition with pronounced variations in attention and alertness.
      b. Recurrent visual hallucinations that are well formed and detailed.
      c. Spontaneous features of parkinsonism, with onset subsequent to the development of cognitive decline.
   2. Suggestive diagnostic features:
      a. Meets criteria for rapid eye movement sleep behavior disorder.
      b. Severe neuroleptic sensitivity.

D. The disturbance is not better explained by cerebrovascular disease, another neurodegenerative disease, the effects of a substance, or another mental, neurological, or systemic disorder.

American Psychiatric Association. (2013). *Diagnostic and statistical manual of mental disorders* (5th ed.). Arlington, VA: American Psychiatric Association.

brain, especially the *cortex*, can suffer potentially severe damage. Vascular disease that results in vascular dementia could also affect only *subcortical* areas of the brain. This can occur from hypertension, diabetes, or heart disease (Jiwa, Garrard, & Hainsworth, 2010).

A stroke is most often caused by blood clots that block a key artery to the brain—an *ischemic* stroke. More unusually, a stroke may be caused by a ruptured blood vessel—a *hemorrhagic* or bleeding stroke (Van der Flier & Cordonnier, 2012). Damage from strokes may be limited, as when a person is treated quickly and perhaps only suffers moderate memory problems. Damage from a stroke can also be severe and lead to paralysis and dementia that resemble symptoms of Alzheimer's disease (Zlokovic, 2011). Severe damage is often the result of multiple strokes.

What is the difference between neurocognitive disorder due to vascular disease versus Alzheimer's disease? The general symptoms of each disorder are quite similar, but

## Table 14.9

### DSM-5 Major or Mild Frontotemporal Neurocognitive Disorder

A. The criteria are met for major or mild neurocognitive disorder.

B. The disturbance has insidious onset and gradual progression.

C. Either (1) or (2):

1. Behavioral variant:
   a. Three or more of the following behavioral symptoms:
      i. Behavioral disinhibition.
      ii. Apathy or inertia.
      iii. Loss of sympathy or empathy.
      iv. Perseverative, stereotyped or compulsive/ritualistic behavior.
      v. Hyperorality and dietary changes.
   b. Prominent decline in social cognition and/or executive abilities.

2. Language variant:
   a. Prominent decline in language ability, in the form of speech production, word finding, object naming, grammar, or word comprehension.

D. Relative sparing of learning and memory and perceptual-motor function.

E. The disturbance is not better explained by cerebrovascular disease, another neurodegenerative disease, the effects of a substance, or another mental, neurological, or systemic disorder.

**Probable frontotemporal neurocognitive disorder** is diagnosed if either of the following is present; otherwise, **possible frontotemporal neurocognitive disorder** should be diagnosed:

1. Evidence of a causative frontotemporal neurocognitive disorder genetic mutation, from either family history or genetic testing.

2. Evidence of disproportionate frontal and/or temporal lobe involvement from neuroimaging.

**Possible frontotemporal neurocognitive disorder** is diagnosed if there is no evidence of a genetic mutation, and neuroimaging has not been performed.

American Psychiatric Association. (2013). *Diagnostic and statistical manual of mental disorders* (5th ed.). Arlington, VA: American Psychiatric Association.

**Korsakoff's syndrome** is a problem associated with chronic alcohol use. Ongoing memory problems of people with this syndrome can be severe and linked to confusion and disorientation. Many people with Korsakoff's syndrome engage in *confabulation*, or the creation of fables or stories to fill memory gaps and hide memory problems (Race & Verfaellie, 2012). Korsakoff's syndrome is caused by lack of *thiamine* because a person drinks alcohol instead of eating a balanced diet. Blood vessel hemorrhages and damage to neurons can thus occur (Kril & Harper,

2012). Some but not complete improvement in symptoms may result when a person withdraws from alcohol use and resumes appropriate nutrition (Sadock & Sadock, 2007).

## Epidemiology of Neurocognitive Disorders

The U.S. Census Bureau reports that people aged 65 years and older currently represent 12.4 percent of the total American population, but this percentage is expected to rise to 20.7 percent by 2050. Percentages of people aged 85+ years will more than triple from 1.5 percent of the population in 2000 to 5 percent in 2050, or from 3 million to 13 million people. This oldest age group will be the fastest growing age group in the country! This trend in aging occurs in many other countries as well. The prevalence of neurocognitive disorders increases with age, so we can expect many more people to experience problems of delirium and dementia over the next decades.

Delirium is a disorder that can affect anyone because the problem can result from various medical conditions, substances, and other variables. The prevalence of delirium does increase with age, however: 0.4 percent for people aged 18+ years, 1.1 percent for people aged 55+ years, and 13.6 percent for people aged 85+ years (Burns, Gallagley, & Byrne, 2004). Medication is a common variable that results in delirium. Patients medicated for a stroke-related condition often experience delirium (Dahl, Ronning, & Thommessen, 2010). About 20 percent of people in a hospital, especially those leaving surgery, have delirium (Ryan et al., 2013). People living in geriatric hospitals and nursing homes may also have relatively high rates of delirium (range, 1.4 to 70.3 percent; de Lange, Verhaak, & van der Meer, 2013).

The rate of dementia also increases with age, especially after age 80 years, and some estimate that everyone would have Alzheimer's disease if they lived to age 140 years (**Figure 14.2**) (Roses, 1997)! Most elderly persons are still *unaffected*, however—only about 5 to 7 percent of people aged 60+ years have dementia (Prince et al., 2013). Rates of dementia increase sharply among persons in long-term care facilities, however (58 percent; Seitz, Purandare, & Conn, 2010). The cost of treating Americans with dementia was $200 billion in 2012 and is estimated to be $1.1 trillion in 2050 (Alzheimer's Association, 2013).

Rates of Alzheimer's disease closely follow rates of general dementia because Alzheimer's disease comprises most cases of dementia (**Figure 14.3**). Risk of Alzheimer's disease may increase with age if other factors are present, however. Studies of people with Alzheimer's disease have samples that are 64.2 percent female, although others have found no gender differences (Plassman et al., 2007; Ropacki & Jeste, 2005).

The prevalence of Alzheimer's disease does vary somewhat across cultures. A common finding is that Alzheimer's disease is diagnosed more in Western countries, where about 50 to 75 percent of all dementias are attributed to this disorder. Vascular dementia is diagnosed more in Eastern countries and especially Asia, however, where about 30 to 60 percent of all dementias are attributed to this disorder (Graves, 2004). This discrepancy may be due to genetic, diagnostic, or cultural differences. People in Eastern countries may find it more acceptable to have an obvious physical problem account for a mental disorder.

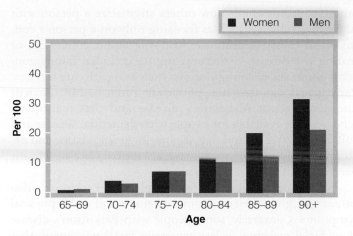

**FIGURE 14.2** **PREVALENCE OF ALL DEMENTIA BY GENDER AND AGE** *Source: "Frequency and impact of neurologic diseases in the elderly of Europe: A collaborative study of population-based cohorts" by L. Launer and A. Hofman, Neurology Vol. 54(11) Supplement. 5 June 2000. S4-S9, Figure 3.*

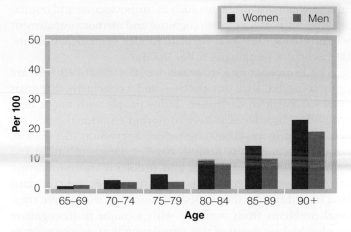

**FIGURE 14.3** **PREVALENCE OF ALZHEIMER'S DISEASE BY GENDER AND AGE** *Source: "Frequency and impact of neurologic diseases in the elderly of Europe: A collaborative study of population-based cohorts" by L. Launer and A. Hofman, Neurology Vol. 54(11) Supplement. 5 June 2000. S4-S9, Figure 5.*

Alzheimer's disease is more prevalent among African Americans than Nigerian Africans (Hall et al., 2006). In the United States, risk for Alzheimer's disease is higher for African Americans and Hispanics than European Americans and Asian Americans, and lower for Native Americans (Manly & Mayeux, 2004).

Vascular dementia also increases with age, but men generally display vascular dementia more than women, especially for ages 90+ years (**Figure 14.4**; Plassman et al., 2007). The general prevalence of vascular dementia is about 1.6 to 2.4 percent, and about 24 percent of those who experience a stroke eventually develop dementia (Allan et al., 2011; Jungehulsing et al., 2008; Plassman et al., 2007). Unlike Alzheimer's disease, vascular dementia appears more common to people living in East Asia than to European and North American populations. Such differences

may be due to, in addition to the reasons noted earlier, different dementia definitions, health care facilities, and frequency of vascular problems (Qiu, De Ronchi, & Fratiglioni, 2007).

Dementia due to Parkinson's disease does not affect men and women differently, but prevalence of the neurocognitive disorder does increase with age. The prevalence of dementia due to Parkinson's disease is 0.5 percent in people aged 65+ years (Aarsland, Zaccai, & Brayne, 2005). Men and women show equal rates of *dementia* due to Parkinson's disease, but prevalence of the disease itself is twice as common among men as women (Shulman, De Jager, & Feany, 2011). This difference may be partly due to effects of sex hormones or X-linked factors, but this remains unclear (Tanner & Marder, 2004). Racial differences for Parkinson's disease have been noted as well, with rates per 100,000 higher for Hispanics (16.6) than European Americans (13.6), Asian Americans (11.3), and African Americans (10.2). Parkinson's disease is seen much less in Asia and Africa than Europe and North America (Muangpaisan, Hori, & Brayne, 2009; Van Den Eeden et al., 2003).

Frontotemporal dementias, which include Pick's disease, are presenile problems that often occur at ages 35 to 75 years but have a median age of onset of 58 years. Men may display the disorders more so than women, but other studies indicate no gender difference. The prevalence of frontotemporal dementia may be as high as 15 to 22 cases per 100,000 people, although others report figures as low as 3.6 to 9.4 per 100,000 (Seelaar, Rohrer, Pijnenburg, Fox, & van Swieten, 2011). Data are scarce regarding cultural differences, but frontotemporal dementia may be less common in Japan than Western nations and less common in African Americans and Hispanics than European Americans (Hou, Yaffe, Perez-Stable, & Miller, 2006; Ikeda, Ishikawa, & Tanabe, 2004).

Korsakoff's syndrome does appear more in males (75 percent of cases) who are divorced. Korsakoff's syndrome is associated

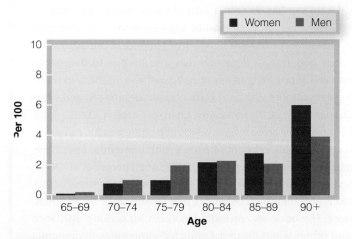

**FIGURE 14.4** **PREVALENCE OF VASCULAR DEMENTIA BY GENDER AND AGE** *Source: "Frequency and impact of neurologic diseases in the elderly of Europe: A collaborative study of population-based cohorts" by L. Launer and A. Hofman, Neurology Vol. 54(11) Supplement. 5 June 2000. S4-S9, Figure 7.*

with many physical problems such as cardiovascular and respiratory illnesses as well as severe cognitive and memory impairment including dementia (Oscar-Berman, Kirkley, Gansler, & Couture, 2004; Schepers, Koopmans, & Bor, 2000).

The neurocognitive disorders we have described here are highly comorbid with one another, and a conclusive diagnosis is often difficult to determine. Many people with major neurocognitive disorder also have comorbid emotional problems such as apathy, psychosis, agitation, aggression, depression, and anxiety (Budson & Kowall, 2011). Changes in eating and sleeping patterns, wandering, and problems communicating with others are also common. Family members and clinicians often have difficulty distinguishing someone with severe emotional problems from someone with a major neurocognitive disorder. Maltreatment of this population is often a concern as well (see **Box 14.1**).

## Stigma Associated with Neurocognitive Disorders

Stigma often affects those who care for people with neurocognitive disorders such as Alzheimer's disease. Werner and colleagues (2010) found that family stigma associated with Alzheimer's disease included caregiver, lay public, and structural stigma. Caregiver stigma included the caregiver's concerns about the inability of the person with Alzheimer's disease to remember information or to engage in self-care such as toileting. Shame, embarrassment, and disgust were also commonly reported by caregivers. Lay public stigma included

family concerns about how others stigmatize a person with Alzheimer's disease such as focusing only on a person's confusion or messy appearance, worrying about contagion, or fearing the disease. Structural stigma included family concerns about social configurations such as health care services. Participants reported that physicians often had insufficient knowledge about Alzheimer's disease and that inadequate services were available for people with dementia. Werner and colleagues (2012) found that stigma, including shame and declining involvement in caregiving, accounted for a significant percentage of caregiver burden.

Stigma can obviously affect people with Parkinson's disease as well, given their sometimes extensive and visible physical symptoms. Conversely, some people with Parkinson's disease show facial masking, or less expressive facial movement, that may give the appearance of apathy or social disengagement. People with high facial masking, especially women, may be seen by others as more depressed, less sociable, and less cognitively competent than those with low facial masking (Tickle-Degnen, Zebrowitz, & Ma, 2011). Such negative judgments may cause some people with Parkinson's disease to withdraw from others or to seek less treatment.

### INTERIM SUMMARY

▶ Normal memory and cognitive changes occur with age and do not interfere with daily functioning. These changes may progress to more serious sets of neurocognitive disorders such as delirium and dementia.

▶ Delirium is an often temporary and reversible condition where a person is disoriented and has trouble with attention,

---

## BOX 14.1   Focus on Violence

### Maltreatment of the Elderly

Substantial media and research attention has focused on maltreatment toward children and domestic violence. One form of cruelty that receives less attention, however, is *maltreatment of the elderly*. Maltreatment of the elderly involves psychological or physical harm, neglect, or exploitation of an older person. Examples include physical and sexual aggression, neglect of basic needs, and theft of assets. About 2 to 10 percent of elderly people are maltreated in some way. Some of this maltreatment occurs in nursing homes and related settings, but much is done by family members at home. The most significant risk factors for elder maltreatment are shared living situations, social isolation of families, and abuser psychopathology (Lachs & Pillemer, 2004).

Maltreatment of an elderly person is also much more likely if a person has dementia. Part of the reason for this may be the elderly person's agitation or aggression toward a caregiver or a caregiver's exhaustion or lack of patience. Maltreatment of elderly people with dementia may also be due to their problems communicating needs or pain to others, inability to make decisions about living arrangements, and depression and stress (Cooper et al., 2010; Hansberry, Chen, & Gorbien, 2005).

Some researchers have advocated strategies for caregivers to combat maltreatment of people with dementia. Anetzberger and colleagues (Anetzberger, 2012; Anetzberger et al., 2000) developed a handbook to help caregivers identify stressful situations and their own behaviors that set the stage for maltreatment. The book also provides resources for seeking assistance from others when needed. Caring for someone with dementia can be difficult, so providing extensive support and respite is crucial to prevent maltreatment.

concentration, and memory. Delirium may result from substance intoxication or medical situations such as anesthesia.

▶ Dementia is a more serious type of neurocognitive disorder that includes chronic and irreversible declines in memory and other cognitive processes. Neurocognitive disorders can be mild or major.

▶ The most common form of neurocognitive disorder is Alzheimer's disease, a progressive condition marked by cognitive deficits such as aphasia, apraxia, and agnosia and deficits in executive functioning.

▶ Neurocognitive disorder due to Lewy bodies occurs when masses of proteins create neuron damage.

▶ Vascular dementia is a neurocognitive disorder caused by a blood vessel problem, especially a stroke. People with vascular dementia often face a more abrupt and acute onset of symptoms but less cognitive impairment than people with Alzheimer's disease.

▶ Neurocognitive disorder may be due to Parkinson's disease, a progressive neurological disorder involving severe problems in motor functioning.

▶ Neurocognitive disorder due to Pick's disease is the most well-known of the frontotemporal dementias, meaning deterioration occurs in the frontal and temporal brain lobes.

▶ Neurocognitive disorders can also be caused by substances or medical conditions. Korsakoff's syndrome involves intense memory problems resulting from long-term alcohol use and thiamine deficiency.

▶ Dementia occurs in about 5 to 8 percent of older persons, and many people with one form of dementia also have another form of dementia.

▶ Caregiver, public, and structural stigma are often associated with neurocognitive disorders.

## REVIEW QUESTIONS

1. What normal changes in memory and general cognitive functioning occur with age?
2. Define and contrast delirium and dementia.
3. What problems commonly lead to dementia or neurocognitive disorder?
4. What is mixed dementia?
5. How common are different neurocognitive disorders in the general population?

# Neurocognitive Disorders: Causes and Prevention

Most disorders we have covered in this textbook generally involve a complex combination of biological and environmental risk factors. With neurocognitive disorders, however, biological changes play a dominant role. We thus concentrate on genetics, neurochemical changes, and major brain changes related to neurocognitive disorders. We do, however, discuss some evidence for environmental risk factors; awareness of these factors may help with prevention efforts regarding neurocognitive disorders.

## Biological Risk Factors for Neurocognitive Disorders

### GENETICS

A genetic link to neurocognitive disorders appears to be clearer in early-onset cases. Wingo and colleagues (2012) examined thousands of people with probable Alzheimer's disease. People with late-onset Alzheimer's disease had an estimated heritability rate of 64.6 to 75.0 percent, but people with early onset Alzheimer's disease (onset age <61 years) had an estimated heritability rate of 92 to 100 percent. The authors concluded that late-onset Alzheimer's disease likely has several environmental components but that early-onset Alzheimer's disease is almost purely a biological problem.

Another way of assessing genetic influence for Alzheimer's disease and other dementias is to evaluate twins. Two important studies from Scandinavia revealed concordance rates for Alzheimer's disease among monozygotic, or identical, twins to be 75 percent and 83 percent, respectively. This compares with much lower concordance rates for dizygotic, or nonidentical, twins: 25.9 percent and 46 percent, respectively (Bergem, Engedal, & Kringlen, 1997; Gatz et al., 1997). A more detailed twin analysis also revealed the concordance rate for Alzheimer's disease varied greatly among monozygotic twins (59 percent), same-gender dizygotic twins (32 percent), and different-gender dizygotic twins (24 percent; Gatz et al., 2005). These data suggest a genetic link to this neurocognitive disorder.

Four main genetic factors seem related to Alzheimer's disease:

- amyloid precursor protein and chromosome 21
- apolipoprotein E and chromosome 19
- presenilin 1 and chromosome 14
- presenilin 2 and chromosome 1

Amyloid precursor protein is a normal brain substance related to a specific gene on chromosome 21. This gene undergoes changes, or *mutations*, in some people (Weggen & Beher, 2012). As these gene mutations occur, devastating brain changes can result because large amounts of this protein are produced (see brain features section). Alzheimer's disease is found in a high percentage of people with Down syndrome (Chapter 13). People with Down syndrome usually have three #21 chromosomes and thus substantial overproduction of this protein (Ness et al., 2012).

Apolipoprotein E (APOE) is a protein related to a specific gene on chromosome 19. APOE, and especially one type of allele (gene part), APOE-4, are highly predictive of Alzheimer's disease in general and declines in episodic memory in particular (Donix, Small, & Bookheimer, 2012). APOE-4 is present in about 22 percent of the general population but in about 60 percent of people with Alzheimer's disease (Ashford & Mortimer, 2002). Like the amyloid precursor protein, APOE-4 causes severe brain changes, and the two substances likely interact in some way (O'Brien & Wong, 2011).

Other key influences to Alzheimer's disease include the presenilin 1 gene on chromosome 14 and the presenilin 2 gene

**THE CONTINUUM VIDEO PROJECT**

*Myriam:* **Alzheimer's Disease**

*"I'm going to forget their names. I'm going to forget who they are. Alzheimer's is eating away at my brain."*

Access the Continuum Video Project in MindTap at **www.cengagebrain.com**.

on chromosome 1 (Bekris, Yu, Bird, & Tsuang, 2010). These genes also mutate in some people and lead to massive brain changes. Approximately 180 mutations have been charted on the presenilin 1 gene alone (Chau, Crump, Villa, Scheinberg, & Li, 2012). Mutations of presenilin 1 may be associated with earlier onset of Alzheimer's disease, whereas mutations of presenilin 2 may be associated with later onset cases (Jayadev et al., 2010). Dozens of other genes also relate to Alzheimer's disease, and the true cause of the disorder likely involves the interaction of these many different genes (Bertram, Lill, & Tanzi, 2010).

What about other forms of dementia? Many single-gene disorders such as sickle cell disease predispose people toward stroke, a major cause of vascular dementia (Meschia, Brott, & Brown, 2005). Researchers have also identified genes that predispose people specifically toward strokes (Markus, 2011). Family history and twin studies suggest a genetic link for stroke as well (Kennedy et al., 2012). Others believe genetic factors implicated in Alzheimer's disease, including APOE-4, are likely present in vascular dementia as well. This may help explain *mixed dementia*, or the presence of Alzheimer's disease and vascular dementia in a person (Korczyn, Vakhapova, & Grinberg, 2012).

Other neurocognitive disorders have some genetic basis as well. Early forms of Parkinson's disease may relate to mutations in certain genes, called *parkin genes*, that cause neuron loss as well as harmful accumulation of proteins in the brain's substantia nigra region (Hardy, Lewis, Revesz, Lees, & Paisan-Ruiz, 2009). Frontotemporal dementias such as Pick's disease may relate to problems of the *tau gene* on chromosome 17. This gene is responsible for a protein that helps keep neurons from breaking apart, so mutations of the gene can lead to neuron disintegration (Seelaar, et al., 2011). Problems such as Korsakoff's syndrome may have some genetic basis as well, but conclusive evidence remains elusive (Thomson, Guerrini, & Marshall, 2012).

## NEUROCHEMICAL FEATURES

Neurochemical changes also influence the development of different neurocognitive disorders. Dementias are often marked by low levels of neurotransmitters, especially *acetylcholine*, *serotonin*, and *norepinephrine*. These neurotransmitter deficits may be especially pertinent to key brain areas such as the limbic system, as well as connections between the frontal

cortex and other brain areas (Weiner & Lipton, 2012). This may help explain some key features of dementia, including problems of memory and other cognitive functioning, motor behavior, and emotional and personality changes. Low levels of these neurotransmitters would also help explain symptoms that commonly occur with dementia, including apathy and depression (Chen, Reese, Kim, Rapoport, & Rao, 2011).

Another neurotransmitter lower among people with dementias, especially those with Parkinson's disease and dementia with Lewy bodies, is *dopamine*. People with Parkinson's disease show progressively lower levels of dopamine in the substantia nigra and other areas of the brain (Kansara, Trivedi, Chen, Jankovic, & Le, 2013). Lowered dopamine clearly relates to motor symptoms of Parkinson's disease and may influence Parkinson's-related dementia (Bohnen & Albin, 2011). People with Lewy body dementia also have lowered dopamine levels, though some overlap with Parkinson's disease is likely (Colloby, McParland, O'Brien, & Attems, 2012).

Other neurochemicals may occur in *excess* in people with dementia. One such substance is *L-glutamate*, which is an excitatory neurotransmitter in the brain. High levels of L-glutamate activity are present in people with Alzheimer's disease and may be high after an ischemic stroke, which could lead to vascular dementia (Beart & O'Shea, 2007). L-glutamate activity is important for normal learning and memory, but excessively high levels have been linked to neuron damage (Hu, Ondrejcak, & Rowan, 2012).

## BRAIN FEATURES

Genetic predispositions and neurochemical changes likely lead to massive brain changes in people with dementia, especially the following:

- *neurofibrillary tangles*, or twisted fibers inside nerve cells of the brain
- *senile* or *neuritic plaques*, or clusters of dead nerve cells and accumulations of amyloid proteins in the brain
- *Lewy bodies*, or deposits of alpha-synuclein proteins inside nerve cells of the brain
- *atrophy*, or gradual deterioration of different brain areas
- *oxidative stress* and *free radicals*, or damage to brain cells via oxygen exposure

**Neurofibrillary tangles** are a key aspect of dementia in general and Alzheimer's disease in particular. Neurons consist of a *microtubule*, or skeleton structure held together by a protein substance called *tau* (Spillantini & Goedert, 2013). Think of the neuron microtubule as the rails of a train track and the tau proteins as the railroad ties that hold the tracks together. The tau protein may become changed chemically and so the individual "railroad ties" become twisted around each other and eventually collapse (Bulic, Pickhardt, Mandelkow, & Mandelkow, 2010). The "tracks" of the neuron thus also collapse, and all of these pieces eventually snarl to form neurofibrillary tangles. The neurons in the brain begin to fall apart; and these fragments eventually collect in spheres and other shapes.

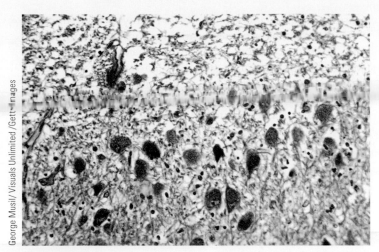

Neurofibrillary tangles, implicated in neurocognitive disorder in general and Alzheimer's disease in particular, impair various brain functions.

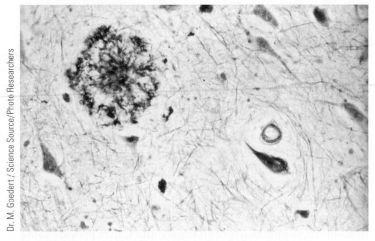

Neuritic plaques are a key aspect of Alzheimer's disease.

As neurofibrillary tangles occur more frequently and affect multiple areas, the brain's ability to coordinate behavior and communicate with the body becomes severely impaired (Mrak, 2012). A person with neurofibrillary tangles will have enormous problems with higher-order behaviors such as thinking and memory because the cortex and hippocampus of the brain are quite susceptible to this process (Lai, Chen, Hope, & Esiri, 2010). Lower-order behaviors such as motor skills and, eventually, life-support functions, become impaired as well. This process is a slow and gradual but irreversible one and helps explain much of the progressive deterioration of functioning in people with dementia like Mr. Ponder.

Another common brain change in people with dementia is **senile or neuritic plaques**. These plaques are made of certain proteins—*beta-amyloid proteins*—that accumulate in spaces between neurons in the brain (Lobello, Ryan, Liu, Rippon, & Black, 2012). Many proteins in the brain are *soluble*, meaning they can be dissolved or broken down by enzymes in the brain, but beta-amyloid proteins become *insoluble*. The proteins thus gradually accumulate into globs that eventually thicken by

combining with other immune and support cells in the brain. This process eventually causes massive damage and an inability to process information or even resist minor infections.

Beta-amyloid proteins are formed from a larger protein called amyloid precursor protein, or APP. Recall that large amounts of APP relate to mutations of chromosome 21. Senile or neuritic plaques are most common to the temporal and occipital brain lobes and somewhat common to the parietal lobe (Cummings, 2003). Another plaque often found in the brains of people with Alzheimer's disease is *diffuse plaque*, which is marked less by amyloid protein accumulations and is common to many elderly people and those with Down syndrome. Diffuse plaques may be a precursor to senile/neuritic plaques, but more research remains needed (Rudolph & Vegrzyn, 2012).

Lewy bodies also represent collections of proteins in the brain that cause damage and are found in many people with dementia. Lewy bodies are not beta-amyloid proteins but rather *alpha-synuclein proteins* (Bennett, 2005). Alpha-synuclein proteins can also become insoluble, accumulate on the synapses of neurons and block effective transmission of information. Lewy body accumulation is likely due to genetic changes (Ho et al., 2011). Such accumulation has been implicated most in people with Alzheimer's disease, Parkinson's disease, and, of course, dementia with Lewy bodies (Lundvig, Lindersson, & Jensen, 2005).

Other brain changes in people with dementia involve gradual **atrophy**, or deterioration, of key areas related to thinking, memory, personality, and other important functions. A gradual withering of the frontal and temporal lobes is seen in people with frontotemporal dementia such as Pick's disease. This atrophy is likely the result of key genetic changes, especially on chromosome 17, and involves intense deterioration of the neurons in these areas (Goedert & Jakes, 2005). *Pick bodies* may infest these areas as well and comprise various tau fibrils similar to what happens in neurofibrillary tangles (Uematsu, Adachi, Nakamura, Tsuchiya, & Uchihara, 2012).

Brain atrophy also affects the substantia nigra in people with Parkinson's disease, which is a main dopamine pathway

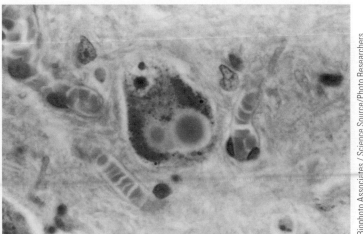

Many cases of neurocognitive disorder involve Lewy bodies, proteins that accumulate in the brain.

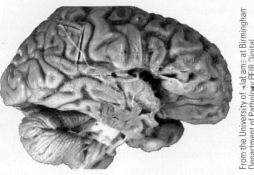

Atrophy of the frontotemporal regions of the brain occurs in people with Pick's disease. A healthy brain would not have the large gaps seen in this photo.

controlling motor behavior (Lehericy, Sharman, Santos, Paquin, & Gallea, 2012). Fewer neurons appear over time. We mentioned earlier that Lewy bodies may also be found in people with Parkinson's disease. Atrophy in Parkinson's disease likely relates to the specific chromosomal changes we mentioned earlier.

Effects of a stroke or other cerebrovascular disease can vary tremendously in people with vascular dementia. These effects may include cortical as well as subcortical areas of the brain. Key brain areas that can be affected, other than the cortex, include the angular gyrus, caudate nucleus, thalamus, basal ganglia, and white matter (Askin-Edgar et al., 2004). These areas are especially important for coordinating visual and auditory information, language comprehension, and motor behavior.

Other brain changes in people with dementia involve **oxidative stress** and **free radicals.** Brain cells are normally exposed to oxygen, which can damage the cells, but antioxidants in vitamins and other substances help prevent major damage. Oxidative stress involves general cell or tissue damage and brain inflammation that can occur when antioxidants are insufficient (Bennett, Grant, & Aldred, 2009). Oxidative stress relates closely to release of free radicals in the brain; free radicals are aggressive substances possibly produced to fight

viruses and bacteria. Oxidative stress from very high amounts of free radicals can be caused by many things, including stroke, brain injury, pollution, smoking, or excessive alcohol use (Willcox, Ash, & Catignani, 2004). Oxidative stress with resulting brain injury appears to be a significant risk factor in people with dementia (Behl, 2012). For the major brain areas implicated in dementia, see **Figure 14.5.**

## Environmental Risk Factors for Neurocognitive Disorders

Biological risk factors clearly predominate in people with neurocognitive disorders, but some evidence suggests that environmental risk factors can be influential as well. We next cover issues of diet, alcohol and tobacco use, aluminum, and cultural factors.

### DIET

Diet may be a risk factor for certain cases of Alzheimer's disease or other dementias. Dementia is probably not connected to one type of nutrient but perhaps to different food substances (Luchsinger & Mayeux, 2004). Medications or vitamins rich in *antioxidants* may help slow the progression of dementia. We are exposed daily to various oxidants, such as ozone ($O_3$), but over time these can lead to beta-amyloid protein accumulation and neuron cell damage in the brain (Munoz, Sole, & Coma, 2005). Ingesting antioxidants from yellow-orange fruits such as cantaloupe and green vegetables (for beta-carotene), and taking vitamins C and E, which have antioxidant qualities, are thus especially important.

High levels of antioxidants may slow (although not stop) the progression of Alzheimer's disease, perhaps lower the risk for developing dementia, or protect against cognitive decline, though data remain mixed (Crichton, Bryan, & Murphy, 2013). In addition, supplements of vitamin E and C may provide some protection from vascular and other dementia (von Arnim et al., 2012). Other researchers have examined effects of other nutrients on cognitive functioning, especially vitamins B6, B12, and folic acid. Data are mixed, however, as to whether levels of these substances relate to the presence of Alzheimer's disease and whether supplements of these nutrients help improve symptoms of dementia (Balk et al., 2007). Vitamin B12 and folic acid help reduce *homocysteine*, high levels of which can cause artery damage (Lamberti et al., 2005).

A diet including ample amounts of fish, fruit, and vegetables, known as the "Mediterranean diet," may reduce risk for neurocognitive disorder.

Loss of neurons in the substantia nigra is a main feature of Parkinson's disease.

2010). Flavonoids are common to certain kinds of alcohol such as red wine.

Early studies indicated that tobacco use may be associated with reduced risk of dementia because nicotine increases acetylcholine, reduces stress, and enhances attention and general cognitive functioning (Swan & Lessov-Schlagger, 2007). Others have found heavy smoking related to *increased* risk for Alzheimer's disease, however (Rusanen, Kivipelto, Quesenberry, Zhou, & Whitmer, 2011). Smoking to prevent dementia would be pointless anyway given the substantial health risks of the behavior (Chapter 9).

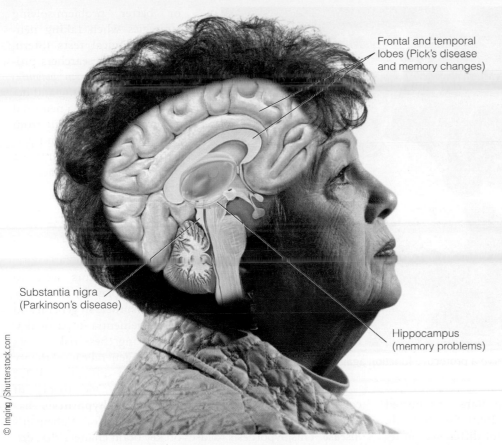

Frontal and temporal lobes (Pick's disease and memory changes)

Substantia nigra (Parkinson's disease)

Hippocampus (memory problems)

© Imging /Shutterstock.com

**FIGURE 14.5** MAJOR BRAIN AREAS IMPLICATED IN NEUROCOGNITIVE DISORDERS
Copyright © Cengage Learning®

## ALUMINUM

Another possible environmental risk factor for dementia is exposure to various toxins. Some researchers have focused on *aluminum*, a common metal ingested from air, food, or water (Mohammadirad & Abdollahi, 2011). Aluminum toxicity, which produces oxidation effects and increased beta-amyloid proteins and free radicals, could result in brain tissue damage and onset of age-related cognitive decline (Shcherbatykh & Carpenter, 2007).

Some researchers found that eating foods with high levels of aluminum, such as pancakes, biscuits, and American cheese, was more common among people with Alzheimer's disease than those without the disorder. Aluminum is also present in neurofibrillary tangles (Frisardi et al., 2010).

People who eat high amounts of curry, such as people from India, those who ingest fluoride, and those with increased melatonin may have lower rates of Alzheimer's disease because these substances reduce aluminum absorption (Jansson, 2005). Others claim no conclusive link can yet be made between aluminum exposure and Alzheimer's disease (Bondy, 2010).

Increased saturated fat and cholesterol intake has sometimes been found related to cognitive decline (Okereke et al., 2012), although not always (Engelhart et al., 2002b). Increased fish or seafood intake seems related to lower risk of dementia as well (Devore et al., 2009). A healthy diet heavy in fruits, vegetables, and fish will also help prevent cardiovascular conditions that could produce vascular dementia. These conditions include diabetes, hypertension, obesity, stroke, and coronary artery disease (Perez, Heim, Sherzai, Jaceldo-Siegl, & Sherzai, 2012). A heart-healthy diet also seems useful as a brain-healthy diet. Your mom was right all along: Eat your veggies!

## ALCOHOL AND TOBACCO USE

People who drink *moderate* amounts of alcohol are less likely to experience dementia compared to people who abstain from alcohol (Anstey, Mack, & Cherbuin, 2009). This finding may apply only to people without substantial genetic predisposition for dementia (Luchsinger, Tang, Siddiqui, Shea, & Mayeux, 2004). People who drink *large* amounts of alcohol are clearly at risk for memory and cognitive deficits, however.

Moderate alcohol use may protect some people from vascular damage, reduce stress, enhance acetylcholine release from the hippocampus to improve memory, and increase social interaction among older adults (Mukamal et al., 2003; Takahashi, Caldwell, & Targonski, 2011). A key element of alcohol—*flavonoids*—has excellent antioxidant properties as well (Grassi, Desideri, & Ferri,

## CULTURAL FACTORS

Recall that Alzheimer's disease may be more prevalent among Western nations and vascular dementia may be more prevalent among Asian and other non-Western nations. This may be partly explained by how dementia is considered within a cultural context and whether shame and stigma are associated with severe cognitive dysfunction (Poveda, 2003). Native Americans tend to view dementia as a normal part of aging and as an expected part of one's transition to the next world (Jervis & Manson, 2002). Asians often emphasize more socially acceptable physical factors to explain dementia, resulting in more reported cases of vascular dementia than Alzheimer's disease. Dementia among Nigerians is seen as a debilitating condition that prevents one from completing prayer and

Keith morris / Alamy

Flavonoids such as those in red wine may serve a protective function against neurocognitive disorder.

work that requires higher-level cognition. Rates of reported dementia are thus quite low (Ineichen, 2000; Suh & Shah, 2001). Stigma may thus be a key reason for differences in reported dementia. Genetic and dietary differences across the world can also be fairly large and help explain cultural differences in dementia (Kalaria et al., 2008).

Cultural factors may also apply to caregivers of those with dementia. Minority caregivers often report more unmet service needs for family members with dementia. This may be due to lack of information about available diagnostic and treatment services, inaccurate diagnosis, poor feedback from physicians, and less membership in support groups (Lampley-Dallas, 2002). Other reasons may include insensitivity of assessments (as discussed later in the chapter) to cultural differences in cognition, reluctance to use medical and social services perceived as racist, and language barriers (Daker-White, Beattie, Gilliard, & Means, 2002). On the other hand, African Americans generally view the caregiver role as less stressful and burdensome than European Americans, perhaps because of greater reliance on religion and extended family support (Janevic & Connell, 2001).

## OTHER FACTORS

Many other environmental risk factors could lead to dementia, including viral infections such as HIV and accidents leading to brain injury (Deeks, 2011). Other significant risk factors could include poverty, malnutrition, poor parental education, and low socioeconomic status. Family history of dementia appears to be a better predictor of whether someone will acquire dementia than these variables, however (Graves, 2004).

Stronger educational background is often linked to less dementia, possibly because cognitive decline is harder to identify. Highly educated people may have more *cognitive reserve,*

or better problem-solving strategies when taking neuropsychological tests (Stern, 2012). Some researchers propose that *long-term potentiation, or strengthening and development* of new neuronal connections, can result from enhanced education and perhaps help reduce dementia onset (Valenzuela & Sachdev, 2009). So, study hard!

## Causes of Neurocognitive Disorders

Many risk factors seem to come into play for neurocognitive disorders in general and severe dementia in particular. Organizing these risk factors into one general causal theory has been a difficult task for researchers. One theory of cognitive disorders—the **amyloid cascade hypothesis**—has received great research attention, especially for Alzheimer's disease. This hypothesis focuses on key brain changes that can cascade or result from various genetic and environmental factors and which, in the end, help produce a state of dementia (Reitz, 2012). **Figure 14.6** illustrates a version of the amyloid cascade hypothesis.

A central aspect of the amyloid cascade hypothesis is that progressive dementias are at least partly caused by a toxic buildup of beta-amyloid proteins that lead to neuron damage and senile plaques. Amyloid precursor protein is a normal protein that the body regularly splices into shorter pieces. This splicing process is done by different enzymes called *secretases* and, in particular, *alpha-secretase, beta-secretase,* and *gamma-secretase* (O'Brien & Wong, 2011). This is a normal process for all of us.

For reasons still unclear, beta-secretase and gamma-secretase often combine to produce the protein A-beta, or beta-amyloid (Quigley, Colloby, & O'Brien, 2011). Again, this process is normal and not usually harmful because beta-amyloid is often soluble and dissolves quickly. Beta-amyloid becomes insoluble, or fails to dissolve, in some people, however. Large deposits of beta-amyloid thus collect and form senile plaques, contribute to the development of neurofibrillary tangles and neurotransmitter changes, and perhaps force the overproduction of free radicals (Reddy, 2009). These toxic effects help lead to the brain damage central to dementia.

A key question in this model is what factors lead initially to changes in amyloid precursor protein splicing and toxic buildup of beta-amyloid. The answer, although still not definitive, may involve a combination of genetic and dietary or other environmental factors. We mentioned earlier that changes in chromosome 21 and presenilin genes may lead to

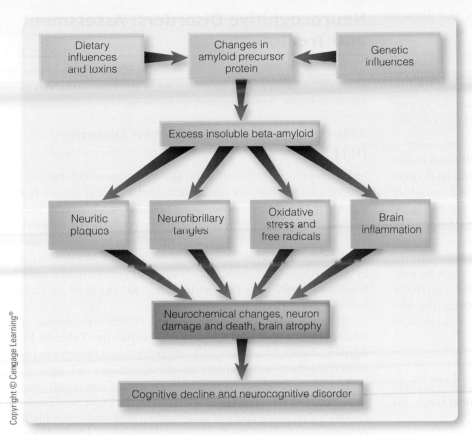

**FIGURE 14.6** **SCHEMATIC OF THE AMYLOID CASCADE HYPOTHESIS**

overproduction of amyloid precursor protein, such that huge amounts of beta-amyloid are also produced. The APOE-4 gene has also been closely linked to amyloid buildup and neurofibrillary tangles (Karran, Mercken, & De Strooper, 2011).

Diet likely intersects with genetic factors to act as a contributor to neurocognitive disorders via toxic amyloid buildup but also as a protective factor via high antioxidants. The interaction of diet and genes may help explain why people of some cultures experience less Alzheimer's disease and other neurocognitive disorders. Those whose diets are rich in fish, fruits, vegetables, and curry may experience fewer cognitive problems than those whose diets are rich in fat, cholesterol, and possibly aluminum, although studies vary (Smith & Blumenthal, 2010).

The amyloid cascade hypothesis was largely designed as an explanation for Alzheimer's disease. Still, genetic changes that lead to certain body and brain alterations are likely main characteristics of other neurocognitive disorders as well. Many people are genetically predisposed to hypertension, diabetes, obesity, and stroke and possible vascular dementia (Kalaria, 2012). Genetic changes are also important for aggressive neurocognitive disorders such as Pick's disease as well as alcoholism that can lead to Korsakoff's syndrome (Seelaar et al., 2011). Some cases of Parkinson's disease are likely related to mutations in parkin genes that help create neuron damage and atrophy to brain areas such as the substantia nigra (Dawson & Dawson, 2010).

Discovering the true cause of these devastating and tragic disorders will likely be a high priority for future researchers given the substantially greater number of people who will be living lengthy lives. The debilitating nature of neurocognitive disorders also means a high priority for prevention, a topic we discuss next.

## Prevention of Neurocognitive Disorders

We mentioned earlier one factor likely important for preventing Alzheimer's disease and other neurocognitive disorders: *diet*. People whose diets are healthy will be at less risk for cerebrovascular problems that could lead to dementia. General recommendations include diets that restrict calories and are rich in antioxidants, folic acid, fish oils, cereals, and *moderate* amounts of red wine—the so-called Mediterranean diet (Feart, Samieri, Alles, & Barberger-Gateau, 2013). Diet may reduce risk of dementia but not necessarily its course in people strongly genetically predisposed to neurocognitive disorder, however (Barberger-Gateau et al., 2013).

People with high-cholesterol diets or whose cholesterol is set genetically to a high level may benefit from a class of drugs called *statins*. These drugs help lower cholesterol levels. Statin drugs have not prevented onset of Alzheimer's disease or other forms of dementia, however (McGuinness et al., 2013). People with high cholesterol will benefit from *exercise* as well. Some animal data indicate that exercise can increase a protective substance known as *brain-derived neurotrophic factor* that may enhance hippocampus activity and memory (Gomez-Pinilla, Zhuang, Feng, Ying, & Fan, 2011). Physical activity in humans may help prevent cognitive decline but not necessarily dementia (Rolland, van Kan, & Vellas, 2010).

Another focus of prevention involves *cognitively stimulating environments*, which include surroundings that constantly challenge the brain and help develop new neuronal connections. Social interactions with others and new intellectual stimulation seem particularly important for preventing cognitive decline (Stern, 2012). To help prevent cognitive decline:

- Continue to stay as socially active as possible and meet new people.
- Continue reading and writing, but try new publications such as detective novels.
- Take a new class to learn a skill such as carpentry or mechanics.
- Learn to play a musical instrument or speak a foreign language.
- Play mentally challenging games such as chess, and assemble puzzles.
- Travel and learn about new cultures.

- Seek treatment for stress and psychological and medical problems.
- Keep regular lists of things to do as well as a detailed daily calendar.
- Challenge your memory by recalling recent events on a regular basis, such as what you had for dinner three nights ago or the name of a new person you met yesterday.

Various drugs may also help reduce beta-amyloid build-up and prevent the cascade of problems that lead to dementia. These drugs include nonsteroidal anti-inflammatory drugs and aspirin, hormone replacement therapy using estrogen, and immunizations to clear beta-amyloid buildup in the brain (Lobello et al., 2012). Lack of tobacco use as well as drugs to reduce the chance of stroke, such as antihypertension and anticlotting medications, are important as well. *Gene therapy* will likely be the approach to revolutionize the prevention of Alzheimer's disease and other dementias, and we discuss this more in the later treatment section (Nilsson et al., 2010).

## INTERIM SUMMARY

▶ Biological risk factors for neurocognitive disorders include genetics; identical twins display more concordance for Alzheimer's disease than nonidentical twins.

▶ Genetic changes in neurocognitive disorders include chromosome 21 and amyloid precursor protein, chromosome 19 and apolipoprotein E, and chromosomes 14 and 1 and presenilin 1 and 2.

▶ Neurochemical changes in neurocognitive disorders include low levels of acetylcholine, serotonin, norepinephrine, and dopamine and high levels of L-glutamate.

▶ Brain changes in neurocognitive disorders often include neurofibrillary tangles, senile plaques, Lewy bodies, atrophy, and oxidative stress and free radicals.

▶ Environmental factors may also influence neurocognitive disorders, especially diets high in antioxidants and fish and low in fat and cholesterol.

▶ Moderate alcohol use may be related to less dementia, but aluminum intake may relate to more dementia.

▶ The amyloid cascade hypothesis refers to various brain changes cascading from genetic and environmental factors to produce neurocognitive disorder.

▶ Prevention of neurocognitive disorder will likely hinge on diet, exercise, cognitive stimulation, medications, and perhaps gene therapy.

## REVIEW QUESTIONS

1. Describe genetic mutations associated with neurocognitive disorders.
2. What neurochemical and brain changes are central to dementia?
3. What dietary factors might relate closely to dementia?
4. Describe the amyloid cascade hypothesis.
5. Outline a strategy for preventing dementia.

# Neurocognitive Disorders: Assessment and Treatment

We have covered some of the major features and causes of neurocognitive disorders, so we turn next to different strategies to assess and treat these devastating problems.

## Assessment of Neurocognitive Disorders

### INTERVIEWS

Interviews to gather information about someone with possible neurocognitive disorder could include the person herself but will likely also include close family members and friends. This is especially so in cases involving severe cognitive or memory problems. Interviews of significant others can be especially useful if a person is currently in a state of delirium. Interviews for people with possible dementia are often designed to determine whether a problem is the result of normal aging or an early form of severe neurocognitive disorder.

Interviews for people with possible Alzheimer's disease or other dementia will often cover some key topics (see **Table 14.10**; Agronin, 2008). An assessor will search for recent changes in behavior, thinking, and memory as well as changes in long-term skills such as language or ability to recognize others. Mr. and Mrs. Ponder's interview led the neuropsychologist to initially conclude that some form of neurocognitive disorder was likely occurring given their confusion and memory problems. Interviews are also commonly used in this population to assess for comorbid problems such as depression, anxiety, and psychosis.

Interviews with people with possible neurocognitive disorder are generally done to conduct a **mental status examination.** A mental status examination involves detailed questioning and observation of key areas of functioning such as appearance, mood, orientation, and odd behaviors, speech, or thoughts (Mitchell, 2009). A clinician may pay close attention to disorganized attire, incoherent speech, agitation, bizarre thought patterns, aphasic speech, motor problems, and flat affect. A person's ability to be oriented to person, place, and time is also assessed. A clinician may ask someone to state her name, where she is, and current day and year. Failure to answer these basic questions appropriately may indicate a neurocognitive disorder.

Interviewing caregivers of people with neurocognitive disorder is also an extremely important assessment area. Key topics to be covered here include family history of neurocognitive disorder, a person's need for help in various areas such as dressing, financial and other resources for care, knowledge about dementia, physical and emotional health of the caregiver, social support, and quality of life of the family (Mittelman, Epstein, & Pierzchala, 2003). Recall that Mrs. Ponder said her quality of life was diminishing because her health was dwindling and she could no longer fully care for her husband.

### QUESTIONNAIRES

Mental status examinations and assessment of cognitive functioning can also be done via questionnaires, which may be administered in interview format. A commonly used measure to screen

---

**Table 14.10**

| **Possible Early Signs and Symptoms of Dementia** | |
|---|---|
| Sign | Symptoms |
| Forgetfulness | Commonly manifested as short-term memory loss for recently learned names, appointments, purpose of activities, points of conversation, and completed tasks or errands. An individual may repeat questions or requests. The degree of forgetfulness begins to interfere with daily activities and responsibilities. |
| Disorientation | Episodic confusion regarding the exact day, date, or location. |
| Impaired performance on daily tasks | Difficulty performing everyday tasks, such as preparing meals, running household appliances, cleaning, and hygiene (e.g., bathing, toileting, brushing teeth). |
| Impaired language | Increasing difficulty with selecting and using words. Sentences may become simpler or fragmented. |
| Impaired recognition | Diminished ability to remember or identify familiar faces, objects, sounds, and locations. |
| Impaired abstract thinking | Diminished ability to think clearly about issues, to discuss complex issues and to make logical connections between them, or to comprehend fully things that were previously understood. |
| Impaired judgment | Impairment in the ability to organize and plan and to make appropriate decisions or selections among several possibilities. A person may act in ways that were previously deemed uncharacteristic or inappropriate. |
| Changes in mood or behavior | Change in mood and behavior that may take many forms, including increased irritability, loss of emotional control (e.g., intense anger, frustration, tearfulness), abusive or inappropriate language, loss of pleasure in particular activities, and apathetic attitudes. |
| Changes in personality | The person may seem less sociable or more self-centered and may act out in disruptive or disinhibited ways. He or she may also seem more suspicious, fearful, or bothered by others, and reactions to everyday stress may be out of proportion. |

From M.E. Agronin, *Alzheimer Disease and Other Dementias: A Practical Guide* (2nd ed.), p. 19. Copyright © 2008 by Lippincott Williams and Wilkins. Reprinted by permission.

---

for neurocognitive disorder is the *Mini-Mental State Examination* (MMSE-2), a 30-item questionnaire that covers orientation, verbal and written comprehension, concentration, learning, writing and copying, and memory (**Figure 14.7**; Folstein, & Folstein, 2010). The MMSE-2 takes only 10 to 15 minutes to administer and can distinguish people with or without dementia. Other commonly used screening tests include the *Mini-Cog* (Lorentz, Scanlan, & Borson, 2002), *Dementia Rating Scale* (Jurica, Leitten, & Mattis, 2001), *Delirium Rating Scale-Revised* (Trzepacz et al., 2001), and *Confusion Assessment Method*, the latter of which can assess delirium even in the presence of dementia (Inouye et al., 2005).

Screening tests for dementia can also be very brief and include asking a person to draw a clock face for a given time (**Figure 14.8**), tell time, make change for a dollar, and spell various words backward (Ismail, Rajji, & Shulman, 2010). Many questionnaires are also available to assess conditions related to delirium and dementia that we covered in previous chapters. Particularly important conditions include anxiety, depression, and adaptive behavior.

## COGNITIVE ASSESSMENT

More formal tests can also be used to assess symptoms of neurocognitive disorders, especially if a screening questionnaire indicates delirium or dementia or if memory problems are clearly evident. A common example is the *Wechsler Memory Scale* (WMS-IV; Wechsler, 2009). The WMS consists of various subtests that measure immediate and delayed memory for visual and auditory stimuli as well as working memory. A person may be asked to immediately recall different words (*tree, table, dime*) and then, later in the test, be asked to recall them again. The WMS is often used in research and clinical settings to assess Alzheimer's disease and other dementias and was used for Mr. Ponder (Hori, Sanjo, Tomita, & Mizusawa, 2013).

We covered other formal tests of cognitive functioning in previous chapters and so just mention them here. These primarily include intelligence tests such as the *Wechsler Adult Intelligence Scale* and neuropsychological tests such as the *Halstead-Reitan* (Chapters 12 and 13). These tests are useful for charting changes in cognitive ability over time to determine whether these changes are normal or an early form of neurocognitive disorder. Certain subtests of these scales are also useful for determining the extent of damage following a stroke. A clinician can examine certain "hold" tests such as vocabulary that tend to remain stable even after brain damage. Other methods include examining a specific profile of scores that seem predictive of people with Alzheimer's disease (Oosterman & Scherder, 2006).

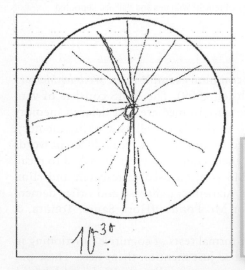

Orientation to time

"What is the date?"

Registration

"Listen carefully. I am going to say three words. You say them back after I stop.

Ready? Here they are...

APPLE (pause), PENNY (pause), TABLE (pause). Now repeat those words back to me." [Repeat up to 5 times, but score only the first trial.]

Naming

"What is this?" [Point to a pencil or pen.]

Reading

"Please read this and do what it says." [Show examinee the words on the stimulus form.]

CLOSE YOUR EYES

**FIGURE 14.7** THE MINI-MENTAL STATE EXAMINATION (MMSE) SAMPLE ITEMS *Reproduced by special permission of the publisher, Psychological Assessment Resources, Inc., 16204 North Florida Avenue, Lutz, Florida 33549, from the Mini-Mental State Examination, by Marshal Folstein and Susan Folstein, Copyright 1975, 1998, 2001 by Mini Mental LLC, Inc. Published 2001 by Psychological Assessment Resources, Inc. Further reproduction is prohibited without permission of PAR, Inc. The MMSE can be purchased from PAR, Inc. by calling (813) 968-3003.*

**Patient**
Male, 75 years old
MMSE = 28 points

**Clinical diagnosis:**
Probable AD

**Autopsy 4 yrs later:**
Definite AD

**FIGURE 14.8** CLOCK DRAWING TEST FOR A 75-YEAR-OLD MALE WITH PROBABLE ALZHEIMER'S DISEASE *From Taylor, K.I., & Monsch, A.U. (2004). The neuropsychology of Alzheimer's disease. In R.W. Richter & B.Z. Richter (Eds.), Alzheimer's disease: A physician's guide to practical management (p. 119). Reprinted by permission of Springer/Humana Press.*

## MEDICAL AND LABORATORY ASSESSMENT

People who may have a neurocognitive disorder are often referred first to a physician for evaluation. A medical examination will likely include tests for cardiovascular and thyroid problems, substance intoxication, HIV and other infections, dehydration,

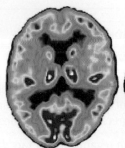 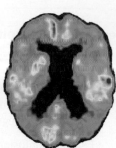 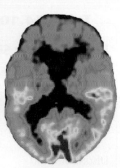

Courtesy, Dr. Arthur W. Toga, Laboratory of Neuro Imaging at UCLA

**FIGURE 14.9** PET SCANS OF BRAINS OF A NORMAL ELDERLY PERSON, LEFT; A PERSON WITH ALZHEIMER'S DISEASE, MIDDLE; AND A PERSON WITH FRONTOTEMPORAL DEGENERATION, RIGHT. *Courtesy, Dr. Arthur W. Toga, Laboratory of Neuro Imaging at UCLA.*

and other basic factors that could explain delirium or dementia (Agronin, 2008). A medical examination could also include more extensive laboratory procedures we discussed in Chapters 4 and 12: *computerized tomography* (CT scan), *magnetic resonance imaging* (MRI scan), *positron emission tomography* (PET scan), and *single photon emission computed tomography* (SPECT). MRI and PET scans are usually recommended as more definitive ways of determining Alzheimer's disease and other dementias (Marcus, Fotenos, Csernansky, Morris, & Buckner, 2010; Quigley, Colloby, & O'Brien, 2011; **Figure 14.9**).

## Biological Treatments of Neurocognitive Disorders

### MEDICATION

Neurocognitive disorders are clearly affected by many biological variables and will certainly become more common given the rapidly aging population around the globe. The search for medical cures for neurocognitive disorder thus remains a high priority for researchers. Many drugs for people with other mental disorders we described in this textbook are given to people with dementia. These drugs include antidepressants and mood stabilizers (Chapter 7) and antipsychotics (Chapter 12). These medications are useful for easing behavioral problems (such as delusions/hallucinations) associated with dementia, or depression or delirium, but are not too useful for changing severe cognitive and memory deficits brought on by Alzheimer's disease and other dementias (Gentile, 2010; Nelson & Devanand, 2011).

Researchers have thus focused on **cholinesterase inhibitors**. These drugs enhance the neurotransmitter acetylcholine, which is deficient in people with dementia and memory problems. These drugs inhibit enzymes in the brain from breaking down acetylcholine so more of the neurotransmitter is available. The primary cholinesterase inhibitors that have been studied include *physostigmine, tacrine, metrifonate, donepezil, rivastigmine*, and *galantamine*, and especially the latter three (Hyde et al., 2013). These drugs produce only a modest increase in functioning for people with mild to moderate neurocognitive disorder, however, and work better if given sooner in the disease process (Small & Bullock, 2011).

Another drug, *memantine*, helps control excess L-glutamate activity. Memantine has some beneficial cognitive effect for people with moderate to severe neurocognitive disorder (Hermann, Li, & Lanctot, 2011). People with Parkinson's disease, a disorder that could lead to dementia, often take the drug *levodopa* (*L-dopa*) to increase dopamine levels in the brain, sometimes in concert with surgical strategies (Huot, Johnston, Koprich, Fox, & Brotchie, 2013). Overall, a combination of medications is often used to treat dementia (Tjia et al., 2010). Over time, however, the steady progression of dementia eventually overwhelms drug effectiveness.

### GENE THERAPY

A revolutionary approach to future treatment of neurocognitive disorder will likely include **gene therapy**, or introduction of genes to a person to help increase neuron growth and regeneration. Healthy genes are generally introduced not to replace but to compensate for dysfunctions from problematic genes. Gene therapy is highly experimental now but has the potential to address some of the most devastating mental and physical disorders in humans. Some success has been shown in animal studies, but the approach requires pinpoint accuracy to prevent adverse effects (Nilsson et al., 2010).

### RESIDENTIAL AND NURSING HOME CARE

Many biological treatments for people with dementia are given in hospitals, residential hospices, and nursing homes. Psychiatric care in these settings often consists of managing behavior problems such as hypersexuality, easing emotional issues such as depression, and reducing infections and pain (Collet, de Vugt, Verhey, & Schols, 2010). Hospice care is especially beneficial to people experiencing later, end-of-life stages of dementia. A family's decision to place a loved one in hospice or nursing home care can be excruciating, however, as it was for the Ponder family. Some questions for family members in this difficult position include the following (adapted from Mittelman et al., 2003):

- What would the person with dementia have wanted?

- What is the recommendation of the person's medical doctor?

- Will entry into a hospice or nursing home help reduce a person's suffering?

- What are the financial and emotional burdens of home care versus hospice/nursing home care?

- Do most family members feel a certain way in this decision?

- Do family members feel comfortable giving control of a person's care to others?

- What services are offered at the hospice or nursing home?

- What provisions are in place at the hospice or nursing home to maximize safety?

## Psychological Treatments of Neurocognitive Disorders

Biological approaches to neurocognitive disorders are a popular area of research, but their general ineffectiveness at this stage means psychological approaches to improve a person's quality of life remain extremely important. Psychological treatments may be divided into two groups: those that target the person with neurocognitive disorder and those that focus on the person's caregivers.

### PSYCHOLOGICAL APPROACHES FOR PEOPLE WITH NEUROCOGNITIVE DISORDERS

Psychological approaches targeted toward people with neurocognitive disorders are generally conducted in earlier stages of the disorder when confusion and disorientation are not yet severe. These approaches are designed to improve a person's quality of life and enhance cognitive functioning to delay onset of more severe symptoms. We described some of these approaches previously in this textbook, including *reminiscence therapy* (Chapter 7). Reminiscence therapy involves a thorough review of a person's life to impart a sense of meaning and resolve remaining interpersonal conflicts or regrets. A person with dementia will likely lose the ability to interact with others, so such reflection will hopefully enhance present well-being and provide a positive sense of closure to one's life (Subramaniam & Woods, 2012).

Another popular psychological therapy aimed toward people with neurocognitive disorder is **reality orientation**. This

Reality orientation kits are often used to help guide people with moderate Alzheimer's disease. The reality orientation clock this woman is holding, which includes the time and days, is frequently pointed out and used in conversations with her.

David hancock / Alamy

is a technique to reduce confusion in people with dementia and often involves constant feedback about time, place, person, and recent events (Spector, Orrell, & Hall, 2012). A person may be consistently reminded about his daily events, settings, and identity. Often this consists of placing clocks and calendars around the living environment, directional arrows to places such as the refrigerator, and pictures to remind a person of loved ones. Reality orientation could be done by staff members at a nursing home or by family members at home. Reality orientation may have some initial benefits on cognitive functioning and may even delay nursing home placement, but these benefits are likely best for people in early and intermediate stages of neurocognitive disorder (Van Mierlo, Van der Roest, Meiland, & Droes, 2010).

**Memory training** is used for people with neurocognitive disorders as well. A person is taught to enhance memory performance by repeatedly practicing various skills such as using a microwave oven, relying on external cues and mnemonic strategies to jog memory, increasing social interaction, and simplifying her living environment so less needs to be remembered. Common strategies include a "memory wallet" that contains written reminders and pictures of loved ones a person can refer to when faced with loss of memory and painting various rooms in bright, different colors and cues for easy identification (e.g., "blue" for bedroom with a picture of a bed; Mahendra, Scullion, & Hamerschlag, 2011). Obstacles that interfere with memory, such as depression, apathy, or cognitive distortions, are addressed as well (Gates, Sachdev, Singh, & Valenzuela, 2011). Memory training is likely best for people in the early stages of a neurocognitive disorder.

*Behavior therapy* is another common form of treatment for people with neurocognitive disorder but one that focuses on reducing behavior problems and increasing frequency of self-care skills. Behavior problems typically addressed in this population include wandering alone, hypersexuality, depression, verbal and physical aggression, and agitation. Self-care skills typically addressed in this population include feeding, dressing, toileting, and grooming (Buchanan, Christenson, Houlihan, & Ostrom, 2011). Family members are taught to positively reward appropriate behaviors and redirect or ignore (if possible) inappropriate behaviors. This approach is often used in combination with reality orientation and memory training as well as music, art, and movement therapies to increase cognitive stimulation (Aguirre, Woods, Spector, & Orrell, 2013).

## PSYCHOLOGICAL APPROACHES FOR CAREGIVERS OF PEOPLE WITH NEUROCOGNITIVE DISORDERS

Other psychological approaches for addressing people with neurocognitive disorder focus more on caregivers such as spouses and other family members. A critical first step when addressing caregivers is to provide *information* about the nature of dementia and provide extensive social support and other resources (Gallagher-Thompson et al., 2010). Information about dementia should include its major symptoms, cause, and course over time. Caregivers should know what to expect of a person in coming weeks and months, such as serious cognitive decline, and begin to plan accordingly. This often involves creating living wills and power of attorney documents, as well as resolving current or past conflicts (Robinson et al., 2012; see **Box 14.2**).

Resources should also be established so caregivers are relieved of the everyday burden of caring for someone with dementia. Arrangements can be made to rotate or add family

---

## BOX 14.2  Focus on Gender

### Grief in the Spouse Caregiver

Treatment for people with dementia often falls to spouses who care for their loved one—most people with dementia live at home. Much has been written about the difficulty of such treatment and how support and respite care are so important, but little has been written about the general grief spouses go through when encountering this tragic situation. Such grief often includes thoughts about gradual isolation from one's life partner, increasing realization of the shortness of life, and sense of meaninglessness and hopelessness about the current situation (Chan, Livingston, Jones, & Sampson, 2013). Grief of this nature usually accompanies strong feelings of anxiety, anger, sadness, and guilt, especially among wives of husbands with dementia (Noyes et al., 2010).

Spousal caregivers and child caregivers differ in their approach to grief (Conde-Sala, Garre-Olmo, Turro-Garriga, Vilalta-Franch, & Lopez-Pousa, 2010). Children who care for a parent with dementia tend to deny the presence of dementia and focus on how a parent's dementia affects them. Spousal caregivers, however, tend to be more open about accepting their spouse's dementia and the burdens of care to come. Spousal caregivers also tend to focus on how a person's dementia affects that person and not themselves. They worry and are sad about their partner's loss of cognitive and memory abilities and grieve over the eventual loss of companionship. Child caregivers respond to nursing home placement of their parent with dementia with a sense of relief, but spousal caregivers feel extensive sadness, anger, and frustration. In either case, attention to a caregiver's grief before a person's death is likely an important aspect of intervention in this population.

members to daily care, provide expert respite care, and consider when placement in a nursing home or hospice might be most appropriate (Beinart, Weinman, Wade, & Brady, 2012). Spouses and caregivers of people with dementia are particularly prone to stress, burnout, and other psychological and physical problems, so easing the burden of care is crucial for their long term health (Brodaty & Donkin, 2009).

*Support groups* for caregivers of people with neurocognitive disorders are crucial as well. These groups allow members to share information about daily care and express frustrations and sadness about their current situation. Online support groups are also available and might be particularly important for caregivers largely confined to their home (Marziali & Garcia, 2011). If a caregiver has substantial depression or other psychological problems, then referral to a psychiatrist and psychologist for more formal intervention may be best.

Living with a person with Alzheimer's disease or other form of severe neurocognitive disorder can be extremely difficult. The Mayo Clinic has provided some practical tips for caregivers in this situation (see **Table 14.11**). These tips focus on assessing the independence of a person with dementia, creating a safe environment, adjusting expectations, limiting distractions, and promoting communication. A key aspect of this day-to-day strategy is to frequently rethink what a person with dementia can still do and what she can no longer do. Incorporating psychological interventions for people with dementia we mentioned earlier would also be important in this process.

## What If Someone I Know Has a Neurocognitive Disorder?

If you suspect someone you know might be experiencing symptoms of a neurocognitive disorder, referring him for a full medical and neuropsychological examination is important. Catching these symptoms early on may be helpful to reverse delirium or slow the progression of dementia and improve someone's quality of life as long as possible. If someone you know does have Alzheimer's disease or another severe neurocognitive disorder, sharing and enjoying what time that person has left is essential. Resolve conflicts with the person while you can and try to fully understand what he would like you to do in later stages of his disorder (see **Box 14.3**). Neurocognitive disorders are among the most vicious disorders we discuss in this textbook. Pursuing what precious quality of life remains is imperative.

## Long-Term Outcome for People with Neurocognitive Disorders

You may have guessed from the tone of this chapter that the long-term outcome for people with Alzheimer's disease and other major neurocognitive disorders is bleak. A person's life span is generally about 3 to 9 years following onset of dementia. Mortality rates differ for people with vascular dementia (53.2 percent), Alzheimer's disease (43.7 percent), and mixed dementia (18.5 percent). People with vascular dementia live only 3.9 years after onset of their neurocognitive disorder.

## Table 14.11

### Practical Tips for Caregivers of Those with Alzheimer's Disease

| | |
|---|---|
| **Assess independence** | Involve loved one in tasks as much as possible. *Give your mother two choices for an outfit rather than asking her to choose from a closet full.* <br> Reassess the level of assistance that is required daily. *Can your husband shave by himself if you set out the supplies? Or can he shave by himself if you turn on an electric razor and put it in his hand? Or does he need you to provide assistance with the entire task?* |
| **Create a safe environment** | Remove throw rugs, extension cords, and any clutter. Avoid rearranging furniture. <br> Install locks on cabinets. <br> Make sure there is a first-aid kit, a fire extinguisher, and working smoke alarms. *If your husband is a smoker, don't allow him to smoke alone.* <br> Remove plug-in appliances. Set the temperature on the water heater no higher than 120° F to prevent burns. |
| **Adjust your expectations** | Allow more time to accomplish everyday tasks. <br> Try not to worry about the way things should be done. *If no danger results from your father's actions, refrain from correcting him.* <br> Try to stay flexible. *If your wife refuses to do something, back off and try again later using a different approach.* |
| **Limit distractions** | Shut off the television and limit background noise. <br> Encourage visitors to call before they come. |
| **Promote communication** | To understand a behavior, consider what your loved one may be feeling. *If your wife is pacing, it may mean she is tired, feels hungry, or needs to use the bathroom.* |

Source: Adapted from the © 2005 Mayo Foundation for Medical Education and Research.

## BOX 14.3 Focus on Law and Ethics

### Ethical Issues and Dementia

As you might guess, serious ethical issues arise when addressing people with cognitive decline and dementia. One key question is whether people who qualify for a diagnosis of major neurocognitive disorder should be told of this diagnosis. Arguments in favor of doing so include respect for the person, his participation in care decisions while still able, and acceptance of limitations. Arguments against doing so include the fact that treatment options are few, the person may not understand the diagnosis, knowledge of the diagnosis could lead to depression and other psychological problems, and insurance may be lost (Mattsson, Brax, & Zetterberg, 2010). Would you want to know?

Another set of ethical issues in this population arises when conducting research. Key questions include use of stem cells, ability of a person to give informed consent, genetic testing for risk factors for dementia such as APOE-4, and treatment and feeding of a person with dementia who refuses such help (Teper & Hughes, 2011). Would you want to know that you have the APOE-4 gene even though this does not necessarily mean you would develop Alzheimer's disease? Should the general population be tested for this gene?

The eventual incapacitation of people with dementia has thrown new light onto the area of *advance directives* such as living wills. In these directives, a person states ahead of time under what conditions food and water and medical treatment should be given. For example, the person may direct that if he were to eventually decline to a profoundly ill state, he would no longer want extensive lifesaving practices such as ventilators to be used. The creation of a living will also help reduce the stress of family members who may be otherwise burdened with such decisions.

---

This compares less favorably to people with mixed dementia (5.4 years), Alzheimer's disease (7.1 years), and people without dementia (11 years; Fitzpatrick et al., 2005).

Many people who experience mild cognitive impairment eventually experience dementia. Geslani and colleagues (2005) examined 161 people with a 3-month history of memory problems and found 35 percent to have mild cognitive impairment. Many of those with mild cognitive impairment progressed to Alzheimer's disease after 1 year (41 percent) or 2 years (64 percent). Several researchers have tried to identify exactly which cognitive impairments are most likely to predict Alzheimer's disease and other major neurocognitive disorders. Initial problems related to episodic memory (memory of recent personal events) and language are possibly related to later onset of dementia (Gallagher & Koh, 2011; Verma & Howard, 2012). People with problems with attention, naming, and psychomotor and visuospatial tasks also seem at risk for later onset of dementia (Benke, 2011).

Others report that strong predictors of the onset of major neurocognitive disorder, especially Alzheimer's disease, include age, less education, depression, stroke, poor health, presence of APOE-4, and poor blood flow to the left frontal cortex (Borenstein et al., 2005; Byers & Yaffe, 2011; Carbranes et al., 2004; Tilvis et al., 2004). The presence of delirium is also a risk factor for older people to develop dementia (Davis et al., 2012). People who have had a stroke and eventually progress to vascular dementia are generally those who have had less cognitive and memory ability, greater depression, and three or more cardiovascular risk factors (Allan et al., 2011). Predictors of eventual dementia in people with Parkinson's disease include age, severe postural and gait problems, mild cognitive impairment, and visual hallucinations (Aarsland & Kurz, 2010).

## INTERIM SUMMARY

- ▶ Interviews are commonly used to assess people with neurocognitive disorders and their caregivers, and topics often include recent changes in behavior, thinking, memory, and long-term skills such as language or ability to recognize others.

- ▶ Questionnaires are also used to screen for delirium and dementia and typically cover orientation, verbal and written comprehension, concentration, learning, writing and copying, and memory.

- ▶ Cognitive tests such as neuropsychological and intelligence tests also evaluate strengths and weaknesses of people with neurocognitive disorders.

- ▶ Medical and laboratory tests, including neuroimaging techniques, can often be used to assess the development of neurocognitive disorders.

- ▶ Biological treatments for people with neurocognitive disorders include cholinesterase inhibitors to increase acetylcholine in the brain, memantine to control L-glutamate activity, and L-dopa to quell symptoms of Parkinson's disease.

- ▶ Gene therapy may be a key future way of treating people with neurocognitive disorders.

- ▶ Many biological treatments for people with neurocognitive disorders are conducted in hospice or nursing home settings.

- Psychological treatments for people with neurocognitive disorders include reminiscence therapy, reality orientation, memory training, and behavior therapy.
- Psychological treatments for caregivers of people with neurocognitive disorders include education about dementia and providing support and respite care to prevent caregiver burnout and improve quality of life.
- The long-term outcome for people with major neurocognitive disorders is bleak; most die within 3 to 9 years of onset of the disorder.

## REVIEW QUESTIONS

1. Describe various methods of assessing a person with neurocognitive disorder and devise an assessment strategy you think might be most helpful.
2. What medications might be best for people with neurocognitive disorders?
3. What questions might family members ask themselves when considering whether to admit a loved one to a nursing home?
4. Describe psychological treatments commonly used for people with neurocognitive disorders and their caregivers.
5. Outline the long-term outcome for people with neurocognitive disorders.

## Final Comments

No cure exists for many major neurocognitive disorders, so preventing these problems and improving quality of life seems most important. You may find it easy to wait to worry about such problems until much later in life, but consider ways you can live a healthy lifestyle that will allow you substantial independence and ability to function later in life. In the meantime, enjoy every day you have and make the most of it. *Carpe diem*: Seize the day!

## Thought Questions

1. Think about famous people (Ronald Reagan, Charlton Heston) or even your own family members who have had Alzheimer's disease—what about their condition seems most tragic?

2. What do you think the future will bring with respect to treating people with major neurocognitive disorders?
3. What would you say to a friend who told you a parent or grandparent seems to be developing symptoms of a neurocognitive disorder?
4. What separates "normal aging" from dementia? At what point does one "cross the line" from regular changes in thinking and memory to more serious problems?
5. What do you think can be done to reduce the prevalence of neurocognitive disorder in the general population?

## Key Terms

delirium 435
dementia 436
neurocognitive disorders 436
major neurocognitive disorder 438
mild neurocognitive disorder 438
Alzheimer's disease 439
Lewy bodies 441
vascular disease 441
Parkinson's disease 443
Pick's disease 442
Korsakoff's syndrome 444
neurofibrillary tangles 448
senile or neuritic plaques 449
atrophy 449
oxidative stress 450
free radicals 450
amyloid cascade hypothesis 452
mental status examination 454
cholinesterase inhibitors 456
gene therapy 457
reality orientation 457
memory training 458

## Media Resources

### MindTap

MindTap for Kearney and Trull's *Abnormal Psychology and Life: A Dimensional Approach* is a highly personalized fully online learning platform of authoritative content, assignments, and services offering you a tailored presentation of course curriculum created by your instructor. MindTap guides you through the course curriculum via an innovative learning path where you will complete reading assignments, annotate your readings, complete homework, and engage with quizzes and assessments. MindTap includes the Continuum Video Project.

Go to **cengagebrain.com** to access MindTap.

# Consumer Guide to Abnormal Psychology

Introduction to the Consumer Guide

Becoming a Mental Health Professional

Becoming a Client

Treatment at the Individual Level
Interim Summary
Review Questions

Treatment at the Community Level
Interim Summary
Review Questions

Limitations and Caveats About Treatment

Ethics
Interim Summary
Review Questions

FINAL COMMENTS
THOUGHT QUESTIONS
KEY TERMS
MEDIA RESOURCES

## SPECIAL FEATURES

PERSONAL NARRATIVE 15.1 Julia Martinez,
Graduate Student in Clinical Psychology   470-471

PERSONAL NARRATIVE 15.2
Tiffany S. Borst, M.A., L.P.C.   474-475

BOX 15.1 | Focus on Gender: Graduate School and
Mentors   469

BOX 15.2 | Focus on Law and Ethics: Rights of Those
Hospitalized for Mental Disorder   477

BOX 15.3 | Focus on Diversity: Lack of Diversity in
Research   478

PERSONAL NARRATIVE 15.3
Christopher A. Kearney, Ph.D.   480

BOX 15.4 | Focus on Law and Ethics: Sexual Intimacy and
the Therapeutic Relationship   483

## Introduction to the Consumer Guide

We covered many unusual, harmful, and distressing behaviors in this textbook. We also discussed various treatment strategies for people with different types of mental disorder. You might be wondering more, though, about people who conduct therapy and what it is about treatment that helps people change their behavior. You may also have questions about providing or seeking therapy services yourself.

We focus in this chapter even more on the treatment process, with special emphasis on information most relevant to you, the consumer. We first discuss different types of mental health professionals and what to consider if you want to become a mental health professional or a client. We also review important components of treatment at individual and community levels, caveats about treatment, and ethics.

## Becoming a Mental Health Professional

Perhaps you have been so intrigued by the material in this textbook that you are thinking of becoming a mental health professional. Good for you! In this section, we discuss different types of therapists and their qualifications and offer suggestions for preparing yourself to become a mental health professional.

### Types of Therapists and Qualifications

Professionals who assess and treat people with mental disorders include psychologists, psychiatrists, psychiatric nurses, marriage and family therapists, social workers, and special education teachers. Various kinds of psychologists (e.g., clinical, counseling, educational, and school) address people with mental

disorders (see **Table 15.1**). **Clinical psychologists** often have a doctoral degree (Ph.D.) that allows them to serve both as *scientists*, or someone who conducts research on abnormal behavior, and as *practitioners*, or someone who conducts a wide range of psychological testing and provides diagnoses and treatment to people with mental disorders. Some clinical psychologists attend Psy.D. graduate programs that may focus less on research and more on developing clinical skills. A state licensing board must certify clinical psychologists to practice independently.

Clinical psychologists obtain an undergraduate degree, usually in psychology, and then attend graduate school for at least 4 years (usually 5) in addition to a 1-year internship. Many clinical psychologists also work in postdoctoral research positions after internship to further specialize in a given area such as neuropsychology or substance use disorder. Many psychologists also become professors.

Clinical psychologists are often trained to work with people with severe behavior problems, and often do so using a *change-oriented* approach in which behavior change is the primary goal (O'Donohue & Fisher, 2012). Clinical psychologists often rely on verbal treatment strategies to change problematic emotions, thoughts, and behaviors. They do not currently prescribe medication in most areas, but do in some states, and other jurisdictions are considering whether to give prescription privileges to clinical psychologists (McGrath, 2012).

**Counseling psychologists** tend to focus on people with less severe problems, such as those needing vocational counseling or marriage and family therapy (Neukrug, 2012). Counseling psychologists usually have a doctoral degree and are licensed as well. Many counseling psychologists adopt a *choice-oriented* approach in which the primary goal is to help a client make the right choices in her life. A client may need help deciding what career to pursue, for example, or whether to get a divorce.

Educational and school psychologists focus on children and learning-based issues. These psychologists often have a master's or doctoral degree. **Educational psychologists** tend to be more research-based and focus on developing effective strategies to teach children (and adults) different concepts like reading or arithmetic. **School psychologists** are usually affiliated with elementary, junior, and high schools and often assess children at risk for learning, developmental, and other mental disorders that could interfere with academic achievement.

**Psychiatrists** are medical doctors who can prescribe medication for people with mental disorders. Their training and background is typically from a biological perspective, so psychiatrists often rely on finding the right medication or other somatic treatment such as electroconvulsive therapy (Chapter 7) to

Clinical and counseling psychologists often work in private practice settings.

Paul Doyle–Alamy

School psychologists often assess youth with learning problems.

reduce suffering. Psychiatrists are usually trained in premedical, medical, and residency programs for at least 11 years. Psychologists and psychiatrists often work together so that different aspects of mental disorder, especially severe mental disorders like schizophrenia or depression, can be treated. A combination of psychological treatment and medication is best for many people. A psychologist or psychiatrist with specialized training in Freudian-based psychoanalysis may be referred to as a **psychoanalyst**.

**Psychiatric nurses** (R.N.s) are those who receive specialized training in addressing the needs of people with severe mental disorders like schizophrenia. These professionals often work in hospital-based, inpatient psychiatric units and are usually responsible for daily management of the unit as well as administering medications.

Bruce Ayres/Stone/Getty Images

Psychiatrists are medical doctors who usually ascribe to a biological approach to mental disorder.

**Marriage and family therapists** can be licensed as a separate entity in several states (check yours) and often have a master's degree in clinical or counseling psychology. These therapists concentrate on couples with marital or relationship problems as well as families with communication or problem-solving difficulties. **Social workers** usually have a master's degree (M.S.W.) and are licensed as well. The traditional role of this profession has been to focus on social and cultural factors of psychopathology and link disadvantaged persons with mental disorders to community resources such as residential programs or unemployment benefits that could improve quality of life. Many social workers could thus be found working in prisons, hospitals, schools, and social service agencies. The role of social workers has now expanded, and many work closely with psychologists and psychiatrists and/or practice therapy independently (Healy & Link, 2012).

**Special education teachers** usually have a master's degree and often work closely with persons with developmental disorders such as severe intellectual disability or autism. These teachers are responsible for designing and implementing specialized educational plans for these children and are often found in unique schools or segregated units of regular schools.

Many people also work with those with mental disorders in other ways. **Paraprofessionals** are those without advanced degrees who conduct assessments and interventions with people with mental disorders under the supervision of a mental health professional. One of your authors has an on-campus research-based clinic staffed by undergraduate and graduate students who assist with assessment and treatment sessions. Students with a bachelor's degree in psychology may also work as paraprofessionals in hospitals and other community-based organizations for people with mental disorders. In addition, **psychotherapist** is a term sometimes used for a mental health professional who practices therapy under supervision but who is not yet licensed.

## Preparing to Be a Mental Health Professional

What should you do if you want to become a mental health professional? A good first strategy is to talk to professors in different departments on campus such as psychology, counseling, and social work. *Do not be afraid to do this!* A professor's job includes counseling students about career options and helping them determine which options fit best for them. Talk to the instructor of the course about her background and ask what advice she has. Think about areas you might be most interested

## Table 15.1

### Common Types of Psychologists

**Clinical psychologists** assess and treat mental, emotional, and behavioral disorders. These range from short-term crises, such as difficulties resulting from adolescent rebellion, to more severe, chronic conditions such as schizophrenia. Some clinical psychologists treat specific problems exclusively, such as phobias or depression. Others focus on specific populations: young people, ethnic minority groups, gays and lesbians, and the elderly, for instance. They also consult with physicians on physical problems that have underlying psychological causes.

**Cognitive and perceptual psychologists** study human perception, thinking, and memory. Cognitive psychologists are interested in questions such as: How does the mind represent reality? How do people learn? How do people understand and produce language? Cognitive psychologists also study reasoning, judgment, and decision making. Cognitive and perceptual psychologists frequently collaborate with behavioral neuroscientists to understand the biological bases of perception or cognition or with researchers in other areas of psychology to better understand the cognitive biases in the thinking of people with depression, for example.

**Counseling psychologists** help people recognize their strengths and resources to cope with their problems. Counseling psychologists do counseling/psychotherapy, teaching, and scientific research with individuals of all ages, families, and organizations (e.g., schools, hospitals, businesses). Counseling psychologists help people understand and take action on career and work problems. They pay attention to how problems and people differ across life stages. Counseling psychologists have great respect for the influence of differences among people (such as race, gender, sexual orientation, religion, disability status) on psychological well-being. They believe that behavior is affected by many things, including qualities of the individual (e.g., psychological, physical, or spiritual factors) and factors in the person's environment (e.g., family, society, and cultural groups).

**Developmental psychologists** study the psychological development of the human being that takes place throughout life. Until recently, the primary focus was on childhood and adolescence, the most formative years. But as life expectancy in this country approaches 80 years, developmental psychologists are becoming increasingly interested in aging, especially in researching and developing ways to help elderly people stay as independent as possible.

**Educational psychologists** concentrate on how effective teaching and learning take place. They consider a variety of factors, such as human abilities, student motivation, and the effect on the classroom of the diversity of race, ethnicity, and culture that makes up America.

**Engineering psychologists** conduct research on how people work best with machines. For example, How can a computer be designed to prevent fatigue and eye strain? What arrangement of an assembly line makes production most efficient? What is a reasonable workload? Most engineering psychologists work in industry, but some are employed by the government, particularly the Department of Defense. They are often known as human factors specialists.

**Evolutionary psychologists** study how evolutionary principles such as mutation, adaptation, and selective fitness influence human thought, feeling, and behavior. Because of their focus on genetically shaped behaviors that influence an organism's chances of survival, evolutionary psychologists study mating, aggression, helping behavior, and communication. Evolutionary psychologists are particularly interested in paradoxes and problems of evolution. For example, some behaviors that were highly adaptive in our evolutionary past may no longer be adaptive in the modern world.

**Experimental psychologists** are interested in a wide range of psychological phenomena, including cognitive processes, comparative psychology (cross-species comparisons), learning and conditioning, and psychophysics (the relationship between the physical brightness of a light and how bright the light is perceived to be, for example). Experimental psychologists study both human and nonhuman animals with respect to their abilities to detect what is happening in a particular environment and to acquire and maintain responses to what is happening. Experimental psychologists work with the empirical method (collecting data) and the manipulation of variables within the laboratory as a way of understanding certain phenomena and advancing scientific knowledge. In addition to working in academic settings, experimental psychologists work in places as diverse as manufacturing settings, zoos, and engineering firms.

**Forensic psychologists** apply psychological principles to legal issues. Their expertise is often essential in court. They can, for example, help a judge decide which parent should have custody of a child or evaluate a defendant's mental competence to stand trial. Forensic psychologists also conduct research on jury behavior or eyewitness testimony. Some forensic psychologists are trained in both psychology and the law.

**Health psychologists** specialize in how biological, psychological, and social factors affect health and illness. They study how patients handle illness; why some people don't follow medical advice; and the most effective ways to control pain or to change poor health habits. They also develop health care strategies that foster emotional and physical well-being. Health psychologists team up with medical personnel in private practice and in hospitals to provide patients with complete health care.

## Table 15.1

### Common Types of Psychologists—cont'd

They educate medical staff about psychological problems that arise from the pain and stress of illness and about symptoms that may seem to be physical in origin but actually have psychological causes. Health psychologists also investigate issues that affect a large segment of society, and develop and implement programs to deal with these problems. Examples are teenage pregnancy, excessive substance use, risky sexual behaviors, smoking, lack of exercise, and poor diet.

**Industrial/organizational psychologists** apply psychological principles and research methods to the workplace in the interest of improving productivity and the quality of work life. Many serve as human resources specialists, helping organizations with staffing, training, and employee development. Others work as management consultants in such areas as strategic planning, quality management, and coping with organizational change.

**Neuropsychologists** (and behavioral neuropsychologists) explore the relationships between brain systems and behavior. For example, behavioral neuropsychologists may study the way the brain creates and stores memories, or how various diseases and injuries of the brain affect emotion, perception, and behavior. They design tasks to study normal brain functions with new imaging techniques, such as positron emission tomography (PET), single photon emission computed tomography (SPECT), and functional magnetic resonance imaging (fMRI). Clinical neuropsychologists also assess and treat people; and many work with health teams to help brain-injured people resume productive lives.

**Quantitative and measurement psychologists** focus on methods and techniques for designing experiments and analyzing psychological data. Some develop new methods for performing analysis; others create research strategies to assess the effect of social and educational programs and psychological treatment. They develop and evaluate mathematical models for psychological tests. They also propose methods for evaluating the quality and fairness of the tests.

**Rehabilitation psychologists** work with stroke and accident victims, people with intellectual disability and autism, and those with developmental disabilities caused by such conditions as cerebral palsy. They help clients adapt to their situation, frequently working with other health care professionals. They address issues of personal adjustment, interpersonal relations, the work world, and pain management. Rehabilitation psychologists are also involved in public health programs to prevent disabilities, including those caused by violence and excessive substance use. They also testify in court as expert witnesses about the causes and effects of a disability and a person's rehabilitation needs.

**School psychologists** work directly with public and private schools. They assess and counsel students, consult with parents and school staff, and conduct behavioral interventions when appropriate. Most school districts employ psychologists full time.

**Social psychologists** study how a person's mental life and behavior are shaped by interactions with other people. They are interested in all aspects of interpersonal relationships, including individual and group influences, and seek ways to improve such interactions. For example, their research helps us understand how people form attitudes toward others, and when these are harmful—as in the case of prejudice—suggests ways to change them. Social psychologists are found in a variety of settings, from academic institutions (where they teach and conduct research), to advertising agencies (where they study consumer attitudes and preferences), to businesses and government agencies (where they help with a variety of problems in organization and management).

**Sports psychologists** help athletes refine their focus on competition goals, become more motivated, and learn to deal with the anxiety and fear of failure that often accompany competition. The field is growing as sports of all kinds become more competitive and attract younger children than ever.

Source: American Psychological Association (www.apa.org/topics/psychologycareer.html#aparesources). Reprinted with permission.

in, such as children or depression, and discuss with the professor what kinds of courses you might wish to take in the future to further develop your interests.

Next, examine different courses in these areas and see which ones appeal most to you. Take these varied courses and see if the content matches what you think you might like to do. Talk to the instructors of each course about their background, training, and advice for future work. As you do, you might find yourself drawn to a particular area of interest. If not, that is fine. Keep searching!

Check also to see which professors in different departments are actively engaged in clinical research. Your current instructor may be a good person to ask first. One usually needs diverse clinical and research experience or internships to enter graduate school to become a mental health professional. Engage in this kind of research with different people as early as possible in your undergraduate career—do not wait until your senior year! In addition to gaining valuable clinical and research experience, you will find people who might be willing to write future letters of recommendation for you. Remember, good grades and standardized test scores are only part of the equation for getting accepted into graduate school. Some other recommendations:

- Get involved in Psi Chi, the national honor society for psychology students.

- Develop contacts with on-campus social groups for certain majors, such as a psychology club.

- Talk with directors of community mental health agencies about openings for volunteers and paraprofessionals. Donate your time conducting assessments, observing treatment sessions, and engaging in telephone work, perhaps at a suicide hotline.

- Get ongoing advice from one or more faculty mentors about deciding on career options, writing a letter of intent, and choosing graduate schools of interest.

- Engage in some clinical research and, if possible, present a paper at a psychology conference.

- Do your homework. Find out which schools might best fit your interests, and tailor your application toward a specific faculty member or two who would best match your interests.

- Review information provided for students by the American Psychological Association (Washington, DC) such as the book *Graduate Study in Psychology* and the "Careers in Psychology" brochure (www.apa.org/topics/psychologycareer. html#aparesources).

- Read the books *What Can You Do with a Major in Psychology: Real People, Real Jobs, Real Rewards* (New York: Wiley) by Shelley O'Hara, and *Insider's Guide to Graduate Programs in Clinical and Counseling Psychology* by Tracy Mayne, John Norcross, and Michael Sayette (New York: Guilford).

- Above all, ask questions and get as much information as possible!

Becoming a mental health professional is exhausting but exciting work. Think carefully about the commitment you will make and how this will affect your life. But above all, do not get discouraged if the work seems challenging at times! Being a mental health professional is among the most rewarding professions we know of, and we strongly recommend the profession to all those who feel they have such a calling.

## Becoming a Client

Perhaps you are more interested in *consuming* mental health services than providing such services. What should you or someone you know do if seeking treatment for a psychological problem? An important idea to consider when seeking treatment is what goal you wish to accomplish in therapy. Are you going through a crisis that needs immediate attention? Are you entering an important life transition and need some direction? Do you have troublesome thoughts or behaviors that need change? Do you have a problem that seems to occur for no reason and might be responsive to medication? The answers to these questions might help you decide what type of mental health professional to choose, such as a crisis intervention counselor, counseling or clinical psychologist, or psychiatrist.

When seeking treatment, one should also get referrals from knowledgeable people such as psychologists in the community. Most mental health professionals focus their practice in key areas, such as anxiety disorders or marital therapy, so find out who in your community specializes in a given area. Find out which agencies offer low-cost services if that is what you desire. Many universities offer community-based, sliding-scale cost treatment. Following this process, ask the mental health professional you are considering several questions before scheduling the first appointment:

- What is your fee, and does my insurance cover this fee or some portion of it and for how many sessions?

- Do you offer sliding-scale fees (based on one's ability to pay) for those with limited financial resources or multiple dependents?

- What should I expect during the first session, and what type of assessment procedures do you use?

- What is the nature of the type of therapy you do, and what are its limits?

If you are interested in a career in psychology, a discussion with your instructor might be a good place to start gathering information.

## BOX 15.1  Focus on Gender

### Graduate School and Mentors

Graduate programs in psychology have experienced a strong surge in applications from females in the past 20 years, and approximately 77.5% of current students in a clinical or counseling doctoral program are female. However, only about 45% of faculty members in clinical doctoral programs are female (American Psychological Association, 2012). This disparity raises the question of whether female graduate students receive sufficient or effective mentoring during their education process. This is important because well-mentored students tend to have more productive careers compared with those who have less mentoring.

Williams-Nickelson (2009) surveyed women in graduate school to determine if they had a mentor and what those experiences were like. Several examples of effective mentoring practices were provided. Effective mentors provided advancement opportunities such as networking with other professionals and inviting a mentee to participate in a special project. Good mentors also provided support and helped the mentee develop self-assurance, especially during times of stress or transition. Mentors help mentees focus on goals and a vision for the future and give constructive feedback about a student's development and progress. Mentors help facilitate independent thinking and help mentees experiment with different professional roles (e.g., as a therapist or researcher). Good mentors are also positive role models, especially with respect to maintaining balance in life (i.e., family and work) and engaging in proper self-care. Mentors help students realize their potential and allow them a good amount of autonomy to challenge the ideas of the mentor. If you are considering graduate school, talk to professors in your discipline who can help mentor you. Once you are in graduate school, look for mentors who have the characteristics mentioned here.

---

- What are your procedures regarding informed consent and confidentiality? (discussed later in this chapter)
- What types of problems do you specialize in addressing?
- What is your theoretical orientation and educational background?
- What is your status as a provider? Are you, for example, a licensed clinical psychologist, board-certified psychiatrist, or graduate student?
- Where are you located, and what are your hours?
- What is your policy for speaking with clients after normal business hours?

Remember, you are a *consumer* of treatment services and therefore entitled to specific answers to these and other relevant questions. Do not be afraid to ask these questions and find a good fit with a therapist.

## Treatment at the Individual Level

Whether you want to provide or consume mental health services, you could find yourself in one of many settings. Some of these settings involve treatment at the individual level, as many mental health professionals conduct therapy one-on-one in private practices. Other settings involve therapy within larger community-based institutions such as group homes, hospitals, prisons, or schools. We next discuss important factors related to one-on-one therapy as well as practices in community-based settings.

We begin with work that largely applies to treatment at the individual level. We discuss common factors that enhance successful outcome regarding treatment. These factors are often described as active treatment ingredients and process variables. We also discuss whether therapy itself is effective for people.

### Active Ingredients of Treatment

We have talked much in this textbook about different kinds of treatment for mental disorders, but what is it about treatment that makes it work? You have seen that mental disorders consist of three components: unsettling physical feelings or emotions, troublesome thoughts, and maladaptive behaviors. Effective treatment strategies must therefore affect these areas in positive ways. One active treatment ingredient is enhancing

David Buffington/Digital Vision/Getty Images

A warm, supportive therapist–client relationship is essential for successful treatment.

**self-control** (Dobson, 2010). People with mental disorders learn in therapy to control their own maladaptive (1) physical responses, such as in relaxation training for panic symptoms (Chapter 5); (2) thoughts, such as in cognitive therapy for depression (Chapter 7); and (3) behaviors, such as in the stop-start procedure for premature ejaculation (Chapter 11). Self-control will lead to **mastery** of certain symptoms and less distress from them (Beck, 2011).

Effective therapies and therapists also require clients to continually *practice* new skills. Examples include a child with learning disorder practicing reading or writing or a person with social anxiety disorder practicing conversations at a party. Practicing new skills may also mean a client has to *take risks*, perhaps by abandoning safety-seeking behaviors or doing things not previously done . A therapist will often encourage a client to boldly attempt different ways of behaving and continue to work toward treatment goals by practicing in real life what was learned in session (Hayes, Strosahl, & Wilson, 2012).

As a client works in therapy, a key goal is to help him gain greater **insight** into why he continues to behave in a maladaptive way (Sommers-Flanagan & Sommers-Flanagan, 2012). This is especially important when personality traits interfere with success in different areas of life. A client should gain greater knowledge about himself and how his behavior affects other people. A client should also gain greater knowledge about how to control his behavior or what to do if behavior seems problematic. If a person finds herself becoming depressed, she may wish to consult friends, become more socially active, and practice cognitive skills to reduce maladaptive thoughts.

A client should also engage in constant *self-exploration* or *introspection* to challenge internal assumptions and enjoy positive life experiences. A therapist will also help a client *work through* hypothetical and real-life problems using more adaptive strategies (Davies, 2010). For example, a therapist might help someone with schizotypal personality disorder interact with others in more socially acceptable ways and solve problems more effectively.

As a client improves in therapy, *ongoing successes* will hopefully and naturally lead to other positive, self-reinforcing events. A person who learns new interviewing skills may land a great job. Or a child who learns social skills and how to follow rules may be better able to make new friends and achieve in school. Ongoing *feedback* from the therapist and significant others will be helpful as well (Norcross, 2011). Success in therapy and life in general often comes from one's ability to behave effectively in life situations, to resolve or come to terms with past negative experiences, to have realistic expectations for change, to control extremes of emotion and behavior, to seek advice from others about appropriate life choices, and to make good choices.

---

## Personal Narrative 15.1

### Julia Martinez, Graduate Student in Clinical Psychology

I was the first in my family to go to college, so I have always thought of graduate school as a very special challenge and opportunity. On the general academic level, I see it as a place where there are no limits to learning or thought. It becomes your job to think critically about everything, and to formulate research and ideas that have the potential to move us all forward. With respect to clinical psychology, it seems to be a relatively new field, with a lot of work to be done. I find this fact both inspiring and daunting. Lastly, I would never deny that graduate school is very difficult. You make a lot of emotional investments, both in your work and in your own personal development. Frustrations and victories are part of everyday life. Balance, tenacity, and maybe a sense of humor are all important.

Before I started graduate school, I thought a lot about what I might expect. Actually, I expected a lot of

Julia Martinez

*Courtesy of Julia Martinez*

awful things that have not come to pass, perhaps because I made some preparations. For example, I knew that graduate school would be a lot of hard work, but I was dead set against pulling all-nighters and then feeling terrible (a familiar experience from my undergraduate years). I thought about how I could improve my work style so I could get a decent night's sleep. Also, a wise person, Dr. Karen Gillock, told me that graduate school would be filled with wonderful opportunities—but that if you did not prioritize well, you could easily find yourself overwhelmed, with the result of getting fewer things done (really important things, like your master's thesis). This advice turned out to be completely true, and it was helpful to expect this at the start. I guess the biggest thing that I did not expect was learning all the great things that I have learned. Going in, I had no idea what exactly I would learn. For instance, I was afraid of statistics, but I have learned to love them. I did not expect to grow and change so much.

And I have changed. I used to be really sensitive about psychology being called a "pseudo-science" or a "soft science," but I did not have enough knowledge about the field to dispute this claim. Over time, I have learned a lot about the impact that well-executed

## Process Variables in Treatment

**Process variables**, also known as *nonspecific factors*, are those common to all treatments that also contribute to treatment success. One powerful process variable is the **placebo effect**, which refers to improvement in treatment due to a client's expectation of help (Wampold, 2012). Many clients, once they know a therapist has diagnosed their problem and has a potential solution, become much more motivated in therapy and expect good progress. This enhances treatment effectiveness. The placebo effect can be quite stable; placebo control group improvement is sometimes greater than no-treatment conditions (Wampold and Budge, 2012).

Other process variables involve the therapist specifically.

John Slater/Digital Vision (RF)/Jupiter Images

One's ability to self-examine thoughts and behaviors is a key aspect of therapy.

research in psychology can have on the public good, which is clearly of importance. I have also changed personally. I wanted graduate school to be a well-rounded and scholarly experience. Although I spend a great deal of time in the lab, I also have sought other ways to broaden my horizons. I have read a lot of classic novels, taken a fencing class, practiced foreign languages with friends, traveled to Spain, recorded my own music, taken up the banjo, and learned to Irish jig and flamenco dance. To me, these are not unessential things; they have helped me to better understand and to love my work.

I would like to share four tips for those preparing for graduate school:

1. *Know what you want going in.* More specifically, some people want a lot of guidance from their advisors; others want to be left alone until they really need their advisors. Also, some advisors enjoy closely mentoring their students, while others prefer giving students more independence. It saves a lot of time and energy to identify what type of learner you are, what type of advisor would be best suited to your working style, and how you want to carry out your graduate school experience.

2. *Make your cultural differences known (in a constructive way).* Sometimes we differ culturally, which is fine. It is particularly important to understand and to be sensitive to cultural differences in psychology. Yet lines of thinking, work habits, and interpersonal exchanges can sometimes be misunderstood, regarded negatively, or not appreciated as being related to cultural differences. If you ever feel that this is the case, never be afraid to tactfully and constructively share your thoughts about relevant cultural differences. This will help everyone involved to be more informed and to be a better psychologist.

3. *Know about "shining star" syndrome.* That is, a lot of students come into graduate school having been the shining star in their high school and college. All of a sudden, graduate school seems horrible because everyone is smart and outstanding. Some people get really depressed, thinking they have lost their identity as the "smart one." This is not so. We all build from each other's abilities. It really is a time to learn about everyone's individual skills, and how we can all work together to make the world a better place. With this in mind, please also remember the next point:

4. *You are not an imposter.* I definitely have felt intimidated, feeling as if my peers had a better feel for how to do things, or how to go about life in graduate school. The truth is that everyone has a lot to learn. Never be afraid to clarify things you do not completely understand. You will learn and grow as long as you do not give too much importance to your doubts.

Such variables include *experience of the therapist* as well as her ability to make the therapy session a *warm and respectful* place. Experienced therapists do not necessarily provide better treatment than less experienced therapists, but therapists who specialize in a given area such as substance use disorders tend to have much knowledge about how to best treat clients with that particular problem. More experienced therapists also develop more detailed case formulations and treatment plans (Eells et al., 2011).

A client will also feel free to communicate private thoughts without fear of rejection or ridicule if his therapist establishes an environment based on *respect*, *empathy*, and *full acceptance* of his expressions (Clark, 2010). Another important therapist variable is *reassurance*, or regularly indicating to a client that solutions to problems can be solved if he puts forward the work to do so. Providing a *rationale* to a client about why a certain treatment is important, and how it should work, is often crucial as well. People with anxiety disorders who must "face their fears" should be given a full explanation as to why, for example (Abramowitz, Deacon, & Whiteside, 2011).

Other process variables involve the therapist–client relationship. An important one is interactions of the therapist and client, or **therapeutic alliance**, which should be productive, free flowing, and honest. The relationship should be a positive one built on trust, full disclosure from the client, and hard work toward treatment goals. In other cases, the mere fact a client comes to treatment and interacts with someone is important. For these clients, who may be alone or feel rejected during the week, therapy is often an excellent means of unburdening themselves or relieving the stress of isolation. Therapeutic alliance is a good predictor of treatment outcome (Del Re, Fluckiger, Horvath, Symonds, & Wampold, 2012).

**Therapeutic alignment** is also an important process variable in marital and family therapy. This can refer to how a therapist supports certain members of a marriage or family to "balance out" differences in power. A therapist might align herself slightly more with a dependent spouse or an intimidated child to ease communication or problem solving. This must be done carefully, however, so as not to alienate someone in therapy (Tuerk, McCart, & Henggeler, 2012).

Some process variables involve the client as well. Many clients report progress in therapy when they experience a release of emotions, or **catharsis** (Greenberg, 2012). For some clients, this may involve a strong grief or anger reaction, and for others it may represent admissions of things long-kept secret, such as child maltreatment or a previous rape. Certain personality characteristics of clients may be important as well. Dependent and less defensive clients often do better in group therapy situations when more structure is provided by a therapist, but independent-minded people may benefit more from less therapist direction. People with very low self-esteem, paranoia, or high hostility may do better in individual therapy than group therapy, where they feel less threatened (Bednar & Kaul, 1994; Karno, Beutler, & Harwood, 2002; Price, Hescheles, & Price, 1999).

Ned Frisk/Blend Images/Jupiter Images

Appropriate expression of strong emotions is sometimes a part of successful treatment.

## Does Treatment Work?

Does treatment actually work for clients? The overall answer is yes—many types of psychotherapy seem effective and better than no treatment at all. One type of therapy has not been shown to be consistently and significantly better than another type of therapy (Budd & Hughes, 2009; Luborsky et al., 2002). A trend in seeing whether treatment works, however, is to examine specific types of treatment for specific types of disorders. We have noted in this textbook that cognitive-behavioral treatments are effective for people with many types of problems, including anxiety, depression, eating disturbances, sexual dysfunction, and schizophrenia. Other therapies are especially useful for other disorders if matched well. Examples include dialectical behavior therapy for borderline personality disorder, behavior modification for autism, and medication for bipolar disorder (Ingram, 2012; Rounsaville & Carroll, 2002).

Another trend in evaluating treatment is the development of *manuals* for clinicians. Manuals provide detailed instructions for addressing clients with a certain problem and what techniques should be used. Researchers usually design manualized treatments for people with a certain type of mental disorder such as obsessive-compulsive disorder (Foa, Yadin, & Lichner, 2012). Manualized treatments have several advantages, including empirical basis, good validity and effectiveness, and specific recommendations for session-by-session assessment and treatment procedures (LeCroy, 2008). Manuals are usually brief, such as 4 to 8 sessions, which is preferred by many clients and insurance companies. Manualized treatments may not apply to all people with a certain disorder, however, because they cannot account for all individual differences in clients (O'Donohue & Fisher, 2012). Also, some clients have multiple mental disorders, which could affect how a treatment manual for one disorder is implemented.

## Prescriptive Treatment

Manuals have been criticized for a "one-size-fits-all" approach, so an important trend in clinical work today (and in new manual development) is to find which treatments are best for groups of people with a certain mental disorder. Researchers evaluate different subtypes of a clinical population and provide a specific treatment to best fit the needs of that subtype. This is sometimes referred to as **prescriptive treatment** (Eisen & Schaefer, 2007). One person with depression may feel sad because of a negative environmental event such as death of a loved one or bankruptcy. Another person may become depressed for little reason, or "out of the blue," because of a neurochemical imbalance. A good prescriptive treatment for the first person might be grief counseling or cognitive-behavioral therapy. A good prescriptive treatment for the second person might be medication. The idea behind prescriptive treatment is that one therapy for all people with a certain mental disorder, or a "single magic bullet," is inadequate. One must consider intricate individual differences when designing the best treatment for a particular client. Sometimes prescriptive treatment is based on form of behavior, sometimes it is based on function or reinforcements of behavior, and sometimes it is based on cause of behavior (Kearney & Albano, 2007).

Prescriptive treatment is important when seeking therapy. Clients should expect a therapist to conduct a thorough assessment of their problem to determine the best treatment. A client should also be open with the therapist when providing important personal information and should ask many questions of the therapist about potential treatments. The therapist and client can thus design an effective and efficient treatment plan together. We next discuss more specific suggestions for seeking treatment.

### INTERIM SUMMARY

▶ Professionals who work with people with mental disorders include psychologists, psychiatrists, psychiatric nurses, marriage and family therapists, social workers, and special education teachers. Paraprofessionals without advanced degrees may also work with special populations under supervision.

▶ Becoming a mental health professional involves gathering different types of experiences, speaking to different people, and taking varied courses.

▶ Finding the right therapist involves asking many important questions and identifying someone that best fits your personal needs.

▶ Active treatment ingredients improve outcome for clients; these include enhancing self-control, gaining mastery of symptoms, practicing new skills, exploring and gaining insight into problems, experiencing ongoing and reinforcing successes, and receiving therapist feedback.

▶ Process variables are general treatment ingredients that improve outcome for clients; these include placebo effect, therapist experience, warm and respectful therapy environment, reassurance, effective therapist–client interactions, and catharsis.

▶ Prescriptive treatment refers to specific therapies that match best with certain types of mental problems. Some clinical manuals have been developed to standardize prescriptive assessment and treatment procedures for clients with specific problems.

### REVIEW QUESTIONS

1. What are different types of psychologists, and how do they focus their work?
2. How might one go about becoming a mental health professional or client?
3. What active treatment ingredients seem to contribute most to therapy success?
4. What nonspecific treatment factors also contribute to therapy success?
5. Does therapy work, and what are advantages and disadvantages of manualized treatments? What is prescriptive treatment?

## Treatment at the Community Level

We mentioned earlier that treatment for mental disorders often involves one-on-one interactions between a therapist and client. Treatment can also occur at a larger, community-based level. Various forms of such treatment are sometimes included under the rubric of **community psychology**, which focuses on enhancing quality of life for people and concentrating on their relationships with different social structures. Examples of such structures include family, work, school, church, neighborhood, and culture (Kloos et al., 2012). We next focus on areas of intervention that often involve groups of people and community structures.

### Self-Help Groups

A **self-help group** is an association of people who share a common problem or mental disorder the group tries to address (Rosner, 2013). Examples include Alcoholics Anonymous and Narcotics Anonymous, in which the goal is to reduce maladaptive behavior such as excessive substance use among the membership. Self-help groups can also be simple neighborhood or church or online meetings for people in grief or isolation, those with a disability, or those who know others with a certain problem such as depression. Groups may also form to protect the cultural, religious, or political values of the membership or advocate for resources. An example of the latter is the National Alliance for the Mentally Ill (Ritter & Lampkin, 2012).

A main advantage of self-help groups is that large numbers of people with problems can be helped. Such help often comes from emotional support and feedback from members, role models for successful recovery, information about a problem, new ideas regarding coping, opportunities for emotional expression, financial aid, self-empowerment, enhanced spirituality, sense of belonging to a group, and realizing one's problems are not unique (Hardiman & Segal, 2003). People

Self-help groups offer support and guidance for people with similar problems.

often find help by listening to others "who have been there" or who can empathize and have experience with the problem in question. Participation in self-help groups enhances treatment outcome for different groups, including those with substance use problems (Chapter 9).

A criticism of self-help groups is that not all have (or wish to have) mental health professionals present. Misinformation about ways to treat or cope with a problem could thus be circulated. Other potential problems with self-help groups include high dropout rates and inadequate help for complicated issues. Still, many people report significant improvements in quality of life from self-help group membership. Membership in self-help groups in addition to professional, individual intervention is an accepted treatment strategy (Bonn-Miller, Zvolensky, & Moos, 2011).

## Aftercare Services for People with Severe Mental Disorders

We described in this textbook various treatment procedures for people with severe mental disorders in inpatient settings. Examples include electroconvulsive therapy for depression, detoxification for substance use disorder, and antipsychotic medication for schizophrenia. Historically, many people with these disorders were treated in hospital settings and then released on their own recognizance once their symptoms subsided. Unfortunately, this led to a situation in which many people eventually relapsed and returned to the hospital—a phenomenon known as the "revolving door" (Botha et al., 2010).

---

**Personal Narrative 15.2**

### Tiffany S. Borst, M.A., L.P.C.

I can't remember a time when I did not want to be a psychologist. From as early as middle school, I dreamed of having my own practice to provide therapy to people in their time of need. I was fascinated with the human mind; the interaction of our behaviors, emotions, and thoughts was always intriguing. I read everything on the subject that I could find and even subscribed to *Psychology Today*, a popular psychology magazine. I remember sitting in the chairs of my childhood living room imagining what it would be like to have my own office, my own clients.

Being sure of my career path from the beginning of my undergraduate program, I sought any information I could get to help me achieve my goal. Repeatedly, I was told I must get a Ph.D., "You can't do anything in the field of psychology without a Ph.D." I did everything

that was recommended to me, including research, publishing articles, and volunteering at local mental health agencies. I made sure that my grade point average was high and worked to get the highest GRE I could get. I knew that getting into a psychology doctoral program was very competitive, but I was willing to do whatever it took to realize my dream. I was devastated when I was an alternate to two programs. Although I was accepted into a master's level program in counseling psychology, I worried what options I would have and planned to eventually get the Ph.D. I was convinced I would need. I never did seek to complete that doctorate. As it turned out, my graduate program provided me with solid basic counseling skills and I soon found I was able to realize my dream of being a therapist without further formal education.

To my surprise, there were plenty of opportunities as a master's level coun-

Tiffany S. Borst, M.A., L.P.C.

selor in the field of psychology. I was fortunate enough to experience a variety of these mental health positions, each further preparing me for the work I do now. First, while still in graduate school, I worked as an intake counselor at a local psychiatric hospital. In this position, I answered crisis calls for a hotline, did

**Aftercare services** have thus been established in many communities to help people with severe mental disorders make the transition between an inpatient setting and independent living. You may have heard the term "halfway house," which refers to an intervention provided "halfway" between a (1) restrictive hospital or rehabilitation setting and (2) a completely independent living environment. A person lives in a supervised setting, often a small home with others with severe mental disorders. Staff at the home provide support and therapy services but residents can enjoy greater personal space, choice, and independence than at a hospital. Aftercare services also include day hospitals where patients live with family members in the evening, as well as supervised work and occupation training centers (Seidler, Garlipp, Machleidt, & Haltenhof, 2005).

Aftercare services are somewhat but not highly effective for people with severe mental disorders such as depression, substance use, and schizophrenia. Little effectiveness has been shown among youth. Much of this may be due to the severity and complexity of symptoms, medication refusal, unmet needs, and family dysfunction. Controversy also remains about how many people use or have access to aftercare services. Concern always exists as well about whether neighborhood residents will accept an aftercare home in their area. Many people with a chronic mental disorder discharged from a hospital thus relapse (recidivism), end up in prison, or become homeless (Daniel, Goldston, Harris, Kelley, & Palmes, 2004; Kallert, Leisse, & Winiecki, 2004; Ramana, Paykel, Melzer, Mehta, & Surtees, 2003).

## Residential Facilities for People with Developmental Disorders

Another area of community-based intervention involves people with pervasive developmental disorders such as severe intellectual disability. People with pervasive developmental disorders were traditionally housed in large residential facilities such as developmental centers, but many have moved to community-oriented and usually smaller facilities that more closely resemble normal life (Lemay, 2009). These smaller facilities, usually group homes or foster-care placements, often involve more daily choice in one's routine, such as what to wear. Job training and work-oriented settings are usually associated with smaller living facilities as well.

Movement to smaller, community-based facilities is based on **normalization** and **social role valorization**, or beliefs that people living in more normal circumstances will behave less unusually and be more valued by others

initial assessments, and recommended levels of treatment for people seeking psychiatric help. I also worked closely with the business office learning how to bill insurance, check benefits, and justify treatment to receive authorization. This experience proved to be invaluable. The business side of a practice was something I did not learn in graduate school and is something I use in my current job every day.

Upon completion of my master's program, as a new and developing therapist, I worked in group settings. I first worked as a therapist at a residential drug and alcohol treatment center for women. I provided individual, family, and group therapy to the women in the center, and play therapy to their children. I later worked in a group private practice, providing play therapy to kids in foster care, as well as seeing adults and adolescents for traditional outpatient therapy. In both settings, I received supervision, participated in staff meetings regarding clients, and consulted with peers frequently. I found it essential to process the work I was doing, to check my conceptualization of clients, and to share ideas with more experienced therapists. If I could give an aspiring therapist only one piece of advice, it would be to seek good supervision and peer consultation throughout your career.

Today I am a licensed professional counselor (L.P.C.), with a master's degree in counseling psychology. I have my own private practice, where my clients and I sit in those very same chairs from my childhood dreams. I treat people of all ages with a variety of mental health problems including depression, obsessive-compulsive disorder, generalized anxiety, panic attacks, posttraumatic stress disorder, and grief. While the majority of my time is spent providing individual or family therapy, I have also run a variety of groups, including expressive arts groups, educational groups, and support groups. As an L.P.C. in the state of Missouri, I am able to practice independently and bill insurance. This allows me flexibility and freedom I might not otherwise have to set my own schedule and to choose the cases I take.

Through the years I have built a successful practice, receiving referrals from doctors, pediatricians, school counselors, clergy, and former clients. I continue to be fascinated by the people I help and am amazed at their strength as they strive for personal healing. While my path was not what I initially thought it would be, I am now doing exactly what I always dreamed of doing and the work is just as rewarding as I imagined.

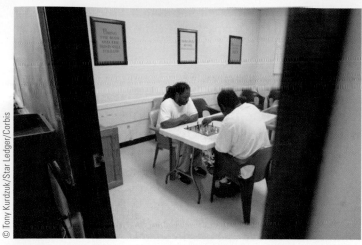

Kyle Leach and Maurice Kellam, residents of The Harbor halfway house, play chess in one of the activity rooms.

(Wolfensberger, 2011). Such movement has led to substantial improvements in self-care skills and general adaptive behavior (Caruso & Osburn, 2011). Some attribute these improvements to better material well-being, staff attention, integration with others and the community, and contact with family members. Personal choice about daily activities is generally higher as well (Kozma, Mansell, & Beadle-Brown, 2009). Some group homes are just as restrictive as larger residential facilities, however, which may hinder certain skills. One should thus assess level of available choice in a living environment for someone with a pervasive developmental disorder.

Forensic psychologist Catherine Howe uses a chart during her testimony at the kidnapping trial of Christian Karl Gerhartsreiter, who calls himself Clark Rockefeller, in Suffolk Superior Court in Boston on Wednesday, June 3, 2009. Gerhartsreiter, originally from Germany, was charged with kidnapping his 7-year-old daughter.

## Criminal Justice System

Other community-based interventions occur in criminal justice settings. **Forensic psychology** is an exciting area involving the interaction of psychological and legal principles. Forensic psychologists are typically involved in many aspects of evaluation and treatment that intersect with the courts and criminal justice system. Many forensic psychologists work in prisons to treat people with severe mental disorders incarcerated for some crime (Shipley & Arrigo, 2012).

Other forensic psychologists conduct assessment, treatment, or research regarding child custody cases, criminal profiling, eyewitness testimony, police interrogations, interpersonal violence, sexual harassment, and jury selection. Forensic psychologists often serve as expert witnesses for specific cases or as general consultants for a court. Forensic work is often based on assessment of individuals, but large groups of people are also studied to identify important patterns of behavior. Examples include prisoners, rape and maltreatment victims, and juvenile offenders. Other key aspects of forensic work include accurately determining whether someone is dangerous to others and whether to commit someone to a hospital (Chapter 2).

## Public Policy and Mental Health

Community-based interventions can also include public health policy regarding people with mental disorders. This policy often comes in the form of sweeping government legislation to improve the quality of life for individuals. Examples include legislation regarding free education for all youth, services for people with severe mental disorders, health promotion and education, prenatal care, child and spousal protective services, discrimination against people with mental disorder, and liability of mental health professionals, among other areas. Public policy can also be affected by individual or groups of mental health professionals who lobby politicians, testify as expert witnesses, or file briefs to inform judges about various mental health issues (Fulero & Wrightsman, 2009). Public policy regarding mental health has a long history in the United States and has shaped key legal rights for people hospitalized with mental disorders (see **Box 15.2**).

### INTERIM SUMMARY

▶ Community psychology treatments focus on enhancing quality of life for people and their relationships with different social structures.

▶ Self-help groups involve people who share a common problem the group tries to address. Advantages include reaching large numbers of people, having people who can empathize with a certain problem, and facilitating therapist–client treatment. Disadvantages include high dropout rate and risk of inadequate information.

▶ Aftercare services represent transitional help for people with severe mental disorders before they pursue independent living.

▶ People with pervasive developmental disorders have gradually moved to community-oriented and usually smaller facilities that more closely resemble normal life.

## BOX 15.2  Focus on Law and Ethics

### Rights of Those Hospitalized for Mental Disorder

A key aspect of public mental health policy involves rights for people hospitalized for mental disorder or severely dangerous behavior (Cohen & Galea, 2011). One basic right is the **right to treatment** itself, which mandates that people in mental health settings receive appropriate care that provides a meaningful chance at some improvement. A person also has the **right to refuse treatment**, meaning he does not have to be subjected to risky psychological or medical procedures such as surgery without proper consent. These rights often conflict with one another, as in the case of someone who wishes to continue hurting himself, or with society's right to be protected from a dangerous person.

Intervention for people with mental disorders is also based on the legal principle of **least restrictive treatment**, meaning a person should be effectively treated in a manner as least restrictive to her freedom as possible. Someone with a pervasive developmental disorder may be effectively treated in a large restrictive developmental center and in a group home. The latter is less restrictive, however, and should thus be chosen. Some people may have a severe mental disorder that requires hospitalization, but this does not mean they have lost basic rights to be treated with respect and dignity.

What do these rights mean for you? If you or someone you know is hospitalized for a mental condition, then ask what the treatment options are, how long a stay is required, and what conditions allow for discharge. If you or someone you know is hospitalized, ask as well about side effects of procedures such as medication and electroconvulsive therapy. If you or someone you know is considering residential care for someone with a chronic medical condition, then explore different options that consider the person's freedom, choice, and quality of life.

---

- ▶ Forensic psychologists address issues that intersect psychology and the legal system, including prisoner treatment, child custody evaluations, criminal profiling, jury selection, and assessment of dangerousness.
- ▶ Treatment at the community level intertwines with social change and public health policy toward people with mental disorders, including rights for those hospitalized.

### REVIEW QUESTIONS

1. What are major advantages and disadvantages of self-help groups?
2. Describe aftercare services and problems potentially associated with them.
3. Outline key concepts related to residential treatment of people with pervasive developmental disorders.
4. What areas comprise forensic psychology?
5. What areas of public health policy have been targeted toward people with mental disorders? What are key rights for people hospitalized with mental disorders?

## Limitations and Caveats About Treatment

Treatment at individual and community levels works for many people with mental disorders, but not everyone. Why not? One possibility is that the most effective treatment was not chosen for a particular client. This relates to the issue of prescriptive treatment we raised earlier, or the idea that treatment should be tailored to meet a client's individual needs. If a therapist uses a general treatment approach for all clients with depression, then some people with broader problems like an additional personality disorder or family conflict may not respond. Inappropriate application of treatment by a therapist can delay progress as well. Therapy may not work for some people because of changes in factors noted earlier; also, some clients may have little expectation for change, another factor that jeopardizes treatment success.

Another limitation on the therapy process is *treatment noncompliance*, when a client fails to put into action the plan developed with the therapist (Westra, 2012). A therapist may instruct a family to design a written contract to solve problems or show a couple how to develop good communication but, if these skills are not practiced during the week, then progress will be difficult. Therapists often have to explore reasons for noncompliance and eliminate obstacles that interfere with treatment. We next describe some specific obstacles to treatment.

### Client–Therapist Differences

One obstacle to treatment success occurs when significant personal differences exist between a client and therapist. If a client has very different *values* than his therapist, then therapy may not be productive (Hecker, 2010). Imagine a client who enters therapy with very set ideas about politics, child rearing, spousal treatment, or abortion and meets a therapist with completely opposite views on these subjects. A psychologist is expected to refrain from projecting his value system onto a client, but some cases involve too much friction to be fruitful. Severe personality conflicts can also exist between a therapist and client. Referral to another therapist is recommended if the therapy process cannot progress because of these conflicts.

## BOX 15.3 Focus on Diversity

### Lack of Diversity in Research

Ethnicity is extremely relevant to the therapy process, but research remains sparse with respect to some mental disorders. Iwamasa, Sorocco, and Koonce (2002) found that only 29.3 percent of published articles in clinical psychology included ethnically diverse participants and only 5.4 percent of published articles focused specifically on ethnically diverse participants. The authors suggested several possible reasons for this, including difficulties accessing diverse samples for research, presence of few diversity-oriented journals, hesitancy of researchers to focus on sensitive issues, and bias on the part of researchers to focus more on the general population and less on individual differences that may be important in the therapy process.

The authors also proposed several possible solutions. First, a commitment must be made to adjust undergraduate and graduate programs so future clinical psychologists are well versed in addressing clients of different cultural backgrounds. Second, researchers must make more effort to examine ethnic, racial, and gender issues in their work. What does this mean for you? As a possible future mental health professional, and one who may be conducting research now, think about how individual differences can affect assessment and treatment procedures. Ask about how your research can include questions about diversity, think about designing a study that specifically focuses on individual differences, and review research in your area of interest that has examined cultural differences. Such practices will allow you to be better prepared to assess and treat people with mental disorders from different backgrounds.

## Cultural Differences

Another important difference that affects therapy is *culture*. A therapist may not fully understand, properly empathize, or adjust to changes in a client's perspective of the world. Differences in language and communication style, beliefs about mental disorder and expression of symptoms, religion, and acculturation can also complicate treatment (Bhugra & Bhui, 2011). Therapists and clients often differ as well with respect to geographical and educational background and income level. These differences are not necessarily related to treatment outcome, but can affect how long a person stays in therapy or whether treatment is sought (Sue, Cheng, Saad, & Chu, 2012). A therapist should thus acknowledge differences with a client at the start of therapy and ask him if he has concerns about the differences. Special efforts to understand the client at multiple levels will also promote therapy progress (see **Box 15.3**).

## Managed Care

*Managed care* is a system of health care delivery that influences the use and cost of medical and psychological procedures. Use of managed care can limit services clients receive under certain coverage plans because insurance companies have essentially set the tone for what type of assessment and therapy a client can receive (Butcher, 2006). Many insurance plans allow a client to see a therapist for only a certain number of sessions, sometimes no more than eight. This forces therapists to use brief therapies when working with clients, a practice that may not be helpful when the problem is severe or complicated (Hansen, Lambert, & Forman, 2002). A therapist may also urge a client to implement treatment plans quickly—perhaps too quickly.

Other insurance plans only cover costs associated with seeing a psychiatrist, not another mental health professional.

This may lead a client toward drug or inpatient treatment for a problem when psychosocial treatment may have been a better long-term alternative (Olfson et al., 2002). Therapists may also be reluctant to treat a problem that is not a formal diagnosis, such as social withdrawal or school refusal behavior, because a diagnosis is often required by insurance companies for reimbursement.

Another possible consequence of managed care is that some clients may end therapy once their insurance company stops payments (O'Donohue & Cucciare, 2008). This could lead to incomplete progress, more referrals to low-cost agencies, more use of support groups and related community services, or greater acceptance of "quick fixes" (see later section). Insurance companies prefer lower costs from treatment providers, so more emphasis may be placed on therapists not trained at the doctoral level, such as master's-level therapists or paraprofessionals (Norcross, Hedges, & Prochaska, 2002).

The focus on managed care raises other ethical questions as well. How much information should a therapist give an insurance company when seeking third-party payments (Rosenberg & DeMaso, 2008)? Information such as a client's name and diagnosis are often needed, and a client must give permission for this information to be released (see later ethics sections). Very personal information such as therapist–client dialogue should not be revealed.

## Differences Between Clinicians and Researchers

Another limitation to treatment is differences between clinicians in private practice and researchers in specialized clinics. Private practitioners are often *eclectic* or *generalist* (Lord & Iudice, 2012; Messer, 2003), which means they use various techniques for various clients, depending on which seems most effective at the time. Researchers, however, often focus on very specific procedures for very specific types of clients to enhance internal validity of their studies. The problem is that many clinicians do not use research-based techniques even though the techniques are quite effective (Rotheram-Borus, Swendeman, & Chorpita, 2012). Why?

Part of the problem is that researchers often exclude the very cases clinicians see in their practice. A researcher may exclude clients with multiple or severe diagnoses, lack of English-speaking skills, low intelligence, medication prescriptions, or treatment compliance problems to boost internal validity of her experiment. Clients with one specific problem, such as obsessive-compulsive disorder only, are thus examined. Private practitioners, however, usually see clients with multiple behavior problems and other complicated issues—they say many published research studies have little to do with their everyday situations. This is a common complaint about treatment manuals as well. Researchers have thus begun to focus on more diverse populations to determine whether their procedures are effective in general community settings.

## Quick Fixes

Managed care and other constraints on therapy have led some people to seek solutions to problems that involve less time or effort. Many people are drawn to the allure of quick but ineffective fixes for a given problem. A popular method of treating a youth with attention-deficit/hyperactivity disorder in the 1970s was to change his diet to include less sugar or additive intake. Subsequent studies found diet changes to be ineffective for treating this disorder (Cormier & Elder, 2007).

Quick fixes for various behavior problems remain with us today. These include drug therapies for obesity, St. John's wort for depression, and facilitated communication for autism. Facilitated communication involves typists who supposedly translate what a nonverbal child with autism wants to communicate to parents and others. Controlled research studies, however, revealed that the so-called communications failed to emerge without biased input of the typist (Mostert, 2012). This false treatment crushes the hopes of parents who want desperately to converse with their child.

## Misuse of Research

Related to the idea of "quick fixes" is misuse of legitimate research for less than honorable purposes. This refers to twisting the meaning of research findings or perhaps citing an isolated result out of context. One of your authors published an article showing that small group homes for people with intellectual disability were *sometimes* as restrictive as large developmental centers. He was surprised the next year to see his article cited by an advocacy group that claimed the article proved large developmental centers to be better than group homes for people with intellectual disability! That was not the conclusion reached in the article, of course, and the author sent a stern letter to the group asking them to stop making this misleading claim.

Another example of misconstrued research was an article published on effects of sexual maltreatment on children (Rind, Tromovitch, & Bauserman, 1998). The authors reviewed various studies and found that many children rebounded from maltreatment and led productive adult lives. Some took this to mean maltreatment toward children is not harmful, which of course is untrue and contrary to what the authors were saying (Ondersma et al., 2001; Rind, Tromovitch, & Bauserman, 2001). You are a consumer of information from the media and other sources, so always consider the entire context of an original writing and do not assume someone's description of it is necessarily accurate.

## Weak Research and How to Judge a Research Article

Another problem with some research, and therefore clinicians' ability to apply it to their own practice, is weak quality. Research articles on treatment procedures could be flawed in many ways, which limits how clinicians use the results to help their clients. A research study may have included clients from particular age, gender, or racial groups, which limits generalizability to the overall population (Chapter 4). Or the study may have involved unusual, expensive, or experimental procedures to which most clinicians do not have access.

What should you look for when judging the quality of a research article on treatment? Consider these questions:

- Is the sample in the study diverse and representative of the general population?
- Were there enough participants in the study to obtain a meaningful effect?
- Are dependent measures in the study varied and of good reliability and validity?
- Did the researchers rely on information gained from different sources, such as clients, parents, teachers, spouses, children, and peers?
- Are treatment procedures defined well, are they understandable, and can they be applied to different clinical settings?
- What was the training of the therapists, and were different therapists used?
- How did the clients respond to treatment, and did they find the treatment acceptable?
- What was the long-term functioning of the clients?

## Negative Therapist Characteristics

Another limitation of treatment may come from negative therapist characteristics. Some therapists, as with some people in any profession, are bad-tempered or abrasive and may not be suitable for certain clients. A client may leave therapy if uncomfortable. A therapist who engages in unethical behavior should also be avoided, especially one who solicits physical contact with a client. Therapists who are evasive about issues such as fees or therapy procedures, who constantly disagree with a client about treatment goals, and who seem uninterested in a client should also be avoided.

## Personal Narrative 15.3

### Christopher A. Kearney, Ph.D.

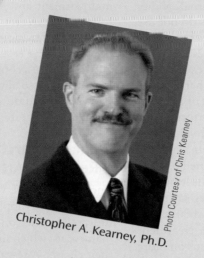

Christopher A. Kearney, Ph.D.

Photo Courtesy of Chris Kearney

I knew I wanted to be a clinical child psychologist the day a former mentor of mine gave a lecture to my undergraduate developmental psychology class. He worked with children with autism in a special on-campus school and told us of one child who threw a huge temper tantrum and ran around the room screaming when a person simply turned a block on its side in the boy's large playroom. When the block was returned to its original position, the boy immediately stopped his tantrum and resumed playing in his own world as if nothing happened. I spent much of the next two years working in that school for children with autism.

I also spent a great deal of time learning about graduate school, and I encourage you to do the same. The most important thing I learned was to talk to many people and be persistent. Consider different areas of psychology and what kinds of people you would like to work with. Get involved with different research labs and make sure people know you are reliable and trustworthy around clients. Get help if you need it on the GRE and retake courses you did not do well in. It's far better to take extra time to fix whatever deficiencies you may have before graduation than to rush toward graduation and have trouble getting into graduate school.

I was excited to enter graduate school and figured I would learn all I could about people with developmental disorders (Chapter 13). I found in graduate school, however, that many different

paths and populations were available, and I eventually extended my clinical and research work to children with anxiety disorders (Chapter 5). Many of the anxious children who came to the clinic I worked at also refused to attend school. No one seemed to know what to do with these kids, so I took them on and developed my dissertation around them. I've been studying kids with school refusal behavior and anxiety disorders ever since!

Today I live a full life as a college professor. I have undergraduate and graduate students who help me in different phases of research. Some have worked in my on-campus clinic for children with school refusal behavior and anxiety disorders, some in a local child protective services unit, some in a hospital setting, some in a truancy court, and some in school settings. My students work on many diverse topics for their theses and dissertations, including posttraumatic

stress disorder, perfectionism, selective mutism (refusal to speak in public situations), school absenteeism, and ethnic variables in clinical child psychology.

I also teach, have seen clients with different psychological problems, publish journal articles and books, and consult across the country and worldwide with school districts and mental health professionals. I supervise graduate students who see clients with various mental disorders, serve as the director of clinical training for our psychology doctoral program, and review articles submitted for publication to clinical journals. I serve on various committees and mentor students as they try to enter graduate programs and full-fledged careers. I think the best job in the world is a college professor!

My main goal in preparing this book was to say many of the things I say to my own students—mental conditions are extraordinary problems that ordinary people have and we all share aspects of the disorders discussed in this textbook. I wanted to convey that we all feel anxious, sad, worried, and even disoriented from time to time. I teach my students to respect people with mental disorder and not refer to them as schizophrenics or bulimics, but people with schizophrenia or people with bulimia. I also wanted to share how many people with mental disorder endure so much suffering. I hope you enjoyed reading the many true stories in this textbook and come away with a greater appreciation of abnormal psychology and its part in life.

## Lack of Access to Treatment

Another reason some people do not benefit from therapy is lack of access to treatment services. Many people cannot afford therapy, do not have insurance to pay for therapy, cannot transport themselves to therapy, or have difficulty finding low-cost services that are right for them or that are culturally sensitive (Mojtabai et al., 2011). People who are members of racial or ethnic minorities have poorer access to mental health care (Snowden, 2012).

Finding a therapist in rural settings can also be difficult, and seeking a therapist in a small town can risk one's privacy.

Some people may also wait until a particular problem is very severe before seeking help, and treatment at an advanced stage of mental disorder can be quite difficult. A person may be so debilitated in very advanced cases that she cannot contact someone for help. Examples include psychosis, substance intoxication, and severe depression.

These scenarios outline the importance of not only developing good treatment strategies but also making sure people have access to them. Establishing home visits, marketing low-cost and self-help services, providing transportation, developing prevention

Finding psychological help in a small town can be difficult and may lead to concerns about violations of confidentiality.

efforts and online-based therapies, and integrating community, psychotherapy, and pharmacological services will likely be an increasingly important part of treatment (Kalucy, Thomas, Lia, Slattery, & Norris, 2004; Prochaska & Norcross, 2013).

# Ethics

All practitioners in the mental health profession are expected to follow highly stringent ethical guidelines. In this section, we outline the general ethical principles that guide work with clients and that you should be aware of when interacting with a therapist.

## General Principles

Psychologists who conduct therapy are expected to follow the American Psychological Association's Ethical Principles of Psychologists and Code of Conduct (American Psychological Association, 2002). These guidelines represent behaviors psychologists should aspire to in their practice, though some states incorporate these guidelines into legal requirements for psychologists. The Ethical Principles are based on several general themes:

- *Beneficence* and *nonmaleficence*, or protecting the welfare of others
- *Fidelity* and *responsibility*, or acting professionally toward others
- *Integrity*, or employing high moral standards in one's work
- *Justice*, or exercising fairness and reasonable judgment
- *Respect for people's rights and dignity*, or valuing others and minimizing conflicts

We next discuss how these themes are specifically implemented with respect to assessment, treatment, and other variables. These sections each relate to a specific area within the Ethical Principles of Psychologists and Code of Conduct.

## Assessment

When assessing clients, psychologists should act in appropriate ways that enhance knowledge about a certain client but at the same time protect the client's privacy. Psychologists using tests to assess clients must be competent in giving a particular test and interpreting test results for clients. These tests should also be kept secure and given only to clients in a professional relationship. Giving a personality test to people at a party, for example, would be unethical. Psychologists should also be familiar with data that support the reliability, validity, and cultural applicability of a given test and should design tests that have good strength in these areas. Psychologists must not use obsolete tests or outdated testing information to make clinical decisions about clients. One should be very careful about examining test information about a child from several years ago because the child may have changed dramatically since then.

When explaining assessment results to others, psychologists are expected to state limitations to their conclusions based on testing. A person with Alzheimer's disease may have had great trouble paying attention to items given during an intelligence test, so the examiner should make this clear in her report. Psychologists must also base their statements or conclusions only on information they have received. This applies especially to child custody evaluations where parents are assessed for their capability to raise a child. If one parent refuses to participate in the evaluation and a second parent consents, then the psychologist could only make conclusions about the fitness of the person who was evaluated. Refusal to take part in an assessment does not necessarily mean a person is unfit or has a mental disorder. Psychologists should also make clear what their role is before an assessment so all those being tested know what is happening.

## Treatment

One of the most delicate areas of psychological endeavor is treatment, which often involves discussing sensitive and personal issues with clients and interacting with other professionals such as medical doctors and educators. Important ethical guidelines impact the therapy process.

### INFORMED CONSENT AND CONFIDENTIALITY

Some of the most important ethical guidelines involve informed consent and confidentiality. **Informed consent** involves educating potential clients about therapy, especially variables that might influence their decision to seek therapy (Hecker, 2010). Important variables to know include nature of therapy, cost, status of a provider, risks, and confidentiality (discussed next). If a person cannot give consent, then psychologists must still provide an explanation of what is to happen, seek the person's verbal agreement or *assent* if possible, consider the person's best interests, and obtain consent from a legally authorized person (Houser & Thoma, 2013). Parents can give consent for children, but many psychologists have children verbally agree to assessment and treatment procedures. Informed consent should be documented and is appropriate as well for participants entering a research project or most testing situations.

**Confidentiality** is based on *privileged communication*, which means discussions between a therapist and client should not be divulged to others unless consent is given. Many relationships enjoy such privilege, including husband–wife, doctor–patient, lawyer–client, and clergy–parishioner relationships. Psychologists are expected to maintain the privacy of their clients, even going as far as to not admit a person is in therapy. Psychologists usually obtain a release of information consent form from a client to speak with others about a particular case. This release permits them to contact teachers, medical professionals, or relevant others (Houser & Thoma, 2013).

Confidentiality is not absolute, however. Psychologists are ethically and legally allowed to break confidentiality under certain conditions. Psychologists are expected to take steps necessary to protect lives when a client is a clear threat to himself or others; this can even include contacting the police and/or someone else who is threatened. Confidentiality does not extend to child or elderly person maltreatment, which a psychologist is legally bound to report to a child protective agency or department of aging. Confidentiality may also be broken when a judge issues a court order for notes or testimony, when a client sues for malpractice, when a client tries to enlist a therapist's help to commit a crime, or when a psychologist seeks

reimbursement for services. Even in these cases, however, a psychologist gives the minimum amount of information necessary about a client and should consult a legal representative. Clients should be informed at the start of therapy about limitations on confidentiality (Hecker, 2010).

## WHO IS THE CLIENT?

An important question that often arises in couple and family therapy is "Who is the client?" In marital cases, one spouse may have initiated therapy for the couple and is paying for it. In family cases, parents usually refer themselves for therapy and pay for it, though a teenager may be the one having behavior problems and seeing the therapist. Who is the client in these situations? Is a spouse or are parents entitled to know what the other party said? Ethically, psychologists should clarify at the outset of therapy her relationship with each person.

A psychologist might say the couple is the client and she will try to be as fair as possible and not allow secrets between a therapist and one partner. A psychologist working with a family might say all information given privately by a child will be kept confidential unless the child is a threat to herself or others or if she allows the therapist to communicate certain information to the parents. If clients disagree with these conditions, then a referral to another therapist may be necessary. Psychologists should also not reveal more information than is needed for third-party payers such as insurance companies.

## SEXUAL INTIMACY

Sexual intimacy with clients is another important ethical issue for psychologists, and the ethics code and legal statutes make clear that such intimacy with current clients is unacceptable. Psychologists should also not accept into therapy anyone with whom they have had a sexual relationship in the past. Psychologists are expected to avoid **dual relationships**, meaning they should not act as a psychologist *and* friend, lover, significant other, or business partner. A psychologist should be unbiased and objective when helping a client, which is difficult to do when emotional feelings are involved.

What about sexual intimacies with *former* clients? The ethics code stipulates that psychologists must wait at least 2 years after the end of therapy before such intimacy can take place. Even if this does happen, a psychologist must show the client has not been exploited. Psychologists should generally avoid sexual and even social contact with former clients. Most cases of malpractice involve inappropriate sexual contact, and such contact is rife with potential for conflicts of interest and harm to a client (see **Box 15.4**).

## ENDING THERAPY

Important ethical guidelines still apply when a client nears the end of therapy. Psychologists should assist a client when she can no longer pay for services. A psychologist could make arrangements to lower the fee, see the client for fewer sessions,

Husband–wife communications are considered privileged in our society, as are communications between a therapist and client.

Andrea Morini/Photodisc/Getty Images

## BOX 15.4  Focus on Law and Ethics

### Sexual Intimacy and the Therapeutic Relationship

Psychologists are expected to follow a strict ethics code in their professional practice. Almost all psychologists do so, but you might wonder what types of ethical violations are referred to the American Psychological Association (APA). Each year, the APA publishes an account of what ethical violations were reported. In 2011, 9 cases were opened before the APA ethics committee. Most cases were allegedly due to sexual misconduct ($n = 5$) and nonsexual dual relationship ($n = 2$). Of the 5 alleged cases of sexual misconduct, 4 involved male psychologist–female client contact and 1 involved female psychologist–female client contact.

An overwhelming percentage of psychologists clearly comply with the ethics code. Some mental health professionals, however, inexplicably cross the line into severe misconduct. Most ethicists agree that touching a client—including hugs, touches of the hand, and two-handed handshakes can be misunderstood. The professional relationship can be undermined if clients become confused about what message is being sent—is a therapist a professional or a friend? Such practice is also a "slippery slope" that can lead to even more dangerous practices such as meeting outside of one's office or sending personal messages. Psychologists empathize with clients and their concerns but usually refrain from physical contact.

---

refer her to a low-cost provider, or make alternative payment arrangements. Therapists are also expected to end treatment when a client is clearly no longer benefiting from, or is being harmed by, the process. Psychologists should not end therapy abruptly but rather prepare clients for termination by discussing the issue with them in previous sessions.

## Public Statements

Psychologists often make public statements through advertisements, printed materials, interviews, lectures, legal proceedings, and interactions with media. Psychologists must ensure that public statements are honest and not deceptive. This includes information about their training, credentials, services, and other public knowledge. Psychologists who provide advice through the media, such as through a radio program, are expected to base their statements on available scientific literature and practice and perhaps remind listeners that their advice does not

Dr. Phil is a popular media psychologist. Psychologists who speak via the media are still expected to comply with ethical guidelines.

necessarily substitute for formal therapy. These principles are important to remember when you hear public figures such as Dr. Phil speak and dole out advice. Pay close attention to how often they refer to scientific literature to support their statements.

## Research

Ethical guidelines such as informed consent apply to research as well as clinical practice. Psychologists are expected to refrain from deceptive research unless the study is justified from a scientific perspective *and* if participants know about important and harmful aspects of the study that might influence their decision to participate. Psychologists engaging in research must also humanely care for animals, honestly report results, and give proper credit for sources of information and authorship of publications.

## Resolving Ethical Issues

What should a psychologist do if she becomes aware of an ethical violation by a colleague? The psychologist should first speak with the colleague to informally address the issue. This might apply to a situation, for example, in which a colleague accidentally left a client's file on a receptionist's desk. If the problem is very serious, however, or cannot be addressed satisfactorily by informal means, then the psychologist should refer the matter to a state licensing board or national ethics committee. Client confidentiality must still be protected in these cases, however. If a client reveals a serious ethical violation by a previous therapist but insists on confidentiality, then the client's request must generally be honored. Psychologists are also expected to fully cooperate in ethics proceedings involving themselves or others.

Donna Ward/Getty Images

## INTERIM SUMMARY

▶ Treatment for mental disorders is generally but not always effective. Ineffectiveness may be due to poor therapist–client relationship, poor choice of treatment, treatment noncompliance, and therapist–client differences.

▶ Increased use of managed care means mental health services and confidentiality are often limited.

▶ Clinicians and researchers often differ in type of clients seen and treatments used, which has led to a gap in clinical practice between the two.

▶ Managed care and other constraints on therapy have led some people to seek quick fixes to problems.

▶ Misuse of research sometimes occurs, so one should always consult original sources of information when making clinical decisions.

▶ Published research articles are sometimes flawed, so one should always judge a study according to its methodological strength and applicability to the general population.

▶ Limitations on treatment may come in the form of negative therapist characteristics and lack of access to treatment.

▶ Psychologists are expected to adhere to a strict code of ethics in their clinical practice, and this code is based on several key themes surrounding fairness and respect.

▶ Psychologists are expected to use assessment devices properly and explain limitations regarding their evaluation results.

▶ Psychologists are expected to provide informed consent to potential clients and research participants and keep information confidential. Confidentiality may be breached with the client's permission or under certain conditions.

▶ An important ethical question in marital and family therapy is "Who is the client?" A therapist's relationship with each party should be clarified at the outset of therapy.

▶ Sexual intimacy with clients is unethical, and psychologists are advised to avoid dual relationships.

▶ Important ethical guidelines also apply to termination of therapy, public statements made by psychologists, research practices, and resolution of ethical issues.

## REVIEW QUESTIONS

1. Outline major limitations on treatment and caveats one should be aware of when conducting therapy.
2. What questions apply when judging the content of a research article on treatment?
3. What general ethical principles are psychologists expected to follow?
4. What ethical principles regarding assessment are psychologists expected to follow?
5. What ethical principles regarding treatment are psychologists expected to follow?

## Final Comments

We have discussed in this textbook many issues related to mental disorders, clients, and therapists. The symptoms and disorders and problems clients face are many, but there remain basic ways in which people with mental disorders should be seen. People with mental disorders are often ordinary people with extraordinary problems, so remember that anyone can develop a mental disorder. A person should always be viewed first and his disorder second. Individuals with a particular mental disorder are always quite different, and these differences must be honored and respected. Try to avoid terms such as "schizophrenic" and favor terms like "a person with schizophrenia." People with mental disorders, especially youth, often need advocates who can work hard and ethically on their behalf. As a possible future mental health professional, keep in mind you hold enormous responsibility for the welfare of your clients.

## Thought Questions

1. Think about television shows or films that involve therapists and their relationships with their clients. What strikes you as realistic or not realistic about these relationships? Why?
2. If you were to see a therapist, what questions would you want to ask and what do you think the process would be like? If you have been in therapy or are currently seeing a therapist, what aspects of treatment have you appreciated most and least?
3. What are advantages and disadvantages of self-help groups, especially in contrast to seeing a mental health professional?
4. When should people be institutionalized for mental problems? What kinds of restrictions, if any, would you place on people with severe mental disorders?
5. Would you add or change anything to the ethics code that psychologists are asked to follow? Why?

## Key Terms

clinical psychologists 464
counseling psychologists 464
educational
     psychologists 464
school psychologists 464
psychiatrists 464
psychoanalyst 465
psychiatric nurses 465
marriage and family
     therapists 465
social workers 465
special education
     teachers 465
paraprofessionals 465
psychotherapist 465
self-control 470
mastery 470
insight 470
process variables 471

placebo effect 471
therapeutic alliance 472
therapeutic alignment 472
catharsis 472
prescriptive treatment 473
community psychology 473
self-help group 473
aftercare services 475
normalization 475
social role valorization 475
forensic psychology 476
right to treatment 477
right to refuse
     treatment 477
least restrictive
     treatment 477
informed consent 483
confidentiality 484
dual relationships 484

## Media Resources

### MindTap

MindTap for Kearney and Trull's *Abnormal Psychology and Life: A Dimensional Approach* is a highly personalized fully online learning platform of authoritative content, assignments, and services offering you a tailored presentation of course curriculum created by your instructor. MindTap guides you through the course curriculum via an innovative learning path where you will complete reading assignments, annotate your readings, complete homework, and engage with quizzes and assessments. MindTap includes the Continuum Video Project.

   Go to **cengagebrain.com** to access MindTap.

# Stress-Related Problems

## CASE: *Ben*

Normal Stress and Unhealthy Stress-Related
   Problems: What Are They?

Stress-Related Problems: Features and Epidemiology

Stress-Related Problems: Causes and Prevention

Stress-Related Problems: Assessment and Treatment

What If I or Someone I Know Has a Stress-Related
   Problem?

Long-Term Outcome for People with Stress-Related
   Problems

KEY TERMS

MEDIA RESOURCES

## CASE: Ben

**Ben** is a 47-year-old man who is employed as a middle manager at a large corporation. He has experienced considerable stress at his job during the past 2 years, having endured downsizing of his staff, pay cuts, mandatory furloughs, and reduced benefits in the sour economy. Ben has thus been forced to take on additional responsibilities, and new rumors are swirling that his position may be cut soon. His work-related stress is beginning to cause problems at home. Ben is forced to work extended hours and thus has less time to spend with his family. His relationships with his wife and children have become strained in recent months.

Ben was able to expertly balance his responsibilities and adjust to a new pay scale initially, but the ongoing stress of his situation has begun to take a physical toll. He visited his primary doctor recently and complained of trouble sleeping, abdominal pain, and headaches. Ben has gained considerable weight during the past few months because of a poor diet and little exercise. His blood pressure has risen since his last visit to the doctor, which is a concern given Ben's family history of heart disease. After several tests, Ben's doctor told him that he appears to be in the early stages of developing a stomach ulcer and that he must reduce his stress or face potentially more serious physical symptoms.

## Normal Stress and Unhealthy Stress-Related Problems: What Are They?

**Stress** is a construct that means different things. Stress can be *external*, meaning events in our daily lives that are taxing for us. Examples include relationship problems, financial worries, and academic pressures. Stress can also be *internal*, meaning we perceive events as demanding and thus experience bodily changes such as muscle tension, trouble sleeping, and headaches. Ben was clearly experiencing external and internal aspects of stress. Everyone experiences stress at some level, so stress is normal and even adaptive. Stress can make us more alert and can help motivate us to prepare for upcoming tasks.

Stress can obviously become excessive, however. We have all been through times when stress was intense, such as taking final exams, planning a wedding, or losing someone. In most cases, intense stress eventually dissipates as time passes, and we readjust to everyday living. In other cases, however, stress continues for lengthy periods and can become physically and otherwise harmful. Ben's ongoing and intense stress at work was clearly leading to several maladaptive physical symptoms and a lower quality of life.

A popular model for understanding acute and chronic stress and its effects on us was proposed by Hans Selye, who referred to the *general adaptation syndrome*. This model of stress consists of three stages (see **Figure A.1**). The first stage is *alarm*, which refers to the body's initial reaction to something stressful. This reaction may be in the form of higher adrenaline and cortisol, substances that allow the body to become energized and fight or flee a stressful stimulus. You may have noticed during final exams that you become quite energized by the stress of having to work so hard to study and concentrate and balance many demands in your life. As final exams pass and your intense stress level declines, so too do your body's physical reactions.

In some periods of our life, however, intense stress continues past this initial point. Some intense stressors can be chronic, such as worries about job loss or pay cuts or a child's severe illness. The body tries to increase *resistance* to stress in stage 2 but, over time, physical resources to do so become depleted. Over a longer period of time, a person enters the *exhaustion* phase, the third level of Selye's model, where physical resources and resistance to stress decline dramatically. This can set the stage for various stress-related physical problems that we discuss here. Ben's chronic stress and new physical problems perhaps meant he was near the end of the resistance stage or entering the exhaustion stage.

Stress-related physical problems have been traditionally referred to as **psychophysiological disorders**. Psychophysiological disorders specifically refer to organ dysfunction or physical symptoms that may be at least partly caused by psychological factors such as stress. Dysfunction often occurs in gastrointestinal, cardiovascular, immune, or respiratory systems, although other areas could be affected as well. The modern terminology for these problems is *psychological factors affecting other medical conditions* (see **Table A.1**; American Psychiatric Association, 2013). This refers to a true medical condition that is influenced to some extent by a psychological factor such as anxiety, stress, or depression. The psychological factor can affect the course or treatment of the medical condition. A person may experience such intense stress that stomach problems develop very quickly, or depression in another

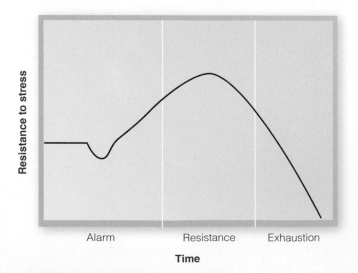

**FIGURE A.1** **HANS SELYE'S GENERAL ADAPTATION SYNDROME** (From David G. Myers, *Exploring Psychology* 7th ed., p. 398. Reprinted by permission.)

## Table A.1

**DSM-5  Psychological Factors Affecting Other Medical Conditions**

A. A medical symptom or condition (other than a mental disorder) is present.

B. Psychological or behavioral factors adversely affect the medical condition in one of the following ways:
 1. The factors have influenced the course of the medical condition as shown by a close temporal association between the psychological factors and the development or exacerbation of, or delayed recovery from, the medical condition.
 2. The factors interfere with the treatment of the medical condition (e.g., poor adherence).
 3. The factors constitute additional well-established health risks for the individual.
 4. The factors influence the underlying pathophysiology, precipitating or exacerbating symptoms or necessitating medical attention.

C. The psychological and behavioral factors in Criterion B are not better explained by another mental disorder (e.g., panic disorder, major depressive disorder, posttraumatic stress disorder).

*Specify* current severity:
 **Mild:** Increases medical risk (e.g., inconsistent adherence with antihypertension treatment).
 **Moderate:** Aggravates underlying medical condition (e.g., anxiety aggravating asthma).
 **Severe:** Results in medical hospitalization or emergency room visit.
 **Extreme:** Results in severe, life-threatening risk (e.g., ignoring heart attack symptoms).

person may cause him to delay visiting a physician for medical symptoms, which then worsen. Psychological factors can also pose additional health risks, as when a fear of needles prevents someone from taking a needed medication. Finally, stress-related physical responses, such as those noted in Selye's model, could help cause or exacerbate a medical problem such as breathing difficulties.

Stress-related physical problems are often studied by **health psychologists** who specialize in examining the interaction of biological, psychological, and social variables on traditional medical disorders. Health psychologists are often employed in health and human service agencies, medical settings, or universities affiliated with a hospital. Health psychologists may intersect with the area of **behavioral medicine**, which refers to a larger multidisciplinary approach to understanding the treatment and prevention of medical problems that may include a psychological approach. Health psychology and behavioral medicine may also overlap with the area of *psychoneuroimmunology*, which refers to the study of the interaction of psychological variables such as stress on the nervous and immune systems of the body.

# Stress-Related Problems: Features and Epidemiology

We next discuss various physical problems that may be partly caused or affected by psychological factors such as stress. Keep in mind that many physical problems can be affected by psychological factors, such as HIV/AIDS, cancer, and chronic fatigue syndrome. We concentrate the following material on those medical problems that tend to be more common and that have a strong research base regarding contributing psychological factors. These medical problems include ulcers, irritable bowel syndrome, headache, asthma, sleep disorders, hypertension, and coronary heart disease.

## Ulcers and Irritable Bowel Syndrome

Stress-related problems often affect the gastrointestinal area of the body. **Ulcers** refer to inflammation or erosion of a part of the body, and often occur in gastrointestinal areas such as the esophagus, stomach, or duodenum (part of the small intestine). A *peptic ulcer* refers to an ulcer that occurs in the stomach or intestine that can create severe abdominal pain (Lau et al., 2011). Recall that Ben appeared to be in the early stages of developing a stomach ulcer, perhaps from his ongoing stress. The prevalence of ulcers is 8.4%, and the problem is more frequent among older and obese persons, African Americans, tobacco users, and those with lung and cardiovascular diseases (Garrow & Delegge, 2010).

**Irritable bowel syndrome (IBS)** refers to a chronic gastrointestinal disorder involving alternating and recurrent constipation and diarrhea as well as abdominal pain. The prevalence of IBS in the general population is difficult to determine but is likely about 8 to 23 percent (Eisenbruch, 2011). In addition, 30 percent of people who visit a physician for gastrointestinal complaints appear to have the disorder. IBS is much more common in women than men and is comorbid with anxiety, depression, and insomnia (Grundmann & Yoon, 2010). Symptoms of IBS may be more common among Afro-Caribbean Americans than Whites (Kang, 2005).

## Headache

Stress-related problems can also result in headaches, as they did for Ben. *Tension headaches* are most common and refer to short-term mild to moderate head pain that may feel as if muscles are contracting, although the actual cause of tension headaches remains unclear. Chronic tension headaches are unusual in the general population (3 percent), but about 20 to 40 percent of people experience a tension headache at least occasionally. Tension headaches are generally more common in women than men (Manzoni & Stovner, 2010; Rasmussen, 2001).

*Migraine headaches* refer to chronic and severe headaches that can last hours to days. Migraine headaches are often concentrated in one area, such as one side of the head or around the eye, and many people with a migraine headache are extremely sensitive to light and crave total darkness. Migraines are sometimes preceded by an *aura*, or early warning signs such as light flashes or tingling in the limbs. Migraines can be quite debilitating and may be associated with nausea and vomiting. About 5 to 9 percent of men and 12 to 15 percent of women experience migraines, and 20 percent of those with migraines experience more than one episode per month (Manzoni & Stovner, 2010; Rasmussen, 2001). Migraine headaches appear to be more common among persons with lower income (Winter, Berger, Buring, & Kurth, 2012). *Cluster headaches* refer to a cyclical pattern of very severe head pain that can last weeks to months at a time. The prevalence of cluster headaches is 0.2 to 0.3 percent (Stovner & Andree, 2010).

## Asthma

**Asthma** refers to a chronic respiratory disease involving inflamed or constricted airways, tightening of the bronchial walls, and excess mucus, all of which hinders breathing. Asthma can involve regular or occasional attacks of wheezing, coughing, shortness of breath, and tightness in the chest. Asthma attacks can begin suddenly and can lead to decreased oxygen intake, lowered alertness, chest pain, and even death. Asthma attacks can last for minutes or much longer and can be triggered by allergens such as dust, animals, cold air, exercise, pollen, and tobacco smoke as well as stress (Murphy, 2011). The prevalence of asthma in the general population is 7.8 percent. Asthma rates are generally higher for children, women, and Puerto Rican Hispanics and African Americans compared with the general population. About 3,500 to 4,000 Americans die from asthma each year (Barnett & Nurmagambetov, 2011; Moorman, Zahran, Truman, & Molla, 2011).

## Sleep Disorders

**Sleep disorders** include dyssomnias and parasomnias. **Dyssomnias** refer to abnormalities in the amount, quality, or timing of sleep. Dyssomnias include problems initiating or maintaining sleep or excessive sleepiness. One of the most common dyssomnias is *insomnia*, which refers to difficulties falling asleep and staying asleep during the night as well as poor quality of sleep. Insomnia may or may not be related to a medical condition and is often the result of excessive stress or depression. Chronic insomnia can result in excessive sleepiness during the day, irritability or moodiness, difficulty concentrating, and poor alertness. Insomnia can be irregular, occurring some nights but not others, or could last for several weeks to months at a time (Green, Espie, Hunt, & Benzeval, 2012). Insomnia affects 13.5 percent of adults, 9.5 percent of college students, and 20 percent of older adults, and occurs in women at twice the rate for men. Insomnia is unrelated to ethnicity but tends to occur more in people with less education (Sivertsen, Krokstad, Overland, & Mykletun, 2009; Taylor, Bramoweth, Grieser, Tatum, & Roane, 2013).

Another dyssomnia is *hypersomnia* that refers to excessive sleepiness. Episodes of sleep may last 8 to 12 hours or longer with difficulty rising from bed in the morning. Frequent napping is common as well. The disorder must interfere with work and social relationships. The prevalence of hypersomnia is unclear, but the disorder occurs in 5 to 10 percent of people at sleep disorder clinics and 10 to 40 percent of people with depressive disorders (Kaplan & Harvey, 2009). The disorder occurs more frequently in men than women (Billiard, Jaussent, Dauvilliers, & Besset, 2011).

In contrast, *narcolepsy* refers to a neurological disorder involving an irresistible desire to sleep during the daytime, especially during times of low activity and often after a strong emotion. People with narcolepsy often have "sleep attacks" that happen suddenly and involve quick entry into REM sleep with sleep-related hallucinations or vivid dreams. Narcolepsy may occur with *cataplexy*, or sudden loss of muscle tone, and a person may experience inability to move upon wakening. The prevalence of the disorder is 0.02 percent (Raggi, Plazzi, Pennisi, Tasca, & Ferri, 2011).

*Circadian rhythm sleep–wake disorders* refer to a collection of sleep problems that affect the timing of sleep and a person's sleep-wake system. As such, a person has difficulty sleeping at the times required for normal functioning at work or in other areas. This disorder could be influenced by environmental factors such as shift work (Sack et al., 2007). Prevalence is 7 percent in adolescents and younger adults but higher among older adults (Sharkey, Carskadon, Figuerio, Zhu, & Rea, 2011). *Breathing-related sleep disorder* refers to sleep disruption caused by abnormal ventilation, such as *sleep apnea* in which a person repeatedly stops breathing for a few seconds or more during sleep. The disorder affects about 3 to 7 percent of men and 2 to 5 percent of women (Punjabi, 2008).

**Parasomnias** refer to abnormal behavioral or physiological events that occur throughout sleep and include nightmare disorder, sleep terrors, and sleepwalking. *Nightmare disorder* refers to repeated awakenings following frightening dreams. Nightmares are common in problems such as posttraumatic stress disorder (Chapter 5). About 85 percent of adults report one nightmare in the past year and 2 to 6 percent of adults report one nightmare per week (Levin & Nielsen, 2009). Repeated nightmares alone, without a concurrent mental disorder, that cause significant interference in daily functioning are uncommon, however. *Sleep terrors* refer to behavioral events during sleep involving screams, fear, and panicked behavior. A person, usually a child, with sleep terrors is difficult to awaken and has little recollection of the event. The prevalence of sleep terrors is about 2.7 percent. *Sleepwalking* refers to rising from bed and walking about during sleep. A person who is sleepwalking is difficult to awaken and has little recollection of the event. The prevalence of sleepwalking is about 1.7 percent (Bjorvatn, Gronli, & Pallesen, 2010).

## Hypertension

**Hypertension** refers to high blood pressure and is commonly identified if *systolic pressure* inside your blood vessels (created when your heart beats) is greater than 140 millimeters of mercury and/or if *diastolic pressure* inside your blood vessels (when your heart is at rest) is greater than 90 millimeters of mercury (i.e., a reading of 140 over 90, or 140/90, or greater). Pressures below 120/80 are preferred (although not too low). Hypertension has few outward symptoms but is a serious risk factor for problems affecting the heart, brain, and kidneys such as heart attack, stroke, and renal failure (Kaplan & Victor, 2010). *Essential hypertension* refers to high blood pressure caused by physical and psychological factors. Hypertension affects people of different cultures quite differently, from 3.4 percent of men from India to 72.5 percent of women in Poland (Kearney, Whelton, Reynolds, Whelton, & He, 2004). Approximately 29.9 percent of Americans have hypertension, with rates especially high for African Americans (42.0 percent), those not completing high school (37.3 percent), and those aged 65+ years (70.3 percent, Keenan & Rosendorf, 2011).

## Coronary Heart Disease

**Coronary heart disease** refers to a narrowing of the small blood vessels that supply blood and oxygen to the heart. Coronary heart disease may be manifested by *angina* (chest pain or discomfort) or *myocardial infarction/heart attack* (blockage of blood vessels to the heart) when advanced. Blood vessels may become blocked when plaque and other material clog the arteries and slow or prevent blood flow. Coronary heart disease is the leading cause of death in the United States, accounting for 1 of 6 deaths per year. Prevalence rates of angina in the United States differ for women who are African American (5.4 percent), Mexican American (4.8 percent), and White (4.5 percent); these rates also differ for men who are African American (4 percent), Mexican American (2.9 percent), and White (4.7 percent). Prevalence rates of coronary heart disease in general in the United States also differ for women who are African American (7.8 percent), Mexican American (6.6 percent), and White (6.9 percent); coronary heart disease rates also differ for men who are African American (7.8 percent), Mexican American (5.3 percent), and White (9.4 percent; American Heart Association, 2010).

## Stress-Related Problems: Causes and Prevention

The stress-related problems described here all have biological factors that help cause the damaging symptoms. Stomach ulcers, for example, often involve a bacterial infection from *Helicobacter pylori* that requires treatment with antibiotics and anti-inflammatory medication. In addition, genetics, poor diet, smoking, allergens, plaque accumulation, and medical problems that affect sleep are common factors that help cause stress-related problems. The following sections concentrate on psychosocial factors that often affect these medical conditions.

## Sociocultural Variables

Stress-related problems appear to manifest differently and for different reasons among people of varying ages, gender, and race, as noted earlier. A particularly strong risk factor for many stress-related problems is socioeconomic status, which includes economic resources, social standing, and education. People with lower socioeconomic status are at increased risk of stress-related problems, especially coronary heart disease (Albus, 2010). People of lower socioeconomic status may have less access to medical care, experience poor nutrition and living conditions, engage in less physical activity and more alcohol and tobacco use, and have less control over decisions in the workplace (Krantz & McCeney, 2002).

## Emotional Difficulties

Several physical problems appear to be related to emotional difficulties such as worry, sadness, and low self-esteem. Ulcers, irritable bowel syndrome, and pain in the head, neck, and back have long been related to stress, anxiety, depression, and lower quality of life (Jones, 2006; Murison, 2001). Pain and headache are particularly related to passive coping, fear, self-perceived poor health, poor emotional well-being, and cognitive distortions about the negative consequences of pain (Linton, 2000; Smitherman & Ward, 2011). Headaches in college students, especially women, are closely related to level of emotional functioning and perception of stress (Labbe, Murphy, & O'Brien, 1997).

Asthma is clearly related to stress in many cases, which exacerbates autonomic function and constriction of the bronchial tubes (Wright, 2011). Asthma is linked to anxiety and depression in children and adults, especially panic symptoms. People with asthma may also assess and manage their asthma symptoms poorly in more severe cases (Bourdin et al., 2012).

Insomnia has also been linked to mood disorders such as depression (Roth, Roehrs, & Pies, 2007). Kappler and Hohagen (2003) found that two thirds of people could correctly be viewed as having insomnia based on an examination of increased age, conflicts with relatives, professional overload, housekeeping overload, illness of relatives, and social and psychiatric status. Insomnia also appears closely related to excessive worry (about daily events and about not being able to sleep), stress and life change, and overarousal (Bonnet & Arand, 2010; Espie, 2002).

Psychosocial risk factors for hypertension include worry about job stability (as with Ben), feeling less competent at one's job, anger, and symptoms of anxiety and depression (Player & Peterson, 2011; Rutledge & Hogan, 2002). Depression also appears to be a significant risk factor for coronary heart disease, especially somatic symptoms of depression (Carney & Freedland, 2012). People with depression may engage in more high-risk behavior, such as using substances excessively and exercising less, and may experience greater arterial thickening and less heart rate variability, which are associated with poor cardiac outcomes (Krantz & McCeney, 2002). People with depression are also likely to experience higher levels of bereavement and anxiety, which may be risk factors for cardiac problems as well (Everson-Rose & Lewis, 2005).

## Personality Type

Personality type may be a key psychosocial cause of some stress-related problems. The traditional focus with respect to personality type was *type A personality*, which refers to someone who is overachieving and hostile and who aggressively and impatiently tries to accomplish more tasks in less time (Everson-Rose & Lewis, 2005). Researchers have since focused more on hostility as a key psychosocial risk factor for coronary heart disease, especially in men (Williams, Steptoe, Chambers, & Kooner, 2011). Impatience and hostility have also been linked to hypertension (Williams, 2010).

Other work has focused on **type D personality**. Type D personality refers to a distressed personality pattern marked by negative affectivity and social inhibition. This means that some people experience increased distress across many different situations but do not express this distress in social interactions. People with type D personality tend to worry excessively, experience tension and unhappiness, feel irritable and pessimistic, and are uncomfortable around strangers. They experience few positive emotions, have few friends, and fear rejection and disapproval from others.

Type D personality has been linked to several stress-related problems such as fatigue, irritability, depression, and low self-esteem. More important, people with type D personality seem to be at greater risk for cardiac problems compared with people without type D personality. The specific reason for this link remains under study, but some evidence indicates that people with type D personality who are socially inhibited tend to have higher blood pressure reactivity to certain stressful events. Type D personality also appears related to lower quality of life and feelings of exhaustion following a medical procedure to address a cardiac problem (O'Dell, Masters, Speilmans, & Maisto, 2011; Pedersen & Denollet, 2003).

## Social Support

Social support, or one's access to friends and family members and others who can be of great comfort during times of trouble, is clearly linked to several stress-related problems. Low social and family support contribute to asthma, for example, whereas enhanced support improves asthma outcomes (Klinnert et al., 2001; Rhee, Belyea, & Brasch, 2010). Social support may ease the ill effects of coronary problems because it helps promote medication use and compliance, positive coping with illness-related stress, and reduced overarousal and worry (MacMahon & Lip, 2002). In contrast, social isolation, being unmarried, or experiencing marital distress or low levels of emotional support are risk factors for coronary heart disease. Good social support may help calm aspects of the autonomic nervous system and reduce activation of serotonin and fear/anxiety centers in the brain such as the hypothalamic-pituitary-adrenal axis (Chapter 5) that could help prevent hypertension and later coronary problems (Everson-Rose & Lewis, 2005).

## Causes of Stress-Related Problems

The stress-related problems described here are largely the result of a combination of biological problems exacerbated by psychological and social factors. A *biopsychosocial model* reflects the idea that biological, psychological (emotions, thoughts, and behaviors), and social factors combine to cause and influence a medical condition. This model is similar to the diathesis-stress model discussed in several chapters of this textbook. A biopsychosocial model is particularly relevant to psychophysiological disorders because of the unique combination of medical and nonmedical factors.

Let's consider coronary heart disease as an example. Several physiological factors predispose people to coronary heart disease, including genetics, inflammation, hormonal changes, elevated lipids, and restriction of arteries, among others. Several psychological factors can, however, combine with these predispositions to increase the likelihood of cardiac effects such as unstable electrical signals or blocked blood flow. These psychological factors include chronic anger, hostility, depression, and exhaustion as well as poor diet, little exercise, inadequate coping, and other unhealthy behaviors. Physiological and psychological factors can be worsened as well by social factors such as isolation from others, job stress, and low socioeconomic status. These factors increasingly interact over time to predispose a person to heart attack, angina, stroke, or death (Hjemdahl, Rosengren, & Steptoe, 2012).

Other psychophysiological disorders can also be understood from a similar biopsychosocial perspective. Biological predispositions can interact with stress, anxiety, and depression as well as social variables to help produce ulcers and IBS, cause headaches or other pain, aggravate respiratory problems such as asthma or sleep problems such as insomnia, and raise blood pressure toward hypertension. Think about someone who has experienced an injury and develops chronic pain aggravated by depression, lack of social support, and trouble sleeping. Preventing these serious and chronic problems from developing requires a focus on several different variables, and this process is illustrated next.

## Prevention of Stress-Related Problems

Prevention of stress-related problems focuses on wide-ranging programs to improve healthy practices and reduce the prevalence of these problems in the general population. Many of these programs focus on primary prevention of the leading cause of death in the United States: coronary heart disease. The American Heart Association published guidelines for preventing cardiovascular disease and stroke that involve behaviors that should begin at age 20 years. These guidelines include recommendations for screening for potential risk factors such as family history, smoking, alcohol use, diet, physical activity, blood pressure, waist circumference, cholesterol and blood glucose level, management of diabetes, and regular use of aspirin.

Other prevention programs for coronary heart disease as well as ulcers and hypertension have focused on improving lifestyle choices such as proper diet, exercise regimens, and smoking cessation (Labarthe, 2011). These programs are not as effective as medications to control high levels of cholesterol and blood pressure (Ebrahim, Beswick, Burke, & Smith, 2006). This may be due to lack of compliance, however. Women who *do* adhere to lifestyle guidelines for diet, exercise, and smoking cessation dramatically lower their risk of sudden cardiac death (Chiuve et al., 2011).

Other primary prevention programs are tailored more specifically to an individual medical condition. Prevention of asthma attacks in children, for example, involves medication and stress management, early breast-feeding, and avoidance of household dust, pets, exposure to tobacco smoke, and other allergens (Chan-Yeung et al., 2005). Other psychophysiological disorders such as IBS, headache, and insomnia are usually treated after a person complains of symptoms or may be prevented by a program for another disorder. A program to prevent depression, for example, may help prevent sleep problems such as insomnia (Sivertsen et al., 2012).

## Stress-Related Problems: Assessment and Treatment

Stress-related problems require a detailed medical assessment to determine the extent of biological causes for the conditions as well as a course of medical treatment. Mental health professionals who specialize in psychophysiological disorders have, however, developed an array of assessment and treatment strategies that focus on the psychological factors that impact these problems. Some of these strategies overlap with those discussed in other chapters, but some are unique to psychophysiological disorders and are summarized next.

### Psychological Assessment of Stress-Related Problems

Psychological assessment of stress-related problems often comes in the form of daily behavior records. Researchers will ask participants to record daily symptoms such as severity of pain and discomfort (for ulcer and headache), bowel function (for IBS), blood pressure (for hypertension), number of hours slept (for sleep disorders), and respiratory distress (for asthma; Kaniecki, 2003; Robinson et al., 2003). Researchers may also focus on intermittent records for variables such as weight and cholesterol level (for coronary heart disease; Stampfer & Colditz, 2004).

Questionnaires are often administered as well. Risk assessment questionnaires assess the degree to which a person is at risk for a certain psychophysiological disorder. A risk assessment questionnaire for ulcer, hypertension, or coronary heart disease, for example, might include screening questions about weight, diet, cholesterol level, blood pressure, exercise, stress, alcohol and tobacco use, and occupation. Other questionnaires such as the *Health Assessment Questionnaire* focus on broader health-related issues such as pain and disability, quality of life, drug side effects, and medical costs (Bruce & Fries, 2005). Questionnaires regarding anxiety, somatization, and depression are also helpful for people with psychophysiological disorders and were covered at length in Chapters 5, 6, and 7.

Other assessment procedures for stress-related problems have involved more specific areas of focus. Assessment of pain, for example, involves not just how intense pain is but also how the pain interferes with a person's daily life and how a person thinks about a pain (e.g., "I can handle the pain"), feels about a pain (e.g., "I am really worried about my pain"), and behaves following a pain (e.g., complaining to others, using medication heavily). Pain quality may be assessed as well and refers to specific descriptors such as sharp, aching, hot, and cramping (Molton & Raichle, 2010).

Assessment measures can also target personality factors related to psychophysiological disorders. Measures are available to evaluate type A and type D personality, anger, and hostility. Another personality variable that has received substantial attention from researchers is *stress reactivity,* which refers to increased physical responses to daily stressful events (Boyce & Ellis, 2005). Inventories that cover key personality variables associated with psychophysiological disorders were described in Chapter 4.

Stressful life events are also assessed by researchers because they impact physical problems so intensely. Smyth and colleagues (2008) surveyed thousands of college students to evaluate which types of life events were most prevalent and stressful or emotionally upsetting. The researchers found that 84.5 percent of college students experienced an adverse life event at some time in their lives. Adverse life events primarily involved death of a loved one (62.7 percent), academic issue (39.6 percent), parental divorce or separation (24.4 percent), and traumatic sexual experience (18.4 percent).

Other researchers have examined daily hassles that college students encounter, such as traffic, missing class, time pressure, or disagreement with a friend. Brougham and colleagues (2009) found that daily hassles were more stressful for college students than academic, family, or financial problems, especially among women. Ross and colleagues (1999) examined the prevalence of recent stressful life events and hassles among college students; their results are shown in **Table A.2**. You can see that the most common stressors for college students included such things as interpersonal conflict, sleep difficulties, public speaking, increased workload, grades, and even breaks from school!

### Psychological Treatment of Stress-Related Problems

As with assessment, psychological treatment for stress-related problems typically accompanies medical treatments such as medication or surgery. Psychological treatment for stress-related problems often consists of relaxation training, biofeedback, stress management, cognitive therapy, and support groups. Note that some of these treatments, such as relaxation training and biofeedback, are often used in combination.

#### RELAXATION TRAINING

We discussed relaxation training in Chapter 5 as a key treatment for physical symptoms of anxiety-related disorders. *Relaxation training* often consists of tensing and releasing different muscle groups to achieve a sense of warmth and rest. Relaxation training may also consist of diaphragmatic breathing in which a person practices appropriate deep breathing to achieve a greater sense of ease and control over physical anxiety symptoms. *Meditation* and *hypnosis* are sometimes a key part of relaxation training as well. Meditation refers to practicing focused attention and minimizing distraction, and hypnosis refers to a state of focused attention with heightened suggestibility. Relaxation training has also been used extensively to reduce stress in people with psychophysiological disorders, especially IBS,

**Table A.2**

## College Students Reporting Each Source of Stress

| Category | Percentage | Category | Percentage |
|---|---|---|---|
| **Interpersonal** | | Severe injury | 5 |
| Change in social activities | 71 | Engagement/marriage | 2 |
| Roommate conflict | 61 | **Academic** | |
| Work with people you don't know | 57 | Increased class workload | 73 |
| Fight with boyfriend/girlfriend | 41 | Lower grade than anticipated | 68 |
| New boyfriend/girlfriend | 36 | Change of major | 24 |
| Trouble with parents | 21 | Search for graduate school/job | 21 |
| **Intrapersonal** | | Missed too many classes | 21 |
| Change in sleeping habits | 89 | Anticipation of graduation | 20 |
| Change in eating habits | 74 | Serious argument with instructor | 11 |
| New responsibilities | 73 | Transferred schools | 3 |
| Financial difficulties | 71 | **Environmental** | |
| Held a job | 65 | Vacations/breaks | 82 |
| Spoke in public | 60 | Waited in long line | 69 |
| Change in use of alcohol or drugs | 39 | Computer problems | 69 |
| Outstanding personal achievement | 35 | Placed in unfamiliar situation | 51 |
| Started college | 32 | Messy living conditions | 50 |
| Decline in personal health | 26 | Put on hold for extended period of time | 47 |
| Minor law violation | 14 | Change in living environment | 46 |
| Change in religious beliefs | 13 | Car trouble | 42 |
| Death of a family member | 12 | Quit job | 8 |
| Death of a friend | 6 | Divorce between parents | 1 |

Source: Ross et al. (1999).

hypertension, sleep disorders, and headache and other pain (Dickinson et al., 2008; Lackner, Morley, Dowzer, Mesmer, & Hamilton, 2004; Morgenthaler et al., 2006).

## BIOFEEDBACK

**Biofeedback** refers to a procedure that allows a person to monitor internal physiological responses and learn to control or modify these responses over time. A person is attached to one or more devices that provide feedback to the person about his brain wave patterns, respiration rate, muscle tension, blood pressure, heart rate, or skin temperature. The person can learn to control these responses by relaxing, using positive imagery, and thinking more flexibly. As the person does so, he can see on a monitor that his physiological responses such as heart rate are easing. With extended practice, the person learns to lower physiological arousal even without being attached to a biofeedback machine.

Biofeedback has been used most for people with migraine headaches and sleep problems. People with migraine headaches are encouraged to engage in *thermal biofeedback,* which involves feedback about skin temperature and warming the extremities (hands, feet) to improve blood flow and reduce throbbing head pain. People with tension headaches are encouraged to engage in *EMG (electromyography) feedback,* which involves feedback about muscle contraction and physically relaxing to ease tension and reduce head pain (Rains, Penzein, McCrory, & Gray, 2005). EMG biofeedback has also been used to help people relax to reduce insomnia and hypertension (Ebben & Spielman, 2009; Greenhalgh, Dickson, & Dundar, 2010). Biofeedback appears to be best

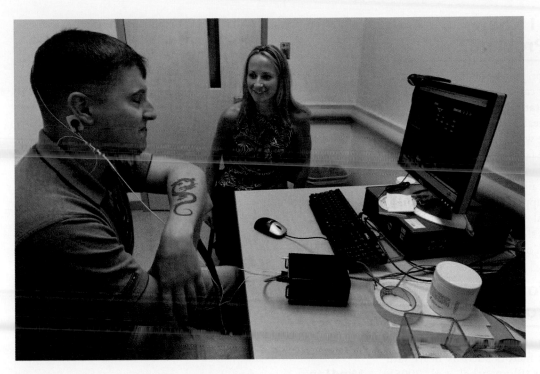

Biofeedback is an essential treatment component for stress-related problems.

## COGNITIVE THERAPY

We discussed cognitive therapy throughout this textbook as an effective treatment for many different mental disorders. Cognitive therapy generally consists of helping people think more flexibly and realistically about their environment and interactions with others. Cognitive therapy may be useful for reducing anxiety and depression, which are key elements of many stress-related problems.

Cognitive therapy for people with psychophysiological disorders also involves correcting misperceptions about certain events. Edinger and colleagues (2001) helped people with insomnia in part by correcting misperceptions about sleep requirements, circadian rhythms, and sleep loss. This was combined with a behavioral approach that consisted of a standard wake-up time, rising from bed after a period of sleeplessness, avoiding behaviors incompatible with sleep in the bedroom, and eliminating napping during the day. Combined cognitive-behavioral treatment greatly improved maintenance of sleep.

Another type of cognitive therapy for this population is *self-instruction training* (Meichenbaum, 2009). Self-instruction training refers to identifying negative thoughts that may occur during a painful episode (e.g., "This pain is so awful") and replacing these thoughts with more adaptive coping ones (e.g., "I have to allow my pain to escape my body and move forward"). Self-instruction training for pain is often accompanied by techniques to educate people about pain, distract oneself from pain, reduce anxiety, and have family members and others reinforce active and positive coping behaviors (Hechler et al., 2010).

## SUPPORT GROUPS

*Support groups* are also a key aspect of treatment for people with psychophysiological disorders. We discussed support groups in different chapters but most notably in Chapter 9 for substance-related disorders. Support groups refer to meetings of people who share a common problem, including a physical problem such as an ulcer. Support groups are useful for sharing information and tips on coping, venting frustration, developing social support and friendships, and practicing stress management and other techniques. Support groups for the stress-related problems discussed here are conducted by the Crohn's and Colitis Foundation of America (for ulcerative colitis), Irritable Bowel Syndrome Association, National Migraine Association, Asthma and Allergy Foundation of America, American Sleep Association (for sleep disorders), and American Heart Association (for cardiac problems).

for people who are open to the approach, who cannot tolerate or do not respond to medication, and who have problematic coping skills (Penzien, Rains, & Andrasik, 2002).

## STRESS MANAGEMENT

**Stress management** refers to a collection of techniques to help people reduce the chronic effects of stress on a daily basis as well as problematic physical symptoms. Stress management can involve using relaxation techniques such as those described earlier, understanding stress better, managing workload effectively, incorporating spirituality and empathy, improving diet and exercise regimens, practicing good sleep hygiene, complying with a medication regimen, scheduling recreational activities, resolving interpersonal conflicts, and managing hostility and anger toward others (Hjemdahl et al., 2012). *Anger management* often consists of identifying triggers to anger, understanding what personal physical responses lead to anger, practicing techniques to lower physical arousal, managing social and work situations more effectively to reduce the chances of anger, and removing oneself from situations in which anger is building (Burns et al., 2008; Schell, Theorell, Hasson, Arnetz, & Saraste, 2008).

Another stress management technique is *mindfulness*, which we discussed in previous chapters. Recall that mindfulness refers to greater daily awareness and acceptance of one's symptoms and how the symptoms can be experienced without severe avoidance or other impairment. A person is asked to engage in moment-by-moment awareness of her mental state including thoughts, emotions, imagery, and perceptions. Mindfulness may be especially useful for people with chronic pain as well as those with intense daily stress that can aggravate most physical disorders (Reiner, Tibi, & Lipsitz, 2013).

## What If I or Someone I Know Has a Stress-Related Problem?

If you suspect that you or someone you know has a physical problem that may be at least partly caused by stress or another psychological variable, then consultation with a physician and a psychologist who specializes in health issues may be best. In addition, many people do not share with their physician details about the stress of their lives, or the fact that they are depressed or lack social support. But these are important factors that may affect treatment, so share these details with your medical doctor. You may also wish to explore support groups or begin daily stress management to ease physical symptoms and adhere to sound practices such as healthy diet, sleep and exercise regimens, periods of relaxation, and resolution of interpersonal conflicts.

## Long-Term Outcome for People with Stress-Related Problems

Stress management is an effective strategy for reducing distress as well as cardiovascular risk factors such as heart rate variability and ventricular problems (Blumenthal et al., 2005). Stress management also helps lower long-term mortality rates among people with cardiovascular problems such as hypertension (Schneider et al., 2005). Stress management and relaxation training may be particularly useful for people with IBS and perhaps ulcer as well (Ford, Talley, Schoenfeld, Quigley, & Moayyedi, 2009).

Other stress-related disorders appear responsive to psychological therapies. As noted earlier, relaxation training and biofeedback are especially useful for headache. Relaxation, family therapy, medication compliance, stress reduction, and

education are particularly important for resolving asthma, especially in children (Yorke, Fleming, & Shuldman, 2007). Insomnia is also commonly treated successfully using cognitive-behavioral approaches, relaxation, and sleep restriction (Carney, Berry, & Geyer, 2012). In general, long-term outcome for stress-related problems is good as long as medication as well as stress, depression, and related psychological variables are appropriately managed.

## Key Terms

stress  488
psychophysiological disorders  488
health psychologists  489
behavioral medicine  489
ulcers  489
irritable bowel syndrome (IBS)  489
asthma  490

sleep disorders  490
dyssomnias  490
parasomnias  490
hypertension  490
coronary heart disease  491
type D personality  492
biofeedback  494
stress management  495

## Media Resources

### MindTap

MindTap for Kearney and Trull's *Abnormal Psychology and Life: A Dimensional Approach* is a highly personalized fully online learning platform of authoritative content, assignments, and services offering you a tailored presentation of course curriculum created by your instructor. MindTap guides you through the course curriculum via an innovative learning path where you will complete reading assignments, annotate your readings, complete homework, and engage with quizzes and assessments. MindTap includes the Continuum Video Project.

Go to **cengagebrain.com** to access MindTap.

# Glossary

**abnormal psychology** The scientific study of troublesome feelings, thoughts, and behaviors associated with mental disorders to better understand and predict mental disorder and help those who are in distress.

**active phase** A phase of schizophrenia marked by full-blown psychotic features such as delusions and hallucinations.

**acute stress disorder** A mental disorder marked by anxiety and dissociative symptoms following a traumatic experience.

**adaptive functioning** A person's ability to carry out daily tasks that allow her to be independent.

**aftercare services** Community-based services for people with severe mental disorders to ease the transition between hospital settings and independent living.

**agonists** Medications to treat substance-related disorders that have a similar chemical composition as an addictive drug.

**agoraphobia** A mental disorder marked by avoidance of places in which one might have an embarrassing or intense panic attack.

**alogia** Speaking very little to other people.

**Alzheimer's disease** A neurocognitive disorder often marked by severe decline in memory and other cognitive functioning.

**amyloid cascade hypothesis** A theory that genetic and environmental factors interact to produce substantial brain changes and dementia.

**analogue experiment** An alternative experimental design that involves simulating a real-life situation under controlled conditions.

**anhedonia** Lack of pleasure or interest in life activities.

**anorexia nervosa** An eating disorder marked by refusal to maintain a minimum, normal body weight, intense fear of gaining weight, and disturbance in perception of body shape and weight.

**antagonists** Medications to treat substance-related disorders that block pleasurable effects and cravings for an addictive drug.

**antecedents** Stimuli or events that precede a behavior.

**antisocial personality disorder** Personality disorder marked by extreme disregard for and violation of the rights of others and impulsive behavior.

**anxiety** An emotional state that occurs as a threatening event draws close and is marked by aversive physical feelings, troublesome thoughts, and avoidance and other maladaptive behaviors.

**anxiety-related disorder** A mental disorder involving overwhelming worry, anxiety, or fear that interferes with a person's daily functioning.

**anxiety sensitivity** A risk factor for anxiety-related disorders involving fear of the potential dangerousness of one's physical symptoms.

**asthma** A chronic respiratory disease involving inflamed or constricted airways, tightening of the bronchial walls, and excess mucus.

**asylums** Places reserved to exclusively treat people with mental disorder, usually separate from the general population.

**atrophy** Gradual deterioration or shrinkage of a brain area in people with dementia.

**attention-deficit/hyperactivity disorder (ADHD)** A mental disorder marked by severe problems of inattention, hyperactivity, and impulsivity.

**atypical antipsychotics** A newer class of drugs to treat schizophrenia and related psychotic disorders.

**autism** A pervasive developmental disorder marked by severe impairments in social relationships and communication as well as bizarre behavior patterns.

**automatic thoughts** Cognitive distortions of the negative cognitive triad that are constantly repeated and often associated with depression.

**aversion treatment** A treatment for paraphilias that involves associating paraphilic stimuli with unpleasant stimuli.

**aversive drugs** Medications to treat substance-related disorders that make ingestion of an addictive drug quite uncomfortable.

**avoidance conditioning** A theory of fear development that combines classical and operant conditioning with internal states such as driving or motivating factors.

**avoidant personality disorder** Personality disorder marked by anxiousness and feelings of inadequacy and socially ineptness.

**avolition** An inability or unwillingness to engage in goal-directed activities.

**basal ganglia** Brain structures that control posture and motor activity.

**behavior genetics** A research specialty that evaluates genetic and environmental influences on development of behavior.

**behavioral assessment** An assessment approach that focuses on measuring overt behaviors or responses.

**behavioral avoidance test** An assessment technique for anxiety-related disorders that measures how close one can approach a feared object or situation.

**behavioral inhibition** A risk factor for anxiety-related disorders involving withdrawal from things that are unfamiliar or new.

**behavioral medicine** A multidisciplinary approach to understanding the treatment and prevention of medical problems that may include a psychological approach.

**behavioral perspective** A perspective of abnormal behavior that assumes that problematic symptoms develop because of the way we learn or observe others.

**binge eating** Eating an amount of food in a limited amount of time that is much larger than most people would eat in that circumstance.

**binge eating disorder** An eating disorder marked by recurrent episodes of binge eating but no compensatory behavior.

**biofeedback** A procedure that allows a person to monitor internal physiological responses and learn to control or modify these responses over time.

**biological model** A perspective of mental disorder that assumes that mental states, emotions, and behaviors arise from brain function and processes.

**bipolar disorder** A mental disturbance sometimes characterized by depression and mania.

**bipolar I disorder** A mental disorder marked by one or more manic episodes.

**bipolar II disorder** A mental disorder marked by episodes of hypomania that alternate with episodes of major depression.

**blood alcohol level** Concentration of alcohol in the blood.

**body dissatisfaction** Negative self-evaluation of what one's body looks like.

**body dysmorphic disorder** A disorder marked by excessive preoccupation with some perceived body flaw.

**borderline personality disorder** Personality disorder marked by impulsivity, difficulty controlling emotions, and self-mutilation or suicidal behavior.

**breathing retraining** A treatment technique for physical anxiety symptoms that involves inhaling slowly and deeply through the nose and exhaling slowly though the mouth.

**brief psychotic disorder** A psychotic disorder marked by features of schizophrenia lasting 1 day to 1 month.

**bulimia nervosa** An eating disorder marked by binge eating, inappropriate methods to prevent weight gain, and self-evaluation greatly influenced by body shape and weight.

**case study method** In-depth examination and observation of one person over time.

**catastrophizing** A cognitive distortion involving the assumption that terrible but incorrect consequences will result from an event.

**catatonic** Tendency to remain in a fixed stuporous state for long periods.

**catatonic behavior** Unusual motor behaviors in people with schizophrenia.

**category** An approach to defining mental disorder by examining large classes of behavior.

**catharsis** A nonspecific factor in treatment that refers to venting emotions and release of tension in a client.

**central nervous system** The brain and spinal cord, which are necessary to process information from our sensory organs and prompt our body into action if necessary.

**cerebral cortex** Gray matter of the brain that covers almost all of each hemisphere.

**cholinesterase inhibitors** A class of drugs to treat people with dementia that help increase levels of acetylcholine in the brain.

**cirrhosis of the liver** A severe medical condition in which scar tissue in the liver replaces functional tissue.

**civil commitment** Involuntary hospitalization of people at serious risk for harming themselves or others or who cannot care for themselves.

**classical conditioning** Pairing of an unconditioned stimulus so the future presentation of a conditioned stimulus results in a conditioned response.

**classification** Arranging mental disorders into broad categories or classes based on similar features.

**client-centered therapy** A humanistic therapy that relies heavily on unconditional positive regard and empathy.

**clinical assessment** Evaluating a person's strengths and weaknesses and formulating a problem to develop a treatment plan.

**clinical psychologists** Mental health professionals with a Ph.D. or Psy.D. who promote behavioral change usually via psychological interventions.

**codependency** Dysfunctional behaviors that significant others of a person with substance-related disorder engage in to care for and cope with the person.

**cognitive-behavioral therapy** A type of treatment that focuses on the connection between thinking patterns, emotions, and behavior and uses cognitive and behavioral techniques to change dysfunctional thinking patterns.

**cognitive distortions** Irrational, inaccurate thoughts that people have about environmental events.

**cognitive perspective** A perspective of abnormal behavior that assumes that problematic symptoms develop because of the way we perceive and think about our present and past experiences.

**cognitive schema** Set of beliefs or expectations that represent a network of already accumulated knowledge.

**cognitive therapy** A treatment technique for cognitive symptoms of anxiety that involves helping a person think more realistically and develop a sense of control over anxious situations.

**cohort effects** Significant differences in the expression of a disorder depending on age.

**community psychology** A branch of psychology that focuses on enhancing quality of life for people and concentrating on their relationships with different social structures.

**community reinforcement approach** Encouraging a person to change environmental conditions to make them more reinforcing than drug use.

**comorbidity** Two or more disorders in one person.

**compensatory behaviors** Inappropriate behaviors to prevent weight gain.

**competency to stand trial** Whether a person can participate meaningfully in his or her own defense and can understand and appreciate the legal process that is involved.

**compulsions** Ongoing and bizarre ritualistic acts performed after an obsession to reduce arousal. These may involve checking, hand washing, ordering, counting, repeating words or phrases, or seeking reassurance from others.

**computerized axial tomography (CT scan)** A neuroimaging technique that uses X-rays to identify structural abnormalities.

**concurrent validity** Whether current test or interview results relate to an important feature or characteristic at the present time.

**conditional positive regard** An environment in which others set conditions or standards for one's life.

**conduct disorder** A childhood mental disorder marked by antisocial conduct in the form of aggression, property destruction, deceitfulness, theft, and serious rule violations.

**confidentiality** The idea that discussions between a therapist and a client should not be divulged to other people unless consent is given.

**confounds** Factors that may account for group differences on a dependent variable.

**consequences** Outcomes or events that follow a behavior.

**construct validity** Whether test or interview results relate to other measures or behaviors in a logical, theoretically expected fashion.

**content validity** Degree to which test or interview items actually cover aspects of the variable or diagnosis under study.

**contingency management** A behavioral treatment technique in which family members and friends reward appropriate behavior in an individual.

**control group** Those who do not receive the active independent variable in an experiment.

**controlled observation** A behavioral assessment technique that involves analogue tests or tasks to approximate situations people face in real life and that may elicit a certain problem behavior.

**conversion disorder** A somatic symptom disorder marked by odd pseudoneurological symptoms that have no discoverable medical cause.

**coronary heart disease** Narrowing of the small blood vessels that supply blood and oxygen to the heart.

**correlational study** A study that allows researchers to make some statements about the association or relationship between variables based on the extent to which they change together in a predictable way.

**counseling psychologists** Mental health professionals with an M.A. or Ph.D. who help clients make choices to improve quality of life.

**covert sensitization** A treatment that involves associating imaginal paraphilic scenes with descriptions of negative consequences or unpleasant events.

**criminal commitment** Involuntary hospitalization of people charged with a crime, either for determination of competency to stand trial or after acquittal by reason of insanity.

**cross-sectional study** A developmental design examining different groups of people at one point in time.

**cross-tolerance** Tolerance for a drug one has never taken because of tolerance to another drug with a similar chemical composition.

**cue exposure therapy** Exposure of a person to drug cues to help him or her control urges to use the drug.

**cultural-familial intellectual disability** Intellectual disability linked less to physical factors and more to environmental ones, such as poor language stimulation and parents with low intelligence.

**cultural syndrome** A problem caused by culturally shared beliefs and ideas that lead to high levels of stress and mental disorder.

**culture** The unique behavior and lifestyle shared by a group of people.

**cyclothymic disorder** A mental disorder marked by fluctuating symptoms of hypomania and depression for at least 2 years.

**defense mechanisms** Strategies used by the ego to stave off threats from the id or superego.

**delayed ejaculation** Delay or absence of orgasm in males during sexual activity with a partner.

**delirium** A neurocognitive disorder marked by usually temporary and reversible problems in thinking and memory.

**delusional disorder** A psychotic disorder marked by one or more delusions without other features of schizophrenia.

**delusions** Irrational beliefs involving a misinterpretation of perceptions or life experiences.

**dementia** A neurocognitive problem marked by usually chronic, progressive, and irreversible problems in thinking and memory.

**dependent personality disorder** Personality disorder marked by extreme submissiveness and a strong need to be liked and be taken care of by others.

**dependent variable** Variables that measure a certain outcome that a researcher is trying to explain or predict.

**depersonalization/derealization disorder** A dissociative disorder marked by chronic episodes of detachment from one's body and feelings of derealization.

**depressant** A class of drugs that inhibit the central nervous system.

**depressive disorder** A mental disorder marked by substantial sadness and related characteristic symptoms.

**detoxification** Withdrawing a person from an addictive drug under medical supervision.

**developmental disorder** A mental disorder marked by delay in key areas of cognitive, adaptive, and academic functioning.

**diagnosis** A category of mental disorder defined by certain rules that outline how many and what features of a disorder must be present.

**dialectical behavior therapy** Cognitive-behavioral treatment for suicidal behavior and related features of borderline personality disorder.

**diathesis** A biological or psychological predisposition to disorder.

**dimension** An approach to defining mental disorder along a continuum.

**discrete-trial training** A structured and repetitive method of teaching various skills to a child.

**disinhibition** The state that occurs when alcohol inhibits key inhibitory systems of the brain.

**disorganized speech** Disconnected, fragmented, interrupted, jumbled, and/or tangential speech.

**disruptive behavior disorders** A class of childhood mental disorders that involve serious acting-out behavior problems and often include attention-deficit/hyperactivity, oppositional defiant, and conduct disorders.

**dissociation** A feeling of detachment or separation from oneself.

**dissociative amnesia** A dissociative disorder marked by severe memory loss for past and/or recent events.

**dissociative disorder** A class of mental disorders marked by disintegration of memory, consciousness, or identity.

**dissociative fugue** A dissociative problem marked by severe memory loss and sudden travel away from home or work.

**dissociative identity disorder** A dissociative disorder marked by multiple personalities in a single individual.

**distal factors** Causal factors that indirectly affect a particular mental disorder.

**double-blind design** An experimental condition meaning that neither the experimenter nor the participants know who received a placebo or an active treatment.

**Down syndrome** A chromosomal condition often caused by an extra chromosome 21 and that leads to characteristic physical features and intellectual disability.

**dream analysis** A psychodynamic technique to access unconscious material thought to be symbolized in dreams.

**dual relationships** A client who is also a significant other in the therapist's life; ethics standards dictate that this practice is to be avoided.

**dyssomnias** Abnormalities in the amount, quality, or timing of sleep.

**eating disorder** A class of mental disorder involving severe body dissatisfaction, weight concerns, and eating problems as well as significant distress, excessive limits on activities, or increased risk for medical problems.

**eating problems** Restricting eating/excessive dieting and lack of control of eating.

**educational psychologists** Psychologists typically with a Ph.D. who work in school settings or academia to study and improve learning strategies for youth and adults.

**ego** The organized, rational component of the personality.

**electrocardiogram** A psychophysiological measure that provides a graphical description of heart rate.

**electroconvulsive therapy (ECT)** A procedure in which an electrical current is introduced to the brain to produce a seizure to alleviate severe depression.

**electroencephalogram (EEG)** A psychophysiological measure of brain activity.

**electronic diaries** Electronic devices for self-monitoring.

**emotional processing** A person's ability to think about a past anxiety-provoking event without significant anxiety.

**emotional reasoning** A cognitive distortion involving the assumption that one's physical feelings reflect how things really are.

**endogenous opioids** Chemicals produced by the body that reduce pain, enhance positive mood, and suppress appetite.

**epidemiologists** Scientists who study the incidence, prevalence, and risk factors of disorders.

**epidemiology** The study of patterns of diseases, disorders, and other health-related behavior in a population of interest.

**erectile disorder** A sexual dysfunction involving difficulty obtaining and maintaining an erection during sexual relations.

**ethnicity** Clusters of individuals who share cultural traits that distinguish themselves from others.

**etiology** Cause of mental disorders.

**exhibitionistic disorder** A paraphilic disorder in which the predominant focus of sexual activity is exposure of one's genitals to others such as strangers.

**experiment** A research method that allows scientists to draw cause-and-effect conclusions.

**exposure-based practices** Treatment techniques for behavioral symptoms of anxiety that involve reintroducing a person to situations she commonly avoids.

**expressed emotion** Family interactions characterized by high levels of emotional overinvolvement, hostility, and criticism.

**external validity** Ability to generalize results from one investigation to the general population.

**extrapyramidal effects** A group of side effects from antipsychotic medication involving involuntary movements of different parts of the body.

**factitious disorder** A mental disorder marked by deliberate production of physical or psychological symptoms to assume the sick role.

**family systems perspective** The idea that each family has its own structure and rules that can affect the mental health of individual family members.

**fear** An immediate and negative reaction to imminent threat that involves fright, increased arousal, and an overwhelming urge to escape.

**female orgasmic disorder** A sexual dysfunction marked by delay or absence of orgasm during sexual activity.

**female sexual interest/arousal disorder** A sexual dysfunction marked by lack of interest in, or arousal during, sexual activity.

**fetal alcohol syndrome** A condition caused by prenatal alcohol use that results in facial abnormalities and learning problems in children.

**fetishistic disorder** A paraphilic disorder in which the predominant focus of sexual activity is a nonliving object or nongenital body part.

**fixation** Frustration and anxiety at a psychosexual stage that can cause a person to be arrested at that level of development.

**flat affect** Lack of variety in emotional expression and speech.

**flooding** An exposure-based therapy technique involving exposure to, and eventual extinction of, one's most intense fear.

**forensic psychology** A branch of psychology involving the interaction of psychological and legal principles.

**fragile X syndrome** A genetic condition that involves damage to the X chromosome and that often leads to intellectual disability, especially in males.

**free association** A psychodynamic technique in which a client speaks continuously without censorship.

**free radicals** Aggressive substances produced by the body possibly to fight viruses and bacteria but that, in excess, may lead to dementia.

**frontal lobe** An area in front of the brain that is responsible for movement, planning, organizing, inhibiting behavior, and decision making.

**frotteuristic disorder** A paraphilic disorder in which the predominant focus of sexual activity is physical contact with an unsuspecting person.

**functional analysis** A behavioral assessment strategy to understand antecedents and consequences of behavior.

**functional MRI (fMRI)** A neuroimaging technique that assesses brain structure and function as well as metabolic changes.

**galvanic skin conductance** A psychophysiological measure of the electrical conductance of skin.

**gender dysphoria** A mental disorder marked by strong desire to be of the opposite gender and identifying oneself as a person of the opposite gender.

**generalized anxiety disorder** A mental disorder marked by constant worry about nondangerous situations and physical symptoms of tension.

**gene therapy** Insertion of genes into an individual's cells and tissues to treat a disorder.

**genito-pelvic pain/penetration disorder** A sexual dysfunction involving pain during vaginal penetration and/or fear of pain before penetration.

**genotype** The genetic composition of an individual that is fixed at birth and received from one's parents.

**hallucinations** Sensory experiences a person believes to be true when actually they are not.

**hallucinogens** A class of drugs that produce psychosis-like symptoms.

**health psychologists** Psychologists who specialize in examining the interaction of biological, psychological, and social variables on traditional medical disorders.

**histrionic personality disorder** Personality disorder marked by excessive need for attention, superficial and fleeting emotions, and impulsivity.

**hopelessness** A feeling of despair often related to severe depression and suicide.

**hopelessness theory** A theory of depression that people are more likely to become depressed if they make global, internal, and stable attributions about negative life events.

**humanistic model** A model of abnormal behavior that emphasizes personal growth, free will, and responsibility.

**hypertension** High blood pressure commonly identified if systolic pressure is greater than 140 millimeters of mercury and/or if diastolic pressure is greater than 90 millimeters of mercury.

**hypomanic episode** A period during which a person experiences manic symptoms but without significant interference in daily functioning.

**hypothalamus** A region of the brain below the thalamus that influences body temperature, food intake, sleep, and sex drive.

**id** The deep, inaccessible portion of the personality that contains instinctual urges.

**illness anxiety disorder** A somatic symptom disorder marked by excessive preoccupation with fear of having a disease.

**Inappropriate affect** Emotion not appropriate for a given situation.

**incidence** Rate of new cases of a disorder that occur or develop during a specific time period such as a month or year.

**independent variable** A variable manipulated by a researcher that is hypothesized to be the cause of the outcome.

**indicated prevention** Preventive intervention targeting individuals at high risk for developing extensive problems in the future.

**induction defects** Problems in closure of the neural tube, proper development of the forebrain, and completion of the corpus callosum, all of which may lead to developmental disorder.

**informant report** Assessment methodology in which individuals who know a person well complete ratings of his or her personality traits and behavior.

**informed consent** The practice of educating potential clients about the therapy process, especially variables that might influence their decision to seek therapy.

**insanity** A legal term that refers to mental incapacity at the time of the crime, perhaps because a person did not understand right from wrong or because he or she was unable to control personal actions at the time of the crime.

**insight** (1) An active treatment ingredient in which a client comes to understand reasons for his maladaptive behavior and how to address it. (2) Understanding the unconscious determinants of irrational feelings, thoughts, or behaviors that create problems or distress.

**intellectual disability** A pervasive developmental disorder marked by below average intelligence, poor adaptive behavior, and onset before age 18 years.

**intelligence tests** Measures of cognitive functioning that provide estimates of intellectual ability.

**internal consistency reliability** Extent to which test items appear to be measuring the same thing.

**internal validity** Extent to which a researcher can be confident that changes in the dependent variable are truly the result of manipulation of the independent variable.

**interoceptive exposure** A treatment technique involving exposure to, and eventual control of, physical symptoms of anxiety.

**interpretation** A method in which a psychodynamic theorist reveals unconscious meanings of a client's thoughts and behaviors to help the person achieve insight.

**interrater reliability** Extent to which two raters or observers agree about their ratings or judgments of a person's behavior.

**irritable bowel syndrome (IBS)** A chronic gastrointestinal disorder involving alternating and recurrent constipation and diarrhea as well as abdominal pain.

**Korsakoff's syndrome** A problem marked by confusion, memory loss, and coordination problems.

**lack of control over eating** A feeling of poor control when eating such that excessive quantities of food are consumed.

**latent content** The symbolic meaning of a dream's events.

**learned helplessness** A theory related to depression that people act in a helpless, passive fashion upon learning their actions have little effect on their overall environment.

**learning disorder** A limited developmental disorder marked by academic problems in reading, spelling, writing, arithmetic, or some other important area.

**least restrictive treatment** A principle according to which people with mental disorders should receive effective treatment that impinges least on their freedom.

**lethal dose** Dose of a substance that kills a certain percentage of test animals.

**Lewy bodies** Clusters of alpha-synuclein proteins that accumulate in the brain and may lead to dementia.

**lifetime prevalence** Proportion of those who exhibit symptoms of a disorder up to the point they were assessed.

**limbic system** An area of the brain in the forebrain that regulates emotions and impulses and is responsible for basic drives like thirst, sex, and aggression.

**limited developmental disorders** A developmental disorder in which one area but not many areas of functioning are affected.

**longitudinal study** A developmental design examining the same group of people over a long period of time.

**magnetic resonance imaging (MRI)** A neuroimaging technique that can produce high-resolution images of brain structure.

**major depressive disorder** A mental disorder often marked by multiple major depressive episodes.

**major depressive episode** A period of time, two weeks or longer, marked by sad or empty mood most of the day, nearly every day, and other symptoms.

**major neurocognitive disorder** A mental disorder marked by severe problems in thinking and memory.

**maladaptive behavior** A behavior that interferes with a person's life, including ability to care for oneself, have good relationships with others, and function well at school or at work.

**male hypoactive sexual desire disorder** A sexual dysfunction involving a lack of fantasies or desire to have sexual relations.

**malingering** Deliberate production of physical or psychological symptoms with some external motivation.

**manic episode** A period during which a person feels highly euphoric or irritable.

**manifest content** The literal meaning of a dream.

**marijuana** A drug produced from the hemp plant that contains THC.

**marriage and family therapists** Mental health professionals with an M.A. or Ph.D. who specialize in working with couples and families.

**mastery** An active treatment ingredient involving strong control over one's symptoms to the point they are not problematic to the individual.

**masturbation training** A treatment for people with paraphilic disorder that involves practicing effective masturbation and stimulation to enhance orgasm.

**memory training** A psychological treatment to enhance a person's memory by repeatedly practicing skills relying on external cues and mnemonic strategies to jog memory, increasing social interaction, and simplifying a living environment.

**mental disorder** A group of emotional (feelings), cognitive (thinking), or behavioral symptoms that cause distress or significant problems.

**mental hygiene** The science of promoting mental health and thwarting mental disorder through education, early treatment, and public health measures.

**mental status examination** An assessment strategy involving evaluation of appearance, mood, orientation, and odd behaviors, speech, or thoughts.

**mesolimbic system** A reward-based area in the brain implicated in substance-related disorders.

**metabolites** By-products of neurotransmitters that can be detected in urine, blood, and cerebral spinal fluid.

**migration defects** Problems in cell growth and distribution in the second to fifth month of pregnancy, which can lead to underdeveloped brain areas and developmental disorder.

**mild neurocognitive disorder** A mental disorder marked by emerging problems in thinking and memory.

**milieu therapy** An inpatient treatment approach involving professionals and staff members encouraging a person with a severe mental disorder to engage in prosocial and therapeutic activities.

**mindfulness** A therapy technique that emphasizes how a person can accept symptoms but still function in a given situation.

**MMPI-2 clinical scales** Subscales of the MMPI-2 used to identify various problematic behaviors and personality styles.

**MMPI-2 validity scales** Subscales of the MMPI-2 used to identify a person's defensiveness during testing and response sets.

**model** A systematic way of viewing and explaining what we observe.

**modeling** Learning a new skill or set of behaviors by observing another person perform the skill or behavior.

**molecular genetics** Analysis of deoxyribonucleic acid (DNA) to identify links between specific genetic material and mental disorders.

**monoamine oxidase inhibitor (MAOI)** A class of antidepressant drug that inhibits monoamine oxidase, which breaks down neurotransmitters, to increase levels of those neurotransmitters.

**mood-stabilizing drugs** Medications used to help people control rapid shifts in mood.

**motivational interviewing** A type of interview for substance-related disorders that focuses on obtaining information and propelling a person to change behavior.

**multidimensional family therapy** A family-based treatment approach that focuses on developing a strong parent–adolescent bond and correcting related problems.

**multisystemic treatment** An intensive family- and community-based treatment program designed to address conduct-related problems in children.

**Munchausen syndrome** A severe factitious disorder in which a person causes symptoms and claims he has a physical or mental disorder.

**narcissistic personality disorder** Personality disorder marked by grandiosity, arrogance, and a tendency to exploit others.

**natural experiment** An observational study in which nature itself helps assign groups.

**naturalistic observation** A behavioral assessment technique that involves observing a person in his or her natural environment.

**negative cognitive triad** Cognitive distortions involving the self, world, and the future.

**negative correlation** Two variables highly related to one another such that an increase in one variable is accompanied by a decrease in the other variable.

**negative reinforcement** Removing an aversive event following a behavior to increase frequency of the behavior.

**negative symptoms** Symptoms such as flat affect and alogia that represent significant deficits in behavior.

**neurochemical assessment** Biological assessment of dysfunctions in specific neurotransmitter systems.

**neurodevelopmental hypothesis** An etiological model for psychotic disorders that assumes early changes in key brain areas and gradual progression over the life span to full-blown symptoms.

**neurofibrillary tangles** Twisted fibers inside nerve cells of the brain that may lead to dementia.

**neuron** The basic unit of the nervous system that comprises a cell body, dendrites, axon, and terminal buttons.

**neuropsychological assessment** Indirect measures of brain and physical function by evaluating a person's performance on standardized tests and tasks that indicate brain–behavior relationships.

**neurotransmitters** Chemical messengers that allow a nerve impulse to cross the synapse.

**normalization** The idea that people with mental disorders in regular living environments will behave more appropriately than those in large institutions.

**objective personality measures** Measures of personality that involve administering a standard set of questions or statements to which a person responds using set options.

**obsessions** Ongoing and bizarre ideas, thoughts, impulses, or images that a person cannot control.

**obsessive-compulsive disorder** A mental disorder marked by ongoing obsessions and compulsions lasting more than 1 hour per day.

**obsessive-compulsive personality disorder** Personality disorder marked by rigidity, perfectionism, and strong need for control.

**occipital lobe** An area of the brain behind the parietal and temporal lobes and associated with vision.

**operant conditioning** A learning principle that behavior followed by positive or pleasurable consequences is likely to be repeated but behavior followed by negative consequences is not likely to be repeated.

**opiates** A class of drugs commonly used to relieve pain.

**oppositional defiant disorder** A childhood mental disorder marked by hostile and negative behavior that includes noncompliance, argumentativeness, anger, spitefulness, and annoyance of others.

**organismic variables** A person's physiological or cognitive characteristics important for understanding a problem and determining treatment.

**orgasmic reconditioning** A treatment for paraphilic disorders that involves initial masturbation to a paraphilic stimulus and later masturbation to more appropriate sexual stimuli.

**oxidative stress** Damage to the brain from extensive exposure to oxygen and related matter.

**panic attack** A brief episode of intense fear and physical symptoms that increases and decreases suddenly in intensity. These symptoms are often accompanied by worry about their dangerousness and negative consequences.

**panic disorder** A mental disorder marked by ongoing and uncued panic attacks, worry about the consequences of these attacks, and, sometimes, agoraphobia.

**paranoid personality disorder** Personality disorder marked by general distrust and suspiciousness of others.

**paraphilias** Preferential, intense, and/or persistent sexual interests that may be odd but are not a mental disorder.

**paraphilic disorders** A class of mental disorder involving problems arising from sexual behavior or fantasies of highly unusual activities.

**paraprofessionals** Persons without advanced degrees who often work in mental health settings and assist with assessment and treatment procedures.

**parasomnias** Abnormal behavioral or physiological events that occur throughout sleep.

**parietal lobe** An area of the brain behind the frontal lobe that is associated with the sensation of touch.

**Parkinson's disease** A progressive neurological disorder marked by abnormal movements that may lead to a neurocognitive disorder.

**partial agonists** Medications to treat substance-related disorders that may act as an agonist or antagonist depending on how much of a certain neurotransmitter is produced.

**pedophilic disorder** A paraphilic disorder in which the predominant focus of sexual activity is with children.

**peripheral nervous system** The somatic and autonomic nervous system that controls muscles and voluntary movement, impacts the cardiovascular and endocrine system, assists with digestion, and regulates body temperature.

**personality assessment** Instruments measuring different traits or aspects of character.

**personality disorders** Mental disorders involving dysfunctional personality traits and

associated problems such as relationship disturbances and impulsive behavior.

**peripartum depression** Symptoms of depression or a major depressive episode that occurs during pregnancy.

**persistent depressive disorder (dysthymia)** A depressive disorder involving a chronic feeling of depression for at least 2 years.

**pervasive developmental disorders** A developmental disorder in which many areas of functioning are affected.

**phenomenological approach** An assumption that one's behavior is determined by perceptions of herself and others.

**phenotype** Observable characteristics of an individual.

**phenylketonuria (PKU)** An autosomal recessive disorder that leads to buildup of phenylalanine and possible intellectual disability.

**Pick's disease** A neurocognitive disorder characterized mainly by deterioration in the frontal and temporal brain lobes.

**placebo** A nonspecific factor involving a client's expectation of improvement in treatment.

**pleasure principle** The rule of conduct by the id to seek pleasure and avoid pain.

**positive correlation** Two variables highly related to one another such that an increase in one variable is accompanied by an increase in the other variable.

**positive reinforcement** Presenting a pleasant event or consequence after a behavior to increase frequency of the behavior.

**positive symptoms** Symptoms such as delusions and hallucinations that are obvious and excessive.

**positron emission tomography (PET scan)** An invasive neuroimaging procedure to assess brain structure and functioning.

**postpartum depression** A major depressive episode during weeks following childbirth.

**postpartum psychosis** A mental condition marked by psychotic symptoms in a mother following the birth of her child.

**posttraumatic stress disorder** A mental disorder marked by a traumatic event and the reexperiencing of the event through unwanted memories, nightmares, flashbacks, and images.

**predictive validity** Whether test or interview results accurately predict some behavior or event in the future.

**premature (early) ejaculation** A sexual dysfunction in men marked by orgasm that occurs before the person wishes.

**premenstrual dysphoric disorder** A mental disorder marked by depressive symptoms during most menstrual periods.

**prescriptive treatment** Assigning a specific treatment to an individual with a specific mental health problem or subtype of a problem.

**prevalence** Rate of new and existing cases of a condition observed during a specific time period.

**prevention** Interventions intended to arrest the development of later problems.

**primary prevention** A type of prevention targeting large groups of people who have not yet developed a disorder.

**primary process** The irrational and impulsive type of thinking that characterizes the id.

**process variables** General ingredients common to most psychological treatments that promote mental health in a client.

**prodromal phase** An initial phase of schizophrenia marked by peculiar thoughts and behaviors but without active psychotic features.

**projection** A defense mechanism used when a person attributes his or her unconscious feelings to someone else.

**projective hypothesis** The assumption that, when faced with unstructured or ambiguous stimuli or tasks, individuals impose their own structure and reveal something of themselves.

**projective tests** Psychological testing techniques based on the assumption that people faced with an ambiguous stimulus such as an inkblot will project their own needs, personality, conflicts, and wishes.

**protective factor** A factor that buffers one against the development of a mental disorder.

**proximal factors** Causal factors that more directly affect a particular mental disorder.

**pseudoseizures** Seizure-like activity such as twitching or loss of consciousness without electrical disruptions in the brain.

**psychiatric nurses** Specialized nurses with an R.N. who often work on inpatient psychiatric wards and have training specific to mental disorders.

**psychiatrists** Mental health professionals with an M.D. who often adopt a medical or biological model to treat people with mental disorders.

**psychic determinism** An assumption of psychodynamic theory that everything we do has meaning and purpose and is goal-directed.

**psychoanalyst** A mental health professional that specializes in Freudian psychoanalysis to treat people with mental disorders.

**psychodynamic model** A model of abnormal behavior that assumes all mental states, emotions, and behaviors arise from unconscious motives and intrapsychic conflicts.

**psychoeducation** A treatment technique that involves educating a person about the physical, cognitive, and behavioral components of anxiety or other problems and how these components occur in sequence for that person.

**psychopathologists** Professionals who study mental problems to see how disorders develop and continue and how they can be prevented or alleviated.

**psychopathy** Diagnostic construct related to antisocial personality disorder that focuses on problematic interpersonal styles such as arrogance, lack of empathy, and manipulativeness.

**psychophysiological assessment** Evaluating bodily changes possibly associated with certain mental conditions.

**psychophysiological disorders** Organ dysfunction or physical symptoms that may be at least partly caused by psychological factors such as stress.

**psychosexual stages of development** A series of developmental stages marked by a particular erogenous zone of the body.

**psychotherapist** A generic mental health professional, or one not currently licensed as a psychologist or psychiatrist.

**psychotic disorders** A class of mental disorder marked by schizophrenia and/or related problems.

**psychotic prephase** A phase of schizophrenia between the prodromal and active phases involving the onset of the first positive symptom of schizophrenia.

**public health model** A model that focuses on promoting good health and good health practices to avert disease.

**purging** Ridding oneself of food or bodily fluids (and thus weight) by self-induced vomiting or misuse of laxatives or diuretics.

**quasi-experimental method** A study in which an independent variable is manipulated but people are not randomly selected or assigned to groups.

**race** A socially constructed category typically based on physical characteristics.

**randomization** Selecting and assigning people to groups so each person has the same chance of being assigned to any one group.

**rational restructuring** A set of techniques to teach individuals to examine their assumptions about situations or the world in general and think more realistically.

**reality orientation** A psychological treatment to reduce confusion in people using constant feedback about time, place, person, and recent events.

**reality principle** The rule of conduct by the ego that defers gratification of instinctual urges until a suitable object and mode of satisfaction are discovered.

**regression** A defense mechanism that occurs when a person returns to a life stage that once provided substantial gratification.

**rehabilitation** Regarding substance-related disorders, treatment involving complete abstinence, education about drugs and consequences of their use, and relapse prevention.

**relaxation training** A treatment technique for physical anxiety symptoms that may involve having a person tense and release (relax) different muscle groups.

**reliability** Consistency of test scores or diagnoses.

**reminiscence therapy** A treatment procedure for older adults with depression involving a systematic review of one's life and resolution of regrets.

**repetitive transcranial magnetic stimulation (rTMS)** A procedure to treat depressive and bipolar disorders that involves rapidly changing magnetic fields.

**repression** A defense mechanism that involves keeping highly threatening sexual or aggressive material out of conscious awareness.

**residual phase** A phase of schizophrenia usually after the active phase involving peculiar thoughts and behaviors similar to the prodromal phase.

**resilience** Ability of an individual to withstand and rise above extreme adversity.

**response (or ritual) prevention** A treatment technique for obsessive-compulsive disorder involving exposure to an obsession such as thoughts of dirty hands without engaging in a related compulsion such as hand washing.

**restricted eating/dieting** Deliberate attempts to limit quantity of food intake or change types of foods that are eaten.

**restricting behaviors** Eating less overall, avoiding foods with high calories, and engaging in excessive exercise.

**reuptake** A feedback mechanism that informs a neuron about the amount of neurotransmitter needed to be released in the future.

**reward deficiency syndrome** The theory that some people may not be able to derive much reward from everyday events and so resort to excesses such as drug use.

**right to refuse treatment** A principle according to which clients have the right to refuse risky or unconventional or discomfiting treatments.

**right to treatment** A principle according to which clients have the right to receive treatment that provides a meaningful chance of improvement in their condition.

**risk factor** An individual, contextual, or environmental characteristic correlated with an outcome or condition such as a mental disorder that precedes the development of the disorder.

**satiety** Feeling of fullness from eating.

**schizoaffective disorder** A psychotic disorder marked by symptoms of schizophrenia and depression or mania.

**schizoid personality disorder** Personality disorder marked by social isolation and restricted emotional expression.

**schizophrenia** A psychotic disorder marked by positive symptoms such as delusions and hallucinations, negative symptoms such as flat affect and withdrawal, and disorganized behavior.

**schizophreniform disorder** A psychotic disorder marked by symptoms of schizophrenia that last 1 to 6 months.

**schizotypal personality disorder** Personality disorder marked by social anxiety, paranoid fears, and eccentric behavior, perceptions, and thoughts.

**school psychologists** Psychologists with an M.A. or Ph.D. who typically work in school settings to evaluate youth with learning and behavioral problems.

**school refusal behavior** A child-motivated refusal to attend school and/or difficulties remaining in classes for an entire day.

**scientific method** A set of agreed-upon rules for systematically gathering information that involves generating a hypothesis, developing a research design, and analyzing and interpreting data to test the hypothesis.

**screening interview** A type of assessment that helps clinicians obtain information about recent and lifetime use of alcohol and other drugs.

**secondary prevention** A type of prevention that addresses emerging problems while they are still manageable and before they become resistant to intervention.

**secondary process** The rational and self-preservative type of thinking that characterizes the ego.

**selective prevention** Preventive intervention targeting subgroups of people at risk for a particular problem.

**selective serotonin reuptake inhibitor (SSRI)** A class of antidepressant medication that specifically affects serotonin levels and has fewer side effects than other antidepressants.

**self-actualization** Striving to be the best one can be.

**self-control** An active treatment ingredient whereby a client learns to control wayward impulses or emotions to improve quality of life.

**self-help group** An association of people who share a common problem such as a mental disorder that the group tries to address.

**self-monitoring** A behavioral assessment technique in which individuals observe and record their own emotions, thoughts, and behaviors.

**senile or neuritic plaques** Clusters of dead nerve cells and accumulations of amyloid proteins in the brain that may lead to dementia.

**sensate focus** A treatment for sexual dysfunction that helps couples reestablish intimacy while gradually rebuilding pleasurable sexual behaviors.

**separation anxiety disorder** A mental disorder marked by extreme and developmentally inappropriate distress when separation from home or close family members occurs or is anticipated.

**sequential design** A developmental design involving aspects of longitudinal and cross-sectional studies.

**serotonin** A major neurotransmitter that influences the way we process information and that regulates our behavior and mood.

**sex reassignment surgery** A treatment for people with gender dysphoria that involves physical transformation to the opposite gender.

**sexual dysfunction** A mental disorder involving disturbance of the normal sexual response cycle.

**sexual masochism** A paraphilic disorder in which the predominant focus of sexual activity is a desire to be humiliated or made to suffer.

**sexual sadism** A paraphilic disorder in which the predominant focus of sexual activity is a desire to humiliate or make suffer.

**sickle cell disease** A genetic condition that leads to damaged red blood cells, poor oxygenation of cells, and potential intellectual disability.

**single-subject experimental design** Experimental designs that involve one person or a small group of persons who are examined under certain conditions.

**skills training** A treatment for substance-related disorders involving functional analysis of drug use and skills to avoid or cope with high-risk situations.

**social phobia/social anxiety disorder** A mental disorder marked by panic attacks in, and avoidance of, situations involving performance before others or possible negative evaluation.

**social role valorization** The idea that people, especially those with mental disorders, behave less deviantly if valued by others in their environment.

**social workers** Mental health professionals with an M.A. or Ph.D. who work to improve quality of life for people with mental disorders.

**sociocultural perspective** A perspective of abnormal behavior that focuses on influences that other people, social institutions, and social forces exert on a person's mental health.

**somatic control exercises** Treatment techniques to help people with anxiety-related disorders decrease severity of their aversive physical feelings.

**somatic symptom disorder** A mental disorder in which a person experiences physical symptoms that may or may not have a discoverable physical cause, as well as distress.

**somatization** A tendency to communicate distress through physical symptoms and to pursue medical help for these symptoms.

**special education teachers** Specialized teachers with an M.A. or Ph.D. who work primarily with youth with developmental disorders in academic settings.

**specific phobia** A mental disorder marked by panic attacks surrounding, and avoidance of, objects and situations other than those involving social interaction and/or performance before others.

**spectator role** The process of attending more to, and worrying about, sexual behavior and performance than the enjoyment and pleasure of sexual activity.

**standardization** Administering or conducting clinical assessment measures in the same way for all examinees.

**stigma** A characterization by others of disgrace or reproach based on an individual characteristic.

**stimulants** A class of drugs that activate the central nervous system.

**stop–start procedure** A treatment for premature ejaculation that involves pinching the tip of the penis when sexual stimulation becomes intense.

**stress** External events in our daily lives that are taxing for us as well as internal events such as perceptions that external events are demanding as well as certain physical symptoms.

**stress-induced relapse** Relapse to excessive substance use following stress and a period of abstinence.

**stress management** A collection of techniques to help people reduce the chronic effects of stress on a daily basis as well as problematic physical symptoms.

**structured interviews** A type of clinical interview that requires an interviewer to ask standardized questions in a specified sequence.

**substance intoxication** A usually reversible condition triggered by excessive alcohol or other drug use.

**substance-related disorder** A class of mental disorders characterized by substance use disorder as well as substance intoxication and withdrawal.

**substance use** A nonmaladaptive use of alcohol or other drug.

**substance use disorder** A mental disorder involving repeated use of substances to the point that recurring problems are evident.

**substance withdrawal** Maladaptive behavioral changes that result when a person stops using a particular drug.

**suicide** The act of killing oneself.

**superego** A component of the personality representing the ideals and values of society as conveyed by parents.

**synapse** A small gap between ends of neurons.

**syndrome** Symptoms that cluster or group together within individuals.

**systematic desensitization** An exposure-based treatment technique involving gradual exposure to feared objects or situations and relaxation/breathing training.

**Tay-Sachs disease** A genetic condition leading to severe motor and sensory disabilities as well as intellectual disability and early death.

**temporal lobe** A middle area of the brain associated with auditory discrimination.

**teratogen** A potentially harmful agent that affects fetuses during the prenatal stage and which may lead to developmental disorders.

**tertiary prevention** A type of prevention aimed to reduce the severity, duration, and negative effects of a mental disorder after it has occurred.

**test–retest reliability** Extent to which a person provides similar answers to the same test items across time.

**thalamus** A structure within the forebrain that relays sensory information to the cerebral cortex.

**theory of mind** An understanding of the thoughts and beliefs of others.

**therapeutic alignment** A nonspecific factor in treatment in which a therapist sides with a particular individual to balance communications or power.

**therapeutic alliance** A nonspecific factor in treatment that refers to the relationship between the therapist and a client.

**thought-action fusion** A risk factor for obsessive-compulsive disorder involving a belief that thinking something is the same as doing it.

**token economy** An operant conditioning system in which desired behaviors are promoted through reinforcements.

**tolerance** The need to ingest greater amounts of a drug to achieve the same effect.

**transference** A key phenomenon in psychodynamic therapy in which a client reacts to the therapist as if the latter represented an important figure from the client's past.

**transvestic disorder** A paraphilic disorder in which the predominant focus of sexual activity is cross-dressing.

**tricyclic antidepressants** A class of antidepressant medication that affects different neurotransmitter systems and often comes with many side effects.

**triple-blind design** Experiments in which participants, experimenters, independent raters of outcome, and data managers are unaware of who received a placebo or active treatment.

**type D personality** A distressed personality pattern marked by negative affectivity and social inhibition.

**typical antipsychotics** A class of older drugs to treat schizophrenia and related psychotic disorders primarily by reducing excess levels of dopamine in the brain.

**ulcer** Inflammation or erosion of a part of the body such as the esophagus, stomach, or duodenum.

**unconditional positive regard** An environment in which a person is fully accepted as she is and allowed to pursue her own desires and goals.

**unconscious motivation** Motivation that resides outside conscious awareness.

**undifferentiated schizophrenia** A subtype of schizophrenia marked by a mixture of symptoms that do not clearly match other subtypes.

**unipolar mood disorder** A mood disturbance usually marked by depression only.

**universal prevention** Preventive intervention targeting large groups of people not afflicted by a particular problem.

**unstructured interview** A type of clinical interview in which clinicians ask any questions in any order.

**validity** Extent to which an assessment technique measures what it is supposed to measure.

**vascular dementia** A form of neurocognitive disorder caused by a cerebrovascular problem such as a stroke.

**voyeuristic disorder** A paraphilic disorder in which the predominant focus of sexual activity is secretly watching others undress or engage in sexual activity without being seen.

**weight concerns** A focus on, and often negative evaluation of, one's weight.

**worry** A largely cognitive construct that refers to concern about possible future threat.

**worry exposure** A treatment technique for generalized anxiety disorder involving extensive concentration on an anxious thought and alternatives to the worst-case scenario.

# References

Aarsland, D., Ballard, C., Rongve, A., Broadstock, M., & Svenningsson, P. (2012). Clinical trials of dementia with Lewy bodies and Parkinson's disease dementia. *Current Neurology and Neuroscience Reports, 12*, 492-501.

Aarsland, D. & Kurz, M.W. (2010). The epidemiology of dementia associated with Parkinson disease. *Journal of the Neurological Sciences, 289*, 19-22.

Aarsland, D., Zaccai, J., & Brayne, C. (2005). A systematic review of prevalence studies of dementia in Parkinson's disease. *Movement Disorders, 20*, 1255-1263.

Aarsland, D., Andersen, K., Larsen, J.P., Lolk, A., & Kragh-Sorensen, P. (2003). Prevalence and characteristics of dementia in Parkinson disease: An 8-year prospective study. *Archives of Neurology, 60*, 387-392.

Abdo, C.H.N., Hounie, A., de Tubino Scanavino, M., & Miguel, E.C. (2001). OCD and transvestism: Is there a relationship? *Acta Psychiatrica Scandinavica, 103*, 471-473.

Abler, B., Seeringer, A., Hartmann, A., Gron, G., Metzger, C., Walter, M., & Stingl, J. (2011). Neural correlates of antidepressant-related sexual dysfunction: A placebo-controlled fMRI study on healthy males under subchronic paroxetine and bupropion. *Neuropsychopharmacology, 36*, 1837-1847.

Ablon, J.S., & Jones, E.E. (2005). On analytic process. *Journal of the American Psychoanalytic Association, 53*, 541-568.

Abramowitz, J.S., Deacon, B.J., & Whiteside, S.P.H. (2011). *Exposure therapy for anxiety: Principles and practice.* New York: Guilford.

Abramson, L.Y., Alloy, L.B., Hankin, B.L., Haeffel, G.J., MacCoon, D.G., & Gibb, B.E. (2002). Cognitive vulnerability-stress models of depression in a self-regulatory and psychobiological context. In I.H. Gotlib & C.L. Hammen (Eds.), *Handbook of depression* (pp. 268-294). New York: Guilford.

Abramson, L.Y., Alloy, L.B., Hogan, M.E., Whitehouse, W.G., Donovan, P., Rose, D.T., Panzarella, C., & Raniere, D. (1999). Cognitive vulnerability to depression: Theory and evidence. *Journal of Cognitive Psychotherapy: An International Quarterly, 13*, 5-20.

Achenbach, T.M., & Rescorla, L.A. (2001). *Manual for the ASEBA school-age forms & profiles.* Burlington, VT: University of Vermont Research Center for Children, Youth, & Families.

Acosta, F.J., Bosch, E., Sarmeinto, G., Juanes, N., Caballero-Hidalgo, A., & Mayans, T. (2009). Evaluation of noncompliance in schizophrenia patients using electronic monitoring (MEMS) and its relationship to sociodemographic, clinical and psychopathological variables. *Schizophrenia Research, 107*, 213-217.

Addington, J., & Addington, D. (2005). Patterns of premorbid functioning in first episode psychosis: Relationship to 2-year outcome. *Acta Psychiatrica Scandinavica, 112*, 40-46.

Addis, M.E., Wade, W.A., & Hatgis, C. (1999). Barriers to dissemination of evidenced-based practices: Addressing practitioners' concerns about manual-based psychotherapies. *Clinical Psychology: Science and Practice, 6*, 430-441.

Addy, P.H., Radhakrishnan, R., Cortes, J.A., & D'Souza, D.C. (2012). Comorbid alcohol, cannabis, and cocaine use disorders in schizophrenia: Epidemiology, consequences, mechanisms, and treatment. *Focus, 10*, 140-153.

Aderibigbe, Y.A., Bloch, R.M., & Walker, W.R. (2001). Prevalence of depersonalization and derealization experiences in a rural population. *Social Psychiatry and Psychiatric Epidemiology, 36*, 63-69.

Adinoff, B. (2004). Neurobiologic processes in drug reward and addiction. *Harvard Review of Psychiatry, 12*, 305-320.

Agras, W.S., & Apple, R.F. (2007). *Overcoming eating disorders: A cognitive-behavioral therapy approach for bulimia nervosa and binge-eating disorder* (2nd ed.). New York: Oxford.

Agronin, M.E. (2004). *Dementia: A practical guide.* Philadelphia: Lippincott.

Aguilera, A., Lopez, S.R., Breitborde, N.J.K., Kopelowicz, A., & Zarate, R. (2010). Expressed emotion and sociocultural moderation in the course of schizophrenia. *Journal of Abnormal Psychology, 119*, 875-885.

Aguirre, E., Woods, R.T., Spector, A., & Orrell, M. (2013). Cognitive stimulation for dementia: A systematic review of the evidence of effectiveness from randomised controlled trials. *Ageing Research Reviews, 12*, 253-262.

Ahlers, C.J., Schaefer, G.A., Mundt, I.A., Roll, S., Englert, H., Willich, S.N., & Beier, K.M. (2011). How unusual are the contents of paraphilias? Paraphilia-associated sexual arousal patterns in a community-based sample of men. *Journal of Sexual Medicine, 8*, 1362-1370.

Ahmed, U., Gibbon, S., Jones, H., Huband, N., Ferriter, M., Vollm, B.A., Stoffers, J.M., Lieb, K., Dennis, J.A., & Duggan, C. (2012). Psychological interventions for avoidant personality disorder. *Cochrane Database of Systematic Reviews*, Issue 1.

Akerman, G., & Beech, A.R. (2012). A systematic review of measures of deviant sexual interest and arousal. *Psychiatry, Psychology and Law, 19*, 118-143.

Akiskal, K.K., & Akiskal, H.S. (2005). The theoretical underpinnings of affective temperaments: Implications for evolutionary foundations of bipolar disorder and human nature. *Journal of Affective Disorders, 85*, 231-239.

Albus, C. (2010). Psychological and social factors in coronary heart disease. *Annals of Medicine, 42*, 487-494.

Aleman, A., Kahn, R.S., & Selten, J.-P. (2003). Sex differences in the risk of schizophrenia: Evidence from meta-analysis. *Archives of General Psychiatry, 60*, 565-571.

Alex, K.D., Yavanian, G.J., McFarlane, H.G., Pluto, C.P., & Pehek, E.A. (2005). Modulation of dopamine release by striatal 5-HT2C receptors. *Synapse, 55*, 242-251.

Allan, L.M., Rowan, E.N., Firbank, M.J., Thomas, A.J., Parry, S.W., Polvikoski, T.M., O'Brien, J.T., & Kalaria, R.N. (2011). Long term incidence of dementia, predictors of mortality and pathological diagnosis in older stroke survivors. *Brain, 134*, 3713-3724.

Allen, D.N., Goldstein, G., & Weiner, C. (2001). Differential neuropsychological patterns of frontal- and temporal-lobe dysfunction in patients with schizophrenia. *Schizophrenia Research, 48*, 7-15.

Allen, L.A., & Woolfolk, R.L. (2010). Cognitive behavioral therapy for somatoform disorders. *Psychiatric Clinics of North America, 33*, 579-593.

Allen, N.B., & Badcock, P.B. (2003). The social risk hypothesis of depressed mood: Evolutionary, psychosocial, and neurobiological perspectives. *Psychological Bulletin, 129*, 887-913.

Allet, J.L., & Allet, R.E. (2006). Somatoform disorders in neurological practice. *Current Opinion in Psychiatry, 19*, 413-420.

Alloy, L.B., Urosevic, S., Abramson, L.Y., Jager-Hyman, S., Nusslock, R., Whitehouse, W.G., & Hogan, M. (2012). Progression along the bipolar spectrum: A longitudinal study of predictors of conversion from bipolar spectrum conditions to bipolar I and II disorders. *Journal of Abnormal Psychology, 121*, 16-27.

Almeida, O.P., Garrido, G.J., Lautenschlager, N.T., Hulse, G.K., Jamrozik, K., & Flicker, L. (2008). Smoking is associated with reduced cortical regional gray matter density in brain regions associated with incipient Alzheimer disease. *American Journal of Geriatric Psychiatry, 16*, 92-98.

Althof, S.E. (2005). Psychological treatment strategies for rapid ejaculation: Rationale, practical aspects, and outcome. *World Journal of Urology, 23*, 89-92.

Alzheimer's Association. (2013). *2013 Alzheimer's disease facts and figures.* Washington, DC: Author.

American Anthropological Association. (1999). AAA statement on race. *American Anthropologist, 100*, 712-713.

American Psychiatric Association. (2000). *Diagnostic and statistical manual of mental disorders* (4th ed.). Washington, DC: Author.

American Psychiatric Association. (2000). Practice guideline for the treatment of patients with major depressive disorder (revision). *American Journal of Psychiatry, 157* (Suppl. 4), 1-45.

American Psychiatric Association. (2001). *The practice of electroconvulsive therapy: Recommendations* for treatment, training, and privileging (2nd. ed.). Washington, DC: Author.

American Psychiatric Association (2006). *Treatment of patients with eating disorders* (3rd ed.). Washington, DC: Author.

American Psychiatric Association. (2013). *Diagnostic and statistical manual of mental disorders* (5th ed.). Arlington, VA: American Psychiatric Publishing.

American Psychological Association. (2002). Ethical principles of psychologists and code of conduct. *American Psychologist, 57,* 1060-1073.

American Psychological Association. (2012). *5-year summary report: Commission on Accreditation.* Washington, DC: Author.

Amieva, H., Phillips, L.H., Della Sala, S., & Henry, J.D. (2004). Inhibitory functioning in Alzheimer's disease. *Brain, 127,* 949-964.

Amminger, G.P., Henry, L.P., Harrigan, S.M., Harris, M.G., Alvarez-Jimenez, M., Herrman, H., Jackson, H.J., & McGorry, P.D. (2011). Outcome in early-onset schizophrenia revisited: Findings from the Early Psychosis Prevention and Intervention Centre long-term follow-up study. *Schizophrenia Research, 131,* 112-119.

Anagnostou, E. (2012). Translational medicine: Mice and men show the way. *Nature, 491,* 196-197.

Ananth, J., Parameswaran, S., & Gunatilake, S. (2004). Side effects of atypical antipsychotic drugs. *Current Pharmaceutical Design, 10,* 2219-2229.

Anderson, N.E., & Kiehl, K.A. (2012). The psychopath magnetized: Insights from brain imaging. *Trends in Cognitive Sciences, 16,* 52-60.

Anderson, R.N. (2002). Deaths: Leading causes for 2000. *National Vital Statistics Reports 50 (16).* Hyattsville, MD: National Center for Health Statistics.

Anderson, R.N., & Smith, B.L. (2003). Deaths: Leading causes for 2001. *National Vital Statistics Reports, 52(9).* Hyattsville, MD: National Center for Health Statistics.

Anderson, V.A., & Taylor, H.G. (2000). Meningitis. In K.O. Yeates, M.D. Ris, & H.G. Taylor (Eds.), *Pediatric neuropsychology: Research, theory, and practice* (pp. 117-148). New York: Guilford.

Andreasen, N.C., Nopoulos, P., Magnotta, V., Pierson, R., Ziebell, S., & Ho, B.-C. (2011). Progressive brain change in schizophrenia: A prospective longitudinal study of first-episode schizophrenia. *Biological Psychiatry, 70,* 672-679.

Anestis, M.D., Bagge, C.L., Tull, M.T., & Joiner, T.E. (2011). Clarifying the role of emotion dysregulation in the interpersonal-psychological theory of suicidal behavior in an undergraduate sample. *Journal of Psychiatric Research, 45,* 603-611.

Anetzberger, G.J. (2012). An update on the nature and scope of elder abuse. *Generations, 36,* 12-20.

Anetzberger, G.J., Palmisano, B.R., Sanders, M., Bass, D., Dayton, C., Eckert, S., & Schimer, M.R. (2000). A model intervention for elder abuse and dementia. *Gerontologist, 40,* 492-497.

Anglesea, M.M., Hoch, H., & Taylor, B.A. (2008). Reducing rapid eating in teenagers with autism: Use of a pager prompt. *Journal of Applied Behavior Analysis, 41,* 107-111.

Angermeyer, M.C., & Schulze, B. (2001). Reducing the stigma of schizophrenia: Understanding the process and options for interventions. *Epidemiologia e Psichiatria Sociale, 10,* 1-7.

Anglin, M.D., Conner, B.T., Annon, J.J., & Longshore, D. (2008). Longitudinal effects of LAAM and methadone maintenance on heroin addict behavior. *Journal of Behavioral Health Services and Research, 36,* 267-282.

Annen, S., Roser, P., & Brune, M. (2012). Nonverbal behavior during clinical interviews: Similarities and dissimilarities among schizophrenia, mania, and depression. *Journal of Nervous and Mental Disease, 200,* 26-32.

Anstey, K.J., Mack, H.A., & Cherbuin, N. (2009). Alcohol consumption as a risk factor for dementia and cognitive decline: Meta-analysis of prospective studies. *American Journal of Geriatric Psychiatry, 17,* 542-555.

Antonius, D., Prudent, V., Rebani, Y., D'Angelo, D., Ardekani, B.A., Malaspina, D., & Hoptman, M.J. (2011). White matter integrity and lack of insight in schizophrenia and schizoaffective disorder. *Schizophrenia Research, 128,* 76-82.

Antshel, K.M., & Remer, R. (2003). Social skills training in children with attention deficit hyperactivity disorder: A randomized-controlled clinical trial. *Journal of Clinical Child and Adolescent Psychology, 32,* 153-165.

Apil, S.R.A., Hoencamp, E., Haffmans, P.M.J., & Spinhoven, P. (2012). A stepped care relapse prevention program for depression in older people: A randomized controlled trial. *International Journal of Geriatric Psychiatry, 27,* 583-591.

Apostolova, L.G., & Cummings, J.L. (2012). Neuropsychiatric aspects of Alzheimer's Disease and other dementing illnesses. In S.C. Yudofsky & R.E. Hales (Eds.), *Manual of clinical neuropsychiatry* (pp. 311-338). Washington, DC: American Psychiatric Publishing.

Aragona, M., Tarsitani, L., De Nitto, S., & Inghilleri, M. (2008). DSM-IV-TR "pain disorder associated with psychological factors" as a nonhysterical form of somatization. *Pain Research and Management, 13,* 13-18.

Aragones, E., Labad, A., Pinol, J.L., Lucena, C., & Alonso, Y. (2005). Somatized depression in primary care attenders. *Journal of Psychosomatic Research, 58,* 145-151.

Arbisi, P.A. (1995). Review of the Schedule for Affective Disorders and Schizophrenia, third edition. In J.C. Conoley & J.C. Impara (Eds.), *The twelfth mental measurements yearbook* (pp. 917-918). Lincoln, NE: Buros Institute of Mental Measurements.

Arcelus, J., Mitchell, A.J., Wales, J., & Nielsen, S. (2011). Mortality rates in patients with anorexia nervosa and other eating disorders: A meta-analysis of 36 studies. *Archives of General Psychiatry, 68,* 724-731.

Armfield, J.M. (2007). Manipulating perceptions of spider characteristics and predicted spider fear: Evidence for the cognitive vulnerability model of the etiology of fear. *Journal of Anxiety Disorders, 21,* 691-703.

Armstrong, J.G., Putnam, F.W., Carlson, E.B., Libero, D.Z., & Smith, S. (1997). Development and validation of a measure of adolescent dissociation: The Adolescent Dissociative Experiences Scale. *Journal of Nervous and Mental Disease, 185,* 491-497.

Arnone, D., McIntosh, A.M., Ebmeier, K.P., Munafo, M.R., & Anderson, I.M. (2012). Magnetic resonance imaging studies in unipolar depression: Systematic review and meta-regression analyses. *European Neuropsychopharmacology, 11,* 1-16.

Aronoff, G.M., Mandel, S., Genovese, E., Maitz, E.A., Dorto, A.J., Klimek, E.H., & Staats, T.E. (2007). Evaluating malingering in contested injury or illness. *Pain Practice, 7,* 178-204.

Arroll, B., Macgillivray, S., Ogston, S., Reid, I., Sullivan, F., Williams, B., & Crombie, I. (2005). Efficacy and tolerability of tricyclic antidepressants and SSRIs compared with placebo for treatment of depression in primary care: A meta-analysis. *Annals of Family Medicine, 3,* 449-456.

Arsenault-Lapierre, G., Kim, C., & Turecki, G. (2004). Psychiatric diagnoses in 3275 suicides: A metaanalysis. *BMC Psychiatry, 4,* 37.

Asami, T., Bouix, S., Whitford, T.J., Shenton, M.E., Salisbury, D.F., & McCarley, R.W. (2012). Longitudinal loss of gray matter volume in patients with first-episode schizophrenia: DARTEL automated analysis and ROI validation. *NeuroImage, 59,* 986-996.

Aseltine, R.H., & DeMartino, R. (2004). An outcome evaluation of the SOS Suicide Prevention Program. *American Journal of Public Health, 94,* 446-451.

Ashford, J.W., & Mortimer, J.A. (2002). Non-familial Alzheimer's disease is mainly due to genetic factors. *Journal of Alzheimer's Disease, 4,* 169-177.

Asher, M.I., Montefort, S., Bjorksten, B., Lai, C.K.W., Strachan, D.P., Weiland, S.K., & Williams, H. (2006). Worldwide time trends in the prevalence of symptoms of asthma, allergic rhinoconjunctivitis, and eczema in childhood: ISAAC Phases One and Three repeat multicountry cross-sectional surveys. *Lancet, 368,* 733-743.

Askin-Edgar, S., White, K.E., & Cummings, J.L. (2004). Neuropsychiatric aspects of Alzheimer's disease and other dementing illnesses. In S.C. Yudofsky & R.E. Hales (Eds.), *Essentials of neuropsychiatry and clinical neurosciences* (pp. 421-456). Washington, DC: American Psychiatric Publishing.

Aubin, S., Heiman, J.R., Berger, R.E., Murallo, A.V., & Yung-Wen, L. (2009). Comparing sildenafil alone vs. sildenafil plus brief couple sex therapy on erectile dysfunction and couples' sexual and marital quality of life: A pilot study. *Journal of Sex and Marital Therapy, 35*, 122-143.

Avena, N.M., & Bocarsly, M.E. Dysregulation of brain reward systems in eating disorders: Neurochemical information from animal models of binge eating, bulimia nervosa, and anorexia nervosa. *Neuropharmacology, 35*, 87-96.

Aviram, R.B., Brodsky, B.S., & Stanley, B. (2006). Borderline personality disorder, stigma, and treatment implications. *Harvard Review of Psychiatry, 14*, 249-256.

Aybek, S., Kanaan, R.A., & David, A.S. (2008). The neuropsychiatry of conversion disorder. *Current Opinion in Psychiatry, 21*, 275-280.

Aytug, S., Laws, E.R., & Vance, M.L. (2012). Assessment of the utility of the high-dose dexamethasone suppression test in confirming the diagnosis of Cushing disease. *Endocrine Practice, 18*, 152-157.

Babe, K.S., Peterson, A.M., Loosen, P.T., & Geracioti, T.D. (1992). The pathogenesis of Munchausen syndrome: A review and case report. *General Hospital Psychiatry, 14*, 273-276.

Babin, P.R. (2003). Diagnosing depression in persons with brain injuries: A look at theories, the DSM-IV and depression measures. *Brain Injury, 17*, 889-900.

Bachar, E., Canetti, L., & Berry, E.M. (2005). Lack of long-lasting consequences of starvation on eating pathology in Jewish Holocaust survivors of Nazi concentration camps. *Journal of Abnormal Psychology, 114*, 165-169.

Bachmann, S., Bottmer, C., & Schroder, J. (2008). One-year outcome and its prediction in first-episode schizophrenia: A naturalistic study. *Psychopathology, 41*, 115-123.

Backman, L., Lindenberger, U., Li, S.-C., & Nyberg, L. (2010). Linking cognitive aging to alterations in dopamine neurotransmitter functioning: Recent data and future avenues. *Neuroscience and Biobehavioral Reviews, 34*, 670-677.

Bagby, R.M., Ryder, A.G., & Cristi, C. (2002). Psychosocial and clinical predictors of response to pharmacotherapy for depression. *Journal of Psychiatry and Neuroscience, 27*, 250-257.

Bailey, J.E., Argyropoulos, S.V., Lightman, S.L., & Nutt, D.J. (2003). Does the brain noradrenaline network mediate the effects of the CO2 challenge? *Journal of Psychopharmacology, 17*, 252-259.

Baker, J.H., Maes, H.H., Lissner, L., Aggen, S.H., Lichtenstein, P., & Kendler, K.S. (2009). Genetic risk factors for disordered eating in adolescent males and females. *Journal of Abnormal Psychology, 118*, 576-586.

Baker, J.H., Mitchell, K.S., Neale, M.C., & Kendler, K.S. (2010). Eating disorder symptomatology and substance use disorders: Prevalence and shared risk in a population-based twin sample. *International Journal of Eating Disorders, 43*, 648-658.

Baldessarini, R.J. (2013). *Chemotherapy in psychiatry* (3rd ed.). New York: Springer.

Baldessarini, R.J., Perry, R., & Pike, J. (2008). Factors associated with treatment nonadherence among

US bipolar disorder patients. *Human Psychopharmacology, 23*, 95-105.

Baldwin, R.C. (2000). Poor prognosis of depression in elderly people: Causes and actions. *Annals of Medicine, 32*, 252-256.

Balk, E.M., Raman, G., Tatsioni, A., Chung, M., Lau, J., & Rosenberg, I.H. (2007). Vitamin B6, B12, and folic acid supplementation and cognitive function: A systematic review of randomized trials. *Archives of Internal Medicine, 167*, 21-30.

Ball, J.R., Mitchell, P.B., Corry, J.C., Skillecorn, A., Smith, M., & Malhi, G.S. (2006). A randomized controlled trial of cognitive therapy for bipolar disorder: Focus on long-term change. *Journal of Clinical Psychiatry, 67*, 277-286.

Ball, S.A. (2005). Personality traits, problems, and disorders: Clinical applications to substance use disorders. *Journal of Research in Personality, 39*, 84-102.

Balling, K., Jones, R.S.P., Noone, S.J., & Hastings, R.P. (2012). Identification of appropriate social interaction by adolescents with autism. *International Journal of Developmental Disabilities, 58*, 1-11.

Balon, R., & Segraves, R.T. (Eds.). (2009). *Clinical manual of sexual disorders*. Washington, DC: American Psychiatric Publishing.

Bandelow, B., Seidler-Brandler, U., Becker, A., Wedekind, D., & Ruther, E. (2007). Meta-analysis of randomized controlled comparisons of psychopharmacological and psychological treatments for anxiety disorders. *World Journal of Biological Psychiatry, 8*, 175-187.

Barberger-Gateau, P., Lambert, J.-C., Feart, C., Peres, K., Ritchie, K., Dartigues, J.-F., & Alperovitch, A. (2013). From genetics to dietetics: The contribution of epidemiology to understanding Alzheimer's disease. *Journal of Alzheimer's Disease, 33 (Suppl 1)*, S457-S463.

Bardone-Cone, A. M., & Cass, K. M. (2007). What does viewing a pro-anorexia website do?: An experimental examination of website exposure and moderating effects. *International Journal of Eating Disorders, 40*, 537-548.

Bargiota, A., Dimitropoulos, K., Tzortzis, V., & Koukoulis, G.N. (2011). Sexual dysfunction in diabetic women. *Hormones, 10*, 196-206.

Barkhof, E., Meijer, C.J., de Sonneville, L.M.J., Linszen, D.H., & de Haan, L. (2012). Interventions to improve adherence to antipsychotic medication in patients with schizophrenia: A review of the past decade. *European Psychiatry, 27*, 9-18.

Barkley, R.A. (2000). *Taking charge of ADHD: The complete, authoritative guide for parents.* New York: Guilford.

Barkovich, A.J., Guerrini, R., Kuzniecky, R.I., Jackson, G.D., & Dobyns, W.B. (2012). A developmental and genetic classification for malformations of cortical development: Update 2012. *Brain, 135*, 1348-1369.

Bari, M., Battista, N., Pirazzi, V., & Maccarrone, M. (2011). The manifold actions of endocannabinoids on female and male reproductive events. *Frontiers in Bioscience, 16*, 498-516.

Barkley, R.A, Murphy, K.R., & Fischer, M. (2010). *ADHD in adults: What the science says.* New York: Guilford.

Barlow, D.H. (2002). *Anxiety and its disorders: The nature and treatment of anxiety and panic* (2nd ed.). New York: Guilford.

Barlow, D.H. (Ed.). (2007). *Clinical handbook of psychological disorders: A step-by-step treatment manual* (4th ed.). New York: Guilford.

Barnett, S.B.L., & Nurmagambetov, T.A. (2011). Costs of asthma in the United States: 2002-2007. *Journal of Allergy and Clinical Immunology, 127*, 145-152.

Barnicot, K., Katsakou, C., Bhatti, N., Savill, M., Fearns, N., & Priebe, S. (2012). Factors predicting the outcome of psychotherapy for borderline personality disorder: A systematic review. *Clinical Psychology Review, 32*, 400-412.

Barnicot, K., Katsakou, C., Marougka, S., & Priebe, S. (2011). Treatment completion in psychotherapy for borderline personality disorder—a systematic review and meta-analysis. *Acta Psychiatrica Scandinavica, 123*, 327-338.

Barrera, T.L., Wilson, K.P., & Norton, P.J. (2010). The experience of panic symptoms across racial groups in a student sample. *Journal of Anxiety Disorders, 24*, 873-878.

Barrett, P.M., Farrell, L.J., Ollendick, T.H., & Dadds, M. (2006). Long-term outcomes of an Australian universal prevention trial of anxiety and depression symptoms in children and youth: An evaluation of the Friends Program. *Journal of Clinical Child and Adolescent Psychology, 35*, 403-411.

Barrett, P.M., & Pahl, K.M. (2006). School based intervention: Examining a universal approach to anxiety management. *Australian Journal of Guidance and Counselling, 16*, 55-75.

Barsky, A.J. (2001). Palpitations, arrhythmias, and awareness of cardiac activity. *Annals of Internal Medicine, 134*, 832-837.

Basheer, C. (2011). Recent analytical strategies on "Date-Rape" Drugs and its metabolites. *Journal of Applied Pharmaceutical Science, 1*, 21-28.

Bass, J.L., Corwin, M., Gozal, D., Moore, C., Nishida, H., Parker, S., Schonwald, A., Wilker, R.E., Stehle, S., & Kinane, T.B. (2004). The effect of chronic or intermittent hypoxia on cognition in childhood: A review of the evidence. *Pediatrics, 114*, 805-816.

Batstra, L., & Frances, A. (2012). DSM-5 inflates attention deficit hyperactivity disorder. *Journal of Nervous and Mental Disease, 200*, 486-488.

Battaglia, A. (2003). Neuroimaging studies in the evaluation of developmental delay/mental retardation. *American Journal of Medical Genetics Part C, 117C*, 25-30.

Battaglia, A., & Carey, J.C. (2003). Diagnostic evaluation of developmental delay/mental retardation: An overview. *American Journal of Medical Genetics Part C, 117C*, 3-14.

Bauermeister, J.J., Canino, G., Polanczyk, & Rohde, L.A. (2010). ADHD across cultures: Is there evidence for a bidimensional organization of symptoms? *Journal of Clinical Child and Adolescent Psychology, 39,* 362-372.

Bauman, M.L., & Kemper, T.L. (2005). Neuroanatomic observations of the brain in autism: A review and future directions. *International Journal of Developmental Neuroscience, 23,* 183-187.

Baumeister, H., & Harter, M. (2007). Prevalence of mental disorders based on general population surveys. *Social Psychiatry and Psychiatric Epidemiology, 42,* 537-546.

Baumeister, R.F., Vohs, K.D., DeWall, C.N., & Zhang, L. (2007). How emotion shapes behavior: Feedback, anticipation, and reflection, rather than direct causation. *Personality and Social Psychology Review, 11,* 167-203.

Bayley, N. (2005). *Bayley Scales of Infant and Toddler Development-Third edition.* San Antonio, TX: Harcourt.

Beardslee, W.R., Gladstone, T.R.G., & O'Connor, E.E. (2011). Transmission and prevention of mood disorders among children of affectively ill parents: A review. *Journal of the American Academy of Child and Adolescent Psychiatry, 50,* 1098-1109.

Beart, P.M., & O'Shea, R.D. (2007). Transporters for L-glutamate: An update on their molecular pharmacology and pathological involvement. *British Journal of Pharmacology, 150,* 5-17.

Beauchaine, T.P., Hinshaw, S.P., & Pang, K.L. (2010). Comorbidity of attention-deficit/hyperactivity disorder and early-onset conduct disorder: Biological, environmental, and developmental mechanisms. *Clinical Psychology: Science and Practice, 17,* 327-336.

Beauchaine, T.P., Webster-Stratton, C., & Reid, M.J. (2005). Mediators, moderators, and predictors of 1-year outcomes among children treated for early-onset conduct problems: A latent growth curve analysis. *Journal of Consulting and Clinical Psychology, 73,* 371-388.

Beck, A.T. (2005). The current state of cognitive therapy: A 40-year retrospective. *Archives of General Psychiatry, 62,* 953-959.

Beck, A.T., & Dozois, D.J.A. (2011). Cognitive therapy: Current status and future directions. *Annual Review of Medicine, 62,* 397-409.

Beck, A.T., Freeman, A.M., and Associates. (1990). *Cognitive therapy of personality disorders.* New York: Guilford.

Beck, A.T., Freeman, A., Davis, D.D., and Associates (2004). *Cognitive therapy of personality disorders* (2nd ed.). New York: Guilford.

Beck, A.T., Rush, A.J., Shaw, B.F., & Emery, G. (1979). *Cognitive therapy of depression.* New York: Guilford.

Beck, A.T., & Steer, R.A. (1988). *Manual for the Beck Hopelessness Scale.* San Antonio, TX: The Psychological Corporation.

Beck, A.T., Steer, R.A., & Brown, G.K. (1996). *Manual for the Beck Depression Inventory-II.* San Antonio, TX: The Psychological Corporation.

Beck, J.S. (2011). *Cognitive behavior therapy: Basics and beyond* (2nd ed.). New York: Guilford.

Becker, T.M., Cicero, D.C., Cowan, N., & Kerns, J.G. (2012). Cognitive control components and speech symptoms in people with schizophrenia. *Psychiatry Research, 196,* 20-26.

Bedics, J.D., Atkins, D.C., Comtois, K.A., & Linehan, M. (2012). Treatment differences in the therapeutic relationship and introject during a 2-year randomized controlled trial of dialectical behavior therapy versus nonbehavioral psychotherapy experts for borderline personality disorder. *Journal of Consulting and Clinical Psychology, 80,* 66-77.

Bednar, R.L., & Kaul, T.J. (1994). Experiential group research: Can the canon fire? In A.E. Bergin & S.L. Garfield (Eds.), *Handbook of psychotherapy and behavior change* (4th ed.; pp. 631-663). New York: Wiley.

Behl, C. (2012). Brain aging and late-onset Alzheimer's disease: Many open questions *International Psychogeriatrics, 24 (Suppl 1),* S3-S9.

Beinart, N., Weinman, J., Wade, D., & Brady, R. (2012). Caregiver burden and psychoeducational interventions in Alzheimer's disease: A review. *Dementia and Geriatric Cognitive Disorders, 2,* 638-648.

Beitchman, J.H., Wilson, B., Johnson, C.J., Atkinson, L., Young, A., Adlaf, E., Escobar, M., & Douglas, L. (2001). Fourteen-year follow-up of speech/ language-impaired and control children: Psychiatric outcome. *Journal of the American Academy of Child and Adolescent Psychiatry, 40,* 75-82.

Bekris, L.M., Yu, C.-E., Bird, T.D., & Tsuang, D.W. (2010). Genetics of Alzheimer's disease. *Journal of Geriatric Psychiatry and Neurology, 23,* 213-227.

Belardinelli, C., Hatch, J.P., Olvera, R.L., Fonseca, M., Caetano, S.C., Nicoletti, M., Pliszka, S., & Soares, J.C. (2008). Family environment patterns in families with bipolar children. *Journal of Affective Disorders, 107,* 299-305.

Bellack, A.S., Mueser, K.T., Gingerich, S., & Agresta, J. (2004). *Social skills training for schizophrenia: A step-by-step guide.* New York: Guilford.

Belujon, P., & Grace, A.A. (2011). Hippocampus, amygdala, and stress: Interacting systems that affect susceptibility to addiction. *Annals of the New York Academy of Sciences, 1216,* 114-121.

Ben-Porath, Y.S., Graham, J.R., Archer, R.P., Tellegen, A., & Kaemmer, B. (2006). *Supplement to the MMPI-A Manual for Administration, Scoring, and Interpretation: The Content Component Scales; the Personality Psychopathology Five (PSY-5) Scales, and the Critical Items.* Minneapolis: University of Minnesota Press.

Benke, T. (2011). The role of neuropsychology in prodromal dementia. *Neurodegenerative Disease Management, 1,* 323-333.

Bennett, M.C. (2005). The role of αsynuclein in neurodegenerative diseases. *Pharmacology & Therapeutics, 105,* 311-331.

Bennett, S., Grant, M.M., & Aldred, S. (2009). Oxidative stress in vascular dementia and Alzheimer's disease: A common pathology. *Journal of Alzheimer's Disease, 17,* 245-257.

Bergem, A.L., Engedal, K., & Kringlen, E. (1997). The role of heredity in late-onset Alzheimer disease and vascular dementia: A twin study. *Archives of General Psychiatry, 54,* 264-270.

Berk, M., Dodd, S., & Berk, L. (2005). The management of bipolar disorder in primary care: A review of existing and emerging therapies. *Psychiatry and Clinical Neurosciences, 59,* 229-239.

Berkman, N.D., Lohr, K.N., & Bulik, C.M. (2007). Outcomes of eating disorders: A systematic review of the literature. *International Journal of Eating Disorders, 40,* 293-309.

Berkout, O.V., Young, J.N., & Gross, A.M. (2011). Mean girls and bad boys: Recent research on gender differences in conduct disorder. *Aggression and Violent Behavior, 16,* 503-511.

Berle, D., & Starcevic, V. (2005). Thought-action fusion: A review of the literature and future directions. *Clinical Psychology Review, 25,* 263-284.

Berlim, M.T., Van den Eynde, F., & Daskalakis, Z.J. (2012). A systematic review and meta-analysis on the efficacy and acceptability of bilateral repetitive transcranial magnetic stimulation (rTMS) for treating major depression. *Psychological Medicine, 2012,* 1-10.

Bernstein, H.-G., Dobrowolny, H., Schott, B.H., Gorny, X., Becker, V., Steiner, J., Seidenbecher, C.I., & Bogerts, B. (2013). Increased density of AKAP5-expressing neurons in the anterior cingulate cortex of subjects with bipolar disorder. *Journal of Psychiatric Research, 47,* 699-705.

Berridge, K.C. (2009). "Liking" and "wanting" food rewards: Brain substrates and roles in eating disorders. *Physiology and Behavior, 97,* 537-550.

Bertholet, N., Daeppen, J.-B., Wietlisbach, V., Fleming, M., & Burnand, B. (2005). Reduction of alcohol consumption by brief alcohol intervention in primary care: Systematic review and meta-analysis. *Archives of Internal Medicine, 165,* 986-995.

Bertram, L., Lill, C.M., & Tanzi, R.E. (2010). The genetics of Alzheimer's disease: Back to the future. *Neuron, 68,* 270-281.

Bertram, L., & Tanzi, R.E. (2004). The current status of Alzheimer's disease genetics: What do we tell the patients? *Pharmacological Research, 50,* 385-396.

Beynon, S., Soares-Weiser, K., Woolacott, N., Duffy, S., & Geddes, J.R. (2008). Psychosocial interventions for the prevention of relapse in bipolar disorder: Systematic review of controlled trials. *British Journal of Psychiatry, 192,* 5-11.

Bhugra, D. (2003). Migration and depression. *Acta Psychiatrica Scandinavica Supplement, 418,* 67-72.

Bhugra, D. (2005). Cultural identities and cultural congruency: A new model for evaluating mental distress in immigrants. *Acta Psychiatrica Scandinavica, 111,* 84-93.

Bhugra, D., & Bhui, K. (2011). *Textbook of cultural psychiatry*. Cambridge: Cambridge University Press.

Bhugra, D., & Gupta, S. (Eds.) (2011). *Migration and mental health*. Cambridge: Cambridge University Press.

Bhugra, D., & Mastrogianni, A. (2004). Globalisation and mental disorders: Overview with relation to depression. *British Journal of Psychiatry, 184*, 10-20.

Biancosino, B., Picardi, A., Marmai, L., Biondi, M., & Grassi, L. (2010). Factor structure of the Brief Psychiatric Rating Scale in unipolar depression. *Journal of Affective Disorders, 124*, 329-334.

Biederman, J. (2005). Attention-deficit/hyperactivity disorder: A selective overview. *Biological Psychiatry, 57*, 1215-1220.

Biederman, J., & Faraone, S.V. (2005). Attention-deficit hyperactivity disorder. *Lancet, 366*, 237-248.

Biederman, J., Faraone, S.V., & Monuteaux, M.C. (2002). Differential effect of environmental adversity by gender: Rutter's Index of Adversity in a group of boys and girls with and without ADHD. *American Journal of Psychiatry, 158*, 1556-1562.

Biederman, J. Hirshfeld-Becker, D.R., Rosenbaum, J.F., Herot, C., Friedman, D., Snidman, N., Kagan, J., & Faraone, S.V. (2001). Further evidence of association between behavioral inhibition and social anxiety in children. *American Journal of Psychiatry, 158*, 1673-1679.

Biederman, J., Petty, C.R., Dolan, C., Hughes, S., Mick, E., Monuteaux, M.C., & Faraone, S.V. (2008). The long-term longitudinal course of oppositional defiant disorder and conduct disorder in ADHD boys: Findings from a controlled 10-year prospective longitudinal follow-up study. *Psychological Medicine, 38*, 1027-1036.

Bieling, P.J., Hawley, L.L., Boch, R.T., Corcoran, K.M., Levitan, R.D., Young, L.T., MacQueen, G.M., & Segal, Z.V. (2012). Treatment-specific changes in decentering following mindfulness-based cognitive therapy versus antidepressant medication or placebo for prevention of depressive relapse. *Journal of Consulting and Clinical Psychology, 80*, 365-372.

Bienvenu, O.J., & Ginsburg, G.S. (2007). Prevention of anxiety disorders. *International Review of Psychiatry, 19*, 647-654.

Billiard, M., Jaussent, I., Dauvilliers, Y., & Besset, A. (2011). Recurrent hypersomnia: A review of 339 cases. *Sleep Medicine Reviews, 15*, 247-257.

Billstedt, E., Gillberg, C., & Gillberg, C. (2005). Autism after adolescence: Population-based 13- to 22-year follow-up study of 120 individuals with autism diagnosed in childhood. *Journal of Autism and Developmental Disorders, 35*, 351-360.

Binik, Y.M. (2010). The DSM diagnostic criteria for dyspareunia. *Archives of Sexual Behavior, 39*, 292-303.

Bird, V., Premkumar, P., Kendall, T., Whittington, C., Mitchell, J., & Kuipers, E. (2010). Early intervention services, cognitive-behavioural therapy and family intervention in early psychosis: Systematic review. *British Journal of Psychiatry, 197*, 350-356.

Birgden, A., & Cucolo, H. (2011). The treatment of sex offenders: Evidence, ethics, and human rights. *Sexual Abuse, 23*, 295-313.

Birley, A.J., James, M.R., Dickson, P.A., Montgomery, G.W., Heath, A.C., Martin, N.G., & Whitfield, J.B. (2009). ADH single nucleotide polymorphism associations with alcohol metabolism in vivo. *Human Molecular Genetics, 18*, 1533-1542.

Birmaher, B. (2012). Pediatric bipolar disorder—clinical picture and longitudinal course. *International Clinical Psychopharmacology, 28*, e27.

Birnbaum, M.H., & Thomann, K. (1996). Visual function in multiple personality disorder. *Journal of the American Optometric Association, 67*, 327-334.

Bisht, J., Sankhyan, N., Kaushal, R.K., Sharma, R.C., & Grover, N. (2008). Clinical profile of pediatric somatoform disorders. *Indian Pediatrics, 45*, 111-115.

Bjorvatn, B., Gronli, J., & Pallesen, S. (2010). Prevalence of different parasomnias in the general population. *Sleep Medicine, 11*, 1031-1034.

Bjorgvinsson, T., Hart, J., & Heffelfinger, S. (2007). Obsessive-compulsive disorder: Update on assessment and treatment. *Journal of Psychiatric Practice, 13*, 362-372.

Black, D.N., Seritan, A.L., Taber, K.H., & Hurley, R.A. (2004). Conversion hysteria: Lessons from functional imaging. *Journal of Neuropsychiatry and Clinical Neuroscience, 16*, 245-251.

Black, D.W., Noyes, R., Goldstein, R.B., & Blum, N. (1992). A family study of obsessive-compulsive disorder. *Archives of General Psychiatry, 49*, 362-368.

Black, K., & Lobo, M. (2008). A conceptual review of family resilience factors. *Journal of Family Nursing, 14*, 33-55.

Black, S.E. (2005). Vascular dementia: Stroke risk and sequelae define therapeutic approaches. *Postgraduate Medicine, 117*, 19-25.

Blackburn, R. (2009). Subtypes of psychopath. In M. McMurran & R. Howard (Eds.), *Personality, personality disorder and violence* (pp. 113-132). Malden, MA: Wiley.

Blackford, J.U., & Pine, D.S. (2012). Neural substrates of childhood anxiety disorders: A review of neuroimaging findings. *Child and Adolescent Psychiatric Clinics of North America, 21*, 501-525.

Blair, R.J.R. (2010). Neuroimaging of psychopathy and antisocial behavior: A targeted review. *Current Psychiatry Reports, 12*, 76-82.

Blakely, T.A., Collings, S.C., & Atkinson, J. (2003). Unemployment and suicide: Evidence for a causal association? *Journal of Epidemiology and Community Health, 57*, 594-600.

Blanchard, R. (2010a). The *DSM* diagnostic criteria for pedophilia. *Archives of Sexual Behavior, 39*, 304-316.

Blanchard, R. (2010b). The *DSM* diagnostic criteria for transvestic fetishism. *Archives of Sexual Behavior, 39*, 363-372.

Blanco, C., Okuda, M., Markowitz, J.C., Liu, S.-M., Grant, B.F., & Hasin, D.S. (2010). The epidemiology of chronic major depressive disorder and dysthymic disorder: Results from the National Epidemiologic Survey on alcohol and related conditions. *Journal of Clinical Psychiatry, 71*, 1645-1656.

Blashill, A.J. (2011). Gender roles, eating pathology, and body dissatisfaction in men: A meta-analysis. *Body Image, 8*, 1-11.

Blau, N., van Spronsen, F.J., & Levy, H.L. (2010). Phenylketonuria. *Lancet, 376*, 1417-1427.

Blazei, R.W., Iacono, W.G., & Krueger, R.F. (2006). Intergenerational transmission of antisocial behavior: How do kids become antisocial adults? *Applied and Preventive Psychology, 11*, 230-253.

Blazei, R.W., Iacono, W.G., & McGue, M. (2008). Father-child transmission of antisocial behavior: The moderating role of father's presence in the home. *Journal of the American Academy of Child and Adolescent Psychiatry, 47*, 406-415.

Blazer, D. (2002). *Depression in late life* (3rd. ed.). New York: Springer.

Blazer, D.G., & van Nieuwenhuizen, A.O. (2010). Evidence for the diagnostic criteria of delirium: An update. *Current Opinion in Psychiatry, 25*, 239-243.

Bleichhardt, G., Timmer, B., & Rief, W. (2004). Cognitive-behavioural therapy for patients with multiple somatoform symptoms: A randomised controlled trial in tertiary care. *Journal of Psychosomatic Research, 56*, 449-454.

Bloom, J.S., Garcia-Barrera, M.A., Miller, C.J., Miller, C.J., & Hynd, G.W. (2013). Planum temporale morphology in children with developmental dyslexia. *Neuropsychologia, 51*, 1684-1692.

Bloomfield, K., Stockwell, T., Gmel, G., & Rehn, N. (2003). International comparisons of alcohol consumption. *Alcohol Research and Health, 27*, 95-109.

Blum, K., Gardner, E., Oscar-Berman, M., & Gold, M. (2012). "Liking" and "wanting" linked to reward deficiency syndrome (RDS): Hypothesizing differential responsivity in brain reward circuitry. *Current Pharmaceutical Design, 18*, 113-118.

Blumberg, H.P., Stern, E., Martinez, D., Ricketts, S., de Asis, J., White, T., Epstein, J., McBride, A., Eidelberg, D., Kocsis, J.H., & Silbersweig, D.A. (2000). Increased anterior cingulate and caudate activity in bipolar mania. *Biological Psychiatry, 48*, 1045-1052.

Blumenthal, J.A., Sherwood, A., Babyak, M.A., Watkins, L.L., Waugh, R., Georgiades, A., Bacon, S.L., Hayano, J., Coleman, R.E., & Hinderliter, A. (2005). Effects of exercise and stress management training on markers of cardiovascular risk in patients with ischemic heart disease: A randomized controlled trial. *Journal of the American Medical Association, 293*, 1626-1634.

Bo, S., Abu-Akel, A., Kongerslev, M., Haahr, U.H., & Simonsen, E. (2011). Risk factors for violence among patients with schizophrenia. *Clinical Psychology Review, 31,* 711-726.

Bob, P. (2008). Pain, dissociation and subliminal self-representations. *Consciousness and Cognition, 17,* 355-369.

Boden, J.M., Fergusson, D.M., & Horwood, L.J (2010). Risk factors for conduct disorder and oppositional/defiant disorder: Evidence from a New Zealand birth cohort. *Journal of the American Academy of Child and Adolescent Psychiatry, 49,* 1125-1133.

Bogaerts, S., Daalder, A., Vanhoule, S., Desmet, M., & Leeuw, F. (2008). Personality disorders in a sample of paraphilic and nonparaphilic child molesters: A comparative study. *International Journal of Offender Therapy and Comparative Criminology, 52,* 21-30.

Bogenschutz, M.P., Geppert, C.M.A., & George, J. (2006). The role of twelve-step approaches in dual diagnosis treatment and recovery. *American Journal on Addictions, 15,* 50-60.

Bohnen, N.I., & Albin, R.L. (2011). White matter lesions in Parkinson disease. *Nature Reviews Neurology, 7,* 229-236.

Bolea, P.S., Grant, G., Burgess, M., & Plasa, O. (2003). Trauma of children of the Sudan: A constructivist exploration. *Child Welfare, 82,* 219-233.

Bondolfi, G., Jermann, F., Van der Linden, M., Gex-Fabry, M., Bizzini, L., Rouget, B.W., Myers-Arrazola, L., Gonzalez, C., Segal, Z., Aubry, J.-M., & Bertschy, G. (2010). Depression relapse prophylaxis with mindfulness-based cognitive therapy: Replication and extension in the Swiss health care system. *Journal of Affective Disorders, 122,* 224-231.

Bondy, S.C. (2010). The neurotoxicity of environmental aluminum is still an issue. *Neurotoxicology, 31,* 575-581.

Bonn-Miller, M.O., Zvolensky, M.J., & Moos, R.H. (2011). 12-step self-help group participation as a predictor of marijuana abstinence. *Addiction Research and Theory, 19,* 76-84.

Bonnet, M.H., & Arand, D.L. (2010). Hyperarousal and insomnia: State of the science. *Sleep Medicine Reviews, 14,* 9-15.

Bora, E., & Pantelis, C. (2011). Structural trait markers of bipolar disorder: Disruption of white matter integrity and localized gray matter abnormalities in anterior fronto-limbic regions. *Biological Psychiatry, 69,* 299-300.

Bordnick, P.S., Traylor, A., Copp, H.L., Graap, K.M., Carter, B., Ferrer, M., & Walton, A.P. (2008). Assessing reactivity to virtual reality alcohol-based cues. *Addictive Behaviors, 33,* 743-756.

Borenstein, A.R., Wu, Y., Mortimer, J.A., Schellenberg, G.D., McCormick, W.C., Bowen, J.D., McCurry, S., & Larson, E.B. (2005). Developmental and vascular risk factors for Alzheimer's disease. *Neurobiology of Aging, 26,* 325-334.

Borge, L., Angel, O.H., & Rossberg, J.I. (2013). Learning through cognitive milieu therapy among inpatients with dual diagnosis: A qualitative study of interdisciplinary collaboration. *Issues in Mental Health Nursing, 34,* 229-239.

Bornovalova, M.A., Lejuez, C.W., Daughters, S.B., Rosenthal, M.Z., & Lynch, T.R. (2005). Impulsivity as a common process across borderline personality and substance use disorders. *Clinical Psychology Review, 25,* 790-812.

Bornstein, R.F., & Gold, S.H. (2008). Comorbidity of personality disorders and somatization disorder: A meta-analytic review. *Journal of Psychopathology and Behavioral Assessment, 30,* 154-161.

Bornstein, R.F., & Malka, I.L. (2009). Dependent and histrionic personality disorders. In P.H. Blaney & Millon, T. (Eds.), *Oxford textbook of psychopathology* (2nd ed.) (pp. 602-621). New York: Oxford University Press.

Borras-Valls, J.J., & Gonzales-Correales, R. (2004). Specific aspects of erectile dysfunction in sexology. *International Journal of Impotence Research, 16,* S3-S6.

Both, S., & Laan, E. (2003). Directed masturbation: A treatment of female orgasmic disorder. In W. O'Donohue, J.E. Fisher, & S.C. Hayes (Eds.), *Cognitive behavior therapy: Applying empirically supported techniques in your practice* (pp. 144-151). New York: Wiley.

Botha, U.A., Koen, L., Joska, J.A., Parker, J.S., Horn, N., Hering, L.M., & Oosthuizen, P.P. (2010). The revolving door phenomenon in psychiatry: Comparing low-frequency and high-frequency users of psychiatric inpatient services in a developing country. *Social Psychiatry and Epidemiology, 45,* 461-468.

Boucher, J. (2012). Structural language in autistic spectrum disorder: Characteristics and causes. *Journal of Child Psychology and Psychiatry, 53,* 219-233.

Bounthavong, M., & Okamoto, M.P. (2007). Decision analysis model evaluating the cost-effectiveness of risperidone, olanzapine and haloperidol in the treatment of schizophrenia. *Journal of Evaluation in Clinical Practice, 13,* 453-460.

Bourdin, A., Halimi, L., Vachier, I., Paganin, F., Lamouroux, A., Gouitaa, M., Vairon, E., Godard, P., & Chanez, P. (2012). Adherence in severe asthma. *Clinical and Experimental Allergy, 42,* 1566-1574.

Boutros, N.N., & Peters, R. (2012). Internal gating and somatization disorders: Proposing a yet un-described neural system. *Medical Hypotheses, 78,* 174-178.

Bouvard, M., Vuachet, M., & Marchand, C. (2011). Examination of the screening properties of the Personality Diagnostic Questionnaire-4+ (PDQ-4+) in a non-clinical sample. *Clinical Neuropsychiatry, 8,* 151-158.

Bowen, S., Chawla, N., Collins, S.E., Witkiewitz, K., Hsu, S., Grow, J., Clifasefi, S., Garner, M., Douglass, A., Larimer, M.E., & Marlatt, A. (2009). Mindfulness-based relapse prevention for substance use disorders: A pilot efficacy trial. *Substance Abuse, 30,* 295-305.

Boyce, W.T., & Ellis, B.J. (2005). Biological sensitivity to context: I. An evolutionary-developmental theory of the origins and functions of stress reactivity. *Development and Psychopathology, 17,* 271-301.

Boyd, B.A., McDonough, S.G., & Bodfish, J.W. (2012). Evidence-based behavioral interventions for repetitive behaviors in autism. *Journal of Autism and Developmental Disorders, 42,* 1236-1248.

Boyd, C.J., McCabe, S.E., & Morales, M. (2005). College students' alcohol use: A critical review. *Annual Review of Nursing Research, 23,* 179-211.

Boyle, J.R., & Boekeloo, B.O. (2006). Perceived parental approval of drinking and its impact on problem drinking behaviors among first-year college students. *Journal of American College Health, 54,* 238-244.

Boyle, C.A., Boulet, S., Schieve, L.A., Cohen, R.A., Blumberg, S.J., Yeargin-Allsopp, M., Visser, S., & Kogan, M.D. (2011). Trends in the prevalence of developmental disabilities in US children, 1997-2008. *Pediatrics, 127,* 1034-1042.

Brabant, C., Alleva, L., Quertemont, E., & Tirelli, E. (2010). Involvement of the brain histaminergic system in addiction and addiction-related behaviors: A comprehensive review with emphasis on the potential therapeutic use of histaminergic compounds in drug dependence. *Progress in Neurobiology, 92,* 421-441.

Bracha, H.S. (2004). Freeze, flight, fight, fright, faint: Adaptionist perspectives on the acute stress response spectrum. *CNS Spectrums, 9,* 679-685.

Bracha, H.S., Yoshioka, D.T., Masukawa, N.K., & Stockman, D.J. (2005). Evolution of the human fear circuitry and acute sociogenic pseudoneurological symptoms: The Neolithic balanced-polymorphism hypothesis. *Journal of Affective Disorders, 88,* 119-129.

Bradley, R., & Westen, D. (2005). The psychodynamics of borderline personality disorder: A view from developmental psychopathology. *Development and Psychopathology, 17,* 927-957.

Bradshaw, J.L. (2001). *Developmental disorders of the frontostriatal system: Neuropsychological, neuropsychiatric, and evolutionary perspectives.* Philadelphia: Taylor & Francis.

Braff, D.L., Freedman, R., Schork, N.J., & Gottesman, I.I. (2007). Deconstructing schizophrenia: An overview of the use of endophenotypes in order to understand a complex disorder. *Schizophrenia Bulletin, 33,* 21-32.

Bragin, V., Chemodanova, M., Dzhafarova, N., Bragin, I., Czerniawski, J.L., & Aliev, G. (2005). Integrated treatment approach improves cognitive function in demented and clinically depressed patients. *American Journal of Alzheimer's Disease and Other Dementias, 20,* 21-26.

Braitman, A.L., Kelley, M.L., Ladage, J., Schroeder, V., Gumienny, L.A., Morrow, J.A., & Klostermann, K. (2009). Alcohol and drug use among college student adult children of alcoholics. *Journal of Alcohol and Drug Education, 53,* 69-88.

Brand, B.L., Classen, C.C., McNary, S.W., & Zaveri, P. (2009). A review of dissociative disorders treatment studies. *Journal of Nervous and Mental Disease, 197*, 646-654.

Brand, B.L., Myrick, A.C., Loewenstein, R.J., Classen, C.C., Lanius, R., McNary, S.W., Pain, C., & Putnam, F.W. (2012). A survey of practices and recommended treatment interventions among expert therapists treating patients with dissociative identity disorder and dissociative disorder not otherwise specified. *Psychological Trauma: Theory, Research, Practice, and Policy, 4*, 490-500.

Brandes, B.M., & Mesrobian, H.-G. O. (2005). Evaluation and management of genital anomalies in two patients with Klinefelter syndrome and review of literature. *Urology, 65*, 976-979.

Brandt, J., & Van Gorp, W.G. (2006). Functional ("psychogenic") amnesia. *Seminars in Neurology, 26*, 331-340.

Brandt, R., Hundelt, M., & Shahani, N. (2005). Tau alteration and neuronal degeneration in tauopathies: Mechanisms and models. *Biochimica et Biophysica Acta, 1739*, 331-354.

Brannigan, G.G., & Decker, S.L. (2006). The Bender-Gestalt II. *American Journal of Orthopsychiatry, 76*, 10-12.

Braswell, H., & Kushner, H.I. (2012). Suicide, social integration, and masculinity in the U.S. military. *Social Science and Medicine, 74*, 530-536.

Bratland-Sanda, S., & Sundgot-Borgen, J. (2013). Eating disorders in athletes: Overview of prevalence, risk factors and recommendations for prevention and treatment. *European Journal of Sport Science, 13(5)*, 499-508.

Braunstein, G.D. (2006). Androgen insufficiency in women. *Growth Hormone and IGF Research, 16 (Suppl. A)*, S109-S117.

Bremner, J.D., Krystal, J.H., Putnam, F.W., Sothwick, S.M., Marmar, C., Charney, D.S., & Mazure, C.M. (1998). Measurement of dissociative states with the Clinician-Administered Dissociative States Scale (CADSS). *Journal of Traumatic Stress, 11*, 125-136.

Brennan, P.A., Mednick, S.A., & Hodgins, S. (2000). Major mental disorders and criminal violence in a Danish birth cohort. *Archives of General Psychiatry, 57*, 494-500.

Brewin, C.R., & Holmes, E.A. (2003). Psychological theories of posttraumatic stress disorder. *Clinical Psychology Review, 23*, 339-376.

Briere, J. (1996). *Trauma symptom checklist for children*. Lutz, FL: Psychological Assessment Resources.

Briken, P., Habermann, N., Berner, W., & Hill, A. (2006). XYY chromosome abnormality in sexual homicide perpetrators. *American Journal of Medical Genetics Part B, 141*, 198-200.

Brindis, C.D. (2006). A public health success: Understanding policy changes related to teen sexual activity and pregnancy. *Annual Review of Public Health, 27*, 277-295.

Brock, G.B., Benard, F., Casey, R., Elliot, S.L., Gajewski, J.B., & Lee, J.C. (2009). Canadian Male Sexual Health Council survey to assess prevalence and treatment of premature ejaculation in Canada. *Journal of Sexual Medicine, 6*, 2115-2123.

Brodaty, H., & Donkin, M. (2009). Family caregivers of people with dementia. *Dialogues in Clinical Neuroscience, 11*, 217-228.

Brody, G.H., Ge, X., Kim, S.Y., Murry, V.M., Simons, R.L., Gibbons, F.X., Gerrard, M., & Conger, R.D. (2003). Neighborhood disadvantage moderates associations of parenting and older sibling problem attitudes and behavior with conduct disorders in African American children. *Journal of Consulting and Clinical Psychology, 71*, 211-222.

Brody, J.F. (2001). Evolutionary recasting: ADHD, mania and its variants. *Journal of Affective Disorders, 65*, 197-215.

Broft, A.I., Berner, L.A., Martinez, D., & Walsh, B.T. (2011). Bulimia nervosa and evidence for striatal dopamine dysregulation: A conceptual review. *Physiology and Behavior, 104*, 122-127.

Brogan, P. (2006, July 2). Meth tops in public treatment programs. Retrieved from www.deseretnews.com.

Brohan, E., Gauci, D., Sartorius, N., Thornicroft, G., and for the GAMIAN-Europe Study Group. (2011). Self-stigma, empowerment and perceived discrimination among people with bipolar disorder or depression in 13 European countries: The GAMIAN-Europe study. *Journal of Affective Disorders, 129*, 56-63.

Brook, D.W. (2008). Group therapy. In M. Galanter & H.D. Kleber (Eds.), *Textbook of substance abuse treatment* (4th ed.) (pp. 413-428). Washington, DC: American Psychiatric Press.

Brook, D.W., Brook, J.S., Rubenstone, E., Zhang, C., & Gerochi, C. (2006). Cigarette smoking in the adolescent children of drug-abusing fathers. *Pediatrics, 117*, 1339-1347.

Broome, M.R., Woolley, J.B., Tabraham, P., Johns, L.C., Bramon, E., Murray, G.K., Pariante, C., McGuire, P.K., & Murray, R.M. (2005). What causes the onset of psychosis? *Schizophrenia Research, 79*, 23-34.

Brotto, L.A. (2010a). The DSM diagnostic criteria for hypoactive sexual desire disorder in women. *Archives of Sexual Behavior, 39*, 221-239.

Brotto, L.A. (2010b). The DSM diagnostic criteria for sexual aversion disorder. *Archives of Sexual Behavior, 39*, 271-277.

Brougham, R.R., Zail, C.M., Mendoza, C.M., & Miller, J.R. (2009). Stress, sex differences, and coping strategies among college students. *Current Psychology, 28*, 85-97.

Broussard, B., Goulding, S.M., Talley, C.L., & Compton, M.T. (2012). Social distance and stigma toward individuals with schizophrenia: Findings in an urban, African-American community sample. *Journal of Nervous and Mental Disease, 200*, 935-940.

Brown, A.M., & Whiteside, S.P. (2008). Relations among perceived parental rearing behaviors, attachment style, and worry in anxious children. *Journal of Anxiety Disorders, 22*, 263-272.

Brown, A.S. (2011). The environment and susceptibility to schizophrenia. *Progress in Neurobiology, 93*, 23-58.

Brown, G.W., & Harris, T.O. (1989). Depression. In G.W. Brown & T.O. Harris (Eds.), *Life events and illness* (pp. 49-93). New York: Guilford.

Brown, I., & Brown, R.I. (2009). Choice as an aspect of quality of life for people with intellectual disabilities. *Journal of Policy and Practice in Intellectual Disabilities, 6*, 11-18.

Brown, R.J. (2004). Psychological mechanisms of medically unexplained symptoms: An integrative conceptual model. *Psychological Bulletin, 130*, 793-812.

Brown, R.J., Schrag, A., & Trimble, M.R. (2005). Dissociation, childhood interpersonal trauma, and family functioning in patients with somatization disorder. *American Journal of Psychiatry, 162*, 899-905.

Brown, T.A., Campbell, L.A., Lehman, C.L., Grisham, J.R., & Mancill, R.B. (2001). Current and lifetime comorbidity of the DSM-IV anxiety and mood disorders in a large clinical sample. *Journal of Abnormal Psychology, 110*, 585-599.

Brown, T.A., DiNardo, P.A., & Barlow, D.H. (2004). *Anxiety Disorders Interview Schedule (ADIS-IV) specimen set*. New York: Oxford.

Brownson, C., Drum, D.J., Smith, S.E., & Denmark, A.B. (2011). Differences in suicidal experiences of male and female undergraduate and graduate students. *Journal of College Student Psychotherapy, 25*, 277-294.

Bruce, B., & Fries, J.F. (2003). The Stanford Health Assessment Questionnaire: A review of its history, issues, progress, and documentation. *Journal of Rheumatology, 30*, 167-178.

Bruce, B., & Fries, J.F. (2005). The Health Assessment Questionnaire (HAQ). *Clinical and Experimental Rheumatology, 23 (Suppl 39)*, S14-S18.

Brucki, T.M., Wittchen, H.U., Hofler, M., Pfister, H., Schneider, S., & Lieb, R. (2007). Childhood separation anxiety disorder and the risk of subsequent psychopathology: Results from a community study. *Psychotherapy and Psychosomatics, 76*, 47-56.

Brune, M. (2004). Schizophrenia—an evolutionary enigma? *Neuroscience and Biobehavioral Reviews, 28*, 41-53.

Bryant, R.A. (1995). Autobiographical memory across personalities in dissociative identity disorder: A case report. *Journal of Abnormal Psychology, 104*, 625-631.

Bryant, R.A., Brooks, R., Silove, D., Creamer, M., O'Donnell, M., & McFarlane, A.C. (2011). Peritraumatic dissociation mediates the relationship between acute panic and chronic posttraumatic stress disorder. *Behaviour Research and Therapy, 49*, 346-351.

Bryant, R.A., Creamer, M., O'Donnell, M.L., Silove, D., & McFarlane, A.C. (2008). A multisite study of the capacity of acute stress disorder diagnosis to predict posttraumatic stress disorder. *Journal of Clinical Psychiatry, 69,* 923-929.

Bryant, R.A., & Das, P. (2012). The neural circuitry of conversion disorder and its recovery. *Journal of Abnormal Psychology, 121,* 289-296.

Buchanan, J.A., Christenson, A., Houlihan, D., & Ostrom, C. (2011). The role of behavior analysis in the rehabilitation of persons with dementia. *Behavior Therapy, 42,* 9-21.

Buckley, P.F., Miller, B.J., Lehrer, D.S., & Castle, D.J. (2009). Psychiatric comorbidities and schizophrenia. *Schizophrenia Bulletin, 35,* 383-402.

Budd, R., & Hughes, I. (2009). The dodo bird verdict: Controversial, inevitable, and important: A commentary on 30 years of meta-analyses. *Clinical Psychology and Psychotherapy, 16,* 510-522.

Budson, A.E., & Kowall, N.W. (2011). *The handbook of Alzheimer's disease and other dementias.* New York: Wiley-Blackwell.

Bufkin, J.L., & Luttrell, V.R. (2005). Neuroimaging studies of aggressive and violent behavior: Current findings and implications for criminology and criminal justice. *Trauma, Violence, and Abuse, 6,* 176-191.

Buhler, M., & Mann, K. (2011). Alcohol and the human brain: A systematic review of different neuroimaging methods. *Alcoholism: Clinical and Experimental Research, 35,* 1771-1793.

Bulic, B., Pickhardt, M., Mandelkow, E.-M., & Mandelkow, E. (2010). Tau protein and tau aggregation inhibitors. *Neuropharmacology, 59,* 276-289.

Bulik, C.M., & Reichborn-Kjennerud, T. (2003). Medical morbidity in binge eating disorder. *International Journal of Eating Disorders, 34,* S39-S46.

Bulik, C.M., Reba, L., Siega-Riz, A., & Reichborn-Kjennerud, T. (2005). Anorexia nervosa: Definition, epidemiology, and cycle of risk. *International Journal of Eating Disorders, 37,* S2-S9.

Bulik, C.M., Slof-Op't Landt, M.C.T., van Furth, E.F., & Sullivan, P.F. (2007). The genetics of anorexia nervosa. *Annual Review of Nutrition, 27,* 263-275.

Bulik, C.M., Sullivan, P.F., & Kendler, K.S. (1998). Heritability of binge-eating and broadly defined bulimia nervosa. *Biological Psychiatry, 44,* 1210-1218.

Bulik, C.M., Thornton, L., Pinheiro, A.P., Plotnicov, K., Klump, K.L., Brandt, H., Crawford, S., Fichter, M.M., Halmi, K.A., Johnson, C., Kaplan, A.S., Mitchell, J., Nutzinger, D., Strober, M., Treasure, J., Woodside, D.B., Berrettini, W.H., & Kaye, W.H. (2008). Suicide attempts in anorexia nervosa. *Psychosomatic Medicine, 70,* 378-383.

Bulik, C.M., Thornton, L., Root, T.L., Pisetsky, E.M., Lichtenstein, P., & Pedersen, N.L. (2010). Understanding the relation between anorexia nervosa and bulimia nervosa in a Swedish national twin sample. *Biological Psychiatry, 67,* 71-77.

Burack, J.A., Hodapp, R.M., Iarocci, G., & Zigler, A. (Eds.). (2012). *The Oxford handbook of intellectual disability and development.* New York: Oxford.

Burd, L., Deal, E., Rios, R., Adickes, E., Wynne, J., & Klug, M.G. (2007). Congenital heart defects and fetal alcohol spectrum disorders. *Congenital Heart Disease, 2,* 250-255.

Burgy, M. (2011). Successful treatment of ultradian or ultra-ultra-rapid cycling: A case report. *Journal of Affective Disorders, 133,* 655-656.

Burke, H.M., Davis, M.C., Otte, C., & Mohr, D.C. (2005). Depression and cortisol responses to psychological stress: A meta-analysis. *Psychoneuroendocrinology, 30,* 846-856.

Burke, J.D., Loeber, R., & Birmaher, B. (2002). Oppositional defiant disorder and conduct disorder: A review of the past 10 years, part II. *Journal of the American Academy of Child and Adolescent Psychiatry, 41,* 1275-1293.

Burns, A., Gallagley, A., & Byrne, J. (2004). Delirium. *Journal of Neurology, Neurosurgery and Psychiatry, 75,* 362-367.

Burns, G.L., & Walsh, J.A. (2002). The influence of ADHD-hyperactivity/impulsivity symptoms on the development of oppositional defiant disorder symptoms in a 2-year longitudinal study. *Journal of Abnormal Child Psychology, 30,* 245-256.

Burri, A.V., Cherkas, L.M., & Spector, T.D. (2009). The genetics and epidemiology of female sexual dysfunction: A review. *Journal of Sexual Medicine, 6,* 646-657.

Burton, C. (2003). Beyond somatisation: A review of the understanding and treatment of medically unexplained physical symptoms (MUPS). *British Journal of General Practice, 53,* 233-241.

Burton, N., & Lane, R.C. (2001). The relational treatment of dissociative identity disorder. *Clinical Psychology Review, 21,* 301-320.

Busby, K.K., & Sajatovic, M. (2010). Patient, treatment, and systems-level factors in bipolar disorder nonadherence: A summary of the literature. *CNS Neuroscience and Therapeutics, 16,* 308-315.

Bush, G., Valera, E.M., & Seidman, L.J. (2005). Functional neuroimaging of attention-deficit/hyperactivity disorder: A review and suggested future directions. *Biological Psychiatry, 57,* 1273-1284.

Butcher, J.N. (2006). Assessment in clinical psychology: A perspective on the past, present challenges, and future prospects. *Clinical Psychology: Science and Practice, 13,* 205-209.

Butcher, J.N. (2011). *A beginner's guide to the MMPI-2* (3rd ed.). Washington, DC: American Psychological Association.

Butcher, J.N., Graham, J.R., Williams, C.L. & Ben-Porath, Y.S. (1990). *Development and use of the MMPI–2 content scales.* Minneapolis: University of Minnesota Press.

Butler, A.C., Chapman, J.E., Forman, E.M., & Beck, A.T. (2006). The empirical status of cognitive-behavioral therapy: A review of meta-analyses. *Clinical Psychology Review, 26,* 17-31.

Butterworth, B., Varma, S., & Laurillard, D. (2011). Dyscalculia: From brain to education. *Science, 332,* 1049-1053.

Byers, A.L., & Yaffe, K. (2011). Depression and risk of developing dementia. *Nature Reviews Neurology, 7,* 323-331.

Cabeza, R., Ciaramelli, E., & Moscovitch, M. (2012). Cognitive contributions of the ventral parietal cortex: An integrative theoretical account. *Trends in Cognitive Science, 16,* 338-352.

Cacchioni, T., & Wolkowitz, C. (2011). Treating women's sexual difficulties: The body work of sexual therapy. *Sociology of Health and Illness, 33,* 266-279.

Cacciola, J.S., Alterman, A.I., Habing, B., & McLellan, A.T. (2011). Recent status scores for version 6 of the Addiction Severity Index (ASI-6). *Addiction, 106,* 1588-1602.

Calabrese, J.R., Bowden, C.L., Sachs, G., Yatham, L.N., Behnke, K., Mehtonen, O.-P., Montgomery, P., Paska, W., Earl, N., & DeVeaugh-Geiss, J. (2003). A placebo controlled 18-month trial of lamotrigine and lithium maintenance treatment in recently depressed patients with bipolar I disorder. *Journal of Clinical Psychiatry, 64,* 1013-1024.

Caldwell-Harris, C.L., & Aycicegi, A. (2006). When personality and culture clash: The psychological distress of allocentrics in an individualist culture and idiocentrics in a collectivist culture. *Transcultural Psychiatry, 43,* 331-361.

Callaghan, R.C., Cunningham, J.K., Allebeck, P., Arenovich, T., Sajeev, G., Remington, G., Boileau, I., & Kish, S.J. (2012). Methamphetamine use and schizophrenia: A population-based cohort study in California. *American Journal of Psychiatry, 169,* 389-396.

Callanan, V.J., & Davis, M.S. (2012). Gender differences in suicide methods. *Social Psychiatry and Psychiatric Epidemiology, 47,* 857-869.

Calvo, R., Lazaro, L., Castro, J., Morer, A., & Toro, J. (2007). Parental psychopathology in child and adolescent obsessive-compulsive disorder. *Social Psychiatry and Psychiatric Epidemiology, 42,* 647-655.

Camilleri, J.A., & Quinsey, V.L. (2011). Appraising the risk of sexual and violent recidivism among intellectually disabled offenders. *Psychology, Crime and Law, 17,* 59-74.

Camisa, K.M., Bockbrader, M.A., Lysaker, P., Rae, L.L., Brenner, C.A., & O'Donnell, B.F. (2005). Personality traits in schizophrenia and related personality disorders. *Psychiatry Research, 133,* 23-33.

Campbell, J.C., Webster, D., Koziol-McLain, J., Block, C., Campbell, D., Curry, M.A., Bary, F., Glass, N., McFarlane, J., Sachs, C., Sharps, P., Ulrich, Y., Wilt, S.A., Manganello, J., Xu, X., Schollenberger, J., Frye, V., & Laughon, K. (2003). Risk factors for femicide in abusive relationships: Results from a multisite case control study. *American Journal of Public Health, 93,* 1089-1097.

Campbell, W.K., & Miller, J.D. (Eds.). (2011). *The handbook of narcissism and narcissistic personality* disorder: Theoretical approaches, empirical findings, and treatments. Hoboken, NJ: Wiley.

Campo, J.A., Nijman, H., Merckelbach, H., & Evers, C. (2003). Psychiatric comorbidity of gender identity disorders: A survey among Dutch psychiatrists. American Journal of Psychiatry, 160, 1332-1336.

Campo, J.V., & Fritsch, S.L. (1994). Somatization in children and adolescents. Journal of the American Academy of Child and Adolescent Psychiatry, 33, 1223-1235.

Cannell, J., Hudson, J.I., & Pope, H.G. (2001). Standards for informed consent in recovered memory therapy. Journal of the American Academy of Psychiatry and the Law, 29, 138-147.

Cannon, M., Jones, P.B., & Murray, R.M. (2002). Obstetric complications and schizophrenia: Historical and meta-analytic review. American Journal of Psychiatry, 159, 1080-1092.

Cantor-Graae, E., & Pedersen, C.B. (2007). Risk for schizophrenia in intercountry adoptees: A Danish population-based cohort study. Journal of Child Psychology and Psychiatry, 48, 1053-1060.

Cappadocia, M.C., Desrocher, M., Pepler, D., & Schroeder, J.H. (2009). Contextualizing the neurobiology of conduct disorder in an emotion dysregulation framework. Clinical Psychology Review, 29, 506-518.

Carbranes, J.A., De Juan, R., Encinas, M., Marcos, A., Gil, P., Fernandez, C., De Ugarte, C., & Barabash, A. (2004). Relevance of functional neuroimaging in the progression of mild cognitive impairment. Neurological Research, 26, 496-501.

Cardno, A.G., & McGuffin, P. (2006). Genetics and delusional disorder. Behavioral Sciences and the Law, 24, 257-276.

Cardno, A.G., Thomas, K., & McGuffin, P. (2002). Clinical variables and genetic loading for schizophrenia: Analysis of published Danish adoption study data. Schizophrenia Bulletin, 28, 393-400.

Carlat, D.J., Camargo, C.A., & Herzog, D.B. (1997). Eating disorders in males: A report on 135 patients. American Journal of Psychiatry, 154, 1127-1132.

Carlson, E.B., Putnam, F.W., Ross, C.A., Torem, M., Coons, P., Dill, D.L., Loewenstein, R.J., & Braun, B.G. (1993). Validity of the Dissociative Experiences Scale in screening for multiple personality disorder: A multicenter study. American Journal of Psychiatry, 150, 1030-1036.

Carlson, G.A. (2005). Early onset bipolar disorder: Clinical and research considerations. Journal of Clinical Child and Adolescent Psychology, 34, 333-343.

Carlsson, A. (2006). The neurochemical circuitry of schizophrenia. Pharmacopsychiatry, 39 (Suppl. 1), S10-S14.

Carney, P.R., Berry, R.B., & Geyer, J.D. (2012). Clinical sleep disorders (2nd ed.). Philadelphia, PA: Lippincott Williams & Wilkins.

Carney, R.M., & Freedland, K.E. (2012). Are somatic symptoms of depression better predictors of cardiac events than cognitive symptoms in coronary heart disease? Psychosomatic Medicine, 74, 33-38.

Carpenter, R.W., Tomko, R.L., Trull, T.J., & Boomsma, D.I. (2013). Gene-environment studies and borderline personality disorder: A review. Current Psychiatry Reports, 15, 336.

Carroll, K.M. (2008). Cognitive-behavioral therapies. In M. Galanter & H.D. Kleber (Eds.), Textbook of substance abuse treatment (4th ed.; pp. 349-360). Washington, DC: American Psychiatric Press.

Carson, K.V., Brinn, M.P., Robertson, T.A., To-A-Nan, R., Esterman, A.J., Peters, M., & Smith, B.J. (2013). Current and emerging pharmacotherapeutic options for smoking cessation. Substance Abuse, 7, 85-105.

Carta, M.G., Bernal, M., Hardoy, M.C., & Haro-Abad, J.M. (2005). Migration and mental health in Europe (the state of the mental health in Europe working group: Appendix 1). Clinical Practice and Epidemiology in Mental Health, 1, 13.

Carter, J.D., Luty, S.E., McKenzie, J.M., Mulder, R.T., Frampton, C.M., & Joyce, P.R. (2011). Patient predictors of response to cognitive behaviour therapy and interpersonal psychotherapy in a randomised clinical trial for depression. Journal of Affective Disorders, 128, 252-261.

Caruso, G.A., & Osburn, J.A. (2011). The origins of "best practices" in the principle of normalization and social role valorization. Journal of Policy and Practice in Intellectual Disabilities, 8, 191-196.

Carvalho, J.P., & Hopko, D.R. (2011). Behavioral theory of depression: Reinforcement as a mediating variable between avoidance and depression. Journal of Behavior Therapy and Experimental Psychiatry, 42, 154-162.

Casadio, P., Fernandes, C., Murray, R.M., & Di Forti, M. (2011). Cannabis use in young people: The risk for schizophrenia. Neuroscience and Biobehavioral Reviews, 35, 1779-1787.

Casiero, D., & Frishman, W.H. (2006). Cardiovascular complications of eating disorders. Cardiology in Review, 14, 227-231.

Castagnini, A., & Berrios, G.E. (2011). The relationship of acute transient psychoses and schizophrenia. In M.S. Ritsner (Ed.), Handbook of schizophrenia spectrum disorders, Volume II (pp. 367-387). New York: Springer.

Castle, D.J. (2008). Anxiety and substance use: Layers of complexity. Expert Review of Neurotherapeutics, 8, 493-501.

Catts, H.W., Fey, M.E., Zhang, X., & Tomblin, J.B. (2001). Estimating the risk of future reading difficulties in kindergarten children: A research-based model and its clinical implementation. Language, Speech, and Hearing Services in Schools, 32, 38-50.

Cayan, S., Akbay, E., Bozlu, M., Canpolat, B., Acar, D., & Ulusoy, E. (2004). The prevalence of female sexual dysfunction and potential risk factors that may impair sexual function in Turkish women. Urologia Internationalis, 72, 52-57.

Cechnicki, A., Bielanska, A., Hanuszkiewicz, I., & Daren, A. (2013). The predictive validity of expressed emotions (EE) in schizophrenia: A 20-year prospective study. Journal of Psychiatric Research, 47, 208-214.

Cederbaum, S. (2002). Phenylketonuria: An update. Current Opinion in Pediatrics, 14, 702-706.

Cerezuela, G.P., Tejero, P., Choliz, M., Chisvert, M., & Monteagudo, M.J. (2004). Wertheim's hypothesis on 'highway hypnosis': Empirical evidence from a study on motorway and conventional road driving. Accident Analysis and Prevention, 36, 1045-1054.

Chadman, K.K., Guariglia, S.R., & Yoo, J.H. (2012). New directions in the treatment of autism spectrum disorders from animal model research. Expert Opinion on Drug Discovery, 7, 407-416.

Chai, Y.-G., Oh, D.-Y., Chung, E.K., Kim, G.S., Kim, L., Lee, Y.-S., & Choi, I.-G. (2005). Alcohol and aldehyde dehydrogenase polymorphisms in men with Type I and Type II alcoholism. American Journal of Psychiatry, 162, 1003-1005.

Chakrabarti, S. (2011). Thyroid functions and bipolar affective disorder. Journal of Thyroid Research, 2011, 1-13.

Chakrabarti, S., & Fombonne, E. (2005). Pervasive developmental disorders in preschool children: Confirmation of high prevalence. American Journal of Psychiatry, 162, 1133-1141.

Chamberlain, S.R., Fineberg, N.A., Blackwell, A.D., Clark, L., Robbins, T.W., & Sahakian, B.J. (2007). A neuropsychological comparison of obsessive-compulsive disorder and trichotillomania. Neuropsychologia, 45, 654-662.

Chamberland, L., & Saewyc, E. (2011). Stigma, vulnerability, and resilience: The psychosocial health of sexual minority and gender diverse people in Canada. Canadian Journal of Community Mental Health, 30, 1-5.

Chan, D., Livingston, G., Jones, L., & Sampson, E.L. (2013). Grief reactions in dementia careers: A systematic review. International Journal of Geriatric Psychiatry, 28, 1-17.

Chan, R.C.K., Xu, T., Heinrichs, R.W., Yu, Y., & Wang, Y. (2010). Neurological soft signs in schizophrenia: A meta-analysis. Schizophrenia Bulletin, 36, 1089-1104.

Chanen, A.M., Jovev, M., McCutcheon, L.K., Jackson, H.J., & McGorry, P.D. (2008). Borderline personality disorder in young people and the prospects for prevention and early intervention. Current Psychiatry Reviews, 4, 48-57.

Chanen, A.M., & McCutcheon, L. (2013). Prevention and early intervention for borderline personality disorder: current status and recent evidence. British Journal of Psychiatry, 202, s24-s29.

Chan-Yeung, M., Ferguson, A., Watson, W., Dimich-Ward, H., Rousseau, R., Lilley, M., DyBuncio, A., & Becker, A. (2005). The Canadian Childhood Asthma Primary Prevention Study: Outcomes at 7 years of age. Journal of Allergy and Clinical Immunology, 116, 49-55.

Chang, C.-M., Sato, S., & Han, C. (2013). Evidence for the benefits of nonantipsychotic pharmacological augmentation in the treatment of depression. *CNS Drugs, 27 (Suppl 1)*, 21-27.

Chau, D.M., Crump, C.J., Villa, J.C., Scheinberg, D.A., & Li, Y.-M. (2012). Familial Alzheimer disease presenilin-1 mutations alter the active site conformation of γ-secretase. *Journal of Biological Chemistry, 287*, 17288-17296.

Chen, K.H., Reese, E.A., Kim, h.-W., Rapoport, S.I., & Rao, J.S. (2011). Disturbed neurotransmitter transporter expression in Alzheimer disease brain. *Journal of Alzheimer's Disease, 26*, 755-766.

Chen, X., Riley, B., & Kendler, K.S. (2009). Genetics of schizophrenia. In D.S. Charney & E.J. Nestler (Eds.), *Neurobiology of mental illness* (3rd ed.). (pp. 252-265). New York: Oxford.

Chen, Y., Nettles, M.E., & Chen, S.-W. (2009). Rethinking dependent personality disorder: Comparing different human relatedness in cultural contexts. *Journal of Nervous and Mental Disease, 197*, 793-800.

Chenu, F., & Bourin, M. (2006). Potentiation of antidepressant-like activity with lithium: Mechanism involved. *Current Drug Targets, 7*, 159-163.

Cherpitel, C.J., Borges, G.L., & Wilcox, H.C. (2004). Acute alcohol use and suicidal behavior: A review of the literature. *Alcoholism-Clinical and Experimental Research, 28*, 18S-28S.

Chertkow, H., Feldman, H.H., Jacova, C., & Massoud, F. (2013). Definitions of dementia and predementia states in Alzheimer's disease and vascular cognitive impairment: consensus from the Canadian conference on diagnosis of dementia. *Alzheimer's Research and Therapy, 5 (Suppl 1)*, 1-8.

Cheung, S.K., & Sun, S.Y. (2001). Helping processes in a mutual aid organization for persons with emotional disturbance. *International Journal of Group Psychotherapy, 51*, 295-308.

Chew, K.K., Bremner, A., Stuckey, B., Earle, C., & Jamrozik, K. (2009). Is the relationship between cigarette smoking and male erectile dysfunction independent of cardiovascular disease? Findings from a population-based cross-sectional study. *Journal of Sexual Medicine, 6*, 222-231.

Chiang, K.-J., Chu, H., Chiang, H.-J., Chung, M.-H., Chen, C.-H., Chiou, H.-Y., & Chou, K.-R. (2010). The effects of reminiscence therapy on psychological well-being, depression, and loneliness among the institutionalized aged. *International Journal of Geriatric Psychiatry, 25*, 380-388.

Chiles, J.A., & Strosahl, K.D. (2005). *Clinical manual for assessment and treatment of suicidal patients.* Washington, DC: American Psychiatric Press.

Chiuve, S.E., Fung, T.T., Rexrode, K.M., Spiegelman, D., Manson, J.E., Stampfer, M.J., & Albert, C.M. (2011). Adherence to a low-risk, healthy lifestyle and risk of sudden cardiac death among women. *Journal of the American Medical Association, 306*, 62-69.

Choi-Kain, L.W., Zanarini, M.C., Frankenburg, F.R., Fitzmaurice, G.M., & Reich, D.B. (2010). A longitudinal study of the 10-year course of interpersonal features in borderline personality disorder. *Journal of Personality Disorders, 24*, 365-376.

Chorpita, B.F., & Barlow, D.H. (1998). The development of anxiety: The role of control in the early environment. *Psychological Bulletin, 124*, 3-21.

Chouinard, G. (2004). Issues in the clinical use of benzodiazepines: Potency, withdrawal, and rebound. *Journal of Clinical Psychiatry, 65 (Suppl. 5)*, 7-12.

Chronis-Tuscano, A., Degnan, K.A., Pine, D.S., Perez-Edgar, K., Henderson, H.A., Diaz, Y., Raggi, V.L., & Fox, N.A. (2009). Stable early maternal report of behavioral inhibition predicts lifetime social anxiety disorder in adolescence. *Journal of the American Academy of Child and Adolescent Psychiatry, 48*, 928-935.

Cisler, J.M., & Koster, E.H.W. (2010). Mechanisms of attentional biases towards threat in the anxiety disorders: An integrative review. *Clinical Psychology Review, 30*, 203-216.

Claes, L., Vandereycken, W., & Vertommen, H. (2004). Family environment of eating disordered patients with and without self-injurious behaviors. *European Psychiatry, 19*, 494-498.

Clark, A.J. (2010). Empathy: An integral model in the counseling process. *Journal of Counseling and Development, 88*, 348-356.

Clark, D.M., & McManus, F. (2002). Information processing in social phobia. *Biological Psychiatry, 51*, 92-100.

Clark, L.A. (2007). Assessment and diagnosis of personality disorder: Perennial issues and an emerging reconceptualization. *Annual Review of Psychology, 58*, 227-257.

Clark, L.A. (2010). Emergent issues in assessing personality pathology: Illustrations from two studies of adolescent personality and related pathology. *Journal of Psychopathology and Behavioral Assessment, 32*, 537-543.

Clarke, G.N., Hornbrook, M., Lynch, F., Polen, M., Gale, J., Beardslee, W., O'Connor, E., & Seeley, J. (2001). A randomized trial of a group cognitive intervention for preventing depression in adolescent offspring of depressed parents. *Archives of General Psychiatry, 58*, 1127-1134.

Clarke, M.C., Tanskanen, A., Huttunen, M., Leon, D.A., Murray, R.M., Jones, P.B., & Cannon, M. (2011). Increased risk of schizophrenia from additive interaction between infant motor developmental delay and obstetric complications: Evidence from a population-based longitudinal study. *American Journal of Psychiatry, 168*, 1295-1302.

Clauss, J.A., & Blackford, J.U. (2012). Behavioral inhibition and risk for developing social anxiety disorder: A meta-analytic study. *Journal of the American Academy of Child and Adolescent Psychiatry, 51*, 1066-1075.

Clayton, A., & Ramamurthy, S. (2008). The impact of physical illness on sexual dysfunction. *Advances in Psychosomatic Medicine, 29*, 70-88.

Clements, R., & Heintz, J.M. (2002). Diagnostic accuracy and factor structure of the AAS and APS scales of the MMPI-2. *Journal of Personality Assessment, 79*, 564-582.

Cleveland, H.H., & Wiebe, R.P. (2008). Understanding the association between adolescent marijuana use and later serious drug use: Gateway effect or developmental trajectory? *Development and Psychopathology, 20*, 615-632.

Clifford, P.R., Maisto, S.A., Stout, R.L., McKay, J.R., & Tonigan, J.S. (2006). Long-term posttreatment functioning among those treated for alcohol use disorders. *Alcoholism: Clinical and Experimental Research, 30*, 311-319.

Cobia, D.J., Smith, M.J., Wang, L., & Csernansky, J.G. (2012). Longitudinal progression of frontal and temporal lobe changes in schizophrenia. *Schizophrenia Research, 139*, 1-6.

Coccaro, E.F., Sripada, C.S., Yanowitch, R.N., & Phan, K.L. (2011). Corticolimbic function in impulsive aggressive behavior. *Biological Psychiatry, 69*, 1153-1159.

Cocozza, J.J., Veysey, B.M., Chapin, D.A., Dembo, R., Walters, W., & Farina, S. (2005). Diversion from the juvenile justice system: The Miami-Dade Juvenile Assessment Center Post-Arrest Diversion Program. *Substance Use and Misuse, 40*, 935-951.

Coelho, H.F., Canter, P.H., & Ernst, E. (2007). Mindfulness-based cognitive therapy: Evaluating current evidence and informing future research. *Journal of Consulting and Clinical Psychology, 75*, 1000-1005.

Coelho, H.F., Cooper, P.J., & Murray, L. (2007). A family study of co-morbidity between generalized social phobia and generalized anxiety disorder in a non-clinic sample. *Journal of Affective Disorders, 100*, 103-113.

Coelho, C.M., & Purkis, H. (2009). The origins of specific phobias: Influential theories and current perspectives. *Review of General Psychology, 13*, 335-348.

Cohen, L.J., & Galynker, I.I. (2002). Clinical features of pedophilia and implications for treatment. *Journal of Psychiatric Practice, 8*, 276-289.

Cohen, L.J., Gans, S.W., McGeoch, P.G., Poznansky, O., Itskovich, Y., Murphy, S., Klein, E., Cullen, K., & Galynker, I.I. (2002). Impulsive personality traits in male pedophiles versus healthy controls: Is pedophilia an impulsive-aggressive disorder? *Comprehensive Psychiatry, 43*, 127-134.

Cohen, L.J., McGeoch, P.G., Watras-Gans, S., Acker, S., Poznansky, O., Cullen, K., Itskovich, Y., & Galynker, I. (2002). Personality impairment in male pedophiles. *Journal of Clinical Psychiatry, 63*, 912-919.

Cohen, N., & Galea, S. (Eds.). (2011). *Population mental health: Evidence, policy, and mental health practice.* New York: Routledge.

Cohen-Kettenis, P.T. (2001). Gender identity disorder in DSM? *Journal of the American Academy of Child and Adolescent Psychiatry, 40,* 391.

Cohen-Kettenis, P.T., & Pfafflin, F. (2003). *Transgenderism and intersexuality in childhood and adolescence: Making choices.* Thousand Oaks, CA: Sage.

Coid, J., & Ullrich, S. (2010). Antisocial personality disorder is on a continuum with psychopathy. *Comprehensive Psychiatry, 51,* 426-433.

Coller, J., de Vugt, M.E., Verhey, F.R.J., & Schols, J.M.G.A. (2010). Efficacy of integrated interventions combining psychiatric care and nursing home care for nursing home residents: A review of the literature. *International Journal of Geriatric Psychiatry, 25,* 3-13.

Colloby, S.J., McParland, S., O'Brien, J.T., & Attems, J. (2011). Neuropathological correlates of dopaminergic imaging in Alzheimer's disease and Lewy body dementias. *Brain, 135,* 2798-2808.

Combs, D.R., Penn, D.L., Michael, C.O., Basso, M.R., Wiedeman, R., Siebenmorgan, M., Tiegreen, J., & Chapman, D. (2009). Perceptions of hostility by persons with and without persecutory delusions. *Cognitive Neuropsychiatry, 14,* 30-52.

Compton, M.T., & Walker, E.F. (2009). Physical manifestations of neurodevelopmental disruption: Are minor physical anomalies part of the syndrome of schizophrenia? *Schizophrenia Bulletin, 35,* 425-436.

Compton, M.T., Weiss, P.S., West, J.C., & Kaslow, N.J. (2005). The associations between substance use disorders, schizophrenia-spectrum disorders, and Axis IV psychosocial problems. *Social Psychiatry and Psychiatric Epidemiology, 40,* 939-946.

Compton, W.M., Thomas, Y.F., Conway, K.P., & Colliver, J.D. (2005). Developments in the epidemiology of drug use and drug use disorders. *American Journal of Psychiatry, 162,* 1494-1502.

Conde-Sala, J.L., Garre-Olmo, J., Turro-Garriga, O., Vilalta-Franch, J., & Lopez-Pousa, S. (2010). Quality of life of patients with Alzheimer's disease: Differential perceptions between spouse and adult child caregivers. *Dementia and Geriatric Cognitive Disorders, 29,* 97-108.

Conduct Problems Prevention Research Group. (2002). Evaluation of the first 3 years of the Fast Track prevention trial with children at high risk for adolescent conduct problems. *Journal of Abnormal Child Psychology, 30,* 19-35.

Conner, K.R., Beautrais, A.L., Brent, D.A., Conwell, Y., Phillips, M.R., & Schneider, B. (2011). The next generation of psychological autopsy studies. *Suicide and Life-Threatening Behavior, 41,* 594-613.

Conners, C.K. (2008). *Conners Third Edition (Conners 3).* Los Angeles: Western Psychological Services.

Conners, C.K., & MHS Staff. (2000). *Conners Continuous Performance Test II (CPT II).* Tonawanda, NY: Multi-Health Systems.

Conners, N.A., Bradley, R.H., Mansell, L.W., Liu, J.Y., Roberts, T.J., Burgdorf, K., & Herrell, J.M. (2004). Children of mothers with serious substance abuse problems: An accumulation of risks. *American Journal of Drug and Alcohol Abuse, 30,* 85-100.

Constant, E.L., Adam, S., Seron, X., Bruyer, R., Seghers, A., & Daumerie, C. (2006). Hypothyroidism and major depression: A common executive dysfunction? *Journal of Clinical and Experimental Neuropsychology, 28,* 790-807.

Cookson, J., & Elliott, B. (2006). The use of anticonvulsants in the aftermath of mania. *Journal of Psychopharmacology, 20 (Suppl. 2),* 23-30.

Coons, P.M. (1999). Psychogenic or dissociative fugue: A clinical investigation of five cases. *Psychological Reports, 84,* 881-886.

Cooper, H., Friedman, S.R., Tempalski, B., Friedman, R., & Keem, M. (2005). Racial/ ethnic disparities in injection drug use in large US metropolitan areas. *Annals of Epidemiology, 15,* 326-334.

Cooper, J., Carty, J., & Creamer, M. (2005). Pharmacotherapy for posttraumatic stress disorder: Empirical review and clinical recommendations. *Australian and New Zealand Journal of Psychiatry, 39,* 674-682.

Cooper, L.D., Balsis, S., & Oltmanns, T.F. (2012). Self- and informant-reported perspectives on symptoms of narcissistic personality disorder. *Personality Disorders: Theory, Research, and Treatment, 3,* 140-154.

Corey, K., Galvin, D., Cohen, M., Bekelman, A., Healy, H., & Edberg, M. (2005). Impact of the September 11 attack on flight attendants: A study of an essential first responder group. *International Journal of Emergency Mental Health, 7,* 227-240.

Cormier, E., & Elder, J.H. (2007). Diet and child behavior problems: Fact or fiction? *Pediatric Nursing, 33,* 138-143.

Corrigan, P. (2004). How stigma interferes with mental health care. *American Psychologist, 59,* 614-625.

Corrigan, P.W., & Penn, D.L. (1999). Lessons from social psychology on discrediting psychiatric stigma. *American Psychologist, 54,* 765-776.

Corrigan, P.W., Watson, A.C., Gracia, G., Slopen, N., Rasinski, K., & Hall, L.L. (2005). Newspaper stories as measures of structural stigma. *Psychiatric Services, 56,* 551-556.

Corsello, C.M. (2005). Early intervention in autism. *Infants and Young Children, 2,* 74-85.

Cosci, F., Schruers, K.R., Abrams, K., & Griez, E.J. (2007). Alcohol use disorders and panic disorder: A review of the evidence of a direct relationship. *Journal of Clinical Psychiatry, 68,* 874-880.

Costello, E.J., Egger, H., & Angold, A. (2005). 10-year research update review: The epidemiology of child and adolescent psychiatric disorders: I. Methods and public health burden. *Journal of the American Academy of Child and Adolescent Psychiatry, 44,* 972-986.

Counts, C.A., Nigg, J.T., Stawicki, J.A., Rappley, M.D., & von Eye, A. (2005). Family adversity in DSM-IV ADHD combined and inattentive subtypes and associated disruptive behavior problems. *Journal of the American Academy of Child and Adolescent Psychiatry, 44,* 690-698.

Courchesne, E., Campbell, K., & Solso, S. (2011). Brain growth across the life span in autism: Age-specific changes in anatomical pathology. *Brain Research, 1380,* 138-145.

Court, A., Mulder, C., Hetrick, S.E., Purcell, R., & McGorry, P.D. (2008). What is the scientific evidence for the use of antipsychotic medication in anorexia nervosa? *Eating Disorders, 16,* 217-223.

Courtney, K.E., & Polich, J. (2009). Binge drinking in young adults: Data, definitions, and determinants. *Psychological Bulletin, 135,* 142-156.

Couture, S., & Penn, D.L. (2003). Contact and the stigma of mental illness: A review of the literature. *Journal of Mental Health, 12,* 291-305.

Couturier, J.L. (2005). Efficacy of rapid-rate repetitive transcranial magnetic stimulation in the treatment of depression: A systematic review and meta-analysis. *Journal of Psychiatry and Neuroscience, 30,* 83-90.

Cowen, E.L., Hightower, A.D., Pedro-Carroll, J.L., Work, W.C., Wyman, P.A., & Haffey, W.G. (1996). *School-based prevention for children at risk: The Primary Mental Health Project.* Washington, DC: American Psychological Association.

Cox, B.J., McWilliams, L.A., Enns, M.W., & Clara, I.P. (2004). Broad and specific personality dimensions associated with major depression in a nationally representative sample. *Comprehensive Psychiatry, 45,* 246-253.

Cox, B.J., Pagura, J., Stein, M.B., & Sareen, J. (2009). The relationship between generalized social phobia and avoidant personality disorder in a national mental health survey. *Depression and Anxiety, 26,* 354-362.

Craddock, N., & Jones, I. (1999). Genetics of bipolar disorder. *Journal of Medical Genetics, 36,* 585-594.

Craig, L.A., & Beech, A.R. (2009). Psychometric assessment of sexual deviance. In A. Beech, L. Craig, & K. Browne (Eds.), *Assessment and treatment of sex offenders: A handbook* (pp. 89-109). New York: Wiley.

Craig, W.M., & Pepler, D.J. (2003). Identifying and targeting risk for involvement in bullying and victimization. *Canadian Journal of Psychiatry, 48,* 577-582.

Craighead, W.E., & Miklowitz, D.J. (2000). Psychosocial interventions for bipolar disorder. *Journal of Clinical Psychiatry, 61 (Suppl. 13),* 58-64.

Cramer, V., Torgersen, S., & Kringlen, E. (2006). Personality disorders and quality of life: A population study. *Comprehensive Psychiatry, 47,* 178-184.

Craske, M.G. (1999). *Anxiety disorders: Psychological approaches to theory and treatment.* New York: Basic.

Craske, M.G., Antony, M.M., & Barlow, D.H. (2006). *Mastering your fears and phobias: Workbook* (2nd ed.). New York: Oxford.

Craske, M.G., & Barlow, D.H. (2007). *Mastery of your anxiety and panic: Therapist guide* (4th ed.). New York: Oxford.

Craske, M.G., Barlow, D.H., & Meadows, E. (2000). *Mastery of your anxiety and panic: Therapist guide for anxiety, panic, and agoraphobia* (MAP-3). San Antonio, TX: The Psychological Corporation.

Craske, M.G., & Hazlett-Stevens, H. (2002). Facilitating symptom reduction and behavior change in GAD: The issue of control. *Clinical Psychology. Science and Practice, 9*, 69-75.

Craske, M.G., Rauch, S.L., Ursano, R., Prenoveau, J., Pine, D.S., & Zinbarg, R.E. (2009). What is an anxiety disorder? *Depression and Anxiety, 26*, 1066-1085.

Craske, M.G., & Waters, A.M. (2005). Panic disorder, phobias, and generalized anxiety disorder. *Annual Review of Clinical Psychology, 1*, 197-225.

Craven, R.M., Priddle, T.H., Crow, T.J., & Esiri, M.M. (2005). The locus coeruleus in schizophrenia: A postmortem study of noradrenergic neurones. *Neuropathology and Applied Neurobiology, 31*, 115-126.

Creed, F., & Barsky, A. (2004). A systematic review of the epidemiology of somatisation disorder and hypochondriasis. *Journal of Psychosomatic Research, 56*, 391-408.

Creed, F.H., Davies, I., Jackson, J., Littlewood, A., Chew-Graham, C., Tomenson, B., Macfarlane, G., Barsky, A., Katon, W., & McBeth, J. (2012). The epidemiology of multiple somatic symptoms. *Journal of Psychosomatic Research, 72*, 311-317.

Crerand, C.E., Menard, W., & Phillips, K.A. (2010). Surgical and minimally invasive cosmetic procedures among persons with body dysmorphic disorder. *Annals of Plastic Surgery, 65*, 11-16.

Crichton, G.E., Bryan, J., & Murphy, K.J. (2013). Dietary antioxidants, cognitive function and dementia: A systematic review. *Plant Foods for Human Nutrition, 68*, 279-292.

Crisp, A. (2005). Stigmatization of and discrimination against people with eating disorders including a report of two nationwide surveys. *European Eating Disorders Review, 13*, 147-152.

Crocker, A.G., Cote, G., Toupin, J., & St-Onge, B. (2007). Rate and characteristics of men with an intellectual disability in pre-trial detention. *Journal of Intellectual and Developmental Disability, 32*, 143-152.

Cronce, J.M., & Larimer, M.E. (2011). Individual-focused approaches to the prevention of college student drinking. *Alcohol Research and Health, 34*, 210-221.

Crosby, A.E., Han, B., Ortega, L.A.G., Parks, S.E., & Gfroerer, J. (2011). Suicidal thoughts and behaviors among adults aged 18 years: United States, 2008-2009. *Surveillance Summaries, 60*, 1-22.

Crossley, N.A., Constante, M., McGuire, P., & Power, P. (2010). Efficacy of atypical v. typical antipsychotics in the treatment of early psychosis: Meta-analysis. *British Journal of Psychiatry, 196*, 434-439.

Crow, S.J., Mitchell, J.E., Roerig, J.D., & Steffen, K. (2009). What potential role is there for medication in anorexia nervosa? *International Journal of Eating Disorders, 42*, 1-8.

Crow, T.J. (2004). Auditory hallucinations as primary disorders of syntax: An evolutionary theory of the origins of language. *Cognitive Neuropsychiatry, 9*, 125-145.

Crow, T.J. (2008). The emperors of the schizophrenia polygene have no clothes. *Psychological Medicine, 38*, 1681-1685.

Crowe, M. (2012). Couple relationship problems and sexual dysfunctions: Therapeutic guidelines. *Advances in Psychiatric Treatment, 18*, 154-159.

Crunelle, C.L., Miller, M.L., Booij, J., & van den Brink, W. (2010). The nicotinic acetylcholine receptor partial agonist varenicline and the treatment of drug dependence: A review. *European Neuropsychopharmacology, 20*, 69-79.

Cubillo, A., Halari, R., Smith, A., Taylor, E., & Rubia, K. (2012). A review of fronto-striatal and fronto-cortical brain abnormalities in children and adults with Attention Deficit Hyperactivity Disorder (ADHD) and new evidence for dysfunction in adults with ADHD during motivation and attention. *Cortex, 48*, 194-215.

Cui, L., Li, M., Deng, W., Guo, W., Ma, X., Huang, C., Jiang, L., Wang, Y., Collier, D.A., Gong, Q., & Li, T. (2011). Overlapping clusters of gray matter deficits in paranoid schizophrenia and psychotic bipolar mania with family history. *Neuroscience Letters, 489*, 94-98.

Cuijpers, P., Geraedts, A.S., van Oppen, P., Andersson, G., Markowitz, J.C., & van Straten, A. (2011). Interpersonal psychotherapy for depression: A meta-analysis. *American Journal of Psychiatry, 168*, 581-592.

Culverhouse, R., Bucholz, K.K., Crowe, R.R., Hesselbrock, V., Nurnberger, J.I., Porjesz, B., Schuckit, M.A., Reich, T., & Bierut, L.J. (2005). Long-term stability of alcohol and other substance dependence diagnoses and habitual smoking: An evaluation after 5 years. *Archives of General Psychiatry, 62*, 753-760.

Cummings, J.L. (2003). *The neuropsychiatry of Alzheimer's disease and related dementias*. London: Dunitz.

Cunningham, J.A., Neighbors, C., Wild, T.C., Humphreys, K. (2012). Normative misperceptions about alcohol use in a general population sample of problem drinkers from a large metropolitan city. *Alcohol and Alcoholism, 47*, 63-66.

Curnoe, S., & Langevin, R. (2002). Personality and deviant sexual fantasies: An examination of the MMPIs of sex offenders. *Journal of Clinical Psychology, 58*, 803-815.

Cutrona, C.E., Wallace, G., & Wesner, K.A. (2006). Neighborhood characteristics and depression: An examination of stress processes. *Current Directions in Psychological Science, 15*, 188-192.

Daban, C., Martinez-Aran, A., Torrent, C., Tabares-Seisdedos, R., Balanza-Martinez, V., Salazar-Fraile, J., Selva-Vera, G., & Vieta, E. (2006). Specificity of cognitive deficits in bipolar disorder versus schizophrenia: A systematic review. *Psychotherapy and Psychosomatics, 75*, 72-84.

Dadds, M.R., Davey, G.C.L., & Field, A.P. (2001). Developmental aspects of conditioning processes in anxiety disorders. In M.W. Vasey & M.R. Dadds (Eds.), *The developmental psychopathology of anxiety* (pp. 205-230). New York: Oxford.

Dadds, M.R., & Roth, J.H. (2001). Family processes in the development of anxiety problems. In M.W. Vasey & M.R. Dadds (Eds.), *The developmental psychopathology of anxiety* (pp. 278-303). New York: Oxford.

Dahl, M.H., Ronning, O.M., & Thommessen, B. (2010). Delirium in acute stroke: Prevalence and risk factors. *Acta Neurologica Scandinavica, 122 (Suppl. 190)*, 39-43.

Dahl, R.E., Birmaher, B., Williamson, D.E., Dorn, L., Perel, J., Kaufman, J., Brent, D.A., Axelson, D.A., & Ryan, N.D. (2000). Low growth hormone response to growth hormone-releasing hormone in child depression. *Biological Psychiatry, 48*, 981-988.

Daker-White, G., Beattie, A.M., Gilliard, J., & Means, R. (2002). Minority ethnic groups in dementia care: A review of service needs, service provision and models of good practice. *Aging and Mental Health, 6*, 101-108.

Daley, D., & Birchwood, J. (2010). ADHD and academic performance: Why does ADHD impact on academic performance and what can be done to support ADHD children in the classroom? *Child: Care, Health and Development, 36*, 455-464.

Dalle Grave, R., Calugi, S., & Marchesini, G. (2008). Is amenorrhea a clinically useful criterion for the diagnosis of anorexia nervosa? *Behaviour Research and Therapy, 46*, 1290-1294.

Daniel, S.S., Goldston, D.B., Harris, A.E., Kelley, A.E., & Palmes, G.K. (2004). Review of literature on aftercare services among children and adolescents. *Psychiatric Services, 55*, 901-912.

Darke, S. (2010). Scales for research in the addictions. In P.G. Miller, J. Strang, & P.M. Miller (Eds.), *Addiction research methods* (pp. 127-146). Ames, IA: Wiley.

Daugherty, R., & Van Tubergen, N. (2002). A comparison of two measures of low response to alcohol among heavy drinking male college students: Implications for indicated prevention. *Prevention Science, 3*, 267-273.

Daughton, J.M., & Kratochvil, C.J. (2009). Review of ADHD pharmacotherapies: Advantages, disadvantages, and clinical pearls. *Journal of the American Academy of Child and Adolescent Psychiatry, 48*, 240-248.

Davidson, K.M., Tyrer, P., Tata, P., Cooke, D., Gumley, A., Ford, I., Walker, A., Bezlyak, V., Seivewright, H., Robertson, H., & Crawford, M.J. (2009). Cognitive behaviour therapy for violent men with antisocial personality disorder in the community: An exploratory randomized controlled trial. *Psychological Medicine, 39*, 569-577.

Davidson, R.J., Pizzagalli, D., & Nitschke, J.B. (2002). The representation and regulation of emotion in depression: Perspectives from affective neuroscience. In I.H. Gotlib & C.L. Hammen (Eds.), *Handbook of depression* (pp. 219-244). New York: Guilford.

Davidson, R.J., Pizzagalli, D.A., & Nitschke, J.B. (2010). Representation and regulation of emotion in depression. In I.H. Gotlib & C.L. Hammen (Eds.), *Handbook of depression* (2nd ed.) (pp. 218-248). New York: Guilford.

Davies, G., Welham, J., Chant, D., Torrey, E.F., & McGrath, J. (2003). A systematic review and meta-analysis of Northern Hemisphere season of birth studies in schizophrenia. *Schizophrenia Bulletin, 29*, 587-593.

Davies, H.A. (2010). *The use of psychoanalytic concepts in therapy with families.* London: Karnac.

Davies, S., Clarke, M., Hollin, C., & Duggan, C. (2007). Long-term outcomes after discharge from medium secure care: A cause for concern. *British Journal of Psychiatry, 191*, 70-74.

Davis, B., Sheeber, L., Hops, H., & Tildesley, E. (2000). Adolescent responses to depressive parental behaviors in problem-solving interactions: Implications for depressive symptoms. *Journal of Abnormal Child Psychology, 28*, 451-465.

Davis, D.H.J., Terrera, G.M., Keage, H., Rahkonen, T., Oinas, M., Matthews, F.E., Cunningham, C., Polvikoski, T., Sulkava, R., MacLullich, A.M.J., & Brayne, C. (2012). Delirium is a strong risk factor for dementia in the oldest-old: A population-based cohort study. *Brain, 135*, 2809-2816.

Davis, L., Uezato, A., Newell, J.M., & Frazier, E. (2008). Major depression and comorbid substance use disorders. *Current Opinion in Psychiatry, 21*, 14-18.

Davis, M. (2004). Functional neuroanatomy of anxiety and fear. In D.S Charney & E.J. Nestler (Eds.), *Neurobiology of mental illness* (2nd ed.; pp. 584-604). New York: Oxford.

Dawson, T.M., & Dawson V.L. (2010). The role of parking in familial and sporadic Parkinson's disease. *Movement Disorders, 25 (Suppl. 1)*, S32 -39.

Dawson, R., Lavori, P.W., Coryell, W.H., Endicott, J., & Keller, M.B. (1998). Maintenance strategies for unipolar depression: An observational study of levels of treatment and recurrence. *Journal of Affective Disorders, 49*, 31-44.

Deacon, B., & Abramowitz, J.S. (2008). Is hypochondriasis related to obsessive-compulsive disorder, panic disorder, or both? An empirical evaluation. *Journal of Cognitive Psychotherapy, 22*, 115-127.

Deacon, B.J., & Valentiner, D.P. (2000). Substance use and non-clinical panic attacks in a young adult sample. *Journal of Substance Abuse, 11*, 7-15.

Deault, L.C. (2010). A systematic review of parenting in relation to the development of comorbidities and functional impairments in children with attention-deficit/ hyperactivity disorder (ADHD). *Child Psychiatry and Human Development, 41*, 168-192.

de Bildt, A., Sytema, S., Ketelaars, C., Kraijer, D., Mulder, E., Volkmar, F., & Minderaa, R. (2004). Interrelationship between Autism Diagnostic Observation Schedule-Generic (ADOS-G), Autism Diagnostic Interview-Revised (ADI-R), and the Diagnostic and Statistical Manual of Mental Disorders (DSM-IV-TR) classification in children and adolescents with mental retardation. *Journal of Autism and Developmental Disorders, 34*, 129-137.

De Boer, A.G., Wijker, W., & De Haes, H.C. (1997) Predictors of health care utilization in the chronically ill: A review of the literature. *Health Policy, 42*, 101-115.

De Brito, S.A., & Hodgins, S. (2009). Antisocial personality disorder. In M. McMurran & R. Howard (Eds.), *Personality, personality disorder and violence* (pp. 133-153). Malden, MA: Wiley.

De Bruijn, C., Van Den Brink, W., De Graaf, R., & Vollebergh, W.A.M. (2005). Alcohol abuse and dependence criteria as predictors of a chronic course of alcohol use disorders in the general population. *Alcohol and Alcoholism, 40*, 441-446.

de Lange, E., Verhaak, P.F.M., & van der Meer, K. (2013). Prevalence, presentation and prognosis of delirium in older people in the population, at home and in long term care: review. *International Journal of Geriatric Psychiatry, 28*, 127-134.

Deeks, S.G. (2011). HIV infection, inflammation, immunosenescence, and aging. *Annual Review of Medicine, 62*, 141-155.

Delgado, C. (2004). Evaluation of needle exchange programs. *Public Health Nursing, 21*, 171-178.

Delis, D.C., Kramer, J.H., Kaplan, E., & Ober, B.A. (2000). *California Verbal Learning Test—Second Edition.* San Antonio, TX: The Psychological Corporation.

del Campo, N., Chamberlain, S.R., Sahakian, B.J., & Robbins, T.W. (2011). The roles of dopamine and noradrenaline in the pathophysiology and treatment of attention-deficit/hyperactivity disorder. *Biological Psychiatry, 69*, e145-e157.

Del Re, A.C., Fluckiger, C., Horvath, A.O., Symonds, D., & Wampold, B.E. (2012). Therapist effects in the therapeutic alliance-outcome relationship: A restricted-maximum likelihood meta-analysis. *Clinical Psychology Review, 32*, 642-649.

Dembo, R., Jainchill, N., Turner, C., Fong, C., Farkas, S., & Childs, K. (2007). Levels of psychopathy and its correlates: A study of incarcerated youths in three states. *Behavioral Sciences and the Law, 25*, 717-738.

Demirkan, A., Penninx, B.W.J.H., Hek, K., Wray, N.R., Amin, N., Aulchenko, Y.S., van Dyck, R., de Geus, E.J.C., Hofman, A., Uitterlinden, A.G., Hottenga, J.-J., Nolen, W.A., Oostra, B.A., Sullivan, P.F., Willemsen, G., Zitman, F.G., Tiemeier, H., Janssens, A.C.J.W., Boomsma, D.I., van Duijn, C.M., & MIddeldorp, C.M. (2011). Genetic risk profiles for depression and anxiety in adult and elderly cohorts. *Molecular Psychiatry, 16*, 773-783.

Denys, D., & de Geus, F. (2005). Predictors of pharmacotherapy response in anxiety disorders. *Current Psychiatry Reports, 7*, 252-257.

Depla, M.F., ten Have, M.L., van Balkom, A.J., & de Graaf, R. (2008). Specific fears and phobias in the general population: Results from the Netherlands Mental Health Survey and Incidence Study (NEMESIS). *Social Psychiatry and Psychiatric Epidemiology, 43*, 200-208.

de Portugal, E., Gonzalez, N., Miriam, V., Haro, J.M., Usall, J., & Cervilla, J.A. (2010). Gender differences in delusional disorder: Evidence from an outpatient sample. *Psychiatry Research, 177*, 235-239.

Derogatis, L.R. (1994). *SCL-90-R Symptom Checklist 90-R: Administration, scoring, and procedures manual.* Minneapolis: National Computer Systems.

DeRubeis, R. J., & Crits-Christoph, P. (1998). Empirically supported individual and group psychological treatments for adult mental disorders. *Journal of Consulting and Clinical Psychology, 66*, 37-52.

DesJardins, J.R., & Duska, R. (2003). Drug testing in employment. In W.H. Shaw (Ed.), *Ethics at work: Basic readings in business ethics.* New York: Oxford.

Desmond, D.W. (2004). The neuropsychology of vascular cognitive impairment: Is there a specific cognitive deficit? *Journal of the Neurological Sciences, 226*, 3-7.

Desrochers, G., Bergeron, S., Landry, T., & Jodoin, M. (2008). Do psychosexual factors play a role in the etiology of provoked vestibulodynia? *Journal of Sex and Marital Therapy, 34*, 198-226.

Detrich, R., & Higbee, T.S. (2010). Teaching functional life skills to children with developmental disabilities: Acquisition, generalization, and maintenance. In G.G. Peacock, R.A. Ervin, E.J. Daly, & K.W. Merrell (Eds.), *Practical handbook of school psychology: Effective practices for the 21st century* (pp. 371-389). New York: Guilford.

Deveci, A., Taskin, O., Dinc, G., Yilmaz, H., Demet, M.M., Erbay-Dundar, P., Kaya, E., & Ozmen, E. (2007). Prevalence of pseudoneurologic conversion disorder in an urban community in Manisa, Turkey. *Social Psychiatry and Psychiatric Epidemiology, 42*, 857-864.

Devore, E.E., Grodstein, F., van Rooij, F.J.A., Hofman, A., Rosner, B., Stampfer, M.J., Witteman, J.C.M., & Breteler, M.M.B. (2009). Dietary intake of fish and omega-3 fatty acids in relation to long-term dementia risk. *American Journal of Clinical Nutrition, 90*, 170-176.

Devoto, P., Flore, G., Saba, P., Cadeddu, R., & Gessa, G.L. (2012). Disulfiram stimulates dopamine release from noradrenergic terminals and potentiates cocaine-induced dopamine release in the prefrontal cortex. *Psychopharmacology, 219*, 1153-1164.

Diamond, G.S., Wintersteen, M.B., Brown, G.K., Diamond, G.M., Gallop, R., Shelef, K., & Levy, S. (2010). Attachment-based family therapy for adolescents with suicidal ideation: A randomized controlled trial. *Journal of the American Academy of Child and Adolescent Psychiatry, 49,* 122-131.

Di Ceglie, D. (2000). Gender identity disorder in young people. *Advances in Psychiatric Treatment, 6,* 458-466.

Di Ceglie, D., & Thummel, E.C. (2006). An experience of group work with parents of children and adolescents with gender identity disorder. *Clinical Child Psychology and Psychiatry, 11,* 387-396.

Dick, D.M., & Bierut, L.J. (2006). The genetics of alcohol dependence. *Current Psychiatry Reports, 8,* 151-157.

Dick, D.M., Viken, R.J., Kaprio, J., Pulkkinen, L., & Rose, R.J. (2005). Understanding the covariation among childhood externalizing symptoms: Genetic and environmental influences on conduct disorder, attention deficit hyperactivity disorder, and oppositional defiant disorder symptoms. *Journal of Abnormal Child Psychology, 33,* 219-229.

Dickerson, D.L., & Johnson, C.L. (2012). Mental health and substance abuse characteristics among a clinical sample of urban American Indian/Alaska Native youths in a large California metropolitan area: A descriptive study. *Community Mental Health Journal, 48,* 56-62.

Dickerson, F.B., Sommerville, J., Origoni, A.E., Ringel, N.B., & Parente, F. (2002). Experiences of stigma among outpatients with schizophrenia. *Schizophrenia Bulletin, 28,* 143-155.

Dickerson, F.B., Tenhula, W.N., & Green-Paden, L.D. (2005). The token economy for schizophrenia: Review of the literature and recommendations for future research. *Schizophrenia Research, 75,* 405-416.

Dickinson, D., Tenhula, W., Morris, S., Brown, C., Peer, J., Spencer, K., Li, L., Gold, J.M., & Bellack, A.S. (2010). A randomized, controlled trial of computer-assisted cognitive remediation for schizophrenia. *American Journal of Psychiatry, 167,* 170-180.

Dickinson, H.O., Campbell, F., Beyer, F.R., Nicolson, D.J., Cook, J.V., Ford, G.A., & Mason, J.M. (2008). Relaxation therapies for the management of primary hypertension in adults: A Cochrane review. *Journal of Human Hypertension, 22,* 809-822.

Dickstein, D.P., & Leibenluft, E. (2006). Emotion regulation in children and adolescents: Boundaries between normalcy and bipolar disorder. *Developmental Psychopathology, 18,* 1105-1131.

Di Ciommo, V., Forcella, E., & Cotugno, G. (2012). Living with phenylketonuria from the point of view of children, adolescents, and young adults: A qualitative study. *Journal of Developmental and Behavioral Pediatrics, 33,* 229-235.

Diefenbach, G.J., Robison, J.T., Tolin, D.F., & Blank, K. (2004). Late-life anxiety disorders among Puerto Rican primary care patients: Impact on well-being, functioning, and service utilization. *Journal of Anxiety Disorders, 18,* 841-858.

Dierssen, M., & De La Torre, R. (Eds.). (2012). *Down syndrome: From understanding the neurobiology to therapy.* New York: Elsevier.

Diflorio, A., & Jones, I. (2010). Is sex important? Gender differences in bipolar disorder. *International Review of Psychiatry, 22,* 437-452.

DiLalla, L. F. (2004). Behavior genetics: Background, current research, and goals for the future. In L. F. DiLalla (Ed.), *Behavior genetics principles: Perspectives in development, personality, and psychopathology* (pp. 3-15). Washington, DC: American Psychological Association.

Dilsaver, S.C., & Akiskal, H.S. (2005). High rate of unrecognized bipolar mixed states among destitute Hispanic adolescents referred for "major depressive disorder." *Journal of Affective Disorders, 84,* 179-186.

Dindo, L., & Fowles, D.C. (2008). The skin conductance orienting response to somatic stimuli: Significance can be independent of arousal. *Psychophysiology, 45,* 111-118.

Di Paola, F., Faravelli, C., & Ricca, V. (2010). Perceived expressed emotion in anorexia nervosa, bulimia nervosa, and binge-eating disorder. *Comprehensive Psychiatry, 51,* 401-405.

Dirks, M.A., De Los Reyes, A., Briggs-Gowan, M., Cella, D., & Wakschlag, L.S. (2012). Annual research review: Embracing not erasing contextual variability in children's behavior: Theory and utility in the selection and use of methods and informants in developmental psychopathology. *Journal of Child Psychology and Psychiatry, 53,* 558-574.

Dishion, T.J., & Tipsord, J.M. (2011). Peer contagion in child and adolescent social and emotional development. *Annual Review of Psychology, 62,* 189-214.

Diwadkar, V.A., Segel, J., Pruitt, P., Murphy, E.R., Keshavan, M.S., Radwan, J., Rajan, U., & Zajac-Benitez, C. (2011). Hypo-activation in the executive core of the sustained attention network in adolescent offspring of schizophrenia patients mediated by premorbid functional deficits. *Psychiatry Research: Neuroimaging, 192,* 91-99.

Dobkin, R.D., Leiblum, S.R., Rosen, R.C., Menza, M., & Marin, H. (2006). Depression and sexual functioning in minority women: Current status and future directions. *Journal of Sex and Marital Therapy, 32,* 23-36.

Dobson, K.S. (Ed.). (2010). *Handbook of cognitive-behavioral therapies* (3rd ed.). New York: Guilford.

Docherty, N.M., St-Hillaire, A., Aakre, J.M., & Seghers, J.P. (2009). Life events and high-trait reactivity together predict psychotic symptom increases in schizophrenia. *Schizophrenia Bulletin, 35,* 638-645.

Dodge, K.A., Godwin, J., and the Conduct Problems Prevention Research Group. (2013). Social-information-processing patterns mediate the impact of preventive intervention on adolescent antisocial behavior. *Psychological Science, 24,* 456-465.

Dodge, K.A., & Pettit, G.S. (2003). A biopsychosocial model of the development of chronic conduct problems in adolescence. *Developmental Psychology, 39,* 349-371.

Dodson, W.W. (2005). Pharmacotherapy of adult ADHD. *Journal of Clinical Psychology, 61,* 589-606.

Dogan, O., Onder, Z., Dogan, S., & Akyuz, G. (2004). Distribution of symptoms of conduct disorder and antisocial personality disorder in Turkey. *Psychopathology, 37,* 285-289.

Dominguez, D.V., Cohen, M., & Brom, D. (2004). Trauma and dissociation in psychiatric outpatients. *Israel Journal of Psychiatry and Related Sciences, 41,* 98-110.

Donaldson, K.I., & Meana, M. (2011). Early dyspareunia experience in young women: Confusion, consequences, and help-seeking barriers. *Journal of Sexual Medicine, 8,* 814-823.

Donix, M., Jurjanz, L., Meyer, S., Amanatidis, E.C., Baeumler, D., Huebner, T., Poettrich, K., Smolka, M.N., & Holthoff, V.A. (2013). Functional imaging during recognition of personally familiar faces and places in Alzheimer's disease. *Archives of Clinical Neuropsychology, 28,* 72-80.

Donix, M., Small, G.W., & Bookheimer, S.Y. (2012). Family history and APOE-4 genetic risk in Alzheimer's disease. *Neuropsychology Review, 22,* 298-309.

Donny, E.C., Caggiula, A.R., Weaver, M.T., Levin, M.E., & Sved, A.F. (2011). The reinforcement-enhancing effects of nicotine: Implications for the relationship between smoking, eating and weight. *Physiology and Behavior, 104,* 143-148.

Donovan, C.L., & Spence, S.H. (2000). Prevention of childhood anxiety disorders. *Clinical Psychology Review, 20,* 509-531.

Dorahy, M.J. (2001). Dissociative identity disorder and memory dysfunction: The current state of experimental research and its future directions. *Clinical Psychology Review, 21,* 771-795.

Dorahy, M.J., Irwin, H.J., & Middleton, W. (2004). Assessing markers of working memory function in dissociative identity disorder using neutral stimuli: A comparison with clinical and general population samples. *Australian and New Zealand Journal of Psychiatry, 38,* 47-55.

Dorahy, M.J., Middleton, W., & Irwin, H.J. (2005). The effect of emotional context on cognitive inhibition and attentional processing in dissociative identity disorder. *Behaviour Research and Therapy, 43,* 555-568.

Doty, T.J., Japee, S., Ingvar, M., & Ungerleider, L.G. (2013). Fearful face detection sensitivity in healthy adults correlates with anxiety-related traits. *Emotion, 13,* 183-188.

Dour, H.J., & Theran, S.A. (2011). The interaction between the superhero ideal and maladaptive perfectionism as predictors of unhealthy eating attitudes and body esteem. *Body Image, 8,* 93-96.

Drake, R.E., Wallach, M.A., & McGovern, M.P. (2005). Future directions in preventing relapse to substance abuse among clients with severe mental illnesses. *Psychiatric Services, 56,* 1297-1302.

Drevets, W.C., Gadde, K.M., & Krishnan, K.R.R. (2004). Neuroimaging studies of mood disorders. In D.S. Charney & E.J. Nestler (Eds.),

*Neurobiology of mental illness* (2nd. ed.; pp. 461-490). New York: Oxford.

Drummond, K.D., Bradley, S.J., Peterson-Badali, M., & Zucker, K.J. (2008). A follow-up study of girls with gender identity disorder. *Developmental Psychology, 44*, 34-45.

D'Souza, R., Piskulic, D., & Sundram, S. (2010). A brief dyadic group based psychoeducation program improves relapse rates in recently remitted bipolar disorder: A pilot randomised controlled trial. *Journal of Affective Disorders, 130*, 272-276.

Du Rocher Schudlich, T.D., Youngstrom, E.A., Calabrese, J.R., & Findling, R.L. (2008). The role of family functioning in bipolar disorder in families. *Journal of Abnormal Child Psychology, 36*, 849-863.

Duberstein, P.R., Conwell, Y., Conner, K.R., Eberly, S., Evinger, J.S., & Caine, E.D. (2004). Poor social integration and suicide: Fact or artifact? A case-control study. *Psychological Medicine, 34*, 1331-1337.

Dubovsky, S.L., & Dubovsky, A.N. (2002). *Concise guide to mood disorders.* Washington, DC: American Psychiatric Publishing.

Duerden, E.G., Szatmari, P., & Roberts, S.W. (2012). Toward a better understanding of self injurious behaviors in children and adolescents with autism spectrum disorders. *Journal of Autism and Developmental Disorders, 42*, 2515-2518.

Duffy, C., & Healy, O. (2011). Spontaneous communication in autism spectrum disorder: A review of topographies and interventions. *Research in Autism Spectrum Disorders, 5*, 977-983.

Dunkley, D.M., Masheb, R.M., & Grilo, C.M. (2010). Childhood maltreatment, depressive symptoms, and body dissatisfaction in patients with binge eating disorder: The mediating role of self-criticism. *International Journal of Eating Disorders, 43*, 274-281.

Dunn, H.G., Stoessl, A.J., Ho, H.H., MacLeod, P.M., Poskitt, K.J., Doudet, D.J., Schulzer, M., Blackstock, D., Dobko, T., Koop, B., & de Amorim, G.V. (2002). Rett syndrome: Investigation of nine patients, including PET scan. *Canadian Journal of Neurological Sciences, 29*, 345-357.

DuPaul, G.J., Anastopoulos, A.D., Power, T.J., Reid, R., Ikeda, M., & McGoey, K. (1998). Parent ratings of attention-deficit/hyperactivity disorder symptoms: Factor structure and normative data. *Journal of Psychopathology and Behavioral Assessment, 20*, 83-102.

DuPaul, G.J., Gormley, M.J., & Laracy, S.D. (2013). Comorbidity of LD and ADHD: Implications of DSM-5 for assessment and treatment. *Journal of Learning Disabilities, 46*, 43-51.

Durkin, M. (2002). The epidemiology of developmental disabilities in low-income countries. *Mental Retardation and Developmental Disabilities Research Reviews, 8*, 206-211.

Durlak, J.A. (1997). *Successful prevention programs for children and adolescents.* New York: Plenum.

Durlak, J.A., & Wells, A.M. (1997). Primary prevention mental health programs for children and adolescents: A meta-analytic review. *American Journal of Community Psychology, 25*, 115-152.

Dutra, L., Stathapoulou, G., Basden, S.L., Leyro, T.M., Powers, M.B., & Otto, M.W. (2008). A meta-analytic review of psychosocial interventions for substance use disorders. *American Journal of Psychiatry, 165*, 179-187.

Dyck, R., de Geus, E.J.C., Hofman, A., Uitterlinden, A.G., Hottenga, J.-J., Nolen, W.A., Oostra, B.A., Sullivan, P.F., Willemsen, G., Zitman, F.G., Tiemeier, H., Janssens, A.C.J.W., Boomsma, D.I., van Duijn, C.M., & Middeldorp, C.M. (2011). Genetic risk profiles for depression and anxiety in adult and elderly cohorts. *Molecular Psychiatry, 16*, 773-783.

Dykens, E.M., & Cassidy, S.B. (1999). Prader-Willi syndrome. In S. Goldstein & C.R.Reynolds (Eds.), *Handbook of neurodevelopmental and genetic disorders in children* (pp. 525-554). New York: Guilford.

Dziegielewski, S.F. (2005). *Understanding substance addictions: Assessment and intervention.* Chicago: Lyceum.

Dzokoto, V.A., & Adams, G. (2005). Understanding genital-shrinking epidemics in West Africa: Koro, juju, or mass psychogenic illness? *Culture, Medicine and Psychiatry, 29*, 53-78.

Eastwood, S., & Bisson, J.I. (2008). Management of factitious disorders: A systematic review. *Psychotherapy and Psychosomatics, 77*, 209-218.

Eaton, W.W., Shao, H., Nestadt, G., Lee, B.H., Bienvenu, O.J., & Zandi, P. (2008). Population-based study of first onset and chronicity in major depressive disorder. *Archives of General Psychiatry, 65*, 513-520.

Ebben, M.R., & Spielman, A.J. (2009). Non-pharmacological treatments for insomnia. *Journal of Behavioral Medicine, 32*, 244-254.

Ebmeier, K.P., Donaghey, C., & Steele, J.D. (2006). Recent developments and current controversies in depression. *Lancet, 367*, 153-167.

Ebrahim, S., Beswick, A., Burke, M., & Davey Smith, G. (2006). Multiple risk factor interventions for primary prevention of coronary heart disease. *Cochrane Database of Systematic Reviews, 18*, CD001561.

Edersheim, J.G., Brendel, R.W., & Price, B.H. (2012). Neuroimaging, diminished capacity and mitigation. In J.R. Simpson (Ed.), *Neuroimaging in forensic psychiatry: From the clinic to the courtroom* (pp. 163-194). New York: Wiley.

Edinger, J.D., Wohlgemuth, W.K., Radtke, R.A., Marsh, G.R., & Quillian, R.E. (2001). Cognitive behavioral therapy for treatment of chronic primary insomnia: A randomized controlled trial. *Journal of the American Medical Association, 285*, 1856-1864.

Eells, T.D., Lombart, K.G., Salsman, N., Kendjelic, E.M., Schneiderman, C.T., & Lucas, C.P. (2011). Expert reasoning in psychotherapy case formulation. *Psychotherapy Research, 21*, 385-399.

Eells, T.D., Lombart, K.G., Kendjelic, E.M., Turner, L.C., & Lucas, C.P. (2005). The quality of psychotherapy case formulations: A comparison of expert, experienced, and novice cognitive-behavioral and psychodynamic therapists. *Journal of Consulting and Clinical Psychology, 73*, 579-589.

Ehlers, C.L., Gizer, I.R., Gilder, D.A., & Wilhelmsen, K.C. (2011). Linkage analyses of stimulant dependence, craving, and heavy use in American Indians. *American Journal of Medical Genetics Part B, 156*, 772-780.

Elzinga, T., Szeimies, A. K., & Schaffrick, C. (2009). An experimental analogue study into the role of abstract thinking in trauma-related rumination. *Behaviour Research and Therapy, 47*, 285-293.

Einfeld, S.L., Ellis, L.A., & Emerson, E. (2011). Comorbidity of intellectual disability and mental disorder in children and adolescents: A systematic review. *Journal of Intellectual and Developmental Disability, 36*, 137-143.

Eisen, A.R., & Schaefer, C.E. (2007). *Separation anxiety in children and adolescents: An individualized approach to assessment and treatment.* New York: Guilford.

Eisen, M.L., Qin, J., Goodman, G.S., & Davis, S.L. (2002). Memory and suggestibility in maltreated children: Age, stress arousal, dissociation, and psychopathology. *Journal of Experimental Child Psychology, 83*, 167-212.

Eisenberg, D., Downs, M.F., Golberstein, E., & Zivin, K. (2009). Stigma and help seeking for mental health among college students. *Medical Care Research and Review, 66*, S220541.

Eisenberg, D., & Schneider, H. (2007). Perceptions of academic skills of children diagnosed with ADHD. *Journal of Attention Disorders, 10*, 390-397.

Eisenbruch, S. (2011). Abdominal pain in Irritable Bowel Syndrome: A review of putative psychological, neural and neuro-immune mechanisms. *Brain, Behavior, and Immunity, 25*, 386-394.

Elhanbly, S., Elkholy, A., Elbayomy, Y., Elsaid, M., & Abdel-gaber, S. (2009). Nocturnal penile erections: The diagnostic value of tumescence and rigidity activity units. *International Journal of Impotence Research, 21*, 376-381.

Ellason, J.W., & Ross, C.A. (1996). Millon Clinical Multiaxial Inventory-II: Follow-up of patients with dissociative identity disorder. *Psychological Reports, 78*, 483-490.

Ellason, J.W., & Ross, C.A. (1997). Two-year follow-up of inpatients with dissociative identity disorder. *American Journal of Psychiatry, 154*, 832-839.

Elliot, L., Orr, L., Watson, L., & Jackson, A. (2005). Secondary prevention interventions for young drug users: A systematic review of the evidence. *Adolescence, 40*, 1-22.

Ellis, A. (1962). *Reason and emotion in psychotherapy.* New York: Lyle Stuart.

Ellis, A. (2000). A critique of the theoretical contributions of nondirective therapy. *Journal of Clinical Psychology, 56*, 897-905.

Ellis, A. (2005). Why I (really) became a therapist. *Journal of Clinical Psychology, 61*, 945-948.

Ellison, J.W., Rosenfeld, J.A., & Shaffer, L.G. (2013). Genetic basis of intellectual disability. *Annual Review of Medicine, 64*, 441-450.

Elsabbagh, M., Divan, G., Koh, Y.-J., Kim, Y.S., Kauchali, S., Marcín, C., Montiel-Nava, C., Patel, V., Paula, C.S., Wang, C., Yasamy, M.T., & Fombonne, E. (2012). Global prevalence of autism and other pervasive developmental disorders. *Autism Research, 5*, 160-179.

Emsley, R., Chiliza, B., & Schoeman, R. (2008). Predictors of long-term outcome in schizophrenia. *Current Opinion in Psychiatry, 21*, 173-177.

Engel, S.M., Berkowitz, G.S., Wolff, M.S., & Yehuda, R. (2005). Psychological trauma associated with the World Trade Center attacks and its effect on pregnancy outcome. *Paediatric and Perinatal Epidemiology, 19*, 334-341.

Engelhart, M.J., Geerlings, M.I., Ruitenberg, A., van Swieten, J.C., Hofman, A., Witteman, J.C.M., & Breteler, M.M.B. (2002a). Dietary intake of antioxidants and risk of Alzheimer disease. *Journal of the American Medical Association, 287*, 3223-3229.

Engelhart, M.J., Geerlings, M.I., Ruitenberg, A., van Swieten, J.C., Hofman, A., Witteman, J.C.M., & Breteler, M.M.B. (2002b). Diet and risk of dementia: Does fat matter?: The Rotterdam study. *Neurology, 59*, 1915-1921.

Engin, E., & Treit, D. (2007). The role of hippocampus in anxiety: Intracerebral infusion studies. *Behavioural Pharmacology, 18*, 365-374.

Engle, D.E., & Arkowitz, H. (2006). *Ambivalence in psychotherapy: Facilitating readiness to change.* New York: Guilford.

Eranti, S.V., MacCabe, J.H., Bundy, H., & Murray, R.M. (2013). Gender difference in age at onset of schizophrenia: A meta-analysis. *Psychological Medicine, 43*, 155-167.

Eriksson, C.J.P. (2001). The role of acetaldehyde in the actions of alcohol (update 2000). *Alcoholism: Clinical and Experimental Research, 25 (Suppl.)*, 15S-32S.

Escobar, J.I. (2004). Transcultural aspects of dissociative and somatoform disorders. *Psychiatric Times, 21.*

Escobar, J.I., & Gureje, O. (2007). Influence of cultural and social factors on the epidemiology of idiopathic somatic complaints and syndromes. *Psychosomatic Medicine, 69*, 841-845.

Espejo, E.P., Hammen, C., & Brennan, P.A. (2012). Elevated appraisals of the negative impact of naturally occurring life events: A risk factor for depressive and anxiety disorders. *Journal of Abnormal Child Psychology, 40*, 303-315.

Esper, C.D., & Factor, S.A. (2008). Failure of recognition of drug-induced parkinsonism in the elderly. *Movement Disorders, 23*, 401-404.

Espie, C.A. (2002). Insomnia: Conceptual issues in the development, persistence, and treatment of sleep disorder in adults. *Annual Review of Psychology, 53*, 215-243.

Essau, C.A., Lewinsohn, P.M., Seeley, J.R., & Sasagawa, S. (2010). Gender differences in the developmental course of depression. *Journal of Affective Disorders, 127*, 185-190.

Estrada, A.L. (2005). Health disparities among African-American and Hispanic drug injectors—HIV, AIDS, hepatitis B virus and hepatitis C virus: A review. *AIDS, 19 (Suppl. 3)*, S47-S52.

Evans, D.L., Foa, E.B., Gur, R.E., Hendlin, H., O'Brien, C.P., Seligman, M.E.P., & Walsh, B.T. (2005). *Treating and preventing adolescent mental health disorders. What we know and what we don't know. A research agenda for improving the mental health of our youth.* New York: Oxford University Press.

Evans, K.E., & Demuth, K. (2012). Individual differences in pronoun reversal: Evidence from two longitudinal case studies. *Journal of Child Language, 39*, 162-191.

Even, C., Schroder, C.M., Friedman, S., & Rouillon, F. (2008). Efficacy of light therapy in nonseasonal depression: A systematic review. *Journal of Affective Disorders, 108*, 11-23.

Everson-Rose, S.A., & Lewis, T.T. (2005). Psychosocial factors and cardiovascular diseases. *Annual Review of Public Health, 26*, 469-500.

Evmenova, A.S., Graff, H.J., Jerome, M.K., & Behrmann, M.M. (2010). Word prediction programs with phonetic spelling support: Performance comparisons and impact on journal writing for students with writing difficulties. *Learning Disabilities Research, 25*, 170-182.

Ewald, H., Rogne, T., Ewald, K., & Fink, P. (1994). Somatization in patients newly admitted to a neurological department. *Acta Psychiatrica Scandinavica, 89*, 174-179.

Fadem, B. (2013). *Behavioral science in medicine* (2nd ed.). Philadelphia: Lippincott, Williams, & Wilkins.

Faggiano, F., Vigla-Taglianti, F.D., Versino, E., Zambon, A., Borraccino, A., & Lemma, P. (2008). School-based prevention for illicit drugs use: A systematic review. *Preventive Medicine, 46*, 385-396.

Fairburn, C.G. (2005). Evidence-based treatment of anorexia nervosa. *International Journal of Eating Disorders, 37*, S26-S30.

Fairburn, C.G., Cooper, Z., & O'Connor, M. (2008). Eating Disorder Examination (Edition 16.0D). In C.G. Fairburn (Ed.), *Cognitive behavior therapy and eating disorders* (pp. 265-308). New York: Guilford.

Fairchild, G., Passamonti, L., Hurford, G., Hagan, C.C., von dem Hagen, E.A.H., van Goozen, S.H.M., Goodyer, I.M., & Calder, A.J. (2011). Brain structure abnormalities in early-onset and adolescent-onset conduct disorder. *American Journal of Psychiatry, 168*, 624-633.

Falkenburg, J., & Tracy, D.K. (2012). Sex and schizophrenia: A review of gender differences. *Psychosis: Psychological, Social, and Integrative Approaches*, 1-9.

Fallon, B.A. (2004). Pharmacotherapy of somatoform disorders. *Journal of Psychosomatic Research, 56*, 455-460.

Fallon, B.A., Qureshi, A.I., Schneier, F.R., Sanchez-Lacay, A., Vermes, D., Feinstein, R., Connelly, J., & Liebowitz, M.R. (2003). An open trial of fluvoxamine for hypochondriasis. *Psychosomatics, 44*, 298-303.

Fanous, A.H., & Kendler, K.S. (2008). Genetics of clinical features and subtypes of schizophrenia: A review of the recent literature. *Current Psychiatry Reports, 10*, 164-170.

Farahmand, F.K., Grant, K.E., Polo, A.J., Duffy, S.N., & DuBois, D.L. (2011). School-based mental health and behavioral programs for low-income, urban youth: A systematic and meta-analytic review. *Clinical Psychology: Science and Practice, 18*, 372-390.

Faraone, S.V., Tsuang, M.T., & Tsuang, D.W. (1999). *Genetics of mental disorders: A guide for students, clinicians, and researchers.* New York: Guilford.

Faravelli, C., Salvatori, S., Galassi, F., Aiazzi, L., Drei, C., & Cabras, P. (1997). Epidemiology of somatoform disorders: A community survey in Florence. *Social Psychiatry and Psychiatric Epidemiology, 32*, 24-29.

Farmer, A., Elkin, A., & McGuffin, P. (2007). The genetics of bipolar affective disorder. *Current Opinion in Psychiatry, 20*, 8-12.

Farooque, R.S., Stout, R.G., & Ernst, F.A. (2005). Heterosexual intimate partner homicide: Review of ten years of clinical experience. *Journal of Forensic Sciences, 50*, 648-651.

Farrugia, D. (2009). Exploring stigma: Medical knowledge and the stigmatisation of parents of children diagnosed with autism spectrum disorder. *Sociology of Health and Illness, 31*, 1011-1027.

Fava, G.A., Sonino, N., & Wise, T.N. (Eds.). (2012). *The psychosomatic assessment: Strategies to improve clinical practice.* Basel, Switzerland: Karger.

Fazel, S., & Danesh, J. (2002). Serious mental disorder in 23000 prisoners: A systematic review of 62 surveys. *Lancet, 359*, 545-550.

Fazel, S., & Seewald, K. (2012). Severe mental illness in 33588 prisoners worldwide: Systematic review and meta-regression analysis. *British Journal of Psychiatry, 200*, 364-373.

Feart, C., Samieri, C., Alles, B., & Barberger-Gateau, P. (2013). Potential benefits of adherence to the Mediterranean diet on cognitive health. *Proceedings of the Nutrition Society, 72*, 140-152.

Federal Interagency Forum on Child and Family Services Statistics. (2005). *America's Children: Key National Indicators of Well-Being, 2005.* Washington, DC: U.S. Government Printing Office.

Fehr, S.S., & De Piano, F. (2003). *Introduction to group therapy: A practical guide.* Philadelphia, PA: Haworth.

Feldman, H.H., & Jacova, C. (2007). Primary prevention and delay of onset of AD/dementia. *Canadian Journal of Neurological Sciences, 34 (Suppl. 1)*, S84-S89.

Ferguson, C.J. (2010a). Genetic contributions to antisocial personality and behavior: A meta-analytic review from an evolutionary perspective. *Journal of Social Psychology, 150,* 160-180.

Ferguson, C.J. (2010b). A meta-analysis of normal and disordered personality across the life span. *Journal of Personality and Social Psychology, 98,* 659-667.

Ferrell, C.B., Beidel, D.C., & Turner, S.M. (2004). Assessment and treatment of socially phobic children: A cross cultural comparison. *Journal of Clinical Child and Adolescent Psychology, 33,* 260-268.

Fichter, M.M., & Quadflieg, N. (2007). Long-term stability of eating disorder diagnoses. *International Journal of Eating Disorders, 40,* 561-566.

Fichter, M.M., Quadflieg, N., & Hedlund, S. (2006). Twelve-year course and outcome predictors of anorexia nervosa. *International Journal of Eating Disorders, 39,* 87-100.

Fichter, M.M., Quadflieg, N., & Hedlund, S. (2008). Longterm course of binge eating disorder and bulimia nervosa: Relevance for nosology and diagnostic criteria. *International Journal of Eating Disorders, 41,* 577-586.

Field, M., Munafo, M.R., & Franken, I.H.A. (2009). A meta-analytic investigation of the relationship between attentional bias and subjective craving in substance abuse. *Psychological Bulletin, 135,* 589-607.

Fineberg, A.M., Ellman, L.M., Buka, S., Yolken, R., & Cannon, T.D. (2013). Decreased birth weight in psychosis: Influence of prenatal exposure to serologically determined influenza and hypoxia. *Schizophrenia Bulletin, 39,* 1037-1044.

Fineberg, N.A., & Gale, T.M. (2004). Evidence-based pharmacotherapy of obsessive-compulsive disorder. *International Journal of Neuropsychopharmacology, 8,* 107-129.

Fink, P., Hansen, M.S., & Oxhoj, M.-L. (2004). The prevalence of somatoform disorders among internal medical inpatients. *Journal of Psychosomatic Research, 56,* 413-418.

Fink, P., Ornbol, E., Toft, T., Sparle, K.C., Frostholm, L., & Oleson, F. (2004). A new, empirically established hypochondriasis diagnosis. *American Journal of Psychiatry, 161,* 1680-1691.

First, M.B., Spitzer, R.L., Gibbon M., & Williams, J.B.W. (2002). *Structured Clinical Interview for DSM-IV-TR Axis I Disorders, Research Version, Patient Edition (SCID-I/P).* New York: Biometrics Research, New York State Psychiatric Institute.

Fisak, B., Jr., & Grills-Taquechel, A.E. (2007). Parental modeling, reinforcement, and information transfer: Risk factors in the development of child anxiety? *Clinical Child and Family Psychology Review, 10,* 213-231.

Fisher, C.A., Hetrick, S.E., & Rushford, N. (2010). *Family therapy for anorexia nervosa.* Cochrane Database of Systematic Reviews, Issue 6.

Fitzpatrick, A.L., Kuller, L.H., Lopez, O.L., Kawas, C.H., & Jagust, W. (2005). Survival following dementia onset: Alzheimer's disease and vascular dementia. *Journal of the Neurological Sciences, 43,* 229-230.

Flament, M.F., Bissada, H., & Spettigue, W. (2012). Evidence-based pharmacotherapy of eating disorders. *International Journal of Neuropsychopharmacology, 15,* 189-207.

Flanagan, N.M., Jackson, A.J., & Hill, A.E. (2003). Visual impairment in childhood: Insights from a community-based survey. *Child Care Health and Development, 29,* 493-499.

Floyd, R.L., Weber, M.K., Denny, C., & O'Connor, M.J. (2009). Prevention of fetal alcohol spectrum disorders. *Developmental Disabilities Research Reviews, 15,* 193-199.

Foa, E.B., Yadin, E., & Lichner, T.K. (2012). *Exposure and response (ritual) prevention for obsessive-compulsive disorder: Therapist guide* (2nd ed.). New York: Oxford.

Fogelson, D.L., Asarnow, R.A., Sugar, C.A., Subotnik, K.L., Jacobsen, K.C., Neale, M.C., Kendler, K.S., Kuppinger, H., & Nuechterlein, K.H. (2010). Avoidant personality disorder symptoms in first-degree relatives of schizophrenia patients predict performance on neurocognitive measures: The UCLA Family Study. *Schizophrenia Research, 120,* 113-120.

Foley, S.R., Kelly, B.D., Clarke, M., McTigue, O., Gervin, M., Kamali, M., Larkin, C., O'Callaghan, E., & Browne, S. (2005). Incidence and clinical correlates of aggression and violence at presentation in patients with first episode psychosis. *Schizophrenia Research, 72,* 161-168.

Folstein, M.F., & Folstein, S.E. (2010). *Mini-Mental® State Examination, 2nd Edition™ (MMSE®-2™).* Lutz, FL: PAR.

Ford, A.C., Talley, N.J., Schoenfeld, P.S., Quigley, E.M.M., & Moayyedi, P. (2009). Efficacy of antidepressants and psychological therapies in irritable bowel syndrome: Systematic review and meta-analysis. *Gut, 58,* 367-378.

Fossati, P., Guillaume, L.B., Ergis, A.-M., & Allilaire, J.-F. (2003). Qualitative analysis of verbal fluency in depression. *Psychiatry Research, 117,* 17-24.

Foster, L.M., Hynd, G.W., Morgan, A.E., & Hugdahl, K. (2002). Planum temporale asymmetry and ear advantage in dichotic listening in developmental dyslexia and attention deficit/hyperactivity disorder (ADHD). *Journal of the International Neuropsychological Society, 8,* 22-36.

Fountoulakis, K.N., Lecht, S., & Kaprinis, G.S. (2008). Personality disorders and violence. *Current Opinion in Psychiatry, 21,* 84-92.

Fournier, J.C., DeRubeis, R.J., Hollon, S.D., Dimidjian, S., Amsterdam, J.D., Shelton, R.C., & Fawcett, J. (2010). Antidepressant drug effects and depression severity: A patient-level meta-analysis. *Journal of the American Medical Association, 303,* 47-53.

Fournier, J.C., DeRubeis, R.J., Shelton, R.C., Hollon, S.D., Amsterdam, J.D., & Gallop, R. (2009). Prediction of response to medication and cognitive therapy in the treatment of moderate to severe depression. *Journal of Consulting and Clinical Psychology, 77,* 775-787.

Foussias, G., & Remington, G. (2010). Negative symptoms in schizophrenia: Avolition and Occam's razor. *Schizophrenia Bulletin, 36,* 359-369.

Fox, N.A., Henderson, H.A., Marshall, P.J., Nichols, K.E., & Ghera, M.M. (2005). Behavioral inhibition: Linking biology and behavior within a developmental framework. *Annual Review of Psychology, 56,* 235-262.

Fox, N.C., & Schott, J.M. (2004). Imaging cerebral atrophy: Normal ageing to Alzheimer's disease. *Lancet, 363,* 392-394.

Francis, J.L., Moitra, E., Dyck, I., & Keller, M.B. (2012). The impact of stressful life events on relapse of generalized anxiety disorder. *Depression and Anxiety, 29,* 386-391.

Frank, J.E., Mistretta, P., & Will, J. (2008). Diagnosis and treatment of female sexual dysfunction. *American Family Physician, 77,* 635-642.

Franke, B., Neale, B.M., & Faraone, S.V. (2009). Genome-wide associations studies in ADHD. *Human Genetics, 126,* 13-50.

Franko, D.L., Becker, A.E., Thomas, J.J., & Herzog, D.B. (2007). Cross-ethnic differences in eating disorder symptoms and related distress. *International Journal of Eating Disorders, 40,* 156-164.

Frazier, T.W., Keshavan, M.S., Minshew, N.J., & Harden, A.Y. (2012). A two-year longitudinal MRI study of the corpus callosum in autism. *Journal of Autism and Developmental Disorders, 42,* 2312-2322.

Frederickson, B., & Roberts, T.A. (1997). Objectification theory: Toward understanding women's lived experiences and mental health risks. *Psychology of Women Quarterly, 21,* 173-206.

Freides, D. (2002). *Developmental disorders: A neuropsychological approach.* New York: Wiley.

Freidl, M., Spitzl, S.P., & Aigner, M. (2008). How depressive symptoms correlate with stigma perception of mental illness. *International Review of Psychiatry, 20,* 510-514.

Freidl, M., Spitzl, S.P., Prause, W., Zimprich, F., Lehner-Baumgartner, E., Baumgartner, C., & Aigner, M. (2007). The stigma of mental illness: Anticipation and attitudes among patients with epileptic, dissociative or somatoform pain disorder. *International Review of Psychiatry, 19,* 123-129.

Freund, K., & Seto, M.C. (1998). Preferential rape in the theory of courtship disorder. *Archives of Sexual Behavior, 27,* 433-443.

Frick, P.J. (2012). Developmental pathways to conduct disorder: Implications for future directions in research, assessment, and treatment. *Journal of Clinical Child and Adolescent Psychology, 41,* 378-389.

Friedl, M.C., Draijer, N., & de Jonge, P. (2000). Prevalence of dissociative disorders in psychiatric in-patients: The impact of study characteristics. *Acta Psychiatrica Scandinavica, 102,* 423-428.

Friedman, H.L., & MacDonald, D.A. (2006). Humanistic testing and assessment. *Journal of Humanistic Psychology, 46,* 510-529.

Friedman, R.S., McCarthy, D.M., Forster, J., & Denzler, M. (2005). Automatic effects of alcohol cues on sexual attraction. *Addiction, 100,* 672-681.

Friedrich, W.N., Gerber, P.N., Koplin, B., Davis, M., Giese, J., Mykelbust, C., & Franckowiak, D. (2001). Multimodal assessment of dissociation in adolescents: Inpatients and juvenile sex offenders. *Sexual Abuse: A Journal of Research and Treatment, 13,* 167-177.

Frisardi, V., Solfrizzi, V., Capurso, C., Kehoe, P.G., Imbimbo, B.P., Santamato, A., Dellegrazie, F., Seripa, D., Pilotto, A., Capurso, A., & Panza, F. (2010). Aluminum in the diet and Alzheimer's disease: From current epidemiology to possible disease-modifying treatment. *Journal of Alzheimer's Disease, 20,* 17-30.

Frith, C. (2005). The self in action: Lessons from delusions of control. *Consciousness and Cognition, 14,* 752-770.

Frith, C., & Johnstone, E. (2003). *Schizophrenia: A very short introduction.* New York: Oxford.

Frye, E.M., & Feldman, M.D. (2012). Factitious disorder by proxy in educational settings: A review. *Educational Psychology Review, 24,* 47-61.

Frye, R.E., & Rossignol, D.A. (2012). Metabolic disorders and abnormalities associated with autism spectrum disorder. *Journal of Pediatric Biochemistry, 2,* 181-191.

Fuller, C.M., Borrell, L.N., Latkin, C.A., Galea, S., Ompad, D.C., Strathdee, S.A., & Vlahov, D. (2005). Effects of race, neighborhood, and social network on age at initiation of injection drug use. *American Journal of Public Health, 95,* 689-695.

Fulero, S.M., & Wrightsman, L.S. (2009). *Forensic psychology* (3rd ed.). Belmont, CA: Cengage.

Fyer, A.J., Mannuzza, S., Gallops, M.S., Martin, L.Y., Aaronson, C., Gorman, J.G., Liebowitz, M.R., & Klein, D.F. (1990). Familial transmission of simple phobias and fears: A preliminary report. *Archives of General Psychiatry, 47,* 252-256.

Gabriel, B., Beach, S.R.H., & Bodenmann, G. (2010). Depression, marital satisfaction and communication in couples: Investigating gender differences. *Behavior Therapy, 41,* 306-316.

Gacono, C.B., Meloy, J.R., & Bridges, M.R. (2000). A Rorschach comparison of psychopaths, sexual homicide perpetrators, and nonviolent pedophiles: Where angels fear to tread. *Journal of Clinical Psychology, 56,* 757-777.

Gaebel, W., Janner, M., Frommann, N., Pietzcker, A., Kopcke, W., Linden, M., Muller, P., Muller-Spahn, F., & Tegeler, J. (2002). First vs multiple episode schizophrenia: Two-year outcome of intermittent and maintenance medication strategies. *Schizophrenia Research, 53,* 145-159.

Galderisi, S., Quarantelli, M., Volpe, U., Mucci, A., Cassano, G.B., Invernizzi, G., Rossi, A., Vita, A., Pini, S., Cassano, P., Daneluzzo, E., De Peri, L.,

Stratta, P., Brunetti, A., & Maj, M. (2008). Patterns of structural MRI abnormalities in deficit and nondeficit schizophrenia. *Schizophrenia Bulletin, 34,* 393-401.

Galderisi, S., Piegari, G., Mucci, A., Acerra, A., Luciano, I., Rabasca, A.F., Santucci, F., Valente, A., Volpe, M., Mastantuono, P., & Maj, M. (2010). Social skills and neurocognitive individualized training in schizophrenia: Comparison with structured leisure activities. *European Archives of Psychiatry and Clinical Neuroscience, 260,* 305-315.

Gallagher, M., & Koh, M.T. (2011). Episodic memory on the path to Alzheimer's disease. *Current Opinion in Neurobiology, 21,* 929-934.

Gallagher-Thompson, D., Wang, P.-C., Liu, W., Cheung, V., Peng, R., China, D., & Thompson, L.W. (2010). Effectiveness of a psychoeducational skill training DVD program to reduce stress in Chinese American dementia caregivers: Results of a preliminary study. *Aging and Mental Health, 14,* 263-273.

Gannon, T.A., Collie, R.M., Ward, T., & Thakker, J. (2008). Rape: Psychopathology, theory and treatment. *Clinical Psychology Review, 28,* 982-1008.

Gannon, T.A., & Polaschek, D.L.L. (2006). Cognitive distortions in child molesters: A re-examination of key theories and research. *Clinical Psychology Review, 26,* 1000-1019.

Garakani, A., Murrough, J.W., Charney, D.S., & Bremner, D. (2009). The neurobiology of anxiety disorders. In D.S. Charney & E.J. Nestler (Eds.), *Neurobiology of mental illness* (pp. 655-690). New York: Oxford.

Garb, H.N., Wood, J.M., Nezworski, M.T., Grove, W.M. & Stejskal, W.J. (2001). Toward a resolution of the Rorschach controversy. *Psychological Assessment, 13,* 433-448.

Garcia, F.D., & Thibaut, F. (2011). Current concepts in the pharmacotherapy of paraphilias. *Drugs, 71,* 771-790.

Garcia, L.F., Aluja, A., & Del Barrio, V. (2008). Testing the hierarchical structure of the Children's Depression Inventory: A multigroup analysis. *Assessment, 15,* 153-164.

Garcia-Bueno, B., Caso, J.R., & Leza, J.C. (2008). Stress as a neuroinflammatory condition in brain: Damaging and protective mechanisms. *Neuroscience and Biobehavioral Reviews, 32,* 1136-1151.

Garcia-Campayo, J., Alda, M., Sobradiel, N., Olivan, B., & Pascual, A. (2007). Personality disorders in somatization disorder patients: A controlled study in Spain. *Journal of Psychosomatic Research, 62,* 675-680.

Garcia-Campayo, J., Fayed, N., Serrano-Blanco, A., & Roca, M. (2009). Brain dysfunction behind functional symptoms: Neuroimaging and somatoform, conversive, and dissociative disorders. *Current Opinion in Psychiatry, 22,* 224-231.

Garcia-Toro, M., & Aguirre, I. (2007). Biopsychosocial model in depression revisited. *Medical Hypotheses, 68,* 683-691.

Gardenswartz, C.A., & Craske, M.G. (2001). Prevention of panic disorder. *Behavior Therapy, 32,* 725-737.

Garland, E.L., Boettiger, C.A., & Howard, M.O. (2011). Targeting cognitive-affective risk mechanisms in stress-precipitated alcohol dependence: An integrated, biopsychosocial model of automaticity, allostasis, and addiction. *Medical Hypotheses, 76,* 745-754.

Garmezy, N. (1991). Resilience in children's adaptation to negative life events and stressed environments. *Pediatrics Annals, 20,* 459-460, 463-466.

Garnock-Jones, K.P., & Keating, G.M. (2009). Atomoxetine: A review of its use in attention-deficit hyperactivity disorder in children and adolescents. *Pediatric Drugs, 11,* 203-226.

Garrow, D., & Delegge, M.H. (2010). Risk factors for gastrointestinal ulcer disease in the US population. *Digestive Diseases and Sciences, 55,* 66-72.

Gass, M.L.S., Cochrane, B.B., Larson, J., Manson, J.E., Barnabei, V.M., Brzyski, R.G., Lane, D.S., LaValleur, J., Ockene, J.K., Mouton, C.P., & Barad, D.H. (2011). Patterns and predictors of sexual activity among women in the Hormone Therapy trials of the Women's Health Initiative. *Menopause, 18,* 1160-1171.

Gates, N., Sachdev, P.S., Singh, M.A.F., & Valenzuela, M. (2011). Cognitive and memory training in adults at risk of dementia: A systematic review. *BMC Geriatrics, 11,* 55.

Gatz, M., Fratiglioni, L., Johansson, B., Berg, S., Mortimer, J.A., Reynolds, C.A., Fiske, A., & Pedersen, N.L. (2005). Complete ascertainment of dementia in the Swedish Twin Registry: The HARMONY study. *Neurobiology of Aging, 26,* 439-447.

Gatz, M., Pedersen, N.L., Berg, S., Johansson, B., Johansson, K., Mortimer, J.A., Posner, S.F., Viitanen, M., Winblad, B., & Ahlbom, A. (1997). Heritability for Alzheimer's disease: The study of dementia in Swedish twins. *Journals of Gerontology, Series A, Biological Sciences and Medical Sciences, 52,* M117-125.

Gearon, J.S., Kaltman, S.I., Brown, C., & Bellack, A.S. (2003). Traumatic life events and PTSD among women with substance use disorders and schizophrenia. *Psychiatric Services, 54,* 523-528.

Geiger, T.C., & Crick, N.R. (2010). Developmental pathways to personality disorders. In R.E. Ingram & J.M. Price (Eds.), *Vulnerability to psychopathology: Risk across the lifespan* (2nd ed.) (pp. 57-112). New York: Guilford.

Gejman, P.V., Sanders, A.R., & Kendler, K.S. (2011). Genetics of schizophrenia: New findings and challenges. *Annual Review of Genomics and Human Genetics, 12,* 121-144.

Gelenberg, A.J., & Chesen, C.L. (2000). How fast are antidepressants? *Journal of Clinical Psychiatry, 61,* 712-721.

Geller, B., & DelBello, M.P. (2003). *Bipolar disorder in childhood and early adolescence.* New York: Guilford.

Geller, B., & DelBello, M.P. (Eds.). (2008). *Treatment of bipolar disorder in children and adolescents*. New York: Guilford.

Gellis, L.A., Lichstein, K.L., Scarinci, I.C., Durrence, H., Heith, T., Daniel, J., Bush, A.J., & Riedel, B.W. (2005). Socioeconomic status and insomnia. *Journal of Abnormal Psychology, 114*, 111-118.

Gentile, S. (2010). Second-generation antipsychotics in dementia: beyond safety concerns. A clinical, systematic review of efficacy data from randomised controlled trials. *Psychopharmacology, 212*, 119-129.

George, M.S., Padberg, F., Schlaepfer, T.E., O'Reardon, J.P., Fitzgerald, P.B., Nahas, Z.H., & Marcolin, M.A. (2009). Controversy: Repetitive transcranial magnetic stimulation or transcranial direct current stimulation shows efficacy in treating psychiatric diseases (depression, mania, schizophrenia, obsessive-compulsive disorder, panic, posttraumatic stress disorder). *Brain Stimulation, 2*, 14-21.

Geraerts, E., McNally, R.J., Jelicic, M., Merckelbach, H., & Raymaekers, L. (2008). Linking thought suppression and recovered memories of childhood sexual abuse. *Memory, 16*, 22-28.

Germain, A., & Kupfer, D.J. (2008). Circadian rhythm disturbances in depression. *Human Psychopharmacology, 23*, 571-585.

Geslani, D.M., Tierney, M.C., Herrmann, N., & Szalai, J.P. (2005). Mild cognitive impairment: An operational definition and its conversion rate to Alzheimer's disease. *Dementia and Geriatric Cognitive Disorders, 19*, 383-389.

Geuze, E., Vermetten, E., & Bremner, J.D. (2005). MR-based in vivo hippocampal volumetrics: 2: Findings in neuropsychiatric disorders. *Molecular Psychiatry, 10*, 160-184.

Ghahramanlou-Holloway, M., Wenzel, A., Lou, K., & Beck, A.T. (2007). Differentiating cognitive content between depressed and anxious outpatients. *Cognitive and Behavior Therapy, 36*, 170-178.

Ghosh, A. (2010). Endocrine, metabolic, nutritional, and toxic disorders leading to dementia. *Annals of Indian Academy of Neurology, 13 (Suppl 2)*, S63-S68.

Giakoumaki, S.G., Roussos, P., Pallis, E.G., & Bitsios, P. (2011). Sustained attention and working memory deficits follow a familial pattern in schizophrenia. *Archives of Clinical Neuropsychology, 26*, 687-695.

Gibbon, S., Duggan, C., Stoffers, J., Huband, N., Völlm, B.A., Ferriter, M., & Lieb, K. (2010). Psychological interventions for antisocial personality disorder. *Cochrane Database of Systematic Reviews*, Issue 6.

Gibbons, C.J., Fournier, J.C., Stirman, S.W., DeRubeis, R.J., Crits-Christop, P., & Beck, A.T. (2010). The clinical effectiveness of cognitive therapy for depression in an outpatient clinic. *Journal of Affective Disorders, 125*, 169-176.

Gidron, Y. (2002). Posttraumatic stress disorder after terrorist attacks: A review. *Journal of Nervous and Mental Disease, 190*, 118-121.

Gilbert, P. (2001). Evolution and social anxiety: The role of attraction, social competition, and social hierarchies. *Psychiatric Clinics of North America, 24*, 723-751.

Gill, J.M., & Saligan, L.N. (2008). Don't let SAD get you down this season. *Nurse Practitioner, 33*, 22-26.

Gillum, H., & Camarata, S. (2004). Importance of treatment efficacy research on language comprehension in MR/DD research. *Mental Retardation and Developmental Disabilities Research Reviews, 10*, 201-207.

Giscombe, C.L., & Lobel, M. (2005). Explaining disproportionately high rates of adverse birth outcomes among African Americans: The impact of stress, racism, and related factors in pregnancy. *Psychological Bulletin, 131*, 662-683.

Gitlin, M.J. (2010). Pharmacotherapy and other somatic treatments for depression. In I.H. Gotlib & C.L. Hammen (Eds.), *Handbook of depression* (2nd ed.) (pp. 554-585). New York: Guilford.

Gitlin, M.J. (2002). Pharmacological treatment for depression. In I.H. Gotlib & C.L. Hammen (Eds.), *Handbook of depression* (pp. 360-382). New York: Guilford.

Gizer, I.R., Seaton-Smith, K.L., Ehlers, C.L., Vieten, C., & Wilhelmsen, K.C. (2010). Heritability of MMPI-2 scales in the UCSF Family Alcoholism Study. *Journal of Addictive Diseases, 29*, 84-97.

Gladstone, G.L., Parker, G.B., Mitchell, P.B., Wilhelm, K.A., & Malhi, G.S. (2005). Relationship between self-reported childhood behavioral inhibition and lifetime anxiety disorders in a clinical sample. *Depression and Anxiety, 22*, 103-113.

Glazer, J.L. (2008). Eating disorders among male athletes. *Current Sports Medicine Reports, 7*, 332-337.

Gleason, O.C., & Yates, W.R. (2004). Somatoform disorders. In S.G. Kornstein & A.H. Clayton (Eds.), *Women's mental health: A comprehensive textbook* (pp. 307-322). New York: Guilford.

Gleaves, D.H., May, M.C., & Cardena, E. (2001). An examination of the diagnostic validity of dissociative identity disorder. *Clinical Psychology Review, 21*, 577-608.

Gleaves, D.H., Smith, S.M., Butler, L.D., & Spiegel, D. (2004). False and recovered memories in the laboratory and clinic: A review of experimental and clinical evidence. *Clinical Psychology: Science and Practice, 11*, 3-28.

Gleeson, J.F., Cotton, S.M., Alvarez-Jimenez, M., Wade, D., Crisp, K., Newman, B., Spiliotacopoulos, D., & McGorry, P.D. (2010). Family outcomes from a randomized clinical trial of relapse prevention therapy in first-episode psychosis. *Journal of Clinical Psychiatry, 71*, 475-483.

Glenthoj, A., Glenthoj, B.Y., Mackeprang, T., Pagsberg, A.K., Hemmingsen, R.P., Jernigan, T.L., & Baare, W.F.C. (2007). Basal ganglia volumes in drug-naïve first-episode schizophrenia patients before and after short-term treatment with either a typical or an atypical antipsychotic drug. *Psychiatry Research: Neuroimaging, 154*, 199-208.

Godart, N.T., Perdereau, F., Jeammet, P., & Flament, M.F. (2005). Comorbidity between eating disorders and mood disorders: Review. *Encephale, 31*, 575-587.

Goddard, A.W., Ball, S.G., Martinez, J., Robinson, M.J., Yang, C.R., Russell, J.M., & Shekhar, A. (2010). Current perspectives of the roles of the central norepinephrine system in anxiety and depression. *Depression and Anxiety, 27*, 339-350.

Goedert, M. (2004). Tau protein and neurodegeneration. *Seminars in Cell & Developmental Biology, 15*, 45-49.

Goedert, M., & Jakes, R. (2005). Mutations causing neurodegenerative tauopathies. *Biochimica et Biophysica Acta, 1739*, 240-250.

Goenjian, A.K., Walling, D., Steinberg, A.M., Karayan, I., Najarian, L.M., & Pynoos, R. (2005). A prospective study of posttraumatic stress and depressive reactions among treated and untreated adolescents 5 years after a catastrophic disaster. *American Journal of Psychiatry, 162*, 2302-2308.

Goldberg, J.F., Garno, J.L., & Harrow, M. (2005). Long-term remission and recovery in bipolar disorder: A review. *Current Psychiatry Reports, 7*, 456-461.

Goldberg, J.F., Gerstein, R.K., Wenze, S.J., Welker, T.M., & Beck, A.T. (2008). Dysfunctional attitudes and cognitive schemas in bipolar manic and unipolar depressed outpatients: Implications for cognitively based psychotherapeutics. *Journal of Nervous and Mental Disease, 196*, 207-210.

Goldberg, J.F., & Harrow, M. (1999). Poor-outcome bipolar disorders. In J.F. Goldberg & M. Harrow (Eds.), *Bipolar disorders: Clinical course and outcome* (pp. 1-19). Washington, DC: American Psychiatric Press.

Goldberg, J.F., & Keck, P.E. (1999). Summary of findings on the course and outcome of bipolar disorders. In J.F. Goldberg & M. Harrow (Eds.), *Bipolar disorders: Clinical course and outcome* (pp. 275-288). Washington, DC: American Psychiatric Press.

Golden, C., & Freshwater, S.M. (2002). *Stroop Color and Word Test: Revised examiner's manual*. Lutz, FL: Psychological Assessment Resources.

Goldenberg, I., & Goldenberg, H. (2004). *Family therapy: An overview* (6th ed.). Pacific Grove, CA: Brooks/Cole.

Goldfarb, R., & Bekker, N. (2009). Noun-verb ambiguity in chronic undifferentiated schizophrenia. *Journal of Communication Disorders, 42*, 74-88.

Goldfried, M.R., & Davison, G.C. (1994). *Clinical behavior therapy: Expanded edition*. New York: Wiley.

Goldhammer, D.L., & McCabe, M.P. (2011). Development and psychometric properties of the Female Sexual Desire Questionnaire (FSDQ). *Journal of Sexual Medicine, 8*, 2512-2521.

Goldman, S.A. (2004). Directed mobilization of endogenous neural progenitor cells: The intersection of stem cell biology and gene therapy. *Current Opinion in Molecular Therapeutics, 6*, 166-172.

Goldner, E.M., Hsu, L., Waraich, P., & Somers, J.M. (2002). Prevalence and incidence studies of schizophrenic disorders: A systematic review of the literature. *Canadian Journal of Psychiatry, 47,* 833-843.

Goldstein, G., Shemansky, W.J., & Allen, D.N. (2005). Cognitive function in schizoaffective disorder and clinical subtypes of schizophrenia. *Archives of Clinical Neuropsychology, 20,* 153-159.

Goldstein, J.M., Buka, S.L., Seidman, L.J., & Tsuang, M.T. (2010). Specificity of familial transmission of schizophrenia psychosis spectrum and affective psychoses in the New England Family Study's high-risk design. *Archives of General Psychiatry, 67,* 458-467.

Goldstein, R.Z., & Volkow, N.D. (2011). Dysfunction of the prefrontal cortex in addiction: Neuroimaging findings and clinical implications. *Nature Reviews Neuroscience, 12,* 652-669.

Gomez-Gil, E., Esteva, I., Almaraz, M.C., Pasaro, E., Segovia, S., & Guillamon, A. (2010). Familiality of gender identity disorder in non-twin siblings. *Archives of Sexual Behavior, 39,* 546-552.

Gomez-Pinilla, F., Zhuang, Y., Feng, J., Ying, Z., & Fan, G. (2011). Exercise impacts brain-derived neurotrophic factor plasticity by engaging mechanisms of epigenetic regulation. *European Journal of Neuroscience, 33,* 383-390.

Goodman, A., Fleitlich-Bilyk, B., Patel, V., & Goodman, R. (2007). Child, family, school and community risk factors for poor mental health in Brazilian schoolchildren. *Journal of the American Academy of Child and Adolescent Psychiatry, 46,* 448-456.

Goodman, R.F., Morgan, A.V., Juriga, S., & Brown, E.J. (2004). Letting the story unfold: A case study of client-centered therapy for childhood traumatic grief. *Harvard Review of Psychiatry, 12,* 199-212.

Goodman, S.H. (2008). Depression in mothers. *Annual Review of Clinical Psychology, 3,* 107-135.

Goodnick, P.J. (2006). Anticonvulsants in the treatment of bipolar mania. *Expert Opinion on Pharmacotherapy, 7,* 401-410.

Goodwin, F.K., & Jamison, K.R. (2007). *Manic-depressive illness: Bipolar disorders and recurrent depression* (2nd ed.). New York: Oxford University Press.

Gooren, L.J. (2011). Ethical and medical considerations of androgen deprivation treatment of sex offenders. *Journal of Clinical Endocrinology and Metabolism, 96,* 3628-3637.

Goto, Y., & Lee, Y.-A. (2011). Is schizophrenia developmental adaptation to environmental menaces? *Medical Hypotheses, 77,* 756-762.

Gould, M.S., Greenberg, T., Velting, D.M., & Shaffer, D. (2003). Youth suicide risk and preventive interventions: A review of the past 10 years. *Journal of the American Academy of Child and Adolescent Psychiatry, 42,* 386-405.

Grabe, S., & Hyde, J.S. (2006). Ethnicity and body dissatisfaction among women in the United States: A meta-analysis. *Psychological Bulletin, 132,* 622-640.

Grace, A.A. (2010). Ventral hippocampus, interneurons, and schizophrenia: A new understanding of the pathophysiology of schizophrenia and its implications for treatment and prevention. *Current Directions in Psychological Science, 19,* 232-237.

Grados, M., & Wilcox, H.C. (2007). Genetics of obsessive-compulsive disorder: A research update. *Expert Review of Neurotherapeutics, 7,* 967-980.

Graham, J.R. (2005). *MMPI 2: Assessing personality and psychopathology* (4th ed.). New York: Oxford University Press.

Gralla, O., Knoll, N., Fenske, S., Spivak, I., Hoffmann, M., Ronnebeck, C., Lenk, S., Hoschke, B., & May, M. (2008). Worry, desire, and sexual satisfaction and their association with severity of ED and age. *Journal of Sexual Medicine, 5,* 2646-2655.

Grassi, D., Desideri, G., & Ferri, C. (2010). Blood pressure and cardiovascular risk: What about cocoa and chocolate? *Archives of Biochemistry and Biophysics, 501,* 112-115.

Grattan, L.M., Roberts, S., Mahan, W.T., McLaughlin, P.K., Otwell, W.S., & Morris, J.G. (2011). The early psychological impacts of the Deepwater Horizon oil spill on Florida and Alabama communities. *Environmental Health Perspectives, 119,* 838-843.

Gratz, K.L., Tull, M.T., Baruch, D.E., Bornovalova, A., & Lejuez, C.W. (2008). Factors associated with co-occurring borderline personality disorder among inner-city substance users: The roles of childhood maltreatment, negative affect intensity/ reactivity, and emotion dysregulation. *Comprehensive Psychiatry, 49,* 603-615.

Graves, A.B. (2004). Alzheimer's disease and vascular dementia. In L.M. Nelson, C.M. Tanner, S.K. Van Den Eeden, & V.M. McGuire (Eds.), *Neuroepidemiology: From principles to practice* (pp. 102-130). New York: Oxford.

Gray, D.E. (2002). 'Everybody just freezes. Everybody is just embarrassed': Felt and enacted stigma among parents of children with high functioning autism. *Sociology of Health and Illness, 24,* 734-749.

Gray, P., & Campbell, B. (2005). Erectile dysfunction and its correlates among the Ariaal of northern Kenya. *International Journal of Impotence Research, 17,* 445-449.

Gray, S.A.O., Carter, A.S., Briggs-Gowan, M.J., Hill, C., Danis, B., Keenan, K., & Wakschlag, L.S. (2012). Preschool children's observed disruptive behavior: Variations across sex, interactional context, and disruptive psychopathology. *Journal of Clinical Child and Adolescent Psychology, 41,* 499-507.

Greco, C.M., Navarro, C.S., Hunsaker, M.R., Maezawa, I., Shuler, J.F., Tassone, F., Delany, M., Au, J.W., Berman, R.F., Jin, L.-W., Schumann, C., Hagerman, P.J., & Hagerman, R.J. (2011). Neuropathologic features in the hippocampus and cerebellum of three older men with fragile X syndrome. *Molecular Autism, 2,* 1-13.

Greden, J.F., Valenstein, M., Spinner, J., Blow, A., Gorman, L.A., Dalack, G.W., Marcus, S., & Kees, M. (2010). Buddy-to-Buddy, a citizen soldier peer support program to counteract stigma, PTSD, depression, and suicide. *Annals of the New York Academy of Sciences, 1208,* 90-97.

Green, M.F. (2001). *Schizophrenia revealed: From neurons to social interactions.* New York: Norton.

Green, M.F. (2006). Cognitive impairment and functional outcome in schizophrenia and bipolar disorder. *Journal of Clinical Psychiatry, 67* (Suppl. 9), 3-8.

Green, M.J., Espie, C.A., Hunt, K., & Benzeval, M. (2012). The longitudinal course of insomnia symptoms: Inequalities by sex and occupational class among two different age cohorts followed for 20 years in the West of Scotland. *Sleep, 35,* 815-823.

Green, M.J., Waldron, J.H., Simpson, I., & Coltheart, M. (2008). Visual processing of social context during mental state perception in schizophrenia. *Journal of Psychiatry and Neuroscience, 33,* 34-42.

Green, R., & Kodish, S. (2009). Discussing a sensitive topic: Nurse practitioners and physician assistants' communication strategies in managing patients with erectile dysfunction. *Journal of the American Academy of Nurse Practitioners, 21,* 698-705.

Greenberg, J.L., & Wilhelm, S. (2011). Cognitive-behavioral therapy for body dysmorphic disorder: A review and future directions. *International Journal of Cognitive Therapy, 4,* 349-362.

Greenberg, R.P. (2012). Essential ingredients for successful psychotherapy: Effect of common factors. In M.J. Dewan, B.N. Steenbarger, & R.P. Greenberg (Eds.), *The art and science of brief psychotherapies: An illustrated guide* (2nd ed.) (pp. 15-25). Arlington, VA: American Psychiatric Publishing.

Greenfield, S.F., Brooks, A.J., Gordon, S.M., Green, C.A., Kropp, F., McHugh, R.K., Lincoln, M., Hien, D., & Miele, G.M. (2007). Substance abuse treatment entry, retention, and outcome in women: A review of the literature. *Drug and Alcohol Dependence, 86,* 1-21.

Greenfield, S.F., & Hennessy, G. (2008). Assessment of the patient. In M. Galanter & H.D. Kleber (Eds.), *Textbook of substance abuse treatment* (4th ed.; pp. 55-78). Washington, DC: American Psychiatric Press.

Greenhalgh, J., Dickson, R., & Dundar, Y. (2010). Biofeedback for hypertension: A review. *Journal of Hypertension, 28,* 644-652.

Greenwood, T.A., Nievergelt, C.M., Sadovnick, A.D., Remick, R.A., Keck, P.E., McElroy, S.L., Shekhtman, T., McKinney, R., & Kelsoe, J.R. (2012). Further evidence for linkage of bipolar disorder to chromosomes 6 and 17 in a new independent pedigree series. *Bipolar Disorders, 14,* 71-79.

Gregg, N. (2013). Adults with learning disabilities: Factors contributing to persistence. In H.L. Swanson, K.R. Harris, & S. Graham (Eds.), *Handbook of learning disabilities* (2nd ed.). (pp. 85-103). New York: Guilford.

Gregory, R.J., & Jindal, S. (2006). Factitious disorder on an inpatient psychiatry ward. *American Journal of Orthopsychiatry, 76*, 31-36.

Greicius, M.D., Geschwind, M.D., & Miller, B.L. (2002). Presenile dementia syndromes: An update on taxonomy and diagnosis. *Journal of Neurology, Neurosurgery and Psychiatry, 72*, 691-700.

Greve, K.W., Ord, J.S., Bianchini, K.J., & Curtis, K.L. (2009). Prevalence of malingering in patients with chronic pain referred for physiologic evaluation in a medico-legal context. *Archives of Physical Medicine and Rehabilitation, 90*, 1117-1126.

Grieger, T.A., Waldrep, D.A., Lovasz, M.M., & Ursano, R.J. (2005). Follow-up of Pentagon employees two years after the terrorist attack of September 11, 2001. *Psychiatric Services, 56*, 1374-1378.

Griffiths, K.M., Batterham, P.J., Barney, L., & Parsons, A. (2011). The Generalized Anxiety Stigma Scale (GASS): Psychometric properties in a community sample. *BMC Psychiatry, 11*, 184.

Griffiths, K.M., Christensen, H., Jorm, A.F., Evans, K., & Groves, C. (2004). Effect of web-based depression literacy and cognitive-behavioural therapy interventions on stigmatising attitudes to depression: Randomized controlled trial. *British Journal of Psychiatry, 185*, 342-349.

Griffiths, J., Norris, E., Stallard, P., & Matthews, S. (2011). Living with parents with obsessive-compulsive disorder: Children's lives and experiences. *Psychology and Psychotherapy: Theory, Research and Practice, 85*, 68-82.

Griffiths, J., Ravindran, A.V., Merali, Z., & Anisman, H. (2000). Dysthymia: A review of pharmacological and behavioral factors. *Molecular Psychiatry, 5*, 242-261.

Grigoriadis, S., & Robinson, G.E. (2007). Gender issues in depression. *Annals of Clinical Psychiatry, 19*, 247-255.

Grilo, C.M., Masheb, R.M., Wilson, G.T., Gueorguieva, R., & White, M.A. (2011). Cognitive-behavioral therapy, behavioral weight loss, and sequential treatment for obese patients with binge-eating disorder: A randomized controlled trial. *Journal of Consulting and Clinical Psychology, 79*, 675-685.

Grob, G.N. (1994). *The mad among us: A history of the care of America's mentally ill.* Cambridge, MA: Harvard University Press.

Grossi, D., Marcone, R., Cinquegrana, T., & Gallucci, M. (2013). On the differential nature of induced and incidental echolalia in autism. *Journal of Intellectual Disability Research, 57*, 903-912.

Grover, S., Biswas, P., & Avasthi, A.A. (2007). Delusional disorder: Study from North India. *Psychiatry and Clinical Neurosciences, 61*, 462-470.

Grundmann, O., & Yoon, S.L. (2010). Irritable bowel syndrome: Epidemiology, diagnosis and treatment: An update for health-care practitioners. *Journal of Gastroenterology and Hepatology, 25*, 691-699.

Grunhaus, L., Dannon, P.N., Schreiber, S., Dolberg, O.H., Amiaz, R., Ziv, R., & Lefkifker, E. (2000). Repetitive transcranial magnetic stimulation is as effective as electroconvulsive therapy in the treatment of nondelusional major depressive disorder: An open study. *Biological Psychiatry, 47*, 314-324.

Grunhaus, L., Schreiber, S., Dolberg, O.T., Polak, D., & Dannon, P.N. (2003). A randomized controlled comparison of electroconvulsive therapy and repetitive transcranial magnetic stimulation in severe and resistant nonpsychotic major depression. *Biological Psychiatry, 53*, 324-331.

Grupe, D.W., & Nitschke, J.B. (2013). Uncertainty and anticipation in anxiety: an integrated neurobiological and psychological perspective. *Nature Reviews Neuroscience, 14*, 488-501.

Guarda, A.S. (2008). Treatment of anorexia nervosa: Insights and obstacles. *Physiology and Behavior, 94*, 113-120.

Guisinger, S. (2003). Adapted to flee famine: Adding an evolutionary perspective on anorexia nervosa. *Psychological Review, 110*, 745-761.

Gunderson, J.G. (2001). *Borderline personality disorder. A clinical guide.* Washington, DC: American Psychiatric Press.

Gunderson, J.G., & Links, P.S. (2008). *Borderline personality disorder: A clinical guide* (2nd ed.). Washington, DC: American Psychiatric Publishing.

Gunderson, J.G., Stout, R.L., McGlashan, T.H., Shea, T., Morey, L.C., Grilo, C.M., Zanarini, M.C., Yen, S., Markowitz, J.C., Sanislow, C., Ansell, E., Pinto, A., & Skodol, A.E. (2011). Ten-year course of borderline personality disorder. *Archives of General Psychiatry, 68*, 827-837.

Gunnell, D., Saperia, J., & Ashby, D. (2005). Selective serotonin reuptake inhibitors (SSRIs) and suicide in adults: Meta-analysis of drug company data from placebo controlled, randomised controlled trials submitted to the MHRA's safety review. *BMJ, 330*, 385.

Gureje, O., Simon, G.E., Ustun, T.B., & Goldberg, D.P. (1997). Somatization in cross-cultural perspective: A World Health Organization study in primary care. *American Journal of Psychiatry, 154*, 989-995.

Gutteling, B.M., Montagne, B., Nijs, M., & van den Bosch, L.M.C. (2012). Dialectical behavior therapy: Is outpatient group therapy an effective alternative to individual psychotherapy? Preliminary conclusions. *Comprehensive Psychiatry, 53*, 1161-1168.

Hadjipavlou, G., & Ogrodniczuk, J.S. (2010). Promising psychotherapies for personality disorders. *Canadian Journal of Psychiatry, 55*, 202-210.

Haedt-Matt, A.A., & Keel, P.K. (2011). Revisiting the affect regulation model of binge eating: A meta-analysis of studies using ecological momentary assessment. *Psychological Bulletin, 137*, 660-681.

Hafner, H., & Maurer, K. (2006). Early detection of schizophrenia: Current evidence and future perspectives. *World Psychiatry, 5*, 130-138.

Hagedorn, J., & Omar, H. (2002). Retrospective analysis of youth evaluated for suicide attempt or suicidal ideation in an emergency room setting. *International Journal of Adolescent Medicine and Health, 14*, 55-60.

Hagerman, P.J. (2008). The Fragile X prevalence paradox. *Journal of Medical Genetics, 45*, 498-499.

Haghighi, A., Rezazadeh, J., Shadmehri, A.A., Haghighi, A., Kornreich, R., & Desnick, R.J. (2011). Identification of two HEXA mutations causing infantile-onset Tay-Sachs disease in the Persian population. *Journal of Human Genetics, 56*, 682-684.

Hajek, P., Stead, L.F., West, R., Jarvis, M., & Lancaster, T. (2009). Relapse prevention interventions for smoking cessation. *Cochrane Database of Systematic Reviews*, Issue 1.

Hajek, T., Carrey, N., & Alda, M. (2005). Neuroanatomical abnormalities as risk factors for bipolar disorder. *Bipolar Disorders, 7*, 393-403.

Hajek, T., Hahn, M., Slaney, C., Garnham, J., Green, J., Ruzickova, M., Zvolsky, P., & Alda, M. (2008). Rapid cycling bipolar disorders in primary and tertiary care treated patients. *Bipolar Disorders, 10*, 495-502.

Hale, D.P., & Reck, A. (2010). Somatoform disorder: Understanding hypochondriasis and somatization. *Journal of Health Sciences and Practice, 1*, 1-8.

Hall, G.C.N. (2006). Diversity in clinical psychology. *Clinical Psychology: Science and Practice, 13*, 258-262.

Hall, G.C.N. (2009). *Multicultural psychology* (2nd ed.). Upper Saddle River, NJ: Prentice-Hall.

Hall, J.M. (2003). Dissociative experiences of women child abuse survivors: A selective constructivist review. *Trauma, Violence, and Abuse, 4*, 283-308.

Hall, K., Murrell, J., Ogunniyi, A., Deeg, M., Baiyewu, O., Gao, S., Gureje, O., Dickens, J., Evans, R., Smith-Gamble, V., Unverzagt, F.W., Shen, J., & Hendrie, H. (2006). Cholesterol, APOE genotype, and Alzheimer disease. *Neurology, 66*, 223-227.

Hall, R.C.W., & Hall, R.C.W. (2007). A profile of pedophilia: Definition, characteristics of offenders, recidivism, treatment outcomes, and forensic issues. *Mayo Clinic Proceedings, 82*, 457-471.

Hames, J.L., Hagan, C.R., & Joiner, T.E. (2013). Interpersonal processes in depression. *Annual Review of Clinical Psychology, 9*, 355-377.

Hamet, P., & Tremblay, J. (2005). Genetics and genomics of depression. *Metabolism, 54 (Suppl. 1)*, 10-15.

Hammen, C. (2005). Stress and depression. *Annual Review of Clinical Psychology, 1*, 293-319.

Hammen, C., & Brennan, P.A. (2001). Depressed adolescents of depressed and nondepressed mothers: Tests of an interpersonal impairment hypothesis. *Journal of Consulting and Clinical Psychology, 69*, 284-294.

Hammen, C., & Rudolph, K.D. (2003). Childhood mood disorders. In E.J. Mash & R.A. Barkley (Eds.), *Child psychopathology* (2nd ed.; pp. 233-278). New York: Guilford.

Hammond, D.C. (2005). Neurofeedback with anxiety and affective disorders. *Child and Adolescent Psychiatric Clinics of North America, 14,* 105-123.

Handler, S.M., & Fierson, W.M. (2011). Learning disabilities, dyslexia, and vision. *Pediatrics, 127,* e818-e856.

Hanel, G., Henningsen, P., Herzog, W., Sauer, N., Schaefert, R., Szecsenyi, J., & Lowe, B. (2009). Depression, anxiety, and somatoform disorders: Vague or distinct categories in primary care? Results from a large cross-sectional study. *Journal of Psychosomatic Research, 67,* 189-197.

Hankin, B.L. (2008). Cognitive vulnerability-stress model of depression during adolescence: Investigating depressive symptom specificity in a multi-wave prospective study. *Journal of Abnormal Child Psychology, 36,* 999-1014.

Hanna, A.C., & Bond, M.J. (2006). Relationships between family conflict, perceived maternal verbal messages, and daughters' disturbed eating symptomatology. *Appetite, 47,* 205-211.

Hansberry, M.R., Chen, E., & Gorbien, M.J. (2005). Dementia and elder abuse. *Clinics in Geriatric Medicine, 21,* 315-332.

Hanna, D., White, R., Lyons, K., McParland, M.J., Shannon, C., & Mulholland, C. (2011). The structure of the Beck Hopelessness Scale: A confirmatory factor analysis in UK students. *Personality and Individual Differences, 51,* 17-22.

Hansen, N.B., Lambert, M.J., & Forman, E.M. (2002). The psychotherapy dose-response effect and its implications for treatment delivery systems. *Clinical Psychology: Science and Practice, 9,* 329-343.

Haour, F. (2005). Mechanisms of the placebo effect and of conditioning. *Neuroimmunomodulation, 12,* 195-200.

Harald, B., & Gordon, P. (2012). Meta-review of depressive subtyping models. *Journal of Affective Disorders, 139,* 126-140.

Harciarek, M., & Kertesz, A. (2008). The prevalence of misidentification syndrome in neurodegenerative diseases. *Alzheimer's Disease and Associated Disorders, 22,* 163-169.

Hardiman, E.R., & Segal, S.P. (2003). Community membership and social networks in mental health self-help agencies. *Psychiatric Rehabilitation Journal, 27,* 25-33.

Hardy, J., Lewis, P., Revesz, T., Lees, A., & Paisan-Ruiz, C. (2009). The genetics of Parkinson's syndromes: A critical review. *Current Opinion in Genetics and Development, 19,* 254-265.

Hare, R.D., & Neumann, C.S. (2008). Psychopathy as a clinical and empirical construct. *Annual Review of Clinical Psychology, 4,* 217-246.

Hariri, A.R., Mattay, V.S., Tessitore, A., Fera, F., & Weinberger, D.R. (2003). Neocortical modulation of the amygdala response to fearful stimuli. *Biological Psychiatry, 53,* 494-501.

Haro, J.M., Novick, D., Suarez, D., Alonso, J., Lepine, J.P., & Ratcliffe, M. (2006). Remission and relapse in the outpatient care of schizophrenia: Three-year results from the Schizophrenia Outpatient Health Outcomes study. *Journal of Clinical Psychopharmacology, 26,* 571-578.

Harper, M.L., Rasolkhani-Kalhorn, T., & Drozd, J.F. (2009). On the neural basis of EMDR therapy: Insights from qEEG studies. *Traumatology, 15,* 81-95.

Harrington, R.A., Lee, L.-C., Crum, R.M., Zimmerman, A.W., & Hertz-Picciotto, I. (2013). Serotonin hypothesis of autism: Implications for selective serotonin reuptake inhibitor use during pregnancy. *Autism Research, 6,* 149-168.

Harris, G.T., Lalumiere, M.L., Seto, M.C., Rice, M.E., & Chaplin, T.C. (2012). Explaining the erectile responses of rapists to rape stories: The contributions of sexual activity, non-consent, and violence with injury. *Archives of Sexual Behavior, 41,* 221-229.

Hart, L.M., Granillo, M.T., Jorm, A.F., & Paxton, S.J. (2011). Unmet need for treatment in the eating disorders: A systematic review of eating disorder specific treatment seeking among community cases. *Clinical Psychology Review, 31,* 727-735.

Harter, S.L. (2000). Psychosocial adjustment of adult children of alcoholics: A review of the recent empirical literature. *Clinical Psychology Review, 20,* 311-337.

Hartmann, U., Schedlowski, M., & Kruger, T.H.C. (2005). Cognitive and partner-related factors in rapid ejaculation: Differences between dysfunctional and functional men. *World Journal of Urology, 23,* 93-101.

Hartzler, B., Lash, S.J., & Roll, J.M. (2012). Contingency management in substance abuse treatment: A structured review of the evidence for its transportability. *Drug and Alcohol Dependence, 122,* 1-10.

Harwood, T.M. & L'Abate, L. (2010). *Self-help in mental health: A critical review.* New York: Springer.

Hassett, A.L., & Sigal, L.H. (2002). Unforeseen consequences of terrorism: Medically unexplained symptoms in a time of fear. *Archives of Internal Medicine, 162,* 1809-1813.

Haugaard, J.J. (2004). Recognizing and treating uncommon behavioral and emotional disorders in children and adolescents who have been severely maltreated: Dissociative disorders. *Child Maltreatment, 9,* 146-153.

Havermans, R., Nicolson, N.A., & Devries, M.W. (2007). Daily hassles, uplifts, and time use in individuals with bipolar disorder in remission. *Journal of Nervous and Mental Disease, 195,* 745-751.

Hawgood, J., & De Leo, D. (2008). Anxiety disorders and suicidal behaviour: An update. *Current Opinion in Psychiatry, 21,* 51-64.

Hawke, J.L., Wadsworth, S.J., & DeFries, J.C. (2005). Genetic influences on reading difficulties in boys and girls: The Colorado twin study. *Dyslexia, 12,* 21-29.

Hawke, L.D., & Provencher, M.D. (2012). Early maladaptive schemas among patients diagnosed with bipolar disorder. *Journal of Affective Disorders, 136,* 803-811.

Hawton, K., Comabella, C.C., Haw, C., & Saunders, K. (2013). Risk factors for suicide in individuals with depression: A systematic review. *Journal of Affective Disorders, 147,* 17-28.

Hawton, K., Sutton, L., Haw, C., Sinclair, J., & Deeks, J.J. (2005). Schizophrenia and suicide: Systematic review of risk factors. *British Journal of Psychiatry, 187,* 9-20.

Hayes, R.D. (2011). Circular and linear modeling of female sexual desire and arousal. *Journal of Sex Research, 48,* 130-141.

Hayes, S.C., Strosahl, K.D., & Wilson, K.G. (2012). *Acceptance and commitment therapy: The process and practice of mindful change.* New York: Guilford.

Hayward, C., & Wilson, K.A. (2007). Anxiety sensitivity: A missing piece to the agoraphobia-without-panic puzzle. *Behavior Modification, 31,* 162-173.

Hazlett, E.A., Goldstein, K.E., & Kolaitis, J.C. (2012). A review of structural MRI ad diffusion tensor imaging in schizotypal personality disorder. *Current Psychiatry Reports, 14,* 70-78.

Healy, L.M., & Link, R.J. (2012). *Handbook of international social work: Human rights, development, and the global profession.* New York: Oxford.

Heaton, R.K., & PAR Staff. (2003). *Wisconsin Card Sorting Test: Computer Version 4 (WCST: CV4™) Research Edition.* San Antonio, TX: Pearson.

Hechler, T., Blankenburg, M., Dobe, M., Kosfelder, J., Hubner, B., & Zernikow, B. (2010). Effectiveness of a multimodal inpatient treatment for pediatric chronic pain: A comparison between children and adolescents. *European Journal of Pain, 14,* 97.e1-97.e9.

Hecker, L. (Ed.). (2010). *Ethics and professional issues in couple and family therapy.* New York: Routledge.

Heimberg, R.G., Brozovich, F.A., & Rapee, R.M. (2010). A cognitive behavioral model of social anxiety disorder: Update and extension. In S.G. Hofmann & P.M. DiBartolo (Eds.), *Social anxiety: Clinical, developmental, and social perspectives* (2nd ed., pp. 395-422). San Diego, CA: Elsevier.

Hembree, E.A., & Foa, E.B. (2000). Posttraumatic stress disorder: Psychological factors and psychosocial interventions. *Journal of Clinical Psychiatry, 61,* 33-39.

Hempel, A., Hempel, E., Schonknecht, P., Stippich, C., & Schroder, J. (2003). Impairment in basal limbic function in schizophrenia during affect recognition. *Psychiatry Research: Neuroimaging, 122,* 115-124.

Henderson, J., Kesmodel, U., & Gray, R. (2007). Systematic review of the fetal effects of prenatal binge-drinking. *Journal of Epidemiology and Community Health, 61,* 1069-1073.

Henderson, L, & Zimbardo, P. (2010). Shyness, social anxiety, and social anxiety disorder. In S.G. Hofmann & P.M. DiBartolo (Eds.), *Social anxiety: Clinical, developmental, and social perspectives* (2nd ed., pp. 65-92). San Diego, CA: Elsevier.

Henggeler, S.W. (2011). Efficacy studies to large-scale transport: The development and validation of multisystemic therapy programs. *Annual Review of Clinical Psychology, 7*, 351-381.

Henggeler, S.W., & Sheidow, A.J. (2012). Empirically supported family-based treatments for conduct disorder and delinquency in adolescents. *Journal of Marital and Family Therapy, 38*, 30-58.

Henningsen, P. (2003). The body in the brain: Towards a representational neurobiology of somatoform disorders. *Acta Neuropsychiatrica, 15*, 157-160.

Henningsen, P., Jakobsen, T., Schiltenwolf, M., & Weiss, M.G. (2005). Somatization revisited: Diagnosis and perceived causes of common mental disorders. *Journal of Nervous and Mental Disease, 193*, 85-92.

Henquet, C., Murray, R., Linszen, D., & van Os, J. (2005). The environment and schizophrenia: The role of cannabis use. *Schizophrenia Bulletin, 31*, 608-612.

Hepp, U., Spindler, A., & Milos, G. (2005). Eating disorder symptomatology and gender role orientation. *International Journal of Eating Disorders, 37*, 227-233.

Hermann, N., Li, A., & Lanctot, K. (2011). Memantine in dementia: A review of the current evidence. *Expert Opinion on Pharmacotherapy, 12*, 787-800.

Herring, M., & Kaslow, N.J. (2002). Depression and attachment in families: A child-focused perspective. *Family Process, 41*, 494-518.

Hersen, M. (Ed.). (2006). *Clinician's handbook of child behavioral assessment*. New York: Elsevier.

Heruti, R.J., Reznik, J., Adunski, A., Levy, A., Weingarden, H., & Ohry, A. (2002). Conversion motor paralysis disorder: Analysis of 34 consecutive referrals. *Spinal Cord, 40*, 335-340.

Hesse, M., Guldager, S., & Holm-Linneberg, I. (2012). Convergent validity of MCMI-III clinical syndrome scales. *British Journal of Clinical Psychology, 51*, 172-184.

Hetrick, S., Merry, S., McKenzie, J., Sindahl, P., & Proctor, M. (2007). Selective serotonin reuptake inhibitors (SSRIs) for depressive disorders in children and adolescents. *Cochrane Database of Systematic Reviews, 18*: CD004851.

Hettema, J.M. (2008). The nosologic relationship between generalized anxiety disorder and major depression. *Depression and Anxiety, 25*, 300-316.

Hettema, J.M., Neale, M.C., & Kendler, K.S. (2001). A review and meta-analysis of the genetic epidemiology of anxiety disorders. *American Journal of Psychiatry, 158*, 1568-1578.

Hewett, K., Gee, M.D., Krishen, A., Wunderlich, H.-P., Le Clus, A., Evoniuk, G., & Modell, J.G. (2010). Double blind, placebo-controlled comparison of the antidepressant efficacy and tolerability of bupropion XR and venlafaxine XR. *Journal of Psychopharmacology, 24*, 1209-1216.

Heyerdahl, S., Kvernmo, S., & Wichstrom, L. (2004). Self-reported behavioural/emotional problems in Norwegian adolescents from multiethnic areas. *European Child and Adolescent Psychiatry, 13*, 64-72.

Hickey, M., Elliot, J., & Davison, S.L. (2012). Hormone replacement therapy. *British Medical Journal, 344*, e763.

Higashi, K., Medic, G., Littlewood, K.J., Diez, T., Granstrom, O., & De Hart, M. (2013). Medicaton adherence in schizophrenia: Factors influencing adherence and consequences of nonadherence, a systematic literature review. *Therapeutic Advances in Psychopharmacology*, 1-19.

Higginson, C.B., Martin, C., & Cook, A. (2010). Initial evaluation and management of bacterial meningitis in an emergent setting: A review. *Advanced Emergency Nursing Journal, 32*, 301-313.

Hilbert, A., Martin, A., Zech, T., Rauh, E., & Rief, W. (2010). Patients with medically unexplained symptoms and their significant others: Illness attributions and behaviors as predictors of patient functioning over time. *Journal of Psychosomatic Research, 68*, 253-262.

Hill, A.J. (2006). Motivation for eating behaviour in adolescent girls: The body beautiful. *Proceedings of the Nutrition Society, 65*, 376-384.

Hill, A.J. (2007). The psychology of food craving. *Proceedings of the Nutrition Society, 66*, 277-285.

Hiller, W., & Janca, A. (2003). Assessment of somatoform disorders: A review of strategies and instruments. *Acta Neuropsychiatrica, 15*, 167-179.

Hiller, W., Liebbrand, R., Rief, W., & Fichter, M.M. (2002). Predictors of course and outcome in hypochondriasis after cognitive-behavioral treatment. *Psychotherapy and Psychosomatics, 71*, 318-325.

Hiller, W., Zaudig, M., & Mambour, W. (1996). *International diagnostic checklists for ICD-10 and DSM-IV*. Seattle: Hogrefe and Huber.

Hines, M. (2011). Gender development and the human brain. *Annual Review of Neuroscience, 34*, 69-88.

Hinkelmann, K., Moritz, S., Botzenhardt, J., Muhtz, C., Wiedemann, K., Kellner, M., & Otte, C. (2012). Changes in cortisol secretion during antidepressive treatment and cognitive improvement in patients with major depression: A longitudinal study. *Psychoneuroendocrinology, 37*, 685-692.

Hinton, D.E., & Lewis-Fernandez, R. (2010). Idioms of distress among trauma survivors: Subtypes and clinical utility. *Culture, Medicine and Psychiatry, 34*, 209-218.

Hinton, D.E., Pham, T., Tran, M., Safren, S.A., Otto, M.W., & Pollack, M.H. (2004). CBT for Vietnamese refugees with treatment-resistant PTSD and panic attacks: A pilot study. *Journal of Traumatic Stress, 17*, 429-433.

Hinton, D.E., Pich, V., Chhean, D., Pollack, M.H., & Barlow, D.H. (2004). Olfactory-triggered panic attacks among Cambodian refugees attending a psychiatric clinic. *General Hospital Psychiatry, 26*, 390-397.

Hinton, D.E., Pich, V., Chhean, D., Pollack, M.H., & McNally, R.J. (2005). Sleep paralysis among Cambodian refugees: Association with PTSD diagnosis and severity. *Depression and Anxiety, 22*, 47-51.

Hirsch, C.R., Clark, D.M., Mathews, A., & Williams, R. (2003). Self-images play a causal role in social phobia. *Behaviour Research and Therapy, 41*, 909-921.

Hirschfeld, R.M.A. (2001). When to hospitalize patients at risk for suicide. *Annals of the New York Academy of Sciences, 932*, 188-199.

Hirschfeld, R.M.A., & Russell, J.M. (1997). Assessment and treatment of suicidal patients. *New England Journal of Medicine, 337*, 910-915.

Hirshfeld-Becker, D.R., Biederman, J., & Rosenbaum, J.F. (2004). Behavioral inhibition. In T.L. Morris & J.S. March (Eds.), *Anxiety disorders in children and adolescents* (2nd ed.; pp. 27-58). New York: Guilford.

Hirshfeld-Becker, D.R., Micco, J., Henin, A., Bloomfield, A., Biederman, J., & Rosenbaum, J. (2008). Behavioral inhibition. *Depression and Anxiety, 25*, 357-367.

Hirshfeld-Becker, D.R., Micco, J.A., Simoes, N.A., & Henin, A. (2008). High risk studies and developmental antecedents of anxiety disorders. *American Journal of Medical Genetics, 148*, 99-117.

Hjemdahl, P., Rosengren, A., & Steptoe, A. (Eds.). (2012). *Stress and cardiovascular disease*. New York: Springer.

Ho, B.-C., Nopoulos, P., Flaum, M., Arndt, S., & Andreasen, N.C. (2004). Two-year outcome in first-episode schizophrenia: Predictive value of symptoms for quality of life. *Focus, 2*, 131-137.

Ho, G.J., Liang, W., Waragai, M., Sekiyama, K., Masliah, E., & Hashimoto, M. (2011). Bridging molecular genetics and biomarkers in Lewy body and related disorders *International Journal of Alzheimer's Disease, 2011*, 1-18.

Hoang, A.N., Romero, C., & Hairston, J.C. (2011). Vacuum constriction device: A new paradigm for treatment of erectile dysfunction. In K.T. McVary (Ed.), *Contemporary treatment of erectile dysfunction: A clinical guide* (pp. 151-160). New York: Springer.

Hodapp, R.M., Griffin, M.M., Burke, M.M., & Fisher, M.H. (2011). Intellectual disabilities. In R.J. Sternberg & S.B. Kaufman (Eds.), *The Cambridge handbook of intelligence* (pp. 193-209). New York: Cambridge University Press.

Hodgins, S. (2008). Violent behavior among people with schizophrenia: A framework for investigations of causes, and effective treatment, and prevention. *Philosophical Transactions of the Royal Society of London, Series B, Biological Sciences, 363*, 2505-2518.

Hoffmann, H., Kupper, Z., Zbinden, M., & Hirsbrunner, H.-P. (2003). Predicting vocational functioning and outcome in schizophrenia outpatients attending a vocational rehabilitation program. *Social Psychiatry and Psychiatric Epidemiology, 38*, 76-82.

Hofmann, H. (2012). Considering the role of conditioning in sexual orientation. *Archives of Sexual Behavior, 41*, 63-71.

Hofmann, S. (2000). Treatment of social phobia: Potential mediators and moderators. *Clinical Psychology: Science and Practice, 7*, 3-16.

Hofmann, S.G., & Asmundson, G.J. (2008). Acceptance and mindfulness-based therapy: New wave or old hat? *Clinical Psychology Review, 28*, 1-16.

Hofmann, S.G., Sawyer, A.T., Witt, A.A., & Oh, D. (2010). The effect of mindfulness-based therapy on anxiety and depression: A meta-analytic review. *Journal of Consulting and Clinical Psychology, 78*, 169-183.

Hofmann, S.G., Suvak, M.K., Barlow, D.H., Shear, M.K., Meuret, A.E., Rosenfield, D., Gorman, J.M., & Woods, S.W. (2007). Preliminary evidence for cognitive mediation during cognitive-behavioral therapy of panic disorder. *Journal of Consulting and Clinical Psychology, 75*, 374-379.

Hoge, C.W., Auchterlonie, J.L., & Milliken, C.S. (2006). Mental health problems, use of mental health services, and attrition from military service after returning from deployment to Iraq or Afghanistan. *Journal of the American Medical Association, 295*, 1023-1032.

Holeva, V., Tarrier, N., & Wells, A. (2001). Prevalence and predictors of acute stress disorder and PTSD following road traffic accidents: Thought control strategies and social support. *Behavior Therapy, 32*, 65-83.

Holland, M.L., Gimpel, G.A., & Merrell, K.W. (2001). *ADHD Symptoms Rating Scale*. Wilmington, DE: Wide Range.

Hollon, S.D., Thase, M.E., & Markowitz, J.C. (2002). Treatment and prevention of depression. *Psychological Science in the Public Interest, 3*, 39-77.

Holman, E.A., Silver, R.C., Poulin, M., Andersen, J., Gil- Rivas, V., & McIntosh, D.N. (2008). Terrorism, acute stress, and cardiovascular health: a 3-year national study following the September 11th attacks. *Archives of General Psychiatry, 65*, 73-80.

Holmes, E.A., Brown, R.J., Mansell, W., Fearon, R.P., Hunter, E.C.M., Frasquilho, F., & Oakley, D.A. (2005). Are there two qualitatively distinct forms of dissociation? A review and some clinical implications. *Clinical Psychology Review, 25*, 1-23.

Hope, D.A., Heimberg, R.G., Juster, H.R., & Turk, C.L. (2000). *Managing social anxiety: A cognitive-behavioral therapy approach*. San Antonio, TX: Psychological Corporation.

Hopper, J.W., Frewen, P.A., van der Kolk, B.A., & Lanius, R.A. (2007). Neural correlates of reexperiencing, avoidance, and dissociation in PTSD: Symptom dimensions and emotion dysregulation in responses to script-driven trauma imagery. *Journal of Traumatic Stress, 20*, 713-725.

Hopper, K., Harrison, G., Janca, A., & Sartorius, N. (2001). *Prospects of recovery from schizophrenia-An international investigation: A report from the WHO Collaborative Project, the International Study of Schizophrenia*. Madison, CT: Psychosocial Press.

Hopwood, C.J., Morey, L.C., Edelen, M.O., Shea, M.T., & Grilo, C.M. (2008). A comparison of interview and self-report methods for the assessment of borderline personality disorder criteria. *Psychological Assessment, 20*, 81-85.

Hor, K., & Taylor, M. (2010). Suicide and schizophrenia: A systematic review of rates and risk factors. *Journal of Psychopharmacology, 24 (Suppl 1)*, 81-90.

Hordern, A. (2008). Intimacy and sexuality after cancer: A critical review of the literature. *Cancer Nursing, 31*, E9-17.

Hori, T., Sanjo, N., Tomita, M., & Mizusawa, H. (2013). Visual reproduction on the Wechsler Memory Scale-Revised as a predictor of Alzheimer's disease in Japanese patients with mild cognitive impairments. *Dementia and Geriatric Cognitive Disorders, 35*, 165-176.

Hou, C.E., Yaffe, K., Perez-Stable, E.J., & Miller, B.L. (2006). Frequency of dementia etiologies in four ethnic groups. *Dementia and Geriatric Cognitive Disorders, 22*, 42-47.

Houser, R.A., & Thoma, S. (2013). *Ethics in counseling and therapy: Developing an ethical identity*. Thousand Oaks, CA: Sage.

Howard, M.O., Delva, J., Jenson, J.M., Edmond, T., & Vaughn, M.G. (2005). Substance abuse. In C.N. Dulmus & L.A. Rapp-Paglicci (Eds.), *Handbook of preventive interventions for adults* (pp. 92-124). Hoboken, NJ: Wiley.

Howard, R., Huband, N., & Duggan, C. (2012). Adult antisocial syndrome with comorbid borderline pathology: Association with severe childhood conduct disorder. *Annals of Clinical Psychiatry, 24*, 127-134.

Howard, R.C. (2011). The quest for excitement: A missing link between personality disorder and violence? *Journal of Forensic Psychiatry and Psychology, 22*, 692-705.

Howland, R.H. (2007). Managing common side effects of SSRIs. *Journal of Psychosocial Nursing, 45*, 15-18.

Howlin, P., Goode, S., Hutton, J., & Rutter, M. (2009). Savant skills in autism: Psychometric approaches and parental reports. *Philosophical Transactions of the Royal Society, 364*, 1359-1367.

Hoyer, J., Beesdo, K., Gloster, A.T., Runge, J., Hofler, M., & Becker, E.S. (2009). Worry exposure versus applied relaxation in the treatment of generalized anxiety disorder. *Psychotherapy and Psychosomatics, 78*, 106-115.

Hsu, L., Woody, S.R., Lee, H.-J., Peng, Y., Zhou, X., & Ryder, A.G. (2012). Social anxiety among East Asians in North America: East Asian socialization or the challenge of acculturation? *Cultural Diversity and Ethnic Minority Psychology, 18*, 181-191.

Hu, N.-W., Ondrejcak, T., & Rowan, M.J. (2012). Glutamate receptors in preclinical research on Alzheimer's disease: Update on recent advances. *Pharmacology Biochemistry and Behavior, 100*, 855-862.

Hu, X., Oroszi, G., Chun, J., Smith, T.L., Goldman, D., & Schuckit, M.A. (2005). An expanded evaluation of the relationship of four alleles to the level of response to alcohol and the alcoholism risk. *Alcoholism: Clinical and Experimental Research, 29*, 8-16.

Huang, B., Grant, B.F., Dawson, D.A., Stinson, F.S., Chou, S.P., Saha, T.D., Goldstein, R.B., Smith, S.M., Ruan, W.J., & Pickering, R.P. (2006). Race-ethnicity and the prevalence and co-occurrence of Diagnostic and Statistical Manual of Mental Disorders, Fourth Edition, alcohol and drug use disorders and Axis I and II disorders: United States, 2001 to 2002. *Comprehensive Psychiatry, 47*, 252-257.

Hudson, J.L., Deveney, C., & Taylor, L. (2005). Nature, assessment, and treatment of generalized anxiety disorder in children. *Pediatric Annals, 34*, 97-106.

Hughes, J.R., Peters, E.N., & Naud, S. (2011). Effectiveness of over-the-counter nicotine replacement therapy: A qualitative review of nonrandomized trials. *Nicotine and Tobacco Research, 13*, 512-522.

Huizinga, D., Haberstick, B.C., Smolen, A., Menard, S., Young, S.E., Corley, R.P., Stallings, M.C., Grotpeter, J., & Hewitt, J.K. (2006). Childhood maltreatment, subsequent antisocial behavior, and the role of monoamine oxidase A genotype. *Biological Psychiatry, 60*, 677-683.

Hulshoff Pol, H.E., & Kahn, R.S. (2008). What happens after the first episode?: A review of progressive brain changes in chronically ill patients with schizophrenia. *Schizophrenia Bulletin, 34*, 354-366.

Hummelen, B., Pedersen, G., & Karterud, S. (2012). Some suggestions for the DSM-5 schizotypal personality disorder construct. *Comprehensive Psychiatry, 53*, 341-349.

Hunter, E.C.M., Baker, D., Phillips, M.L., Sierra, M., & David, A.S. (2005). Cognitive-behaviour therapy for depersonalisation disorder: An open study. *Behaviour Research and Therapy, 43*, 1121-1130.

Hunter, E.C.M., Sierra, M., & David, A.S. (2004). The epidemiology of depersonalisation and derealisation: A systematic review. *Social Psychiatry and Psychiatric Epidemiology, 39*, 9-18.

Hunter, J.A., Figueredo, A.J., Malamuth, N.M., & Becker, J.V. (2003). Juvenile sex offenders: Toward the development of a typology. *Sexual Abuse, 15*, 27-48.

Hunter, J.A., Ram, N., & Ryback, R. (2008). Use of satiation therapy in the treatment of adolescent-manifest sexual interest in male children: A single-case, repeated measures design. *Clinical Case Studies, 7*, 54-74.

Huntjens, R.J.C., Peters, M.L., Postma, A., Woertman, L., Effting, M., & van der Hart, O. (2005). Transfer of newly acquired stimulus valence between identities in dissociative identity disorder (DID). *Behaviour Research and Therapy, 43*, 243-255.

Huot, P., Johnston, T.H., Koprich, J.B., Fox, S.H., & Brotchie, J.M. (2013). The pharmacology of L-dopa-induced dyskinesia in Parkinson's disease. *Pharmacological Reviews, 65*, 171-222.

Huprich, S.K., Gacono, C.B., Schneider, R.B., & Bridges, M.R. (2004). Rorschach oral dependency in psychopaths, sexual homicide perpetrators, and nonviolent pedophiles. *Behavioral Sciences and the Law, 22,* 345-356.

Hurlburt, R.T., & Akhter, S.A. (2008). Unsymbolized thinking. *Consciousness and Cognition, 17,* 1364-1374.

Hurwitz, T.A. (2004). Somatization and conversion disorder. *Canadian Journal of Psychiatry, 49,* 172-178.

Hyde, C., Peter, J., Bond, M., Rogers, G., Hoyle, M., Anderson, R., Jeffreys, M., Davis, S., Tholaka, P., & Moxham, T. (2013). Evolution of the evidence on the effectiveness and cost-effectiveness of acetylcholinesterase inhibitors and memantine for Alzheimer's disease: systematic review and economic model. *Age and Ageing, 42,* 14-20.

Hyde, J.S., & DeLameter, J.D. (2011). *Understanding human sexuality* (11th ed.). New York: McGraw-Hill.

Hyde, J.S., Mezulis, A.H., & Abramson, L.Y. (2008). The ABCs of depression: Integrating affective, biological, and cognitive models to explain the emergence of the gender difference in depression. *Psychological Review, 115,* 291-313.

Hyde, T.M. (2004). Cognitive impairment in demyelinating disease. In D.S. Charney & E.J. Nestler (Eds.), *Neurobiology of mental illness* (2nd ed.; pp. 873-880). New York: Oxford.

Hypericum Depression Trial Study Group. (2002). Effect of *Hypericum perforatum* (St John's wort) in major depressive disorder: A randomized controlled trial. *Journal of the American Medical Association, 287,* 1807-1814.

Iezzi, T., Duckworth, M.P., & Adams, H.E. (2001). Somatoform and factitious disorders. In P.B. Sutker & H.E. Adams (Eds.), *Comprehensive handbook of psychopathology* (pp. 211-258). New York: Kluwer Academic/Plenum.

Ikeda, M., Ishikawa, T., & Tanabe, H. (2004). Epidemiology of frontotemporal lobar degeneration. *Dementia and Geriatric Cognitive Disorders, 17,* 265-268.

Ineichen, B. (2000). The epidemiology of dementia in Africa: A review. *Social Science and Medicine, 50,* 1673-1677.

Inouye, S.K., Leo-Summers, L., Zhang, Y., Bogardus, S.T., Leslie, D.L., & Agostini, J.V. (2005). A chart-based method for identification of delirium: Validation compared with interviewer ratings using the Confusion Assessment Method. *Journal of the American Geriatric Society, 53,* 312-318.

Ingenhoven, T., Lafay, P., Rinne, T., Passchier, J., & Duivenvoorden, H. (2010). Effectiveness of pharmacotherapy for severe personality disorders: Meta-analyses of randomized controlled trials. *Journal of Clinical Psychiatry, 71,* 14-25.

Ingersoll, B., & Dvortcsak, A. (2010). *Teaching social communication to children with autism: A manual for parents.* New York: Guilford.

Ingram, B.L. (2012). *Clinical case formulations: Matching the integrative treatment plan to the client* (2nd ed.). New York: Wiley.

Iniesta, R., Ochoa, S., & Usall, J. (2012). Gender differences in service use in a sample of people with schizophrenia and other psychoses. *Schizophrenia Research and Treatment, 2012,* 1-6.

Insel, T.R. (2008). Assessing the economic costs of serious mental illness. *American Journal of Psychiatry, 165,* 663-665.

Institute of Medicine. (2009). *Preventing mental, emotional, and behavioral disorders among young people: Progress and possibilities.* Washington, DC: National Academy Press.

Ipser, J.C., Kariuki, C.M., & Stein, D.J. (2008). Pharmacotherapy for social anxiety disorder: A systematic review. *Expert Review of Neurotherapeutics, 8,* 235-257.

Ipser, J.C., Sander, C., & Stein, D.J. (2009). Pharmacotherapy and psychotherapy for body dysmorphic disorder. *Cochrane Database of Systematic Reviews,* Issue 1.

Isidori, A.M., Giannetta, E., Gianfrilli, D., Greco, E.A., Bonifacio, V., Aversa, A., Isidori, A., Fabbri, A., & Lenzi, A. (2005). Effects of testosterone on sexual function in men: Results of a meta-analysis. *Clinical Endocrinology, 63,* 381-394.

Ismail, Z., Rajji, T.K., & Shulman, K.I. (2010). Brief cognitive screening instruments: An update. *International Journal of Geriatric Psychiatry, 25,* 111-120.

Ito, K., Ahadieh, S., Corrigan, B., French, J., Fullerton, T., & Tensfeldt, T. (2010). Disease progression meta-analysis model in Alzheimer's disease. *Alzheimer's and Dementia, 6,* 39-53.

Ivanov, I., Schulz, K.P., London, E.D., & Newcorn, J.H. (2008). Inhibitory control deficits in childhood and risk for substance use disorders: A review. *American Journal of Drug and Alcohol Abuse, 34,* 239-258.

Iwamasa, G.Y., Sorocco, K.H., & Koonce, D.A. (2002). Ethnicity and clinical psychology: A content analysis of the literature. *Clinical Psychology Review, 22,* 931-944.

Iwata, Y., Suzuki, K., Takei, N., Toulopoulou, T., Tsuchiya, K.J., Matsumoto, K., Takagai, S., Oshiro, M., Nakamura, K., & Mori, N. (2011). Jiko-shisen-kyofu (fear of one's own glance), but not taijin-kyofusho (fear of interpersonal relations), is an East Asian culture-related specific syndrome. *Australian and New Zealand Journal of Psychiatry, 45,* 148-153.

Jaaro-Peled, H., Ayhan, Y., Pletnikov, M.V., & Sawa, A. (2010). Review of pathological hallmarks of schizophrenia: Comparison of genetic models with patients and nongenetic models. *Schizophrenia Bulletin, 36,* 301-313.

Jackson, W.C. (2008). The importance of facilitating adherence in maintenance therapy for bipolar disorder. *Journal of Clinical Psychiatry, 69,* e3.

Jacob, T., & Windle, M. (1999). Family assessment: Instrument dimensionality and correspondence across family reporters. *Journal of Family Psychology, 13,* 339-354.

Jacobi, C., Volker, U., Trockel, M.T., & Taylor, C.B. (2012). Effects of an Internet-based intervention for subthreshold eating disorders: A randomized controlled trial. *Behaviour Research and Therapy, 50,* 93-99.

Jacobs, M.J., Roesch, S., Wonderlich, S.A., Crosby, R., Thornton, L., Wilfley, D.E., Berrettini, W.H., Brandt, H., Crawford, S., Fichter, M.M., Halmi, K.A., Johnson, C., Kaplan, A.S., La Via, M., Mitchell, J.E., Rotondo, A., Strober, M., Woodside, D.B., Kaye, W.H., & Bulik, C.M. (2009). Anorexia nervosa trios: Behavioral profiles of individuals with anorexia nervosa and their parents. *Psychological Medicine, 39,* 451-461.

Jaffe, S.L., & Solhkhah, R. (2004). Substance abuse disorders. In J.M. Weiner & M.K. Dulcan (Eds.), *Textbook of child and adolescent psychiatry* (pp. 795-812). Washington, DC: American Psychiatric Publishing.

Jager, M., Haack, S., Becker, T., & Frasch, K. (2011). Schizoaffective disorder: An ongoing challenge for psychiatric nosology. *European Psychiatry, 26,* 159-165.

James, A., Madeley, R., & Dove, A. (2006). Violence and aggression in the emergency department. *Emergency Medicine Journal, 23,* 431-434.

James, S. (2011). What works in group care? A structural review of treatment models for group homes and residential care. *Children and Youth Services Review, 33,* 308-321.

Janevic, M.R., & Connell, C.M. (2001). Racial, ethnic, and cultural differences in the dementia caregiving experience: Recent findings. *The Gerontologist, 41,* 334-347.

Jang, D.P., Ku, J.H., Choi, Y.H., Wiederhold, B.K., Nam, S.W., Kim, I.Y., & Kim, S.I. (2002). The development of virtual reality therapy (VRT) system for the treatment of acrophobia and therapeutic case. *IEEE Transactions on Information Technology in Biomedicine, 6,* 213-217.

Janssen, E. (2011). Sexual arousal in men: A review and conceptual analysis. *Hormones and Behavior, 59,* 708-716.

Jansson, E.T. (2005). Alzheimer disease is substantially preventable in the United States—Review of risk factors, therapy, and the prospects for an expert software program. *Medical Hypotheses, 64,* 960-967.

Jary, S., De Carli, A., Ramenghi, L.A., & Whitelaw, A. (2012). Impaired brain growth and neurodevelopment in preterm infants with posthaemorrhagic ventricular dilatation. *Acta Paediatrica, 101,* 743-748.

Jaskiw, G.E., & Popli, A.P. (2004). A meta-analysis of the response to chronic L-dopa in patients with schizophrenia: Therapeutic and heuristic implications. *Psychopharmacology, 171,* 365-374.

Jasper, F.J. (2003). Working with dissociative fugue in a general psychotherapy practice: A cautionary tale. *American Journal of Clinical Hypnosis, 45,* 311-322.

Jayadev, S., Leverenz, J.B., Steinbart, E., Stahl, J., Klunk, M., Yu, C.-E., & Bird, T.D. (2010).

Alzheimer's disease phenotypes and genotypes associated with mutations in presenilin 2. *Brain, 133*, 1143-1154.

Jervis, L.L., & Manson, S.M. (2002). American Indians/ Alaska natives and dementia. *Alzheimer Disease and Associated Disorders, 16 (Suppl. 2)*, S89-S95.

Jespersen, A.F., Lalumiere, M.L., & Seto, M.C. (2009). Sexual abuse history among adult sex offenders and non-sex offenders: A meta-analysis. *Child Abuse and Neglect, 33*, 179-192.

Jester, J. M., Nigg, J. T., Adams, K., Fitzgerald, H. E., Puttler, L. I., Wong, M. M., & Zucker, R. A. (2005). Inattention/hyperactivity and aggression from early childhood to adolescence: Heterogeneity of trajectories and differential influence of family environment characteristics. *Development and Psychopathology, 17*, 99-125.

Jiwa, N.S., Garrard, P., & Hainsworth, A.H. (2010). Experimental models of vascular dementia and vascular cognitive impairment: a systematic review. *Journal of Neurochemistry, 115*, 814-828.

Jobe, T.H., & Harrow, M. (2010). Schizophrenia course, long-term outcome, recovery, and prognosis. *Current Directions in Psychological Science, 19*, 220-225.

Johannessen Landmark, C. (2008). Antiepileptic drugs in non-epilepsy disorders: Relations between mechanisms of action and clinical efficacy. *CNS Drugs, 22*, 27-47.

Johnson, A.W. (2013). Eating beyond metabolic need: How environmental cues influence feeding behavior. *Trends in Neurosciences, 36*, 101-109.

Johnson, S.D., Phelps, D.L., & Cottler, L.B. (2004). The association of sexual dysfunction and substance use among a community epidemiological sample. *Archives of Sexual Behavior, 33*, 55-63.

Johnson, S.L. (2004). Defining bipolar disorder. In S.L. Johnson & R.L. Leahy (Eds.), *Psychological treatment of bipolar disorder* (pp. 3-16). New York: Guilford.

Johnson, S.L., & Meyer, B. (2004). Psychosocial predictors of symptoms. In S.L. Johnson & R.L. Leahy (Eds.), *Psychological treatment of bipolar disorder* (pp. 83-105). New York: Guilford.

Jonason, P.K., & Perilloux, C. (2012). Domain-specificity and individual differences in worry. *Personality and Individual Differences, 52*, 228-231.

Jones, C., Hacker, D., Cormac, I., Meaden, A., & Irving, C.B. (2012). Cognitive behavior therapy versus other psychosocial treatments for schizophrenia. *Schizophrenia Bulletin, 38*, 908-910.

Jones, D., Godwin, J., Dodge, K.A., Bierman, K.L., Coie, J.D., Greenberg, M.T., Lochman, J.E., McMahon, R.J., & Pinderhughes, E.E. (2010). Impact of the Fast Track Prevention Program on health services use by conduct-problem youth. *Pediatrics, 125*, e130-e136.

Jones, D.J., Forehand, R., Cuellar, J., Kincaid, C., Parent, J., Fenton, N., & Goodrum, N. (2013). Harnessing innovative technologies to advance children's mental health: Behavioral parent training as an example. *Clinical Psychology Review, 33*, 241-252.

Jones, M.P. (2006). The role of psychosocial factors in peptic ulcer disease: Beyond Helicobacter pylori and NSAIDs. *Journal of Psychosomatic Research, 60*, 407-412.

Jones, R.M., Arlidge, J., Gillham, R., Reagu, S., van den Bree, M., & Taylor, P.J. (2011). Efficacy of mood stabilisers in the treatment of impulsive or repetitive aggression. Systematic review and meta-analysis. *British Journal of Psychiatry, 198*, 93-98.

Jordan, J., Joyce, P.R., Carter, F.A., Horn, J., McIntosh, V.V.W., Luty, S.E., McKenzie, J.M., Frampton, C.M.A., Mulder, R.T., & Bulik, C.M. (2008). Specific and nonspecific comorbidity in anorexia nervosa. *International Journal of Eating Disorders, 41*, 47-56.

Jordan, J.V. (2000). The role of mutual empathy in relational/cultural therapy. *Journal of Clinical Psychology, 56*, 1005-1016.

Jordan, K., Fromberger, P., Stolpmann, G., & Muller, J.L. (2011). The role of testosterone in sexuality and paraphilia—A neurobiological approach. Part II: Testosterone and paraphilia. *Journal of Sexual Medicine, 8*, 3008-3029.

Jorm, A.F., Christensen, H., Griffiths, K.M., Parslow, R.A., Rodgers, B., & Blewitt, K.A. (2004). Effectiveness of complementary and self-help treatments for anxiety disorders. *Medical Journal of Australia, 181 (Suppl. 7)*, S29-S46.

Jorns, C., Ellis, E.C., Nowak, G., Fischler, B., Nemeth, A., Strom, S.C., & Ericzon, B.G. (2012). Hepatocyte transplantation for inherited metabolic diseases of the liver. *Journal of Internal Medicine, 272*, 201-223.

Joshi, G., & Wilens, T. (2009). Comorbidity in pediatric bipolar disorder. *Child and Adolescent Psychiatric Clinics of North America, 18*, 291-319.

Judd, L.L., Schettler, P.J., Solomon, D.A., Maser, J.D., Coryell, W., Endicott, J., & Akiskal, H.S. (2008). Psychosocial disability and work role function compared across the long-term course of bipolar I, bipolar II and unipolar major depressive disorders. *Journal of Affective Disorders, 108*, 49-58.

Judson, R., & Langdon, S.W. (2009). Illicit use of prescription stimulants among college students: Prescription status, motives, theory of planned behaviour, knowledge and self-diagnostic tendencies. *Psychology, Health and Medicine, 14*, 97-104.

Juliano, L.M., Huntley, E.D., Harrell, P.T., & Westerman, A.T. (2012). Development of the Caffeine Withdrawal Symptom Questionnaire: Caffeine withdrawal symptoms cluster into 7 factors. *Drug and Alcohol Dependence, 124*, 229-234.

Jungehülsing, G.J., Müller-Nordhorn, J., Nolte, C.H., Roll, S., Rossnagel, K., Reich, A., Wagner, A., Einhäupl, K.M., Willich, S.N., & Villringer, A. (2008). Prevalence of stroke and stroke symptoms: A population-based survey of 28,090 participants. *Neuroepidemiology, 30*, 51-57.

Jurica, P.J., Leitten, C.L., & Mattis, S. (2001). *Dementia Rating Scale-2: Professional manual.* Lutz, FL: Psychological Assessment Resources.

Kadri, N., Alami, K.H.M., & Tahiri, S.M. (2002). Sexual dysfunction in women: Population-based epidemiological study. *Archives of Women's Mental Health, 5*, 59-63.

Kaduson, H.G., & Schaefer, C.E. (2006). *Short-term play therapy for children* (2nd ed.). New York: Guilford.

Kafka, M.P. (2010a). The *DSM* diagnostic criteria for fetishism. *Archives of Sexual Behavior, 39*, 357-362.

Kafka, M.P. (2010b). The *DSM* diagnostic criteria for paraphilia not otherwise specified. *Archives of Sexual Behavior, 39*, 373-376.

Kagan, J. (2012). The biography of behavioral inhibition. In M. Zentner & R.L. Shiner (Eds.), *Handbook of temperament* (pp. 69-82). New York: Guilford.

Kagan, J. (2001). Temperamental contributions to affective and behavioral profiles in childhood. In S.G. Hofmann & P.M. DiBartolo (Eds.), *From social anxiety to social phobia: Multiple perspectives* (pp. 216-234). Needham Heights, MA: Allyn and Bacon.

Kalaria, R.N., Maestre, G.E., Arizaga, R., Friedland, R.P., Galasko, D., Hall, K., Luchsinger, J.A., Ogunniyi, A., Perry, E.K., Potocnik, F., Prince, M., Stewart, R., Wimo, A., Zhang, Z.-X., & Antuono, P. (2008). Alzheimer's disease and vascular dementia in developing countries: prevalence, management, and risk factors. *Lancet Neurology, 7*, 812-826.

Kalivas, P.W., LaLumiere, R.T., Knackstedt, L., & Shen, H. (2009). Glutamate transmission in addiction. *Neuropharmacology, 56*, 169-173.

Kallert, T.W., Leisse, M., & Winiecki, P. (2004). Needs for care of chronic schizophrenic patients in longterm community treatment. *Social Psychiatry and Psychiatric Epidemiology, 39*, 386-396.

Kalucy, R., Thomas, L., Lia, B., Slattery, T., & Norris, D. (2004). Managing increased demand for mental health services in a public hospital emergency department: A trial of "Hospital-in-the-Home" for mental health consumers. *International Journal of Mental Health Nursing, 13*, 275-281.

Kalueff, A.V., & Nutt, D.J. (2007). Role of GABA in anxiety and depression. *Depression and Anxiety, 24*, 495-517.

Kamatenesi-Mugisha, M., & Oryem-Origa, H. (2005). Traditional herbal remedies used in the management of sexual impotence and erectile dysfunction in western Uganda. *African Health Sciences, 5*, 40-49.

Kanaan, R.A., Craig, T.K., Wessely, S.C., & David, A.S. (2007). Imaging repressed memories in motor conversion disorder. *Psychosomatic Medicine, 69*, 202-205.

Kaner, E.F.S., Dickinson, H.O., Beyer, F., Pienaar, E., Schlesinger, C., Campbell, F., Saunders, J.B., Burnand, B., & Heather, N. (2009). The effectiveness of brief alcohol interventions in primary care settings: A systematic review. *Drug and Alcohol Review, 28,* 301-323.

Kang, J.Y. (2005). Systematic review: The influence of geography and ethnicity in irritable bowel syndrome. *Alimentary Pharmacology and Therapeutics, 21,* 663-676.

Kaniecki, R. (2003). Headache assessment and management. *Journal of the American Medical Association, 289,* 1430-1433.

Kansara, S., Trivedi, A., Chen, S., Jankovic, J., & Le, W. (2013). Early diagnosis and therapy of Parkinson's disease: Can disease progression be curbed? *Journal of Neural Transmission, 120,* 197-210.

Kaplan, K.A., & Harvey, A.G. (2009). Hypersomnia across mood disorders: A review and synthesis. *Sleep Medicine Reviews, 13,* 275-285.

Kaplan, N.M., & Victor, R.G. (2010). *Clinical hypertension* (10th ed.). Philadelphia, PA: Lippincott Williams & Wilkens.

Kappler, C., & Hohagen, F. (2003). Psychosocial aspects of insomnia: Results of a study in general practice. *European Archives of Psychiatry and Clinical Neuroscience, 253,* 49-52.

Karande, S., Sawant, S., Kulkarni, M., Galvankar, P., & Sholapurwala, R. (2005). Comparison of cognition abilities between groups of children with specific learning disability having average, bright normal and superior nonverbal intelligence. *Indian Journal of Medical Sciences, 59,* 95-103.

Karl, A., Muhlnickel, W., Kurth, R., & Flor, H. (2004). Neuroelectric source imaging of steady-state movement-related cortical potentials in human upper extremity amputees with and without phantom limb pain. *Pain, 110,* 90-102.

Karnik-Henry, M.S., Wang, L., Barch, D.M., Harms, M.P., Campanella, C., & Csernansky, J.G. (2012). Medial temporal lobe structure and cognition in individuals with schizophrenia and in their non-psychotic siblings. *Schizophrenia Research, 138,* 128-135.

Karno, M.P., Beutler, L.E., & Harwood, T.M. (2002). Interactions between psychotherapy procedures and patient attributes that predict alcohol treatment effectiveness: A preliminary report. *Addictive Behaviors, 27,* 779-797.

Karran, E., Mercken, M., & De Strooper, B. (2011). The amyloid cascade hypothesis for Alzheimer's disease: An appraisal for the development of therapeutics. *Nature Reviews Drug Discovery, 10,* 698-712.

Kasai, K., Shenton, M.E., Salisbury, D.F., Onitsuka, T., Toner, S.K., Yurgelun-Todd, D., Kikinis, R., Jolesz, F.A., & McCarley, R.W. (2003). Differences and similarities in insular and temporal pole MRI gray matter volume abnormalities in first-episode schizophrenia and affective psychosis. *Archives of General Psychiatry, 60,* 1069-1077.

Kasari, C., & Patterson, S. (2012). Interventions addressing social impairment in autism. *Current Psychiatry Reports, 14,* 713-725.

Kates, W.R., Folley, B.S., Lanham, D.C., Capone, G.T., & Kaufmann, W.E. (2002). Cerebral growth in fragile X syndrome: Review and comparison with Down syndrome. *Microscopy Research and Technique, 57,* 159-167.

Katz, S.J., Conway, C.C., Hammen, C.L., Brennan, P.A., & Najman, J.M. (2011). Childhood social withdrawal, interpersonal impairment, and young adult depression: A mediational model. *Journal of Abnormal Child Psychology, 39,* 1227-1238.

Kawa, I., Carter, J.D., Joyce, P.R., Doughty, C.J., Frampton, C.M., Wells, J.E., Walsh, A.E., & Olds, R.J. (2005). Gender differences in bipolar disorder: Age of onset, course, comorbidity, and symptom presentation. *Bipolar Disorders, 7,* 119-125.

Kawasaki, Y., Suzuki, M., Takahashi, T., Nohara, S., McGuire, P.K., Seto, H., & Kurachi, M. (2008). Anomalous cerebral asymmetry in patients with schizophrenia demonstrated by voxel-based morphometry. *Biological Psychiatry, 63,* 793-800.

Kay, S.R., Fiszbein, A., & Opler, L.A. (1987). The positive and negative symptom scale (PANSS) for schizophrenia. *Schizophrenia Bulletin, 13,* 261-276.

Kaye, A.L., & Shea, M.T. (2000). Personality disorders, personality traits, and defense mechanisms measures. In H.A. Pincus, A.J. Rush, M.B. First, & L.E. McQueen (Eds.). *Handbook of psychiatric measures* (pp. 713-750). Washington, DC: American Psychiatric Association.

Kaye, W. (2008). Neurobiology of anorexia and bulimia nervosa. *Physiology and Behavior, 94,* 121-135.

Kaye, W.H., Bulik, C.M., Thornton, L., Barbarich, N., & Masters, K. (2004). Comorbidity of anxiety disorders with anorexia and bulimia nervosa. *American Journal of Psychiatry, 161,* 2215-2221.

Kayman, D.J., & Goldstein, M.F. (2012). Cognitive deficits in schizophrenia. *Current Translational Geriatrics and Experimental Gerontology Reports, 1,* 45-52.

Kazdin, A. E., & Weisz, J. R. (1998). Identifying and developing empirically supported child and adolescent treatments. *Journal of Consulting and Clinical Psychology, 66,* 19–36.

Kearney, C.A. (2001). *School refusal behavior in youth: A functional approach to assessment and treatment.* Washington, DC: American Psychological Association.

Kearney, C.A. (2005). *Social anxiety and social phobia in youth: Characteristics, assessment, and psychological treatment.* New York: Springer.

Kearney, C.A. (2008). School absenteeism and school refusal behavior in youth: A contemporary review. *Clinical Psychology Review, 28,* 451-471.

Kearney, C.A., & Albano, A.M. (2004). The functional profiles of school refusal behavior: Diagnostic aspects. *Behavior Modification, 28,* 147-161.

Kearney, C.A., Albano, A.M., Eisen, A.R., Allan, W.D., & Barlow, D.H. (1997). The phenomenology of panic disorder in youngsters: An empirical study of a clinical sample. *Journal of Anxiety Disorders, 11,* 49-62.

Kearney, C.A., Alvarez, K., & Vecchio, J. (2005). 3-5-10-15 method for spelling. In M. Hersen, A.M. Gross, & R.S. Drabman (Eds.), *Encyclopedia of behavior modification and cognitive behavior therapy: Vol. II. Child clinical applications* (pp. 1068-1070). Thousand Oaks, CA: Sage.

Kearney, C.A., Durand, V.M., & Mindell, J.A. (1995). It's not where but how you live: Choice and adaptive/ maladaptive behavior in persons with severe handicaps. *Journal of Developmental and Physical Disabilities, 7,* 11-24.

Kearney, P.M., Whelton, M., Reynolds, K., Whelton, K., & He, J. (2004). Worldwide prevalence of hypertension: A systematic review. *Journal of Hypertension, 22,* 11-19.

Keck, P.E. (2006). Long-term management strategies to achieve optimal function in patients with bipolar disorder. *Journal of Clinical Psychiatry, 67 (Suppl. 9),* 19-24, 36-42.

Keck Seeley, S.M., Perosa, S.L., & Perosa, L.M. (2004). A validation study of the Adolescent Dissociative Experiences Scale. *Child Abuse and Neglect, 28,* 755-769.

Keel, P.K., & Brown, T.A. (2010). Update on course and outcome in eating disorders. *International Journal of Eating Disorders, 43,* 195-204.

Keel, P.K., Brown, T.A., Holland, L.A., & Bodell, L.P. (2012). Empirical classification of eating disorders. *Annual Review of Clinical Psychology, 8,* 381-404.

Keel, P.K., & Haedt, A. (2008). Evidence-based psychosocial treatments for eating problems and eating disorders. *Journal of Clinical Child and Adolescent Psychology, 37,* 39-61.

Keel, P.K., & Klump, K.L. (2003). Are eating disorders culture-bound syndromes? Implications for conceptualizing their etiology. *Psychological Bulletin, 129,* 747-769.

Keeley, P., Creed, F., Tomenson, B., Todd, C., Borglin, G., & Dickens, C. (2008). Psychosocial predictors of health-related quality of life and health service utilization in people with chronic low back pain. *Pain, 135,* 142-150.

Keen, D.V., Reid, F.D., & Arnone, D. (2010). Autism, ethnicity and maternal immigration. *British Journal of Psychiatry, 196,* 274-281.

Keenan, N.L., & Rosendorf, K.A. (2011). Prevalence of hypertension and controlled hypertension—United States, 2005-2008. *Morbidity and mortality Weekly Report, 60,* 94-97.

Keenan-Miller, D., & Miklowitz, D.J. (2011). Interpersonal functioning in pediatric bipolar disorder. *Clinical Psychology: Science and Practice, 18,* 342-356.

Kehagia, A.A., Barker, R.A., & Robbins, T.W. (2010). Neuropsychological and clinical heterogeneity of cognitive impairment and dementia in patients with Parkinson's disease. *Lancet Neurology, 9,* 1200-1213.

Kelley, M.L., Braitman, A., Henson, J.M., Schroeder, V., Ladage, J., & Gumienny, L. (2010). Relationships among depressive mood symptoms and parent and peer relations in collegiate children of alcoholics. *American Journal of Orthopsychiatry, 80,* 204-212.

Kelly, B.D. (2005). Erotomania: Epidemiology and management. *CNS Drugs, 19,* 657-669.

Kelly, J.F., Kahler, C.W., & Humphreys, K. (2010). Assessing why substance use disorder patients drop out from or refuse to attend 12-step mutual-help groups: The "REASONS" questionnaire. *Addiction Research and Theory, 18,* 316-325.

Kelly, J.F., & Moos, R. (2003). Dropout from 12-step self-help groups: Prevalence, predictors, and counteracting treatment influences. *Journal of Substance Abuse Treatment, 24,* 241-250.

Kemp, D.E., Gao, K., Ganocy, S.J., Elhaj, O., Bilali, S.R., Conroy, C., Findling, R.L., & Calabrese, J.R. (2009). A 6-month, double-blind, maintenance trial of lithium monotherapy versus the combination of lithium and divalproex for rapid-cycling bipolar disorder and co-occurring substance abuse or dependence. *Journal of Clinical Psychiatry, 70,* 113-121.

Kendler, K. S. (2005). Psychiatric genetics: A methodological critique. *American Journal of Psychiatry, 162,* 3-11.

Kendler, K.S., Aggen, S.H., Knudsen, G.P., Roysamb, E., Neale, M.C., & Reichborn-Kjennerud, T. (2011). The structure of genetic and environmental risk factors for syndromal and subsyndromal common DSM-IV Axis I and all Axis II disorders. *American Journal of Psychiatry, 168,* 29-39.

Kendler, K.S., Aggen, S.H., & Patrick, C.J. (2012). A multivariate twin study of the DSM-IV criteria for antisocial personality disorder. *Biological Psychiatry, 71,* 247-253.

Kendler, K.S., Chen, X., Dick, D., Maes, H., Gillespie, N., Neale, M.C., & Riley, B. (2012). Recent advances in the genetic epidemiology and molecular genetics of substance use disorders. *Nature Neuroscience, 15,* 181-189.

Kendler, K.S., Kuhn, J., & Prescott, C.A. (2004). The interrelationship of neuroticism, sex, and stressful life events in the prediction of episodes of major depression. *American Journal of Psychiatry, 161,* 631-636.

Kendler, K. S., Myers, J., & Prescott, C. A. (2005). Sex differences in the relationship between social support and risk for major depression: A longitudinal study of opposite-sex twin pairs. *American Journal of Psychiatry, 162,* 250-256.

Kendler, K.S., Neale, M.C., Kessler, R.C., Heath, A.C., & Eaves, L.J. (1992). The genetic epidemiology of phobias in women: The interrelationship of agoraphobia, social phobia, situational phobia, and simple phobia. *Archives of General Psychiatry, 49,* 273-281.

Kendler, K.S., & Prescott, C.A. (1999). A population-based twin study of lifetime major depression in men and women. *Archives of General Psychiatry, 56,* 39-44.

Kendrick, D., Barlow, J., Hampshire, A., Polnay, L., & Stewart-Brown, S. (2007). Parenting interventions for the prevention of unintentional injuries in childhood. *Cochrane Database of Systematic Reviews, 17.*

Kennedy, N., Boydell, J., van Os, J., & Murray, R.M. (2004). Ethnic differences in first clinical presentation of bipolar disorder: Results from an epidemiological study. *Journal of Affective Disorders, 83,* 161-168.

Kenny, P.J. (2011). Common cellular and molecular mechanisms in obesity and drug addiction. *Nature Reviews Neuroscience, 12,* 638-651.

Kennedy, R.E., Howard, G., Go, R.C., Rothwell, P.M., Tiwari, H.K., Feng, R., McClure, L.A., Prineas, R.J., Banerjee, A., & Arnett, D.K. (2012). Association between family risk of stroke and myocardial infarction with prevalent risk factors and coexisting diseases. *Stroke, 43,* 974-979.

Kent, J.E., & Rauch, S.L. (2009). Neuroimaging studies of anxiety disorders. In D.S. Charney & E.J. Nestler (Eds.), *Neurobiology of mental illness* (pp. 703-730). New York: Oxford.

Kertesz, S.G., Horton, N.J., Friedmann, P.D., Saitz, R., & Samet, J.H. (2003). Slowing the revolving door: Stabilization programs reduce homeless persons' substance use after detoxification. *Journal of Substance Abuse Treatment, 24,* 197-207.

Kessler, K.C., Sonnega, A., Bromet, E., Hughes, M., & Nelson, C.B. (1995). Posttraumatic stress disorder in the National Comorbidity Survey. *Archives of General Psychiatry, 52,* 1048-1060.

Kessler, R.C. (2002). Epidemiology of depression. In I.H. Gotlib & C.L. Hammen (Eds.), *Handbook of depression* (pp. 23-42). New York: Guilford.

Kessler, R.C. (2003). Epidemiology of women and depression. *Journal of Affective Disorders, 74,* 5-13.

Kessler, R.C., Adler, L.A., Barkley, R., Biederman, J., Conners, C.K., Faraone, S.V., Greenhill, L.L., Jaeger, S., Secnik, K., Spencer, T., Ustun, T.B., & Zaslavsky, A.M. (2005). Patterns and predictors of attention-deficit/hyperactivity disorder persistence into adulthood: Results from the National Comorbidity Survey Replication. *Biological Psychiatry, 57,* 1442-1451.

Kessler, R.C., Amminger, G.P., Aguilar-Gaxiola, S., Alonso, J., Lee, S., & Ustun, T.B. (2007). Age of onset of mental disorders: A review of recent literature. *Current Opinion in Psychiatry, 20,* 359-364.

Kessler, R.C., Angermeyer, M., Anthony, J.C., de Graaf, R., Demyttenaere, K., Gasquet, I., de Girolamo, G., Gluzman, S., Gureje, O., Haro, J.M., Kawakami, N., Karam, A., Levinson, D., Medina Mora, M.E., Oakley Browne, M.A., Posada-Villa, J., Stein, D.J., Adley Tsang, C.H., Aguilar-Gaxiola, S., Alonso, J., Lee, S., Heeringa, S., Pennell, B.E., Berglund, P., Gruber, M.J., Petukhova, M., Chatterji, S., & Ustun, T.B. (2007). Lifetime prevalence and age-of-onset distributions of mental disorders in the World Health Organization's World Mental Health Survey Initiative. *World Psychiatry, 6,* 168-176.

Kessler, R.C., Berglund, P., Demler, O., Jin, R., Koretz, D., Merikangas, K.R., Rush, A.J., Walters, E.E., & Wang, P.S. (2003). The epidemiology of major depressive disorder: Results from the National Comorbidity Survey Replication (NCS-R). *Journal of the American Medical Association, 289,* 3095-3105.

Kessler, R.C., Berglund, P., Demler, O., Jin, R., Merikangas, K.R., & Walters, E.E. (2005). Lifetime prevalence and age-of-onset distributions of DSM-IV disorders in the National Comorbidity Survey Replication. *Archives of General Psychiatry, 62,* 593-602.

Kessler, R.C., Chiu, W.T., Demler, O., & Walters, E.E. (2005). Prevalence, severity, and comorbidity of 12-month DSM-IV disorders in the National Comorbidity Survey Replication. *Archives of General Psychiatry, 62,* 617-627.

Kessler, R.C., Galea, S., Gruber, M.J., Sampson, N.A., Ursano, R.J., & Wessely, S. (2008). Trends in mental illness and suicidality after Hurricane Katrina. *Molecular Psychiatry, 13,* 374-384.

Kessler, R.C., McGonagle, K.A., Zhao, S., Nelson, C.B., Hughes, M., Eshleman, S., Wittchen, H., & Kendler, K.S. (1994). Lifetime and 12-month prevalence of DSM-III-R psychiatric disorders in the United States: Results from the National Comorbidity Survey. *Archives of General Psychiatry, 51,* 8-19.

Kessler, R.C., & Wang, P.S. (2010). Epidemiology of depression. In I.H. Gotlib & C.L. Hammen (Eds.), *Handbook of depression* (2nd ed.) (pp. 5-22). New York: Guilford.

Kessler, R.C., Zhao, S., Katz, S.J., Kouzis, A.C., Frank, R.G., Edlund, M., & Leaf, P. (1999). Past-year use of outpatient services for psychiatric problems in the National Comorbidity Survey. *American Journal of Psychiatry, 156,* 115-123.

Kety, S.S., Wender, P.H., Jacobsen, B., Ingraham, L.J., Jansson, L., Faber, B., & Kinney, D.K. (1994). Mental illness in the biological and adoptive relatives of schizophrenic adoptees: Replication of the Copenhagen study in the rest of Denmark. *Archives of General Psychiatry, 51,* 443-455.

Khalifa, N., & Hardie, T. (2005). Possession and jinn. *Journal of the Royal Society of Medicine, 98,* 351-353.

Khantzian, E.J., Golden-Schulman, S.J., & McAuliffe, W.E. (2004). Group therapy. In M. Galanter & H.D. Kleber (Eds.), *Textbook of substance abuse treatment* (3rd ed.; pp. 391-403). Washington, DC: American Psychiatric Press.

Khashan, A.S., Abel, K.M., McNamee, R., Pedersen, M.G., Webb, R.T., Baker, P.N., Kenny, L.C., & Mortensen, P.B. (2008). Higher risk of offspring schizophrenia following antenatal maternal exposure to severe adverse life events. *Archives of General Psychiatry, 65,* 146-152.

Khouzam, H.R., El-Gabalawi, F., Pirwani, N., & Priest, F. (2004). Asperger's disorder: A review of its diagnosis and treatment. *Comprehensive Psychiatry, 45,* 184-191.

Kiehl, K.A., & Sinnott-Armstrong, W.P. (Eds.). (2013). *Handbook on psychopathy and law.* New York: Oxford.

Kieling, R., & Rohde, L.A. (2010). ADHD in children and adults: Diagnosis and prognosis. In C. Stanford & R. Tannock (Eds.), *Behavioral neuroscience of attention deficit hyperactivity disorder and its treatment* (pp. 1-16). Berlin: Springer-Verlag.

Kiesner, J., Poulin, F., & Dishion, T.J. (2010). Adolescent substance use with friends: Moderating and mediating effects of parental monitoring and peer activity contexts. *Merrill Palmer Quarterly, 56,* 529-556.

Kihlstrom, J.F. (2005). Dissociative disorders. *Annual Review of Clinical Psychology, 1,* 227-253.

Kikuchi, M., Komuro, R., Oka, H., Kidani, T., Hanaoka, A., & Koshino, Y. (2005). Panic disorder with and without agoraphobia: Comorbidity within a half year of the onset of panic disorder. *Psychiatry and Clinical Neurosciences, 59,* 639-643.

Kilian, S., Brown, W.S., Hallam, B.J., McMahon, W., Lu, J., Johnson, M., Bigler, E.D., & Lainhart, J. (2008). Regional callosal morphology in autism and macrocephaly. *Developmental Neuropsychology, 33,* 74-99.

Kim, D., Irwin, K.S., & Khoshnood, K. (2009). Expanded access to naloxone: Options for critical response to the epidemic of opioid overdose mortality. *American Journal of Public Health, 99,* 402-407.

Kim, J., Cicchetti, D., Rogosch, F.A., & Manly, J.T. (2009). Child maltreatment and trajectories of personality and behavioral functioning: Implications for the development of personality disorder. *Development and Psychopathology, 21,* 889-912.

King, D.C., Abram, K.M., Romero, E.G., Washburn, J.J., Welty, L.J., & Teplin, L.A. (2011). Childhood maltreatment and psychiatric disorders among detained youths. *Psychiatric Services, 62,* 1430-1438.

King, S.M., Tsai, J.L., & Chentsova-Dutton, Y. (2002). Psychophysiological studies of emotion and psychopathology. In J.N. Butcher (Ed.), *Clinical personality assessment: Practical approaches* (2nd ed.; pp. 56-75). New York: Oxford University Press.

Kingsberg, S., Shifren, J., Wekselman, K., Rodenberg, C., Koochaki, P., & Derogatis, L. (2007). Evaluation of the clinical relevance of benefits associated with transdermal testosterone treatment in postmenopausal women with hypoactive sexual desire disorder. *Journal of Sexual Medicine, 4,* 1001-1008.

Kingston, T., Dooley, B., Bates, A., Lawlor, E., & Malone, K. (2007). Mindfulness-based cognitive therapy for residual depressive symptoms. *Psychology and Psychotherapy: Theory, Research, and Practice, 80,* 193-203.

Kinscherff, R. (2010). Proposition: A personality disorder may nullify responsibility for a criminal act. *Journal of Law, Medicine and Ethics, 38,* 745-759.

Kirmayer, L.J., Groleau, D., Looper, K.J., & Dao, M.D. (2004). Explaining medically unexplained symptoms. *Canadian Journal of Psychiatry, 49,* 663-672.

Kirmayer, L.J., & Looper, K.J. (2006). Abnormal illness behaviour: Physiological, psychological and social dimensions of coping with distress. *Current Opinion in Psychiatry, 19,* 54-60.

Kirsch, L.G., & Becker, J.V. (2007). Emotional deficits in psychopathy and sexual sadism: Implications for violent and sadistic behavior. *Clinical Psychology Review, 27,* 904-922.

Klein, D.N., Kotov, R., & Bufferd, S.J. (2011). Personality and depression: Explanatory models and review of the evidence. *Annual Review of Clinical Psychology, 7,* 267-295.

Klein, D.N., Shankman, S.A., & Rose, S. (2008). Dysthymic disorder and double depression: Prediction of 10-year course trajectories and outcomes. *Journal of Psychiatric Research, 42,* 408-415.

Kleinman, A. (2012). The art of medicine: Culture, bereavement, and psychiatry. *Lancet, 379,* 608-609.

Kleinplatz, P.J. (2011). Arousal and desire problems: Conceptual, research and clinical considerations of the more things change the more they stay the same. *Sexual and Relationship Therapy, 26,* 3-15.

Klevens, J., & Whitaker, D.J. (2007). Primary prevention of child physical abuse and neglect: Gaps and promising directions. *Child Maltreatment, 12,* 364-377.

Kliem, S., Kroger, C., & Kosfelder, J. (2010). Dialectical behavior therapy for borderline personality disorder: A meta-analysis using mixed-effects modeling. *Journal of Consulting and Clinical Psychology, 78,* 936-951.

Klinger, E., Bouchard, S., Legeron, P., Roy, S., Lauer, F., Chemin, I., & Nugues, P. (2005). Virtual reality therapy versus cognitive behavior therapy for social phobia: A preliminary controlled study. *Cyberpsychology and Behavior, 8,* 76-88.

Klinger, L.G., Dawson, G., & Renner, P. (2003). Autistic disorder. In E.J. Mash & R.A. Barkley (Eds.), *Child psychopathology* (2nd ed.; pp. 409-454). New York: Guilford.

Klinnert, M.D., Nelson, H.S., Price, M.R., Adinoff, A.D., Leung, D.Y.M., & Mrazek, D.A. (2001). Onset and persistence of childhood asthma: Predictors from infancy. *Pediatrics, 108.* e69-e76.

Kloos, B., Hill, J., Thomas, E., Wandersman, A., Elias, M.J., & Dalton, J.H. (2012). *Community psychology: Linking individuals and communities* (3rd ed.). Belmont, CA: Cengage.

Kluft, R.P. (1999). An overview of the psychotherapy of dissociative identity disorder. *American Journal of Psychotherapy, 53,* 289-319.

Klump, K.L., Bulik, C.M., Kaye, W.H., Treasure, J., & Tyson, E. (2009). Academy for eating disorders position paper: Eating disorders are serious mental illnesses. *International Journal of Eating Disorders, 42,* 97-103.

Knight, R.A., & Cerce, D.D. (1999). Validation and revision of the Multidimensional Assessment of Sex and Aggression. *Psychologica Belgica, 39,* 135-161.

Knowles, R., McCarthy-Jones, S., & Rowse, G. (2011). Grandiose delusions: A review and theoretical integration of cognitive and affective perspectives. *Clinical Psychology Review, 31,* 684-696.

Koegel, L.K., Kuriakose, S., Singh, A.K., & Koegel, R.L. (2012). Improving generalization of peer socialization gains in inclusive school settings using initiations training. *Behavior Modification, 36,* 361-377.

Koelkebeck, K., Pedersen, A., Suslow, T., Kueppers, K.A., Arolt, V., & Ohrmann, P. (2010). Theory of mind in first-episode schizophrenia patients: Correlations with cognition and personality traits. *Schizophrenia Research, 119,* 115-123.

Koenigs, M., Baskin-Sommers, A., Zeier, J., & Newman, J.P. (2011). Investigating the neural correlates of psychopathy: A critical review. *Molecular Psychiatry, 16,* 792-799.

Koenigsberg, H.W., Siever, L.J., Lee, H., Pizzarello, S., New, A.S., Goodman, M., Cheng, H., Flory, J., & Prohovnik, I. (2009). Neural correlates of emotion processing in borderline personality disorder. *Psychiatry Research: Neuroimaging, 172,* 192-199.

Kohn, Y., & Lerer, B. (2002). Genetics of schizophrenia: A review of linkage findings. *Israel Journal of Psychiatry and Related Sciences, 39,* 340-351.

Kohnke, M.D. (2008). Approach to the genetics of alcoholism: A review based on pathophysiology. *Biochemical Pharmacology, 75,* 160-177.

Kokai, M., Fujii, S., Shinfuku, N., & Edwards, G. (2004). Natural disaster and mental health in Asia. *Psychiatry and Clinical Neurosciences, 58,* 110-116.

Kolla, N.J., & Brodie, J.D. (2012). Application of neuroimaging in relationship to competence to stand trial and insanity. In J.R. Simpson (Ed.), *Neuroimaging in forensic psychiatry: From the clinic to the courtroom* (pp. 147-162). New York: Wiley.

Kolodziej, M.E., & Johnson, B.T. (1996). Interpersonal contact and acceptance of persons with psychiatric disorders: A research synthesis. *Journal of Consulting and Clinical Psychology, 64,* 1387-1396.

Konrad, K., & Eickhoff, S.B. (2010). Is the ADHD brain wired differently? A review on structural and functional connectivity in attention deficit hyperactivity disorder. *Human Brain Mapping, 31,* 904-916.

Koob, G.F. (2011). Neurobiology of addiction. *Focus, 9,* 55-65.

Kopelman, M.D. (2010). Neurological and psychological forms of amnesia. In K. Myoshi, Y. Morimura, & K. Maeda (Eds.), *Neuropsychiatric disorders* (pp. 77-91). New York: Springer.

Korczyn, A.D., Vakhapova, V., & Grinberg, L.T. (2012). Vascular dementia. *Journal of the Neurological Sciences, 322,* 2-10.

Kotov, R., Gamez, W., Schmidt, F., & Watson, D. (2010). Linking "big" personality traits to anxiety, depressive, and substance use disorders: A meta-analysis. *Psychological Bulletin, 136,* 768-821.

Kovacs, M. (1996). *Children's Depression Inventory manual.* North Tonawanda, NY: Multi-Health Systems.

Kovel, C.C. (2000). Cross-cultural dimensions of sadomasochism in the psychoanalytic situation. *Journal of the American Academy of Psychoanalysis, 28,* 51-62.

Kozma, A., Mansell, J., & Beadle-Brown, J. (2009). Outcomes in different residential settings for people with intellectual disability: A systematic review. *American Journal on Intellectual and Developmental Disabilities, 114,* 193-222.

Krabbenborg, M.A.M., Danner, U.N., Larsen, J.K., van der Veer, N., van Elburg, A.A., de Ridder, D.T.D., Evers, C., Stice, E., & Engels, R.C.M.E. (2012). The Eating Disorder Diagnostic Scale: Psychometric features within a clinical population and a cut-off point to differentiate clinical patients from healthy controls. *European Eating Disorders Review, 20,* 315–320.

Krantz, D.S., & McCeney, M.K. (2002). Effects of psychological and social factors on organic disease: A critical assessment of research on coronary heart disease. *Annual Review of Psychology, 53,* 341-369.

Krem, M.M. (2004). Motor conversion disorders reviewed from a neuropsychiatric perspective. *Journal of Clinical Psychiatry, 65,* 783-790.

Kril, J.J., & Harper, C.G. (2012). Neuroanatomy and neuropathology associated with Korsakoff's syndrome. *Neuropsychology Review, 22,* 72-80.

Krugman, S.D., Lane, W.G., & Walsh, C.M. (2007). Update on child abuse prevention. *Current Opinion in Pediatrics, 19,* 711-718.

Ku, J.H., Park, D.W., Kim, S.W., & Paick, J.S. (2005). Cross-cultural differences for adapting translated five-item version of International Index of Erectile Function: Results of a Korean study. *Urology, 65,* 1179-1182.

Kupelian, V., Link, C.L., Rosen, R.C., & McKinlay, J.B. (2008). Socioeconomic status, not race/ethnicity, contributes to variation in the prevalence of erectile dysfunction: Results from the Boston Area Community Health (BACH) survey. *Journal of Sexual Medicine, 5,* 1325-1333.

Kupka, R.W., Luckenbaugh, D.A., Post, R.M., Leverich, G.S., & Nolen, W.A. (2003). Rapid and non-rapid cycling bipolar disorder: A meta-analysis of clinical studies. *Journal of Clinical Psychiatry, 64,* 1483-1494.

Kurasaki, K.S., Sue, S., Chun, C., & Gee, K. (2000). Ethnic minority intervention and treatment research. In J.F. Aponte & J. Wohl (Eds.), *Psychological intervention and cultural diversity* (2nd ed.; pp. 234-249). Boston: Allyn and Bacon.

Kuroki, N., Shenton, M.E., Salisbury, D.F., Hirayasu, Y., Onitsuka, T., Ersner-Hershfield, H., Yurgelun-Todd, D., Kikinis, R., Jolesz, F.A., & McCarley, R.W. (2006). Middle and inferior temporal gyrus gray matter volume abnormalities in first-episode schizophrenia: An MRI study. *American Journal of Psychiatry, 163,* 2103-2110.

Kurtz, P.F., Boelter, E.W., Jarmolowicz, D.P., Chin, M.D., & Hagopian, L.P. (2011). An analysis of functional communication training as an empirically supported treatment for problem behavior displayed by individuals with intellectual disabilities. *Research in Developmental Disabilities, 32,* 2935-2942.

Kutz, A., Marshall, E., Bernstein, A., & Zvolensky, M.J. (2010). Evaluating emotional sensitivity and tolerance factors in the prediction of panic-relevant responding to a biological challenge. *Journal of Anxiety Disorders, 24,* 16-22.

Kyle, U.G., & Pichard, C. (2006). The Dutch Famine of 1944-1945: A pathophysiological model of long-term consequences of wasting disease. *Current Opinion in Clinical Nutrition and Metabolic Care, 9,* 388-394.

Kymalainen, J.A., & Weisman de Mamani, A.G. (2008). Expressed emotion, communication deviance, and culture in families of patients with schizophrenia: A review of the literature. *Cultural Diversity and Ethnic Minority Psychology, 14,* 85-91.

Labarthe, D.R. (2011). *Epidemiology and prevention of cardiovascular diseases: A global challenge* (2nd ed.). Sudbury, MA: Jones and Bartlett.

Labbe, E.E., Murphy, L., & O'Brien, C. (1997). Psychosocial factors and predictors of headaches in college students. *Headache, 37,* 1-5.

Labrecque, J., Dugas, M.J., Marchand, A., & Letarte, A. (2006). Cognitive-behavioral therapy for comorbid generalized anxiety disorder and panic disorder with agoraphobia. *Behavior Modification, 30,* 383-410.

Lachs, M.S., & Pillemer, K. (2004). Elder abuse. *Lancet, 364,* 1263-1272.

Lackner, J.M., Morley, S., Dowzer, C., Mesmer, C., & Hamilton, S. (2004). Psychological treatments for irritable bowel syndrome: A systematic review and meta-analysis. *Journal of Consulting and Clinical Psychology, 72,* 1100-1113.

Lacy, T., & Mathis, M. (2003). Dissociative symptoms from combined treatment with sertraline and trazodone. *Journal of Neuropsychiatry and Clinical Neuroscience, 15,* 241-242.

Lad, S.P., Jobe, K.W., Polley, J., & Byrne, R.W. (2004). Munchhausen's syndrome in neurosurgery: Report of two cases and review of the literature. *Neurosurgery, 55,* 1436.

LaFerla, F.M., & Oddo, S. (2005). Alzheimer's disease: Aβ, tau and synaptic dysfunction. *Trends in Molecular Medicine, 11,* 170-176.

Lahey, B.B., Pelham, W.E., Loney, J., Lee, S.S., & Willcutt, E. (2005). Instability of the DSM-IV subtypes of ADHD from preschool through elementary school. *Archives of General Psychiatry, 62,* 896-902.

Lahey, B.B., & Waldman, I.D. (2012). Annual research review: Phenotypic and causal structure of conduct disorder in the broader context of prevalent forms of psychopathology. *Journal of Child Psychology and Psychiatry, 53,* 536-557.

Lai, M.K.P., Chen, C.P., Hope, T., & Esiri, M.M. (2010). Hippocampal neurofibrillary tangle changes and aggressive behaviour in dementia. *Clinical Neuroscience and Neuropathology, 21,* 1111-1115.

LaLumiere, R.T., Smith, K.C., & Kalivas, P.W. (2012). Neural circuit competition in cocaine-seeking: Roles of the infralimbic cortex and nucleus accumbens shell. *European Journal of Neuroscience, 35,* 614-622.

Lam, D.H., Hayward, P., Watkins, E.R., Wright, K., & Sham, P. (2005). Relapse prevention in patients with bipolar disorder: Cognitive therapy outcome after 2 years. *American Journal of Psychiatry, 162,* 324-329.

Lam, K., Marra, C., Salzinger, K. (2005). Social reinforcement of somatic versus psychological description of depressive events. *Behaviour Research and Therapy, 43,* 1203-1218.

Lam, K.S., Aman, M.G., & Arnold, L.E. (2005). Neurochemical correlates of autistic disorder: A review of the literature. *Research in Developmental Disabilities, 27,* 254-289.

Lam, R.W. (2012). *Depression* (2nd ed.). Oxford: Oxford University Press.

Lambert, M.V., Sierra, M., Phillips, M.L., & David, A.S. (2002). The spectrum of organic depersonalization: A review plus four new cases. *Journal of Neuropsychiatry and Clinical Neuroscience, 14,* 141-154.

Lamberti, P., Zoccolella, S., Armenise, E., Lamberti, S.V., Fraddosio, A., de Mari, M., Iliceto, G., & Livrea, P. (2005). Hyperhomocysteinemia in L-dopa treated Parkinson's disease patients: Effect of cobalamin and folate administration. *European Journal of Neurology, 12,* 365-368.

Lampley-Dallas, V.T. (2002). Research issues for minority dementia patients and their caregivers: What are the gaps in our knowledge base? *Alzheimer Disease and Associated Disorders, 16,* S46-S49.

Lancon, C., Auquier, P., Nayt, G., & Reine, G. (2000). Stability of the five-factor structure of the Positive and Negative Syndrome Scale (PANSS). *Schizophrenia Research, 42,* 231-239.

Lang, A.J. (2004). Treating generalized anxiety disorder with cognitive-behavioral therapy. *Journal of Clinical Psychiatry, 65 (Suppl. 13),* 14-19.

Lang, U.E., Puls, I., Muller, D.J., Strutz-Seebohm, N., & Gallinat, J. (2007). Molecular mechanisms of schizophrenia. *Cellular Physiology and Biochemistry, 20,* 687-702.

Langevin, R., Langevin, M., & Curnoe, S. (2007). Family size, birth order, and parental age among male paraphilics and sex offenders. *Archives of Sexual Behavior, 36,* 599-609.

Langevin, R., & Paitich, D. (2002). *Clarke Sex History Questionnaire for Males-Revised.* North Tonawanda, NY: Multi-Health Systems.

Langhinrichsen-Rohling, J., Friend, J., & Powell, A. (2009). Adolescent suicide, gender, and culture: A rate and risk factor analysis. *Aggression and Violent Behavior, 14,* 402-414.

Langstrom, N. (2010). The *DSM* diagnostic criteria for exhibitionism, voyeurism, and frotteurism. *Archives of Sexual Behavior, 39,* 317-324.

Langstrom, N., & Seto, M.C. (2006). Exhibitionistic and voyeuristic behavior in a Swedish national population survey. *Archives of Sexual Behavior, 35,* 427-435.

Lanius, R.A., Vermetten, E., Loewenstein, R.J., Brand, B., Schmahl, C., Bremner, J.D., & Spiegel, D. (2010). Emotion modulation in PTSD: Clinical and neurobiological evidence for a dissociative subtype. *American Journal of Psychiatry, 167,* 640-647.

Lansford, J.E., Malone, P.S., Dodge, K.A., Petit, G.S., & Bates, J.E. (2010). Developmental cascades of peer rejection, social information processing biases, and aggression during middle childhood. *Development and Psychopathology, 22,* 593-602.

Lapierre, C.B., Schwegler, A.F., & Labauve, B.J. (2007). Posttraumatic stress and depression symptoms in soldiers returning from combat operations in Iraq and Afghanistan. *Journal of Traumatic Stress, 20,* 933-943.

Lasky, G.B., & Riva, M.T. (2006). Confidentiality and privileged communication in group psychotherapy. *International Journal of Group Psychotherapy, 56,* 455-476.

Latimer, K., Wilson, P., Kemp, J., Thompson, L., Sim, F., Gillberg, C., Puckering, C., & Minnis, H. (2012). Disruptive behavior disorders: A systematic review of environmental antenatal and early years risk factors. *Child: Care, Health, and Development, 38,* 611-628.

Lau, A.S., & Weisz, J.R. (2003). Reported maltreatment among clinic-referred children: Implications for presenting problems, treatment attrition, and long-term outcomes. *Journal of the American Academy of Child and Adolescent Psychiatry, 42,* 1327-1334.

Lau, H.C., & Passingham, R.E. (2007). Unconscious activation of the cognitive control system in the human prefrontal cortex. *Journal of Neuroscience, 27,* 5805-5811.

Lau, J.Y., Sung, J., Hill, C., Henderson, C., Howden, C.W., & Metz, D.C. (2011). Systematic review of the epidemiology of complicated peptic ulcer disease: Incidence, recurrence, risk factors and mortality. *Digestion, 84,* 102-113.

Lauber, C., & Rossler, W. (2007). Stigma towards people with mental illness in developing countries in Asia. *International Review of Psychiatry, 19,* 157-178.

Laugeson, E.A., Frankel, F., Gantman, A., Dillon, A.R., & Mogil, C. (2012). Evidence-based social skills training for adolescents with autism spectrum disorders: The UCLA PEERS program. *Journal of Autism and Developmental Disorders, 42,* 1025-1036.

Laumann, E.O., Das, A., & Waite, L.J. (2008). Sexual dysfunction among older adults: Prevalence and risk factors from a nationally representative U.S. probability sample of men and women 57-85 years of age. *Journal of Sexual Medicine, 5,* 2300-2311.

Laumann, E.O., Paik, A., & Rosen, R.C. (1999). Sexual dysfunction in the United States: Prevalence and predictors. *Journal of the American Medical Association, 281,* 537-544.

Laurent, S.M., & Simons, A.D. (2009). Sexual dysfunction in depression and anxiety: Conceptualizing sexual dysfunction as part of an internalizing dimension. *Clinical Psychology Review, 29,* 573-585.

Lavi, T., & Solomon, Z. (2005). Palestinian youth of the Intifada: PTSD and future orientation. *Journal of the American Academy of Child and Adolescent Psychiatry, 44,* 1176-1183.

Law, S., & Liu, P. (2008). Suicide in China: Unique demographic patterns and relationship to depressive disorder. *Current Psychiatry Reports, 10,* 80-86.

Lawrence, A.A. (2003). Factors associated with satisfaction or regret following male-to-female sex reassignment surgery. *Archives of Sexual Behavior, 32,* 299-315.

Laws, D.R., & O'Donohue, W.T. (Eds.). (2008). *Sexual deviance: Theory, assessment, and treatment* (2nd ed.). New York: Guilford.

Leahy, R.L., Holland, S.J.F., & McGinn, L. (2012). *Treatment plans and interventions for depression and anxiety disorders* (2nd ed.). New York: Guilford.

Lebow, J., Sim, L.A., Erwin, P.J., & Murad, M.H. (2013). The effect of atypical antipsychotic medications in individuals with anorexia nervosa: A systematic review and meta-analysis. *International Journal of Eating Disorders, 46,* 332-339.

LeCroy, C.W. (Ed.). (2008). *Handbook of evidence-based treatment manuals for children and adolescents* (2nd ed.). New York: Oxford.

Ledgerwood, D.M., Goldberger, B.A., Risk, N.K., Lewis, C.E., & Price, R.K. (2008). Comparison between self-report and hair analysis of illicit drug use in a community sample of middle-aged men. *Addictive Behaviors, 33,* 1131-1139.

Lee, C., McGlashan, T.H., & Woods, S.W. (2005). Prevention of schizophrenia: Can it be achieved? *CNS Drugs, 19,* 193-206.

Lee, J.H., Jang, M.K., Lee, J.Y., Kim, S.M., Kim, K.H., Park, J.Y., Lee, J.H., Kim, H.Y., & Yoo, J.Y. (2005). Clinical predictors for delirium tremens in alcohol dependence. *Journal of Gastroenterology and Hepatology, 20,* 1833-1837.

Lee, J.K.P., Jackson, H.J., Pattison, P., & Ward, T. (2002). Developmental risk factors for sexual offending. *Child Abuse and Neglect, 26,* 73-92.

Lee, Y., & Lin, P.-Y. (2010). Association between serotonin transporter gene polymorphism and eating disorders: A meta-analytic study. *International Journal of Eating Disorders, 43,* 498-504.

Leff, J., Vearnals, S., Brewin, C.R., Wolff, G., Alexander, B., Asen, E., Dayson, D., Jones, E., Chisholm, D., & Everitt, B. (2000). The London depression intervention trial: Randomised controlled trial of antidepressants v. couple therapy in the treatment and maintenance of people with depression living with a partner: Clinical outcome and costs. *British Journal of Psychiatry, 177,* 95-100.

Lehericy, S., Sharman, M.A., Santos, C.L.D., Paquin, R., & Gallea, C. (2012). Magnetic resonance imaging of the substantia nigra in Parkinson's disease. *Movement Disorders, 27,* 822-830.

Leifker, F.R., Patterson, T.L., Heaton, R.K., & Harvey, P.D. (2011). Validating measures of real-world outcome: The results of the VALERO expert survey and RAND panel. *Schizophrenia Bulletin, 37,* 334-343.

Lejuez, C.W., Hopko, D.R., Acierno, R., Daughters, S.B., & Pagoto, S.L. (2011). Ten year revision of the brief behavioral activation treatment for depression: Revised treatment manual. *Behavior Modification, 35,* 111-161.

Lejuez, C.W., Hopko, D.R., & Hopko, S.D. (2001). A brief behavioral activation treatment for depression: Treatment manual. *Behavior Modification, 25,* 255-286.

Lemay, R.A. (2009). Deinstitutionalization of people with developmental disabilities: A review of the literature. *Canadian Journal of Community Mental Health, 28,* 181-194.

Lemmens, G.M.D., Eisler, I., Buysse, A., Heene, E., & Demyttenaere, K. (2009). The effects on mood of adjunctive single-family and multi-family group therapy in the treatment of hospitalized patients with major depression: A 15-month follow-up study. *Psychotherapy and Psychosomatics, 78,* 98-105.

Lemstra, M., Bennett, N., Nannapaneni, U., Neudorf, C., Warren, L., Kershaw, T., & Scott, C. (2010). A systematic review of school-based marijuana and alcohol prevention programs targeting adolescents aged 10-15 years. *Addiction Research and Theory, 18,* 84-96.

Lende, D.H., & Smith, E.O. (2002). Evolution meets biopsychosociality: An analysis of addictive behavior. *Addiction, 97,* 447-458.

Lenz, B., Frieling, H., Kornhuber, J., Bleich, S., & Hillemacher, T. (2011). Genetics of the androgen receptor influences craving of men in alcohol withdrawal. *European Psychiatry, 26,* 73.

Lenzenweger, M.F., Lane, M.C., Loranger, A.W., & Kessler, R.C. (2007). DSM-IV personality disorders in the National Comorbidity Survey Replication. *Biological Psychiatry, 62,* 553-564.

Leonard, H., & Wen, X. (2002). The epidemiology of mental retardation: Challenges and opportunities in the new millennium. *Mental Retardation and Developmental Disabilities Research Reviews, 8,* 117-134.

Leonardo, E.D., & Hen, R. (2006). Genetics of affective and anxiety disorders. *Annual Review of Psychology, 57,* 117-137.

Lester, B.M., & Tronick, E.Z. (2004). History and description of the Neonatal Intensive Care Unit Network Neurobehavioral Scale. *Pediatrics, 113,* 634-640.

LeVay, S., & Baldwin, J. (2012). *Human sexuality* (4th ed.). Sunderland, MA: Sinauer Associates

Levensen, J.S., Becker, J., & Morin, J.W. (2008). The relationship between victim age and gender crossover among sex offenders. *Sexual Abuse, 20,* 43-60.

Levenson, J.S. (2003). Policy interventions designed to combat sexual violence: Community notification and civil commitment. *Journal of Child Sexual Abuse, 12,* 17-52.

Levin, R., & Nielsen, T. (2009). Nightmares, bad dreams, and emotional dysregulation: A review and new neurocognitive model of dreaming. *Current Directions in Psychological Science, 18,* 84-88.

Levin, R.J. (2007). Single case studies in human sexuality—Important or idiosyncratic? *Sexual and Relationship Therapy, 22,* 457-469.

Levine, M.P., & Murnen, S.K. (2009). "Everybody knows that mass media are/are not [pick one] a cause of eating disorders:" A critical review of evidence for a causal link between media, negative body image, and distorted eating in females. *Journal of Social and Clinical Psychology, 28,* 9-42.

Levit, K.R., Kassed, C.A., Coffey, R.M., Mark, T.L., McKusick, D.R., King, E.C., Vandivort-Warren, R., Buck, J.A., Ryan, K., & Stranges, E. (2008). *Projections of national expenditures for mental health services and substance abuse treatment 2004-2014.* Rockville, MD: U.S. Department of Health and Human Services.

Levy, A., & Perry, A. (2011). Outcomes in adolescents and adults with autism: A review of the literature. *Research in Autism Spectrum Disorders, 5,* 1271-1282.

Levy, K.N., Edell, W.S., & McGlashan, T.H. (2007). Depressive experiences in inpatients with borderline personality disorder. *Psychiatric Quarterly, 78,* 129-143.

Lewandowski, K.E., DePaola, J., Camsari, G.B., Cohen, B.M., & Ongur, D. (2009). Tactile, olfactory, and gustatory hallucinations in psychotic disorders: A descriptive study. *Annals of the Academy of Medicine of Singapore, 38,* 383-387.

Lewis, A.J., Dennerstein, M., & Gibbs, P.M. (2008). Short-term psychodynamic psychotherapy: Review of recent process and outcome studies. *Australian and New Zealand Journal of Psychiatry, 42,* 445-455.

Lezak, M.D., Howieson, D.B., Bigler, E.D., & Tranel, D. (2012). *Neuropsychological Assessment* (5th ed.). New York: Oxford University Press.

Li, X., Frye, M., & Shelton, R.C. (2012). Review of pharmacological treatment in mood disorders and future directions for drug development. *Neuropsychopharmacology, 37,* 77-101.

Liberzon, I., & Sripada, C.S. (2008). The functional neuroanatomy of PTSD: A critical review. *Progress in Brain Research, 167,* 151-169.

Licence, K. (2004). Promoting and protecting the health of children and young people. *Child Care Health and Development, 30,* 623-635.

Lichtenstein, P., Yip, B.H., Bjork, C., Pawitan, Y., Cannon, T.D., Sullivan, P.F., & Hultman, C.M. (2009). Common genetic determinants of schizophrenia and bipolar disorder in Swedish families: A population-based study. *Lancet, 373,* 234-239.

Liddle, H.A. (2010). Multidimensional family therapy: A science-based treatment system. *Australian and New Zealand Journal of Family Therapy, 31,* 133-148.

Lieb, R., Meinlschmidt, G., & Araya, R. (2007). Epidemiology of the association between somatoform disorders and anxiety and depressive disorders: An update. *Psychosomatic Medicine, 69,* 860-863.

Lieberman, J.A., Stroup, T.S., McEvoy, J.P., Swartz, M.S., Rosenheck, R.A., Perkins, D.O., Keefe, R.S.E., Davis, S.M., Davis, C.E., Lebowitz, B.D., Severe, J., & Hsiao, J.K. (2005). Effectiveness of antipsychotic drugs in patients with chronic schizophrenia. *New England Journal of Medicine, 353,* 1209-1223.

Liechty, A., & Quallich, S.A. (2008). Teaching a patient to successfully operate a penile prosthesis. *Urologic Nursing, 28,* 106-108.

Liederman, J., Kantrowitz, L., & Flannery, K. (2005). Male vulnerability to reading disability is not likely to be a myth: A call for new data. *Journal of Learning Disabilities, 38,* 109-129.

Lifschytz, T., Segman, R., Shalom, G., Lerer, B., Gur, E., Golzer, T., & Newman, M.E. (2006). Basic mechanisms of augmentation of antidepressant effects with thyroid hormone. *Current Drug Targets, 7,* 203-210.

Lilienfeld, S.O., Ammirati, R., & David, M. (2012). Distinguishing science from pseudoscience in school psychology: Science and scientific thinking as safeguards against human error. *Journal of School Psychology, 50,* 7-36.

Lilienfeld, S.O., Wood, J.M., & Garb, H.N. (2000). The scientific status of projective techniques. *Psychological Science in the Public Interest, 1,* 27-66.

Lin, J.H., Rin, R.T., Tai, C.T., Hsieh, C.L., Hsiao, S.F., & Liu, C.K. (2003). Prediction of poststroke dementia. *Neurology, 61,* 343-348.

Lindberg, L., & Hjern, A. (2003). Risk factors for anorexia nervosa: A national cohort study. *International Journal of Eating Disorders, 34,* 397-408.

Linehan, M.M., & Kehrer, C.A. (1993). Borderline personality disorder. In D.H. Barlow (Ed.), *Clinical handbook of psychological disorders: A step-by-step treatment manual* (2nd ed.; pp. 396-441). New York: Guilford.

Ling, C.Y.M., Mak, W.W.S., & Cheng, J.N.S. (2010). Attribution model of stigma toward children with autism in Hong Kong. *Journal of Applied Research in Intellectual Disabilities, 23,* 237-249.

Linhorst, D.M. (2006). *Empowering people with severe mental illness: A practical guide.* New York: Oxford.

Links, P.S., & Eynan, R. (2013). The relationship between personality disorders and Axis I psychopathology: Deconstructing comorbidity. *Annual Review of Clinical Psychology, 9,* 529-554.

Linning, L.M., & Kearney, C.A. (2004). Posttraumatic stress disorder in maltreated youth: A study of diagnostic comorbidity and child factors. *Journal of Interpersonal Violence, 19,* 1087-1101.

Linton, S.J. (2000). A review of psychological risk factors in back and neck pain. *Spine, 25,* 1148-1156.

Lipsanen, T., Korkeila, J., Peltola, P., Jarvinen, J., Langen, K., & Lauerma, H. (2004). Dissociative disorders among psychiatric patients: Comparison with a nonclinical sample. *European Psychiatry, 19,* 53-55.

Lipton, R.B., & Bigal, M.E. (2005). The epidemiology of migraine. *American Journal of Medicine, 118 (Suppl. 1),* 3-10.

Litzinger, S., & Gordon, K.C. (2005). Exploring relationships among communication, sexual satisfaction, and marital satisfaction. *Journal of Sex and Marital Therapy, 31,* 409-424.

Livesley, W.J., & Jang, K.L. (2008). The behavioral genetics of personality disorder. *Annual Review of Clinical Psychology, 4,* 247-274.

Lloyd-Evans, B., Slade, M., Jagielska, D., & Johnson, S. (2009). Residential alternatives to acute psychiatric hospital admission: Systematic review. *British Journal of Psychiatry, 195,* 109-117.

Lobbestael, J., Arntz, A., & Sieswerda, S. (2005). Schema modes and childhood abuse in borderline and antisocial personality disorders. *Journal of Behavior Therapy and Experimental Psychiatry, 36,* 240-253.

Lobello, K., Ryan, J.M., Liu, E., Rippon, G., & Black, R. (2012). Targeting beta amyloid: A clinical review of immunotherapeutic approaches in Alzheimer's disease. *International Journal of Alzheimer's Disease, 2012,* 1-14.

Lobmaier, P.P., Kunoe, N., Gossop, M., & Waal, H. (2011). Naltrexone depot formulations for opioid and alcohol dependence: A systematic review. *CNS Neuroscience and Therapeutics, 17,* 629-636.

Loeber, R., & Burke, J.D. (2011). Developmental pathways in juvenile externalizing and internalizing problems. *Journal of Research on Adolescence, 21,* 34-46.

Loftus, E.F. (2003). Make-believe memories. *American Psychologist, 58,* 867-873.

Lohr, I., & Cook, B.L. (2003). Mood disorders: Bipolar disorders. In M. Hersen & S.M. Turner (Eds.), *Adult psychopathology and diagnosis* (4th. ed.; pp. 313-355). New York: Wiley.

Lopez-Figueroa, A.L., Norton, C.S., Lopez-Figueroa, M.O., Armellini-Dodel, D., Burke, S., Akil, H., Lopez, J.F., & Watson, S.J. (2004). Serotonin 5-HT1A, 5-HT1B, and 5-HT2A Receptor mRNA expression in subjects with major depression, bipolar disorder, and schizophrenia. *Biological Psychiatry, 55,* 225-233.

Lord, S.A., & Iudice, J. (2012). Social workers in private practice: A descriptive study of what they do. *Clinical Social Work Journal, 40,* 85-94.

Lorentz, W.J., Scanlan, J.M., & Borson, S. (2002). Brief screening tests for dementia. *Canadian Journal of Psychiatry, 47,* 723-732.

Lorenzetti, V., Allen, N.B., Fornito, A., & Yucel, M. (2009). Structural brain abnormalities in major depressive disorder: A selective review of recent MRI studies. *Journal of Affective Disorders, 117*, 1-17.

Louria, D. (2004). Mandatory drug testing of high school athletes: Unethical evaluation, unethical policy. *American Journal of Bioethics, 4*, 35-36.

Lovejoy, M.C., Graczyk, P.A., O'Hare, E., & Neuman, G. (2000). Maternal depression and parenting behavior: A meta-analytic review. *Clinical Psychology Review, 20*, 561-592.

Low, N.C., Cui, L., & Merikangas, K.R. (2008). Specificity of familial transmission of anxiety and comorbid disorders. *Journal of Psychiatric Research, 42*, 596-604.

Lu, R.B., Ko, H.C., Lee, J.F., Lin, W.W., Huang, S.Y., Wang, T.J., Wu, Y.S., Lu, T.E., & Chou, Y.H. (2005). No alcoholism-protection effects of ADH1B*2 allele in antisocial alcoholics among Han Chinese in Taiwan. *Alcoholism: Clinical and Experimental Research, 29*, 2101-2107.

Luborsky, L., Rosenthal, R., Diguer, L., Andrusyna, T.P., Berman, J.S., Levitt, J.T., Seligman, D.A., & Krause, E.D. (2002). The dodo bird verdict is alive and well— mostly. *Clinical Psychology: Science and Practice, 9*, 2-12.

Lucantonio, F., Stalnaker, T.A., Shaham, Y., Niv, Y., & Schoenbaum, G. (2012). The impact of orbitofrontal dysfunction on cocaine addiction. *Nature Neuroscience, 15*, 358-366.

Luchsinger, J.A., & Mayeux, R. (2004). Dietary factors and Alzheimer's disease. *Lancet Neurology, 3*, 579-587.

Luchsinger, J.A., Tang, M.-X., Siddiqui, M., Shea, S., & Mayeux, R. (2004). Alcohol intake and risk of dementia. *Journal of the American Geriatrics Society, 52*, 540-546.

Luckasson, R., & Schalock, R.L. (2013). Defining and applying a functionality approach to intellectual disability. *Journal of Intellectual Disability Research, 57*, 657-668.

Lundstrom, M., Stenvall, M., & Olofsson, B. (2012). Symptom profile of postoperative delirium in patients with and without dementia. *Journal of Geriatric Psychiatry and Neurology, 25*, 162-169.

Lundvig, D., Lindersson, E., & Jensen, P.H. (2005). Pathogenic effects of α-synuclein aggregation. *Molecular Brain Research, 134*, 3-17.

Luoma, S., Hakko, H., Ollinen, T., Jarvelin, M.-R., & Lindeman, S. (2008). Association between age at onset and clinical features of schizophrenia. The Northern Finland 1966 birth cohort study. *European Psychiatry, 23*, 331-335.

Luoma, J.B., Twohig, M.P., Waltz, T., Hayes, S.C., Roget, N., Padilla, M., & Fisher, G. (2007). An investigation of stigma in individuals receiving treatment for substance abuse. *Addictive Behaviors, 32*, 1331-1346.

Luthar, S.S., Cicchetti, D., & Becker, B. (2000). The construct of resilience: A critical evaluation and guidelines for future work. *Child Development, 71*, 543-562.

Lykken, D.T. (1995). *The antisocial personalities.* Hillsdale, NJ: Erlbaum.

Lynam, D.R., & Widiger, T.A. (2007). Using a general model of personality to understand sex differences in the personality disorders. *Journal of Personality Disorders, 21*, 583-602.

Lynch, P., & Galbraith, K.M. (2003). Panic in the emergency room. *Canadian Journal of Psychiatry, 48*, 361-366.

Lynch, T.R., Trost, W.T., Salsman, N., & Linehan, M.M. (2007). Dialectical behavior therapy for borderline personality disorder. *Annual Review of Clinical Psychology, 3*, 181-205.

Lyneham, H.J., Abbott, M.J., & Rapee, R.M. (2007). Interrater reliability of the Anxiety Disorders Interview Schedule for DSM-IV: Child and parent version. *Journal of the American Academy of Child and Adolescent Psychiatry, 46*, 731-736.

Lynn, S.J., & Cardena, E. (2007). Hypnosis and the treatment of posttraumatic conditions: An evidence-based approach. *International Journal of Clinical and Experimental Hypnosis, 55*, 167-188.

Lysaker, P.H., Davis, L.W., Bryson, G.J. & Bell, M.D. (2009). Effects of cognitive behavioral therapy on work outcomes in vocational rehabilitation for participants with schizophrenia spectrum disorders. *Schizophrenia Research, 107*, 186-191.

Lysaker, P.H., Dimaggio, G., Buck, K.D., Callaway, S.S., Salvatore, G., Carcione, A., Nicolo, G., & Stanghellini, G. (2011). Poor insight in schizophrenia: Links between different forms of metacognition with awareness of symptoms, treatment need, and consequences of illness. *Comprehensive Psychiatry, 52*, 253-260.

Ma, N., Liu, Y., Li, N., Wang, C.-X., Zhang, H., Jiang, X.-F., Xu, H.-S., Fu, X.-M., Hu, X., & Zhang, D.-R. (2010). Addiction related alteration in resting-state brain connectivity. *NeuroImage, 49*, 738-744.

Ma, S.H., & Teasdale, J.D. (2004). Mindfulness-based cognitive therapy for depression: Replication and exploration of differential relapse prevention effects. *Journal of Consulting and Clinical Psychology, 72*, 31-40.

Maaranen, P., Tanskanen, A., Honkalampi, K., Haatainen, K., Hintikka, J., & Viinamaki, H. (2005). Factors associated with pathological dissociation in the general population. *Australian and New Zealand Journal of Psychiatry, 39*, 387-394.

MacDonald, K., & MacDonald, T. (2009). Peas, please: A case report and neuroscientific review of dissociative amnesia and fugue. *Journal of Trauma and Dissociation, 10*, 420-435.

Machado, L.A., Azevedo, D.C., Capanema, M.B., Neto, T.N., & Cerceau, D.M. (2007). Client-centered therapy vs exercise therapy for chronic low back pain: A pilot randomized controlled trial in Brazil. *Pain Medicine, 8*, 251-258.

MacMahon, K.M.A., & Lip, G.Y.H. (2002). Psychological factors in heart failure: A review of the literature. *Archives of Internal Medicine, 162*, 509-516.

Madras, B.K., Compton, W.M., Avula, D., Stegbauer, T., Stein, J.B., & Clark, H.W. (2009). Screening, brief interventions, referral to treatment (SBIRT) for illicit drug and alcohol use at multiple healthcare sites: Comparison at intake and 6 months later. *Drug and Alcohol Dependence, 99*, 280-295.

Maes, M., De Vos, N., Van Hunsel, F., Van West, D., Westenberg, H., Cosyns, P., & Neels, H. (2001). Pedophilia is accompanied by increased plasma concentrations of catecholamines, in particular epinephrine. *Psychiatry Research, 103*, 43-49.

Magarinos, M., Zafar, U., Nissenson, K., & Blanco, C. (2002). Epidemiology and treatment of hypochondriasis. *CNS Drugs, 16*, 9-22.

Maggi, M. (Ed.). (2012). *Hormonal therapy for male sexual dysfunction.* Hoboken, NJ: Wiley.

Magnusson, A., & Boivin, D. (2003). Seasonal affective disorder: An overview. *Chronobiology International, 20*, 189-207.

Mahan, A.L., & Ressler, K.J. (2012). Fear conditioning, synaptic plasticity, and the amygdala: Implications for posttraumatic stress disorder. *Trends in Neuroscience, 35*, 24-35.

Mahendra, N., Scullion, A., & Hamerschlag, C. (2011). Cognitive-linguistic interventions for persons with dementia: A practitioner's guide to 3 evidence-based techniques. *Topics in Geriatric Rehabilitation, 27*, 278-288.

Mai, F. (2004). Somatization disorder: A practical review. *Canadian Journal of Psychiatry, 49*, 652-662.

Maier, S.F., & Watkins, L.R. (2005). Stressor controllability and learned helplessness: The roles of the dorsal raphe nucleus, serotonin, and corticotropin-releasing factor. *Neuroscience and Biobehavioral Reviews, 29*, 829-841.

Maj, M. (1999). Lithium prophylaxis of bipolar disorder in ordinary clinical conditions: Patterns of longterm outcome. In J.F. Goldberg & M. Harrow (Eds.), *Bipolar disorders: Clinical course and outcome* (pp. 21-37). Washington, DC: American Psychiatric Press.

Maki, P., Veijola, J., Jones, P.B., Murray, G.K., Koponen, H., Tienari, P., Miettunen, J., Tanskanen, P., Wahlberg, K.-E., Koskinen, J., Lauronen, E., & Isohanni, M. (2005). Predictors of schizophrenia: A review. *British Medical Bulletin, 73-74*, 1-15.

Malamuth, N. (1998). Revised Attraction to Sexual Aggression Scale. In C.M. Davis, W.L. Yarber, R. Bauserman, G. Schreer, & S.L. Davis (Eds.), *Handbook of sexuality-related measures* (pp. 52-55). Thousand Oaks, CA: Sage.

Malatesta, V.J., & Adams, H.E. (2001). Sexual dysfunctions. In P.B. Sutker & H.E. Adams (Eds.), *Comprehensive handbook of psychopathology* (pp. 713-748). New York: Kluwer Academic/Plenum.

Maletsky, B.M. (2003). A serial rapist treated with behavioral and cognitive techniques and followed for 12 years. *Clinical Case Studies, 2*, 127-153.

Maletsky, B. M., & Steinhauser, C. (2002). A 25-year follow-up of cognitive/behavioral therapy with 7,275 sexual offenders. *Behavior Modification, 2*, 123-147.

Malhi, G.S., Green, M., Fagiolini, A., Peselow, E.D., & Kumari, V. (2008). Schizoaffective disorder: Diagnostic issues and future recommendations. *Bipolar Disorders, 10*, 215-230.

Malla, A., & Payne, J. (2005). First-episode psychosis: Psychopathology, quality of life, and functional outcome. *Schizophrenia Bulletin, 31*, 650-671.

Manassis, K. (2001). Child-parent relations: Attachment and anxiety disorders. In W.K. Silverman & P.D.A. Treffers (Eds.), *Anxiety disorders in children and adolescents: Research, assessment and intervention* (pp. 255-272). New York: Cambridge University Press.

Manly, J.J., & Mayeux, R. (2004). Ethnic differences in dementia and Alzheimer's disease. In N.B. Anderson, R.A. Bulatao, & B. Cohen (Eds.), *Critical perspectives on racial and ethnic differences in health in late life* (pp. 95-142). Washington, DC: National Academies Press.

Mandel, J.L., & Biancalana, V. (2004). Fragile X mental retardation syndrome: From pathogenesis to diagnostic issues. *Growth Hormone and IGF Research, 14*, S158-S165.

Mann, J.J., Apter, A., Bertolote, J., Beautrais, A., Currier, D., Haas, A., Hegerl, U., Lonnqvist, J., Malone, K., Marusic, A., Mchlum, L., Patton, G., Phillips, M., Rutz, W., Rihmer, Z., Schmidtke, A., Shaffer, D., Silverman, M., Takahashi, Y., Varnik, A., Wasserman, D., Yip, P., & Hendin, H. (2005). Suicide prevention strategies: A systematic review. *Journal of the American Medical Association, 294*, 2064-2074.

Mannie, Z.N., Barnes, J., Bristow, G.C., Harmer, C.J., & Cowen, P.J. (2009). Memory impairment in young women at increased risk of depression: Influence of cortisol and 5-HTT genotype. *Psychological Medicine, 39*, 757-762.

Manzoni, G.C., & Stovner, L.J. (2010). Epidemiology of headache. In M.J. Aminoff, F. Boller, & D.F. Swaab (Eds.), *Handbook of clinical neurology* (Vol. 97, pp. 3-22). Netherlands: Elsevier.

Marcin, M.S., & Nemeroff, C.B. (2003). The neurobiology of social anxiety disorder: The relevance of fear and anxiety. *Acta Psychiatrica Scandinavaca, 108 (Suppl.)*, 51-64.

Marcus, D.S., Fotenos, A.F., Csernansky, J.G., Morris, J.C., & Buckner, R.L. (2010). Open access series of imaging studies: Longitudinal MRI data in nondemented and demented older adults. *Journal of Cognitive Neuroscience, 22*, 2677-2684.

Mark, T.L., Coffey, R.M., McKusick, D.R., Harwood, H., King, E., Bouchery, E., Genuardi, J., Vandivort, R., Buck, J.A., & Dilonardo, J. (2005). *National expenditures for mental health services and substance abuse treatment 1991-2001* (DHHS Publication No. SMA 05-3999). Rockville, MD: Substance Abuse and Mental Health Services Administration.

Markowitsch, H.J. (2003). Psychogenic amnesia. *Neuroimage, 20*, S132-S138.

Markon, K.E., Quilty, L.C., Bagby, R.M., & Krueger, R.F. (2013). The development and psychometric properties of an informant-report form of the Personality Inventory for DSM-5 (PID-5). *Assessment, 20*, 370-383.

Markus, H.S. (2011). Stroke genetics. *Human Molecular Genetics, 20*, R124-R131.

Marlatt, G.A., & Witkiewitz, K. (2010). Update on harm-reduction policy and intervention research. *Annual Review of Clinical Psychology, 6*, 591-606.

Marom, S., Munitz, H., Jones, P.B., Weizman, A., & Hermesh, H. (2005). Expressed emotion: Relevance to rehospiralization in schizophrenia over 7 years. *Schizophrenia Bulletin, 31*, 751-758.

Marshall, W.L., & Marshall, L.E. (2000). Child sexual molestation. In V.B. Van Hasselt & M. Hersen (Eds.), *Aggression and violence: An introductory text* (pp. 67-91). Needham Heights, MA: Allyn and Bacon.

Marshall, W.L., Serran, G.A., & Cortoni, F.A. (2000). Childhood attachments, sexual abuse, and their relationship to adult coping in child molesters. *Sexual Abuse: A Journal of Research and Treatment, 12*, 17-26.

Martel, M.M., Nikolas, M., Jernigan, K., Friderici, K., & Nigg, J.T. (2012). Diversity in pathways to common childhood disruptive behavior disorders. *Journal of Abnormal Child Psychology, 40*, 1223-1236.

Martin, J.K., Pescosolido, B.A., Olafsdottir, S., & McLeod, J.D. (2007). The construction of fear: Americans' preferences for social distance from children and adolescents with mental health problems. *Journal of Health and Social Behavior, 48*, 50-67.

Marziali, E., & Garcia, L.J. (2011). Dementia caregivers' responses to 2 Internet-based intervention programs. *American Journal of Alzheimer's Disease and Other Dementias, 26*, 36-43.

Masho, S.W., & Ahmed, G. (2007). Age at sexual assault and posttraumatic stress disorder among women: Prevalence, correlates, and implications for prevention. *Journal of Women's Health, 16*, 262-271.

Masten, A.S. (2011). Resilience in children threatened by extreme adversity: Frameworks for research, practice, and translational synergy. *Development and Psychopathology, 23*, 493-506.

Masten, A.S., & Coatsworth, J.D. (1998). The development of competence in favorable and unfavorable environments: Lessons from research on successful children. *American Psychologist, 53*, 205-220.

Mathew, S.J., Hoffman, E.J., & Charney, D.S. (2009). In D.S. Charney & E.J. Nestler (Eds.), *Neurobiology of mental illness* (pp. 731-754). New York: Oxford.

Mathew, S.J., Price, R.B., & Charney, D.S. (2008). Recent advances in the neurobiology of anxiety disorders: Implications for novel therapeutics. *American Journal of Medical Genetics, 148*, 89-98.

Mathews, C.A., Nievergelt, C.M., Azzam, A., Garrido, H., Chavira, D.A., Wessel, J., Bagnarello, M., Reus, V.I., & Schork, N.J. (2007). Heritability and clinical features of multigenerational families with obsessive-compulsive disorder and hoarding. *American Journal of Medical Genetics Part B, 144*, 174-182.

Matson, J.L., & Kozlowski, A.M. (2011). The increasing prevalence of autism spectrum disorders. *Research in Autism Spectrum Disorders, 5*, 418-425.

Matson, J.L., & Shoemaker, M. (2009). Intellectual disability and its relationship to autism spectrum disorders. *Research in Developmental Disabilities, 30*, 1107-1114

Matsui, A., & Williams, J.T. (2010). Activation of μ-opioid receptors and block of KIR3 potassium channels and NMDA receptor conductance by l- and d-methadone in rat locus coeruleus. *British Journal of Pharmacology, 161*, 1403-1413.

Matsui, A., & Williams, J.T. (2011). Opioid-sensitive GABA inputs from rostromedial tegmental nucleus synapse onto midbrain dopamine neurons. *Journal of Neuroscience, 31*, 17729-17735.

Mattelaer, J.J., & Jilek, W. (2007). Koro—the psychological disappearance of the penis. *Journal of Sexual Medicine, 4*, 1509-1515.

Matthys, W., Vanderschuren, L.J.M.J., Schutter, D.J.L.G., & Lochman, J.E. (2012). Impaired neurocognitive functions affect social learning processes in oppositional defiant disorder and conduct disorder: Implications for interventions. *Clinical Child and Family Psychology Review, 15*, 234-246.

Mattsson, N., Brax, D., & Zetterberg, H. (2010). To know or not know: Ethical issues related to early diagnosis of Alzheimer's disease. *International Journal of Alzheimer's Disease, 2010*, 1-4.

Mattson, S.N., Crocker, N., & Nguyen, T.T. (2011). Fetal alcohol spectrum disorders: Neuropsychological and behavioral features. *Neuropsychology Review, 21*, 81-101.

Mautone, J.A., Marshall, S.A., Costigan, T.E., Clarke, A.T., & Power, T.J. (2012). Multidimensional assessment of homework: An analysis of students with ADHD. *Journal of Attention Disorders, 16*, 600-609.

Maxwell, C.J., Hicks, M.S., Hogan, D.B., Basran, J., & Ebly, E.M. (2005). Supplemental use of antioxidant vitamins and subsequent risk of cognitive decline and dementia. *Dementia and Geriatric Cognitive Disorders, 20*, 45-51.

Maxwell, M.A., & Cole, D.A. (2009). Weight change and appetite disturbance as symptoms of adolescent depression: Toward an integrative biopsychosocial model. *Clinical Psychology Review, 29*, 260-273.

May, A.L., Kim, J.Y., McHale, S.M., & Crouter, C. (2006). Parent-adolescent relationships and the development of weight concerns from early to late adolescence. *International Journal of Eating Disorders, 39*, 729-740.

Mayberg, H.S., Keightley, M., Mahurin, R.K., & Brannan, S.K. (2004). Neuropsychiatric aspects of mood and affective disorders. In S.C. Yudofsky & R.E. Hales (Eds.), *Essentials of neuropsychiatry and clinical neurosciences* (pp. 489-517). Washington, DC: American Psychiatric Publishing.

Mayer, P., & Hollt, V. (2005). Genetic disposition to addictive disorders—Current knowledge and future perspectives. *Current Opinion in Pharmacology, 5,* 4-8.

Mayer, P., & Hollt, V. (2006). Pharmacogenetics of opioid receptors and addiction. *Pharmacogenetics and Genomics, 16,* 1-7.

Mayes, S.D., Calhoun, S.L., Murray, M.J., & Zahid, J. (2011). Variables associated with anxiety and depression in children with autism. *Journal of Developmental and Physical Disabilities, 23,* 325-337.

Maynard, C.K. (2003). Assess and manage somatization. *The Nurse Practitioner, 28,* 20-29.

Maynard, T.M., Sikich, L., Lieberman, J.A., & LaMantia, A.S. (2001). Neural development, cell-cell signaling, and the "two-hit" hypothesis of schizophrenia. *Schizophrenia Bulletin, 27,* 457-476.

Mayes, S.D., & Calhoun, S.L. (2011). Impact of IQ, age, SES, gender, and race on autistic symptoms. *Research in Autism Spectrum Disorders, 5,* 749-757.

McAlonan, G.M., Cheung, C., Cheung, V., Wong, N., Suckling, J., & Chua, S.E. (2009). Differential effects on white-matter systems in high-functioning autism and Asperger's syndrome. *Psychological Medicine, 39,* 1885-1893.

McAnulty, R., Dillon, J., & Adams, H.E. (2001). Sexual deviation: Paraphilias. In P.B. Sutker & H.E. Adams (Eds.), *Comprehensive handbook of psychopathology* (3rd ed.; pp. 749-773). New York: Kluwer Academic/Plenum.

McBride-Chang, C., Lam, F., Lam, C., Chan, B., Fong, C. Y.-C., Wong, T. T.-Y., & Wong, S. W.-L. (2011). Early predictors of dyslexia in Chinese children: Familial history of dyslexia, language delay, and cognitive profiles. *Journal of Child Psychology and Psychiatry, 52,* 204-211.

McCabe, M., Althof, S.E., Assalian, P., Chevret-Measson, M., Leiblum, S.R., Simonelli, C., & Wylie, K. (2010). Psychological and interpersonal dimensions of sexual function and dysfunction. *Journal of Sexual Medicine, 7,* 327-336.

McCall, K.M., & Meston, C.M. (2007). The effects of false positive and false negative physiological feedback on sexual arousal: A comparison of women with or without sexual arousal disorder. *Archives of Sexual Behavior, 36,* 518-530.

McCance-Katz, E.F., Sullivan, L.E., & Nallani, S. (2009). Drug interactions of clinical importance among the opioids, methadone and buprenorphine, and other frequently prescribed medications: A review. *American Journal on Addictions, 19,* 4-16.

McCarthy, B., & McDonald, D. (2009). Sex therapy failures: A crucial, yet ignored, issue. *Journal of Sex and Marital Therapy, 35,* 320-329.

McCarthy, M.D., & Thompson, S.J. (2010). Predictors of trauma-related symptoms among runaway adolescents. *Journal of Loss and Trauma, 15,* 212-227.

McCaul, M.E., & Petry, N.M. (2003). The role of psychosocial treatments in pharmacotherapy for alcoholism. *American Journal on Addictions, 12,* S41-S52.

McClean, C.P., & Anderson, E.R. (2009). Brave men and timid women? A review of the gender differences in fear and anxiety. *Clinical Psychology Review, 29,* 496-505.

McClure, M.M., Harvey, P.D., Goodman, M., Triebwasser, J., New, A., Koenigsberg, H.W., Sprung, L.J., Flory, J.D., & Siever, L.J. (2010). Pergolide treatment of cognitive deficits associated with schizotypal personality disorder: Continued evidence of the importance of the dopamine system in the schizophrenia spectrum. *Neuropsychopharmacology, 35,* 1356-1362.

McCusker, J., Cole, M., Dendukuri, N., Han, L., & Belzile, E. (2003). The course of delirium in older medical patients: A prospective study. *Journal of General Internal Medicine, 18,* 696-704.

McDermott, B.E., & Feldman, M.D. (2007). Malingering in the medical setting. *Psychiatric Clinics of North America, 30,* 645-662.

McDermott, S., Moran, R., Platt, T., Issac, T., Wood, H., & Dasari, S. (2005). Depression in adults with disabilities, in primary care. *Disability and Rehabilitation, 27,* 117-123.

McElroy, S.L., Guerdjikova, A.I., Mori, N., & O'Melia, A.M. (2012). Pharmacological management of binge eating disorder: Current and emerging treatment options. *Therapeutics and Clinical Risk Management, 8,* 219-241.

McEwen, B.S. (2005). Glucocorticoids, depression, and mood disorders: Structural remodeling in the brain. *Metabolism, 54 (Suppl. 1),* 20-23.

McFarlane, A.C., Barton, C.A., Yehuda, R., & Wittert, G. (2011). Cortisol response to acute trauma and risk of posttraumatic stress disorder. *Psychoneuroendocrinology, 36,* 720-727.

McGlashan, T.H., Grilo, C.M., Sanislow, C.A., Ralevski, E., Morey, L.C., Gunderson, J.G., Skodol, A.E., Shea, M.T., Zanarini, M.C., Bender, D., Stout, R.L., Yen, S., & Pagano, M. (2005). Two-year prevalence and stability of individual DSM-IV criteria for schizotypal, borderline, avoidant, and obsessive-compulsive personality disorders: Toward a hybrid model of Axis II disorders. *American Journal of Psychiatry, 162,* 883-889.

McGorry, P.D., Yung, A.R., Phillips, L.J., Yuen, H.P., Francey, S., Cosgrave, E.M., Germano, D., Bravin, J., McDonald, T., Blair, A., Adlard, S., & Jackson, H. (2002). Randomized controlled trial of interventions designed to reduce the risk of progression to first-episode psychosis in a clinical sample with subthreshold symptoms. *Archives of General Psychiatry, 59,* 921-928.

McGovern, M.P., Wrisley, B.R., & Drake, R.E. (2005). Relapse of substance use disorder and its prevention among persons with co-occurring disorders. *Psychiatric Services, 56,* 1270-1273.

McGrath, J., Saha, S., Chant, D., & Welham, J. (2008). Schizophrenia: A concise overview of incidence, prevalence, and mortality. *Epidemiologic Reviews, 30,* 67-76.

McGrath, R.E. (2010). Prescriptive authority for psychologists. *Annual Review of Clinical Psychology, 6,* 21-47.

McGrath, R.J., Lasher, M.P., & Cumming, G.F. (2012). The Sex Offender Treatment and Intervention Progress Scale (SOTIPS): Psychometric properties and incremental predictive validity with Static-99R. *Sexual Abuse, 24,* 431-458.

McGuinness, B., O'Hare, J., Craig, D., Bullock, R., Malouf, R., & Passmore, P. (2013). Cochrane review on 'Statins for the treatment of dementia'. *International Journal of Geriatric Psychiatry, 28,* 119-126.

McKay, J.R., Van Horn, D.H.A., Oslin, D.W., Lynch, K.G., Ivey, M., Ward, K., Drapkin, M.L., Becher, J.R., & Coviello, D.M. (2010). A randomized trial of extended telephone-based continuing care for alcohol dependence: Within-treatment substance use outcomes. *Journal of Consulting and Clinical Psychology, 78,* 912-923.

McKim, W.A. (2003). *Drugs and behavior: An introduction to behavioral pharmacology* (5th ed.). Upper Saddle River, NJ: Prentice-Hall.

McKim, W.A., & Hancock, S. (2013). *Drugs and behavior: An introduction to behavioral pharmacology* (7th ed.). Upper Saddle River, NJ: Pearson.

McKnight, P.E., & Kashdan, T.B. (2009). The importance of functional impairment to mental health outcomes: A case for reassessing our goals in depression treatment research. *Clinical Psychology Review, 29,* 243-259.

McLaughlin, K.A., Costello, E.J., Leblanc, W., Sampson, N.A., & Kessler, R.C. (2012). Socioeconomic status and adolescent mental disorders. *American Journal of Public Health, 102,* 1742-1750.

McMahon, B., Holly, L., Harrington, R., Roberts, C., & Green, J. (2008). Do larger studies find smaller effects?: The example of studies for the prevention of conduct disorder. *European Child and Adolescent Psychiatry, 17,* 432-437.

McMahon, C.G., Abdo, C., Incrocci, L., Perelman, M., Rowland, D., Waldinger, M., & Xin, Z.C. (2004). Disorders of orgasm and ejaculation in men. *Journal of Sexual Medicine, 1,* 58-65.

MacMillan, H.L., Wathen, C.N., Barlow, J., Fergusson, D.M., Leventhal, J.M., & Taussig, H.N. (2009). Interventions to prevent child maltreatment and associated impairment. *Lancet, 373,* 250-266.

McMurran, M., Huband, N., & Overton, E. (2010). Non-completion of personality disorder treatments: A systematic review of correlates, consequences, and interventions. *Clinical Psychology Review, 30,* 277-287.

McNair, B.G., Highet, N.J., Hickie, I.B., & Davenport, T.A. (2002). Exploring the perspectives of people whose lives have been affected by depression. *Medical Journal of Australia, 176,* S69-S76.

McNeece, C.A., & DiNitto, D.M. (2005). *Chemical dependency: A systems approach* (3rd ed.). New York: Pearson.

Mead, D.E. (2002). Marital distress, co-occurring depression, and marital therapy: A review. *Journal of Marital and Family Therapy, 28,* 299-314.

Meagher, D.J., Leonard, M., Donnelly, S., Conroy, M., Adamis, D., & Trzepacz, P.T. (2012). A longitudinal study of motor subtypes in delirium: Frequency and stability during episodes. *Journal of Psychosomatic Research, 72*, 236-241.

Medalia, A., Revheim, N., & Casey, M. (2000). Remediation of memory disorders in schizophrenia. *Psychological Medicine, 30*, 1451-1459.

Mehler-Wex, C., Romanos, M., Kirchheiner, J., & Schulze, U.M. (2008). Atypical antipsychotics in severe anorexia nervosa in children and adolescents: Review and case reports. *European Eating Disorders Review, 16*, 100-108.

Meichenbaum, D. (2009). Bolstering resilience: Benefiting from lessons learned. In D. Brom, R. Pat-Horenczyk, & J. Ford (Eds.), *Treating traumatized children: Risk, resilience, and recovery* (pp. 183-191). New York: Routledge.

Meichenbaum, D. (2007). Stress inoculation training: A preventative and treatment approach. In P.M. Lehrer, R.L. Woolfolk, & W.E. Sime (Eds.), *Principles and practice of stress management* (3rd ed.; pp. 497-518). New York: Guilford.

Meile, I., Larsen, T.K., Haahr, U., Friis, S., Johannesen, J.O., Opjordsmoen, S., Rund, B.R., Simonsen, E., Vaglum, P., & McGlashan, T. (2008). Prevention of negative symptom psychopathologies in first-episode schizophrenia: Two-year effects of reducing the duration of untreated psychosis. *Archives of General Psychiatry, 65*, 634-640.

Melamed, Y. (2010). Mentally ill persons who commit crimes: Punishment or treatment? *Journal of the American Academy of Psychiatry and the Law, 38*, 100-103.

Meltzer, H.Y. (2013). Update on typical and atypical antipsychotic drugs. *Annual Review of Medicine, 64*, 393-406.

Meltzer, H.Y., & Massey, B.W. (2011). The role of serotonin receptors in the action of atypical antipsychotic drugs. *Current Opinion in Pharmacology, 11*, 59-67.

Mendez, M.F., Joshi, A., Tassniyom, K., Teng, E., & Shapira, J.S. (2013). Clinicopathologic differences among patients with behavioral variant frontotemporal dementia. *Neurology, 80*, 561-568.

Mendlewicz, J. (2009). Sleep disturbances: Core symptoms of major depressive disorder rather than associated or comorbid disorders. *World Journal of Biological Psychiatry, 10*, 269-275.

Mennin, D.S., McLaughlin, K.A., & Flanagan, T.J. (2009). Emotion regulation deficits in generalized anxiety disorder, social anxiety disorder, and their co-occurrence. *Journal of Anxiety Disorders, 23*, 866-871.

Merckelbach, H., Devilly, G.J., & Rassin, E. (2002). Alters in dissociative identity disorder: Metaphors or genuine entities? *Clinical Psychology Review, 22*, 481-497.

Merckelbach, H., & Muris, P. (2001). The causal link between self-reported trauma and dissociation: A critical review. *Behaviour Research and Therapy, 39*, 245-254.

Merikangas, K.R., He, J., Burstein, M., Swanson, S.A., Avenevoli, S., Cui, L., Benjet, C., Georgiades, K., & Swendsen, J. (2010). Lifetime prevalence of mental disorders in U.S. adolescents: Results from the National Comorbidity Survey Replication—Adolescent Supplement (NCS-A). *Journal of the American Academy of Child and Adolescent Psychiatry, 49*, 980-989.

Merikangas, K.R., Jin, R., He, J.-P., Kessler, R.C., Lee, S., Sampson, N.A., Viana, M.C., Andrade, L.H., Hu, C., Karam, E.G., Ladea, M., Medina-Mora, M.E., Ono, Y., Posada-Villa, J., Sagar, R., Wells, J.E., & Zarkov, Z. (2011). Prevalence and correlates of bipolar spectrum disorder in the World Mental Health Survey Initiative. *Archives of General Psychiatry, 68*, 241-251.

Merikangas, K.R., Lieb, R., Wittchen, H.-U., & Avenevoli, S. (2003). Family and high-risk studies of social anxiety disorder. *Acta Psychiatrica Scandinavica, 108*, 28-37.

Merikangas, K.R., Stolar, M., Stevens, D.E., Goulet, J., Preisig, M.A., Fenton, B., Zhang, H., O'Malley, S.S., & Rounsaville, B.J. (1998). Familial transmission of substance use disorders. *Archives of General Psychiatry, 55*, 973-979.

Merikangas, K.R., Zhang, H., Aveneoli, S., Acharyya, S., Neuenschwander, M., & Angst, J. (2003). Longitudinal trajectories of depression and anxiety in a prospective community study: The Zurich cohort study. *Archives of General Psychiatry, 60*, 993-1000.

Mervielde, I., De Clecq, B., De Fruyt, F., & Van Leeuwen, K. (2005). Temperament, personality, and developmental psychopathology as childhood antecedents of personality disorders. *Journal of Personality Disorders, 19*, 171-201.

Meschia, J.F., Brott, T.G., & Brown, R.D. (2005). Genetics of cerebrovascular disorders. *Mayo Clinic Proceedings, 80*, 122-132.

Mesquita, B., & Walker, R. (2003). Cultural differences in emotions: A context for interpreting emotional experiences. *Behavior Research and Therapy, 41*, 777-793.

Messer, S.B. (2003). A critical examination of belief structures in integrative and eclectic psychotherapy. In J.C. Norcross & M.R. Goldfried (Eds.), *Handbook of psychotherapy integration* (pp. 130-165). New York: Oxford.

Meston, C.M., & Derogatis, L.R. (2002). Validated instruments for assessing female sexual function. *Journal of Sex and Marital Therapy, 28 (Suppl. 1)*, 155-164.

Meuret, A.E., Wilhelm, F.H., & Roth, W.T. (2004). Respiratory feedback for treating panic disorder. *Journal of Clinical Psychology, 60*, 197-207.

Meuser, K.T., Deavers, F., Penn, D.L., & Cassisi, J.E. (2013). Psychosocial treatments for schizophrenia. *Annual Review of Clinical Psychology, 9*, 465-497.

Meuser, K.T., & Jeste, D.V. (Eds.). (2008). *Clinical handbook of schizophrenia.* New York: Guilford.

Meuser, T.M., & Marwit, S.J. (2001). A comprehensive, stage-sensitive model of grief in dementia caregiving. *Gerontologist, 41*, 658-670.

Meyer, B., Pilkonis, P.A., Proietti, J.M., Heape, C.L., & Egan, M. (2001). Attachment styles and personality disorders as predictors of symptom course. *Journal of Personality Disorders, 15*, 371-389.

Meyer, J.M. (2007). Antipsychotic safety and efficacy concerns. *Journal of Clinical Psychiatry, 68 (Suppl. 14)*, 20-26.

Meyer-Lindenberg, A., Miletich, R.S., Kohn, P.D., Esposito, G., Carson, R.E., Quarantelli, M., Weinberger, D.R., & Berman, K.F. (2002). Reduced prefrontal activity predicts exaggerated striatal dopaminergic function in schizophrenia. *Nature Neuroscience, 5*, 267-271.

Meyerbroker, K., & Emmelkamp, P.M.G. (2010). Virtual reality exposure therapy in anxiety disorders: A systematic review of process-and-outcome studies. *Depression and Anxiety, 27*, 933-944.

Meyers, R.J., Roozen, H.G., & Smith, J.E. (2011). The community reinforcement approach: An update of the evidence. *Alcohol Research and Health, 33*, 380-388.

Micali, N., Heyman, I., Perez, M., Hilton, K., Nakatani, E., Turner, C., & Mataix-Cols, D. (2010). Long-term outcomes of obsessive-compulsive disorder: Follow-up of 142 children and adolescents. *British Journal of Psychiatry, 197*, 128-134.

Middleboe, T., Schjodt, T., Byrsting, K., & Gjerris, A. (2001). Ward atmosphere in acute psychiatric in-patient care: Patients' perceptions, ideals and satisfaction. *Acta Psychiatrica Scandanavia, 103*, 212-219.

Mihailides, S., Devilly, G.J., & Ward, T. (2004). Implicit cognitive distortions and sexual offending. *Sexual Abuse, 16*, 333-350.

Miklowitz, D.J., & Johnson, S.L. (2006). The psychopathology and treatment of bipolar disorder. *Annual Review of Clinical Psychology, 2*, 199-235.

Miklowitz, D.J., & Scott, J. (2009). Psychosocial treatments for bipolar disorder: Cost-effectiveness, mediating mechanisms, and future directions. *Bipolar Disorders, 11 (Suppl 2)*, 110-122.

Mikton, C., & Grounds, A. (2007). Cross-cultural clinical judgment bias in personality disorder diagnosis by forensic psychiatrists in the UK: A case-vignette study. *Journal of Personality Disorders, 21*, 400-417.

Milad, M.R., & Rauch, S.L. (2012). Obsessive-compulsive disorder: beyond segregated cortico-striatal pathways. *Trends in Cognitive Sciences, 16*, 43-51.

Miles, J.H. (2011). Autism spectrum disorders: A genetics review. *Genetics in Medicine, 13*, 278-294.

Miller, C.J., Johnson, S.L., & Eisner, L. (2009). Assessment tools for bipolar disorder. *Clinical Psychology, 16*, 188-201.

Miller, D.N., Eckert, T.L., & Mazza, J.J. (2009). Suicide prevention programs in the schools: A review and public health perspective. *School Psychology Review, 38*, 168-188.

Miller, L.E., & Stewart, M.E. (2011). The blind leading the blind: Use and misuse of blinding in randomized controlled trials. *Contemporary Clinical Trials, 32,* 240-243.

Miller, M.D., & Solai, L.K. (Eds.). (2013). *Geriatric psychiatry.* New York: Oxford.

Miller, W.R., & Cervantes, E.A. (1997). Gender and patterns of alcohol problems: Pretreatment responses of women and men to the Comprehensive Drinker Profile. *Journal of Clinical Psychology, 53,* 263-277.

Miller, W.R., & Rollnick, S. (2009). Ten things that motivational interviewing is not. *Behavioural and Cognitive Psychotherapy, 37,* 129-140.

Millon, T. (2012). On the history and future study of personality and its disorders. *Annual Review of Clinical Psychology, 8,* 1-19.

Millon, T., Davis, R., Millon, C., & Grossman, S. (2006). *The Millon Clinical Multiaxial Inventory-III, Third Edition.* San Antonio, TX: Pearson.

Miltenberger, R.G. (2012). *Behavior modification: Principles and procedures* (5th ed). Belmont, CA: Wadsworth/Cengage.

Mineka, S., & Ohman, A. (2002). Phobias and preparedness: The selective, automatic, and encapsulated nature of fear. *Biological Psychiatry, 52,* 927-937.

Mineka, S., & Zinbarg, R. (2006). A contemporary learning theory perspective on the etiology of anxiety disorders: It's not what you thought it was. *American Psychologist, 61,* 10-26.

Mitchell, A.J. (2009). A meta-analysis of the accuracy of the mini-mental state examination in the detection of dementia and mild cognitive impairment. *Journal of Psychiatric Research, 43,* 411-431.

Mitchell, I.J., & Beech, A.R. (2011). Towards a neurobiological model of offending. *Clinical Psychology Review, 31,* 872-882.

Mitchell, J.E., Agras, S., Crow, S., Halmi, K., Fairburn, C.G., Bryson, S., & Kraemer, H. (2011). Stepped care and cognitive-behavioural therapy for bulimia nervosa: Randomised trial. *British Journal of Psychiatry, 198,* 391-397.

Mitchell, J.E., Roerig, J., & Steffen, K. (2013). Biological therapies for eating disorders. *International Journal of Eating Disorders, 46,* 470-477.

Mitchell, K.S., Neale, M.C., Bulik, C.M., Aggen, S.H., Kendler, K.S., & Mazzeo, S.E. (2010). Binge eating disorder: A symptom-level investigation of genetic and environmental influences on liability. *Psychological Medicine, 40,* 1899-1906.

Mitelman, A.R., & Buchsbaum, M.S. (2007). Very poor outcome schizophrenia: Clinical and neuroimaging aspects. *International Review of Psychiatry, 19,* 345-357.

Mitte, K. (2005). A meta-analysis of the efficacy of psycho- and pharmacotherapy in panic disorder with and without agoraphobia. *Journal of Affective Disorders, 88,* 27-45.

Mittelman, M.S., Epstein, C., & Pierzchala, A. (2003). *Counseling the Alzheimer's caregiver: A resource for health care professionals.* Chicago: American Medical Association.

Mitter, P.R., Krishnan, S., Bell, P., Stewart, R., & Howard, R.J. (2004). The effect of ethnicity and gender on first-contact rates for schizophrenia-like psychosis in Bangladeshi, Black and White elders in Tower Hamlets, London. *International Journal of Geriatric Psychiatry, 19,* 286-290.

Moch, S. (2011). Dysthymia: More than "minor" depression. *South African Pharmaceutical Journal, 78,* 38-43.

Mody, M. (2003). Phonological basis in reading disability: A review and analysis of the evidence. *Reading and Writing, 16,* 21-39.

Moeller, F.G., Dougherty, D.M., Barratt, E.S., Schmitz, J.M., Swann, A.C., & Grabowski, J. (2001). The impact of impulsivity on cocaine use and retention in treatment. *Journal of Substance Abuse Treatment, 21,* 193-198.

Moeller, K., Fischer, U., Cress, U., & Nuerk, H.-C. (2012). Diagnostics and intervention in developmental dyscalculia: Current issues and novel perspectives. In Z. Breznitz, O. Rubinsten, V.J. Molfese, & D.L. Molfese (Eds.), *Reading, writing, mathematics and the developing brain: Listening to many voices* (pp. 233-275). New York: Springer.

Moffitt, T.E. (2005). The new look of behavioral genetics in developmental psychopathology: Gene-environment interplay in antisocial behaviors. *Psychological Bulletin, 131,* 533-554.

Mohammadirad, A., & Abdollahi, M. (2011). A systematic review on oxidant/antioxidant imbalance in aluminum toxicity. *International Journal of Pharmacology, 7,* 12-21.

Mohan, R., Slade, M., & Fahy, T.A. (2004). Clinical characteristics of community forensic mental health services. *Psychiatric Services, 55,* 1294-1298.

Mohan, T.S.P., Tharyan, P., Alexander, J., & Raveendran, N.S. (2009). Effects of stimulus intensity on the efficacy and safety of twice-weekly, bilateral electroconvulsive therapy (ECT) combined with antipsychotics in acute mania: A randomised controlled trial. *Bipolar Disorders, 11,* 126-134.

Mojtabai, R., Olfson, M., Sampson, N.A., Jin, R., Druss, B., Wang, P.S., Wells, K.B., Pincus, H.A., & Kessler, R.C. (2011). Barriers to mental health treatment: Results from the National Comorbidity Study Replication (NCS-R). *Psychological Medicine, 41,* 1751-1761.

Moller, B., Schreier, H., Li, A., & Romer, G. (2009). Gender identity disorder in children and adolescents. *Current Problems in Pediatric and Adolescent Health Care, 39,* 117-143.

Moller, H.J. (2003). Suicide, suicidality and suicide prevention in affective disorders. *Acta Psychiatrica Scandinavica Supplement, 418,* 73-80.

Molton, I.R., & Raichle, K.A. (2010). Psychophysiological disorders. In D.L. Segal & M. Hersen (Eds.), *Diagnostic interviewing* (4th ed.; pp. 343-369). New York: Springer.

Monroe, S.M. (2008). Modern approaches to conceptualizing and measuring human life stress. *Annual Review of Clinical Psychology, 4,* 33-52.

Montoya, E.R., Terburg, D., Bos, P.A., & van Honk, J. (2011). Testosterone, cortisol, and serotonin as key regulators of social aggression: A review and theoretical perspective. *Motivation and Emotion, 36,* 65-73.

Moore, J.D., & Bona, J.R. (2001). Depression and dysthymia. *Medical Clinics of North America, 85,* 631-643.

Moore, T.M., Elkins, S.R., McNulty, J.K., Kivisto, A.J., & Handsel, V.A. (2011). Alcohol use and intimate partner violence perpetration among college students: Assessing the temporal association using electronic diary technology. *Psychology of Violence, 1,* 315-328.

Moorman, J.E., Zahran, H., Truman, B.I., & Molla, M.T. (2011). Current asthma prevalence—United States, 2006-2008. *Morbidity and Mortality Weekly Report, 60,* 84-86.

Morakinyo, O., & Peltzer, K. (2002). "Brain fag": symptoms in apprentices in Nigeria. *Psychopathology, 35,* 362-366.

Moran, S., Wechsler, H., & Rigotti, N.A. (2004). Social smoking among US college students. *Pediatrics, 114,* 1028-1034.

Moreira, E.D., Kim, S.C., Glasser, D., & Gingell, C. (2006). Sexual activity, prevalence of sexual problems, and associated help-seeking patterns in men and women aged 40-80 years in Korea: Data from the Global Study of Sexual Attitudes and Behaviors (GSSAB). *Journal of Sexual Medicine, 3,* 201-211.

Moreira, E.D., Lbo, C.F., Diament, A., Nicolosi, A., & Glasser, D.B. (2003). Incidence of erectile dysfunction in men 40 to 69 years old: Results from a population-based cohort study in Brazil. *Urology, 61,* 431-436.

Morley, T.E., & Moran, G. (2011). The origins of cognitive vulnerability in early childhood: Mechanisms linking early attachment to later depression. *Clinical Psychology Review, 31,* 1071-1082.

Morgan, C., Colombres, M., Nunez, M.T., & Inestrosa, N.C. (2004). Structure and function of amyloid in Alzheimer's disease. *Progress in Neurobiology, 74,* 323-349.

Morgentaler, A., Barada, J., Niederberger, C., Donatucci, C., Garcia, C.S., Natanegara, F., Ahuja, S., & Wong, D.G. (2006). Efficacy and safety of tadalafil across ethnic groups and various risk factors in men with erectile dysfunction: Use of a novel noninferiority study design. *Journal of Sexual Medicine, 3,* 492-503.

Morgenthaler, T., Kramer, M., Alessi, C., Friedman, L., Boehlecke, B., Brown, T., Coleman, J., Kapur, V., Lee-Chiong, T., Owens, J., Pancer, J., & Swick, T. (2006). Practice parameters for the psychological and behavioral treatment of insomnia: An update. *Sleep, 29,* 1414-1419.

Morin, C.M., Bootzin, R.R., Buysse, D.J., Edinger, J.D., Espie, C.A., & Lichstein, K.L. (2006). Psychological and behavioral treatment of insomnia: Update of the recent evidence (1998-2004). *Sleep, 29,* 1398-1414.

Morris, E.P., Stewart, S.H., & Ham, L.S. (2005). The relationship between social anxiety disorder and alcohol use disorders: A critical review. *Clinical Psychology Review, 25,* 734-760.

Moschetti, K., Cummings, P.L., Sorvillo, F., & Kuo, T. (2012). Burden of Alzheimer's disease-related mortality in the United States, 1999-2008. *Journal of the American Geriatrics Society, 60,* 1509-1514.

Moskowitz, A. (2004). Dissociation and violence: A review of the literature. *Trauma, Violence, and Abuse, 5,* 21-46.

Mostert, M.P. (2012). Facilitated communication: The empirical imperative to prevent further professional malpractice. *Evidence-Based Communication Assessment and Intervention, 6,* 18-27.

Mostert, M.P. (2001). Facilitated communication since 1995: A review of published studies. *Journal of Autism and Developmental Disorders, 31,* 287-313.

Moulden, H.M., Firestone, P., Kingston, D., & Bradford, J. (2009). Recidivism in pedophiles: An investigation using different diagnostic methods. *Journal of Forensic Psychiatry and Psychology, 20,* 680-701.

Moulds, M.L., & Nixon, R.D. (2006). In vivo flooding for anxiety disorders: Proposing its utility in the treatment of posttraumatic stress disorder. *Journal of Anxiety Disorders, 20,* 498-509.

Mrak, R.E. (2012). Microglia in Alzheimer brain: A neuropathological perspective. *International Journal of Alzheimer's Disease, 2012,* 1-6.

Muangpaisan, W., Hori, H., & Brayne, C. (2009). Systematic review of the prevalence and incidence of Parkinson's disease in Asia. *Journal of Epidemiology, 19,* 281-293.

Mueller, C., Moergeli, H., Assaloni, H., Schneider, R., & Rufer, M. (2007). Dissociative disorders among chronic and severely impaired psychiatric outpatients. *Psychopathology, 40,* 470-471.

Mueser, K.T., Curran, P.J., & McHugo, G.J. (1997). Factor structure of the Brief Psychiatric Rating Scale in schizophrenia. *Psychological Assessment, 9,* 196-204.

Muir, A., & Palmer, R.L. (2004). An audit of a British sample of death certificates in which anorexia nervosa is listed as a cause of death. *International Journal of Eating Disorders, 36,* 356-360.

Mukamal, K.J., Kuller, L.H., Fitzpatrick, A.L., Longstreth, W.T., Mittleman, M.A., & Siscovick, D.S. (2003). Prospective study of alcohol consumption and risk of dementia in older adults. *Journal of the American Medical Association, 289,* 1405-1413.

Mulle, J.G. (2012). Schizophrenia genetics: Progress, at last. *Current Opinion in Genetics and Development, 22,* 238-244.

Muller, D.J., Barkow, K., Kovalenko, S., Ohlraun, S., Fangerau, H., Kolsch, H., Lemke, M.R., Held, T., Nothen, M.M., Maier, W., Heun, R., & Rietschel, M. (2005). Suicide attempts in schizophrenia and affective disorders with relation to some specific demographical and clinical characteristics. *European Psychiatry, 20,* 65-69.

Muller, J.E., Wentzel, I., Koen, L., Niehaus, D.J., Seedat, S., & Stein, D.J. (2008). Escitalopram in the treatment of multisomatoform disorder: A double-blind placebo-controlled trial. *International Clinical Psychopharmacology, 23,* 43-48.

Munoz, R.F., Beardslee, W.R., & Leykin, Y. (2012). Major depression can be prevented. *American Psychologist, 67,* 285-295.

Munoz, F.J., Sole, M., & Coma, M. (2005). The protective role of vitamin E in vascular amyloid beta-mediated damage. *Subcellular Biochemistry, 38,* 147-165.

Muntaner, C., Eaton, W.W., Miech, R., & O'Campo, P. (2004). Socioeconomic position and major mental disorders. *Epidemiologic Reviews, 26,* 53-62.

Mura, G., Petretto, D.R., Bhat, K.M., & Carta, M.G. (2012). Schizophrenia: From epidemiology to rehabilitation. *Clinical Practice and Epidemiology in Mental Health, 8,* 52-66.

Murad, M.H., Elamin, M.B., Garcia, M.Z., Mullan, R.J., Murad, A., Erwin, P.J., & Montori, V.M. (2010). Hormonal therapy and sex reassignment: A systematic review and meta-analysis of quality of life and psychosocial outcomes. *Clinical Endocrinology, 72,* 214-231.

Muralidharan, A., Sheets, E.S., Madsen, J., Craighead, L.W., & Craighead, W.E. (2010). Interpersonal competence across domains: Relevance to personality pathology. *Journal of Personality Disorders, 25,* 16-27.

Muralidharan, P., Sarmah, S., Zhou, F.C., & Marrs, J.A. (2013). Fetal alcohol spectrum disorder (FASD) associated neural defects: Complex mechanisms and potential therapeutic targets. *Brain Sciences, 3,* 964-991.

Murdach, A.D. (2006). Social work and malingering. *Health and Social Work, 31,* 155-158.

Muris, P., Rapee, R., Meesters, C., Schouten, E., & Geers, M. (2003). Threat perception abnormalities in children: The role of anxiety disorders symptoms, chronic anxiety, and state anxiety. *Journal of Anxiety Disorders, 17,* 271-287.

Murison, R. (2001). Is there a role for psychology in ulcer disease? *Integrative Physiological and Behavioral Science, 36,* 75-83.

Murphy, K.C. (2002). Schizophrenia and velocardio-facial syndrome. *Lancet, 359,* 426-430.

Murphy, R., Straebler, S., Cooper, Z., & Fairburn, C.G. (2010). Cognitive behavioral therapy for eating disorders. *Psychiatric Clinics of North America, 33,* 611-627.

Murphy, W. (2011). *Asthma.* Minneapolis, MN: Lerner.

Murphy, W.D., & Page, I.J. (2008). Exhibitionism: Psychopathology and theory. In D.R. Laws & W.T. O'Donohue (Eds.), *Sexual deviance: Theory, assessment, and treatment* (2nd ed.) (pp. 61-75). New York: Guilford.

Murray, R.M., Jones, P.B., Susser, E., van Os, J., & Cannon, M. (2003). *The epidemiology of schizophrenia.* Cambridge, UK: Cambridge University Press.

Murray, R.M., Lappin, J., & Di Forti, M. (2008). Schizophrenia: From developmental deviance to dopamine dysregulation. *European Neuropsychopharmacology, 18* (Suppl. 3), S129-S134.

Murrie, D.C., Cornell, D.G., & McCoy, W.K. (2005). Psychopathy, conduct disorder, and stigma: Does diagnostic labeling influence juvenile probation officer recommendations? *Law and Human Behavior, 29,* 323-342.

Muse, K., McManus, F., Hackmann, A., Williams, M., & Williams, M. (2010). Intrusive imagery in severe health anxiety: Prevalence, nature and links with memories and maintenance cycles. *Behaviour Research and Therapy, 48,* 792-798.

Myers, B., Fakier, N., & Louw, J. (2009). Stigma, treatment beliefs, and substance abuse treatment use in historically disadvantaged communities. *African Journal of Psychiatry, 12,* 218-222.

Nacmias, B., Piccini, C., Bagnoli, S., Tedde, A., Cellini, E., Bracco, L., & Sorbi, S. (2004). Brain-derived neurotrophic factor, apolipoprotein E genetic variants and cognitive performance in Alzheimer's disease. *Neuroscience Letters, 367,* 379-383.

Nader, M.A., Czoty, P.W., Gould, R.W., & Riddick, N.V. (2008). Positron emission tomography imaging studies of dopamine receptors in primate models of addiction. *Philosophical Transactions of the Royal Society of London, Series B, Biological Sciences, 363,* 3223-3232.

Nager, A., Sundquist, K., Ramirez-Leon, V., & Johansson, L.M. (2008). Obstetric complications and postpartum psychosis: A follow-up study of 1.1 million first-time mothers between 1975 and 2003 in Sweden. *Acta Psychiatrica Scandanavia, 117,* 12-19.

Nair, M.K.C., & Russell, P. (Eds.). (2012). *Illingworth's the development of the infant and young child: Normal and abnormal* (10th ed.). Oxford: Elsevier.

Nakao, M., Shinozaki, Y., Ahern, D.K., & Barsky, A.J. (2011). Anxiety as a predictor of improvements in somatic symptoms and health anxiety associated with cognitive-behavioral intervention in hypochondriasis. *Psychotherapy and Psychosomatics, 80,* 151-158.

Nanke, A., & Rief, W. (2003). Biofeedback-based interventions in somatoform disorders: A randomized controlled trial. *Acta Neuropsychiatrica, 15,* 249-256.

Naqvi, N.H., & Bechara, A. (2010). The insula and drug addiction: An interoceptive view of pleasure, urges and decision-making. *Brain Structure and Function, 214,* 435-450.

Narita, M., Kato, H., Miyoshi, K., Aoki, T., Yajima, Y., & Suzuki, T. (2005). Treatment for psychological dependence on morphine: Usefulness of inhibiting NMDA receptor and its associated protein kinase in the nucleus accumbens. *Life Sciences, 77,* 2207-2220.

Narrow, W.E., Rae, D.S., Robins, L.N., & Regier, D.A. (2003). Revised prevalence estimates of mental disorders in the United States. *Archives of General Psychiatry, 59,* 115-123.

Neal, D., Matson, J.L., & Belva, B.C. (2013). An examination of the reliability of a new observation measure for autism spectrum disorders: The autism spectrum disorder observation for children. *Research in Autism Spectrum Disorders, 7,* 29-34.

Nelson, J.C., & Devanand, D.P. (2011). A systematic review and meta-analysis of placebo-controlled antidepressant studies in people with depression and dementia. *Journal of the American Geriatrics Society, 59,* 577-585.

Ness, S., Rafii, M., Aisen, P., Krams, M., Silverman, W., & Manji, H. (2012). Down's syndrome and Alzheimer's disease: Towards secondary prevention. *Nature Reviews Drug Discovery, 11,* 655-656.

Nesse, R.M., & Ellsworth, P.C. (2009). Evolution, emotions, and emotional disorders. *American Psychologist, 64,* 129-139.

Neukrug, E. (2012). *The world of the counselor: An introduction to the counseling profession* (4th ed.). Belmont, CA: Cengage.

Neul, J.L. (2012). The relationship of Rett syndrome and MECP2 disorders to autism. *Dialogues in Clinical Neuroscience, 14,* 253-262.

Nevels, R.M., Dehon, E.E., Alexander, K., & Gontkovsky, S.T. (2010). Psychopharmacology of aggression in children and adolescents with primary neuropsychiatric disorders: A review of current and potentially promising treatment options. *Experimental and Clinical Psychopharmacology, 18,* 184-201.

Newberg, A.R., Catapano, L.A., Zarate, C.A., & Manji, H.K. (2008). Neurobiology of bipolar disorder. *Expert Review of Neurotherapeutics, 8,* 93-110.

Newlin, D.B., Regalia, P.A., Seidman, T.I., & Bobashev, G. (2012). Control theory and addictive behavior. In B. Gutkin & S.H. Ahmed (Eds.), *Computational neuroscience of drug addiction* (pp. 57-108). New York: Springer.

Newman, C.F., Leahy, R.L., Beck, A.T., Reilly-Harrington, N.A., & Gyulai, L. (2002). *Bipolar disorder: A cognitive therapy approach*. Washington, DC: American Psychological Association.

Newton, A.W., & Vandeven, A.M. (2005). Update on child maltreatment with a special focus on shaken baby syndrome. *Current Opinion in Pediatrics, 17,* 246-251.

Newton-Howes, G., Weaver, T., & Tyrer, P. (2008). Attitudes of staff towards patients with personality disorder in community mental health teams. *Australian and New Zealand Journal of Psychiatry, 42,* 572-577.

Nichols, H.R., & Molinder, I. (2000). *Multiphasic Sex Inventory II*. Fircrest, WA: Nichols & Molinder Assessments.

Nichols, M.P., & Schwartz, R.C. (2004). *Family therapy: Concepts and methods*. (6th ed.). Boston: Allyn & Bacon.

Nicholson, T.R.J., Stone, J., & Kanaan, R.A.A. (2011). Conversion disorder: A problematic diagnosis. *Journal of Neurology, Neurosurgery and Psychiatry, 82,* 1267-1273.

Nicolosi, A., Moreira, E.D., Shirai, M., Tambi, M.I.I.M., & Glasser, D.B. (2003). Epidemiology of erectile dysfunction in four countries: Cross-national study of the prevalence and correlates of erectile dysfunction. *Urology, 61,* 201-206.

Niemi, L.T., Suvisaari, J.M., Tuulio-Henriksson, A., & Lonnqvist, J.K. (2003). Childhood developmental abnormalities in schizophrenia: Evidence from high-risk studies. *Schizophrenia Research, 60,* 239-258.

Nieratschker, V., Batra, A., & Fallgatter, A.J. (2013). Genetics and epigenetics of alcohol dependence. *Journal of Molecular Psychiatry, 2013,* 1-11.

Nihira, K., Leland, H., & Lambert, N.M. (1993). *Adaptive Behavior Scale-Residential and Community: 2nd Ed.* Lutz, FL: Psychological Assessment Resources.

Nilsson, P., Iwata, N., Muramatsu, S., Tjernberg, L.O., Winblad, B., & Saido, T.C. (2010). Gene therapy in Alzheimer's disease: Potential for disease modification. *Journal of Cellular and Molecular Medicine, 14,* 741-757.

Nishiyori, A., Shibata, A., Ogimoto, I., Uchimura, N., Egami, H., Nakamura, J., Sakata, R., & Fukuda, K. (2005). Alcohol drinking frequency is more directly associated with alcohol use disorder than alcohol metabolizing enzymes among male Japanese. *Psychiatry and Clinical Neurosciences, 59,* 38-44.

Nobis, W.P., Kash, T.L., Silberman, Y., & Winder, D.G. (2011). β-adrenergic receptors enhance excitatory transmission in the bed nucleus of the stria terminalis through a corticotrophin-releasing factor receptor-dependent and cocaine-regulated mechanism. *Biological Psychiatry, 69,* 1083-1090.

Nobre, P.J. (2010). Psychological determinants of erectile dysfunction: Testing a cognitive-emotional model. *Journal of Sexual Medicine, 7,* 1429-1437.

Norcross, J.C. (Ed.). (2011). *Psychotherapy relationships that work: Evidence-based responsiveness* (2nd ed.). New York: Oxford.

Norcross, J.C., Hedges, M., & Prochaska, J.O. (2002). The face of 2010: A Delphi poll on the future of psychotherapy. *Professional Psychology: Research and Practice, 33,* 316-322.

Norko, M.A., & Baranoski, M.V. (2005). The state of contemporary risk assessment research. *Canadian Journal of Psychiatry, 50,* 18-26.

Norman, A.L., Crocker, N., Mattson, S.N., & Riley, E.P. (2009). Neuroimaging and fetal alcohol spectrum disorders. *Developmental Disabilities Research Reviews, 15,* 209-217.

Norris, M.L., Boydell, K.M., Pinhas, L. & Katzman, D.K. (2006). Ana and the Internet: A review of pro-anorexia websites. *International Journal of Eating Disorders, 39,* 443-447.

Norton, G.R., Dorward, J., & Cox, B.J. (1986). Factors associated with panic attacks in nonclinical subjects. *Behavior Therapy, 17,* 239-252.

Norton, P.J., & Price, E.C. (2007). A meta-analytic review of adult cognitive-behavioral treatment outcome across the anxiety disorders. *Journal of Nervous and Mental Disease, 195,* 521-531.

Noyes, B.B., Hill, R.D., Hicken, B.L., Luptak, M., Rupper, R., Dailey, N.K., & Bair, B.D. (2010). The role of grief in dementia caregiving. *American Journal of Alzheimer's Disease and Other Dementias, 25,* 9-17.

Noyes, R., Clarkson, C., Crowe, R.R., Yates, W.R., & McChesney, C.M. (1987). A family study of generalized anxiety disorder. *American Journal of Psychiatry, 144,* 1019-1024.

Nunes, K.P., Labazi, H., & Webb, R.C. (2012). New insights into hypertension-associated erectile dysfunction. *Current Opinion in Nephrology and Hypertension, 21,* 163-170.

Nusbaum, M.R., Braxton, L., & Strayhorn, G. (2005). The sexual concerns of African American, Asian American, and White women seeking routine gynecological care. *Journal of the American Board of Family Practice, 18,* 173-179.

Nusbaum, M.R.H., Gamble, G., Skinner, B., & Heiman, J. (2000). The high prevalence of sexual concerns among women seeking routine gynecological care. *Journal of Family Practice, 49,* 229-232.

Oades, R.D., Sadile, A.G., Sagvolden, T., Viggiano, D., Zuddas, A., Devoto, P., Aase, H., Johansen, E.B., Ruocco, L.A., & Russell, V.A. (2005). The control of responsiveness in ADHD by catecholamines: Evidence for dopaminergic, noradrenergic and interactive roles. *Developmental Science, 8,* 122-131.

Oberg, M., Jaakola, M.S., Woodward, A., Peruga, A., & Pruss-Ustun, A. (2011). Worldwide burden of disease from exposure to second-hand smoke: A retrospective analysis of data from 192 countries. *Lancet, 377,* 139-146.

O'Brien, R.J., & Wong, P.C. (2011). Amyloid precursor protein processing and Alzheimer's disease. *Annual Review of Neuroscience, 34,* 185-204.

O'Dell, K.R., Masters, K.S., Speilmans, G.I., & Maisto, S.A. (2011). Does type-D personality predict outcomes among patients with cardiovascular disease? A meta-analytic review. *Journal of Psychosomatic Research, 71,* 199-206.

O'Donohue, W.T., & Cucciare, M. (Eds.). (2008). *Terminating psychotherapy: A clinician's guide*. New York: Routledge.

O'Donohue, W.T., & Fisher, J.E. (2012). The core principles of cognitive behavior therapy. In W.T. O'Donohue & J.E. Fisher (Eds.), *Cognitive behavior therapy: Core principles for practice* (pp. 1-12). Hoboken, NJ: Wiley.

O'Farrell, T.J., & Clements, K. (2012). Review of outcome research on marital and family therapy in treatment for alcoholism. *Journal of Marital and Family Therapy, 38,* 122-144.

O'Hagan, D.T., & Rappuoli, R. (2004). Novel approaches to vaccine delivery. *Pharmaceutical Research, 21,* 1519-1530.

O'Hara, M.W. (2009). Postpartum depression: What we know. *Journal of Clinical Psychology, 65,* 1258-1269.

Oertel-Knöchel, V., Knöchel, C., Matura, S., Prvulovic, D., Linden, D.E.J., & van de Ven, V. (2013). Reduced functional connectivity and asymmetry of the planum temporale in patients with schizophrenia and first-degree relatives. *Schizophrenia Research, 147,* 331-338.

Offord, D.R., Boyle, M.H., Campbell, D., Goering, P., Lin, E., Wong, M., & Racine, Y.A. (1996). One-year prevalence of psychiatric disorder in Ontarians 15 to 64 years of age. *Canadian Journal of Psychiatry, 41,* 559-563.

Oguru, M., Tachibana, H., Toda, K., Okuda, B., & Oka, N. (2010). Apathy and depression in Parkinson disease. *Journal of Geriatric Psychiatry Neurology 23:*35-41.

Okabe, N., Sato, T., Matsumoto, Y., Ido, Y., Terada, S., & Kuroda, S. (2008). Clinical characteristics of patients with gender identity disorder at a Japanese gender identity disorder clinic. *Psychiatry Research, 157,* 315-318.

Okeahialam, B.N., & Obeka, N.C. (2006). Sexual dysfunction in female hypertensives. *Journal of the National Medical Association, 98,* 638-640.

Okeahialam, B.N., & Obeka, N.C. (2007). Erectile dysfunction in Nigerian hypertensives. *African Journal of Medicine and Medical Sciences, 36,* 221-224.

Okereke, O.I., Rosner, B.A., Kim, D.H., Kang, J.H., Cook, N.R., Manson, J.E., Buring, J.E., Willett, W.C., & Grodstein, F. (2012). Dietary fat types and 4-year cognitive change in community-dwelling older women. *Annals of Neurology, 72,* 124-134.

Olabi, B., & Hall, J. (2010). Borderline personality disorder: Current drug treatments and future prospects. *Therapeutic Advances in Chronic Disease, 1,* 59-66.

Olatunji, B.O., & Wolitsky-Taylor, K.B. (2009). Anxiety sensitivity and the anxiety disorders: A meta-analytic review and synthesis. *Psychological Bulletin, 135,* 974-999.

olde Hartman, T.C., Borghuis, M.S., Lucassen, P.L.B.J., van de Laar, F.A., Speckens, A.E., & van Weel, C. (2009). Medically unexplained symptoms, somatization disorder and hypochondriasis: Course and prognosis. A systematic review. *Journal of Psychosomatic Research, 66,* 363-377.

Olfson, M. (2004). New options on the pharmacological management of attention-deficit/hyperactivity disorder. *American Journal of Managed Care, 10,* S117-S124.

Olfson, M., Marcus, S.C., Druss, B., Elinson, L., Tanielian, T., & Pincus, H.A. (2002). National trends in the outpatient treatment of depression. *Journal of the American Medical Association, 287,* 203-209.

Ollendick, T.H., Lewis, K.M., Cowart, M.J.W., & Davis, T. (2012). Prediction of child performance on a parent-child behavioral approach test with animal phobic children. *Behavior Modification, 36,* 509-524.

Olsen, K.A., & Rosenbaum, B. (2006). Prospective investigations of the prodromal state of schizophrenia: Review of studies. *Acta Psychiatrica Scandanavia, 113,* 247-272.

Ondersma, S.J., Chaffin, M., Berliner, L., Cordon, I., Goodman, G.S., & Barnett, D. (2001). Sex with children is abuse: Comment on Rind, Tromovitch, and Bauserman (1998). *Psychological Bulletin, 127,* 707-714.

Onishi, H., Onose, M., Yamada, T., Mizuno, Y., Ito, M., Sugiura, K., Kato, H., & Nakayama, H. (2003). Brief psychotic disorder associated with bereavement in a patient with terminal-stage uterine cervical cancer: A case report and review of the literature. *Supportive Care in Cancer, 11,* 491-493.

Oosterlaan, J., Geurts, H M., Knol, D.L., & Sergeant, J.A. (2005). Low basal salivary control is associated with teacher-reported symptoms of conduct disorder. *Psychiatry Research, 134,* 1-10.

Oosterman, J.M., & Scherder, E.J. (2006). Distinguishing between vascular dementia and Alzheimer's disease by means of the WAIS: A meta-analysis. *Journal of Clinical and Experimental Neuropsychology, 28,* 1158-1175.

Oscar-Berman, M., Kirkley, S.M., Gansler, D.A., & Couture, A. (2004). Comparisons of Korsakoff and non-Korsakoff alcoholics on neuropsychological tests of prefrontal brain functioning. *Alcoholism: Clinical and Experimental Research, 28,* 667-675.

Osman, A., Gutierrez, P.M., Smith, K., Fang, Q., Lozano, G., & Devine, A. (2010). The Anxiety Sensitivity Index—3: Analyses of dimensions, reliability estimates, and correlates in nonclinical samples. *Journal of Personality Assessment, 92,* 45-52.

Ostrager, B. (2010). SMS. OMG! LOL! TTYL: Translating the law to accommodate today's teens and the evolution from texting to sexting. *Family Court Review, 48,* 712-726.

Oswald, S.H., Heil, K., & Goldbeck, L. (2010). History of maltreatment and mental health problems in foster children: A review of the literature. *Journal of Pediatric Psychology, 35,* 462-472.

Otto, M.W., Pollack, M.H., & Maki, K.M. (2000). Empirically supported treatments for panic disorder: Costs, benefits, and stepped care. *Journal of Consulting and Clinical Psychology, 68,* 556-563.

Ottosson, J.-O., & Fink, M. (2004). *Ethics in electroconvulsive therapy.* New York: Brunner-Routledge.

Ouimet, A.J., Gawronski, B., & Dozois, D.J.A. (2009). Cognitive vulnerability to anxiety: A review and an integrative model. *Clinical Psychology Review, 29,* 459-470.

Owen, M.J., O'Donovan, M.C., Thapar, A., & Craddock, N. (2011). Neurodevelopmental hypothesis of schizophrenia. *British Journal of Psychiatry, 198,* 173-175.

Ozsungur, S., Brenner, D., & El-Sohemy, A. (2009). Fourteen well-described caffeine withdrawal symptoms factor into three clusters. *Psychopharmacology, 201,* 541-548.

Padma-Nathan, H. (2006). Sildenafil citrate (Viagra) treatment for erectile dysfunction: An updated profile of response and effectiveness. *International Journal of Impotence Research, 18,* 423-431.

Page, M.P., & Azar, S.T. (2012). The link between thyroid function and depression. *Journal of Thyroid Research, 2012,* 1-8.

Pais, S. (2009). A systemic approach to the treatment of dissociative identity disorder. *Journal of Family Psychotherapy, 20,* 72-88.

Palha, A.P., & Lourenco, M.F. (2011). Psychological and cross-cultural aspects of infertility and human sexuality. In R. Balon (Ed.), *Sexual dysfunction: Beyond the brain-body connection* (pp. 164-183). Basel: Korgem.

Palmer, B.A., Pankratz, V.S., & Bostwick, J.M. (2005). The lifetime risk of suicide in schizophrenia: A reexamination. *Archives of General Psychiatry, 62,* 247-253.

Pampallona, S., Bollini, P., Tibaldi, G., Kupelnick, B., & Munizza, C. (2004). Combined psychotherapy and psychological treatment for depression: A systematic review. *Archives of General Psychiatry, 61,* 714-719.

Paparelli, A., Di Forti, M., Morrison, P.D., & Murray, R.M. (2011). Drug-induced psychosis: How to avoid star gazing in schizophrenia research by looking at more obvious sources of light. *Frontiers in Behavioral Neuroscience, 5,* 1-9.

Pardini, D., & Frick, P.J. (2013). Multiple developmental pathways to conduct disorder: Current conceptualizations and clinical implications. *Journal of the Canadian Association of Child and Adolescent Psychiatry, 22,* 20-25.

Paradise, J.E. (2001). Current concepts in preventing sexual abuse. *Current Opinion in Pediatrics, 13,* 402-407.

Parent, J., Forehand, R., Merchant, M.J., Edwards, M.C., Conners-Burrow, N.A., Long, N., & Jones, D.J. (2011). The relation of harsh and permissive discipline with child disruptive behaviors: Does child gender make a difference in an at-risk sample? *Journal of Family Violence, 26,* 527-533.

Paris, J. (2003). Personality disorders over time: Precursors, course and outcome. *Journal of Personality Disorders, 17,* 479-488.

Paris, J. (2009). The treatment of borderline personality disorder: Implications of research on diagnosis, etiology, and outcome. *Annual Review of Clinical Psychology, 5,* 277-290.

Park, A., Sher, K.J., Todorov, A.A., & Heath, A.C. (2011). Interaction between the DRD4 VNTR polymorphism and proximal and distal environments in alcohol dependence during emerging and young adulthood. *Journal of Abnormal Psychology, 120,* 585-595.

Park, K.-M., Ku, J., Choi, S.-H., Jang, H.-J., Park, J., Kim, S.I., & Kim, J.-J. (2011). A virtual reality application in role-plays of social skills training for schizophrenia: A randomized, controlled trial. *Psychiatry Research, 189,* 166-172.

Parker, L. (2012). *Health and safety in early years settings.* New York: Routledge.

Parker, R.N. (2004). Alcohol and violence: Connections, evidence and possibilities for prevention. *Journal of Psychoactive Drugs (Suppl. 2),* 157-163.

Pastor, P.N., & Reuben, C.A. (2005). Racial and ethnic differences in ADHD and LD in young school-age children: Parental reports in the National Health Interview Survey. *Public Health Reports, 120,* 383-392.

Pearce, B.D. (2003). *Can a virus cause schizophrenia? Facts and hypotheses.* New York: Kluwer/Academic.

Pedersen, S.S., & Denollet, J. (2003). Type D personality, cardiac events, and impaired quality of life: A review. *European Journal of Cardiovascular Prevention and Rehabilitation, 10,* 241-248.

Penn, D.L., Judge, A., Jamieson, P., Garczynski, J., Hennessey, M., & Romer, D. (2005). Stigma. In M. Seligman (Ed.), *The Annenberg adolescent mental health initiative* (pp. 532-543). Oxford, England: Oxford University Press.

Pennay, A., Cameron, J., Reichart, T., Strickland, H., Lee, N.K., Hall, K., & Lubman, D.I. (2011). A systematic review of interventions for co-occurring substance use disorder and borderline personality disorder. *Journal of Substance Abuse Treatment, 41,* 363-373.

Penzien, D.B., Rains, J.C., & Andrasik, F. (2002). Behavioral management of recurrent headache: Three decades of experience and empiricism. *Applied Psychophysiology and Biofeedback, 27,* 163-181.

Peralta, V., & Cuesta, M.J. (2001). How many and which are the psychopathological dimensions in schizophrenia?: Issues influencing their ascertainment. *Schizophrenia Research, 49,* 269-285.

Perelman, M., Shabsigh, R., Seftel, A., Althof, S., & Lockhart, D. (2005). Attitudes of men with erectile dysfunction: A cross-national survey. *Journal of Sexual Medicine, 2,* 397-406.

Perera, T.D., Coplan, J.D., Lisanby, S.H., Lipira, C.M., Arif, M., Carpio, C., Spitzer, G., Santarelli, L., Scharf, B., Hen, R., Rosoklija, G., Sackeim, H.A., & Dwork, A.J. (2007). Antidepressant-induced neurogenesis in the hippocampus of adult nonhuman primates. *Journal of Neuroscience, 27,* 4894-4901.

Perez, L., Heim, L., Sherzai, A., Jaceldo-Siegl, K., & Sherzai, A. (2012). Nutrition and vascular dementia. *Journal of Nutrition Health and Aging, 16,* 319-324.

Perkins, D.O., Gu, H., Boteva, K., & Lieberman, J.A. (2005). Relationship between duration of untreated psychosis and outcome in first-episode schizophrenia: A critical review and meta-analysis. *American Journal of Psychiatry, 162,* 1785-1804.

Perry, J., & Felce, D. (2005). Factors associated with outcome in community group homes. *American Journal on Mental Retardation, 110,* 121-135.

Perugi, G., Frare, F., & Toni, C. (2007). Diagnosis and treatment of agoraphobia with panic disorder. *CNS Drugs, 21,* 741-764.

Peterson, B., Boivin, J., Norre, J., Smith, C., Thorn, P., & Wischmann, T. (2012). An introduction to infertility counseling: A guide from mental health and medical professionals. *Journal of Assisted Reproduction and Genetics, 29,* 243-248.

Peterson, L., & Brown, D. (1994). Integrating child injury and abuse-neglect research: Common histories, etiologies, and solutions. *Psychological Bulletin, 116,* 293-315.

Petrovich, G.D., Setlow, B., Holland, P.C., & Gallagher, M. (2002). Amygdalo-hypothalamic circuit allows learned cues to override satiety and promote eating. *Journal of Neuroscience, 22,* 8748-8753.

Pettifor, J., Crozier, S., & Chew, J. (2001). Recovered memories: Ethical guidelines to support professionals. *Journal of Child Sexual Abuse, 10,* 1-15.

Peveler, R., Kilkenny, L., & Kinmouth, A.-L. (1997). Medically unexplained physical symptoms in primary care: A comparison of self-report screening questionnaires and clinical opinion. *Journal of Psychosomatic Research, 42,* 245-252.

Pfeiffer, B., Kinnealey, M., Reed, C., & Herzberg, G. (2005). Sensory modulation and affective disorders in children and adolescents with Asperger's disorder. *American Journal of Occupational Therapy, 59,* 335-345.

Pfohl, B., Blum, N., & Zimmerman, M. (1994). *Structured interview for DSM-IV personality (SIDP-IV).* Iowa City, IA: Author.

Philipsen, A., Schmahl, C., & Lieb, K. (2004). Naloxone in the treatment of acute dissociative states in female patients with borderline personality disorder. *Pharmacopsychiatry, 37,* 196-199.

Phillips, K.A. (2004). Body dysmorphic disorder: Recognizing and treating imagined ugliness. *World Psychiatry, 3,* 12-17.

Phillips, K.A., Pagano, M.E., Menard, W., Fay, C., & Stout, R.L. (2005). Predictors of remission from body dysmorphic disorder: A prospective study. *Journal of Nervous and Mental Disease, 193,* 564-567.

Phillips, K.A., Siniscalchi, J.M., & McElroy, S.L. (2004). Depression, anxiety, anger, and somatic symptoms in patients with body dysmorphic disorder. *Psychiatric Quarterly, 75,* 309-320.

Pickens, C.L., Airavaara, M., Theberge, F., Fanous, S., Hope, B.T., & Shaham, Y. (2011). Neurobiology of the incubation of drug craving. *Trends in Neurosciences, 34,* 411-420.

Piet, J., & Hougaard, E. (2011). The effect of mindfulness-based cognitive therapy for prevention of relapse in recurrent major depressive disorder: A systematic review and meta-analysis. *Clinical Psychology Review, 31,* 1032-1040.

Pina, A.A., & Silverman, W.K. (2004). Clinical phenomenology, somatic symptoms, and distress in Hispanic/Latino and European American youths with anxiety disorders. *Journal of Clinical Child and Adolescent Psychology, 33,* 227-236.

Pincus, A.L., & Lukowitsky, M.R. (2010). Pathological narcissism and narcissistic personality disorder. *Annual Review of Clinical Psychology, 6,* 421-446.

Piper, M., Beneyto, M., Burne, T.H.J., Eyles, D.W., Lewis, D.A., & McGrath, J.J. (2012). The neurodevelopmental hypothesis of schizophrenia: Convergent clues from epidemiology and neuropathology. *Psychiatric Clinics of North America, 35,* 571-584.

Pirelli, G., Gottdiener, W.H., & Zapf, P.A. (2011). A meta-analytic review of competency to stand trial research. *Psychology, Public Policy, and Law, 17,* 1-53.

Pirkola, S., Sohlman, B., & Wahlbeck, K. (2005). The characteristics of suicides within a week of discharge after psychiatric hospitalisation—A nationwide register study. *BMC Psychiatry, 5,* 32.

Plaga, S.L., Demareo, R., & Shulman, L.P. (2005). Prenatal diagnostic decision-making in adolescents. *Journal of Pediatric and Adolescent Gynecology, 18,* 97-100.

Plante, D.T., & Winkelman, J.W. (2008). Sleep disturbance in bipolar disorder: Therapeutic implications. *American Journal of Psychiatry, 165,* 830-843.

Plassman, B.L., Langa, K.M., Fisher, G.G., Heeringa, S.G., Weir, D.R., Ofstedal, M.B., Burke, J.R., Hurd, M.D., Potter, G.G., Rodgers, W.L., Steffens, D.C., Willis, R.J., & Wallace, R.B. (2007). Prevalence of dementia in the United States: The aging, demographics, and memory study. *Neuroepidemiology, 29,* 125-132.

Player, M.S., & Peterson, L.E. (2011). Anxiety disorders, hypertension, and cardiovascular risk: A review. *International Journal of Psychiatry in Medicine, 41,* 365-377.

Plessen, K.J., & Peterson, B.S. (2009). The neurobiology of impulsivity and self-regulatory control in children with attention-deficit/hyperactivity disorder. In D.S. Charney & E.J. Nestler (Eds), *Neurobiology of mental illness* (3rd ed.). (pp. 1129-1152). New York: Oxford.

Pliszka, S.R. (2005). The neuropsychopharmacology of attention deficit/hyperactivity disorder. *Biological Psychiatry, 57,* 1385-1390.

Poetter, C.E., & Stewart, J.T. (2012). Treatment of indiscriminate, inappropriate sexual behavior in frontotemporal dementia with carbamazepine. *Journal of Clinical Psychopharmacology, 32,* 137-138.

Poikolainen, K. (1999). Effectiveness of brief interventions to reduce alcohol intake in primary health care populations: A meta-analysis. *Preventive Medicine, 28,* 503-509.

Pole, N., Best, S.R., Metzler, T., & Marmar, C.R. (2005). Why are Hispanics at greater risk for PTSD? *Cultural Diversity and Ethnic Minority Psychology, 11,* 144-161.

Polidori, M.C., Pientka, L., & Mecocci, P. (2012). A review of the major vascular risk factors related to Alzheimer's disease. *Journal of Alzheimer's Disease, 32,* 521-530.

Polimeni, J., Reiss, J.P., & Sareen, J. (2005). Could obsessive-compulsive disorder have originated as a group-selected adaptive trait in traditional societies? *Medical Hypotheses, 65,* 655-664.

Polivy, J., & Herman, C.P. (2002). Causes of eating disorders. *Annual Review of Psychology, 53,* 187-213.

Polosa, R., & Benowitz, N.L. (2011). Treatment of nicotine addiction. Present therapeutic options and pipeline developments. *Trends in Pharmacological Sciences, 32*, 281-289.

Porter, R.J., Douglas, K., & Knight, R.G. (2008). Monitoring of cognitive effects during a course of electroconvulsive therapy: Recommendations for clinical practice. *Journal of ECT, 24*, 25-34

Potuzak, M., Ravichandran, C., Lewandowski, K.E., Ongur, D., & Cohen, B. (2012). Categorical vs dimensional classifications of psychotic disorders. *Comprehensive Psychiatry, 53*, 1118-1129.

Poveda, A.M. (2003). An anthropological perspective of Alzheimer disease. *Geriatric Nursing, 24*, 26-31.

Powell, L.H., Shahabi, L., & Thoresen, C.E. (2003). Religion and spirituality: Linkages to mental health. *American Psychologist, 58*, 36-52.

Powell, M.D., & Ladd, L.D. (2010). Bullying: A review of the literature and implications for family therapists. *American Journal of Family Therapy, 38*, 189-206.

Powell, M.P., & Schulte, T. (1999). Turner syndrome. In S. Goldstein & C.R.Reynolds (Eds.), *Handbook of neurodevelopmental and genetic disorders in children* (pp. 277-297). New York: Guilford.

Powell, R.A., & Powell, A.J. (1998). Treatment outcome for dissociative identity disorder. *American Journal of Psychiatry, 155*, 1304.

Powls, J., & Davies, J. (2012). A descriptive review of research relating to sadomasochism: Considerations for clinical practice. *Deviant Behavior, 33*, 223-234.

Praharaj, S.K., Ram, D., & Arora, M. (2009). Efficacy of high frequency (rapid) suprathreshold repetitive transcranial magnetic stimulation of right prefrontal cortex in bipolar mania: A randomized sham controlled study. *Journal of Affective Disorders, 117*, 146-150.

Pratt, H.D., & Patel, D.R. (2007). Learning disorders in children and adolescents. *Primary Care, 34*, 361-374.

President's New Freedom Commission on Mental Health (2003). *Achieving the promise: Transforming mental health care in America*. Rockville, MD: U.S. Department of Health and Human Services, Substance Abuse and Mental Health Services Administration, Center for Mental Health Services, National Institutes of Health, National Institute of Mental Health.

Price, G.R., Holloway, I., Rasanen, P., Vesterinen, M., & Ansari, D. (2007). Impaired parietal magnitude processing in developmental dyscalculia. *Current Biology, 17*, R1042-1043.

Price, J.L., & Drevets, W.C. (2012). Neural circuits underlying the pathophysiology of mood disorders. *Trends in Cognitive Sciences, 16*, 61-71.

Price, J.R., Hescheles, D.R., & Price, A.R. (1999). Selecting clients for group psychotherapy. In J.R. Price, D.R. Hescheles, & A.R. Price (Eds.), *A guide to starting psychotherapy groups* (pp. 15-19). New York: Academic.

Price, R.K., Risk, N.K., Murray, K.S., Virgo, K.S., & Spitznagel, E.L. (2001). Twenty-five year mortality of US servicemen deployed in Vietnam: Predictive utility of early drug use. *Drug and Alcohol Dependence, 64*, 309-318.

Prince, M., Bryce, R., Albanese, E., Wimo, A., Ribeiro, W., & Ferri, C.P. (2013). The global prevalence of dementia: A systematic review and metaanalysis. *Alzheimer's and Dementia, 9*, 63-75.

Prochaska, J.O., & Norcross, J.C. (2013). *Systems of psychotherapy: A transtheoretical analysis* (8th ed.). Stamford, CT: Cengage.

Prouty, G. (2003). Pre-therapy: A newer development in the psychotherapy of schizophrenia. *Journal of the American Academy of Psychoanalysis and Dynamic Psychiatry, 31*, 59-73.

Pull, C.B. (2008). Recent trends in the study of specific phobias. *Current Opinion in Psychiatry, 21*, 43-50.

Punjabi, N.M. (2008). The epidemiology of adult obstructive sleep apnea. *Proceedings of the American Thoracic Society, 5*, 136-143.

Purdon, C. (2004). Empirical investigations of thought suppression in OCD. *Journal of Behavior Therapy and Experimental Psychiatry, 35*, 121-136.

Puri, B.K., Counsell, S.J., Saeed, N., Bustos, M.G., Treasaden, I.H., & Bydder, G.M. (2008). Regional grey matter volumetric changes in forensic schizophrenia patients: An MRI study comparing the brain structure of patients who have seriously and violently offended with that of patients who have not. *BMC Psychiatry, 8 (Suppl. 1)*, S6.

Putnam, F.W. (2003). Ten-year research update review: Child sexual abuse. *Journal of the American Academy of Child and Adolescent Psychiatry, 42*, 269-278.

Qiu, C., Skoog, I., & Fratiglioni, L. (2002). Occurrence and determinants of vascular cognitive impairment. In T. Erkinjuntti & S. Gauthier (Eds.), *Vascular cognitive impairment* (pp. 61-83). London: Martin Dunitz.

Quayle, E. (2011). Pedophilia, child porn, and cyberpredators. In C.D. Bryant (Ed.), *The Routledge handbook of deviant behavior* (pp. 390-396). New York: Routledge.

Quigley, H., Colloby, S.J., & O'Brien, J.T. (2011). PET imaging of brain amyloid in dementia: a review. *International Journal of Geriatric Psychiatry, 26*, 991-999.

Quinsey, V.L. (2003). The etiology of anomalous sexual preferences in men. *Annals of the New York Academy of Sciences, 989*, 105-117.

Quinsey, V.L. (2012). Pragmatic and Darwinian views of the paraphilias. *Archives of Sexual Behavior, 41*, 217-220.

Quinsey, V.L., Harris, G.T., Rice, M.E., & Cormier, C.A. (1998). *Violent offenders: Appraising and managing risk*. Washington, DC: American Psychological Association.

Rabinerson, D., Kaplan, B., Orvieto, R., & Dekel, A. (2002). Munchausen syndrome in obstetrics and gynecology. *Journal of Psychosomatic Obstetrics and Gynecology, 23*, 215-218.

Race, E., & Verfaellie, M. (2012). Remote memory function and dysfunction in Korsakoff's syndrome. *Neuropsychology Review, 22*, 105-116.

Rachman, S. (2004). *Anxiety* (2nd ed.). New York: Taylor and Francis.

Radenbach, K., Flaig, V., Schneider-Axmann, T., Usher, J., Reith, W., Falkai, P., Gruber, O., & Scherk, H. (2010). Thalamic volumes in patients with bipolar disorder. *European Archives of Psychiatry and Clinical Neuroscience, 260*, 601-607.

Rodemalm, M.G., & Otto, M.W. (2002). The cognitive-behavioral treatment of social anxiety disorder. *Psychiatric Clinics of North America, 24*, 805-816.

Raggi, A., Plazzi, G., Pennisi, G., Tasca, D., & Ferri, R. (2011). Cognitive evoked potentials in narcolepsy: A review of the literature. *Neuroscience and Biobehavioral Reviews, 35*, 1144-1153.

Raguram, R., Weiss, M.G., Channabasavanna, S.M., & Devins, G.M. (1996). Stigma, depression, and somatization in south India. *American Journal of Psychiatry, 153*, 1043-1049.

Rains, J.C., Penzein, D.B., McCrory, D.C., & Gray, R.N. (2005). Behavioral headache treatment: History, review of the empirical literature, and methodological critique. *Headache, 45 (Suppl. 2)*, S92-S109.

Ramana, R., Paykel, E.S., Melzer, D., Mehta, M.A., & Surtees, P.G. (2003). Aftercare of depressed inpatients: Service delivery and unmet needs. *Social Psychiatry and Psychiatric Epidemiology, 38*, 109-115.

Ranjith, G., & Mohan, R. (2006). Dhat syndrome as a functional somatic syndrome: Developing a sociosomatic model. *Psychiatry, 69*, 142-150.

Rao, D., Young, M., & Raguram, R. (2007). Culture, somatization, and psychological distress: Symptom presentation in South Indian patients from a public psychiatric hospital. *Psychopathology, 40*, 349-355.

Rao, P.A., Beidel, D.C., & Murray, M.J. (2008). Social skills interventions for children with Asperger's syndrome or high-functioning autism: A review and recommendations. *Journal of Autism and Developmental Disorders, 38*, 353-361.

Rapee, R.M. (2012). Family factors in the development and management of anxiety disorders. *Clinical Child and Family Psychology Review, 15*, 69-80.

Rapee, R.M., Schniering, C.A., & Hudson, J.L. (2009). Anxiety disorders during childhood and adolescence: Origins and treatment. *Annual Review of Clinical Psychology, 5*, 311-341.

Rapoport, J.L., Giedd, J.N., & Gogtay, N. (2012). Neurodevelopmental model of schizophrenia: Update 2012. *Molecular Psychiatry, 17*, 1228-1238.

Rasmussen, B.K. (2001). Epidemiology of headache. *Cephalagia, 21*, 774-777.

Rastad, C., Ulfberg, J., & Lindberg, P. (2008). Light room therapy effective in mild forms of seasonal affective disorder: A randomized controlled study. *Journal of Affective Disorders, 108*, 291-296.

Rathod, S., Kingdon, D., Weiden, P., & Turkington, D. (2008). Cognitive-behavioral therapy for medication-resistant schizophrenia: A review. *Journal of Psychiatric Practice, 14*, 22-33.

Rathod, S., Kingdon, D., Weiden, P., & Turkington, D. (2010). Cognitive-behavioral therapy for medication-resistant schizophrenia: A review. *Focus, 8*, 626-637.

Ratnavalli, E., Brayne, C., Dawson, K., & Hodges, J.R. (2002). The prevalence of frontotemporal dementia. *Neurology, 58*, 1615-1621.

Rautalinko, E., Lisper, H.O., & Ekehammar, B. (2007). Reflective listening in counseling: Effects of training time and evaluator social skills. *American Journal of Psychotherapy, 61*, 191-209.

Ravenel, M.C., Salinas, C.F., Marlow, N.M., Slate, E.H., Evans, Z.P., & Miller, P.M. (2012). Methamphetamine use and oral health: A pilot study of "meth mouth." *Quintessence International, 43*, 229-237.

Raymond, F.L. (2005). X-linked mental retardation: A clinical guide. *Journal of Medical Genetics, 43*, 193-200.

Rayner, L., Price, A., Evans, A., Valsraj, K., Hotopf, M., & Higginson, I.J. (2011). Antidepressants for the treatment of depression in palliative care: Systematic review and meta-analysis. *Palliative Medicine, 25*, 36-51.

Read, C.Y. (2004). Using the Impact of Event Scale to evaluate psychological response to being a phenylketonuria gene carrier. *Journal of Genetic Counseling, 13*, 207-219.

Reagan, L.P., Grillo, C.A., & Piroli, G.G. (2008). The As and Ds of stress: Metabolic, morphological and behavioral consequences. *European Journal of Pharmacology, 585*, 64-75.

Real, E., Montejo, A., Alonso, P., & Menchón, J.M. (2013). Sexuality and obsessive-compulsive disorder: The hidden affair. *Neuropsychiatry, 3*, 23-31.

Reas, D.L., Kjelsas, E., Heggestad, T., Eriksen, L., Nielsen, S., Gjertsen, F., & Gotestam, K.G. (2005). Characteristics of anorexia nervosa-related deaths in Norway (1992-2000): Data from the National Patient Register and the Causes of Death Register. *International Journal of Eating Disorders, 37*, 181-187.

Reblin, M., & Uchino, B.N. (2008). Social and emotional support and its implications for health. *Current Opinion in Psychiatry, 21*, 201-205.

Rector, N.A., Kamkar, K., Cassin, S.E., Ayearst, L.E., & Laposa, J.M. (2011). Assessing excessive reassurance seeking in the anxiety disorders. *Journal of Anxiety Disorders, 25*, 911-917.

Reddy, P.H. (2009). Amyloid beta, mitochondrial structural and functional dynamics in Alzheimer's disease. *Experimental Neurology, 218*, 286-292.

Regehr, C., Alaggia, R., Dennis, J., Pitts, A., & Saini, M. (2013). Interventions to reduce distress in adult victims of rape and sexual violence: A systematic review. *Research on Social Work Practice, 23*, 257-265.

Rehm, J., Taylor, B., Mohapatra, S., Irving, H., Baliunas, D., Patra, J., & Roerecke, M. (2010). Alcohol as a risk factor for liver cirrhosis: A systematic review and meta-analysis. *Drug and Alcohol Review, 29*, 437-445.

Reichborn-Kjennerud, T. (2010). The genetic epidemiology of personality disorders. *Dialogues in Clinical Neuroscience, 12*, 103-114.

Reichow, B. (2012). Overview of meta-analyses on early intensive behavioral intervention for young children with autism spectrum disorders. *Journal of Autism and Developmental Disorders, 42*, 512-520.

Reichow, B., & Volkmar, F.R. (2010). Social skills interventions for individuals with autism: Evaluation for evidence-based practices within a best evidence synthesis framework. *Journal of Autism and Developmental Disorders, 40*, 149-166.

Reid, R., & Johnson, J. (2012). *Teacher's guide to ADHD*. New York: Guilford.

Reid, R.C., Carpenter, B.N., Spackman, M., & Willes, D.L. (2008). Alexithymia, emotional instability, and vulnerability to stress proneness in patients seeking help for hypersexual behavior. *Journal of Sex and Marital Therapy, 34*, 133-149.

Reid, V., & Meadows-Oliver, M. (2007). Postpartum depression in adolescent mothers: An integrative review of the literature. *Journal of Pediatric Health Care, 21*, 289-298.

Reiner, K., Tibi, L., & Lipsitz, J.D. (2013). Do mindfulness-based interventions reduce pain intensity? A critical review of the literature. *Pain Medicine, 14*, 230-242.

Reitan, R.M., & Wolfson, D. (1993). *The Halstead-Reitan Neuropsychological Test Battery: Theory and clinical interpretation* (2nd ed.). Tucson, AZ: Neuropsychology Press.

Reitz, C. (2012). Dyslipidemia and dementia: Current epidemiology, genetic evidence, and mechanisms behind the associations. *Journal of Alzheimer's Disease, 30 (Suppl. 2)*, S127-S145.

Rellini, A.H., & Clifton, J. (2011). Female orgasmic disorder. In Balon, R. (Ed.), *Sexual dysfunction: Beyond the brain-body connection* (pp. 35-56). Basel: Karger.

Remschmidt, H., & Global ADHD Working Group. (2005). Global consensus on ADHD/HKD. *European Child and Adolescent Psychiatry, 14*, 127-137.

Retzlaff, P., Stoner, J., & Kleinsasser, D. (2002). The use of the MCMI-III in the screening and triage of offenders. *International Journal of Offender Therapy and Comparative Criminology, 46*, 319-332.

Reyes-Rodriguez, M.L., Rivera-Medina, C.L., Camara-Fuentes, L., Suarez-Torres, A., & Bernal, G. (2013). Depression symptoms and stressful life events among college students in Puerto Rico. *Journal of Affective Disorders, 145*, 324-330.

Reynolds, C.R., & Kamphaus, R.W. (2004). *Behavior Assessment System for Children—Second Edition manual*. Circle Pines, MN: American Guidance Service Publishing.

Rhee, H., Belyea, M.J., & Brasch, J. (2010). Family support and asthma outcomes in adolescents: Barriers to adherence as a mediator. *Journal of Adolescent Health, 47*, 472-478.

Rice, M.E., & Harris, G.T. (2011). Is androgen deprivation therapy effective in the treatment of sex offenders? *Psychology, Public Policy, and Law, 17*, 315-332.

Rice, M.L., Warren, S.F., & Betz, S.K. (2005). Language symptoms of developmental language disorders: An overview of autism, Down syndrome, fragile X, specific language impairment, and Williams syndrome. *Applied Psycholinguistics, 26*, 7-27.

Richards, C.S., & Perri, M.G. (Eds.). (2010). *Relapse prevention in depression*. Washington, DC: American Psychological Association.

Richards, D. (2011). Prevalence and clinical course of depression: A review. *Clinical Psychology Review, 31*, 1117-1125.

Richards, D.A., Lovell, K., & McEvoy, P. (2003). Access and effectiveness in psychological therapies: Selfhelp as a routine health technology. *Health and Social Care in the Community, 11*, 175-182.

Richardson, D., & Goldmeier, D. (2005). Premature ejaculation—does country of origin tell us anything about etiology? *Journal of Sexual Medicine, 2*, 508-512.

Richardson, D., Wood, K., & Goldmeier, D. (2006). A qualitative pilot study of Islamic men with lifelong premature (rapid) ejaculation. *Journal of Sexual Medicine, 3*, 337-343.

Richmond, K., Carroll, K., & Denboske, K. (2010). Gender identity disorder: Concerns and controversies. In J.C. Chrisler & D.R. McCreary (Eds.), *Handbook of gender research in psychology* (pp. 111-131). New York: Springer.

Rief, W., & Broadbent, E. (2007). Explaining medically unexplained symptoms: Models and mechanisms. *Clinical Psychology Review, 27*, 821-841.

Rief, W., Hennings, A., Riemer, S., & Euteneuer, F. (2010). Psychobiological differences between depression and somatization. *Journal of Psychosomatic Research, 68*, 495-502.

Rief, W., & Hiller, W. (2003). A new approach to the assessment of the treatment effects of somatoform disorders. *Psychosomatics, 44*, 492-498.

Rief, W., Hiller, W., & Margraf, J. (1998). Cognitive aspects of hypochondriasis and the somatization syndrome. *Journal of Abnormal Psychology, 107*, 587-595.

Rief, W., Ihle, D., & Pilger, F. (2003). A new approach to assess illness behaviour. *Journal of Psychosomatic Research, 54*, 405-414.

Rief, W., Martin, A., Klaiberg, A., & Brahler, E. (2005). Specific effects of depression, panic, and somatic symptoms on illness behavior. *Psychosomatic Medicine, 67*, 596-601.

Rief, W., Nanke, A., Emmerich, J., Bender, A., & Zech, T. (2004). Causal illness attributions on somatoform disorders: Associations with comorbidity and illness behavior. *Journal of Psychosomatic Research, 57,* 367-371.

Rief, W., & Sharpe, M. (2004). Somatoform disorders: New approaches to classification, conceptualization, and treatment. *Journal of Psychosomatic Research, 56,* 387-390.

Riekse, R.G., Leverenz, J.B., McCormick, W., Bowen, J.D., Ten, L., Nochlin, D., Simpson, K., Eugenio, C., Larson, E.B., & Tsuang, D. (2004). Effect of vascular lesions on cognition in Alzheimer's disease: A community-based study. *Journal of the American Geriatrics Society, 52,* 1442-1448.

Riemann, D. (2007). Insomnia and comorbid psychiatric disorders. *Sleep Medicine, 8 (Suppl. 4),* S15-S20.

Rifkin, A., Ghisalbert, D., Dimatou, S., Jin, C., & Sethi, M. (1998). Dissociative identity disorder in psychiatric inpatients. *American Journal of Psychiatry, 155,* 844-845.

Rigaud, D., Brondel, L., Poupard, A.T., Talonneau, I., & Brun, J.M. (2007). A randomized trial on the efficacy of a 2-month tube feeding regimen in anorexia nervosa: A 1-year follow-up study. *Clinical Nutrition, 26,* 421-429.

Riley, E.P., Infante, A., & Warren, K.R. (2011). Fetal alcohol spectrum disorders: An overview. *Neuropsychology Review, 21,* 73-80.

Rinck, M., Becker, E.S., Kellermann, J., & Roth, W.T. (2003). Selective attention in anxiety: Distraction and enhancement in visual search. *Depression and Anxiety, 18,* 18-28.

Rind, B., Tromovitch, P., & Bauserman, R. (1998). A meta-analytic examination of assumed properties of child sexual abuse using college samples. *Psychological Bulletin, 124,* 22-53.

Rind, B., Tromovitch, P., & Bauserman, R. (2001). The validity and appropriateness of methods, analyses, and conclusions in Rind et al. (1998): A rebuttal of victimological critique from Ondersma et al. (2001) and Dallam et al. (2001). *Psychological Bulletin, 127,* 734-758.

Ringham, R., Klump, K., Kaye, W., Stone, D., Libman, S., Stowe, S., & Marcus, M. (2006). Eating disorder symptomatology among ballet dancers. *International Journal of Eating Disorders, 39,* 503-508.

Ritsner, M.S. (Ed.). (2011). *Handbook of schizophrenia spectrum disorders: Vol. 1. Conceptual issues and methodological advances.* New York: Springer.

Ritter, L., & Lampkin, S.M. (2012). *Community mental health.* Sudbury, MA: Jones and Bartlett Learning.

Rivet, T.T., & Matson, J.L. (2011). Review of gender differences in core symptomatology in autism spectrum disorders. *Research in Autism Spectrum Disorders, 5,* 957-976.

Robertson, E., Grace, S., Wallington, T., & Stewart, D.E. (2004). Antenatal risk factors for postpartum depression: A synthesis of recent literature. *General Hospital Psychiatry, 26,* 289-295.

Robertson, G.S., Hori, S.E., & Powell, K.J. (2006). Schizophrenia: An integrative approach to modeling a complex disorder. *Journal of Psychiatry and Neuroscience, 31,* 157-167.

Robichaud, M., Dugas, M.J., & Conway, M. (2003). Gender differences in worry and associated cognitivebehavioral variables. *Journal of Anxiety Disorders, 17,* 501-516.

Robbins, M.S., Liddle, H.A., Turner, C.W., Dakof, G.A., Alexander, J.F., & Kogan, S.M. (2006). Adolescent and parent therapeutic alliances as predictors of dropout in multidimensional family therapy. *Journal of Family Psychology, 20,* 108-116.

Robins, L.N., Locke, B.Z., & Regier, D.A. (1991). An overview of psychiatric disorders in America. In L.N. Robins & D.A. Regier (Eds.), *Psychiatric disorders in America: The Epidemiologic Catchment Area study* (pp. 328-366). New York: Free Press.

Robinson, D.S., Campbell, D.A., Durham, S.R., Pfeffer, J., Barnes, P.J., & Chung, K.F. (2003). Systematic assessment of difficult-to-treat asthma. *European Respiratory Journal, 22,* 478-483.

Robinson, D.L., Zitzman, D.L., & Williams, S.K. (2011). Mesolimbic dopamine transients in motivated behaviors: Focus on maternal behavior. *Frontiers in Psychiatry, 2,* 1-13.

Robinson, J., Sareen, J., Cox, B.J., & Bolton, J.M. (2011). Role of self-medication in the development of comorbid anxiety and substance use disorders: A longitudinal investigation. *Archives of General Psychiatry, 68,* 800-807.

Robinson, L., Dickinson, C., Rousseau, N., Beyer, F., Clark, A., Hughes, J., Howel, D., & Exley, C. (2012). A systematic review of the effectiveness of advance care planning interventions for people with cognitive impairment and dementia. *Age and Ageing, 41,* 263-269.

Robinson, O.J., Charney, D.R., Overstreet, C., Vytal, K., & Grillon, C. (2012). The adaptive threat bias in anxiety: amygdala-dorsomedial prefrontal cortex coupling and aversive amplification. *Neuroimage, 60,* 523-529.

Robinson, S., Curwen, T., & Ryan, T.G. (2012). A review of co-morbid disorders of Asperger's disorder and the transition to adulthood. *International Journal of Special Education, 27,* 4-16.

Robinson, S.J. (2012). Childhood epilepsy and autism spectrum disorders: Psychiatric problems, phenotypic expression, and anticonvulsants. *Neuropsychology Review, 22,* 271-279.

Rodriguez-Murillo, L., Gogos, J.A., & Karayiorgou, M. (2012). The genetic architecture of schizophrenia: New mutations and emerging paradigms. *Annual Review of Medicine, 63,* 63-80.

Roemer, L., & Orsillo, S.M. (2002). Expanding our conceptualization of and treatment for generalized anxiety disorder: Integrating mindfulness/acceptance-based approaches with existing cognitive behavioral models. *Clinical Psychology: Science and Practice, 9,* 54-68.

Roe-Sepowitz, D.E., Bedard, L.E., & Thyer, B.A. (2005). Anxiety. In C.N. Dulmus & L.A. Rapp-Paglicci (Eds.), *Handbook of preventive interventions for adults* (pp. 13-26). Hoboken, NJ: Wiley.

Rogosch, F.A., Dackis, M.N., & Cicchetti, D. (2011). Child maltreatment and allostatic load: Consequences for physical and mental health in children from low-income families. *Development and Psychopathology, 23,* 1107-1124.

Rohan, K.J., Roecklein, K.A., & Haaga, D.A.F. (2009). Biological and psychological mechanisms of seasonal affective disorder: A review and integration. *Current Psychiatry Reviews, 5,* 37-47.

Rohde, L.A., Szobot, C., Polanczyk, G., Schmitz, M., Martins, S., & Tramontina, S. (2005). Attention-deficit/hyperactivity disorder in a diverse culture: Do research and clinical findings support the notion of a cultural construct for the disorder? *Biological Psychiatry, 57,* 1436-1441.

Roizen, N.J., & Patterson, D. (2003). Down's syndrome. *Lancet, 361,* 1281-1289.

Rolland, Y., van Kan, G.A., & Vellas, B. (2010). Healthy brain aging: Role of exercise and physical activity. *Clinics in Geriatric Medicine, 26,* 75-87.

Romera, I., Perez, V., Menchon, J.M., Polavieja, P., & Gilaberte, I. (2011). Optimal cutoff point of the Hamilton Rating Scale for Depression according to normal levels of social and occupational functioning. *Psychiatry Research, 186,* 133-137.

Ropacki, S.A., & Jeste, D.V. (2005). Epidemiology of and risk factors for psychosis of Alzheimer's disease: A review of 55 studies published from 1990 to 2003. *American Journal of Psychiatry, 162,* 2022-2030.

Ropers, H.H. (2010). Genetics of early onset cognitive impairment. *Annual Review of Genomics and Human Genetics, 11,* 161-187.

Rosen, J.L., Miller, T.J., D'Andrea, J.T., McGlashan, T.H., & Woods, S.W. (2006). Comorbid diagnoses in patients meeting criteria for the schizophrenia prodrome. *Schizophrenia Research, 85,* 124-131.

Rosen, R.C., & Althof, S. (2008). Impact of premature ejaculation: The psychological, quality of life, and sexual relationship consequences. *Journal of Sexual Medicine, 5,* 1296-1307.

Rosen, R.C., Cappelleri, J.C., & Gendrano, N. (2002). The International Index of Erectile Function (IIEF): A state-of-the-science review. *International Journal of Impotence Research, 14,* 226-244.

Rosen, R.C., Catania, J.A., Althof, S.E., Pollack, L.M., O'Leary, M., Seftel, A.D., & Coon, D.W. (2007). Development and validation of four-item version of Male Sexual Health Questionnaire to assess ejaculatory dysfunction. *Urology, 69,* 805-809.

Rosenberg, E., & DeMaso, D.R. (2008). A doubtful guest: Managed care and mental health. *Child and Adolescent Psychiatric Clinics of North America, 17,* 53-66.

Rosenhan, D.L. (1973). On being sane in insane places. *Science, 179,* 250-258.

Rosenmann, A., & Safir, M.P. (2006). Forced online: Push factors of Internet sexuality: A preliminary study of online paraphilic empowerment. *Journal of Homosexuality, 51,* 71-92.

Roses, A.D. (1997). Alzheimer's disease: The genetics of risk. *Hospital Practice, 32,* 51-69.

Rosner, R. (Ed.). (2013). *Clinical handbook of adolescent addiction.* New York: Wiley.

Ross, R.O., & Ness, L. (2010). Symptom patterns in dissociative identity disorder patients and the general population. *Journal of Trauma and Dissociation, 11,* 458-468.

Ross, S.E., Niebling, B.C., & Heckert, T.M. (1999). Sources of stress among college students. *College Student Journal, 33,* 312-317.

Rosso, S.M., Kaat, L.D., Baks, T., Joosse, M., de Koning, I., Pijnenburg, Y., de Jong, D., Dooijes, D., Kamphorst, W., Ravid, R., Niermeijer, M.F., Verheij, F., Kremer, H.P., Scheltens, P., van Duijn, C.M., Heutink, P., & van Swieten, J.C. (2003). Frontotemporal dementia in The Netherlands: Patient characteristics and prevalence estimates from a population-based study. *Brain, 126,* 2016-2022.

Roth, T., Roehrs, T., & Pies, R. (2007). Insomnia: Pathophysiology and implications for treatment. *Sleep Medicine Reviews, 11,* 71-79.

Rothbaum, B.O., Houry, D., Heekin, M., Leiner, A.S., Daugherty, J., Smith, L.F., & Gerardi, M. (2008). A pilot study of an exposure-based intervention in the ED designed to prevent posttraumatic stress disorder. *American Journal of Emergency Medicine, 26,* 326-330.

Rotheram-Borus, M.J., Swendeman, D., & Chorpita, B.F. (2012). Disruptive innovations for designing and diffusing evidence-based interventions. *American Psychologist, 67,* 463-476.

Rothlisberger, M., Riecher-Rossler, A., Aston, J., Fusar-Poli, P., Radu, E.-W., & Borgwardt, S. (2012). Cingulate volume abnormalities in emerging psychosis. *Current Pharmaceutical Design, 18,* 495-504.

Rounsaville, B.J., & Carroll, K.M. (2002). Commentary on the dodo bird revisited: Why aren't we dodos yet? *Clinical Psychology: Science and Practice, 9,* 17-20.

Rovet, J., Netley, C., Keenan, M., Bailey, J., & Stewart, D. (1996). The psychoeducational profile of boys with Klinefelter syndrome. *Journal of Learning Disabilities, 29,* 180-196.

Rowe, R., Costello, E.J., Angold, A., Copeland, W.E., & Maughan, B. (2010). Developmental pathways in oppositional defiant disorder and conduct disorder. *Journal of Abnormal Psychology, 119,* 726-738.

Rowe, R., Maughan, B., Worthman, C.M., Costello, E.J., & Angold, A. (2004). Testosterone, antisocial behavior, and social dominance in boys: Pubertal development and biosocial interaction. *Biological Psychiatry, 55,* 546-552.

Rowland, D., & Cooper, S. (2011). Practical tips for sexual counseling and psychotherapy in premature ejaculation. *Journal of Sexual Medicine, 8 (Suppl 4),* 342-352.

Rowles, B.M., & Findling, R.L. (2010). Review of pharmacotherapy options for the treatment of attention-deficit/hyperactivity disorder (ADHD) and ADHD-like symptoms in children and adolescents with developmental disorders.

*Developmental Disabilities Research Reviews, 16,* 273-282.

Roy-Byrne, P.P., Craske, M.G., & Stein, M.B. (2006). Panic disorder. *Lancet, 368,* 1023-1032.

Rubin, D., Lane, W., & Ludwig, S. (2001). Child abuse prevention. *Current Opinion in Pediatrics, 13,* 388-401.

Rudd, M.D., Mandrusiak, M., & Joiner, T.E. (2006). The case against no-suicide contracts: The commitment to treatment statement as a practice alternative. *Journal of Clinical Psychology: In Session, 62,* 243-251.

Rudolph, A.S., & Vegrzyn, R.D. (Eds.). (2012). *Alzheimer's disease: Targets for new clinical diagnostic and therapeutic strategies.* Boca Raton, FL: Taylor and Francis.

Ruggiero, K.J., Morris, T.L., & Scotti, J.R. (2001). Treatment for children with posttraumatic stress disorder: Current status and future directions. *Clinical Psychology: Science and Practice, 8,* 210-227.

Ruiz, M.A., Poythress, N.G., Lilienfeld, S.O., & Douglas, K.S. (2008). Factor structure and correlates of the Dissociative Experiences Scale in a large offender sample. *Assessment, 15,* 511-521.

Ruiz-Perez, I., Plazaola-Castano, J., & Vives-Cases, C. (2007). Methodological issues in the study of violence against women. *Journal of Epidemiology and Community Health, 61 (Suppl. II),* ii26-ii31.

Ruocco, A.C., Amirthavasagam, S., Choi-Kain, L.W., & McMain, S.F. (2013). Neural correlates of negative emotionality in borderline personality disorder: An activation-likelihood-estimation meta-analysis. *Biological Psychiatry, 73,* 153-160.

Rusanen, M., Kivipelto, M., Quesenberry, C.P., Zhou, J., & Whitmer, R.A. (2011). Heavy smoking in midlife and long-term risk of Alzheimer disease and vascular dementia. *Archives of Internal Medicine, 171,* 333-339.

Ruscio, A.M., Brown, T.A., Chiu, W.T., Sareen, J., Stein, M.B., & Kessler, R.C. (2008). Social fears and social phobia in the USA: Results from the National Comorbidity Survey Replication. *Psychological Medicine, 38,* 15-28.

Ruscio, A.M., Lane, M., Roy-Byrne, P., Stang, P.E., Stein, D.J., Wittchen, H.-U., & Kessler, R.C. (2005). Should excessive worry be required for a diagnosis of generalized anxiety disorder? Results from the US National Comorbidity Survey Replication. *Psychological Medicine, 35,* 1761-1772.

Rutherford, L., & Couturier, J. (2007). A review of psychotherapeutic interventions for children and adolescents with eating disorders. *Journal of the Canadian Academy of Child and Adolescent Psychiatry, 16,* 153-157.

Rutledge, T., & Hogan, B.E. (2002). A quantitative review of prospective evidence linking psychological factors with hypertension development. *Psychosomatic Medicine, 64,* 758-766.

Ryan, D.J., O'Regan, N.A., Caoimh, R.O., Clare, J., O'Connor, M., Leonard, M., McFarland, J., Tighe, S., O'Sullivan, K., Trzepacz, P.T., Meagher, D., &

Timmons, S. (2013). Delirium in an adult acute hospital population: predictors, prevalence and detection. *BMJ Open, 3,* e001772.

Ryan, S.M., Jorm, A.F., & Lubman, D.I. (2010). Parenting factors associated with reduced adolescent alcohol use: A systematic review of longitudinal studies. *Australian and New Zealand Journal of Psychiatry, 44,* 774-783.

Sachs, G.S., & Gardner-Schuster, E.E. (2007). Adjunctive treatment of acute mania: A clinical overview. *Acta Psychiatrica Scandinavica, S434,* 27-34.

Sack, R.L., Auckley, D., Auger, R.R., Carskadon, M.A., Wright, K.P., Vitiello, M.V., & Zhdanova, I.V. (2007). Circadian rhythm disorders: Part I, basic principles, shift work and jet lag disorders. *Sleep, 30,* 1460-1483.

Sadock, B.J., & Sadock, V.A. (2003). *Synopsis of psychiatry: Behavioral sciences/clinical psychiatry* (9th ed.). New York: Lippincott Williams & Wilkens.

Sadock, B.J., & Sadock, V.A. (2007). *Synopsis of psychiatry: Behavioral sciences/clinical psychiatry* (10th ed.). Philadelphia, PA: Wolters Kluwer.

Sadowski, C.M., & Friedrich, W.N. (2000). Psychometric properties of the Trauma Symptom Checklist for Children (TSCC) with psychiatrically hospitalized adolescents. *Child Maltreatment, 5,* 364-372.

Safren, S.A., Heimberg, R.G., Lerner, J., Henin, A., Warman, M., & Kendall, P.C. (2000). Differentiating anxious and depressive self-statements: Combined factor structure of the Anxious Self-Statements Questionnaire and the Automatic Thoughts Questionnaire-Revised. *Cognitive Therapy and Research, 24,* 327-344.

Saha, S., Chant, D., & McGrath, J. (2008). Meta-analyses of the incidence and prevalence of schizophrenia: Conceptual and methodological issues. *International Journal of Methods in Psychiatric Research, 17,* 55-61.

Saha, S., Welham, J., Chant, D., & McGrath, J. (2006). Incidence of schizophrenia does not vary with economic status of the country: Evidence from a systematic review. *Social Psychiatry and Psychiatric Epidemiology, 41,* 338-340.

Saigh, P.A., Lee, K.S., Ward, A.M., & Wilson, K. (November, 2005). *The clinical assessment of traumatized children and adolescents.* Workshop presented at the meeting of the Association for Behavioral and Cognitive Therapies, Washington, DC.

Salerno, S. (2005). *SHAM: How the self-help movement made America helpless.* New York: Crown Publishing.

Salthouse, T. (2012). Consequences of age-related cognitive declines. *Annual Review of Psychology, 63,* 201-226.

Sample, L.L. (2011). The need to debate the fate of sex offender community notification laws. *Criminology and Public Policy, 10,* 265-274.

Samuel, D.B., Hopwood, C.J., Ansell, E.B., Morey, L.C., Sanislow, C.A., Markowitz, J.C., Yen, S., Shea, M.T., Skodol, A.E., & Grilo, C.M. (2011). Comparing the temporal stability of self-report and interview assessed personality disorder. *Journal of Abnormal Psychology, 120*, 670-680.

Samuel, D.B., & Widiger, T.A. (2009). Comparative gender biases in models of personality disorder. *Personality and Mental Health, 3*, 12-25.

Sanislow, C.A., Little, T.D., Ansell, E.B., Grilo, C.M., Daversa, M., Markowitz, J.C., Pinto, A., Shea, M.T., Yen, S., Skodol, A.E., Morey, L.C., Gunderson, J.G., Zanarini, M.C., & McGlashan, T.H. (2009). Ten-year stability and latent structure of the DSM-IV schizotypal, borderline, avoidant, and obsessive-compulsive personality disorders. *Journal of Abnormal Psychology, 118*, 507-519.

Santos, M., & Gago, E. (2010). Running towards a different life: A case of dissociative fugue. *European Psychiatry, 25*, 615.

Sar, V., Akyuz, G., Kundakci, T., Kiziltan, E., & Dogan, O. (2004). Childhood trauma, dissociation, and psychiatric comorbidity in patients with conversion disorder. *American Journal of Psychiatry, 161*, 2271-2276.

Sar, V., Unal, S.N., & Ozturk, E. (2007). Frontal and occipital perfusion changes in dissociative identity disorder. *Psychiatry Research, 156*, 217-223.

Sarisoy, G., Boke, O., Arik, A.C., & Sahin, A.R. (2008). Panic disorder with nocturnal panic attacks: Symptoms and comorbidities. *European Psychiatry, 23*, 195-200.

Sartor, C.E., Grant, J.D., Lynskey, M.T., McCutcheon, V.V., Waldron, M., Statham, D.J., Bucholz, K.K., Madden, P.A.F., Heath, A.C., Martin, N.G., & Nelson, E.C. (2012). Common heritable contributions to low-risk trauma, high-risk trauma, posttraumatic stress disorder, and major depression. *Archives of General Psychiatry, 69*, 293-299.

Sassaroli, S., Romero Lauro, L.J., Maria Ruggiero, G., Mauri, M.C., Vinai, P., & Frost, R. (2008). Perfectionism in depression, obsessive-compulsive disorder and eating disorders. *Behaviour Research and Therapy, 46*, 757-765.

Sattler, J.M. (2008). *Assessment of children: Cognitive foundations* (5th ed.). San Diego, CA: Sattler.

Savla, G.N., Twamley, E.W., Delis, D.C., Roesch, S.C., Jeste, D.V., & Palmer, B.W. (2012). Dimensions of executive functioning in schizophrenia and their relationship with processing speed. *Schizophrenia Bulletin, 38*, 760-768.

Scaer, R.C. (2001). The neurophysiology of dissociation and chronic disease. *Applied Psychophysiology and Biofeedback, 26*, 73-91.

Schaffer, M., Jeglic, E., Moster, A., & Wnuk, D. (2010). Cognitive-behavioral therapy in the treatment and management of sex offenders. *Journal of Cognitive Psychotherapy, 24*, 92-103.

Schalet, B.D., Durbin, C.E., & Revelle, W. (2011). Multidimensional structure of the Hypomanic Personality Scale. *Psychological Assessment, 23*, 504-522.

Schell, E., Theorell, T., Hasson, D., Arnetz, B., & Saraste, H. (2008). Impact of a web-based stress management and health promotion program on neck-shoulder-back pain in knowledge workers? 12 month prospective controlled follow-up. *Journal of Occupational and Environmental Medicine, 50*, 667-676.

Schempf, A.H. (2007). Illicit drug use and neonatal outcomes: A critical review. *Obstetrical and Gynecological Survey, 62*, 749-757.

Schennach, R., Musil, R., Moller, H.-J., & Riedel, M. (2012). Functional outcomes in schizophrenia: Employment status as a metric of treatment outcome. *Current Psychiatry Reports, 14*, 229-236.

Schepers, J.P., Koopmans, R.T., & Bor, J.H. (2000). Patients with Korsakoff's syndrome in a nursing home: Characteristics and comorbidity. *Tijdschrift Voor Gerentologie En Geriatrie, 31*, 113-118.

Schepis, T.S., & Rao, U. (2005). Epidemiology and etiology of adolescent smoking. *Current Opinion in Pediatrics, 17*, 607-612.

Scherag, S., Hebebrand, J., & Hinney, A. (2010). Eating disorders: The current status of molecular genetic research. *European Child and Adolescent Psychiatry, 19*, 211-226.

Schermer, C.R. (2006). Alcohol and injury prevention. *Journal of Trauma, 60*, 447-451.

Schiffman, J., Walker, E., Ekstrom, M., Schulsinger, F., Sorensen, H., & Mednick, S. (2004). Childhood videotaped social and neuromotor precursors of schizophrenia: A prospective investigation. *American Journal of Psychiatry, 161*, 2021-2027.

Schmidt, N.B., Keough, M.E., Mitchell, M.A., Reynolds, E.K., MacPherson, L., Zvolensky, M.J., & Lejuez, C.W. (2010). Anxiety sensitivity: Prospective prediction of anxiety among early adolescents. *Journal of Anxiety Disorders, 24*, 503-508.

Schmidt, N.B., Woolaway-Bickel, K., Trakowski, J., Santiago, H., Storey, J., Koselka, M., & Cook, J. (2000). Dismantling cognitive-behavioral treatment for panic disorder: Questioning the utility of breathing retraining. *Journal of Consulting and Clinical Psychology, 68*, 417-424.

Schmitt, R., Gazalle, F.K., de Lima, M.S., Cunha, A., Souza, J., & Kapczinski, F. (2005). The efficacy of antidepressants for generalized anxiety disorder: A systematic review and meta-analysis. *Revista Brasileira de Psiquiatria, 27*, 18-24.

Schneider, R.H., Alexander, C.N., Staggers, F., Rainforth, M., Salerno, J.W., Hartz, A., Arndt, S., Barnes, V.A., & Nidich, S.I. (2005). Long-term effects of stress reduction on mortality in persons 55 years of age with systemic hypertension. *American Journal of Cardiology, 95*, 1060-1064.

Schneiderman, N., Ironson, G., & Siegel, S. D. (2005). Stress and health: Psychological, behavioral, and biological determinants. *Annual Review of Clinical Psychology, 1*, 607-628.

Schopler, E., Van Bourgondien, M.E., Wellman, G.J., & Love, S.R. (2010). *Childhood Autism Rating Scale, Second Edition (CARS2)*. San Antonio, TX: Pearson.

Schuckit, M.A. (2009). An overview of genetic influences in alcoholism. *Journal of Substance Abuse and Treatment, 36*, 5-14.

Schuckit, M.A., & Smith, T.L. (2011). Onset and course of alcoholism over 25 years in middle class men. *Drug and Alcohol Dependence, 113*, 21-28.

Schuckit, M.A., Smith, T.L., Anthenelli, R., & Irwin, M. (1993). Clinical course of alcoholism in 636 male inpatients. *American Journal of Psychiatry, 150*, 786-792.

Schulte, I.E., & Petermann, F. (2011). Somatoform disorders: 30 years of debate about criteria! What about children and adolescents? *Journal of Psychosomatic Research, 70*, 218-228.

Schurhoff, F., Bellivier, F., Jouvent, R., Mouren-Simeoni, M.-C., Bouvard, M., Allilaire, J.-F., & LeBoyer, M. (2000). Early and late onset bipolar disorders: Two different forms of manic-depressive illness? *Journal of Affective Disorders, 58*, 215-221.

Schwab, S.G., Scott, A., & Wildenauer, D.B. (2009). Molecular biology of addiction and substance dependence. *Molecular Biology of Neuropsychiatric Disorders, 23*, 187-204.

Schwalbe, C.S., Gearing, R.E., MacKenzie, M.J., Brewer, K.B., & Ibrahim, R. (2012). A meta-analysis of experimental studies of diversion programs for juvenile offenders. *Clinical Psychology Review, 32*, 26-33.

Schwartz, A.C., Bradley, R.L., Sexton, M., Sherry, A., & Ressler, K.J. (2005). Posttraumatic stress disorder among African Americans in an inner city mental health clinic. *Psychiatric Services, 56*, 212-215.

Schwartz, B.S., Glass, T.A., Bolla, K.I., Stewart, W.F., Glass, G., Rasmussen, M., Bressler, J., Shi, W., & Bandeen-Roche, K. (2004). Disparities in cognitive functioning by race/ethnicity in the Baltimore memory study. *Environmental Health Perspectives, 112*, 314-320.

Schwartz, M.S., & Andrasik, F. (2005). *Biofeedback: A practitioner's guide*. New York: Guilford.

Schwartz, R.H., Silber, T.J., Heyman, R.B., Sheridan, M.J., & Estabrook, D.M. (2003). Urine testing for drugs of abuse: A survey of parent-adolescent dyads. *Archives of Pediatrics and Adolescent Medicine, 157*, 158-161.

Schweitzer, I., Tuckwell, V., Ames, D., & O'Brien, J. (2001). Structural neuroimaging studies in late-life depression: A review. *World Journal of Biological Psychiatry, 2*, 83-88.

Schwitzer, A., Hatfield, T., Jones, A.R., Duggan, M.H., Jurgens, J., & Winninger, A. (2008). Confirmation among college women: The eating disorders not otherwise specified diagnostic profile. *Journal of American College Health, 56*, 607-615.

Scileppi, J.A., Teed, E.L., & Torres, R.D. (2000). *Community psychology: A common sense approach to mental health*. Upper Saddle River, NJ: Prentice-Hall.

Scott-Sheldon, L.A.J., Demartini, K.S., Carey, K.B., & Carey, M.P. (2009). Alcohol interventions for college students improves antecedents of behavioral change: Results from a meta-analysis of

34 randomized controlled trials. *Journal of Social and Clinical Psychology, 28,* 799-823.

Seagraves, R.T. (2010). Considerations for an evidence-based definition of premature ejaculation in the DSM-V. *Journal of Sexual Medicine, 7,* 672-689.

Seedat, S., Stein, M.B., & Forde, D.R. (2003). Prevalence of dissociative experiences in a community sample: Relationship to gender, ethnicity, and substance use. *Journal of Nervous and Mental Disease, 191,* 115-120.

Seelaar, H., Rohrer, J.D., Pijnenburg, Y.A., Fox, N.C., & van Swieten, J.C. (2011). Clinical, genetic and pathological heterogeneity of frontotemporal dementia: a review. *Journal of Neurology, Neurosurgery and Psychiatry, 82,* 476-486.

Seeman, P. (2011). All roads to schizophrenia lead to dopamine supersensitivity and elevated dopamine D2$^{High}$ receptors. *CNS Neuroscience and Therapeutics, 17,* 118-132.

Segal, N.L., & Blozis, S.A. (2002). Psychobiological and evolutionary perspectives on coping and health characteristics following loss: A twin study. *Twin Research, 5,* 175-187.

Segarra, R., Ojeda, N., Zabala, A., Garcia, J., Catalan, A., Eguiluz, J.I., & Gutierrez, M. (2012). Similarities in early course among men and women with a first episode of schizophrenia and schizophreniform disorder. *European Archives of Psychiatry and Clinical Neuroscience, 262,* 95-105.

Segrin, C. (2000). Social skills deficits associated with depression. *Clinical Psychology Review, 20,* 379-403.

Segrin, C.G. (2011). Depressive disorders and interpersonal processes. In L.M. Horowitz & S. Strack (Eds.), *Handbook of interpersonal psychology: Theory, research, assessment, and therapeutic interventions* (pp. 425-448). Hoboken, NJ: Wiley.

Segrin, C., & Flora, J. (2000). Poor social skills are a vulnerability factor in the development of psychosocial problems. *Human Communication Research, 26,* 489-514.

Segrin, C., & Rynes, K.N. (2009). The mediating role of positive relations with others in associations between depressive symptoms, social skills, and perceived stress. *Journal of Research in Personality, 43,* 962-971.

Seidler, K.-P., Garlipp, P., Machleidt, W., & Haltenhof, H. (2005). Treatment concepts of day hospitals for general psychiatric patients. Findings from a national survey in Germany. *European Psychiatry, 21,* 110-117.

Seidman, L.J., Valera, E.M., & Makris, M. (2005). Structural brain imaging of attention-deficit/hyperactivity disorder. *Biological Psychiatry, 57,* 1263-1272.

Seipp, C.M., & Johnston, C. (2005). Mother-son interactions in families of boys with attention-deficit/hyperactivity disorder with and without oppositional behavior. *Journal of Abnormal Child Psychology, 33,* 87-98.

Seitz, D., Purandare, N., & Conn, D. (2010). Prevalence of psychiatric disorders among older adults in long-term care homes: A systematic review. *International Psychogeriatrics, 22,* 1025-1039.

Seligman, M.E.P., & Maier, S.F. (1967). Failure to escape traumatic shock. *Journal of Experimental Psychology, 14,* 1-9.

Selya, A.S., Dierker, L.C., Rose, J.S., Hedeker, D., & Mermelstein, R.J. (2012). Risk factors for adolescent smoking: Parental smoking and the mediating role of nicotine dependence. *Drug and Alcohol Dependence, 124,* 311-318.

Semkovska, M., Bedard, M.A., Godbout, L., Limoge, F., & Stip, E. (2004). Assessment of executive dysfunction during activities of daily living in schizophrenia. *Schizophrenia Research, 69,* 289-300.

Semple, D.M., McIntosh, A.M., & Lawrie, S.M. (2005). Cannabis as a risk factor for psychosis: Systematic review. *Journal of Psychopharmacology, 19,* 187-194.

Seo, D., Patrick, C.J., & Kennealy, P.J. (2008). Role of serotonin and dopamine system interactions in the neurobiology of impulsive aggression and its comorbidity with other clinical disorders. *Aggression and Violent Behavior, 13,* 383-395.

Seto, M.C. (2004). Pedophilia and sexual offenses against children. *Annual Review of Sex Research, 15,* 321-361.

Seto, M.C., & Lalumiere, M.L. (2010). What is so special about male adolescent sexual offending? A review and test of explanations through meta-analysis. *Psychological Bulletin, 136,* 526-575.

Sexton, C., Mackay, C.E., & Ebmeier, K.P. (2013). A systematic review and meta-analysis of magnetic resonance imaging studies in late-life depression. *American Journal of Geriatric Psychiatry, 21,* 184-195.

Shabsigh, R., & Anastasiadis, A.G. (2003). Erectile dysfunction. *Annual Review of Medicine, 54,* 153-168.

Shabsigh, R., Kaufman, J., Magee, M., Creanga, D., Russell, D., & Budhwani, M. (2010). Lack of awareness of erectile dysfunction in many men with risk factors for erectile dysfunction. *BMC Urology, 10,* 18.

Shaffer, D., Fisher, P., Lucas, C.P., Dulcan, M.K., & Schwab-Stone, M.E. (2000). NIMH Diagnostic Interview Schedule for Children Version IV (NIMH DISC-IV): Description, differences from previous versions, and reliability of some common diagnoses. *Journal of the American Academy of Child and Adolescent Psychiatry, 39,* 28-38.

Shah, M., Cork, C., & Chowdhury, U. (2005). ADHD: Assessment and intervention. *Community Practitioner, 78,* 129-132.

Shah, N.R., Jones, J.B., Aperi, J., Shemtov, R., Karne, A., & Borenstein, J. (2008). Selective serotonin reuptake inhibitors for Premenstrual Syndrome and Premenstrual Dysphoric Disorder: A meta-analysis. *Obstetrics and Gynecology, 111,* 1175-1182.

Shamasundar, C. (2001). Love, praxis, and desirable therapist qualities. *American Journal of Psychotherapy, 55,* 273-282.

Shan, G., Xu, S., & Jin, P. (2008). FXTAS: A bad RNA and a hope for a cure. *Expert Opinion on Biological Therapy, 8,* 249-253.

Shane, H.C., Laubscher, E.H., Schlosser, R.W., Flynn, S., Sorce, J.F., & Abramson, J. (2012). Applying technology to visually support language and communication in individuals with autism spectrum disorders. *Journal of Autism and Developmental Disorders, 42,* 1228-1235.

Shapiro, E., & Balthazor, M. (1999). Metabolic and neurodegenerative disorders. In K.O. Yeates, M.D. Ris, & H.G. Taylor (Eds.), *Pediatric neuropsychology: Research, theory, and practice* (pp. 171-205). New York: Guilford.

Shapiro, E.S. (2011). *Academic skills problems: Direct assessment and intervention* (4th ed.). New York: Guilford.

Sharkey, K.M., Carskadon, M.A., Figueiro, M.G., Zhu, Y., & Rea, M.S. (2011). Effects of an advanced sleep schedule and morning short wavelength light exposure on circadian phase in young adults with late sleep schedules. *Sleep Medicine, 12,* 685-692.

Sharpley, M., Hutchinson, G., McKenzie, K., & Murray, R.M. (2001). Understanding the excess of psychosis among the African-Carribean population in England: Review of current hypotheses. *British Journal of Psychiatry, 178 (Suppl 40),* s60-s68.

Shastry, B.S. (2002). Schizophrenia: A genetic perspective (review). *International Journal of Molecular Medicine, 9,* 207-212.

Shaw, D.S., Lacourse, E., & Nagin, D.S. (2005). Developmental trajectories of conduct problems and hyperactivity from ages 2 to 10. *Journal of Child Psychology and Psychiatry, 46,* 931-942.

Shaw, H., Ramirez, L., Trost, A., Randall, P., & Stice, E. (2004). Body image and eating disturbances across ethnic groups: More similarities than differences. *Psychology of Addictive Behaviors, 18,* 12-18.

Shaw, I. (2004). Doctors, "dirty work" patients, and "revolving doors." *Qualitative Health Research, 14,* 1032-1045.

Shaw, R.J., Dayal, S., Hartman, J.K., & DeMaso, D.R. (2008). Factitious disorder by proxy: Pediatric condition falsification. *Harvard Review of Psychiatry, 16,* 215-224.

Shaywitz, S.E., & Shaywitz, B.A. (2012). Psychopathology of dyslexia and reading disorders. In A.S. Davis (Ed.), *Psychopathology of childhood and adolescence: A neuropsychological approach* (pp. 109-126). New York: Springer.

Shaywitz, S.E., & Shaywitz, B.A. (2005). Dyslexia (specific reading disability). *Biological Psychiatry, 57,* 1301-1309.

Shcherbatykh, I., & Carpenter, D.O. (2007). The role of metals in the etiology of Alzheimer's disease. *Journal of Alzheimer's Disease, 11,* 191-205.

Shea, A., Walsh, C., MacMillan, H., & Steiner, M. (2004). Child maltreatment and HPA axis dysregulation: Relationship to major depressive disorder and post-traumatic stress disorder in females. *Psychoneuroendocrinology, 30,* 162-178.

Shea, S.C. (2002). *The practical art of suicide assessment: A guide for mental health professionals and substance abuse counselors.* Hoboken, NJ: Wiley.

Shearer, S.L. (2007). Recent advances in the understanding and treatment of anxiety disorders. *Primary Care, 34,* 475-504.

Shek, D.T. (2005). Paternal and maternal influences on the psychological well-being, substance abuse, and delinquency of Chinese adolescents experiencing economic disadvantage. *Journal of Clinical Psychology, 61,* 219-234.

Shen-Shan, Z., & Le-hua, L. (2004). Comparative study on cognitive function of Alzheimer's disease and vascular dementia. *Chinese Journal of Clinical Psychology, 12,* 272-273.

Shepherd, A.M., Laurens, K.R., Matheson, S.L., Carr, V.J., & Green, M.J. (2012). Systematic meta-review and quality assessment of the structural brain alterations in schizophrenia. *Neuroscience and Biobehavioral Reviews, 36,* 1342-1356.

Sher, L. (2006). Combined dexamethasone suppression–corticotropin-releasing hormone stimulation test in studies of depression, alcoholism, and suicidal behavior. *Scientific World Journal, 6,* 1398-1404.

Sherman, S.L., Allen, E.G., Bean, L.H., & Freeman, S.B. (2007). Epidemiology of Down syndrome. *Mental Retardation and Developmental Disabilities Research Reviews, 13,* 221-227.

Sherrington, J.M., Hawton, K., Fagg, J., Andrew, B., & Smith, D. (2001). Outcome of women admitted to hospital for depressive illness: Factors in the prognosis of major depression. *Psychological Medicine, 31,* 115-125.

Sherry, S.B., Vriend, J.L., Hewitt, P.L., Sherry, D.L., Flett, G.L., & Wardrop, A.A. (2009). Perfectionism dimensions, appearance schemas, and body image disturbance in community members and university students. *Body Image, 6,* 83-89.

Shi, Z., Bureau, J.-F., Easterbrooks, M.A., Zhao, X., & Lyons-Ruth, K. (2012). Childhood maltreatment and prospectively observed quality of early care as predictors of antisocial personality disorder features. *Infant Mental Health Journal, 33,* 55-69.

Shiels, K., & Hawk, L.W. (2010). Self-regulation in ADHD: The role of error processing. *Clinical Psychology Review, 30,* 951-961.

Shih, R.A., Belmonte, P.L., & Zandi, P.P. (2004). A review of the evidence from family, twin and adoption studies for a genetic contribution to adult psychiatric disorders. *International Review of Psychiatry, 16,* 260-283.

Shiner, R.L. (2005). A developmental perspective on personality disorders: Lessons from research on normal personality development in childhood and adolescence. *Journal of Personality Disorders, 19,* 202-210.

Shing, Y.L., Werkle-Bergner, M., Brehmer, Y., Muller, V., Li, S.-C., & Lindenberger, U. (2010).

Episodic memory across the lifespan: The contributions of associative and strategic components. *Neuroscience and Biobehavioral Reviews, 34,* 1080-1091.

Shipley, S.L., & Arrigo, B.A. (2012). *Introduction to forensic psychology: Court, law enforcement, and correctional practices* (3rd ed.). Oxford: Elsevier.

Shochet, I.M., Dadds, M.R., Holland, D., Whitefield, K., Harnett, P.H., & Osgarby, S.M. (2001). The efficacy of a universal school-based program to prevent adolescent depression. *Journal of Clinical Child Psychology, 30,* 303-315.

Shull, R.L. (2005). The sensitivity of response rate to the rate of variable-interval reinforcement for pigeons and rats: A review. *Journal of the Experimental Analysis of Behavior, 84,* 99-110.

Shulman, J.M., De jager, P.L., & Feany, M.B. (2011). Parkinson's disease: Genetics and pathogenesis. *Annual Review of Pathology: Mechanisms of Disease, 6,* 193-222.

Shuttleworth-Edwards, A.B., Donnelly, M.J., Reid, I., & Radloff, S.E. (2004). A cross-cultural study with culture fair normative indications on WAIS-III Digit Symbol-Incidental Learning. *Journal of Clinical and Experimental Neuropsychology, 26,* 921-932.

Shyn, S.I., & Hamilton, S.P. (2010). The genetics of major depression: Moving beyond the monoamine hypothesis. *Psychiatric Clinics of North America, 33,* 125-140.

Sibitz, I., Unger, A., Woppmann, A., Zidek, T., & Amering, M. (2011). Stigma resistance in patients with schizophrenia. *Schizophrenia Bulletin, 37,* 316-323.

Sidman, J. (2006, June 26). A college student's death may help save lives. Retrieved from www.usatoday.com.

Sierra, M. (2008). Depersonalization disorder: Pharmacological approaches. *Expert Review of Neurotherapeutics, 8,* 19-26.

Sierra, M., & Berrios, G.E. (1998). Depersonalization: Neurobiological perspectives. *Biological Psychiatry, 44,* 898-908.

Sierra, M., & David, A.S. (2011). Depersonalization: A selective impairment of self-awareness. *Consciousness and Cognition, 20,* 99-108.

Sierra, M., Gomez, J., Molina, J.J., Luque, R., Munoz, J.F., & David, A.S. (2006). Depersonalization in psychiatric patients: A transcultural study. *Journal of Nervous and Mental Disease, 194,* 356-361.

Signorini, A., De Filippo, E., Panico, S., De Caprio, C., Pasanisi, F., & Contaldo, F. (2007). Long-term mortality in anorexia nervosa: A report after an 8-year follow-up and a review of the most recent literature. *European Journal of Clinical Nutrition, 61,* 119-122.

Silber, T.J. (2011). Somatization disorders: Diagnosis, treatment, and prognosis. *Pediatrics in Review, 32,* 56-64.

Silber, T.J., & Pao, M. (2003). Somatization disorders in children and adolescents. *Pediatrics in Review, 24,* 255-261.

Silk, J.S., Ziegler, M.L., Whalen, D.J., Dahl, R.E., Ryan, N.D., Dietz, L.J., Birmaher, B., Axelson, D.A., & Williamson, D.E. (2009). Expressed emotion in mothers of currently depressed, remitted, high-risk and low-risk youth: Links to child depression status and longitudinal course. *Journal of Clinical Child and Adolescent Psychology, 38,* 36-47.

Sills, T., Wunderlich, G., Pyke, R., Segraves, R.T., Leiblum, S., Clayton, A., Cotton, D., & Evans, K. (2005). The Sexual Interest and Desire Inventory-Female (SIDI-F): Item response analyses of data from women diagnosed with hypoactive sexual desire disorder. *Journal of Sexual Medicine, 2,* 801-818.

Silverman, M. (2004, March). College student suicide prevention: Background and blueprint for action. College Mental Health [Special Issue]. *Student Health Spectrum,* 13-20.

Silverman, M., Meyer, P., Sloane, R., Raffel, M., & Pratt, D. (1997). The Big Ten student suicide study. *Suicide and Life Threatening Behavior, 27,* 285-303.

Silverman, W.K., & Albano, A.M. (1996). *The Anxiety Disorders Interview Schedule for DSM-IV: Child version.* New York: Oxford.

Silverman, W.K., & Ollendick, T.H. (2005). Evidence-based assessment of anxiety and its disorders in children and adolescents. *Journal of Clinical Child and Adolescent Psychology, 34,* 380-411.

Silverstein, S.M., & Bellack, A.S. (2008). A scientific agenda for the concept of recovery as it applies to schizophrenia. *Clinical Psychology Review, 28,* 1108-1124.

Simeon, D., Guralnik, O., Schmeidler, J., & Knutelska, M. (2004). Fluoxetine therapy in depersonalization disorder: Randomised controlled trial. *British Journal of Psychiatry, 185,* 31-36.

Simeon, D., & Knutelska, M. (2005). An open trial of naltrexone in the treatment of depersonalization disorder. *Journal of Clinical Psychopharmacology, 25,* 267-270.

Simeon, D., Kozin, D.S., Segal, K., Lerch, B., Dujour, R., & Giesbrecht, T. (2008). De-constructing depersonalization: Further evidence for symptom clusters. *Psychiatry Research, 157,* 303-306.

Simon, N.M., Safren, S.A., Otto, M.W., Sharma, S.G., Lanka, G.D., & Pollack, M.H. (2002). Longitudinal outcome with pharmacotherapy in a naturalistic study of panic disorder. *Journal of Affective Disorders, 69,* 201-208.

Simon, R.I., & Hales, R.E. (2012). *The American Psychiatric Publishing textbook of suicide assessment and management* (2nd ed.). Arlington, VA: American Psychiatric Publishing.

Simons, J.S., & Carey, M.P. (2001). Prevalence of sexual dysfunctions: Results from a decade of research. *Archives of Sexual Behavior, 30,* 177-219.

Simpson, H.B., Maher, M.J., Wang, Y., Bao, Y., Foa, E.B., & Franklin, M. (2011). Patient adherence predicts outcome from cognitive behavioral therapy in obsessive-compulsive disorder.

*Journal of Consulting and Clinical Psychology, 79,* 247-252.

Sisemore, T.A. (2012). *The clinician's guide to exposure therapies for anxiety spectrum disorders: Integrating techniques and applications from CBT, DBT, and ACT.* Oakland, CA: New Harbinger.

Sivertsen, B., Krokstad, S., Overland, S., & Mykletun, A. (2009). The epidemiology of insomnia: Associations with physical and mental health: The HUNT-2 study. *Journal of Psychosomatic Research, 67,* 109-116.

Sivertsen, B., Salo, P., Mykletun, A., Hysing, M., Pallesen, S., Krokstad, S., Nordhus, I.H., & Overland, S. (2012). The bidirectional association between depression and insomnia: The HUNT study. *Psychosomatic Medicine, 74,* 1-8.

Skinner, B. F. (1953). *Science and human behavior.* New York: Macmillan.

Skodol, A.E. (2012). Personality disorders in DSM-5. *Annual Review of Clinical Psychology, 8,* 317-344.

Skodol, A.E., Grilo, C.M., Keyes, K.M., Geier, T., Grant, B.F., & Hasin, D.S. (2011). Relationship of personality disorders to the course of major depressive disorder in a nationally representative sample. *American Journal of Psychiatry, 168,* 257-264.

Skodol, A.E., Gunderson, J.G., Shea, M.T., McGlashan, T.H., Morey, L.C., Sanislow, C.A., Bender, D.S., Grilo, C.M., Zanarinin, M.C., Yen, S., Pagano, M.E., & Stout, R.L. (2005). The Collaborative Longitudinal Personality Disorders Study (CLPS). *Journal of Personality Disorders, 19,* 487-504.

Skogen, J.C., Overland, S., Knudsen, A.K., & Mykletun, A. (2011). Concurrent validity of the CAGE questionnaire: The Nord-Trondelag Health Study. *Addictive Behaviors, 36,* 302-307.

Slane, J.D., Burt, S.A., & Klump, K.L. (2011). Genetic and environmental influences on disordered eating and depressive symptoms. *International Journal of Eating Disorders, 44,* 605-611.

Slesinger, D., Archer, R.P., & Duane, W. (2002). MMPI-2 characteristics in a chronic pain population. *Assessment, 9,* 406-414.

Small, G., & Bullock, R. (2011). Defining optimal treatment with cholinesterase inhibitors in Alzheimer's disease. *Alzheimer's and Dementia, 7,* 177-184.

Small, S.A., Schobel, S.A., Buxton, R.B., Witter, M.P., & Barnes, C.A. (2011). A pathophysiological framework of hippocampal dysfunction in ageing and disease. *Nature Reviews Neuroscience, 12,* 585-601.

Smallbone, S.W., & Dadds, M.R. (2000). Attachment and coercive sexual behavior. *Sexual Abuse: A Journal of Research and Treatment, 12,* 3-15.

Smedley, A., & Smedley, B. D. (2005). Race as biology is fiction, racism as a social problem is real: Anthropological and historical perspectives in the social construction of race. *American Psychologist, 60,* 16-26.

Smith, E.W.L. (2003). *The person of the therapist.* Jefferson, NC: McFarland.

Smith, J.F., Caan, B.J., Sternfeld, B., Haque, R., Quesenberry, C.P., Quinn, V.P., Shan, J., Walsh, T.J., Lue, T.F., Jacobsen, S.J., & Van Den Eeden, S.K. (2009). Racial disparities in erectile dysfunction among participants in the California Men's Health Study. *Journal of Sexual Medicine, 6,* 3433-3439.

Smith, J.T. (1999). Sickle cell disease. In S. Goldstein & C.R.Reynolds (Eds.), *Handbook of neurodevelopmental and genetic disorders in children* (pp. 368-384). New York: Guilford.

Smith, P.J., & Blumenthal, J.A. (2010). Diet and neurocognition: Review of evidence and methodological considerations. *Current Aging Science, 3,* 57-66.

Smith, V., Reddy, J., Foster, K., Asbury, E.T., & Brooks, J. (2011). Public perceptions, knowledge and stigma towards people with schizophrenia. *Journal of Public Mental Health, 10,* 45-56.

Smith, W., & Ruiz, J.M. (2002). Psychosocial influences on the development and course of coronary heart disease: Current status and implications for research and practice. *Journal of Consulting and Clinical Psychology, 70,* 548-568.

Smitherman, T.A., & Ward, T.N. (2011). Psychosocial factors of relevance to sex and gender studies in headache. *Headache, 51,* 923-931.

Smolak, L., & Murnen, S. (2001). Gender and eating problems. In R.H. Striegel-Moore & L. Smolak (Eds.), *Eating disorders: Innovative directions in research and practice* (pp. 91-110). Washington, D.C.: American Psychological Association.

Smolak, L., Murnen, S.K., & Ruble, A.E. (2000). Female athletes and eating problems: A meta-analysis. *International Journal of Eating Disorders, 27,* 371-380.

Smoller, J.W., & Finn, C.T. (2003). Family, twin, and adoption studies of bipolar disorder. *American Journal of Medical Genetics Part C, 123C,* 48-58.

Smoller, J.W., & Tsuang, M.T. (1998). Panic and phobic anxiety: Defining phenotypes for genetic studies. *American Journal of Psychiatry, 155,* 1152-1162.

Smyth, J.M., Hockemeyer, J.R., Heron, K.E., Wonderlich, S.A., & Pennebaker, J.W. (2008). Prevalence, type, disclosure, and severity of adverse life events in college students. *Journal of American College Health, 57,* 69-76.

Sno, H.N., & Schalken, H.F.A. (1999). Dissociative identity disorder: Diagnosis and treatment in the Netherlands. *European Psychiatry, 14,* 270-277.

Snowden, L.R. (2012). Health and mental health policies' role in better understanding and closing African American-White American disparities in treatment access and quality of care. *American Psychologist, 67,* 524-531.

Snowden, R.J., Craig, R.L., & Gray, N.S. (2011). Indirect behavioral measures of cognition among sexual offenders. *Journal of Sex Research, 48,* 192-217.

Snowling, M.J. (2013). Early identification and interventions for dyslexia: A contemporary review. *Journal of Research in Special Education Needs, 13,* 7-14.

Snyder, C.R., Feldman, D.B., Taylor, J.D., Schroeder, L.L., & Adams, V.H. (2000). The roles of hopeful thinking in preventing problems and enhancing strengths. *Applied and Preventive Psychology, 9,* 249-270.

Snyder, J., Cramer, A., Afrank, J., & Patterson, G.R. (2005). The contributions of ineffective discipline and parental hostile attributions of child misbehavior to the development of conduct problems at home and school. *Developmental Psychology, 41,* 30-41.

Sobue, I., Takeshita, T., Maruyama, S., & Morimoto, K. (2002). The effects of low Km aldehyde dehydrogenase (ALDH2) phenotype on drinking behavior in Japanese university students. *Journal of Studies on Alcohol, 63,* 527-530.

Solarino, B., Rosenbaum, F., Riel-Belmann, B., Buschmann, C.T., & Tsokos, M. (2010). Death due to ingestion of nicotine-containing solution. Case report and review of the literature. *Forensic Science International, 195,* e19-e22.

Soloff, P.H., Price, J.C., Mason, N.S., Becker, C., & Meltzer, C.C. (2010). Gender, personality, and serotonin-2A receptor binding in healthy subjects. *Psychiatry Research, 181,* 77-84.

Solomon, H., Man, J.W., & Jackson, G. (2003). Erectile dysfunction and the cardiovascular patient: Endothelial dysfunction is the common denominator. *Heart, 89,* 251-253.

Solomon, Z., & Lavi, T. (2005). Israeli youth in the Second Intifada: PTSD and future orientation. *Journal of the American Academy of Child and Adolescent Psychiatry, 44,* 1167-1175.

Sommers-Flanagan, J.S., & Sommers-Flanagan, R. (2012). *Counseling and psychotherapy theories in context and practice: Skills, strategies, and techniques* (2nd ed.). New York: Wiley.

Song, S., Wang, W., & Hu, P. (2009). Famine, death, and madness: Schizophrenia in early adulthood after prenatal exposure to the Chinese Great Leap Forward Famine. *Social Science and Medicine, 68,* 1315-1321.

Southwick, S.M., Vythilingham, M., & Charney, D.S. (2005). The psychobiology of depression and resilience to stress: Implications for prevention and treatment. *Annual Review of Clinical Psychology, 1,* 255-291.

Spalletta, G., Piras, F., Rubino, I.A., Caltagirone, C., & Fagioli, S. (2013). Fronto-thalamic volumetry markers of somatic delusions and hallucinations in schizophrenia. *Psychiatry Research: Neuroimaging, 212,* 54-64.

Spanagel, R., & Kiefer, F. (2008). Drugs for relapse prevention of alcoholism: Ten years of progress. *Trends in Pharmacological Sciences, 29,* 109-115.

Sparrow, S.S., Cicchetti, D.V., & Balla, D.A. (2005). *Vineland Adaptive Behavior Scales, Second Edition.* Bloomington, MN: Pearson.

Spector, A., Orrell, M., & Hall, L. (2012). Systematic review of neuropsychological outcomes in dementia from cognition-based psychological interventions. *Dementia and Geriatric Cognitive Disorders, 34*, 244-255.

Spector, A.Z. (2006). Fatherhood and depression: A review of risks, effects, and clinical application. *Issues in Mental Health Nursing, 27*, 867 883.

Sperling, R.A., Aisen, P.S., Beckett, L.A., Bennett, D.A., Craft, S., Fagan, A.M., Iwatsubo, T., Jack, C.R., Kaye, J., Montine, T.J., Park, D.C., Reiman, E.M., Rowe, C.C., Siemers, E., Stern, Y., Yaffe, K., Carillo, M.C., Thies, B., Morrison-Bogorad, M., Wagster, M.V., & Phelps, C.H. (2011). Toward defining the preclinical stages of Alzheimer's disease: Recommendations from the National Institute on Aging-Alzheimer's Association workgroups on diagnostic guidelines for Alzheimer's disease. *Alzheimer's and Dementia, 7*, 280-292.

Sperry, L., Neitzel, J., & Engelhardt-Wells, K. (2010). Peer-mediated instruction and intervention strategies for students with autism spectrum disorders. *Preventing School Failure, 54*, 256-264.

Spillantini, M.G., & Goedert, M. (2013). Tau pathology and neurodegeneration. *Lancet Neurology, 12*, 609-622.

Spillers, C.S. (2007). An existential framework for understanding the counseling needs of clients. *American Journal of Speech and Language Pathology, 16*, 191-197.

Spilt, J.L., Koot, J.M., & van Lier, P.A.C. (2013). For whom does it work? Subgroup differences in the effects of a school-based universal prevention program. *Prevention Science, 14*, 479-488.

Spinelli, M.G. (2009). Postpartum psychosis: Detection of risk and management. *American Journal of Psychiatry, 166*, 405-408.

Spira, E.G., & Fischel, J.E. (2005). The impact of preschool inattention, hyperactivity, and impulsivity on social and academic development: A review. *Journal of Child Psychology and Psychiatry, 46*, 755-773.

Spirito, A., Boergers, J., Donaldson, D., Bishop, D., & Lewander, W. (2002). An intervention trial to improve adherence to community treatment by adolescents after a suicide attempt. *Journal of the American Academy of Child and Adolescent Psychiatry, 41*, 435-442.

Spitzer, C., Klauer, T., Grabe, H.J., Lucht, M., Stieglitz, R.D., Schneider, W., & Freyberger, H.J. (2003). Gender differences in dissociation: A dimensional approach. *Psychopathology, 36*, 65-70.

Spitzer, C., Liss, H., Dudeck, M., Orlob, S., Gillner, M., Hamm, A., & Freyberger, H.J. (2003). Dissociative experiences and disorders in forensic inpatients. *International Journal of Law and Psychiatry, 26*, 281-288.

Sreenath, S., & Barber, R. (2009). Dementia with Lewy bodies. *Clinical Risk, 15*, 115-119.

Stadler, C., Schmeck, K., Nowraty, I., Muller, W.E., & Poustka, F. (2004). Platelet 5-HT uptake in boys with conduct disorder. *Neuropsychobiology, 50*, 244-251.

Staiger, P.K., Kambouropoulos, N., & Dawe, S. (2007). Should personality traits be considered when refining substance misuse treatment programs? *Drug and Alcohol Review, 26*, 17-23.

Stampfer, M.J., & Colditz, G.A. (2004). Estrogen replacement therapy and coronary heart disease: A quantitative assessment of the epidemiologic evidence. *International Journal of Epidemiology, 33*, 445-453.

Starcevic, V., & Berle, D. (2006). Cognitive specificity of anxiety disorders: A review of selected key constructs. *Depression and Anxiety, 23*, 51-61.

Stargardt, T., Weinbrenner, S., Busse, R., Juckel, G., & Gericke, C.A. (2008). Effectiveness and cost of atypical versus typical antipsychotic treatment for schizophrenia in routine care. *Journal of Mental Health Policy and Economics, 11*, 89-97.

Staring, A.B.P., Van der Gaag, M., Van den Berge, M., Duivenvoorden, H.J., & Mulder, C.L. (2009). Stigma moderates the associations of insight with depressed mood, low self-esteem, and low quality of life in patients with schizophrenia spectrum disorders. *Schizophrenia Research, 115*, 363-369.

Starkstein, S.E., & Merello, M. (2002). *Psychiatric and cognitive disorders in Parkinson's Disease.* New York: Cambridge University Press.

Starling, S.P., Patel, S., Burke, B.L., Sirotnak, A.P., Stronks, S., & Rosquist, P. (2004). Analysis of perpetrator admissions to inflicted traumatic brain injury in children. *Archives of Pediatric and Adolescent Medicine, 158*, 454-458.

Startup, M., Bucci, S., & Langdon, R. (2009). Delusions of reference: A new theoretical model. *Cognitive Neuropsychiatry, 14*, 110-126.

Stautz, K., & Cooper, A. (2013). Impulsivity-related personality traits and adolescent alcohol use: A meta-analytic review. *Clinical Psychology Review, 33*, 574-592.

Stein, D.J. (2004). *Clinical manual of anxiety disorders.* Washington, DC: American Psychiatric Publishing.

Stein, D.J., & Hugo, F.J. (2004). Neuropsychiatric aspects of anxiety disorders. In S.C. Yudofsky & R.E. Hales (Eds.), *Essentials of neuropsychiatry and clinical neurosciences* (pp. 519-533). Washington, DC: American Psychiatric Publishing.

Stein, D.J., & Simeon, D. (2009). Cognitive-affective neuroscience of depersonalization. *CNS Spectrums, 14*, 467-471.

Stein, J., & Kapoula, A. (Eds.). (2012). *Visual aspects of dyslexia.* Oxford: Oxford University Press.

Stein, M.B., Jang, K.L., Taylor, S., Vernon, P.A., & Livesley, W.J. (2002). Genetic and environmental influences on trauma exposure and posttraumatic stress disorder symptoms: A twin study. *American Journal of Psychiatry, 159*, 1675-1681.

Steinberg, M. (2000). Advances in the clinical assessment of dissociation: The SCID-D-R. *Bulletin of the Menninger Clinic, 64*, 146-163.

Steinhausen, H.-C., & Weber, S. (2009). The outcome of bulimia nervosa: Findings from one-quarter century of research. *American Journal of Psychiatry, 166*, 1331-1341.

Steketee, G., Siev, J., Fama, J.M., Keshaviah, A., Chosak, A., & Wilhelm, S. (2011). Predictors of treatment outcome in modular cognitive therapy for obsessive-compulsive disorder. *Depression and Anxiety, 28*, 333 341.

Stephen, M., & Suryani, L.K. (2000). Shamanism, psychosis and autonomous imagination. *Culture, Medicine and Psychiatry, 24*, 5-40.

Stern, Y. (2012). Cognitive reserve in ageing and Alzheimer's disease. *Lancet Neurology, 11*, 1006-1012.

Stewart, A. J., & McDermott, C. (2004). Gender in psychology. *Annual Review of Psychology, 55*, 519-544.

Stewart, M. Keel, P. K., & Schiavo, R. S. (2006). Stigmatization of anorexia nervosa. *International Journal of Eating Disorders, 39*, 320-325.

Stewart, R.E., & Chambless, D.L. (2009). Cognitive-behavioral therapy for adult anxiety disorders in clinical practice: A meta-analysis of effectiveness studies. *Journal of Consulting and Clinical Psychology, 77*, 595-606.

Stewart, S.E., Geller, D.A., Jenike, M., Pauls, D., Shaw, D., Mullin, B., & Faraone, S.V. (2004). Long-term outcome of pediatric obsessive-compulsive disorder: A meta-analysis and qualitative review of the literature. *Acta Psychiatrica Scandinavica, 110*, 4-13.

Stice, E., Ng, J., & Shaw, H. (2010). Risk factors and prodromal eating pathology. *Journal of Child Psychology and Psychiatry, 51*, 518-525.

Stice, E., Shaw, H., & Marti, C.N. (2007). A meta-analytic review of eating disorder prevention programs: Encouraging findings. *Annual Review of Clinical Psychology, 3*, 207-231.

Stice, E., Telch, C.F., & Rizvi, S.L. (2000). Development and validation of the Eating Disorder Diagnostic Scale: A brief self-report measure of anorexia, bulimia, and binge-eating disorder. *Psychological Assessment, 12*, 123-131.

Stilo, S.A., Di Forti, M., & Murray, R.M. (2011). Environmental risk factors for schizophrenia: Implications for prevention. *Neuropsychiatry, 1*, 457-466.

Stinson, J.D., Becker, J.V., & Sales, B.D. (2008). Self-regulation and the etiology of sexual deviance: Evaluating causal theory. *Violence and Victims, 23*, 35-51.

Stinson, F.S., Dawson, D.A., Chou, P.S., Smith, S., Goldstein, R.B., June, R.W., & Grant, B.F. (2007). The epidemiology of DSM-IV specific phobia in the USA: Results from the National Epidemiologic Survey on Alcohol and Related Conditions. *Psychological Medicine, 37*, 1047-1059.

Stirling, J. (2007). Beyond Munchausen Syndrome by Proxy: Identification and treatment of child abuse in a medical setting. *Pediatrics, 119*, 1026-1030.

Stolberg, R.A., Clark, D.C., & Bongar, B. (2002). Epidemiology, assessment, and management of suicide in depressed patients. In I.H. Gotlib & C.L. Hammen (Eds.), *Handbook of depression* (pp. 581-601). New York: Guilford.

Stone, W.L., Coonrod, E.E., Pozdol, S.L., & Turner, L.M. (2003). The Parent Interview for Autism-Clinical Version (PIA-CV): A measure of behavioral change for young children with autism. *Autism, 7, 9-30.*

Stone, W.S., & Hsi, X. (2011). Declarative memory deficits and schizophrenia: Problems and prospects. *Neurobiology of Learning and Memory, 96, 544-552.*

Stone-Manista, K. (2009). Protecting pregnant women: A guide to successfully challenging criminal child abuse prosecutions of pregnant drug addicts. *Journal of Criminal Law and Criminology, 99, 823-856.*

Stovner, L.J., & Andree, C. (2010). Prevalence of headache in Europe: A review for the Eurolight project. *Journal of Headache and Pain, 11, 289-299.*

Stowe, G.N., Schlosburg, J.E., Vendruscolo, L.F., Edwards, S., Misra, K.K., Schulteis, G., Zakhari, J.S., Koob, G.F., & Janda, K.D. (2011). Developing a vaccine against multiple psychoactive targets: A case study of heroin. *CNS and Neurological Disorders-Drug Targets, 10, 865-875.*

Strakowski, S.M., DelBello, M.P., Zimmerman, M.E., Getz, G.E., Mills, N.P., Ret, J., Shear, P., & Adler, C.M. (2002). Ventricular and periventricular structural volumes in first- versus multiple-episode bipolar disorder. *American Journal of Psychiatry, 159, 1841-1847.*

Stratford, T.R., & Wirtshafter, D. (2012). Evidence that the nucleus accumbens shell, ventral pallidum, and lateral hypothalamus are components of a lateralized feeding circuit. *Behavioural Brain Research, 226, 548-554.*

Stroud, C.B., Davila, J., & Moyer, A. (2008). The relationship between stress and depression in first onsets versus recurrences: A meta-analytic review. *Journal of Abnormal Psychology, 117, 206-213.*

Stuart, G.L., Treat, T.A., & Wade, W.A. (2000). Effectiveness of an empirically based treatment for panic disorder delivered in a service clinic setting: 1-year follow-up. *Journal of Consulting and Clinical Psychology, 68, 506-512.*

Stuart, S., Noyes, R., Starcevic, V., & Barsky, A. (2008). An integrative approach to somatoform disorders combining interpersonal and cognitive-behavioral theory and techniques. *Journal of Contemporary Psychotherapy, 38, 45-53.*

Sturmey, P. (2009). Behavioral activation is an evidence-based treatment for depression. *Behavior Modification, 33, 818-829.*

Subramaniam, P., & Woods, B. (2012). The impact of individual reminiscence therapy for people with dementia: Systematic review. *Expert Review of Neurotherapeutics, 12, 545-555.*

Suchy, Y., Whittaker, W.J., Strassberg, D.S., & Eastvold, A. (2009). Facial and prosodic affect recognition among pedophilic and nonpedophilic criminal child molesters. *Sexual Abuse, 21, 93-110.*

Sudarov, A. (2013). Defining the role of cerebellar Purkinje cells in autism spectrum disorders. *Cerebellum, 2013.*

Sudi, K., Ottl, K., Payerl, D., Baumgartl, P., Tauschmann, K., & Muller, W. (2004). Anorexia athletica. *Nutrition, 20, 657-661.*

Sue, S., Cheng, J.K.Y., Saad, C.S., & Chu, J.P. (2012). Asian American mental health: A call to action. *American Psychologist, 67, 532-544.*

Suh, G.-H., & Shah, A. (2001). A review of the epidemiological transition in dementia—cross-national comparisons of the indices related to Alzheimer's disease and vascular dementia. *Acta Psychiatrica Scandinavica, 104, 4-11.*

Suicide Prevention Resource Center. (2004). *Promoting mental health and preventing suicide in college and university settings.* Newton, MA: Education Development Center, Inc.

Sullivan, M.M., & Rehm, R. (2005). Mental health of undocumented Mexican immigrants: A review of the literature. *Advances in Nursing Science, 28, 240-251.*

Sullivan, P.F., Daly, M.J., & O'Donovan, M. (2012). Genetic architectures of psychiatric disorders: The emerging picture and its implications. *Nature Reviews Genetics, 13, 537-551.*

Sullivan, P.F., Neale, M.C., & Kendler, K.S. (2000). General epidemiology of major depression: Review and meta-analysis. *American Journal of Psychiatry, 157, 1552-1562.*

Sumathipala, A. (2007). What is the evidence for the efficacy of treatments for somatoform disorders?: A critical review of previous intervention studies. *Psychosomatic Medicine, 69, 889-900.*

Suribhatla, S., Baillon, S., Dennis, M., Marudkar, M., Muhammad, S., Munro, D., Spreadbury, C., & Lindesay, J. (2004). Neuropsychological performance in early and late onset Alzheimer's disease: Comparisons in a memory clinic population. *International Journal of Geriatric Psychology, 19, 1140-1147.*

Sutcliffe, P.A., Dixon, S., Akehurst, R.L., Wilkinson, A., Shippam, A., White, S., Richards, R., & Caddy, C.M. (2009). Evaluation of surgical procedures for sex reassignment: A systematic review. *Journal of Plastic, Reconstructive and Aesthetic Surgery, 62, 294-306.*

Svirko, E., & Hawton, K. (2007). Self-injurious behavior and eating disorders: The extent and nature of the association. *Suicide and Life-Threatening Behavior, 37, 409-421.*

Svrakic, D.M., Zorumski, C.F., Svrakic, N.M., Zwir, I., & Cloninger, C.R. (2013). Risk architecture of schizophrenia: the role of epigenetics. *Current Opinion in Psychiatry, 26, 188-195.*

Swan, G.E., & Lessov-Schlagger, C.N. (2007). The effects of tobacco smoke and nicotine on cognition and the brain. *Neuropsychology Review, 17, 259-273.*

Swanson, M.E., Grosse, S.D., & Kulkarni, R. (2011). Disability among individuals with sickle cell disease: Literature review from a public health perspective. *American Journal of Preventive Medicine, 41, S390-S397.*

Swinbourne, J.M., & Touyz, S.W. (2007). The co-morbidity of eating disorders and anxiety disorders: A review. *European Eating Disorders Review, 15, 253-274.*

Swogger, M.T., Walsh, Z., Lejuez, C.W., & Kosson, D.S. (2010). Psychopathy and risk taking among jailed inmates. *Criminal Justice and Behavior, 37, 439-452.*

Sytema, S., Wunderlink, L., Bloemers, W., Roorda, L., & Wiersma, D. (2007). Assertive community treatment in the Netherlands: A randomized controlled trial. *Acta Psychiatrica Scandanavia, 116, 105-112.*

Tagliapietra, M., Zanusso, G., Fiorini, M., Bonetto, N., Zarantonello, G., Zambon, A., Ermani, M., Monaco, S., Manara, R., & Cagnin, A. (2013). Accuracy of diagnostic criteria for Creutzfeldt-Jakob disease among rapidly progressive dementia. *Journal of Alzheimer's Disease, 34, 231-238.*

Takahashi, P.Y., Caldwell, C.R., & Targonski, P.V. (2012). Effect of vascular burden as measured by vascular indexes upon vascular dementia: A matched case-control study. *Clinical Interventions in Aging, 7, 27-33.*

Tandon, N., Shah, J., Keshavan, M.S., & Tandon, R. (2012). Attenuated psychosis and the schizophrenia prodrome: Current status of risk identification and psychosis prevention. *Neuropsychiatry, 2, 345-353.*

Tandon, R., Keshavan, M.S., & Nasrallah, H.A. (2008). Schizophrenia, "Just the facts" What we know in 2008. 2. Epidemiology and etiology. *Schizophrenia Research, 102, 1-18.*

Tanner, C.M., & Marder, K. (2004). Movement disorders. In L.M. Nelson, C.M. Tanner, S.K. Van Den Eeden, & V.M. McGuire (Eds.), *Neuroepidemiology: From principles to practice* (pp. 131-161). New York: Oxford.

Tantam, D. (2000). Adolescence and adulthood of individuals with Asperger syndrome. In A. Klin, F.R. Volkmar, & S.S. Sparrow (Eds.), *Asperger syndrome* (pp. 367-399). New York: Guilford.

Tarbox, S.I., Brown, L.H., & Haas, G.L. (2012). Diagnostic specificity of poor premorbid adjustment: Comparison of schizophrenia, schizoaffective disorder, and mood disorder with psychotic features. *Schizophrenia Research, 141, 91-97.*

Tarrier, N., Khan, S., Cater, J., & Picken, A. (2007). The subjective consequences of suffering a first episode psychosis: Trauma and suicide behavior. *Social Psychiatry and Psychiatric Epidemiology, 42, 29-35.*

Tarumi, S., Ichimiya, A., Yamada, S., Umesue, M., & Kuroki, T. (2004). Taijin kyofusho in university students: Patterns of fear and predispositions to the offensive variant. *Transcultural Psychiatry, 41, 533-546.*

Tasse, M.J., Schalock, R.L., Balboni, G., Bersani, H., Borthwick-Duffy, S.A., Spreat, S., Thissen, D., Widaman, K.F., & Zhang, D. (2012). The construct of adaptive behavior: Its conceptualization, measurement, and use in the field of intellectual disability. *American Journal on Intellectual and Developmental Disabilities, 117*, 291-303.

Taylor, C.B., Bryson, S., Luce, K.H., Cunning, D., Doyle, A.C., Abascal, L.B., Rockwell, R., Dev, P., Winzelberg, A.J., & Wilfley, D.E. (2006). Prevention of eating disorders in at-risk college-age women. *Archives of General Psychiatry, 63*, 881-888.

Taylor, D.J., Bramoweth, A.D., Grieser, E.A., Tatum, J.I., & Roane, B.M. (2013). Epidemiology of insomnia in college students: Relationship with mental health, quality of life, and substance use difficulties. *Behavior Therapy, 44*, 339-348.

Taylor, E., & Rogers, J.W. (2005). Practitioner review: Early adversity and developmental disorders. *Journal of Child Psychology and Psychiatry, 46*, 451-467.

Taylor, M.A., & Fink, M. (2003). Catatonia in psychiatric classification: A home of its own. *American Journal of Psychiatry, 160*, 1233-1241.

Taylor, S., Zvolensky, M.J., Cox, B.J., Deacon, B., Heimberg, R.G., Ledley, D.R., Abramowitz, J.S., Holaway, R.M., Sandin, B., Stewart, S.H., Coles, M., Eng, W., Daly, E.S., Arrindell, W.A., Bouvard, M., & Cardenas, S.J. (2007). Robust dimensions of anxiety sensitivity: Development and initial validation of the Anxiety Sensitivity Index-3. *Psychological Assessment, 19*, 176-188.

Taylor, S. E., Klein, L. C., Lewis, B. P., Gruenewald, T. L., Gurung, R. A. R., & Updegraff, J. A. (2000). Biobehavioral responses to stress in females: Tend-and-befriend, not fight-or-flight. *Psychological Review, 107*, 411-429.

Taylor, S. E., Lewis, B. P., Gruenewald, T. L., Gurung, R. A. R., Updegraff, J. A., & Klein, L. C. (2002). Sex differences in biobehavioral responses to stress; Reply to Geary and Flinn (2002). *Psychological Review, 109*, 751-753.

Telch, M.J., Kamphuis, J.H., & Schmidt, N.B. (2011). The effects of comorbid personality disorders on cognitive behavioral treatment for panic disorder. *Journal of Psychiatric Research, 45*, 469-474.

Tellegen, A., Ben-Porath, Y.S., McNulty, J.L., Arbisi, P.A., Graham, J.R., & Kaemmer, B. (2003). *The MMPI-2 Restructured Clinical Scales: Development, validation, and interpretation.* Minneapolis: University of Minnesota Press.

Templeman, T.L., & Stinnett, R.D. (1991). Patterns of sexual arousal and history in a "normal" sample of young men. *Archives of Sexual Behavior, 20*, 137-150.

Teper, E.L., & Hughes, J.C. (2011). Clinical and ethical issues in palliative care and dementia: An overview. *US Neurology, 7*, 10-14.

Teplin, L.A., Abram, K.M., McClelland, G.M., Dulcan, M.K., & Mericle, A.A. (2002). Psychiatric disorders in youth in juvenile detention. *Archives of General Psychiatry, 59*, 1133-1143.

Teplin, L.A., McClelland, G.M., Abram, K.M., & Weiner, D.A. (2005). Crime victimization in adults with severe mental illness: Comparison with the National Crime Victimization Survey. *Archives of General Psychiatry, 62*, 911-921.

ter Kuile, M.M., Both, S., & van Lankveld, J.J.D.M. (2010). Cognitive behavioral therapy for sexual dysfunctions in women. *Psychiatric Clinics of North America, 33*, 595-610.

Tessner, K.D., Mittal, V., & Walker, E.F. (2011). Longitudinal study of stressful life events and daily stressors among adolescents at high risk for psychotic disorders. *Schizophrenia Bulletin, 37*, 432-441.

Thaker, G.K., & Carpenter, W.T. (2001). Advances in schizophrenia. *Nature Medicine, 7*, 667-671.

Thapar, A., Cooper, M., Eyre, O., & Langley, K. (2013). Practitioner review: What have we learnt about the causes of ADHD? *Journal of Child Psychology and Psychiatry, 51*, 3-16.

Thase, M.E. (2006). Depression and sleep: Pathophysiology and treatment. *Dialogues in Clinical Neuroscience, 8*, 217-226.

Thase, M.E. (2010). Neurobiological aspects of depression. In I.H. Gotlib & C.L. Hammen (Eds.), *Handbook of depression* (2nd ed.) (pp. 187-217). New York: Guilford.

Thase, M.E., Jindal, R., & Howland, R.H. (2002). Biological aspects of depression. In I.H. Gotlib & C.L. Hammen (Eds.), *Handbook of depression* (pp. 192-218). New York: Guilford.

Thayer, J.F., & Brosschot, J.F. (2005). Psychosomatics and psychopathology: Looking up and down from the brain. *Psychoneuroendocrinology, 30*, 1050-1058.

Theircelin, N., Lechevallier, Z.R., Rusch, E., & Plat, A. (2012). Risk factors for delirium tremens: A literature review. *La Revue de Médecine Interne, 33*, 18-22.

Thoma, R.J., Hanlon, F.M., Moses, S.N., Ricker, D., Huang, M., Edgar, C., Irwin, J., Torres, F., Weisend, M.P., Adler, L.E., Miller, G.A., & Canive, J.M. (2005). M50 sensory gating predicts negative symptoms in schizophrenia. *Schizophrenia Research, 73*, 311-318.

Thomas, J.J., Vartanian, L.R., & Brownell, K.D. (2009). The relationship between eating disorder not otherwise specified (EDNOS) and officially recognized eating disorders: Meta-analysis and implications for DSM. *Psychological Bulletin, 135*, 407-433.

Thomas, M., & Jankovic, J. (2004). Psychogenic movement disorders: Diagnosis and management. *CNS Drugs, 18*, 437-452.

Thomas, R., & Perera, R. (2006). School-based programmes for preventing smoking. *Cochrane Database of Systematic Reviews, 19*.

Thompson, C. (2006). Review of 212 individuals attending a city centre genitourinary medicine clinic following acute sexual assault. *Journal of Clinical Forensic Medicine, 13*, 186-188.

Thompson, J. K., & van den Berg, P. (2002). Measuring body image attitudes among adolescents and adults. In T.F. Cash & T. Pruzinsky (Eds.), *Body image: A handbook of theory, research, and clinical practice* (pp. 142-154). New York: Guilford.

Thompson, P.M., Bartzokis, G., Hayashi, K.M., Klunder, A.D., Lu, P.H., Edwards, N., Hong, M.S., Yu, M., Geaga, J.A., Toga, A.W., Charles, C., Perkins, D.O., McEvoy, J., Hamer, R.M., Tohen, M., Tollefson, G.D., Lieberman, J A , and the HGDH Study Group. (2009). Time-lapse mapping of cortical changes in schizophrenia with different treatments. *Cerebral Cortex, 19*, 1107-1123.

Thomson, A.D., Guerrini, I., & Marshall, E.J. (2012). The evolution and treatment of Korsakoff's syndrome: Out of sight, out of mind? *Neuropsychology Review, 22*, 81-92.

Thornton, D. (2010). Evidence regarding the need for a diagnostic category for a coercive paraphilia. *Archives of Sexual Behavior, 39*, 411-418.

Thornton, L.M., Mazzeo, S.E., & Bulik, C.M. (2010). The heritability of eating disorders: Methods and current findings. In R.A.H. Adan & W.H. Kaye (Eds.), *Behavioral neurobiology of eating disorders* (pp. 141-156). Berlin: Springer-Verlag.

Thrasher, S., Power, M., Morant, N., Marks, I., & Dalgleish, T. (2010). Social support moderates outcome in a randomized controlled trial of exposure therapy and (or) cognitive restructuring for chronic posttraumatic stress disorder. *Canadian Journal of Psychiatry, 55*, 187-190.

Tickle-Degnen, L., Zebrowitz, L.A., & Ma, H. (2011). Culture, gender and health care stigma: Practitioner's response to facial masking experienced by people with Parkinson's disease. *Social Science and Medicine, 73*, 95-102.

Tiggeman, M., & Slater, A. (2001). A test of objectification theory in former dancers and non-dancers. *Psychology of Women Quarterly, 25*, 57-64.

Tija, J., Rothman, M.R., Kiely, D.K., Shaffer, M.L., Holmes, H.M., Sachs, G.A., & Mitchell, S.L. (2010). Daily medication use in nursing home residents with advanced dementia. *Journal of the American Geriatrics Society, 58*, 880-888.

Tillfors, M., Furmark, T., Ekselius, L., & Fredrikson, M. (2001). Social phobia and avoidant personality disorder as related to parental history of social anxiety: A general population study. *Behaviour Research and Therapy, 39*, 289-298.

Tillfors, M., Furmark, T., Marteinsdottir, I., & Fredrikson, M. (2002). Cerebral blood flow during anticipation of public speaking in social phobia: A PET study. *Biological Psychiatry, 52*, 1113-1119.

Tilvis, R.S., Kahonen-Vare, M.H., Jolkkonen, J., Valvanne, J., Pitkala, K.H., & Strandberg, T.E. (2004). Predictors of cognitive decline and mortality of aged people over a 10-year period. *Journal of Gerontology Series A: Biological Sciences and Medical Sciences, 59*, 268-274.

Timko, C., Moos, R.H., Finney, J.W., & Lesar, M.D. (2000). Long-term outcomes of alcohol use disorders: Comparing untreated individuals with those in Alcoholics Anonymous and formal treatment. *Journal of Studies on Alcohol, 61*, 529-540.

Tishler, C.L., & Reiss, N.S. (2009). Inpatient suicide: Preventing a common sentinel event. *General Hospital Psychiatry, 31*, 103-109.

Toneatto, T., & Nguyen, L. (2007). Does mindfulness meditation improve anxiety and mood symptoms?: A review of the controlled research. *Canadian Journal of Psychiatry, 52*, 260-266.

Tonigan, J.S., & Conners, G.J. (2008). Psychological mechanisms in Alcoholics Anonymous. In M. Galanter & H.D. Kleber (Eds.), *Textbook of substance abuse treatment* (4th ed.) (pp. 491-498). Washington, DC: American Psychiatric Press.

Tonna, M., De Panfilis, C., & Marchesi, C. (2012). Mood-congruent and mood-incongruent psychotic symptoms in major depression: The role of severity and personality. *Journal of Affective Disorders, 141*, 464-468.

Torgersen, S. (2005). Epidemiology. In J.M. Oldham, A.E. Skodol, & D.S. Bender (Eds.), *The American Psychiatric Publishing textbook of personality disorders* (pp. 129-142). Washington, DC: American Psychiatric Publishing.

Toriello, H.V. (2011). Genetic evaluation in developmental disabilities. In D.R. Patel, D.E. Graydanus, H.A. Omar, & J. Merrick (Eds.), *Neurodevelopmental disabilities: Clinical care for children and young adults* (pp. 69-78). New York: Springer.

Tough, S.C., Clarke, M., & Clarren, S. (2005). Preventing fetal alcohol spectrum disorders: Preconception counseling and diagnosis help. *Canadian Family Physician, 51*, 1199-1201.

Town, J.M., Abbass, A., & Hardy, G. (2011). Short-term psychodynamic psychotherapy for personality disorders: A critical review of randomized controlled trials. *Journal of Personality Disorders, 25*, 723-740.

Tozzi, F., Thornton, L.M., Klump, K.L., Fichter, M.M., Halmi, K.A., Kaplan, A.S., Strober, M., Woodside, D.B., Crow, S., Mitchell, J., Rotondo, A., Mauri, M., Cassano, G., Keel, P., Plotnicov, K.H., Pollice, C., Lilenfeld, L.R., Berrettini, W.H., Bulik, C.M., & Kaye, W.H. (2005). Symptom fluctuation in eating disorders: Correlates of diagnostic crossover. *American Journal of Psychiatry, 162*, 732-740.

Trace, S.E., Baker, J.H., Penas-Lledo, E., & Bulik, C.M. (2013). The genetics of eating disorders. *Annual Review of Clinical Psychology, 9*, 589-620.

Treasure, J., Schmidt, U., & Macdonald, P. (Eds.). (2010). *The clinician's guide to collaborative caring in eating disorders: The new Maudsley method.* New York: Routledge.

Treffert, D.A. (2009). The savant syndrome. An extraordinary condition. A synopsis: Past, present, future. *Philosophical Transactions of the Royal Society, 364*, 1351-1357.

Tremolizzo, L., Beretta, S., & Ferrarese, C. (2004). Peripheral markers of glutamatergic dysfunction in neurological diseases: Focus on ex vivo tools. *Critical Reviews in Neurobiology, 16*, 141-146.

Treuer, T., & Tohen, M. (2009). Course and outcome of bipolar disorder—focusing on depressive aspects. In C.A. Zarate & H.K. Manji (Eds.), *Bipolar depression: Molecular neurobiology,*

*clinical diagnosis and pharmacotherapy* (pp. 29-46). Boston: Birkhauser.

Treuer, T., & Tohen, M. (2010). Predicting the course and outcome of bipolar disorder: A review. *European Psychiatry, 25*, 328-333.

Troisi, A. (2003). Sexual disorders in the context of Darwinian psychiatry. *Journal of Endocrinological Investigation, 26*, 54-57.

Trull, T.J., & Prinstein, M.J. (2013). *Clinical psychology* (8th ed.) Belmont, CA: Wadsworth/Cengage

Trull, T.J., Jahng, S., Tomko, R.L., Wood, P.K., & Sher, K.J. (2010). Revised NESARC personality disorder diagnoses: Gender, prevalence, and comorbidity with substance dependence disorders. *Journal of Personality Disorders, 24*, 412-426.

Tryon, W.W. (2005). Possible mechanisms for why desensitization and exposure therapy work. *Clinical Psychology Review, 25*, 67-95.

Trzepacz, P.T., Meagher, D.J., & Wise, M.G. (2004). Neuropsychiatric aspects of delirium. In S.C. Yudofsky & R.E. Hales (Eds.), *Essentials of neuropsychiatry and clinical neurosciences* (pp. 141-187). Washington, DC: American Psychiatric Publishing.

Trzepacz, P.T., Mittal, D., Torres, R., Kanary, K., Norton, J., & Jimerson, N. (2001). Validation of the Delirium Rating Scale-revised-98: Comparison with the Delirium Rating Scale and the Cognitive Test for Delirium. *Journal of Neuropsychiatry and Clinical Neurosciences, 13*, 229-242.

Tse, W.S., & Bond, A.J. (2004). The impact of depression on social skills: A review. *Journal of Nervous and Mental Disease, 192*, 260-268.

Tseng, W. (2001). *Handbook of cultural psychiatry.* New York: Academic Press.

Tseng, W.-S. (2003). *Clinician's guide to cultural psychiatry.* San Diego, CA: Academic.

Tsuno, N., Shigeta, M., Hyoki, K., Faber, P.L., & Lehmann, D. (2004). Fluctuations of source locations of EEG activity during transition from alertness to sleep in Alzheimer's disease and vascular dementia. *Neuropsychobiology, 50*, 267-272.

Tuerk, E.H., McCart, M.R., & Henggeler, S.W. (2012). Collaboration in family therapy. *Journal of Clinical Psychology, 68*, 168-178.

Turan, M.K., Moroz, L., & Croteau, N.P. (2012). Comparing the effectiveness of error-correction strategies in discrete trial training. *Behavior Modification, 36*, 218-234.

Tyler, K.A., Cauce, A.M., & Whitbeck, L. (2004). Family risk factors and prevalence of dissociative symptoms among homeless and runaway youth. *Child Abuse and Neglect, 28*, 355-366.

Uematsu, M., Adachi, E., Nakamura, A., Tsuchiya, K., & Uchihara, T. (2012). Atomic identification of fluorescent Q-dots on tau-positive fibrils in 3D-reconstructed Pick bodies. *American Journal of Pathology, 180*, 1394-1397.

Uguz, S., Soylu, L., Unal, M., Diler, R.S., & Evlice, Y.E. (2004). Psychosocial factors and sexual dysfunctions: A descriptive study in Turkish males. *Psychopathology, 37*, 145-151.

Uhl, G.R., Drgon, T., Johnson, C., & Liu, Q.-R. (2009). Addiction genetics and pleiotropic effects of common haplotypes that make polygenic contributions to vulnerability to substance dependence. *Journal of Neurogenetics, 23*, 272-282.

UK ECT Review Group. (2003). Efficacy and safety of electroconvulsive therapy in depressive disorders: A systematic review and meta-analysis. *Lancet, 361*, 799-808.

Ungless, M.A., Argilli, E., & Bonci, A. (2010). Effects of stress and aversion on dopamine neurons: Implications for addiction. *Neuroscience and Biobehavioral Reviews, 35*, 151-156.

Ungvari, G.S., Mann, S.C., & Caroff, S.N. (2013). An outline of the historical and clinical aspects of catatonic schizophrenia. *Current Psychiatry Reviews, 9*, 94-100.

U.S. Census Bureau. (2004). *We the people: Aging in the United States.* Washington, DC: U.S. Department of Commerce.

U.S. Department of Health and Human Services. (1999). *Mental health: A report of the Surgeon General.* Rockville, MD: U.S. Department of Health and Human Services, Substance Abuse and Mental Health Services Administration, Center for Mental Health Services, National Institutes of Health, National Institute of Mental Health.

U.S. Department of Health and Human Services. (2001). *Mental health: culture, race, and ethnicity: A Supplement to Mental Health: A Report of the Surgeon General.* Rockville, MD: U.S. Department of Health and Human Services, Substance Abuse and Mental Health Services Administration, Center for Mental Health Services, National Institutes of Health, National Institute of Mental Health.

Vader, A.M., Walters, S.T., Prabhu, G.C., Houck, J.M., & Field, C.A. (2010). The language of motivational interviewing and feedback: Counselor language, client language, and client drinking outcomes. *Psychology of Addictive Behaviors, 24*, 190-197.

Valenzuela, M., & Sachdev, P. (2009). Can cognitive exercise prevent the onset of dementia? Systematic review of randomized clinical trials with longitudinal follow-up. *American Journal of Geriatric Psychiatry, 17*, 179-187.

Valla, J.P., Bergeron, L., & Smolla, N. (2000). The Dominic-R: A pictorial interview for 6- to 11-year-old children. *Journal of the American Academy of Child and Adolescent Psychiatry, 39*, 85-93.

van Bokhoven, H. (2011). Genetic and epigenetic networks in intellectual disabilities. *Annual Review of Genetics, 45*, 81-104.

Van Deerlin, V.M., Gill, L.H., Farmer, J.M., Trojanowski, J.Q., & Lee, V.M-Y. (2003). Familial frontotemporal dementia: From gene discovery to clinical molecular diagnostics. *Clinical Chemistry, 49*, 1717-1725.

Van Den Eeden, S.K., Tanner, C.M., Bernstein, A.L., Fross, R.D., Leimpeter, A., Bloch, D.A., & Nelson, L.M. (2003). Incidence of Parkinson's disease: Variation by age, gender, and race/ethnicity. *American Journal of Epidemiology, 157*, 1015-1022.

Van der Flier, W.M., & Cordonnier, C. (2012). Microbleeds in vascular dementia: Clinical aspects. *Experimental Gerontology, 47*, 853-857.

van der Flier, W.M., Pijnenburg, Y.A.L., Fox, N.C., & Scheltens, P. (2011). Early-onset versus late-onset Alzheimer's disease: The case of the missing APOE 4 allele. *Lancet Neurology, 10*, 280-288.

Van Gundy, K., & Rebellon, C.J. (2010). A life-course perspective on the "gateway hypothesis." *Journal of Health and Social Behavior, 51*, 244-259.

van den Heuvel, O.A., Veltman, D.J., Groenewegen, H.J., Dolan, R.J., Cath, D.C., Boellaard, R., Mesina, C.T., van Balkom, A.J., van Oppen, P., Witter, M.P., Lammertsma, A.A., & van Dyck, R. (2004). Amygdala activity in obsessive-compulsive disorder with contamination fear: A study with oxygen-15 water positron emission tomography. *Psychiatry Research, 132*, 225-237.

Vanderbilt-Adriance, E., & Shaw, D.S. (2008). Conceptualizing and re-evaluating resilience across levels of risk, time, and domains of competence. *Clinical Child and Family Psychology Review, 11*, 30-58.

van der Hart, O., Bolt, H., & van der Kolk, B.A. (2005). Memory fragmentation in dissociative identity disorder. *Journal of Trauma and Dissociation, 6*, 55-70.

van der Hart, O., & Nijenhuis, E. (2001). Generalized dissociative amnesia: Episodic, semantic and procedural memories lost and found. *Australian and New Zealand Journal of Psychiatry, 35*, 589-600.

Van Duijl, M., Cardena, E., & De Jong, J.T. (2005). The validity of DSM-IV dissociative disorders categories in south-west Uganda. *Transcultural Psychiatry, 42*, 219-241.

Van Gestel, S.V., & Van Broeckhoven, C. (2003). Genetics of personality: Are we making progress? *Molecular Psychiatry, 8*, 840-852.

Vanheule, S., Desmet, M., Groenvynck, H., Rosseel, Y., & Fontaine, J. (2008). The factor structure of the Beck Depression Inventory-II: An evaluation. *Assessment, 15*, 177-187.

Van Houtem, C.M.H.H., Laine, M.L., Boomsma, D.I., Ligthart, L., van Wijk, A.J., & De Jongh, A. (2013). A review and meta-analysis of the heritability of specific phobia subtypes and corresponding fears. *Journal of Anxiety Disorders, 27*, 379-388.

van Lankveld, J. (2009). Self-help therapies for sexual dysfunction. *Journal of Sex Research, 46*, 143-155.

Van Meter, A.R., Youngstrom, E.A., & Findling, R.L. (2012). Cyclothymic disorder: A critical review. *Clinical Psychology Review, 32*, 229-243.

Van Mierlo, L.D., Van der Roest, H.G., Meiland, F.J.M., & Droes, R.M. (2010). Personalized dementia care: Proven effectiveness of psychosocial interventions in subgroups. *Ageing Research Reviews, 9*, 163-183.

Varnick, P. (2012). Suicide in the world. *International Journal of Environmental Research and Public Health, 9*, 760-771.

Vase, L., Nikolajsen, L., Christensen, B., Egsgaard, L.L., Arendt-Nielsen, L., Svensson, P., & Jensen, T.S. (2011). Cognitive-emotional sensitization contributes to wind-up-like pain in phantom limb pain patients. *Pain, 152*, 157-162.

Veale, J.F., Clarke, D.E., & Lomax, T.C. (2010). Biological and psychosocial correlates of adult gender-variant identities: A review. *Personality and Individual Differences, 48*, 357-366.

Vecchio, J., & Kearney, C.A. (2007). Assessment and treatment of a Hispanic youth with selective mutism. *Clinical Case Studies, 6*, 34-43.

Vehmanen, L., Kaprio, J., & Lonnqvist, J. (1995). Twin studies on concordance for bipolar disorder. *Psychiatria Fennica, 26*, 107-116.

Velligan, D.I., Kern, R.S., & Gold, J.M. (2006). Cognitive rehabilitation for schizophrenia and the putative role of motivation and expectancies. *Schizophrenia Bulletin, 32*, 474-485.

Venturello, S., Barzega, G., Maina, G., & Bogetto, F. (2002). Premorbid conditions and precipitating events in early-onset panic disorder. *Comprehensive Psychiatry, 43*, 28-36.

Verdejo-Garcia, A., Lawrence, A.J., & Clark, L. (2008). Impulsivity as a vulnerability marker for substance-use disorders: Review of findings from high-risk research, problem gamblers and genetic association studies. *Neuroscience and Biobehavioral Reviews, 32*, 777-810.

Verma, M., & Howard, R.J. (2012). Semantic memory and language dysfunction in early Alzheimer's disease: A review. *International Journal of Geriatric Psychiatry, 27*, 1209-1217.

Vermeiren, R., Jones, S.M., Ruchkin, V., Deboutte, D., & Schwab-Stone, M. (2004). Juvenile arrest: A crosscultural comparison. *Journal of Child Psychology and Psychiatry, 45*, 567-576.

Verona, E., Sprague, J., & Sadeh, N. (2012). Inhibitory control and negative emotional processing in psychopathy and antisocial personality disorder. *Journal of Abnormal Psychology, 121*, 498-510.

Vicary, J.R., & Karshin, C.M. (2002). College alcohol abuse: A review of the problems, issues, and prevention approaches. *Journal of Primary Prevention, 22*, 299-331.

Vidaeff, A.C., Franzini, L., & Low, M.D. (2003). The unrealized potential of prenatal care: A population health approach. *Journal of Reproductive Medicine, 48*, 837-842.

Videbech, P., & Ravnkilde, B. (2004). Hippocampal volume and depression: A meta-analysis of MRI studies. *American Journal of Psychiatry, 161*, 1957-1966.

Vieira, R., Caixeta, L., Machado, S., Silva, A.C., Nardi, A.E., Arias-Carrion, O., & Carta, M.G. (2013). Epidemiology of early-onset dementia: A review of the literature. *Clinical Practice and Epidemiology in Mental Health, 9*, 88-95.

Viglione, D. J. (1999). A review of recent research addressing the utility of the Rorschach. *Psychological Assessment, 11*, 251-265.

Viglione, D.J., & Hilsenroth, M.J. (2001). The Rorschach: Facts, fictions, and future. *Psychological Assessment, 13*, 452-471.

Vigna-Taglianti, F., Vadrucci, S., Faggiano, F., Burkhart, G., Siliquini, R., Galanti, M.R., & the EU-Dap Study Group. (2009). Is universal prevention against youths' substance misuse really universal? Gender-specific effects in the EU-Dap school based prevention trial. *Journal of Epidemiology and Community Health, 63*, 722-728.

Vilain, J., Galliot, A.M., Durand-Roger, J., Leboyer, M., Llorca, P.M., Schurhoff, F., & Szoke, A. (2013). Environmental risk factors for schizophrenia: A review. *Encephale, 39*, 19-28.

Villodas, M.T., Pfiffner, L.J., & McBurnett, K. (2012). Prevention of serious conduct problems in youth with attention deficit/hyperactivity disorder. *Expert Review of Neurotherapeutics, 12*, 1253-1263.

Vindenes, V., Lund, H.M.E., Andresen, W., Gjerde, H., Ikdahl, S.E., Christophersen, A.S., & Oiestad, E.L. (2012). Detection of drugs of abuse in simultaneously collected oral fluid, urine and blood from Norwegian drug drivers. *Forensic Science International, 219*, 165-171.

Vinkers, D.J., De Beurs, E., Barendregt, M., Rinne, T., & Hoek, H.W. (2011). The relationship between mental disorders and different types of crime. *Criminal Behaviour and Mental Health, 21*, 307-320.

Vismara, L.A., & Rogers, S.J. (2010). Behavioral treatments in autism spectrum disorder: What do we know? *Annual Review of Clinical Psychology, 6*, 447-468.

Visser, S., & Bouman, T.K. (2001). The treatment of hypochondriasis: Exposure plus response prevention vs cognitive therapy. *Behaviour Research and Therapy, 39*, 423-442.

Vocks, S., Tuschen-Caffier, B., Pietrowsky, R., Rustenbach, S.J., Kersting, A., & Herpertz, S. (2010). Meta-analysis of the effectiveness of psychological and pharmacological treatments for binge eating disorder. *International Journal of Eating Disorders, 43*, 205-217.

Volkmar, F., Chawarska, K., & Klin, A. (2005). Autism in infancy and early childhood. *Annual Review of Psychology, 56*, 315-336.

Volkmar, F.R., & Klin, A. (2000). Diagnostic issues in Asperger syndrome. In A. Klin, F.R. Volkmar, & S.S. Sparrow (Eds.), *Asperger syndrome* (pp. 25-71). New York: Guilford.

Volkow, N.D., Fowler, J.S., Wang, G.-J., Telang, F., Logan, J., Jayne, M., Ma, Y., Pradhan, K., Wong, C., & Swanson, J.M. (2010). Cognitive control of drug craving inhibits brain reward regions in cocaine abusers. *NeuroImage, 49*, 2536-2543.

Volkow, N.D., Wang, G.-J., & Baler, R.D. (2011). Reward, dopamine and the control of food intake: Implications for obesity. *Trends in Cognitive Sciences, 15*, 37-46.

Volkow, N.D., Wang, G.-J., Fowler, J.S., Tomasi, D., & Telang, F. (2011). Addiction: Beyond dopamine reward circuitry. *Proceedings of the National Academy of Sciences, 108*, 1-6.

Volkow, N.D., Wang, G.J., Fowler, J.S., & Ding, Y.S. (2005). Imaging the effects of methylphenidate on brain dopamine: New model on its therapeutic actions for attention-deficit/hyperactivity disorder. *Biological Psychiatry, 57*, 1410-1415.

Volkow, N.D., Wang, G.-J., Fowler, J.S., Tomasi, D., & Telang, F. (2011). Addiction: Beyond dopamine reward circuitry. *Proceedings of the National Academy of Sciences, 108*, 1-6.

Volkow, N.D., Wang, G.-J., Maynard, L., Jayne, M., Fowler, J.S., Zhu, W., Logan, J., Gatley, S.J., Ding, Y. S., Wong, C., & Pappas, N. (2003). Brain dopamine is associated with eating behaviors in humans. *International Journal of Eating Disorders, 33*, 136-142.

Vollstadt-Klein, S., Loeber, S., Kirsch, M., Bach, P., Richter, A., Buhler, M., von der Goltz, Hermann, D., Mann, K., & Kiefer, F. (2011). Effects of cue-exposure treatment on neural cue reactivity in alcohol dependence: A randomized trial. *Biological Psychiatry, 69*, 1060-1066.

von Arnim, C.A.F., Herbolsheimer, F., Nikolaus, T., Peter, R., Biesalski, H.K., Ludolph, A.C., Riepe, M., & Nagel, G. (2012). Dietary antioxidants and dementia in a population-based case-control study among older people in South Germany. *Journal of Alzheimer's Disease, 31*, 717-724.

Vreeburg, S.A., Zitman, F.G., van Pelt, J., DrRijk, R.H., Verhagen, J.C.M., van Dyck, R., Hoogendijk, W.J.G., Smit, J.H., & Penninx, B.W.J.H. (2010). Salivary cortisol levels in persons with and without different anxiety disorders. *Psychosomatic Medicine, 72*, 340-347.

Vuilleumier, P. (2005). Hysterical conversion and brain function. *Progress in Brain Research, 150*, 309-329.

Waddell, C., Hua, J.M., Garland, O.M., Peters, R.D., & McEwan, K. (2007). Preventing mental disorders in children: A systematic review to inform policy-making. *Canadian Journal of Public Health, 98*, 166-173.

Wade, T.D., Bergin, J.L., Tiggemann, M., Bulik, C.M., & Fairburn, C.G. (2006). Prevalence and long-term course of lifetime eating disorders in an adult Australian twin cohort. *Australian and New Zealand Journal of Psychiatry, 40*, 121-128.

Wade, T.D., Bulik, C.M., Neale, M., & Kendler, K.S. (2000). Anorexia nervosa and major depression: Shared genetic and environmental risk factors. *American Journal of Psychiatry, 157*, 469-471.

Wade, T.D., Gillespie, N., & Martin, N.G. (2007). A comparison of early family life events amongst monozygotic twin women with lifetime anorexia nervosa, bulimia nervosa, or major depression. *International Journal of Eating Disorders, 40*, 679-686.

Wakefield, J.C. (2012). The DSM-5's proposed new categories of sexual disorder: The problem of false positives in sexual diagnosis. *Clinical Social Work Journal, 40*, 213-223.

Wald, J., & Taylor, S. (2007). Efficacy of interoceptive exposure therapy combined with trauma-related exposure therapy for posttraumatic stress disorder: A pilot study. *Journal of Anxiety Disorders, 21*, 1050-1060.

Waldman, I.D., & Gizer, I.R. (2006). The genetics of attention deficit hyperactivity disorder. *Clinical Psychology Review, 26*, 396-432.

Wallien, M.S., Swaab, H., & Cohen-Kettenis, P.T. (2007). Psychiatric comorbidity among children with gender identity disorder. *Journal of the American Academy of Child and Adolescent Psychiatry, 46*, 1307-1314.

Walterfang, M., Wood, A.G., Reutens, D.C., Wood, S.J., Chen, J., Velakoulis, D., McGorry, P.D., & Pantelis, C. (2008). Morphology of the corpus callosum at different stages of schizophrenia: Cross-sectional study in first-episode and chronic illness. *British Journal of Psychiatry, 192*, 429-434.

Walters, G.D. (2002). The heritability of alcohol abuse and dependence: A meta-analysis of behavior genetic research. *American Journal of Drug and Alcohol Abuse, 28*, 557-584.

Walters, S.T., Vader, A.M., Harris, T.R., Field, C.A., & Jouriles, E.N. (2009). Dismantling motivational interviewing and feedback for college drinkers: A randomized clinical trial. *Journal of Consulting and Clinical Psychology, 77*, 64-73.

Walton, K.M., & Ingersoll, B.R. (2013). Improving social skills in adolescents and adults with autism and severe to profound intellectual disability: A review of the literature. *Journal of Autism and Developmental Disorders, 43*, 594-615.

Wampold, B.E., & Budge, S.L. (2012). The 2011 Leona Tyler Award address: The relationship—and its relationship to the common and specific factors of psychotherapy. *Counseling Psychologist, 40*, 601-623.

Wampold, B.E., Minami, T., Tierney, S.C., Baskin, T.W., & Bhati, K.S. (2005). The placebo is powerful: Estimating placebo effects in medicine and psychotherapy from randomized clinical trials. *Journal of Clinical Psychology, 61*, 835-854.

Wampold, B.E. (2012). Humanism as a common factor in psychotherapy. *Psychotherapy, 49*, 445-449.

Wan, M.W., Abel, K.M., & Green, J. (2008). The transmission of risk to children from mothers with schizophrenia: A developmental psychopathology model. *Clinical Psychology Review, 28*, 613-637.

Wandersman, A., & Nation, M. (1998). Urban neighborhoods and mental health: Psychological contributions to understanding toxicity, resilience, and interventions. *American Psychologist, 53*, 647-656.

Wang, P.S., Angermeyer, M., Borges, G., Bruffaerts, R., Chiu, W.T., de Girolamo, G., Fayyad, J., Gureje, O., Haro, J.M., Huang, Y., Kessler, R.C., Kovess, V., Levinson, D., Nakane, Y., Oakley Browne, M.A., Ormel, J.H., Posada-Villa, J., Aguilar-Gaxiola, S., Alonso, J., Lee, S., Heeringa, S., Pennell, B.-E., Chatterji, S., & Ustun, T.B. (2007). Delay and failure in treatment seeking after first onset of mental disorders in the World Health Organization's World Mental Health Survey Initiative. *World Psychiatry, 6*, 177-185.

Wang, P.S., Berglund, P., Olfson, M., Pincus, H.A., Wells, K.B., & Kessler, R.C. (2005). Failure and delay in initial treatment contact after first onset of mental disorders in the National Comorbidity Survey Replication. *Archives of General Psychiatry, 62*, 603-613.

Wang, P.S., Lane, M., Olfson, M., Pincus, H.A., Wells, K.B., & Kessler, R.C. (2005). Twelve-month use of mental health services in the United States: Results from the National Comorbidity Survey Replication. *Archives of General Psychiatry, 62*, 629-640.

Ward, T., & Beech, A.R. (2008). An integrated theory of sexual offending. In D.R. Laws & W.T. O'Donohue (Eds.), *Sexual deviance: Theory, assessment, and treatment* (2nd ed.) (pp. 21-36). New York: Guilford.

Watanabe, N., Churchill, R., & Furukawa, T.A. (2007). Combination of psychotherapy and benzodiazepines versus either therapy alone for panic disorder: A systematic review. *BMC Psychiatry, 7*, 18.

Watari, K.F., & Brodbeck, C. (2000). Culture, health, and financial appraisals: Comparison of worry in older Japanese and European Americans. *Journal of Clinical Geropsychology, 6*, 25-39.

Waters, F., Allen, P., Aleman, A., Fernyhough, C., Woodward, T.S., Badcock, J.C., Barkus, E., Johns, L., Varese, F., Menon, M., Vercammen, A., & Laroi, F. (2012). Auditory hallucinations in schizophrenia and nonschizophrenia populations: A review and integrated model of cognitive mechanisms. *Schizophrenia Bulletin, 38*, 683-692.

Watson, J. D. (2003). *DNA: The secret of life.* New York: Alfred A. Knopf.

Watson, P.J., & Andrews, P.W. (2002). Toward a revised evolutionary adaptationist analysis of depression: The social navigation hypothesis. *Journal of Affective Disorders, 72*, 1-14.

Watson, R., & O'Brien, J.T. (2012). Differentiating dementia with Lewy bodies and Alzheimer's disease using MRI. *Neurodegenerative Disease, 2*, 411-420.

Waxman, S.E. (2009). A systematic review of impulsivity in eating disorders. *European Eating Disorders Review, 17*, 408-425.

Webb, L., Craissati, J., & Keen, S. (2007). Characteristics of internet child pornography offenders: A comparison with child molesters. *Sexual Abuse, 19*, 449-465.

Webb, S.J., Sparks, B.-F., Friedman, S.D., Shaw, D.W.W., Giedd, J., Dawson, G., & Dager, S.R. (2009). Cerebellar vermal volumes and behavioral correlates in children with autism spectrum disorder. *Psychiatry Research: Neuroimaging, 172*, 61-67.

Webber, S. (2011). Who am I? Locating the neural correlate of the self. *Bioscience Horizons, 4*, 165-173.

Webster-Stratton, C.H., Reid, M.J., & Beauchaine, T. (2011). Combining parent and child training for young children with ADHD. *Journal of Clinical Child and Adolescent Psychology, 40,* 191-203.

Wechsler, D. (2008). *WAIS-IV: Wechsler Adult Intelligence Scale—fourth edition.* San Antonio, TX: Pearson.

Wechsler, D. (2009). *Wechsler Memory Scale—Fourth Edition* (WMS-IV). San Antonio, TX: Pearson.

Wechsler, H., Lee, J., Kuo, M., & Lee, H. (2000). College binge drinking in the 1990s: A continuing problem. Results of the Harvard School of Public Health 1999 College Alcohol Study. *Journal of American College Health, 48,* 199-210.

Wechsler, H., & Wilson, T.F. (2008). What we have learned from the Harvard School of Public Health College Alcohol Study: Focusing attention on college student alcohol consumption and the environmental conditions that promote it. *Journal of Studies on Alcohol and Drugs, 69,* 481-490.

Wedig, M.M., Silverman, M.H., Frankenburg, F.R., Reich, D.B., Fitzmaurice, G., & Zanarini, M.C. (2012). Predictors of suicide attempts in patients with borderline personality disorder over 16 years of prospective follow-up. *Psychological Medicine, 42,* 2395-2404.

Weggen, S., & Beher, D. (2012). Molecular consequences of amyloid precursor protein and presenilin mutations causing autosomal-dominant Alzheimer's disease. *Alzheimer's Research and Therapy, 4,* 9.

Wehmeier, P.M., Barth, N., & Remschmidt, H. (2003). Induced delusional disorder: A review of the concept and an unusual case of folie a famille. *Psychopathology, 36,* 37-45.

Wei, M., Liao, K. Y.-H., Chao, R. C.-L., Mallinckrodt, B., Tsai, P.-C., & Botello-Zamarron, R. (2010). Minority stress, perceived bicultural competence, and depressive symptoms among ethnic minority college students. *Journal of Counseling Psychology, 57,* 411-422.

Weiner, M.F., & Lipton, A.M. (Eds.). (2012). *Clinical manual of Alzheimer disease and other dementias.* Arlington, VA: American Psychiatric Association.

Weiss, R.D., Potter, J.S., & Iannucci, R.A. (2008). Inpatient treatment. In M. Galanter & H.D. Kleber (Eds.), *Textbook of substance abuse treatment* (4th ed.; pp. 445-458). Washington, DC: American Psychiatric Press.

Weissman, M., & Verdeli, H. (2012). Interpersonal psychotherapy: Evaluation, support, triage. *Clinical Psychology and Psychotherapy, 19,* 106-112.

Weissman, M.M. (2007). Recent non-medication trials of interpersonal psychotherapy for depression. *International Journal of Neuropsychopharmacology, 10,* 117-122.

Weissman, M.M., Bland, R., Canino, G., Greenwald, S., Hwo, H., Lee, C., Newman, S., Oakley-Browne, M., Rubio-Stupek, M., Wickramaratne, P., Wittchen, H., & Eng-Kung, Y. (1994). The cross national epidemiology of obsessive compulsive disorder. *Journal of Clinical Psychiatry, 55,* 5-10.

Weissman, M.M., & Markowitz, J.C. (2002). Interpersonal therapy for depression. In I.H. Gotlib

& C.L. Hammen (Eds.), *Handbook of depression* (pp. 404-421). New York: Guilford.

Weissman, M.M., Markowitz, J.C., & Klerman, G.L. (2000). *Comprehensive guide to interpersonal psychotherapy.* New York: Basic.

Weisz, J.R., Sandler, I.N., Durlak, J.A., & Anton, B.S. (2005). Promoting and protecting youth mental health through evidence-based prevention and treatment. *American Psychologist, 60,* 628-640.

Wells, A. (2002). GAD, metacognition, and mindfulness: An information processing analysis. *Clinical Psychology: Science and Practice, 9,* 95-100.

Wemmie, J.A. (2011). Neurobiology of panic and pH chemosensation in the brain. *Dialogues in Clinical Neuroscience, 13,* 475-483.

Werner, F.-M., & Covenas, R. (2010). Classical neurotransmitters and neuropeptides involved in major depression: A review. *International Journal of Neuroscience, 120,* 455-470.

Werner, P., Goldstein, D., & Buchbinder, E. (2010). Subjective experience of family stigma as reported by children of Alzheimer's disease patients. *Qualitative Health Research, 20,* 159-169.

Werner, P., Mittelman, M.S., Goldstein, D., & Heinik, J. (2012). Family stigma and caregiver burden in Alzheimer's disease. *The Gerontologist, 52,* 89-97.

Westen, D. (1998). The scientific legacy of Sigmund Freud: Toward a psychodynamically informed psychological science. *Psychological Bulletin, 124,* 333-371.

Westenberg, H.G., & Sandner, C. (2006). Tolerability and safety of fluvoxamine and other antidepressants. *International Journal of Clinical Practice, 60,* 482-491.

Westra, H.A. (2012). *Motivational interviewing in the treatment of anxiety.* New York: Guilford.

Westrich, L., & Sprouse, J. (2010). Circadian rhythm dysregulation in bipolar disorder. *Current Opinion in Investigational Drugs, 11,* 779-787.

Wetzel, R.D., Brim, J., Guze, S.B., Cloninger, C.R., Martin, R.L., & Clayton, P.J. (1999). MMPI screening scales for somatization disorder. *Psychological Reports, 85,* 341-348.

Whiffen, V.E., & MacIntosh, H.B. (2005). Mediators of the link between childhood sexual abuse and emotional distress: A critical review. *Trauma, Violence, and Abuse, 6,* 24-39.

Whitaker, D.J., Le, B., Hanson, R.K., Baker, C.K., McMahon, P.M., Ryan, G., Klein, A., & Rice, D.D. (2008). Risk factors for the perpetuation of child sexual abuse: A review and meta-analysis. *Child Abuse and Neglect, 32,* 529-548.

Whitty, P., Clarke, M., McTigue, O., Browne, S., Kamali, M., Larkin, C., & O'Callaghan, E. (2005). Diagnostic stability four years after a first episode of psychosis. *Psychiatric Services, 56,* 1084-1088.

Widiger, T.A. (2011). Personality and psychopathology. *World Psychiatry, 10,* 103-106.

Wiegel, M., Meston, C., & Rosen, R. (2005). The Female Sexual Function Index (FSFI): Cross-validation and development of clinical cutoff

scores. *Journal of Sex and Marital Therapy, 31,* 1-20.

Wiegel, M., Scepkowski, L.A., & Barlow, D.H. (2006). Cognitive and affective processes in female sexual dysfunctions. In I. Goldstein, C.M. Meston, S.R. Davis, & A.M. Traish (Eds.), *Women's sexual function and dysfunction: Study, diagnosis and treatment* (pp. 85-92). London: Taylor and Francis.

Wilens, T.E. (2007). The nature of the relationship between attention-deficit/ hyperactivity disorder and substance use. *Journal of Clinical Psychiatry, 68 (Suppl. 11),* 4-8.

Wilk, K., & Hegerl, U. (2010). Time of mood switches in ultra-rapid cycling disorder: A brief review. *Psychiatry Research, 180,* 1-4.

Wilkeson, A., Lambert, M.T., & Petty, F. (2000). Posttraumatic stress disorder, dissociation, and trauma exposure in depressed and nondepressed veterans. *Journal of Nervous and Mental Disease, 188,* 505-509.

Wilkinson, G.S., & Robertson, G.J. (2006). *Wide Range Achievement Test 4.* Lutz, FL: Psychological Assessment Resources.

Willcox, J.K., Ash, S.L., & Catignani, G.L. (2004). Antioxidants and prevention of chronic disease. *Critical Reviews in Food Science and Nutrition, 44,* 275-295.

Williams, C.L., & Butcher, J.N. (2011). *A beginner's guide to the MMPI-A.* Washington, DC: American Psychological Association.

Williams, E.D., Steptoe, A., Chambers, J.C., & Kooner, J.S. (2011). Ethnic and gender differences in the relationship between hostility and metabolic and autonomic risk factors for coronary heart disease. *Psychosomatic Medicine, 73,* 53-58.

Williams, J.E. (2010). Anger/hostility and cardiovascular disease. In M. Potegal, G. Stemmler, & C. Spielberger (Eds.), *International handbook of anger* (pp. 435-447). New York: Springer.

Williams, J.M. (2011). The malingering factor. *Archives of Clinical Neuropsychology, 26,* 280-285.

Williams, R.J., Chang, S.Y., & Addiction Centre Adolescent Research Group. (2000). A comprehensive and comparative review of adolescent substance abuse treatment outcome. *Clinical Psychology: Science and Practice, 7,* 138-166.

Williams, V.S., Baldwin, D.S., Hogue, S.L., Fehnel, S.E., Hollis, K.A., & Edin, H.M. (2006). Estimating the prevalence and impact of antidepressant-induced sexual dysfunction in 2 European countries: A cross-sectional patient survey. *Journal of Clinical Psychiatry, 67,* 204-210.

Williams-Nickelson, C. (2009). Mentoring women graduate students: A model for professional psychology. *Professional Psychology: Research and Practice, 40,* 284-291.

Williamson, E.D., & Martin, A. (2012). Psychotropic medications in autism: Practical considerations for parents. *Journal of Autism and Developmental Disorders, 42,* 1249-1255.

Wilmshurst, L.A. (2002). Treatment programs for youth with emotional and behavioral disorders: An outcome study of two alternate approaches. *Mental Health Services Research, 4*, 85-96.

Wilson, C.T., Fairburn, C.C., Agras, W.S., Walsh, B.T., & Kraemer, H. (2002). Cognitive-behavioral therapy for bulimia nervosa: Time course and mechanisms of change. *Journal of Consulting and Clinical Psychology, 70*, 267-274.

Wilson, G.T. (2005). Psychological treatment of eating disorders. *Annual Review of Clinical Psychology, 1*, 439-465.

Wilson, R.J., Abracen, J., Looman, J., Picheca, J.E., & Ferguson, M. (2011). Pedophilia: An evaluation of diagnostic and risk prediction methods. *Sexual Abuse, 23*, 260-274.

Wincze, J.P. (2009). *Enhancing sexuality: A problem-solving approach to treating dysfunction*. New York: Oxford.

Wincze, J.P., & Carey, M.P. (2001). *Sexual dysfunction: A guide for assessment and treatment* (2nd ed.). New York: Guilford.

Wingo, T.S., Rosen, A., Cutler, D.J., Lah, J.J., & Levey, A.I. (2012). Paraoxonase 1 polymorphisms In Alzheimer's disease, Parkinson's disease, and AD-PD spectrum diseases. *Neurobiology of Aging, 33*, 204.e13-204.e15.

Winter, A.C., Berger, K., Buring, J.E., & Kurth, T. (2012). Associations of socioeconomic status with migraine and non-migraine headache. *Cephalalgia, 32*, 159-170.

Winters, K.C., Botzet, A.M., & Fahnhorst, T. (2011). Advances in adolescent substance abuse treatment. *Current Psychiatry Reports, 13*, 416-421.

Winzelberg, A.J., Eppstein, D., Eldredge, K.L., Wilfley, D., Dasmahapatra, R., Dev, P., Taylor, C.B. (2000). Effectiveness of an Internet-based program for reducing risk factors for eating disorders. *Journal of Consulting and Clinical Psychology, 68*, 346-350.

Wise, R.A. (2009). Roles for nigrostriatal—not just mesocorticolimbic—dopamine in reward and addiction. *Trends in Neurosciences, 32*, 517-524.

Wittchen, H.-U., Gloster, A.T., Beesdo-Baum, K., Fava, G.A., & Craske, M.G. (2010). Agoraphobia: A review of the diagnostic classificatory position and criteria. *Depression and Anxiety, 27*, 113-133.

Witthaus, H., Brune, M., Kaufmann, C., Bohner, G., Ozgurdal, S., Gudlowski, Y., Heinz, A., Klingebiel, R., & Juckel, G. (2008). White matter abnormalities in subjects at ultra high-risk for schizophrenia and first-episode schizophrenic patients. *Schizophrenia Research, 102*, 141-149.

Wojtowicz, A.E., & von Ranson, K.M. (2012). Weighing in on risk factors for body dissatisfaction: A one-year prospective study of middle-adolescent girls. *Body Image, 9*, 20-30.

Wolf, R.C., Thomann, P.A., Sambataro, F., Vasic, N., Schmid, M., & Wolf, N.D. (2012). Orbitofrontal cortex and impulsivity in borderline personality disorder: An MRI study of baseline brain perfusion. *European Archives of Psychiatry and Clinical Neuroscience, 262*, 677-685.

Wolfensberger, W. (2011). An "If this, then that" formulation of decisions related to social role valorization as a better way of interpreting it to people. *Intellectual and Developmental Disabilities, 49*, 456-462.

Wolpe, J. (1990). *The practice of behavior therapy* (4th ed.). New York: Pergamon.

Wong, B.Y.L., & Butler, D.L. (Eds.). (2012). *Learning about learning disabilities* (4th ed.). Waltham, MA: Elsevier.

Wong, C., & Kasari, C. (2012). Play and joint attention of children with autism in the preschool special education classroom. *Journal of Autism and Developmental Disorders, 42*, 2152-2161.

Woodruff-Borden, J., Morrow, C., Bourland, S., & Cambron, S. (2002). The behavior of anxious parents: Examining mechanisms of transmission of anxiety from parent to child. *Journal of Clinical Child and Adolescent Psychology, 31*, 364-374.

Woods, S.W., Morgenstern, H., Saksa, J.R., Walsh, B.C., Sullivan, M.C., Money, R., Hawkins, K.A., Gueorguieva, R.V., & Glazer, W.M. (2010). Incidence of tardive dyskinesia with atypical and conventional antipsychotic medications: Prospective cohort study. *Journal of Clinical Psychiatry, 71*, 463-474.

World Health Organization (2001). *The World Health Report 2001—Mental health: New understanding, new hope*. Geneva: World Health Organization.

Wright, R.J. (2011). Epidemiology of stress and asthma: From constricting communities and fragile families to epigenetics. *Immunology and Allergy Clinics of North America, 31*, 19-39.

Wu, J., McCallum, S.E., Glick, S.D., & Huang, Y. (2011). Inhibition of the mammalian target of rapamycin pathway by rapamycin blocks cocaine-induced locomotor sensitization. *Neuroscience, 172*, 104-109.

Wustmann, T., Pillmann, F., & Marneros, A. (2011). Gender-related features of persistent delusional disorders. *European Archives of Psychiatry and Clinical Neuroscience, 261*, 29-36.

Wykes, T., Huddy, V., Cellard, C., McGurk, S.R., & Czobor, P. (2011). A meta-analysis of cognitive remediation for schizophrenia: Methodology and effect sizes. *American Journal of Psychiatry, 168*, 472-485.

Wylie, F.M., Torrance, H., Seymour, A., Buttress, S., & Oliver, J.S. (2005). Drugs in oral fluid Part II. Investigation of drugs in drivers. *Forensic Science International, 150*, 199-204.

Wylie, K. (2008). Erectile dysfunction. *Advances in Psychosomatic Medicine, 29*, 33-49.

Wylie, K.R., Davies-South, D., Steward, D., Walters, S., Iqbal, M., & Ryles, S. (2006). A comparison between portable ultrasound (MIDUS) and nocturnal RigiScan when confirming the diagnosis of vascular organic erectile disorder. *International Journal of Impotence Research, 18*, 354-358.

Yager, J. (2008). Binge eating disorder: The search for better treatments. *American Journal of Psychiatry, 165*, 4-6.

Yager, Z., & O'Dea, J.A. (2008). Prevention programs for body image and eating disorders on university campuses: A review of large, controlled interventions. *Health Promotion International, 23*, 173-189.

Yamada, M., Hirao, K., Namiki, C., Hanakawa, T., Fukuyama, H., Hayashi, T., & Murai, T. (2007). Social cognition and frontal lobe pathology in schizophrenia: A voxel based morphometric study. *NeuroImage, 35*, 292-298.

Yanez, A.M., Peix, M.A., Atserias, N., Arnau, A., & Brug, J. (2007). Association of eating attitudes between teenage girls and their parents. *International Journal of Social Psychiatry, 53*, 507-513.

Yassa, M.A., Hazlett, R.L., Stark, C.E.L., & Hoehn-Saric, R. (2012). Functional MRI of the amygdala and bed nucleus of the stria terminalis during conditions of uncertainty in generalized anxiety disorder. *Journal of Psychiatric Research, 46*, 1045-1052.

Yau, W.Y.W., Zubieta, J.K., Weiland, B.J., Samudra, P.G., Zucker, R.A., & Heitzeg, M.M. (2012). Nucleus accumbens response to incentive stimuli anticipation in children of alcoholics: Relationships with precursive behavioral risk and lifetime alcohol use. *Journal of Neuroscience, 32*, 2544-2551.

Yeargin-Allsopp, M., Rice, C., Karapurkar, T., Doernberg, N., Boyle, C., & Murphy, C. (2003). Prevalence of autism in a US metropolitan area. *Journal of the American Medical Association, 289*, 49-55.

Yeung, M., Treit, D., & Dickson, C.T. (2012). A critical test of the hippocampal theta model of anxiolytic drug action. *Neuropharmacology, 62*, 155-160.

Yorke, J., Fleming, S.L., & Shuldham, C. (2007). A systematic review of psychological interventions for children with asthma. *Pediatric Pulmonology, 42*, 114-124.

Yoshida, T., McCarley, R.W., Nakamura, M., Lee, K., Koo, M.-S., Bouix, S., Salisbury, D.F., Morra, L., Shenton, M.E., & Niznikiewicz, M.A. (2009). A prospective longitudinal volumetric MRI study of superior temporal gyrus gray matter and amygdalahippocampal complex in chronic schizophrenia. *Schizophrenia Research, 113*, 84-94.

Young, E., & Korszun, A. (2010). Sex, trauma, stress hormones and depression. *Molecular Psychiatry, 15*, 23-28.

Young, S., & Amarasinghe, J.M. (2010). Practitioner review: Non-pharmacological treatments for ADHD: A lifespan approach. *Journal of Child Psychology and Psychiatry, 51*, 116-133.

Youngstrom, E.A., Findling, R.L., Danielson, C.K., & Calabrese, J.R. (2001). Discriminative validity of parent report of hypomanic and depressive symptoms on the General Behavior Inventory. *Psychological Assessment, 13*, 267-276.

Yu, K.K., Cheung, C., Chua, S.E., & McAlonan, G.M. (2011). Can Asperger syndrome be distinguished from autism? An anatomic likelihood meta-analysis of MRI studies. *Journal of Psychiatry and Neuroscience, 36,* 412-421.

Yudofsky, S.C., & Hales, R.E. (Eds.) (2010). *Essentials of neuropsychiatry and behavioral neurosciences* (2nd ed.). Washington, DC: American Psychiatric Publishing.

Yung, A.R., Killackey, E., Hetrick, S.E., Parker, A.G., Schultze-Lutter, F., Klosterkoetter, J., Purcell, R., & Mcgorry, P.D. (2007). The prevention of schizophrenia. *International Review of Psychiatry, 19,* 633-646.

Zaazaa, A., Selim, O., Hosny Awad, H., Soltan, G., & Ghanem, H. (2012). Safety and efficacy of escitalopram in the treatment of premature ejaculation: A double-blind, placebo-controlled, fixed-dose, randomized study. *Human Andrology, 2,* 16-18.

Zahn-Waxler, C., Shirtcliff, E.A., & Marceau, K. (2008). Disorders of childhood and adolescence: Gender and psychopathology. *Annual Review of Clinical Psychology, 4,* 275-303.

Zalenski, R.J., & Raspa, R. (2006). Maslow's hierarchy of needs: A framework for achieving human potential in hospice. *Journal of Palliative Medicine, 9,* 1120-1127.

Zamboanga, B.L., Schwartz, S.J., Ham, L.S., Borsari, B., & Van Tyne, K. (2010). Alcohol expectancies, pregaming, drinking games, and hazardous alcohol use in a multiethnic sample of college students. *Cognitive Research and Therapy, 34,* 124-133.

Zanarini, M.C., Frankenburg, F.R., Hennen, J., Reich, D.B., & Silk, K.R. (2006). Prediction of the 10-year course of borderline personality disorder. *American Journal of Psychiatry, 163,* 827-832.

Zanarini, M.C., Frankenburg, F.R., Reich, D.B., & Fitzmaurice, G. (2010). The 10-year course of psychosocial functioning among patients with borderline personality disorder and axis II comparison subjects. *Acta Psychiatrica Scandinavica, 122,* 103-109.

Zaretsky, A.E., Rizvi, S., & Parikh, S.V. (2007). How well do psychosocial interventions work in bipolar disorder? *Canadian Journal of Psychiatry, 52,* 14-21.

Zhang, Y.P., Ma, C., Wen, Y.Q., & Wang, J.J. (2003) Convergence of gastric vagal and cerebellar fastigial nuclear inputs on glycemia-sensitive neurons of lateral hypothalamic area in the rat. *Neuroscience Research, 45,* 9-16.

Zhou, M., & Bankston, C.L. (1998). *Growing up American: How Vietnamese children adapt to life in the United States.* New York: Russell Sage Foundation.

Zimmerman, K., Rudolph, J., Salow, M., & Skarf, L.M. (2011). Delirium in palliative care patients: Focus on pharmacotherapy. *American Journal of Hospice and Palliative Medicine, 28,* 501-510.

Zimmerman, M., Rothschild, L., & Chelminski, I. (2005). The prevalence of DSM-IV personality disorders in psychiatric outpatients. *American Journal of Psychiatry, 162,* 1911-1918.

Zlokovic, B.V. (2011). Neurovascular pathways to neurodegeneration in Alzheimer's disease and other disorders. *Nature Reviews Neuroscience, 12,* 723-738.

Zucker, K.J., Bradley, S.J., Owen-Anderson, A., Kibblewhite, S.J., Wood, H., Singh, D., & Choi, K. (2012). Demographics, behavior problems, and psychosexual characteristics of adolescents with gender identity disorder or transvestic fetishism. *Journal of Sex and Marital Therapy, 38,* 151-189.

Zucker, K.J., & Lawrence, A.A. (2009). Epidemiology of gender identity disorder: Recommendations for the *Standards of Care* of the World Professional Association for Transgender Health. *International Journal of Transgenderism, 11,* 8-18.

Zucker, K.J., Wood, H., Singh, D., & Bradley, S.J. (2012). A developmental, biopsychosocial model for the treatment of children with gender identity disorder. *Journal of Homosexuality, 59,* 369-397.

Zuroff, D.C., Kelly, A.C., Leybman, M.J., Blatt, S.J., & Wampold, B.E. (2010). Between-therapist and within-therapist differences in the quality of the therapeutic relationship: Effects on maladjustment and self-critical perfectionism. *Journal of Clinical Psychology, 66,* 681-697.

Zvolensky, M.J., Kotov, R., Antipova, A.V., & Schmidt, N.B. (2005). Diathesis stress model for panic-related distress: A test in a Russian epidemiological sample. *Behaviour Therapy and Research, 43,* 521-532.

# Name Index

## A

Aakre, J.M., 379
Aaronson, C., 122
Aarsland, D., 442, 445, 460
Abascal, L.B., 237
Abbass, A., 313
Abbott, M.J., 133
Abdel-Gaber, S., 334
Abdo, C., 327
Abdollahi, M., 451
Abel, G.G., 344
Abel, K.M., 379
Abler, B., 327, 330
Abram, K.M., 374, 422
Abramowitz, J.S., 133, 155, 478
Abrams, K., 120
Abramson, J., 411
Abramson, L.Y., 41, 192, 201, 202
Abu-Akel, A., 374
Acar, D., 327
Acerra, A., 387
Achenbach, T.M., 425
Acierno, R., 214
Acker, S., 345
Acosta, F.J., 387
Adachi, E. 449
Adamis, D., 437
Adams, G., 111
Adams, H.E., 149, 327, 333, 334, 341
Adams, V.H., 62
Addiction Centre Adolescent Research Group., 284
Addington, D., 367
Addington, J., 367
Addy, P.H., 379
Aderibigbe, Y.A., 166
Adickes, E., 405
Adinoff, A.D., 492
Adinoff, B., 267
Adlard, S., 382
Adler, L.A., 429
Adler, L.E., 379
Adley Tsang, C.H., 118
Afrank, J., 421
Aggen, S.H., 122, 153, 232, 270, 304, 305, 306
Agostini, J.V., 455
Agras, S., 244, 246
Agras, W.S., 243
Agresta, J., 387
Agronin, M.E., 454, 455, 456
Aguilar-Gaxiola, S., 118, 119
Aguilera, A., 382
Aguirre, E., 458
Aguirre, I., 204
Ahadieh, S., 441
Ahlbom, A., 448
Ahlers, C.J., 344
Ahmed, G., 119

Ahmed, U., 309, 315
Ahuja, S., 331
Aiazzi, L., 152
Aigner, M., 152, 166
Airavaara, M., 266, 274
Aisen, P., 404, 447
Aisen, P.S., 441
Akbay, E., 327
Akehurst, R.L., 355
Akerman, G., 348, 349
Akhter, S.A., 87
Akiskal, H.S., 192, 204
Akiskal, K.K., 204
Akyuz, G., 166, 418
Alaggia, R., 131
Alami, K.H.M., 331
Albanese, E., 445
Albano, A.M., 117, 133, 473
Albert, C.M., 492
Albin, R.L., 448
Albus, C., 491
Alda, M., 152, 189
Aldred, S., 450
Aleman, A., 363
Alessi, C., 494
Alex, K.D., 378
Alexander, B., 216
Alexander, C.N., 496
Alexander, J., 213
Alexander, J.F., 283
Alexander, K., 426
Allan, L.M., 445, 460
Allebeck, P., 378
Allen, D.N., 379
Allen, E.G., 404
Allen, L.A., 158
Allen, N.B., 198, 204
Allen, P., 363
Alles, B., 453
Allet, J.L., 152
Allet, R.E., 152
Alleva, L., 269
Alloy, L.B., 192, 201, 202
Almaraz, M.C., 353
Almeida, O.P., 268
Alonso, P., 346
Alonso, J., 118, 119
Alonso, Y., 152
Alperovitch, A., 453
Alterman, A.I., 276
Althof, S., 326, 327, 330
Althof, S.E., 331, 334, 336
Aluja, A., 208
Alvarez, K., 412
Alvarez-Jimenez, M., 382, 388
Alzheimer's Association, 444
Amanatidis, E.C., 441
Amarasinghe, J.M., 426
American Anthropological Association, 42
American Heart Association, 491

American Psychiatric Association, 42, 75, 76, 77, 92, 93, 105, 106, 107, 108, 109, 110, 111, 112, 113–115, 116, 117, 119, 146, 147, 148, 149, 150, 151, 161, 162, 164, 165, 166, 179, 181, 182, 183, 185, 186, 187, 188, 189, 190, 213, 223, 224, 225, 228, 230, 241, 255, 256, 257, 293, 296, 297, 298, 299, 300, 301, 302, 303, 305, 306, 312, 316, 322, 323, 324, 325, 326, 327, 331, 337, 338, 340, 341, 342, 351, 352, 362, 365, 366, 367, 368, 370, 371, 396, 397, 398, 399, 400, 401, 415, 416, 417, 418, 419, 420, 436, 438, 439, 440, 441, 442, 443, 444, 488
American Psychological Association, 36, 409, 467, 468, 469, 481, 483
Amering, M., 374
Amirthavasagam, S., 306
Amminger, G.P., 60, 119, 388
Ammirati, R., 85
Amsterdam, J.D., 212, 215, 217
Anagnostou, E., 406
Ananth, J., 386
Anastasiadis, A.G., 331
Anastopoulos, A.D., 425
Anderson, E.R., 119
Anderson, I.M., 198
Anderson, N.E., 271
Anderson, R., 456
Anderson, R.N., 195
Andersson, G., 216
Andrade, L.H., 192
Andrasik, F., 495
Andreasen, N.C., 382, 389
Andree, C., 490
Andrew, B., 218
Andrews, P.W., 204
Andrusyna, T.P., 472
Anestis, M.D., 210
Anetzberger, G.J., 446
Angel, O.H., 386
Angermeyer, M., 118
Angermeyer, M.C., 380
Anglesea, M.M., 97
Anglin, M.D., 280
Angold, A., 57, 417, 423, 424, 427
Annen, S., 208
Annon, J.J., 280
Ansell, E.B., 310, 311, 317, 318
Anstey, K.J., 451
Anthenelli, R., 284
Anthony, J.C., 118
Antipova, A.V., 129
Anton, B.S., 66
Antonius, D., 365
Antuono, P., 452
Aoki, T., 251
Aperi, J., 186
Apil, S.R.A., 206

Apostolova, L.G., 439
Apple, R.F., 243
Apter, A., 195, 206
Aragona, M., 157
Aragones, E., 152
Arand, D.L., 491
Araya, R., 155
Arbisi, P.A., 82, 207, 389
Arcelus, J., 227, 245
Archer, R.P., 82, 157
Ardekani, B.A., 365
Arendt-Nielsen, L., 148
Arenovich, T., 378
Argilli, E., 271
Arias-Carrion, O., 438
Arif, M., 213
Arik, A.C., 105
Arizaga, R., 452
Arlidge, J., 313
Armenise, E., 450
Armfield, J.M., 120
Armstrong, J.G., 172
Arnau, A., 234
Arndt, S., 389, 496
Arnett, D.K., 448
Arnetz, B., 495
Arnone, D., 198, 406
Arntz, A., 303
Arolt, V., 381
Aronoff, G.M., 151
Arora, M., 213
Arrigo, B.A., 476
Arrindell, W.A., 133
Arroll, B., 211
Arsenault-Lapierre, G., 195
Asami, T., 377
Asarnow, R.A., 375
Asbury, E.T., 374
Aseltine, R.H., 68
Asen, E., 216
Ash, S.L., 450
Ashby, D., 210
Ashford, J.W., 447
Askin-Edgar, S., 450
Asmundson, G.J., 140
Assalian, P., 330
Assaloni, H., 166
Aston, J., 377
Atkins, D.C., 313
Atkinson, J., 195
Atserias, N., 234
Attems, J., 448
Au, J.W., 405
Aubin, S., 336
Aubry, J.-M., 206
Auchterlonie, J.L., 121
Auquier, P., 383
Avasthi, A.A., 373
Avena, N.M., 232
Avenevoli, S., 122, 191, 218, 417
Aversa, A., 336

Aviram, R.B., 303, 304
Avula, D., 282
Axelson, D.A., 203
Aybek, S., 146
Aycicegi, A., 303
Ayearst, L.E., 103
Ayhan, Y., 376
Aytug, S., 210
Azar, S.T., 200
Azevedo, D.C., 36
Assam, A., 123

**B**

Baare, W.F.C., 377
Babe, K.S., 151
Babyak, M.A., 496
Bach, P., 283
Bachar, E., 230
Bachmann, S., 381
Backman, L., 435
Bacon, S.L., 496
Badcock, J.C., 363
Badcock, P.B., 204
Baeumler, D., 441
Bagby, R.M., 212, 312
Bagge, C.L., 210
Bagnarello, M., 123
Bailey, J., 405
Bair, B.D., 458
Baiyewu, O., 445
Baker, C.K., 346
Baker, D., 173
Baker, J.H., 230, 232
Baker, P.N., 379
Balanza-Martinez, V., 199
Balboni, G., 396
Baldessarini, R.J., 212
Baldwin, D.S., 331
Baldwin, J., 340, 346
Baler, R.D., 232
Baliunas, D., 259
Balk, E.M., 450
Ball, J.R., 215
Ball, S.G., 124
Balla, D.A., 410
Ballard, C., 443
Balling, K., 398
Balon, R., 336
Balsis, S., 312
Bandelow, B., 39
Banducci, A.N., 313
Banerjee, A., 448
Bankston, C.L., 63
Bao, Y., 141
Barabash, A., 460
Barad, D.H., 334
Barada, J., 331
Baranoski, M.V., 33
Barbarich, N., 229
Barber, R., 441
Barberger-Gateau, P., 453
Barch, D.M., 377
Bardone-Cone, A.M., 243
Barendregt, M., 343
Bargiota, A., 334
Bari, M., 262

Barker, R.A., 442
Barkhof, E., 386, 387
Barkley, R., 429
Barkley, R.A., 425, 427
Barkovich, A.J., 405
Barkow, K., 191
Barkus, E., 363
Barlow, D.H., 128, 129, 133, 136, 138, 141, 331, 336
Barlow, J., 67, 308
Barnabei, V.M., 334
Barnes, C.A., 123
Barnes, J., 200
Barnes, P.J., 493
Barnes, V.A., 496
Barnett, D., 479
Barnett, S.B.L., 490
Barney, L., 120
Barnicot, K., 315
Barrera, T.L., 118
Barrett, P.M., 131
Barsky, A., 152, 155
Barsky, A.J., 155, 158
Barth, N., 371
Barton, C.A., 125
Bartzokis, G., 377
Baruch, D.E., 306
Bary, F., 64
Barzega, G., 128
Basden, S.L., 275, 284
Basheer, C., 345
Baskin-Sommers, A., 305
Bass, D., 446
Basso, M.R., 362
Bates, A., 216
Bates, J.E., 422
Batra, A., 266
Batstra, L., 416
Batterham, P.J., 120
Battista, N., 262
Bauermeister, J.J., 423
Baumeister, H., 61
Baumeister, R.F., 103
Baumgartner, C., 152, 166
Bauserman, R., 479
Bayley, N., 409
Beach, S.R.H., 202
Beadle-Brown, J., 476
Bean, L.H., 404
Beardslee, W., 206
Beardslee, W.R., 197, 203, 205, 206
Beart, P.M., 448
Beattie, A.M., 452
Beauchaine, T.P., 417, 422
Beautrais, A., 195, 206
Beautrais, A.L., 210
Bechara, A., 267
Becher, J.R., 284
Beck, A.T., 38, 39, 126, 137, 138, 201, 202, 208, 209, 215, 305, 306, 307
Beck, J.S., 87
Becker, A., 39, 493
Becker, A.E., 229
Becker, B., 62
Becker, C., 230
Becker, E.S., 126, 140

Becker, J., 341
Becker, J.V., 345, 347
Becker, T., 369
Becker, T.M., 379
Becker, V., 198
Beckett, L.A., 441
Bedard, L.E., 131
Bedard, M.-A., 383
Bedics, J.D., 313
Bednar, R.L., 472
Beech, A.R., 345, 347, 348, 349
Beers, C., 12, 13
Beesdo-Baum, K., 107, 140
Beher, D., 447
Behl, C., 450
Behrmann, M.M., 412
Beidel, D.C., 118
Beier, K.M., 344
Beinart, N., 459
Bekelman, A., 129
Bekker, N., 364
Bekris, L.M., 448
Belardinelli, C., 203
Bell, M.D., 387
Bell, P., 380
Bellack, A.S., 379, 387, 389
Belmonte, P.L., 122, 375
Belujon, P., 267, 269
Belva, B.C., 410
Belyea, M.J., 492
Benard, F., 328
Bender, A., 155
Bender, D., 318
Beneyto, M., 380
Benjet, C., 191, 417
Benke, T., 460
Bennett, D.A., 441
Bennett, M.C., 449
Bennett, N., 276
Bennett, S., 450
Benowitz, N.L., 280
Ben-Porath, Y.S., 82, 157, 172
Benzeval, M., 490
Berg, S., 447
Bergem, A.L., 447
Berger, K., 490
Berger, R.E., 336
Bergeron, L., 410
Bergeron, S., 331
Bergin, J.L., 245
Berglund, P., 55, 56, 57, 58, 60, 61, 117, 118, 191, 192, 268
Berk, L., 212
Berk, M., 212
Berkman, N.D., 246
Berkout, O.V., 417
Berkowitz, D., 374
Berkowitz, G.S., 129
Berle, D., 126
Berlim, M.T., 213
Berliner, L., 479
Berman, J.S., 472
Berman, K.F., 378
Berman, R.F., 405
Bernal, G., 201
Bernal, M., 203
Berner, L.A., 233

Berner, W., 345
Bernstein, A., 134
Bernstein, A.L., 445
Bernstein, H.-G., 198
Berrettini, W.H., 229, 234
Berridge, K.C., 232
Berrios, G.E., 168, 379
Berry, E.M., 230
Berry, R.B., 496
Bersani, H., 396
Bertholet, N., 282
Bertolote, J., 195, 206
Bertram, L., 448
Bertschy, G., 206
Best, S.R., 129
Beswick, A., 492
Betz, S.K., 413
Beutler, L.E., 472
Beyer, F., 282, 458
Beyer, F.R., 494
Beynon, S., 206
Bezlyak, V., 315
Bhat, K.M., 373
Bhatti, N., 318
Bhugra, D., 192, 195, 204, 478
Bhui, K., 478
Bianchini, K.J., 151
Biancosino, B., 207
Biederman, J., 125, 417, 429
Bielanska, A., 382
Bieling, P.J., 206
Bienvenu, O.J., 131, 218
Bierman, K.L., 424
Bierut, L.J., 285
Biesalski, H.K., 450
Bigler, E.D., 91
Bilali, S.R., 212
Billiard, M., 490
Billstedt, E., 413
Binik, Y.M., 328
Biondi, M., 207
Birchwood, J., 426
Bird, T.D., 448
Bird, V., 388
Birgden, A., 350
Birley, A.J., 266
Birmaher, B., 192, 203, 417
Birnbaum, M.H., 162
Bisht, J., 156
Bissada, H., 233
Bisson, J.I., 151
Biswas, P., 373
Bitsios, P., 378
Bizzini, L., 206
Bjorgvinsson, T., 139
Bjork, C., 197
Bjorvatn, B., 490
Black, K., 44
Black, D.N., 153, 155
Black, D.W., 123
Black, R., 449, 454
Black, S.E., 442
Blackford, J.U., 123, 125
Blair, A., 382
Blair, R.J.R., 305, 423
Blakely, T.A., 195
Blanchard, R., 340, 342, 344

Blanco, C., 159, 192
Bland, R., 119
Blank, K., 120
Blashill, A.J., 230
Blau, N., 403
Blazei, R.W., 306
Blazer, D., 215
Blazer, D.G., 436
Bleich, S., 266
Bleichhardt, G., 159
Blewitt, K.A., 136
Bloch, D.A., 445
Bloch, R.M., 166
Block, C., 64
Bloom, J.S., 406
Bloomfield, K., 274
Blow, A., 122
Blozis, S.A., 155
Blum, K., 269, 345
Blum, N., 123, 311
Blumberg, S.J., 401
Blumenthal, J.A., 454, 496
Bo, S., 374
Bob, P., 173
Bobashev, G., 274
Bocarsly, M.E., 232
Boch, R.T., 206
Bodell, L.P., 229
Boden, J.M., 423
Bodenmann, G., 202
Bodfish, J.W., 398
Boehlecke, B., 494
Boekeloo, B.O., 272
Boellaard, R., 123
Boelter, E.W., 411
Boettiger, C.A., 274
Bogaerts, S., 344
Bogardus, S.T., 455
Bogenschutz, M.P., 284
Bogerts, B., 198
Bogetto, F., 128
Bohnen, N.I., 448
Boileau, I., 378
Boivin, J., 328
Boke, O., 105
Bolea, P.S., 129
Bollini, P., 216, 218
Bolt, H., 169
Bolton, J.M., 271
Bonanno, G.A., 63
Bonci, A., 271
Bond, A.J., 202
Bond, M., 456
Bond, M.J., 234
Bondolfi, G., 206
Bondy, S.C., 451
Bonetto, N., 438
Bongar, B., 210
Bonifacio, V., 336
Bonnet, M.H., 491
Bonn-Miller, M.O., 474
Booij, J., 281
Bookheimer, S.Y., 447
Boomsma, D.I., 122, 297
Bor, J.H., 446
Bora, E., 199
Bordnick, P.S., 270

Borenstein, A.R., 460
Borenstein, J., 186
Borge, L., 386
Borges, G.L., 195
Borghuis, M.S., 152, 159
Borglin, G., 149
Borgwardt, S., 377
Bornovalova, A., 306
Bornovalova, M.A., 271
Bornstein, R.F., 152, 310
Borraccino, A., 276
Borras-Valls, J.J., 330
Borrell, L.N., 274
Borsari, B., 270
Borson, S., 455
Borst, T.S., 474–475
Borthwick-Duffy, S.A., 396
Bos, P.A., 420
Bosch, E., 387
Botello-Zamarron, R., 201
Boteva, K., 389
Both, S., 334, 336
Botha, U.A., 474
Bottmer, C., 381
Botzenhardt, J., 200
Botzet, A.M., 284
Boucher, J., 398
Bouchery, E., 58
Bouix, S., 377
Boulet, S., 401
Bouman, T.K., 159
Bounthavong, M., 385
Bourdin, A., 491
Bourin, M., 212
Bourland, S., 127
Boutros, N.N., 149
Bouvard, M., 133, 310
Bowen, J.D., 442, 460
Bowen, S., 283
Boyce, W.T., 493
Boyd, B.A., 398
Boydell, J., 192, 204
Boydell, K.M., 243
Boyle, C.A., 401
Boyle, J.R., 272
Bozlu, M., 327
Brabant, C., 269
Bracha, H.S., 126, 155
Bradford, J., 351
Bradley, R.L.,129
Bradley, R., 28
Bradley, R.H., 273
Bradley, S.J., 352, 353, 354, 355
Brady, R., 459
Braff, D.L., 385
Brahler, E., 154
Braitman, A., 259
Braitman, A.L., 272
Bramoweth, A.D., 490
Brand, B.L., 169, 173, 174
Brandes, B.M., 405
Brandt, H., 229, 234
Brandt, J., 173
Brannan, S.K., 198, 199
Brannigan, G.G., 90
Brasch, J., 492
Braswell, H., 191

Bratland-Sanda, S., 229
Braun, B.G., 172
Bravin, J., 382
Brax, D., 460
Braxton, L., 33, 332
Brayne, C., 445
Brehmer, Y., 435
Breitborde, N.J.K., 382
Bremner, A., 327
Bremner, D., 124
Bremner, J.D., 169, 172, 198
Brendel, R.W., 212
Brennan, P.A., 201, 203, 374
Brent, D.A., 210
Breteler, M.M.B., 451
Brewer, K.B., 428
Brewin, C.R., 127, 216
Bridges, M.R., 345
Briere, J., 172
Briggs-Gowan, M., 424
Briggs-Gowan, M.J., 425
Briken, P., 345
Brim, J., 157
Brindis, C.D., 67
Brim, M.D., 382
Bristow, G.C., 200
Broadbent, E., 156
Broadstock, M., 443
Brock, G.B., 328
Brodaty, H., 459
Brodbeck, C., 119
Brodie, J.D., 69
Brodsky, B.S., 303, 304
Brody, G.H., 418
Brody, J.F., 204
Broft, A.I., 233
Brohan, E., 195, 373
Brom, D., 166
Brondel, L., 241
Brook, D.W., 272, 284
Brook, J.S., 272
Brooks, A.J., 284
Brooks, J., 374
Brooks, R., 169, 170
Brosschot, J.F., 153
Brotchie, J.M., 457
Brott, T.G., 448
Brotto, L.A., 323, 327
Brougham, R.R., 493
Broussard, B., 373
Brown, A.M., 127
Brown, C., 379, 387
Brown, D., 65, 308
Brown, E.J., 36
Brown, G.K., 208, 216
Brown, I., 403
Brown, L.H., 369
Brown, R.D., 448
Brown, R.I., 403
Brown, R.J., 146, 155, 156, 169
Brown, T., 494
Brown, T.A., 121, 133, 229, 246, 379
Browne, S., 373, 374
Brownell, K.D., 226
Brownson, C., 61, 68, 195
Brozovich, F.A., 108, 137
Bruce, B., 493

Brucki, T.M., 120
Brug, J., 234
Brun, J.M., 241
Brune, M., 208, 386
Brunetti, A., 377
Bryan, J., 450
Bryant, R.A., 112, 153, 170, 170
Bryce, R., 445
Bryson, G.J., 387
Bryson, S., 237, 244, 246
Brzyski, R.G., 334
Bucci, G., 363
Buchanan, J.A., 459
Bucholz, K.K., 285
Buchsbaum, M.S., 389
Buck, J.A., 58
Buck, K.D., 365
Buckley, P.F., 372
Buckner, R.L., 456
Budd, R., 472
Budge, S.L., 471
Budhwani, M., 328
Budson, A.E., 446
Bufferd, S.J., 201
Buhler, M., 268, 283
Buka, S., 379
Buka, S.L., 375
Bulic, B., 448
Bulik, C.M., 227, 229, 232, 234, 246
Bullington, S., 356–357
Bullock, R., 453, 456
Bundy, H., 372
Burack, J.A., 401
Burd, L., 405
Bureau, J.-F., 306
Burgdorf, K., 273
Burgess, M., 129
Burgy, M., 189
Buring, J.E., 451, 490
Burke, B.L., 406
Burke, J.D., 417, 423
Burke, J.R., 444
Burke, M., 492
Burke, M.M., 406
Burkhart, G., 276
Burnand, B., 282
Burne, T.H.J., 380
Burns, G.L., 495
Burns, A., 444
Burri, A.V., 327
Burstein, M., 191, 417
Burt, S.A., 233
Burton, C., 154, 155
Burton, N., 173
Busby, K.K., 212
Buschmann, C.T., 259
Busse, R., 386
Bustos, M.G., 377
Butcher, J.N., 82, 157, 172, 478
Butler, A.C., 138
Butler, D.L., 400
Butler, L.D., 173
Butterworth, B., 401
Buttress, S., 280
Buxton, R.B., 123
Buysse, A., 216
Bydder, G.M., 377

Byers, A.L., 460
Byrne, J., 444
Byrne, R.W., 151

## C

Caan, B.J., 331
Caballero-Hidalgo, A., 387
Cabeza, R., 406
Cabras, P., 152
Cacchioni, T., 335
Cacciola, J.S., 276
Caddy, C.M., 333
Cadeddu, R., 281
Cadigan, J., 368–369
Caetano, S.C., 203
Caggiula, A.R., 271
Cagnin, A., 438
Caine, E.D., 195
Caixeta, L., 438
Calabrese, J.R., 203, 209, 212
Calder, A.J., 421
Caldwell, C.R., 451
Caldwell-Harris, C.L., 303
Calhoun, S.L., 401
Callaghan, R.C., 378
Callanan, V.J., 195
Callaway, S.S., 365
Caltagirone, C., 363
Calvo, R., 123
Camara-Fuentes, L., 201
Camargo, C.A., 229
Cambron, S., 127
Cameron, J., 318
Camilleri, J.A., 33
Campanella, C., 377
Campbell, B., 331
Campbell, D., 64
Campbell, D.A., 493
Campbell, F., 282, 494
Campbell, J.C., 64
Campbell, K., 405
Campbell, W.K., 300
Camsari, G.B., 363
Canetti, L., 230
Canino, G., 119, 429
Canive, J.M., 379
Cannell, J., 167
Cannon, M., 379
Cannon, T.D., 197, 379
Canpolat, B., 327
Cantor-Graae, E., 376
Caoimh, R.O., 444
Capanema, M.B., 36
Cappadocia, M.C., 420
Cappelleri, J.C., 333
Capurso, A., 451
Capurso, C., 451
Carbranes, J.A., 460
Carcione, A., 365
Cardena, E., 163, 171, 173
Cardenas, S.J., 133
Cardno, A.G., 373, 376
Carey, K.B., 284
Carey, M.P., 284, 324, 327
Carillo, M.C., 441
Carlat, D.J., 229

Carlson, E.B., 172
Carlsson, A., 378
Carney, P.R., 496
Carney, R.M., 491
Caroff, S.N., 364
Carpenter, B.N., 345
Carpenter, D.O., 451
Carpenter, R.W., 297
Carpenter, W.T., 378
Carpio, C., 213
Carr, V.J., 377
Carroll, K., 354
Carroll, K.M., 283, 472
Carskadon, M.A., 490
Carson, K.V., 282
Carson, R.E., 378
Carta, M.G., 203, 373, 438
Carter, A.S., 425
Carter, B., 270
Carter, F.A., 229
Carter, J.D., 192, 315
Carty, J., 134
Caruso, G.A., 476
Carvalho, J.P., 202
Casadio, P., 379
Casey, R., 328
Caso, J.R., 199
Cass, K.M., 243
Cassano, G., 229
Cassano, G.B., 377
Cassano, P., 377
Cassidy, S.B., 405
Cassin, S.E., 103
Cassisi, J.E., 388
Castagnini, A., 373
Castle, D.J., 120, 372
Castro, J., 123
Catalan, A., 367
Catania, J.A., 334
Catapano, L.A., 200
Cater, J., 374
Cath, D.C., 123
Catignani, G.L., 450
Cauce, A.M., 166
Cayan, S., 327
Cechnicki, A., 382
Cella, D., 424
Cellard, C., 387
Cerce, D.D., 348
Cerceau, D.M., 36
Cerezuela, G.P., 161
Cervantes, E.A., 276
Cervilla, J.A., 373
Chadman, K.K., 410
Chaffin, M., 479
Chai, Y.-G., 274
Chakrabarti, S., 200
Chamberlain, S.R., 120, 420
Chamberland, L., 352
Chambers, J.C., 492
Chambless, D.L., 139
Chan, B., 402
Chan, D., 458
Chan, R.C.K., 383
Chanen, A.M., 309
Chanez, P., 491
Chang, C.-M., 200

Chang, S.Y., 284
Channabasavanna, S.M., 152
Chant, D., 371, 373
Chan-Yeung, M., 493
Chao, R.C.-L., 201
Chapin, D.A., 428
Chaplin, T.C., 345
Chapman, D., 362
Chapman, J.E., 138
Charles, C., 377
Charney, D.R., 123
Charney, D.S., 62, 124, 172
Chatterji, S., 118
Chau, D.M., 448
Chavira, D.A., 123
Chawla, N., 283
Chelminski, I., 295
Chen, C.P., 449
Chen, E., 446
Chen, J., 377
Chen, K.H., 448
Chen, S., 448
Chen, S.-W., 303
Chen, X., 24, 270, 382
Chen, Y., 303
Cheng, J.K.Y., 478
Cheng, J.N.S., 402
Chentsova-Dutton, Y., 90
Chenu, F., 212
Cherbuin, N., 451
Cherkas, L.M., 327
Cherpitel, C.J., 195
Chertkow, H., 441
Cheung, C., 405
Cheung, V., 459
Chevret-Measson, M., 330
Chew, J., 167
Chew, K.K., 327
Chew-Graham, C., 152
Chhean, D., 129
Chiang, K.-J., 215
Childs, K., 271
Chiles, J.A., 190, 194, 195, 205, 217
Chiliza, B., 389
Chin, M.D., 411
China, D., 459
Chisholm, D., 216
Chisvert, M., 161
Chiu, W.T., 2, 55, 56, 57, 117, 118, 191, 192
Chiuve, S.E., 492
Choi, I.-G., 274
Choi, K., 352, 353
Choi, S.-H., 383
Choi-Kain, L.W., 306, 317
Choliz, M., 161
Chorpita, B.F., 128, 479
Chosak, A., 141
Chou, P.S., 118
Chou, S.P., 300
Chou, Y.H., 274
Chouinard, G., 135
Christensen, B., 148
Christensen, H., 136, 195
Christenson, A., 458
Chronis-Tuscano, A., 142
Chu, J.P., 478

Chua, S.E., 405
Chun, J., 284
Chung, E.K., 274
Chung, K.F., 493
Chung, M., 450
Churchill, R., 134
Ciaramelli, E., 406
Cicchetti, D., 62, 269, 308
Cicchetti, D.V., 410
Cicero, D.C., 379
Cinquegrana, T., 398
Ciolur, J.M., 136
Claes, L., 234
Clare, J., 444
Clark, A., 458
Clark, A.J., 472
Clark, D.C., 210
Clark, D.M., 126
Clark, H.W., 282
Clarke, A.T., 410
Clarke, D.E., 353
Clarke, G.N., 206
Clarke, M., 275, 316, 373, 374, 379
Clarke, M.C., 379
Clarkson, C., 122
Clarren, S., 275
Classen, C.C., 173, 174
Clauss, J.A., 125
Clayton, A., 330, 334
Clayton, P.J., 157
Clements, K., 283
Clements, R., 277
Clifasefi, S., 283
Clifford, P.R., 284
Clifton, J., 324
Cloninger, C.R., 157, 376
Coatsworth, J.D., 63
Cobia, D.J., 377
Coccaro, E.F., 305
Cochrane, B.B., 334
Cocozza, J.J., 428
Coelho, C.M., 128
Coelho, H.F., 122
Coffey, R.M., 58
Cohen, B., 367
Cohen, B.M., 363
Cohen, L.J., 341, 345
Cohen, M., 129, 166
Cohen, N., 477
Cohen, R.A., 401
Cohen-Kettenis, P.T., 352, 353, 354, 355
Coid, J., 297
Coie, J.D., 424
Colditz, G.A., 493
Coleman, J., 494
Coleman, R.E., 496
Coles, M., 133
Collet, J., 457
Collier, D.A., 198, 199
Collings, S.C., 195
Collins, S.E., 283
Colliver, J.D., 273
Colloby, S.J., 448, 452, 456
Coltheart, M., 379
Coma, M., 450
Comabella, C.C., 210

Combs, D.R., 362
Compton, M.T., 373, 380, 381
Compton, W.M., 273, 282
Comtois, K.A., 313
Conde-Sala, J.L., 458
Conduct Problems Prevention
    Research Group, 422, 424
Conger, R.D., 418
Conn, D., 444
Connell, C.M., 452
Connelly, J., 158
Conner, B.T., 280
Conner, K.R., 195, 210
Conners, C.K., 384, 425, 429
Conners, G.J., 284
Conners, N.A., 273
Conners-Burrow, N.A., 421
Connor-Greene, P., 2
Conroy, C., 212
Conroy, M., 437
Constante, M., 385
Contaldo, F., 227
Conway, C.C., 203
Conway, K.P., 273
Conway, M., 119
Conwell, Y., 195, 210
Cook, A., 406
Cook, J.V., 494
Cook, N.R., 451
Cooke, D., 315
Cookson, J., 212
Coon, D.W., 334
Coonrod, E.E., 410
Coons, P., 172
Coons, P.M., 174
Cooper, A., 271, 446
Cooper, H., 274
Cooper, J., 134
Cooper, L.D., 312
Cooper, M., 421
Cooper, P.J., 122
Cooper, S., 334
Cooper, Z., 238, 243
Copeland, W.E., 417, 423, 427
Coplan, J.D., 213
Copp, H.L., 270
Corcoran, K.M., 206
Cordon, I., 479
Cordonnier, C., 441
Corey, K., 129
Corley, R.P., 306
Cormac, I., 386
Cormier, E., 479
Cornell, D.G., 420
Corrigan, B., 441
Corrigan, P., 15, 16
Corrigan, P.W., 15, 16
Corry, J.C., 215
Cortes, J.A., 379
Coryell, W., 192
Cosci, F., 120
Cosgrave, E.M., 382
Costello, E.J., 57, 417, 422, 423,
    424, 427
Costigan, T.E., 410
Cote, G., 33
Cottler, L.B., 330

Cotton, D., 334
Cotton, S.M., 388
Cotugno, G., 403
Counsell, S.J., 377
Counts, C.A., 421
Courchesne, E., 405
Courtney, K.E., 256
Couture, A., 446
Couture, S., 16
Couturier, J., 243
Couturier, J.L., 214
Covenas, R., 199, 452
Coviello, D.M., 284
Cowan, N., 379
Cowart, M.J.W., 134
Cowen, E.L., 67
Cowen, P.J., 200
Cox, B.J., 118, 120, 133, 271
Craddock, N., 380
Craft, S., 441
Craig, D., 453
Craig, L.A., 348
Craig, R.J., 257, 280
Craig, R.L., 346
Craig, T.K., 153
Craig, W.M., 422
Craighead, L.W., 309
Craighead, W.E., 309
Craissati, J., 345
Cramer, A., 421
Cramer, V., 295
Craske, M.G., 69, 103, 107, 109, 119,
    122, 131, 136, 138
Craven, R.M., 378
Crawford, M.J., 315
Crawford, S., 229, 234
Creamer, M., 112, 134, 170
Creanga, D., 328
Creed, F., 149, 152
Creed, F.H., 152
Crerand, C.E., 111
Cress, U., 413
Crichton, G.E., 450
Crick, N.R., 303, 304
Crisp, A., 231
Crisp, K., 388
Cristi, C., 212
Crits-Christoph, P., 39
Crocker, A.G., 33
Crocker, N., 259, 407
Crombie, I., 211
Cronce, J.M., 275
Crosby, A.E., 194
Crosby, R., 234
Crossley, N.A., 385
Croteau, N.P., 411
Crouter, C., 234
Crow, S., 229, 244, 246
Crow, T.J., 376, 378, 380
Crowe, M., 334
Crowe, R.R., 122, 285
Crozier, S., 167
Crum, R.M., 405
Crump, C.J., 448
Crunelle, C.L., 281
Czornansky, J.G., 377, 456
Cubillo, A., 421

Cucciare, M., 478
Cucolo, H., 350
Cui, L., 122, 191, 198, 199, 417
Cuijpers, P., 216
Cullen, K., 345
Culverhouse, R., 285
Cumming, G.F., 348
Cummings, J.L., 439, 449
Cummings, P.L., 441
Cunha, A., 134
Cunning, D., 237
Cunningham, J.A., 270
Cunningham, J.K., 378
Curnoe, S., 345
Curran, P.J., 383
Currier, D., 195, 206
Curry, M.A., 64
Curtis, K.L., 151
Curwen, T., 399, 413
Cutler, D.J., 447
Cutrona, C.E., 44
Czobor, P., 387

**D**

Daalder, A., 344
Daban, C., 199
Dackis, M.N., 269
Dadds, M., 131
Dadds, M.R., 128, 206
Daeppen, J.-B., 282
Dager, S.R., 405
Dahl, M.H., 444
Dahl, R.E., 203
Dailey, N.K., 458
Daker-White, G., 452
Dakof, G.A., 283
Dalack, G.W., 122
Daley, D., 426
Dalgleish, T., 141
Dalton, J.H., 473
Daly, E.S., 133
Daly, M.J., 197, 270
D'Andrea, J.T., 372
Daneluzzo, E., 377
Danesh, J., 299, 376
D'Angelo, D., 365
Daniel, S.S., 475
Danielson, C.K., 209
Danis, B., 425
Danner, U.N., 238
Dao, M.D., 153
Daren, A., 382
Darke, S., 276, 277
Dartigues, J.-F., 453
Das, A., 327, 331
Das, P., 153
Daskalakis, Z.J., 213
Dasmahapatra, R., 237
Daugherty, J., 131
Daugherty, R., 266
Daughters, S.B., 214, 271
Daughton, J.M., 425
Dauvilliers, Y., 490
Davenport, T.A., 195
Daversa, M., 318
Davey, G.C.L., 128

Davey Smith, G., 492
David, A.S., 146, 153, 166, 167, 169,
    171, 173
David, M., 85
Davidson, K.M., 315
Davidson, R.J., 198
Davies, S., 316
Davies, H.A., 470
Davies, I., 152
Davies, J., 341
Davila, J., 201
Davis, D.D., 305, 306, 307
Davis, D.H.J., 460
Davis, L., 192
Davis, L.W., 387
Davis, M., 172
Davis, M.S., 195
Davis, R., 310
Davis, S., 456
Davis, S.L., 167
Davis, T., 134
Davison, G.C., 39
Dawe, S., 271
Dawson, T.M., 453
Dawson, V.L., 453
Dawson, D.A., 118, 300
Dawson, G., 405
Dayal, S., 151
Dayson, D., 216
Dayton, C., 446
Deacon, B., 133, 155
Deacon, B.J., 118, 478
Deal, E., 405
Deault, L.C., 423
Deavers, F., 388
De Beurs, E., 343
de Bildt, A., 410
De Boer, A.G., 149
Deboutte, D., 418
De Brito, S.A., 315
De Bruijn, C., 284
De Caprio, C., 227
De Carli, A., 405
Decker, S.L., 90
De Clecq, B., 307
Deeg, M., 445
Deeks, S.G., 452
De Filippo, E., 227
DeFries, J.C., 404
De Fruyt, F., 307
de Geus, F., 135
de Girolamo, G., 118
Degnan, K.A., 142
de Graaf, R., 118
De Graaf, R., 284
de Haan, L., 386, 387
De Haes, H.C., 149
De Hart, M., 386
Dehon, E.E., 426
De Jager, P.L., 445
De Jong, J.T., 171
de Jonge, P., 166
De Jongh, A., 122
De Juan, R., 460
Dekel, A., 151
DeLamater, J.D., 346, 347, 350
de Lange, E., 445

Delany, M., 405
De La Torre, R., 404
Del Barrio, V., 209
DelBello, M.P., 206
del Campo, N., 420
Delegge, M.H., 489
De Leo, D., 120
Delgado, C., 275
de Lima, M.S., 134
Delis, D.C., 378, 384
Dellegrazie, F., 451
De Los Reyes, A., 424
Del Re, A.C., 472
Delva, J., 275
de Mari, M., 450
Demartini, K.S., 284
DeMartino, R., 68
DeMaso, D.R., 151, 478
Dembo, R., 271, 428
Demet, M.M., 152
Demirkan, A., 197
Demler, O., 2, 55, 56, 57, 60, 61, 117, 118, 191, 192, 268
Demuth, K., 398
Demyttenaere, K., 118, 216
Denboske, K., 354
Deng, W., 198, 199
De Nitto, S., 157
Denmark, A.B., 61, 68, 194
Dennerstein, M., 32
Dennis, J.A., 131, 309, 315
Denny, C., 275
Denollet, J., 492
Denys, D., 135
De Panfilis, C., 181
DePaola, J., 363
De Peri, L., 377
Depla, M.F., 118
de Portugal, E., 373
de Ridder, D.T.D., 238
Derogatis, L.R., 333, 336, 383, 384
DeRubeis, R.J., 39, 212, 215, 217
DesJardins, J.R., 281
Desmet, M., 208, 344
Desmond, D.W., 442
Desnick, R.J., 404
de Sonneville, L.M.J., 386, 387
Desrocher, M., 420
Desrochers, G., 331
De Strooper, B., 453
Detrich, R., 412
De Ugarte, C., 460
Dev, P., 237
Devanand, D.P., 456
Deveci, A., 152
Deveney, C., 110
Devilly, G.J., 163, 346
Devine, A., 133
Devins, G.M., 152
Devore, E.E., 451
Devoto, P., 281
Devries, M.W., 201
de Vugt, M.E., 457
DeWall, C.N., 103
Diament, A., 331
Diamond, G.M., 216

Diamond, G.S., 216
Diaz, Y., 142
Di Ceglie, D., 353, 354
Di Ciommo, V., 403
Dick, D., 24, 270
Dick, D.M., 427
Dickens, C., 149
Dickens, J., 445
Dickerson, D.L., 273
Dickerson, F.B., 386
Dickinson, C., 458
Dickinson, D., 387
Dickinson, H.O., 282, 494
Dickson, C.T., 124
Dickson, P.A., 266
Dickson, R., 494
Didziulis, V., 164
Diefenbach, G.J., 120
Dierker, L.C., 272
Dierssen, M., 404
Dietz, L.J., 203
Diez, T., 386
Diflorio, A., 192
Di Forti, M., 378, 379, 383
Diguer, L., 472
DiLalla, L.F., 24
Diler, R.S., 331
Dill, D.L., 172
Dillon, A.R., 412
Dillon, J., 341
Dilonardo, J., 58
Dilsaver, S.C., 204
Dimaggio, G., 365
Dimatou, S., 166
Dimich-Ward, H., 493
Dimidjian, S., 212
Dimitropoulos, K., 334
DiNardo, P.A., 133
Dinc, G., 152
Dindo, L., 134
DiNitto, D.M., 274
Di Paola, F., 234
Dirks, M.A., 424
Dishion, T.J., 271, 422
Divan, G., 401
Diwadkar, V.A., 378
Dix, D., 12
Dixon, S., 355
Dobrowolny, H., 198
Dobson, K.S., 470
Dobyns, W.B., 405
Docherty, N.M., 379
Dodd, S.., 212
Dodge, K.A., 28, 422, 424, 428
Dodson, W.W., 425
Dogan, O., 166, 418
Dogan, S., 418
Dolan, C., 429
Dolan, R.J., 123
Dominguez, D.V., 166
Donaghey, C., 195
Donaldson, R.L., 328, 330
Donatucci, C., 331
Donix, M., 441, 447
Donkin, M., 459
Donnelly, M.J., 82
Donnelly, S., 437

Donny, E.C., 271
Donovan, C.L., 130
Donovan, P., 201
Dooley, B., 216
Dorahy, M.J., 164, 169
Dorto, A.J., 151
Dorward, J., 118
Doty, T.J., 126
Doughty, C.J., 192
Douglas, K., 213
Douglas, K.S., 172
Douglass, A., 283
Dour, H.J., 230
Dove, A., 272
Downs, M.F., 15
Dowzer, C., 494
Doyle, A.C., 237
Dozois, D.J.A., 103, 126, 137, 138, 201
Draijer, N., 166
Drake, R.E., 275
Drapkin, M.L., 284
Drei, C., 152
Drevets, W.C., 198
Droes, R.M., 458
Drozd, J.F., 139
DrRijk, R.H., 125
Drum, D.J., 61, 68, 194
Drummond, K.D., 355
Druss, B., 478, 480
Desideri, G., 451
D'Souza, D.C., 217, 379
Dua, T., 401
Duane, W., 157
Duberstein, P.R., 195
DuBois, D.L., 426
Dubovsky, A.N., 197, 218
Dubovsky, S.L., 197, 218
Duckworth, M.P., 149
Dude, K., 70–71
Dudeck, M., 172
Duerden, E.G., 398
Duffy, C., 411
Duffy, S., 206
Duffy, S.N., 426
Dugas, M.J., 119, 134
Duggan, C., 296, 309, 316
Duggan, M.H., 227
Duivenvoorden, H., 312
Duivenvoorden, H.J., 374
Dujour, R., 166
Dulcan, M.K., 425
Dundar, Y., 494
Dunkley, D.M., 234
DuPaul, G.J., 402, 425
Durand-Roger, J., 373
Durbin, C.E., 209
Durham, S.R., 493
Durkheim, E., 191
Durlak, J.A., 66, 67
Du Rocher Schudlich, T.D., 203
Duska, R., 281
Dutra, L., 275, 284
Dvortcsak, A., 411
Dwork, A.J., 213
DyBuncio, A., 493
Dyck, I., 141

Dykens, E.M., 405
Dziegielewski, S.F., 282
Dzokoto, V.A., 111

**E**

Earle, C., 327
Easterbrooks, M.A., 306
Eastvold, A., 340, 345
Eastwood, S., 151
Eaton, W.W., 218, 373
Eaves, L.J., 122
Ebben, M.R., 494
Eberly, S., 195
Ebmeier, K.P., 195, 198
Ebrahim, S., 492
Eckert, S., 446
Eckert, T.L., 206
Edberg, M., 129
Edelen, M.O., 310
Edell, W.S., 192
Edersheim, J.G., 312
Edgar, C., 379
Edin, H.M., 331
Edinger, J.D., 495
Edlund, M., 118, 268
Edmond, T., 275
Edwards, G., 129
Edwards, M.C., 421
Edwards, N., 377
Eells, T.D., 472
Effting, M., 164
Egami, H., 274
Egan, M., 307
Egger, H., 57, 417
Egsgaard, L.L., 148
Eguiluz, J.I., 367
Ehlers, C.L., 153, 277
Ehring, T., 96
Eickhoff, S.B., 421
Einfeld, S.L., 401
Einhäupl, K.M., 445
Eisen, A.R., 473
Eisen, M.L., 167
Eisenberg, D., 15, 419
Eisenbruch, S., 489
Eisler, I., 216
Eisner, L., 209
Ekehammar, B., 35
Ekselius, L., 122
Ekstrom, M., 381
Elamin, M.B., 355
Elbayomy, Y., 334
Elder, J.H., 479
Eldredge, K.L., 237
El-Gabalawi, F., 413
Elhaj, O., 212
Elhanbly, S., 334
Elias, M.J., 473
Elinson, L., 478
Elkholy, A., 334
Elkin, A., 197
Elkins, S.R., 28
Ellason, J.W., 174
Elliot, L., 67
Elliot, S.L., 328
Elliott, B., 212

Ellis, A., 40
Ellis, B.J., 493
Ellis, E.C., 403
Ellis, L.A., 401
Ellison, J.W., 405
Ellman, L.M., 379
Ellsworth, P.C., 204
Elsabbagh, M., 401
Elsaid, M., 334
Emerson, E., 401
Emery, G., 38
Emmelkamp, P.M.G., 139
Emmerich, J., 155
Emsley, R., 389
Encinas, M., 460
Endicott, J., 192
Eng, W., 133
Engedal, K., 447
Engel, S.M., 129
Engelhardt-Wells, K., 412
Engelhart, M.J., 451
Engels, R.C.M.E., 238
Eng-Kung, Y., 119
Englera, H., 344
Eppstein, D., 237
Epstein, C., 454, 457
Eranti, S.V., 372
Erbay-Dundar, P., 152
Ericzon, B.G., 403
Eriksen, L., 227
Eriksson, C.J.P., 274
Ermani, M., 438
Ernst, F.A., 272
Erwin, P.J., 241, 355
Escobar, J.I., 152
Eshleman, S., 43, 60, 119
Esiri, M.M., 378, 449
Espejo, E.P., 201
Esper, C.D., 378
Espie, C.A., 490
Espie, C.A., 491
Esposito, G., 378
Essau, C.A., 192
Estabrook, D.M., 281
Esterman, A.J., 282
Esteva, I., 353
Estrada, A.L., 274
EU-Dap Study Group, 276
Eugenio, C., 441
Euteneur, F., 153
Evans, D.L., 64, 66, 67
Evans, K., 195, 334
Evans, K.E., 398
Evans, R., 445
Evans, Z.P., 260
Even, C., 214
Everitt, B., 216
Evers, C., 238
Everson-Rose, S.A., 491, 492
Evinger, J.S., 195
Evlice, Y.E., 331
Evmenova, A.S., 412
Evoniuk, G., 212
Ewald, H., 152
Ewald, K., 152
Exley, C., 458
Eyles, D.W., 380

Eynan, R., 295
Eyre, O., 421

F

Fabbri, A., 336
Faber, P.L., 442
Factor, S.A., 378
Fadem, B., 150, 151
Fagan, A.M., 441
Fagg, J., 718
Faggiano, F., 276
Fagioli, S., 363
Fagiolini, A., 373
Fahnhorst, T., 284
Fairburn, C.G., 238, 243, 244, 245, 246
Fairchild, G., 421
Fakier, N., 265
Falkai, P., 199
Falkenburg, J., 372
Fallgatter, A.J., 266
Fallon, B.A., 158
Fama, J.M., 141
Fan, G., 453
Fang, Q., 133
Fangerau, H., 191
Fanous, A.H., 375
Fanous, S., 266, 274
Farahmand, F.K., 426
Faraone, S.V., 125, 375, 419, 427, 429
Faravelli, C., 152, 234
Farina, S., 428
Farkas, S., 271
Farmer, A., 197
Farooque, R.S., 272
Farrell, L.J., 131
Farrugia, D., 402
Fava, G.A., 107, 157
Fawcett, J., 212
Fay, C., 159
Fayed, N., 153
Fazel, S., 299, 374
Feany, M.B., 445
Fearns, N., 318
Fearon, R.P., 169
Feart, C., 453
Federal Interagency Forum on Child and Family Services Statistics, 57
Fehnel, S.E., 331
Feinstein, R., 158
Feldman, D.B., 62
Feldman, H.H., 66, 446
Feldman, M.D., 151
Feng, J., 453
Feng, R., 448
Fenske, S., 330
Fenton, B., 266
Ferguson, A., 493
Ferguson, C.J., 306, 315
Fergusson, D.M., 308, 423
Fernandes, C., 379
Fernandez, C., 460
Fernyhough, C., 363
Ferrell, C.B., 118
Ferrer, M., 270
Ferri, C., 451, 490

Ferri, C.P., 445
Ferriter, M., 309, 316
Fichter, M.M., 159, 229, 234, 246
Field, A.P., 128
Field, C.A., 277, 284
Field, M., 270
Fierson, W.M., 400
Figueredo, A.J., 345
Figuerio, M.G., 490
Findling, R.L., 192, 203, 209, 212, 410
Fineberg, A.M., 379
Fineberg, N.A., 134
Fink, M., 214
Fink, P., 150, 152
Finn, C.T., 197
Finney, J.W., 284
Fiorini, M., 438
Firbank, M.J., 445, 460
Firestone, P., 351
First, M.B., 80, 157, 207, 238
Fisak, B., Jr., 127
Fischel, J.E., 417
Fischer, M., 427
Fischer, U., 110
Fischler, B., 403
Fisher, G.G., 444
Fisher, J.E., 137, 464, 472
Fisher, M.H., 406
Fisher, P., 425
Fiszbein, A., 383
Fitzgerald, P.B., 213
Fitzmaurice, G., 300, 317
Fitzpatrick, A.L., 442, 451, 460
Flaig, V., 199
Flament, M.F., 229, 233
Flanagan, T.J., 120
Flannery, K., 401
Flaum, M., 389
Fleitlich-Bilyk, B., 44, 203
Fleming, M., 282
Fleming, S.L., 496
Flett, G.L., 235
Flicker, L., 268
Flor, H., 153
Flore, G., 281
Flory, J.D., 304
Floyd, R.L., 275
Fluckiger, C., 472
Flynn, S., 411
Foa, E.B., 64, 66, 67, 141, 478
Fogelson, D.L., 375
Foley, S.R., 374
Folstein, M.F., 455
Folstein, S.E., 455
Fombonne, E., 401
Fong, C., 271
Fong, C.Y.-C., 402
Fonseca, M., 203
Fontaine, J., 208
Forbes, D., 278–280
Forbes, T., 278–280
Forcella, E., 403
Ford, A.C., 496
Ford, G.A., 494
Ford, I., 315
Forde, D.R., 166

Forehand, R., 421
Forman, E.M., 138, 478
Fornito, A., 198
Foster, K., 374
Fotenos, A.F., 456
Fountoulakis, K.N., 300
Fournier, J.C., 212, 215, 217
Foussias, G., 365
Fowler, J.S., 268, 274
Fowles, D.C., 134
Fox, S.H., 445, 448, 454
Fox, M.A., 142
Fox, N.C., 438
Fox, S.H., 457
Fraddosio, A., 450
Frampton, C.M., 192, 315
Frampton, C.M.A., 229
Frances, A., 416
Francey, S., 382
Francis, J.L., 141
Franckowiak, D., 172
Frank, J.E., 336
Frank, R.G., 118, 268
Franke, B., 419
Frankel, F., 412
Franken, I.H.A., 270
Frankenburg, F.R., 300, 317
Franklin, M., 141
Franko, D.L., 229
Franzini, L., 407
Frare, F., 107
Frasch, K., 369
Frasquilho, F., 169
Fratiglioni, L., 445, 447
Frazier, E., 192
Frazier, T.W., 405
Frederickson, B., 230
Fredrikson, M., 122, 123
Freedland, K.E., 491
Freedman, R., 385
Freeman, A., 305, 306, 307
Freeman, A.M., 305, 307
Freeman, S.B., 404
Freides, D., 25
Freidl, M., 152, 166
French, J., 441
Freshwater, S.M., 384
Freud, S., 29
Freund, K., 346
Frewen, P.A., 168
Freyberger, H.J., 166, 172
Frick, P.J., 421, 423, 427
Friderici, K., 421
Friedl, M.C., 166
Friedland, R.P., 452
Friedman, D., 125
Friedman, H.L., 35
Friedman, L., 494
Friedman, R., 274
Friedman, S., 214
Friedman, S.D., 405
Friedman, S.R., 274
Friedrich, W.N., 172
Frieling, H., 266
Friend, J., 191
Fries, J.F., 493
Friis, S., 382

Frisardi, V., 451
Frith, C., 362, 364
Fromberger, P., 345, 349
Frommann, N., 389
Fross, R.D., 445
Frost, R., 233
Frostholm, L., 150, 152
Frye, E.M., 151
Frye, M., 212
Frye, R.E., 403
Frye, V., 64
Fu, X. M., 266
Fujii, G., 129
Fukuda, K., 274
Fukuyama, H., 377
Fulero, S.M., 33, 476
Fuller, C.M., 274
Fullerton, T., 441
Fung, T.T., 492
Furmark, T., 122, 123
Furukawa, T.A., 134
Fusar-Poli, P., 377
Fyer, A.J., 122

G
Gabriel, B., 202
Gacono, C.B., 345
Gaebel, W., 389
Gago, E., 162
Gajewski, J.B., 328
Galanti, M.R., 276
Galasko, D., 452
Galassi, F., 152
Galbraith, K.M., 118
Galderisi, S., 377, 387
Gale, J., 206
Gale, T.M., 134
Galea, S., 129, 274, 477
Gallagher, M., 460
Gallagher-Thompson, D., 458
Gallagley, A., 444
Gallea, C., 450
Galliot, A.M., 373
Gallop, R., 215, 216, 217
Gallops, M.S., 122
Gallucci, M., 398
Galvin, D., 129
Galynker, I.I., 341, 345
Gamble, G., 327
Gamez, W., 271
GAMIAN-Europe Study Group, 195
Gannett News Service, 261
Gannon, T.A., 341
Ganocy, S.J., 212
Gans, S.W., 345
Gansler, D.A., 446
Gantman, A., 412
Gao, K., 212
Gao, S., 445
Garakani, A., 124
Garb, H.N., 85, 86
Garcia, C.S., 331
Garcia, F.D., 349
Garcia, J., 367
Garcia, L.F., 208
Garcia, L.J., 459

Garcia, M.Z., 355
Garcia-Barrera, M.A., 406
Garcia-Bueno, B., 199
Garcia-Campayo, J., 152, 153
Garcia-Toro, M., 204
Garczynski, J., 15
Gardenswartz, C.A., 69, 131
Gardner, E., 269, 345
Garland, E.L., 274
Garland, O.M., 205
Garlipp, P., 475
Garmezy, N., 63
Garner, M., 283
Garnham, J., 189
Garno, J.L., 218
Garnock-Jones, K.P., 425
Garrard, P., 441
Garre-Olmo, J., 458
Garrido, G.J., 268
Garrido, H., 123
Garrow, D., 489
Gasquet, I., 118
Gass, M.L.S., 334
Gates, N., 458
Gatz, M., 447
Gauci, D., 195
Gawronski, B., 103
Gazalle, F.K., 134
Ge, X., 418
Geaga, J.A., 377
Gearing, R.E., 428
Gearon, J.S., 379
Geddes, J.R., 206
Gee, M.D., 212
Geerlings, M.I., 451
Geers, M., 126
Geier, T., 318
Geiger, T.C., 303, 304
Gejman, P.V., 376
Geller, B., 207
Geller, B., 206
Gendrano, N., 333
Genovese, E., 151
Gentile, S., 456
Genuardi, J., 58
George, J., 284
George, M.S., 213
Georgiades, A., 496
Georgiades, K., 191, 417
Geppert, C.M.A., 284
Geracioti, T.D., 151
Geraedts, A.S., 216
Geraerts, E., 167
Gerardi, M., 131
Gerber, P.N., 172
Gericke, C.A., 386
Germain, A., 200
Germano, D., 382
Gerochi, C., 272
Gerrard, M., 418
Gerstein, R.K., 201
Gervin, M., 374
Geslani, D.M., 460
Gessa, G.L., 281
Geuze, E., 198
Gex-Fabry, M., 206
Geyer, J.D., 496

Gfroerer, J., 194
Ghahramanlou-Holloway, M., 126
Ghanem, H., 334
Ghisalbert, D., 166
Ghosh, A., 438
Giakoumaki, S.G., 378
Gianfrilli, D., 336
Giannetta, E., 336
Gibb, B.E., 201, 202
Gibbon, S., 309, 316
Gibbon M., 80, 157, 207
Gibbons, C.J., 215
Gibbons, F.X., 418
Gibbs, P.M., 32
Gidron, Y., 129
Giedd, J., 405
Giedd, J.N., 377, 382
Giesbrecht, T., 165
Giese, J., 172
Gil, P., 460
Gilaberte, I., 207
Gilbert, P., 126
Gilder, D.A., 273
Gill, J.M., 182
Gillberg, C., 413, 422
Gillespie, N., 24, 234, 270
Gillham, R., 313
Gilliard, J., 452
Gillner, M., 172
Gimpel, G.A., 425
Gingell, C., 331
Gingerich, S., 387
Ginsburg, G.S., 131
Giscombe, C.L., 129
Gitlin, M.J., 212
Gizer, I.R., 153, 277, 419
Gjertsen, F., 227
Gladstone, G.L., 125
Gladstone, T.R.G., 197, 203
Glass, N., 64
Glasser, D., 332
Glasser, D.B., 331
Glazer, J.L., 229
Glazer, W.M., 386
Gleason, O.C., 152
Gleaves, D.H., 163, 173
Gleeson, J.F., 388
Glenthoj, A., 377
Glenthoj, B.Y., 377
Glick, S.D., 267
Global ADHD Working Group., 425
Gloster, A.T., 107, 140
Gluzman, S., 118
Gmel, G., 274
Go, R.C., 448
Godard, P., 491
Godart, N.T., 229
Godbout, L., 383
Goddard, A.W., 124
Godwin, J., 422, 424
Goedert, M., 448, 449
Goenjian, A.K., 129
Gogos, J.A., 376
Gogtay, N., 377, 382
Golberstein, E., 15
Gold, J.M., 387
Gold, M., 269, 345

Gold, S.H., 152
Goldbeck, L., 422
Goldberg, D.P., 152
Goldberg, J.F., 201, 218
Goldberger, B.A., 280
Golden, C., 384
Goldenberg, H., 44, 45
Goldenberg, I., 44, 45
Golden-Schulman, S.J., 284
Goldfarb, R., 364
Goldfried, M.R., 39
Goldhammer, D.L., 333
Goldman, D., 284
Goldmeier, D., 331
Goldner, E.M., 373
Goldstein, D., 446
Goldstein, G., 379
Goldstein, J.M., 375
Goldstein, K.E., 304
Goldstein, M.F., 379
Goldstein, R.B., 118, 123, 300
Goldstein, R.Z., 267, 269
Goldston, D.B., 475
Gomez, J., 167
Gomez-Gil, E., 353
Gomez-Pinilla, F., 453
Gong, Q., 198, 199
Gontkovsky, S.T., 426
Gonzales-Correales, R., 330
Gonzalez, C., 206
Gonzalez, N., 373
Goode, S., 398
Goodman, A., 44, 203
Goodman, G.S., 167, 479
Goodman, M., 304
Goodman, R., 44, 203
Goodman, R.F., 35
Goodman, S.H., 199
Goodnick, P.J., 212
Goodwin, F.K., 200
Goodyer, I.M., 421
Gooren, L.J., 349
Gorbien, M.J., 446
Gordon, K.C., 333
Gordon, P., 180
Gordon, S.M., 284
Gorman, J.G., 122
Gorman, J.M., 141
Gorman, L.A., 122
Gormandy, K., 184–185
Gormley, M.J., 402
Gorny, X., 198
Gossop, M., 281
Gotestam, K.G., 227
Goto, Y., 381
Gottdiener, W.H., 33
Gottesman, I.I., 385
Gouitaa, M., 491
Gould, M.S., 195, 206
Goulding, S.M., 373
Goulet, J., 266
Graap, K.M., 270
Grabe, H.J., 166
Grabe, S., 222, 236
Grace, A.A., 267, 269, 381
Grace, S., 187
Gracia, G., 15

Grados, M., 123
Graff, H.J., 412
Graham, J.R., 82, 83, 157, 172
Gralla, O., 330
Granillo, M.T., 227
Granstrom, O., 386
Grant, B.F., 118, 192, 300, 318
Grant, G., 129
Grant, K.E., 426
Grant, M.M., 450
Grassi, D., 451
Grassi, L., 207
Grattan, L.M., 96
Gratz, K.L., 306
Graves, A.B., 444, 452
Gray, D.E., 402
Gray, N.S., 346
Gray, P., 331
Gray, R.N., 494
Gray, S.A.O., 425
Greco, C.M., 405
Greco, E.A., 336
Greden, J.F., 122
Green, C.A., 284
Green, J., 67, 189
Green, M., 373
Green, M.F., 218
Green, M.J., 490
Green, M.J., 377, 379
Green, R., 328
Greenberg, J.L., 158
Greenberg, M.T., 424
Greenberg, R.P., 472
Greenberg, T., 195, 206
Greenfield, S.F., 281, 284
Greenhalgh, J., 494
Greenhill, L.L., 429
Green-Paden, L.D., 386
Greenwald, S., 119
Greenwood, T.A., 197
Gregg, N., 413
Gregory, R.J., 151
Greve, K.W., 151
Grieger, T.A., 129
Grieser, E.A., 490
Griez, E.J., 120
Griffin, M.M., 406
Griffiths, J., 121
Griffiths, K.M., 120, 136, 195
Grigoriadis, S., 192
Grillo, C.A., 125
Grillon, C., 123
Grills-Taquechel, A.E., 127
Grilo, C.M., 234, 245, 310, 311, 317, 318
Grinberg, L.T., 448
Grob, G.N., 10
Grodstein, F., 451
Groenvynck, H., 208
Groleau, D., 153
Gron, G., 327, 330
Gronenewegen, H.J., 123
Gronli, J., 490
Gross, A.M., 417
Grosse, S.D., 404
Grossi, D., 398
Grossman, S., 310

Grotpeter, J., 306
Grounds, A., 311
Grover, N., 156
Grover, S., 373
Groves, C., 195
Grow, J., 283
Gruber, M.J., 118, 129
Gruber, O., 199
Gruenewald, T.L., 44
Grundmann, O., 489
Grupe, D.W., 123
Gu, H., 389
Guarda, A.S., 241
Guariglia, S.R., 410
Gueorguieva, R., 245
Gueorguieva, R.V., 386
Guerdjikova, A.I., 241
Guerrini, I., 448
Guerrini, R., 405
Guillamon, A., 353
Guisinger, S., 229
Guldager, S., 277
Gumienny, L., 259
Gumienny, L.A., 272
Gumley, A., 315
Gunatilake, S., 386
Gunderson, J.G., 313, 317, 318
Gunnell, D., 210
Guo, W., 198, 199
Gupta, S., 204
Gur, R.E., 64, 66, 67
Guralnik, O., 172
Gureje, O., 118, 152, 445
Gurung, R.A.R., 44
Gutierrez, M., 367
Gutierrez, P.M., 133
Gutteling, B.M., 314
Guze, S.B., 157
Gyulai, L., 202, 215

## H

Haack, S., 369
Haaga, D.A.F., 181
Haalu, U., 382
Haahr, U.H., 374
Haas, A., 195, 206
Haas, G.L., 369
Haatainen, K., 166
Habermann, N., 345
Haberstick, B.C., 306
Habing, B., 276
Hacker, D., 386
Hackmann, A., 155
Hadjipavlou, G., 315
Haedt, A., 241
Haedt-Matt, A.A., 240
Haeffel, G.J., 201, 202
Haffey, W.G., 67
Haffmans, P.M.J., 206
Hafner, H., 366
Hagan, C.C., 421
Hagan, C.R., 202
Hagedorn, J., 210
Hagerman, P.J., 402, 405
Hagerman, R.J., 405
Haghighi, A., 404

Hagopian, L.P., 411
Hahn, M., 189
Hainsworth, A.H., 441
Hairston, J.C., 334
Hajek, P., 275
Hajek, T., 189
Hakko, H., 265, 371
Halari, R., 421
Hale, D.P., 152
Hales, R.E., 210, 439
Halimi, L., 491
Hall, G.C.N., 14, 16
Hall, J., 313
Hall, J.M., 169
Hall, K., 318, 445, 452
Hall, L., 458
Hall, L.L., 15
Hall, R.C.W., 344, 351
Halmi, K., 244, 246
Halmi, K.A., 229, 234
Haltenhof, H., 475
Ham, L.S., 120, 270
Hamer, R.M., 377
Hamerschlag, C., 458
Haines, J.L., 202
Hamet, P., 197
Hamilton, M., 208
Hamilton, S., 494
Hamilton, S.P., 197
Hamm, A., 172
Hammen, C., 45, 201
Hammen, C.L., 203
Hammond, D.C., 140
Hampshire, A., 67
Han, B., 194
Han, C., 200
Hanakawa, T., 377
Hanaoka, A., 107
Hancock, S., 255, 270
Handler, S.M., 400
Handsel, V.A., 28
Hanel, G., 155
Hankin, B.L., 201, 202
Hanlon, F.M., 379
Hanna, A.C., 234
Hanna, D., 209
Hansberry, M.R., 446
Hansen, M.S., 152
Hansen, N.B., 478
Hanson, R.K., 346
Hanuszkiewicz, I., 382
Haque, R., 331
Harald, B., 180
Harciarek, M., 441
Harden, A.Y., 405
Hardie, T., 167
Hardiman, E.R., 473
Hardoy, M.C., 203
Hardy, G., 313
Hardy, J., 448
Hare, R.D., 300
Harmer, C.J., 200
Harms, M.P., 377
Harnett, P.H., 206
Haro, J.M., 118, 379
Haro-Abad, J.M., 203
Harper, C.G., 259, 444

Harper, M.L., 139
Harrell, P.T., 259
Harrigan, S.M., 382
Harrington, R., 67
Harrington, R.A., 405
Harris, A.E., 475
Harris, G.T., 345, 349
Harris, M.G., 382
Harris, T.R., 277
Harrison, G., 389
Harrow, M., 218, 366
Hart, L.M., 277
Harter, M., 61
Harter, S.L., 273
Hartman, J.K., 151
Hartmann, A., 327, 330
Hartmann, U., 330
Hartz, A., 496
Hartzler, B., 283
Harvey, A.G., 490
Harvey, P.D., 304, 383
Harwood, H., 58
Harwood, T.M., 14, 472
Hashimoto, M., 449
Hasin, D.S., 192, 318
Hassett, A.L., 156
Hasson, D., 495
Hastings, R.P., 398
Hatch, J.P., 203
Hatfield, T., 227
Haugaard, J.J., 173
Havermans, R., 201
Haw, C., 210
Hawgood, J., 120
Hawk, L.W., 425
Hawke, J.L., 404
Hawke, L.D., 183
Hawkins, K.A., 386
Hawley, L.L., 206
Hawton, K., 210, 218, 229
Hayano, J., 496
Hayashi, K.M., 377
Hayashi, T., 377
Hayes, R.D., 322
Hayes, S.C., 470
Hayward, C., 127
Hayward, P., 215
Hazlett, E.A., 304
Hazlett, R.L., 124
Hazlett-Stevens, H., 109
He, J., 191, 417, 491
He, J.-P., 192
Healy, H., 129
Healy, L.M., 465
Healy, O., 411
Heape, C.L., 307
Heath, A.C., 122, 270, 274
Heather, N., 282
Heaton, R.K., 383, 384
Hebebrand, J., 232
Hechler, T., 495
Hecker, L., 477, 482
Heckert, T.M., 493, 494
Hedeker, D., 272
Hedges, M., 478
Hedlund, S., 246
Hoskin, M., 131

Heene, E., 216
Heeringa, S., 118
Heeringa, S.G., 444
Heffelfinger, S., 139
Hegerl, U., 189, 195, 206
Heggestad, T., 227
Heil, K., 422
Heim, L., 451
Heiman, J., 327
Heiman, J.R., 336
Heimberg, R.G., 108, 133, 137, 209
Heinik, J., 446
Heinrichs, R.W., 300
Heintz, J.M., 277
Heitzeg, M.M., 259
Held, T., 191
Hemmingsen, R.P., 377
Hempel, A., 364
Hempel, E., 364
Hen, R., 213
Henderson, C., 489
Henderson, H.A., 142
Henderson, L., 118
Hendin, H., 195, 206
Hendlin, H., 64, 66, 67
Hendrie, H., 445
Henggeler, S.W., 416, 427, 472
Henin, A., 120, 125, 209
Hennen, J., 317
Hennessey, M., 15
Hennessy, G., 281
Hennings, A., 153
Henningsen, P., 154
Henry, L.P., 382
Henson, J.M., 259
Hepp, U., 43
Herbolsheimer, F., 450
Hering, L.M., 474
Hermann, D., 283
Hermann, N., Li, A., 457
Hermesh, H., 45
Heron, K.E., 493
Herot C., 125
Herpertz, S., 241
Herrell, J.M., 273
Herrman, H., 382
Herrmann, N., 460
Hersen, M., 86
Hertz-Picciotto, I., 405
Herzog, D.B., 229
Hescheles, D.R., 472
Hesse, M., 277
Hesselbrock, V., 285
Hetrick, S., 210
Hetrick, S.E., 66
Hettema, J.M., 122
Heun, R., 191
Hewett, K., 212
Hewitt, J.K., 306
Hewitt, P.L., 235
Heyerdahl, S., 418
Heyman, I., 142
Heyman, R.B., 281
HGDH Study Group, 377
Hicken, B.L., 458
Hickie, I.B., 195
Hickey, M., 334

Hien, D., 284
Higashi, K., 386
Higbee, T.S., 412
Higginson, C.B., 406
Highet, N.J., 195
Hightower, A.D., 67
Hilbert, A., 155
Hill, A., 345
Hill, A.J., 233, 235
Hill, C., 425, 489
Hill, J., 473
Hill, R.D., 458
Hillemacher, T., 266
Hiller, W., 157, 159
Hilsenroth, M.J., 85
Hilton, K., 142
Hinderliter, A., 496
Hines, M., 353
Hinkelmann, K., 200
Hinney, A., 232
Hinshaw, S.P., 417
Hintikka, J., 166
Hinton, D.E., 129, 155
Hippocrates, 10–11
Hirao, K., 377
Hiripi, E., 228
Hirsbrunner, H.-P., 389
Hirsch, C.R., 126
Hirschfeld, R.M.A., 210, 217
Hirshfeld-Becker, D.R., 120, 125
Hjemdahl, P., 492, 495
Hjern, A., 43
Ho, B.-C., 382, 389
Ho, G.J., 449
Hoang, A.N., 334
Hoch, H., 97
Hockemeyer, J.R., 493
Hodapp, R.M., 401, 406
Hodgins, S., 315, 374, 376
Hoehn-Saric, R., 124
Hoek, H.W., 343
Hoencamp, E., 206
Hof, P.R., 28
Hofler, M., 140
Hoffman, E.J., 124
Hoffmann, H., 389
Hoffmann, M., 330
Hofman, A., 445, 446, 451
Hofmann, H., 346
Hofmann, S.G., 140, 141
Hogan, M., 192, 491
Hogan, M.E., 201
Hoge, C.W., 121
Hogue, S.L., 331
Hohagen, F., 491
Holaway, R.M., 133
Holeva, V., 112
Holland, D., 206
Holland, L.A., 229
Holland, M.L., 425
Holland, S.J.F., 136, 137
Hollis, K.A., 331
Hollon, S.D., 209, 212, 215, 217
Hollt, V., 266
Holly, L., 67
Holmes, E.A., 127, 169
Holmes, H.M., 457

Holm-Linneberg, I., 277
Holthoff, V.A., 441
Honea, R., 376
Hong, M.S., 377
Honkalampi, K., 166
Hoogendijk, W.J.G., 125
Hope, B.T., 266, 274
Hope, T., 449
Hopko, D.R., 202, 214
Hopper, J.W., 168
Hopper, K., 389
Hopman, M.J., 365
Hopwood, C.J., 310, 311, 313
Hor, K., 373
Hordern, A., 330
Hori, T., 445, 455
Horn, J., 229
Horn, N., 474
Hornbrook, M., 206
Horvath, A.O., 472
Horwood, L.J., 423
Hoschke, B., 330
Hosny Awad, H., 334
Hou, C.E., 445
Houck, J.M., 284
Hougaard, E., 216
Houlihan, D., 458
Houry, D., 131
Houser, R.A., 482
Howard, G., 448
Howard, M.O., 274, 275
Howard, R., 296
Howard, R.C., 300
Howard, R.J., 380, 460
Howden, C.W., 489
Howel, D., 458
Howieson, D.B., 90, 91
Howland, R.H., 210
Howlin, P., 398
Hoyer, J., 140
Hoyle, M., 456
Hsi, X., 378
Hsu, L., 303, 373
Hsu, S., 283
Hu, C., 192
Hu, N.-W., 448
Hu, P., 379
Hu, X., 266, 284
Hua, J.M., 205
Huang, B., 300
Huang, C., 198, 199
Huang, M., 379
Huang, S.Y., 274
Huang, Y., 267
Huband, N., 296, 309, 316
Huddy, V., 387
Hudson, J.I., 167
Hudson, J.L., 110, 127
Huebner, T., 441
Hughes, I., 472
Hughes, J., 458
Hughes, J.C., 460
Hughes, J.R., 280
Hughes, M., 43, 60, 119
Hughes, S., 429
Huizinga, D., 306
Hulse, G.K., 268

Hulshoff Pol, H.E., 389
Hultman, C.M., 197
Hummelen, B., 294
Humphreys, K., 270, 284
Hunsaker, M.R., 405
Hunt, K., 490
Hunter, E.C.M., 166, 169, 173
Hunter, J.A., 345, 350
Huntjens, R.J.C., 163
Huntley, E.D., 259
Huot, P., 457
Huprich, S.K., 345
Hurd, M.D., 444
Hurford, G., 421
Hurlburt, R.T., 87
Hurley, R.A., 153, 155
Hurwitz, T.A., 146, 150, 154
Hutchinson, G., 380
Hutton, J., 398
Huttunen, M., 379
Hwo, H., 119
Hyde, C., 456
Hyde, J.S., 41, 192, 222, 236, 346, 347, 350
Hyler, S.E., 311
Hynd, G.W., 406
Hyoki, K., 442
Hypericum Depression Trial Study Group, 212
Hysing, M., 493

I

Iacono, W.G., 306
Iannucci, R.A., 282
Iarocci, G., 401
Ibrahim, R., 428
Ichimiya, A., 120
Ido, Y., 353
Iezzi, T., 149, 153, 159
Ihle, D., 157
Ikeda, M., 425, 445
Iliceto, G., 450
Imbimbo, B.P., 451
Incrocci, L., 327
Ineichen, B., 452
Infante, A., 259, 407
Ingenhoven, T., 312
Ingersoll, B., 411
Ingersoll, B.R., 411
Inghilleri, M., 157
Ingram, B.L., 472
Ingvar, M., 125
Iniesta, R., 373
Inouye, S.K., 455
Insel, T.R., 58
Institute of Medicine., 66
Invernizzi, G., 377
Ipser, J.C., 134, 158
Ironson, G., 45
Irving, C.B., 386
Irving, H., 259
Irwin, H.J., 169
Irwin, J., 379
Irwin, K.S., 281
Irwin, M., 284
Ishikawa, T., 445

Isidori, A.M., 336
Ismail, Z., 455
Isohanni, M., 381
Ito, K., 441
Itskovich, Y., 345
Iudice, J., 478
Ivanov, I., 271
Ivey, M., 284
Iwamasa, G.Y., 478
Iwata, N., 454, 457
Iwata, Y., 111
Iwatsubo, T., 441

**J**

Jaakola, M.S., 272
Jaaro-Peled, H., 376
Jaceldo-Siegl, K., 451
Jack, C.R., 441
Jackson, A., 67
Jackson, G.D., 405
Jackson, H., 382
Jackson, H.J., 345, 382
Jackson, J., 152
Jackson, W.C., 35
Jacob, T., 44
Jacobi, C., 237
Jacobs, M.J., 234
Jacobsen, K.C., 375
Jacobsen, S.J., 331
Jacova, C., 66, 446
Jaeger, S., 429
Jaffe, S.L., 273
Jager, M., 369
Jager-Hyman, S., 192
Jagielska, D., 388
Jagust, W., 442, 460
Jahng, S., 291, 295, 300, 303
Jainchill, N., 271
Jakes, R., 449
Jakobsen, T., 154
James, A., 272
James, M.R., 266
James, S., 427
Jamieson, P., 15
Jamison, K.R., 200
Jamrozik, K., 268, 327
Janca, A., 157, 389
Janevic, M.R., 452
Jang, H.-J., 383
Jang, K.L., 123, 304, 306, 307
Jankovic, J., 158, 448
Janner, M., 389
Janssen, E., 331
Jansson, E.T., 451
Japee, S., 126
Jarmolowicz, D.P., 411
Jarvelin, M.-R., 265, 371
Jarvinen, J., 166
Jarvis, M., 275
Jary, S., 405
Jaskiw, G.E., 378
Jasper, F.J., 173
Jaussent, I., 490
Jayadev, S., 448
Jayne, M., 268
Jeammet, P., 229

Jeffreys, M., 456
Jeglic, E., 348, 350
Jelicic, M., 167
Jensen, P.H., 449
Jensen, T.S., 148
Jenson, J.M., 275
Jermann, F., 206
Jernigan, K., 421
Jernigan, T.L., 377
Jerome, M.K., 412
Jervis, L.L., 451
Jespersen, A.F., 343, 346
Jeste, D.V., 378, 388, 444
Jiang, L., 198, 199
Jiang, X.-F., 266
Jilek, W., 120
Jimerson, N., 455
Jin, C., 166
Jin, L.-W., 405
Jin, R., 55, 56, 57, 60, 61, 117, 118, 191, 192, 268, 480
Jindal, S., 151
Jiwa, N.S., 442
Jobe, K.W., 151
Jobe, T.H., 300
Jodoin, M., 331
Johannesen, J.O., 382
Johannessen Landmark, C., 212
Johansson, B., 447
Johansson, K., 448
Johns, L., 363
Johnson, A.W., 232
Johnson, B.T., 16
Johnson, C., 229, 234
Johnson, C.L., 273
Johnson, J., 426
Johnson, S., 388
Johnson, S.D., 330
Johnson, S.L., 192, 195, 209
Johnston, C., 422
Johnston, T.H., 457
Johnstone, E., 364
Joiner, T.E., 202, 210, 217
Jolkkonen, J., 460
Jonasen, P.K., 103
Jones, A.R., 227
Jones, C., 386
Jones, D., 424
Jones, D.J., 421
Jones, E., 216
Jones, H., 309, 315
Jones, I., 192
Jones, J.B., 186
Jones, M.P., 491
Jones, P.B., 45, 381, 385
Jones, R.M., 313
Jones, R.S.P., 398
Jones, S.M., 418
Jordan, J., 229
Jordan, J.V., 35
Jordan, K., 345, 349
Jorm, A.F., 136, 195, 227, 273
Jorns, C., 403
Joshi, A., 443
Joshi, G., 192
Joska, J.A., 474
Jouriles, E.N., 277

Joyce, P.R., 192, 229, 315
Juanes, N., 387
Juckel, G., 386
Judd, L.L., 192
Judge, A., 15
Judson, J.I., 228
Judson, R., 425
Juliano, L.M., 259
June, R.W., 118
Jungehülsing, G.J., 445
Jurgens, I., 227
Jurica, P.J., 155
Juriga, S., 36
Jurjanz, L., 441

**K**

Kadri, N., 331
Kaemmer, B., 82
Kafka, M.P., 339, 342, 344
Kagan, J., 125
Kahler, C.W., 284
Kahn, R.S., 389
Kahonen-Vare, M.H., 460
Kalaria, R.N., 445, 452, 453, 460
Kales, A., 388
Kalivas, P.W., 269
Kallert, T.W., 475
Kaltman, S.I., 379
Kalucy, R., 481
Kalueff, A.V., 124
Kamali, M., 373, 374
Kamatenesi-Mugisha, M., 331
Kambouropoulos, N., 271
Kamkar, K., 103
Kamphaus, R.W., 425
Kamphuis, J.H., 315
Kanaan, R.A., 146, 153
Kanaan, R.A.A., 155
Kanary, K., 455
Kaner, E.F.S., 282
Kang, J.H., 451
Kang, J.Y., 489
Kaniecki, R., 493
Kansara, S., 448
Kantrowitz, L., 401
Kapczinski, F., 134
Kaplan, A.S., 229, 234
Kaplan, B., 151
Kaplan, E., 384
Kaplan, K.A., 490
Kaplan, N.M., 491
Kapoula, A., 401
Kappler, C., 491
Kaprinis, G.S., 300
Kaprio, J., 197, 427
Kapur, V., 494
Karam, A., 118
Karam, E.G., 192
Karayan, I., 129
Karayiorgou, M., 376
Kariuki, C.M., 134
Karl, A., 153
Karne, A., 186
Karnik-Henry, M.S., 377
Karno, M.P., 472
Karran, E., 433

Karshin, C.M., 67
Karterud, S., 294
Kasari, C., 398
Kash, T.L., 267
Kashdan, T.B., 192
Kaslow, N.J., 380
Kassed, C.A., 58
Kato, H., 251
Katon, W., 152
Katsakou, C., 315
Katz, S.J., 118, 203, 268
Katzman, D.K., 243
Kauchali, S., 401
Kaufman, J., 328
Kaul, T.J., 472
Kaushal, R.K., 156
Kawa, I., 192
Kawakami, N., 118
Kawas, C.H., 442, 460
Kay, S.R., 383
Kaya, E., 152
Kaye, J., 441
Kaye, W., 229
Kaye, W.H., 229, 232, 234
Kayman, D.J., 379
Kazdin, A.E., 39
Kearney, C.A., 97, 117, 125, 127, 128, 129, 412, 473, 480
Kearney, P.M., 491
Keating, G.M., 425
Keck, P.E., 197, 218
Keck Seeley, S.M., 172
Keel, P.K., 229, 231, 240, 241, 246
Keeley, P., 149
Keem, M., 274
Keen, D.V., 406
Keen, S., 345
Keenan, K., 425
Keenan, M., 405
Keenan, N.L., 491
Keenan-Miller, D., 203
Kees, M., 122
Kehagia, A.A., 442
Kehoe, P.G., 451
Kehrer, C.A., 314, 315
Keightley, M., 198, 199
Keller, M.B., 141
Kellermann, J., 126
Kelley, A.E., 475
Kelley, M.L., 259, 272
Kellner, M., 200
Kelly, B.D., 373, 374
Kelly, J.F., 284
Kelsoe, J.R., 197
Kemp, D.E., 212
Kemp, J., 422
Kendall, P.C., 209
Kendall, T., 388
Kendjelic, E.M., 472
Kendler, K.S., 24, 43, 44, 60, 119, 122, 123, 153, 197, 198, 230, 232, 270, 304, 305, 306, 376, 381, 382
Kendrick, D., 67
Kennedy, N., 192, 204
Kennedy, R.E., 448
Kenny, L.C., 379
Kenny, P.J., 267

Kent, J.E., 123
Keogh, F., 379
Keough, M.E., 127
Kern, R.S., 387
Kerns, J.G., 379
Kershaw, T., 276
Kersting, A., 241
Kertesz, A., 441
Keshavan, M.S., 366, 371, 378, 405
Keshaviah, A., 141
Kessler, R.C., 2, 43, 55, 56, 57, 58, 60,
61, 117, 118, 119, 122, 129, 191,
192, 202, 228, 264, 295, 300, 422,
429, 480
Ketelaars, C., 410
Keyes, K.M., 318
Khalifa, N., 167
Khan, S., 374
Khantzian, E.J., 284
Khashan, A.S., 379
Khoshnood, K., 281
Khouzam, H.R., 413
Kibblewhite, S.J., 352, 353
Kidani, T., 107
Kiefer, F., 275, 281, 283
Kiehl, K.A., 271, 296
Kieling, R., 427
Kiely, D.K., 457
Kiesner, J., 271
Kihlstrom, J.F., 170
Kikuchi, M., 107
Kilkenny, L., 152
Killackey, E., 66
Kim, C., 195
Kim, D., 281
Kim, D.H., 451
Kim, G.S., 274
Kim, H.-W., 448
Kim, J., 308
Kim, J.-J., 383
Kim, J.Y., 234
Kim, L., 274
Kim, S.C., 332
Kim, S.I., 383
Kim, S.W., 331
Kim, S.Y., 418
Kim, Y.S., 401
King, D.C., 422
King, E., 58
King, E.C., 58
King, S.M., 90
Kingdon, D., 39, 387
Kingsberg, S., 336
Kingston, D., 351
Kingston, T., 216
Kinmouth, A.-L., 152
Kinscherff, R., 312
Kinsella, A., 379
Kirchheiner, J., 241
Kirkley, S.M., 446
Kirmayer, L.J., 152, 153
Kirsch, L.G., 345
Kirsch, M., 283
Kish, S.J., 378
Kivipelto, M., 451
Kivisto, A.J., 28
Kiziltan, E., 166

Kjelsas, E., 227
Klaiberg, A., 154
Klauer, T., 166
Klein, A., 345
Klein, D.F., 122
Klein, D.N., 182, 201
Klein, E., 346
Klein, L.C., 44
Kleinman, A., 77
Kleinplatz, P.J., 327
Kleinsasser, D., 277
Klerman, G.L., 158
Klevens, J., 67
Kliem, S., 315
Klimek, E.H., 151
Klin, A., 413
Klinnert, M.D., 492
Kloos, B., 473
Klosterkoetter, J., 66
Klostermann, K., 272
Kluft, R.P., 173
Klug, M.G., 405
Klump, K., 229
Klump, K.L., 229, 232, 233
Klunder, A.D., 377
Klunk, M., 448
Knackstedt, L., 269
Knight, R.A., 348
Knight, R.G., 213
Knöchel, C., 377
Knoll, N., 330
Knowles, R., 362
Knudsen, A.K., 277
Knudsen, G.P., 122, 153, 232, 270,
304, 305, 306
Knutelska, M., 172
Ko, H.C., 274
Kodish, S., 328
Koegel, L.K., 411
Koegel, R.L., 411
Koelkebeck, K., 381
Koen, L., 158, 474
Koenigs, M., 305
Koenigsberg, H.W., 304
Kogan, M.D., 401
Kogan, S.M., 283
Koh, M.T., 460
Koh, Y.-J., 401
Kohn, P.D., 378
Kokai, M., 129
Kolaitis, J.C., 304
Kolla, N.J., 69
Kolodziej, M.E., 16
Kolsch, H., 191
Komuro, R., 107
Kongerslev, M., 374
Konrad, K., 421
Koob, G.F., 270
Koonce, D.A., 478
Kooner, J.S., 492
Koopmans, R.T., 446
Koot, J.M., 423
Kopcke, W., 389
Kopelman, M.D., 443
Kopelowicz, A., 382
Koplin, B., 172
Koponen, H., 381

Koprich, J.B., 457
Korczyn, A.D., 448
Koretz, D., 192
Korkeila, J., 166
Kornhuber, J., 266
Kornreich, R., 404
Korszun, A., 192
Kosfelder, J., 315
Koshino, Y., 107
Koskinen, J., 381
Kosson, D.S., 271
Koster, F.H.W., 126
Kotov, R., 129, 201, 271
Koukoulis, G.N., 334
Kouzis, A.C., 118, 268
Kovacs, M., 209
Kovalenko, S., 191
Kovel, C.C., 347
Kowall, N.W., 446
Kozin, D.S., 165
Koziol-McLain, J., 64
Kozlowski, A.M., 401
Kozma, A., 476
Krabbenborg, M.A.M., 238
Kraemer, H., 244, 246
Kraepelin, E., 23
Kraijer, D., 410
Kramer, J.H., 384
Kramer, M., 494
Krams, M., 404, 447
Krantz, D.S., 491
Kratochvil, C.J., 425
Krause, E.D., 472
Krem, M.M., 158
Kril, J.J., 259, 444
Kringlen, E., 295, 447
Krishen, A., 212
Krishnan, S., 380
Kroger, C., 315
Krokstad, S., 490, 493
Kropp, F., 284
Krueger, R.F., 306, 312
Kruger, T.H.C., 330
Krugman, S.D., 65
Krystal, J.H., 172
Ku, J., 383
Ku, J.H., 331
Kueppers, K.A., 381
Kuipers, E., 388
Kulkarni, R., 404
Kuller, L.H., 442, 451, 460
Kumari, V., 373
Kundakci, T., 166
Kunoe, N., 281
Kuo, M., 67
Kuo, T., 441
Kupelian, V., 327
Kupelnick, B., 216, 218
Kupfer, D.J., 200
Kupper, Z., 389
Kuppinger, H., 375
Kuriakose, S., 411
Kuroda, S., 353
Kuroki, T., 120
Kurth, R., 153
Kurth, T., 490
Kurtz, P.F., 411

Kurz, M.W., 442, 460
Kushner, H.I., 191
Kutz, A., 134
Kuzniecky, R.I., 405
Kvernmo, S., 418
Kymalainen, J.A., 382

L

Laan, E., 336
Labad, A., 152
Labarthe, D.R., 492
L'Abate, L., 14
Labauve, B.J., 129
Labazi, H., 327
Labbe, E.E., 491
Labrecque, J., 134
Lachs, M.S., 446
Lackner, J.M., 494
Lacourse, E., 422
Lacy, T., 172
Lad, S.P., 151
Ladage, J., 259, 272
Ladd, L.D., 422
Ladea, M., 192
Lafay, P., 312
Lah, J.J., 447
Lahey, B.B., 416, 427
Lai, M.K.P., 449
Laine, M.L., 122
Lalumiere, M.L., 345, 346, 347, 348,
349
LaLumiere, R.T., 269
Lam, C., 402
Lam, D.H., 215
Lam, F., 402
Lam, K., 152
Lam, R.W., 180
Lambert, J.-C., 453
Lambert, M.J., 478
Lambert, M.T., 166
Lambert, M.V., 171
Lambert, N.M., 410
Lamberti, P., 450
Lamberti, S.V., 450
Lammertsma, A.A., 123
Lamouroux, A., 491
Lampkin, S.M., 473
Lampley-Dallas, V.T., 452
Lancaster, T., 275
Lancon, C., 383
Lanctot, K., 457
Landry, T., 331
Lane, D.S., 334
Lane, M., 55, 57, 118
Lane, M.C., 295, 300
Lane, R.C., 173
Lane, W., 171
Lane, W.G., 65
Langa, K.M., 444
Langdon, R., 363
Langdon, S.W., 425
Langen, K., 166
Langevin, M., 345
Langevin, R., 345, 348
Langhinrichsen-Rohling, J., 191
Langley, K., 421

Langstrom, N., 338, 340, 342, 344, 346
Lanius, R.A., 169, 173
Lanka, G.D., 135
Lansford, J.E., 422
Lapierre, C.B., 129
Laposa, J.M., 103
Lappin, J., 378
Laracy, S.D., 402
Larimer, M.E., 275, 283
Larkin, C., 373, 374, 376
Laroi, F., 363
Larsen, J.K., 238
Larsen, T.K., 382
Larson, E.B., 442, 460
Larson, J., 334
Lash, S.J., 283
Lasher, M.P., 348, 464
Latimer, K., 422
Latkin, C.A., 274
Lau, H.C., 29
Lau, J., 450
Lau, J.Y., 489
Lauber, C., 152
Laubscher, E.II., 411
Lauerma, H., 166
Laugeson, E.A., 412
Laughon, K., 64
Laumann, E.O., 327, 329, 331
Launer, L., 445, 446
Laurens, K.R., 377
Laurent, S.M., 327, 331
Laurillard, D., 401
Lauronen, E., 381
Lautenschlager, N.T., 268
LaValleur, J., 334
Lavi, T., 129
La Via, M., 234
Law, S., 191, 195
Lawlor, E., 216
Lawrence, A.A., 353, 355
Laws, D.R., 343, 344, 347, 348, 349, 350
Laws, E.R., 210
Lazaro, L., 123
Lbo, C.F., 331
Le, B., 346
Le, W., 448
Leaf, P., 118, 268
Leahy, R.L., 136, 137, 202, 215
Leblanc, W., 422
Lebow, J., 241
Leboyer, M., 373
Lechevallier, Z.R., 253
Lecht, S., 300
Le Clus, A., 212
LeCroy, C.W., 472
Ledgerwood, D.M., 280
Ledley, D.R., 133
Lee, H., 67
Lee, J., 67
Lee, B.H., 218
Lee, C., 67, 119
Lee, H.-J., 303
Lee, J.C., 328
Lee, J.F., 274
Lee, J.K.P., 345

Lee, K.S., 129
Lee, L.-C., 405
Lee, N.K., 318
Lee, S., 118, 119, 192
Lee, S.S., 427
Lee, Y., 233
Lee, Y.-A., 381
Lee, Y.-S., 274
Lee-Chiong, T., 494
Lees, A., 448
Leeuw, F., 341
Leff, J., 216
Lehericy, S., 450
Lehmann, D., 442
Lehner-Baumgartner, E., 152, 166
Lehrer, D.S., 372
Le-hua, L., 442
Leiblum, S.R., 330, 331
Leifker, F.R., 383
Leimpeter, A., 445
Leiner, A.S., 131
Leisse, M., 475
Leitten, C.L., 455
Lejuez, C.W., 127, 214, 271, 275, 306, 313
Leland, H., 410
Lemay, R.A., 475
Lemke, M.R., 191
Lemma, P., 276
Lemmens, G.M.D., 216
Lemstra, M., 276
Lende, D.H., 274
Lenk, S., 330
Lenz, B., 266
Lenzenweger, M.F., 295, 299
Lenzi, A., 336
Leon, D.A., 379
Leonard, H., 401
Leonard, M., 437, 444
Leo-Summers, L., 455
Lerch, B., 165
Lerner, J., 209
Lesar, M.D., 284
Leslie, D.L., 455
Lessov Schlagger, C.N., 451
Lester, B.M., 409
Letarte, A., 134
Leung, D.Y.M., 492
LeVay, S., 340, 346
Levensen, J.S., 341
Levenson, J.S., 33
Leventhal, J.M., 308
Leverenz, J.B., 442, 448
Levey, A.I., 447
Levin, M.E., 271
Levin, R., 63, 490
Levine, M.P., 235
Levinson, D., 118
Levit, K.R., 58
Levitan, R.D., 206
Levitt, J.T., 472
Levy, A., 413
Levy, H.L., 403
Levy, K.N., 192
Levy, S., 216
Lewandowski, K.E., 363, 367
Lewinsohn, P.M., 192

Lewis, A.J., 32
Lewis, B.P., 44
Lewis, C.E., 280
Lewis, D.A., 380
Lewis, K.M., 134
Lewis, P., 448
Lewis, T.T., 491, 492
Lewis-Fernandez, R., 155
Leykin, Y., 205, 206
Leyro, T.M., 275, 284
Leza, J.C., 199
Lezak, M.D., 30, 31
Li, A., 354
Li, L., 387
Li, M., 198, 199
Li, N., 266
Li, S.-C., 435
Li, T., 198, 199
Li, X., 212
Li, Y.-M., 448
Lia, B., 481
Liang, W., 449
Liao, K.Y.-H., 201
Libero, D.Z., 172
Libman, S., 229
Lichner, T.K., 472
Lichtenstein, P., 197, 232
Liddle, H.A., 283
Lieb, K., 172, 313, 316
Lieb, R., 122, 155, 218
Liebbrand, R., 159
Lieberman, J.A., 377, 389
Liebowitz, M.R., 122, 158
Liechty, A., 334
Liederman, J., 401
Ligthart, L., 122
Lilenfeld, L.R., 229
Lilienfeld, S.O., 85, 86, 172
Lill, C.M., 448
Lilley, M., 493
Limoge, F., 383
Lin, P.-Y., 233
Lin, W.W., 274
Lincoln, M., 284
Lindberg, L., 43
Lindberg, P., 214
Lindeman, S., 265, 371
Linden, D.E.J., 377
Linden, M., 389
Lindenberger, U., 435
Lindersson, E., 449
Linehan, M., 310, 313, 314
Ling, C.Y.M., 402
Link, C.L., 327
Link, R.J., 465
Links, P.S., 295, 313
Linning, L.M., 127
Linszen, D.H., 386, 387
Linton, S.J., 491
Lip, G.Y.H., 492
Lipira, C.M., 213
Lipsanen, T., 166
Lipsitz, J.D., 495
Lipton, A.M., 448
Lisanby, S.H., 213
Lisper, H.O., 35
Liss, H., 172

Lissner, L., 232
Little, T.D., 318
Littlewood, A., 152
Littlewood, K.J., 386
Litzinger, S., 333
Liu, E., 449, 454
Liu, J.Y., 273
Liu, P., 191, 195
Liu, S.-M., 192
Liu, W., 459
Liu, Y., 266
Livesley, W.J., 123, 304, 306, 307
Livingston, G., 265, 458
Livrea, P., 450
Llorca, P.M., 373
Lloyd-Evans, B., 388
Lobbestael, J., 303
Lobel, M., 129
Lobello, K., 449, 454
Lobmaier, P.P., 281
Lobo, M., 44
Lochman, J.E., 420, 424
Locke, B.Z., 60
Lockhart, D., 331
Loeber, R., 417, 423
Loeber, S., 283
Loewenstein, R.J., 169, 172, 173
Loftus, E.F., 166
Logan, J., 268
Lohr, K.N., 246
Lomax, T.C., 353
Lombart, K.G., 472
London, E.D., 271
Loney, J., 427
Long, N., 421
Longshore, D., 280
Longstreth, W.T., 451
Lonnqvist, J., 195, 197, 206
Lonnqvist, J.K., 381
Looman, J., 348
Looper, K.J., 152, 153
Loosen, P.T., 151
Lopez, O.L., 442, 460
Lopez, S.R., 382
Lopez-Pousa, S., 458
Loranger, A.W., 295, 300
Lord, S.A., 478
Lorentz, W.J., 455
Lorenzetti, V., 198
Lou, K., 126
Lourenco, M.F., 328
Louria, D., 281
Louw, J., 265
Lovasz, M.M., 129
Love, S.R., 410
Low, M.D., 107
Low, N.C., 122
Lozano, G., 133
Lu, P.H., 377
Lu, R.B., 274
Lu, T.E., 274
Lubman, D.I., 273, 318
Luborsky, L., 472
Lucantonio, F., 267
Lucas, C.P., 425, 472
Lucassen, P.L.B.J., 152, 159
Luce, K.H., 237

Lucena, C., 152
Luchsinger, J.A., 450, 451
Lucht, M., 166
Luciano, L., 387
Luckasson, R., 397
Ludolph, A.C., 450
Ludwig, S., 171
Lue, T.F., 331
Lukowitsky, M.R., 299, 306
Lundstrom, M., 437
Lundvig, D., 449
Luoma, J.B., 265
Luoma, S., 265, 371
Luptak, M., 458
Luque, R., 167
Luthar, S.S., 62
Luty, S.E., 229, 315
Lykken, D.T., 296
Lynam, D.R., 295, 299, 300
Lynch, F., 206
Lynch, K.G., 284
Lynch, P., 118
Lynch, T.R., 271
Lyneham, H.J., 133
Lynn, S.J., 173
Lyons, K., 209
Lyons-Ruth, K., 306
Lysaker, P.H., 365, 387

**M**

Ma, H., 446
Ma, N., 267
Ma, S.H., 216
Ma, X., 198, 199
Ma, Y., 268
Maaranen, P., 166
MacCabe, J.H., 372
Maccarrone, M., 262
MacCoon, D.G., 201, 202
MacDonald, D.A., 35
MacDonald, K., 174
Macdonald, P., 234
MacDonald, T., 174
Macfarlane, G., 152
Macgillivray, S., 211
Machado, L.A., 36
Machado, S., 438
Machleidt, W., 475
MacIntosh, H.B., 169
Mack, H.A., 451
Mackay, C.E., 198, 376
MacKenzie, M.J., 428
Mackeprang, T., 377
MacMahon, K.M.A., 492
MacMillan, H., 127
MacMillan, H.L., 308
MacPherson, L., 127
MacQueen, G.M., 206
Madeley, R., 272
Madras, B.K., 282
Madsen, J., 309
Maes, H., 24, 270
Maes, H.H., 232
Maestre, G.E., 452
Maezawa, I., 405
Magarinos, M., 159

Magee, M., 328
Maggi, M., 334, 349, 351
Magnotta, V., 382
Mahan, A.L., 123
Mahendra, N., 458
Maher, M.J., 141
Mahurin, R.K., 198, 199
Mai, F., 149, 151, 153, 154, 155
Maier, S.F., 202
Maier, W., 191
Maina, G., 128
Maisto, S.A., 284, 492
Maitz, E.A., 151
Maj, M., 212, 377, 387
Mak, W.W.S., 402
Maki, P., 381
Malamuth, N.M., 345, 348
Malaspina, D., 365
Malatesta, V.J., 327, 333, 334
Maletsky, B.M., 349, 350
Malhi, G.S., 125, 215, 373
Malka, I.L., 306
Malla, A., 389
Mallinckrodt, B., 201
Malmon, A., 16–17
Malone, K., 195, 206, 216
Malone, P.S., 422
Malouf, R., 453
Mambour, W., 157
Manara, R., 438
Manassis, K., 127
Mandel, S., 151
Mandelkow, E., 448
Mandelkow, E.-M., 448
Manderscheid, R.W., 386
Mandrusiak, M., 217
Manganello, J., 64
Manji, H., 404, 447
Manji, H.K., 200
Manly, J.J., 445
Manly, J.T., 308
Mann, J.J., 195, 206
Mann, K., 268, 283
Mann, S.C., 364
Mannie, Z.N., 200
Mannuzza, S., 122
Mansell, J., 476
Mansell, L.W., 273
Mansell, W., 169
Manson, J.E., 334, 451, 492
Manson, S.M., 451
Manzoni, G.C., 489, 490
Marceau, K., 192
Marchand, A., 134
Marchand, C., 310
Marchesi, C., 181
Marcín, C., 401
Marcolin, M.A., 213
Marcone, R., 398
Marcos, A., 460
Marcus, D.S., 456
Marcus, M., 229
Marcus, M.D., 245
Marcus, S., 122
Marcus, S.C., 478
Marder, K., 445
Margraf, J., 157

Mark, T.L., 58
Markon, K.E., 312
Markowitsch, H.J., 169
Markowitz, J.C., 192, 216, 310, 311, 317, 318
Marks, I., 141
Markus, H.S., 448
Marlatt, A., 283
Marlatt, G.A., 275
Marlow, N.M., 260
Marmai, L., 207
Marman, C., 172
Marmar, C.R., 129
Marneros, A., 371
Marom, S., 45
Maroughka, S., 315
Marra, C., 152
Marrs, J.A., 268
Marsh, G.R., 495
Marshall, E., 134
Marshall, E.J., 448
Marshall, S.A., 110
Marteinsdottir, I., 123
Martel, M.M., 421
Marti, C.N., 237
Martin, A., 154, 155, 410
Martin, C., 406
Martin, J.K., 420
Martin, L.Y., 122
Martin, N.G., 234, 266
Martin, R.L., 157
Martinez, D., 233
Martinez, J., 124, 470–471
Martinez-Aran, A., 199
Martins, S., 417
Marusic, A., 195, 206
Maruyama, S., 274
Marx, R.F., 164
Marziali, E., 459
Mascarenhas, M.N., 401
Maser, J.D., 192
Masheb, R.M., 234, 245
Masho, S.W., 119
Masliah, E., 449
Maslow, A., 33, 34
Mason, J.M., 494
Mason, N.S., 230
Massey, B.W., 386
Massoud, F., 441
Mastantuono, P., 387
Masten, A.S., 63
Masters, K., 229
Masters, K.S., 492
Mastrogianni, A., 192, 195
Masukawa, N.K., 155
Mataix-Cols, D., 142
Mathers, C.D., 401
Matheson, S.L., 377
Mathew, S.J., 124
Mathews, A., 126
Mathews, C.A., 123
Mathis, M., 172
Matson, J.L., 396, 398, 401, 410
Matsui, A., 269, 280
Matsumoto, K., 111
Matsumoto, Y., 353
Mattelaer, J.J., 120

Matthews, S., 121
Matthys, W., 420
Mattis, S., 455
Mattson, S.N., 259, 407
Mattsson, N., 460
Matura, S., 377
Matusiewicz, A.K., 313
Maughan, B., 417, 423, 427
Maulik, P.K., 401
Maurer, K., 366
Mauri, M., 229
Mauri, M.C., 233
Mautone, J.A., 410
May, A.L., 234
May, M., 330
May, M.C., 163
May, R., 33, 35
Mayans, T., 387
Mayberg, H.S., 198, 199
Mayer, P., 266
Mayes, S.D., 401
Mayeux, R., 445, 450, 451
Maynard, C.K., 157
Mazure, C.M., 172
Mazza, J.J., 206
Mazzeo, S.E., 232
McAlonan, G.M., 405
McAnulty, R., 341
McAuliffe, W.E., 284
McBeth, J., 152
McBride-Chang, C., 402
McBurnett, K., 423
McCabe, M.P., 330, 333
McCall, K.M., 331
McCallum, S.E., 267
McCance-Katz, E.F., 281
McCarley, R.W., 377
McCart, M.R., 472
McCarthy, B., 332
McCarthy, M.D., 166
McCarthy-Jones, S., 362
McCaul, M.E., 282
McCeney, M.K., 493
McChesney, C.M., 122
McClean, C.P., 119
McClelland, G.M., 374
McClure, L.A., 448
McClure, M.M., 304
McCormick, W., 442
McCormick, W.C., 460
McCoy, W.K., 420
McCrory, D.C., 494
McCurry, S., 460
McCutcheon, L., 309
McDermott, C., 43
McDermott, B.E., 151
McDonald, D., 332
McDonald, T., 382
McDonough, S.G., 398
McElroy, S.L., 152, 197, 241
McEvoy, J., 377
McEwan, K., 205
McFarland, J., 444
McFarlane, A.C., 112, 125, 170
McFarlane, H.G., 378
McFarlane, J., 64
McGeoch, P.G., 345

McGinn, L., 136, 137
McGlashan, T., 382
McGlashan, T.H., 67, 192, 317, 318, 372
McGoey, K., 425
McGonagle, K.A., 43, 60, 119
McGorry, P.D., 66, 377, 382, 388
McGovern, M.P., 275
McGrath, J., 371, 373
McGrath, J.J., 380
McGrath, R.J., 340, 464
McGue, M., 306
McGuffin, P., 197, 379, 382
McGuinness, B., 453
McGuire, P., 385
McGurk, S.R., 387
McHale, S.M., 234
Mchlum, L., 195, 206
McHugh, R.K., 284
McHugo, G.J., 383
McIntosh, A.M., 198
McIntosh, V.V.W., 229
McKay, J.R., 284
McKenzie, J., 211
McKenzie, J.M., 229, 315
McKenzie, K., 380
McKim, W.A., 255, 270
McKinlay, J.B., 327
McKinney, R., 197
McKnight, P.E., 192
McKusick, D.R., 58
McLaughlin, K.A., 120, 422
McLellan, A.T., 276
McMahon, B., 67
McMahon, C.G., 327
McMahon, P.M., 346
McMahon, R.J., 424
McMain, S.F., 306
McManus, F., 126, 155
McMurran, M., 315
McNair, B.G., 195
McNally, R.J., 129, 167
McNamee, R., 379
McNary, S.W., 173, 174
McNeece, C.A., 274
McNulty, J.K., 28
McNulty, J.L., 82
McParland, M.J., 209
McParland, S., 448
McTigue, O., 373, 374
Mead, D.E., 216
Meaden, A., 386
Meadows, E., 136
Meadows-Oliver, M., 187
Meagher, D., 444
Meagher, D.J., 437, 438
Meana, M., 328, 330
Means, R., 452
Mecocci, P., 442
Medic, G., 386
Medina-Mora, M.E., 118, 192
Mednick, S., 381
Mednick, S.A., 374
Meesters, C., 126
Mehler-Wex, C., 241
Melita, M.A., 475
Meichenbaum, D., 138, 495

Meiland, F.J.M., 458
Meile, I., 382
Meinischmidt, G., 155
Melamed, Y., 312
Meloy, J.R., 345
Meltzer, C.C., 230
Meltzer, H.Y., 386
Melzer, D., 475
Menard, S., 306
Menard, W., 111, 159
Menchón, J.M., 207, 346
Mendez, M.F., 443
Mendoza, C.M., 493
Mennin, D.S., 120
Menon, M., 363
Merchant, M.J., 421
Merckelbach, H., 163, 167, 170
Mercken, M., 453
Merello, M., 442
Merikangas, K.R., 24, 55, 56, 57, 60, 61, 117, 118, 122, 191, 192, 218, 266, 268, 417
Mermelstein, R.J., 272
Merrell, K.W., 425
Merry, S., 211
Mervielde, I., 307
Meschia, J.F., 448
Mesina, C.T., 123
Mesmer, C., 494
Mesquita, B., 5
Mesrobian, H.-G.O., 405
Messer, S.B., 478
Meston, C.M., 331, 333
Metz, D.C., 489
Metzger, C., 327, 330
Metzler, T., 129
Meuret, A.E., 140, 141
Meuser, K.T., 388
Meyer, B., 307
Meyer, P., 61
Meyer, S., 441
Meyerbroker, K., 139
Meyer-Lindenberg, A., 378
Meyers, R.J., 283
Mezulis, A.H., 41, 192
MHS Staff, 384, 425
Micali, N. 142
Micco, J.A., 120, 125
Michael, C.O., 362
Mick, E., 429
Middeldorp, C.M., 197
Middleton, W., 169
Miech, R., 373
Miele, G.M., 284
Miettunen, J., 381
Mihailides, S., 346
Miklowitz, D.J., 195, 203, 216
Mikton, C., 311
Milad, M.R., 123, 124
Miles, J.H., 404
Miletich, R.S., 378
Miller, B.J., 372
Miller, B.L., 445
Miller, C.J., 209, 406
Miller, D.N., 206
Miller, G.A., 379
Miller, J.D., 300

Miller, J.R., 493
Miller, L.E., 94
Miller, M.D., 438
Miller, M.L., 281
Miller, P.M., 260
Miller, T.J., 372
Miller, W.R., 276, 277
Milliken, C.S., 121
Millon, C., 310
Millon, T., 304, 310
Milos, G., 43
Miltenberger, R.G., 86
Minderaa, R., 410
Mineka, S., 126, 128
Minnis, H., 422
Minshew, N.J., 405
Miriam, V., 373
Mistretta, P., 336
Mitchell, A.J., 227, 245, 454
Mitchell, I.J., 347
Mitchell, J., 229
Mitchell, J.E., 234, 241, 244, 246
Mitchell, K.S., 230, 232
Mitchell, M.A., 127
Mitchell, P.B., 216
Mitchell, P.B., 125
Mitchell, S.L., 457
Mitelman, A.R., 389
Mittal, D., 455
Mittal, V., 371
Mitte, K., 134
Mittelman, M.S., 446, 454, 457
Mitter, P.R., 380
Mittleman, M.A., 451, 454
Miyoshi, K., 251
Mizusawa, H., 455
Moayyedi, P., 496
Moch, S., 182
Modell, J.G., 212
Moeller, K., 413
Moergeli, H., 166
Moffitt, T.E., 423
Mogil, C., 412
Mohammadirad, A., 451
Mohan, R., 42
Mohan, T.S.P., 213
Mohapatra, S., 259
Moitra, E., 141
Mojtabai, R., 480
Molina, J.J., 167
Molinder, I., 348
Molla, M.T., 490
Moller, B., 354
Moller, H.-J., 389
Molton, I.R., 493
Monaco, S., 438
Money, R., 386
Monroe, S.M., 201
Monsch, A.U., 456
Montagne, B., 314
Monteagudo, M.J., 161
Montejo, A., 346
Montgomery, G.W., 266
Montiel-Nava, C., 401
Montine, T.J., 441
Montori, V.M., 355
Montoya, E.R., 420

Monuteaux, M.C., 427, 429
Moore, T.M., 28
Moorman, J.E., 490
Moos, R.H., 284, 474
Morakinyo, O., 42
Moran, G., 203
Moran, P., 379
Moran, S., 259
Morant, N., 141
Moreira, E.D., 331, 332
Morer, A., 123
Morey, L.C., 310, 311, 317, 318
Morgan, A.V., 35
Morgenstern, H., 386
Morgentaler, A., 331
Morgenthaler, T., 494
Mori, N., 111, 241
Morimoto, K., 274
Morin, J.W., 341
Moritz, S., 200
Morley, S., 494
Morley, T.E., 203
Moroz, L., 411
Morris, E.P., 120
Morris, J.C., 456
Morris, M., 379
Morris, S., 387
Morris, T.L., 115
Morrison, P.D., 383
Morrison-Bogorad, M., 441
Morrow, C., 127
Morrow, J.A., 272
Mortensen, P.B., 379
Mortimer, J.A., 447, 460
Moschetti, K., 441
Moscovitch, M., 406
Moses, S.N., 379
Moskowitz, A., 170
Moster, A., 348, 350
Mostert, M.P., 479
Moulden, H.M., 351
Moulds, M.L., 139
Mouton, C.P., 334
Moxham, T., 456
Moyer, A., 201
Mrak, R.E., 449
Mrazek, D.A., 492
Muangpaisan, W., 445
Mucci, A., 377, 387
Mueller, C., 166
Mueser, K.T., 383, 387
Muhlnickel, W., 153
Muhtz, C., 200
Mukamal, K.J., 451
Mulder, C.L., 374
Mulder, E., 410
Mulder, R.T., 229, 315
Mulholland, C., 209
Mullan, R.J., 355
Mulle, J.G., 376
Muller, D.J., 191
Muller, J.E., 158
Muller, J.L., 345, 349
Muller, P., 389
Muller, V., 435
Müller-Nordhorn, J., 445
Muller Spahn, F., 389

Munafo, M.R., 198, 274
Mundt, I.A., 344
Munitz, H., 45
Munizza, C., 216, 218
Munoz, F.J., 450
Munoz, J.F., 167
Munoz, R.F., 205, 206
Muntaner, C., 373
Mura, G., 373
Murad, A., 355
Murad, M.H., 241, 355
Murai, T., 377
Muralidharan, A., 309
Muralidharan, P., 268
Murallo, A.V., 336
Muramatsu, S., 454, 457
Murdach, A.D., 151
Muris, P., 126, 170
Murison, R., 493
Murnen, S.K., 229, 235
Murphy, E.R., 378
Murphy, K.C., 381
Murphy, K.J., 450
Murphy, K.R., 427
Murphy, L., 493
Murphy, R., 243
Murphy, S., 345
Murphy, W., 490
Murphy, W.D., 338
Murray, G.K., 381
Murray, H.A., 86
Murray, K.S., 270
Murray, L., 122
Murray, M.J., 401
Murray, R.M., 192, 204, 372, 378,
    379, 380, 383
Murrell, J., 445
Murrie, D.C., 420
Murrough, J.W., 124
Murry, V.M., 418
Muse, K., 155
Musil, R., 389
Myers, B., 265
Myers, J., 44
Myers-Arrazola, L., 206
Mykelbust, C., 172
Mykletun, A., 277, 490, 493
Myrick, A.C., 173

N

Nagel, G., 450
Nagin, D.S., 422
Nahas, Z.H., 213
Nair, M.K.C., 405
Najarian, L.M., 129
Najman, J.M., 203
Nakamura, A., 449
Nakamura, J., 274
Nakamura, K., 111
Nakao, M., 159
Nakatani, E., 142
Nallani, S., 281
Namiki, C., 377
Nanke, A., 155, 158
Nannapaneni, U., 276
Naqvi, N.H., 267

Nardi, A.E., 438
Narita, M., 251
Nasrallah, H.A., 371
Natanegara, F., 331
Nation, M., 44
Naud, S., 280
Navarro, C.S., 405
Nayt, G., 383
Neal, D., 410
Neale, B.M., 419
Neale, M.C., 24, 122, 123, 153, 230,
    232, 270, 304, 305, 306, 381
Neighbors, C., 270
Neitzel, J., 412
Nelson, C.B., 43, 60, 119
Nelson, H.S., 492
Nelson, J.C., 456
Nelson, L.M., 445
Nemeth, A., 403
Ness, L., 162
Ness, S., 404, 447
Nesse, R.M., 204
Nestadt, G., 218
Netley, C., 405
Neto, T.N., 36
Nettles, M.E., 303
Neudorf, C., 276
Neukrug, E., 464
Neul, J.L., 405
Neumann, C.S., 300
Nevels, R.M., 426
New, A., 304
Newberg, A.R., 200
Newcorn, J.H., 271
Newell, J.M., 192
Newlin, D.B., 274
Newman, B., 388
Newman, C.F., 202, 215
Newman, J.P., 305
Newman, S., 119
Newton, A.W., 406
Newton-Howes, G., 304
Ng, J., 235
Nguyen, L., 140
Nguyen, T.T., 259, 407
Nichols, H.R., 348
Nichols, M.P., 44, 45
Nicholson, T.R.J., 155
Nicoletti, M., 203
Nicolo, G., 365
Nicolosi, A., 331
Nicolson, D.J., 494
Nicolson, N.A., 201
Nidich, S.I., 496
Niebling, B.C., 493, 494
Niederberger, C., 331
Niehaus, D.J., 158
Nielsen, S., 227, 245
Nielsen, T., 490
Niemi, L.T., 381
Nieratschker, V., 266
Nievergelt, C.M., 123, 197
Nigg, J.T., 421
Nihira, K., 410
Nijenhuis, E., 162
Nijs, M., 314
Nikolajsen, L., 148

Nikolas, M., 421
Nikolaus, T., 450
Nilsson, P., 454, 457
Nishiyori, A., 274
Nissenson, K., 159
Nitschke, J.B., 123, 198
Niv, Y., 267
Nixon, R.D., 139
Nobis, W.P., 267
Nobre, P.J., 331
Nochlin, D., 442
Nolte, C.H., 445
Noone, S.J., 398
Nopoulos, P., 382, 389
Norcross, J.C., 46, 470, 478, 481
Nordhus, I.H., 493
Norko, M.A., 33
Norre, J., 328
Norris, D., 481
Norris, E., 121
Norris, M.L., 243
Norton, G.R., 118
Norton, J., 455
Norton, P.J., 118
Nothen, M.M., 191
Nowak, G., 403
Noyes, B.B., 458
Noyes, R., 122, 123, 155
Nuechterlein, K.H., 375
Nuerk, H.-C., 413
Nunes, K.P., 327
Nurmagambetov, T.A., 490
Nurnberger, J.I., 285
Nusbaum, M.R., 327, 331, 332
Nusslock, R., 192
Nutzinger, D., 229
Nyberg, L., 435

O

Oakley, D.A., 169
Oakley Browne, M.A., 118, 119
Obeka, N.C., 331
Ober, B.A., 384
Oberg, M., 272
O'Brien, C., 491
O'Brien, C.P., 64, 66, 67
O'Brien, J.T., 441, 445, 448, 452,
    456, 460
O'Brien, R.J., 447, 452
O'Callaghan, E., 373, 374, 379
O'Campo, P., 373
Ochoa, S., 373
Ockene, J.K., 334
O'Connor, E., 206
O'Connor, E.E., 197, 203
O'Connor, M., 238, 444
O'Connor, M.J., 275
O'Dea, J.A., 237
O'Dell, K.R., 492
O'Donnell, M., 170
O'Donnell, M.L., 112
O'Donohue, W.T., 137, 343, 344,
    347, 348, 349, 350, 472, 478
O'Donovan, M., 197, 270
O'Donovan, M.C., 380
Oertel- Knöchel, V., 377

O'Farrell, T.J., 283
Offord, D.R., 119
Ofstedal, M.B., 444
Ogimoto, I., 274
Ogrodniczuk, J.S., 315
Ogston, S., 211
Ogunniyi, A., 445, 452
Oguru, M., 443
Oh, D.-Y., 141, 274
O'Hagan, D.T., 407
O'Hara, M.W., 181
O'Hare, J., 433
Ohlraun, S., 191
Ohrmann, P., 381
Ojeda, N., 367
Oka, H., 107
Oka, N., 443
Okabe, N., 353
Okamoto, M.P., 385
Okeahialam, B.N., 331
Okereke, O.I., 451
Okuda, D., 443
Okuda, M., 192
Olabi, B., 313
Olatunji, B.O., 127
olde Hartman, T.C., 152, 159
Olds, R.J., 192
O'Leary, M., 334
Oleson, F., 150, 152
Olfson, M., 55, 57, 58, 425, 478,
    480
Olivan, B., 152
Oliver, J.S., 280
Ollendick, T.H., 131, 133, 134
Ollinen, T., 265, 371
Olofsson, B., 437
Oltmanns, T.F., 312
Olvera, R.L., 203
O'Malley, S.S., 266
Omar, H., 210
O'Melia, A.M., 241
Ompad, D.C., 274
Onder, Z., 418
Ondersma, S.J., 479
Ondrejcak, T., 448
Ongur, D., 363, 367
Ono, Y., 192
Oosterman, J.M., 455
Oosthuizen, P.P., 474
Opjordsmoen, S., 382
Opler, L.A., 383
Ord, J.S., 151
O'Reardon, J.P., 213
O'Regan, N.A., 444
Orlob, S., 172
Ornbol, E., 150, 152
Oroszi, G., 284
Orr, L., 67
Orrell, M., 458
Orsillo, S.M., 140
Ortega, L.A.G., 194
Orvieto, R., 151
Oryem-Origa, H., 331
Osborn, C.A., 344
Osburn, J.A., 476
Oscar-Berman, M., 269, 345, 446
Osgarby, S.M., 206

O'Shea, R.D., 448
Oshiro, M., 111
Oslin, D.W., 284
Osman, A., 133
Ostrager, B., 340
Ostrom, C., 458
O'Sullivan, K., 444
Oswald, S.H., 422
Otte, C., 200
Otto, M.W., 135
Ottosson, J.-O., 214
Ouimet, A.J., 103
Overland, S., 277, 492, 493
Overstreet, C., 123
Overton, E., 315
Owen, M.J., 380
Owen-Anderson, A., 352, 353
Owens, J., 494
Oxhoj, M.-L., 152
Ozmen, E., 152
Ozturk, E., 169

**P**

Padberg, F., 213
Padma-Nathan, H., 336
Paganin, F., 491
Pagano, M., 318
Pagano, M.E., 159
Page, I.J., 338
Page, M.P., 200
Pagoto, S.L., 214
Pagsberg, A.K., 377
Pagura, J., 120
Pahl, K.M., 131
Paick, J.S., 331
Paik, A., 327, 329
Pain, C., 173
Pais, S., 173
Paisan-Ruiz, C., 448
Paitich, D., 348
Palha, A.P., 328
Pallesen, S., 490, 493
Pallis, E.G., 378
Palmen, J.M.C., 28
Palmer, B.W., 378
Palmes, G.K., 475
Palmisano, B.R., 446
Pampallona, S., 216, 218
Pancer, J., 494
Pang, K.L., 417
Panico, S., 227
Pantelis, C., 199, 377
Panza, F., 451
Panzarella, C., 201
Pao, M., 152, 156
Paparelli, A., 383
Paquin, R., 450
Paracelsus, 11
Paradise, J.E., 171
Parameswaran, S., 386
Pardini, D., 423, 427
Parent, J., 421
Parikh, S.V., 216
Paris, J., 313, 315, 316, 317
Park, A., 274
Park, D.C., 441

Park, D.W., 331
Park, J., 383
Park, K.-M., 383
Parker, A.G., 66
Parker, G.B., 125
Parker, J.S., 474
Parker, L., 408
Parker, R.N., 272
Parks, S.E., 194
Parry, S.W., 445, 460
Parslow, R.A., 136
Parsons, A., 120
PAR Staff, 384
Pasanisi, F., 227
Pasaro, E., 353
Pascual, A., 152
Passamonti, L., 421
Passchier, J., 312
Passingham, D., 376
Passingham, R.E., 29
Passmore, P., 453
Pastor, P.N., 401
Patel, D.R., 413
Patel, S., 406
Patel, V., 44, 203, 407
Patra, J., 259
Patrick, C.J., 306
Patterson, G.R., 421
Patterson, S., 398
Patterson, T.L., 383
Pattison, P., 345
Patton, G., 195, 206
Paula, C.S., 401
Pavlov, I., 36–37, 128
Pawitan, Y., 197
Paxton, S.J., 227
Paykel, E.S., 475
Payne, J., 389
Pedersen, A., 381
Pedersen, C.B., 376
Pedersen, G., 294
Pedersen, M.G., 379
Pedersen, N.L., 232, 447
Pedersen, S.S., 492
Pedro-Carroll, J.L., 67
Peer, J., 387
Pehek, E.A., 378
Peix, M.A., 234
Pelham, W.E., 427
Peltola, P., 166
Peltzer, K., 42
Penas-Lledo, E., 232
Peng, R., 459
Peng, Y., 303
Penn, D.L., 15, 16, 368, 388
Pennay, A., 315
Pennebaker, J.W., 493
Pennell, B.E., 118
Penninx, B.W.J.H., 125
Pennisi, G., 492
Penzein, D.B., 494, 495
Pepler, D., 420
Pepler, D.J., 422
Perdereau, F., 229
Perera, R., 67
Perera, T.D., 213

Peres, K., 453
Perez, L., 451
Perez, M., 142
Perez, V., 207
Perez-Edgar, K., 142
Perez-Stable, E.J., 445
Perilloux, C., 103
Perkins, D.O., 377, 389
Perosa, L.M., 172
Perosa, S.L., 172
Perri, M.G., 206
Perry, A., 413
Perry, E.K., 452
Perry, R., 212
Peruga, A., 272
Perugi, G., 107
Peselow, E.D., 373
Peter, J., 456
Peter, R., 450
Petermann, F., 153, 156
Peters, E.N., 280
Peters, M., 282
Peters, M.L., 163
Peters, R., 149
Petti, R.D., 205
Peterson, A.M., 151
Peterson, B., 328
Peterson, B.S., 421
Peterson, L., 65, 308
Peterson, L.E., 491
Peterson-Badali, M., 355
Petir, G.S., 422
Petretto, D.R., 373
Petry, N.M., 282
Pettifor, J., 167
Pettit, G.S., 28
Petty, C.R., 429
Petty, F., 166
Petukhova, M., 118
Peveler, R., 152
Pfafflin, F., 353, 354
Pfeffer, J., 493
Pfiffner, L.J., 423
Pfohl, B., 311, 315
Pham, T., 129
Phan, K.L., 305
Phelps, C.H., 441
Phelps, D.L., 330
Philipsen, A., 172
Phillips, K.A., 111, 152, 159
Phillips, L.J., 382
Phillips, M., 195, 206
Phillips, M.L., 171, 173
Phillips, M.R., 210
Picardi, A., 207
Pich, V., 129
Picken, A., 374
Pickens, C.L., 266, 274
Pickering, R.P., 300
Pickhardt, M., 448
Piegari, G., 387
Pienaar, E., 282
Pientka, L., 442
Pierson, R., 382
Pierzchala, A., 454, 457
Pies, R., 491
Piet, J., 216

Pietrowsky, R., 241
Pietzcker, A., 389
Pijneneburg, Y.A.L., 438, 445, 448, 454
Pike, J., 212
Pike, K.M., 240
Pilger, F., 157
Pilkonis, P.A., 307
Pillemer, K., 446
Pillmann, F., 371
Pilotto, A., 451
Pina, A.A., 118
Pincus, A.L., 299, 306
Pincus, H.A., 55, 57, 58, 478, 480
Pinderhughes, E.E., 424
Pine, D.S., 103, 123, 142
Pinel, P., 11, 12
Pinhas, L., 243
Pinheiro, A.P., 229
Pini, S., 377
Pinol, J.L., 152
Pinto, A., 317, 318
Piper, M., 380
Piras, F., 363
Pirazzi, V., 262
Pirelli, G., 33
Pirkola, S., 218
Piroli, G.G., 125
Pirwani, N., 413
Pisetsky, E.M., 232
Piskulic, D., 217
Pitkala, K.H., 460
Pitts, A., 131
Pizzagalli, D.A., 198
Plante, D.T., 200–201
Plasa, O., 129
Plassman, B.L., 444
Plat, A., 253
Player, M.S., 491
Plazaola-Castano, J., 119
Plazzi, G., 492
Plessen, K.J., 421
Pletnikov, M.V., 376
Pliszka, S., 203
Plotnicov, K., 229
Plotnicov, K.H., 229
Pluto, C.P., 378
Poetter, C.E., 345
Poettrich, K., 441
Polanczyk, G., 417, 423
Polaschek, D.L.L., 341
Polavieja, P., 207
Pole, N., 129
Polen, M., 206
Polich, J., 256
Polidori, M.C., 442
Polimeni, J., 126
Pollack, L.M., 334
Pollack, M.H., 129, 135
Polley, J., 151
Pollice, C., 229
Polnay, L., 67
Polo, A.J., 426
Polosa, R., 280
Polvikoski, T.M., 445, 460
Pope, H.G., 167, 228

Popli, A.P., 378
Porjesz, B., 285
Porter, R.J., 213
Posada-Villa, J., 118, 192
Posner, S.F., 448
Postma, A., 163
Potocnik, F., 452
Potter, G.G., 444
Potter, J.S., 282
Potuzak, M., 367
Poulin, F., 271
Poupard, A.T., 241
Povada, A.M., 151
Powell, A., 191
Powell, A.J., 174
Powell, L.H., 63
Powell, M.D., 422
Powell, M.P., 405
Powell, R.A., 174
Power, M., 141
Power, P., 385
Power, T.J., 410, 425
Powers, M.B., 275, 284
Powls, J., 341
Poythress, N.G., 172
Pozdol, S.L., 410
Poznansky, O., 345
Prabhu, G.C., 284
Pradhan, K., 268
Praharaj, S.K., 213
Pratt, D., 61
Pratt, H.D., 413
Prause, W., 152, 166
Preisig, M.A., 266
Premkumar, P., 388
Prenoveau, J., 103
Prescott, C.A., 44, 197, 198
President's New Freedom Commission on Mental Health, 15, 59
Price, A.R., 472
Price, B.H., 312
Price, J.C., 230
Price, J.L., 198
Price, J.R., 472
Price, M.R., 492
Price, R.K., 270, 280
Priddle, T.H., 378
Priebe, S., 315
Priest, F., 413
Prince, M., 445, 452
Prineas, R.J., 448
Prinstein, M.J., 77, 311
Prochaska, J.O., 478, 481
Proctor, M., 210–211
Proietti, J.M., 307
Prouty, G., 35
Provencher, M.D., 183
Prudent, V., 365
Pruitt, P., 378
Pruss-Ustun, A., 272
Prvulovic, D., 377
Puckering, C., 422
Pulkkinen, L., 427
Pull, C.B., 118
Punjabi, N.M., 492
Purandare, N., 444
Purcell, R., 66

Purdon, C., 126
Puri, B.K., 377
Purkis, H., 128
Putnam, F.W., 172, 173, 346
Pyke, R., 334
Pynoos, R., 129

**Q**

Qin, J., 167
Qiu, C., 445
Quadflieg, N., 246
Quallich, G.A., 334
Quarantelli, M., 377
Quarantelli, M., 378
Quayle, E., 340, 341
Quertemont, E., 269
Quesenberry, C.P., 331, 451
Quigley, E.M.M., 496
Quigley, H., 452, 456
Quillian, R.E., 495
Quilty, L.C., 312
Quinn, V.P., 331
Quinsey, V.L., 33, 347
Qureshi, A.I., 158

**R**

Rabasca, A.F., 387
Rabinerson, D., 151
Race, E., 444
Rachman, S., 127
Radenbach, K., 199
Radhakrishnan, R., 379
Radloff, S.E., 82
Radtke, R.A., 495
Radu, E.-W., 377
Radwan, J., 378
Raffel, M., 61
Rafii, M., 404, 447
Raggi, A., 492
Raggi, V.L., 142
Raguram, R., 152
Raichle, K.A., 493
Rainforth, M., 496
Rains, J.C., 494, 495
Rajan, U., 378
Rajji, T.K., 455
Ralevski, E., 318
Ram, D., 213
Ram, N., 350
Ramamurthy, S., 330
Raman, G., 450
Ramana, R., 475
Ramenghi, L.A., 405
Ramirez, L., 229, 235
Randall, P., 229, 235
Raniere, D., 201
Ranjith, G., 42
Rao, D., 152
Rao, J.S., 448
Rapee, R., 126
Rapee, R.M., 108, 127, 133, 137
Rapoport, J.L., 377, 382
Rapoport, S.I., 448
Rappley, M.D., 421
Rappuoli, R., 407
Rasinski, K., 15

Rasmussen, B.K., 489, 492
Rasolkhani-Kalhorn, T., 139
Rassin, E., 163
Rastad, C., 214
Rathod, S., 39, 387
Rathus, S., 29
Rauch, S.L., 103, 123, 124
Rauh, E., 155
Rautalinko, E., 35
Raveendran, N.S., 213
Ravenel, M.C., 260
Ravichandran, C., 367
Ray, O., 256
Raymaekers, L., 167
Raymond, F.L., 403
Rayner, L., 211
Rea, M.S., 492
Reagan, L.P., 125
Reagu, S., 313
Real, E., 346
Reas, D.L., 227
Reba, I., 227
Rebani, Y., 365
Rebellon, C.J., 262
Reblin, M., 62
Reck, A., 152
Rector, N.A., 103
Reddy, J., 374
Reddy, P.H., 452
Reese, E.A., 448
Regalia, P.A., 274
Regehr, C., 131
Regier, D.A., 60
Rehm, J., 259
Rehm, R., 203
Rehn, N., 274
Reich, A., 445
Reich, D.B., 300, 317
Reich, T., 285
Reichart, T., 318
Reichborn-Kjennerud, T., 122, 153, 227, 232, 246, 270, 304, 305, 306
Reichow, B., 408, 412
Reid, F.D., 406
Reid, I., 82, 211
Reid, M.J., 422
Reid, R., 425, 426
Reid, R.C., 345
Reid, V., 187
Reilly-Harrington, N.A., 202, 215
Reiman, E.M., 441
Reine, G., 383
Reiner, K., 495
Reiss, J.P., 126
Reiss, N.S., 217
Reitan, R.M., 384
Reith, W., 199
Reitz, C., 452
Rellini, A.H., 324
Remick, R.A., 197
Remington, G., 365, 378
Remschmidt, H., 371, 425
Rescorla, L.A., 425
Ressler, K.J., 123
Retzlaff, P., Stoner, J., 277
Reuben, C.A., 401

Reus, V.I., 123
Reutens, D.C., 377
Revelle, W., 209
Revesz, T., 448
Rexrode, K.M., 492
Reyes-Rodriguez, M.L., 201
Reynolds, C.R., 425
Reynolds, E.K., 127
Reynolds, K., 491
Rezazadeh, J., 404
Rhee, H., 492
Ribeiro, W., 445
Ricca, V., 234
Rice, D.D., 346
Rice, M.E., 345, 349
Rice, M.L., 413
Richards, C.S., 206
Richards, D., 195, 218
Richards, R., 355
Richardson, D., 331
Richmond, K., 354
Richter, A., 283
Ricker, D., 379
Riecher-Rossler, A., 377
Riedel, M., 389
Rief, W., 153, 154, 155, 156, 157, 158, 159
Riekse, R.G., 442
Riel-Belmann, B., 259
Riemann, D., 200
Riemer, S., 153
Riepe, M., 450
Rietschel, M., 191
Rifkin, A., 166
Rigaud, D., 241
Rigotti, N.A., 259
Rihmer, Z., 195, 206
Riley, B., 24, 270, 382
Riley, E.P., 259, 407
Rinck, M., 126
Rind, B., 479
Ringham, R., 229
Rinne, T., 312, 343
Rios, R., 405
Rippon, G., 449, 454
Risch, N., 24
Risk, N.K., 270, 280
Ritchie, K., 453
Ritsner, M.S., 372
Ritter, L., 473
Rivera-Medina, C.L., 201
Rivet, T.T., 401
Rizvi, S., 216
Rizvi, S.L., 238, 240
Roane, B.M., 492
Robbins, M.S., 283
Robbins, T.W., 420, 442
Roberts, C., 67
Roberts, S.W., 398
Roberts, T.-A., 230
Roberts, T.J., 273
Robertson, E., 187
Robertson, G.J., 384, 409–410
Robertson, H., 315
Robertson, T.A., 282
Robichaud, M., 119
Robins, L.N., 60, 61

Robinson, D.L., 267
Robinson, D.S., 493
Robinson, G.E., 192
Robinson, J., 271
Robinson, L., 458
Robinson, M.J., 124
Robinson, O.J., 123
Robinson, S., 399, 413
Robinson, S.J., 410
Roca, M., 153
Rockwell, R., 237
Rodenberg, C., 336
Rodgers, B., 136
Rodgers, W.L., 444
Rodriguez-Murillo, L., 376
Roecklein, K.A., 181
Roehrs, T., 491
Roemer, L., 140
Roerecke, M., 259
Roerig, J., 241
Roesch, S., 234
Roesch, S.C., 378
Roe-Sepowitz, D.E., 131
Rogers, C., 33, 34, 35
Rogers, G., 456
Rogers, S.J., 411
Rogne, T., 152
Rogosch, F.A., 269, 308
Rohan, K.J., 181
Rohde, L.A., 417, 423, 427
Rohrer, J.D., 445, 448, 454
Roll, J.M., 283
Roll, S., 344, 445
Rolland, Y., 453
Rollnick, S., 277
Romanos, M., 241
Romer, D., 15
Romer, G., 354
Romera, I., 207
Romero, C., 334
Romero, E.G., 422
Romero Lauro, L.J., 233
Rongve, A., 443
Ronnebeck, C., 330
Ronning, O.M., 444
Root, T.L., 232
Roozen, H.G., 283
Ropacki, S.A., 444
Ropers, H.H., 404
Rorschach, H., 85
Rose, D.T., 201
Rose, J.S., 272
Rose, R.J., 427
Rose, S., 182
Rosen, A., 447
Rosen, J.L., 372
Rosen, R., 333
Rosen, R.C., 326, 327, 333
Rosenbaum, F., 259
Rosenbaum, J.F., 125
Rosenberg, E., 478
Rosenberg, I.H., 450
Rosendorf, K.A., 491
Rosenfeld, J.A., 405
Rosenfield, D., 141
Rosengren, A., 492, 495
Rosenhan, D.L., 380

Rosenmann, A., 342
Rosenthal, M.Z., 271
Rosenthal, R., 472
Roser, P., 208
Roses, A.D., 445
Rosner, B.A., 451
Rosner, R., 473
Rosoklija, G., 213
Rosquist, P., 406
Ross, C.A., 172, 174
Ross, S.E., 493, 494
Rossberg, J.I., 386
Rosseel, Y., 208
Rossi, A., 377
Rossignol, D.A., 403
Rossler, W., 152
Rossnagel, K., 445
Roth, J.H., 128
Roth, T., 491
Roth, W.T., 126, 140
Rothbaum, B.O., 131
Rotheram-Borus, M.J., 479
Rothlisberger, M., 377
Rothman, M.R., 457
Rothschild, L., 295
Rothwell, P.M., 448
Rotondo, A., 229, 234
Rouget, B.W., 206
Rouillon, F., 214
Rounsaville, B.J., 266, 472
Rousseau, N., 458
Rousseau, R., 493
Roussos, P., 378
Rovet, J., 405
Rowan, E.N., 445, 460
Rowan, M.J., 448
Rowe, C.C., 441
Rowe, R., 418, 423, 427
Rowland, D., 327, 334
Rowles, B.M., 410
Rowse, G., 362
Roy-Byrne, P., 118
Roysamb, E., 122, 153, 232, 270, 304, 305, 306
Ruan, W.J., 300
Rubenstone, E., 272
Rubia, K., 421
Rubin, D., 171
Rubino, I.A., 363
Rubio-Stupek, M., 119
Ruble, A.E., 229
Ruchkin, V., 418
Rudd, M.D., 217
Rudolph, A.S., 449
Rudolph, J., 436
Rufer, M., 166
Ruggiero, K.J., 115
Ruitenberg, A., 451
Ruiz, M.A., 172
Ruiz-Perez, I., 119
Rund, B.R., 382
Runge, J., 140
Ruocco, A.C., 306
Rupper, R., 458
Rusanen, M., 451
Rusch, D., 253
Ruscio, A.M., 118

Rush, A.J., 38, 192
Rush, B., 12
Russell, D., 328
Russell, J.M., 124, 210, 217
Russell, P., 405
Rustenbach, S.J., 241
Ruther, E., 39
Rutherford, L., 243
Rutledge, 491
Rutter, M., 398
Rutz, W., 195, 206
Ruzickova, M., 189
Ryan, D.J., 444
Ryan, G., 346
Ryan, J.M., 449, 454
Ryan, K., 58
Ryan, N.D., 203
Ryan, S.M., 273
Ryan, T.G., 399, 413
Ryback, R., 350
Ryder, A.G., 212, 303
Rynes, K.N., 202

**S**

Saad, C.S., 478
Saba, P., 281
Sachdev, P., 452
Sachdev, P.S., 458
Sachs, C., 64
Sachs, G.A., 457
Sack, R.L., 492
Sackeim, H.A., 213
Sadeh, N., 297
Sadock, B.J., 124, 443, 444
Sadock, V.A., 124, 443, 444
Sadovnick, A.D., 197
Sadowski, C.M., 172
Saeed, N., 377
Saewyc, E., 352
Safir, M.P., 342
Safren, S.A., 135, 209
Sagar, R., 192
Saha, S., 371, 373
Saha, T.D., 300
Sahakian, B.J., 120, 420
Sahin, A.R., 105
Saido, T.C., 454, 457
Saigh, P.A., 129
Saini, M., 131
Sajatovic, M., 212
Sajeev, G., 378
Sakata, R., 274
Saksa, J.R., 386
Salazar-Fraile, J., 199
Salerno, J.W., 496
Salerno, S., 14
Sales, B.D., 347
Saligan, L.N., 182
Salinas, C.F., 260
Salisbury, D.F., 377
Salo, P., 493
Salow, M., 436
Salsman, N., 472
Salthouse, T., 435
Salvatore, G., 365
Salvatori, S., 152

Salzinger, K., 152
Sambataro, F., 305
Samieri, C., 453
Sample, L.L., 350
Sampson, E.L., 458
Sampson, N.A., 129, 192, 422, 480
Samudra, P.G., 259
Samuel, D.B., 300, 310, 311
Sanchez-Lacay, A., 158
Sander, C., 158
Sanders, A.R., 376
Sanders, M., 446
Sandin, B., 133
Sandler, I.N., 66
Sandner, C., 135
Sanislow, C.A., 310, 311, 317, 318
Sanjo, N., 455
Sankhyan, N., 156
Santamato, A., 451
Santarelli, L., 213
Santos, C.L.D., 450
Santos, M., 162
Santucci, F., 387
Saperia, J., 210
Sar, V., 166, 169
Saraste, H., 495
Sareen, J., 120, 126, 271
Sarisoy, G., 105
Sarmah, S., 268
Sarmeinto, G., 387
Sartor, C.E., 123
Sartorius, N., 195, 389
Sasagawa, S., 192
Sassaroli, S., 233
Sato, S., 200
Sato, T., 353
Sattler, J.M., 82, 409
Saunders, J.B., 282
Saunders, K., 210
Savill, M., 318
Savla, G.N., 378
Sawa, A., 376
Sawyer, A.T., 141
Saxena, S., 401
Scaer, R.C., 168
Scanlan, J.M., 455
Scepkowski, L.A., 331
Schaefer, C.E., 473
Schaefer, G.A., 344
Schaffer, M., 348, 350
Schaffrick, C., 96
Schalet, B.D., 209
Schalken, H.F.A., 173
Schalock, R.L., 396, 397
Scharf, B., 213
Schedlowski, M., 330
Scheinberg, D.A., 448
Schell, E., 495
Schellenberg, G.D., 460
Scheltens, P., 438
Schempf, A.H., 405
Schennach, R., 389
Schepers, J.P., 446
Scherag, S., 232
Scherder, E.J., 455
Scherk, H., 199

Schermer, C.R., 257
Schettler, P.J., 192
Schiavo, R.S., 231
Schieve, L.A., 401
Schiffman, J., 381, 382
Schiltenwolf, M., 154
Schimer, M.R., 446
Schlaepfer, T.E., 213
Schlesinger, C., 282
Schlosser, R.W., 411
Schmahl, C., 169, 172
Schmeidler, J., 172
Schmid, M., 505
Schmidt, F., 271
Schmidt, N.B., 127, 129, 315
Schmidt, U., 234
Schmidtke, A., 195, 206
Schmitt, R., 134
Schmitz, C., 28
Schmitz, M., 417
Schneider, B., 210
Schneider, H., 419
Schneider, R., 166
Schneider, R.B., 345
Schneider, R.H., 496
Schneider, W., 166
Schneider-Axmann, T., 199
Schneiderman, C.T., 472
Schneiderman, N., 45
Schneier, F.R., 158
Schniering, C.A., 127
Schobel, S.A., 123
Schoeman, R., 389
Schoenbaum, G., 267
Schoenfeld, P.S., 496
Schollenberger, J., 64
Schols, J.M.G.A., 457
Schonknecht, P., 364
Schopler, E., 410
Schork, N.J., 123, 385
Schott, B.H., 198
Schouten, E., 126
Schrag, A., 146
Schreier, H., 354
Schroder, C.M., 214
Schroder, J., 364, 381
Schroeder, J.H., 420
Schroeder, L.L., 62
Schroeder, V., 259, 272
Schruers, K.R., 120
Schuckit, M.A., 266, 281, 285
Schulsinger, F., 381
Schulte, I.E., 153, 156
Schulte, T., 405
Schultze-Lutter, F., 66
Schulz, K.P., 271
Schulze, B., 380
Schulze, U.M., 241
Schumann, C., 405
Schurhoff, F., 373
Schutter, D.J.L.G., 420
Schwab, S.G., 41, 270
Schwab-Stone, M., 418
Schwab-Stone, M.E., 425
Schwalbe, C.S., 428
Schwartz, A.C., 129
Schwartz, R.C., 44, 45

Schwartz, R.H., 281
Schwartz, S.J., 270
Schwegler, A.F., 129
Schwitzer, A., 227
Scott, A., 41, 270
Scott, C., 276
Scott, J., 216
Scotti, J.R., 115
Scott-Sheldon, L.A.J., 284
Scullion, A., 458
Seagraves, R.T., 328
Seaton-Smith, K.T., 153
Secnik, K., 429
Seedat, S., 158, 166
Seelaar, 445, 448, 453
Seeley, J., 206
Seeley, J.R., 192
Seeman, P., 378
Seeringer, A., 327, 330
Seewald, K., 374
Seftel, A., 331
Seftel, A.D., 334
Segal, K., 165
Segal, N.L., 155
Segal, S.P., 473
Segal, Z., 206
Segal, Z.V., 206
Segarra, R., 367
Segel, J., 378
Seghers, J.P., 379
Segovia, S., 353
Segraves, R.T., 334, 336
Segrin, C., 202
Segrin, C.G., 202
Seidenbecher, C.I., 198
Seidler, K.-P., 475
Seidler-Brandler, U., 39
Seidman, L.J., 274, 375
Seipp, C.M., 422
Seitz, D., 444
Seivewright, H., 315
Sekiyama, K., 449
Seligman, D.A., 472
Seligman, M.E.P., 64, 66, 67, 202
Selim, O., 334
Selva-Vera, G., 199
Selya, A.S., 272
Selye, H., 488
Semkovska, M., 383
Seripa, D., 451
Seritan, A.L., 153, 155
Serrano-Blanco, A., 153
Sethi, M., 166
Seto, M.C., 345, 346, 347, 348, 349
Sexton, C., 198
Sexton, M., 129
Seymour, A., 280
Shabsigh, R., 328, 331
Shadmehri, A.A., 404
Shaffer, D., 195, 206, 425
Shaffer, L.G., 405
Shaffer, M.L., 457
Shah, A., 452
Shah, J., 366
Shah, N.R., 186
Shahabi, L., 63

Shaham, Y., 266, 267, 274
Sham, P., 215
Shamasundar, C., 35
Shan, J., 331
Shane, H.C., 411
Shankman, S.A., 182
Shannon, C., 209
Shao, H., 218
Shapira, J.S., 443
Shapiro, E.S., 412
Sharkey, K.M., 492
Sharma, R.C., 156
Sharma, S.G., 135
Sharman, M.A., 450
Sharpe, M., 159
Sharpley, M., 380
Sharps, P., 64
Shaw, B.F., 38
Shaw, D.S., 63, 422
Shaw, D.W.W., 405
Shaw, H., 229, 235, 237
Shaw, R.J., 151
Shaywitz, B.A., 401, 404, 406
Shaywitz, S.E., 401, 404, 406
Shcherbatykh, I., 451
Shea, M.T., 127, 310, 311, 318
Shea, S., 451
Shea, T., 317
Shear, M.K., 141
Shearer, S.L., 138
Sheets, E.S., 309
Sheidow, A.J., 416
Shek, D.T., 418
Shekhar, A., 124
Shekhtman, T., 197
Shelef, K., 216
Shelton, R.C., 212, 215, 217
Shemansky, W.J., 379
Shemtov, R., 186
Shen, H., 269
Shen, J., 445
Shen-Shan, Z., 442
Shenton, M.E., 377
Shepherd, A.M., 377
Sher, K.J., 274, 291, 295, 300, 303
Sher, L., 210
Sheridan, M.J., 281
Sherman, S.L., 404
Sherrington, J.M., 218
Sherry, A., 129
Sherry, D.L., 235
Sherry, S.B., 235
Sherwood, A., 496
Sherzai, A., 451
Shi, Z., 306
Shibata, A., 274
Shiels, K., 425
Shifren, J., 336
Shigeta, M., 442
Shih, R.A., 122, 375
Shiner, R.L., 303
Shinfuku, N., 129
Shing, Y.L., 435
Shipley, S.L., 476
Shippam, A., 355
Shirai, M., 331
Shirtcliff, E.A., 192

Shochet, I.M., 206
Shoemaker, M., 396, 398
Shuldham, C., 496
Shuler, J.F., 405
Shull, R.L., 37
Shulman, J.M., 445
Shulman, K.I., 455
Shuttleworth-Edwards, A.B., 82
Shyn, S.I., 197
Sibitz, I., 374
Siddiqui, M., 451
Siebenmorgan, M., 362
Siega-Riz, A., 227
Siegel, S.D., 45
Siemers, E., 441
Sierra, M., 166, 167, 168, 169, 171, 173
Sieswerda, S., 303
Siev, J., 141
Siever, L.J., 304
Sigal, L.H., 156
Signorini, A., 227
Silber, T.J., 152, 153, 156, 281
Silberman, Y., 267
Siliquini, R., 276
Silk, J.S., 203
Silk, K.R., 317
Sills, T., 333
Silove, D., 112, 170
Silva, A.C., 438
Silverman, M., 61, 195, 206
Silverman, M.H., 300
Silverman, W., 404, 447
Silverman, W.K., 118, 133
Silverstein, S.M., 389
Sim, F., 422
Sim, L.A., 241
Simeon, D., 165, 169, 172
Simoes, N.A., 120, 125
Simon, G.E., 152
Simon, N.M., 135
Simonelli, C., 330
Simons, A.D., 327, 331
Simons, J.S., 327
Simons, R.L., 418
Simonsen, E., 374, 382
Simpson, H.B., 141
Simpson, I., 379
Simpson, K., 442
Sindahl, P., 211
Singh, A.K., 411
Singh, D., 352, 353, 354
Singh, M.A.F., 458
Siniscalchi, J.M., 152
Sinnott-Armstrong, W.P., 296
Sirotnak, A.P., 406
Siscovick, D.S., 451
Sisemore, T.A., 138
Sivertsen, B., 492, 493
Skarf, L.M., 436
Skillecorn, A., 215
Skinner, B., 327
Skodol, A.E., 291, 310, 311, 315, 317
Skogen, J.C., 277
Skoog, I., 446
Slade, M., 388
Slane, J.D., 233

Slaney, C., 189
Slate, E.H., 260
Slater, A., 229
Slattery, T., 481
Slesinger, D., 157
Sloane, R., 61
Slopen, N., 15
Small, G., 456
Small, G.W., 447
Small, S.A., 123
Smedley, A., 42, 45
Smedley, B.D., 42, 45
Smit, J.H., 125
Smith, A., 421
Smith, B.J., 282
Smith, C., 328
Smith, D., 218
Smith, E.O., 274
Smith, J.E., 283
Smith, J.F., 331
Smith, K., 133
Smith, K.C., 269
Smith, L.S., 131
Smith, M., 215
Smith, M.J., 377
Smith, P.J., 453
Smith, S., 118, 172
Smith, S.E., 61, 68, 194
Smith, S.M., 173, 300
Smith, T.L., 284
Smith, V., 374
Smitherman, T.A., 491
Smith-Gamble, V., 445
Smolak, L., 229
Smolen, A., 306
Smolka, M.N., 441
Smolla, N., 410
Smoller, J.W., 122, 197
Smyth, J.M., 493
Snidman, N., 125
Sno, H.N., 173
Snow, J., 55
Snowden, L.R., 480
Snowden, R.J., 346
Snowling, M.J., 401
Snyder, C.R., 62
Snyder, J., 421
Soares, J.C., 203
Soares-Weiser, K., 206
Sobradiel, N., 152
Sobue, I., 274
Sohlman, B., 218
Solai, L.K., 438
Solarino, B., 259
Sole, M., 450
Solfrizzi, V., 451
Solhkhah, R., 273
Soloff, P.H., 230
Solomon, D.A., 192
Solomon, Z., 129
Solso, S., 405
Soltan, G., 334
Somers, J.M., 373
Sommers-Flanagan, J.S., 470
Sommers-Flanagan, R., 470
Song, S., 379
Sonino, N., 157

Sorce, J.F., 411
Sorensen, H., 381
Sorocco, K.H., 478
Sorvillo, F., 441
Sothwick, S.M., 172
Southwick, S.M., 62
Souza, J., 134
Soylu, L., 331
Spackman, M., 345
Spalletta, G., 363
Spanagel, R., 275, 281
Sparks, B.-F., 405
Sparle, K.C., 150, 152
Sparrow, S.S., 410
Speckens, A.E., 152, 159
Spector, A., 458
Spector, A.Z., 203
Spector, T.D., 327
Speilmans, G.I., 492
Spence, S.H., 130
Spencer, K., 387
Spencer, T., 429
Sperling, R.A., 441
Sperry, L., 412
Spettigue, W., 233
Spiegel, D., 169, 173
Spiegelman, D., 492
Spielman, A.J., 494
Spiliotacopoulos, D., 388
Spillantini, M.G., 448
Spillers, C.S., 35
Spilt, J.L., 423
Spindler, A., 43
Spinelli, M.G., 371, 373
Spinhoven, P., 206
Spinner, J., 122
Spira, E.G., 417
Spitzer, C., 166, 172, 238
Spitzer, G., 213
Spitzer, R.L., 80, 157, 207
Spitzl, S.P., 152, 166
Spitznagel, E.L., 270
Spivak, I., 330
Sprague, J., 297
Spreat, S., 396
Sprouse, J., 201
Sprung, L.J., 304
Sreenath, S., 441
Sripada, C.S., 309
Staats, T.E., 151
Staggers, F., 496
Stahl, J., 448
Staiger, P.K., 271
Stallard, P., 121
Stallings, M.C., 306
Stalnaker, T.A., 267
Stampfer, M.J., 492, 493
Stang, P.E., 118
Stanghellini, G., 365
Stanley, B., 303, 304
Starcevic, V., 126, 155
Stargardt, T., 386
Staring, A.B.P., 374
Stark, C.E.L., 124
Starkstein, S.E., 442
Starling, S.P., 406
Startup, M., 363

Stathapoulou, G., 275, 284
Stautz, K., 271
Stawicki, J.A., 421
Stead, L.F., 275
Steele, J.D., 195
Steer, R.A., 208, 209
Steffen, K., 241
Steffens, D.C., 444
Stegbauer, T., 282
Stein, D.J., 118, 134, 158, 169
Stein, J., 401
Stein, J.B., 282
Stein, M.B., 120, 123, 166
Steinbart, E., 448
Steinberg, A.M., 129
Steiner, J., 198
Steiner, M., 127
Steinhausen, H.-C., 246
Steinhauser, C., 350
Steketee, G., 141
Stenvall, M., 437
Stephen, M., 77
Steptoe, A., 492, 495
Stern, Y., 441, 452, 453
Sternfeld, B., 331
Stevens, D.E., 266
Stewart, A.J., 43
Stewart, D., 405
Stewart, D.E., 187
Stewart, J.T., 345
Stewart, M., 231
Stewart, M.E., 94
Stewart, R., 380, 452
Stewart, R.E., 139
Stewart, S.H., 120, 133
Stewart-Brown, S., 67
St-Hillaire, A., 379
Stice, E., 229, 235, 237, 238, 240
Stieglitz, R.D., 166
Stilo, S.A., 379
Stingl, J., 327, 330
Stinnett, R.D., 343
Stinson, F.S., 118, 300
Stinson, J.D., 347
Stip, E., 383
Stippich, C., 364
Stirling, J., 151
Stirman, S.W., 215
Stockman, D.J., 155
Stockwell, T., 274
Stoffers, J.M., 309, 316
Stolar, M., 266
Stolberg, R.A., 210
Stolpmann, G., 345, 349
Stone, D., 229
Stone, J., 155
Stone, W.L., 410
Stone, W.S., 378
Stone-Manista, K., 281
St-Onge, B., 33
Stout, R.G., 272
Stout, R.L., 159, 284, 317, 318
Stovner, L.J., 489, 490
Stowe, G.N., 282
Stowe, S., 229
Straebler, S., 243

Strandberg, T.E., 460
Stranges, E., 58
Strassberg, D.S., 340, 345
Stratford, T.R., 232
Strathdee, S.A., 274
Stratta, P., 377
Strayhorn, G., 331, 332
Strickland, H., 318
Strober, M., 229, 234
Strom, S.C., 403
Stronks, S., 406
Strosahl, K.D., 190, 194, 195, 205, 217, 470
Stroud, C.B., 201
Stroup, A.L., 386
Stuart, S., 155
Stuckey, B., 327
Sturmey, P., 214
Suarez-Torres, A., 201
Subotnik, K.L., 375
Subramaniam, P., 457
Suchy, Y., 340, 345
Sudarov, A., 405
Sue, S., 478
Suenens, L.J.C., 71
Sugar, C.A., 375
Suh, G.-H., 452
Suicide Prevention Resource Center, 61, 68
Sullivan, F., 211
Sullivan, M.C., 386
Sullivan, M.M., 203
Sullivan, P.F., 197, 270, 281, 295
Sumathipala, A., 158
Sundgot-Borgen, J., 229
Sundram, S., 217
Sung, J., 489
Surtees, P.G., 475
Suryani, L.K., 77
Suslow, T., 381
Sutcliffe, P.A., 355
Suvak, M.K., 141
Suvisaari, J.M., 381
Suzuki, K., 111
Suzuki, T., 251
Sved, A.F., 271
Svenningsson, P., 443
Svensson, P., 148
Svirko, E., 229
Svrakic, D.M., 376
Svrakic, N.M., 376
Swaab, H., 352
Swan, G.E., 451
Swanson, J.M., 268
Swanson, M.E., 404
Swanson, S.A., 191, 417
Swendeman, D., 479
Swendsen, J., 191, 417
Swick, T., 494
Swinbourne, J.M., 120
Swogger, M.T., 271
Symonds, D., 472
Sytema, S., 410
Szalai, J.P., 460
Szatmari, P., 398
Szeimies, A.-K., 96

Szobot, C., 417
Szoke, A., 373

T

T., Hart, J., 139
Tabares-Seisdedos, R., 199
Taber, K.H., 153, 155
Tachibana, H., 443
Tagliapietra, M., 438
Tahiri, S.M., 331
Takagai, S., 111
Takahashi, D.Y., 151
Takahashi, Y., 195, 206
Takei, N., 111
Takeshita, T., 274
Talley, C.L., 373
Talley, N.J., 496
Talonneau, I., 241
Tambi, M.I.I.M., 331
Tanabe, H., 445
Tandon, N., 366
Tandon, R., 366, 371
Tang, M.-X., 451
Tanielian, T., 478
Tanner, C.M., 445
Tanskanen, A., 166, 385
Tanskanen, P., 381
Tantam, D., 413
Tanzi, R.E., 448
Tarbox, S.I., 369
Targonski, P.V., 451
Tarrier, N., 112, 374
Tarsitani, L., 157
Tarumi, S., 120
Tasca, D., 492
Taskin, O., 152
Tasse, M.J., 396
Tassniyom, K., 443
Tassone, F., 405
Tata, P., 315
Tatsioni, A., 450
Tatum, J.I., 492
Taussig, H.N., 308
Taylor, B., 259
Taylor, B.A., 97
Taylor, C.B., 237
Taylor, D.J., 492
Taylor, E., 421
Taylor, J.D., 62
Taylor, K.I., 456
Taylor, L., 110
Taylor, M., 373
Taylor, P.J., 313
Taylor, S., 123, 133, 139
Taylor, S.E., 44
Teasdale, J.D., 216
Tegeler, J., 389
Tejero, P., 161
Telang, F., 268, 274
Telch, C.F., 238, 240
Telch, M.J., 315
Tellegen, A., 82
Tempalski, B., 274
Templeman, T.L., 343
Ten, L., 442
Teng, E., 443

ten Have, M.L., 118
Tenhula, W., 387
Tenhula, W.N., 386
Tensfeldt, T., 441
Teper, E.L., 460
Teplin, L.A., 374, 422
Terada, S., 353
Terburg, D., 420
ter Kuile, M.M., 334
Tessner, K.D., 371
Thaker, G.K., 378
Thapar, A., 380, 421
Tharyan, P., 213
Thase, M.E., 200
Thayer, J.F., 153
Theberge, F., 266, 274
Theircelin, N., 253
Theorell, T., 495
Theran, S.A., 230
Thibaut, F., 349
Thies, B., 441
Thissen, D., 396
Tholaka, P., 456
Thoma, R.J., 379
Thoma, S., 482
Thomann, K., 163
Thomann, P.A., 305
Thomas, A.J., 445, 460
Thomas, E., 473
Thomas, J.J., 226, 229
Thomas, K., 376
Thomas, L., 481
Thomas, M., 158
Thomas, R., 67
Thomas, Y.F., 273
Thommessen, B., 444
Thompson, C., 257
Thompson, L., 422
Thompson, L.W., 459
Thompson, P.M., 377
Thompson, S.J., 166
Thomson, A.D., 448
Thoresen, C.E., 63
Thorn, P., 328
Thornicroft, G., 195
Thornton, D., 344
Thornton, L., 229, 232, 234
Thornton, L.M., 229, 232
Thrasher, S., 141
Thummel, E.C., 354
Thyer, B.A., 131
Tibaldi, G., 216, 218
Tibi, L., 495
Tickle-Degnen, L., 446
Tiegreen, J., 362
Tienari, P., 381
Tierney, M.C., 460
Tiggeman, M., 229
Tiggemann, M., 245
Tighe, S., 444
Tija, J., 457
Tillfors M., 122
Tilvis, R.S., 460
Timko, C., 284
Timmer, B., 159
Timmons, S., 444
Tipsord, J.M., 422

Tirelli, E., 269
Tishler, C.L., 217
Tiwari, H.K., 448
Tjernberg, L.O., 454, 457
To-A-Nan, R., 282
Toda, K., 443
Todd, C., 149
Todorov, A.A., 274
Toft, T., 150, 152
Toga, A.W., 377, 456
Tohen, M., 205, 218, 377
Tolin, D.F., 120
Tollefson, G.D., 377
Tomasi, D., 268, 274
Tomenson, B., 149, 152
Tomita, M., 455
Tomko, R.L., 291, 295, 297, 300, 303
Toneatto, T., 140
Toni, C., 107
Tonigan, J.S., 284, 284
Tonna, M., 181
Torem, M., 172
Torgersen, S., 295
Toriello, H.V., 407
Toro, J., 123
Torrance, H., 280
Torrent, C., 199
Torres, F., 379
Torres, R., 455
Tough, S.C., 275
Toulopoulou, T., 111
Toupin, J., 33
Touyz, S.W., 120
Town, J.M., 313
Tozzi, F., 229
Trace, S.E., 232
Tracy, D.K., 372
Tramontina, S., 417
Tranel, D., 91
Traylor, A., 270
Treasaden, I.H., 377
Treasure, J., 229, 232, 234
Treffert, D.A., 398
Treit, D., 124
Tremblay, J., 197
Treuer, T., 205, 218
Triebwasser, J., 304
Trimble, M.R., 146
Trivedi, A., 448
Trockel, M.T., 237
Troisi, A., 347
Tromovitch, P., 479
Tronick, E.Z., 409
Trost, A., 229, 235
Trull, T.J., 77, 85, 96, 291, 295, 297, 299, 300, 302, 303, 311
Truman, B.I., 492
Trzepacz, P.T., 438, 444, 455
Tsai, J.L., 90
Tsai, P.-C., 201
Tse, W.S., 202
Tseng, W., 91, 92
Tseng, W.-S., 42, 43, 91, 167
Tsokos, M., 259
Tsuang, D., 442
Tsuang, D.W., 375, 448
Tsuang, M.T., 122, 375, 381

Tsuchiya, K.J., 111, 449
Tsuno, N., 442
Tuerk, E.H., 472
Tuke, W., 12
Tull, M.T., 210, 306
Turan, M.K., 411
Turecki, G., 195
Turkington, D., 39, 387
Turner, C., 142, 271
Turner, C.W., 283
Turner, J.M., 110
Turner, S.M., 118
Turro-Garriga, O., 458
Tuschen-Caffier, B., 241
Tuulio-Henriksson, A., 381
Twamley, E.W., 378
Tyler, K.A., 166
Tyrer, P., 304, 315
Tyson, E., 232
Tzortzis, V., 334

U

Uchihara, T., 449
Uchimura, N., 274
Uchino, B.N., 62
Uematsu, M., 449
Uezato, A., 192
Uguz, S., 331
UK ECT Review Group, 213
Ulfberg, J., 214
Ullrich, S., 297
Ulrich, Y., 64
Ulusoy, E., 327
Umesue, M., 120
Unal, M., 331
Unal, S.N., 169
Unger, A., 374
Ungerleider, L.G., 126
Ungless, M.A., 271
Ungvari, G.S., 364
Unverzagt, F.W., 445
Updegraff, J.A., 44
Upp, H.E., 164–165
Urosevic, S., 192
Ursano, R., 103
Ursano, R.J., 129
Usall, J., 373
USA Today, 258
U.S. Census Bureau., 435
U.S. Department of Health and Human Services, 15, 57, 60, 61, 63
Usher, J., 199
Ustun, T.B., 60, 118, 119, 152, 429

V

Vachier, I., 491
Vader, A.M., 277, 284
Vadrucci, S., 276
Vaglum, P., 382
Vairon, E., 491
Vakhapova, V., 448
Valenstein, M., 122
Valente, A., 387
Valentiner, D.P., 118
Valenzuela, M., 452, 458
Valla, J.P., 410

Valvanne, J., 460
van Balkom, A.J., 118, 123
van Bokhoven, H., 411
Van Bourgondien, M.E., 410
Van Broeckhoven, C., 306
Vance, M.L., 210
van de Laar, F.A., 152, 159
Van den Berge, M., 374
van den Bosch, L.M.C., 314
van den Bree, M., 313
Van Den Brink, W., 201, 204
Van Den Eeden, S.K., 331, 445
Van den Eynde, F., 213
Vanderbilt-Adriance, E., 63
Vandereycken, W., 234
van der Flier, W.M., 438
Van der Flier, W.M., 441
Van der Gaag, M., 374
van der Hart, O., 162, 163, 169
van der Kolk, B.A., 168, 169
Van der Linden, M., 206
van der Meer, K., 445
Van der Roest, H.G., 458
Vanderschuren, L.J.M.J., 100
van der Veer, N., 238
Vandeven, A.M., 406
van de Ven, V., 377
Vandivort, R., 58
Vandivort-Warren, R., 58
Van Duijl, M., 171
van Dyck, R., 123, 125
van Elburg, A.A., 238
van Engeland, H., 28
Van Gestel, S.V., 306
van Goozen, S.H.M., 421
Van Gorp, W.G., 173
Van Gundy, K., 262
Vanheule, S., 208, 344
van Honk, J., 420
Van Horn, D.H.A., 284
van Houtem, C.M.H.H., 122
van Kan, G.A., 453
van Lankveld, J.J.D.M., 334, 335
Van Leeuwen, K., 307
van Lier, P.A.C., 423
Van Meter, A.R., 192
Van Mierlo, L.D., 458
van Nieuwehuizen, A.O., 436
van Oppen, P., 123, 216
van Os, J., 192, 204
van Pelt, J., 125
van Spronsen, F.J., 403
van Straten, A., 216
van Swieten, J.C., 445, 451, 448, 454
Van Tubergen, N., 266
Van Tyne, K., 270
van Weel, C., 152, 159
van Wijk, A.J., 122
Varese, F., 363
Varma, S., 401
Varnick, P., 194
Varnik, A., 195, 206
Vartanian, L.R., 226
Vase, L., 149
Vasic, N., 305
Vaughn, M.G., 275
Veale, J.F., 353

Vearnals, S., 216
Vecchio, J., 97, 412
Vegrzyn, R.D., 449
Vehmanen, L., 197
Veijola, J., 381
Velakoulis, D., 377
Vellas, B., 453
Velligan, D.I., 387
Velting, D.M., 195, 206
Veltman, D.J., 123
Venturello, S., 128
Vercammen, A., 363
Verdeli, H., 216
Verfaellie, M., 444
Verhaak, P.F.M., 445
Verhagen, J.C.M., 125
Verhey, F.R.J., 457
Verma, M., 460
Vermeiren, R., 418
Vermes, D., 158
Vermetten, E., 169, 198
Vernon, P.A., 123
Verona, E., 297
Versino, E., 276
Vertommen, H., 234
Veysey, B.M., 428
Viana, M.C., 192
Vicary, J.R., 67
Vidaeff, A.C., 407
Vieira, R., 438
Vieta, E., 199
Vieten, C., 153
Vigla-Taglianti, F.D., 276
Viglione, D.J., 85
Vigna-Taglianti, F., 276
Viinamaki, H., 166
Viitanen, M., 448
Viken, R.J., 427
Vilain, J., 373
Vilalta-Franch, J., 458
Villa, J.C., 448
Villodas, M.T., 423
Villringer, A., 445
Vinai, P., 233
Vindenes, V., 280
Vinkers, D.J., 343
Virgo, K.S., 270
Vismara, L.A., 411
Visser, S., 159, 407
Vita, A., 377
Vives-Cases, C., 119
Vlahov, D., 274
Vocks, S., 241
Vohs, K.D., 103
Volker, U., 237
Volkmar, F., 410
Volkmar, F.R., 412, 413
Volkow, N.D., 232, 267, 268, 269, 274
Vollebergh, W.A.M., 284
Vollm, B.A., 309, 316
Vollstadt-Klein, S., 283
Volpe, M., 387
Volpe, U., 377
von Arnim, C.A.F., 450
von dem Hagen, E.A.H., 421

von Eye, A., 421
von Ranson, K.M., 222
Vreeburg, S.A., 125 Vriend, J.L., 235
Vuachet, M., 310
Vuilleumier, P., 153
Vytal, K., 123
Vythilingham, M., 62

**W**

Waal, H., 281
Waddell, C., 203
Wade, D., 388, 459
Wade, T.D., 234, 245
Wadsworth, S.J., 404
Wagner, A., 445
Wagster, M.V., 441
Wahlbeck, K., 218
Wahlberg, K.-E., 381
Waite, L.J., 327, 331
Wakefield, J.C., 292
Wakschlag, L.S., 424, 425
Wald, J., 139
Waldinger, M., 327
Waldman, I.D., 416, 419
Waldrep, D.A., 129
Waldron, J.H., 379
Wales, J., 227, 245
Walker, R., 5
Walker, A., 315
Walker, E., 381
Walker, E.F., 371, 381
Walker, W.R., 166
Wallace, G., 44
Wallace, R.B., 444
Wallach, M.A., 275
Wallien, M.S., 352, 355
Walling, D., 129
Wallington, T., 187
Walsh, A.E., 192
Walsh, B.C., 386
Walsh, B.T., 64, 66, 67, 233
Walsh, C., 127, 271
Walsh, C.M., 65
Walsh, D., 379
Walsh, T.J., 331
Walter, M., 327, 330
Walterfang, M., 377
Walters, E.E., 2, 55, 56, 57, 60, 61, 117, 118, 191, 192, 268
Walters, G.D., 266
Walters, S.T., 277, 284
Walters, W., 428
Walton, A.P., 270
Walton, K.M., 411
Wampold, B.E., 471
Wandersman, A., 44, 473
Wang, C., 401
Wang, C.-X., 266
Wang, G.-J., 232, 268, 274
Wang, L., 377
Wang, P.-C., 459
Wang, P.S., 55, 57, 58, 191, 192, 480
Wang, T.J., 274
Wang, W., 379
Wang, Y., 141, 198, 199, 389
Waragai, M., 449

Waraich, P., 373
Ward, A.M., 129
Ward, K., 284
Ward, T., 345, 346, 347
Ward, T.N., 491
Wardrop, A.A., 235
Warman, M., 209
Warren, K.R., 259, 407
Warren, L., 276
Warren, S.F., 413
Washburn, J.J., 422
Wasserman, D., 195, 206
Watanabe, N., 134
Watari, K.F., 119
Waters, A.M., 109
Waters, F., 363
Wathen, C.N., 308
Watkins, E.R., 215
Watkins, L.L., 496
Watkins, L.R., 202
Watras-Gans, S., 345
Watson, A.C., 15
Watson, D., 271
Watson, J.D., 23
Watson, J., 67
Watson, P.J., 204
Watson, R., 441
Watson, W., 493
Waugh, R., 496
Waxman, S.E., 234
Weaver, M.T., 271
Weaver, T., 304
Webb, L., 345
Webb, R., 239
Webb, R.C., 327
Webb, R.T., 379
Webb, S.J., 405
Webber, S., 171
Weber, M.K., 275
Weber, S., 246
Webster, D., 64
Webster-Stratton, C., 422
Wechsler, D., 81, 384, 455
Wechsler, H., 67, 257, 259
Wedekind, D., 39
Wedig, M.M., 300
Weggen, S., 447
Wehmeier, P.M., 371
Wei, M., 201
Weiden, P., 39, 387
Weiland, B.J., 259
Weinberger, D.R., 378
Weinbrenner, S., 386
Weiner, C., 379
Weiner, D.A., 374
Weiner, M.F., 448
Weinman, J., 459
Weir, D.R., 444
Weisend, M.P., 379
Weisman de Mamani, A.G., 382
Weiss, M.G., 152, 154
Weiss, P.S., 380
Weiss, R.D., 282
Weissman, M., 216
Weissman, M.M., 119, 216
Weisz, J.R., 39, 66
Weizman, A., 15

Wekselman, K., 336
Welham, J., 371, 373
Welker, T.M., 201
Wellman, G.J., 410
Wells, A., 109, 112
Wells, A.M., 66, 67
Wells, J.E., 192
Wells, K.B., 55, 57, 58, 480
Welty, L.J., 422
Wemmie, J.A., 124
Wen, X., 401
Wentzel, I., 158
Wenze, O.J., 201
Wenzel, A., 126
Werkle-Bergner, M., 435
Werner, F.-M., 199, 452
Werner, P., 446
Wesner, K.A., 44
Wessel, J., 123
Wessely, S., 129
Wessely, S.C., 153
West, J.C., 380
West, R., 275
Westen, D., 28
Westenberg, H.G., 135
Westerman, A.T., 259
Westin, A., 226–227
Westin, K., 226–227
Westra, H.A., 477
Westrich, L., 201
Wetzel, R.D., 157
Whalen, D.J., 203
Whelton, K., 491
Whelton, M., 491
Whiffen, V.E., 169
Whitaker, D.J., 67, 346
Whitbeck, L., 166
White, E., 36
White, K.E., 450
White, M.A., 245
White, R., 209
White, S., 355
Whitefield, K., 206
Whitehouse, W.G., 192, 201
Whitelaw, A., 405
Whiteside, S.P., 127
Whiteside, S.P.H., 472
Whitfield, J.B., 266
Whitford, T.J., 377
Whitmer, R.A., 451
Whittaker, W.J., 340, 345
Whittington, C., 388
Whitty, P., 373
Wichstrom, L., 418
Wickramaratne, P., 119
Widaman, K.F., 396
Widiger, T.A., 295, 299, 300
Wiedeman, R., 362
Wiedemann, K., 200
Wiegel, M., 331, 333
Wietlisbach, V., 282
Wijker, W., 149
Wilcox, H.C., 123, 195
Wild, T.C., 270
Wildenauer, D.B., 41, 270
Wilens, T., 192
Wilens, T.E., 417

Wilfley, D., 237
Wilfley, D.E., 234, 237
Wilhelm, F.H., 140
Wilhelm, K.A., 125
Wilhelm, S., 141, 158
Wilhelmsen, K.C., 153, 277
Wilk, K., 189
Wilkeson, A., 166
Wilkinson, A., 355
Wilkinson, G.S., 384, 409, 410
Will, J., 336
Willcox, J.K., 450
Willcutt, E., 427
Willes, D.L., 345
Willett, W.C., 451
Williams, B., 211
Williams, C.L., 82, 151, 157, 172
Williams, E.D., 492
Williams, J.B.W., 80, 157, 207, 238
Williams, J.E., 492
Williams, J.T., 269, 280
Williams, M., 155
Williams, R., 126
Williams, R.J., 284
Williams, S.K., 266
Williams, V.S., 331
Williams-Nickelson, C., 469
Williamson, D.E., 203
Williamson, E.D., 410
Willich, S.N., 344, 445
Willis, R.J., 444
Wilmshurst, L.A., 427
Wilson, G.T., 245, 246
Wilson, J.F., 24
Wilson, K., 129
Wilson, K.A., 127
Wilson, K.G., 470
Wilson, K.P., 118
Wilson, P., 422
Wilson, T.F., 257
Wilt, S.A., 64
Wimo, A., 445, 452
Winblad, B., 448, 454, 457
Wincze, J.P., 324, 327, 331, 333, 335
Winder, D.G., 267
Windle, M., 44
Wingo, T.S., 447
Winiecki, P., 475
Winkelman, J.W., 200–201
Winninger, A., 227
Winter, A.C., 492
Winters, K.C., 284
Wintersteen, M.B., 216
Winzelberg, A.J., 237
Wirtshafter, D., 232
Wischmann, T., 328
Wise, R.A., 269
Wise, T.N., 157
Witkiewitz, K., 275, 283
Witt, A.A., 141
Wittchen, H., 43, 60, 119
Wittchen, H.-U., 107, 118, 122, 218
Wittchen, H.U., 122
Witteman, J.C.M., 451
Witter, M.P., 123
Wittert, G., 125

Wnuk, D., 348, 350
Woertman, L., 163
Wohlgemuth, W.K., 495
Wojtowicz, A.E., 222
Wolf, N.D., 305
Wolf, R.C., 305
Wolfensberger, W., 476
Wolff, G., 216
Wolff, M.S., 129
Wolfson, D., 384
Wolitsky-Taylor, K.B., 127
Wolkowitz, C., 333
Wonderlich, S.A., 234, 493
Wong, B.Y.L., 400
Wong, C., 268, 398
Wong, D.G., 331
Wong, P.C., 447, 452
Wong, S.W.-L., 402
Wong, T.T.-Y., 402
Wood, A.G., 377
Wood, H., 352, 353, 354
Wood, J.M., 85, 86
Wood, K., 331
Wood, P.K., 291, 295, 300, 303
Wood, S.J., 377
Wood, T., 428–429
Woodruff-Borden, J., 127
Woods, B., 457
Woods, R.T., 458
Woods, S.W., 67, 141, 372, 386
Woodside, D.B., 229, 234
Woodward, A., 272
Woodward, T.S., 363
Woody, S.R., 303
Woolacott, N., 206
Woolfolk, R.L., 158
Woppmann, A., 374
Work, W.C., 67
World Health Organization, 58, 60
Wright, K., 215
Wright, R.J., 491
Wrightsman, L.S., 33, 476
Wrisley, B.R., 275
Wu, J., 267
Wu, Y., 460
Wu, Y.S., 274
Wunderlich, G., 334
Wunderlich, H.-P., 212
Wustmann, T., 371
Wykes, T., 387
Wylie, F.M., 280
Wylie, K., 327, 330
Wyman, P.A., 67
Wynne, J., 405
Wyshak, G., 158

**X**

Xin, Z.C., 327
Xu, H.-S., 266
Xu, T., 383
Xu, X., 64

**Y**

Yadin, E., 472
Yaffe, K., 441, 445, 460
Yager, J., 229

Yager, Z., 237
Yajima, Y., 251
Yamada, M., 377
Yamada, S., 120
Yanez, A.M., 234
Yang, C.R., 124
Yanowitch, R.N., 305
Yasamy, M.T., 401
Yassa, M.A., 124
Yates, W.R., 122, 152
Yau, W.-Y.W., 259
Yavanian, G.J., 378
Yeargin-Allsopp, M., 401
Yehuda, R., 125, 129
Yen, S., 310, 311, 317, 318
Yeung, M., 124
Yilmaz, H., 152
Ying, Z., 453
Yip, B.H., 197
Yip, P., 195, 206
Yolken, R., 379
Yoo, J.H., 410
Yoon, S.L., 489
Yorke, J., 496
Yoshioka, D.T., 155
Young, E., 192
Young, J.N., 417
Young, L.T., 206
Young, M., 152
Young, S., 426
Young, S.E., 306
Youngstrom, E.A., 192, 203, 209
Yu, C.-E., 448
Yu, K.K., 405
Yu, M., 377
Yu, Y., 383
Yucel, M., 198
Yudofsky, S.C., 439
Yuen, H.P., 382
Yung, A.R., 66, 382
Yung-Wen, L., 336

**Z**

Zaazaa, A., 334
Zabala, A., 367
Zaccai, J., 445
Zafar, U., 159
Zahid, J., 401
Zahn-Waxler, C., 192
Zahran, H., 492
Zail, C.M., 493
Zajac-Benitez, C., 378
Zamboanga, B.L., 270
Zambon, A., 276, 438
Zanarini, M.C., 300, 317, 318
Zandi, P., 218
Zandi, P.P., 122, 375
Zanusso, G., 438
Zapf, P.A., 33
Zarantonello, G., 438
Zarate, C.A., 200
Zarate, R., 382
Zaretsky, A.E., 216
Zarkov, Z., 192
Zaslavsky, A.M., 429
Zaudig, M., 157

Zaveri, P., 173, 174
Zbinden, M., 389
Zebrowitz, L.A., 446
Zech, T., 155
Zeier, J., 305
Zetterberg, H., 460
Zhang, C., 272
Zhang, D., 396
Zhang, D.-R., 266
Zhang, H., 266
Zhang, L., 109

Zhang, Y., 455
Zhang, Z.-X., 452
Zhao, S., 43, 60, 118, 119, 268
Zhao, X., 306
Zhou, F.C., 268
Zhou, J., 451
Zhou, M., 63
Zhou, X., 303
Zhu, Y., 492
Zhuang, Y., 453
Zidek, T., 374

Ziebell, S., 382
Ziegler, M.L., 203
Zigler, A., 401
Zimbardo, P., 118
Zimmerman, A.W., 405
Zimmerman, K., 436
Zimmerman, M., 295, 311
Zimprich, F., 152, 166
Zinbarg, R.E., 103, 128
Zitzman, D.I., 267
Zitman, F.G., 125

Zivin, K., 15
Zlokovic, B.V., 441
Zoccolella, S., 450
Zorumski, C.F., 376
Zubieta, J.-K., 259
Zucker, K.J., 352, 353, 354, 355
Zucker, R.A., 259
Zvolensky, M.J., 127, 129, 133, 134, 474
Zvolsky, P., 189
Zwir, I., 376

# Subject Index

## A

Abnormal behavior
  assessing, 77
  classifying, 76
  criteria for determining, 3–6
  defining, 74–76
  forms, 74
  studying, 93–98
Abnormality
  defining, 6
  statistical definition, 3–4, 4f
Abnormal psychology
  definitions, 2, 7t
  features continuum, 8f
  history, 10–13
  introduction to, 2
  themes, 12–17
  types of prevention, 13–14
Academic skills training
  developmental disorders and, 412
  disruptive behavior disorders and, 426
Acetylcholine, 25t
Achievement test, 409–410
Acquaintance rape, 345
Acrotomophilia, 344t
Active schizophrenic phase, 366, 366f
Acute stress disorder, 112, 116t
Acute transient psychosis, 373
Adaptation difficulties, 4–5
*Adaptive Behavior Scale-Residential and Community:*
  *Second Edition,* 410
Adaptive functioning, 396
Addiction Potential Scale, 277
Addictions Acknowledgement Scale, 277
Addiction Severity Index, 276
ADHD. *See* Attention deficit hyperactivity
  disorder (ADHD)
ADHD Rating Scale-IV, 425
ADHD Symptoms Rating Scale, 425
Adolescent Dissociative Experiences Scale
  (A-DES), 172, 172t
Adverse life events and schizophrenia, 379, 380f
Age
  mental disorders and, 60, 62t
  neurocognitive disorders and, 445
  normal neurocognitive changes, 435–436
  Parkinson's disease and, 445
  sexual dysfunction and, 327
Aggression, 28. *See also* Violence
Agonist
  partial, 281
  substance-related disorders and, 280
Agoraphobia
  features, 107, 107t
  gender and, 119f
  prevalence rates, 118f
  treatment seekers, 118f
Al-Anon, 284
Alateen, 284

Alcohol
  blood levels of. *See* Blood alcohol level
  blood test and, 277, 280
  drug interactions, 258t
  effects, 253, 255
  epidemiology, 263, 263f
  gender and blood alcohol level, 256t
  genetics and, 266
  intoxication, 252t
  neurocognitive disorders and, 451
  tolerance, 252
  violence and, 272
  withdrawal, 252–253, 253t
Alcohol abuse
  diagnostic categories, 254t–255t
  diathesis-stress model, 53f
  effects, 255–257, 259
  gender differences, 41
  prevention, 67–68
Alcoholics Anonymous, 284, 285t, 473
Alcoholism
  brain and, 266–267, 268f
  defined, 257
  stigmas, 231t
Alcohol use disorder, 251–252, 251t
Alogia, 364, 365
Altruistic suicide, 191
Aluminum, and dementia, 451
Alzheimer's disease
  assessing, 454–456, 456f
  features, 439–441, 441t
  genetics and, 446
  long-term outcomes, 459–460
  prevalence rates, 444, 445f
  reality orientation and, 457–458
  tips for caregivers, 458–459, 459t
  video about, 448
Amnesia
  anterograde, 443
  dissociative, 161–162, 162t
  retrograde, 443
Amniocentesis, 407
"Amok, running," 42
Amphetamines
  abusing, 260
  diagnostic categories of abuse, 254t–255t
Amygdala
  anxiety-related disorders and, 123–124
  substance-related disorders and, 266, 266f
Amyloid cascade hypothesis, 452, 453f
Analogue experiments, 96–97
Angelman syndrome, 405t
Anhedonia, 362t, 365
Anomic suicide, 191
Anorexia nervosa
  defined, 43, 43f
  features, 223–224, 224t
  genetics and, 232t
  prevalence rates, 226–227, 228t

Antagonists, and substance related disorders, 281
Antecedent, 86
Anterior cingulate
  obsessive-compulsive behavior and, 124
  substance-related disorders and, 266–267, 266f
Anthrophobia, 42, 42f
Antianxiety medication, 134–135, 136t
Antidepressant
  anxiety-related disorders and, 134, 136t
  for depressive and bipolar disorders, 210–212
Antipsychotic medication
  compliance, 387
  ethics and, 385–386
  psychotic disorders and, 385–386, 385t, 386f
Antisocial personality disorder
  epidemiology, 299–300
  features, 296–297, 297t
Anxiety
  continuum, 104f
  defined, 103
  Freudian theory and, 30
  GABA and, 25
  hierarchy, 138, 140f
  sensitivity, 127
Anxiety-related disorder. *See also specific types*
  age of onset, 56–57
  assessing, 132–134
  biological risk factors, 122–125
  brain and, 123f
  causes, 129–130
  comorbidity, 120, 121t
  continuum, 104f–105f
  cultural factors, 128–129
  defined, 104
  environmental risk factors, 126–129
  epidemiology, 117–120
  evolution and, 125
  family-based contributions, 127–128
  features, 104–112
  gender and, 118, 119, 119f
  genetics and, 122–123
  global, 119–120
  interview and, 133
  learning experiences, 128
  medications for, 136t
  prevalence rates, 118f
  preventing, 130–131
  prognosis, 141–142
  screening questions, 142t
  self-evaluating, 141
  somatic symptom disorders and, 151–152
  stigma associated with, 120–122
  treatment, 134–141
  treatment seekers, 118, 118f
Anxiety-related disorders Interview Schedule
  (ADIS), 133
Anxiety Sensitivity Index, 133, 134t
Anxiolytic, diagnostic categories of abuse,
  254t–255t

Anxious/fearful personality disorder
  biological risk factors, 306–307
  causes, 308, 308f
  cognition examples, 307t
  environmental risk factors, 307
  epidemiology, 302–303
  features, 292, 300–303
Aphasia, 439
Apotemnophilia, 344t
Arbitrary inference, 38
Asperger's disorder features, 399
Asphyxiophilia, 341
Assessment
  behavioral, 86–87
  biological, 87–88
  clinical, and culture, 92
  ethics and, 481
  neurochemical, 88, 90
  neuropsychological, 90–91
  personality, 82–86
  stress, 493
Assessment technique
  intelligence test, 81–82
  interview, 80–81
  MMPI-2 clinical scale, 83–84, 84f
  MMPI-2 validity scale, 82–83
  neuroimaging, 88
  objective personality measure, 82–83
  observation, 86–87
  projective personality measure, 85–86
  Rorschach test, 85
  self-monitoring, 87
Asthma, and stress, 490
Asylum, 11
Ataque de nervios, 91–92, 120
Atrophy, brain, 449
Attention deficit hyperactivity disorder (ADHD)
  brain changes and, 420–421
  causes, 423
  culture and, 422–423
  defined, 414–415
  features, 415–416, 418t
  genetics and, 419–420
  long-term outcomes, 427, 429
  neurochemical changes and, 420
  sample multifactorial model, 423, 423f
  treatment (biological), 425–426
Attraction to Sexual Aggression Scale (revised), 348
Attribution theory, 201–202
Attrition, in longitudinal studies, 97
Autagonistophilia, 344t
Authenticity in psychology, 35
Autism Diagnostic Interview-Revised, 410
Autism spectrum disorder
  CARS2 rating sheet sample items, 410t
  concordance rate, 404
  epidemiology, 401
  features, 398t
  severity of, 397–399, 400t
  video about, 411
Autistic disorder. See Autism spectrum disorder
Autogynephilia, 341
Automatic thoughts, 201
Automatic Thoughts Questionnaire-Revised, 209, 209t
Autonepiophilia, 344t
Autosomal recessive disorder, 403
Autosuggestibility, 150

Aversion treatment, and paraphilias, 349
Aversive drug, 281
Avoidance conditioning, 38–39, 39f
Avoidant personality disorder, 301t
  environmental risk factors, 307
  features, 301
  gender and, 303
Avolition, 361, 365

B

Basal ganglia
  function, 25
  obsessive-compulsive behavior and, 124
  schizophrenia and, 377
Bayley Scales of Infant and Toddler Development-Third
    Edition, 409
Beck Anxiety Inventory, 135t
Beck Depression Inventory-II, 208
Beck Hopelessness Scale, 209
Beck's cognitive theory, 38
Behavior
  blood alcohol level and, 257t
  continuum, 10f–11f
  criteria for abnormal, 3–6
  degree of normality, 6–8
  maladaptive, 4
Behavioral activation, for depression, 214
Behavioral assessment, 86–87
Behavioral avoidance test, and anxiety-related
    disorders, 134
Behavioral inhibition, and anxiety-related
    disorders, 125
Behavioral observation
  developmental disorders and, 410
  disruptive behavior disorders and, 425
Behavioral perspective, 36–37
Behavior Assessment System for Children, Second
    Edition, 425
Behavior genetics, 24
Behavior management (school-based), 426
Behavior problem, addressing, 413
Behavior therapy. See also Cognitive-behavioral
    therapy (CBT)
  neurocognitive disorders and, 458
  somatic symptom disorders and,
      158–159
  substance-related disorders and, 283
Bender Visual-Motor Gestalt Test
    (Bender-Gestalt II), 90
Benton Visual Retention Test, 90, 91f
Benzodiazepine, 134, 136t
Biastophilia, 344t
Binge drinking
  defined, 67
  effects, 255–257, 256–257
Binge eating, 225
Binge eating disorder
  compensatory behaviors, 228t
  features, 225–226, 228t
  genetics and, 232t
  prevalence rates, 228t
  questionnaires for assessing, 240t
Binge Eating Scale, 240t
Biofeedback, 494–495
  and anxiety-related disorders, 140
  and stress, 494
Biological assessment, 87–88

Biological model
  evaluating, 25–26
  mental disorders and, 22, 23
Biological risk factor
  for anxiety-related disorders, 122–125
  for anxious/fearful personality disorders, 306–307
  for depressive and bipolar disorders, 196–201
  for developmental disorders, 402–404
  for disruptive behavior disorders, 419–421
  for dissociative disorders, 168–169
  for dramatic personality disorders, 305–306
  for eating disorders, 232–234
  for gender dysphoria, 353
  for neurocognitive disorders, 447–450
  for odd or eccentric personality disorders, 304
  for paraphilic disorder, 345
  for sexual dysfunctions, 330
  for somatic symptom disorders, 153
  for substance-related disorders, 266–268
  for suicide, 196–201
Biopsychosocial model, 47
Bipolar disorder. See also Depressive disorders
  defined, 179
  mood-stabilizing drugs, 212
  schizophrenia and, 199f
Bipolar I disorder
  cycle, 190f
  features, 185, 189, 189t
  prevalence rates, 191f
  transcultural variation and, 194f
Bipolar II disorder
  cycle, 190f
  features, 185, 189, 190t
  prevalence rates, 191f
  transcultural variation and, 194f
Bipolar mood disorder
  mood-stabilizing drugs, 212t
  stigma associated with, 195
  video about, 206
Bipolar schizoaffective disorder, 369
Bleeding stroke, 441
Blood alcohol level
  defined, 255
  expected behavior and, 257t
  relationships among variables, 256t
Blood test, for substance-related disorders, 277, 280
Body dissatisfaction
  continuum, 223, 224f–225f
  defined, 222, 235
  questionnaires for assessing, 240t
Body dysmorphic disorder, 111
  diagnostic criteria, 111t
  response prevention for, 140
Body Image Avoidance Questionnaire, 240t
Body image disturbance
  defined, 235
  questionnaires for assessing, 240t
Body mass index (BMI), and eating disorders,
    240, 242t
Body Shape Questionnaire (BSQ), 240t
Borderline personality disorder, 298t
  epidemiology, 300
  features, 297–298
Brain
  Alzheimer's disease and, 448
  anxiety-related disorders and, 123–124
  assessing function, 88, 90

Brain (Continued)
  assessing metabolic changes, 88
  assessing structural abnormalities, 88
  bipolar disorder and, 199f
  conversion disorder and, 155f
  dementia and, 448–450, 451f
  depressive and bipolar disorders and, 198–199,
    198f, 199f
  developmental disorders and, 406f
  disruptive behavior disorders and changes,
    419–421
  dissociative disorders and, 168–169, 168f
  DTB and, 441
  eating disorders and, 232, 233f
  imaging techniques, 88, 89f
  intellectual disability and, 405–406
  major depression and, 200f
  major features, 26f–27f
  memory and, 435–436
  normal changes during aging, 435
  overview, 25
  paraphilias and, 346, 346f
  Parkinson's disease and, 449–450
  personality disorders and, 305–306
  Pick's disease and, 443
  schizophrenia and, 376–378, 377f, 378f
  somatic symptom disorders and, 153, 154f
  substance-related disorders and, 266–268, 267f,
    268f, 269f
  symmetry and developmental disorders, 406
  vascular disease and, 441–442
Brain fag, 42
Breathalyzer, 280
Breathing-related sleep disorder, 490
Breathing retraining, for anxiety-related disorders,
  136–137
Brief Psychiatric Rating Scale, 207, 383
Brief psychotic disorder
  epidemiology, 373
  features, 361t, 371, 371t
Bulimia nervosa
  binge-purge cycle, 243, 244f
  CBT monitoring sheet, 244f
  features, 224–225, 228t
  genetics and, 232t
  prevalence rates, 226–227, 228t
  sample maintenance plan, 245f
  video about, 233

C

Caffeine
  abusing, 259
  diagnostic categories of abuse, 254t–255t
CAGE alcohol measure, 277
California Verbal Learning Test-II, 384
Cannabis diagnostic categories of abuse,
  254t–255t
Cannabis sativa, 262
Case
  abnormal behavior (Travis), 2
  alcohol abuse (DeShawn), 52
  antisocial personality disorder (Duane), 296
  anxiety-related disorders (Angelina), 102
  bulimia nervosa (Lisa), 224
  delusional disorder (Jody), 370
  dependent personality disorder (Betty), 301

depressive and bipolar disorders and suicide
    (Katey), 178
  developmental behavior disorder (Robert), 394
  diagnosis and assessment (Professor Smith), 74
  disruptive behavior disorder (Will), 415
  dissociative disorders (Erica), 160
  drug use (Elon), 250
  eating disorder (Sooki), 222
  gender dysphoria (Austin), 351
  indecent exposure (Tom), 338–339
  learning disorder (Alison), 399
  mental disorder risk factors (Juan), 59
  neurocognitive disorders (William and Laura
    Ponder), 434
  obsessive-compulsive disorder (Jonathan), 110
  personality disorder (Michelle), 290
  personality disorder (Treva Thorneberry), 3
  perspectives (Mariella), 22
  posttraumatic stress (Marcus), 112
  schizophrenia (James), 360
  schizotypal personality disorder (Jackson), 294
  sexual dysfunction (Douglas and Stacy), 322
  somatization (Gisela), 146–147
  stress (Ben), 488
Case study
  advantages, 97t
  as study tool, 97
Catalepsy, 364
Catastrophizing, 126
Catatonia, 361
Catatonic behavior, and schizophrenia, 364, 365
Catatonic schizophrenia, 367f
Categorical approach, to behavioral definitions, 75
Catharsis, 472
Caudate nucleus, 124
CBT. See Cognitive-behavioral therapy (CBT)
Central nervous system function, 24
Cerebellum
  function, 25
  schizophrenia and, 377
Cerebral cortex function, 25
Cerebrovascular disease, 441
Child Behavior Checklist, 425
Childhood Autism spectrum disorder Rating
  Scale, Second Edition (CARS2), 410, 410t
Child maltreatment, preventing, 65t, 308, 308t
Child molestation, 340
Children's Depression Inventory, 208, 209t
Children's Manifest Anxiety Scale, 135t
Cholera deaths, 55f
Cholinesterase inhibitor, 456
Chorionic villus sampling, 407
Chromosomal aberration, and developmental
  disorders, 404, 405t
Chromosome, defined, 23
Chromosome, and depressive and bipolar
  disorders, 200
Circadian rhythm sleep-wake disorders, 490
Cirrhosis, of the liver, 257
Civil commitment, 33
Clang association, 364
Clarke Sex History Questionnaire for Males
  (Revised), 348
Classical conditioning theory, 36, 37, 37f
Classification, defined, 76
Client-centered therapy, 34–35
Client identification, 482

Clinical assessment
  culture and, 91–93
  defined, 77
Clinical interview, for personality disorder
  assessment, 311t
Clinical psychologist
  job description, 466t
  qualifications, 464
Clinician
  compared to researcher, 478–479
  cultural responsibilities, 92
Clinician-Administered Dissociative States Scale, 172
Clinician rating and depressive and bipolar
  disorders, 207–208
Club drugs, 262–263
Cocaine
  abusing, 260, 261
  brain and, 268f
Cocaine Anonymous, 284
Codeine, 261
Codependency, and substance-related disorders,
  273
Cognition
  disruptive behavior disorders and, 422
  normal changes during aging, 435–436
Cognitions about Body and Health
  Questionnaire, 157
Cognitive assessment, of psychotic disorders, 384
Cognitive-behavioral model
  assessment, 39
  evaluating, 40–41
  example, 38–39
  learning principles, 36–37
  overview, 36–41
  treatment, 39–40
Cognitive-behavioral therapy (CBT)
  defined, 39
  eating disorders and, 243–245, 244f
  for personality disorders, 313
  psychotic disorders and, 386–387
  sample maintenance plan, 245f
  substance-related disorders and, 282–283
Cognitive beliefs
  dramatic personality disorders and, 306, 307t
  of odd/eccentric personality disorders, 304, 305t
Cognitive deficit, and schizophrenia, 378–379
Cognitive distortion
  anxiety-related disorders and, 126
  defined, 38
  depressive and bipolar disorders and, 201–202
  eating disorders and, 235
  paraphilic disorders and, 346
  for substance-related disorders, 269–270
Cognitive perspective, 36, 37–38
Cognitive principles, 37–38
Cognitive psychologist, job description, 466t
Cognitive rehearsal, 39
Cognitive risk factor, for anxiety-related disorders,
  126–127
Cognitive schema, 37–38
Cognitive test, for developmental disorders, 408–409
Cognitive therapy
  anxiety-related disorders and, 137–138
  depressive and bipolar disorders and, 214–215
  paraphilic disorders and, 350
  somatic symptom disorders and, 158–159
  for stress, 495

Cohort effect
   children and, 57
   in cross-sectional studies, 97
Collectivist culture, 45
College Alcohol Study, 256–257
College student
   alcohol use disorders and, 67–68
   suicide and, 61
Commitment
   civil, 33
   criminal, 33
Commitment, to a treatment statement, 217
Community
   mental disorders and, 44
   psychotic disorder interventions, 388, 388f
Community psychology, 473
Community reinforcement, and substance-related
   disorders, 283
Comorbidity, 56
Compartmentalization, 169
Compensatory behavior
   for binge eating, 228t
   bulimia nervosa and, 225
Competency to stand trial, 33
Composite International Diagnostic Interview,
   157
Comprehensive Drinker Profile, 276
Compulsion, 110–111
Computerized axial tomography (CT) scan
   as assessment tool, 88
   neurocognitive disorders and, 456
Concordance, and developmental disorders, 404
Concurrent validity, 80, 80t
Conditional positive regard, 34
Conditioned response (CR), 37
Conditioned stimulus (CS), 37
Conditioning, and anxiety-related disorders, 128,
   128f
Conduct disorder
   defined, 415
   features, 416–417, 420t
   genetics and, 419–420
   neurochemical changes and, 420
   sample multifactorial model, 423–424, 424f
Confabulation, 444
Confidentiality, 481–482
Confound, 96
Confusion Assessment Method, 455
Conners ADHD/DSM-IV Scales, 425, 425t
Conners Rating Scales (Conners 3), 425
Conscience, 30
Consequence, 86
Construct validity, 80, 80t
Content validity, 80, 80t
Contingency management
   for depression, 214
   somatic symptom disorders and, 158
   substance-related disorders and, 283
Continuous Performance Test, 425
Continuous Performance Test II, 384
Continuum of intervention, 66, 66f
Control delusion, 362
Control group, 94
Controlled observation, 86–87
Controlled weight gain, 241
Conversion disorder, 150, 150t
   behavior therapy and, 158

brain changes and, 153, 155f
   features, 150
Coping, and depression, 214
Coprophilia, 344t
Coronary heart disease, and stress, 491
Corpus callosum, 377
Correlation
   advantages, 97t
   defined, 95
Correlational studies, 95
Correlation coefficient, 95, 96f
Cortisol, and anxiety-related disorders, 124–125
Counseling psychologist
   job description, 466t
   qualifications, 464
Couples therapy. See Marital therapy
Courtship stages, and paraphilic disorders, 346
Craving, 266
Criminal commitment, 33
Criminal insanity, 33, 69
Criterion-referenced test, 409
Cross-dressing
   gender and, 330
   transvestic fetishism and, 342
Cross-sectional study, 97
Cross-tolerance, 280
Cue exposure therapy, 283
Cultural-familial intellectual disability, 406
Cultural idioms of distress, 155
Culture
   bipolar disorder and, 194f
   clinical assessment and, 91–93
   defined, 42
   depression and, 193f
   depressive and bipolar disorders and, 203–204
   diagnosis and, 77
   disruptive behavior disorders and, 422–423
   dissociation and, 167
   dissociative disorders and, 170
   eating disorders and, 235–236
   emotion and, 5
   expression and, 5
   gender identity and, 353
   mental disorder development and, 91–92
   mental disorders and, 43t
   neurocognitive disorders and, 451–452
   paraphilic disorders and, 346–347
   schizophrenia and, 380
   sexual dysfunction and, 331–332, 332t
   somatic symptom disorders and, 155
   substance-related disorders and, 273–274
Culture-bound syndrome, 42–43, 229
Cyclothymia. See Cyclothymic disorder
Cyclothymic disorder
   cycle, 190f
   features, 185, 189, 190t

# D

Dangerousness and commitment, 33
Date rape, 345
Date rape drugs, 263
Day hospital, 475
Decatastrophizing, 138
Defense mechanism
   examples, 31t
   overview, 30
   use, 29

Delayed ejaculation, 324, 326t
Deliberate self-harm, 191
Delirium
   causes, 436–438
   defined, 435
   differential diagnosis, 439t
   features, 437, 437t
Delirium Rating Scale-Revised, 455
Delirium tremens (DT), 253
Delusion. See also specific types
   defined, 361
   schizophrenia and, 362–363
Delusional disorder
   epidemiology, 373
   features, 361t, 370–371, 370t
Dementia
   advanced directives, 460
   Alzheimer's type, 439–441, 445. See also
      Alzheimer's disease
   brain and, 451f
   brain changes and, 448–450
   defined, 436
   differential diagnosis, 439t
   due to Parkinson's disease, 443, 446
   ethics and, 460
   features, 436–437
   with Lewy bodies (DLB), 441, 448–450
   long-term outcomes, 459–460
   Pick's disease, and, 443
   prevalence rates, 444, 445f
   signs and symptoms, 455t
   types, 438–439
Dementia Rating Scale, 455
Deoxyribonucleic acid (DNA) and mental
   disorders, 24
Dependent personality disorder, 302t
   environmental risk factors, 307
   example assessment questions, 312t
   features, 301
   gender and, 303
Dependent variable, 93
Depersonalization disorder, 165–166, 166t
Depressant abuse, 253, 255–257, 259
Depression. See also Major depression
   associated disorders, 207t
   biologically oriented, 205
   brain activity and, 198f
   brain and, 199f, 200f
   continuum, 180f–181f
   defined, 179
   developmental pathway, 204f
   differential diagnosis, 439t
   elderly people and, 215
   endogenous, 205
   environmentally oriented, 205
   exogenous, 202, 205
   family factors, 203
   gender differences, 41
   Hamilton Rating Scale, 208t
   interpersonal factors, 202–203
   medications for, 25, 212t
   nonbiological, 202
   prevalence rates, 193f
   somatic symptom disorders and, 151–152
   stigmas, 231t
   twin studies and, 198f
   women and, 186–187

Depressive disorders, 183. *See also* Depression
  assessing, 207–210
  biological risk factors, 196–201
  brain and, 199f
  causes, 204–205
  cognitive factors, 201–202
  culture and, 203–204
  environmental risk factors, 201–204
  epidemiology, 191–192
  evolution and, 204
  genetics and, 196–198
  interview and, 207–208
  long term outcomes, 217–218
  persistent, 183f, 187t
  prevalence rates, 191f
  prevention, 205–206
  screening questions, 217, 217t
  stigma associated with, 195
  treatment (biological), 210–214
  treatment (psychological), 214–217
  treatment seekers, 194f
  types, 179–189
Depressive schizoaffective disorder, 369
Derealization disorder, 165–166, 166t
Derogatis Sexual Functioning Inventory, 333
Designer drugs, 262–263
Detoxification, 282
Development
  continuum, 394f–395f
  normal, 395, 414
Developmental design, 97
Developmental disability. *See* Developmental
  disorder
Developmental disorder. *See also* specific types
  addressing problem behaviors, 413
  assessing, 408–410
  biological risk factors, 402–406
  causes, 406–407
  environmental risk factors, 406
  epidemiology, 401–402
  ethics and, 403
  features, 397–399
  genetics and, 402–404
  interview and, 410
  long-term outcomes, 413
  normalization, 475
  patient residential facilities, 475–476
  prevention, 407–408
  sample final common pathway, 407f
  social role valorization, 475
  stigma associated with, 402
  testing for and ethics, 409
  treatment (biological), 410–411
  treatment (psychological), 411–413
  types, 394–395
Developmental psychologist, job description, 466t
Deviance from the norm as abnormal behavior,
  3–4
Dexamethasone suppression test (DST), 210, 210f
*Dhat*, 119
*Dhat* syndrome, 42
Diagnosis
  advantages, 75–76
  categorical, 75
  culture and, 77
Diagnostic and Statistical Manual of Mental
  Disorders *(DSM-V). See DSM-V*

Dialectical behavior therapy, 313–314
Diathesis, 47, 53
Diathesis-stress model
  anxiety-related disorders and, 129
  defined, 47
  eating disorders and, 236
  implications, 54
  mental disorders and, 59, 79
  overview, 52–54
  substance-related disorders and, 274
Diet
  dementia and, 450
  neurocognitive disorders and, 450
Dietary restraint questionnaires, 240t
Dieting, 223
Diffuse plaque, 449
Dimensional approach, to behavioral definitions,
  74–75
Directionality, 95
Direct learning and anxiety-related disorders, 128
Disability, 59f
Discrete-trial training, 411
Disengaged family, 44
Disinhibition, 255
Disorganized schizophrenia, 367f
Disorganized schizophrenic dimension, 367f
Disorganized speech, 364
Disorientation, 436
Disruptive behavior disorder
  assessing, 425
  biological risk factors, 419–421
  causes, 423
  continuum, 416f–417f
  defined, 414, 415
  environmental risk factors, 421–423
  epidemiology, 417–418
  features, 417–418
  genetics and, 419–420
  interview and, 424–425
  long-term outcomes, 427, 429
  neurochemical changes and, 420
  prevention, 423–424
  screening questions, 427t
  stigma associated with, 418–419
  treatment (biological), 425–426
  treatment (multisystemic), 427
  treatment (psychological), 426–427
  treatment (residential), 426–427
  violence and, 428
Disruptive mood dysregulation disorder, 188t
Dissociation, 162f–163f, 161
Dissociative amnesia, 161–162, 162t
Dissociative disorder
  assessing, 172
  biological risk factors, 168–169
  brain and, 168f
  causes, 171
  continuum, 162f–163f
  cultural factors, 170
  defined, 161
  environmental risk factors, 169–170
  epidemiology, 166
  gender and, 166, 167
  historical introduction, 146
  interview and, 172
  long-term outcomes, 174
  prevention, 171

  stigma associated with, 166–167
  treatment (biological), 172–173
  treatment (psychological), 173
  types, 161
  violence and, 170
Dissociative Experiences Scale (DES), 172
Dissociative fugue, 162
Dissociative identity disorder
  defined, 42
  features, 163t
Dissociative trance disorder, 170
Distal factor, 274
Distress, as abnormal behavior, 5–6
Distress tolerance skills training, 314
Diversity, 14–15. *See also* Ethnicity
  anxiety-related disorders, sociocultural factors
    and, 119–120
  culture and diagnosis, 77
  depression and, 215
  influence on emotion, 5
  influence on expression, 5
  research limitations, 478
  schizophrenia and, 373
Dopamine
  functions, 25t
  schizophrenia and, 25, 378
Double-blind designs, 94
Double depression, 182
Double Trouble in Recovery, 284
Down syndrome, 404
Dramatic personality disorder
  biological risk factors, 305–306
  causes, 306
  cognition examples, 306
  environmental risk factors, 306
  epidemiology, 299–300
  features, 296
Dream analysis, 31
Driving factor, 39
Drug cue, 266
Drugs, 259–263, 264f. *See also* Substance-related
  disorder
  alcohol interactions, 258t
  categories of abused, 253–263
  first-time use, 264, 265f
  testing for and ethics, 281
  type of illicit use, 264, 264t
*DSM-V*
  acute stress disorder and, 112, 116t
  ADHD, 418t
  agoraphobia and, 107t
  alcohol intoxication, 252t
  alzheimer's disease, 441t
  anorexia nervosa, 224t
  anxiety-related disorders and, 135t
  autistic disorder, 398t
  behavioral definition and, 75
  binge eating disorder, 228t
  brief psychotic disorder, 371t
  bulimia nervosa features, 228t
  causes of delirium, 438t
  conduct disorder, 420t
  culture and, 92, 93t
  cyclothymic disorder features, 190t
  delirium, 437t
  delusional disorder, 370t
  depersonalization disorder symptoms, 166t

dissociative amnesia, 162t
dissociative identity disorder, 163t
dysthymia, 187t
eating disorder diagnostic scale, 238
exhibitionism, 338t
fetishism, 339t
frotteurism, 340t
generalized anxiety order and, 109, 109t
hypomanic episode, 189t
intellectual disability features, 396
learning disorder specific, 401t
Lewy body, 441t
major depressive disorder, 182t
manic episode features, 188t
mood-stabilizing drugs for bipolar disorder, 212
obsessive-compulsive disorder and, 110, 110t
oppositional defiant disorder, 419t
panic disorder, 105, 106t
paraphilic disorders, 338t
Parkinson's disease, 443t
pedophilia, 341t
persistent depressive disorder, 187t
personality disorder organization, 292t
posttraumatic stress disorder and, 111–112,
    113t–115t
premature ejaculation, 326t
schizoaffective disorder, 370t
schizophrenia, 366t
schizophreniform disorder features, 367t
separation anxiety-related disorder and, 117, 117t
sexual masochism, 342t
social anxiety-related disorder and, 107, 108t
somatization disorder classification, 148t
specific phobia and, 108, 108t
transvestic fetishism, 343t
voyeurism, 343t
DTs (Delirium tremens), 253
Dual relationships, 482
Durham rule, 69
Dutch Eating Behavior Questionnaire (DEBQ),
    240t
Dyscalculia, 401
Dysfunctional Thought Record, 87, 87f
Dyslalia, 401
Dyslexia, 401
Dysnomia, 401
Dysphasia, 401
Dyspraxia, 401
Dyssomnias, 490
Dysthymia
    cycle of, 183f
    features, 182, 187t
    prevalence rates, 193f

E

Early ejaculation. See Premature ejaculation
Early morning wakening, 180
Eating disorder
    assessing, 238–240
    biological risk factors, 232–234
    causes, 236, 237f
    cognitive factors, 235
    continuum, 223, 224f–225f
    culture and, 235–236
    defined, 222
    diagnostic scale sample items, 240t
    environmental risk factors, 234–235

epidemiology, 226–230
features, 223–226
genetics and, 232
interview and, 238
long-term outcomes, 245–246
prevalence rates, 226–227, 228t
prevention, 237
questionnaires for assessing, 240t
screening questions, 246t
self-monitoring, 239–240
stigma associated with, 231, 231t
treatment (biological), 241
treatment (psychological), 241, 243–245
Eating Disorder Diagnostic Scale, 238, 240t
Eating Disorders Examination (EDE), 238
Eating Disorders Inventory-2 (EDI-2), 240t
Echolalia, 364, 398
Echopraxia, 364
Education, and mental disorders, 61, 62t
Educational psychologist
    job description, 466t
    qualifications, 464
Ego, 29–30
Ego ideal, 30
Ejaculation
    delayed, 324, 326t
    premature. See Premature ejaculation
Electrocardiogram, 88, 90
Electroconvulsive therapy (ECT)
    for depression, 212–213
    ethical dilemmas, 214
Electroencephalogram (EEG), 90, 90f
Electronic diary, and eating disorders,
    239–240
Emotion
    continuum, 10f–11f
    culture and, 5
Emotional dysregulation, 309
Emotional personality disorder, 292
Emotional processing, 127
Emotional reasoning, 126
Emotional regulation skills training, 313
Emotion regulation training, 309, 310t
Emphysema, 270–271
Employment and mental disorders, 62t
Endogenous opioid, 233
Engineering psychologist, job description, 466t
Enlarged ventricle
    developmental disorders and, 405
    psychotic disorders and, 376
    schizophrenia and, 376f
Enmeshed family, 44
Environmental risk factors
    anxiety-related disorders and, 126–129
    anxious/fearful personality disorders and, 307
    avoidant personality disorder and, 307
    dependent personality disorder and, 307
    depressive and bipolar disorders and, 201–204
    developmental disorders and, 406
    disruptive behavior disorders and, 421–423
    dissociative disorders and, 169–170
    dramatic personality disorders and, 306
    eating disorders and, 234–235
    neurocognitive disorders and, 450–452
    odd or eccentric personality disorders and,
        304–305
    paraphilic disorders and, 345–346

psychotic disorders and, 379–380
somatic symptom disorders and, 153–155
substance-related disorders and, 268–274
Epidemiologist, 54
Epidemiology, 54
Episodic memory and aging, 435
Erectile disorder/dysfunction, 310, 323–324
    culture and, 331–332
    model, 332f
    treatment (biological), 334
Erogenous zone, 30
Erotomanic delusion, 370
Erratic personality disorder, 292
Esteem needs, 34
Ethical Principles of Psychologists and Code of
    Conduct, 481
Ethics
    antipsychotic medication and, 385t
    dementia and, 460
    developmental disorders and, 403, 409
    drug testing and, 281
    electroconvulsive therapy and, 214
    ending therapy, 482–483
    exposure-based practices and, 142
    humanistic perspective and, 36
    mental disorder treatment and, 481–483
    mental health professionals and, 481–483
    pro-anorexia websites, 243
    recovered memories and suggestibility, 167
    resolving issues, 483
    rights of the hospitalized, 477
    sex offenders and, 350
    sexual intimacy with clients, 482, 483
Ethnicity. See also Diversity
    ADHD and, 422–423
    defined, 42
    mental disorders and, 60, 62t
    research limitations, 380
    schizophrenia and, 373
    substance-related disorders and, 273, 273f
Etiology, 54
Euphoria, 179
Evening people, 353
Evidence examination, and anxiety-related
    disorders, 137–138
Evolution
    anxiety-related disorder and, 125
    depressive and bipolar disorders and, 204
    paraphilic disorders and, 347
    schizophrenia and, 380
    somatic symptom disorders and, 155
    substance-related disorders and, 274
Excess dopamine hypothesis, 378
Exhibitionism, 337–338
    features, 337, 338t
    focus of arousal, 338t
    gender and, 330
Existential psychology, 35
Exorcism, 10
Expectancy, 38
Experiment
    advantages of, 97t
    analogue, 96–97
    natural, 96
    as study tool, 93–95
Experimental designs, 96–97
Experimental group, 94

Experimental psychologist, job description, 466t
Exposure-based practices
    anxiety-related disorders and, 138–140
    ethics and, 142
Exposure treatment, 40
Expressed emotion
    defined, 44
    eating disorders and, 234
    schizophrenia and, 382
Expressive speech, 411
External validity, 95
Extrapyramidal effect, 388
Eye movement desensitization and reprocessing (EMDR), 139

**F**

*Fa'afafine*, 353
Factitious disorder, 150–151
    imposed on others, 151t
    self-imposed, 151t
*Fakaletti*, 353
Family
    activity, 44
    affect, 44
    anxiety-related disorders and, 122, 127–128
    control, 44
    depression and, 203
    depressive and bipolar disorders and, 196–197
    disruptive behavior disorders and, 421–422, 426
    eating disorders and, 234
    environment, 44–45
    mental disorders and, 44
    paraphilic disorders and, 345–346
    problematic environments, 44–45
    problematic relationships, 44–45
    substance-related disorders and, 266, 271–273, 275–276
Family suicide, 42
Family systems perspective, 44
Family therapy
    defined, 45
    for depressive and bipolar disorders, 216–217
    eating disorders and, 241, 243
    psychotic disorders and, 388
    substance-related disorders and, 283
Fantasy training, 334
Fast Track model for disruptive behavior prevention, 424
Fatalistic suicide, 191
Fear
    brain and, 123, 124f
    conditioning model, 128f
    continuum, 104f
    defined, 103–104
    as learned response, 128
Fear Questionnaire, 135t
Fear Survey Schedule for Children-Revised, 135t
Female orgasmic disorder, 324, 325t
Female Sexual Desire Questionnaire, 333
Female Sexual Function Index, 333, 335t
Female sexual interest/arousal disorder, 323, 325t
Femicide, 64
Fetal alcohol effects, 405

Fetal alcohol syndrome, 259, 259f, 268, 269f
Fetishism, 338, 338t, 339t
Final common pathway, 406
First-degree relative, and anxiety-related disorders, 122
Fixation, 30
Flashing, 337
Flat affect, 361, 365
Flavonoid, 451, 452f
Flight of ideas, 183–184
Flooding
    anxiety-related disorders and, 139
    defined, 40
    example, 141f
Focal testing, 90
*Folie à deux*, 371
Forensic psychologist, job description, 466t
Forensic psychology, 476
Fragile X syndrome, 402–403
Free association, 31
Free radicals, 450
Freudian slip, 28, 31
Freudian theory
    defined, 28
    psychosexual stages, 30, 30t
FRIENDS workbook, 131
Frontal lobe
    function, 25
    normal changes during aging, 435
Frontotemporal dementia
    features, 443, 444t
    genetics and, 448
    prevalence rates, 445
Frotteurism
    features, 340–341, 340t
    focus of arousal, 338t
Functional analysis, 39, 86
Functional MRI (fMRI), 88
Functional somatization, 148

**G**

GABA. *See* Gamma-aminobutyric acid (GABA)
Galvanic skin conductance, 90
Gamma-aminobutyric acid (GABA)
    anxiety and, 25
    anxiety-related disorders and, 124
    functions, 25t
Gender
    anxiety-related disorder and, 118, 119, 119f
    date rape drugs and, 263
    dementia caregivers and grief, 458
    depression and, 186–187
    dysthymia and, 193f
    eating disorders and, 229, 230
    graduate school mentoring programs, 469
    major depression and, 193f
    mental disorders and, 41, 43–44, 60, 62t
    neurocognitive disorders and, 445
    personality disorders and, 303
    sexual dysfunction and, 328t–329t, 330
    suicide and, 196f–197f
Gender development, 351
Gender dysphoria, 352–355
    in adolescents, 352t
    in adults, 352t
    assessing, 354–355
    causes, 353

    in children, 352t
    defined, 351
    features, 351–353
    long-term outcomes, 355
    prevention, 353
    treatment (biological), 354
    treatment (psychological), 354
    video about, 355
Gender expectation, 43
Gender identity, 43
Gene, defined, 23, 24
Gene damage, and developmental disorders, 402–404
General Behavior Inventory and Hypomanic Personality Scale, 209
Generalized anxiety-related disorder
    causes, 130
    cognitive therapy examples for, 137t
    exposure-based therapy examples for, 139t
    features, 109–110, 109t
    gender and, 119f
    genetics and, 122
    prevalence rates, 118f
    psychoeducation example for, 136t
    somatic control exercise example for, 136t
    treatment seekers, 118f
Gene therapy
    dementia and, 457
    developmental disorders and, 411
Genetics
    alcohol and, 266
    Alzheimer's disease and, 448
    anorexia nervosa and, 232t
    anxiety-related disorders and, 122–123
    behavior genetics, 24
    binge eating disorder and, 232t
    bulimia nervosa and, 232t
    conduct disorder and, 419–420
    depressive and bipolar disorders and, 196–198
    developmental disorders and, 402–404
    disruptive behavior disorders and, 419–420
    eating disorders and, 232, 232t
    mental disorders and, 23–24
    molecular genetics, 24
    neurocognitive disorders and, 447–448
    obsessive-compulsive disorder and, 122–123
    panic disorder and, 122
    Parkinson's disease and, 447–448
    posttraumatic stress disorder and, 123
    psychotic disorders and, 375–376
    social anxiety-related disorder and, 122
    somatic symptom disorders and, 153
    specific phobia and, 122
    stroke and, 448–448
    substance-related disorders and, 266
Genito-pelvic pain/penetration disorder, 327, 327t
Genotype, 24
Ghost dance, 295
Glutamate, 25t
Graduate school mentoring programs, 469
Grandiose delusion, 362, 371
Grandiosity, 179, 188t
Gray matter, and schizophrenia, 377, 378f
Grossly disorganized behavior, 364
Group therapy for substance-related disorders, 283–284
Gynemimetophilia, 344t

## H

Hair analysis, for substance-related disorders, 280
Halfway house, 475
Hallucination
    defined, 361
    schizophrenia and, 363–364
Hallucinogens
    abusing, 261–262
    diagnostic categories of abuse, 254t–255t
Halstead-Reitan Neuropsychological Test Battery, 90, 384, 455
Hamilton Rating Scale for Depression, 207, 208t
Headaches, and stress, 489–490
Health psychologist, DSM-V job description, 467t
Hemorrhagic stroke, 441
Heritability, 24, 24f
Heroin
    abusing, 261
    Vietnam soldiers and, 270
Heteromodal association cortex, 377
Hierarchy of needs, 34f
High school student suicide prevention, 68
Hippocampus and substance-related disorders, 267, 267f
Histrionic personality disorder, 299t
    epidemiology, 300
    features, 297
Home and School Situations Questionnaire, 425t
Hopelessness, 210
Hopelessness theory, 201–202
Hormonal features of depressive and bipolar disorders, 200
Humanistic assessment, 35
Humanistic model, 33–36
Humanistic treatment, 35
Hypersomnia, 180, 490
Hypertension, 490–491
Hypnosis, and dissociative disorders, 173
Hypnotics, 254t–255t
Hypoactive sexual desire disorder, 323, 324t
Hypomanic episode, 185, 188t, 189t
Hypothalamic-pituitary-adrenal (HPA) system
    and anxiety-related disorders, 124–126
Hypothalamus
    eating disorders and, 232, 233f
    function, 25
Hypothesis
    anxiety-related disorders and, 138
    as experimental tool, 93
Hypoxic ischemia, and psychotic disorders, 379
Hypoxyphilia, 341

## I

Id, 29
Illness anxiety-related disorder, 149–150, 150t
    cognitive therapy and, 158
    features, 149
    prevalence rate, 152t
Illness Attitude Scales, 157
Illness attribution, 154–155
Illness behavior and somatic symptom disorders, 154
Illness Behaviour Questionnaire, 157
Illness belief, 154–155
Impact of Event Scale, 135t
Impotence, 323–324

Impulsivity
    defined, 53
    eating disorders and, 233–234
    substance-related disorders and, 271
Inappropriate affect, 361, 364
Incidence, 54
Indecent exposure, 337
Independent variable, treatment as, 93
Indicated prevention, 67
Induction defect, 405
Industrial psychologist, job description, 467t
Infantile autism. See Autism spectrum disorder
Inflexible family, 44
Informant report for personality disorder assessment, 311t, 312
Information transfer, and anxiety-related disorders, 128
Informed consent, 142, 481–482
Inhalants
    defined, 263
    diagnostic categories of abuse, 254t–255t
Insanity
    competency to stand trial, 33
    criminal, 33, 69
Insight, 32
Insomnia, and stress, 490
Insula, and substance-related disorders, 266f, 267
Insular cortex, and substance-related disorders, 266f, 267
Integrative psychotherapy, 46
Intellectual disability
    chromosomal aberrations and, 405t
    epidemiology, 401
    features, 395–398, 396t
    severity subtypes, 397
Intelligence test
    as assessment technique, 81–82
    developmental disorders and, 409
Internal consistency reliability, 78t, 79
Internal validity, 95
International Diagnostic Checklists, 157
International Index of Erectile Dysfunction, 333
Interoceptive exposure, 139
Interpersonal effectiveness skills training, 313
Interpersonal factors, and depressive and bipolar disorders, 202–203
Interpersonal therapy (IPT), for depression, 216
Interpretation in psychodynamic therapy, 32
Interrater reliability, 78t, 79
Intervention, brief, and substance-related disorders, 282–283
Interview
    anxiety-related disorders and, 133
    as assessment technique, 80–81
    depressive and bipolar disorders and, 207–208
    developmental disorders and, 410
    disruptive behavior disorders and, 424–425
    dissociative disorders and, 172
    eating disorders and, 238
    neurocognitive disorders and, 454
    paraphilic disorders and, 348
    personality disorders and, 311–312, 311t
    psychotic disorders and, 383
    sexual dysfunction and, 333

somatic symptom disorders and, 157
structured interview(s), 80. See also specific types
substance-related disorders and, 276–277
unstructured interview, 80
Intimate partner violence, 28
Intrapsychic, 28
Irresistible impulse, 69
Irritable bowel syndrome (IBS), and stress, 489
Ischemic stroke, 441

## J

Jealous delusion, 371
Jinn, 167
Juvenile delinquency, 416

## K

Kathoey, 353
Kegel exercises, 335
Kids Eating Disorders Survey (KEDS), 240t
Kleptophilia, 344t
Klinefelter syndrome, 405t
Klismaphilia, 344t
Koro, 119, 120
Korsakoff's syndrome
    alcohol use and, 257, 259
    features, 444
    prevalence rates, 444

## L

La belle indifference
    conversion disorder and, 154
    defined, 150
Laboratory assessment
    of depressive and bipolar disorders, 210
    of neurocognitive disorders, 456
    of substance-related disorders, 277, 280
Lack of control over eating, 223
Lack of insight, and schizophrenia, 365
Language training, and developmental disorders, 411
Latah, 120
Latent content, of dreams, 32
Learned helplessness, 202
Learning disorder
    concordance rate, 404
    epidemiology, 401–402
    features, 399–401
    specific, 400t
Learning experience
    anxiety-related disorders and, 128
    paraphilic disorders and, 346
    substance-related disorders and, 270–271
Lethal dose (LD), 255
Lewy body
    defined, 441
    dementia and, 441, 448–450
    features, 441t
    Parkinson's disease and, 443
Lifetime prevalence
    defined, 54–55
    of mental disorders, 57f
    rates, 56, 56f
Light therapy for SAD, 213–214
Limbic system, 25
Limited developmental disorder, 395
Longitudinal study, 97

Long-term memory and aging, 435
Loose association, 364
Lycanthropy, 11

## M

MacAndrew Alcoholism Scale, 277
Magnetic resonance imaging (MRI)
    as assessment tool, 88
    function, 25
    healthy, 28f
    neurocognitive disorders and, 456
    schizophrenic, 28f
Major depression
    brain and, 200f
    cycle, 183f
    features, 181–182
    prevalence rates, 193f
Major depressive disorder
    cycle, 183f
    features, 181–182, 182t
Major depressive episode, 179–181, 181–182
Maladaptive behavior, 4
Male erectile disorder, 325t. See also Erectile
    disorder/dysfunction
Male Sexual Health Questionnaire, 333
Malingering, 151
Maltreatment
    anxiety-related disorders and, 127–128, 127f
    disruptive behavior disorders and, 422
Managed care, 478
Mania, 179
Manic depression. See Bipolar I disorder
Manic episode, 183–185, 188t
Manifest content, of dreams, 31
MAOI, for depression, 211–212, 212t
Marijuana abuse, 262
Marital status, and mental disorders, 61, 62t
Marital therapy, 45
    depressive and bipolar disorders and, 216–217
    substance-related disorders and, 283
Marriage and family therapist qualifications, 465
Maslow's hierarchy of needs, 34f
Mass madness, 11
Masturbation training, 335
Masturbatory reconditioning, 349
Masturbatory satiation, 350
Maudsley Obsessional-Compulsive Inventory, 135t
Meaninglessness, defined, 35
Measurement psychologist, job description,
    467t
Media
    eating disorders and, 234–235
    mental disorders and, 97
Medication. See also specific types
    for depressive and bipolar disorders, 25,
        210–212, 212t
    for eating disorders, 241
    for neurocognitive disorders, 456
    token economy and compliance with, 387
Medulla, function, 25
Megan's laws, 350
Melancholia, 180
Memory
    change and dissociative disorders, 169, 169f
    problems continuum, 436f–437f
    training, 458

Mental disorder
    age of onset, 56–57, 57f
    assessing, 77
    biological assessment, 25
    biological model, 22, 23
    classifying, 76
    consumer perspective, 14
    criminal justice system and, 476
    defined, 2, 3–10
    defining, 74–76
    dimensional perspective, 13
    disability and, 59t
    features, 75
    genetics as cause, 23
    heritability, 24, 24f
    media research, 97
    models describing, 22–23
    prevalence rates, 55–57, 57f
    prevention, 64–69
    prevention perspective, 13–14
    protective factors, 61–63, 63t
    psychogenic perspectives, 12
    relevance of understanding, 6–9
    research method advantages, 97t
    research use and quality, 479
    rights of the hospitalized, 477
    risk factors, 59–61, 62t
    severe, and aftercare services, 474–475
    severity rates, 56f
    somatogenic perspectives, 12
    studying, 93–98
    treatment. See Mental disorder treatment
Mental disorder treatment
    active ingredients, 468–469
    aftercare services, 474–475
    biological, 25
    caveats, 477
    client-therapist differences, 477
    clinicians vs. researchers, 478–479
    cost, 58
    cultural differences, 478
    effectiveness, 472
    ethics and, 481–483
    lack of access, 480–481
    managed care, 478
    manualized, 472
    noncompliance, 477
    nonspecific factors, 471
    prescriptive, 473
    for preventing child maltreatment, 65t
    process variables, 471–472
    quick fixes, 479
    rights of the hospitalized, 477
    seekers, 468–469
    seeking, 57–58
    self-help groups, 473–474
Mental health, public policy, 476
Mental health professional
    ethics and, 481–483
    preparation, 465, 467–468
    seeking treatment from, 468–469
    types, 464–465
Mental hygiene, 13
Mental hygiene movement, 12
Mental status examination, 454
Mesolimbic system, and substance-related disor-
    ders, 266, 266f

Metabolite and neurochemical assessment, 88
Methadone treatment, 280
Methamphetamine abuse, 260
Miami-Dade Juvenile Assessment Center
    Post-Arrest Diversion Program, 428
Michigan Alcohol Screening Test, 277
Migraine headaches, 489–490
Migration defect, 405
Milieu therapy, 386
Millon Clinical Multiaxial Inventory-III, 277, 310
Mind
    Freud's structure, 29f
    structure and mental disorders, 29–30
Mindfulness
    anxiety-related disorders and, 140–141
    personality disorders and, 314
    as treatment for depression, 215–216
Mini-Cog dementia screening test, 455
Mini-Mental State Examination (MMSE-2),
    455, 456f
Minnesota Multiphasic Personality Inventory-2
    (MMPI-2), 157, 277, 310
Mixed dementia, 442
Mixed design study, 95–96, 97t
MMPI-2 clinical scale, 83–84, 83t, 84f
MMPI-2 validity scale, 82–83
M'Naghten rule, 69
Mobility Inventory, 135t
Modeling
    anxiety-related disorders and, 140
    defined, 38
Model(s). See also specific types
    defined, 22
    uses, 23f
Molecular genetics, 24
Monoamine oxidase inhibitor (MAOI), 211–212,
    212t
Mood
    continuum, 180f–181f
    cycling, 185, 189
    disorder, age of onset of, 56–57
    normal changes, 179
Mood-stabilizing drugs
    for bipolar disorder, 212, 212t
    for depression, 212, 212t
Morphine abuse, 261
Motivating factor, 39
MRI. See Magnetic resonance imaging (MRI)
Mukhannathun, 353
Multicultural psychology, 14–15
Multidimensional Anxiety Scale for Children, 135t
Multidimensional Assessment of Sex and
    Aggression (Revised), 348
Multiphasic Sex Inventory II, 348
Multiple personality disorder. See Dissociative
    identity disorder
Munchausen syndrome, 151
Myograph, 348

## N

Nar-Anon, 284
Narcissistic personality disorder, 299t
    epidemiology, 300
    features, 298–300
Narcolepsy, 490
Narcotics abuse. See Substance abuse
Narcotics Anonymous, 284, 473

Narratophilia, 344t
National Alliance for the Mentally Ill, 473
National Eating Disorders Awareness Week, 237
National Institute of Mental Health
    Diagnostic Interview Schedule for
    Children (Version IV), 425
Natural experiments, 96
Natural incidental training, 411
Naturalistic observation, 86–87
Necrophilia, 344t
Needs, human, 34
Negative affectivity, 120
Negative cognitive triad, 201, 202f, 364
Negative correlation, 95
Negative reinforcement, 37
Negative schizophrenic dimension, 367f
Negative thought pattern, and anxiety-related
    disorders, 126
Neighborhood and mental disorders, 44
Neologism, 364
Neonatal Intensive Care Unit Network
    Neurobehavioral Scale, 409
Nervous system, and mental disorders, 24
Neuritic plaque, 448–449
Neurochemical assessment, of neurotransmitter
    systems, 88
Neurochemical change
    ADHD and, 420
    neurocognitive disorders and, 448–449
Neurochemical features
    of depressive and bipolar disorders, 199–200
    of eating disorders, 233
    of schizophrenia, 378
    of substance-related disorders, 268
Neurocognitive assessment, 455–456
Neurocognitive disorder. See also specific types
    aging and, 435
    assessing, 454–456
    biological risk factors, 447–450
    case study, 434
    causes, 452–453
    continuum, 436f–437f
    environmental risk factors, 450–452
    epidemiology, 445–446
    features, 436–444, 440t
    genetics and, 447
    interview and, 454
    long-term outcomes, 459–460
    major disorders, 440t
    maltreatment of patients, 447
    minor disorders, 440t
    prevention, 453–454
    stigma associated with, 446
    treatment (biological), 456–457
    treatment (nursing home), 457
    treatment (psychological), 457–458
    treatment (residential), 457
Neurodevelopmental hypothesis, 380–381
Neurofibromatosis, 405t
Neurofibromatosis tangles, 448
Neuroimaging, 88
Neuron, 24f
Neuropsychological assessment, 90–91
Neuropsychological problems, and rape, 345
Neuropsychological testing, 409–410
Neuropsychologist, DSM-V job description, 467t

Neurosis, 361
Neurotic disorder, 361
Neurotransmitter
    anxiety-related disorders and, 124
    defined, 24
    mental disorders and, 25t
Nicotine abuse, 259–260
Nicotine replacement therapy, 280
Nightmare disorder, 490
Nocturnal penile testing, 333
Nonassociative theory of fear, 128
Nondirective treatment, 35
Noonan syndrome, 405t
Norepinephrine
    anxiety-related disorders and, 124
    depression and, 25
    functions, 25t
Normal behavior, defined, 3
Normal impulsivity, 290f–291f
Normalization, 475
Normal mood change, 179
Normal rambunctious behavior, 414
Norm-referenced test, 409
No-suicide contract, 217

O
Objective personality measure, 82–83
Observation
    as assessment technique, 86–87
    controlled, 86–87
    of depressive and bipolar disorders, 209
    of developmental disorders, 410
    of disruptive behavior disorders, 425
    naturalistic, 86–87
    of psychotic disorders, 383–384
    of substance-related disorders, 277
Obsession, 110
Obsessive-compulsive disorder, 111. See also
    Anxiety-related disorder
    brain features and, 124
    cognitive distortions and, 126–127
    cognitive therapy examples for, 137t
    exposure-based therapy examples for, 139t
    features, 110–111, 110t
    gender and, 119f
    genetics and, 122–123
    prevalence rates, 118f
    psychoeducation example for, 136t
    somatic control exercise example for, 136t
    stigma associated with, 120–122
Obsessive-compulsive personality disorder, 302t
    environmental risk factors, 307
    features, 301–302
Occipital lobe
    function, 25
    schizophrenia and, 377
Odd/eccentric personality disorder
    biological risk factors, 304
    causes, 305, 305f
    environmental risk factors, 304–305
    epidemiology, 295
    features, 293–295
Olfactophilia, 344t
Oligogenic transmission, 197
Operant conditioning, 37, 38f
Opiate/Opioid abuse, 254t–255t, 261

Oppositional defiant disorder
    defined, 416–417
    features, 416–417, 419t
    sample multifactorial model, 423–424, 424f
Orbitofrontal cortex
    obsessive-compulsive behavior and, 124
    substance-related disorders and, 266f, 267
Organismic variable, 86
Organizational psychologist, DSM-V job
    description, 467t
Orgasmic reconditioning, 349
Other-centeredness, 35
Oxidative stress, 450

P
Painkiller abuse, 261
Pa-leng, 119
Panic and Agoraphobia Scale, 135t
Panic attack, 105, 106t
Panic disorder
    causes, 130
    cognitive therapy examples for, 137t
    diagnostic criteria, 106t
    exposure-based therapy examples for, 139t
    features, 106–107
    gender and, 119f
    genetics and, 122
    prevalence rates, 118f
    prevention, 69
    psychoeducation example for, 136t
    somatic control exercise example for, 136t
    treatment seekers, 118f
Paranoid personality disorder, 293t, 293, 372f
Paraphilic disorder, 337–340
    assessing, 348–351
    atypical, 342, 344t
    causes, 347
    defined, 337
    deviant sexual interest and, 344t
    environmental risk factors, 345–346
    epidemiology, 342–345
    evolution and, 347
    features, 337–345, 338t
    interview and, 348
    long-term outcomes, 350–351
    physiological assessment, 348–349
    prevalence rates, 342–344, 344t
    prevention, 347–348
    sample developmental pathway, 347, 347f
    screening questions, 350t
    treatment (biological), 349
    treatment (psychological), 349–350
Paraprofessional qualifications, 465
Parasomnias, 490
Parasuicidal behavior, 191
Parent Interview for Autism spectrum disorder-Clinical
    Version, 410
Parietal lobe
    function, 25
    learning disorders and, 406
    schizophrenia and, 377
Parkin gene, 448
Parkinson's disease, 442–443
    brain atrophy and, 450
    dementia and, 442–443, 445
    features, 444t

Parkinson's disease (Continued)
  genetics and, 448
  prevalence rates, 445
Partial agonist, and substance-related disorders, 282
Partialism, 344t
Pedophilic disorder
  features, 340–341, 341t
  focus of arousal, 338t
  Screening Scale for Pedophilic Interests, 349t
  subtypes, 341
Peer influence, and disruptive behavior disorders, 422
Peer-mediated intervention, 412
Penetration disorder, 327, 327t
Penile plethysmograph, 348
Penn State Worry Questionnaire, 135t
Perceptual psychologist, job description, 466t
Peresecutory delusion, 371
Perfectionism, and eating disorders, 233
Perinatal complication, and developmental disorders, 405
Peripheral nervous system, 24
Permissive hypothesis, 200, 200f
Persecutory delusion, 362
Persistent depressive disorder
  cycle of, 183f
  features, 187t
Personal distress as abnormal behavior, 5–6
Personal Journal of Body Image, 237
Personal narrative
  ADHD (Toni Wood), 428–429
  anorexia nervosa (Kitty Westin), 226–227
  anxiety-related disorders (anonymous), 132–133
  author's note (Christopher Kearney), 480
  borderline personality disorder (anonymous), 316–317
  clinical psychology study (Julia Martinez), 470–471
  counseling psychologist (Tiffany Borst), 474–475
  depression (anonymous), 78–79
  depression (Karen Gormandy), 184–185
  dissociative fugue (Hannah Emily Upp), 164–165
  eating disorders (Rachel Webb), 239
  integrative psychology (Dr. J. C. Norcross), 46
  schizophrenia (John Cadigan), 368–369
  substance-related disorders, 278–279
  suicide (Alison Malmon), 16
  transsexuality (Sam), 356–357
  Wellness Resource Center (Kim Dude), 70–71
Personality
  disruptive behavior disorders and, 421
  substance-related disorders and, 271
  trait, 291
Personality assessment
  as assessment technique, 82–86
  somatic symptom disorders and, 157
Personality Diagnostic Questionnaire-4 (PDQ-4), 310, 311t
Personality disorder, 293t. See also specific types
  assessing, 309, 311–312
  assessment method comparison, 311t
  cognitive-behavioral therapy and, 313
  dialectical behavior therapy and, 313–314
  dimensional model of, 292–293

features, 291–292
gender and, 303
impulsivity continuum, 290f–291f, 291
interview and, 311–312, 311t
long-term outcomes, 315–316, 318
organization, 292
paraphilic disorders and, 330
prevalence rates, 295
prevention, 308–309
screening questions, 315, 315t
short-term psychodynamic therapy and, 313
stigma associated with, 303–304
treatment (biological), 312–313
treatment (psychological), 313–315
violence and, 298
Personalization, 38
Perspective
  defined, 22
  uses, 23f
Pervasive developmental disorder, 395
PET scan. See Positron emission tomography (PET scan)
Phallometric testing, 348
Phencyclidine abuse, 254t–255t
Phenomenological approach, 33
Phenotype, 24
Phenylketonuria (PKU), 403
Phii bob, 167
Phong tap, 155
Physical assessment and eating disorders, 240
Physiological assessment
  of anxiety-related disorders, 134
  of psychotic disorders, 384–385
  of sexual dysfunctions, 333–334
Physiological needs, 34
Pick's disease
  brain atrophy and, 450
  dementia and, 443
  features, 443
Placebo effect, 94, 471
Planum temporale, and learning disorders, 406
Plastic surgery, guidelines, 157
Playboy bunnies, and eating disorders, 234, 236f
Pleasure principle, 29
Plethysmography, 349
Pons, 25
Positive and Negative Syndrome Scale, 383
Positive correlation, 95
Positive psychology, 35
Positive regard, 34
Positive reinforcement, 37
Positron emission tomography (PET scan)
  as assessment tool, 88
  neurocognitive disorders and, 456, 456f
Possession disorder, and culture, 167
Possession trance disorder, 170
Postpartum depression, 187
Postpartum psychosis, 371
Posttraumatic stress disorder (PTSD)
  culture and, 128–129
  dissociation, 169–170
  exposure-based therapy examples for, 139t
  features, 111–112, 113t–115t
  gender and, 119f
  genetics and, 123
  prevalence rates, 118f

psychoeducation example for, 136t
somatic control exercise example for, 136t
stigma associated with, 120–122
treatment seekers, 118f
Poverty, and disruptive behavior disorders, 422
Prader-Willi syndrome, 405t
Predictive validity, 80
  defined, 80t
Preferential rape, 346
Prefrontal cortex
  anxiety-related disorders and, 121
  substance-related disorders and, 266f, 267
Premature ejaculation
  features, 326, 326t
  treatment, 334
Premenstrual dysmorphic disorder, 186t
Prenatal complication
  developmental disorders and, 405
  schizophrenia and, 379, 379f
Preparedness and anxiety-related disorders, 125
Presenile dementia, 438
Presenting somatization, 149
Pretherapy, 35
Prevalence rates, of major mental disorders., 56, 56f. See also specific disorders
Prevention, of mental disorders, 64–69
Primary gain, 154
Primary prevention
  of alcohol use disorders, 67–68
  defined, 66
  of suicidal behavior, 68
Priming, 266
Privileged communication, 482
Pro-anorexia websites, 243
Problem behavior, addressing, 413
Problem-solving skills training, 214
Process variable, 35
Prodromal schizophrenic phase, 365–366, 366f
Prognosis, 141
Projection, 30
Projective hypothesis, 31
Projective personality measure, 85–86
Projective technique, 31
Protective factor
  for children, 64–65
  mental disorders and, 61–63, 63t
Proximal factor, 274
Pseudoseizure, 150
Psychiatric nurse (R.N.) qualifications, 465
Psychiatrist qualifications, 464–465
Psychic determinism, 29
Psychoanalyst qualifications, 465
Psychobiological theory, of personality disorders, 304
Psychodynamic model
  assessment, 31–32
  evaluating, 32
  mental disorders and, 28–32
  overview, 29–32
  treatment, 32
Psychodynamic perspective principles, 28–29
Psychoeducation and anxiety-related disorders, 135–137, 136t
Psychological autopsy, and suicide, 210
Psychological drug dependence, 251
Psychological factors affecting medical conditions, 489t

Psychological predisposition, 53
Psychological risk factor
    for gender dysphoria, 353–354
    for sexual dysfunctions, 330–331
Psychological testing, and substance-related
    disorders, 277
Psychological treatment, of anxiety-related
    disorders, 135–141
Psychologist
    public statements by, 483
    types, 464, 466t
Psychopathologist, 6
Psychopathy, 271, 296
Psychophysiological assessment, 88, 90
Psychophysiological disorders, 488–489
Psychosexual development stages, 30, 30t
Psychosis, 361, 365
Psychosomatic, 148
Psychotherapist qualifications, 465
Psychotherapy, and dissociative disorders, 173
Psychotic disorder. See also specific types
    adverse life events and, 379
    alternatives to hospital care, 388f
    antipsychotic medication and, 386f
    assessing, 383–385
    biological risk factors, 375–379
    causes, 380–382
    continuum, 362f–363f
    environmental risk factors, 379–380
    epidemiology, 371–373
    examples, 361
    features, 361–371
    interview and, 383
    long term outcomes, 389
    prevention, 382
    sample developmental pathway, 381f
    screening questions, 389t
    substance abuse and, 379
    treatment (biological), 385–386
    treatment (psychological), 386–388
    types, 361t
Psychoticism subscale, 384t
Psychotic schizophrenic dimension, 367f
Psychotic schizophrenic prephase, 366, 366f
PTSD. See Posttraumatic stress disorder
Public health model, and abnormal
    psychology, 13
Public policy, 476, 477
Public stigma, 15, 15f
Purging
    anorexia nervosa and, 223, 224t
    bulimia nervosa and, 225
Purkinje cell, 405

Q

Qualitative assessment, 35
Quantitative psychologist, DSM-V job description,
    467t
Quasi-experimental method, 95–96, 97t
Questionnaire
    for anxiety-related disorder assessment, 133, 135t
    for dissociative disorders assessment, 172
    for eating disorder assessment, 238, 240t
    for mood disorder assessment, 208–209
    for neurocognitive disorders, 454–455
    paraphilias and, 348
    for personality disorder assessment, 311, 311t

for sexual dysfunction assessment, 333
    for somatic symptom disorder assessment, 157

R

Race
    anxiety-related disorder and, 118–119
    defined, 42
    eating disorders and, 229
    mental disorders and, 60, 62t
    personality disorders and, 295
    suicide and, 196f–197f
Randomization, 94
Rape
    preferential, 346
    violence and, 345
Rapid-eye-movement (REM) sleep, and depressive
    and bipolar disorders, 200–201
Rating scale
    developmental disorders and, 410
    disruptive behavior disorders and, 425
Rational restructuring, 40
Reaction formation, 30
Reality orientation, 457–458
Reality principle, 30
Recidivism rate, 351
Referential delusion, 363
Regression, 30
Rehabilitation
    psychotic disorders and, 387
    substance-related disorders and, 282
Rehabilitation psychologist, DSM-V job
    description, 467t
Relapse prevention
    paraphilic disorders and, 347
    substance-related disorders and, 275
Relaxation training, 136, 493–494
Reliability of assessment measures, 78–79, 78t
Religion, as a protective factor, 63, 64f
Reminiscence therapy
    for dementia, 457
    for depression, 215
REM-sleep, and depressive and bipolar disorders,
    200–201
Repetitive transcranial magnetic stimulation
    (rTMS), 213
Repression, 30
Research design, 93
Researcher vs. clinician, 478–479
Residual schizophrenic phase, 366, 366f
Resilience, 62–63, 63t
Resiliency factor, 63
Resourceful Adolescent Program-Adolescents
    (RAP-A), 205–206
Resourceful Adolescent Program-Family (RAP-F),
    205–206
Response prevention, in obsessive-compulsive
    behavior, 139
Restricted eating, 223
Restricting behavior, and anorexia nervosa, 223,
    224t
Reticular activating system, 25
Retrospective analysis, and suicide, 210
Rett's disorder, 405t
Reuptake, 24
Reward deficiency syndrome, 268, 345
Right to least restrictive treatment, 477
Right to refuse treatment, 477

Right to treatment, 477
Risk factor. See also specific types
    for depression, 330–331
    for depressive and bipolar disorders, 196–204
    for gender dysphoria, 353–354
    for mental disorders, 59–61, 62t
    for suicide, 196–204
Risky drug use, 252
Ritual prevention, and obsessive-compulsive
    behavior, 139
Roofie, 345
Rorschach test
    as assessment technique, 85
    continuum, 85f
    psychodynamic assessment and, 31
"Running amok," 42

S

SAD. See Seasonal affective disorder (SAD)
Sadism
    features, 341
    focus of arousal, 338t
    rape, 345
Sadness continuum, 180f–181f
Sadomasochism, 341
Safety/security needs, 34
St. Vitus's dance, 11
Saliva test, for substance-related disorders, 280
Satiety, 233
Scale for the Assessment of Illness Behavior, 157
Scatterplot, 96f
Schedule for Affective Disorders and Schizophrenia
    (SADS), 207, 383
Schizoaffective disorder
    epidemiology, 373
    features, 361t, 368–369, 370t
Schizoid personality disorder, 293, 294t, 372f
Schizophrenia
    adverse life events and, 379, 380f
    bipolar disorder and, 199f
    brain and, 376–378, 376f, 377f, 378f
    cognitive deficits, 378–379
    culture and, 380
    differential diagnosis, 439t
    dimensions, 367f
    dopamine and, 25
    epidemiology, 371–373
    evolution and, 380
    features, 361–362, 362t, 366t
    labeling and, 380
    MRI results, 28f
    negative symptoms, 361–362, 362t, 364–365, 372f
    neurochemical features, 378
    other criteria, 365
    phases, 365–366, 366f
    positive symptoms, 361, 362–364, 362t
    prenatal complications, 379, 379f
    prevalence rates, 375–376, 375f
    spectrum disorders, 372f
    stigma associated with, 373–375
    substance abuse and, 379, 380t
    two-hit model for prevention, 382
    video about, 382
    violence and, 374
Schizophreniform disorder
    epidemiology, 373
    features, 361t, 367, 367t

Schizotypal personality disorder, 293–295, 295t, 372f
School psychologist
  *DSM-V* job description, 467t
  qualifications, 464, 465
School Refusal Assessment Scale-Revised, 135t
School refusal behavior, 117
Scientific method, 93–97
Screening for Somatoform Disorders (SOMS), 157
Screening for Somatoform Disorders-7 (SOMS-7), 157
Screening Scale for Pedophilic Interests (SSPI), 348, 349t
Seashore rhythm test, 90
Seasonal affective disorder (SAD)
  features, 181
  light therapy, 213–214
Secondary gain, 154
Secondary prevention
  defined, 66
  of panic disorder, 69
Sedative
  abusing, 253, 255–257, 259
  diagnostic categories of abuse, 254t–255t
Selective prevention
  defined, 66–67
  of panic disorder, 69
Selective serotonin reuptake inhibitor (SSRI)
  for depression, 210–212, 212t
  for eating disorders, 241
Self-actualization, 34, 34f
Self-care skills training, 412
Self-control therapy
  for depression, 214
  as treatment, 469–470
Self-help group
  mental disorders and, 473–474
  substance-related disorders and, 284
Self-injurious behavior, 402
Self-monitoring
  as assessment technique, 87, 133–134
  depressive and bipolar disorders and, 209
  eating disorders and, 239–240
  sexual dysfunction and, 333
  substance-related disorders and, 283
Self-report questionnaire
  as assessment technique, 133, 135t
  depressive and bipolar disorders and, 208–209
  eating disorders and, 238
  personality disorders and, 310
Self-stigma, 15, 15f
Senile dementia, 438
Senile plaque, 448
Sensate focus, 334
Separation anxiety-related disorder
  cognitive therapy examples for, 137t
  exposure-based therapy examples for, 139t
  features, 115, 117, 117t
  gender and, 119f
  prevalence rates, 118f
  psychoeducation example for, 136t
  somatic control exercise example for, 136t
Septal-hippocampal system, and anxiety-related disorders, 123–124
Sequential design, 97

Serotonin
  anxiety-related disorders and, 124, 125f
  depression and, 24
  functions, 25t
Sex offender, 340, 350–351
Sex Offender Treatment Intervention and Progress Scale, 348
Sex reassignment surgery, 354
Sex therapy, 334
Sexual behavior
  continuum, 322f–323f, 336f–337f
  factors affecting, 333f
  normal, 322, 337
Sexual desire, normal, 337
Sexual disorder/dysfunction. *See also specific types*
  age and, 327, 328t–329t
  assessing, 333–334
  biological risk factors, 330
  causes, 331, 332f, 333f
  continuum, 322f–323f, 336f–337f
  culture and, 331–332, 332t
  defined, 322
  epidemiology, 327
  features, 323–329
  gender and, 328, 328t–329t, 332t
  interview and, 333
  long-term outcomes, 336
  prevalence rates, 328t–329t
  prevention, 331–332
  psychological risk factors, 330–331
  screening questions, 336t
  stigma associated with, 327–328
  treatment (biological), 334
  treatment (physiological), 333–334
  treatment (psychological), 334–335
Sexual fantasy, 338
Sexual Interest and Desire Inventory, 333
Sexual intimacy, with clients, 482, 483
Sexual masochism, 338t, 341, 342t
Sexual response cycle, 323
Shame therapy, 349
Shock therapy
  for depression, 212–213
  ethical dilemmas, 214
Short-term memory, normal changes, 435–436
Short-term psychodynamic therapy, 313
Sickle cell disease, 403–404
Sign language, 411
Single photon emission computed tomography (SPECT), 456
Single-subject experimental designs, 97
Skills training. *See also specific types*
  depressive and bipolar disorders and, 214
  developmental disorders and, 412–413
  disruptive behavior disorders and, 426
  for emotion regulation, 309, 310t
  personality disorders and, 308–309, 313–314
  psychotic disorders and, 382, 387
  schizophrenia and, 387
  substance-related disorders and, 283
Sleep deficiency, and depressive and bipolar disorders, 200
Sleep disorders, 490
Sleep terrors, 490
Sleepwalking, 490
Smith-Magenis syndrome, 405t

Social anxiety-related disorder
  behavioral inhibition and, 125
  characteristics, 8
  example, 7–8
  features, 107–108, 108t
  gender and, 119f
  genetics and, 122
  prevalence rates, 118f
  sample developmental pathway, 129f
  treatment seekers, 118f
Social Anxiety Scale for Children-Revised, 135t
Social impairment from substance use, 251–252
Social Interaction Anxiety Scale, 135t
Socialization differences, 43
Socialization training, for developmental disorders, 411–412
Social needs, 34
Social norming, and substance abuse prevention, 67
Social phobia. *See also* Social anxiety-related disorder
  cognitive therapy examples for, 137t
  exposure-based therapy examples for, 139t
  psychoeducation example for, 136t
  somatic control exercise example for, 136t
Social Phobia and Anxiety Inventory, 135t
Social play group, 411–412
Social psychologist, *DSM-V* job description, 467t
Social role valorization, 475
Social skills training
  for depression, 214
  disruptive behavior disorders and, 426
  for schizophrenia, 387
Social worker qualifications, 465
Sociocultural assessment, 45
Sociocultural model, 41–47
Sociocultural perspective, 41
Sociocultural treatment, 45, 47
Socioeconomic status, and mental disorders, 61
Somatic control exercises, 136, 136t
Somatic delusion, 363, 371
Somatic symptom disorder, 147–149. *See also specific types*
  assessing, 157
  biological risk factors, 153
  brain and, 154f
  causes, 155–156
  continuum, 148f–149f
  defined, 147
  environmental risk factors, 153–155
  epidemiology, 151–152
  evolution and, 155
  features, 148–152, 148t
  guidelines, 157t
  historical introduction, 146
  interview and, 157
  prevalence rates, 152t
  prevention, 155–156
  stigma associated with, 152
  treatment (biological), 157–158
  treatment (psychological), 158–159
Somatization, 146
Somatoform disorder. *See* Somatic symptom disorder
Somatoform Disorders Schedule, 157
Somatosensory Amplification Scale (SAS), 157, 158t
Somatosensory awareness, 155

Special education teacher qualifications, 465
Specific phobia
    causes, 130
    cognitive therapy examples for, 137t
    exposure-based therapy examples for, 139t
    features, 108, 108t
    gender and, 119f
    genetics and, 122
    prevalence rates, 118f
    psychoeducation example for, 136t
    somatic control exercise example for, 136t
    treatment seekers, 118f
SPECT (single photon emission computed
    tomography), 456
Speech imitation, 411
Spirituality, as a protective factor, 63, 64f
Sports psychologist, DSM-V job description,
    467t
SSRI. See Selective serotonin reuptake inhibitor
    (SSRI)
Standardization, of assessment measures, 80
State-Trait Anxiety Inventory, 135t
Steroids, 263
Stigma, 15–16, 15f. See also specific disorders
Stimulant abuse, 259–260
    diagnostic categories of, 254t–255t
Stress
    assessing, 493
    causes, 491–492
    college students, 494t
    culture and, 91–92
    defined, 47, 488
    depressive and bipolar disorders and, 201
    diathesis and, 53
    long-term outcomes, 496
    management of, 495
    prevention, 492–493
    substance-related disorders and, 269
    treatment, 493–494
Stress-induced relapse, 269
Stress inoculation training, 138
Stria terminalis
    anxiety-related disorders and, 124
    substance-related disorders and, 266f, 267
Stroke
    causes, 441–442
    genetics and, 448
    vascular disease and, 441
Stroop Color and Word Test, 384
Structured Clinical Interview, 207, 238
Structured Clinical Interview for Dissociative
    Disorders-Revised (SCID-D-R), 172
Structured Clinical Interview for DSM-V, 157
Structured interview, 80
Structured Interview for DSM-IV Personality
    (SIDP-IV), 312, 312t
Student Bodies, 237
Subcortical dementia, 442
Substance abuse, 261–262
    continuum, 252f–253f
    diagnostic categories, 254t–255t
    features, 251
    schizophrenia and, 379
    social norming and prevention, 67
    stigma associated with, 265
    stimulant abuse. See Stimulant abuse
    street names, 254t

Substance dependence, 251
Substance intoxication, 252
Substance-related disorder, 251–252, 251t
    assessing, 276–277, 280
    biological risk factors, 266–268
    causal model, 275f
    causes, 274–275
    comorbidity, 265
    continuum, 252f–253f
    defined, 251
    environmental risk factors, 269–274
    epidemiology, 263–265
    evolution and, 274
    features, 251–263
    genetics and, 266
    interview and, 276–277
    long-term outcomes, 284–285
    prevalence rates, 264, 273, 273f
    prevention, 275–276
    stigma associated with, 265
    treatment (biological), 280–282
    treatment (inpatient), 282
    treatment (psychological), 282–284
    treatment (residential), 282
    treatment seekers, 265
    urinalysis and, 277, 280t
Substance tolerance, 252
Substance use
    age of onset, 56–57
    categories of, 253–263
    normal, 250–251
    schizophrenia and, 380t
Substance withdrawal, 252–253
Suicidal behavior
    defined, 189–191
    prevention, 68
Suicidal ideation, 190
Suicidality
    assessing, 210
    long-term outcomes, 218
    multidimensional model, 205
    schematic for assessing, 210, 211f
    spectrum, 189–191, 191f
    treatment, 217
Suicide
    attempt, 191
    biological risk factors, 196–201
    college students and, 61
    completion, 191
    depressive and bipolar disorders and,
        189–191
    epidemiology, 194–195
    gender and, 195
    prevalence rates, 196f–197f
    prevention, 206
    transcultural variation and, 195f
Superego, 30
Supervised training center, 475
Support groups, 495
Supportive psychotherapy, 386–387
Sweat test, for substance-related disorders, 280
Symphorophilia, 344t
Symptom Checklist 90-R Crime-Related PTSD
    Scale, 135t
Symptom Checklist-90-Revised (SCL-90-R), 383,
    384t
Synapses, and mental disorders, 24

Syndrome, defined, 23, 75
Systematic desensitization
    anxiety-related disorders and, 138
    defined, 40

T

Tactual performance test, 90
Taijin kyofusho, 119, 120
Tangentiality, 364
Tarantism, 11
Tardive dyskinesia, 386
TAT. See Thematic Apperception Test (TAT)
Tay-Sachs disease, 404
Teacher Report Form, 425
Telephone scatalogia, 338
Temporal lobe
    function, 25
    schizophrenia and, 377
Tension headaches, 489
Teratogen
    developmental disorders and, 405
    disruptive behavior disorders and, 421
Terrorism, and medically unexplained symptoms,
    156
Tertiary prevention, 67
Test-retest reliability, 78, 78t
Thalamus
    function, 25
    obsessive-compulsive behavior and, 124
    schizophrenia and, 377
Thematic Apperception Test (TAT)
    as assessment technique, 85–86, 86f
    psychodynamic assessment and, 31
Theory of mind, 381
Therapeutic alignment, 472
Therapeutic alliance, 472
Therapeutic relationship, 482, 483
Therapist
    client-therapist differences, 477
    clinicians vs. researchers, 478–479
    negative characteristics, 479
    types, 464–465
Therapy. See specific types
Thinking problems continuum, 436f–437f
Third variable problem, 95
Thought
    continuum, 10f–11f
    primary process and id, 29
    secondary process and ego, 30
Thought-action fusion, 127
Three-Factor Eating Questionnaire (TFEQ-R),
    240t
Tip-of-the-tongue phenomenon, 435
Tobacco
    diagnostic categories of abuse, 254t–255t
    epidemiology, 263–264
    neurocognitive disorders and, 451
Token economy
    defined, 40
    medication compliance and, 387
    milieu therapy and, 386
Transference, 32
Transsexualism. See Gender dysphoria
Transvestic fetishism
    features, 342, 343t
    focus of arousal, 338t
    gender and, 330

Transvestism, 342
Trauma
    dissociative disorders and, 169–170
    resilience and, 63, 63t
    stigma associated with, 120–122
Trauma Symptom Checklist for Children, 172t
Trephination, 10
Triangular relationship, 44
Trichotillomania, 120
Tricyclic antidepressant, 211
    for depression, 212t
Triple-blind designs, 94
Troilism, 344t
Turner syndrome, 405t
Twin study
    anxiety-related disorders and, 122
    depression and, 198f
    depressive and bipolar disorders and, 197
    eating disorders and, 232
    schizophrenia and, 375–376
Two-hit model for schizophrenia, 382
Type D personality, 492

U

Ulcers, and stress, 489
Unconditional positive regard, 34
Unconditioned stimulus (UCS), 37
Unconscious, 28–29
Unconscious motivation, 29
Unipolar depression, 181–182, 183f
Unipolar disorder, 179
Universal prevention
    of alcohol use disorders, 67–68
    defined, 66
    of suicidal behavior, 68
Unstructured interview, 80
Urinalysis, and substance-related disorders, 277, 280t
Urophilia, 344t

V

Vaginal photoplethysmograph, 348, 349f
Validity
    of assessment measures, 79–80
    of experimental studies, 95
    types, 80t
Variable (experimental), 93–94
Vascular dementia, 443t
Vascular disease
    features, 441–442
    prevalence rates, 445–446, 445f
Vascular neurological disorder, 441–442, 443t
Vicarious conditioning, 38
Vineland Adaptive Behavior Scales, Second Edition
    (VABS-II), 410
Violence, 28
    alcohol and, 272
    dissociative disorders and, 170
    elder abuse, 446
    juvenile arrests and diversion, 428
    personality disorders and, 298
    predisposition to, 28
    prevention, 64
    rape, 345
    schizophrenia and, 374
    somatic symptom disorders and, 155, 156
Virtual reality therapy, 139
Voyeurism, 338t, 342, 343t
Vulnerability
    to anxiety-related disorders, 129–130, 129f
    to depressive and bipolar disorders, 204–205
    to dramatic personality disorders, 305, 307f
    to eating disorders, 236

W

Washington University in St. Louis Kiddie Sched-
    ule for Affective Disorders and Schizophrenia,
    207
Waxy flexibility, 364
Wechsler Adult Intelligence Scale-Fourth Edition
    (WAIS-IV)
    neurocognitive disorders and, 455
    overview, 81–82
    psychotic disorders and, 384
    simulated examples, 81t, 82f
Wechsler Memory Scale (WMS-III), neurocogni-
    tive disorders and, 455
Wechsler Memory Scale (WMS-IV), psychotic
    disorders and, 384
Weight, percentage of expected, 236f
Weight concern
    continuum, 223, 224f–225f
    defined, 222
Whiteley Index, 157
Wide Range Achievement Test (4th edition) (WRAT-4),
    384, 409–410
Williams syndrome, 405t
Wisconsin Card Sorting Test, 384
Worry
    continuum, 104f
    defined, 103
Worry exposure, 140
Write-say spelling method, 412–413

Z

Zoophilia, 344t

# DSM-5 CLASSIFICATIONS

## Neurodevelopmental Disorders

### Intellectual Disabilities

Intellectual Disability (Intellectual Developmental Disorder)/Global Developmental Delay/Unspecified Intellectual Disability (Intellectual Developmental Disorder)

### Communication Disorders

Language Disorder/Speech Sound Disorder/Childhood-Onset Fluency Disorder (Stuttering)/Social (Pragmatic) Communication Disorder/Unspecified Communication Disorder

### Autism Spectrum Disorder

Autism Spectrum Disorder

### Attention-Deficit/Hyperactivity Disorder

Attention-Deficit/Hyperactivity Disorder/Other Specified Attention-Deficit/Hyperactivity Disorder/Unspecified Attention-Deficit/Hyperactivity Disorder

### Specific Learning Disorder

### Motor Disorders

Developmental Coordination Disorder/Stereotypic Movement Disorder

### Tic Disorders

Tourette's Disorder/Persistent (Chronic) Motor or Vocal Tic Disorder/Provisional Tic Disorder/Other Specified Tic Disorder/Unspecific Tic Disorder

### Other Neurodevelopmental Disorders

Other Specified Neurodevelopmental Disorder/Unspecified Neurodevelopmental Disorder

## Schizophrenia Spectrum and Other Psychotic Disorders

Schizotypal (Personality) Disorder
Delusional Disorder
Brief Psychotic Disorder
Schizophreniform Disorder
Schizophrenia
Schizoaffective Disorder
Substance/Medication-Induced Psychotic Disorder
Psychotic Disorder Due to Another Medical Condition
Catatonia Associated with Another Mental Disorder
Catatonic Disorder Due to Another Medical Condition
Unspecified Catatonia
Other Specified Schizophrenia Spectrum and Other Psychotic Disorder
Unspecified Schizophrenia Spectrum and Other Psychotic Disorder

## Bipolar and Related Disorders

Bipolar I Disorder/Bipolar II Disorder/Cyclothymic Disorder/Substance/Medication-Induced Bipolar and Related Disorder/Bipolar and Related Disorder Due to Another Medical Condition/Other Specified Bipolar and Related Disorder/Unspecified Bipolar and Related Disorder

## Depressive Disorders

Disruptive Mood Dysregulation Disorder/Major Depressive Disorder/Persistent Depressive Disorder (Dysthymia)/Premenstrual Dysphoric Disorder/Substance/Medication-Induced Depressive Disorder/Depressive Disorder Due to Another Medical Condition/Other Specified Depressive Disorder/Unspecified Depressive Disorder

## Anxiety Disorders

Separation Anxiety Disorder/Selective Mutism/Specific Phobia/Social Anxiety Disorder (Social Phobia)/Panic Disorder/Panic Attack Specifier/Agoraphobia/Generalized Anxiety Disorder/Substance/Medication-Induced Anxiety Disorder/Anxiety Disorder Due to Another Medical Condition/Other Specified Anxiety Disorder/Unspecified Anxiety Disorder

## Obsessive-Compulsive and Related Disorders

Obsessive-Compulsive Disorder/Body Dysmorphic Disorder/Hoarding Disorder/Trichotillomania (Hair-Pulling Disorder)/Excoriation (Skin-Picking) Disorder/Substance/Medication-Induced Obsessive-Compulsive and Related Disorder/Obsessive-Compulsive and Related Disorder Due to Another Medical Condition/Other Specified Obsessive-Compulsive and Related Disorder/Unspecified Obsessive-Compulsive and Related Disorder

## Trauma- and Stressor-Related Disorders

Reactive Attachment Disorder/Disinhibited Social Engagement Disorder/Posttraumatic Stress Disorder (includes Posttraumatic Stress Disorder for Children 6 Years and Younger)/Acute Stress Disorder/Adjustment Disorders/Other Specified Trauma- and Stressor-Related Disorder/Unspecified Trauma- and Stressor-Related Disorder

## Dissociative Disorders

Dissociative Identity Disorder/Dissociative Amnesia/Depersonalization/Derealization Disorder/Other Specified Dissociative Disorder/Unspecified Dissociative Disorder

## Somatic Symptom and Related Disorders

Somatic Symptom Disorder/Illness Anxiety Disorder/Conversion Disorder (Functional Neurological Symptom Disorder)/Psychological Factors Affecting Other Medical Conditions/Factitious Disorder (includes Factitious Disorder Imposed on Self, Factitious Disorder Imposed on Another)/Other Specified Somatic Symptom and Related Disorder/Unspecified Somatic Symptom and Related Disorder

## Feeding and Eating Disorders

Pica/Rumination Disorder/Avoidant/Restrictive Food Intake Disorder/Anorexia Nervosa (Restricting type, Binge-eating/Purging type)/Bulimia Nervosa/Binge-Eating Disorder/Other Specified Feeding or Eating Disorder/Unspecified Feeding or Eating Disorder

## Elimination Disorders

Enuresis/Encopresis/Other Specified Elimination Disorder/Unspecified Elimination Disorder

## Sleep-Wake Disorders

Insomnia Disorder/Hypersomnolence Disorder/Narcolepsy

## Breathing-Related Sleep Disorders

Obstructive Sleep Apnea Hypopnea/ Central Sleep Apnea/Sleep-Related Hypoventilation/Circadian Rhythm Sleep-Wake Disorders

## Parasomnias

Non-Rapid Eye Movement Sleep Arousal Disorders/Nightmare Disorder/Rapid Eye Movement Sleep Behavior Disorder/ Restless Legs Syndrome/Substance/ Medication-Induced Sleep Disorder/ Other Specified Insomnia Disorder/ Unspecified Insomnia Disorder/Other Specified Hypersomnolence Disorder/ Unspecified Hypersomnolence Disorder/ Other Specified Sleep-Wake Disorder/ Unspecified Sleep-Wake Disorder

## Sexual Dysfunctions

Delayed Ejaculation/Erectile Disorder/ Female Orgasmic Disorder/Female Sexual Interest/Arousal Disorder/ Genito-Pelvic Pain/Penetration Disorder/Male Hypoactive Sexual Desire Disorder/Premature (Early) Ejaculation/ Substance/Medication-Induced Sexual Dysfunction/Other Specified Sexual Dysfunction/Unspecified Sexual Dysfunction

## Gender Dysphoria

Gender Dysphoria/Other Specified Gender Dysphoria/Unspecified Gender Dysphoria

## Disruptive, Impulse-Control, and Conduct Disorders

Oppositional Defiant Disorder/Intermittent Explosive Disorder/Conduct Disorder/ Antisocial Personality Disorder/ Pyromania/Kleptomania/Other Specified Disruptive, Impulse-Control, and Conduct Disorder/Unspecified Disruptive, Impulse-Control, and Conduct Disorder

## Substance-Related and Addictive Disorders

### Substance-Related Disorders

Alcohol-Related Disorders: Alcohol Use Disorder/Alcohol Intoxication/Alcohol Withdrawal/Other Alcohol-Induced Disorders/Unspecified Alcohol-Related Disorder

Caffeine-Related Disorders: Caffeine Intoxication/Caffeine Withdrawal/Other Caffeine-Induced Disorders/Unspecified Caffeine-Related Disorder

Cannabis-Related Disorders: Cannabis Use Disorder/Cannabis Intoxication/ Cannabis Withdrawal/Other Cannabis-Induced Disorders/Unspecified Cannabis-Related Disorder

Hallucinogen-Related Disorders: Phencyclidine Use Disorders/ Other Hallucinogen Use Disorder/ Phencyclidine Intoxication/Other Hallucinogen Intoxication/Hallucinogen Persisting Perception Disorder/Other Phencyclidine-Induced Disorders/ Other Hallucinogen-Induced Disorders/ Unspecified Phencyclidine-Related Disorders/Unspecified Hallucinogen Related Disorders

Inhalant-Related Disorders: Inhalant Use Disorder/Inhalant Intoxication/Other Inhalant-Induced Disorders/Unspecified Inhalant-Related Disorders

Opioid-Related Disorders: Opioid Use Disorder/Opioid Intoxication/Opioid Withdrawal/Other Opioid-Induced Disorders/Unspecified Opioid-Related Disorder

Sedative-, Hypnotic-, or Anxiolytic-Related Disorders: Sedative, Hypnotic, or Anxiolytic Use Disorder/Sedative, Hypnotic, or Anxiolytic Intoxication/ Sedative, Hypnotic, or Anxiolytic Withdrawal/Other Sedative-, Hypnotic-, or Anxiolytic-Induced Disorders/ Unspecified Sedative-, Hypnotic-, or Anxiolytic-Related Disorder

Stimulant-Related Disorders: Stimulant Use Disorder/Stimulant Intoxication/ Stimulant Withdrawal/Other Stimulant-Induced Disorders/Unspecified Stimulant-Related Disorder

Tobacco-Related Disorders: Tobacco Use Disorder/Tobacco Withdrawal/Other Tobacco-Induced Disorders/Unspecified Tobacco-Related Disorder

Other (or Unknown) Substance-Related Disorders: Other (or Unknown) Substance Use Disorder/Other (or Unknown) Substance Intoxication/Other (or Unknown) Substance Withdrawal/ Other (or Unknown) Substance-Induced Disorders/Unspecified Other (or Unknown) Substance-Related Disorder

## Non-Substance-Related Disorders

Gambling Disorder

## Neurocognitive Disorders

Delirium

### Major and Mild Neurocognitive Disorders

Major or Mild Neurocognitive Disorder Due to Alzheimer's Disease

Major or Mild Frontotemporal Neurocognitive Disorder

Major or Mild Neurocognitive Disorder with Lewy Bodies

Major or Mild Vascular Neurocognitive Disorder

Major or Mild Neurocognitive Disorder Due to Traumatic Brain Injury

Substance/Medication-Induced Major or Mild Neurocognitive Disorder

Major or Mild Neurocognitive Disorder Due to HIV Infection

Major or Mild Neurocognitive Disorder Due to Prion Disease

Major or Mild Neurocognitive Disorder Due to Parkinson's Disease

Major or Mild Neurocognitive Disorder Due to Huntington's Disease

Major or Mild Neurocognitive Disorder Due to Another Medical Condition

Major and Mild Neurocognitive Disorders Due to Multiple Etiologies

Unspecified Neurocognitive Disorder

## Personality Disorders

### Cluster A Personality Disorders

Paranoid Personality Disorder/Schizoid Personality Disorder/Schizotypal Personality Disorder

### Cluster B Personality Disorders

Antisocial Personality Disorder/Borderline Personality Disorder/Histrionic Personality Disorder/Narcissistic Personality Disorder

### Cluster C Personality Disorders

Avoidant Personality Disorder/Dependent Personality Disorder/Obsessive-Compulsive Personality Disorder

### Other Personality Disorders

Personality Change Due to Another Medical Condition/Other Specified Personality Disorder/Unspecified Personality Disorder